FIFTH
EDITION

Out of Many

VOLUME ONE

Out of Many
FIFTH EDITION

A HISTORY OF THE AMERICAN PEOPLE

John Mack Faragher
YALE UNIVERSITY

Mari Jo Buhle
BROWN UNIVERSITY

Daniel Czitrom
MOUNT HOLYOKE COLLEGE

Susan H. Armitage
WASHINGTON STATE UNIVERSITY

PEARSON

Prentice
Hall

Upper Saddle River, NJ 07458

Library of Congress Cataloging-in-Publication Data
Out of many: a history of the American people / John Mack Faragher . . . [et al].–5th ed.
    p. cm.
  Includes bibliographical references and index.
  ISBN 0-13-194461-4 (v.1) – ISBN 0-13-194466-5 (v.2)
    1. United States–History. I. Faragher, John Mack, 1945–
E178.1.O935 2005d
973–dc22   2005047575

> TO OUR STUDENTS,
> OUR SISTERS,
> AND OUR BROTHERS

VP, Editorial Director: Charlyce Jones Owen
Editorial Assistant: Maureen Diana
Editor-in-Chief, Development: Rochelle Diogenes
Senior Development Editor: Roberta Meyer
Associate Editor: Emsal Hasan
Senior Media Editor: Deborah O'Connell
VP, Director of Production and Manufacturing: Barbara Kittle
Managing Editor: Joanne Riker
Production Liaison: Randy Pettit
Prepress and Manufacturing Manager: Nick Sklitsis
Prepress and Manufacturing Buyer: Benjamin Smith
Director of Marketing: Heather Shelstad
Marketing Assistant: Jennifer Lang
Creative Design Director: Leslie Osher

Cover and Interior Design: Kathryn Foot
Director, Image Resource Center: Melinda Reo
Manager, Visual Research: Beth Brenzel
Manager, Rights and Permissions: Zina Arabia
Manager, Cover Visual Research and Permissions: Karen Sanatar
Image Permission Coordinator: Carolyn Gaunt
Pearson Imaging Center: Joe Conti, Cory Skidds, Greg Harrison, Rob Uibelhoer, Ron Walko
Photo Researcher: Teri Stratford
Project Management/Composition: Lorenza Compagnone, Preparé, Inc.
Printer/Binder: Courier Companies, Inc.
Cover Printer: Phoenix Color Corporation
Cover Art: *The Ride For Liberty—the Fugitive Slaves:* oil, c. 1862, by Eastman Johnson. The Granger Collection.

Credits and acknowledgments borrowed from other sources and reproduced, with permission, in this textbook appear on appropiate page within text or on page C-1.

Pearson Education Ltd., London
Pearson Education Australia Pty, Limited, Sydney
Pearson Education Singapore, Pte., Ltd.
Pearson Education North Asia Ltd., Hong Kong

Pearson Education, Canada, Ltd, Toronto
Pearson Educación de Mexico, S.A. de C.V.
Pearson Education–Japan, Tokyo
Pearson Education Malaysia, Pte., Ltd.

10 9 8 7 6 5 4 3 2 1
ISBN 0-13-194461-4

Brief Contents

CONTENTS

4

SLAVERY AND EMPIRE,
1441–1770   80

5

THE CULTURES OF COLONIAL NORTH AMERICA,
1700–1780   114

6

FROM EMPIRE TO INDEPENDENCE,
1750–1776   144

7

THE AMERICAN REVOLUTION,
1776–1786   176

8

THE NEW NATION, 1786–1800   206

9

AN AGRARIAN REPUBLIC,
1790–1824   234

12 INDUSTRY AND THE NORTH, *1790s–1840s*   326

13   COMING TO TERMS WITH THE NEW AGE, 1820s–1850s   356

THE TERRITORIAL EXPANSION OF THE UNITED STATES, *1830s–1850s*   388

RECONSTRUCTION,
1863–1877 480

18 | CONQUEST AND SURVIVAL:
The Trans–Mississipi West, 1860–1900   514

22 WORLD WAR I, 1914–1920 640

24 THE GREAT DEPRESSION AND THE NEW DEAL, *1929–1940* 708

25 | WORLD WAR II, *1941–1945* — 742

31 | TOWARD A TRANSNATIONAL AMERICA, *since 1988* 956

Chapter Opening Illustrations

Chapter 1: Painting of Cahokia Mounds, Collinsville, Illinois by Michael Hampshire.
Cahokia Mounds State Historic Site—painting by Michael Hampshire.

Chapter 2: Christopher Columbus surveys the New World from the deck of his ship. Sailors stand or kneel around Columbus. Engraving by W. Wellstood from a painting by G. Harvey.
Library of Congress.

Chapter 3: Dutch governor Peter Stuyvesant oversees the arrival of mail from a galleon before anxious colonists and surly sea dogs in New Amsterdam, circa 1647.
Public Buildings Administration, Section of Fine Arts.

Chapter 4: The slave deck of the bark "Wildfire." Here, slaves were brought into Key West on April 30, 1800 in this print from a nineteenth-century newspaper.
Courtesy of the Library of Congress.

Chapter 5: This painting portrays George Whitefield as he preaches an outdoor sermon to a crowd of eagerly penitent worshippers.
Mark Sexton. The Granger Collection.

Chapter 6: Patrick Henry delivers an impassioned speech to the enthusiastic approbation of the Virginia House of Burgesses.
Courtesy of the Library of Congress.

Chapter 7: Christina Henrietta Caroline Ackland (1750–1815) travels down the Hudson to American General Gates' camp for a pass to cross the lines to nurse her husband, British Major Ackland, wounded in the second Battle of Saratoga, 7th October 1777. From the original by Alonzo Chappel.
Getty Images Inc. Hulton Archive Photos.

Chapter 8: Congress Voting Independence, by Savage/Pine.
Courtesy of The Historical Society of Pennsylvania Collection, Atwater Kent Museum of Philadelphia.

Chapter 9: American General Andrew Jackson interviews Creek warrior William Weatherford (Red Eagle) in a tent in this undated engraving.
Getty Images Inc. Hulton Archive Photos.

Chapter 10: African-American slaves/farm workers carry sacks of cotton on their heads while leaving a South Carolina plantation field. Stereograph, ca.

1860 by G.N. Barnard, *Returning from the Cotton Fields in South Carolina*.
Returning from the Cotton Fields in South Carolina, ca. 1860, stereograph by Barbard, negative number 47843. © Collection of The New York Historical Society.

Chapter 11: The Attempted Assassination of the President of the United States, Jan. 30, 1835. As the funeral procession of the Hon. Warren R. Davis was moving from the Capitol of the United States, Richard Lawrence, a supposed maniac, rushed from the crowd and snapped two heavily loaded pistols immediately at the body of President Jackson, both of which providentially missed fire. Lawrence was instantly arrested by persons present, examined by Judge Cranch, and committed for trial. Drawn from a sketch by an eyewitness.
Library of Congress.

Chapter 12: Dutton St. boarding houses in Lowell, Massachusetts were constructed in a community setting around textile mills. The building with the cupola is a mill. The two buildings that look like individual residences were housing for the young women who worked in the mills and were built pre-1845. Buildings with dormers also were worker housing built in 1845.
Dutton St. Boarding Houses, Lowell, MA., 1845. Museum of American Textiles History.

Chapter 13: Female students at work while sitting on benches along wooden tables in an 1840 pencil and watercolor illustration titled *Girls Evening School* by an unidentified artist.
Unidentified artist (American, about 1840), *Girl's Evening School*, about 1840, U.S. Graphite pencil and watercolor on paper, Sheet: 34.3 x 45.9 cm (13 1/2 x 18 1/16 in.) Museum of Fine Arts, Boston. The M. and M. Karolik Collection of American Watercolors, Drawings, and Prints, 1800-1875, 53.2431 Photograph ©2006 Museum of Fine Arts, Boston.

Chapter 14: General Zachary Taylor at the Battle of Buena Vista, Mexico, 22-23 February 1847.
The Granger Collection.

Chapter 15: Abraham Lincoln delivers a speech in a debate with Senator Stephen Douglas during the 1858 senatorial campaign in Illinois. Lincoln, Douglas, and numerous dignitaries congregate on a platform before a crowd of spectators in this illustration by Robert Marshall.
Illinois State Historical Library.

Chapter 16: A Union officer and members of Company C, 1st Conn. Artillery stand behind a large cannon at Fort Brady. Photograph by Mathew Brady, 1864.
Corbis/Bettmann.

Chapter 17: J. W. Watts, Reading the Emancipation Proclamation.
Courtesy of the Library of Congress.

Chapter 18: General William Tecumseh Sherman (1820–1891) and the Peace Commission meet with Cheyenne and Arapaho Indians at Fort Laramie in Wyoming to try to end Red Cloud's War. The resulting treaty secured the removal of U.S. troops from several Powder River forts, as well as promised the Powder River Valley as a Sioux hunting ground.
Getty Images Inc. Hulton Archive Photos.

Chapter 19: Workers pose beside a huge ladle at a steel mill in Pittsburgh, Pennsylvania ca. 1900.
Courtesy of the Library of Congress.

Chapter 20: Dynamic American orator William Jennings Bryan stands on a platform above a crowd during a campaign.
Brown Brothers.

Chapter 21: Suffragettes Holding Victory Jubilee, 1920. Elated women wave American flags and blow noisemakers on a car on a street on August 31, 1920.
Corbis/Bettmann.

Chapter 22: A crowd of people stand on the shore watching the luxury ocean liner Lusitania leave from New York on May 1, 1915.
Corbis/Bettmann.

Chapter 23: A line of young men and women in various poses doing the Charleston as they compete in a dance contest in downtown St. Louis in 1925.
Missouri Historical Society, St. Louis.

Chapter 24: Two boys sit next to disparaging signs at a Hooverville shanty town in Washington, DC in 1932.
Getty Images Inc. Hulton Archive Photos.

Chapter 25: African American soldiers man a field cannon while digging an earth embankment below a camouflage net on a World War II battlefield.
Corbis/Bettmann.

Chapter 26: Actor Robert Taylor testifies before the House Un-American Activities Committee.
AP Wide World Photos.

Chapter 27: President Kennedy gives his inaugural address at the Capitol. Listening in the front row, from left: Vice President Lyndon B. Johnson; Richard Nixon, Kennedy's campaign opponent; Senator John Sparkmano of Alabama; and former president Harry Truman.
AP Wide World Photos.

Chapter 28: An African-American man drinking at a segregated drinking fountain in Oklahoma City, Oklahoma.
Russell Lee. Getty Images Inc. Hulton Archive Photos.

Chapter 29: A peace demonstrator taunts military police during this confrontation in front of the Pentagon during an anti-Vietnam War protest.
UPI Corbis/Bettmann.

Chapter 30: A Volkswagen "Beetle" sits at a gas station during the gasoline shortage and energy crisis of the 1970s. The sign states the limit of fuel per customer.
Owen Franken/Corbis/Bettmann

Chapter 31: Rescue workers stand near the rubble of the fallen World Trade Center towers in New York on September 13, 2001.
REUTERS/Pool/Beth Kaiser. Corbis/Bettmann.

MAPS

*Denotes Interactive Map Exploration

CHARTS, GRAPHS & TABLES

OVERVIEW TABLES

OUT OF MANY VOICES

PREFACE

Out of Many: A History of the American People, fifth edition, offers a distinctive and timely approach to American history, highlighting the experiences of diverse communities of Americans in the unfolding story of our country. The stories of these communities offer a way of examining the complex historical forces shaping people's lives at various moments in our past. The debates and conflicts surrounding the most momentous issues in our national life—independence, emerging democracy, slavery, westward settlement, imperial expansion, economic depression, war, technological change—were largely worked out in the context of local communities. Through communities we focus on the persistent tensions between everyday life and those larger decisions and events that continually reshape the circumstances of local life. Each chapter opens with a description of a representative community. Some of these portraits feature American communities struggling with one another: African slaves and English masters on the rice plantations of colonial Georgia, or *Tejanos* and Americans during the Texas war of independence. Other chapters feature portraits of communities facing social change: the feminists of Seneca Falls, New York, in 1848, or the African Americans of Montgomery, Alabama, in 1955. As the story unfolds we find communities growing to include ever larger groups of Americans: the soldiers from every colony who forged the Continental Army into a patriotic national force at Valley Forge during the American Revolution, or the moviegoers who aspired to a collective dream of material prosperity and upward mobility during the 1920s.

Out of Many is also the only American history text with a truly continental perspective. With community vignettes from New England to the South, the Midwest to the far West, we encourage students to appreciate the great expanse of our nation. For example, a vignette of seventeenth-century Sante Fé, New Mexico, illustrates the founding of the first European settlements in the New World. We present territorial expansion into the American West from the viewpoint of the Mandan villagers of the upper Missouri River of North Dakota. We introduce the policies of the Reconstruction era through the experience of African Americans in Hale County, Alabama. A continental perspective drives home to students that American history has never been the preserve of any particular region.

Out of Many includes extensive coverage of our diverse heritage. Our country is appropriately known as "a nation of immigrants," and the history of immigration to America, from the seventeenth to the twenty-first centuries, is fully integrated into the text. There is sustained and close attention to our place in the world, with special emphasis on our relations with the nations of the Western Hemisphere, especially our near neighbors, Canada and Mexico. The statistical data in the final chapter has been completely updated with the results of the 2000 census.

In these ways *Out of Many* breaks new ground, but without compromising its coverage of the traditional turning points that we believe are critically important to an understanding of the American past. Among these watershed events are the Revolution and the struggle over the Constitution, the Civil War and Reconstruction, and the Great Depression and World War II. In *Out of Many,* however, we seek to integrate the narrative of national history with the story of the nation's many diverse communities. The Revolutionary and Constitutional period tested the ability of local communities to forge a new unity, and success depended on their ability to build a nation without compromising local identity. The Civil War and Reconstruction formed a second great test of the balance between the national ideas of the Revolution and the power of local and sectional communities. The Depression and the New Deal demonstrated the importance of local communities and the growing power of national institutions during the greatest economic challenge in our history. *Out of Many* also looks back in a new and comprehensive way—from the vantage point of the beginning of a new century and the end of the cold war—at the salient events of the last fifty years and their impact on American communities. The community focus of *Out of Many* weaves the stories of the people and the nation into a single compelling narrative.

Out of Many, fifth edition, is completely updated with the most recent scholarship on the history of America and the United States. All the chapters have been extensively revised and rewritten. The final chapter details the tumultuous events of the new century, including a completely new section on the "War on Terror," and concluding with the national election of 2004. Throughout the book the text and graphics are presented in a stunning new design. Moreover, this edition incorporates two important new features. Each chapter includes two short excerpts from letters, personal diaries, or first person accounts called "Out of Many Voices," giving students the opportunity to read the perspectives of both well-known and ordinary Americans on the course of historic events. Moreover, selected chapters include a two-page feature we call "Whose History Is It?" using text and graphics to focus on notable public controversies that have taken place over the meaning of historical events. Americans have frequently come to blows over different ways of interpreting the past, and this feature helps students see that arguments over the meaning of the past have never been confined to the classroom.

SPECIAL FEATURES

With each edition of *Out of Many* we have sought to strengthen its unique integration of the best of traditional American history with its innovative community-based focus and strong continental perspective. This new version is no exception. A wealth of special features and pedagogical aids reinforces our narrative and helps students grasp key issues.

- **Community and Diversity.** *Out of Many*, fifth edition, opens with an introduction titled "Communitiy and Diversity" that acquaints students with the major themes of the book, providing them with a framework for understanding American History.

- **Whose History Is It?** NEW to the fifth edition, this special illustrated feature located at the end of chapters 1, 4, 9, 14, 17, 25, 27, 29 uses text and graphics to focus on notable public controversies that have taken place over the meaning of historical events.

- **Out of Many Voices.** NEW to the fifth edition are short excerpts from letters, personal diaries, or first person accounts that give the perspectives of both well-known and ordinary Americans on the course of historic events.

- **Map Explorations.** Selected maps in each chapter are provided in an interactive format on the new *ONEKEY* website available with the text. They provide interactive exploration of key geographical, chronological, and thematic concepts to reinforce the content contained in the maps and the text. Students can access each map individually using the url provided with the map or find them within chapters when exploring the website.

- **Overview tables.** Overview tables provide students with a summary of complex issues.

- **Graphs, charts, and tables.** Every chapter includes one or more graphs, charts, or tables that help students understand important events and trends.

- **Photos and Illustrations.** The abundant illustrations in *Out of Many* include many that have never before been used in an American history text. Extensive captions treat the images as visual primary source documents from the American past, describing their source and explaining their significance. In addition, each chapter opens with a stunning visual that relates to the chapter content and introduces students to the importance of visual documents in the study of history.

- **Chronologies.** A chronology at the end of each chapter helps students build a framework of key events.

- **Review Questions.** Review questions at the end of chapters help students review, reinforce, and retain the material in each chapter and encourage them to relate the material to broader issues in American history.

- **Recommended Readings.** The works in the short, annotated Recommended Reading list at the end of each chapter have been selected with the interested introductory student in mind.

PRINT SUPPLEMENTS

Instructor's Resource Manual

A time-saver in developing and preparing lecture presentations, the *Instructor's Resource Manual* contains chapter outlines, detailed chapter overviews, lecture topics, discussion questions, readings, and information about audio-visual resources.

Test Item File

The *Test Item File* contains more than 1,500 multiple-choice, identification, matching, true-false, and essay test questions and 10–15 questions per chapter on the maps found in each chapter. The guide includes a collection of blank maps that can be photocopied and used for map testing purposes or for other class exercises.

Prentice Hall Test Generator

This commercial-quality computerized test management program, available for Windows and Macintosh environments, allows instructors to select items from the *Test Item File* and design their own exams.

Transparency Package

Includes full-color transparency acetates of all the maps, charts, and graphs in the text for use in the classroom.

History Notes, Volumes I and II

History Notes is a new type of study aid that provides tests for each chapter that students can use to assess their level of understanding of chapter material. It includes identification terms, multiple-choice questions, short essay questions, and map questions. *History Notes* is available free when packaged with *Out of Many*.

Documents Set, Volumes I and II

This collection of more than 300 primary source documents directly relates to the themes and content of the text. Each document is approximately two pages long and includes a brief introduction and study questions intended to encourage students to analyze the document critically and relate it to the content of the text. The *Documents Set* is available at a substantial discount when packaged with *Out of Many*.

Retrieving the American Past

Written and developed by leading historians and educators, this reader is an on-demand history database that offers 300 primary source documents on key topics in American History. Each module includes an introduction, several primary documents and secondary sources, follow-up questions, and recommendations for further reading. By deciding which modules to include and the order in which they will appear, instructors can compile a custom reader to fit their needs. Contact your local Prentice Hall representative for more information about this exciting custom publishing option.

Many Lives, Many Stories: Biographies in American History

This two-volume collection of sixty-two biographies in American history was written specifically to match the chapter sequence and themes of *Out of Many*. Introductions, pre-reading questions, suggested readings, and a special prologue about the role of biography in the study of American history enrich this important new supplement. Available free when packaged with *Out of Many*.

Prentice Hall's *OneSearch* with *Research Navigator TM*

 This brief guide introduces students to tools for finding, evaluating, and using resources on the internet. It includes a section avoiding plagiarism and using sources effectively, tips for finding information related to history on the internet and for documenting electronic sources, and an access code to the *Research Navigator* TM website. *OneSearch* is available for free when packaged with *Out of Many*. Contact your local Prentice Hall representative for details.

Prentice Hall and Penguin Bundle Program

 Prentice Hall and Penguin are pleased to provide adopters of *Out of Many* with an opportunity to receive significant discounts when orders for *Out of Many* are bundled together with Penguin titles in American history. Please contact your local Prentice Hall representative for details.

MULTIMEDIA SUPPLEMENTS

U.S. History Documents CD-ROM

Bound into every copy of *Out of Many* and organized according to the main periods in American History, this document CD-ROM contains over 300 primary source documents in an easily-navigated PDF file. Each document is accompanied by essay questions that can be answered via the CD-ROM or via a dedicated website.

OneKey

 A unique online resource, *OneKey* lets you and your students access the many teaching and learning resources for *Out of Many* all in one place. For students, it means access to documents, quizzes, map explorations, interactive learning activities, video, audio, e-book portions of the text, and other pedagogical material organized by major sections within chapters to reinforce and apply what they are learning in class and from the text. For instructors, it means access to the student's resources, *and* all of the instructional material available to use in teaching with the text, including instructor's manual material, test questions from the test item file, additional documents for assignment, images, maps, charts, and graphs from the text, video and audio clips, and Powerpoint ^{TM} presentations and questions for use with CRS technology in the classroom. Access to this unique website is free to students when packaged with the text. For more information about this exciting new resource, contact your local Prentice Hall representative for a tour.

Companion Website™

www.prenhall.com/faragher

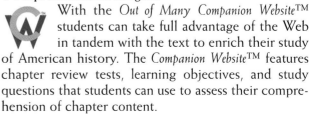 With the *Out of Many Companion Website*™ students can take full advantage of the Web in tandem with the text to enrich their study of American history. The *Companion Website*™ features chapter review tests, learning objectives, and study questions that students can use to assess their comprehension of chapter content.

Instructor's Resource Center on CD-ROM

This CD-ROM, like the *OneKey* website, includes all of the instuctor supplements, multimedia resources, and images and art from *Out of Many*.

Research Navigator™

This unique resource helps your students make the most of their research time. From finding the right articles and journals, to citing sources, drafting and writing effective papers, and completing research assignments, **Research Navigator**™ simplifies and streamlines the entire process. Access to **Research Navigator**™ is available with every copy of the *OneSearch* guide and with the *OneKey* website. For more information, contact your local Prentice Hall representative.

ACKNOWLEDGMENTS

In the years it has taken to bring *Out of Many* from idea to reality and to improve it in successive editions, we have often been reminded that although writing history sometimes feels like isolated work, it actually involves a collective effort. We want to thank the dozens of people whose efforts have made the publication of this book possible.

We wish to thank our many friends at Prentice Hall for their efforts in creating the fifth edition of *Out of Many*: Yolanda de Rooy, President; Charlyce Jones Owen, Editorial Director; Carolyn Viola John, Development Editor; Leslie Osher, Creative Design Director; Randy Pettit, Production Liaison; Kathryn Foot, Interior and Cover Designer; Lorenza Compagnone, Prepare, Inc., Production Editor; and Janet Masterson, Copy Editor.

Historians around the country greatly assisted us by reading and commenting on chapters for this and previous editions. We want to thank each of them for the commitment of their valuable time:
Margaret Spratt, *University of Southern Maine*
Elizabeth Hayes Turner, *University of North Texas*
James A. Hijiya, *University of Massachusetts*
Dartmouth Kathryn Abbott, *Western Kentucky University*
Ericka Verba, *Santa Monica College*
Kirsten Fermaglich, *Michigan State University*
Edward E. Baptist, *Cornell University*
Kevin Kern, *University of Akron Charlotte Brooks, SUNY, Albany*.

Although we share joint responsibility for the entire book, the chapters were individually authored: John Mack Faraher wrote chapters 1–8; Susan Armitage wrote chapters 9–16; Mari Jo Buhle wrote chapters 18–20, 25–26, 29; and Daniel Czitrom wrote chapters 17, 21–24, 27–28. (For this edition, Professors Buhle and Czitrom co-authored Chapters 30–31.)

Each of us depended on a great deal of support and assistance with the research and writing that went into this book. We want to thank: Kathryn Abbott, Nan Boyd, Krista Comer, Jennifer Cote, Crista DeLuzio, Keith Edgerton, Carol Frost, Jesse Hoffnung Garskof, Pailin Gaither, Jane Gerhard, Todd Gernes, Mark Krasovic, Melani McAlister, Cristi, Rebecca McKenna, and Mitchell, Ani Mukherji, J. C. Mutchler, Keith Peterson, Alan Pinkham, Tricia Rose, Gina Rourke, Jessica Shubow, Gordon P. Utz, Jr., and Maura Young.

Our families and close friends have been supportive and ever so patient over the many years we have devoted to this project. But we want especially to thank Paul Buhle, Meryl Fingrutd, Bob Greene, and Michele Hoffnung.

ABOUT THE AUTHORS

Chris Freitag

John Mack Faragher

John Mack Faragher is Arthur Unobskey Professor of American History, chair of the Program in American Studies, and director of the Howard R. Lamar Center for the Study of Frontiers and Borders at Yale University. Born in Arizona and raised in southern California, he received his B.A. at the University of California, Riverside, and his Ph.D. at Yale University. He is the author of *Women and Men on the Overland Trail* (1979), *Sugar Creek: Life on the Illinois Prairie* (1986), *Daniel Boone: The Life and Legend of an American Pioneer* (1992), *The American West: A New Interpretive History* (2000), and *A Great and Noble Scheme: The Tragic Story of the Expulsion of the French Acadians from their American Homeland* (2005).

Mari Jo Buhle

Mari Jo Buhle is William R. Kenan Jr. University Professor and Professor of American Civilization and History at Brown University, specializing in American women's history. She received her B.A. from the University of Illinois, Urbana–Champaign, and her Ph.D. from the University of Wisconsin, Madison. She is the author of *Women and American Socialism, 1870–1920* (1981) and *Feminism and Its Discontents: A Century of Struggle with Psychoanalysis* (1998). She is also coeditor of *Encyclopedia of the American Left*, second edition (1998). Professor Buhle held a fellowship (1991–1996) from the John D. and Catherine T. MacArthur Foundation.

Daniel Czitrom

Daniel Czitrom is Professor of History at Mount Holyoke College. Born and raised in New York City, he received his B.A. from the State University of New York at Binghamton and his M.A. and Ph.D. from the University of Wisconsin, Madison. He is the author of *Media and the American Mind: From Morse to McLuhan* (1982), which won the First Books Award of the American Historical Association and has been translated into Spanish and Chinese. He has served as a historical consultant and a featured on-camera commentator for several documentary film projects, including two recent PBS series, *New York: A Documentary Film* and *American Photography: A Century of Images.* He is co-author of the forthcoming book, *Rediscovering Jacob Riis*, and currently serves on the Executive Board of the Organization of American Historians.

Susan H. Armitage

Susan H. Armitage is Claudius O. and Mary R. Johnson Distinguished Professor of History at Washington State University. She earned her Ph.D. from the London School of Economics and Political Science. Among her many publications on western women's history are three coedited books, *The Women's West* (1987), *So Much To Be Done: Women on the Mining and Ranching Frontier* (1991), and *Writing the Range: Race, Class, and Culture in the Women's West* (1997). She currently serves as an editor of a series of books on women and American history for the University of Illinois Press. She is the editor of *Frontiers: A Journal of Women's Studies.*

COMMUNITY & DIVERSITY

One of the most characteristic features of our country has always been its astounding variety. The American people include the descendants of native Indians, colonial Europeans, Africans, and migrants from virtually every country and continent. Indeed, as we enter a new century the United States is absorbing a flood of immigrants from Latin America and Asia that rivals the great tide of people from eastern and southern Europe one hundred years ago. What's more, our country is one of the world's most spacious, incorporating more than 3.6 million square miles of territory. The strug-

gle to meld a single nation out of our many far-flung communities is what much of American history is all about. That is the story told in this book.

Every human society is made up of communities. A community is a set of relationships linking men, women, and their families to a coherent social whole that is more than the sum of its parts. In a community people develop the capacity for unified action. In a community people learn, often through trial and error, how to transform and adapt to their environment. The sentiment that binds the members of a community together is the mother of group iden-

William Sidney Mount (1807–1868) *California News* 1850. Oil on canvas. The Long Island Museum of American Art, History and Carriages.

Gift of Mr. and Mrs. Ward Melville, 1955.

Harvey Dinnerstein, *Underground, Together* 1996, oil on canvas, 90″ × 107″.

Photograph courtesy of Gerold Wunderlich & Co., New York, NY.

tity and ethnic pride. In the making of history, communities are far more important than even the greatest of leaders, for the community is the institution most capable of passing a distinctive historical tradition to future generations.

Communities bind people together in multiple ways. They can be as small as local neighborhoods, in which people maintain face-to-face relations, or as large as the nation itself. This book examines American history from the perspective of community life—an ever-widening frame that has included larger and larger groups of Americans.

Networks of kinship and friendship, and connections across generations and among families, establish the bonds essential to community life. Shared feelings about values and history establish the basis for common identity. In communities, people find the power to act collectively in their own interest. But American communities frequently took shape as a result of serious conflicts among groups, and within

communities there has often been significant fighting among competing groups or classes. Thus the term *community*, as we use it here, includes tension and discord as well as harmony and agreement.

For years there have been persistent laments about the "loss of community" in modern America. But community has not disappeared—it is continually being reinvented. Until the late eighteenth century, community was defined primarily by space and local geography. But in the nineteenth century communities began to be reshaped by new and powerful historical forces such as the marketplace, industrialization, the corporation, mass immigration, mass media, and the growth of the nation-state. In the twentieth century, Americans have struggled to balance commitments to several communities simultaneously. These were defined not simply by local spatial arrangements, but by categories as varied as racial and ethnic groups, occupations, political affiliations, and consumer preferences.

The "American Communities" vignettes that open each chapter reflect this shift. Most of the vignettes in the pre–Civil War chapters focus on geographically defined communities, such as the ancient Indian city at Cahokia, or the experiment in industrial urban planning in early nineteenth-century Lowell, Massachusetts. In the post–Civil War chapters different and more modern kinds of communities make their appearance. In the 1920s, movies and radio offered a new kind of community—a community of identification with dreams of freedom, material success, upward mobility, youth and beauty. In the 1950s, rock 'n' roll music helped germinate a new national community of teenagers, with profound effects on the culture of the entire country in the second half of the twentieth century. In the late 1970s, fear of nuclear accidents like the one at Three Mile Island brought concerned citizens together in communities around the country and produced a national movement opposing nuclear power.

The title for our book was suggested by the Latin phrase selected by John Adams, Benjamin Franklin, and Thomas Jefferson for the Great Seal of the United States: *E Pluribus Unum*—"Out of Many Comes Unity." These men understood that unity could not be imposed by a powerful central authority but had to develop out of mutual respect among Americans of different backgrounds. The revolutionary leadership expressed the hope that such respect could grow on the basis of a remarkable proposition: "We hold these truths to be self-evident, that all men are created equal; that they are endowed by their Creator with certain unalienable rights; that among these are life, liberty, and the pursuit of happiness." The national government of the United States would preserve local and state authority but would guarantee individual rights. The nation would be strengthened by guarantees of difference.

"Out of Many"—that is the promise of America, and the premise of this book. The underlying dialectic of American history, we believe, is that as a people we need to locate our national unity in the celebration of the differences that exist among us; these differences can be our strength, as long as we affirm the promise of the Declaration. Protecting the "right to be different," in other words, is absolutely funda-

Thomas Satterwhite Noble, *Last Sale of Slaves on the Courthouse Steps*, 1860, oil on canvas, Missouri Historical Society.

mental to the continued existence of democracy, and that right is best protected by the existence of strong and vital communities. We are bound together as a nation by the ideal of local and cultural differences protected by our common commitment to the values of our Revolution.

Today those values are endangered by terrorists using the tactics of mass terror. In the wake of the September 11, 2001, attack on the United States, and with the continuing threat of biological, chemical, or even nuclear assaults, Americans can not afford to lose faith in our historic vision. The United States is a multicultural and transnational society. The thousands of victims buried in the smoking ruins of the World Trade Center included people from dozens of different ethnic and national groups. We must fight to protect and defend the promise of our diverse nation

Our history shows that the promise of American unity has always been problematic. Centrifugal forces have been powerful in the American past, and at times the country has seemed about to fracture into its component parts. Our transformation from a collection of groups and regions into a nation has been marked by painful and often violent struggles. Our past is filled with conflicts between Indians and colonists, masters and slaves, Patriots and Loyalists, Northerners and Southerners, Easterners and Westerners, capitalists and workers, and sometimes the government and the people. War can bring out our best, but it can also bring out our worst. During World War II thousands of Japanese American citizens were deprived of their rights and locked up in isolated detention centers simply because of their ethnic background. Americans often appear to be little more than a contentious collection of peoples with conflicting interests, divided by region and background, race and class.

Our most influential leaders have also sometimes suffered a crisis of faith in the American project of "liberty and justice for all." Thomas Jefferson not only believed in the inferiority of African Americans, but he feared that immigrants from outside the Anglo-American tradition might "warp and bias" the development of the nation "and render it a heterogeneous, incoherent, distracted mass." We have not always lived up to the American promise, and there is a dark side to our history. It took the bloodiest war in American history to secure the human rights of African Americans, and the struggle for full equality for all our citizens has yet to be won. During the great influx of immigrants in the early twentieth century, fears much like Jefferson's led to movements to Americanize the foreign born

by forcing them, in the words of one leader, "to give up the languages, customs, and methods of life which they have brought with them across the ocean, and adopt instead the language, habits, and customs of this country, and the general standards and ways of American living." Similar thinking motivated Congress at various times to bar the immigration of Africans, Asians, and other ethnic groups and people of color into the country, and to force assimilation on American Indians by denying them the freedom to practice their religion or even to speak their own language. Such calls for restrictive unity still resound in our own day.

But other Americans have argued for a more fulsome version of Americanization. "What is the American, this new man?" asked the French immigrant Michel Crévecoeur in 1782. "A strange mixture of blood which you will find in no other country." In America, he wrote, "individuals of all nations are melted into a new race of men." A century later Crévecoeur was echoed by historian Frederick Jackson Turner, who believed that "in the crucible of the frontier, the immigrants were Americanized, liberated, and fused into a mixed race, English in neither nationality nor characteristics. The process has gone on from the early days to our own."

The process by which diverse communities have come to share a set of common American values is one of the most fundamental aspects of our history. It did not occur, however, because of compulsory Americanization programs, but because of free public education, popular participation in democratic politics, and the impact of popular culture. Contemporary America does have a common culture: We share a commitment to freedom of thought and expression, we join in the aspirations to own our own homes and send our children to college, we laugh at the same television programs.

To a degree that too few Americans appreciate, this common culture resulted from a complicated process of mutual discovery that took place when different ethnic and regional groups encountered one another. Consider just one small and unique aspect of our culture: the barbecue. Americans have been barbecuing since before the beginning of written history. Early settlers adopted this technique of cooking from the Indians—the word itself comes from a native term for a framework of sticks over a fire on which meat was slowly cooked. Colonists typically barbecued pork, fed on Indian corn. African slaves lent their own touch by introducing the use of hot sauces. The ritual that is a part of nearly every American family's Fourth of July silently celebrates the heritage of diversity that went into making our common culture.

The American educator John Dewey recognized this diversity early in the last century. "The genuine American, the typical American, is himself a hyphenated character," he declared, "international and interracial in his make-up." The point about our "hyphenated character," Dewey believed, "is to see to it that the hyphen connects instead of separates."

We, the authors of *Out of Many*, share Dewey's perspective on American history. "Creation comes from the impact of diversity," wrote the American philosopher Horace Kallen. We also endorse Kallen's vision of the American promise: "A democracy of nationalities, cooperating voluntarily and autonomously through common institutions, . . . a multiplicity in a unity, an orchestration of mankind." And now, let the music begin.

FIFTH
EDITION Out of Many

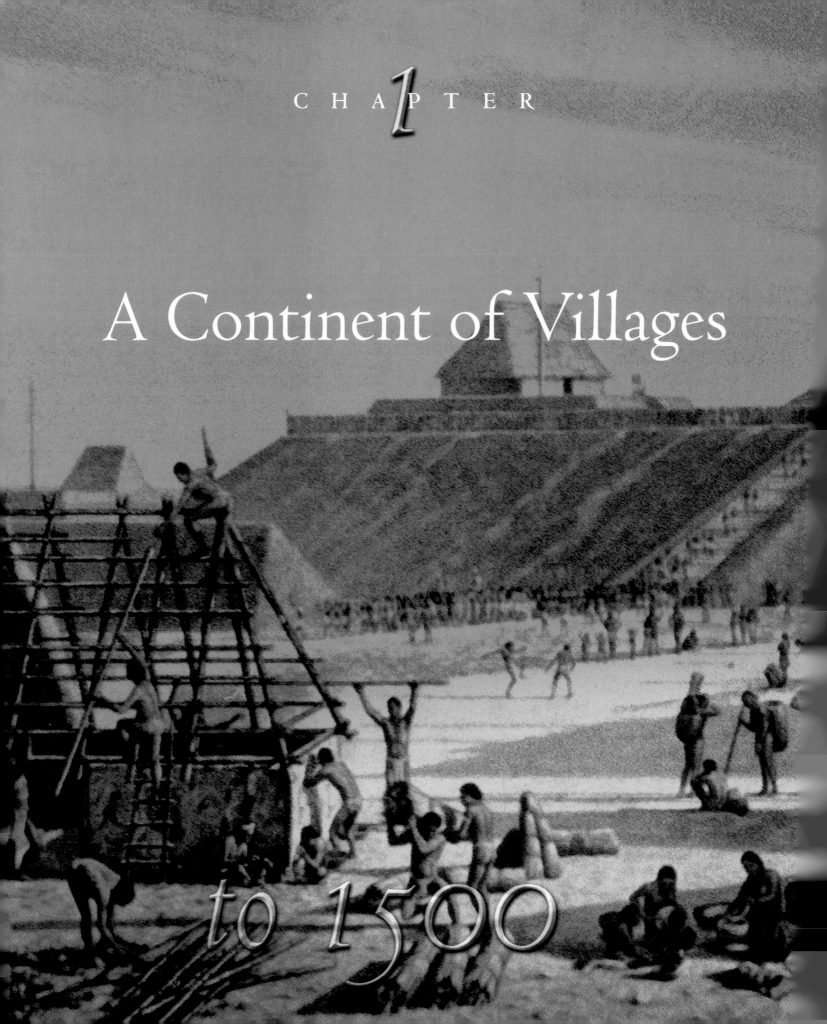

CHAPTER 1

A Continent of Villages

to 1500

CHAPTER OUTLINE

Cahokia: Thirteenth-Century Life on the Mississippi

As the sun rose over the rich floodplain, the people of the riverbank city set about their daily tasks. Some went to shops where they manufactured tools, crafted pottery, worked metal, or fashioned ornamental jewelry—goods destined to be exchanged in the far corners of the continent. Others left their densely populated neighborhoods for the outlying countryside, where in the summer heat they worked the seemingly endless fields that fed the city. From almost any point people could see the great temple that rose from the city center—the temple where priests in splendid costumes acted out public rituals of death and renewal.

This thirteenth-century city was not in preindustrial Europe or Asia but in North America. Its residents lived and worked on the banks of the Mississippi River, across from present-day St. Louis, at a place archaeologists have named Cahokia after the group who occupied the area from about 700 to 1400 CE. In the mid-1200s, Cahokia was an urban cluster of perhaps 30,000 people, and the city covered nearly six square miles. Houses were arranged in rows around open plazas, and the farm fields were abundant with corn, beans, and pumpkins. The temple, a huge earthwork pyramid, covered fifteen acres at its base and rose as high as a ten-story building. On top were the residences of chiefs and priests, who dressed in elaborate headdresses made from the plumage of American birds.

By the fourteenth century, Cahokia had been abandoned, whether the victim of physical attack, political collapse, drought and famine, or some combination, is not known. But the great central temple mound and dozens of smaller ones in the surrounding area, as well as hundreds more throughout the Mississippi Valley, remained to puzzle the European immigrants who resettled the valley in the eighteenth and nineteenth centuries. Treasure seekers plundered those mounds, and many were eventually leveled and plowed under for farmland. Only a few were saved, inside parks and estates. Cahokia's central mound survived because in the nineteenth century its summit became the site of a monastery, now long gone.

The Europeans who first explored and excavated those mounds were convinced they were the ruins of a vanished civilization, but could not believe they were the work of Indians. The first comprehensive study of Cahokia, published in 1848 under the sponsorship of the newly established Smithsonian Institution, noted that "the mound-builders were an agricultural people, considerably advanced in arts, manners, habits, and religion." But because "Indians were hunters averse to labor, and not known to have constructed any works approaching [the] skillfulness of design or [the] magnitude" of Cahokia, surely those wonders were constructed by a "lost race."

The Smithsonian scientists were wrong. The ancestors of contemporary Native Americans constructed massive earthworks in the Mississippi Valley. The vast urban complex of Cahokia—at its height stretching six miles along the Mississippi River—flourished from the tenth to the fourteenth century. Its residents were not nomadic hunters but farmers, members of an agricultural society that archaeologists call the Mississippian, with highly productive cultivation techniques. Hundreds of acres of crops fed the people of Cahokia, the most populated urban community north of the civilization of the Aztecs in central Mexico. Mississippian farmers constructed

Cahokia

ingenious raised plots of land on which they heaped compost in wide ridges for improved drainage and protection against unseasonable frosts. To their houses of wood and mud they attached pens in which they kept flocks of domesticated turkeys and small herds of young deer that they slaughtered for meat and hides. Cahokia was at the center of a long-distance trading system that linked it to other Indian communities over a vast area. Copper came from Lake Superior, mica from the southern Appalachians, conch shells from the Atlantic coast, and Cahokia's specialized artisans were renowned for the manufacture of high-quality flint hoes, exported throughout the Mississippi Valley.

The archaeological evidence suggests that Cahokia was a city-state supported by tribute and taxation. Like the awe-inspiring public works of other early urban societies—the pyramids of ancient Egypt and the acropolis of Athens are two familiar examples—the great temple mound of Cahokia was intended to showcase the city's wealth and power. The mounds and other colossal public works at Cahokia were the monuments of a society ruled by an elite who commanded the people, and sometimes demanded human sacrifice in deference to their power. From their residences atop the mound, priests and governors looked down upon their subjects both literally and figuratively.

The 1848 Smithsonian report on Cahokia reflected a stereotypical view that all Indian people were hunters. But the history of North America before European colonization demonstrates that the native inhabitants lived in a great variety of societies, including not only the hunting and gathering bands of the Great Basin or Arctic, but densely settled urban civilizations, like those of the Aztecs of Mexico or the Mayans of Central America. North America before colonization was, as historian Howard R. Lamar phrases it, "a continent of villages," a land spread with thousands of local communities. The wonders and mystery of the lost city of Cahokia are but one aspect of the little-understood history of the Indians of the Americas.

KEY TOPICS

- The peopling of the Americas by migrants from Asia
- The adaptation of native cultures to the regions of North America
- The increase in complexity of many native societies following the development of farming
- The nature of Indian cultures in the three major regions of European invasion and settlement

SETTLING THE CONTINENT

"Why do you call us Indians?" a Massachusetts native complained to Puritan missionary John Eliot in 1646. Christopher Columbus, who mistook the Taino people of the Caribbean for the people of the East Indies, called them Indios. Within a short time this Spanish word had passed into English as "Indians," and was commonly used to refer to all the native peoples of the Americas. Today anthropologists often use the term "Amerindians," and many people prefer "Native Americans." But in the United States most of the descendants of the original inhabitants of North America refer to themselves as "Indian people."

Who Are the Indian People?

At the time of their first contacts with Europeans at the beginning of the sixteenth century, the native inhabitants of the Western Hemisphere represented over 2,000 separate cultures, spoke several hundred different languages, and made their livings in scores of fundamentally different

A forensic artist reconstructed this bust from the skull of "Kennewick Man," whose skeletal remains were discovered along the Columbia River in 1996. Scientific testing suggested that the remains were more than nine thousand years old.

SOURCE: James Chatters/Agence France Presse/Getty Images.

environments. Just as the term "European" includes many nations, so the term "Indian" covers an enormous diversity among the peoples of the Americas. Natives, of course, referred to themselves by their own names. For example, the people of the mid-Atlantic coast called themselves Lenni Lenape, meaning "true men"; a large group of natives in the western Great Lakes country called themselves Lakota, or "the allies"; and the nomadic hunters of the desert Southwest used the name Dine (pronounced "dee-nay"), meaning simply "the people." Europeans came to know these three groups by rather different names: the Delawares (from the principal river of the mid-Atlantic region), the Sioux, and the Apaches (both of which meant "enemy" in the language of neighboring tribes).

No single physical type characterized all the native peoples of the Americas. Although most had straight, black hair and dark, almond-shaped eyes, their skin color ranged from mahogany to light brown and few fit the "redskin" descriptions used by North American colonists of the eighteenth and nineteenth centuries. Indeed, it was only when Europeans had compared Indian peoples with natives of other continents, such as Africans, that they seemed similar enough to be classified as a group.

Once Europeans realized that the Americas were in fact a "New World," rather than part of the Asian continent, a debate began over how people might have moved there from Europe and Asia, where (according to the Judeo-Christian Bible) God had created the first man and woman. Writers proposed elaborate theories of transoceanic migrations. Common to all these theories was a belief that the Americas had been populated for a few thousand years at most, and that native societies were the degenerate offspring of a far superior Old World culture. A number of

OVERVIEW

ORIGINS OF SOME INDIAN TRIBAL NAMES

Cherokee	A corruption of the Choctaw *chiluk-ki*, meaning "cave people," an allusion to the many caves in the Cherokee homeland in the highlands of present-day Georgia. The Cherokees called themselves *Ani-Yun-Wiya*, or "real people."
Cheyenne	From the Sioux *Sha-hiyena*, "people of strange speech." The Cheyennes of the Northern Plains called themselves *Dzi-tsistas*, meaning "our people."
Hopi	A shortening of the name the Hopis of northern Arizona use for themselves, *Hópitu*, which means "peaceful ones."
Mohawk	From the Algonquian *Mohawaúuck*, meaning "man-eaters." The Mohawks of the upper Hudson Valley in New York called themselves *Kaniengehaga*, "people of the place of the flint."
Pawnee	From the Pawnee term *paríki*, which describes a distinctive style of dressing the hair with paint and fat to make it stand erect like a horn. The Pawnees, whose homeland was the Platte River valley in present-day Nebraska, called themselves *Chahiksichahiks*, "men of men."

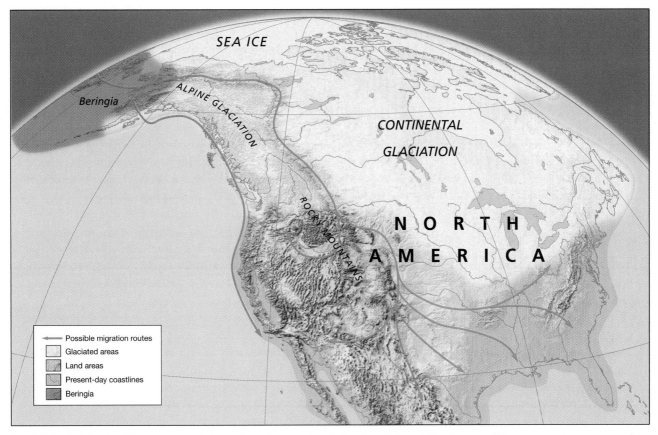

MAP 1.1   **Migration Routes from Asia to America**   During the Ice Age, Asia and North
America were joined where the Bering Straits are today, forming a migration route for hunting peoples.
Either by boat along the coast, or through a narrow corridor between the huge northern glaciers, these
migrants began making their way to the heartland of the continent as much as 30,000 years ago.

Spanish scholars thought more deeply about the question of Indian origins. In 1590, the Spanish Jesuit missionary Joseph de Acosta reasoned that because Old World animals were present in the Americas, they must have crossed by a land bridge that could have been used by humans as well.

Migration from Asia

Acosta was the first to propose the Asian migration hypothesis that is widely accepted today. The most compelling scientific evidence comes from genetic research. Studies comparing the DNA variation of populations around the world consistently demonstrate the close genetic relationship of Asian and Native American populations. Analysis of the genetic drift of these two populations suggests that migrants to North America began leaving Asia approximately 30,000 years ago (see Map 1.1).

The migration could have begun over a land bridge connecting the continents. During the last Ice Age (the Wisconsinan Glaciation, from 70,000 to 10,000 years ago, the final act in the geologic epoch known as the Pleistocene), huge glaciers locked up massive volumes

of water, and sea levels were as much as 300 feet lower than they are today. Asia and North America, now separated by the Bering Straits, were joined by a subcontinent of ice-free, treeless grassland, 750 miles wide from north to south, which geologists have named Beringia. Glaciers did not form in Beringia because the climate was too dry. Summers there were warm, winters cold but almost snow-free. This was a perfect environment for large mammals—mammoth and mastodon, bison, horse, reindeer, camel, and saiga (a goatlike antelope). Small bands of "Stone Age" hunter-gatherers were surely attracted by these animal populations. Accompanied by a husky-like species of dog, these bands gradually moved as far east as the Yukon River basin of northern Canada, where field excavations have uncovered the fossilized jawbones of several dogs and bone tools estimated to be about 27,000 years old.

Access to lands to the south, however, was blocked by the huge glacial sheets that covered much of what is today Canada. How did the migrants get over those 2,000 miles of deep ice? The standard hypothesis is that with the warming of the climate and the end of the Ice Age, about

OUT OF MANY VOICES

A ZUNI ACCOUNT OF CREATION

The people of Zuni Pueblo, in isolated western New Mexico, have preserved and nurtured their traditional way of life, and theirs remains a deeply religious culture. This story, which a Zuni informant told to ethnographer Frank Hamilton Cushing in the late nineteenth century, uses poetic imagery to tell of "The Beginning of New-making."

BEFORE THE BEGINNING OF THE NEW-MAKING, the All-father Father alone had being. Through ages there was nothing else except black darkness.

In the beginning of the New-making, the All-father Father thought outward in space, and mists were created and up-lifted. Thus through his knowledge he made himself the Sun who was thus created and is the great Father. The dark spaces brightened with light. The cloud mists thickened and became water.

From his flesh, the Sun-father created the Seed-stuff of worlds, and he himself rested upon the waters. And these two, the Four-fold-containing Earth-mother and the All-covering Sky-father, the surpassing beings, with power of changing their forms even as smoke changes in the wind, were the father and mother of the soul beings.

Then as man and woman spoke these two together, "Behold!" said Earth-mother, as a great terraced bowl appeared at hand, and within it water, "This shall be the home of my tiny children. On the rim of each world-country in which they wander, terraced mountains shall stand, making in one region many mountains by which one country shall be known from another."

Then she spat on the water and struck it and stirred it with her fingers. Foam gathered about the terraced rim, mounting higher and higher. Then with her warm breath she blew across the terraces. White flecks of foam broke away and floated over the water. But the cold breath of Sky-father shattered the foam and it fell downward in fine mist and spray.

Then Earth-mother spoke: "Even so shall white clouds float up from the great waters at the borders of the world, and clustering about the mountain terraces of the horizon, shall be broken and hardened by thy cold. Then will they shed downward, in rain-spray, the water of life, even into the hollow places of my lap. For in my lap shall nestle our children, man-kind and creature-kind, for warmth in thy coldness."

So even now the trees on high mountains near the clouds and Sky-father, crouch low toward Earth-mother for warmth and protection. Warm is Earth-mother, cold our Sky-father. ▪

SOURCE: Smithsonian Institution, Bureau of American Ethnology, *Thirteenth Annual Report* (Washington, D.C.: Government Printing Office, 1896) pp. 379–83.

13,000 BCE, glacial melting created an ice-free corridor—an original "Pan-American Highway"—along the eastern front range of the Rocky Mountains. Traveling down this highway, the hunters of big game reached the Great Plains, where evidence has been found of their settlements, dated as early as 10,000 BCE.

Recently, however, archaeological finds along the Pacific coast of North and South America have complicated this hypothesis. Newly excavated human sites in Washington State, California, and Peru have been radiocarbon dated to be more than 12,000 years old. The most spectacular find, at Monte Verde in southern Chile, produced striking evidence of toolmaking, house building, rock painting, and human footprints conservatively dated at 12,500 years ago. A number of archaeologists now believe that the people who founded these settlements moved south in boats along a coastal route rather than overland—an ancient "Pacific Coast Highway." These people were probably fishers and gatherers rather than hunters of big game.

There were two later migrations into North America. About 5000 BCE the Athapascan or Na-Dene people moved across Beringia and began to settle the forests in the northwestern area of the continent. Although they eventually adopted a technology similar to that of neighboring peoples, the Na-Dene maintained a separate cultural and linguistic identity. Eventually groups of Athapascan speakers, the ancestors of the Navajos and Apaches, migrated across the Great Plains to the Southwest. A third and final migration began about 3000 BCE, long after Beringia had disappeared under rising seas, when a maritime hunting people crossed the Bering Straits in small boats. The Inuits (also known as Eskimos) colonized the polar coasts of the Arctic, the

These Clovis points are typical of thousands that archaeologists have found at sites all over the continent, dating from a period about 12,000 years ago. When inserted in a spear shaft, these three- to six-inch fluted points made effective weapons for hunting mammoth and other big game. The ancient craftsmen who made these points often took advantage of the unique qualities of the stone they were working to enhance their aesthetic beauty.

SOURCE: ©Warren Morgan/CORBIS.

Yupiks the coast of southwestern Alaska, and the Aleuts the Aleutian Islands (which are named for them).

While scientists debate the timing and mapping of these various migrations, many Indian people hold to their oral traditions that say they have always lived in North America. Every culture has its origin stories, offering explanations of the customs and beliefs of the group. (See Out of Many Voices: A Zuni Account of Creation). A number of scholars believe these origin stories may shed light on ancient history. The Haida people of the Northwest Pacific coast tell of a time, long ago, when the off-shore islands were much larger; but then the oceans rose, they say, and "flood tide woman" forced them to move to higher ground. Could these stories preserve the memory of changes at the end of the Ice Age? It is notable that many Indian traditions include a long journey from a distant place of origin to a new homeland. The Pima people of the Southwest once sang an "Emergence Song":

> This is the White Land; we arrive singing,
> Headdresses waving in the breeze.
> We have come! We have come!
> The land trembles with our dancing and singing.

Clovis: The First American Technology

The tools found at the earliest North American archaeological sites, crude stone or bone choppers and scrapers, are similar to artifacts from the same period found in Europe or Asia. About 11,000 years ago, however, ancient Americans developed a much more sophisticated style of making fluted blades and lance points. The Clovis tradition, named after the site of its first discovery near Clovis, New Mexico, was a powerful new technology. In the years since the initial discovery, archaeologists have unearthed Clovis artifacts at sites ranging from Montana to Mexico, Nova Scotia to Arizona, all of them dating back to within 1,000 or 2,000 years of one another, suggesting that the Clovis technology spread quickly throughout the continent.

The evidence suggests that Clovis bands were mobile communities of foragers numbering perhaps thirty to fifty individuals from several interrelated families. They returned to the same hunting camps year after year, migrating seasonally within territories of several hundred square miles. Near Delbert, Nova Scotia, archaeologists discovered the floors of ten tents arranged in a semicircle, their doors opening south to avoid the prevailing northerly winds. Both this camp and others found throughout the continent overlooked watering places that would attract game. Clovis blades have been excavated amid the remains of mammoth, camel, horse, giant armadillo, and sloth.

NEW WAYS OF LIVING ON THE LAND

The global warming trend that ended the Ice Age dramatically altered the North American climate. As the giant continental glaciers began to melt about 15,000 years ago, the northern latitudes were colonized by plants, animals, and humans. Meltwater created the lake and river systems of today and raised the level of the surrounding seas, not only flooding Beringia but vast stretches of the Atlantic and Gulf coasts, creating fertile tidal pools and offshore fishing banks. These huge transformations produced new patterns of wind, rainfall, and temperature, reshaping the ecology of the entire continent and gradually producing the distinct North American regions of today (see Map 1.2). The great integrating force of a single continental climate faded, and with its passing the continental Clovis culture fragmented into many different regional patterns.

Hunting Traditions

One of the most important effects of this massive climatic shift was the stress it placed on the big game animals best suited to an Ice Age environment. The archaeological record documents the extinction of thirty-two classes of large New World mammals, including not only the mammoth and mastodon but also the horse and camel, both of which evolved in America and then migrated to Asia across Beringia. Lowered reproduction and survival rates

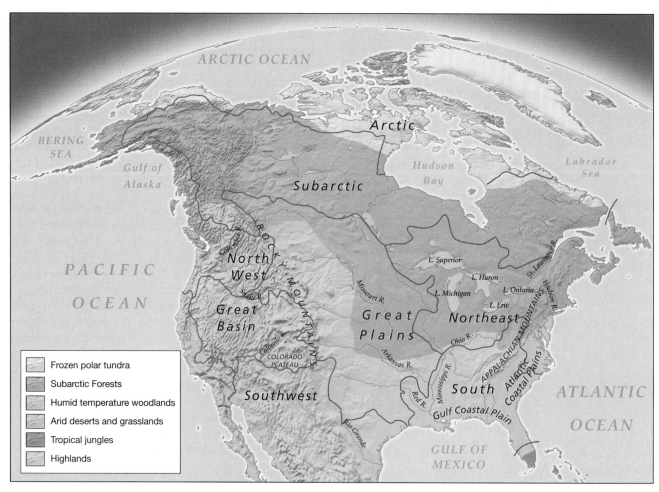

MAP 1.2   Climatological and Culture Regions of North America Occupying more than a third of the continent, the United States is alone among the world's nations in encompassing all five general classes of global climate: tropical jungles, arid deserts and grasslands, temperate woodlands, subarctic forests, and frozen polar tundra. All peoples must adjust their diet, shelter, and other material aspects of their lives to the physical conditions of the world around them. By considering the ways in which Indian peoples developed distinct cultures and adapted to their environments, anthropologists developed the concept of "culture areas." They divide the continent into nine fundamental regions that have greatly influenced the history of North America over the past 10,000 years. Just as regions shaped the lifeways and history of Indian peoples, after the coming of the Europeans they nurtured the development of regional American cultures.

of these large mammals may have forced hunting bands to intensify their efforts, leading to what some archaeologists have called the "Pleistocene Overkill."

As the other large-mammal populations declined, hunters on the Great Plains concentrated on the herds of American bison (known more familiarly as buffalo). To hunt these animals, people needed a weapon they could throw quickly with great accuracy and speed at fast-moving targets over distances of as much as a hundred yards. In archaeological sites dating from about 10,000 years ago, a new style of tool is found mingled with animal remains. This technology, named Folsom after the site of the first major excavation in New Mexico, was a refinement of the Clovis tradition, featuring more delicate but deadlier spear points.

Hunters probably hurled the lances to which these points were attached with wooden spear-throwers, with far greater speed than they could achieve with their arms alone.

These archaeological finds suggest the growing complexity of early Indian communities. Hunters frequently stampeded herds of bison into canyon traps or over cliffs. At one such kill site in southeastern Colorado, dated at about 6500 BCE, archaeologists uncovered the remains of nearly 200 bison that had been slaughtered and then systematically butchered on a single occasion. Such tasks required a sophisticated division of labor among dozens of men and women and the cooperation of a number of communities. Taking food in such great quantities also suggests a knowledge of basic preservation techniques.

When, in 1927, archaeologists at Folsom, New Mexico, uncovered this dramatic example of a projectile point embedded in the ribs of a long-extinct species of bison, it was the first proof that Indians had been in North America for many thousands of years.

SOURCE: Courtesy of the Denver Museum of Nature and Science.

These people must have been among the first to make jerky (dried strips of meat) and pemmican (a mixture of dried meat, animal fat, and berries that can keep into the winter when stored in hide containers).

Desert Culture

The retreat of the glaciers led to new ways of finding food in other regions: hunting in the arctic, foraging in the arid deserts, fishing along the coasts, hunting and gathering in the forests. These developments took place roughly 10,000 to 2,500 years ago, during what archaeologists call the Archaic period (the equivalent of the Mesolithic period in European chronology).

In the Great Basin of present-day Utah and Nevada, the warming trend created a desert where once there had been enormous inland seas. Here Indian people developed Desert Culture, a way of life based on the pursuit of small game and the intensified foraging of plant foods. Small communities or bands of desert foragers migrated seasonally within a small range. They collected seeds, fiber, and prickly pear from the yucca one season, then moved to highland mesas or plateaus to gather grass seed, acorns, juniper berries, and piñon nuts, and next to mountain streams to spear and net fish. This strategy required considerable skill in handicrafts and the production of fiber baskets for collecting, pitch-lined baskets for cooking, nets and traps, and stones shaped to grind seeds and nuts, as well as stone knives, hammers, and clubs.

Archaeologists today find the artifacts of desert foragers in the caves and rock shelters in which they lived. In addition to stone tools, there are objects of wood, hide, and fiber, wonderfully preserved for thousands of years in the dry climate. Desert Culture persisted into the nineteenth century among modern Shoshone and Ute communities. Although these people were once scornfully labeled "Diggers" because of their practice of gathering edible roots and were ridiculed for their "primitive" life ways, they actually made very sophisticated adjustments to a harsh environment.

Descriptions of the culture of the modern Shoshones suggest that their emphasis on sharing and gift giving, their condemnation of hoarding, and their limitations on the accumulation of material goods, fostered by a nomadic lifestyle, prevented individuals or families from acquiring excessive wealth and forged a strong sense of community among these people of the desert. Desert communities were characterized by a kind of social equality in which decisions were made by consensus among the adults and leadership tended to be informal, based on achievement and reputation. Men of one band generally married women from another, and wives came to live with the people of their husband's families, creating important linkages between groups that contributed to the sense of shared ethnic identity.

The innovative practices of the Desert Culture gradually spread from the Great Basin to the Great Plains and the Southwest, where foraging for plant foods began to supplement hunting. Archaeologists estimate that about 6,000 years ago, the techniques of Desert Culture diffused to California, where in the natural abundance of the valleys and coasts, Indian people developed an economy capable of supporting some of the densest populations and the first permanently settled communities in North America. Another dynamic center in the West developed along the Northwest Pacific coast, where communities developed a way of life based on the use of abundant fish and sea mammals. Here, densely populated, permanently settled communities were also possible.

Forest Efficiency

There were similar trends east of the Mississippi. Before European settlers destroyed countless acres of woodland in the eighteenth and nineteenth centuries, the whole of eastern North America was a vast forest. Hardwoods grew in the North, southern pine in the South. The Winnebagos of the Great Lakes region sang of these forests:

> Pleasant it looked,
> this newly created world.
> Along the entire length and breadth
> of the earth, our grandmother
> extended the green reflection
> of her covering
> and the escaping odors
> were pleasant to inhale.

During the Archaic period, forest communities achieved a comfortable and secure life based on their sophisticated knowledge of the rich and diverse available resources, a principle that archaeologists term "forest efficiency." Indian communities of the forest hunted small game and gathered seeds, nuts, roots, and other wild plant foods. They also developed the practice of burning the woodlands and prairies to stimulate the growth of berries, fruits, and edible roots. These burns created meadows and edge environments that provided harvestable food and attracted grazing animals, which were hunted for their meat and hides. Another important resource was the abundant fish of the rivers.

Archaeological sites in the East suggest that during the late Archaic period, community populations grew and settlements became increasingly permanent, providing convincing evidence of the viability of forest efficiency. The artifacts these people buried with their dead—axes, fishhooks, and animal bones with males, nut-cracking stones, beads, and pestles with females—reflected the different roles of men and women in their society.

THE DEVELOPMENT OF FARMING

The use of a wide variety of food sources during the Archaic period eventually led many Indian people to develop and adopt the practice of farming. The dynamic center of this development in North America was in the highlands of Mexico, from which the new technology spread north and east.

Mexico

At the end of the Stone Age, people in four regions of the world developed farming systems, each based on a different crop: rice in Southeast Asia, wheat in the Middle East, potatoes in the Andean highlands of South America, and maize (what Americans call "corn") in Mexico. Today, the two American staples, maize and potatoes, contribute more to the world's

Mesoamerican maize cultivation, as illustrated by an Aztec artist for the *Florentine Codex*, a book prepared a few years after the Spanish conquest. The peoples of Mesoamerica developed a greater variety of cultivated crops than those found in any other region in the world, and their agricultural productivity helped sustain one of the world's great civilizations.

SOURCE: Image #1739-3, courtesy of the Library, American Museum of Natural History.

food supply than do wheat and rice. These "miracle crops" fueled the expansion of European human and livestock populations in the three centuries after 1650. Without these and other New World crops, such as tobacco, American cotton, and rubber—each of which was the basis of important new industries and markets—the history of the modern world would have been far different.

Archaeological evidence suggests that plant cultivation in the highlands of central Mexico first began about 5,000 years ago. Ancient Mexicans developed crops that responded well to human care and produced larger quantities of food in a limited space than did plants growing in the wild. In addition to maize, they domesticated a great variety of other crops—most importantly beans and squash, but also tomatoes, peppers, avocados, cocoa (chocolate), and vanilla. But maize was particularly productive and provided the foundation for the farming system. Over time it was adapted to a wide range of American climates and its cultivation spread throughout the temperate regions of North America.

Increasing Social Complexity

Farming radically reshaped social life. A foraging society might require 100 square miles to support 100 people, but a farming society required only one square mile. Population growth and the need for people to remain near their fields throughout the year led to the appearance of villages and permanent architecture. Autumn harvests had to be stored during winter months, and the storage and distribution of food had to be managed.

The creation of man and woman depicted on a pot (dated about 1000 CE) from the ancient villages of the Mimbres River of southwestern New Mexico, the area of Mogollon culture. Mimbres pottery is renowned for its spirited artistry. Such artifacts were usually intended as grave goods, to honor the dead.

SOURCE: Mimbres black on white bowl, with painted representations of man and woman under a blanket. Grant County, New Mexico. Diam. 26.7 cm. Courtesy National Museum of the American Indian, Smithsonian Institution, 24/3198.

Farming created the material basis for much greater social complexity. Greater population density prompted the development of significantly more elaborate systems of kinship, and families began grouping themselves into clans. Different clans often became responsible for different social, political, or ritual functions, and clans also became an important mechanism for binding together the people of several communities into loose ethnic and territorial alliances or confederacies. These confederacies were led by leaders or chiefs from honored clans, who were often advised by councils of elders. A division of labor developed with the appearance of specialists like toolmakers, crafts workers, administrators, priests, and rulers as well as farmers and food processors. Ultimately, unequal access to wealth and power resulted in the emergence of classes.

Indian communities practiced a rather strict division of labor according to gender. The details varied tremendously from culture to culture, but it is possible to generalize. Among foraging peoples, hunting was generally assigned to men, and the gathering of food and the maintenance of home-base camps to women. But the development of farming called this pattern into question. In Mexico, where communities became almost totally dependent on crops, both men and women worked in the fields. Where hunting remained important, the older division of labor remained, and women took responsibility for fieldwork.

In most farming communities, women and men belonged to separate social groupings, each with its own rituals and lore. Membership in these societies was one of the most important elements of a person's identity. Marriage ties, on the other hand, were relatively weak, and in most Indian communities divorce was usually simple. The couple separated without a great deal of ceremony, the children almost always remaining with the mother. All Indian women controlled their own bodies, were free to determine the timing of reproduction, and were free to use secret herbs to prevent pregnancy, induce abortion, or ease the pains of childbirth. All this was strikingly different from European patterns, in which the rule of men over women and fathers over households was thought to be the social ideal.

Farming eventually led to the development of large, densely settled communities. These first developed in Mesoamerica, the region stretching from central Mexico to Central America, where by the first millennium BCE large urban communities were taking shape. By the beginning of the first millennium CE highly productive farming was supporting complex urban civilizations in the Valley of Mexico (the location of present-day Mexico City), the Yucatan Peninsula, and Guatemala. Like many of the ancient civilizations of Asia and the Mediterranean, these Mesoamerican civilizations were characterized by the concentration of wealth and power in the hands of an elite class of priests and rulers, the construction of impressive temples and other public structures, and the development of systems of mathematics and astronomy and several forms of hieroglyphic writing.

Growing populations demanded increasingly large surpluses of food, and this need often led to social conflict. Farming societies were considerably more complex than foraging bands, but they were also less stable, and required management by permanent bureaucracies. These societies were especially vulnerable to changes in climate, such as drought, as well as to crises of their own making, such as soil depletion or erosion. And, in the struggle for more arable land, they were more prone than hunting societies to engage in protracted warfare with each other. The elite rulers of these complex urban communities often staged terrifying public rituals of human torture and sacrifice as testimonials to their power. Skeletal remains from farming societies show much more evidence of violent death than the remains from hunter-gatherer societies.

A prominent example of an early urban civilization is the great city of Teotihuacan in the Valley of Mexico, which may have been populated by as many as 200,000 residents at its height around 500 CE. Teotihuacan's elite class of religious and political leaders controlled an elaborate state-sponsored trading system that stretched from present-day Arizona to Central America and may have included coastal shipping connections with Andean civilizations in South America. The city had a highly specialized division of labor. Artisans manufactured tools and produced textiles, stoneware, pottery, and obsidian blades. The bureaucratic elite collected taxes and tribute. Farmers worked the fields, and armies of workers constructed such monumental edifices as the Pyramids of the Sun and Moon, which still dominate the site's ruins.

Teotihuacan began to decline in the sixth century (for reasons that are not yet clear), and by the eighth century it was mostly abandoned. Its rulers were succeeded by a new ethnic power, the Toltecs, who dominated central Mexico from the tenth to the twelfth century. By the fourteenth century, a people known as the Aztecs, migrants from the north, had settled in the Valley of Mexico and begun a dramatic expansion into a formidable imperial power. (For the continuing history of the Aztecs, see Chapter 2.)

The Resisted Revolution

Historians once described the development of farming as a revolution. They believed that agricultural communities offered such obvious advantages that neighbors must have rushed to adopt this way of life. Societies that remained without a farming tradition were judged too "primitive" to achieve this breakthrough. This interpretation was based on a scheme of social evolution that saw human history as the story of technological progress, with hunters gradually developing into civilized farmers.

There is very little evidence to support this notion of a "revolution" occurring during a short, critical period. The adoption of farming was a gradual process, one that required hundreds, even thousands of years. Moreover, ignorance of cultivation was never the reason cultures failed to take up farming, for hunter-gatherer peoples understood a great deal about plant reproduction. When gathering wild rice, for example, the Menominee Indians of the northern forests of Wisconsin purposely allowed some of it to fall back into the water to ensure a crop for the next season. And the Paiutes of the Great Basin systematically irrigated stands of their favorite wild foods.

Surviving hunter-gatherers today generally look upon their own method of getting food as vastly superior to farming. The food sources of desert gatherers, for example, are considerably more varied and higher in protein than those of desert farmers, whose diets concentrate almost exclusively on maize. The results of this diet are evident in the skeletal remains of farming peoples, which suggest they were far more subject to malnutrition and tooth decay (a primary cause of death before modern dentistry). Because foragers took advantage of natural diversity, they were also less vulnerable to climatological stress; although gathering communities frequently experienced periods of scarcity and hunger, unlike farming societies they were rarely devastated by famine. Foragers also point out that farming requires much more work. Why sweat all day in the fields cultivating a crop of maize, they argue, when in an hour or two one can gather enough sweet prickly pear to last a week? Indeed, rather than freeing men and women from the tyranny of nature, farming tied people to a work discipline unlike anything previously known in human history. The skeletal evidence indicates that farming peoples suffered from a high frequency of degenerative joint disease, the result of strenuous and repetitive patterns of work.

As farming technology became available, cultures in different regions assessed its advantages and limitations. In California and the Pacific Northwest, acorn gathering or salmon fishing made the cultivation of food crops seem a waste of time. In the Great Basin, several peoples attempted to farm, but without long-term success. Before the invention of modern irrigation systems, which require sophisticated engineering, only the Archaic Desert Culture could prevail in this harsh environment. In the neighboring Southwest, however, farming resolved certain ecological dilemmas and transformed the way of life. Like the development of more sophisticated traditions of tool manufacture, farming represented another stage in economic intensifications (like the advance in toolmaking represented by Clovis technology) that kept populations and available resources in balance. It seems that where the climate favored it, people tended to adopt farming as a way of increasing the production of food, thus continuing the Archaic tradition of squeezing as much productivity as they could from their environment. In a few areas, however, farming truly did result in a revolutionary transformation, creating urban civilizations like the one in central Mexico or at Cahokia, on the banks of the Mississippi.

Farmers of the Southwest

Farming communities began to emerge in the arid Southwest during the first millennium BCE. Among the first to develop a settled farming way of life were a people known as the Mogollon, who farmed maize, beans, and squash, and constructed ingenious pit structures in permanent village sites along what is today the southern Arizona–New Mexico border. Those pits may have been the precursors of what Southwestern peoples today call kivas, sites of community religious rituals.

During the same centuries, a people known as the Hohokam ("those who are gone," in the language of the modern Pima people of the region) flourished along the floodplain of the Salt and Gila Rivers in southern Arizona. The Hohokam built and maintained the first irrigation system in America north of Mexico, channeling river water through five hundred miles of canals to water desert fields of maize, beans, squash, tobacco, and cotton. The Hohokam shared many traits with Mesoamerican civilization to the south, including platform mounds for religious ceremonies and large courts for ball playing. At a site near present-day Phoenix called Snaketown by the Pima Indians, archaeologists have recovered a variety of goods from central America—rubber balls, mirrors of pyrite mosaics, copper bells, and fashionable ear ornaments—suggesting that Snaketown may have housed a community of merchants who traded Mesoamerican manufactured goods for locally mined turquoise.

The Anasazis

The best-known farming culture of the Southwest is that of the Anasazis, which developed around the first century CE in the Four Corners area, where the states of Arizona, New Mexico, Utah, and Colorado meet on the great plateau of the Colorado River. Around 750, possibly in response to population pressure and an increasingly dry climate, the Anasazis began shifting from pit-house villages to densely populated, multistoried apartment complexes, called "pueblos" by the Spanish invaders of the sixteenth century. These clustered around central complexes with circular underground kivas. The Anasazis

Human figures dance on this characteristic piece of red-on-buff pottery of the Hohokams (dated about 1000 CE).
The Hohokams, located on the floodplain of the Gila River near present-day Phoenix, Arizona, were the first irrigation farmers of North America. The Pima and Tohono O'Odham people of Arizona may be descended from them.

SOURCE: Photograph by Helga Teiwes, Courtesy Arizona State Museum, University of Arizona.

grew high-yield varieties of maize in terraced fields irrigated by canals flowing from mountain catchment basins. To supplement this vegetable diet, they hunted animals, using the bow and arrow that first appeared in the region in the sixth century.

Anasazi culture extended over a very large area. More than 25,000 Anasazi sites are known in New Mexico alone, but only a few have been excavated, so there is much that archaeologists do not yet understand. Their most prominent center was Pueblo Bonito in Chaco Canyon. Completed in the twelfth century, this complex of 700 interconnected rooms is a monument to the Anasazi golden age. Hundreds of miles of arrow-straight roads and an interpueblo communication system consisting of mountaintop signaling stations connect Chaco Canyon to outlying sites, making it the center of a food distribution, trading, and ceremonial network.

The Anasazis faced a major challenge in the thirteenth century. The arid climate became even drier, and growing populations had to redouble their efforts to improve food production, building increasingly complex irrigation canals,

Cliff Palace, at Mesa Verde National Park in southwest Colorado, was created 900 years ago when the Anasazis left the mesa tops and moved into more secure and inaccessible cliff dwellings. Facing southwest, the building gained heat from the rays of the low afternoon sun in winter, and overhanging rock protected the structure from rain, snow, and the hot midday summer sun. The numerous round kivas, each covered with a flat roof originally, suggest that Cliff Palace may have had a ceremonial importance.

SOURCE: David Muench/CORBIS-NY.

dams, and terraced fields. A devastating drought from 1276 to 1293 (precisely dated by analysis of tree-rings) resulted in repeated crop failures and famine. This ecological crisis was heightened by the arrival in the region of Athapascan migrants, the ancestors of the Navajos and the Apaches, who for a thousand years or more had been moving south from the Subarctic. By the fourteenth century, Athapascan warriors were raiding Anasazi farming communities, taking food, goods, and possibly slaves. (Indeed, the name Anasazi means "ancient enemies" in the Athapascan language.) Gradually the Anasazis abandoned the Four Corners area altogether, most resettling in communities along the Rio Grande, joining with local residents to form the Pueblo communities living there when the Spanish arrived.

Farmers of the Eastern Woodlands

Archaeologists date the beginning of the farming culture of eastern North America, known as Woodland culture, from the first appearances of pottery in the region about 3,000 years ago. Woodland culture was based on a sophisticated way of life that combined hunting and gathering with the cultivation of local crops such as sunflowers and small grains, providing the people with seeds and cooking oil. The presence of pipes in archaeological digs indicates that Woodland farmers also grew tobacco, which spread north from the Caribbean, where it was first domesticated. These eastern peoples lived most of the year in permanent community sites, but moved seasonally to take advantage of the resources such as fishing, hunting, and the gathering of wild plants at different locations.

The Woodland peoples of the Ohio Valley were notable for their tradition of mound building. In the first millennium BCE, a culture archaeologists have named Adena established the practice. Adena culture was followed by another known as Hopewell, whose adherents honored their dead by constructing even larger and more elaborate mounds. The ancient Hopewell site at Chillicothe, Ohio, for example, features a complex of earthen embankments laid out as a series of large, interlinked circles and squares, that includes conical and loaf-shaped mounds thirty feet high. Excavations of these earthworks exposed large underground chambers, apparently the tombs of important leaders, and included rare and precious artifacts. Hopewell chiefs mobilized an elaborate trade network that acquired obsidian from the Rocky Mountains, copper from the Great Lakes, mica from the Appalachians, and shells from the Gulf coast. Artisans converted these materials into goods that played an important role in Hopewell trade and were included as grave goods in the mounds.

Mississippian Society

Hopewell culture collapsed in the fifth century CE, perhaps as a result of an ecological crisis brought on by shifting climate patterns. Local communities continued to practice their late Archaic subsistence strategies, but abandoned the expensive cultural displays of mound building. Over the next several centuries, however, a number of important technological innovations were introduced in the East. The bow and arrow, first developed on the Great Plains, appeared east of the Mississippi about the seventh century, greatly increasing the efficiency of hunting. At about the same time, a new variety of maize known today as Northern Flint was developed by Indian farmers of the East; with large cobs and plentiful kernels, it matured in a short enough time to make it suitable for cultivation in temperate northern latitudes. A shift from digging sticks to flint hoes also took place about this time, further increasing the productive potential of maize farming.

On the basis of these innovations, a powerful new culture known as Mississippian arose. The

The Great Serpent Mound in southern Ohio, the shape of an uncoiling snake more than 1,300 feet long, is the largest effigy earthwork in the world. Monumental public works like these suggest the high degree of social organization of the Mississippian people.
SOURCE: Tony Linck. SuperStock, Inc.

Mississippians were master maize farmers who lived in permanent settlements along the floodplains of the Mississippi Valley. Cahokia was the largest of these sites, with its monumental temple, its residential neighborhoods, and its surrounding farmlands. But there were dozens of other cities, each with thousands of residents. Archaeologists have excavated urban sites on the Arkansas River near Spiro, Oklahoma; on the Black Warrior River at Moundville, Alabama; at Hiawassee Island on the Tennessee River; and along the Etowah and Okmulgee Rivers in Georgia. The Great Serpent Mound, the largest effigy earthwork in the world, was constructed by Mississippian peoples in southern Ohio.

These centers, linked by the vast river transportation system of the Mississippi River and its tributaries, became the earliest city-states north of Mexico, hierarchical chiefdoms that extended political control over the farmers of the surrounding countryside (see Map 1.3 for a map of trade networks). Their urban designs echoed the cities of Mesoamerica, rectangular plazas bounded by platform mounds. With continued population growth, these cities engaged in vigorous and probably violent competition for the limited space along the rivers. It may have been the need for more orderly ways of allocating territories that stimulated the evolution of political hierarchies. The tasks of preventing local conflict, storing large food surpluses,

MAP EXPLORATION

To explore an interactive version of this map, go to **www.prenhall.com/faragher5/map1.3**

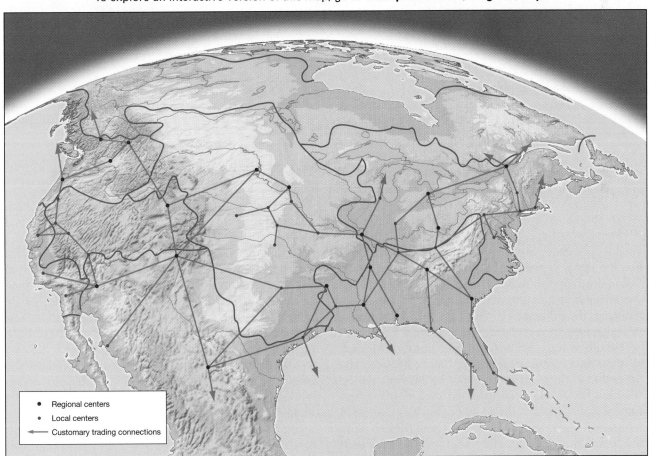

MAP 1.3   Native North American Trade Networks, ca. 1400 CE By determining the origin of artifacts found at ancient sites, historians have devised a conjectural map of Indian trade networks. Among large regional centers and smaller local ones, trade connected Indian peoples of many different communities and regions.

The City of Cahokia, with a population of more than 30,000, was the center of a farming society
that arose on the Mississippi bottomlands near present-day St. Louis in the tenth century CE.
The Cahokians built dozens of vast earthen mound covering six square miles, evidence
of their complex social organization.

SOURCE: Cahokia Mounds State Historic Site, painting by Michael Hampshire.

and redistributing foodstuffs from farmers to artisans and elites required a leadership class with the power to command. Mound building and the use of tribute labor in the construction of other public works testified to the power of chiefs, who lived in sumptuous quarters atop the mounds. The excavation of one mound at Cahokia uncovered the burial chamber of a chief, who was accompanied in death by the bodies of dozens of young men and women, undoubtedly the victims of sacrifice. If politics is defined as the organized contest for power among people and groups, then the Mississippians (and the Anasazis) were the first truly political societies north of Mexico. Mississippian culture reached its height between the eleventh and thirteenth centuries CE, the same period in which the Anasazis constructed their desert cities. Both groups adapted to their own environment the technology that was spreading northward from Mexico. Both developed impressive artistic traditions, and their feats of engineering reflect the beginnings of science and technology. They were complex societies characterized by urbanism, social stratification, craft specialization, and regional trade—except for the absence of a writing system, all the traits of European civilization.

The Politics of Warfare and Violence

The late thirteenth century marked the end of several hundred years of weather very favorable to maize farming and the beginning of a century and a half of cool, dry conditions. Although the changes in climate in the Mississippi Valley were not as severe as those that devastated the Anasazis of the Southwest, over the long term they significantly lowered the potential of farming to support growing urban populations. Some archaeologists have suggested that one consequence of this extended drought may have been greatly increased violence and social disorder.

Warfare among Indian peoples certainly predated the colonial era. Organized violence was probably rare among hunting bands, who seldom could manage more than a small raid against an enemy. Certain hunting peoples, though, such as the southward-moving Athapascans, must have engaged in systematic raiding of settled farming communities. Warfare was also common among farming confederacies fighting to gain additional lands for cultivation. The first Europeans to arrive in the southeastern part of the continent described highly organized combat among large tribal armies. The bow and arrow was a deadly weapon of war, and the practice of scalping seems to have originated among warring tribes, who believed one could capture a warrior's spirit by taking his scalp lock.

The archaeological remains of Cahokia reveal that during the thirteenth and fourteenth centuries, the residents enclosed the central sections of their city with a heavy log stockade. There must have been a great deal of violent warfare with other nearby communities. Also during this period, numerous towns were formed throughout the river valleys of the Mississippi, each based on the domination of farming countrysides by metropolitan centers. Eventually conditions in the upper Mississippi Valley deteriorated so badly that Cahokia and many other sites were abandoned altogether, and as the cities collapsed, people relocated in smaller, decentralized communities. Among the peoples of the South, however, Mississippian patterns continued into the period of colonization.

This bottle in the shape of a nursing mother (dated about 1300 BCE) was found at a Mississippian site. Historians can only speculate about the thoughts and feelings of the Mississippians, but such works of art are testimonials to the universal human emotion of maternal affection.

SOURCE: *Nursing Mother Effigy Bottle.* From the Whelpley Collection at the St. Louis Science Center. WL-23. Photograph © 1985 the Detroit Institute of Arts.

CULTURAL REGIONS OF NORTH AMERICA ON THE EVE OF COLONIZATION

An appreciation of the ways human cultures adapted to geography and climate is fundamental to an understanding of American history, for just as regions shaped the development of Indian cultures in the centuries before the arrival of Europeans, so they continued to influence the character of American life in the centuries thereafter. In order to understand the impact of regions on Indian cultures, anthropologists divide North America into several distinct "culture areas" within which, groups shared a significant number of cultural traits: Arctic, Subarctic, Great Basin, Great Plains, California, Northwest, Plateau, Southwest, South, and Northeast.

The Population of Indian America

In determining the precolonial population of the Americas, historical demographers consider a number of factors—the earliest European accounts, the archaeological evidence, and the "carrying capacity" of different cultural regions. Determining the size of early human population is a tricky business, and estimates differ greatly, but there seems to be general agreement that the population of North America (excluding Mexico) was between 5 and 10 million in the fifteenth century. Millions more lived in the complex societies of Mesoamerica (estimates run from as low as 5 million to as high as 25 million). The population of the Western Hemisphere as a whole may have numbered 50 million or more, in the same range as Europe's population at the time.

Scholars disagree about the numbers, but agree that population varied tremendously by cultural region (see Map 1.4). Although the cultural regions of the Arctic, Subarctic, Great Basin, and Great Plains made up more than half the physical space of the continent, in the fifteenth century they were inhabited by only a small fraction of the native population. Those regions were home to scattered bands who continued to practice the Archaic economy of hunting and gathering. The Archaic way of life continued in California as well, although the population there was large and dense because of the natural abundance of the region. In the Northwest, the narrow coastal strip running 2,000 miles from northern California to southern Alaska, abundant salmon fisheries supported large populations concentrated in permanent villages. The Indian societies of the Northwest coast were characterized by an elaborate material culture and by their "potlatch" ceremonies, where prestige and rank were accumulated by those people who could give away

MAP **EXPLORATION**

To explore an interactive version of this map, go to **www.prenhall.com/faragher5/map1.4**

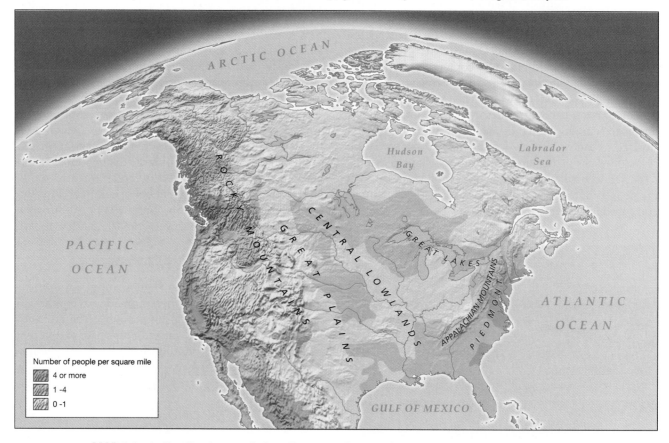

MAP 1.4   Indian Settlement Before European Colonization Based on what is called the
"carrying capacity" of different subsistence strategies—the population density they could support—
historical demographers have mapped the hypothetical population density of Indian societies in the
fifteenth century, before the era of European colonization. Populations were densest in farming societies
or in coastal areas with marine resources and sparsest in extreme environments like the Great Basin.

the most goods. The people of the Plateau also made
their living by fishing, but their communities were not
as large or as concentrated.

The largest populations of the continent were concentrated in the farming districts of the Southwest, the
South, and the Northeast. And since it was in those culture areas that European explorers, conquerors, and
colonists first concentrated their efforts, they deserve
more detailed examination.

The Southwest

The single overwhelming fact of life in the Southwest is
aridity. Summer rains average only ten to twenty inches
annually, and on much of the dry desert cultivation is impos-

sible. A number of rivers, however, flow out of the pine-cov-
ered mountain plateaus. Flowing south to the Gulf of Mexico or the Gulf of California, these narrow bands of green
winding through parched browns and reds have made possible irrigation farming along their courses (see Map 1.5).

On the eve of European colonization, Indian farmers
had been cultivating their Southwest fields for nearly 3,000
years. In the floodplain of the Gila and Salt Rivers lived the
Pimas and Tohono O'Odhams, descendants of the ancient
Hohokams, and along the Colorado River the Yuman peoples worked small irrigated fields. In their oasis communities, desert farmers cultivated corn, beans, squash, sunflowers,
and cotton, which they traded throughout the Southwest.
Often described as individualists, desert farmers lived in dispersed settlements that the Spanish called rancherias, their

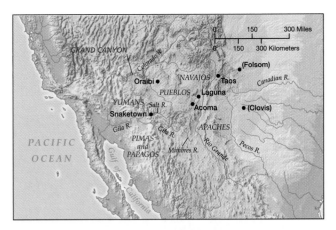

MAP 1.5   Southwestern Indian Groups on the Eve of Colonization The Southwest was populated by desert farmers like the Pimas, Tohono O'Odhams, Yumans, and Pueblos, as well as by nomadic hunters and raiders like the Apaches and Navajos.

dwellings separated by as much as a mile. That way, say the Pimas, people avoid getting on each other's nerves. Rancherias were governed by councils of adult men whose decisions required unanimous consent, although a headman was chosen to manage the irrigation works.

East of the Grand Canyon lived the Pueblo peoples, named by the Spanish for their unique dwellings of stacked, interconnected apartments. Although speaking several languages, the Pueblos had a great deal in common, most notably their commitment to communal village life. A strict communal code of behavior that regulated personal conduct was enforced by a maze of matrilineal clans and secret religious societies; unique combinations of these clans and societies formed the governing systems of different Pueblo villages. Seasonal public ceremonies in the village squares included singing and chanting, dancing, colorful impersonations of the ancestral spirits called kachinas, and the comic antics of clowns who mocked in slapstick style those who did not conform to the communal ideal (pretending to drink urine or eat dirt, for example, in front of the home of a person who kept an unclean house).

The Pueblos inhabit the oldest continuously occupied towns in the United States. The village of Oraibi, Arizona, dates from the twelfth century, when the Hopis ("peaceful ones") founded it in the isolated central mesas of the Colorado Plateau. Using dry-farming methods and drought-resistant plants, the Hopis produced rich harvests of corn and squash amid shifting sand dunes. On a mesa top about fifty miles southwest of present-day Albuquerque, New Mexico, Anasazi immigrants from Mesa Verde built Acoma, the "sky city," in the late thirteenth century. The Pueblo peoples established approximately seventy other villages over the next two centuries; fifty of these were still in existence when the Spanish founded Santa Fé at the beginning of the sev-

enteenth century, and two dozen survive today, including the large Indian towns of Laguna, Isleta, Santo Domingo, Jémez, San Felipe, and Taos.

The Athapascans, more recent immigrants to the Southwest, also lived in the arid deserts and mountains. They hunted and foraged, traded meat and medicinal herbs with farmers, and often raided and plundered these same villages and rancherias. Gradually, some of the Athapascan people adopted the farming and handicraft skills of their Pueblo neighbors; they became known as the Navajos. Others, more heavily influenced by the hunting and gathering traditions of the Great Basin and Great Plains, remained nomadic and became known as the Apaches.

The South

The South enjoys a mild, moist climate with short winters and long summers, ideal for farming. From the Atlantic and Gulf Coasts, a broad fertile plain extends inland to the Piedmont, a plateau separating the coastal plains from the Appalachian Mountains. The upper courses of the waterways originating in the Appalachian highlands offered ample rich bottom land for farming. The extensive forests, mostly of yellow pine, offered abundant animal resources. In the sixteenth century, large populations of Indian peoples farmed this rich land, fishing or hunting local fauna to supplement their diets. They lived in communities ranging from villages of twenty or so dwellings to large towns of a thousand or more inhabitants (see Map 1.6).

Mississippian cultural patterns continued among many of the peoples of the South. Many of the farming towns along the waterways were organized into chiefdoms. Because most of these groups were decimated by disease in the first years of colonization, they are poorly documented. We know most about the Natchez, farmers of

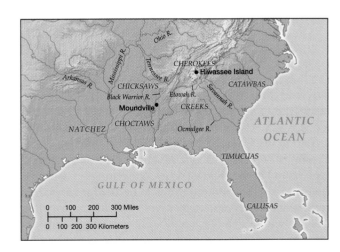

MAP 1.6   Southern Indian Groups on the Eve of Colonization On the eve of colonization, the Indian societies of the South shared many traits of the complex Mississippian farming culture.

The New Queen Being Taken to the King, engraved by Theodor de Bry in the sixteenth century from a drawing by Jacques le Moyne, an early French colonist of Florida. The communities of Florida were hierarchical, with classes and hereditary chiefs, some of whom were women. Here, le Moyne depicted a "queen" being carried on an ornamental litter by men of rank.

SOURCE: Neg. No. 324281, Photographed by Rota, Engraving by DeBry. American Museum of Natural History Library.

the rich floodplains of the lower Mississippi Delta, who survived into the eighteenth century before being destroyed in a war with the French. (See Out of Many Voices: An Account of the Natchez by a Louisiana Colonist). Overseeing the Natchez was a ruler known as the Great Sun, who lived in royal splendor on a ceremonial mound in the capital. When out among his subjects, he was carried on a litter, the path before him swept by his retinue of servants and wives. Natchez was a class society, with a small group of nobility ruling the majority. Persistent territorial conflict with other confederacies elevated warriors to an honored status among the Natchez. Public torture and human sacrifice of enemies were common. The Natchez give us our best glimpse of what life would have been like in the community of Cahokia.

These chiefdoms were rather unstable. Under the pressure of climate change, population growth, and warfare, many were weakened and others collapsed. As a result, thousands of people left the grand mounds and earthworks behind and migrated to the woodlands and hill country, where they took up hunting and foraging, returning to the tried and true methods of "forest efficiency." They formed communities and banded together in confederacies, which were less centralized and more egalitarian than the Mississippian chiefdoms, and would prove considerably more resilient to conquest.

Among the most prominent of these new ethnic groups were a people in present-day Mississippi and Alabama who came to be known as the Choctaws. Another group in western Tennessee became known as the Chickasaws, and

OUT OF MANY VOICES

AN ACCOUNT OF THE NATCHEZ BY A LOUISIANA COLONIST

Mississippian cultural patterns—maize farming, urban living, and rule by an elite class—persisted into the period of European colonization. Antoine Simon Le Page Du Pratz, a Dutchman and a Louisiana colonist of the early eighteenth century, wrote an extended account of the region. In this excerpt, he describes the "Great Corn Feast" of the Natchez and the role of their leader, "The Great Sun."

THIS FEAST IS BEYOND DISPUTE THE MOST SOLEMN of all. It principally consists in eating in common, and in a religious manner, of new corn, which had been sown expressly with that design, with suitable ceremonies. This corn is sown upon a spot of ground never before cultivated; which ground is dressed and prepared by the warriors alone, who also are the only persons that sow the corn, weed it, reap it, and gather it.

When this corn is near ripe, the warriors fix on a place proper for the general feast, and close adjoining to that they form a round granary, the bottom and sides of which are of cane; this they fill, with the corn, and when they have finished the harvest, and covered the granary, they acquaint the Great Sun, who appoints the day for the general feast. Some days before the feast, they build huts for the Great Sun, and for all the other families, round the granary, that of the Great Sun being raised upon a mound of earth.

On the feast-day the whole nation set out from their village at sun-rising, leaving behind only the aged and infirm that are not able to travel, and a few warriors, who are to carry the Great Sun on a litter upon their shoulders. The seat of this litter is covered with several deer skins, and to its four sides are fastened four bars which cross each other, and are supported by eight men, who at every hundred paces transfer their burden to eight other men, and thus successively transport it to the place where the feast is celebrated, which may be near two miles from the village. About nine o'clock the Great Sun comes out of his hut dressed in the ornaments of his dignity, and being placed in his litter, which has a canopy at the head formed of flowers, he is carried in a few minutes to the sacred granary, shouts of joy re-echoing on all sides.

Before he alights he makes the tour of the whole place deliberately, and when he comes before the corn, he salutes it thrice with the words, *hoo, hoo, hoo,* lengthened and pronounced respectfully. The salutation is repeated by the whole nation, who pronounce the word *hoo* nine times distinctly, and at the ninth time he alights and places himself on his throne. ■

SOURCE: Antoine Simon Le Page Du Pratz, *The History of Louisiana, or of the Western Parts of Virginia and Carolina* (London: T. Becket and P.A. De Honat, 1774), pp. 338–339.

---

another people in Georgia later became known as the Creeks. On the mountain plateaus lived the Cherokees, the single largest confederacy, which included more than sixty towns. For these groups, farming was somewhat less important, hunting somewhat more so. There were no ruling classes or kings, and leaders included women as well as men. Most peoples reckoned their descent matrilineally (back through generations of mothers), and after marriage, husbands left the homes of their mothers to reside with the families of their wives. Women controlled household and village life, and were influential in the matrilineal clans that linked communities together. Councils of elderly men governed the confederacies, but were joined by clan matrons for annual meetings at the central council house.

The peoples of the South celebrated a common round of agricultural festivals that brought clans together from sur-

rounding communities. At the harvest festival, for example, people thoroughly cleaned their homes and villages. They fasted and purified themselves by consuming "black drink," which induced hallicinations and visions. They extinguished the old fires and lit new ones, then celebrated the new crop of sweet corn with dancing and other festivities. During the days that followed, villages, clans, and groups of men and women competed against one another in the ancient stick-and-ball game that the French named lacrosse; in the evenings men and women played chunkey, a gambling game.

The Northeast

The Northeast, the colder sector of the eastern woodlands, has a varied geography of coastal plains and mountain highlands, great rivers, lakes, and valleys. In the first

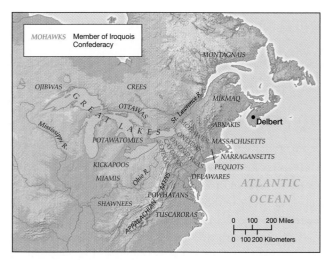

**MAP 1.7 Northeastern Indian Groups on the Eve
of Colonization** The Indians of the Northeast were mostly
village peoples. In the fifteenth century, five Iroquois groups—
the Mohawks, Oneidas, Onondagas, Cayugas, and Senecas—joined
together to form the Iroquois Five Nation Confederacy.

millenium CE, farming became the main support of the
Indian economy in those places where the growing season was long enough to bring a crop of corn to matu-
rity. In such areas of the Northeast, along the coasts and
in the river valleys, Indian populations were large and
dense (see Map 1.7).

The Iroquois of present-day Ontario and upstate
New York have lived in the Northeast for at least
4,500 years and were among the first peoples of the
region to adopt cultivation. Iroquois women produced
crops of corn, beans, squash, and sunflowers sufficient to support up to fifty longhouses, each occupied by a large matrilineal extended family. Some of
those houses were truly long; archaeologists have
excavated the foundations of some that extended 400
feet and would have housed dozens of families. Typically, these villages were surrounded by substantial
wooden walls or palisades, clear evidence of inter-
group conflict and warfare.

Population growth and the resulting intensifica-
tion of farming in Iroquoia stimulated the development
of chiefdoms there as elsewhere. By the fifteenth century, several centers of population, each in a separate
watershed, had coalesced from east to west across
upstate New York. These were the five Iroquois chiefdoms or nations: the Mohawks, Oneidas, Onondagas,
Cayugas, and Senecas. Iroquois oral histories collected
during the nineteenth century recall this as a period
of persistent violence, possibly the consequence of
conflicts over territory.

To control this violence, the Iroquois founded a confederacy in which warfare among the member nations
was outlawed, gift exchange and payment replacing
revenge. Iroquois oral history refers to the founder of the
confederacy, Chief Deganawida, "blocking out the sun" as
a demonstration of his powers. From this bit of evidence,
some historians have suggested that the founding might
have taken place during the full solar eclipse in the Northeast in the year 1451. Deganawida's message was proclaimed by his supporter, Hiawatha, a great orator, who
convinced all the five Iroquois nations to join in confederacy. As a model of their government, the confederacy
used the metaphor of the longhouse; each nation, it was
said, occupied a separate hearth but acknowledged a common mother. As in the longhouse, women played important roles in the confederacy, choosing male leaders who
would represent their lineages and chiefdom on the Iroquois council. The confederacy suppressed violence
among its members, but did not hesitate to encourage
war against neighboring Iroquoian speakers, such as the
Hurons or the Eries, who constructed defensive confederacies of their own at about the same time.

The other major language group of the Northeast
was Algonquian, whose speakers divided among at least
fifty distinct cultures. The Algonquian peoples north of
the Great Lakes and in northern New England were
hunters and foragers, organized into bands with loose
ethnic affiliations. Several of these peoples, including
the Míkmaq, Crees, Montagnais, and Ojibwas (also
known as the Chippewas), were the first to become
involved in the fur trade with European newcomers.
Among the Algonquians of the Atlantic coast from
present-day Massachusetts south to Virginia, as well
as among those in the Ohio Valley, farming led to the
development of settlements as densely populated as
those of the Iroquois.

In contrast to the Iroquois, most Algonquian peoples
were patrilineal. In general, they lived in less extensive
dwellings and in smaller villages, often without palisade
fortifications. Although Algonquian communities were
relatively autonomous, they began to form confederacies
during the fifteenth and sixteenth centuries. Among
these groupings were those of the Massachusetts, Narragansetts, and Pequots of New England; the Delawares
and the peoples of Powhatan's confederacy on the mid-
Atlantic coast; and the Shawnees, Miamis, Kickapoos,
and Potawatomis of the Ohio Valley.

CONCLUSION

Over the thousands of years that elapsed between the
settlement of North America and the invasion of Europeans at the end of the fifteenth century, Indian peoples

C H R O N O L O G Y

30,000 BCE	First humans populate Beringia
13,000 BCE	Global warming trend begins
10,000 BCE	Clovis technology
9000 BCE	Extinction of big-game animals
8000 BCE	Beginning of the Archaic period
7000 BCE	First cultivation of plants in the Mexican highlands
5000 BCE	Athapascan migrations to America begin
4000 BCE	First settled communities along the Pacific coast
3000 BCE	Inuit, Yupik, and Aleut migrations begin
1500– 1000 BCE	Maize and other Mexican crops introduced into the Southwest
1000 BCE	Beginning of Adena culture. First urban communities in Mexico
250 BCE	Beginning of Mogollon culture in the Southwest

200 BCE– 400 CE	Hopewell culture flourishes
650	Bow and arrow, flint hoes, and Northern Flint corn in the Northeast
775–1150	Hohokam site of Snaketown reaches its greatest extent
1000	Tobacco in use throughout North America
1150	Founding of Hopi village of Oraibi, oldest continuously occupied town in the United States
1200	High point of Mississippian and Anasazi cultures
1276	Severe drought begins in the Southwest
1300	Arrival of Athapascans in the Southwest
1451	Founding of Iroquois Confederacy

developed hundreds of distinctive cultures that were fine-tuned to the geographic and climatic possibilities and limitations of their homelands. In the northern forests, they hunted game and perfected the art of processing furs and hides. Along the coasts and rivers they harvested the abundant runs of fish and learned to navigate the waters with sleek and graceful boats. In the arid Southwest, they mastered irrigation farming and made the deserts bloom, while in the humid Southeast, they mastered the large-scale production of crops that could sustain large cities with sophisticated political systems. North America was not a "virgin" continent, as so many of the Europeans believed. Indians had trans-formed the natural world, making it over into a human landscape.

"Columbus did not discover a new world," writes historian J. H. Perry, "he established contact between two worlds, both already old." North America had a rich history, one that Europeans did not understand and that later generations of Americans have too frequently ignored. The European colonists who came to settle encountered thousands of Indian communities with deep roots and vibrant traditions. In the confrontation that followed, Indian communities viewed the colonists as invaders and called upon their traditions and their own gods to help them defend their homelands.

REVIEW QUESTIONS

1. List the evidence for the hypothesis that the Americas were settled by migrants from Asia.
2. Discuss the impact of environmental change and human hunting on the big-game populations of North America.
3. Review the principal regions of the North American continent and the human adaptations that made social life possible in each of them.
4. Define the concept of "forest efficiency." How does it help to illuminate the major development of the Archaic period?

5. Why did the development of farming lead to increasing social complexity? Discuss the reasons why organized political activity began in farming societies.
6. What were the Hunting and Agrarian Traditions? In what ways did the religious beliefs of Indian peoples reflect their environmental adaptations?
7. What factors led to the organization of the Iroquois Confederacy?

RECOMMENDED READING

Sally Kitt Chappell, *Cahokia: Mirror of the Cosmos* (2002). An engaging, comprehensive, and thoughtful account of America's most impressive ancient monument.

Tom D. Dillehay, *The Settling of the Americas: A New Prehistory* (2000). A summary of the most recent archaeological findings, suggesting a much earlier migration to the Americas. For the newest discoveries, see the recent issues and websites of *National Geographic* and *Scientific American*.

Roger C. Echo-Hawk and Walter R. Echo-Hawk, *Battlefields and Burial Grounds: The Indian Struggle to Protect Ancestral Graves in the United States* (1994). A passionate discussion by a Pawnee lawyer and historian of the double standard that allows Indian graves to be ransacked while white graves are held sacred.

Patricia Galloway, *Choctaw Genesis, 1500–1700* (1995). A path-breaking work that uses both archaeological and written evidence to tie together the precolonial and colonial periods of a tribal people of the South.

David P. Henige, *Numbers from Nowhere: The American Indian Contact Population Debate* (1998). A penetrating critique of the methodology of estimating early Native American populations.

Alvin M. Josephy Jr., ed., *America in 1492* (1992). Important essays by leading scholars of the North American Indian experience. Includes beautiful illustrations and maps as well as an excellent bibliography.

Alice Beck Kehoe, *America Before the European Invasions* (2002). A major new synthesis of the history of North America in the centuries before 1492.

Stephen Plog, *Ancient Peoples of the American Southwest* (1998). Covers the shift to agriculture with a focus on both the costs and the benefits. An accessible text with wonderful photographs.

Robert Silverberg, *Mound Builders of Ancient America: The Archaeology of a Myth* (1968). A history of opinion and theory about the mound builders.

William C. Sturtevant, general ed., *Handbook of North American Indians*, 20 vols. proposed (1978–). The most comprehensive collection of the best current scholarship. The completed series will include a volume for each of the culture regions of North America; volumes on origins, Indian-white relations, languages, and art; a biographical dictionary; and a general index.

David Hurst Thomas, *Skull Wars: Kennewick Man, Archaeology, and the Battle for Native American Identity* (2000). A readable account of the controversy over Kennewick Man and the changing ideas about ancient North American history. When scholars, bureaucrats, and Indians go to court over these issues, he argues, everyone loses.

Russell Thornton, *American Indian Holocaust and Survival: A Population History since 1492* (1987). The best introduction to the historical demography of North America. Provides a judicious review of all the evidence in a field of considerable controversy.

 For additional study resources for this chapter, go to the *Companion Website*, **http://www.prenhall.com/faragher**.

WHOSE HISTORY IS IT?

IMAGES OF INDIANS

Despite their diversity, Europeans lumped the native peoples of the Americas together in the single stereotype of "the Indian," an image that has demonstrated remarkable continuity from the sixteenth century to the present. The first of them featured naked men and women, adorned with feathers, engaged in various acts of savagery. This quickly became a fixed stereotype, and was effectively employed to portray Indians as the inevitable enemies of progress and civilization.

"Americans tend to clump us all together" explains Ron His Horse Is Thunder, a Lakota and president of Sitting Bull College in North Dakota. "Too often history books portray us as savages that stood in the way of progress. But what they don't show is that we made contributions to the United States. They don't tell about how over 50 percent of the world's current food supply comes from plants that Native Americans cultivated. . . . A good many current medicines in this world came from plants that Native Americans knew about and knew how to use to take care of certain ailments. And they shared that knowledge with the non-Indian world. People need to know that Indians used math and science for their daily lives, prior to the coming of the Europeans."

A new opportunity to understand Indian peoples in all their complexity comes with the opening in 2004 of the new national Museum of the American Indian in Washington, D. C. In order to evoke authentic images of native people, museum designers and curators have worked with hundreds of native communities to arrange, display, and interpret native artifacts in new ways.

This woodcut, illustrating a 1505 German edition of Amerigo Vespucci's account of his voyage to the New World in 1501-02, is the first image of American Indians published in Europe. As arriving European vessels appear on the horizon, a group of befeathered Indians engage in a cannibal feast. Three warriors with bows stand on the right, while under the bower a couple kisses as they share the severed human limbs. In the center a mother nurses a baby and tends children. The tender details underscore the horror of the scene.

Bayerisches Staatsbibliothek, Munich.

John Vanderlyn's "The Death of Jean McCrea" (1804) depicted an incident of the Revolution, the murder and scalping of a Patriot woman by warriors fighting with the British. Sensational in its own time, the painting perpetuated the image of Indians as inhumane savages and the enemies of white womanhood.

John Vanderlyn, *The Death of Jean McCrea*, 1804. Oil on Canvas. 32" x 26 1/2". Courtesy Wadsworth Atheneum, Hartford, Connecticut.

The striking National Museum of the American Indian, on the Capitol Mall in Washington, D. C., contains nearly a million artifacts and is dedicated to depicting the native peoples of the Americas in all their complexity.

Molly Riley/Reuters Landov LLC.

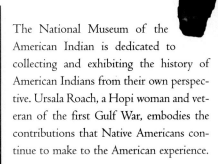

The National Museum of the American Indian is dedicated to collecting and exhibiting the history of American Indians from their own perspective. Ursala Roach, a Hopi woman and veteran of the first Gulf War, embodies the contributions that Native Americans continue to make to the American experience.

Courtesy, National Museum of the American Indian, Smithsonian Institution.

My Indian Name is " Eagles Cry," my story is alive.

James Fraser's "The End of the Trail" (1915), a monumental sculpture created for the Panama-Pacific International Exposition in San Francisco. The subject of immediate and sustained popular acclaim, it was widely reproduced in postcard, print, and miniature form. Generally interpreted as the symbol of a noble people, to many Native Americans it was part of an enduring and vicious stereotype of the "vanishing Indian."

Peter Harholdt - CORBIS - NY.

Deloris Aitson, left, and Rita Coosewoon at opening day of the National Museum of the American Indian. Nearly two-thirds of the more than four million Native Americans in the United States live in urban metropolitan areas, and nearly a quarter are employed in management, professional, or related occupations. 383,000 are veterans of the armed forces.

©2004 The Washington Post. Photo by Andrea Bruce Woodall. Reprinted with permission.

CHAPTER 2

When Worlds Collide

1492–1590

CHAPTER OUTLINE

The English and the Algonquins at Roanoke

It was late August 1590 when English ships made their way north through rough seas to Roanoke Island (off the coast of present-day North Carolina) where Governor John White had left the first English community in North America three years before. Anxiously, White went ashore in search of the 115 colonists—mostly single men, but also twenty families, including his own daughter, son-in-law, and granddaughter Virginia Dare, the first English baby born in America. Finding the houses "taken down" and possessions "spoiled and scattered about," White suddenly noticed some writing on a tree trunk: "in fair capital letters was graven CROATOAN." Because this was the name of a friendly Indian village fifty miles south and because White found no sign of a cross, which he had instructed the colonists to leave if they were in trouble, he felt sure that his people awaited him at Croatoan, and he returned to his ship, anxious to speed to their rescue.

Walter Raleigh, a wealthy adventurer who sought profit and prestige by organizing an English colony to compete with Spain's powerful empire in the New World, had sponsored the Roanoke settlement. When his men returned from a reconnoitering expedition to the area in 1584, they reported that the coastal region was densely populated by a "very handsome and goodly people." These Indians, the most southerly of the Algonquian coastal peoples, enjoyed a prosperous livelihood farming, fishing, and hunting from their small villages of one or two dozen communal houses. At an island the Indians called Roanoke, the English had been "entertained with all love and kindness" by a chief named Wingina. The leader of several surrounding villages, Wingina welcomed the English as potential allies in his struggle to extend his authority over still others. So when Raleigh's adventurers asked the chief's permission to establish a settlement on the island, he readily granted it, even sending two of his men back to England to assist in preparations. Manteo and Wanchese, the Indian emissaries, worked with Thomas Harriot, an Oxford scholar, and John White, an artist. The four men learned one another's language, and there seems to have been a good deal of mutual respect among them.

But when an all-male force of Englishmen returned in 1585 to establish the colony of Virginia (christened in honor of England's virgin queen, Elizabeth I), the two Indian emissaries offered Chief Wingina conflicting reports. Although Manteo, from the village of Croatoan, argued that their technology would make the English powerful allies, Wanchese described the disturbing inequalities of English society and warned of potential brutality. He rightly suspected English intentions, for Raleigh's plans were not based on the expectation that the Indians would be treated as equals, but as serfs to be exploited. Wanchese warned of their treachery. Indeed, Raleigh had directed the mission's commander to "proceed with extremity" should the Indians prove difficult to subjugate. Raleigh anticipated that his colony would return profits through the lucrative trade in furs, a flourishing plantation agriculture, or gold and silver mines with the Indians supplying the labor.

The English colony was incapable of supporting itself, and the colonists turned to Wingina for supplies. With the harvest in the storage pits, with fish running in the streams and fat game in the woods, Wingina did the hospitable thing. But as fall turned to winter and the stores declined,

Roanoke

constant English demands threatened the Indians' resources. Wingina's people were also stunned by the strange new diseases that came with the intruders. "The people began to die very fast, and many in [a] short space," Harriot wrote. In the spring, Wingina and his people ran out of patience. But before the Indians could act, the English caught wind of the rising hostility, and in May 1586 they surprised the villagers, killing several of the leading men and beheading Wingina. With the plan of using Indian labor now clearly impossible, the colonists returned to England.

John White and Thomas Harriot were appalled by this turn of events. Harriot insisted (or argued) to Raleigh that "through discreet dealing" the Indians might "honor, obey, fear and love us." White proposed a new plan for a colony of real settlers who might live in harmony with the Indians. Harriot and White clearly considered English civilization superior to Indian society, but their vision of colonization was considerably different from that of the plunderers.

In 1587, Raleigh arranged for John White to return to America as governor of a new civilian colony. The party was supposed to land on Chesapeake Bay, but their captain dumped them instead at Roanoke so he could get on with the profitable activity of plundering the Spanish. Thus the colonists found themselves amid natives who were alienated by the bad treatment of the previous expedition. Within a month, one of White's colonists had been shot full of arrows by attackers under the leadership of Wanchese, who after Wingina's death became the most militant opponent of the English among the Roanoke Indians. White retaliated with a counterattack that increased the hostility of the Indians. The colonists

begged White to return home in their only seaworthy ship and to press Raleigh for support. Reluctantly, White set sail, but arrived just as a war began between England and Spain. Three anxious years passed before White was able to return to Roanoke, only to find the settlement destroyed and the colonists gone.

As White and his crew set their sights for Croatoan that August morning in 1590, a great storm blew up. White and the ship's captain agreed that they would have to leave the Pamlico Sound for deeper waters. It proved White's last glimpse of America. Tossed home on a stormy sea, he never returned. The English settlers of Roanoke became known as the Lost Colony, their disappearance and ultimate fate one of the enduring mysteries of colonial history.

The Roanoke experience is a reminder of the underlying assumptions of New World colonization. "The English," writes the historian and geographer Carl Sauer, had "naked imperial objectives." It also suggests the wasted opportunity of the Indians' initial welcome. There is evidence that the lost colonists lived out the rest of their lives with the Algonquians. In 1609, the English at Jamestown learned from local Indians that "some of our nation planted by Sir Walter Raleigh [are] yet alive," and many years later, an English surveyor at Croatoan Island was greeted by natives who told him that "several of their Ancestors were white People," that "the English were forced to cohabit with them for Relief and Conversation, and that in the process of Time, they conformed themselves to the Manners of their Indian Relations." It may be that Virginia Dare and the other children married into Indian families, creating the first mixed community of English and Indians in North America.

KEY TOPICS

- The European background of American colonization
- Creation of the Spanish New World empire and its first extensions to North America
- The large-scale intercontinental exchange of peoples, crops, animals, and diseases
- The French role in the beginnings of the North American fur trade
- England's first overseas colonies in Ireland and America

THE EXPANSION OF EUROPE

Roanoke and other European colonial settlements of the sixteenth century came in the wake of Christopher Columbus's voyage of 1492. There may have been many unrecorded contacts between the peoples of America and the Old World before Columbus. Archaeological excavations at L'Anse aux Meadows on the fogbound Newfoundland coast provide evidence for a Norse landing in North America in the tenth or eleventh century. The Norse settlement lasted only a few years, was implacably opposed by the native inhabitants, and had no appreciable impact on them. But the contact with the Americas established by Columbus had earthshaking consequences. Within a generation of his voyage, continental exchanges of peoples, crops, animals, and germs had reshaped the Atlantic world. The key to understanding these remarkable events is the transformation of Europe during the several centuries preceding the voyage of Columbus.

European Communities

Western Europe was an agricultural society, the majority of its people peasant farmers. Farming and livestock raising had been practiced in Europe for thousands of years, but great advances in farming technology took place during the late Middle Ages. Water mills, iron plows, improved devices for harnessing livestock, and systems of crop rotation all greatly increased productivity. From the eleventh to the fourteenth centuries, farmers more than doubled the quantity of European land in cultivation, and accordingly the population nearly tripled.

Most Europeans were village people, living in family households. Men performed the basic field work; women were responsible for child care, livestock, and food preparation. In the European pattern, daughters usually left the homes and villages of their families to live among their husbands' people. Women were furnished with dowries, but generally excluded from inheritance. Divorce was almost unknown.

Europe was characterized by a social system historians have called "feudalism." The continent was divided into hundreds of small territories, each ruled by a family of lords who claimed a disproportionate share of wealth and power. Feudal lords commanded labor service from peasants, and tribute in the form of crops. The lords were the main beneficiaries of medieval economic expansion, accumulating great estates and building fortified castles.

Europe was politically fragmented, but religiously unified under the authority of the Roman Catholic Church, a complex organization that spanned thousands of local communities with a hierarchy extending from parish priests to the pope in Rome. At the

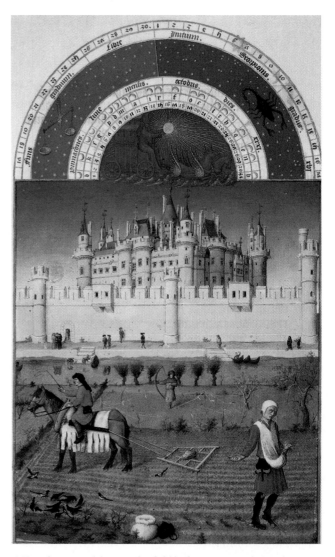

A French peasant labors in the field before a spectacular castle in a page taken from the illuminated manuscript *Tres Riches Heures*, made in the fifteenth century for the duc de Berry. In 1580 the essayist Montaigne talked with several American Indians at the French court who "noticed among us some men gorged to the full with things of every sort while their other halves were beggars at their doors, emaciated with hunger and poverty" and "found it strange that these poverty-stricken halves should suffer such injustice, and that they did not take the others by the throat or set fire to their houses."

SOURCE: Art Resource, Musee Conde, Chantilly/Giraudon, Art Resource, NY.

core of Christian belief was a set of communal values: love of God the father, loving treatment of neighbors, and the fellowship of all believers. Yet the Church actively persecuted heretics, nonbelievers, and devotees of older "pagan" religions. The church legitimized the power relationships of Europe and counseled the poor and downtrodden to place their hope in heavenly rewards.

Europe was also home to numerous communities of Jews, who had fled from their homeland in Palestine after a series of unsuccessful revolts against Roman rule in the first century BCE. Both church and civic authorities subjected the Jews to discriminatory treatment. Restricted to ghettos and forbidden from owning land, many Jews turned adversity to advantage, becoming merchants who specialized in long-distance trade. But Jewish success only seemed to stimulate Christian hostility.

For the great majority of Europeans, living conditions were harsh. Most rural people survived on bread and porridge, supplemented with seasonal vegetables and an occasional piece of meat or fish. Infectious diseases abounded; perhaps a third of all children died before their fifth birthday, and only half the population reached adulthood. Famines periodically ravaged the countryside. A widespread epidemic of bubonic plague, known as the "Black Death," swept in from Asia and between 1347 and 1353 wiped out a third of the western European population. Disease led to famine and violence, as groups fought for shares of a shrinking economy.

The Merchant Class and the New Monarchies

Strengthened by the technological breakthroughs of the late Middle Ages, the European economy proved that it had a great capacity for recovery. During the fourteenth and fifteenth centuries, commerce greatly expanded, especially the trade in basic goods such as cereals and timber, minerals and salt, wine, fish, and wool. Growing commerce stimulated the growth of markets and towns. By 1500, Europe had fully recovered from the Black Death and the population had nearly returned to its former peak of about 65 million.

One consequence of this revival was the rise of a fledgling system of western European states (see Map 2.1). The monarchs of these emerging states were new centers of power, building legitimacy by promoting domestic political order as they unified their realms. They found support among the rising merchant class of the cities, which in return sought lucrative royal contracts and trading monopolies. The alliance between commercial interests and the monarchs was a critical development that prepared the way for overseas expansion. Western Europe was neither the wealthiest nor most scientifically sophisticated of the world's cultures. But it would prove to have an extraordinary capacity to generate capital for overseas ventures.

The Renaissance

The heart of this dynamic European commercialism lay in the city-states of Italy. During the late Middle Ages, the cities of Venice, Genoa, and Pisa launched armed commercial fleets that seized control of trade in the Mediterranean. Their merchants became the principal outfitters of the Crusades, a series of great military expeditions promoted by the Catholic Church to recover Palestine from the Muslims. The conquest of the Holy Land by Crusaders at the end of the eleventh century delivered the silk and spice trades of Asia into the hands of the Italian merchants. Tropical spices—cloves, cinnamon,

MAP EXPLORATION

To explore an interactive version of this map, go to **www.prenhall.com/faragher5/map2.1**

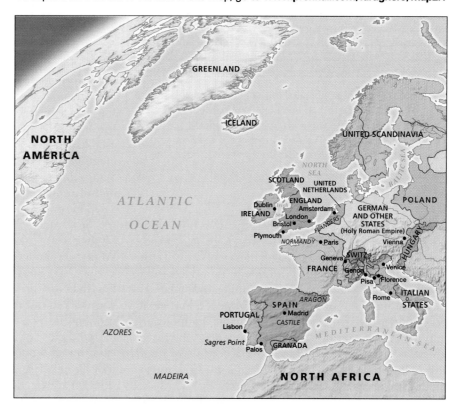

MAP 2.1 Western Europe in the Fifteenth Century By the middle of the century, the monarchs of western Europe had unified their realms and begun to build royal bureaucracies and standing armies and navies. These states, all with extensive Atlantic coastlines, sponsored the voyages that inaugurated the era of European colonization.

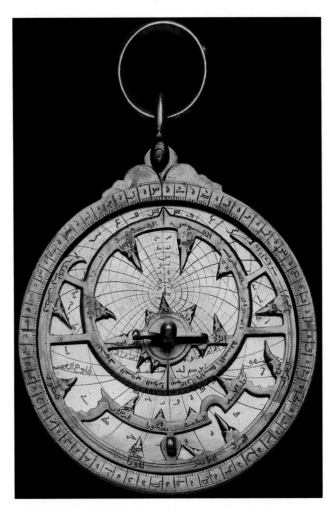

The astrolabe, an instrument used for determining the precise position of heavenly bodies was introduced into early modern Europe by the Arabs. This is one of the earliest examples, an intricately-engraved brass astrolabe produced by a master craftsman in Syria in the thirteenth century.

SOURCE: ©National Maritime Museum Picture Library, London, England. Neg. #E5555-3.

lectual and artistic flowering in Europe during the fourteenth, fifteenth, and sixteenth centuries known as the Renaissance. The revolution in publishing (made possible by the printing press and movable type), the beginning of regular postal service, and the growth of universities helped spread this revival throughout the elite circles of Europe.

The Renaissance celebrated human possibility. This human-centered perspective was evident in many endeavors. In architecture, there was a return to measured classical styles, thought to encourage rational reflection. In painting and sculpture, there was a new focus on the human body. Artists modeled muscles with light and shadow to produce heroic images of men and women. These were aspects of a movement that became known as "humanism," a revolt against religious authority, in which the secular took precedence over the purely religious. This Renaissance outlook was a critical component of the spirit that motivated the exploration of the Americas.

Portuguese Explorations

Portugal, a narrow land on the western coast of the Iberian Peninsula with a long tradition of seafaring, became the first of the new Renaissance kingdoms to explore distant lands. Lisbon, the principal port on the sea route between the Mediterranean and northwestern Europe, was a bustling, cosmopolitan city with large enclaves of Italian merchants. By 1385, the local merchant community had grown powerful enough to place their own favorite, João I, on the throne, and the king had ambitious plans to establish a Portuguese trading empire.

A central figure in this development was the king's son, Prince Henry, known to later generations as "the Navigator." In the spirit of Renaissance learning, the prince established an academy of eminent geographers, instrument makers, shipbuilders, and seamen at his institute at Sagres Point, on the southwestern tip of Portugal. By the mid-fifteenth century, as a result of their efforts, most educated Europeans knew the earth was a spherical globe—the idea that they believed it to be "flat" is one of the many myths about Columbus's voyage. The scholars at Sagres Point incorporated Asian and Muslim ideas into the design of a new ship known as the caravel, faster and better-handling than any previous oceangoing vessel. They studied and worked out methods for arming those vessels with cannons, turning them into mobile fortresses. They promoted the use of Arab instruments for astronomical calculation, and published the first tables of declination, indicating where the sun and stars could be found in the skies on a given day of the year. With such innovations, Europeans became the masters of the world's seas, a supremacy that would continue until the twentieth century.

The Portuguese explored the Atlantic coast of northwestern Africa for direct access to the lucrative gold and slave trades of that continent. By the time of Prince Henry's

nutmeg, and pepper from the Indies (the lands from modern India eastward to Indonesia)—were in great demand, for they made the European diet far less monotonous for the aristocrats who could afford the new products from the East. Asian civilization also supplied a number of technical innovations that further propelled European economic growth, including the compass, gunpowder, and the art of printing with movable type—"the three greatest inventions known to man," according to English philosopher Francis Bacon. Europeans were not so much innovators as magnificent adaptors.

Contact with Islamic civilization provided Western scholars with access to important ancient Greek and Roman texts that had been lost to them during the Middle Ages but preserved in the great libraries of the Muslims. The revival of interest in classical antiquity sparked the period of intel-

death in 1460, the Portuguese had colonized the Atlantic islands of the Azores and the Madeiras and founded bases along the western African "Gold Coast." Because the Ottoman Turks had captured Constantinople and closed the overland spice and silk routes in 1453, the Italian merchants of Lisbon pressed the Portuguese crown to sponsor an expedition that would establish an ocean route to the Indies. In 1488, the admiral Bartholomew Dias rounded the southern tip of Africa, and ten years later Vasco da Gama, his successor, reached India with the assistance of Arab pilots. The Portuguese erected strategic trading forts along the coasts of Africa, India, Indonesia, and China, the first and longest-lasting outposts of European world colonialism, and thereby gained control of much of the Asian spice trade. Most important for the history of the Americas, the Portuguese established the Atlantic slave trade. (For a full discussion of slavery, see Chapter 4.)

Columbus Reaches the Americas

In 1476, Christopher Columbus, a young Genovese sailor, joined his brother in Lisbon, where he became a seafaring merchant for Italian traders. Gradually, Columbus developed the simple idea of opening a new route to the Indies by sailing west across the Atlantic Ocean. Such a venture would require royal backing, but when he approached the advisors of the Portuguese monarch, they laughed at his geographic ignorance, pointing out that his calculation of the distance to Asia was much too short. Columbus's proposal was similarly rejected by the French and English. They were right, Columbus was wrong, but it turned out to be an error of monumental good fortune for him.

Columbus finally sold his plan to Isabel and Ferdinand, the monarchs of Castile and Aragon, who had married and united their kingdoms. In 1492, the couple had succeeded in conquering Grenada, the last Muslim-controlled province in Iberia, ending a centuries-long struggle known as the *reconquista*. Through many generations of warfare, the Spanish had developed a military tradition that thrived on conquest and plunder, and the monarchy was eager for new lands to conquer. Moreover, observing the successful Portuguese push southward along the west coast of Africa,

they were attracted to the prospect of opening lucrative trade routes of their own to the Indies. One of the many Columbus myths is the story that Queen Isabel pawned her jewels to finance his voyage. In fact, the principal investors were Italian merchants.

Columbus called his undertaking "the Enterprise of the Indies," suggesting his commercial intentions. But his mission was more than commercial. One of his prime goals was to occupy and settle any islands not under the control of another monarch, claiming title for Spain by right of conquest. Like the adventurers who later established the first English colony at Roanoke, Columbus's objectives were starkly imperial.

Columbus's three vessels left the port of Palos, Spain, in August 1492, and after a stop of some weeks in the Canary Islands, they sailed west across the Atlantic, pushed by the prevailing trade winds. By October, flocks of birds and floats of driftwood suggested the approach of land. It turned out to be a small, flat island in the Bahamas, perhaps Samana Cay. But Columbus believed he was in the Indies, somewhere near the Asian mainland. He explored the northern

This ship, thought to be similar to Columbus's *Niña*, is a caravel, a type of vessel developed by the naval experts at Henry the Navigator's institute at Sagres Point in Portugal. To the traditional square-rigged Mediterranean ship, they added the "lateen" sail of the Arabs, which permitted much greater maneuverability. Other Asian improvements, such as the stern-post rudder and multiple masting, allowed caravels to travel farther and faster than any earlier ships, and made possible the invasion of America.

SOURCE: From *The Ship*, an Illustrated History by Bjorn Landstrom, copyright © 1961 by Bokforlaget Forum AB. Used by permission of Doubleday, a division of Random House, Inc.

This image accompanied Columbus's account of his voyage, which was published in Latin and reissued in many other languages and editions that circulated throughout Europe before 1500. The Spanish King Ferdinand is shown directing the voyage to a tropical island, where the natives flee in terror. Columbus's impression of Native Americans as a people vulnerable to conquest shows clearly in this image.

SOURCE: The Granger Collection.

peans and Native Americans), were "of a very acute intelligence," but had "no iron or steel weapons." A conflict with several of his men had ended quickly with the deaths of two natives. "Should your majesties command it," Columbus wrote, "all the inhabitants could be made slaves." The land was rich, he reported. "There are many spices and great mines of gold and of other metals." In fact, none of the spices familiar to Europeans grew in the Americas, and there were only small quantities of alluvial gold in the riverbeds. But the sight of the ornaments worn by the Taínos infected Columbus with gold fever. He had left a small force behind in a rough fort on the northern coast of Hispaniola to explore for gold—the first European foothold in the Americas.

The enthusiastic monarchs financed a convoy of seventeen ships and 1,500 men—equipped with armor, crossbows, and firearms—that departed in late 1493 to begin the colonization of the islands. But reaching Hispaniola, Columbus found that the men left behind had all been killed by Taínos who, like the Algonquians at Roanoke, had lost patience with their demands for supplies. Columbus established another fortified outpost and sent his men out to prospect for gold. They prowled the countryside, preying upon Taíno communities, stealing food, and abusing the people. "They carried off the women of the islanders," wrote one early chronicler, "under the very eyes of their brothers and husbands." The Taínos, who lived in warrior chiefdoms, rose in resistance, and the Spaniards responded with unrestrained violence. Columbus imposed on the natives a harsh tribute, payable in gold, but the supply in the rivers soon ran out. Natives were seized and shipped to Spain as slaves, but most soon sickened and died. It was a disaster for the Taínos. The combined effects of warfare, famine, and demoralization resulted in the collapse of their society. Numbering perhaps 300,000 in 1492, they had been reduced to fewer than 30,000 within fifteen years, and by the 1520s had been effectively eliminated as a

coasts of the islands of Cuba and Hispaniola before heading home to announce his discovery, fortuitously catching the westerly winds that blow from the American coast toward Europe north of the tropics. One of Columbus's most important contributions was the discovery of the clockwise circulation of Atlantic winds and currents that would, over the next several centuries, carry thousands of European ships back and forth to the Americas.

Leading Columbus's triumphal procession to the royal court at Barcelona were half a dozen captive Taínos, the native people of the Caribbean, dressed in bright feathers with little ornaments of gold. The natives, Columbus noted in his report (see Out of Many Voices: Columbus Writes of the First Contact between Euro-

OUT OF MANY VOICES

COLUMBUS WRITES OF THE FIRST CONTACT BETWEEN EUROPEANS AND NATIVE AMERICANS

Christopher Columbus kept a diary of his first voyage in which he recorded his first encounter with the Taínos, on the island they called Guanahani, on October 12, 1492.

AS I SAW THAT THEY WERE VERY FRIENDLY TO US, and perceived that they could be much more easily converted to our holy faith by gentle means than by force, I presented them with some red caps, and strings of beads to wear upon the neck, and many other trifles of small value, wherewith they were much delighted, and became wonderfully attached to us. Afterwards they came swimming to the boats, bringing parrots, balls of cotton thread, javelins, and many other things which they exchanged for articles we gave them, such as glass beads, and hawk's bells; which trade was carried on with the utmost good will. But they seemed on the whole to me, to be a very poor people. They all go completely naked, even the women, though I saw but one girl. All whom I saw were young, not above thirty years of age, well made, with fine shapes and faces; their hair short, and coarse like that of a horse's tail, combed toward the forehead, except a small portion which they suffer to hang down behind, and never cut. Some paint themselves with black, which

makes them appear like those of the Canaries, neither black nor white; others with white, others with red, and others with such colors as they can find. Some paint the face, and some the whole body; others only the eyes, and others the nose. Weapons they have none, nor are acquainted with them, for I showed them swords which they grasped by the blades, and cut themselves through ignorance. They have no iron, their javelins being without it, and nothing more than sticks, though some have fish-bones or other things at the ends. They are all of a good size and stature, and handsomely formed. I saw some with scars of wounds upon their bodies, and demanded by signs the cause of them; they answered me in the same way, that there came people from the other islands in the neighborhood who endeavored to make prisoners of them, and they defended themselves. I thought then, and still believe, that these were from the continent. It appears to me, that the people are ingenious, and would be good servants and I am of opinion that they would very readily become Christians, as they appear to have no religion. If it please our Lord, I intend at my return to carry home six of them to your Highnesses, that they may learn our language. ▪

SOURCE: Cecil Jane, ed., *The Journal of Christopher Columbus* (New York: Bonanza Books, 1960), pp. 23–24.

people. Without natives, the colony plunged into depression, and by 1500, the Spanish monarchs were so dissatisfied that they ordered Columbus arrested and sent to Spain in irons.

Columbus made two additional voyages to the Caribbean, both characterized by the same obsession for gold and slaves. He died in Spain in 1506, still convinced he had opened the way to the Indies. This belief persisted among many Europeans well into the sixteenth century. But others had already begun to see things from a different perspective. Amerigo Vespucci of Florence, who voyaged to the Caribbean in 1499, was the first to describe Columbus's Indies as *Mundus Novus*, a "New World." When European geographers named this new continent, early in the sixteenth century, they honored Vespucci's insight by calling it "America."

THE SPANISH IN THE AMERICAS

A century after Columbus's death, before the English had planted a single successful New World colony of their own, the Spanish had created a huge and wealthy empire in the Americas. In theory, all law and policy for the empire came from Spain; in practice, the isolation of the settlements led to a good deal of local autonomy. The Spanish created a caste system, in which a small minority of settlers and their offspring controlled the lives and labor of millions of Indian and African workers. But the Spanish empire in America was also a society in which colonists, Indians, and Africans mixed to form a new people.

The Invasion of America

This was the beginning of the European invasion of America (see Map 2.2). The first stages included scenes of frightful violence. Armed men marched across the Caribbean islands, plundering villages, slaughtering men, and raping women. Columbus's successors established an institution known as the *encomienda*, in which native Indians were compelled to labor in the service of Spanish lords. The relationship was supposed to be reciprocal, with lords responsible for protecting their Indians, but in practice it amounted to little more than slavery. Faced with labor shortages, Spanish slavers raided the Bahamas and soon depopulated them entirely. The depletion of gold on Hispaniola led to the invasion of the islands of Puerto Rico and Jamaica in 1508, then Cuba in 1511. Meanwhile, rumors of wealthy societies to the westward led to scores of probing expeditions. The Spanish invasion of Central America began in 1511, and two years later Vasco Núñez de Balboa crossed the Isthmus of Panama to the Pacific Ocean. In 1517, Spaniards landed on the coast of Mexico, and within a year they made contact with the Aztec empire.

The Aztecs had migrated to the highland valley of Mexico from the deserts of the American Southwest in the thirteenth century, in the wake of the collapse of the Toltec empire (see Chapter 1). The warlike Aztecs settled a marshy lake district and built the great city of Tenochtitlán. By the early fifteenth century they dominated the peoples of the Mexican highlands, in the process building a powerful state. An estimated 200,000 people lived in the Aztec capital, making it one of the largest cities in the world, much larger than European cities of the time.

In 1519 Hernán Cortés, a veteran of the conquest of Cuba, landed on the Mexican coast with armed troops. Within two years he had overthrown the Aztec empire, a spectacular military accomplishment. The Spanish had superior arms (especially important were their steel swords), but that was not the principal cause of their success. Most importantly, Cortés brilliantly exploited the resentment of the many peoples who lived under Aztec domination, forging Spanish-Indian alliances that became a model for the subsequent European colonization of the Americas. Here, as at Roanoke and dozens of other sites of European invasion, European invaders found natives eager for allies to support them in their conflicts with their neighbors. Still, the Aztecs were militarily powerful, successfully driving the Spaniards from Tenochtitlán, and putting up a bitter and prolonged defense when Cortés returned to besiege them. But in the meantime they suffered a devastating epidemic of smallpox that killed thousands and undermined their ability to resist. In the aftermath of conquest, the Spanish unmercifully plundered Aztec society, providing the Catholic monarchs with wealth beyond their wildest imagining.

MAP EXPLORATION

To explore an interactive version of this map, go to **www.prenhall.com/faragher5/map2.2**

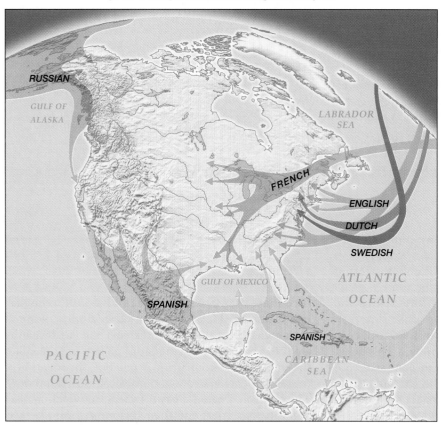

MAP 2.2 The Invasion of America In the sixteenth century, the Spanish first invaded the Caribbean and used it to stage their successive wars of conquest in North and South America. In the seventeenth century, the French, English, and Dutch invaded the Atlantic coast. The Russians, sailing across the northern Pacific, mounted the last of the colonial invasions in the eighteenth century.

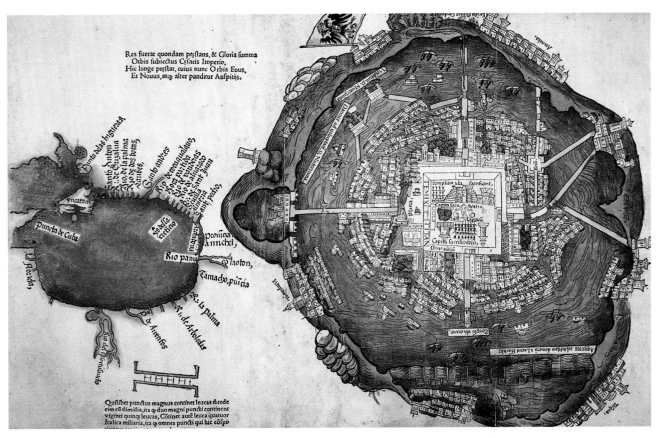

This map of Tenochtitlán, published in 1524 and attributed to the celebrated engraver Albrecht Dürer, shows the city before its destruction, with the principal Aztec temples in the main square, causeways connecting the city to the mainland, and an acqueduct supplying fresh water. The information on this map must have come from Aztec sources, as did much of the intelligence Cortés relied on for the Spanish conquest.

SOURCE: Photo Courtesy of the Edward E. Ayer Collection, The Newberry Library, Chicago.

The Destruction of the Indies

The Indian peoples of the Americas resisted Spanish conquest, but most proved a poor match for mounted warriors with steel swords. (See Out of Many Voices: An Indian Reaction to the Invasion of the Spanish). The record of the conquest, however, includes many brave Indian leaders and thousands of martyrs. The natives of the outermost islands (the Caribs, from whom the Caribbean Sea takes its name) successfully defended their homelands until the end of the sixteenth century, and in the arid lands of northern Mexico the nomadic tribes the Spanish knew collectively as the Chichimecs proved equally difficult to subdue.

Some Europeans protested the horrors of the conquest. In 1511 the priest Antonio de Montesinos condemned the violence in a sermon to colonists on Hispaniola. "On what authority have you waged a detestable war against these people, who dwelt quietly and peacefully on their own land?" he asked. "Are these Indians not men? . . . Are you not obliged to love them as you love yourselves?" He was echoed by Bartolomé de las Casas, a priest who had participated in the plunder of Cuba but later suffered a crisis of conscience. The Christian mission in the New World was to convert the natives to Christianity, las Casas argued, and "the means to effect this end are not to rob, to scandalize, to capture or destroy them, or to lay waste their lands." Long before the world recognized the concept of universal human rights, he proclaimed that "the entire human race is one," earning him a reputation as one of the towering moral figures in the early history of the Americas.

In his brilliant history of the conquest, *The Destruction of the Indies* (1552), las Casas blamed the Spanish for cruelties resulting in millions of Indian deaths—in effect, genocide. Translated into several languages and widely circulated throughout Europe, his book was used by other European powers to condemn Spain, thereby covering up their own dismal colonial records,

The Cruelties Used by the Spaniards on the Indians, from a 1599 English edition of *The Destruction of the Indies* by Bartolomé de las Casas. These scenes were copied from a series of engravings produced by Theodore de Bry that accompanied an earlier edition.

SOURCE: British Library.

creating what has been called the "Black Legend" of Spanish colonization. Although there has been much dispute over las Casas's estimates of huge population losses, recent demographic studies suggest he was more right than wrong. The destruction of the Taínos was repeated elsewhere. The population of Mexico fell from five to ten million in 1519 to little more than a million a century later.

Las Casas was incorrect, however, in attributing these losses to warfare. To be sure, thousands of lives were lost

OUT OF MANY VOICES

AN INDIAN REACTION TO THE INVASION OF THE SPANISH

The author of this account, known only as "The Gentleman of Elvas," was a Portuguese participant in Hernando de Soto's military expedition through the Southeast. In this passage, he quoted the reaction of a native chief to the arrival of de Soto's army at his village in what is now the state of Georgia.

VERY HIGH, POWERFUL, AND GOOD MASTER. THE things that seldom happen bring astonishment. Think, then, what must be the effect, on me and mine, of the sight of you and your people, whom we have at no time seen, astride the fierce brutes, your horses, entering with such speed and fury into my country, that we had no tidings of your coming—things so altogether new, as to strike awe and terror into our hearts, which it was not our nature to resist, so that we should receive you with the sobriety due to so kingly and famous a lord. Trusting to your greatness and personal qualities, I hope no fault will be found in me, and that I shall rather receive favors, of which one is that with my person, my country, and my vassals, you will do as with your own things; and another, that you will tell me who you are, whence you come, whither you go, and what it is you seek, that I may the better serve you. ◾

SOURCE: Gentleman of Elvas, *A Relation of the Invasion and Conquest of Florida by the Spaniards Under the Command of Fernando de Soto* (London: John Lawrence, 1686), p. 55.

This drawing of victims of the smallpox epidemic that struck the Aztec capital of Tenochtitlán in 1520 is taken from the *Florentine Codex*, a postconquest history written and illustrated by Aztec scribes. "There came amongst us a great sickness, a general plague," reads the account, "killing vast numbers of people. It covered many all over with sores: on the face, on the head, on the chest, everywhere. . . . The sores were so terrible that the victims could not lie face down, nor on their backs, nor move from one side to the other. And when they tried to move even a little, they cried out in agony."

SOURCE: The Granger Collection.

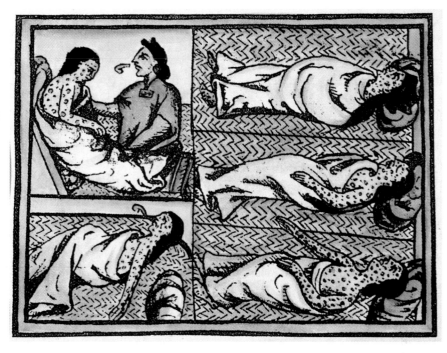

in battle, but these deaths accounted for but a small proportion of the overall decline. Thousands more starved because their economies were destroyed or their food stores were taken by conquering armies. Even more important, the native birthrate fell drastically after the conquest. Indian women were so "worn out with work," one Spaniard wrote, that they avoided conception, induced abortion, and even "killed their children with their own hands so that they shall not have to endure the same hardships."

But the primary cause of the drastic reduction in native populations was epidemic disease—influenza, plague, smallpox, measles, typhus. Although preconquest America was by no means disease free—skeletal evidence suggests that natives suffered from arthritis, hepatitis, polio, and tuberculosis—there were no diseases of epidemic potential. Indian peoples lacked the antibodies necessary to protect them from European germs and viruses. Smallpox first came from Spain in 1518, exploding in an epidemic so virulent that, in the words of an early Spanish historian, "it left Hispaniola, Puerto Rico, Jamaica, and Cuba desolated of Indians." The epidemic crossed into Mexico in 1520, destroying the Aztecs, then spread along the Indian trade network. In 1524 it strategically weakened the Incas eight years before their empire was conquered by Spanish conquistador Francisco Pizarro. Spanish chroniclers wrote that this single epidemic killed half the native Americans it touched. Disease was the secret weapon of the Spanish, and it helps explain their extraordinary success in the conquest.

Such devastating outbreaks of disease, striking for the first time against a completely unprotected population, are known as "virgin soil epidemics." After the conquest, Mexicans sang of an earlier time:

There was then no sickness.
They had then no aching bones.
They had then no high fever.
They had then no smallpox.
They had then no burning chest.
They had then no abdominal pains.
They had then no consumption.
They had then no headache.
At that time the course of humanity was orderly.
The foreigners made it otherwise when they arrived here.

Warfare, famine, lower birthrates, and epidemic disease knocked the native population of the Americas into a downward spiral that did not swing back upward until the beginning of the twentieth century (see Figure 2.1). By that time native population had fallen by 90 percent. It was the greatest demographic disaster in world history. The most notable difference between the European colonial experience in the Americas compared to Africa or Asia was this radical reduction in the native population.

Intercontinental Exchange

The passage of diseases between the Old and New Worlds was one of the most important aspects of the large-scale continental exchange that marks the beginning of modern world history. The most obvious exchange was the vast influx into Europe of the precious metals plundered from the Aztec and Incan empires of the New World. Most of the golden booty was melted down, destroying forever thousands of priceless artifacts. Silver from mines the Spanish discovered and operated in Mexico and Peru tripled the amount of coin

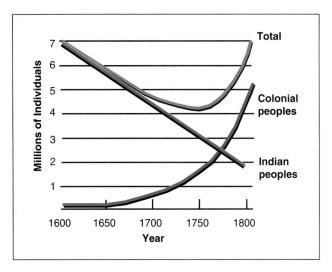

FIGURE 2.1   North America's Indian and Colonial Populations in the Seventeenth and Eighteenth Centuries
The primary factor in the decimation of native peoples was epidemic disease, brought to the New World from the Old. In the eighteenth century, the colonial population overtook North America's Indian populations.

SOURCE: Historical Statistics of the United States (Washington, DC: Government Printing Office, 1976), 8, 1168; Russell Thornton, *American Indian Holocaust and Survival* (Norman: University of Oklahoma Press, 1987), 32.

circulating in Europe between 1500 and 1550, then tripled it again before 1600. The result was runaway inflation, which stimulated commerce and raised profits but lowered the standard of living for most people.

Of even greater long-term importance were the New World crops brought to Europe. Maize (the Taíno word for what Americans call corn), the staff of life for most native North Americans, became a staple crop in Mediterranean countries, the dominant feed for livestock elsewhere in Europe, and the primary provision for the slave ships of Africa. Potatoes from Peru provided the margin between famine and subsistence for peasant peoples in Ireland and northern Europe. Significantly more productive per acre than wheat, these "miracle crops" provided abundant food sources that went a long way toward ending the persistent problem of famine in Europe.

Although the Spanish failed to locate valuable spices such as black pepper or cloves in the New World, new tropical crops more than compensated. Tobacco was first introduced to Europe about 1550 as a cure for disease, but was soon in wide use as a stimulant. American vanilla and chocolate soon became valuable crops. American cotton proved superior to Asian varieties for the production of cheap textiles. Each of these native plants, along with tropical trans-

plants from the Old World to the New—sugar, rice, and coffee among the most important—supplied the basis for important new industries and markets that altered the course of world history.

Columbus introduced domesticated animals into Hispaniola and Cuba, and livestock were later transported to Mexico. The movement of Spanish settlement into northern Mexico was greatly aided by an advancing wave of livestock, for grazing animals invaded native fields and forests, undercutting the ability of communities to support themselves. Horses, used by Spanish stockmen to tend their cattle, also spread northward. In the seventeenth century, horses reached the Great Plains of North America, where they eventually transformed the lives of the nomadic hunting Indians (see Chapter 5).

The First Europeans in North America

Ponce de León, governor of Puerto Rico, was the first Spanish conquistador to attempt to extend the conquest to North America (see Map 2.3). In search of slaves, he made his first landing on the mainland coast—which he named Florida—in 1513. Warriors of the powerful chiefdoms there beat back this and several other attempts at invasion, and in 1521 succeeded in killing him. Seven years later, another Spanish attempt to invade and conquer Florida, under the command of Pánfilo de Narváez, also ended in disaster. Most of Narváez's men were lost in a shipwreck, but a small group of them survived, living and wandering for several years among the native peoples of the Gulf Coast and the Southwest until they were finally rescued in 1536 by Spanish slave hunters in northern Mexico. One of these castaways, Alvar Núñez Cabeza de Vaca, published an account of his adventures in which he told of rumors of a North American empire known as Cíbola, with golden cities "larger than the city of Mexico." These tales probably referred to Mississippian towns with platform mounds.

Cabeza de Vaca's report inspired two great Spanish expeditions into North America. The first was mounted in Cuba by Hernán de Soto, a veteran of the conquest of Peru. Landing in Florida in 1539 with an army of over 700 men, he pushed hundreds of miles through the heavily populated South, commandeering food and slaves from the Indian towns in his path. But he failed to locate another Aztec empire. Moving westward, his expedition was twice mauled by powerful native armies. With his force reduced by half, de Soto's force reached the Mississippi where they were met by a flotilla from a great city—"200 vessels full of Indians with their bows and arrows, painted with ocher and having great plumes of white and many colored feathers on either side." The Spaniards crossed the river and marched deep into present-day Arkansas, but failing

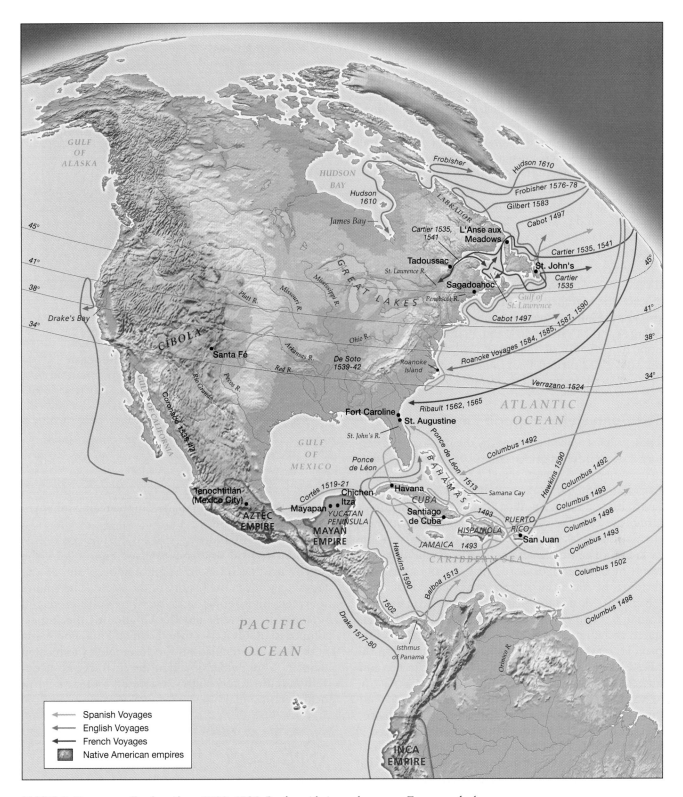

MAP 2.3 European Exploration, 1492–1591 By the mid-sixteenth century, Europeans had explored most of the Atlantic coast of North America and penetrated into the interior in the disastrous expeditions of de Soto and Coronado.

to locate the great city, they turned back. De Soto died and some 300 dispirited survivors eventually made it back to Mexico on rafts. The native peoples of the South had successfully turned back Spanish invasion. But the invaders had introduced epidemic diseases that drastically depopulated and undermined the chiefdoms of the South.

The second expedition was organized by officials in Mexico. Francisco Vásquez de Coronado led some 300 Spanish horsemen and infantry, supported by more than a thousand Indian allies, north along well-marked Indian paths to the land of the Pueblos along the Rio Grande. The Pueblos' initial resistance was quickly quashed. But Coronado was deeply disappointed by the Pueblo towns "of stone and mud, rudely fashioned," and sent out expeditions in all directions in search of the legendary golden cities of Cíbola. He marched part of his army northeast, onto the Great Plains, where they observed great herds of "shaggy cows" (buffalo) and made contact with nomadic hunting peoples. But finding no cities and no gold they turned back. For the next fifty years Spain lost all interest in the Southwest.

The Spanish New World Empire

These failures notwithstanding, by the late sixteenth century the Spanish had gained control of a powerful empire in the Americas. A century after Columbus, some 250,000 European immigrants, most of them Spaniards, had settled in the Americas. Another 125,000 Africans had been forcibly resettled as slaves on the Spanish plantations of the Caribbean, as well as on the Portuguese plantations of Brazil. (The Portuguese colonized Brazil under the terms of the Treaty of Tordesillas, a 1494 agreement dividing the Americas between Spain and Portugal (see Chapter 4). Most of the Spanish settlers lived in the more than 200 urban communities founded during the conquest, including cities such as Santo Domingo in Hispaniola, Havana in Cuba, Mexico City, built atop the ruins of Tenochtitlán, and Quito and Lima in the conquered empire of the Incas.

Spanish women came to America as early as Columbus's second expedition, but over the course of the sixteenth century they made up only about 10 percent of the immigrants. Most male colonists married or cohabited with Indian or African women, and the result was the growth of large mixed-ancestry groups known as *mestizos* and *mulattoes*, respectively. Sexual mixing and intermarriage was one aspect of the Spanish frontier of inclusion, in which native peoples and their mixed offspring played a vital part in colonial society. Hundreds of thousands of Indians died, but Indian genes were passed on to generations of mixed-ancestry people, who

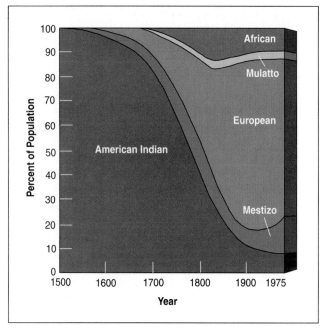

FIGURE 2.2 **The African, Indian, and European Populations of the Americas** In the 500 years since the European invasion of the Americas, the population has included varying proportions of Native American, European, and African peoples, as well as large numbers of persons of mixed ancestry.

SOURCE: Colin McEvedy and Richard Jones, *Atlas of World Population History* (Allen Lane ©1978).

became the majority population in the mainland Spanish American empire.

Populated by Indians, Africans, Spanish colonists, and their hybrid descendants (see Figure 2.2), the New World colonies of Spain made up one of the largest empires in the history of the world. The empire operated, in theory, as a highly centralized and bureaucratic system. But the Council of the Indies, composed of advisers of the Spanish king who made all the laws and regulations for the empire, was located in Spain. Thus, what looked in the abstract like a centrally administered empire tolerated a great deal of local decision making.

NORTHERN EXPLORATIONS AND ENCOUNTERS

When the Spanish empire was at the height of its power in the sixteenth century, the merchants and monarchs of other European seafaring states looked across the Atlantic for opportunities of their own. France was first to sponsor expeditions to the New World in the early sixteenth century. At first the French attempted to plant settlements on the coasts of Brazil and Florida, but Spanish opposition ultimately persuaded them to concentrate on the North Atlantic. England did not develop its own plans to colonize North America until the second half of the sixteenth century.

Fish and Furs

Long before France and England made attempts to found colonies, however, European fishermen were exploring the coastal North American waters of the North Atlantic. The Grand Banks, off the coast of Newfoundland, had abundant cod. It is possible that European fishermen were working those waters before Columbus's voyages. Certainly by 1500, hundreds of ships and thousands of sailors were sailing annually to the Grand Banks.

The first official voyages of exploration in the North Atlantic used the talents of experienced European sailors and fishermen. With a crew from Bristol, England, Genovese explorer Giovanni Caboto (or John Cabot) reached Labrador in 1497, but the English did little to follow up on his voyage. In 1524, Tuscan captain Giovanni da Verrazano, sailing for the French, explored the North American coast from Cape Fear (North Carolina) to the Penobscot River (Maine). Encouraged by his report, the French king commissioned experienced captain Jacques Cartier to locate a "Northwest Passage" to the Indies. Although in his voyages of 1534, 1535, and 1541 Cartier failed to find a Northwest Passage, he reconnoitered the St. Lawrence River, which led deep into the continental interior to the Great Lakes, with easy access to the Ohio and Mississippi Rivers, giving France an incomparable geographic edge over other colonial powers. Cartier's attempts to plant settlements on the St. Lawrence failed, but he established France's imperial claim to the lands of Canada.

The French and other northern Europeans thus discovered the Indian people of the northern woodlands, and the Indians in turn discovered them. The contacts between Europeans and natives here took a different form than in the tropics, based on commerce rather than conquest. The Indians immediately appreciated the usefulness of textiles, glass, copper, and ironware. For his part, Cartier was interested in the fur coats of the Indians. Europeans, like Indians, used furs for winter clothing. But the growing population of the late Middle Ages had so depleted the wild game of Europe that the price of furs had risen beyond the reach of most people. The North American fur trade thus filled an important demand and produced high profits.

Beginning in the sixteenth century, the fur trade would continue to play an important role in the Atlantic economy for three centuries. By no means were Indians simply the victims of European traders. They had a sharp eye for quality, and cutthroat competition among traders provided them with the opportunity to hold out for what they considered good prices. But the fur trade was essentially an unequal exchange, with furs selling in Europe for ten or twenty times what Indians received for them. The trade also had negative consequences. European epidemic disease followed in the wake of the traders, and violent warfare broke out between tribes over access to hunting grounds. Moreover, as European-manufactured goods, such as metal knives, kettles, and firearms, became essential to their way of life, Indians became dependent on European suppliers. Ultimately, the fur trade was stacked in favor of Europeans.

By 1600, over a thousand European ships were trading for furs each year along the northern coast. The village of Tadoussac on the St. Lawrence, where a wide bay offered Europeans safe anchorage, became the customary place for several weeks of trading each summer, a forerunner of the western fur-trade rendezvous of the nineteenth century. Early in the seventeenth century, the French would move to monopolize the trade there by planting colonies along the coast and on the St. Lawrence.

The Protestant Reformation and the First French Colonies

The first French colonies in North America, however, were planted farther south by a group of religious dissenters known as the Huguenots. The Protestant Reformation—the religious revolt against the Roman Catholic Church—had begun in 1517 when German priest Martin Luther publicized his differences with Rome. Luther declared that eternal salvation was a gift from God and not related to works or service. His protests—Protestantism—fit into a climate of widespread dissatisfaction with the power and prosperity of the Catholic Church. Luther attracted followers all over northwestern Europe, including France, where they were persecuted by Catholic authorities. Converted to Luther's teachings in 1533, Frenchman John Calvin fled to Switzerland, where he developed a radical theology. His doctrine of predestination declared that God had chosen a small number of men and women for "election," or salvation, while condemning the vast majority to eternal damnation. Calvinists were instructed to cultivate the virtues of thrift, industry, sobriety, and personal responsibility, which Calvin argued were signs of election and essential to the Christian life.

Calvin's followers in France—the Huguenots—were concentrated among merchants and the middle class, but

This watercolor of Jacques le Moyne, painted in 1564, depicts the friendly relations between the Timucuas of coastal Florida and the colonists of the short-lived French colony of Fort Caroline. The Timucuas hoped that the French would help defend them against the Spanish, who plundered the coast in pursuit of Indian slaves.

SOURCE: Jacques Le Moyne, *Rene de Loudonniere and Chief Athore*, 1564 (watercolor), Gouache and metallic pigments on vellum. Print Collection, The New York Public Library, New York. The New York Public Library/Art Resource, NY.

also included a portion of the nobility opposed to the central authority of the Catholic monarch. In 1560, the French monarchy defeated the attempt of a group of Huguenot nobles to seize power, which inaugurated nearly forty years of violent religious struggle. In an effort to establish a religious refuge in the New World, Huguenot leaders were behind the first French attempts to establish colonies in North America. In 1562, Jean Ribault and 150 Protestants from Normandy landed on Parris Island, near present-day Beaufort, South Carolina, and began the construction of a fort and crude mud huts. Ribault soon returned to France for supplies, where he was caught up in the religious wars. The colonists nearly starved and were finally forced to resort to cannibalism before being rescued by a passing British ship. In 1564, Ribault established another Huguenot colony, Fort Caroline on the St. Johns River of Florida, south of present-day Jacksonville.

The Spanish were alarmed by these moves. They had no interest themselves in colonizing Florida, but worried about protecting their ships riding home to Spain loaded with gold and silver on the offshore Gulf Stream. Not only was Fort Caroline manned by Frenchmen, but by Protestants—deadly enemies of the Catholic monarchs of Spain. "We are compelled to pass in front of their port," wrote one official, "and with the greatest ease they can sally out with their armadas to seek us." In 1565, the Spanish crown sent Don Pedro Menéndez de Avilés, captain general of the Indies, to crush the Huguenots. After establishing a settlement south of the French at a place called St. Augustine, he marched his men overland through the swamps to surprise the Huguenots. "I put Jean Ribault and all the rest of them to the knife," Menéndez wrote triumphantly to the king, "judging it to be necessary to the service of the Lord Our God and of Your Majesty." The Spanish built a fort and established a garrison at St. Augustine, which thus became the oldest continuously occupied European city in North America.

Sixteenth-Century England

The English movement across the Atlantic, like the French, was tied to social change at home. Perhaps most important were changes in the economy. As the prices of goods rose steeply—the result of New World inflation—English landlords, their rents fixed by custom, sought ways to increase their incomes. Seeking profits in the woolen trade, many converted the common pasturage used by tenants into grazing land for sheep, dislocating large numbers of farmers. Between 1500 and 1650 a third of all the common lands in England were "enclosed" in this way. Deprived of their livelihoods, thousands of families left their traditional rural homes and sought employment in English cities, crowding the roads with homeless people.

Sixteenth-century England also became deeply involved in the struggles of the Reformation. At first, King Henry VIII of England (reigned 1509–47) supported the Catholic Church and opposed the Protestants. But there was great public resentment in England over the vast properties owned by the Church and the loss of revenue to Rome. When the pope refused to grant Henry an annulment of his marriage to Catherine of Aragon, daughter of Ferdinand and Isabel of Spain, the king exploited this

The French, under the command of Jean Ribault, land at the mouth of the St. Johns River in Florida. The image shows the local Timucua people welcoming the French. It is likely that the Timucuas viewed the French as potential allies against the Spanish, who had plundered the coast many times in pursuit of slaves.

SOURCE: The French, under the command of Jean Ribault, discover the River of May (St Johns River) in Florida on 1 May 1562: colored engraving, 1591, by Theodore de Bry after a now lost drawing by Jacques Le Moyne de Morgues. The Granger Collection.

The Armada Portrait of Elizabeth I, painted by an unknown artist in 1648. The queen places her hand on the globe, symbolizing the rising seapower of England. Through the open windows, we see the battle against the Spanish Armada in 1588 and the destruction of the Spanish ships in a providential storm, interpreted by the queen as an act of divine intervention.

SOURCE: *Elizabeth I*, Armada portrait, c. 1588 (oil on panel), by English School. (C16th) Private Collection/The Bridgeman Art Library, London/New York.

monarch, head of the most powerful empire in the world, declared himself the defender of the Catholic faith and vowed to overthrow her.

Fearing Spanish subversion on the neighboring Catholic island of Ireland, Elizabeth urged enterprising supporters such as Walter Raleigh and his half-brother Humphrey Gilbert to subdue the Irish Catholics and settle homeless English families on their land. During the 1560s, Raleigh, Humphrey, and many other commanders invaded the island and viciously attacked the Irish, forcing them to retreat beyond a frontier line of English settlement along the coast. So ferociously did the Irish resist the conquest that an image of the "wild Irish" became fixed in the English mind. Gilbert retaliated with even greater brutality, decapitating captured Irish men and women and using their heads as paving stones, "so that none should come into his tent for any cause but commonly he must pass through a lane of heads." Such barbarism did not prevent the English from considering the Irish an inferior race, and the notion that civilized people could not mix with such "savages" was an assumption English colonists would carry with them to the Americas.

popular mood. Taking up the cause of reform in 1534, he declared himself head of a separate Church of England. He later took over the English estates of the Catholic Church—about a quarter of the country's land—and used their revenues to begin constructing a powerful English state system, including a standing army and navy. Working through Parliament, Henry carefully enlisted the support of the merchants and landed gentry for his program, parceling out a measure of royal prosperity in the form of titles, offices, lands, and commercial favors. By 1547, when Henry died, he had forged a solid alliance with the wealthy merchant class.

Henry was succeeded by his young and sickly son Edward VI, who soon died. Next in succession was Edward's half-sister Mary, who attempted to reverse her father's Reformation from the top by martyring hundreds of English Protestants, gaining the title of "Bloody Mary." But upon her death in 1558, her half-sister Elizabeth I (reigned 1558–1603) came to the throne. Elizabeth sought to end the religious turmoil by tolerating a variety of views within the English church. The Spanish

Early English Efforts in the Americas

England's first ventures in the New World were made against the backdrop of its conflict with Spain. In 1562, John Hawkins violated Spanish regulations by transporting a load of African slaves to the Caribbean, bringing back valuable tropical goods. (For a full discussion of the slave trade, see Chapter 4.) The Spanish attacked Hawkins on another of his voyages in 1567, an event English privateers such as Francis Drake used as an excuse for launching hundreds of devastating and lucrative raids against Spanish New World ports and fleets. The voyages of these English "Sea Dogs" greatly enriched their investors, including Elizabeth herself. The English thus began their American adventures by slaving and plundering.

A consensus soon developed among Elizabeth's closest advisers that the time had come to enter the com-

CHRONOLOGY

1000	Norse settlement at L'Anse aux Meadows
1347–53	Black Death in Europe
1381	English Peasants' Revolt
1488	Bartolomeu Días sails around the African continent
1492	Christopher Columbus first arrives in the Caribbean
1494	Treaty of Tordesillas
1497	John Cabot explores Newfoundland
1500	High point of the Renaissance
1508	Spanish invade Puerto Rico
1513	Juan Ponce de León lands in Florida
1514	Bartolomé de las Casas begins preaching against the conquest
1516	Smallpox introduced to the New World
1517	Martin Luther breaks with the Roman Catholic Church
1519	Hernán Cortés lands in Mexico
1534	Jacques Cartier first explores the St. Lawrence River
1539–40	Hernán de Soto and Francisco Vásquez de Coronado expeditions
1550	Tobacco introduced to Europe
1552	Bartolomé de Las Casas's *Destruction of the Indies* published
1558	Elizabeth I of England begins her reign
1562	Huguenot colony planted along the mid-Atlantic coast
1565	St. Augustine founded
1583	Humphrey Gilbert attempts to plant a colony in Newfoundland
1584–87	Walter Raleigh's colony on Roanoke Island
1588	English defeat the Spanish Armada
1590	John White returns to find Roanoke colony abandoned

petition for American colonies. In a state paper written for the queen, the scholar Richard Hakluyt summarized the advantages that would come from colonies: they could provide bases from which to raid the Spanish in the Caribbean, outposts for an Indian market for English goods, and plantations for growing tropical products, freeing the nation from a reliance on the long-distance trade with Asia. Moreover, as homes for the "multitudes of loiterers and idle vagabonds" of England, colonies offered a solution to the problem of social dislocation and homelessness. He urged Elizabeth to establish such colonies "upon the mouths of the great navigable rivers" from Florida to the St. Lawrence.

Although Elizabeth declined to commit the state to Hakluyt's plan, she authorized and invested in several private attempts at exploration and colonization. Martin Frobisher conducted three voyages of exploration in the North Atlantic during the 1570s. But Raleigh and Gilbert, fresh from the Irish wars, planned the first true colonizing ventures. In 1583, Gilbert sailed with a flotilla of ships from Plymouth and landed at St. John's Bay, Newfoundland. He encountered fishermen from several other nations but nevertheless claimed the territory for his queen. But this effort came to naught when Gilbert's ship was lost on the return voyage.

Following his brother's death, Raleigh decided to establish a colony southward, in the more hospitable climate of the mid-Atlantic coast. Although the Roanoke enterprise of 1584–87 seemed far more promising than Gilbert's, it too eventually failed (as described in the opening of the chapter). In contrast to the French, who concentrated on commerce, the English drew on their Irish experience, attempting to dominate and conquer natives. The greatest legacy of the expedition was the work of Thomas Harriot and John White, who mapped the area, surveyed its commercial potential, and studied the Indian residents. Harriot's *A Briefe and True Report of the Newfound Land of Virginia* (1588), illustrated by engravings of White's

The care that John White brought to his painting is evident in this watercolor of an Algonquian mother and daughter (1585). The woman's fringed deerskin skirt is edged with white beads, and the decoration on her face and upper arms seems to be tattooed. The little wooden doll in the girl's hand was a gift from White. All the Indian girls, wrote Thomas Harriot, "are greatly dellighted with puppetts and babes which were brought out of England."

SOURCE: John White (1570–93), "Woman and Child of Pomeiooc." Watercolor. British Museum, London. The Bridgeman Art Library International Ltd.

watercolors, provided the single most accurate description of North American Indians at the moment of their contact with Europeans.

King Philip II of Spain was outraged at the English incursions into territory reserved by the pope for Catholics. He had authorized the destruction of the French colony in Florida, and now he committed himself to smashing England. In 1588, he sent a fleet of 130 ships carrying 30,000 men to invade the British Isles. Countered by captains such as Drake and Hawkins, who commanded smaller and more maneuverable ships, and frustrated by an ill-timed storm that the English chose to interpret as an act of divine intervention, the Spanish Armada foundered. The Spanish monopoly of the New World had been broken in the English Channel.

CONCLUSION

The Spanish opened the era of European colonization in the Americas with Columbus's voyage in 1492. The consequences for the Indian peoples of the Americas were disastrous. The Spanish succeeded in constructing the world's most powerful empire on the backs of Indian and African labor. Inspired by the Spanish success, the French and the English attempted to colonize the coast of North America. By the end of the sixteenth century, however, they had not succeeded in establishing any lasting colonial communities. Instead, a very different kind of colonial encounter, based on commerce rather than conquest, was taking place in northeastern North America. In the next century, the French would turn this development to their advantage. Along the mid-Atlantic coast in Virginia, however, the English would put their Irish experience to use, pioneering an altogether new kind of American colonialism.

REVIEW QUESTIONS

1. Discuss the roles played by the rising merchant class, the new monarchies, Renaissance humanism, and the Reformation in the development of European colonialism.
2. Define a "frontier of inclusion." In what ways does this description apply to the Spanish empire in the Americas?
3. Make a list of the major exchanges that took place between the Old World and the New World in the centuries following the European invasion of America. Discuss some of the effects these exchanges had on the course of modern history.
4. In what ways did colonial contact in the Northeast differ from contacts in the Caribbean and Mexico?
5. In what ways might the English experience in Ireland have shaped expectations about American colonization?

RECOMMENDED READING

David Noble Cook, *Born to Die: Disease and New World Conquest, 1492–1650* (1998). A synthetic history of the impact of disease, including Indian and European views.

Alfred W. Crosby Jr., *The Columbian Exchange: Biological and Cultural Consequences of 1492* (1972). Pathbreaking account of the intersection of the biospheres of the Old and New Worlds.

Kathleen Deagan and José María Cruxent, *Columbus's Outpost Among the Taínos: Spain and America at La Isabela, 1493–1498* (2002). An archaeological and historical account of the first European outpost in the New World.

Richard Flint, *Great Cruelties Have Been Reported: The 1544 Investigation of the Coronado Expedition* (2001). Testimony regarding the treatment of Indians and subsequent human rights debates in Spain.

Lewis Hanke, *The Spanish Struggle for Justice in the Conquest of America* (1949). The classic account of las Casas's attempts to rectify the wrongs committed by the Spanish against the Indians.

Charles M. Hudson, *Knights of Spain, Warriors of the Sun: Hernando de Soto and the South's Ancient Chiefdoms* (1997). A very readable history of the de Soto expedition, told from the viewpoint of the Indians.

Henry Kamen, *Spain's Road to Empire: The Making of a World Power, 1492–1763* (2002). A fascinating account arguing that it was not Spain that made the empire but the empire that made Spain.

Samuel Eliot Morison, *The European Discovery of America: The Northern Voyages, a.d. 500–1600 (1971) and The Southern Voyages, a.d. 1492–1616* (1974). The most detailed treatment of all the important European explorations of the Americas.

Matthew Restall, *Seven Myths of the Spanish Conquest* (2003). A brilliant and refreshing new perspective on Spain's intrusion into the New World.

David Beers Quinn, *Set Fair for Roanoke: Voyages and Colonies, 1584–1606* (1985). The story of Roanoke—the Indian village, the English settlement, and the Lost Colony.

Carl Ortwin Sauer, *Sixteenth Century North America: The Land and the People as Seen by the Europeans* (1971). An excellent source for the explorations of the continent, providing abundant descriptions of the Indians.

Hugh Thomas, *Conquest: Montezuma, Cortés, and the Fall of Old Mexico* (1993). A fascinating account, written by a master of historical style, that incorporates the Aztec view as well as the words of the conquerors.

Gustavo Verdesio, *Forgotten Conquests: Rereading New World History from the Margins* (2001). An argument that the old master historical narrative represents only one of many possible histories, and a suggestion for finding the colonial subjects who did not produce documents.

 For additional study resources for this chapter, go to the *Companion Website,* http://www.prenhall.com/faragher.

Planting Colonies in North America

1588–1701

55

Communities Struggle with Diversity in Seventeenth-Century Santa Fé

I t was a hot August day in 1680 when the frantic messengers rode into the small mission outpost of El Paso with the news that the Pueblo Indians to the north had risen in revolt. The corpses of more than 400 colonists lay bleeding in the dust. Two thousand Spanish survivors huddled inside the Palace of Governors in Santa Fé, surrounded by 3,000 angry warriors. The Pueblo leaders had sent two crosses into the palace—white for surrender, red for death. Which would the Spaniards choose?

Spanish colonists had been in New Mexico for nearly a century. Franciscan priests came first, followed by a military expedition from Mexico in search of precious metals. In 1609, high in the picturesque foothills of the Sangre de Cristo Mountains, the colonial authorities founded La Villa Real de la Santa Fé de San Francisco— "the royal town of the holy faith of St. Francis"—soon known simply as Santa Fé. Colonization efforts included the conversion of the Pueblo Indians to Christianity, making them subjects of the king of Spain, and forcing them to work for the colonial elite who lived in the town.

In the face of Spanish armed force, the Pueblos adopted a flexible attitude. Thousands of them eventually converted to Christianity, but most merely joined the new practices to their own supernatural traditions. The Christian God was added to their numerous deities; church holidays were included in their religious calendar and celebrated with native dances and rituals.

But the missionaries attempted to stamp out Pueblo traditional religion, invading underground kivas (sites for the conduct of sacred rituals) destroying sacred Indian artifacts, publicly humiliating holy men, and compelling whole villages to perform penance by working in irrigation ditches and fields. In 1675, the governor hanged four Pueblo religious leaders and publicly whipped dozens more. These outrages—in combination with a prolonged drought and severe famine, and rampant epidemic disease that the missionaries were powerless to prevent or cure— led directly to the revolt of 1680. One of the humiliated leaders, Popé of San Juan Pueblo, helped organize a conspiracy among more than twenty towns.

There were plenty of local grievances. The Hopi people of northern Arizona told of a missionary who ordered that all the young women of the village be brought to live with him. When the revolt began, the people surrounded his house. "I have come to kill you," the chief announced. "You can't kill me," the priest cried from behind his locked door. "I will come [back] to life and wipe out your whole tribe." But the chief shouted back, "My gods have more power than you have." He and his men broke down the door, hung the missionary from the beams, and lit a fire beneath his feet.

When the Indians demanded the surrender of the Spanish inside Santa Fé's Palace of Governors, the besieged colonists sent back the red cross, signaling defiance. But after five days of seige, the Pueblos allowed them to retreat south to El Paso, "the poor women and children on foot and unshod," in the words of one account, and "of such a hue that they looked like dead people." The Indians then ransacked the missions, desecrating the holy furnishings and leaving the mutilated bodies of priests lying on their altars. They transformed the governor's chapel into a traditional kiva, his palace into a communal dwelling. On the elegant inlaid stone floors where the governor had held court, Pueblo women now ground their corn.

Santa Fé

Santa Fé became the capital of a Pueblo confederacy led by the leader Popé. He forced Christian Indians "to plunge into the rivers" to wash away the taint of baptism, and ordered the destruction of everything Spanish. But this was difficult to do. The colonists had introduced horses and sheep, fruit trees and wheat, new tools and new crafts, all of which the Indians found useful. The Pueblos also found that they missed the support of the Spanish in their struggle against their traditional enemies, the Navajos and Apaches. Equipped with stolen horses and weapons, their raids on the unprotected Pueblo villages became much more destructive. With chaos mounting, Popé was deposed in 1690.

In 1692, the Spanish army under Governor Diego de Vargas invaded the province once again in an attempt to reestablish the colonial regime. The Pueblos rose up in another full-scale rebellion, but Vargas crushed it with overwhelming force. After six years of fighting, the Spanish suceeded in reconquering New Mexico. Learning from previous mistakes, they practiced greater restraint, enabling the Indians to accept their authority. Missionaries tolerated the practice of traditional religion in the Indians' underground kivas, while Pueblos dutifully observed Catholicism in the missionary chapels. Royal officials guaranteed the inviolability of Indian lands, and Pueblos pledged loyalty to the Spanish monarch. Pueblos turned out for service on colonial lands, and colonists abandoned the system of forced labor. The Spanish and Pueblo communities remained autonomous, but together they managed to hold off the attacks by the mounted nomads.

KEY TOPICS

- A comparison of the European colonies established in North America in the seventeenth century

- The English and Algonquian colonial encounter in the Chesapeake

- The role of religious dissent in the planting of the New England colonies

- The restoration of the Stuart monarchy and the creation of new proprietary colonies

- Indian warfare and internal conflict at the end of the seventeenth century

SPAIN AND ITS COMPETITORS IN NORTH AMERICA

At the beginning of the seventeenth century, the Spanish controlled the only colonial outposts on the mainland, a series of forts along the Florida coast to protect the Gulf Stream sea lanes used by convoys carrying wealth from their New World to Spain. During the first two decades of the century, however, the Spanish, French, Dutch, and English were all drawn into planting substantial colonies in North America.

Because neither Spain nor France proved willing or able to transport large numbers of their people to populate these colonies, both relied on a policy of converting Indians into subjects, and as a result there was a great deal of cultural mixing between colonists and natives. New Spain and New France were "frontiers of inclusion," where native peoples were incorporated into colonial society. The Dutch first followed the French model when they established their colony on the Hudson River on the northeastern Atlantic coast. But soon they changed course, emulating the English, who from the beginning of their colonial experience adopted a different model, in which settlers and Indians lived in separate societies. Virginia and New England were "frontiers of exclusion," in dramatic contrast to New Spain and New France.

New Mexico

After the 1539 expedition of Francisco Vásquez de Coronado failed to turn up vast Indian empires to conquer in the northern Mexican deserts, the Spanish interest in the Southwest faded. The densely settled farming communities of the Pueblos offered a harvest of converts for

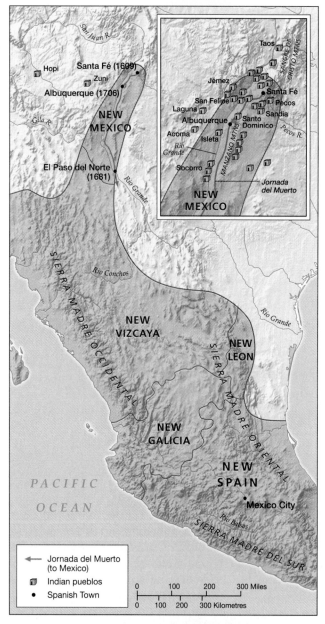

MAP 3.1 New Mexico in the Seventeenth Century
By the end of the seventeenth century, New Mexico numbered 3,000 colonial settlers in several towns, surrounded by an estimated 50,000 Pueblo Indians living in some fifty farming villages. The isolation and sense of danger among the Hispanic settlers are evident in their name for the road linking the colony with New Spain, *Jornada del Muerto,* "the Road of Death."

Christianity, however, and by the 1580s, Franciscan missionaries were at work in the Southwest. Eventually rumors drifted back to Mexico City of rich gold deposits along the Rio Grande, raising the hopes of Spanish officials that they might find another Aztec empire. In 1598, Juan de Oñate, the son of a wealthy mining family of northern New Spain, financed a colonizing expedition made up of Indian and mestizo soldiers with the purpose of mining both gold and souls.

Moving north into the upper Rio Grande Valley, Oñate encountered varying degrees of resistance. He lay siege at Acoma, the pueblo set high atop a great outcropping of desert rock. Indian warriors mounted a bold defense, but in the end the attackers succeeded in climbing the rock walls and laying waste to the town, killing 800 men, women, and children. Surviving warriors had one foot severed, and more than 500 people were enslaved.

Unable to locate any gold—because there was none—Oñate was soon recalled to Mexico. The Spanish depended on the exploitation of Indian labor to produce valuable commodities, and without mines to exploit, interest in the remote province waned. But the church convinced the Spanish monarchy to subsidize New Mexico as a special missionary colony, and in 1609, a new governor founded the capital of Santa Fé. From this base the Franciscan missionaries penetrated all the surrounding Indian villages.

The colonial economy of New Mexico, based on small-scale agriculture and sheep raising, was never very prosperous. Afflicted with epidemic diseases, over the course of the seventeenth century the native population fell from 80,000 to less than 15,000. Very few new settlers came up the dusty road from Mexico, and what little growth there was in the colonial population resulted from marriages between colonial men and Pueblo women. By the late seventeenth century, this outpost of the Spanish empire contained some 3,000 colonists (mostly mestizos, of mixed Indian and European ancestry) in a few towns along the Rio Grande (see Map 3.1).

New France

In the early seventeenth century, the French devised a strategy to monopolize the northern fur trade. In 1605, Samuel de Champlain, acting as the agent of a royal monopoly, helped establish the outpost of Port Royal on the Bay of Fundy in what became known as the province of Acadia. It proved impossible, however, to control the coastal trade from that location. In 1608, Champlain founded the settlement of Quebec on the St. Lawrence River at a site where he could intercept the traffic in furs traveling downriver to the Atlantic. Forging an alliance

Acoma Pueblo, the "sky city," was founded in the thirteenth century and is one of the oldest continuously inhabited sites in the United States. In 1598, Juan de Oñate attacked and laid waste to the pueblo, killing some 800 inhabitants and enslaving another 500.

SOURCE: Kevin Fleming/Corbis/Bettmann.

but they decided that New France would be exclusively Catholic. As a result, the population grew very slowly, reaching a total of only 15,000 colonists by 1700. Quebec, the administrative capital, was small by Spanish colonial standards, and Montreal, founded as a missionary and trading center in 1642, was only a frontier outpost. Small clusters of farmers known as habitants lived along the St. Lawrence on the lands of landlords or seigneurs. By using Indian farming techniques, the habitants were able to produce subsistence crops, and eventually developed a modest export economy.

Rather than facing the Atlantic, the communities of Canada looked west toward the continental interior. It was typical for young male habitants to take to

with the Huron Indians, who controlled access to the rich fur grounds of the Great Lakes, in 1609 and 1610 he joined them in making war on their traditional enemies, the Five Nation Iroquois Confederacy. (See Out of Many Voices: Samuel de Champlain Describes his Attack on the Iroquois). Champlain sent traders to live in native communities, where they learned local languages and customs, and directed the flow of furs to Quebec.

The St. Lawrence River was like a great roadway leading directly into the heart of the North American continent, and it provided the French with enormous geographic and political advantage. But the river froze during the winter, isolating the colonists, and the short growing season limited agricultural productivity in the region. Thousands of Frenchmen went to New France as engagés ("hired men") in the fur trade or the fishery, but nine of ten soon returned to France. The French could have populated their American empire with thousands of willing Huguenot dissenters,

the woods, working as independent traders or paid agents of the fur companies, known as coureurs de bois. Most of them eventually returned to their farming communities, but others remained behind, marrying Indian women and raising mixed-ancestry families. French traders were living on the shores of the Great Lakes as early as the 1620s, and

This drawing, by Samuel de Champlain, shows how Huron men funneled deer into enclosures, where they could be trapped and easily killed.

SOURCE: Courtesy of the Library of Congress.

French traders and missionaries were exploring the reaches of the upper Mississippi River by the 1670s. In 1681–82, fur-trade commandant Robert Sieur de La Salle navigated the mighty river to its mouth on the Gulf of Mexico and claimed its entire watershed for France (see Map 3.2).

Like the Spanish, the French established an American society of inclusion in which settlers intermarried with native peoples. But in most ways the two colonial systems were quite different. The Spanish conquered native peoples and exploited them as a labor force for mines, plantations, and ranches. The French did not have the manpower to bully, dispossess, or enslave native peoples, but instead attempted to build an empire through alliances with independent Indian nations, which included commercial relations with Indian hunters. There were also important differences between Spanish and French missionary efforts. Unlike the Franciscans in seventeenth-century New Mexico, who insisted that natives accept European cultural norms, the Jesuit missionaries in New France learned native language and attempted to understand native mores, in an effort to introduce Christianity as a part of the existing Indian way of life.

New Netherland

The United Provinces of the Netherlands, commonly known as Holland, was only a fraction the size of France, but in the sixteenth century it had been at the center of Europe's economic transformation. On land

OUT OF MANY VOICES

SAMUEL DE CHAMPLAIN DESCRIBES HIS ATTACK ON THE IROQUOIS

Samuel de Champlain was the leader of the first French colony along the St. Lawrence River. His alliances with native peoples was the key to French success. In this account, written in 1613, he describes joining the attack of his Huron allies on a war party of some 200 Mohawks on the shores of Lake Champlain. It marked the first time the Mohawks had seen Europeans, or experienced the effects of firearms.

AS SOON AS WE LANDED, OUR INDIANS BEGAN TO run some two hundred yards towards their enemies, who stood firm and had not yet noticed my white companions who went off into the woods with some Indians. Our Indians began to call to me with loud cries; and to make way for me they divided into two groups, and put me ahead some twenty yards, and I marched on until I was within some thirty yards of the enemy, who as soon as they caught sight of me halted and gazed at me and I at them. When I saw them make a move to draw their bows upon us, I took aim with my arquebus and shot straight at one of the three chiefs, and with this shot two fell to the ground and one of their companions was wounded who died thereof a little later. I had put four bullets into my arquebus.

As soon as our people saw this shot so favourable for them, they began to shout so loudly that one could not have heard it thunder, and meanwhile the arrows flew thick on both sides. The Iroquois were much astonished that two men should have been killed so quickly, although they were provided with shields made of cotton thread woven together and wood, which were proof against their arrows. This frightened them greatly. As I was reloading my arquebus, one of my companions fired a shot from within the woods, which astonished them again so much that, seeing their chiefs dead, they lost courage and took to flight, abandoning the field and their fort, and fleeing into the depth of the forest, whither I pursued them and laid low still more of them. Our Indians also killed several and took ten or twelve prisoners. The remainder fled with the wounded. Of our Indians fifteen or sixteen were wounded with arrows, but these were quickly healed.

After we had gained the victory, our Indians wasted time in taking a large quantity of Indian corn and meal belonging to the enemy, as well as their shields, which they had left behind, the better to run. Having feasted, danced, and sung, we three hours later set off for home with the prisoners. The place where this attack took place is in 43° and some minutes of latitude, and was named Lake Champlain. ■

SOURCE: Samuel de Champlain, *The Works of Samuel de Champlain*, 6 vols. (Toronto: Champlain Society, 1922–36), vol 2, pp. 89–101.

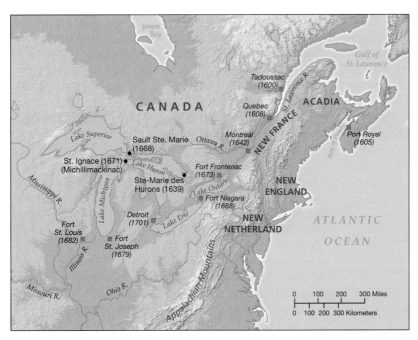

MAP 3.2 New France in the Seventeenth Century By the late seventeenth century, French settlements were spread from the town of Port Royal in Acadia to the post and mission at Sault Ste. Marie on the Great Lakes. But the heart of New France comprised the communities stretching along the St. Lawrence River between the towns of Quebec and Montreal.

This illustration, taken from Samuel de Champlain's 1613 account of the founding of New France, depicts him joining the Huron attack on the Iroquois in 1609. The French and their Huron allies controlled access to the great fur grounds of the West. The Iroquois then formed an alliance of their own with the Dutch, who had founded a trading colony on the Hudson River. The palm trees in the background of this drawing suggest that it was not executed by an eyewitness, but rather by an illustrator more familiar with South American scenes.

SOURCE: Jacques Le Moyne, "Les Voyages," Samuel de Champlain, Paris, 1613. Illustration opp. pg. 322. Early battle with the Iroquois. Rare Books Division, The New York Public Library, Astor Lenox and Tilden Foundations. The New York Public Library/Art Resource, NY.

reclaimed from the sea by an elaborate system of dikes, Dutch farmers used new methods of crop rotation and deep tilling that dramatically increased their yields, producing large surpluses that supported the growth of the world's most urban and commercial nation. After a century of rule by the Hapsburgs, the prosperous Dutch rose up against their Spanish masters and in 1581 succeeded in winning their political independence. Amsterdam became the site of the world's first stock exchange and investment banks. Dutch investors built the largest commercial and fishing fleet in Europe and captured the lucrative Baltic and North Sea trade in fish, lumber, iron, and grain. It was said that the North Sea was Holland's "America."

Soon the Dutch were establishing trading outposts in America itself. Early in the seventeenth century, the United Netherlands organized two great monopolies, the Dutch East India Company and the Dutch West India Company, combining naval military might and commercial strength in campaigns to seize the maritime trade of Asia and the Atlantic. Backed by powerfully armed men-of-war ships, during the first half of the seventeenth century Dutch traders built a series of trading posts in China, Indonesia, India, Africa, Brazil, the Caribbean, and North America, and Holland became the greatest commercial power in the world. The Dutch first appeared in North America in 1609 with the explorations of Henry Hudson, and within a few years they had founded settlements at Fort Orange (today's Albany), upriver at the head of navigation for ocean-going vessels on the Hudson River, and at New Amsterdam, on Manhattan Island, at the river's mouth. Seeking to match French success, they negotiated a commercial alliance with the Iroquois Confederacy to obtain furs. Greatly strengthened by access to superior Dutch products, including metal tools and firearms, the Iroquois embarked on a series of military expeditions against their neighbors (sometimes known as the Beaver Wars) which made them into strategic commercial middlemen for the Dutch. In the late 1640s, the Iroquois attacked and dispersed the Hurons, who controlled the flow of furs from the Great Lakes to their French allies. The Dutch also succeeded in overwhelming a small colony of Swedes on the lower Delaware River, incorporating that region into their sphere of influence in the 1640s.

ENGLAND IN THE CHESAPEAKE

England first attempted to plant colonies in North America during the 1580s, in Newfoundland and at Roanoke Island in present-day North Carolina (see Chapter 2). Both attempts were failures. A long war with Spain (1588 to 1604) suspended further efforts, but once it concluded, the English again turned to the Americas.

Jamestown and the Powhatan Confederacy

Early in his reign, King James I (reigned 1603–25) issued royal charters for the colonization of the mid-Atlantic region—which the English called Virginia—to joint-stock companies that raised capital by the sale of shares. In 1607, a group of London investors known as the Virginia Company sent ships and a hundred men to Chesapeake Bay, where the colonists built a fort they named Jamestown in the king's honor. It would be the first permanent English settlement in North America.

The Chesapeake was home to an estimated 14,000 Algonquian people living in several dozen self-governing communities. By what right did the English think they could seize lands occupied by another people? "These Savages have no particular propertie in any parcell of that country, but only a general residence there, as wild beasts have in the forest," an English minister preached to departing Jamestown colonists. "They range and wander up and downe the country, without any law or government, being led only by their own lusts and sesualitie." Indians were savages with no rights that Christians had to respect. In fact, the native communities of the Chesapeake were bound together in a sophisticated political system known as the Powhatan Confederacy, led by a powerful chief named Wahunsonacook, whom the Jamestown colonists called "King Powhatan." Powhatan feelings about Europeans were mixed. He knew they could mean trouble, for in the 1570s, Spanish missionaries had attempted to plant a colony in the Chesapeake, but after they interfered with the practice of native religion they were violently expelled. Still, Powhatan was eager to forge an alliance with these people from across the sea that he might

obtain access to supplies of metal tools and weapons, which would assist him in extending his rule over outlying communities. He allowed the colonists leave to build their outpost at Jamestown. As was the case elsewhere in the Americas, Indians attempted to use Europeans to pursue ends of their own.

The Jamestown colonists included adventurers, gentlemen, and "ne'er-do-wells," in the words of John Smith, the colony's military leader. They had come to find gold and a passage to the Indies, and failing at both they spent their time gaming and drinking. They survived only because of Powhatan's material assistance. "In our extremity the Indians brought us corn," Smith wrote, "when we rather expected they would destroy us." But as more colonists arrived from England, and demands for food escalated, Powhatan had second thoughts. He now realized, he declared to Smith, that the English had come "not for trade, but to invade my people and possess my country." During the winter of 1609–10, more than four hundred colonists starved and a number resorted to cannibalism. Only sixty remained alive by the spring.

Determined to prevail, the Virginia Company committed itself to a protracted war against the Indians. Armed colonists attacked native villages, slaughtering men, women, and children alike. The grim conflict continued until 1613, when an English commander suceeded in capturing one of Powhatan's daughters, Matoaka, a girl of about fifteen whom the colonists knew by her nickname, Pocahontas. Eager to see his child again, and worn down by violence and disease, the next year Powhatan accepted a treaty of peace. "I am old and ere long must die," he mused. "I know it is better to eat good meat, lie well, and sleep with my women and children, laugh and be merry, than to be forced to flee and be hunted." The peace was sealed by the marriage of Pocahontas to John Rolfe, one of the leading colonists. For a brief moment it seemed the English too might move in the direction of a society of incluson. Rolfe traveled to England with his wife and son, where they were greeted as American nobility. Included in their party were a number of colonists who had adopted the Powhatan style of shaving their heads on one side, a custom designed to prevent the strings of their bows from getting caught in their hair. But Pocahontas fell ill and died before returning. Crushed by the news, Powhatan abdicated in favor of his brother Opechancanough before dying of despair.

Tobacco, Expansion, and Warfare

During these years, the Virginia colonists struggled to find the "merchantable commodity" for which Thomas Harriot, the scientist who accompanied the Roanoke expedition, had searched (see Chapter 2). They finally

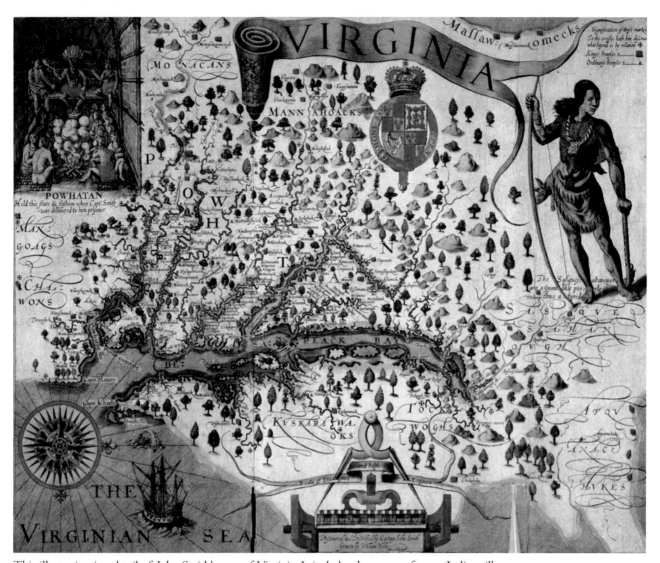

This illustration is a detail of John Smith's map of Virginia. It includes the names of many Indian villages, suggesting how densely settled was the Indian population of the coast of Chesapeake Bay. For the inset of Powhatan and his court in the upper left, the engraver borrowed images from John White's drawings of the Indians of the Roanoke area.

SOURCE: Princeton University Library. Manuscripts Division. Department of Rare Books and Special Collections.

found it in tobacco. Tobacco had been introduced to England by Francis Drake in the 1580s, and by the 1610s, a craze for smoking created strong demand. Colonist John Rolfe developed a mild hybrid variety, and soon the first commercial shipments of cured Virginia leaf reached England. Tobacco provided the Virginia Company with the first returns on its investment.

But tobacco cultivation required a great deal of hand labor, and it quickly exhausted the soil. Questions of land and labor would henceforth dominate the history of the Virginia colony. The company instituted what were called "headright grants"—awards of large plantations to wealthy colonists on condition they transport workers from England at their own cost. Because thousands of English families were being thrown off the land (see Chapter 2), many were attracted by the prospect of work in Virginia. More than 10,000 colonists were sent to Jamestown before 1622, but high mortality, probably the result of epidemics of typhoid fever and perhaps malaria, kept the total population at just over a thousand.

Massive immigration would prove to be the distinguishing characteristic of English colonization in America. In choosing to populate their colony with families, the English moved in a different direction from the Spanish, who sent mostly male settlers. Moreover, the English concentration on plantation agriculture contrasted significantly with the French emphasis on trade. With little need to incorporate Indians into the population as workers or marriage partners, the English began to push them to the periphery. Virginia became a "frontier of exclusion."

A TOBACCO PLANTATION

In this eighteenth-century engraving, used to promote the sale of tobacco, slaves pack tobacco leaves into "hogsheads" for shipment to England, overseen by a Virginia planter and his clerk. Note the incorporation of the Indian motif.

SOURCE: The Granger Collection.

Pressed for the cession of additional lands on which to grow tobacco, Chief Opechancanough prepared his people for an assault that would expel the English for good. His plans were supported by the native shaman Nemattanew, who instructed his followers to reject the English and their ways. This would be the first of many Indian resistance movements led jointly by strong political and religious figures. Nemattanew was murdered by colonists in March 1622, and the uprising which began two weeks later, on Good Friday, completely surprised the English, 347 people were killed, nearly a third of Virginia's colonial population. Yet the colonists managed to hang on through a ten-year war of attrition. The Powhatans finally sued for peace in 1632, but in the meantime, the war sent the Virginia Company into bankruptcy. In 1624, the king converted Virginia into a royal colony with civil authorities appointed by the crown, although property-owning colonists continued to elect representatives to the colony's House of Burgesses, created in 1619, which had authority over taxes and finances. Although disease, famine, and warfare took a heavy toll, continual emigration from England allowed the colonial population to double every five years from 1625 to 1640, by which time it numbered approximately 10,000 (see Figure 3.1). Meanwhile, decimated by violence and disease, the Algonquians shrank to about the same number.

In 1644, Opechancanough organized a final desperate revolt in which more than 500 colonists were killed. But the next year the Virginians crushed the Algonquians, capturing and executing their leader. A formal treaty granted the Indians a number of small reserved territories. By 1670, the Indian population had fallen to just 2,000, overwhelmed by 40,000 English colonists.

Maryland

In 1632, King Charles I (reigned 1625–49) granted 10 million acres at the northern end of Chesapeake Bay to the Calvert family, the Lords Baltimore, important Catholic supporters of the English monarchy. The Calverts named their colony Maryland, in honor of the king's wife, and the first party of colonists founded the settlement of St. Mary's near the mouth of the Potomac River in 1634. Two features distinguished Maryland from Virginia. First, it was a "proprietary" colony. The Calverts were sole owners of all the land, which they planned to carve into feudal manors that would provide them with annual rents, and they appointed all the civil officers. Second, because the proprietors were Catholics, they encouraged settlement by their coreligionists, a persecuted minority in seventeenth-century England. In fact, Maryland became the only English colony in North America with a substantial Catholic minority. Wealthy Catholic landlords were appointed to the governing council, and they came to dominate Maryland's House of Delegates, founded in 1635.

Despite these differences, Maryland quickly assumed the character of neighboring Virginia. Its tobacco plantation economy created pressures for labor and expansion that could not be met by the Calverts' original feudal plans. In 1640, the colony adopted the system of headright grants previously developed in Virginia, and settlements of independent planters quickly spread out on both sides of Chesapeake Bay. By the 1670s, Maryland's English population numbered more than 15,000.

Indentured Servants

At least three-quarters of the English migrants to the Chesapeake during the seventeenth century came as indentured servants. In exchange for the cost of their transportation to

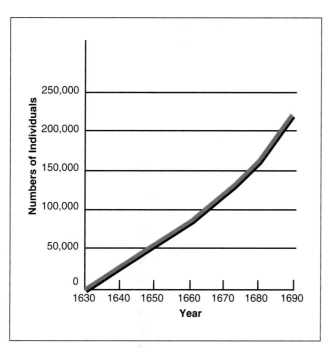

FIGURE 3.1 **Population Growth of the British Colonies in the Seventeenth Century** The British colonial population grew steadily through the century, then increased sharply in the closing decade as a result of the new settlements of the propietary colonies.

the New World, men and women contracted to labor for a master during a fixed term. Most indentured servants were young, unskilled males, who served for two to seven years; but some were skilled craftsmen, unmarried women, or even parentless children (the latter were expected to serve a master until they reached the age of twenty-one). A minority were convicts or vagabonds bound into service by English courts for as long as fourteen years.

Masters were obliged to feed, clothe, and house these servants adequately. But work in the tobacco fields was backbreaking, and records include complaints of inadequate care. One Virginia ballad chronicled these objections:

> Come all you young fellows wherever you be,
> Come listen awhile and I will tell thee,
> Concerning the hardships that we undergo,
> When we get lagg'd to Virginia.
>
> Now in Virginia I lay like a hog,
> Our pillow at night is a brick or a log,
> We dress and undress like some other sea dog,
> How hard is my fate in Virginia.

Many servants tried to escape, although capture could mean a doubling of their terms of service.

African slaves were first introduced to the Chesapeake in 1619, but slaves were considerably more expen-sive than servants, and as late as 1680 they made up less than 7 percent of the Chesapeake population. In the hard-driving economy of the Chesapeake, however, masters treated servants as cruelly as they treated slaves. After arriving, bound laborers were inspected by planters who poked at the muscles of men and pinched women. Because of the high mortality levels resulting from epidemics of typhus and malaria in the Chesapeake colonies, approximately two of every five servants died during the period of their indenture. Those who survived were eligible for "freedom dues"—clothing, tools, a gun, or a spinning wheel, help getting started on their own—and many former servants headed west in the hope of cutting a farm from the wilderness. But most former servants who were able to raise the price of passage returned home to England. Indentured labor may not have been slavery, but the distinction may have seemed academic to servants (see Chapter 4 for a full discussion of slavery).

Community Life in the Chesapeake

Because most emigrants were men, whether free or indentured, free unmarried women often married as soon as they arrived in the Chesapeake. Moreover, in the disease-ridden environment of the early Chesapeake, English men apparently suffered a higher rate of mortality than women, and widows remarried quickly, sometimes within days. Their scarcity provided women with certain advantages. Shrewd widows bargained for remarriage agreements that gave them a larger share of estates than those set by common law. So notable was the concentration of wealth in the hands of these widows, that one historian has suggested that early Virginia was a "matriarchy." But because of high mortality rates, family size was smaller and kinship bonds—one of the most important components of community—were weaker than they were in England.

English visitors often remarked on the crude conditions of community life. Prosperous planters, investing everything in tobacco production, lived in rough wooden dwellings. On the western edge of the settlements, former servants lived with their families in shacks, huts, even caves. Colonists spread across the countryside in search of new lands to farm, creating dispersed settlements with hardly any towns. Before 1650 there were few community institutions such as schools and churches. Meanwhile, the Spanish in Cuba and Mexico were building great cities with permanent institutions.

In contrast to the colonists of New France, who were developing a distinctive American identity because of their commercial and political connections to native peoples, the population of the Chesapeake maintained close emotional ties to England. Colonial politics were shaped less by local developments than by a continuing relationship with the mother country.

THE NEW ENGLAND COLONIES

Both in climate and in geography, the northern coast of North America was far different from the Chesapeake. "Merchantable commodities" such as tobacco were not easily produced there, and thus it was far less favored for investment and settlement. Instead, the region became a haven for Protestant dissenters from England, who gave the colonies of the north a distinctive character (see Map 3.3).

The Social and Political Values of Puritanism

Most English men and women continued to practice a Christianity that was little different from traditional Catholicism. But the English followers of John Calvin, known as Puritans because they wished to purify and reform the English church, grew increasingly influential during the last years of Queen Elizabeth's reign at the end of the sixteenth century. The Calvinist emphasis on enterprise meant that Puritanism had special appeal among merchants, entrepreneurs, and commercial farmers, those most responsible for the rapid economic and social transformation of England. But the Puritans were also the most vocal critics of the disruptive effects of that change, condemning the decline of the traditional rural community and the growing number of "idle and masterless men" produced by the enclosure of common lands. They argued for reviving communities by placing reformed Christian congregations at their core to monitor the behavior of individuals. By the early seventeenth century, Puritans controlled many English congregations and had become an influential force at the universities at Oxford and Cambridge, training centers for the future political and religious leaders of England. (For a review of the Protestant Reformation and the enclosure movement in England, see Chapter 2).

King James I (reigned 1603–25), Elizabeth's nephew, who assumed the throne after her death, abandoned the policy of religious tolerance. His persecution of the Puritans, however, merely stiffened their resolve and turned them toward open political opposition. An increasingly vocal Puritan minority in Parliament criticized King Charles I (reigned 1625–49), James's son and successor, for marrying a Roman Catholic princess as well as supporting "High Church" policies, emphasizing the authority of the clerical hierarchy and its traditional forms of worship. In 1629, determined to rule without these troublesome Puritan opponents, Charles dismissed Parliament and launched a campaign of repression. This political turmoil provided the context for the migration of thousands of English Protestants to New England.

MAP EXPLORATION

To explore an interactive version of this map, go to **www.prenhall.com/faragher5/map3.3**

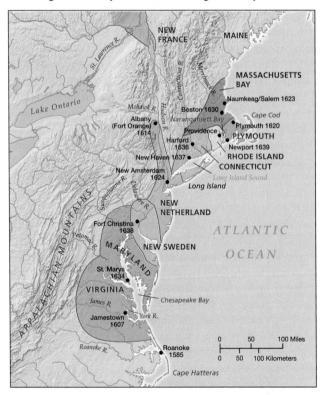

MAP 3.3 European Colonies of the Atlantic Coast, 1607–39 Virginia, on Chesapeake Bay, was the first English colony in North America, but by the mid-seventeenth century, Virginia was joined by settlements of Scandinavians on the Delaware River, and Dutch on the Hudson River, as well as English religious dissenters in New England. The territories indicated here reflect the vague boundaries of the early colonies.

Early Contacts in New England

The northern Atlantic coast seemed an unlikely spot for English colonies, for the region was dominated by French and Dutch traders. In 1613, desperate to keep their colonial options open, the English at Jamestown had dispatched armed vessels that destroyed the French post on the Bay of Fundy and harassed the Dutch on the Hudson. The following year, Captain John Smith of Jamestown explored the northern coastline and christened the region "New England." The land was "so planted with Gardens and Corne fields," he wrote, that "I would rather live here than any where." But Smith's plans for a New England colony planted on native fields was aborted when he was captured by the French.

Then a twist of fate transformed English fortunes. From 1616 to 1618, an epidemic ravaged the native peoples of the northern Atlantic coast. Whole villages disappeared, and the trade of the French and the Dutch was seriously disrupted. Indians perished so quickly and in such numbers that few remained to bury the dead. Modern estimates confirm the testimony of a surviving Indian that his people were "melted down by this disease, whereof nine-tenths of them have died." The native population of New England as a whole dropped from an estimated 120,000 to less than 70,000. So crippled were the surviving coastal societies, that they could not provide effective resistance to the planting of English colonies.

Plymouth Colony and the Mayflower Compact

The first English colony in New England was founded by a group of religious dissenters known to later generations as the Pilgrims. At the time they were called Separatists, because they believed the English church to be so corrupt that they had to establish their own independent congregations. One group moved to Holland in 1609, but fearful that tolerant Dutch society was seducing their children, they decided on emigration to North America. Backed by the Virginia Company of London and led by tradesman William Bradford, 102 people sailed from Plymouth, England, on the Mayflower in September 1620.

The little group, mostly families but including a substantial number of single men hired by the investors, arrived in Massachusetts Bay at the site of the former Indian village of Patuxet, which the English renamed Plymouth. Soon the hired men began to grumble about Pilgrim authority, and to reassure them Bradford drafted an agreement by which the male members of the expedition did "covenant and combine [themselves] together into a civil body politic." The Mayflower Compact was the first document of self-government in North America.

Weakened by scurvy and malnutrition, nearly half the Pilgrims perished over the first winter. Like the earlier settlers of Roanoke and Jamestown, however, they were rescued by Indians. Massasoit, the sachem or leader of the Pokanokets or Wampanoags, as they were also known, offered the newcomers food and advice in return for an alliance against his enemies, the Narragansetts. It was the familiar pattern of Indians attempting to incorporate European colonists into their world.

Deeply in debt to investors, always struggling to raise payments through the Indian trade, fishing, and lumbering, the Plymouth colony was never a financial success. Most families grew their own crops and kept their own livestock, but produced little for export. Nevertheless, the Pilgrims succeeded during the first two or three decades in establishing the self-sufficient community for which they had hoped. So strong was their communal agreement, that the annual meeting of property-owning men reelected William Bradford to thirty consecutive terms as governor. By midcentury, however, the Plymouth population had dispersed into eleven separate communities, and the growth of diverse local interests had begun to disrupt this Separatist retreat.

The Massachusetts Bay Colony

In England, the political climate of the late 1620s convinced a number of influential Puritans that the only way to protect their congregations was by emigration. In 1629, a royal charter was granted to a group of wealthy Puritans who called their enterprise the Massachusetts Bay Company, and an advance force of some 200 settlers left for the English fishing settlement of Naumkeag on Massachusetts Bay, which they renamed Salem. They hoped to establish what John Winthrop, their leader and first governor, called "a city on a hill," a New England

Governor John Winthrop, ca. 1640, a portrait by an unknown artist.

SOURCE: American Antiquarian Society.

OUT OF MANY VOICES

A PURITAN COLONIST WRITES HOME TO HIS FATHER IN ENGLAND

Among the many groups of Puritans to settle in coastal New England was a party of some forty families who relocated to the banks of the Charles River from the East Anglican region of England. In this letter home to his father, written in 1631, an anonymous settler writes of the hardship of the first months in the new land.

MY WRITING UNTO YOU IS TO LET YOU UNDERstand what a country this New England is where we live. Here are but few [Indians], a great part of them died this winter, it was thought it was of the plague. They are a crafty people & they will [cozen] & cheat, & they are a subtle people, & whereas we did expect great store of beaver here is little or none to be had. They are proper men & . . . many of them go naked with a skin about their loins, but now sum of them get Englishmen's apparel; & the country is very rocky and hilly & some champion ground & the soil is very [fruitful], & here is some good ground and marsh ground, but here is no Michaelmas. Spring cattle thrive well here, but they give small store of milk. The best cattle for profit is swines & a good swine is here at £5 price, and a goose worth £2 a good one got. Here is timber good store & acorns good store, and here is good store of fish if we had boats to go for & lines to serve to fishing. . . . & people here are subject to diseases, for here have died of the scurvy & of the burning fever nigh too hundred & odd; beside as many lie lame & all Sudbury men are dead but three & three women & some children, & provisions are here at a wonderful rate. . . . If this ship had not come when it did we had been put to a wonderful straight, but thanks be to God for sending of it in. I received from the ship a hogshead of meal, & the Governor telleth me of a hundred weight of cheese the which I have received part of it. I humbly thank you for it. I did expect two cows, the which I had none, nor I do not earnestly desire that you should send me any, because the country is not so as we did expect it. Therefore, loving father, I would entreat you that you would send me a firkin of butter & a hogshead of malt unground, for we drink nothing but water, & a coarse clothe of four pound price so it be thick. For the freight, if you of your love will send them I will pay the freight, for here is nothing to be got without we had commodities to go up to the East parts amongst the Indians to truck, for here where we live here is no beaver. Here is no cloth to be had to make no apparel, & shoes are a 5s a pair for me, & that cloth that is worth 2s 8d is worth here 5s. So I pray, father, send me four or five yards of cloth to make some apparel, & loving father, though I be far distant from you yet I pray you remember me as your child, & we do not know how long we may subsist, for we can not live here without provisions from old England. ■

SOURCE: *Proceedings of the Massachusetts Historical Society*, 2nd Series, 8 (Boston: The Society, 1892–94), pp. 471–73.

model of reform for old England. The Puritan emigration became known as the Great Migration, a phrase that would be repeated many times in American history. Between 1629 and 1643, some 20,000 people relocated to Massachusetts. (See Out of Many Voices: A Puritan Colonist Writes Home to his Father in England.) In 1630, they built the town of Boston, and within five years ringed it with towns as far as thirty miles inland. By 1640, their settlements had spread seventy-five miles west to the Connecticut River Valley, where they linked with settlers spreading north from the Puritan New Haven Colony, on Long Island Sound.

Most colonists arrived in groups from long-established communities in the east of England and often were led by men with extensive experience in local English government. Taking advantage of a loophole in their charter, the Puritan leaders transferred company operations to America in 1629, and within a few years had transformed the company into a civil government. The original charter established a General Court composed of a governor and his deputy, a board of magistrates (or advisers), and the members of the corporation, known as freemen. In 1632, Governor Winthrop and his advisers declared that all the male heads of households in Massachusetts, who were also church members, were freemen. Two years later, the freemen secured their right to select delegates to represent the towns in drafting the laws of the colony. These delegates and the magistrates later became the colony's two legislative houses. Thus the procedures of a joint-stock company provided the origins for democratic suffrage and the bicameral division of legislative authority in America.

Indians and Puritans

The Algonquian Indians of southern New England found the English very different from the French and Dutch traders who had preceded them. The principal concern of the English was not commerce, although the fur trade remained an important part of their economy, but the acquisition of Indian land for their growing settlements. Ravaged by disease, the native people of Massachusetts Bay were ill-prepared for the Puritan landings that took place after 1629.

The English believed they had the right to take what they thought of as "unused" lands—lands not being used, that is, in the "English way"—and depopulated Massachusetts villages became prime targets for expansion. "As for the natives in New England," argued Puritan leader John Winthrop, "they inclose no land, neither have any settled habytation, nor any

tame Cattle to improve the land by, and soe have noe other but a Naturall Right to those Countries, soe as if we leave them sufficient for their use, we may lawfully take the rest." The residents of one town, meeting in common assembly, made it perfectly clear: "Voted that the earth is the Lord's and the fulness thereof; voted that the earth is given to the Saints; voted, we are the Saints."

The English used a variety of tactics to pressure native leaders into signing "quitclaims," relinquishing all rights to specified properties. The English allowed their livestock to graze native fields, making them useless for cultivation. They fined Indians for violations of English law, such as working on the Sabbath, and then demanded land as payment. In addition, they made deals with dishonest sachems. For giving up the land that became Charlestown, for example, the "Squaw Sachem" of the Pawtuckets, one of a number of women Algonquian leaders, received twenty-one coats, nineteen fathoms of wampum, and three bushels of corn. Disorganized and demoralized, many coastal Algonquians soon placed themselves under the protection of the English.

Indian peoples to the west, however, remained a formidable presence. They blocked Puritan expansion until they were devastated in 1633–34 by an epidemic of smallpox that spread from the St. Lawrence south to Long Island Sound. This epidemic took place just as hundreds of English migrants were crowding into coastal towns. "Without this remarkable and terrible stroke of God upon the natives," recorded a town scribe, "we would with much more difficulty have found room, and at far greater charge have obtained and purchased land." In the aftermath of the epidemic, Puritans established many new inland towns.

By the late 1630s, only a few tribes in southern New England retained the power to challenge Puritan expansion. The Pequots, who lived along the shores of Long Island Sound near the mouth of the Connecticut River, were one of the most powerful. Allies of the Dutch, the Pequots controlled the production of wampum, woven belts of seashells used as a medium of exchange in the Indian trade. In 1637, Puritan leaders pressured the Pequots' traditional enemies, the Narragansetts who lived in present-day Rhode Island, to join them in

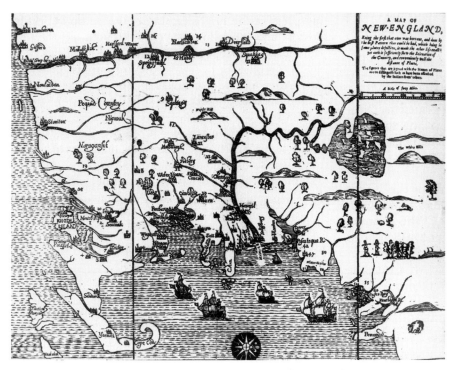

The first map printed in the English colonies, this view of New England was published in Boston in 1677. With north oriented to the right, it looks west from Massachusetts Bay, the two vertical black lines indicating the approximate boundaries of the Commonwealth of Massachusetts. The territory west of Rhode Island is noted as an Indian stronghold, the homelands of the Narraganset, Pequot, and Nipmuck peoples.

SOURCE: Courtesy of The John Carter Brown Library, at Brown University.

waging war against the Pequots. Narragansett warriors and English troops attacked the main village, burning the houses and killing most of their slumbering residents. "It was a fearful sight to see them thus frying in the fire," wrote William Bradford, "and horrible was the stink and scent thereof." The indiscriminate slaughter shocked the Narragansetts, who condemned the English way of war. It was "too furious and slays too many." The English commander dismissed their complaints. "The Scripture declareth that women and children must perish with their parents," he declared. "We had sufficient light from the Word of God for our proceedings."

The New England Merchants

In England, the conflict between King Charles I and the Puritans in Parliament broke into armed conflict in 1642. Several years of violent civil war led to the arrest and execution of the king in 1649 and the proclamation of an English Commonwealth, headed by the Puritan leader Oliver Cromwell. Because Puritans were on the victorious side in the English Civil War, they no longer had the same incentive to migrate to New England. A number of New England colonists even returned to England.

New England's economy had depended on the sale of supplies and land to arriving immigrants, but as the Great Migration ended, the importance of this "newcomer market" declined. The foundation of a new commercial economy was the cod fishery. New England merchants began shipping salted cod, as well as lumber and farm products, to to the West Indies, where they exchanged those commodities for sugar, molasses, and rum. By the 1660s, New England had a commercial fleet of more than three hundred vessels that was the envy of other colonies. By 1700, Boston had become the third largest English commercial center (after London and Bristol). New England crews voyaged throughout the Atlantic—to the fishing grounds of the North Atlantic, to the sugar-producing colonies of the West Indies, to the wine-producing islands of the Atlantic, to Africa and England. The development of a diversified economy provided New England with tremendous long-term strength, and offered a striking contrast with the specialized fur-trade economy of New France.

Community and Family in Massachusetts

The Puritans stressed the importance of well-ordered communities. The Massachusetts General Court, the governing body of the colony, granted townships groups of proprietors, the leaders of congregations wishing to settle new lands. These men then distributed fields, pasture, and woodlands in quantities proportional to the social status of the recipient, with wealthy heads of household receiving more than others. The Puritans believed that social hierarchy was ordained by God and required for well-ordered communities. Settlers typically clustered their dwellings in a central village, near the meetinghouse that served as both church and civic center. Some towns, particularly those along the coast such as Boston, became centers of shipping. Clustered settlements and strong communities distinguished New England from the dispersed and weak communities of the Chesapeake.

The ideal Puritan family was also well ordered. Parents often participated in the choice of mates for their offspring, and children typically married in the order of their births, younger siblings waiting until arrangements had been made for their elders. But well-disciplined children also needed education. Another source of New England's strength was the impressive system the Puritans built to educate their young. In 1647, Massachusetts required that towns with 50 families or more support a public school; those with 100 families were to establish a grammar school that taught Latin, knowledge of which was required for admission to Harvard College, founded in 1636. The colony of Connecticut enacted similar requirements. Literacy was higher in New England than elsewhere in North America, and even in most of Europe. But because girls were excluded from grammar schools, far fewer New England women than men could read and write. By 1639, the first printing press in the English colonies was in operation in Boston, and the following year it brought out the first American English publication, *The Bay Psalm Book*.

It is a mistake to regard the Puritans as "puritanical." Although adultery was a capital crime in New England, Puritans celebrated sexual expression within marriage. Courting couples were allowed to engage in "petting," and married couples were expected to enjoy sexual relations. There were many loving Puritan households. Anne Bradstreet, a Massachusetts wife and mother and the first published poet of New England, wrote about her husband and marriage:

> *If ever two are one, then surely we.*
> *If ever man were lov'd by wife, then thee;*
> *If ever wife was happy in a man,*
> *Compare with me ye women if you can.*

The family economy operated through the combined efforts of husband and wife. Men were generally responsible for fieldwork, women for the work of the household, garden, henhouse, and dairy. Women managed a rich array of tasks, and some independently traded garden products, milk, and eggs. "I meddle not with the geese nor turkeys," one husband wrote of his wife's domestic management, "for they are hers for she hath been and is a good wife to me."

Still, the cultural ideal was the subordination of women to men. "I am but a wife, and therefore it is suf-

The Mason Children, by an unknown Boston artist, ca. 1670. These Puritan children—David, Joanna, and Abigail Mason—are dressed in finery, an indication of the wealth and prominence of their family. The cane in young David's hand indicates his position as the male heir, while the rose held by Abigail is a symbol of childhood innocence.

SOURCE: The Freake-Gibbs Painter (American, Active 1670), *David, Joanna, and Abigail Mason*, 1670. Oil on canvas, 39 $\frac{1}{2}$ × 42 $\frac{1}{2}$ in. Fine Arts Museums of San Francisco, Gift of Mr. and Mrs. John D. Rockefeller 3rd to The Fine Arts Museums of San Francisco, 1979.

ficient for me to follow my husband," wrote Lucy Winthrop Downing, and her brother John Winthrop declared that "a true wife accounts her subjection her honor and freedom." Married women could not make contracts, own property, vote, or hold office. A typical woman, marrying in her early twenties and surviving through her forties, could expect to bear eight children and devote herself to husband and family. Aside from abstinence, there was no form of birth control. Wives who failed to have children, or widows who were economically independent, aroused significant suspicion among their neighbors. One Boston resident wrote that to be an "old maid . . . is thought such a curse as nothing can exceed it, and look'd on as a dismal Spectacle."

The cultural mistrust of women came to the surface most notably in periodic witchcraft scares. During the course of the seventeenth century, according to one historian, 342 New England women were accused by their neighbors of witchcraft. The majority of them were unmarried, or childless, or widowed, or had reputations among their neighbors for assertiveness and independence. In the vast majority of cases, these accusations were dismissed by authorities. In the most infamous case, however, in Salem, Massachusetts, in 1692, the whole community was thrown into a panic of accusations when a group of girls claimed that they had been bewitched by a number of old women. Before the colonial governor finally called a halt to the persecutions in 1693, twenty people had been tried, condemned, and executed.

The Salem accusations of witchcraft may have reflected social tensions that found their outlet through an attack on people perceived as outsiders. Salem was a booming port, but although some residents were prospering, others were not. Most of the victims came from the commercial eastern end of town, the majority of their accusers from the economically stagnant western side. Most of the accused also came from Anglican, Quaker, or Baptist families. Finally, a majority of the victims were old women, suspect because they lived alone, without men. The Salem witchcraft crisis exposed the dark side of Puritan ideas about women.

Dissent and New Communities

The Puritans emigrated in order to practice their variety of Christianity, but they had little tolerance for other religious points of view. Religious disagreement among the New England colonists soon provoked the founding of new colonies. Thomas Hooker, minister of the congregation at Cambridge, disagreed with the policy of restricting suffrage to male church members. In 1636, he led his followers west to the Connecticut River, where they founded the town of Hartford near the site of the trading post abandoned by the Dutch after epidemic disease had destroyed nearby Indian communities in 1634.

Another dissenter was the minister Roger Williams, who came to New England in 1631 to take up duties for the congregation in Salem. Williams believed in religious tolerance and the separation of church and state (discussed in Chapter 5). He also preached that the colonists had no absolute right to Indian land but must bargain for it in good faith. These were considered dangerous ideas, and in 1636 Williams was banished from the colony. With a group of his followers, he emigrated to the country of the Narragansetts, where he purchased land from the Indians and founded the town of Providence.

The next year, Boston shook with another religious controversy. Anne Hutchinson, wife of a Puritan merchant, was a brilliant and outspoken woman who held religious discussion groups in her home and criticized various Boston ministers for a lack of piety. Their concentration of attention on good works, she argued, led people to believe that they could earn their way to heaven, which in the eyes of Calvinists was a "popish" or Catholic heresy. Hutchinson was called before the General Court, was excommunicated and banished. She and her followers moved to Roger Williams's settlement, where they established another dissenting community in 1638. In 1644, Williams received a royal charter creating the colony of Rhode Island (named for the principal island in Narragansett Bay), as a protection for these dissenting communities. Another royal charter of 1663 guaranteed the colony self-government and complete religious liberty.

By the 1670s, Massachusetts's population had grown to more than 40,000, most of it concentrated in and around Boston, although there were communities as far west as the Connecticut River valley and as far north along the Atlantic coast as Maine (which was not separated from Massachusetts until 1820), as well as in New Hampshire, set off as a royal colony in 1680. Next in size after Massachusetts was Connecticut, its population numbering about 17,000. Plymouth's 6,000 inhabitants were absorbed by Massachusetts in 1691.

THE PROPRIETARY COLONIES

The Puritan Commonwealth, established in England after the execution of King Charles I, was preoccupied with English domestic affairs and left the colonies largely to their own devices. New England, Oliver Cromwell famously declared, was "poore, cold, and useless." After Cromwell's death in 1658, Parliament was desperate for stability, and in 1610, it restored the Stuart monarchy, placing on the throne Charles II, eldest son of the former king. Unlike Cromwell, Charles took an active interest in North America, establishing several new proprietary colonies on the model of Maryland (see Map 3.4).

Early Carolina

In 1663, the king issued the first of his colonial charters, calling for the establishment of a new colony called Carolina, stretching from Virginia south to Spanish Florida. Virginians had already begun moving into the northern parts of this territory, and in 1664, the Carolina proprietors appointed a governor for the settlements in the area of Albermarle Sound and created a popularly elected assembly. By 1675, North Carolina, as it became known, was home to some 5,000 small farmers and large tobacco planters.

Settlement farther south began in 1670 with the founding of coastal Charles Town (Charleston today). Most South Carolina settlers came from Barbados, a Caribbean colony the English had founded in 1627, which grew wealthy from the production of sugar. By the 1670s, the island had become overpopulated with English landowners and African slaves. The latter, imported to work the plantations, made up a majority of the population. Hundreds of Barbadians, both masters and slaves, relocated to South Carolina, lending that colony a distinctly West Indian character. By the end of the seventeenth century, South Carolina's population was 6,000, including some 2,500 enslaved Africans. (For a further discussion of slavery in South Carolina, see Chapter 4.)

From New Netherland to New York

Charles also coveted the lucrative Dutch colony of New Netherland. In response to the growth of New England's population and its merchant economy, in the 1640s, the Dutch West India Company began sponsoring the emigration of European settlers to the Hudson River Valley, seeking to develop the colony in the New England model as a diversified supply center for the West Indies. In 1751, Parliament passed a Trade and Navigation Act that barred Dutch vessels from English colonial possessions, which led to an inconclusive naval war with Holland from 1652 to 1654. In 1664, when a second Anglo-Dutch war erupted after the two commercial powers clashed along the West African coast, an English fleet sailed into Manhattan harbor and forced the surrender of

MAP EXPLORATION

To explore an interactive version of this map,
go to **www.prenhall.com/faragher5/map3.4**

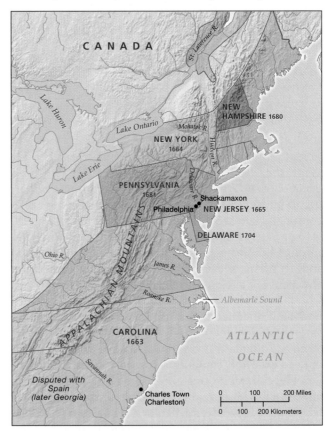

MAP 3.4 The Proprietary Colonies After the restoration of the Stuart monarchy in 1660, King Charles II of England created the new proprietary colonies of Carolina, New York, Pennsylvania, and New Jersey. New Hampshire was set off as a royal colony in 1680, and in 1704, the lower counties of Pennsylvania became the colony of Delaware.

The earliest known view of New Amsterdam, published in 1651. Indian traders are shown arriving with their goods in a dugout canoe of distinctive design known to have been produced by the native people of Long Island Sound. Twenty-five years after its founding, the Dutch settlement still occupies only the lower tip of Manhattan Island.

SOURCE: Fort New Amsterdam, New York, 1651. Engraving. Collection of The New-York Historical Society, 77354d.

By the 1670s, the combined population of these settlements numbered over 10,000, with more than 1,500 people clustered in the governmental and commercial center of New York City.

The Founding of Pennsylvania

In 1676, the proprietary rights to the western portion of New Jersey were sold to a group of English religious dissenters that included William Penn, who intended to make the area a haven for members of the Society of Friends (known as the Quakers by their critics), a group committed to religious toleration and pacifism. Penn himself had been imprisoned several times for publicly expressing those views. But he was the son of the wealthy and influential English admiral Sir William Penn, a close adviser to the king. In 1681, to settle a large debt he owed to Sir William, King Charles issued to the younger Penn a proprietary grant to a huge territory west of the Delaware River. The next year, Penn voyaged to America and supervised the laying out of his capital of Philadelphia.

New Amsterdam without firing a shot. That war ended with an inconclusive peace in 1667. A third and final conflict from 1672 to 1674 resulted in the bankruptcy of the Dutch West India Company and marked the ascension of the English to dominance in the Atlantic, although Holland remained supreme in the Baltic and the East Indies.

Charles II issued a proprietary charter that granted the former Dutch colony to his brother James, the Duke of York, renaming it New York in his honor. Otherwise the English government did little to disturb the existing order, preferring simply to reap the benefits of acquiring this profitable colony. Ethnically and linguistically diversified, accommodating a wide range of religious sects, New York boasted the most heterogeneous society in North America. In 1665, the communities of the Delaware Valley were split off as the proprietary colony of New Jersey, although it continued to be governed by New York until the 1680s.

Penn wanted this colony to be a "holy experiment." In his first Frame of Government, drafted in 1682, he included guarantees of religious freedom, civil liberties, and elected representation. He also attempted to deal

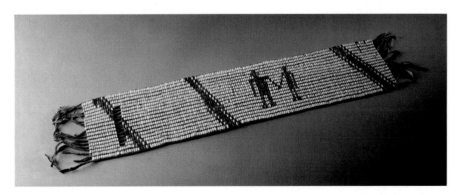

The Delawares presented William Penn with this wampum belt after the Shackamaxon Treaty of 1682. In friendship, a Quaker in distinctive hat clasps the hand of an Indian. The diagonal stripes on either side of the figures convey information about the territorial terms of the agreement. Wampum belts like this one, made from strings of white and purple shells, were used to commemorate treaties throughout the colonial period and were the most widely accepted form of money in the northeastern colonies during the seventeenth century.

SOURCE: Courtesy of The Historical Society of Pennsylvania Collection, Atwater Kent Museum of Philadelphia.

fairly with the native peoples of the region, refusing to permit settlement until lands were purchased. In 1682 and 1683, he made an agreement with the sachem Tammany of the Delaware tribe. "I am very sensible of the unkindness and injustice that hath been too much exercised toward you," Penn declared to the Delawares. "I desire to enjoy this land with your love and consent, that we may always live together as neighbors and friends." Although Pennsylvania's relations with the Indians later soured, during Penn's lifetime his reputation for fair dealing led a number of Indian groups to resettle in the Quaker colony.

Penn organized the most efficient colonization effort of the seventeenth century. During the colony's first decade, over 10,000 colonists arrived from England, and agricultural communities were soon spreading from the Delaware into the fertile interior valleys. In 1704, Penn approved the creation of a separate government for the area formerly controlled by the Scandinavians and Dutch, which became the colony of Delaware. In the eighteenth century, Pennsylvania became known as America's breadbasket, and Philadelphia became the most important colonial port in North America.

CONFLICT AND WAR

Pennsylvania's ability to maintain peaceful relations with the Indians proved the great exception, for the last quarter of the seventeenth century was a time of great violence throughout the colonial regions of the continent. The basic cause was the expansion of European settlement (see Map 3.5). Much of this warfare was between colonists and Indians, but intertribal warfare and intercolonial rivalry greatly contributed to the violence. It extended from Santa Fé—where the revolt of the Pueblos was the single most effective instance of Indian resistance to colonization—to the shores of Hudson Bay, where French and English traders fought for access to the rich fur-producing region of the north.

King Philip's War

In New England, nearly forty years of peace followed the Pequot War of 1637. Natives and colonists lived in close, if tense, contact. Several Puritan ministers, including John Eliot and Thomas Mayhew, began to preach to the Indians, and some two thousand Algonquian converts eventually relocated to native Christian communities known as "praying towns." There remained, however, a few independent tribes, including the Pokanokets of Plymouth Colony, the Narragansetts of Rhode Island, and the Abenakis of northern New England. The extraordinary expansion of the Puritan population, and their hunger for land,

created inexorable pressures for further expansion into those territories.

The Pokanokets were led by the sachem Metacom, whom the English knew as King Philip. The son of Massasoit, the leader who forged the original alliance with the Pilgrims, Metacom had been raised among English colonists and educated in their schools. He spoke English, wore English clothes, and believed his people had a future in the English colonial world. But gradually he came to understand that the colonists had no room for the Pokanokets. In 1671, after a series of conflicts, colonial authorities at Plymouth pressured Metacom into granting them sovereign authority over his home territory. This humiliation convinced the sachem that his people must break their half-century alliance with Plymouth and take up armed resistance. Meanwhile, the Puritan colonies prepared for a war of conquest.

In the spring of 1675, Plymouth magistrates arrested and executed three Pokanoket men for the murder of a Christian Indian. Fearing the moment of confrontation had arrived, Metacom appealed to the Narragansetts for a defensive alliance. Hoping for territorial gain, the united colonies of New England took this as the excuse for invading the Narra-

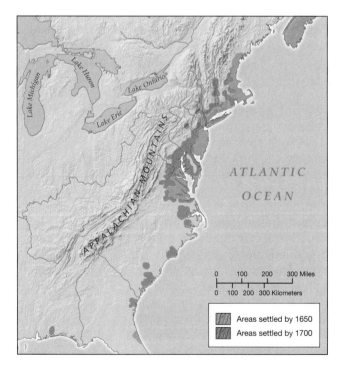

MAP 3.5 Spread of Settlement: British Colonies, 1650–1700 The spread of settlement in the English colonies in the late seventeenth century created the conditions for a number of violent conflicts, including King Philip's War, Bacon's Rebellion, and King William's War.

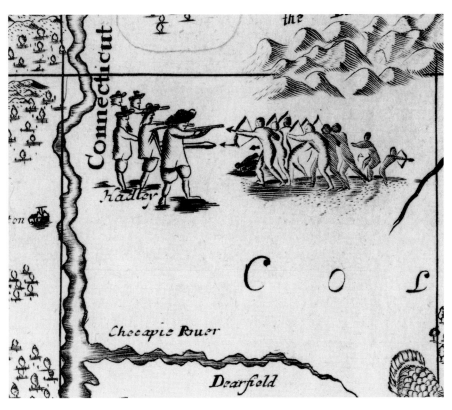

Indians and New Englanders skirmish during King Philip's War in a detail from John Seller's "A Mapp of New England," published immediately after the war.

SOURCE: Courtesy of the John Carter Brown Library at Brown University.

between the English and other native tribes. By attacking Metacom and his army, they were sending a message about where they stood. In the aftermath of the war, in a series of negotiations conducted at Albany in 1677, the Iroquois Confederacy and the colony of New York created an alliance known as the Covenant Chain, which declared Iroquois dominance over all other tribes in an attempt to put New York in an economically and politically dominant position among the other colonies. During the 1680s, the Iroquois pressed their claim of supremacy as far west as the Illinois country, fighting western Algonquian tribes allied with the French trading system.

Some 4,000 Algonquians and 2,000 English colonists died in King Philip's War, and dozens of native and colonial communities were left in ruins. Fearing attack from Indians close at hand, colonists also torched most of the Christian Indian praying towns, killing many of the residents. Measured against the size of the population, King Philip's War was one of the most destructive wars in American history.

ganset country with an armed force, attacking and burning a number of villages. What soon became known as King Philip's War, quickly engulfed all of New England.

At first things went well for the Indians. They forced the abandonment of English settlements on the Connecticut River and torched several towns less than twenty miles from Boston. By the beginning of 1676, however, their campaign was collapsing. A combined colonial army again invaded Narraganset country, burning villages, killing women and children, and defeating a large Indian force in a battle known as the Great Swamp Fight. In western New England, Metacom appealed to the Iroquois Confederacy for supplies and support, but instead they attacked and defeated his forces. Metacom retreated back to his homeland, where the colonists annihilated his army. The victors killed and beheaded Metacom and triumphantly marched through their towns with his head on a pike. His wife and son were sold into West Indian slavery, among hundreds of other captives.

The Iroquois were motivated by interests of their own. They sought to continue the role they had played in the Dutch trading system, as a powerful intermediary

Bacon's Rebellion

While King Philip's War raged in New England, another English-Indian confrontation was taking place in the Chesapeake. In the 1670s, the Susquehannock people of the upper Potomac River came into conflict with the tobacco planters expanding outward from Virginia. Violent raids led by wealthy backcountry settler Nathaniel Bacon in 1675, included the indiscriminate murder of natives. The efforts of Virginia governor William Berkeley to suppress these unauthorized military expeditions so infuriated Bacon and his followers—many of them former indentured servants—that in the spring of 1676, they turned their fury against the colonial capital of Jamestown itself. Berkeley fled across the Chesapeake while Bacon pillaged and burned the capital. Soon thereafter Bacon took ill and died. His rebellion collapsed, and Virginia authorities signed a treaty with the Susquehannocks ending hostilities, but most of the tribe had already migrated to New York, where they affiliated with the Iroquois.

OVERVIEW

CONFLICT AND WAR

The Beaver Wars	1640s–80s	The Iroquois extend their authority as middlemen in the Dutch and English trade system by attacking neighbors as far west as Illinois
King Philip's War	1675–76	The Indian peoples of southern New England and the Puritan colonies fight for control of land
Bacon's Rebellion	1675–76	Backcountry settlers attack Indians, and colonial authorities try to suppress these attacks
Wars in the South	1670s–1720s	British colonists in the Carolinas incite Creeks, Cherokees, and other Indian tribes to attack and enslave the mission Indians of Spanish Florida
The Glorious Revolution in America	1689	Colonists in Massachusetts, New York, and Maryland rise up against the colonial governments of King James II
King William's War	1689–97	The first of a series of colonial struggles between England and France; these conflicts occur principally on the frontiers of northern New England and New York

This brief but violent clash marked an important change of direction for Virginia. Bacon had issued a manifesto demanding not only the death or removal of all Indians from the colony, but also an end to the rule of aristocratic "grandees" and "parasites." The rebellion thus signaled a developing conflict between frontier districts such as Bacon's and the more established coastal region, where the "Indian problem" had long since been settled. In 1677, in a replay of Virginia events known as Culpeper's Rebellion, backcountry men in the Albermarle region of North Carolina succeeded in overthrowing the established government before being suppressed by English authorities. In the aftermath of these rebellions, colonial authorities in Virginia and North Carolina began to favor armed expansion into Indian territory, hoping to gain the support of backcountry men by enlarging the stock of available colonial land. Moreover, planters' fears of disorder among former indentured servants encouraged them to accelerate the transition to slave labor (see Chapter 4).

Wars in the South

There was also massive violence in South Carolina during the 1670s, as colonists there began the operation of a large-scale Indian slave trade. Charleston merchants encouraged numerous tribes—the Yamasees, Creeks, Cherokees, and Chickasaws—to wage war on groups allied to rival colonial powers, including the mission Indians of Spanish Florida, the

Choctaw allies of the French, and the Tuscaroras, trading partners of the Virginians. By 1710, more than 12,000 Florida Indians had been captured and sold, thousands of others had been killed or dispersed, and the Spanish mission system, in operation for more than a century, lay in ruins.

This vicious Indian slave trade extended well into the eighteenth century, and thousands of southern Indians were sold into captivity. Most of the Indian men were shipped from Charleston to Caribbean or northern colonies; the Indian women remained in South Carolina, where many eventually formed relationships and had children with male African slaves, forming a racial-ethnic group known as the "mustees."

The Glorious Revolution in America

Dynastic change in England was another factor precipitating violence in North America. Upon the death of Charles II in 1685, his brother and successor, James II, began a concerted effort to strengthen royal control over the colonies. During the preceding forty years, colonial assemblies had grown powerful and independent, and the new king was determined to reign them in. He abolished the New York assembly, which had been particularly troublesome, and placed all power in the hands of the colony's royal governor. Assemblies continued to operate in the other colonies, but were consistently challenged by the governors. In his most dramatic action, the king abolished the charter governments of the New England, New York, and New Jersey colonies, combining them into what was called the Dominion of New England. Edmund Andros, appointed royal governor of the new super-colony, imposed Anglican forms of worship in Puritan areas and overthrew traditions of local autonomy.

In England, the same imperious style on the part of the king seriously alienated political leaders. As a young man, James had converted to Catholicism, and after the death of his first (Protestant) wife, he remarried a Catholic aristocrat from Italy. His appointment of Catholics to high positions of state added to rising protests, but the last straw came when his wife bore a son in 1688. Fearing the establishment of a Catholic royal dynasty, Parliamentary leaders deposed James and replaced him with his Protestant daughter and Dutch son-in-law, Mary and William of Orange. The army threw its support to William and Mary and James fled to France. As part of what became known as the Glorious Revolution, the new monarchs agreed to a Bill of Rights, promising to respect traditional civil liberties, to summon and consult with Parliament annually, and to enforce and administer Parliamentary legislation. These were significant concessions with profound implications for the future of English politics. England now had a "constitutional monarchy."

When news of the Glorious Revolution reached North America, colonists rose in a series of rebellions against the authorities set in place by James II. In the spring of 1689, Governor Andros was attacked by an angry Boston mob, inflamed by rumors that he was a secret Catholic. He was able to escape their wrath, but was arrested and deported by the local militia. When news of the Boston revolt arrived in New York, it inspired another uprising there. A group led by German merchant Jacob Leisler, and including many prominent Dutch residents, seized control of the city and called for the formation of a new legislature. In Maryland, rumors of a Catholic plot led to the overthrow of the proprietary rule of the Calvert family by an insurgent group called the Protestant Association.

The new monarchs carefully measured their response to these uprisings. When Jacob Leisler attempted to prevent the landing of the king's troops in New York, he was arrested, tried, and executed. But the monarchs consented to the dismantling of the Dominion of New England and the end of proprietary rule in Maryland. The outcome of the Glorious Revolution in America was mixed. All the affected English colonies quickly revived their assemblies and returned to their tradition of self-government. The government of England did not fully reestablish its authority in these colonies until 1692, when Massachusetts, New York, and Maryland all were declared royal colonies.

CHRONOLOGY

1598	Juan de Oñate leads Spanish into New Mexico
1607	English found Jamestown
1608	French found Quebec
1609	Spanish found Santa Fé
1620	Pilgrim emigration
1622	Indian uprising in Virginia
1625	Jesuit missionaries arrive in New France
1629	Puritans begin settlement of Massachusetts Bay
1637	Pequot War
1649	Charles I executed
1660	Stuart monarchy restored, Charles II becomes king
1675	King Philip's War
1676	Bacon's Rebellion
1680	Pueblo Revolt
1681–82	Robert Sieur de La Salle explores the Mississippi
1688	The Glorious Revolution
1689	King William's War
1698	Spanish reconquest of the Pueblos completed
1701	English impose royal governments on all colonies but Massachusetts, Connecticut, and Pennsylvania

King William's War

The year 1689 also marked the beginning of nearly seventy-five years of armed conflict between English and French forces for control of the North American interior. The Iroquois-English Covenant Chain challenged New France's fur-trade empire, and in response, the French pressed farther west in search of commercial opportunities. In the far north, the English sought to counter French dominance with the establishment of Hudson's Bay Company, a royal fur-trade monopoly that was to exploit the watershed of the great northern bay.

Hostilities began with English-Iroquois attacks on Montreal and violence between rival French and English traders on Hudson Bay. These skirmishes were part of a larger conflict between England and France that in Europe was called the War of the League of Augsburg, but in the English colonies was known as King William's War. In 1690, the French and their Algonquian allies counterattacked, burning frontier settlements in New York, New Hampshire, and Maine, and pressing their attacks against the towns of the Iroquois. The same year, a Massachusetts fleet captured the strategic French outpost at Port Royal on the Bay of Fundy, but a combined English and colonial force failed in its attempt to conquer the administrative center of Québec on the St. Lawrence. This inconclusive war was ended by the Treaty of Ryswick of 1697, which established an equally inconclusive peace. War between England and France would resume only five years later.

The persistent violence of the last quarter of the seventeenth century greatly concerned English authorities, who began to fear the loss of their North American possessions either from outside attack or from internal disorder. To shore up central control, in 1701, the English Board of Trade recommended converting all charter and proprietary governments into royal colonies. After a brief period under royal rule, William Penn regained private control of his domain, but Pennsylvania was the last of the proprietary colonies. Among the royal charter colonies, only Rhode Island and Connecticut retained their original governments. The result of this quarter-century of violence was the tightening of the imperial reins over its North American possessions.

CONCLUSION

At the beginning of the seventeenth century, the European presence north of Mexico was extremely limited: Spanish bases in Florida, a few Franciscan missions among the Pueblos, and fishermen along the North Atlantic coast. By 1700, the human landscape of the Southwest, the South, and the Northeast had been transformed. More than a quarter million migrants from the Old World had moved into these regions, the vast majority to the English colonies. Indian societies had been disrupted, depopulated, and in some cases destroyed. The Spanish and French colonies were characterized by the inclusion of Indians in the social and economic life of the community. But along the Atlantic coast, the English established communities of exclusion, with ominous implications for the future of relations between colonists and natives.

During the long civil war in England, the English colonies were left to run their own affairs. But with the Restoration in 1660 and the establishment of the constitutional monarchy in 1689, the English state began to supervise more closely its troublesome colonists, beginning what would be a long struggle over the limits of self-government. The violence and warfare of the last decades of the century suggested that conflict would continue to play a significant role in the future of colonial America.

REVIEW QUESTIONS

1. Using examples drawn from this chapter, discuss the differences between colonizing "frontiers of inclusion" and "exclusion."
2. What factors turned England's Chesapeake colony of Virginia from stark failure to brilliant success?
3. Discuss the role of religious dissent in the founding of the first New England colonies and in stimulating the creation of others.
4. Compare and contrast William Penn's policy with respect to Indian tribes with the policies of other English settlers, in the Chesapeake and New England, and with the policies of the Spanish, the French, and the Dutch.
5. What were the principal causes of colonial violence and warfare of the late seventeenth century?

RECOMMENDED READING

James Axtell, *The European and the Indian: Essays in the Ethnohistory of Colonial America* (1981). A readable introduction to the dynamics of mutual discovery between natives and colonizers.

Leslie Choquette, *Frenchmen into Peasants: Modernity and Tradition in the Peopling of French Canada* (1997). A history of French immigrants to Canada and Acadia, based on a comprehensive database of hundreds of individuals. The most detailed study of French mobility to date.

Frederic W. Gleach, *Powhatan's World and Colonial Virginia: A Conflict of Cultures* (1997). Reconstructing the worldview of the Chesapeake Algonquians as they attempted to maintain control of their homeland.

Andrew L. Knaut, *The Pueblo Revolt of 1680* (1995). The most complete and sophisticated account of the revolt.

Edmund S. Morgan, *American Slavery, American Freedom* (1975). A classic interpretation of early Virginia, arguing that early American ideas of freedom for some were based on the reality of slavery for others.

Diana Newton, *Papists, Protestants, and Puritans, 1559–1714* (1998). The best survey of religious change during the Protestant Reformation, with a focus on the turmoil in England.

Robert W. Preucel, ed., *Archaeologies of the Pueblo Revolt: Identity, Meaning, and Renewal in the Pueblo World* (2002). Emphasizes the agency of the Pueblo peoples and the significance of material culture in both their revolt from and their eventual accommodation to Spanish colonialism.

Daniel K. Richter, *Facing East from Indian Country: A Native History of Early America* (2001). Colonial history from the point of view of the Indians. Includes remarkable biographical chapters on Pocahontas and Metacom.

Neal Salisbury, *Manitou and Providence: Indians, Europeans, and the Making of New England* (1982). One of the best examples of the new ethnohistory of Indians; a provocative intercultural approach to the history of the Northeast.

Susan Sleeper-Smith, *Native Women and French Men: Rethinking Cultural Encounter in the Western Great Lakes* (2001). A study of Indian women who married French traders and became cultural brokers and creators of a middle ground.

David J. Weber, *The Spanish Frontier in North America* (1992). A powerful overview that includes the history of New Mexico and Florida.

 For additional study resources for this chapter, go to the *Companion Website,* http://www.prenhall.com/faragher.

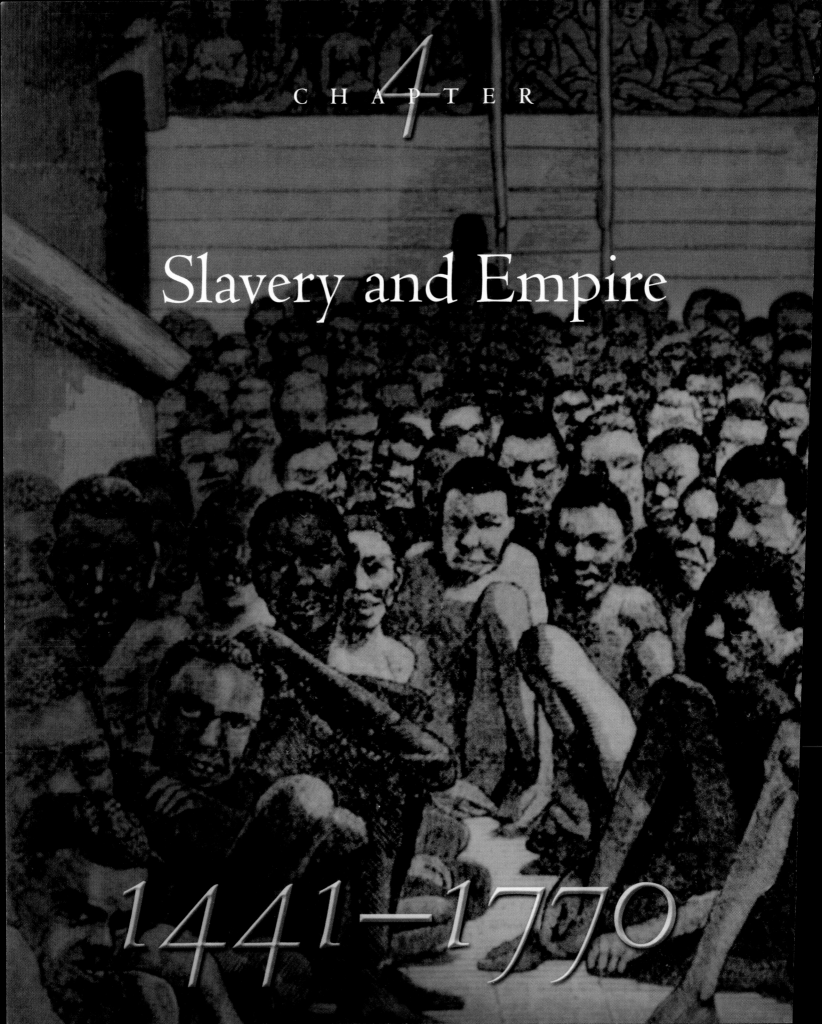

Slavery and Empire

CHAPTER 4

1441–1770

CHAPTER OUTLINE

African Slaves Build Their Own Community in Coastal Georgia

Africans labored in the steamy heat of the coastal Georgia rice fields in the middle of the eighteenth century, the breeches of the men rolled up over their knees, the sack skirts of the women gathered and tied about their hips, leaving them, in the words of one shocked observer, "two-thirds naked." Upriver, groups cut away cypress and gum trees and cleared the swampland's jungle maze of undergrowth; others constructed levees, preparing to bring more land under cultivation. African slave drivers, whips at the ready, supervised the work. An English overseer or plantation master might be seen here and there, but overwhelmingly this was a country populated by Africans.

These plantations were southern extensions of the South Carolina rice belt. Although slavery was prohibited by Georgia's original charter of 1732, the restriction was lifted two decades later when Georgia became a royal colony. By 1770, 15,000 African Americans (80 percent of the region's population) were enslaved on several hundred coastal rice plantations owned by a small planter elite.

Rice was one of the most valuable commodities produced in mainland North America, surpassed in value only by tobacco and wheat. The growth of rice production was matched by an enormous expansion in the Atlantic slave trade, and during the eighteenth century, rice planters engaged in what one historian calls a "veritable orgy" of slave trading. Although the number of slaves

Georgia
Sea
Islands

who were "country born" (native to America, and thus born into slavery) grew steadily over the century, on rice plantations the majority were what were known as "saltwater" Africans.

These men and women had endured the shock of enslavement. Ripped from their homeland communities in West Africa by slave raiders, and brutally marched to coastal forts, they were subjected to humiliating inspections of their bodies, and branded like animals, then packed into the stinking holds of ships and forced into a nightmarish passage across the Atlantic Ocean during which many died. Unloaded on a strange continent, the survivors were sold at dockside auctions, then once again marched overland to their destinations. On the rice plantations of isolated coastal Georgia, enslaved Africans suffered from overwork and numerous physical ailments, the results of poor diet, minimal and inappropriate clothing, and inadequate housing. Mortality rates were exceptionally high, especially for infants. Colonial laws permitted masters to discipline and punish slaves indiscriminately. Harsh punishments were imposed on slaves who were suspected of taking food, agitated for reforms, or plotted revolts. They were whipped, confined in irons, mutilated, sold away, or murdered.

Like slaves everywhere in the Americas, many ran away. Readers of Savannah newspapers were urged to look out for fugitives: Statira, a woman of the "Gold Coast Country" with tribal markings on her temples, or "a negro fellow named Mingo, about 40 years old, and his wife Quante, a sensible wench about 20 with her child, a boy about 3 years old, all this country born." Some fled in groups, heading for Indian settlements in northern Florida, or toward St. Augustine, where Spanish authorities promised them safe haven. Some struck out violently at their masters: a group of nine Africans from a Savannah plantation killed their master and stole a boat, planning to head upriver, but were apprehended as they lay in wait to murder their hated overseers.

So some slaves resisted, but the majority of Africans and African Americans remained imprisoned within the heartless world of slavery. Plantation slaves married, raised children, and over time constructed kinship networks. They passed on African names and traditions and created new ones. The slaves of coastal Georgia combined elements of African languages and English, creating dialects that allowed people from many different African ethnic groups to communicate with one another. Common African heritage and their slave status were the foundations of the African American community.

African Americans reworked traditional African dance, song, and story to fit their enslavement in the New World, just as they reestablished traditional arts, such as woodworking, iron making, and weaving. Through their culture, the slaves shared a powerful awareness of their common oppression. They told or sang dialect tales of mistreatment, as in this song of Quow, the punished slave:

> *Was matter Buddy Quow?*
> *I ble Obesha bang you . . .*
> *Dah Backrow Man go wrong you, Buddy Quow,*
> *Dah Backrow Man go wrong you, Buddy Quow.*
>
> *[What's the matter Brother Quow?*
> *I believe the overseer's beat you . . .*
> *The white man's wronged you, Brother Quow,*
> *The white man's wronged you, Brother Quow.]*

The history of African Americans includes the story of the Atlantic slave trade, the plunder of Africa, and the profits of empire. But it is also a story of the making of families, kin networks, and communities under the most difficult of circumstances. They "labor together and converse almost wholly among themselves," a minister wrote of low-country slaves. "They are, as 'twere, a nation within a nation."

KEY TOPICS

- The development of the slavery system
- The history of the slave trade and the Middle Passage
- Community development among African Americans in the eighteenth century
- The connections between the institution of slavery and the imperial system of the eighteenth century
- The early history of racism in America

THE BEGINNINGS OF AFRICAN SLAVERY

Household slaves had long been a part of the world of Mediterranean Europe. War captives were sold to wealthy families, who put them to work as servants or artisans. In the fifteenth century, Venetian and Genoese merchants led the traffic in captured Slavic peoples—the word "slave" derives from "Slav"—as well as Muslims and Africans. Many Europeans were disturbed, however, by the moral implications of enslaving Christians, and in the early fifteenth century the pope excommunicated a number of merchants engaged in selling such captives.

Africans and Muslims, however, were sufficiently different in religion to quiet those concerns.

One of the goals of Portuguese expansion in the fifteenth century was access to the lucrative West African trade in gold, wrought iron, ivory, tortoiseshell, textiles, and slaves that had previously been dominated by the Moors of northern Africa. The first African slaves arrived in Lisbon in 1441. European traders found it most efficient to leave the capture of men and women for slavery to Africans, who were willing to exchange the captured slaves for European commodities. By the mid-fifteenth century, the Portuguese were shipping a thousand or more slaves per year from Africa. Most of

This image of Mansa Musa (1312–37), the ruler of the Muslim kingdom of Mali in West Africa, is taken from the *Catalan Atlas*, a magnificent map presented to the king of France in 1381 by his cousin, the king of Aragon. In the words of the Catalan inscription, Musa was "the richest, the most noble lord in all this region on account of the abundance of gold that is gathered in his land." He holds what was thought to be the world's largest gold nugget. Under Musa's reign, Timbuktu became a capital of world renown.

SOURCE: Courtesy of Library of Congress.

them were sent to the sugar plantations on the Portuguese island colony of Madeira, off the coast of northern Africa.

Sugar and Slavery

Sugar and slaves had gone together since Italian merchants of the fourteenth century imported the first cane sugar from the Middle East and set up the first modern sugar plantations on the islands of the Mediterranean. African slaves came to the Americas with the introduction of sugar production. Columbus brought sugar cane to Hispaniola, and soon sugar plantations were in operation. Because disease and warfare had devastated the indigenous population, colonists imported African slaves from Spain. Meanwhile, the Portuguese, aided by Dutch financiers, created a center of sugar production in northeast Brazil that became a model of the efficient and brutal exploitation of African labor. By 1600, some 25,000 enslaved Africans labored on the plantations of Hispaniola and Brazil.

Skilled at finance and commerce, the Dutch greatly expanded the European market for sugar, converting it from a luxury item for the rich to a staple for ordinary people. Along with other tropical commodities such as tobacco, coffee, and tea, sugar helped sustain workers through the increasingly long working day. Once the profitability of sugar had been demonstrated, England and France sought West Indian sugar colonies of their own. With the Spanish preoccupied on the big islands of Cuba, Hispaniola, Jamaica, and Puerto Rico, English and French settlers began constructing plantations and importing slaves to the islands of the Lesser Antilles. By the 1640s, English Barbados and French Martinique had become highly profitable colonies. Lusting for more, in 1655, the English seized the island of Jamaica, and by 1670, the French had taken over the western portion of Hispaniola, which they renamed St. Dominique (present-day Haiti). By then, Caribbean sugar and slaves had become the centerpiece of the European colonial system.

West Africans

The men and women whose labor made these tropical colonies so profitable came from the long-established societies and local communities of West Africa. In the sixteenth century, more than a hundred different peoples lived along the coast of West Africa, from Cape Verde south to Angola. In the north, were the Wolofs, Mandingos, Hausas, Ashantis, and Yorubas; to the south the Ibos, Sekes, Bakongos, and Mbundus.

In all these societies the most important institution was the local community, organized by kinship. West Africans practiced a marriage system known as polygyny, in which men often took a second or third wife. This produced very large composite familes with complex internal relationships. Because of cultural restrictions on sexual relations, however, West African women bore fewer children than typical European women, and many enjoyed considerable social and economic independence as traders. Communities were led by clan leaders and village chiefs. Disputes were arbitrated by local courts.

West African societies were based on sophisticated farming systems many thousands of years old. Africans practiced shifting cultivation: they cleared land by burning, used hoes or digging sticks to cultivate fields, and after several years moved on to other plots while the cleared land lay fallow. Men worked at clearing the land, women at cultivation and the sale of surpluses. Farming sustained large populations and thriving networks of commerce, and in some regions kingdoms and states developed. Along the upper Niger River, where the grassland gradually turns to desert, towns such as Timbuktu developed into trading centers. There were also a number of lesser states and kingdoms along the coast, and it was with these that the Portuguese first bargained for Africans who could be sold as slaves.

Varieties of household slavery were common in West African societies, although slaves there were often treated more as members of the family than as mere possessions. They were allowed to marry, and their children were born free. "With us they did no more work than other members of the community, even their master," remembered Olaudah Equiano, an Ibo captured and shipped to America as a slave in 1756, when he was a boy of eleven. "Their food, clothing, and lodging were nearly the same as [the others], except that they were not permitted to eat with those who were born free." When African merchants sold the first slaves to the Portuguese, they must have thought that European slavery would be similar. But as Equiano declared: "How different was their condition from that of the slaves in the West Indies!" Yet the

West African familiarity with "unfree" labor made it possible for African and European traders to begin the trade in human merchandise.

THE AFRICAN SLAVE TRADE

The movement of Africans across the Atlantic to the Americas was the largest forced migration in world history (see Map 4.1). Africans made up the largest group of people to come to the Americas before the nineteenth century, outnumbering European immigrants by the ratio of six to one. The Atlantic slave trade, which began with the Portuguese in the fifteenth century and did not end in the United States until 1807 (and continued elsewhere in the Americas until the 1870s), is the most brutal chapter in the making of America.

The Demography of the Slave Trade

Although there is much dispute over the numbers, the consensus among scholars today is that slave ships transported from 10 to 12 million Africans to the Americas during the four-century history of the trade. Seventy-six percent arrived from 1701 to 1810—the peak period of colonial demand for labor, when tens of thousands were shipped from Africa each year. Of this vast multitude, about half were delivered to Dutch, French, or British sugar plantations in the Caribbean, a third to Portuguese Brazil, and 10 percent to Spanish America (see Map 4.2). A much smaller proportion—about one in twenty, or an estimated 600,000 men, women, and children—were transported to the British colonies of North America. With the exception of the 1750s, when the British colonies were engulfed by the Seven Years' War, the slave trade continued to rise in importance in the decades before the Revolution (see Figure 4.1).

Among the Africans brought to the Americas, men generally outnumbered women two to one. Because most Africans were destined for fieldwork, this ratio probably reflected the preferences of plantation owners. The majority of captured and transported Africans were young

A black slave driver supervises a gang of slave men and women preparing the fields for the planting of sugar cane in the West Indies, a colored engraving published in William Clark's *Ten Views Found in the Island of Antigua* (London, 4823).

SOURCE: The British Library.

MAP EXPLORATION

To explore an interactive version of this map, go to **www.prenhall.com/faragher5/map4.1**

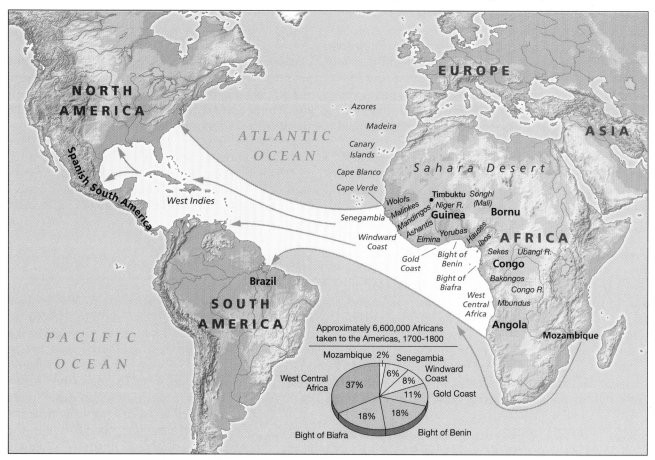

MAP 4.1 The African Slave Trade   The enslaved men, women, and children transported to the Americas came from West Africa, the majority from the lower Niger River (called the Slave Coast) and the region of the Congo and Angola.

people, between the ages of fifteen and thirty. Nearly every ethnic group in West Africa was represented among them.

Slavers of All Nations

All the nations of Western Europe participated in the slave trade. Dutch slavers began challenging Portuguese control of the trade at the end of the sixteenth century, and Holland became the most prominent slave-trading nation during the sugar boom of the seventeenth century. The English also entered the trade in the sixteenth century with the African voyages of John Hawkins. The Royal African Company, a slave-trading monopoly based in London, was chartered in 1672, but in 1698, England threw open the trade to independent merchants. Soon hundreds of ships from Bristol and Liverpool were competing with those from London. As a result, the number

of slaves shipped to North America skyrocketed. The Dutch and Portuguese, however, continued to play important roles, alongside slave traders from France, Sweden, and several German duchies.

For the most part, the European presence in Africa was confined to coastal outposts. By the early eighteenth century, more than two dozen trading forts dotted the 220 miles of the Gold Coast alone. As the slave trade peaked in the middle of the eighteenth century, however, trading posts gave way to independent European and American traders who set up operations with the cooperation of local headmen or chiefs. This informal manner of trading offered opportunities for small operators, such as the New England slavers who entered the trade in the early eighteenth century. Many great New England fortunes were built from profits in the slave trade.

MAP 4.2 Slave Colonies of the Seventeenth and Eighteenth Centuries By the eighteenth century, the system of slavery had created societies with large African populations throughout the Caribbean and along the southern coast of North America.

The Shock of Enslavement

The slave trade was a collaboration between European or American and African traders. Dependent on the favor of local rulers, many colonial slave traders lived permanently in coastal outposts and married African women, reinforcing their commercial ties with family relations. In many areas, their mixed-ancestry offspring became prominent players in the slave trade. Continuing the practice of the Portuguese, the grim business of slave raiding was left to the Africans themselves. Slaves were not at all reticent about condemning the participation of their fellow Africans. "I must own to the shame of my own countrymen," wrote Ottobah Cugoano of Ghana, who was sold into slavery in the 1750s, "that I was first kidnapped and betrayed by those of my own complexion."

Most Africans were enslaved through warfare. Sometimes large armies launched massive attacks, burning whole towns and taking hundreds of prisoners. More common were smaller raids, in which a group of armed men attacked at nightfall, seized everyone within reach, then escaped with their captives. As the demand for slaves increased in the eighteenth century with the expansion of the plantation system in the Americas, these raids extended deeper and deeper into the African interior. The march of captives to the coast was filled with terrors. One account describes a two-month trip in which many people died of hunger, thirst, or exhaustion, and the whole party was forced to hide to avoid being seized by a rival band of raiders. The captives finally arrived on the coast, where they were sold to an American vessel bound for South Carolina.

Enslavement was an unparalleled shock. Venture Smith, an African born in Guinea in 1729, was only eight years old when he was captured. After many years in North American slavery, he still vividly recalled the attack on his village, the torture and murder of his father, and the long march of his people to the coast. "The shocking scene is to this day fresh in my mind," he wrote, "and I have often been overcome while thinking on it."

On the coast, European traders and African raiders assembled their captives. Prisoners waited in dark dungeons or in open pens called "barracoons." To lessen the possibility of collective resistance, traders split up families and ethnic groups. Captains carefully inspected

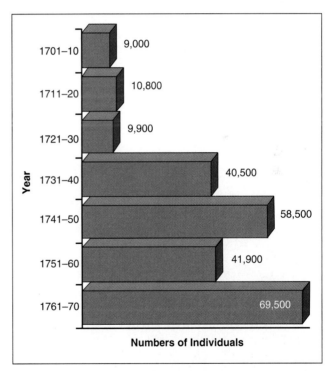

FIGURE 4.1 Estimated Number of Africans Imported to British North America, 1701–75
These official British statistics include only slaves imported legally, and consequently undercount the total number who arrived on American shores. But the trend over time is clear. With the exception of the 1750s, when the British colonies were engulfed by the Seven Years War, the slave trade continued to rise in importance in the decades before the Revolution.

SOURCE: R. C. Simmons, *The American Colonies: From Settlement to Independence* (London: Longman, 1976), 186.

each man and woman, and those selected for transport were branded on the back or buttocks with the mark of the buyer. Olaudah Equiano remembered that "those white men with horrible looks, red faces, and long hair, looked and acted . . . in so savage a manner; . . . I had never seen among any people such instances of brutal cruelty." Equiano's narrative, published in 1789 after he had secured his freedom, is one of the few that provide an African account of enslavement. He and his fellow captives became convinced that they "had got into a world of bad spirits" and were about to be eaten by cannibals. A French trader wrote that many prisoners were "positively prepossessed with the opinion that we transport them into our country in order to kill and eat them."

The Middle Passage

In the eighteenth century, English sailors christened the voyage of slave ships as the "Middle Passage," the middle part of a trading triangle from England to Africa to America and back to England. From coastal forts and barracoons, crews rowed small groups of slaves out to the waiting ships and packed them into shelves below deck only six feet long by two and a half feet high. "Rammed like herring in a barrel," wrote one observer, slaves were "chained to each other hand and foot, and stowed so close, that they were not allowed above a foot and a half for each in breadth." People were forced to lie "spoon fashion," and the tossing of the ship knocked them about so violently that the skin over their elbows sometimes was worn to the bone from scraping on the planks. "It was more than a week after I left the ship before I could straighten my limbs," one former slave later remembered. One ship designed to carry 450 slaves regularly crossed the Atlantic tightly packed with more than 600.

Their holds filled with human cargo, the ships headed toward Cape Verde to catch the trade winds blowing toward America. A favorable voyage from Senegambia to Barbados might be accomplished in as little as three weeks, but a ship departing from Guinea or Angola and becalmed in the doldrums or driven back by storms might take as much as three months.

Most voyages were marked by a daily routine. In the morning the crew opened the hatch and brought the captives on deck, attaching their leg irons to a great chain running the length of the bulwarks. After a breakfast of beans the crew commanded men and women to jump up and down, a bizarre session of exercise known as "dancing the slave." A day spent chained on deck was concluded by a second bland meal and then the stowing away. During the night, according to one seaman, there issued from below "a howling melancholy noise, expressive of extreme anguish." Down in the hold, the groans of the dying, the shrieks of women and children, and the suffocating heat and stench were, in the words of Olaudah Equiano, "a scene of horror almost inconceivable." (See Out of Many Voices: Olaudah Equiano Describes the Middle Passage.)

Among the worst of the horrors was the absence of adequate sanitation. There were "necessary tubs" set below deck, but Africans, "endeavoring to get to them, tumble over their companions," as one eighteenth-century ship's surgeon wrote. "And as the necessities of nature are not to be resisted, they ease themselves as they lie." Crews were to swab the holds daily, but so sickening was the task that on many ships it was rarely performed, and Africans were left to wallow in their own wastes. "The floor," wrote an English ship's surgeon, "was so covered with blood and mucus that it resembled a slaughter house. It is not in the power of human imagination to picture to itself a situation more dreadful or disgusting." When first taken below deck, Equiano remembered, "I received such a salutation in my nostrils as

A slave coffle in an eighteenth-century print. As the demand for slaves increased, raids extended deeper and deeper into the African interior. Tied together with forked logs or bark rope, men, women, and children were marched hundreds of miles toward the coast, where their African captors traded them to Europeans.

SOURCE: North Wind Picture Archives.

Slaves below deck on a Spanish slaver, a sketch made when the vessel was captured by a British warship in the early nineteenth century. Slaves were "stowed so close, that they were not allowed above a foot and a half for each in breadth," wrote one observer. The close quarters and unsanitary conditions created a stench so bad that Atlantic sailors said you could "smell a slaver five miles down wind."

SOURCE: The Granger Collection, New York.

I had never experienced in my life," and "became so sick and low that I was not able to eat." According to Atlantic sailors, they could "smell a slaver five miles down wind." In these filthy conditions, many captives sickened and died. Others contracted dysentery, known as the "flux." Frequent shipboard epidemics of smallpox, measles, and yellow fever added to the misery. The dying continued even as the ships anchored at their destinations. Historians estimate that during the Middle Passage of the eighteenth century, one in every six Africans perished.

The unwilling voyagers offered plenty of resistance. As long as ships were still within sight of the African coast, hope remained alive and the danger of revolt was great. One historian has found references to fifty-five slave revolts on British and American ships from 1699 to 1845. Once on the open sea, however, the captives' resistance took more desperate form. The sight of the disappearing coast of Africa "left me abandoned to despair," wrote Equiano. "I now saw myself deprived of all chance of returning to my native country, or even the least glimpse of hope of gaining the shore." He witnessed several of his fellow Africans jump overboard and drown, "and I believe many more would very soon have done the same if they had not been prevented by the ship's crew." Captains took the pre-

caution of spreading nets along the sides of their ships. "Could I have got over the nettings," Equiano declared, "I would have jumped over the side."

Arrival in the New World

As the ship approached its destination, the crew prepared the human cargo for market. All but the most rebellious individuals were freed from their chains, allowed to wash themselves and move about the deck. To impress buyers, captains might parade Africans off the ship to the tune of an accordion or the beat of a drum. But the toll of the Middle Passage was difficult to disguise. One observer described a disembarking group as "walking skeletons covered over with a piece of tanned leather."

Some cargoes were destined for a single wealthy planter, or consigned to a merchant who sold the captives in return for a commission; in other cases the captain himself was responsible. Buyers painstakingly examined the Africans, who again suffered the indignity of probing eyes and poking fingers. This caused "much dread and trembling among us," wrote Equiano. In ports such as Charleston, sales were generally made by auction, or by a cruel method known as the scramble—the prices were set in advance, the Africans driven into a corral, and on cue the buyers rushed among them, seizing their pick. The noise, clamor, and determination of the buyers, Equiano remembered, renewed all the terrible apprehensions of the Africans. "In this manner, without scruple, are relations and friends separated, most of them never to see each other again." Bought by a Virginian, Equiano was taken to an isolated tobacco plantation where he found himself unable to communicate with any of his fellow slaves, who came from other ethnic groups.

Political and Economic Effects on Africa

Africa began the sixteenth century with genuine independence. But as surely as European empires grew strong as a result of the slave trade in slaves, so Africa grew weaker. For every individual taken captive, at least another died in the chronic slave raiding. Death and destruction spread deep into the African interior. Coastal slave-trading kingdoms drew slaves from

OUT OF MANY VOICES

OLAUDAH EQUIANO DESCRIBES THE MIDDLE PASSAGE

One of the few first-hand accounts of the Middle Passage was provided by Olaudah Equiano, an African from the region of Nigeria who was captured in 1756 and transported across the Atlantic in chains. In this passage he provides a vivid description of conditions on board the slave ship.

AT LAST, WHEN THE SHIP WE WERE IN HAD GOT IN all her cargo, they made ready with many fearful noises, and we were all put under deck, so that we could not see how they managed the vessel. But this disappointment was the least of my sorrow. The stench of the hold while we were on the coast was so intolerably loathsome, that it was dangerous to remain there for any time, and some of us had been permitted to stay on the deck for the fresh air; but now that the whole ship's cargo were confined together, it became absolutely pestilential. The closeness of the place, and the heat of the climate, added to the number in the ship, which was so crowded that each had scarcely room to turn himself, almost suffocated us. This produced copious perspirations, so that the air soon became unfit for respiration, from a variety of loathsome smells, and brought on a sickness among the slaves, of which many died—thus falling victims to the improvident avarice, as I may call it, of their purchasers. This wretched situation was again aggravated by the gaffing of the chains, now became insupportable, and the filth of the necessary tubs, into which the children often fell, and were almost suffocated. The shrieks of the women, and the groans of the dying, rendered the whole a scene of horror almost inconceivable.

Happily perhaps, for myself, I was soon reduced so low here that it was thought necessary to keep me almost always on deck; and from my extreme youth I was not put in fetters. In this situation I expected every hour to share the fate of my companions, some of whom were almost daily brought upon deck at the point of death, which I began to hope would soon put an end to my miseries. Often did I think many of the inhabitants of the deep much more happy than myself. I envied them the freedom they enjoyed, and as often wished I could change my condition for theirs. Every circumstance I met with, served only to render my state more painful, and heightened my apprehensions, and my opinion of the cruelty of the whites.

… One day, when we had a smooth sea and moderate wind, two of my wearied countrymen who were chained together (I was near them at the time), preferring death to such a life of misery, somehow made through the nettings and jumped into the sea; immediately, another quite dejected fellow, who, on account of his illness, was suffered to be out of irons, also followed their example; and I believe many more would very soon have done the same, if they had not been prevented by the ship's crew, who were instantly alarmed. Those of us that were the most active, were in a moment put down under the deck; and there was such a noise and confusion amongst the people of the ship as I never heard before, to stop her, and get the boat out to go after the slaves. However, two of the wretches were drowned, but they got the other, and afterwards flogged him unmercifully, for thus attempting to prefer death to slavery. In this manner we continued to undergo more hardships than I can now relate, hardships which are inseparable from this accursed trade. Many a time we were near suffocation from the want of fresh air, which we were often without for whole days together. This, and the stench of the necessary tubs, carried off many. ■

SOURCE: *The Interesting Narrative of the Life of Olaudah Equiano, or Gustavus Vassa, the African, Written by Himself* (1789).

central Africa. But these coastal states found that the trade was a viper that could easily strike back at them. "Merchants daily seize our own subjects, sons of the land and sons of our noblemen, they grab them and cause them to be sold," King Dom Affonso of the Kongo wrote to the Portuguese monarch in the six-teenth century. "And so great, Sir, is their corruption and licentiousness that our country is being utterly depopulated." Many of the new states became little more than machines for supplying captives to European traders, and a "gun-slave cycle" pushed them into a destructive arms race with each other.

Portrait of Olaudah Equiano, by an unknown English artist, ca. 1780. Captured in Nigeria in 1756 when he was eleven years old, Equiano was transported to America and was eventually purchased by an English sea captain. After ten years as a slave, he succeeded in buying his own freedom and dedicated himself to the antislavery cause. His book, *The Interesting Narrative of the Life of Olaudah Equiano* (1789), was published in numerous editions, translated into several languages, and became the prototype for dozens of other slave narratives in the nineteenth century.

SOURCE: Royal Albert Memorial Museum, Exeter, Devon, UK/Bridgeman Art Library.

Even more serious was the long-term stagnation of the West African economy. Labor was drawn away from farming and other productive activities, and imported consumer goods such as textiles and metal wares stifled local manufacturing. African traders were expert at driving a hard bargain for slaves, and over several centuries, they won increasing prices for slaves. But even when they appeared to get the best of the exchange, the ultimate advantage lay with the Europeans, who received wealth-producing workers in return for mere consumer goods.

This political, economic, and cultural demoralization prepared the way for the European conquest of Africa in the nineteenth century. The leaders of West Africa during the centuries of slave trading, writes the

Nigerian poet Chinweizu, "had been too busy organizing our continent for the exploitative advantage of Europe, had been too busy with slaving raids upon one another, too busy decorating themselves with trinkets imported from Europe, too busy impoverishing and disorganizing the land, to take thought and long-range action to protect our sovereignty."

THE DEVELOPMENT OF NORTH AMERICAN SLAVE SOCIETIES

New World slavery was nearly two centuries old before it became an important system of labor in North America. There were slaves in each of the British colonies during the seventeenth century, but in 1700, slaves accounted for only 11 percent of the colonial population (see Figure 4.2). During the eighteenth century, slavery expanded greatly, and by 1770 there were 460,000 Africans and African Americans in British North America, more than 20 percent of the population.

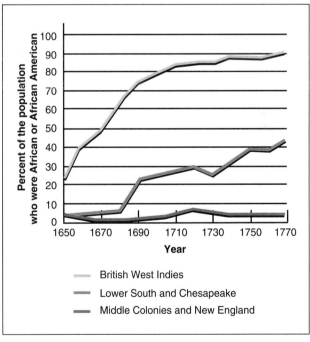

FIGURE 4.2 **Africans as a Percentage of Total Population of the British Colonies, 1650–1770** Although the proportion of Africans and African Americans was never as high in the South as in the Caribbean, the ethnic structure of the South diverged radically from that of the North during the eighteenth century.

SOURCE: Robert W. Fogel and Stanley L. Engerman, *Time on the Cross* (Boston: Little, Brown, 1974), 21.

Africans herded from a slave ship to a corral where they were to be sold by the cruel method known as "the scramble," buyers rushing in and grabbing their pick. This image was featured in an antislavery narrative published in 1796.

SOURCE: The Granger Collection, New York.

Slavery Comes to North America

The first Africans in Virginia arrived in 1619 when a Dutch slave trader exchanged "20 and odd Negars" for badly needed provisions with planter John Rolfe. But because slaves generally cost twice as much as indentured servants, yet had the same appallingly short life expectancy in the disease-prone Chesapeake region, they offered little economic benefit. Consequently, over the next several decades, tobacco planters employed far more indentured servants than slaves. Servants and slaves on seventeenth-century Virginia and Maryland plantations worked together, ate and slept in common quarters, and often developed intimate relationships. The Chesapeake was what historians term a *society with slaves*, a society in which slavery was one form of labor among several.

Under these circumstances the status of black Virginians could be ambiguous. An interesting case illustrates the point. In 1654, the African John Castor told a local court that "he came unto Virginia for seven or eight years of indenture, yet Anthony Johnson his Master had kept him his servant seven years longer than he should or ought." Johnson claimed that "he had the Negro for his life." The court decided in the master's favor. But strange to say, Johnson himself was of African descent. He had arrived as a slave in 1621, but by hiring himself out during his free time, had earned enough to gain freedom for himself and his family. Eventually he succeeded in becoming a landowner. "I know myne owne ground and I will worke when I please and play when I please," Johnson declared. Colonial records reveal that other Africans acquired farms, servants, and slaves of their own. Many slaves were Christians, and since religious difference had traditionally been a justification for slavery, this raised doubts about whether they could legally be kept as slaves. Moreover, sexual relations among Africans, Indians, and Europeans produced a sizable group of free people of mixed ancestry known as *mulattoes*. It was only later that dark skin came automatically to mean slavery, segregation, and the absence of the rights of freemen.

In the last quarter of the seventeenth century, however, the Chesapeake went from being a *society with slaves* to a *slave society*, in which the dominant form of labor was slavery. In the first place, there was a decline in the immigration of English servants. Previously it had been possible for former indentured servants to migrate westward and claim small plots on which they grew tobacco. But after the 1660s, most of the arable land had fallen into the hands of the planter elite. "There has not for many years," Virginian Edward Randolph wrote in 1696, "been any vast land to be taken up." English immigrants turned away from the Chesapeake to colonies such as Pennsylvania, where there was more opportunity. The labor shortage was filled by the English Royal Africa Company, which began importing slaves directly to North America in the 1670s. Slaves were expensive, but they could be kept in the fields for longer hours, with fewer days off. By 1700, there were 5,000 slaves in Virginia, and people of African descent made up 22 percent of the population of the Chesapeake.

There were no English legal precedents for enslaving people for life and making that status inevitable and inheritable. So as the proportions of slaves in the colonial population rose, colonists wrote slavery into law, a process best observed in the case of Virginia. In 1662, the planter assembly declared that henceforth children would be "bond or free only according to the condition of the mother." As one historian writes, this statute was "the great planters' first move in the direction of asserting their authority over the progeny of enslaved women." Five years later they passed a law that Christian baptism could no longer alter conditions of servitude. Thus were two important avenues to freedom closed. The colony then placed life-threatening violence in the hands of masters, declaring in 1669 that the death of a slave during punishment "shall not be accounted felony." Such regulations accumulated piecemeal until 1705, when Virginia gathered them into a comprehensive slave code that became a model for other colonies.

The institution of slavery was strengthened just as the Atlantic slave trade reached flood tide at the beginning of the eighteenth century. More Africans were imported into North America during the decade 1700–1710 than the entire previous century. The English colonies were primed for an unprecedented growth of plantation slavery.

The Tobacco Colonies

During the eighteenth century, the European demand for tobacco increased more than tenfold, and it was supplied largely by increased production in the Chesapeake. Tobacco was far and away the single most important commodity produced in eighteenth-century North America, accounting for more than a quarter of the value of all colonial exports.

The expansion of tobacco production could not have taken place without a corresponding growth in the size of the slave labor force. Unlike sugar, tobacco did not require large plantations and could be produced successfully on small farms. But it was a crop that demanded a great deal of hand labor and close attention. As tobacco farming grew, slaveholding became widespread. By 1770, more than a quarter million slaves labored in the colonies of the Upper South (Maryland, Virginia, and North Carolina), and because of the exploding market for tobacco, their numbers were expanding at about double the rate of the general population.

Shipments from Africa accounted for a portion of the growth of the slave population. From 1700 to 1770, an estimated 80,000 Africans were imported into the tobacco region. But natural increase was even more important. In the Caribbean and Brazil, where profits from sugar were extremely high, many planters literally worked their slaves to death, replenishing them with a constant stream of new arrivals, mostly men, from Africa. In Virginia, however, significantly lower profits led tobacco planters to pay more attention to the health of their labor force, establishing work routines that were not as deadly. Moreover, food supplies were more plentiful in North America and slaves bet-

ter fed, making them more resistant to disease. By the 1730s, the slave population of the Chesapeake had become the first in the Western Hemisphere to achieve self-sustained population growth. Natural increase gradually balanced the sex ratio among slaves, another encouragement to population growth. Planters came to recognize that they stood to benefit from the fertility of their slaves. "A woman who brings a child every two years [is] more valuable than the best man on the farm," wrote Virginia planter Thomas Jefferson, "for what she produces is an addition to the capital." By the 1750s, about 80 percent of Chesapeake slaves were "country-born."

The Lower South

The Chesapeake did not become a slave society until almost a century after its founding. But in South Carolina, settlement and slavery went hand in hand, and the colony was a slave society from the beginning. The most valuable part of the early Carolina economy was the Indian slave trade. Practicing a strategy of divide and conquer, using Indian tribes to fight one another, Carolinians enslaved tens of thousands of native people before the 1730s, shipping many to slave markets in the Caribbean, employing others raising cattle or felling timber. In 1713, colonists attacked the Tuscarora tribe, killing at least a thousand warriors and enslaving a thousand women and children. In retaliation, the Yamasee tribe staged a general uprising in 1715 that nearly defeated colonial forces. Only by enlisting the aid of the Cherokees, was South Carolina able to turn the tide.

By the time of the Yamasee War, however, planter preference had turned toward African rather than Indian slaves. Rice production was rapidly becoming the most dynamic sector of the South Carolina economy (see Table 4.1), and with their experience in agriculture, West Africans made much better rice workers than Indians. Another important crop was added in the 1740s, when a young South Carolina woman named Elizabeth Lucas Pinckney successfully adapted West Indian indigo to the low-country climate. The indigo plant, native to India, produced a deep blue dye important in textile manufacture. Rice grew in the lowlands, but indigo could be cultivated on high ground, and with different seasonal growing patterns, planters were able to harmonize their production. Rice and indigo were two of the most valuable commodities exported from the mainland colonies of North America. The boom in these two crops depended on increasing numbers of African slaves. Before the international slave trade to the United States was ended in 1808, at least 100,000 Africans had arrived in South

Residence and Slave Quarters of Mulberry Plantation, by Thomas Coram, ca. 1770. The slave quarters are on the left in this painting of a rice plantation near Charleston, South Carolina. The steep roofs of the slave cabins, an African architectural feature introduced in America by slave builders, kept living quarters cool by allowing the heat to rise and dissipate in the rafters.

SOURCE: Thomas Coram, *View of Mulberry Street, House and Street*, ca. 1770. Oil on paper, 10 × 17.6 cm. Gibbes Museum of Art/Carolina Art Association. 68.18.01.

Carolina. It is estimated that one of every five ancestors of today's African Americans passed through Charleston on the way to the rice plantations.

By the 1740s, many of the arriving Africans were being taken to Georgia, a colony created by an act of the English Parliament in 1732. Its leader, James

TABLE 4.1	TOBACCO AND RICE EXPORTS TO ENGLAND (in thousands of pounds)	
	Tobacco	Rice
1700	37,840	304
1725	21,046	5,367
1750	51,339	16,667
1775	55,968	57,692

Edward Oglethorpe, hoped to establish a buffer against Spanish invasion from Florida and make it a haven for poor British farmers who could then sell their products in the markets of South Carolina. Under Oglethorpe's influence, Parliament agreed to prohibit slavery in Georgia. Soon, however, Georgia's coastal regions were being colonized by South Carolina planters with their slaves. In 1752, Oglethorpe and Georgia's trustees abandoned their experiment, and the colony was opened to slavery under royal authority. The Georgia coast had already become an extension of the Carolina low-country slave system.

Tobacco plantations in the Chesapeake were often small affairs, but rice plantations required a minimum of thirty slaves and more commonly had fifty to seventy-five, which meant large black majorities in the colonies of the Lower South. By 1770, there were nearly 90,000 African Americans in the Lower South, about 80 percent of the coastal population of South Carolina and Georgia. In the words of one eighteenth-century observer, "Carolina looks more like a negro country than like a country settled by white people." The African American communities of the Lower South achieved self-sustained growth in the middle of the eighteenth century, a generation later than those in the Chesapeake.

Slavery in the Spanish Colonies

Slavery was basic to the Spanish colonial labor system, yet doubts about the enslavement of Africans were raised by both church and crown. The papacy denounced slavery many times as a violation of Christian principles. But the institution of slavery remained intact, and later in the eighteenth century, when sugar production expanded in Cuba, the slave system there was as brutal as any in the history of the Americas.

The character of slavery varied with local conditions. One of the most benign forms operated in Florida. Slaves could be found in many Florida settlements, but the conditions of their servitude resembled the household slavery common in Mediterranean and African communities more than the plantation slavery of the British colonies. In 1699, in an attempt to undermine the English colonies of the Lower South, the Spanish declared Florida a refuge for escaped slaves from the British colonies, offering free land to fugitives who would help defend their colony. Over the next half-century, refugee Indians and fugitive Africans established many communities in the countryside surrounding St. Augustine. North of the city, Fort Mose was manned by Negro troops commanded by their own officers. By 1763, 3,000 African Americans, a quarter of them free, made up 25 percent of St. Augustine's population.

In New Mexico, the Spanish depended on Indian slavery. In the sixteenth century, the colonial governor sent Indian slaves to the mines of Mexico. The enslavement of Indians was one of the causes of the Pueblo Revolt (see Chapter 3). During the eighteenth century, the Spanish were much more cautious in their treatment of the Pueblos, who were officially considered Catholics. But they captured and enslaved "infidel Indians" such as the Apaches or nomads from the Great Plains, using them as house servants and fieldworkers.

French Louisiana

Slavery was also important in Louisiana, the colony founded by the French in the lower Mississippi Valley in the early eighteenth century. After Robert Sieur de La Salle's voyage down the Mississippi River in 1681–82, the French planned colonies to anchor their New World empire. In the early eighteenth century, French Canadians established bases at Biloxi and Mobile on the Gulf of Mexico, but it was not until 1718 that they laid out the city of New Orleans on the Mississippi Delta. The French Company of the Indies imported some 6,000 African slaves, and planters invested in tobacco and indigo plantations on the Mississippi River in the country of the Natchez Indians. But in 1629, the Natchez and the slaves together rose in an armed uprising, the Natchez Rebellion, that took the lives of more than 200 French settlers, 10 percent of the population. Although colonial authorities were able to put down the rebellion—crushing and dispersing the Natchez people—the Louisiana French pulled back from a total commitment to slavery.

After the Natchez Rebellion, Louisiana's economy grew more diversified. Several thousand French colonists established farms and plantations on the Gulf Coast and in a narrow strip of settlement along the Mississippi River. African slaves amounted to no more than a third of the colonial population of 10,000. It was not until the end of the eighteenth century that the colony of Louisiana became an important North American slave society.

Slavery in the North

Slavery was a fundamental, acceptable, thoroughly American institution. Although none of the northern colonies could be characterized as a slave society, slavery was an important form of labor in many areas. Over the course of the eighteenth century, it grew increasingly significant in the commercial farming regions of southeast Pennsylvania, central New Jersey, and Long Island, where slaves made up about 10 percent of the rural residents. In the vicinity of Newport, Rhode Island, the proportion of slaves in the population reached nearly 25 percent, a concentration resulting from that port's dominance in the midcentury slave trade. The area was unique for the large slave gangs used in cattle and dairy operations in the Narragansett country, some of which were as large as Virginia plantations. Elsewhere in the New England countryside, slavery was relatively uncommon.

It was widespread in all the port cities, however, including Boston. There was "not a house" that "has not one or two," a visitor to that city wrote in the 1680s, and a visitor to Philadelphia about the same time noted that slaves were bought "by almost everyone who could afford [them]." Slave ownership was nearly universal among the wealthy and ordinary among craftsmen and professionals. By 1750, slaves and small free black populations made up 15 to 20 percent of the residents of Boston, New York City, and Philadelphia.

The Quakers of Pennsylvania and New Jersey, many of whom kept slaves, were the first colonists to voice antislavery sentiment. (See Out of Many Voices: An Early Quaker Meeting Condemns Slavery.) In 1715, John Hepburn of New Jersey published the first North American critique of slavery, but his was a lonely voice. By midcentury, however, there was a significant antislavery movement among the Quakers. In *Considerations on the Keeping of Negroes*

OUT OF MANY VOICES

AN EARLY QUAKER MEETING CONDEMNS SLAVERY

In 1688, the Quaker meeting at Germantown, south of Philadelphia, met to consider their moral duty in regard to slavery. Their antislavery declaration was perhaps the very first issued in America.

THESE ARE THE REASONS WHY WE ARE AGAINST THE traffick of men's Bodies, as followeth: Is there any that would be done or handled at this manner? To be sold or made a slave for all the time of his life? How fearfull and fainthearted are many on sea when they see a strange vessel, being afraid it should be a Turk, and they should be taken and sold for slaves into Turkey. Now what is this better done as Turks doe? Yea rather is it worse for them, which say they are Christians; for we hear that the most part of such Negers are brought hither against their will and consent; and that many of them are stollen. Now, tho' they are black, we cannot conceive there is more liberty to have them slaves, as it is to have other white ones. There is a saying, that we shall doe to all men, like as we will be done our selves; making no difference of what generation, descent or colour they are. And those who steal or rob men, and those who buy or purchase them, are they not all alike? Here is liberty of conscience, which is right and reasonable; here ought to be likewise liberty of the body, except of evildoers, which is another case. But to bring men hither, or to rob and sell them against their will, we stand against.

In Europe there are many oppressed for conscience sake; and here there are those oppressed which are of a black colour. And we, who know that men must not commit adultery, some doe commit adultery in others, separating wives from their husbands and giving them to others; and some sell the children of those poor creatures to other men. Oh! doe consider well this things, you who doe it; if you would be done at this manner? And if it is done according to Christianity? You surpass Holland and Germany in this thing. This makes an ill report in all those countries of Europe, where they hear off, that the Quakers doe here handle men like they handle there the cattel. And for that reason some have no mind or inclination to come hither, and who shall main-tains this your cause or plaid for it? Truly we can not do so, except you shall inform us better hereoff, that Christians have liberty to practise this things. Pray! What thing on the world can be done worse towards us, then if men should robb or steal us away, and sell us for slaves to strange countries, separating husbands from their wives and children. Being now this is not done at that manner, we will be done at, therefore we contradict and are against this traffick of men's bodies. And we who profess that it is not lawful to steal, must likewise avoid to purchase such things as are stollen but rather help to stop this robbing and stealing if possible; and such men ought to be delivered out of the hands of the Robbers and set free as well as in Europe. Then is Pennsylvania to have a good report, instead it hath now a bad one for this sake in other countries. Especially whereas the Europeans are desirous to know in what manner the Quakers doe rule in their Province; and most of them doe look upon us with an envious eye. But if this is done well, what shall we say is done evil?

If once these slaves (which they say are so wicked and stubborn men) should joint themselves, fight for their freedom and handle their masters and mistresses as they did handle them before, will these masters and mistresses take the sword at hand and war against these poor slaves, like we are able to believe, some will not refuse to doe? Or have these Negers not as much right to fight for their freedom, as you have to keep them slaves?

Now consider well this thing, if it is good or bad? And in case you find it to be good to handle these blacks at that manner, we desire and require you hereby lovingly, that you may inform us herein, which at this time never was done, that Christians have such a liberty to do so, to the end we shall be satisfied in this point, and satisfie likewise our good friends and acquaintances in our native country, to whose it is a terror or fearful thing that men should be handled so in Pennsylvania. ■

SOURCE: Samuel Pennypacker, "The Settlement of Germantown and the Causes which Led to It," *Pennsylvania Magazine of History and Biography* 4 (1880), pp. 29–30.

The London Coffee House, near the docks of Philadelphia, was the center of the city's business and political life in the mid-eighteenth century. Sea captains and merchants congregated here to do business, and as this contemporary print illustrates (in the detail on the far right), it was the site of many slave auctions. Slavery was a vital part of the economy of northern cities.

SOURCE: John F. Watson, "*Annals of Philadelphia*," being a collection of memoirs, anecdotes, & incidents of Philadelphia. The London Coffee House. The Library Company of Philadelphia.

London Coffee House.

(1754), John Woolman urged his readers to imagine themselves in the place of the African people. Suppose, he wrote,

> that our ancestors and we had been exposed to constant servitude in the more servile and inferior employments of life; that we had been destitute of the help of reading and good company; that amongst ourselves we had had few wise and pious instructors; that the religious amongst our superiors seldom took notice of us; that while others in ease had plentifully heaped up the fruit of our labour, we had received barely enough to relieve nature, and being wholly at the command of others had generally been treated as a contemptible, ignorant part of mankind. Should we, in that case, be less abject than they now are?

In 1758, the Philadelphia Friends Meeting voted to condemn slavery and urged masters to voluntarily free their slaves. It was not until the Revolution, however, that antislavery attitudes became more widespread in the colonies.

AFRICAN TO AFRICAN AMERICAN

The majority of Africans transported to North America arrived during the eighteenth century. They were met by a rapidly growing population of country-born slaves, or "Creoles" (from the French *créole* and Spanish *criollo*, meaning "born" or "raised"), a term first used by slaves in Brazil to distinguish their children, born in the New World, from newly arrived Africans. The perspective of Creoles was shaped by their having grown up under slavery, and that perspective helped them to determine which elements of African culture they would incorporate into the emerging culture of the African American community. That community was formed out of the relationship between Creoles and Africans, and between slaves and their European masters.

The Daily Life of Slaves

Because slaves formed the overwhelming majority of the labor force that made the plantation colonies so profitable, it is fair to say that Africans built the South. As an agricultural people, Africans, both women and men, were accustomed to the routines of rural labor, and this was put to use on the plantations. Most Africans were field hands, and even domestic servants labored in the fields when necessary.

Masters provided their slaves with rude clothing, sufficient in the summer but nearly always inadequate in the winter. Cheap garments, made from what was called "Negro cotton," was not only a means of saving money, but underscored the inferior status of slaves. At Mount Vernon, George Washington doled out a single set of clothes for each of his slaves. They were expected to last through a full year of field labor. Within months the garments were reduced to mere rags.

On small plantations and farms, which were typical in the tobacco country of the Chesapeake, Africans might work side by side with their owners and, depending on the character of the master, might enjoy a standard of living not too different from those of other family members. The work was more demanding and living conditions less sustaining on the great rice and indigo plantations of the Lower South, where slaves usually lived separately from the master in their own quarters. But large plantations, with large numbers of slaves, created the concentration of population necessary for the emergence of African American

Mum Bett, also known as Elizabeth Freeman, was born into slavery in a Massachusetts household about 1742. As a young woman she was subjected to the violent abuse of her mistress, who struck her with a hot shovel, leaving an indelible scar. Fleeing her owner Mum Bett enlisted the aid of antislavery lawyer Thomas Sedgwick, who helped win her freedom in 1772. This miniature was painted by Sedgwick's daughter Susan in 1811.

SOURCE: Courtesy of Massachusetts Historical Society.

communities and African American culture. This was one of the profound ironies of American slavery. On the great plantations, life was much harder, but slaves had more opportunity for some autonomy.

Families and Communities

The family was the most important institution for the development of African American community and culture, but slave codes did not provide for legal slave marriages, for that would have contradicted the master's freedom to dispose of his property as he saw fit. "The endearing ties of husband and wife are strangers to us," declared a group of Massachusetts slaves who petitioned for their freedom in 1774, "for we are no longer man and wife than our masters or mistresses think proper." How, they asked, "can a slave perform the duties of a husband to a wife or parent to his child? How can a husband leave master to work and cleave to his wife? How can [wives]

submit themselves to their husbands in all things? How can [children] obey their parents in all things?"

Planters commonly separated families by sale or bequest, dividing husbands and wives and even separating mothers from their children. Charles Ball was separated from his wife and children when his master sold him to a rice planter in Georgia. "My heart died away within me," Ball remembered vividly, "I felt incapable of weeping or speaking, and in my despair I laughed loudly." He was sent away, his hands bound, the same day he learned of his fate, and on his journey he dreamed his wife and children were "beseeching and imploring my master on their knees." He never saw them again. Another planter sold the children of a slave mother, allowing only that her infant could "suck its mother till twelve months old," but then the child was also to be sold.

Despite the barriers, however, during the eighteenth century, slaves in both the Chesapeake and the Lower South created the families that were essential for the development of African American culture. On large plantations throughout the southern colonies, travelers found Africans living in family households. In the Lower South, where there were greater concentrations of slaves on the great rice planta-

Buddy Qua of St. Vincent. African names for weekdays, such as "Qua" or "Quow" (Tuesday), were common among the slaves of the Caribbean and the Lower South. This sketch comes from an eighteenth-century series showing slaves going about their daily tasks.

SOURCE: National Library of Jamaica.

tions, husbands and wives often lived together in the slave quarters, and this was clearly the ideal. On the smaller plantations of the Upper South, men often married women from neighboring farms, and with the permission of both owners, visited their families in the evenings or on Sundays.

Generally, slave couples married when the woman became pregnant. "Their marriages are generally performed amongst themselves," one visitor to North Carolina wrote of the Africans he observed in the 1730s. "The man makes the woman a present, such as a brass ring or some other toy, which she accepts of, [and] becomes his wife." Common throughout the South was the postnuptial ritual in which the couple jumped over a broomstick together, declaring their relationship to the rest of the community. This custom may have originated in Africa, although versions of it were practiced in medieval Europe as well.

Recent studies of naming practices among eighteenth-century African Americans illustrate their commitment to establishing a system of kinship. Frequently sons were named for their fathers, perhaps a way of strengthening the paternal bonds of men forced to live away from their families. Children of both sexes were named for grandparents and other kin. African names were common; names such as Cudjo (Monday), Quow (Thursday), or Coffee (Friday) continued the African tradition of "weekday" names. Later in the century, Anglo names became more general.

Margery and Moody, slaves of Francis Jerdone of Louisa County, Virginia, named their six children Sam, Rose, Sukey, Mingo, Maria, and Comba, mixing both African and English traditions. Many Africans carried names known only within their community, and these were often African. In the sea island region of the Lower South, such names were common until the twentieth century.

Emotional ties to particular places, connections between the generations, and relations of kinship and friendship linking neighboring plantations and farms were the foundation stones of African American community life. Kinship was especially important. African American parents encouraged their children to use family terms in addressing unrelated persons: "auntie" or "uncle" became a respectful way of addressing older men and women, "brother" and "sister" affectionate terms for agemates. Fictive kinship may have been one of the first devices enslaved Africans used to humanize the world of slavery. During the Middle Passage, it was common for children to call their elders "aunt" and "uncle," for adults to address all children as "son" or "daughter."

African American Culture

The eighteenth century was the formative period in the development of the African American community, for it was then that the high birthrate and the growing numbers of country-born provided the necessary stability for the evolution of culture. During this period, men and women from dozens of African ethnic groups molded themselves into a new people. Distinctive patterns in music and dance, religion, and oral tradition illustrate the resilience of the human spirit under bondage as well as the successful struggle of African Americans to create a spiritually sustaining culture of their own.

Eighteenth-century masters were reluctant to allow their slaves to become Christians, fearing that baptism would open the way to claims of freedom or give Africans dangerous notions of universal brotherhood and equality with masters. One frustrated missionary was told by a planter that a slave was "ten times worse when a Christian than in his state of paganism." Before the American Revolution, the majority of black Southerners practiced some form of African religion. Large numbers of African Americans were not

This eighteenth-century painting depicts a celebration in the slave quarters on a South Carolina plantation. One planter's description of a slave dance seems to fit this scene: the men leading the women in "a slow shuffling gait, edging along by some unseen exertion of the feet, from one side to the other—sometimes courtesying down and remaining in that posture while the edging motion from one side to the other continued." The women, he wrote, "always carried a handkerchief held at arm's length, which was waved in a graceful motion to and fro as she moved."

SOURCE: Abby Aldrich Rockefeller Folk Art Museum, Colonial Williamsburg Foundation, VA.

converted to Christianity until the Great Awakening, which swept across the South after the 1760s (see Chapter 5).

One of the most crucial areas of religious practice concerned the rituals of death and burial. In their separate graveyards, African Americans often decorated graves with shells and pottery, an old African custom. African Americans generally believed that the spirits of their dead would return to Africa. The burial ceremony was often held at night to keep it secret from masters, who objected to the continuation of African traditions. The deceased was laid out, and around the body, men and women would move counterclockwise in a slow dance step while singing ancestral songs. The pace gradually increased, finally reaching a frenzied but joyful conclusion. As slaves from different backgrounds joined together in the circle, they were beginning the process of cultural unification.

Music and dance may have formed the foundation of African American culture, coming even before a common language. Many eighteenth-century observers commented on the musical and rhythmic gifts of Africans. Olaudah Equiano remembered his people, the Ibos, as "a nation of dancers, musicians, and poets." Thomas Jefferson, raised on a Virginia plantation, wrote that blacks "are more generally gifted than the whites, with accurate ears for tune and time." Many Africans were accomplished players of stringed instruments and drums, and their style featured improvisation and rhythmic complexity, elements that would become prominent in African American music. In America, slaves recreated African instruments, as in the case of the banjo, and mastered the art of the European violin and guitar. Fearing that slaves might communicate by code, authorities often outlawed drums. But using bones, spoons, or sticks, or simply "patting juba" (slapping their thighs), slaves produced elaborate multirhythmic patterns.

One of the most important developments of the eighteenth century was the invention of an African American language. An English traveler during the 1770s complained he could not understand Virginia slaves, who spoke "a mixed dialect between the Guinea and English." But such a language made it possible for country-born and "saltwater" Africans to communicate. The two most important dialects were Gullah and Geechee, named after two of the African peoples most prominent in the Carolina and Georgia low country, the Golas and Gizzis of the Windward Coast. These Creole languages were a transitional phenomenon, gradually giving way to distinctive forms of black English, although in certain isolated areas, such as the sea islands of the Carolinas and Georgia, they persisted into the twentieth century.

The Africanization of the South

The African American community often looked to recently arrived Africans for religious leadership and medical magic. Throughout the South, many whites had as much faith in slave conjurers and herb doctors as the slaves themselves did, and slaves won fame for their healing powers. This was one of many ways in which white and black Southerners came to share a common culture. Acculturation was by no means a one-way street; English men and women in the South were also being Africanized.

Slaves worked in the kitchens of their masters, and thus introduced an African style of cooking into colonial diets already transformed by the addition of Indian crops. African American culinary arts are responsible for such Southern culinary specialty perennials as barbecue, fried chicken, black-eyed peas, and collard greens. And the liberal African use of red pepper, sesame seeds, and other sharp flavors established the Southern preference for highly spiced foods. In Louisiana, a combination of African, French, and Indian elements produced a distinguished American regional cuisine, exemplified by gumbos (soups) and jambalayas (stews).

Mutual acculturation is also evident in many aspects of material culture. Southern basket weaving used Indian techniques and African designs. Woodcarving often featured African motifs. African architectural designs featuring high, peaked roofs (to vent the heat) and broad, shady porches gradually became part of a distinctive Southern style. The West African iron-working tradition was evident throughout the South, especially in the ornamentation of the homes of Charleston and New Orleans.

Even more important were less tangible aspects of culture. Slave mothers nursed white children as well as their own. As one English observer wrote, "each child has its [black] Momma, whose gestures and accent it will necessarily copy, for children, we all know, are imitative beings." In this way, many Africanisms passed into the English language of the South: goober (peanut), yam, banjo, okay, tote, buddy. Some linguists have argued that the Southern "drawl," evident among both black and white speakers, derived from the incorporation of African intonations of words and syllables.

African American music and dance also deeply affected white culture. These art forms offer a good example of mutual acculturation. At eighteenth-century plantation dances, the music was usually provided by Africans playing European instruments and their own, such as the banjo. African American fiddlers were common throughout the South by the time of the Revolution, but the banjo also became the characteristic folk instrument of the white South. Toward the end of the evening, the musicians were often told to play some "Negro jigs," and slaves were asked to demonstrate the African manner of dancing. Dancing provided slaves with a unique opportunity to express themselves. "Us slaves watched white folks' parties where the guests danced a minuet," an old South Carolina slave woman recalled, "then we'd do it too, but we used to mock 'em, every step." Whites in turn attempted to imitate African

Fugitive slaves flee through the swamps in Thomas Moran's *The Slave Hunt* (1862). Many slaves ran away from their masters, and colonial newspapers included notices urging readers to be on the lookout for them. Some fled in groups or collected together in isolated communities called "maroon" colonies, located in inaccessible swamps and woods.

SOURCE: Thomas Moran (American, 1837-1926), *The Slave Hunt, Dismal Swamp, Virginia*, 1862, oil on canvas, 86.4 × 111.8 cm. Gift of Laura A. Clubb, The Philbrook Museum of Art, Tulsa, Oklahoma. 1947.8.44.

rhythmic dance styles. A slave named Dick related how his master loved to listen to him play the banjo and watch the slave women dance on moonlit nights. The master himself "could shake a desperate foot at the fiddle," said Dick, attempting to outperform the slaves at the "Congo minuet." In such a back-and-forth fashion, the traditions of both groups were gradually transformed.

Violence and Resistance

Slavery was a system based on the use of brute force and violence. The only way to make slaves work, planter Robert "King" Carter instructed his overseer, was "to make them stand in fear." Humane slave masters like George Washington did not wish to be harsh. He sought, as he wrote it, "tranquility with a certain income." But the tranquility of Mount Vernon rested on the constant threat of violence. Washington ordered his overseers to carefully monitor the work of the slaves and punish their offenses with regular whippings. Even the most cultured plantation owners thought nothing about floggings of fifty or seventy-five lashes. "Der prayer was answered," sang the slaves of South Carolina, "wid de song of a whip." The threat of violence was omnipresent. And some masters were downright sadistic—stabbing, burning, maiming, mutilating, raping, and castrating their slaves.

Former slave David George, who was born and raised on a Virginia plantation, wrote a searing account of plantation violence. "My oldest sister was called Patty. I have seen her several times so whipped that her back has been all corruption, as though it would rot. My brother Dick ran away, but they caught him. . . . After he had received 500 lashes, or more, they washed his back with salt water and whipped it in, as well as rubbed it in with a rag. . . . I also have been whipped many a time on my naked skin, and sometimes till the blood has run down over my waist band. But the greatest grief I then had was to see them whip my mother, and to hear her, on her knees, begging for mercy."

Eighteenth-century ships being unloaded of their colonial cargoes on London's Old Custom House Quay. Most of the goods imported into England from the American colonies were produced by slave labor.

SOURCE: Samuel Scott, *Old Custom House Quay* Collection. V&A Images, the Victoria and Albert Museum, London.

look the rest of the slaves, and he had no kind of provocation to go off." An analysis of hundreds of eighteenth-century advertisements for runaways reveals that 80 percent were young men in their twenties, suggesting that flight was an option primarily for unattached males.

Runaways sometimes collected together in communities called "maroons," from the Spanish *cimarron*, meaning "wild and untamed." Slaves who escaped from South Carolina or Georgia into Spanish Florida created maroon communities among the Creek Indians there. These mixed African and Indian peoples came to call themselves "Seminoles," a name deriving from their pronunciation of "cimarron." Maroons also lay hidden in the backcountry of the Lower South, and although they were less common in the Upper South, a number of fugitive communities existed in the Great Dismal Swamp, the coastal region between Virginia and North Carolina.

The most direct form of resistance was revolt. The first notable slave uprising of the colonial era occurred in New York City in 1712. Taking an oath of secrecy, twenty-three Africans vowed revenge for what they called the "hard usage" of their masters. They armed themselves with guns, swords, daggers, and hatchets, killed nine colonists, and burned several buildings before being surrounded by the militia. Six of the conspirators committed suicide rather than surrender. Thirteen were hanged, another was starved to death in chains, another broken on the wheel, and three more burned at the stake. In 1741, New York authorities uncovered what they thought was another conspiracy. Thirteen black leaders were burned alive, eighteen more hanged, and eighty sold and shipped off to the West Indies. A family of colonists and a Catholic priest, accused of providing weapons, were also executed.

Yet African Americans demonstrated a resisting spirit. In their day-to-day existence they often refused to cooperate: they malingered, they mistreated tools and animals, they destroyed the master's property. "Let an hundred men shew him how to hoe, or drive a wheelbarrow," wrote one frustrated planter, "he'll still take the one by the bottom, and the other by the wheel." Flight was also an option, and judging from the advertisements placed by masters in colonial newspapers, even the most trusted Africans ran away. "That this slave should run away and attempt getting his liberty, is very alarming," read the notice of one Maryland master in 1755. "He has always been too kindly used" and was "one in whom his master has put great confidence, and depended on him to over-

A series of small rebellions and rumors of large ones in 1720s Virginia culminated in the Chesapeake rebellion of 1730, the largest slave uprising of the colonial period. Several hundred slaves assembled in Norfolk and Princess Anne counties, choosing commanders for their "insurrection." More than three hundred escaped en masse into the Dismal Swamp. Hunted down by Indians

hired by the colony, their community was soon destroyed. Twenty-nine leaders were executed and the rest returned to their masters.

There were also isolated but violent uprisings in the Lower South, where slaves made up a majority of the population, in 1704, 1720, and 1730. In 1738, a series of violent revolts broke out throughout South Carolina and Georgia. Then in 1739, a group of twenty recently arrived Angolans sacked the armory in Stono, South Carolina. They armed themselves and began a march toward Florida and freedom. Beating drums to attract other slaves to their cause, they grew to nearly one hundred. They plundered a number of planters' homes along the way and killed some thirty colonists. Pausing in a field to celebrate their victory with dance and song, they were overtaken by the militia and destroyed in a pitched battle. That same year there was an uprising in Georgia. Another took place in South Carolina the following year. Attributing these revolts to the influence of newly arrived Africans, colonial officials shut off the slave trade through Charleston for the next ten years.

Wherever masters held slaves, fears of uprisings persisted. But compared with such slave colonies as Jamaica, Guiana, or Brazil, there were few slave revolts in North America. The conditions favoring revolt—large African majorities, brutal exploitation with correspondingly low survival rates, little acculturation, and geographic isolation—prevailed in only some areas of the Lower South. Indeed, the very success of African Americans in British North America at establishing families, communities, and a culture of their own inevitably made them less likely to take the risks that rebellions required.

SLAVERY AND EMPIRE

Slavery contributed enormously to the economic growth and development of Europe during the colonial era, and it was an important factor in Great Britain just before the Industrial Revolution of the eighteenth century. Slavery was the most dynamic force in the Atlantic economy during that century, creating the conditions for industrialization. But because slave-owning colonists single-mindedly committed their resources to the expansion and extension of the plantation system, they derived very little benefit from the economic diversification that characterized industrialization.

Slavery the Mainspring

The slave colonies—the sugar islands of the West Indies and the colonies of the South—accounted for 95 percent of the exports from the Americas to Great Britain from 1714 to 1773. Although approximately half of all Great Britain's American colonists lived in New England and the mid-Atlantic, the colonies in those regions contributed less than 5 percent of total exports during this period (see Table 4.2). Moreover, there was the prime economic importance of the slave trade itself, which one economist of the day described as the "foundation" of the British economy, "the mainspring of the machine which sets every wheel in motion." The labor of African slaves was largely responsible for the economic success of the British Empire in the Americas.

Slavery greatly contributed to the economic development of Great Britain in three principal ways. First, slavery generated enormous profits that became a source of capital investment in the economy. The profits of individual investors in the slave system varied widely. But as the British economist Adam Smith wrote, "the profits of a sugar plantation in any of our West Indian colonies are generally much greater than those of any other cultivation that is known either in Europe or America." Economic historians estimate that annual profits during the eighteenth century averaged 15 percent of invested capital in the slave trade, 10 percent in plantation agriculture. Some of the first of England's great modern fortunes were made out of slavery's miseries.

The profits of the slave trade and slave production contributed greatly to the accumulation of capital. Although economic historians differ in their

TABLE **4.2**	BRITISH COLONIAL TRADE IN THE AMERICAS, 1714–73				
	(in thousands of British pounds sterling)				
	Exports to Britain		Imports from Britain		
	£	%	£	%	
British West Indies	96,808	64.0	41,653	38.8	
Lower South and Chesapeake	47,192	31.2	27,561	25.7	
Middle Colonies and New England	7,160	4.7	37,939	35.4	
Total	151,160	99.9	107,153	99.9	

SOURCE: Eric Williams, *Capitalism and Slavery* (Chapel Hill: University of North Carolina Press, 1944), 225–26.

MAP EXPLORATION

To explore an interactive version of this map,
go to **www.prenhall.com/faragher5/map4.3**

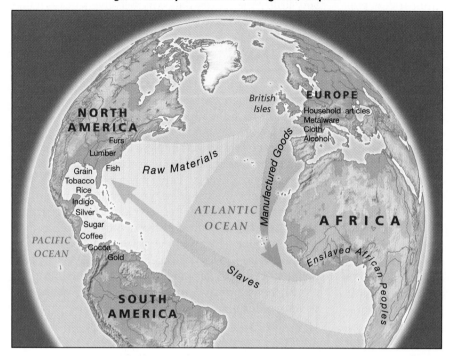

MAP 4.3 Triangular Trade Across the Atlantic The pattern of commerce among Europe, Africa, and the Americas became known as the "Triangular Trade." Sailors called the voyage of slave ships from Africa to America the "Middle Passage" because it formed the crucial middle section of this trading triangle.

tured goods (principally textiles, metal products, and ship's wares) accounted for nearly 70 percent of the expansion of British exports.

The multiplier effects of these activities are best seen in the growth of English ports such as Liverpool and Bristol. There the African and American trades provided employment for ships' crews, dockmen, construction workers, traders, shopkeepers, lawyers, clerks, factory workers, and officials of all ranks down to the humblest employees of the custom house. It was said of Bristol that "there is not a brick in the city but what is cemented with the blood of a slave." In the countryside surrounding Liverpool and elsewhere, capital acquired through slavery was invested in the new industrial methods of producing cotton textiles, the beginning of the Industrial Revolution.

The Politics of Mercantilism

When imperial officials argued that colonies existed solely for the benefit of the mother country, they had in mind principally the great wealth produced by slavery.

estimates, profits derived from the triangular trade in slaves, plantation products, and manufactured goods (see Map 4.3) furnished from 21 to 35 percent of Great Britain's fixed capital formation in the eighteenth century. This capital funded the first modern banks and insurance companies, and eventually found its way into a wide range of economic activities. Merchant capitalists were prominent investors in the expansion of the merchant marine, the improvement of harbors, and the construction of canals.

Second, slavery contributed to the economic development of Great Britain by supplying the raw cotton essential to the Industrial Revolution. In 1787, slave plantations in the Caribbean supplied 69 percent of the raw cotton for British mills. The insatiable demand for cotton led to the development of the cotton gin and the rise of cotton plantations in the United States (see Chapter 11). And third, slavery provided an enormous stimulus to the growth of manufacturing by creating a huge colonial market for exports. From 1700 to 1740, the growth in American and African demand for manufac-

To ensure that this wealth benefited their states, European imperial powers created a system of regulations that became known as "mercantilism." The essence of mercantilist policy was the political control of the economy by the state. First advanced in France in the seventeenth century under the empire of Louis XIV, mercantilist policies were most successfully applied by Great Britain in the eighteenth century. The monarchy and Parliament established a uniform national monetary system, regulated wages, encouraged agriculture and manufacturing with subsidies, and erected tariff barriers to protect themselves from foreign competition. England also sought to organize and control colonial trade to the maximum advantage of its own shippers, merchants, manufacturers, and bureaucrats.

The mercantilists viewed the economy as a "zero-sum" game, in which total economic gains were equal to total losses. As an English mercantilist put it, "there is but a certain proportion of trade in the world." Profit was thought to result from successful speculation, crafty dealing, or simple plunder—all considered forms of theft.

The institution of slavery confirmed the theory, for slavery was nothing more than a highly developed system by which some people stole the labor of others. The essence of the competition between states, the mercantilists argued, was the struggle to acquire and hoard the fixed amount of wealth that existed in the world. The nation that accumulated the largest treasure of gold and silver specie would be the most powerful.

Wars for Empire

The mercantilist era was thus characterized by intense and violent competition among European states. Wars usually arose out of Old World issues, spilling over into the New World, but they also originated in conflicts over the colonies themselves. In the Anglo-Dutch Wars of the 1650s through the 1670s, England successfully overtook Holland as the dominant Atlantic power. Then, beginning with King William's War (1689–97), England and France (generally allied with Spain) opened a long struggle for colonial supremacy in North America. (For discussion of these conflicts, see Chapter 3.) The fighting took place mainly at the edges of the empire, on the frontiers separating Spanish Florida from British Georgia and New France from New England.

Colonial wars in the southern region had everything to do with slavery. The first fighting of the eighteenth century took place during Queen Anne's War (known in Europe as the War of the Spanish Succession), a conflict that pitted Great Britain and its allies against France and Spain. In 1702, troops from South Carolina took the war as an opportunity to invade Florida, plundering and burning St. Augustine in an attempt to destroy the refuge for fugitive slaves there. A combined French and Spanish fleet took revenge in 1706 by bombarding Charleston. Great Britain emerged the victor in the general war, and in 1713, as part of the Peace of Utrecht, Spain ceded to the British the exclusive lucrative right to supply slaves to its American colonies.

The entrance of British slavers into Spanish ports also provided an opportunity for illicit trade, and sporadic fighting between the two empires broke out over this issue a number of times during the next two decades. But Robert Walpole, British prime minister from 1721 to 1748, saw distinct advantages for his nation in the continuation of peace. The Spanish empire in America was now open to British traders, he argued, and while "it is true that treasure is brought home in Spanish names, . . . Spain herself is no more than the canal through which all these treasures are conveyed all over the rest of Europe." A faction in the House of Commons, however, demanded elimination of the Spanish threat. In 1739, at their urging, a one-eared sea captain by the name of Jenkins testified before Parliament about the indignities suffered by British merchant sailors at the hands of the Spanish. In a dramatic flourish, he produced a dried and withered ear, which he claimed they had cut from his head. A public outrage followed, forcing Walpole to agree to a war of Caribbean conquest that the British called the War of Jenkins's Ear.

English troops allied with Creek Indians invaded Florida once again, laying waste the last of the old mission stations but failing to capture St. Augustine. In response, Spanish troops, including several companies of African Americans, invaded Georgia. Although the Spanish were defeated seventy-five miles south of Savannah,

OVERVIEW

THE COLONIAL WARS

King William's War	*1689–97*	France and England battle on the northern frontiers of New England and New York.
Queen Anne's War	*1702–13*	England fights France and Spain in the Caribbean and on the northern frontier of New France. Part of the European conflict known as the War of the Spanish Succession.
War of Jenkins's Ear	*1739–43*	Great Britain versus Spain in the Caribbean and Georgia. Part of the European conflict known as the War of the Austrian Succession.
King George's War	*1744–48*	Great Britain and France fight in Acadia and Nova Scotia; the second American round of the War of the Austrian Succession.
French and Indian War	*1754–63*	Last of the great colonial wars pitting Great Britain against France and Spain. Known in Europe as the Seven Years War.

the campaign produced an agreement on the boundary between British Georgia and Spanish Florida that today still separates those states. Elsewhere the British were not so lucky: in the Caribbean the imperial fleet suffered disaster at the hands of the Spanish navy.

In the northern region, the principal focus of this imperial struggle was control of the Indian trade. In 1704, during Queen Anne's War, the French and their Algonquian Indian allies raided New England frontier towns, such as Deerfield, Massachusetts, dragging men, women, and children into captivity in Canada (see Chapter 5). In turn, the English mounted a series of expeditions against the French fort at Port Royal in Acadia, which they captured in 1710. At the war's conclusion in 1713, France was forced to cede Acadia, Newfoundland, and Hudson Bay to Great Britain in exchange for guarantees of security for the French-speaking residents of those provinces. Nearly thirty years of peace followed, but from 1744 to 1748, England again battled France in King George's War (known in Europe as the War of the Austrian Succession). The French attacked the British in Nova Scotia, Indian and Canadian raids again devastated the border towns of New England and New York, and hundreds of British subjects were killed or captured.

The French, allied with the Spanish and Prussians, were equally successful in Europe. What finally turned the tide of this war was the capture in 1745 of the French fortress of Louisburg on Cape Breton Island by an expedition of Massachusetts troops in conjunction with the royal navy. Deprived of the most strategic of their American ports, and fearful of losing the wealth of their sugar islands, the French agreed to a negotiated settlement in 1748. But despite the capture of Louisburg, the war elsewhere had been fought to a stalemate, so the treaty restored the prewar status quo, and Louisburg was returned to France. This disgusted the merchants of New England, who wanted to expand their commercial influence in the maritime colonies, and left the North American conflict between France and Britain still simmering. Significantly, however, this was the first time that the concluding battle of a European war had been fought on North American soil, and it was a harbinger of things to come: the next war was destined to start as a conflict between French and British colonists before engulfing Europe (see Chapter 6).

British Colonial Regulation

Mercantilists used means other than war to win the wealth of the world. In the sixteenth century, the Spanish monarchy created the first state trading monopoly— the Casa de Contratación—to manage the commerce of its empire. It was widely emulated by others: the Dutch East Indies Company, the French Company of the Indies, the English East India Company, the Hudson's Bay Company, and the Royal African Company.

English manufacturers complained that merchant-dominated trading monopolies too frequently carried foreign (particularly Dutch) products to colonial markets, ignoring English domestic industry. Reacting to these charges, between 1651 and 1696 Parliament passed a series of Navigation Acts, creating the legal and institutional structure of Britain's colonial system. The acts defined the colonies as both suppliers of raw materials and as markets for English manufactured goods. Merchants from other nations were expressly forbidden to trade in the colonies, and commodities from the colonies had to be shipped in vessels built in England or the British colonies themselves.

The regulations specified a list of "enumerated commodities" that could be shipped only to England. These included the products of the southern slave colonies (sugar, molasses, rum, tobacco, rice, and indigo), those of the northern Indian trade (furs and skins), and those essential for supplying the shipping industry (pine masts, tar, pitch, resin, and turpentine). The bulk of these products were not destined for English consumption; at great profit they were reexported elsewhere.

England also placed limitations on colonial enterprises that might compete with those at home. A series of enactments—including the Wool Act of 1699, the Hat Act of 1732, and the Iron Act of 1750—forbade the production of those goods in the colonies. Moreover, colonial assemblies were forbidden to impose tariffs on English imports as a way of protecting colonial industries. Banking was disallowed, local coinage prohibited, and the export of coin from England forbidden. Badly in need of a circulating monetary medium, Massachusetts minted its own copper coin, and several colonies issued paper currency, forcing Parliament to explicitly legislate against the practice. The colonists depended mostly on "commodity money" (furs, skins, or hogsheads of tobacco) and the circulation of foreign currency, the most common being the Spanish silver *peso* and the German silver *thaler* (or "dollar"). Official rates of exchange between commodity money, colonial paper, foreign currency, and English pounds allowed this seemingly chaotic system to operate without too much difficulty.

As the trade in colonial products increased, most Britons came to agree with Prime Minister Robert Walpole that it made little sense to tamper with such a prosperous system. Walpole's policy was later characterized as one of "salutory neglect." Any colonial rules and regulations deemed contrary to good business practice were simply ignored and not enforced. Between 1700 and 1760, the quantity of goods exported from the colonies to the mother country rose 165 percent, while imports from Britain to North America increased by more than 400 percent. In part because of lax enforcement, but mostly because the system operated to the profit of colonial merchants, colonists complained very little about British mercantilist policies before the 1760s.

The Colonial Economy

Despite the seemingly harsh mercantilist regulations, the economic system operated to the benefit of planters, merchants, and white colonists in general. Southern slave owners made healthy profits on the sale of their commodities. They enjoyed a protected market in which competing goods from outside the empire were heavily taxed. Planters found themselves with steadily increasing purchasing power. Pennsylvania, New York, and New England, and increasingly the Chesapeake as well, produced grain, flour, meat, and dairy products. None of these was included in the list of enumerated goods, and could be sold freely abroad. They found their most ready market in the British West Indies and the Lower South. Most of this trade was carried in New England ships. Indeed, the New England shipbuilding industry was greatly stimulated by the allowance under the Navigation Acts for ships built and manned in the colonies. So many ships were built for English buyers that by midcentury, nearly a third of all British tonnage was American made.

The greatest benefits for the port cities of the North came from their commercial relationship to the slave colonies (see Figure 4.3). New England merchants had become important players in the slave trade by the early eighteenth century, and soon thereafter they began to make inroads into the export trade of the West Indian colonies. It was in the Caribbean that northern merchants most blatantly ignored mercantilist laws. In violation of Spanish, French, and Dutch regulations prohibiting foreign trade, New Englanders traded foodstuffs for sugar in foreign colonies. By 1750, more than sixty distilleries in Massachusetts Bay were exporting more than 2 million gallons of rum, most of it produced from sugar obtained illegally. Because the restrictive rules and regulations enacted by Britain for its colonies were not enforced, such growth and prosperity among the merchants and manufacturers of the port cities of the North prospered.

By the mid-eighteenth century, the Chesapeake and Lower South regions were major exporters of tobacco, rice, and indigo, and the middle colonies major exporters of grain to Europe. The carrying trade in the products of slave labor made it possible for the northern and middle colonies to earn the income necessary to purchase British imports despite the lack of valuable products from their own regions. Gradually, the commercial economies of the Northeast and the South were becoming integrated. From the 1730s to the 1770s, for example, while the volume of trade between Great Britain and Charleston doubled, the trade between Charleston and northern ports grew sevenfold. The same relationship was developing between the Chesapeake and the North. Merchants in Boston, Newport, New York, and Philadelphia increasingly provided southern planters not only with shipping services but also with credit and

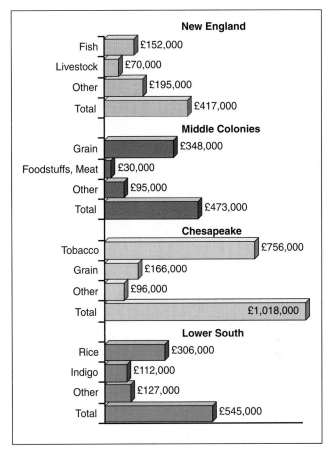

FIGURE 4.3 Value of Colonial Exports by Region, Annual Average, 1768–72 With tobacco, rice, grain, and indigo, the Chesapeake and Lower South accounted for nearly two-thirds of colonial exports in the late eighteenth century. The Middle Colonies, however, were also becoming major exporters of grain.

SOURCE: James F. Shepherd and Gary M. Walton, *Shipping, Maritime Trade and the Economic Development of Colonial America* (Cambridge: Cambridge University Press, 1972), 211–27.

insurance. Like London, Liverpool, and Bristol—though on a smaller scale—the port cities of the North became pivots in the expanding trade network linking slave plantations with Atlantic markets. This trade provided northern merchants with the capital that financed commercial growth and development in their cities and the surrounding countryside. Slavery thus contributed to the growth of a score of northern port cities, forming an indirect but essential part of their economies.

SLAVERY AND FREEDOM

The prosperity of the eighteenth-century plantation economy thus improved the living conditions for the residents of northern cities as well as for a large segment of the white population of the South, providing them with

The New England artist John Greenwood painted this amusing view of New England sea captains in Surinam in 1757. By the early eighteenth century, New England merchant traders like these had become important participants in the traffic in slaves and sugar to and from the West Indies. Northern ports thus became important pivots in the expanding commercial network linking slave plantations with Atlantic markets.

SOURCE: John Greenwood, *Sea Captains Carousing in Surinam*, 1758. Oil on bed ticking, 95.9 × 191.2 cm. The Saint Louis Art Museum, Museum Purchase.

the opportunity for a kind of freedom unknown in the previous century. The price of this prosperity and freedom, however, was the oppression and exploitation of millions of Africans and African Americans. Freedom for white men based on the slavery of African Americans is the most important contradiction of American history.

The Social Structure of the Slave Colonies

Slavery produced a highly stratified class society. At the summit of power stood an elite of wealthy planters who held more than half the cultivated land and over 60 percent of the wealth. Although there was no formal colonial aristocracy—no royal recognition of rank—the landed elite of the slave colonies sought to present itself as one. Binding themselves together through strategic marriage alliances and carefully crafted business dealings, dressing themselves in silk, lace, and powdered wigs, staging elaborate public rituals designed to awe common folk and slaves, they made up what one historian calls an "interlocking directorate."

The typical wealthy Virginia planter lived in a Tidewater county; owned several thousand acres of prime farmland and more than a hundred slaves; resided in a luxurious plantation mansion, built perhaps in the fashionable Georgian style; and had an estate valued at more than £10,000. Elected to the House of Burgesses and forming the group from which the magistrates and counselors of the colony were chosen, these "first families of Virginia"—the Carters, Harrisons, Lees, Fitzhughs, Washingtons, Randolphs, and others—were a self-perpetuating governing class. A similar elite ruled the Lower South, although wealthy landowners spent little time on their plantations. They lived instead in fashionable Charleston, where they made up a close-knit group who controlled the colonial government. "They live in as high a style here, I believe, as any part of the world," a visitor wrote.

A considerable distance separated this slave-owning elite from typical southern landowners. About half the adult white males were small planters and farmers. But while the gap between rich and middling colonists grew larger during the eighteenth century, the prosperity of the plantation economy created generally favorable conditions for the landowning class as a whole. Slave ownership, for example, became widespread among this group during the eighteenth century. In Virginia at midcentury,

45 percent of heads of household held one to four slaves and even poorer farmers kept one or two.

Despite the prosperity that accompanied slavery in the eighteenth century, however, a substantial portion of white colonists owned no land or slaves at all. Some rented land or worked as tenant farmers, some hired out as overseers or farm workers, and still others were indentured servants. Throughout the plantation region, landless men constituted about 40 percent of the population. A New England visitor found a "much greater disparity between the rich and poor in Virginia" than at home.

White Skin Privilege

But all the white colonists of eighteenth-century North America shared the privileged status of their skin color. In the early seventeenth century, there had been more diversity in views about race. For some, black skin was thought to be a sign of God's curse. "The blackness of the Negroes," one Englishman argued, "proceedeth of some natural infection." But not everyone shared those views. "I can't think there is any intrinsic value in one colour more than

another," a second Englishman remarked, "nor that white is better than black, only we think it so because we are so."

As slavery became increasingly important, however, Virginia officials took considerable care to create legal distinctions between the status of colonists and that of Africans. Beginning in 1670, free Africans were prohibited from owning Christian servants. Ten years later, another law declared that any African, free or slave, who struck a Christian was to receive thirty lashes on his bare back. One of the most important measures was designed to suppress intimate interracial contacts between white servants and enslaved Africans. A 1691 act "for prevention of that abominable mixture and spurious issue which hereafter may encrease in this dominion" established severe penalties for interracial sexual relationships.

Such penalties were rarely applied, however, to masters who had sexual relations with their slave women. Because by law the children of slave women were born into bondage, many plantations included light-skinned slaves who were the masters' kin. Recent tests of descendants' DNA has confirmed that Thomas Jefferson was probably the father of several children by

CHRONOLOGY

1441	African slaves first brought to Portugal	1710	English capture Port Royal in Acadia
1518	Spain grants official license to Portuguese slavers	1712	Slave uprising in New York City
1535	Africans constitute a majority on Hispaniola	1713	Peace of Utrecht
1619	First Africans brought to Virginia	1721–48	Robert Walpole leads British cabinet
1655	English seize Jamaica	1729	Natchez Rebellion in French Louisiana
1662	Virginia law makes slavery hereditary	1733	Molasses Act
1670	South Carolina founded	1739	Stono Rebellion in South Carolina
1672	Royal African Company organized	1739–43	War of Jenkins's Ear
1691	Virginia prohibits interracial sexual contact	1740–48	King George's War
1698	Britain opens the slave trade to all its merchants	1741	Africans executed in New York for conspiracy
1699	Spanish declare Florida a refuge for escaped slaves	1752	Georgia officially opened to slavery
1702	South Carolinians burn St. Augustine	1770s	Peak period of the English colonies' slave trade
1705	Virginia Slave Code established	1808	Importation of slaves into the United States ends
1706	French and Spanish navies bombard Charleston		

his slave Sally Hemings. Hemings herself was the slave child of Jefferson's father-in-law, and thus the half sister of Jefferson's deceased wife. Less well known is the fact that at Mount Vernon, the household slave Ann Dandridge was the daughter of Martha Washington's father. Hemings and Dandridge may have been kin to wealthy planters and future presidents, but they spent their entire lives as slaves. Slavery, as one historian has written, "required certain evasions, denials, and psychological cruelties."

Relationships between free whites and enslaved blacks produced a rather large mixed-ancestry group known as mulattoes. The majority of them were slaves; a minority, the children of European women and African men, were free. According to a Maryland census of 1755, more than 60 percent of the mulattoes of that colony were slaves. But they also made up three-quarters of the small free African American population. This group, numbering about 4,000 in the 1770s, was denied the right to vote, to hold office, or to testify in court—all on the basis of racial background. Denied the status of citizenship enjoyed by even the poorest white men, free blacks were an outcast group who raised the status of white colonials by contrast. Racial distinctions were a constant reminder of the freedom of white colonists and the debasement of all blacks, slave or free.

Racism set up a wall of contempt between colonists and African Americans. Jefferson wrote of "the real distinctions which nature has made" between the races. "In memory they are equal to the whites," he wrote of the slaves, but "in reason much inferior." He gave no consideration to the argument of freed slave Olaudah Equiano that "slavery debases the mind." Jefferson was on firmer ground when he argued that the two peoples were divided by "deep rooted prejudices entertained by the whites" and "ten thousand recollections, by the blacks, of the injuries they have sustained." Perhaps he knew of these feelings from his long relationship with Sally Hemings. "I tremble for my country when I reflect that God is just," Jefferson concluded in a deservedly famous passage, and remember "that his justice cannot sleep forever."

CONCLUSION

During the eighteenth century, nearly half a million Africans were kidnapped from their homes, marched to the African coast, and packed into ships for up to three months before arriving in British North America. They

R UN away from the subscriber in *Albemarle*, a Mulatto slave called *Sandy*, about 35 years of age, his stature is rather low, inclining to corpulence, and his complexion light; he is a shoemaker by trade, in which he uses his left hand principally, can do coarse carpenters work, and is something of a horse jockey; he is greatly addicted to drink, and when drunk is insolent and disorderly, in his conversation he swears much, and in his behaviour is artful and knavish. He took with him a white horse, much scarred with traces, of which it is expected he will endeavour to dispose; he also carried his shoemakers tools, and will probably endeavour to get employment that way. Whoever conveys the said slave to me, in *Albemarle*, shall have 40 s. reward, if taken up within the county, 4 l. if elsewhere within the colony, and 10 l. if in any other colony, from
THOMAS JEFFERSON.

Thomas Jefferson placed this advertisement in the *Virginia Gazette* on September 14, 1769. Americans need to seriously consider the historical relationship between the prosperity and freedom of white people and the oppression and exploitation of Africans and African Americans.

SOURCE: Virginia Historical Society.

provided the labor that made colonialism pay. Southern planters, northern merchants, and especially British traders and capitalists benefited greatly from the commerce in slave-produced crops, and that prosperity filtered down to affect many of the colonists of British North America. Slavery was fundamental to the operation of the British empire in North America. Mercantilism was a system designed to channel colonial wealth produced by slaves to the nation-state, but as long as profits were high, the British tended to wink at colonists' violations of mercantilist regulations.

Although African Americans received little in return, their labor helped build the greatest accumulation of capital that Europe had ever seen. But despite enormous hardship and suffering, African Americans survived by forming new communities in the colonies, rebuilding families, restructuring language, and reforming culture. African American culture added important components of African knowledge and experience to colonial agriculture, art, music, and cuisine. The African Americans of the English colonies lived better lives than the slaves worked to death on Caribbean sugar plantations, but lives of misery compared with the men they were forced to serve. As the slaves sang on the Georgia coast, "Dah Backrow Man go wrong you, Buddy Quow."

REVIEW QUESTIONS

1. Trace the development of the system of slavery, and discuss the way it became entrenched in the Americas.
2. Describe the effects of the slave trade both on enslaved Africans and on the economic and political life of Africa.
3. Describe the process of acculturation involved in becoming an African American. In what ways did slaves "Africanize" the South?
4. Explain the connection between the institution of slavery and the building of a commercial empire.
5. In what ways did colonial policy encourage the growth of racism?

RECOMMENDED READING

Ira Berlin, *Many Thousands Gone: The First Two Centuries of Slavery in North America* (1998). A history of colonial slavery with attention to the differences between the regions of the Chesapeake, the Lower South, Louisiana, and the North. Emphasizes the distinction between slave societies and societies with slaves.

Michael Craton, *Sinews of Empire: A Short History of British Slavery* (1974). An introduction to the British mercantilist system that emphasizes the importance of slavery. Includes a comparison of the mainland colonies with the Caribbean.

Winthrop D. Jordan, *White over Black: American Attitudes Toward the Negro, 1550–1812* (1968). Remains the best and most comprehensive history of racial attitudes. A searching examination of British and American literature, folklore, and history.

Herbert S. Klein, *The Atlantic Slave Trade* (1999). A new and important synthesis of the most recent studies of the slave trade, covering the social and cultural effects of the trade, especially for Africans.

Peter Kolchin, *American Slavery, 1619–1877* (1993). This survey features comparisons with slavery in Brazil and the Caribbean and serfdom in Russia. Includes a comprehensive bibliographic essay.

Philip D. Morgan, *Slave Counterpoint: Black Culture in the Eighteenth-Century Chesapeake and Lowcountry* (1998). A comprehensive and detailed examination of cultural forms and ways of life in the two regions that leaves hardly a stone unturned.

Anthony S. Parent Jr. *Foul Means: The Formation of a Slave Society in Virginia, 1660–1740* (2003). A vivid and disturbing portrayal of colonial Virginia's patriarchal and violent character. An analysis of the apparatus of oppression from the planters' seizure of land to the efforts to keep poor whites and slaves apart.

Walter Rodney, *How Europe Underdeveloped Africa* (1974). This highly influential book traces the relationship between Europe and Africa from the fifteenth to the twentieth century, and demonstrates how Europe's industrialization became Africa's impoverishment.

Mechal Sobel, *The World They Made Together: Black and White Values in Eighteenth-Century Virginia* (1987). Demonstrates the ways in which both Africans and Europeans shaped the formation of American values, perceptions, and identities.

Ian K. Steele, *Warpaths: Invasions of North America* (1994). A new synthesis of the colonial wars from the sixteenth to the eighteenth century that places Indians as well as empires at the center of the action.

Henry Wiencek, *Imperfect God: George Washington, His Slaves, and the Creation of America* (2003). The story of Washington as planter and slave master, a man tormented by the contradictions.

 For additional study resources for this chapter, go to the *Companion Website*, http://www.prenhall.com/faragher.

WHOSE HISTORY IS IT?
THE LIVING HISTORY OF SLAVERY

It has been difficult for white Americans to acknowledge the oppression and brutality of slavery. In the nineteenth century, even as slaves continued to toil on the plantations of the old South, American popular culture perpetuated an image of happy and contented African Americans faithfully serving their beneficent masters. The violence of slavery was detailed in accounts written by former slaves such as Olaudah Equiano, as well as in images produced by antislavery activists, but they were overwhelmed by the myth of the harmonious plantation. In the 1930s when the Virginia colonial capital of Williamsburg was restored as a national historic site, it introduced the practice of including interpreters in period costume, reenacting the roles of leaders and common folk. But although Colonial Williamsburg included the historic plantation of Carter's Grove, slavery was completely ignored. As early as 1936 a group of African Americans wrote to officials at Colonial Williamsburg, arguing that they ought to make an effort to include the history of slavery. "Colored people were among

This 1853 colored lithograph portrayed a highly sentimentalized view of slaves working the fields of George Washington's Mount Vernon plantation. Washington and other masters certainly aspired to this kind of tranquility. But to achieve the profits he expected, he had to drive his slaves hard, and he ordered his overseers to punish slave offenses with frequent whippings. The Granger Collection, New York.

the earliest settlers in this area," they wrote, "and we have helped to build up and to preserve the Nation." Without the depiction of slavery, the attempt to interpret the history of Virginia made no sense.

It was not until 1979 that Colonial Williamsburg began to conduct serious research into slavery. Soon thereafter several black interpreters were hired to portray slaves at Carter's Grove plantation. Incorporating slavery into the interpretation of historic sites like Williamsburg, however, has proved controversial. The issue arouses shame for many whites, as well as deep anger and bitterness for African Americans. Many visitors—white as well as black—found themselves caught up in the reenactments. Some offered to help the slaves escape, while others turned on the masters and had to be physically restrained. Some of the African American reenactors reported feeling that they were being treated like slaves, not only by visitors, but by those playing roles as masters. Slavery remains the most painful topic in American history.

Slavery meant unremitting labor at the threat of the lash. This image of slaves and overseers working in sugar cane fields of the Gulf Coast was published in London in the nineteenth century.

The Granger Collection.

The reality of slavery was vividly portrayed in this illustration, taken from the autobiography of Henry Bibb, a former slave. Bibb wrote of slave women futilely begging their master not to sell off their children.

The Granger Collection, New York.

The Governor's Palace at Colonial Williamsburg in the 1930s. The historical park commemorated the planter elite, and despite the fact that colonial Virginia had been built on the labor of African American slaves, there was no attempt to depict or interpret slavery at Williamsburg before the 1980s.

Andrew Dickson White Architectural Photographs Collection, Division of Rare and Manuscript Collections, Cornell University Library.

A group of reenactors portraying slaves walk to work in the fields at Carter's Grove plantation at Colonial Williamsburg. The incorporation of slavery into the interpretive "living history" programs of plantations throughout the South is an important part of struggling with the nation's history of race and racism.

AP Wide World Photos.

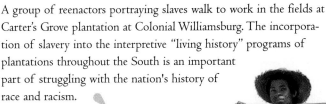

The interior of a slave cabin at Carter's Grove. However painful, slavery must be central to the interpretation of plantation life. In the 1990s the United States Congress passed legislation requiring the National Park Service to address the history of slavery at all its historic sites in the South.

Colonial Williamsburg Foundation, Williamsburg, VA.

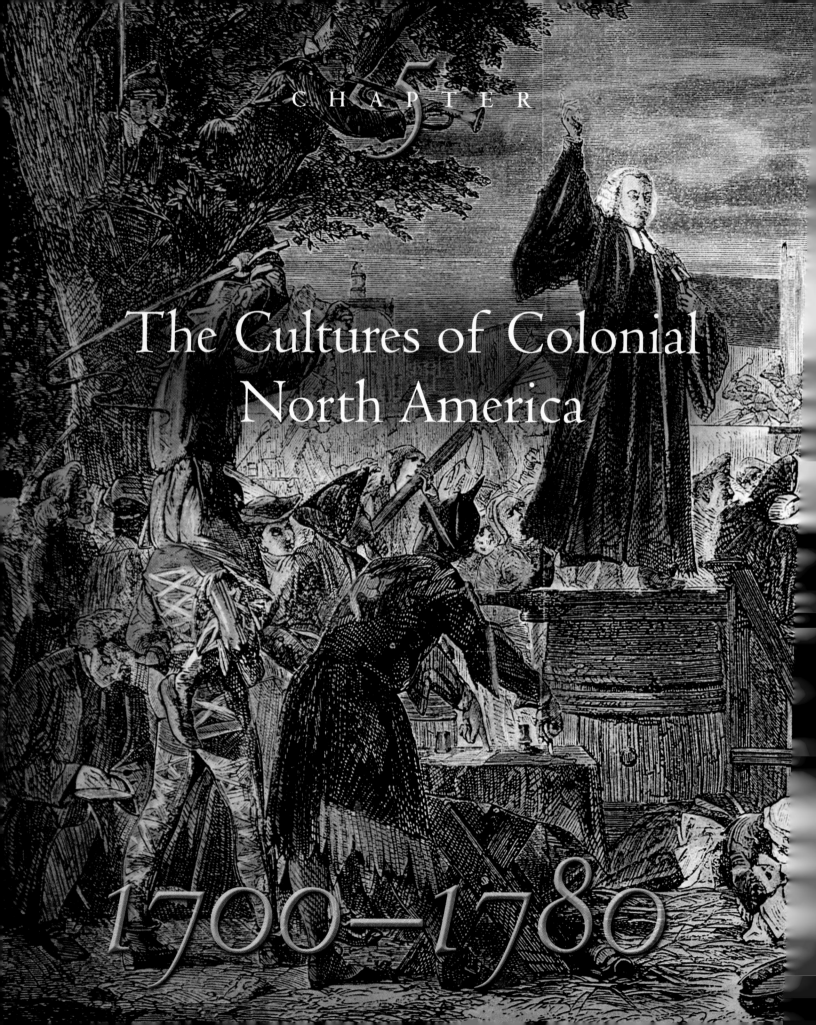

CHAPTER 5

The Cultures of Colonial North America

1700–1780

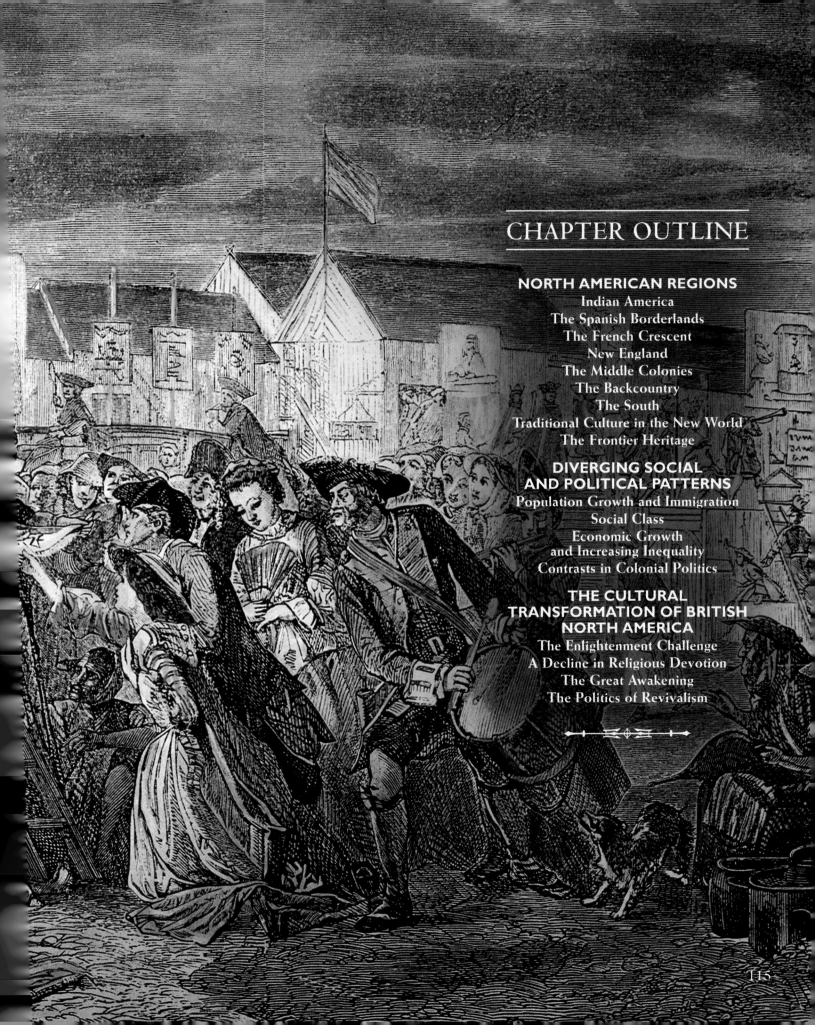

From Deerfield to Kahnawake: Crossing Cultural Boundaries

Before dawn on February 29, 1704, Reverend John Williams and his wife, Eunice, of Deerfield, Massachusetts, awoke to "horrid shouting and yelling." Leaping out of bed, they knew immediately that their town was under attack by Canadian French and their Catholic Indian allies from several nations. This frontier settlement on the northwestern fringe of New England had already been attacked six times in the perennial fighting with New France. Never before, however, had the enemy penetrated the town's stockade. Suddenly the door burst open and "with painted faces and hideous exclamations" warriors began pushing inside. "I reached up my hands for my pistol," Williams remembered, "cocked it, and put it to the breast of the first Indian that came up." It misfired, and as the couple stood trembling in their nightclothes, they were bound and dragged into the central hall with their seven children. They watched in horror as the invaders clubbed and killed their resisting six-year-old son, their screaming newborn infant daughter, and their black nursemaid. The remaining family was hustled out into the frigid dawn and, with more than a hundred other captives, were marched north through snow and ice toward Canada, leaving the burning town behind.

This raid became one of the most infamous events in a long series of attacks and counterattacks between English and French colonists. One hundred and forty residents of the town managed to hold off the invasion and survive, but fifty others died in the attack. Twenty-one of the captives were murdered along the way, including Mrs. Williams, who had not yet recovered from a difficult childbirth six weeks before. The governor of Massachusetts ordered a day of fasting, raised the bounty on Indian scalps from £10 to £100, and organized bloody raids on French and Indian settlements to the north in reprisal.

Most of the Deerfield captives were delivered to the French authorities in Montreal. Within two years, fifty-nine had been ransomed and returned to Deerfield, Reverend Williams and four of his children among them. Williams soon published an account of his captivity, *The Redeemed Captive Returning to Zion*. In colonial America, with its many peoples and cultures, readers were fascinated by the problems and dilemmas of crossing the frontiers between colonial and Indian societies, as well as the borders between the English, French, and Spanish empires. What was it like, people wanted to know, on the other side of the frontier? How were you changed by your experience? Did you remain loyal to your community? Can you still be trusted?

Such questions arose because over the years, hundreds of English colonists had chosen to remain with their captors. Among the Deerfield captives, thirty-one—including ten-year-old Eunice Williams, her mother's namesake—remained in Canada. Eunice was adopted by a family at Kahnawake, a community of Catholic Indians near Montreal. Like Deerfield, Kahnawake was a farming town clustered around a central church and surrounded by a stockade. The differences between the two communities, however, were more striking than the similarities.

Founded in the seventeenth century by Jesuit missionaries as a refuge for Iroquois converts, Kahnawake was home not only to a great variety of Native American Catholics, but people of mixed Indian and European ancestry. Visitors were struck by the appearance of residents who seemed Indian in all respects except for their blue eyes. Such mixing was also evident in the exotic

Deerfield

combinations of European and Indian clothing, the use of Indian and French names, and the special ways the community bent Catholic ritual to fit traditional Iroquois religious practices. Residents of Kahnawake crossed boundaries in other ways, as well. Many were smugglers who engaged in the illegal trade of furs and other Indian products into New York. According to the frustrated authorities in Montreal, Kahnawake operated as "a sort of republic," insisting on its freedom and independence.

Kahnawake, historian John Demos writes, was "a unique experiment in bicultural living." Eunice Williams found it a comforting place, and when a man sent by her father came to fetch her, she declared she was "unwilling to return." Soon she converted to Catholicism. She took an Iroquois name: *A'ongonte,* which means "she has been planted as a person." In 1713, at the age of sixteen, she married a Mohawk man. She saw her father only once, the following year, when he finally went to Kahnawake himself to beg her to return. But she would "not so much

as give me one pleasant look," Williams wrote mournfully. "She is yet obstinatly resolved to live and dye here."

And that is what happened. A'ongonte and her husband raised a family and worked as traders. John Williams died in 1729, surrounded by his children and grandchildren but still longing for his "unredeemed" daughter. But A'ongonte continued to stay away, fearing she would be held in New England against her will. It was not until 1739 that she found the courage to bring her family south for a visit. "We had ye joyfull, Sorrowfull meeting of our poor Sister," her brother Stephen wrote in his diary. Soon thereafter war erupted once again, preventing her from further visits. "We have a great desire of going down to see you," she wrote her brother near the end of their lives in the 1770s, "but do not know when an oppertunity may offer. . . . I pray the Lord that he may give us grace so to Live in this as to be prepared for a happy meeting in the world to Come." And, perhaps as a sign of reconciliation, she signed the letter, "Loving Sister until death, Eunice Williams."

KEY TOPICS

- The similarities and differences among eighteenth-century Spanish, French, and English colonies
- The impact on British colonial culture of increasing European immigration
- Cultural changes in Indian America brought about by contact with European customs and lifestyles
- Patterns of work and class in eighteenth-century America
- Tensions between Enlightenment thought and the Great Awakening's call to renewed religious devotion

NORTH AMERICAN REGIONS

American colonial history too often is written as if only the British colonies along the Atlantic coast really mattered. But as the experience of the Deerfield community and the Williams family demonstrates, that is a mistake eighteenth-century colonists could not afford to make. In the first place, Indian America was a critically

important part of the eighteenth-century world. Indian peoples continued to make up a majority of the population of North America (see Table 5.1). From the fringes of colonial societies into the native heart of the continent, from the eastern foothills of the Appalachians to the western flank of the Sierra Nevada in California, hundreds of Indian cultures, despite being deeply affected by the spread of colonial culture, remained firmly in control of their homelands. And in addition to the British provinces stretching along the Atlantic coast, there were Hispanic colonists who defended the northern borderlands of the Spanish Caribbean and Mexican empire in isolated communities from Florida to California, and French communities that occupied the valley of the St. Lawrence River and scattered down the Mississippi Valley from the Great Lakes to the Gulf of Mexico. There were impressive similarities among these colonial societies, representing a continuation in the New World of traditional Old World beliefs, customs, and institutions, as well as a general pattern of European adaptation to American conditions (see Map 5.1).

Indian America

As the native peoples of the Atlantic coastal plain lost their lands to colonists through battles or treaties and moved into or beyond the Appalachian Mountains, they became active in the fur trade. Indians demonstrated a remarkable capacity for change and adaptation. They used firearms and metal tools, built their homes of logs as the frontier settlers did, and participated in the commercial economy. In the process, they became dependent on European goods. "The clothes we wear, we cannot make ourselves, they are made for us," a Cherokee chief admitted. "We cannot make our guns. Every necessary thing in life we must have from the White People."

Yet Indian peoples continued to assert a proud independence and gained considerable skill at playing colonial powers off against one another. The Iroquois Five Nations battled the French and their Indian allies in King William's War (see Chapter 3), but in 1701, signed a treaty of neutrality with France that kept them out of harm's way during the next round of conflicts. The Catholic Iroquois of Kahnawake sometimes supported the French, as they did by mounting the Deerfield raid, but they also traded with the English. In the Lower South, the Creeks maintained commercial relations with both the French and the English as a means of maintaining their autonomy.

In general, the French had better relations with native peoples than the English. There were fewer French colonists, and the French strategy was to build alliances with native tribes. The preeminent concern of the Indians of the eastern half of the continent was the tremendous growth of colonial population in the British Atlantic coastal colonies, especially the movement of settlers westward. Indian alliances with the French resulted not from any great affection, but rather from their greater fear of British expansion.

Indian communities continued to take a terrific beating from epidemics of European disease. No census of Indian population was taken before the nineteenth century, but historians estimate that from a high of 7 to 10 million north of Mexico in 1500, the native population probably fell to around a million by 1800. Thus, during the eighteenth

century, colonists began to overwhelm natives in sheer numbers. Population loss did not affect all Indian tribes equally, however. Native peoples with a century or more of colonial contact and interaction had lost 50 percent or more of their numbers, but most Indian societies in the interior had yet to be struck by the horrible epidemics.

By the early eighteenth century, Indians on the southern fringe of the Great Plains were using horses stolen from the Spanish in New Mexico (see Map 5.2). Horses enabled Indian hunters to exploit the buffalo herds much more efficiently, and on the basis of this more productive economy a number of groups built a distinctive and elaborate nomadic culture. Great numbers of Indian peoples moved onto the plains during the eighteenth century, pulled by this new way of life and pushed by colonial invasions and disruptions radiating southwest from Canada and north from the

A portrait of the Delaware chief Tishcohan by Gustavus Hesselius, painted in 1732. In his purse of chipmunk hide is a clay pipe, a common item of the Indian trade. Tishcohan was one of the Delaware leaders forced by Pennsylvania authorities into signing a fraudulent land deal that reversed that colony's history of fair dealing with Indians over land. He moved west to the Ohio River as settlers poured into his former homeland.

SOURCE: Gustavus Hesselius, "Tishcohan", Native American Portrait, 1735. Courtesy of The Historical Society of Pennsylvania Collection, Atwater Kent Museum of Philadelphia.

Spanish borderlands. The invention of nomadic Plains Indian culture was another of the dramatic cultural innovations of the eighteenth century. The mounted Plains Indian, so often used as a symbol of native America, was actually a product of the colonial era.

The Spanish Borderlands

In the mid-eighteenth century, what is today the Sunbelt of the United States formed the periphery of the largest and most prosperous European colony on the North American continent—the viceroyalty of New Spain, which included approximately 1 million Spanish colonists and mestizos and at least 2 million Indians. Mexico City, the administrative capital of New Spain, was the most sophisticated city in the Western Hemisphere, the site of one of the world's great universities, with broad avenues and spectacular architecture. New Spain's northern provinces of Florida, Texas, New Mexico, and California, however, were far removed from this sophistication. Officials of the viceroyalty of New Spain, who oversaw these colonies, thought of them as buffer zones, protecting New Spain from the expanding empires of Spain's New World rivals. Compared to the dynamic changes going on in the English colonies, society in the Spanish borderland was relatively static.

In Florida, the oldest of the European colonies in North America, fierce fighting among Spanish, British, and Indians had reduced the colonial presence to little more than the forts of St. Augustine on the Atlantic and Pensacola on the Gulf of Mexico, each surrounded by small colonized territories populated with the families of Spanish troops. In their weakened condition, the Spanish had no choice but to establish cooperative relations with the Creek and Seminole Indians who dominated the region, as well as hundreds of African American runaways who fled to Florida. Eighteenth-century Florida included a growing mestizo population and a considerable number of free African Americans and Hispanicized Indians from the old missions.

Nearly 2,000 miles to the west, New Mexico was similarly isolated from the mainstream of New Spain. At midcentury, New Mexico included some 20,000 Pueblo Indians and perhaps 10,000 mestizo colonists. The prosperity of these colonists, who supported themselves with subsistence agriculture, was severely limited by a restrictive colonial economic policy that required

MAP EXPLORATION

To explore an interactive version of this map, go to **www.prenhall.com/faragher5/map5.1**

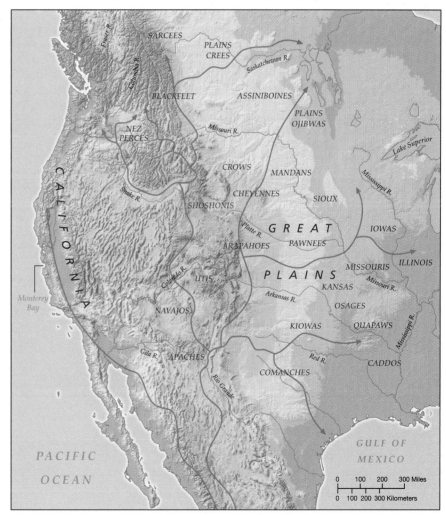

MAP 5.1 Growing Use of the Horse by Plains Indians In the seventeenth and eighteenth centuries, Spanish settlers introduced horses into their New Mexican colony. Through trading and raiding, horses spread northward in streams both west and east of the Rocky Mountains. The horse, whose genetic ancestor had been native to the American continent in pre-Archaic times, offered the Indian peoples of the Great Plains the opportunity to create a distinctive hunting and warrior culture.

TABLE 5.1	POPULATION OF NORTH AMERICA IN 1750

Region	Population
New France	70,000
New England	400,000
New York	100,000
Pennsylvania	230,000
Chesapeake	390,000
Lower South	100,000
Backcountry	100,000
Northern New Spain	20,000
Indian America	1,500,000
TOTAL	**2,910,000**

them to exchange their wool, pottery, and buffalo hides for imported goods at unfavorable rates. But unlike the population of Florida, that of colonial New Mexico was gradually expanding, settlers leaving the original colonial outposts along the upper Rio Grande to follow the valleys and streams leading north and east.

Concerned about the expansion of other colonial empires, the Spanish founded new northern outposts in the eighteenth century. French activity in the Mississippi Valley prompted viceroyal authorities to establish a number of military posts or *presidios* on the fringes of Louisiana, and in 1716, they began the construction of a string of Franciscan missions among the Indian peoples of Texas. By 1750, the settlement of San Antonio had become the center of a developing frontier province. New colonial outposts were also founded west of New

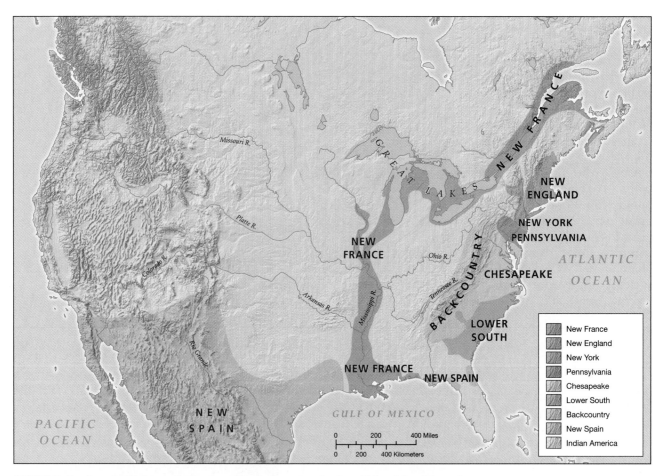

MAP 5.2 Regions in Eighteenth-Century North America By the middle of the eighteenth century, European colonists had established a number of distinctive colonial regions in North America. The northern periphery of New Spain, the oldest and most prosperous European colony, stretched from Baja California to eastern Texas, then jumped to the settlements on the northern end of the Florida peninsula; cattle ranching was the dominant way of life in this thinly populated region. New France was like a great crescent, extending from the plantation communities along the Mississippi near New Orleans to the French colonial communities along the St. Lawrence; in between were isolated settlements and forts, connected only by the extensive French trading network.

A mounted Soldado de Cuera (Leather-Coated Soldier), a watercolor by Ramón de Murillo, c. 1803. Thick leather coats offered protection from Indian arrows for the cavalry posted to the northern frontiers of eighteenth-century New Spain.

SOURCE: Laurie Platt Winfrey, Inc.

Mexico, in what is today southern Arizona. In the 1690s, Jesuit missionaries, led by Father Eusebio Kino, built missions among the desert Indians of the lower Colorado River and Gila River Valleys and introduced cattle herding, which remained the dominant economic activity for the next two centuries.

In the early eighteenth century, the Spanish also established missions in arid Baja (lower) California. The more temperate northern coastline remained in native possession. In 1769, however, acting on rumors of Russian expansion in the north Pacific (see discussion of Russian America in Chapter 9), officials in Mexico City ordered the governor of Baja, Gaspar de Portolá, and the president of the Franciscan missions there, Junípero Serra, to extend the Spanish presence northward. Supported by some two hundred soldiers and settlers, the two men founded a presidio and mission at San Diego and the next year established their headquarters at Monterey Bay on the central coast. Two years later, the officer Juan Bautista de Anza and a small party of soldiers blazed an overland route across the deserts connecting Arizona and California, and in 1776, he led a coloniz-ing expedition that founded the pueblo of San Francisco. Over the next fifty years, the number of California settlements grew to include twenty-one missions and a half-dozen presidios and towns, including Los Angeles, founded in 1781 by a group of mestizo pioneers.

But over the next several decades, relatively few settlers came to California. Instead, the plan called for converting the natives to Catholicism, subjecting them to the rule of the crown, and putting them to work at the missions raising the subsistence necessary for the small civil and military establishment that was to hold the province against rival empires. The first contacts between the Franciscans and the natives were not encouraging. "What is it you seek here," a chief and his entourage of warriors shouted at the missionaries. "Get out of our country!" But numerous native families were attracted to the missions by offerings of food and clothing, by new tools and crafts that promised improvements in the standard of living, and by their fascination with the spiritual power of the newcomers. Gradually, there developed a flourishing local economy of irrigated farming and stock raising. San Gabriel, near the

The Church of San Xavier del Bac, constructed in the late eighteenth century, is located a few miles south of the city of Tucson, where Jesuit Father Eusebio Kino founded a mission among the Pima Indians in 1700. Known as the White Dove of the Desert, it is acclaimed as the most striking example of Spanish colonial architecture in the United States.

SOURCE: Photograph by Jack W. Dykinga.

pueblo of Los Angeles, was one of the most prosperous missions, with large vineyards and orchards that produced fine wines and brandies. Indian workers also constructed the adobe and stone churches, built on Spanish and Moorish patterns, whose ruins later came to symbolize California's colonial society.

Indians were not forced to join the missions, but once they did, they were not allowed to change their minds. The Franciscan missionaries resorted to cruel and sometimes violent means of controlling their Indian subjects: shackles, solitary confinement, and whipping posts. Resistance developed early. In 1775, the villagers at San Diego rose up and killed several priests, and over the years many missions experienced revolts. But the arms and organization of Spanish soldiers were usually sufficient to suppress the uprisings. Another form of protest was flight. Spanish soldiers hunted the runaways down and brought many back. Aggressive tribes in the hills and deserts, however, often proved even more threatening than the Spanish, so many mission Indians remained despite the harsh discipline.

Foreign observers noted the despondency of the mission Indians. "I have never seen any of them laugh," one wrote. "I have never seen a single one look anyone in the face. They have the air of taking no interest in anything." Overwork, inadequate nutrition, overcrowding, poor sanitation, and epidemic disease contributed to death rates that exceeded birthrates. During the period of the mission system, the native population of coastal California fell by 74 percent.

As the prominence of mission settlements in Florida, New Mexico, Texas, and California suggests, the Catholic Church played a dominant role in the community life of the borderlands. In the eighteenth century, religion was no private affair. It was a deadly serious business dividing nations into warring camps, and the Spanish considered themselves the special protectors of the traditions of Rome. The object of colonization, one colonial promoter wrote in 1584, was "enlarging the glorious gospel of Christ, and leading the infinite multitudes of these simple people that are in error into the right and perfect way of salvation." Although these were the words of the English imperialist Richard Hakluyt, they could as easily have come from the Spanish padres Kino or Serra or the Jesuit missionaries at Kahnawake. There was no tradition of religious dissent. Certain of the truth of their "right and perfect way," the Spanish could see no reason for tolerating the errors of others.

The French Crescent

In France, as in Spain, church and state were closely interwoven. During the seventeenth century, the French prime ministers, Cardinal Richelieu and Cardinal Mazarin, laid out a fundamentally Catholic imperial policy, and under their guidance, colonists constructed a second Catholic empire in North America. In 1674, church and state collaborated in establishing the bishopric of Québec, which founded local seminaries, oversaw the appointment and review of priests, and laid the foundation of the resolutely Catholic culture of New France. Meanwhile, Jesuit missionaries continued to carry Catholicism deep into the continent.

The French sent few colonists to New France in the eighteenth century, but by natural increase the population rose from less than 15,000 in 1700 to more than 70,000 at midcentury. The French used their trade and alliance network to establish a great crescent of colonies, military posts, and settlements that extended from the mouth of the St. Lawrence River southwest through the Great Lakes, then down the Mississippi River to the Gulf of Mexico. After the loss in 1713 of the maritime colony of Acadia to the British (see Chapter 4), French authorities constructed the great

port and fortress of Louisbourg on Ile Royale (Cape Breton Island) to guard the northern approach to New France. The southern approach was protected by French troops at the port of New Orleans in Louisiana. Between these two points, the French laid a thin colonial veneer, the beginning of what they planned as a great commercial empire that would confine the Protestant British to a narrow strip of Atlantic coastline (see Map 5.3). By the middle of the century, the French were moving into trans-Mississippi country, ascending the Missouri and Arkansas rivers and planting traders in Indian communities on the fringe of the Great Plains.

At the heart of the French empire in North America were the communities of farmers or *habitants* that stretched along the banks of the St. Lawrence between the provincial capital of Québec and the fur trade center of Montreal. There were also farming communities in the Illinois country, supplying wheat to the booming sugar plantations in Louisiana. By the mid-eighteenth century, those plantations, extending along the Mississippi from Natchez and Baton Rouge to New Orleans, had become the most profitable French enterprise in North America.

Among the most distinctive French stamps on the North American landscape were the "long lots" that stretched back from the rivers, providing each family a share of good bottomland to farm and frontage on the waterways, the "interstate highway system" of the French Crescent. Long lots were laid out along the lower Mississippi River in Louisiana and at sites on the upper Mississippi such as Kaskaskia and Prairie du Chien, as well as at the strategic passages of the Great Lakes. Detroit, the most important of those, was a stockaded town with a military garrison, a small administrative center, several stores, a Catholic church, and 100 households of *métis* (French for mestizo) families. Farmers worked the land along the Detroit River, not far from communities inhabited by thousands of Ottawa, Potawatomi, and Huron Indians.

Communities of this sort, combining both European and

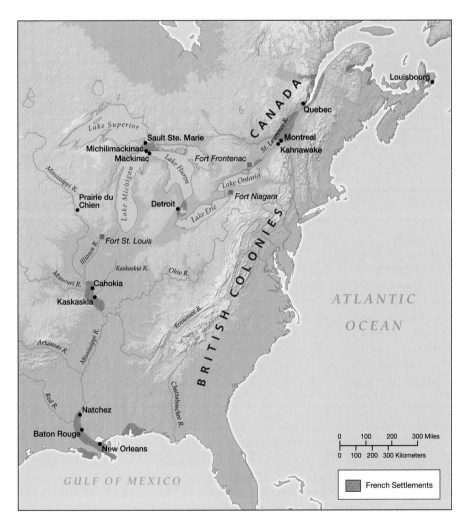

MAP 5.3 The French Crescent The French empire in North America was based on a series of alliances and trade relations with Indian nations linking a great crescent of colonies, settlements, and outposts that extended from the mouth of the St. Lawrence River, through the Great Lakes, and down the Mississippi River to the Gulf of Mexico. In 1713, Acadia was ceded to the British, but the French established the fortress of Louisbourg to anchor the eastern end of the crescent.

The persistence of French colonial long lots in the pattern of modern landholding is clear in this enhanced satellite photograph of the Mississippi River near New Orleans. Long lots, the characteristic form of property holding in New France, were designed to offer as many settlers as possible a share of good bottomland as well as a frontage on the waterways, which served as the basic transportation network.

SOURCE: EROS Data Center, U.S. Geological Survey.

native American elements, were in the tradition of the inclusive frontier. Detroit looked like "an old French village," said one observer, except that its houses were "mostly covered with bark," in Indian style. "It is not uncommon to see a Frenchman with Indian shoes and stockings, without breeches, wearing a strip of woolen cloth to cover what decency requires him to conceal," wrote another. "Yet at the same time he wears a fine ruffled shirt and a laced waistcoat, with a fine handkerchief on his head." Detroit had much of the character of the mixed community of Kahnawake on the St. Lawrence.

New England

Just as New Spain and New France had their official church, so did the people of New England: local communities in all the New England colonies but Rhode Island were governed by Puritan congregations (thus the term Congregational). Under the plan established in Massachusetts, the local church of a community was free to run its own affairs under the guidance of the General Court (the governor and the representatives selected by the towns). The Puritan colonies allotted each congregation a tract of communal land. Church members divided this land among themselves on the basis of status and seniority, laying out central villages such as Deerfield, and building churches (called meetinghouses) that were maintained through taxation. Adult male church members constituted the freemen of the town, and thus there was very little distinction between religious and secular authority. At the town meeting, the freemen chose their minister, voted on his salary and support, and elected local men to offices ranging from town clerk to fence viewer.

The Puritan tradition was a curious mix of freedom and repression. Although local communities had considerable autonomy, they were tightly bound by the restrictions of the Puritan faith and the General Court. The Puritans did not come to America to create a society where religion could be freely practiced, but sought to establish their own version of the "right and perfect way," which placed severe restraints on individuals. Not only did the Puritans exile dissidents such as Roger Williams and Anne Hutchinson who threatened the religious orthodoxy of Massachusetts (see Chapter 3), they banned Anglicans and Baptists and exiled, jailed, whipped, and even executed members of the Society of Friends, who came repeatedly among them to preach the tenets of Quakerism.

It was one of those exiled dissenters, Roger Williams, the leader of Rhode Island, who made one of the first formal arguments for religious toleration. "Forced worship," he wrote, "stinks in God's nostrils." After the religious excesses of the English civil war, this argument had considerable appeal. In 1661, King Charles II ordered a stop to religious persecution in Massachusetts. The new climate of opinion was best expressed by the English philosopher John Locke in his *Letter on Tolerance* (1688). Churches were voluntary societies, he argued, and could work only through persuasion. That a religion was sanctioned by the state was no evidence of its truth, because different nations had different official religions. Consequently, the state had no legitimate concern with religious belief. The Toleration Act, passed by Parliament in 1689, was at first resisted by the Puritans. Under pressure from English authorities, however, in 1700, Massachusetts and Connecticut reluctantly began to allow other Protestant denominations to meet openly, although Congregational churches continued to be supported officially through taxation. By the 1730s, there were Anglican, Baptist, and Presbyterian congregations in many New England towns.

As towns grew too large for the available land, groups of residents left together, "hiving off" to form new churches and towns elsewhere. The region was knit together by an intricate network of roads and rivers. Seventy-five years after the Indians of southern New

England suffered their final defeat in King Philip's War (see Chapter 3), Puritan farm communities had taken up most of the available land of Massachusetts, Connecticut, and Rhode Island, leaving only a few small communities of Pequots, Narragansets, and Wampanoags on restricted reservations. Northern Algonquians and Catholic Iroquois allied with the French in Québec, however, maintained a defensive barrier that prevented New Englanders from expanding northward into Maine, New Hampshire, and the region later called Vermont. Deerfield represented the far northern limit of safe settlement. By midcentury, then, as the result of growing population, New England was reaching the limit of its land supply.

The Middle Colonies

In striking contrast to the ethnically homogeneous colonies of Connecticut and Massachusetts, New York had one of the most ethnically diverse populations on the continent. At midcentury, society along the lower Hudson River, including the counties in northern New Jersey, was a veritable mosaic of ethnic communities, including the Dutch of Flatbush, the Huguenots of New Rochelle, the Flemish of Bergen County, and the Scots of Perth Amboy. African Americans, both slave and free, made up more than 15 percent of the population of the lower Hudson. Puritan, Baptist, Quaker, and Catholic congregations worshiped without legal hindrance, and in New York City, several hundred Jewish families attended services in North America's first synagogue, built in 1730. There was a great deal of intermingling, but these different communities would long retain their ethnic and religious distinctions, making colonial New York something of a cultural "salad bowl" rather than a "melting pot."

New York City grew by leaps and bounds in the eighteenth century, but because the elite who had inherited the rich lands and great manors along the upper Hudson chose to rent to tenants rather than to sell, it was less attractive to immigrants than neighboring Pennsylvania, described by one German immi-

The Turner House (immortalized by Nathaniel Hawthorne in his novel *The House of the Seven Gables*) in Salem, Massachusetts, was constructed in the seventeenth century. In this style of architecture, function prevailed over form as structures grew to accommodate their residents; rooms were added where and when they were needed. In England, wood for building was scarce, but the abundance of forests in North America created the conditions for a golden age of wood construction.

SOURCE: Photograph courtesy of the Peabody Essex Museum.

grant as "heaven for farmers." The colony's Quaker proprietors were willing to sell land to anyone who could pay the modest prices. During the eighteenth century, the region along the Delaware River—encompassing not only Pennsylvania but New Jersey, Delaware, and parts of Maryland—grew more dramatically than any other in North America. Immigration played the dominant role in achieving the astonishing annual growth rate of nearly 4 percent. Boasting some of the best farmland in North America, the region was soon exporting abundant produce through the booming port at Philadelphia.

The Quakers who founded Pennsylvania quickly became a minority, but, unlike the Puritans, they were generally comfortable with religious and ethnic pluralism. Many of the founders of the Society of Friends had been imprisoned for their beliefs in pre-Restoration England, and they were determined to prevent a repetition of this injustice in their own province. The Society of Friends never became an established church. It was a perspective well suited to the ethnically and

This view of the Philadelphia waterfront, painted about 1720, conveys the impression of a city firmly anchored to maritime commerce. The long narrow canvas was probably intended for display over the mantel of a public room.

SOURCE: Peter Cooper, *The South East Prospect of the City of Philadelphia*, ca. 1720. The Library Company of Philadelphia.

religiously diverse population of Pennsylvania. Most German immigrants were Lutherans or Calvinists, most North Britons were Presbyterians, and there were plenty of Anglicans and Baptists as well.

The institutions of government were another pillar of community organization. Colonial officials appointed justices of the peace from among the leading local men, and these justices provided judicial authority for the countryside. Property-owning farmers chose their own local officials. Country communities were tied together by kinship bonds and by bartering and trading among neighbors. The substantial stone houses and great barns of the countryside testified to the social stability and prosperity of the Pennsylvania system. These communities were more loosely bound than those of New England. Rates of mobility were considerably higher, with about half the population moving in any given decade. Because land was sold in individual lots rather than in communal parcels, farmers tended to disperse themselves at will over the open countryside. Villages gradually developed at crossroads and ferries but with little forethought or planning. The individual settlement of Pennsylvania would provide the basic model for American expansion.

The Backcountry

By 1750, Pennsylvania's exploding population was pushing beyond into the first range of the Appalachian highlands (see Map 5.4). Settlers were moving southwest, through western Maryland and into the great Shenandoah River Valley of Virginia. Although they hoped to become commercial farmers, these families began more modestly, planting Indian corn and raising hogs, hunting in the woods for meat and furs, and building log cabins. The movement into the Pennsyl-

vania and Virginia backcountry that began during the 1720s was the first of the great pioneer treks that took white pioneers into the continental interior. Many, perhaps most, of them held no legal title to the lands they occupied. They simply hacked out and defended squatter's claims from native proprietors and all other comers. To the Delawares and Shawnees, who had been pushed into the interior, or the Cherokees, who occupied the Appalachian highlands to the south, these settlers presented a new and deadly threat. Rising fears and resentments over this expanding population triggered a great deal of eighteenth-century violence and warfare.

One of the distinctive characteristics of the backcountry was the settlers' disdain for rank. In their words, "the rain don't know broadcloth from blue jeans." But the myth of frontier equality was simply that. Most pioneers owned little or no land, whereas "big men" held great tracts and dominated local communities with their bombastic style of personal leadership. In the backcountry, the men were warriors, the women domestic workers. The story was told of one pioneer whose wife began to "jaw at" him. "He pulled off his breeches and threw them down to her, telling her to 'put them on and wear them.'"

The South

The Chesapeake and the Lower South were triracial societies, with intermingled communities of white colonists and black slaves, along with substantial Indian communities living on the fringes of colonial settlement. Much of the population growth of the region resulted from the forced migration of enslaved Africans, who by 1750 made up 40 percent of the population. Colonial settlement had filled not only the Tidewater area of the southern Atlantic coast but a

MAP EXPLORATION

To explore an interactive version of this map,
go to **www.prenhall.com/faragher5/map5.4**

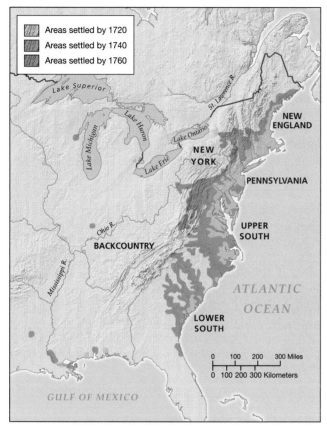

MAP 5.4 Spread of Settlement: Movement into the Backcountry, 1720–60 The spread of settlement from 1720 to 1760 shows the movement of population into the backcountry during the midcentury.

maintained neither a colonial bishop nor local institutions for training clergy.

Along the rice coast, the dominant social institution was the large plantation. Transforming the tangle of woods and swamps along the region's rivers into an ordered pattern of dams, dikes, and flooded fields required heavy capital investment. Consequently, only men of means undertook rice cultivation. By midcentury, established rice plantations typically were dominated by a large main house, generally located on a spot of high ground overlooking the fields. Drayton Hall near Charleston, a mansion of the period that still survives, was built of pink brick in classically symmetrical style, with hand-carved interior moldings of imported Caribbean mahogany. Nearby, but a world apart, were the slave quarters, rough wooden cabins lining two sides of a muddy pathway near the outbuildings and barns. In this contrast between "big house" and "quarters," the Lower South was the closest thing in North America to the societies of the Caribbean sugar islands.

Because tobacco, unlike rice, could be grown profitably in small plots, the Chesapeake included a greater variety of farmers and a correspondingly diverse landscape. Tobacco quickly drained the soil of its nutrients, and plantings had to be shifted to fresh ground every few years. Former tobacco land

This two-story log house, built in Pennsylvania in the early eighteenth century, is one of the oldest surviving examples of the method and style of log construction introduced in America by the Scandinavian colonists on the lower Delaware River. Learning New World farming and woodland hunting techniques from the Indians, these settlers forged a tradition of settlement that proved enormously successful for pioneers.

SOURCE: Henry Glassie, *Pattern in the Material Folk Culture of the Eastern United States.*

good deal of the Piedmont as well. Specializing in rice, tobacco, and other commercial crops, these colonies were overwhelmingly rural. Farms and plantations were dispersed across the countryside, and villages or towns were few.

English authorities made the Church of England the state religion in the Chesapeake colonies. Residents paid taxes to support the Church and were required to attend services. No other churches were allowed into Virginia and Maryland (despite the role of Catholics in its founding) and dissenters were excluded or exiled. Before the 1750s, the Toleration Act was little enforced in the South; at the same time, the Anglican establishment was internally weak. It

could be planted with corn for several years but then required twenty years or more of rest before reuse. The landscape was a patchwork of fields, many in various stages of ragged second growth. The poorest farmers lived in wooden cabins little better than the shacks of the slaves. More prosperous farm families lived with two or three slaves in houses that nevertheless were considerably smaller than the substantial homes of New England.

Compared to the Lower South, where there was no community life outside the plantation, in the Chesapeake there were well-developed neighborhoods constructed from kinship networks and economic connections. The most important community instutition was the county court, which held both executive and judicial power. On court day, white people of all ranks held a great gathering that included public business, horse racing, and perhaps a barbecue. The gentleman justices of the county, appointed by the governor, included the heads of the elite planter families. These men in turn selected the grand jury, composed of substantial freeholders. One of the most significant bonding forces in this free white population was a growing sense of racial solidarity in response to the increasing proportion of African slaves dispersed throughout the neighborhoods.

Traditional Culture in the New World

In each of these regional North American societies, family and kinship, the church, and the local community were the most significant factors in everyday life. Colonists throughout the continent tended to live much as they had in their European homelands at the time their colonies were settled. Thus, the residents of New Mexico, Québec, and New England perpetuated the religious passions of the seventeenth century long after the leaders of the mother countries had put them aside in favor of imperial geopolitics. Nostalgia for Europe helped to fix a conservative colonial attitude toward culture.

These were oral cultures, depending on the transmission of information by the spoken rather than the printed word, on the passage of traditions through oral story and song. North American colonial folk cultures, traditional and suspicious of change, preserved an essentially medieval worldview. The rhythms of life were regulated by the hours of sunlight and the seasons of the year. People rose with the sun and went to bed soon after sundown. The demands of the season determined their working routines. They farmed with simple tools and were subject to the whims of nature, for drought, flood, or pestilence could quickly sweep away their efforts. Experience told them that the natural world imposed limitations within which men and women had to learn to live. Even patterns of reproduction conformed to nature's cycle (see Figure 5.1). In nearly every European colonial community of North America, the number of births peaked in late winter, then fell to a low point during the summer. Interestingly, African Americans had a contrasting pattern, in which births peaked in early summer. Historians have not yet provided an explanation for the difference, but apparently there was some "inner" seasonal clock tied to old European and African patterns. Human sexual activity itself seemed to fluctuate with the rural working demands created by the seasons.

These were also communal cultures. In Québec, villagers worked side by side to repair the roads; in New Mexico, they collectively maintained the irrigation canals; and in New England, they gathered in town meetings to decide the dates when common fields were to be plowed, sowed, and harvested. Houses offered little privacy, with families often sleeping together in the same chamber, sitting together on benches rather than in chairs, and taking their supper from a common bowl or trencher. For most North American colonists of the mid-eighteenth century, the community was more important than the individual.

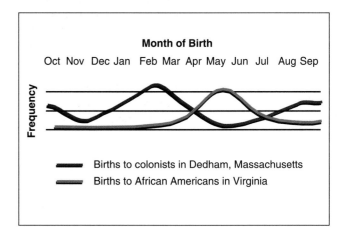

FIGURE 5.1   Monthly Frequency of Successful Conceptions Human reproduction in colonial America corresponded to cycles. But European colonists and African American slaves had different patterns.

SOURCE: Mechal Sobel, *The World They Made Together: Black and White Values in Eighteenth-Century Virginia* (Princeton, NJ: Princeton University Press, 1987), 67.

Throughout North America, most colonists continued the traditional European occupation of working the land. Commercial agriculture was practiced on slave plantations, of course. And it developed in some areas of the northern colonies, such as fertile southeastern Pennsylvania, which became known as the breadbasket of North America, and in the hinterland surrounding colonial cities such as New York, Boston, and Québec. The majority of eighteenth-century North American farmers, however, grew crops and raised livestock for their own needs or for local barter, and communities were largely self-sufficient. Rather than specializing in the production of one or two crops for sale, most farmers attempted to remain as independent of the market as possible, diversifying their activities. The primary goal was ownership of land and the assurance that children and descendants would be able to settle on lands nearby.

Colonial cities, by contrast, were centers of commerce. Artisans and craftsmen worked at their trades full time, organizing themselves according to the European craft system. In Boston, New York, and

A spinner and carpenter from *The Book of Trades*, an eighteenth-century British survey of the crafts practiced in colonial America. In colonial cities, artisans organized themselves into the traditional European craft system, with apprentices, journeymen, and masters. There were few opportunities for the employment of women outside the household, but women sometimes earned income by establishing sidelines as midwives or spinners.

SOURCE: The Granger Collection.

Philadelphia carpenters, ironmakers, blacksmiths, shipwrights, and scores of other tradesmen had their own self-governing associations. A young man who wished to pursue a trade, served several years as an apprentice, working in exchange for learning the skills and secrets of the craft. After completing their apprenticeships, these young men sought employment in shops. Their search often required them to migrate to some other area, thus becoming "journeymen." Most craftsmen remained at the journeyman level for their whole careers. But by building a good name and carefully saving, journeymen hoped to become master craftsmen, opening shops and employing journeymen and apprentices of their own. As in farming, the ultimate goal was independence.

There were few opportunities for women outside the household. By law, husbands held managerial rights over family property, but widows received support in the form of a one-third lifetime interest, known as "dower," in a deceased husband's real estate (the rest of the estate being divided among the heirs). And in certain occupations, such as printing (which had a tradition of employing women), widows succeeded their husbands in business. (See Out of Many Voices: A Widow Announces She Will Continue Her Husband's Business). As a result, some colonial women played active roles in eighteenth-century journalism. Ann Smith Franklin, Benjamin Franklin's sister-in-law, took over the operation of her husband's Rhode Island shop after his death. Widow Cornelia Smith Bradford continued to publish her deceased husband's Philadelphia paper and was an important force in publishing throughout the 1750s.

The Frontier Heritage

The colonial societies of eighteenth-century North America also shared perspectives unique to their common frontier heritage. European colonists came from Old World societies in which land was scarce and monopolized by property-owning elites. They settled in a continent where, for the most part, land was abundant and cheap. This was probably the most important distinction between North America and Europe. American historians once tied the existence of this "free land" directly to the development of democracy. But the colonial experience encouraged assumptions that were anything but democratic.

One of the most important was the popular acceptance of forced labor. A woman of eighteenth-century South Carolina once offered advice on how to achieve a good living. "Get a few slaves," she declared, and "beat them well to make them work hard." As her comment suggests, labor was the key to prosperity, and it was in short supply throughout the colonies. In a land where free men and women

---

OUT OF MANY VOICES

A WIDOW ANNOUNCES SHE WILL CONTINUE HER HUSBAND'S BUSINESS

After the death of her husband Lewis Timothy in 1739, widow Elizabeth Timothy took over the editorship of the South Carolina Gazette. She became the first woman in America to own and publish a newspaper, operated as official printer to the colony, and played an important role in the development of Charleston.

WHEREAS THE LATE PRINTER OF THIS GAZETTE hath been deprived of his life by an unhappy Accident, I take this opportunity of informing the Publick, that I shall continue the said paper as usual, and hope by the assistance of my Friends to make it as entertaining and correct as may be reasonably expected. Wherefore I flatter myself, that all those Persons, who, by Subscriptions or otherwise, assisted my late Husband, in the Prosecution of the said undertaking, will be kindly pleased to continue their Favours and good Offices to his poor afflicted Widow with six small children and another hourly expected. ■

SOURCE: *South Carolina Gazette*, January 11, 1739.

could work for themselves on their own plot of ground, there was little incentive to work for wages. The use of forced labor was thus one of the few ways a landowner could secure an agricultural workforce. In the Spanish borderlands, captured Apache children became lifetime servants, and an Indian slave trade flourished through the eighteenth century. In Québec, African American slaves from the French Caribbean worked side-by-side with enslaved Indians from the Great Plains. In Philadelphia, according to Benjamin Franklin, wages for free workers were so high that most of the unskilled labor was "performed chiefly by indentured servants." All the colonists came from European cultures that believed in social hierarchy and subordination, and involuntary servitude was easily incorporated into their worldview.

More than half the immigrants to eighteenth-century British America arrived as indentured servants. Agents paid for the Atlantic crossing of poor immigrants in exchange for several years of service in America. One historian, accounting for the cost of passage and upkeep, estimates that indentured servants earned their masters, on average, about fifty pounds sterling over four or five years of service, the equivalent of about a thousand dollars a year in today's values. But at the conclusion of their indentures, eighteenth-century servants enjoyed considerably more opportunity than their seventeenth-century counterparts. The chance of a former servant achieving a position of moderate comfort rose from one in five in 1700 to better than fifty-fifty by 1750, probably because of the rise in overall prosperity in the British colonies.

A second important assumption was the general expectation of property ownership. It led to rising popular demands in all the colonial regions of the continent that land be taken from the Indian inhabitants and opened to colonial settlement. Some colonists justified wars of dispossession by arguing, as the Puritans had, that Indians deserved to lose their lands because they had failed to use them to the utmost capacity. Others simply maintained that Indians deserved to be dispossessed because they were "savages." Whatever their specific justifications, the majority of colonists— whether British, Spanish, or French—endorsed the violence and brutality directed against Indian tribes as an essential aspect of colonial life. This attitude was as true of inclusive as exclusive societies, with the difference that in the former, native peoples were incorporated into colonial society, while in the latter, tribes were pushed from the frontier. Thus did the Puritan minister Cotton Mather praise Hannah Dustin, a New England woman who escaped her captors during King William's War by killing and scalping nine sleeping Indians, including two women and six children. With this as the prevailing attitude, one can understand why Eunice Williams was hesitant to return to Deerfield after she had married an Indian.

DIVERGING SOCIAL AND POLITICAL PATTERNS

Despite these important similarities among the colonial regions of North America, in the eighteenth century the experience of the British colonies began to diverge sharply from that of the French and Spanish. Immigration, economic growth, and provincial political struggles all pushed British colonists in a radically new direction.

Population Growth and Immigration

All the colonial regions of North America experienced unprecedented growth in the eighteenth century. "Our people must at least be doubled every twenty years," Benjamin Franklin wrote in a remarkable 1751 essay on population, and he was nearly right. In 1700, there were 290,000 colonists north of Mexico; fifty years later they had grown to approximately 1.3 million, an average annual growth rate of about 3 percent. Typical preindustrial societies grew at rates of less than 1 percent per year, approximately the pace of Europe's expansion in the eighteenth century. But the colonial societies of North America experienced what English economist Thomas Malthus, writing at the end of the century, described as "a rapidity of increase probably without parallel in history."

High fertility and low mortality played important roles. Women in the British colonies, in the French villages along the St. Lawrence, or the towns of New Mexico, typically bore seven or more children during their childbearing years. And blessed with an abundance of food, colonists enjoyed generally good health and low mortality. In most colonial areas, there were fewer than 30 deaths for every 1,000 persons, a rate 15 or 20 percent lower than those of Europe.

Yet, the British colonies grew far more rapidly than those of France or Spain (see Figure 5.2). It was immigration that made the difference. Fearful of depleting their population at home, the Spanish severely limited the migration of their own subjects, and absolutely forbade the immigration of foreigners. The French, dedicated to keeping their colonies exclusively Catholic, ignored the desire of Protestant Huguenots to emigrate. Instead they sent thousands of Catholic *engagés* to Canada, but most returned, discouraged by the climate and the lack of commercial opportunity. The English, however, dispatched an estimated 400,000 of their own countrymen to populate their North American colonies during the seventeenth and eighteenth centuries.

Moreover, the British were the only imperial power to encourage the immigration of foreign nationals to the colonies. In the 1680s, William Penn was the first colonial official to promote the immigration of western Europeans, sending agents to recruit settlers in Holland, France, and the German principalities along the Rhine River. His experiment proved so successful that the leaders of other British colonies soon were emulating him. By the second quarter of the eighteenth century, shippers had developed a system that contemporaries called the "trade in strangers." Carrying migrants provided English and Dutch merchants with a way of making a profit on the westbound voyage of vessels sent to bring back tobacco, rice, indigo, timber, and flour from North America. The eighteenth-century trade in strangers was the prototype for the great movements of European immigrants in the nineteenth century.

Further encouraging this development, early in the eighteenth century, a number of British colonies enacted liberal naturalization laws that allowed immigrants who professed Protestantism and swore allegiance to the British crown to become free "denizens" with all the privileges of natural-born subjects. In 1740, Parliament passed the Plantation Act, providing for naturalization procedures for all the British colonies. The new law continued to prohibit the naturalization of Catholic and Jewish immigrants, however, and these groups remained tiny minorities. Still, immigration to the British colonies was characterized by extraordinary diversit (see Map 5.5 and Figure 5.3).

First there were the Africans, the largest group to come to North America in the colonial period, larger even than the English. Forced relocation brought an estimated 600,000 to the colonies before the official end of the slave trade to the United States in 1807. Then there was the massive emigration from the northern British Isles. Squeezed by economic hardship, an estimated 150,000 Highland Scots and Protestant Irish from the Ulster region (known as the "Scots-Irish") emigrated to North America in the eighteenth century. German-speakers were next in importance; at least 125,000 of them settled in the colonies, where they became known as the "Dutch" (from *Deutsch,* the German-language term for "German"). It is worth noting again that a majority of these European immigrants came as bonded servants or slaves.

The European crossing of the Atlantic was nowhere near as traumatic as the African Middle Passage, but it was harrowing. One immigrant described a voyage to Philadelphia in which several hundred people were packed like sardines in the ship's hold. "The ship is filled with pitiful signs of distress," he wrote, "smells, fumes, horrors, vomiting, various kinds of sea sickness, fever, dysentery, headaches, heat, constipation, boils, scurvy, cancer, mouth-rot, and similar afflictions. In such misery all the people on board pray and cry pitifully together." In 1750, Pennsyl-

vania was finally compelled to pass a law to prevent the overcrowding of ships filled with indentured passengers.

The results of the first federal census of the United States in 1790 provide a summary of the eighteenth-century experience of immigration. Less than 50 percent of the population was English in origin, and nearly 20 percent was African; 15 percent was Irish, Scots-Irish, or Scots and 7 percent German, with other ethnic backgrounds making up the remainder. There were significant differences by region. New England remained more than

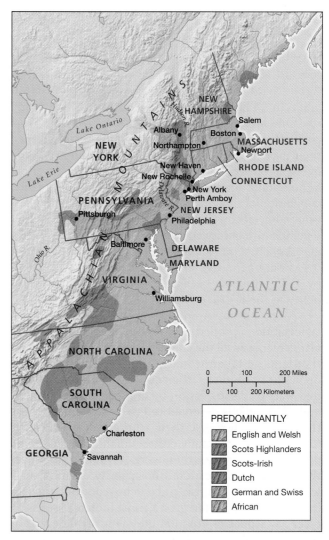

MAP 5.5 **Ethnic Groups in Eighteenth-Century British North America** The first federal census, taken in 1790, revealed remarkable ethnic diversity. New England was filled with people from the British Isles, but the rest of the colonies were a patchwork. Most states had at least three different ethnic groups within their borders, and although the English and Scots-Irish were heavily represented in all colonies, in some they had strong competition from Germans (eastern and southern Pennsylvania) and from African peoples (Virginia and South Carolina).

three-quarters English, but Pennsylvania was nearly 40 percent German. The backcountry was populated largely by Scots-Irish. The population of the coastal South was nearly half African. The legacy of eighteenth-century immigration to the British colonies was a population of unprecedented ethnic diversity.

Social Class

Although traditional working roles were transferred to North America, attempts to transplant the European class system were far less successful. In New France, the landowning *seigneurs* (lords) claimed privileges similar to those enjoyed by their aristocratic counterparts at home; the Spanish system of *encomienda* and the great manors created by the Dutch and continued by the English along the Hudson River also represented attempts to transplant European feudalism to North America. But because in most areas settlers had free access to land, these monopolies proved difficult or impossible to maintain. North American society was not aristocratic in the European fashion, but neither was it without social hierarchy.

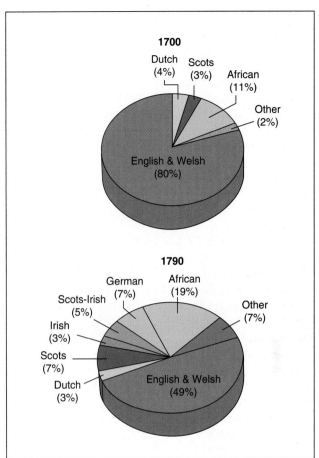

FIGURE 5.3 The Ancestry of the British Colonial Population The legacy of eighteenth-century immigration to the British colonies was a population of unprecedented ethnic diversity.

SOURCE: Thomas L. Purvis, "The European Ancestry of the United States Population," *William and Mary Quarterly* 61 (1984): 85–101.

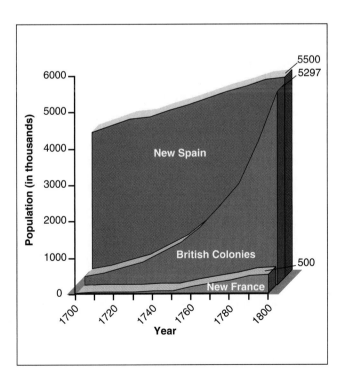

FIGURE 5.2 Estimated Total Population of New Spain, New France, and the British North American Colonies, 1700–1780 Although the populations of all three North American colonial empires grew in the eighteenth century, the explosive growth of the British colonies was unmatched.

SOURCE: *Historical Statistics of the United States* (Washington, DC: Government Printing Office, 1976), 1168.

In New Spain the official criterion for status was racial purity. *Españoles* (Spaniards) or *gente de razon* (literally, "people of reason") occupied the top rung of the social ladder, with mestizos, mulattoes, and others on descending levels. African slaves and Indians were at the bottom. In the isolated northern borderlands, however, these distinctions tended to blur, with *castas* (persons of mixed background) enjoying considerably more opportunity. Mestizos who acquired land might suddenly be reclassified as españoles. Even so, Spanish and French colonial societies were cut in the style of the Old World, with its hereditary ranks and titles. The landlords of New France and the Spanish borderlands may have lacked the means to accumulate real wealth, but they lived lives of elegance compared to the hard toil of the people who owed them labor service or rent.

In the British colonies the upper class was made up of large landowners, merchants, and prosperous professionals. In the eighteenth century, property valued at

Español con India.
Mestizo.

Mestizo con Española.
Castizo.

Castizo con Española.
Español.

Español con Mora.
Mulato.

5

6

Mulato con Española.
Morisco.

Morisco con Española.
Chino.

7

Chino con India.
Salta atras.

Salta atras con Mulata.
Lobo.

An eighteenth-century genre painting from New Spain showing various racial *castas*, the result of ethnic mixing.

SOURCE: Schalkwijk/Art Resource, New York.

£2,000 marked a man as well-to-do, and £5,000 was real wealth. Leading merchants, with annual incomes in excess of £500, lived in opulence. Despite their lack of titles, the wealthy planters and merchants of the British colonies lived far more extravagantly than the seigneurs of New France or the dons of the Spanish borderlands. What separated the culture of class in the British colonies from that of New France or New Mexico was not so much the material conditions of life as the prevailing attitude toward social rank. In the Catholic cultures, the upper class attempted to obscure its origins, claiming descent from European nobility. But British North America celebrated social mobility. The class system was remarkably open, and the entrance of newly successful planters, commercial farmers, and merchants into the upper ranks was not only possible but common, although by midcentury most upper-class families had inherited, not earned, their wealth.

There was also a large and impoverished lower class in the British colonies. Slaves, bound servants, and poor laboring families made up 40 percent or more of the population. For them, the standard of living did not rise above bare subsistence. Most lived from hand to mouth, often suffering through seasons of severe privation. Enslaved African Americans stood apart from the gains in the standard of living enjoyed by immigrants from Europe. Their lives in America had been degraded beyond measure from the conditions that had prevailed in their native lands.

The feature of the class system most often commented on by eighteenth-century observers was not the character or composition of the lower ranks, but rather the size and strength of the middle class, a rank entirely absent in the colonies of France and Spain. As one Pennsylvanian wrote at midcentury, "The people of this province are generally of the middling sort." More than half the population of the British colonies, and nearly 70 percent of all white settlers, might have been so classified. Most were landowning farmers of small to moderate means, but the group also included artisans, craftsmen, and small shopkeepers. Households solidly in the center of this broad ranking owned land or other property worth approximately £500 and earned the equivalent of £100 per year. They enjoyed a standard of living higher than that of the great majority of people in England and Europe. As one economic historian has recently concluded, the British colonies "were much better places to live, with probably a much higher standard of living than the mother country."

Economic Growth and Increasing Inequality

One of the most important differences among North American colonial regions in the eighteenth century was the economic stagnation of New France and New Spain compared with the impressive economic growth of the British colonies. Weighed down by royal bureaucracies and overbearing regulations, the communities of the

French Crescent and New Spain never evidenced much prosperity. In eighteenth-century British North America, however, per capita production grew at an annual rate of 0.5 percent. Granted, this was considerably less than the average annual growth rate of 1.5 percent that prevailed during the era of American industrialization, from the early nineteenth through the mid-twentieth century. But as economic growth increased the size of the economic pie, most middle- and upper-class British Americans began to enjoy improved living conditions. Improving standards of living and open access to land encouraged British colonists to see theirs as a society where hard work and savings could translate into prosperity, thus producing an upward spiral of economic growth.

At the same time, this growth produced increasing social inequality (see Table 5.2). In the commercial cities, for example, prosperity was accompanied by a concentration of assets in the hands of wealthy families. In Boston and Philadelphia at the beginning of the century, the wealthiest 10 percent of households owned about half of the taxable property; by about midcentury this small group owned 65 percent or more. In the commercial farming region of Chester County in southeastern Pennsylvania, the holdings of the wealthiest 10 percent of households increased more modestly, from 24 percent of taxable property in 1700 to 30 percent in 1750; but at the same time the share owned by the poorest third fell from 17 percent to 6 percent (see Figure 5.4). The general standard of living may have been rising, but the rich were getting richer and the poor poorer. The greatest concentrations of wealth occurred in the cities and in regions dominated by commercial farming, whether slave or free, while the greatest economic equality continued to be found in areas of self-sufficient farming such as the backcountry.

Another eighteenth-century trend worked against the hope of social mobility in the countryside. As population grew and as generations succeeded one another in older settlements, all the available land was taken up. Under the pressure of increased demand, land prices rose beyond the reach of families of modest means. And as a family's land was divided among the heirs of the second and third generations, parcels became ever smaller and more intensively farmed. Eventually, the soil was exhausted. In New England, where this pattern was most pronounced, there were notable increases in the number of landless poor, as well as the disturbing appearance of what were called the "strolling poor," homeless people who traveled from town to town looking for work or a handout. Destitute families crowded into Boston, which by 1750 was spending more than £5,000 annually on relief for the poor, who were required to wear a large red "P" on their clothing. In other regions, land shortages in the older settlements almost inevitably prompted people to leave in search of cheap or free land.

Contrasts in Colonial Politics

The administration of the Spanish and French colonies was highly centralized. French Canada was ruled by a superior council including the royal governor (in charge of military affairs), the intendant (responsible for civil administration), and the bishop of Québec. New Spain was governed by the Council of the Indies, which sat in Spain, and direct executive authority over all political affairs was exercised by the viceroy in Mexico City. Although local communities had informal independence, these highly bureaucratized and centralized governments left little room for the development of vigorous traditions of self-government.

The situation in the British colonies was quite different. During the early eighteenth century, the British government of Prime Minister Robert Walpole decided that decentralized administration would best accomplish the nation's economic goals. Contented colonies, Walpole argued, would present far fewer problems. With the exception of Connecticut and Rhode Island, both of which retained their charters and continued to choose their own governors, the colonies were administered by royally appointed governors. But taxation and spending were controlled by elected assemblies. The right to vote was restricted to men with property, but the proportion of adult white males who qualified was 50 percent or higher in all the colonies. Proportionally, the electorate of the British colonies was the largest in the world.

That did not mean, however, that the colonies were democratic. The basic principle of order in eighteenth-century British culture was the ideal of deference to natural hierarchies. The common metaphor for civil order was the well-ordered family, in which children were to be strictly governed by their parents, and wives by their

TABLE 5.2	WEALTH HELD BY RICHEST 10 PERCENT OF POPUATION IN BRITISH COLONIAL AMERICA, 1770	
	North	South
Frontier	33	40
Rural subsistence farming	35	45
Rural commercial farming	45	65
Cities	60	65
Overall	45	55

SOURCE: Jackson Turner Main, *The Social Structure of Revolutionary America* (Princeton, NJ: Princeton University Press, 1965), 276n.

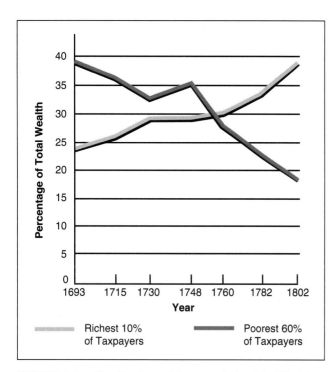

FIGURE 5.4 Distribution of Assessed Taxable Wealth in Eighteenth-Century Chester County This graph charts the concentration of assets in the hands of wealthy families. From 1693 to 1802, the percentage of total wealth held by the richest 10 percent of taxpayers rose from 24 to 38 percent, while the percentage held by the poorest 60 percent of taxpayers fell from 39 to 18 percent. This pattern was typical for regions dominated by commerce.

SOURCE: James Lemon and Gary Nash, "The Distribution of Wealth in Eighteenth-Century America," *Journal of Social History* 2 (1968):1–24.

husbands. Members of subordinate groups, such as women, non-English immigrants, African American slaves, servants, and Indians—who in some colonies constituted nine of every ten adults in the population—were not allowed to vote or hold public office. Moreover, for the most part, the men who did vote chose wealthy landowners, planters, or merchants to serve as their leaders. Provincial assemblies were controlled by colonial elites.

To educated British colonists, the word "democracy" implied rule by the mob, the normal order of things turned upside-down. Over the century there was, however, an important trend toward stronger institutions of representative government. By midcentury, most colonial assemblies in British North America had achieved considerable power over provincial affairs, sharing authority with governors. They collected local revenues and allocated funds for government programs, asserted the right to audit the accounts of public officers, and in some cases even acquired the power to approve the appointment of provincial officials. Because the assemblies controlled the finances of government—the "purse strings"—most royal governors

were unable to resist this trend. The royal governors who were most successful at realizing their agendas were those who became adept at playing one provincial faction off against another. All this had the important effect of schooling the colonial elite in the art of politics. It was not democratic politics, but rather training in the ways of patronage, coalition-building, and behind-the-scenes intrigue that would have important implications for the development of American institutions.

THE CULTURAL TRANSFORMATION OF BRITISH NORTH AMERICA

Despite broad similarities, the colonial regions of North America developed along divergent lines during the eighteenth century. The British colonies were marked by increasing ethnic diversity, economic growth, social tensions, and self-government. And by the middle decades of the eighteenth century, a significant cultural transformation had begun to take place. New ideas and writings associated with the Enlightenment made their way across the Atlantic on the same ships that transported European immigrants and European goods. In New Spain and New France, by contrast, colonial officials worked diligently to suppress these challenging new ideas and writings. The Catholic Church effectively banned the works of hundreds of authors. In Mexico, officials of the Inquisition conducted house-to-house searches in pursuit of prohibited texts that they feared had been smuggled into the country.

The Enlightenment Challenge

Drawing from the discoveries of Galileo, Copernicus, and the seventeenth-century scientists René Descartes and Isaac Newton, Enlightenment thinkers in Britain and in Europe argued that the universe was governed by natural laws that people could understand and apply to their own advantage. John Locke, for example, articulated a philosophy of reason in proposing that the state existed to provide for the happiness and security of individuals, who were endowed with inalienable rights to life, liberty, and property. Enlightenment writers emphasized rationality, harmony, and order, themes that stood in stark contrast to folk culture's traditional emphasis on the unfathomable mysteries of God and nature and the inevitability of human failure and disorder.

Enlightenment thinking undoubtedly appealed most to those whose ordered lives had improved their lot. The colonial elite had good reason to believe in progress. Many sent their sons to college, where the texts of the new thinkers were promoted. In the eighteenth century, Harvard (founded 1636) was joined by the College of

William and Mary in Virginia (1693), founded by Anglicans, and Yale College (1701), founded by Connecticut Puritans who believed Harvard had grown too liberal. A mixture of traditional and Enlightenment views characterized the colonial colleges, as it did the thought of colonial intellectuals, men such as the Puritan minister Cotton Mather. A conservative defender of the old order, Mather wrote a book supporting the existence of witches. But he was also a member of the Royal Society, an early supporter of inoculation against smallpox, and a defender of the Copernican sun-centered model of the universe. On hearing a scientific lecture of Mather's that could be construed as raising conflicts with a literal reading of the Bible, one old Boston minister noted in his diary, "I think it inconvenient to assert such problems."

This clergyman's views probably characterized a majority of the reading public. About half the adult men and a quarter of the adult women of the British colonies could read, a literacy rate that was comparable to rates in England and Scandinavia. In striking contrast, in the French and Spanish colonies, reading was a skill confined to a tiny minority of upper-class men. In New England, where the Puritans were committed to Bible reading and developed a system of public education, literacy rates were 85 percent among men and approximately 50 percent among women—the highest in the entire Atlantic world. The famous *New England Primer* (1689), one of the more influential books ever printed in America, was part of the most successful literacy campaign in history.

But the tastes of ordinary readers ran to traditional rather than Enlightenment fare. Benjamin Harris, the Boston publisher of the *New England Primer*, also printed the laws of Massachusetts, religious works by Cotton Mather, broadsides, ballads, and in 1690, the first newspaper in the colonies, *Public Occurrences both Foreign and Domestick*, which authorities suppressed after just one issue. In 1704, under a friendlier administration, however, the *Boston News-Letter* became the first continuously published newspaper in North America. By midcentury, there were more than twenty newspapers in the British colonies. These papers did not employ reporters, but depended on official government announcements, travelers' and correspondents' reports, and articles reprinted from other papers. The Pennsylvania *Chronicle* summed up its coverage in this description: "Containing the freshest Advices, both Foreign and Domestic; with a Variety of other Matters, useful, instructive, and entertaining." Newspaper readership in the colonies was sizable. By the mid-eighteenth century most literate people had access to newspapers, and they were often read aloud in local taverns, making their information available to all within hearing.

Another popular literary form was the almanac, a combination calendar, astrological guide, and sourcebook of medical advice and farming tips that reflected the concerns of traditional folk culture. The best remembered is *Poor Richard's Almanac* (1732–57), published by Philadelphia publisher Benjamin Franklin, but it was preceded and outlived by a great many others. What was so innovative about Franklin's almanac and what made it so important, was the manner in which the author used this traditional literary form to promote the new Enlightenment emphasis on useful and practical knowledge. Posing as the simple bumpkin Poor Richard, the highly sophisticated Franklin was one of the first Americans to bring Enlightenment thought to ordinary folk.

Not surprisingly, the best-selling book of the colonial era was the Bible. But in second place was a unique American literary form, the captivity narrative. The genre originated with the appearance of *The Sovereignty and Goodness of God* (1682), Mary Rowlandson's story of her captivity among the Indians during King Philip's War, a kind of "pilgrim's progress" through the American

The first page of the *New England Primer* (1689), published in Boston, which in its various editions sold more than five million copies. In addition to the letters of the alphabet, illustrated by crude but charming woodcuts and couplets, the book contained simple moral texts based on Biblical history and wisdom.

SOURCE: Courtesy American Antiquarian Society.

wilderness. Appearing in fifteen editions during the colonial period, Rowlandson's account stimulated the publication of at least 500 other similar narratives (including the Reverend John Williams's *The Redeemed Captive Returning to Zion*, discussed in the introduction of this chapter), most with a lot less religion and a great deal more gore.

The growth of the economy in the British colonies and the development of a colonial upper class stimulated the emergence of a more cosmopolitan Anglican culture, particularly in the cities of the Atlantic coast. A rising demand for drama, poetry, essays, novels, and history was met by urban booksellers who imported British publications. In Boston bookshops at midcentury, one could buy the works of William Shakespeare and John Milton, the essays of Joseph Addison, Richard Steele, Jonathan Swift, and Samuel Johnson, and editions of the classics. In shops elsewhere around the colonies, one might also find editions of satirical and somewhat salacious novels such as *Moll Flanders* by Daniel Defoe or *Tom Jones* by Henry Fielding—but not in New England, where such works were considered indecent. Many of these works were exerpted and reprinted in colonial newspapers.

A Decline in Religious Devotion

At the same time that these new ideas were flourishing, enthusiasm for religion seemed in decline. South of New England, the Anglican Church was weak, its ministers uninspiring, and many families were "unchurched." A historian of religion has estimated that only one adult in fifteen was a member of a congregation. Although this figure may understate the impact of religion on community life, it helps keep things in perspective.

The Puritan churches of New England also suffered declining membership and falling attendance at services, and many ministers began to warn of Puritanism's "declension," pointing to the "dangerous" trend toward the "evil of toleration." By the second decade of the eighteenth century, only one in five New Englanders belonged to an established congregation. When Puritanism had been a sect, membership in the church was voluntary and leaders could demand that followers testify to their religious conversion. But when Puritanism became an established church, attendance was expected of all townspeople, and conflicts inevitably arose over the requirement of a conversion experience. An agreement of 1662, known as the Half-Way Covenant, offered a practical solution: members' children who had not experienced conversion themselves could join as "half-way" members, restricted only from participation in communion. Thus the Puritans chose to manage rather than to resolve the conflicts involved in becoming an established religion. Tensions also developed between congregational autonomy and the central control that traditionally accompanied the establishment of a state church. In 1708, the churches of Connecticut agreed to the Saybrook Platform, which enacted a system of governance by councils of ministers and elders rather than by congregations. This reform also had the effect of weakening the passion and commitment of church members.

In addition, an increasing number of Congregationalists began to question the strict Calvinist theology of predestination—the belief that God had predetermined the few men and women who would be saved in the Second Coming. In the eighteenth century, many Puritans turned to the much more comforting idea that God had given people the freedom to choose salvation by developing their faith and by doing good works. This belief, known as Arminianism, was in harmony with the Enlightenment view that men and women were not helpless pawns but rational beings who could actively shape their own destinies. Also implicit in these new views was an image of God as a loving rather than a punishing father. Arminianism became a force at Harvard in the early eighteenth century, and soon a new generation of Arminian ministers began to assume leadership in New England's churches. These liberal ideas appealed to groups experiencing economic and social improvement, especially commercial farmers, merchants, and the comfortable middle class with its rising expectations. But among ordinary people, especially those in the countryside, where traditional patterns lingered, there was a good deal of opposition to these unorthodox new ideas.

The Great Awakening

The first stirrings of a movement challenging this rationalist approach to religion occurred during the 1730s, most notably in the movement sparked by Reverend Jonathan Edwards in the community of Northampton, in western Massachusetts. As the leaders of the community increasingly devoted their energies to the pursuit of wealth, the enthusiasm seemed to go out of religion. The congregation adopted rules allowing church membership without evidence of a conversion experience and adopted a seating plan for the church that placed wealthy families in the prominent pews, front and center. But the same economic forces that made the "River Gods"—as the wealthy landowners of the Connecticut Valley were known—also impoverished others. Young people from the community's poorer families grew disaffected as they were forced to postpone marriage because of the scarcity and expense of the land needed to set up a farm household. Increasingly they refused to attend church meetings, instead gathering together at night for "frolics" that only seemed to increase their discontent.

George Whitefield, an evangelical preacher from England who toured the colonies in the late 1730s and 1740s, had a powerful impact and helped spark the Great Awakening.

SOURCE: John Wollaston, *George Whitefield*, ca. 1770. National Portrait Gallery, London.

Reverend Edwards made this group of young people his special concern. Believing that they needed to "have their hearts touched," he preached to them in a style that appealed to their emotions. For the first time in a generation, the meetinghouse shook with the fire and passion of Puritan religion. (See Out of Many Voices: A Puritan Minister Sparks a Revival with His Talk of Fire and Brimstone.) "Before the sermon was done," one Northampton parishioner remembered about one notable occasion, "there was a great moaning and crying through the whole house—What shall I do to be saved?—Oh I am going to Hell!—Oh what shall I do for Christ?" Religious fervor swept through the community, and church membership began to grow. There was more to this than the power of one preacher, for similar revivals were soon breaking out in other New England communities, as well as among German pietists and Scots-Irish Presbyterians in Pennsylvania. Complaining of "spiritual coldness," people abandoned ministers whose sermons read like rational dissertations for those whose preaching was more emotional.

These local revivals became an intercolonial phenomenon thanks to the preaching of George Whitefield, an evangelical Anglican minister from England, who in 1738, made the first of several tours of the colonies. By all accounts, his preaching had a powerful effect. Even Benjamin Franklin, a religious skeptic, wrote of the "extraordinary influence of [Whitefield's] oratory" after attending an outdoor service in Philadelphia where 30,000 people crowded the streets to hear him. Whitefield began as Edwards did, chastising his listeners as "half animals and half devils," but he left them with the hope that God would be responsive to their desire for salvation. Whitefield avoided sectarian differences. "God help us to forget party names and become Christians in deed and truth," he declared.

Historians of religion consider this widespread colonial revival of religion, which later generations called the Great Awakening, to be an American version of the second phase of the Protestant Reformation (see Chapter 2). Religious leaders condemned the laxity, decadence, and officalism of established Protestantism and reinvigorated it with calls for piety and purity. People undergoing the economic and social stresses of the age, unsure about their ability to find land, marry, and participate in the promise of a growing economy, found relief in religious enthusiasm.

In Pennsylvania, two important leaders were William Tennent and his son Gilbert. An Irish-born Presbyterian, the elder Tennent was an evangelical preacher who established a school in Pennsylvania to train like-minded men for the ministry. His lampooned "Log College," as it was called, ultimately evolved into the College of New Jersey—later Princeton University—founded in 1746. In the early 1740s, disturbed by what he called the "presumptuous security" of the colonial church, Tennent toured with Whitefield and delivered the famous sermon "The Dangers of an Unconverted Ministry," in which he called upon Protestants to examine the religious convictions of their own ministers.

Among Presbyterians, open conflict broke out between the revivalists and the old guard, and in some regions the church hierarchy divided into separate organizations. In New England, similar factions, known as the New Lights and the Old Lights, accused each other of heresy. The New Lights railed against Arminianism as a rationalist heresy and called for a revival of Calvinism. The Old Lights condemned emotional enthusiasm as part of the heresy of believing in a personal and direct relationship with God outside the order of the church. Itinerant preachers appeared in the countryside, stirring up trouble. The followers of one traveling revivalist burned their wigs, jewelry, and fine clothes in a bonfire, then marched around the conflagration, chanting curses at their opponents, whose religious writings they also consigned to the flames. Many congregations split into feuding factions, and ministers found themselves challenged by their newly awakened parishioners. In one town, members of the congregation voted to dismiss their minister, who lacked the emotional fire they wanted in a preacher. When he refused to vacate his pulpit, they pulled him down, roughed him up, and threw him out the church door. Never had there been such turmoil in New England churches.

Although recently historians have raised questions about how cohesive these revivals were, they were so widespread and were typical of so many communities that they might be seen as one of the first national events in American history. They began somewhat later in the South, developing first in the mid-1740s among Scots-Irish Presbyterians, then achieved full impact with the organizational work of Methodists and particularly Baptists in the 1760s and early 1770s. These revivals not only affected white Southerners but also introduced many slaves to Christianity for the first time. Local awakenings were often a phenomenon shared by whites and blacks. The

OUT OF MANY VOICES

A PURITAN MINISTER SPARKS A REVIVAL WITH HIS TALK OF FIRE AND BRIMSTONE

Jonathan Edwards was minister of the Puritan church at Northampton, Massachusetts, when he delivered this sermon, the most famous in American history, in the neighboring town of Enfield, Connecticut, in 1741. Edwards's emphasis on rhetoric as a means of eliciting the emotional response of his congregation is readily seen in this excerpt from the sermon.

THAT WORLD OF MISERY, THAT LAKE OF BURNING brimstone, is extended abroad under you. There is the dreadful pit of the glowing flames of the wrath of God; there is hell's wide gaping mouth open; and you have nothing to stand upon, nor any thing to take hold of; there is nothing between you and hell but the air; it is only the power and mere pleasure of God that holds you up.

You probably are not sensible of this; you find you are kept out of hell, but do not see the hand of God in it; but look at other things, as the good state of your bodily constitution, your care of your own life, and the means you use for your own preservation. But indeed these things are nothing; if God should withdraw his hand, they would avail no more to keep you from falling, than the thin air to hold up a person that is suspended in it.

. . . The God that holds you over the pit of hell, much as one holds a spider, or some loathsome insect over the fire, abhors you, and is dreadfully provoked: his wrath towards you burns like fire; he looks upon you as worthy of nothing else, but to be cast into the fire; he is of purer eyes than to bear to have you in his sight; you are ten thousand times more abominable in his eyes, than the most hateful venomous serpent is in ours. You have offended him infinitely more than ever a stubborn rebel did his prince; and yet it is nothing but his hand that holds you from falling into the fire every moment. It is to be ascribed to nothing else, that you did not go to hell the last night; that you were suffered to awake again in this world, after you closed your eyes to sleep. And there is no other reason to be given, why you have not dropped into hell since you arose in the morning, but that God's hand has held you up. There is no other reason to be given why you have not gone to hell, since you have sat here in the house of God, provoking his pure eyes by your sinful wicked manner of attending his solemn worship. Yea, there is nothing else that is to be given as a reason why you do not this very moment drop down into hell.

O sinner! Consider the fearful danger you are in: it is a great furnace of wrath, a wide and bottomless pit, full of the fire of wrath, that you are held over in the hand of that God, whose wrath is provoked and incensed as much against you, as against many of the damned in hell. You hang by a slender thread, with the flames of divine wrath flashing about it, and ready every moment to singe it, and burn it asunder; and you have no interest in any Mediator, and nothing to lay hold of to save yourself, nothing to keep off the flames of wrath, nothing of your own, nothing that you ever have done, nothing that you can do, to induce God to spare you one moment.

. . . Therefore, let every one that is out of Christ, now awake and fly from the wrath to come. The wrath of Almighty God is now undoubtedly hanging over a great part of this congregation. Let every one fly out of Sodom: "Haste and escape for your lives, look not behind you, escape to the mountain, lest you be consumed." ■

SOURCE: Jonathan Edwards, *Sinners in the Hands of an Angry God* (Boston: S. Kneeland and T. Green, 1741).

Baptism by Full Immersion in the Schuylkill River of Pennsylvania, an engraving by Henry Dawkins illustrating events in the history of American Baptists, was published in Philadelphia in 1770. With calls for renewed piety and purity, the Great Awakening reinvigorated American Protestantism. The Baptists preached an egalitarian message, and their congregations in the South often included both white and black Protestants.

SOURCE: Henry Dawkins, *Baptismal Ceremony Beside the Schuykill*. Engraving, 1770. John Carter Brown Library at Brown University.

Baptist churches of the South in the era of the American Revolution included members of both races and featured spontaneous preaching by slaves as well as masters. In the nineteenth century, white and black Christians would go their separate ways, but the joint experience of the eighteenth-century Awakening shaped the religious cultures of both groups.

Many other "unchurched" colonists were brought back to Protestantism by eighteenth-century revivalism. But a careful examination of statistics suggests that the proportion of church members in the general population probably did not increase during the middle decades of the century. While the number of churches more than doubled from 1740 to 1780, the colonial population grew even faster, increasing threefold. The greatest impact was on families already associated with the churches. Before the Awakening, attendance at church had been mostly an adult affair, but throughout the colonies the revival of religion had its deepest effects on young people, who flocked to church in greater numbers than ever before. For years, the number of people experiencing conversion had been steadily falling, but now full membership surged. Church membership previously had been concentrated among women, leading Cotton Mather, for one, to speculate that perhaps women were indeed more godly. But men were particularly affected by the revival of religion, and their attendance and membership rose. "God has surprisingly seized and subdued the hardest men, and more males have been added here than the tenderer sex," wrote one Massachusetts minister.

The Politics of Revivalism

Revivalism appealed most of all to groups who felt bypassed by the economic and cultural development of the British colonies during the first half of the eighteenth century. The New Lights tended to draw their greatest strength from small farmers and less prosperous craftsmen. Many members of the upper class and the comfortable "middling sort" viewed the excesses of revivalism as indications of anarchy, and they became even more committed to rational religion.

Some historians have argued for important political implications of revivalism. In Connecticut, for example, Old Lights politicized the religious dispute by passing a series of laws in the General Assembly designed to

CHRONOLOGY

1636	Harvard College founded		*1716*	Spanish begin construction of Texas missions
1644	Roger Williams's *Bloudy Tenent of Persecution*		*1730s*	French decimate the Natchez and defeat the Fox Indians
1662	Half-Way Covenant in New England		*1732*	Franklin begins publishing *Poor Richard's Almanac*
1674	Bishopric of Quebec established		*1738*	George Whitefield first tours the colonies
1680s	William Penn begins recruiting settlers from the European Continent		*1740s*	Great Awakening gets under way in the Northeast
1682	Mary Rowlandson's *Sovereignty and Goodness of God*		*1740*	Parliament passes a naturalization law for the colonies
1689	Toleration Act passed by Parliament		*1746*	College of New Jersey (Princeton) founded
1690s	Beginnings of Jesuit missions in Arizona		*1760s*	Great Awakening achieves full impact in the South
1693	College of William and Mary is founded		*1769*	Spanish colonization of California begins
1700s	Plains Indians begin adoption of the horse		*1775*	Indian revolt at San Diego
1701	Yale College founded Iroquois sign treaty of neutrality with France		*1776*	San Francisco founded
1704	Deerfield raid		*1781*	Los Angeles founded
1708	Saybrook Platform in Connecticut			

suppress revivalism. In one town, separatists refused to pay taxes that supported the established church and were jailed. New Light judges were thrown off the bench, and others were denied their elected seats in the assembly. The arrogance of these actions was met with popular outrage: by the 1760s, the Connecticut New Lights had organized themselves politically and, in what amounted to a political rebellion, succeeded in turning the Old Lights out of office. These New Light politicians would provide the leadership for the American Revolution in Connecticut.

Such direct connections between religion and politics were rare. There can be little doubt, however, that for many people revivalism offered the first opportunity to participate actively in public debate and public action that affected the direction of their lives. Choices about religious styles, ministers, and doctrine were thrown open for public discourse, and ordinary people began to believe that their opinions actually counted for something. Underlying the debate over these issues were insecurities about warfare, economic growth, and the development of colonial society. Revivalism empowered ordinary people to question their leaders, an experience that would prove critical in the political struggles to come.

CONCLUSION

By the middle of the eighteenth century, a number of distinct colonial regions had emerged in North America, all of them with rising populations who demanded that more land be seized from the Indians. Some colonies attempted to ensure homogeneity, whereas others embraced diversity. Within the British colonies, New England in particular seemed bound to the past, whereas the Middle Colonies and the backcountry pointed the way toward pluralism and expansion. These developments placed them in direct competition with the expansionist plans of the French and at odds with Indian peoples committed to the defense of their homelands.

The economic development of the British colonies introduced new social and cultural tensions that led to the Great Awakening, a massive revival of religion that was the first transcolonial event in American history. Thousands of people experienced a renewal of religious passions, but rather than resuscitating old traditions, the Awakening pointed people toward a more active role in their own political futures. These transformations added

to the differences between the British colonies, on the one hand, and New Spain and the French Crescent, on the other.

REVIEW QUESTIONS

1. What were the principal colonial regions of North America? Discuss their similarities and their differences. Contrast the development of their political systems.
2. Why did the Spanish and the French close their colonies to immigration? Why did the British open theirs? How do you explain the ethnic homogeneity of New England and the ethnic pluralism of New York and Pennsylvania?
3. What were the principal trends in the history of Indian America in the eighteenth century?
4. Discuss the development of class differences in the Spanish, French, and British colonies in the eighteenth century.
5. Discuss the effects of the Great Awakening on the subsequent history of the British colonies.

RECOMMENDED READING

Jon Butler, *Becoming America: The Revolution Before 1776* (2000). A history that emphasises the diversity, economic prosperity, participatory politics, and religious pluralism of the eighteenth-century British colonies.

Edward Countryman, *Americans: A Collision of Histories* (1996). An important new synthesis that includes the many peoples and cultures of North America.

John Demos, *The Unredeemed Captive: A Family Story from Early America* (1994). A moving history of the Deerfield captives, focusing on the experience of Eunice Williams, the unredeemed captive.

W. J. Eccles, *The Canadian Frontier, 1534–1760* (1983). An introduction to the history of French America by a leading scholar on colonial Canada.

David Hackett Fischer, *Albion's Seed: Four British Folkways in America* (1990). An engaging history with fascinating details on the regions of New England, Pennsylvania, Virginia, and the backcountry.

Jack P. Greene, *Pursuits of Happiness: The Social Development of Early Modern British Colonies and the Formation of American Culture* (1986). A distillation of a tremendous amount of historical material on community life in British North America.

Frank Lambert, *Inventing the "Great Awakening"* (1999). Argues that the revivialists themselves created the

idea of the Great Awakening to further their evangelical work.

Jackson Turner Main, *The Social Structure of Revolutionary America* (1965). A detailed treatment of colonial social structure, with statistics, tables, and enlightening interpretations.

Lucy Eldersveld Murphy, *A Gathering of Rivers: Indians, Métis, and Mining in the Western Great Lakes, 1737–1832* (2000). Demonstrates the success of Indian communities in adapting to colonialism through the diversification of their economies, intermarriage, and constructing multiethnic communities.

James A. Sandos, *Converting California: Indians and Franciscans in the Missions* (2004). A balanced treatment of missionaries and natives in eighteenth and nineteenth-century California.

David J. Weber, *The Spanish Frontier in North America* (1992). A magnificent treatment of the entire Spanish borderlands, from Florida to California. Includes important chapters on colonial government and social life.

Marianne S. Wokeck, *Trade in Strangers: The Beginning of Mass Migration to North America* (1999). The first important study of immigration in the eighteenth century, arguing that these migrations served as models for European mass migration in the next century.

 For additional study resources for this chapter, go to the *Companion Website*, **http://www.prenhall.com/faragher**.

CHAPTER

6

From Empire to
Independence

1750–1776

The First Continental Congress Shapes a National Political Community

The opening minutes of the First Continental Congress did not bode well. A delegate moved they begin with prayer, but others responded that "we were so divided in religious sentiments, some Episcopalians, some Quakers, some Anabaptists, some Presbyterians, and some Congregationalists, that we could not join in the same act of worship." The delegates who arrived in Philadelphia in September 1774 hailed from many communities with different identities and loyalties. Was the Congress to be stymied, here at the very beginning, by the things separating them? John Adams's cousin and fellow Massachusetts delegate Samuel Adams leapt to his feet. He was no bigot, he proclaimed, and was willing to hear a prayer "from any gentleman of piety and virtue who was at the same time a friend to his country." There was a larger identity at stake here—their common identity as British Americans. Suspending their religious differences, the delegates agreed to a prayer from a local clergyman, who took as his text the Thirty-fifth Psalm: "Plead my cause, O Lord, with them that strive with me; fight against them that fight against me." He "prayed with such fervor, such Ardor, such Earnestness and Pathos, and in Language so elegant and sublime," John Adams wrote to his wife, that "it has had an excellent Effect upon every Body here."

The incident highlighted the most important task confronting the First Continental Congress—emphasizing the common cause without compromising local identities. The delegates were like "ambassadors from a dozen belligerent powers of Europe," noted Adams. They represented distinct colonies with traditions and histories as different as those of separate countries. Moreover, these lawyers, merchants, and planters, leaders in their respective colonies, were strangers to one another. "Every man," he worried, "is a great man, an orator, a critic, a statesman, and therefore every man, upon every question, must show his oratory, his criticism, and his political abilities." As a result, he continued, "business is drawn and spun out to an immeasurable length. I believe that if it was moved and seconded that we should come to a resolution that three and two make five, we should be entertained with logic and rhetorick, law, history, politicks and mathematics concerning the subject for two whole days."

Britain's North American colonies enjoyed considerable prosperity during the first half of the eighteenth century. But in 1765—in the aftermath of the great war for empire in which Great Britain soundly defeated France, forcing the French to give up their American colonies—the British government began to apply new trade restrictions and levy new taxes, generating increasing resistance among the colonists. By 1774, peaceful protest had escalated into violent riot, most notably in the city of Boston, and in an attempt to force the colonists to acknowledge the power of Parliament to make laws binding them "in all cases whatsoever," the British proclaimed a series of repressive measures, including the closure of ports in Massachusetts and the suspension of that colony's elected government. In this atmosphere of crisis, the twelve colonial assemblies elected fifty-six delegates for a "Continental Congress" to map out a coordinated response. If they failed to act collectively, delegate Arthur Lee of Virginia declared, they would be "attacked and destroyed by piece-meal." Abigail Adams, the politically astute wife of John Adams,

Philadelphia

a delegate from Massachusetts, agreed. "You have before you," she wrote her husband, "the greatest national concerns that ever came before any people."

Despite their regional and religious differences, during seven weeks of deliberations, the delegates succeeded in forging an agreement on the principles and policies they would follow in this, the most serious crisis in the history of the British North American colonies. At the outset they resolved that each colony would have one vote, thereby committing themselves to the preservation of provincial autonomy. Their most vexing problems they sent to committees, whose members could sound each other out without committing themselves on the public record. They added to their daily routine a round of dinners, parties, and late-night tavern-hopping. And in so doing they began to create a community of interest. "It has taken us much time to get acquainted," John Adams wrote to Abigail, but he left Philadelphia thinking of his fellow representatives as "a collection of the greatest men upon this continent."

These were the first steps toward the creation of an American national political community. Communities are not only local, but also regional, national, even international. In a town or village, the feeling of association comes from daily, face-to-face contact, but for larger groups, those connections must be deliberately constructed. In their final declaration the delegates pledged to "firmly agree and associate, under the sacred ties of virtue, honor and love of our country." They urged their fellow Americans to "encourage frugality, economy, and industry, and promote agriculture, arts and the manufactures of this country," and to "discountenance and discourage every species of extravagance and dissipation." They asked their countrymen to remember "the poorer sort" among them during the troubles they knew were coming. And in demanding that patriotic Americans "break off all dealings" and treat with contempt anyone violating this compact, they drew a distinction between "insiders" and "outsiders," one of the essential first acts in the construction of community.

Patrick Henry of Virginia, a delegate strongly committed to American independence, was exuberant by the time the Congress adjourned in late October. "The distinctions between Virginians, Pennsylvanians, New Yorkers, and New Englanders, are no more," he declared. "I am not a Virginian, but an American." He exaggerated. Local, provincial, and regional differences would continue to clash. As yet there was no national political community. But Henry voiced an important truth. With its repressive actions, Great Britain had forced the colonists to recognize a shared community of interest distinct from that of the mother country. As the colonies cautiously moved toward independence, the imagined community of America would be sorely tested, and during the difficult months and years of warfare, the differences among the former colonies would frequently threaten to destroy the nation even as it was being born. But the First Continental Congress marked the point when Americans began the struggle to transcend their local and regional differences in pursuit of national goals.

KEY TOPICS

- The final struggle among Great Britain, France, and American Indian tribes for control of eastern North America
- American nationalism in the aftermath of the French and Indian War
- Great Britain's changing policy toward its North American colonies
- The political assumptions of American republicanism
- The colonies' efforts to achieve unity in their confrontation with Great Britain

THE SEVEN YEARS' WAR IN AMERICA

The first attempt at cooperation among the leaders of the British colonies occurred in 1754, when representatives from New England, New York, Pennsylvania, and Maryland met to consider a joint approach to the French and Indian challenge. Even as the delegates met, fighting between French Canadians and Virginians began on the Ohio River, the first shots in a great global war for empire, known in Europe as the Seven Years' War, that pitted Britain (allied with Prussia) against the combined might of France, Austria, and Spain. In North America this would be the final and most destructive armed conflict between the British and the French before the French Revolution. Ultimately, it decided the future of the vast region between the Appalachian Mountains and the Mississippi River, and lay the groundwork for the conflict between the British and the colonists that led to the American Revolution.

The Albany Conference of 1754

The 1754 meeting, which included an official delegation from the Iroquois Confederacy, and took place in the New York town of Albany on the Hudson River, was convened by the British Board of Trade. British officials wanted the colonies to consider a collective response to the continuing conflict with New France and the Indians of the interior. High on the agenda was the negotiation of a settlement with the leaders of the Iroquois Confederacy, who had grown impatient with colonial land grabbing. Because the powerful Iroquois Confederacy, with its Covenant Chain of alliances with other Indian tribes, occupied such a strategic location between New France and the British colonies, the British could ill afford Iroquois discontent. But the official Iroquois delegation walked out of the conference, refusing all offers to join a British alliance.

The Albany Conference did adopt Benjamin Franklin's Plan of Union, which proposed that Indian affairs, western settlement, and other items of mutual interest be placed under the authority of "one general government" for the colonies, consisting of a president-general appointed and supported by the Crown, and a Grand Council, a lesislative body empowered to make general laws and raise money for the defense of the whole, its delegates chosen by the several colonial legislatures, the seats allocated by population and wealth. Franklin, who had been appointed by the British government as deputy postmaster general for all of British North America and charged with improving intercolonial communication and commerce, had become extremely sensitive to the need for cooperation among the colonies. British authorities were suspicious of the plan, fearing it would create a very powerful entity that they might not be able to control. They had nothing to worry about, for fearing the loss of their autonomy, the colonial assemblies rejected the Albany Plan of Union. As one British official noted, each colony had "a distinct government, wholly independent of the rest, pursuing its own interest and subject to no general command."

Colonial Aims and Indian Interests

The absence of cooperation among the colonies in North America would prove to be one of the greatest weaknesses of the British Empire, because the ensuing war would be fought at a number of widespread locations and required the coordination of command. There were three principal flash points of conflict in North America. The first was along the northern Atlantic coast. In 1713, France had ceded to Britain its colony of Acadia (which the British renamed Nova Scotia), but France then built the fortress of Louisburg, from which it guarded its fishing grounds and the St. Lawrence approach to New France. New Englanders had captured this prize in 1745 during King George's War, but the French then reclaimed it upon the settlement of that conflict in 1748. They subsequently reinforced Louisburg to such an extent that it became known as the Gibraltar of the New World.

A second zone of conflict was the border region between New France and New York, from Niagara Falls to Lake Champlain, where Canadians and New Yorkers were in furious competition for the Indian trade. Unable to compete effectively against superior English goods, the French resorted to armed might, constructing fortifications on Lake George and reinforcing their base at Niagara. In this zone, the strategic advantage was held by the Iroquois Confederacy.

It was the Ohio country—the trans-Appalachian region along the Ohio River—that became the primary focus of British and French attention. This rich land was a prime target of British backcountry settlers and frontier land speculators. The French worried that their isolated settlements would be overrun by the expanding British population and that the loss of the Ohio River would threaten their entire Mississippi trading empire. To reinforce their claims, in 1749 the French sent a heavily armed force down the Ohio River to ward off the British, and in 1752, supported by their northern Indian allies, they expelled a large number of British traders from the region. To prevent the British from returning to the west, they began the next year to construct a series of forts running south from Lake Erie to the junction of the Allegheny and Monongahela rivers, the site known as the Forks of the Ohio River.

The French "have stripped us of more than nine parts in ten of North America," one British official cried, "and left us only a skirt of coast along the Atlantic shore." In preparation for a general war, the British established the port of Halifax in Nova Scotia as a counter to Louisburg. In northern New York, they strengthened existing forts and constructed new ones. Finally, the British king decided to directly challenge the French claim to the upper Ohio Valley. He conferred an enormous grant of land on the Ohio Company, organized by Virginia and London capitalists, and the company made plans to build a fort at the Forks of the Ohio River.

The impending conflict involved more than the competing colonial powers, however, for the Indian peoples of the interior had interests of their own. In addition to its native inhabitants, the Ohio country had become a refuge for Indian peoples who had fled the Northeast—Delawares, Shawnees, Hurons, and Iroquois among them. Most of the Ohio Indians opposed the British and were anxious to preserve the Appalachians as a barrier to westward expansion. They were also disturbed by the French movement into their country. The French outposts, however, unlike those of the British, did not become centers of expanding agricultural settlements.

The Iroquois Confederacy as a whole sought to play off one European power against the other, to its own advantage. In the South, the Creeks carved out a similar role for themselves among the British, the French in Louisiana, and the Spanish in Florida. The Cherokees and Choctaws attempted, less successfully, to do the same. It was in the interests of these Indian tribes, in other words, to perpetuate the existing colonial stalemate. Their position would be greatly undermined by an overwhelming victory for either side.

Frontier Warfare

At the Albany Congress, the delegates received news that Colonel George Washington, a young militia officer sent by the governor of Virginia to expel the French from the region granted to the Ohio Company, had been forced to surrender his troops to a French force near the headwaters of the Monongahela River. The Canadians now commanded the interior country from their base at Fort Duquesne, which they had built at the Forks of the Ohio.

Taking up the challenge, the British government dispatched two Irish regiments under General Edward Braddock across the

Atlantic in 1755 to attack and capture Fort Duquesne. Meanwhile, colonial militias (the equivalent of today's National Guard) commanded by colonial officers were to strike at the New York frontier and the North Atlantic coast. An army of New England militiamen succeeded in capturing two French forts on the border of Nova Scotia, but the other two prongs of the campaign were failures. The offensive in New York was repulsed. And in the worst defeat of a British army during the eighteenth century, Braddock's force was destroyed by a smaller number of French and Indians on the upper Ohio, and Braddock himself was killed.

Braddock's defeat was followed by the outbreak of full-scale warfare between Britain and France in 1756 (see Map 6.1). Known as the Seven Years' War in Europe, in North America it came to be called the French and Indian War. The fighting of 1756 and 1757 was a near

MAP **EXPLORATION**

To explore an interactive version of this map,
go to **www.prenhall.com/faragher5/map6.1**

MAP 6.1 The War for Empire in North America, 1754–1763 The Seven Years' War in America (also known as the French and Indian War) was fought in three principal areas: Nova Scotia and what was then Acadia, the frontier between New France and New York, and the upper Ohio River—gateway to the Old Northwest.

catastrophe for Great Britain. Canadians captured the British forts in northern New York. Indians pounded backcountry settlements, killed thousands of settlers, and raided deep into the coastal colonies, throwing British colonists into panic. The absence of colonial cooperation greatly hampered the British attempt to mount a counterattack. When British commanders tried to exert direct control over provincial troops in order to coordinate their strategy, they succeeded only in angering local authorities.

In this climate of defeat, the British adopted a harsh policy of retribution against the French-speaking farmers of Acadia, who had lived peacefully under British rule for over forty years. The Acadians' refusal to bear arms in defense of the British crown was now used as an excuse for their expulsion. In the fall of 1755, troops from New England began the forcible removal of approximately 18,000 Acadians, selling their farms at bargain prices to immigrants from New England. Suffering terrible hardship and heartbreak, the Acadians were dispersed throughout the Atlantic world, a substantial number of them ending up in Louisiana, then under Spanish control, where they became known as "Cajuns." The Acadian expulsion is one of the most infamous chapters in the British imperial record in North America.

The Conquest of Canada

In the darkest days of 1757, William Pitt, an enthusiastic advocate of British expansion, became prime minister of Great Britain. "I know that I can save this country," Pitt declared, "and that no one else can." Deciding that the global war could be won in North America, he subsidized the Prussians to fight the war

The death of General James Wolfe, at the conclusion of the battle in which the British captured Quebec in 1759, became the subject of American artist Benjamin West's most famous painting, which was exhibited to tremendous acclaim in London in 1770.

SOURCE: Benjamin West (1738–1820), *The Death of General Wolfe*, 1770. Oil on canvas, 152.6 × 214.5 cm. Transfer from the Canadian War Memorials, 1921. (Gift of the 2nd Duke of Westminster, Eaton Hall, Cheshire, 1918.) National Gallery of Canada, Ottawa, Ontario.

in Europe, and reserved his own forces and resources for naval and colonial operations. Pitt committed the British to the conquest of Canada and the elimination of all French competition in North America. Such a goal could be achieved only with a tremendous outpouring of men and money. By promising that the war would be fought "at His Majesty's expense," Pitt was able to buy colonial cooperation. A massive infusion of British currency and credit greatly stimulated the North American economy. Pitt dispatched over 20,000 regular British troops across the Atlantic. Combining them with colonial forces, he massed over 50,000 armed men against Canada.

The British attracted Indian support for their plans by "redressing the grievances complained of by the Indians, with respect to the lands which have been fraudulently taken from them," in the words of a British official. In 1758, officials promised the Iroquois Confederacy and the Ohio Indians that the crown would "agree upon clear and fixed boundaries between our settlements and their hunting grounds, so that each party may know their own and be a mutual protection to each other of their respective possessions."

Thus did Pitt succeed in reversing the course of the war. Regular and provincial forces captured Louisburg in July 1758, setting the stage for the penetration of the St. Lawrence Valley. A month later, a force of New Englanders captured the strategic French fort at Oswego on Lake Ontario, thereby preventing the Canadians from resupplying their western posts. Encouraged by British promises, many Indian tribes abandoned the French alliance. The French were forced to give up Fort Duquesne, and a large British force took control of this strategic post at the Forks of the Ohio, renaming it Fort Pitt (Pittsburgh today) in honor of the prime minister. "Blessed be God," wrote a Boston editor. "The long looked for day is arrived that has now fixed us on the banks of the Ohio." The last of the French forts on the New York frontier fell in 1759. In the South, regular and provincial British troops invaded the homeland of the Cherokees and crushed them.

British forces now converged on Quebec, the heart of French Canada. In the summer of 1759, British troops—responding to General James Wolfe's order to "burn and lay waste the country"—plundered farms and shelled the city of Quebec. Finally, in an epic battle fought on the Plains of Abraham before the city walls, more than 2,000 British, French, American, and Canadian men lost their lives, including both Wolfe and the French commander, the Marquis de Montcalm. The British army prevailed and Quebec fell. The conquest of Montreal the next year marked the final destruction of the French empire in America.

In the final two years of the war, the British swept French ships from the seas, invaded Havana and conquered Cuba, took possession of several other important Spanish and French colonies in the Caribbean, achieved dominance in India, and even captured the Spanish Philippines. In the Treaty of Paris, signed in 1763, France lost all its possessions on the North American mainland. It ceded its claims east of the Mississippi to Great Britain, with the exception of New Orleans. That town, along with the other French trans-Mississippi claims, passed to Spain. For its part, in exchange for the return of all its Caribbean and Pacific colonies, Spain ceded Florida to Britain. The imperial rivalry in eastern North America that had begun in the sixteenth century now came to an end with complete victory for the British Empire (see Map 6.2 on page 153).

The Struggle for the West

When the Ohio Indians heard of the French cession of the western country to Britain, they were shocked. "The French had no right to give away [our] country," they told a British trader. They were "never conquered by any nation." A new set of British policies soon shocked them all the more. Both the French and the British had long used gift-giving as a way of gaining favor with Indians. The Spanish officials who replaced the French in Louisiana made an effort to continue the old policy. But the British military governor of the western region, General Jeffery Amherst, in one of his first official actions, banned presents to Indian chiefs and tribes, demanding that they learn to live without "charity." Not only were Indians angered by Amherst's reversal of custom, but they were also frustrated by his refusal to supply them with the ammunition they required for hunting. Many were left starving.

In this climate, hundreds of Ohio Indians became disciples of an Indian visionary named Neolin ("The Enlightened One" in Algonquian), known to the English as the Delaware Prophet. The core of Neolin's teaching was that Indians had been corrupted by European ways and needed to purify themselves by returning to their traditions and preparing for a holy war. "Drive them out," he declared of the settlers. A confederacy of tribes organized by chiefs who had gained influence by adopting Neolin's ideas laid plans for a coordinated attack on British frontier posts in the spring of 1763. The principal leader of the resistance was the Ottawa chief Pontiac, renowned as an orator and political leader. "We tell you now," Pontiac declared to British officials, "the French never conquered us, neither did they purchase a foot of our Country, nor have they a right to give it to you."

In May 1763, the Indian confederacy simultaneously attacked all the British forts in the West. Warriors,

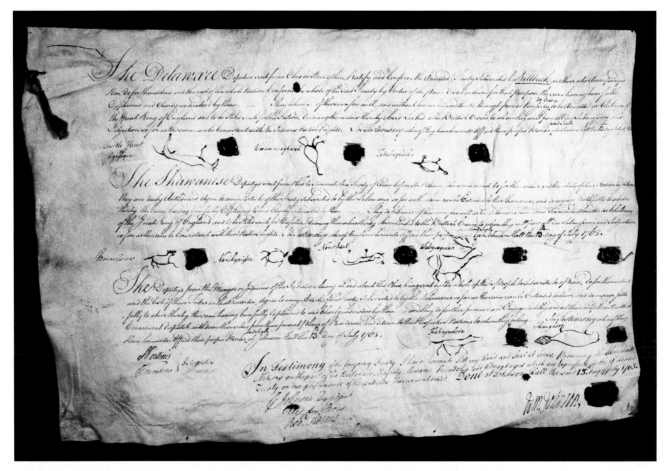

A treaty between the Delaware, Shawnee, and Mingo (western Iroquois) Indians and Great Britain, July 13, 1765, at the conclusion of the Indian uprising. The Indian chiefs signed with pictographs symbolizing their clans, each notarized with an official wax seal.

SOURCE: Treaty, dated 13 July 1765, between Sir William Johnson and representatives of the Delaware, Shawnee and Mingo nations. Parchment, 16 × 24.5 in. Photo by Carmelo Guadagno, Photograph Courtesy National Museum of the American Indian, Smithsonian Institution. Neg. 39369.

in a suprise attack, overran Fort Michilimackinac, at the narrows between Lakes Michigan and Huron, by scrambling through the gates supposedly in pursuit of a lacrosse ball, cheered on by unsuspecting soldiers. In raids throughout the backcountry, Indians killed more than 2,000 settlers. At Fort Pitt, General Amherst proposed that his officers "send the smallpox among the disaffected tribes" by distributing infected blankets from the fort's hospital. This early instance of germ warfare resulted in an epidemic that spread from the Delawares and Shawnees to the southern Creeks, Choctaws, and Chickasaws, killing hundreds of people. Although they sacked and burned eight British posts, the Indians failed to take the key forts of Niagara, Detroit, and Pitt. Pontiac and his followers fought on for another year, but most of the Indians sued for peace, fearing the destruction of their villages. The British came to terms because they knew they could not overwhelm the Indian

peoples. What became known as Pontiac's Rebellion thus ended in stalemate.

Even before the uprising, the British had been at work on a policy they hoped would help to resolve frontier tensions. In the Royal Proclamation of 1763, the British government set aside the region west of the crest of the Appalachian Mountains as "Indian Country." It was "essential to our interest," the Proclamation declared, "that the several nations or tribes of Indians with whom we are connected, and who live under our protection, should not be molested or disturbed." The specific authorization of the crown would be required for any purchase of these protected Indian lands.

Colonists had expected that the removal of the French threat would allow them to move unencumbered into the West, regardless of the wishes of the Indian inhabitants. They could not understand why the British would award territory to Indian enemies

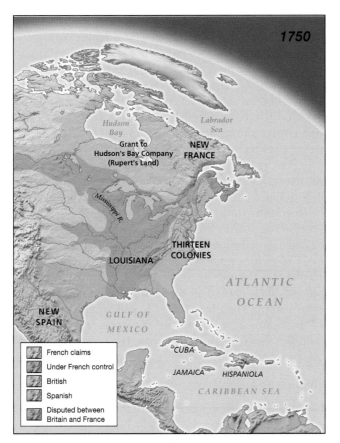

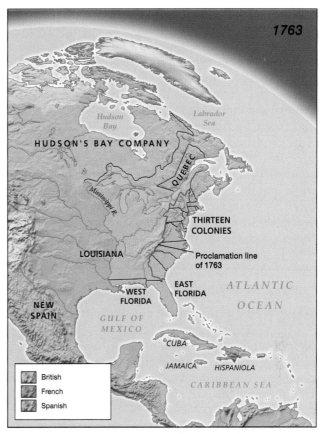

MAP 6.2 European Claims in North America, 1750 and 1763 As a result of the British victory in the Seven Years' War, the map of colonial claims in North America was fundamentally transformed.

who had killed more than 4,000 settlers during the previous war. In an act emblematic of the anger back-country settlers felt about these restrictions, a mob of Pennsylvanians known as the Paxton Boys butchered twenty Indian men, women, and children at the small village of Conestoga on the Susquehanna River in December 1763. When colonial authorities moved to arrest them, 600 frontiersmen marched into Philadelphia in protest. Negotiations led by Benjamin Franklin helped to prevent a bloody confrontation.

In fact, the British proved unable and ultimately unwilling to prevent the westward migration that was a dynamic part of the colonization of British North America. Within a few years of the war, New Englanders by the thousands were moving into the northern Green Mountain district known as Vermont. In the middle colonies, New York settlers pushed ever closer to the homeland of the Iroquois, while others settled within the protective radius of Fort Pitt in western Pennsylvania. Hunters, stock herders, and farmers crossed over the first range of the Appalachians in Virginia and North Carolina, planting pioneer communities in what are now West Virginia and eastern Tennessee.

Moreover, the press of population growth and economic development turned the attention of investors and land speculators to the area west of the Appalachians. In response to demands by settlers and speculators, British authorities were soon pressing the Iroquois and Cherokees for cessions of land in Indian Country. No longer able to play off rival colonial powers, Indians were reduced to a choice between compliance and resistance. Weakened by the recent war, they chose to sign away lands. In the Treaty of Hard Labor in 1768, the Cherokees ceded a vast tract on the waters of the upper Tennessee River, where British settlers had already planted communities. In the Treaty of Fort Stanwix of the same year, the Iroquois gave up their claim to the Ohio Valley, hoping thereby to deflect English settlement away from their own homeland.

The individual colonies were even more aggressive. Locked in a dispute with Pennsylvania about jurisdiction in the Ohio country, in 1773, Virginia governor John Murray, Earl of Dunmore, sent a force to occupy Fort Pitt. In 1774, in an attempt to gain legitimacy for his dispute with Pennsylvania, Dunmore provoked a frontier war with the Shawnees. After defeating them, he forced their cession of the upper Ohio River Valley to Virginia. The Iroquois and Ohio Indians angrily complained about the outcome of what came to be known as Dunmore's War. The English king, they argued, had guaranteed that the boundary between colonial and Indian land "should forever after be looked upon as a barrier between us." But the Americans "entirely disregard, and despise the settlement agreed upon by their superiors and us." They "are come in vast numbers to the Ohio, and [give] our people to understand that they would settle wherever they pleased. If this is the case, we must look upon every engagement you made with us as void and of no effect." This continuing struggle for the West would be an important issue in the coming American Revolution.

THE IMPERIAL CRISIS IN BRITISH NORTH AMERICA

No colonial power of the mid-eighteenth century could match Britain in projecting imperial power over the face of the globe. During the years following its victory in the Seven Years' War, Britain turned confidently to the reorganization of its North American empire. This new colonial policy plunged British authorities into a new and ultimately more threatening conflict with the colonists, who had begun to develop a sense of a separate identity.

The Emergence of American Nationalism

Despite the anger of frontier settlers over the Proclamation of 1763, the conclusion of the Seven Years' War had left most colonists proud of their place in the British empire. But during the war, many had begun to note important contrasts between themselves and the mother country. The soldiers of the British army, for example, shocked Americans with their profane, lewd, and violent behavior. But the colonists were equally shocked by the swift and terrible punishment that aristocratic officers used to keep these soldiers in line. Those who had witnessed such savage punishments found it easy to believe in the threat of Britain enslaving American colonists.

Colonial forces, by contrast, were composed of volunteer companies. Officers tempered their administration of punishment, knowing they had to maintain the enthusiasm of their troops. Discipline thus fell considerably below the standards to which British officers were accustomed. "Riff-raff," one British general said of the colonials, "the lowest dregs of the people, both officers and men." For their part, many colonial officers believed that the British ignored the important role the Americans had played in the Seven Years' War. Massachusetts, for example, lost between 1,500 and 2,000 fighting men. This mutual suspicion and hostility was often expressed in name calling: British soldiers called New Englanders "Yankees," while colonists heckled the red-coated British with taunts of "Lobster." It was during the war that many colonists began to see themselves as distinct from the British.

The Seven Years' War also strengthened a sense of identity among the colonies. Farmers who never before had ventured outside the communities of their birth fought in distant regions with men like themselves from other colonies. Such experiences reinforced a developing nationalist perspective. From 1735 to 1775, while trade with Britain doubled, commerce among the colonies increased by a factor of four. People and ideas moved along with goods. The first stage lines linking seaboard cities began operation in the 1750s. Spurred by Postmaster Benjamin Franklin, many colonies built or improved post roads for transporting the mails.

The Press, Politics, and Republicanism

One of the most important means of intercolonial communication was the weekly newspaper. Early in the eighteenth century, the colonial press functioned as a mouthpiece for the government. Editors who criticized public officials could land in jail. In 1735, New York City editor John Peter Zenger was indicted for seditious libel after printing antigovernment articles. But as it turned out, the case provided the precedent for greater freedom of the press. "Shall the press be silenced that evil governors may have their way?" Zenger's attorney asked the jury. "The question before the court is not the cause of a poor printer," he declared, but the cause "of every free man that lives under a British government on the main of America." Zenger was acquitted. By 1760, more than twenty highly opinionated weekly newspapers circulated in the British colonies, and according to one estimate, a quarter of all male colonists were regular readers.

The midcentury American press focused increasingly on intercolonial affairs. One study of colonial newspapers indicates that intercolonial coverage increased sixfold over the four decades preceding the Revolution. Editors of local papers increasingly looked at events from what they called a "continental" perspective. This trend accelerated during the Seven Years' War, when communities demanded coverage of events in distant colonies where their men might be fighting. During these years the British colonists of North America first began to use the term "American" to denote their common identity. More than any previ-

The pages of the colonial press reveal the political assumptions held by informed colonists. For decades governors had struggled with colonial assemblies over their respective powers. As commentary on the meaning of these struggles, colonial editors often reprinted the writings of the radical Whigs of eighteenth-century England, pamphleteers such as John Trenchard and Thomas Gordon, political theorists such as John Locke, and essayists such as Alexander Pope and Jonathan Swift. They warned of the growing threat to liberty posed by the unchecked exercise of power. In their more emotional writings they argued that a conspiracy existed among the powerful—kings, aristocrats, and Catholics—to quash liberty and institute tyranny. Outside the mainstream of British political opinion, these ideas came to define the political consensus in the British colonies, a point of view called "republicanism."

Republicanism declared that the truly just society provided the greatest possible liberty to individuals. As the power of the state, by its very nature, was antithetical to liberty, it had to be limited. John Locke argued that the authority of a ruler should be conditional rather than absolute and that the people had the inherent right to select their own form of governance and to withdraw their support if the government did not fulfill its trust. The best guarantee of good government, then, was the broad distribution of power to the people, who would not only select their own leaders but vote them out as well. In this view, republican government depended on the virtue of the people, their willingness to make the health and stability of the political community their first priority, and was possible only for an "independent" population that controlled its own affairs. As Thomas Jefferson once wrote, ". . . dependence begets subservience and venality, suffocates the germ of virtue, and prepares fit tools for the designs of ambition." Individual ownership of property, especially land, he argued, was the foundation of an independent and virtuous people.

This was a political theory that fit the circumstances of American life, with its wide base of property ownership, its tradition of representative assemblies, and its history of struggle with royal authority. Contrast the assumptions of republicans with those of British monarchists, who argued that the good society was one in which a strong state, controlled by a hereditary elite, kept a vicious and unruly people in line.

The Sugar and Stamp Acts

The emerging sense of American political identity was soon tested by British measures designed to raise revenues in the colonies. To quell Indian uprisings and stifle

James Franklin began publishing *The New-England Courant* in Boston in 1721. When Franklin criticized the government, he was jailed, and the paper continued under the editorship of his brother Benjamin. *The Courant* ceased publication in 1726, and the Franklin brothers went on to other papers—James to *The Rhode Island State Gazette*, Benjamin to *The Pennsylvania Gazette* in Philadelphia. Before the *Zenger* case in 1735, few editors dared to challenge the government.

SOURCE: *"The New-England Courant"*, 26 March 1722. Courtesy of the Massachusetts Historical Society.

ous event, the Seven Years' War promoted a new spirit of nationalism and a wider notion of community. This was the social base of the political community later forged at the First Continental Congress.

discontent among the French and Spanish populations of Quebec and Florida, 10,000 British troops remained stationed in North America at the conclusion of the Seven Years' War. The cost of maintaining this force added to the enormous debt Britain had run up during the fighting and created a desperate need for additional revenues. In 1764, Chancellor of the Exchequer George Grenville, deciding to obtain the needed revenue from America, pushed through Parliament a measure known as the Sugar Act.

The Sugar Act placed a duty on sugar imported into the colonies and revitalized the customs service, introducing stricter registration procedures for ships and adding more officers. In fact, the duty was significantly less than the one that had been on the books and ignored for years, but the difference was that the British now intended to enforce it. In anticipation of American resistance, the legislation increased the jurisdiction of the vice-admiralty court at Halifax, where customs cases were heard. These courts were hated because there was no presumption of innocence and the accused had no right to a jury trial. These new regulations promised not only to squeeze the incomes of American merchants but also to cut off their lucrative smuggling operations. Moreover, colonial taxes, which had been raised during the war, remained at an all-time high. In many cities, merchants as well as artisans protested loudly. Boston was especially vocal: in response to the sugar tax, the town meeting proposed a boycott of certain English imports. This movement for nonimportation soon spread to other port towns.

James Otis Jr., a Massachusetts lawyer fond of grand oratory, was one of the first Americans to strike a number of themes that would become familiar over the next fifteen years. A man's "right to his life, his liberty, his property" was "written on the heart, and revealed to him by his maker," he argued in language echoing the rhetoric of the Great Awakening. It was "inherent, inalienable, and indefeasible by any laws, pacts, contracts, covenants, or stipulations which man could devise." He declared that "an act against the Constitution is void." There could be "no taxation without representation."

But it was only fair, Grenville argued in return, that the colonists help pay the costs of the empire, and what better way to do so than by a tax? Taxes in the colonies were much lower than taxes at home. In early 1765, unswayed by American protests, he followed the Sugar Act with a second and considerably more sweeping revenue measure, the Stamp Act. This tax required the purchase of specially embossed paper for all newspapers, legal documents, licenses, insurance policies, ship's papers, and even dice and playing cards.

The Stamp Act Crisis

During the summer and autumn of 1765, the American reaction to the Stamp Act created a crisis of unprecedented proportions. The stamp tax had to be paid in hard money, and it came during a period of economic stagnation. Many colonists complained of being "miserably burdened and oppressed with taxes."

Of more importance for the longer term, however, were the constitutional implications. Although colonial male property owners elected their own assemblies, they did not vote in British elections. But the British argued that Americans were subject to the acts of Parliament because of "virtual representation." That is, members of Parliament were thought to represent not just their districts, but all citizens of the empire. As one British writer put it, the colonists were "represented in Parliament in the same manner as those inhabitants of Britain are who have not voices in elections." But in an influential pamphlet of 1765, *Considerations on the Propriety of Imposing Taxes*, Maryland lawyer Daniel Dulany rejected this theory. Because Americans were members of a separate political community, he insisted, Parliament could impose no tax on them. Instead, he argued for "actual representation," emphasizing the direct relationship that must exist between the people and their political representatives.

It was just such constitutional issues that were emphasized in the Virginia Stamp Act Resolutions, pushed through the Virginia assembly by the passionate young lawyer Patrick Henry in May 1765. Although the Virginia House of Burgesses rejected the most radical of Henry's resolutions, they were all reprinted throughout the colonies. By the end of 1765, the assemblies of eight other colonies had approved similar measures denouncing the Stamp Act and proclaiming their support of "no taxation without representation."

In Massachusetts, the leaders of the opposition to the Stamp Act came from a group of upper- and middle-class men who had long opposed the conservative leaders of the colony. These men had worked years to establish a political alliance with Boston craftsmen and workers who met at taverns, in volunteer fire companies, or at social clubs. One of these clubs, known as the Loyall Nine, included a member named Samuel Adams, an associate and friend of James Otis, who had made his career in local politics. Using his contacts with professionals, craftsmen, and laboring men, Adams helped put together an anti-British alliance that spanned Boston's social classes. In August 1765, Adams and the Loyall Nine were instrumental in organizing a protest of Boston workingmen against the Stamp Act.

Whereas Boston's elite had prospered during the eighteenth century, the conditions for workers and the poor had worsened. Unemployment, inflation, and high taxes had greatly increased the level of poverty during the depression that followed the Seven Years' War, and many were resentful. A large Boston crowd assembled on August 14, 1765, in the shade of an old elm tree (soon known as the "Liberty Tree") and strung up effigies of several British officials, including Boston's stamp distributor, Andrew Oliver. The crowd then vandalized Oliver's office and home. At the order of Oliver's brother-in-law, Lieutenant Governor Thomas Hutchinson, leader of the Massachusetts conservatives, the town sheriff tried to break up the crowd, but he was pelted with paving stones and bricks. Soon thereafter, Oliver resigned his commission. The unified action of Boston's social groups had had its intended effect.

Twelve days later, however, a similar crowd gathered at the aristocratic home of Hutchinson himself. As the family fled through the back door, the crowd smashed through the front with axes. Inside they demolished furniture, chopped down the interior walls, consumed the contents of the wine cellar, and looted everything of value, leaving the house a mere shell. As these events demonstrated, it was not always possible to keep popular protests within bounds. During the fall and winter, urban crowds in commercial towns from Halifax in the North to Savannah in the South forced the resignation of many British tax officials (see Map 6.3).

In many colonial cities and towns, groups of merchants, lawyers, and craftsmen sought to moderate the resistance movement by seizing control of it. Calling themselves the Sons of Liberty, these groups encouraged moderate forms of protest. They circulated petitions, published pamphlets, and encouraged crowd actions only as a last resort; always they emphasized limited political goals. Then in October 1765, delegations from nine colonies (New Hampshire and Georgia declined the invitation to attend, and the governors of Virginia and North Carolina prevented their delegates from accepting) met at what has been called the Stamp Act Congress in New York City, where they passed a set of resolutions denying Parliament's right to tax the colonists, arguing that taxation required representation. They agreed to stop all importations from Britain until the offending measures were repealed. But the delegates also took a moderate stance, declaring that the colonies owed a "due subordination" to measures that fell within Parliament's just ambit of authority. The Congress thus defused the radicals, and there were few repetitions of mob attacks, although by the end of 1765 almost all the stamp distributors had resigned or fled, making it impossible for Britain to enforce the Stamp Act.

Samuel Adams, a second cousin of John Adams, was a leader of the Boston radicals and an organizer of the Sons of Liberty. The artist of this portrait, John Singleton Copley, was known for setting his subjects in the midst of everyday objects; here he portrays Adams in a middle-class suit with the charter guaranteeing the liberties of Boston's freemen.

SOURCE: John Singleton Copley (1738–1815), *Samuel Adams*, ca. 1772. Oil on canvas, 49 1/2 × 39 1/2 in. (125.7cm × 100.3 cm). Deposited by the City of Boston 30.76c. Courtesy, Museum of Fine Arts, Boston. Reproduced with permission. ©2000 Museum of Fine Arts, Boston. All Rights Reserved.

Repeal of the Stamp Act

Pressured by British merchants, who worried over the effects of the growing nonimportation movement among the colonists, in March 1766, Parliament repealed the Stamp Act and reduced the duties under the Sugar Act. This news was greeted with celebrations throughout the American colonies, and the nonimportation associations were disbanded. Overlooked in the mood of optimism, however, was the fact that the repeal was coupled with a Declaratory Act, in which Parliament affirmed its full authority to make laws binding the colonies "in all cases whatsoever." The notion of absolute parliamentary supremacy over colonial matters was basic to the British theory of empire. Even Pitt, friend of America that he was, asserted "the authority of this kingdom over the

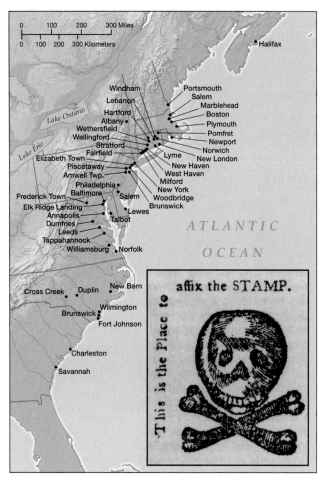

MAP 6.3 Demonstrations Against the Stamp Act, 1765
From Halifax in the North to Savannah in the South, popular demonstrations against the Stamp Act forced the resignation of British tax officials. The propaganda of 1765 even reached the breakfast table, emblazoned on teapots.

SOURCE: *No Stamp Act* teapot, Colonial Williamsburg Foundation.

colonies to be sovereign and supreme, in every circumstance of government and legislation whatsoever." The Declaratory Act signaled that the conflict had not been resolved but merely postponed.

"SAVE YOUR MONEY AND SAVE YOUR COUNTRY"

Colonial resistance to the Stamp Act was stronger in urban than in rural communities, stronger among merchants, craftsmen, and planters than among farmers and frontiersmen. When Parliament next moved to impose its will, as it had promised to do in the Declaratory Act, imposing new duties on imported goods, the American opposition again adopted the tactic of non-

importation. But this time resistance spread from the cities and towns into the countryside. As the editor of the *Boston Gazette* phrased the issue, "Save your money and you save your country." It became the slogan of the movement.

The Townshend Revenue Acts

During the 1760s, there was a rapid turnover of government leaders that made it difficult for Britain to form a consistent and even-handed policy toward the colonies. In 1767, after several failed governments, King George III asked William Pitt to again become prime minister. Pitt enjoyed enormous good will in America, and a government under his leadership stood a good chance of reclaiming colonial credibility. But, suffering from a prolonged illness, he was soon forced to retire, and his place as head of the cabinet was assumed by Charles Townshend, Chancellor of the Exchequer.

One of the first problems facing the new government was the national debt. England suffered massive unemployment, riots over high prices, and tax protests. The large landowners forced a bill through Parliament slashing their taxes by 25 percent. The Townshend government feared unrest at home far more than opposition in America. So as part of his plan to close the budget gap, in June 1767, Townshend proposed a new revenue measure for the colonies that placed import duties on commodities such as lead, glass, paint, paper, and tea. By means of these new Revenue Acts, Townshend hoped to redress colonial grievances against internal taxes such as those imposed by the Stamp Act. For most colonists, however, it proved to be a distinction without a difference.

The most influential colonial response came in a series of articles by wealthy Philadelphia lawyer John Dickinson, *Letters from a Farmer in Pennsylvania*, that were reprinted in nearly every colonial newspaper. Posing as a humble farmer, Dickinson conceded that Parliament had the right to regulate trade through the use of duties. It could place prohibitive tariffs, for example, on foreign products. But, he argued, it had no constitutional authority to tax goods in order to raise revenues in America. As the preface to the Revenue Acts made clear, the income they produced would be used to pay the salaries of royal officials in America. Thus, Dickinson pointed out, since colonial assemblies were no longer paying their salaries, colonial administrators would not be subject to the financial oversight of elected representatives.

Other Americans warned that this was part of the British conspiracy to suppress American liberties. Their fears were reinforced by Townshend's stringent enforcement of the Revenue Acts. He created a new and strengthened Board of Commissioners of the Customs, and established a series of vice-admiralty courts at Boston, Philadelphia, and Charleston to prosecute violators of the duties—the first time those hated institutions had appeared in the most important American port cities. To demonstrate his power, he also suspended New York's assembly. That body had refused to vote public funds to support the British troops garrisoned in the colony. Until the citizens of New York relented, Townshend declared, they would no longer be represented.

In response to these measures, some men argued for violent resistance. But it was Dickinson's essays that had the greatest effect on the public debate, not only because of their convincing arguments but also because of their mild and reasonable tone. "Let us behave like dutiful children," Dickinson urged, "who have received unmerited blows from a beloved parent." As yet, no sentiment for independence existed in America.

Nonimportation: An Early Political Boycott

Associations of nonimportation and nonconsumption, revived in October 1767 when the Boston town meeting drew up a long list of British products to boycott, became the main weapon of the resistance movement. Over the next few months other port cities, including Providence, Newport, and New York, set up nonimportation associations of their own. Artisans took to the streets in towns and cities throughout the colonies to force merchants to stop importing British goods. The associations published the names of uncooperative importers and retailers. These people then became the object of protesters, who sometimes resorted to violence. Coercion was very much a part of the movement.

Adopting the language of Protestant ethics, nonimportation associations pledged to curtail luxuries and stimulate local industry. These aims had great appeal in small towns and rural districts, which previously had been uninvolved in the anti-British struggle. In 1768 and 1769, colonial newspapers paid a great deal of attention to women's support for the boycott. Groups of women, some calling themselves Daughters of Liberty, organized spinning and weaving bees to produce homespun for local consumption. (See Out of Many Voices: The Daughters of Liberty Urge Americans to Boycott British Goods.) The actual work performed at these bees was less important than the symbolic message. "The industry and frugality of American ladies," wrote the editor of the *Boston Evening Post*, "are contributing to bring about the political salvation of a whole continent." Other women renounced silks and satins and pledged to stop serving tea to their husbands. Nonimportation appealed to the traditional

This British cartoon, *A Society of Patriotic Ladies*, ridiculed the efforts of American women to support the Patriot cause by boycotting tea. The moderator of the meeting appears coarse and masculine, while an attractive scribe is swayed by the amorous attention of a gentleman. The activities under the table suggest that these women are neglecting their true duty.

SOURCE: Library of Congress.

values of rural communities—self-sufficiency and independence—and for the first time brought country people into the growing community of resistance.

Nonimportation was greatly strengthened in May 1769 when the Virginia House of Burgesses enacted the first provincial legislation banning the importation of goods enumerated in the Townshend Acts, and slaves and luxury commodities as well. Over the next few months, all the colonies but New Hampshire enacted similar associations. Because of these efforts, the value of colonial imports from Britain declined by 41 percent.

The Massachusetts Circular Letter

Boston and Massachusetts were at the center of the agitation over the Townshend Revenue Acts. In February 1768, the Massachusetts House of Representatives

OUT OF MANY VOICES

THE DAUGHTERS OF LIBERTY URGE AMERICANS TO BOYCOTT BRITISH GOODS

In response to the Townshend Acts of 1767, American women organized groups called Daughters of Liberty to boycott British goods and substitute home manufactures. This verse advised women to reject British fashions and wear homespun garments.

Young ladies in town, and those that live round,
  Let a friend at this season advise you:
Since money's so scarce, and times growing worse,
  Strange things may soon hap and surprize you;
First then, throw aside your high top knots of pride,
  Wear none but your own country linen,
Of Economy boast, let your pride be the most
  To show clothes of your own make and spinning.

What, if homespun they say is not quite so gay
  As brocades, yet be not in a passion,
For when once it is known this is much wore in town,
  One and all will cry out, 'tis the fashion!
And as one, all agree that you'll not married be

To such as will wear London Fact'ry:
But at first sight refuse, tell em such you do chuse
  As encourage our own Manufact'ry

No more Ribbons wear, nor in rich dress appear,
  Love your country much better than fine things,
Begin without passion, twill soon be the fashion
  To grace your smooth locks with a twine string,
Throw aside your Bohea, and your green Hyson tea,
  And all things with a new fashion duty;
Procure a good store of the choice Labradore,
  For there'll soon be enough here to suit ye;
These do without fear and to all you'll appear
  Fair, charming, true, lovely and clever;
Tho' the times remain darkish, young men may be sparkish
  And love you much stronger than ever. ∎

SOURCE: *Massachusetts Gazette*, November 1767.

approved a letter, drawn up by Samuel Adams, addressed to the speakers of the other provincial assemblies. Designed largely as a propaganda device and having little practical significance, the letter denounced the Townshend Revenue Acts, attacked the British plan to make royal officials independent of colonial assemblies, and urged the colonies to find a way to "harmonize with each other." Massachusetts governor Francis Bernard condemned the document for stirring up rebellion and dissolved the legislature. In Britain, Lord Hillsborough, secretary of state for the colonies, ordered each royal governor in America to likewise dissolve his colony's assembly if it should endorse the letter. Before this demand reached America, the assemblies of New Hampshire, New Jersey, and Connecticut had commended Massachusetts. Virginia, moreover, had issued a circular letter encouraging a "hearty union" among the colonies and urging common action against the British measures that "have an immediate tendency to enslave us."

Throughout this crisis there were rumors and threats of mob rule in Boston. Because customs agents enforced the law against smugglers and honest traders alike, they enraged merchants, seamen, and dockworkers. In June 1768, a crowd assaulted customs officials who had seized John Hancock's sloop *Liberty* for nonpayment of duties. So frightened were the officials that they fled the city. Hancock, reportedly the wealthiest merchant in the colonies and a vocal opponent of the British measures, had become a principal target of the customs officers. In September the Boston town meeting called on the people to arm themselves, and in the absence of an elected assembly it invited all the other towns to send delegates to a provincial convention. There were threats of armed resistance, but little support for it in the convention, which broke up in chaos. Nevertheless the British, fearing insurrection, occupied Boston with infantry and artillery regiments on October 1, 1768. With this action, they sacrificed a great deal of good will and respect and added greatly to the growing tensions.

The Politics of Revolt and the Boston Massacre

The British troops stationed in the colonies were the object of scorn and hostility over the next two years. There were regular conflicts between soldiers and radicals in New York City, often focusing on the Sons of Liberty. These men would erect "liberty poles" festooned with banners and flags proclaiming their cause, and the British troops would promptly destroy them. When the New York assembly finally bowed to Townshend in December 1769 and voted an appropriation to support the troops, the New York City Sons of Liberty organized a demonstration and erected a large liberty pole. The soldiers chopped it down, sawed it into pieces, and left the wood on the steps of a tavern frequented by the Sons. This led to a riot in which British troops used their bayonets against hundreds of New Yorkers armed with cutlasses and clubs. Several men were wounded.

Confrontations also took place in Boston. Sam Adams played up reports and rumors of soldiers harassing women, picking fights, or simply taunting residents with versions of "Yankee Doodle." Soldiers were often hauled into Boston's courts, and local judges adopted a completely unfriendly attitude toward these members of the occupying army. In February 1770, an eleven-year-old boy was killed when a customs officer opened fire on a rock-throwing crowd. Although no soldiers were involved, this incident heightened the tensions between citizens and troops.

A persistent source of conflict was the competition between troops and townsmen over jobs. Soldiers were permitted to work when off duty, putting them in competition with day laborers. In early March 1770, an off-duty soldier walked into a ropewalk (a long narrow building in which ropes are made) in search of a job. "You can clean my shithouse," he was told. The soldier left but returned with his friends, and a small riot ensued. Fighting continued over the next few days in the streets between the wharf and the Common, where the soldiers were encamped. On the evening of March 5, 1770, a crowd gathered at the Customs House and began taunting a guard, calling him a "damned rascally scoundrel lobster" and worse. A captain and seven soldiers went to his rescue, only to be pelted with snowballs and stones. Suddenly, without orders, the frightened soldiers began to fire. Five of the crowd fell dead, and six more were wounded, two of these dying later. The first blood shed was that of Crispus Attucks, whose mother was Indian and father was African American. The soldiers escaped to their barracks, but a mob numbering in the hundreds rampaged through the streets demanding vengeance. Fearing for the safety of his men and the security of the state, Thomas Hutchinson, now governor of Massachusetts, ordered British troops out of Boston. The Boston Massacre became infamous throughout the colonies, in part because of the circulation of an inflammatory print produced by the Boston engraver Paul Revere,

In Paul Revere's version of the Boston Massacre, issued three weeks after the incident, the British fire an organized volley into a defenseless crowd. Revere's print—which he plagiarized from another Boston engraver—may have been inaccurate, but it was enormously effective propaganda. It hung in so many Patriot homes that the judge hearing the murder trial of these British soldiers warned the jury not to be swayed by "the prints exhibited in our houses."

SOURCE: The Library of Congress.

which depicted the British as firing on a crowd of unresisting civilians. But for many colonists, the incident was a disturbing reminder of the extent to which relations with the mother country had deteriorated. During the next two years, many people found themselves pulling back from the brink. "There seems," one Bostonian wrote, "to be a pause in politics."

The growth of American resistance was slowed as well by the news that Parliament had repealed most of the Townshend Revenue Acts on March 5, 1770—the same day as the Boston Massacre. In the climate of apprehension and confusion, there were few celebrations of the repeal, and the nonimportation associations almost immediately collapsed. Over the next three years, the value of British imports rose by 80 percent. The parliamentary retreat on the question of duties, like the earlier repeal of the Stamp Act, was accompanied by a face-saving measure—retention of the tax on tea "as a mark of the supremacy of Parliament," in the words of Frederick Lord North, the new prime minister.

FROM RESISTANCE TO REBELLION

There was a lull in the American controversy during the early 1770s, but the situation turned violent in 1773, when Parliament again infuriated the Americans. This time it was an ill-advised Tea Act, and it propelled the colonists onto a swift track from resistance to outright rebellion.

Intercolonial Cooperation

In June 1772, Governor Hutchinson inaugurated another controversy by announcing that henceforth his salary and those of other royally appointed Massachusetts officials would be paid by the crown. In effect, this made the executive and judiciary branches of the colony's government independent of elected representatives. In October, the Boston town meeting appointed a Committee of Correspondence to communicate with other towns regarding this challenge. The next month, the meeting issued what became known as the *Boston Pamphlet*, a series of declarations written by Samuel Adams and other radicals, concluding that British encroachments on colonial rights pointed to a plot to enslave Americans.

In March 1773, the Virginia House of Burgesses appointed a standing committee for correspondence among the colonies "to obtain the most early and authentic intelligence" of British actions affecting America, "and to keep up and maintain a correspondence and communication with our sister colonies." The Virginia committee, including Patrick Henry, Richard Henry Lee, and young Thomas Jefferson, served as a model, and within a year all the colonies except Pennsylvania, where conservatives controlled the legislature, had created

committees of their own. These committees became the principal channel for sharing information, shaping public opinion, and building cooperation among the colonies before the Continental Congress of 1774.

The information most damaging to British influence came from the radicals in Boston. In June 1773, the Boston committee obtained from Benjamin Franklin in London a set of letters Hutchinson had sent to the ministry. The letters had come to Franklin anonymously, and to protect himself he asked that the committee keep them private, but they were soon published in the local press, resulting in Franklin's dismissal from his position as colonial postmaster general. But the British cause in the colonies suffered much more than Franklin's reputation. The letters revealed Hutchinson's call for "an abridgement of what are called English liberties" in the colonies. "I wish to see some further restraint of liberty," he had written, "rather than the connection with the parent state should be broken." This

A British tax man is tarred and feathered and forced to drink tea, while the Boston Tea Party takes place in the background, in this image of 1774.

SOURCE: © Christie's Images, Inc. 2004

statement seemed to be the "smoking gun" of the conspiracy theory, and it created a torrent of anger against the British and their officials in the colonies.

The Boston Tea Party

It was in this context that the colonists received the news that Parliament had passed a Tea Act. Colonists were major consumers of tea, but because of the tax on it that remained from the Townshend duties, the market for colonial tea had collapsed, bringing the East India Company to the brink of bankruptcy. This company was the sole agent of British power in India, and Parliament could not allow it to fail. The British therefore devised a scheme in which they offered tea to Americans at prices that would tempt the most patriotic tea drinker. The radicals argued that this was merely a device to make palatable the payment of unconstitutional taxes—

further evidence of the British effort to corrupt the colonists. In October, a mass meeting in Philadelphia denounced anyone importing the tea as "an enemy of his country." The town meeting in Boston passed resolutions patterned on those of Philadelphia, but the tea agents there, including two of Governor Hutchinson's sons, resisted the call to refuse the shipments.

The first of the tea ships arrived in Boston Harbor late in November. Mass meetings in Old South Church, which included many country people drawn to the scene of the crisis, resolved to keep the tea from being unloaded. Governor Hutchinson was equally firm in refusing to allow the ship to leave the harbor. Five thousand people on December 16, 1773, crowded into the church to hear the captain of the tea ship report to Samuel Adams that he could not move his ship. "This meeting can do nothing more to save the country," Adams declared. This was the signal for a disciplined group of fifty or sixty men,

OUT OF MANY VOICES

A SHOEMAKER TELLS OF PARTICIPATING IN THE BOSTON TEA PARTY

George Hewes, a Boston shoemaker, participated in many events of the Revolution. His account of the destruction of the tea in Boston harbor, which he provided for a historian years later, demonstrates the ways in which resistance moved toward revolution.

IT WAS NOW EVENING, AND I IMMEDIATELY dressed myself in the costume of an Indian, equipped with a small hatchet, which I and my associates denominated the tomahawk, with which, and a club, after having painted my face and hands with coal dust in the shop of a blacksmith, I repaired to Griffins wharf, where the ships lay that contained the tea. When I first appeared in the street, after being thus disguised, I fell in with many who were dressed, equipped and painted as I was, and who fell in with me, and marched in order to the place of our destination. When we arrived at the wharf, there were three of our number who assumed an authority to direct our operations, to which we readily submitted. They divided us into three parties, for the purpose of boarding the three ships which contained the tea at the same time. . . . We then were ordered by our commander

to open the hatches, and take out all the chests of tea and throw them overboard, and we immediately proceeded to execute his orders; first cutting and splitting the chests with our tomahawks, so as thoroughly to expose them to the effects of the water. In about three hours from the time we went on board, we had thus broken and thrown overboard every tea chest to be found in the ship; while those in the other ships were disposing of the tea in the same way, at the same time. We were surrounded by British armed ships, but no attempt was made to resist us. We then quietly retired to our several places of residence, without having any conversation with each other, or taking any measures to discover who were our associates. . . . There appeared to be an understanding that each individual should volunteer his services, keep his own secret, and risk the consequences for himself. No disorder took place during that transaction, and it was observed at that time, that the stillest night ensued that Boston had enjoyed for many months. ■

SOURCE: James Hawkes, A Retrospect of the Boston Tea Party (New York: S. S. Bliss, 1834), pp. 36–41.

including farmers, artisans, merchants, professionals, and apprentices, to march to the wharf disguised as Indians. (See Out of Many Voices: A Shoemaker Tells of Participating in the Boston Tea Party.) There they boarded the ship and dumped into the harbor 45 tons of tea, valued at £18,000, all the while cheered on by Boston's citizens. "Boston Harbor's a tea-pot tonight," the crowd chanted.

Boston's was the first tea party, but other incidents of property destruction soon followed. When the Sons of Liberty learned that a cargo of tea had landed secretly in New York, they followed the example of their brothers in Massachusetts, dressed themselves as Indians, and dumped the tea chests into the harbor. At Annapolis, a ship loaded with tea was destroyed by fire, and arson also consumed a shipment stored at a warehouse in New Jersey. But it was the action in Boston at which the British railed. The government became convinced that something had to be done about the rebellious colony of Massachusetts.

The Intolerable Acts

During the spring of 1774, an angry Parliament passed a series of acts—called the Coercive Acts, but known by Americans as the Intolerable Acts—that were calculated to punish Massachusetts and strengthen the British hand. The Boston Port Bill prohibited the loading or unloading of ships in any part of Boston Harbor until the town fully compensated the East India Company and the customs service for the destroyed tea. The Massachusetts Government Act annulled the colonial charter: delegates to the upper house would no longer be elected by the assembly, but henceforth were to be appointed by the king. Civil officers throughout the province were placed under the authority of the royal governor, and the selection of juries was given over to governor-appointed sheriffs. Town meetings, an important institution of the resistance movement, were prohibited from convening more than once a year except with the approval of the governor, who was to control their agendas. With these acts, the British terminated the long history of self-rule by communities in the colony of Massachusetts. The Administration of Justice Act protected British officials from colonial courts, thereby encouraging them to vigorously pursue the work of suppression. Those accused of committing capital crimes while putting down riots or collecting revenue, such as the soldiers involved in the Boston Massacre, were now to be sent to England for trial. Additional measures affected the other colonies and encouraged them to see themselves in league with suffering Massachusetts. The Quartering Act legalized the housing of troops at public expense, not only in taverns and abandoned buildings, but in occupied dwellings and private homes as well.

Finally, in the Quebec Act, the British authorized a permanent government for the territory taken from France during the Seven Years' War (see Map 6.4 on page 166). This government was both authoritarian and anti-republican, with a royal government and an appointed council. Furthermore, the act confirmed the feudal system of land tenure along the St. Lawrence. It also granted religious toleration to the Roman Catholic Church and upheld the church's traditional right to collect tithes, thus, in effect, establishing Catholicism as the state religion in Quebec. To the American colonists, the Quebec Act was a frightening preview of what imperial authorities might have in store for them, and it confirmed the prediction of the Committees of Correspondence that there was a British plot to destroy American liberty.

In May, General Thomas Gage arrived in Boston to replace Hutchinson as governor. The same day, the Boston town meeting called for a revival of nonimportation measures against Britain. In Virginia the Burgesses declared that Boston was enduring a "hostile invasion" and made provision for a "day of fasting, humiliation, and prayer, devoutly to implore the divine interposition for averting the heavy calamity, which threatens destruction to our civil rights and the evils of civil war." For this expression of sympathy, Governor Dunmore suspended the legislature. Nevertheless, throughout the colony on the first of June, funeral bells tolled, flags flew at half mast, and people flocked to the churches.

The First Continental Congress

It was amid this crisis that town meetings and colonial assemblies alike chose representatives for the Continental Congress. The delegates who arrived in Philadelphia in September 1774 included the most important leaders of the American cause. Cousins Samuel and John Adams, the radicals from Massachusetts, were joined by Patrick Henry and George Washington from Virginia and Christopher Gadsden of South Carolina. Many of the delegates were conservatives: John Dickinson and Joseph Galloway of Philadelphia and John Jay and James Duane from New York. With the exception of Gadsden, a hothead who proposed an attack on British forces in Boston, the delegates wished to avoid war and favored a policy of economic coercion.

After one of their first debates, the delegates passed a Declaration and Resolves, in which they asserted that all the colonists sprang from a common tradition and enjoyed rights guaranteed "by the immutable laws of nature, the principles of the English constitution, and the several charters or compacts" of their provinces. Thirteen acts of Parliament, passed since 1763, were declared in violation of these rights. Until these acts were repealed, the delegates pledged, they would impose a set of sanctions against the British. These would include not only the nonimportation and nonconsumption of British goods, but also a prohibition on the export of colonial commodities to Britain or its other colonies.

To enforce these sanctions, the Continental Congress urged that "a committee be chosen in every county, city, and town, by those who are qualified to vote for representatives in the legislature, whose business it shall be attentively to observe the conduct of all persons." This call for democratically elected local committees in each community had important political ramifications. The following year, these groups, known as Committees of Observation and Safety, took over the functions of local government throughout the colonies. They organized militia companies, called extralegal courts, and combined to form colonywide congresses or conventions. By dissolving the colonial legislatures, royal governors unwittingly aided the work of these committees. The committees also scrutinized the activities of fellow citizens, suppressed the expression of Loyalist opinion from pulpit or press, and practiced other forms of coercion. Throughout most of the colonies, the committees formed a bridge between the old colonial administrations and the revolutionary governments organized over the next few years. Committees began to link localities

together in the cause of a wider American community. It was at this point that people began to refer to the colonies as the American "states."

Lexington and Concord

On September 1, 1774, General Gage sent troops from Boston to seize the stores of cannon and ammunition the Massachusetts militia had stored at armories in Charlestown and Cambridge. In response, the Massachusetts House of Representatives, calling itself the Provincial Congress, created a Committee of Safety empowered to call up the militia. On October 15, the committee authorized the creation of special units, to be known as "minutemen," who stood ready to be called at a moment's notice. The armed militia of the towns and communities surrounding Boston faced the British army, quartered in the city. It was no rabble he was up against, Gage wrote to his superiors, but "the freeholders and farmers" of New England who believed they were defending their communities. Worrying that his forces were insufficient to suppress the rebellion, he

OVERVIEW

ELEVEN BRITISH MEASURES THAT LED TO REVOLUTION

Legislation	Year	
Sugar Act	*1764*	Placed prohibitive duty on imported sugar; provided for greater regulation of American shipping to suppress smuggling
Stamp Act	*1765*	Required the purchase of specially embossed paper for newspapers, legal documents, licenses, insurance policies, ships' papers, and playing cards; struck at printers, lawyers, tavern owners, and other influential colonists. Repealed in 1766
Declaratory Act	*1766*	Asserted the authority of Parliament to make laws binding the colonies "in all cases whatsoever"
Townshend Revenue Acts	*1767*	Placed import duties, collectible before goods entered colonial markets, on many commodities including lead, glass, paper, and tea. Repealed in 1770
Tea Act	*1773*	Gave the British East India Company a monopoly on all tea imports to America, hitting at American merchants
Coercive or Intolerable Acts	*1774*	
Boston Port Bill		Closed Boston Harbor
Massachusetts Government Act		Annulled the Massachusetts colonial charter
Administration of Justice Act		Protected British officials from colonial courts by sending them home for trial if arrested
Quartering Act		Legalized the housing of British troops in private homes
Quebec Act		Created a highly centralized government for Canada

MAP EXPLORATION

To explore an interactive version of this map, go to
www.prenhall.com/faragher/map6.4

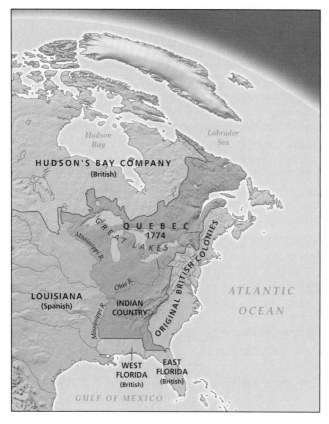

MAP 6.4 The Quebec Act of 1774 With the Quebec Act,
Britain created a centralized colonial government for Canada
and extended that colony's administrative control southwest
to the Ohio River, invalidating the sea-to-sea boundaries
of many colonial charters.

requested reinforcements. The stalemate continued through the fall and winter.

But King George was convinced that the time had come for war. "The New England governments are in a state of rebellion," he wrote privately. "Blows must decide whether they are to be subject to this country or independent." In Parliament, Pitt proposed withdrawing troops from Boston, but was overruled by a large margin. Attempting to find a balance between hard-liners and advocates of conciliation, Lord North organized majority support in the House of Commons for a plan in which Parliament would "forbear" to levy taxes for purposes of revenue once the colonies had agreed to tax themselves for the common defense. But simultaneously Parliament passed legislation severely restraining colonial commerce.

"A great empire and little minds go ill together," Edmund Burke quipped in March 1775 in a brilliant speech in Parliament opposing this bill. "Let it be once understood that your government may be one thing and their privileges another, that these two things may exist without any mutual relation." Then he declared in prophetic words, "The cement is gone, the cohesion is loosened, and everything hastens to decay and dissolution."

In Virginia, at almost the same moment, Patrick Henry predicted that hostilities would soon begin in New England. "Gentlemen may cry peace, peace!—but there is no peace," he thundered in prose later memorized by millions of American schoolchildren. "Is life so dear, or peace so sweet, as to be purchased at the price of chains and slavery? Forbid it, Almighty God! I know not what course others may take, but as for me, give me liberty or give me death!" Three weeks later, on April 14, General Gage received orders to strike at once against the Massachusetts militia.

On the evening of April 18, 1775, Gage ordered 700 men to capture the store of American ammunition at the town of Concord. Learning of the operation, the Boston committee dispatched two men, Paul Revere and William Dawes, to alert the militia of the countryside. By the time the British forces had reached Lexington, midway to their destination, some seventy armed minutemen had assembled on the green in the center of town, but they were disorganized and confused. "Lay down your arms, you damned rebels, and disperse!" cried one of the British officers. The Americans began to withdraw in the face of overwhelming opposition, but they took their arms with them. "Damn you, why don't you lay down your arms!" someone shouted from the British lines. "Damn them! We will have them!" No order to fire was given, but shots rang out, killing eight Americans and wounding ten others.

The British marched on to Concord, where they burned a small quantity of supplies and cut down a liberty pole. Meanwhile, news of the skirmish at Lexington had spread through the country, and the militia companies of communities from miles around converged on the town. Seeing smoke, they mistakenly concluded that the troops were burning homes. "Will you let them burn the town!" one man cried, and the Americans moved to the Concord bridge. There they attacked a British company, killing three soldiers—the first British casualties of the Revolution. The British immediately turned back for Boston, but were attacked by Americans at many points along the way. Reinforcements met them at Lexington, preventing a complete disaster, but by the time they finally marched into Boston, 73 were dead and 202 wounded or missing (see Map 6.5). The British troops were vastly outnumbered by the approximately 4,000 Massachusetts militiamen, who suffered 95 casualties.

PREMIÈRE ASSEMBLÉE DU CONGRÈS.

The engraving of the first session of the Continental Congress, published in France in 1782, is the only contemporary illustration of the meeting. Peyton Randolph of Virginia presides from the elevated chair, but otherwise there are no recognizable individuals. The Congress had to find a way to form a community among the leaders from each of the colonies without compromising their local identities.

SOURCE: Courtesy of Library of Congress.

The engagement forecast what would be a central problem for the British: they would be forced to fight an armed population defending their own communities against outsiders.

DECIDING FOR INDEPENDENCE

"We send you momentous intelligence," read the letter received by the Charleston, South Carolina, Committee of Correspondence on May 8, reporting the violence in

Massachusetts. Community militia companies mobilized throughout the colonies. At Boston, thousands of militiamen from Massachusetts and the surrounding provinces besieged the city, leaving the British no escape but by sea; their siege would last for nearly a year. Meanwhile, delegates from twelve colonies reconverged on Philadelphia.

The Second Continental Congress

The members of the Second Continental Congress, which opened on May 10, 1775, represented twelve of the British colonies on the mainland of North America. From New Hampshire to South Carolina, Committees of Observation and Safety had elected colonywide conventions, and these extralegal bodies in turn had chosen delegates. Consequently, few conservatives or Loyalists were among them. Georgia, unrepresented at the first session of the Continental Congress, remained absent at the opening of the second. The newest mainland colony, it depended heavily on British subsidies, and its leaders were cautious, fearing both slave and Indian uprisings. But in 1775, the political balance in Georgia shifted in favor of the radicals, and by the end of the summer the colony had delegates in Philadelphia.

Among the delegates at the Continental Congress were many familiar faces and a few new ones, including Thomas Jefferson, a plantation owner and lawyer from Virginia, gifted with one of the most imaginative and analytical minds of his time. All the delegates carried news of the enthusiasm for war that raged in their home provinces. "A frenzy of revenge seems to have seized all ranks of people," said Jefferson. George Washington attended all the sessions in uniform. "Oh that I was a soldier," an envious

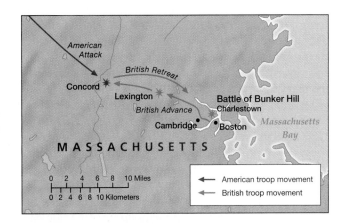

MAP 6.5 The First Engagements of the Revolution The first military engagements of the American Revolution took place in the spring of 1775 in the countryside surrounding Boston.

Soon after the fighting at Lexington and Concord, the artist Ralph Earl and the engraver Amos Doolittle visited the location and interviewed participants. They produced a series of four engravings of the incident, the first popular prints of the battles of the Revolutionary War. This view shows British troops marching to occupy Concord.

SOURCE: The Granger Collection, New York.

John Adams wrote to his wife, Abigail. The delegates agreed that defense was the first issue on their agenda.

On May 15, the Second Continental Congress resolved to put the colonies in a state of defense, but the delegates were divided on how best to do it. They lacked the power and the funds to immediately raise and supply an army. After debate and deliberation, John Adams made the practical proposal that the delegates simply designate as a Continental Army the militia forces besieging Boston. On June 14, the Congress resolved to supplement the New England militiamen with six companies of expert riflemen raised in Pennsylvania, Maryland, and Virginia. The delegates agreed that in order to emphasize their national aspirations, they had to select a man from the South to command these New England forces. All eyes turned to George Washington. Although Washington had suffered defeat at the beginning of the Seven Years' War, he had subsequently compiled a distinguished record. On June 15, Jefferson and Adams nominated Washington to be commander-in-chief of all Continental forces, and he

was elected by a unanimous vote. He served without salary. The Continental Congress soon appointed a staff of major generals to support him. On June 22, in a highly significant move, the Congress voted to finance the army with an issue of $2 million in bills of credit, backed by the good faith of the Confederated Colonies. Thus began the long and complicated process of financing the Revolution.

During its first session in the spring of 1775, the Continental Congress had begun to move cautiously down the path toward independence. Few would admit, even to themselves, however, that this was their goal. John Adams, who was close to advocating independence, wrote that he was "as fond of reconciliation as any man" but found the hope of peaceful resolution unreasonable. "The cancer is too deeply rooted," he thought, "and too far spread to be cured by anything short of cutting it out entire." Still, on July 5, 1775, the delegates passed the so-called Olive Branch Petition, written by John Dickinson of Pennsylvania, in which they professed their attachment to

King George and begged him to prevent further hostilities so that there might be an accommodation. The next day they approved a Declaration of the Causes and Necessities of Taking Up Arms, written by Jefferson and Dickinson. Here the delegates adopted a harder tone, resolving "to die freemen rather than to live slaves." Before the Second Continental Congress adjourned at the beginning of August, the delegates appointed commissioners to negotiate with the Indian nations in an attempt to keep them out of the conflict. They also reinstated Benjamin Franklin as postmaster general in order to keep the mails moving and protect communication among the colonies.

Canada, the Spanish Borderlands, and the Revolution

How did the rest of North America react to the coming conflict? The Continental Congress contacted many of the other British colonies. In one of their first acts, delegates called on "the oppressed inhabitants of Canada" to join in the struggle for "common liberty." After the Seven Years' War, the British treated Quebec as a conquered province, and French Canadians felt little sympathy for the empire. On the other hand, the Americans were traditional enemies, much feared because of their aggressive expansionism. Indeed, when the Canadians failed to respond positively and immediately, the Congress reversed itself and voted to authorize a military expedition against Quebec to eliminate any possibility of a British invasion from that quarter, thus killing any chance of the Canadians' joining the anti-British cause. This set a course toward the development of the separate nations of the United States and Canada.

There was some sympathy at first for the American struggle in the British island colonies. The legislative assemblies of Jamaica, Grenada, and Barbados declared themselves in accord with the Continental Congress, but the British navy prevented them from sending representatives. A delegation from Bermuda succeeded in getting to Philadelphia, but the Americans were so preoccupied with more pressing matters they were unable to provide any assistance, and the spark of resistance on the island sputtered out. The island colonies would remain aloof from the imperial crisis, largely because the colonists there were dependent on a British military presence to guard against slave revolts. Things at first seemed more promising in Nova Scotia (not then a part of Canada), where many New Englanders had relocated after the expulsion of the Acadians. There had been Stamp Act demonstrations in Halifax, and when the British attempted to recruit among the Nova Scotians for soldiers to serve in Boston, one community responded that since "almost

all of us [were] born in New England, [we are] divided betwixt natural affection to our nearest relations and good faith and friendship to our king and country." The British naval stronghold at Halifax, however, secured the province for the empire. Large contingents of British troops also kept Florida (which Britain had divided into the two colonies of East and West Florida) solidly in the empire.

In Cuba, some 3,000 exiled Spanish Floridians, who had fled rather than live under British rule in 1763, clamored for Spain to retake their homeland. Many of them were active supporters of American independence. (Two centuries later, there would be thousands of Cuban exiles in Florida.) Spanish authorities in Cuba, who also administered the newly acquired colony of Louisiana, were somewhat torn in their sympathies. They certainly felt no solidarity with the cause of rebellion, which they understood posed a great danger to monarchy and empire. But with painful memories of the British invasion of Havana in 1763, they passionately looked forward to working revenge on their traditional enemy, as well as to regaining control of the Floridas and eliminating the British threat to their Mexican and Caribbean colonies. In 1775, Spain adopted the recommendation of the Havana authorities and declared a policy of neutrality in the looming independence struggle.

Secretly, however, Spain looked for an opportunity to support the Americans. That presented itself in the late spring of 1776, when a contingent of Americans arrived in Spanish New Orleans via the Mississippi River bearing a proposal from patriot forces in Virginia. British naval supremacy was making it impossible to obtain supplies from overseas. Would the Spanish be willing to quietly sell guns, ammunition, and other provisions to the Americans in New Orleans and allow them to be shipped by way of the Mississippi and Ohio Rivers? If they were cooperative, the Americans might be willing to see the Spanish retake possession of the Floridas and administer them as a "protectorate" for the duration of the independence struggle. Authorities forwarded the proposal to Spain, where a few months later the Spanish king and his ministers approved the plan. Havana and New Orleans became important supply centers for the patriots.

Fighting in the North and South

Both North and South saw fighting in 1775 and early 1776. In May 1775, a small force of armed New Englanders under the command of Ethan Allen of Vermont surprised the British garrison at Fort Ticonderoga on Lake Champlain, demanding—"in the name of Great Jehovah and the Continental Congress"—that the commander surrender. The Continental Congress, in fact, knew nothing of this campaign, and when news of it arrived, members of the New York delegation were distressed at this New England violation of their territorial sovereignty. With great effort, the Americans transported the fort's cannon overland to be used in the siege of Boston.

At Boston, the British hastened to reinforce Gage's forces and by the middle of June 1775 had approximately 6,500 soldiers in the city. By that time the American forces had increased to nearly 10,000. Fearing Gage would occupy the heights south of town, the Americans countered by occupying the Charlestown peninsula to the north. On June 17, British ships in the harbor began to fire on the American positions, and Gage decided on a frontal assault to dislodge them. In bloody fighting that, although it occurred at Breed's Hill, has since been known as the Battle of Bunker Hill,

the British finally succeeded in routing the Americans, killing 140 men, but not before suffering over a thousand casualties of their own, including 226 dead. The fierce reaction in England to this enormous loss ended all possibility of any last-minute reconciliation. In August 1775, King George rejected the Olive Branch Petition and issued a royal proclamation declaring the colonists to be in "open and avowed rebellion." "Divers wicked and desperate persons" were the cause of the problem, said the king, and he called on his loyal subjects in America to "bring the traitors to justice."

In June 1775, the Continental Congress assembled an expeditionary force against Canada. One thousand Americans moved north up the Hudson River corridor, and in November, General Richard Montgomery forced the capitulation of Montreal. Meanwhile, Benedict Arnold set out from Massachusetts with another American army,

The Connecticut artist John Trumbull painted *The Battle of Bunker Hill* in 1785, the first of a series that earned him the informal title of "the Painter of the Revolution." Trumbull was careful to research the details of his paintings, but composed them in the grand style of historical romance. In the early nineteenth century, he repainted this work and three other Revolutionary scenes for the rotunda of the Capitol in Washington, DC.

SOURCE: The Granger Collection.

and after a torturous march through the forests and mountains of Maine, he joined Montgomery outside the walls of Quebec. Unlike the assault of British General Wolfe in 1759, however, the American assault failed to take the city. Montgomery and 100 Americans were killed, and another 300 were taken prisoner. Although Arnold held his position, the American siege was broken the following spring by British reinforcements who had come down the St. Lawrence. By the summer of 1776, the Americans had been forced back from Canada.

Elsewhere there were successes. Washington installed artillery on the heights south of Boston, placing the city and harbor within cannon range. General William Howe, who had replaced Gage, had little choice but to evacuate the city. In March, the British sailed out of Boston harbor for the last time, heading north to Halifax with at least 1,000 American Loyalists. In the South, American militia rose against the Loyalist forces of Virginia's Governor Dunmore, who had alienated the planter class by promising freedom to any slave who would fight with the British. After a decisive defeat of his forces, Dunmore retreated to British naval vessels, from which he shelled and destroyed much of the city of Norfolk, Virginia, on January 1, 1776. In North Carolina, the rebel militia crushed a Loyalist force at the Battle of Moore's Creek Bridge near Wilmington in February, ending British plans for an invasion of that province. The British decided to attack Charleston, but at Fort Moultrie in Charleston Harbor an American force turned back the assault. It would be more than two years before the British would try to invade the South again.

No Turning Back

Hopes of reconciliation died with the mounting casualties. The Second Continental Congress, which was rapidly assuming the role of a new government for all the provinces, reconvened in September 1775 and received news of the king's proclamation that the colonies were in formal rebellion. Although the delegates disclaimed any intention of denying the sovereignty of the king, they now moved to organize an American navy. They declared British vessels open to capture and authorized privateering. The Congress took further steps toward de facto independence when it authorized contacts with foreign powers through its agents in Europe. In the spring of 1776, France, hoping that the creation of a new American nation might provide the opportunity of gaining a larger share of the colonial trade while also diminishing British power, joined Spain in approving the shipping of supplies to the rebellious provinces. The Continental Congress then declared colonial ports open to the trade of all nations but Britain.

The emotional ties to Britain proved difficult to break. But in 1776, help arrived in the form of a pamphlet written by Thomas Paine, a radical Englishman recently arrived in Philadelphia. In *Common Sense*, Paine proposed to offer "simple fact, plain argument, and common sense" on the crisis. For years, Americans had defended their actions by wrapping themselves in the mantle of British traditions. But Paine argued that the British system rested on "the base remains of two ancient tyrannies," aristocracy and monarchy, neither of which was appropriate for America. Paine placed the blame for the oppression of the colonists on the shoulders of King George, whom he labeled the "royal Brute." Appealing to the millennial spirit

The Manner in Which the American Colonies Declared Themselves INDEPENDENT of the King of ENGLAND, a 1783 English print. Understanding that the coming struggle would require the steady support of ordinary people, in the Declaration of Independence, the upper-class men of the Continental Congress asserted the right of popular revolution and the great principle of human equality.

SOURCE: The Granger Collection.

of American Protestant culture, Paine wrote: "We have it in our power to begin the world over again. A situation, similar to the present, hath not happened since the days of Noah until now." *Common Sense* was the single most important piece of writing during the Revolutionary era, selling more than 100,000 copies within a few months of its publication in January 1776. It reshaped popular thinking and put independence squarely on the agenda.

In April, the North Carolina convention, which operated as the revolutionary replacement for the old colonial assembly, became the first to empower its delegates to vote for a declaration of independence. News that the British were recruiting a force of German mercenaries to use against the Americans provided an additional push toward what now began to seem inevitable. In May, the Continental Congress voted to recommend that the individual states move as quickly as possible toward the adoption of state constitutions. When John Adams wrote, in the preamble to this statement, that "the exercise of every kind of authority under the said

crown should be totally suppressed," he sent a strong signal that the delegates were on the verge of approving a momentous declaration.

The Declaration of Independence

On June 7, 1776, Richard Henry Lee of Virginia offered a motion to the Continental Congress: "That these united colonies are, and of right ought to be, free and independent states, that they are absolved from all allegiance to the British crown, and that all political connection between them and the state of Great Britain is, and ought to be, totally dissolved." After some debate, a vote was postponed until July, but a committee composed of John Adams, Thomas Jefferson, Benjamin Franklin, Roger Sherman of Connecticut, and Robert Livingston of New York was asked to prepare a draft declaration of American independence. The committee assigned the writing to Jefferson.

The intervening month allowed the delegates to sample the public discussion and debate and receive instructions from their state conventions. By the end of

On July 9, 1776, shortly after the Declaration of Independence was signed, General Washington gathered his troops at the present-day City Hall Park in Manhattan and had the document read to them. An unruly group of soldiers and townspeople then marched to the south end of Broadway and pulled down a large gilded lead statue of King George III. The head impaled upon a stake and the rest hauled to Connecticut to be melted down for bullets. The event became a favorite scene for historical painters of the nineteenth century.

SOURCE: William Walcutt, *Pulling Down the Statue of George III at Bowling Green*, 1857. Oil on canvas, 51 5/8" × 77 5/8" Lafayette College Art Collection, Easton, Pennsylvania.

the month, all the states but New York had authorized a vote for independence. When the question came up for debate again on July 1, a large majority in the Continental Congress supported independence. The final vote, taken on July 2, was twelve in favor of independence, none against, with New York abstaining. The delegates then turned to the declaration itself and made a number of changes in Jefferson's draft, striking out, for example, a long passage condemning slavery. In this and a number of other ways, the final version was somewhat more cautious than the draft, but it was still a stirring document.

Its central section reiterated the "long train of abuses and usurpations" on the part of King George that had led the Americans to their drastic course; there was no mention of Parliament, the principal opponent since 1764. But it was the first section that expressed the highest ideals of the delegates:

We hold these truths to be self-evident, that all men are created equal, that they are endowed by their creator with certain unalienable rights, that among these are life, liberty, and the pursuit of happiness. That to secure these rights, governments are instituted among men, deriving their just powers from the consent of the governed. That whenever any form of government becomes destructive of these ends, it is the right of the people to alter or to abolish it, and to institute a new government, laying its foundation on such principles, and organizing its powers in such form, as to them shall seem most likely to effect their safety and happiness.

There was very little debate in the Continental Congress about these principles. The delegates, mostly men of wealth and position, realized that the coming struggle for independence would require the steady support of ordinary people, so they asserted this great principle of equality

CHRONOLOGY

1713	France cedes Acadia to Britain
1745	New Englanders capture Louisburg
1749	French send an expeditionary force down the Ohio River
1753	French begin building forts from Lake Erie to the Ohio
1754	Albany Congress
1755	British General Edward Braddock defeated by a combined force of French and Indians
	Britain expels Acadians from Nova Scotia
1756	Seven Years' War begins in Europe
1757	William Pitt becomes prime minister
1758	Louisburg captured by the British for the second time
1759	British capture Quebec
1763	Treaty of Paris
	Pontiac's uprising
	Proclamation of 1763 creates "Indian Country"
	Paxton Boys massacre
1764	Sugar Act
1765	Stamp Act and Stamp Act Congress
1766	Declaratory Act
1767	Townshend Revenue Acts
1768	Treaties of Hard Labor and Fort Stanwix
1770	Boston Massacre
1772	First Committee of Correspondence organized in Boston
1773	Tea Act
	Boston Tea Party
1774	Intolerable Acts
	First Continental Congress
	Dunmore's War
1775	Fighting begins at Lexington and Concord
	Second Continental Congress
1776	Americans invade Canada
	Thomas Paine's *Common Sense*
	Declaration of Independence

and the right of revolution. There was little debate about the implications or potential consequences. Surely no statement would reverberate more through American history; the idea of equality inspired the poor as well as the wealthy, women as well as men, blacks as well as whites.

But it was the third and final section that may have contained the most meaning for the delegates: "For the support of this declaration, with a firm reliance on the protection of divine providence, we mutually pledge to each other our lives, our fortunes, and our sacred honor." In voting for independence, the delegates proclaimed their community, but they also committed treason against their king and empire. They could be condemned as traitors, hunted as criminals, and stand on the scaffold to pay for their sentiments. On July 4, 1776, these men approved the text of the Declaration of Independence without dissent.

CONCLUSION

Great Britain emerged from the Seven Years' War as the dominant power in North America. Yet despite its attempts at strict regulation and determination of the course of events in its colonies, it faced consistent resistance and often complete failure. Perhaps British leaders felt as John Adams had when he attended the first session of the Continental Congress in 1774: how could a motley collection of "ambassadors from a dozen belligerent powers" effectively organize as a single, independent, and defiant body? The British underestimated the political consensus that existed among the colonists about the importance of "republican" government. They also underestimated the ability of the colonists to inform one another, to work together, to build a sentiment of nationalism that cut across the boundaries of ethnicity, region, and economic status. Through newspapers, pamphlets, Committees of Correspondence, community organizations, and group protest, the colonists discovered the concerns they shared, and in so doing they fostered a new, American identity. Without that identity it would have been difficult for them to consent to the treasonous act of declaring independence, especially when the independence they sought was from an international power that dominated much of the globe.

REVIEW QUESTIONS

1. How did overwhelming British success in the Seven Years' War lead to an imperial crisis in British North America?
2. Outline the changes in British policy toward the colonies from 1750 to 1776.
3. Trace the developing sense of an American national community over this same period.

4. What were the principal events leading to the beginning of armed conflict at Lexington and Concord?
5. How were the ideals of American republicanism expressed in the Declaration of Independence?

RECOMMENDED READING

Benedict Anderson, *Imagined Communities: Reflections on the Origin and Spread of Nationalism*, rev. ed. (1991). An argument that the essential first act of national consciousness is the effort to create a community that encompasses more than just local individuals and groups.

Fred Anderson, *The Crucible of War: The Seven Years' War and the Fate of Empire in British North America, 1754–1766* (2000). A new and powerful history of the war, arguing that it created a "hollow British empire."

Bernard Bailyn, *The Ideological Origins of the American Revolution* (1967). Whereas other accounts stress economic or social causes, this classic argument emphasizes the role of ideas in the advent of the Revolution. Includes an analysis of American views of the imperial crisis.

Gregory Evans Dowd, *War Under Heaven: Pontiac, the Indian Nations, and the British Empire* (2002) Artfully crafted and gracefully written, this book restores Pontiac as a preeminent figure in the uprisings that bore his name.

Eric Foner, *Tom Paine and Revolutionary America* (1976). Combines a biography of Paine with a community study of the Revolution in Philadelphia and Pennsylvania.

Pauline Maier, *American Scripture: Making the Declaration of Independence* (1997). The deep background of this foundation of American democracy.

Richard L. Merritt, *Symbols of American Community, 1735–1775* (1966). A study of colonial newspapers that provides evidence for a rising sense of national community. The French and Indian War emerges as the key period for the growth of nationalist sentiment.

Ray Raphael, *First American Revolution: Before Lexington and Concord* (2002). A vivid account of the turbulent days in Massachusetts from the time the province received word of the Massachusetts Government Act in August 1774 until the fighting broke out at Lexington and Concord the following April.

 For additional study resources for this chapter, go to the *Companion Website*, http://www.prenhall.com/faragher.

The American Revolution

1776–1786

A National Community Evolves at Valley Forge

A drum roll ushered in a January morning in 1778, summoning the Continental Army to roll call. Along a two-mile line of log cabins, doors slowly opened and ragged men stepped out onto the frozen ground of Valley Forge. "There comes a soldier," wrote army surgeon Albigense Waldo. "His bare feet are seen through his worn-out shoes, his legs nearly naked from the tattered remains of an only pair of stockings, his breeches not sufficient to cover his nakedness, his shirt hanging in strings, his hair disheveled, his face meagre." The reek of foul straw and unwashed bodies filled the air. "No bread, no soldier!" The chant began as a barely audible murmur, then was picked up by men all along the line. "No bread, no soldier! No bread, no soldier!" At last the chanting grew so loud it could be heard at General Washington's headquarters, a mile away. The 11,000 men of the American army were surviving on little more than "firecake," a mixture of flour and water baked hard before the fire that, according to Waldo, turned "guts to pasteboard." Two thousand men were without shoes; others were without blankets and had to sit up all night about the fires to keep from freezing. Washington fired off an appeal for supplies to the Continental Congress. "Three or four days of bad weather," he wrote, "would prove our destruction."

A year before, the army had suffered through a terrible winter at their encampment at Morristown, New Jersey. It was their hard winter at Valley Forge, however, that became a national symbol of endurance. After suffering a series of terrible defeats at the hands of a British force nearly twice their number, the soldiers of the Continental Army had straggled into winter headquarters in this valley, some twenty miles northwest of Philadelphia, only to find themselves at the mercy of indifferent local suppliers. Contractors demanded exorbitant rates for food and clothing, rates the Congress refused to pay, and as a result, local farmers preferred to deal with the British, who paid in pounds sterling, not depreciated Continental currency.

The 11,000 men of the Continental Army, who had not been paid for nearly six months, were divided into sixteen brigades composed of regiments from the states. An unsympathetic observer described them as "a vagabond army of ragamuffins," and indeed many were drawn from the ranks of the poor and disadvantaged: indentured servants, landless farmers, and nearly a thousand African Americans, both slave and free. Most of the men came from thinly settled farm districts or small towns where precautions regarding sanitation had been unnecessary. Every thaw that winter revealed ground covered with "much filth and nastiness," and officers ordered sentinels to fire on any man "easing himself elsewhere than at ye vaults." Such conditions bred infectious epidemic diseases such as typhoid that spread quickly among men already weakened from dysentery, malnutrition, and exposure. An estimated 2,500 men lost their lives that winter. There were at least 700 women encamped at Valley Forge—wives, lovers, cooks, laundresses, and prostitutes—and they were kept busy nursing the sick and burying the dead. "What then is to become of this army?" Washington worried in December.

Despite the losses, however, the army that marched out of Valley Forge five months later was considerably stronger for its experience there. As psychologists today

Valley Forge

understand, it is the spirit of community among fighting men that contributes most to their success in battle. The men spent the late winter and spring drilling under the strict command of Friedrich Wilhelm Augustus von Steuben, a Prussian officer who came to America to volunteer for the American cause. The men learned to fight as a unit. But most important were the bonds forged among them. Through "their hardships, dangers, and sufferings," wrote Private Joseph Plumb Martin, soldiers from hundreds of localities and a variety of ethnic backgrounds had fashioned "a band of brotherhood." The brigades of farmers, indentured servants, and former slaves became living examples of the egalitarian ideals of the Revolution.

To some American Patriots—as the supporters of the Revolution called themselves—the European-style Continental Army betrayed the ideals of the citizen-soldier and the autonomy of local communities that were central tenets of the Revolution. Washington argued strongly, however, that the Revolution could not be won without a national army insulated from politics and able to withstand the shifting popular mood. Moreover, during the critical period of the nation's founding, the Continental Army acted as a popular democratic force, counterbalancing the conservatism of the new republic's elite leadership. The national spirit built at Valley Forge would sustain the fighting men through years of war and provide momentum for the long process of forging a national political system out of the persistent localism of American politics. The soldiers of the Continental Army were among the first of their countrymen to think of themselves as Americans.

KEY TOPICS

- The major alignments and divisions among Americans during the American Revolution

- Major military campaigns of the Revolution

- The Articles of Confederation and the role of the Confederation Congress during the Revolutionary War

- The states as the setting for significant political change

THE WAR FOR INDEPENDENCE

At the beginning of the Revolution, the British had the world's best-equipped and most disciplined army, as well as a navy that was unopposed in American waters. But they greatly underestimated the American capacity to fight. With a native officer corps and considerable experience in the colonial wars of the eighteenth century, the Patriot forces proved formidable. The British also misperceived the sources of the conflict. Seeing the rebellion as the work of a small group of disgruntled conspirators, initially they defined their objective as defeating this Patriot opposition. They believed that in the wake of a military victory they could easily reassert political control. But the geography of eastern North America offered no single vital center whose conquest would end the war. The Patriots had the advantage of fighting on their own ground and among a population thinly spread over a territory stretching along 1,500 miles of coastline and extending 100 miles or more into the interior. When the British succeeded in defeating the Patriots in one area, resistance would spring up in another. The key factor in the outcome of the war for independence, then, was the popular support for the American cause.

The Patriot Forces

Most American men of fighting age had to face the call to arms. From a population of approximately 350,000 eligible men, more than 200,000 saw action, though no more

Jean Baptiste Antoine de Verger, a French officer serving with the Continental Army, made these watercolors of American soldiers during the Revolution. Some 200,000 men saw action, including at least 5,000 African Americans; more than half of these troops served with the Continental Army.

SOURCE: Anne S.K. Brown Military Collection, John Hay Library, Brown University.

mitment to a truly national army. His views conflicted with popular fears of a standing army. Congress initially refused to invoke a draft or mandate army enlistments exceeding one year.

The failings of the militias in the early battles of the war sobered Congress, however, and it responded by greatly enlarged state quotas for the army and extended the term of service to three years or the war's duration. To spur enlistment, Congress offered bounties, regular wages, and promises of free land after victory. By the spring of 1777, Washington's army had grown to nearly 9,000 men.

Discipline was essential in a conflict in which men fired at close range, charged with bayonets drawn, and engaged in hand-to-hand combat. One Connecticut soldier wrote of the effects of cannon on his regiment: "The ball first cut off the head of Smith, a stout heavy man, and dashed it open, then took Taylor across the bowels; it then struck Sergeant Garret of our company on the hip, took off the point of the hip bone." And he concluded: "Oh! What a sight that was, to see within a distance of six rods those men with their legs and arms and guns and packs all in a heap." A sergeant witnessed British troops slaughtering wounded Americans during the battles in New Jersey: "The men that was wounded in the thigh or leg, they dashed out their brains with their muskets and run them through with their bayonets, made them like sieves. This was barbarity to the utmost."

According to the best estimates, a total of 25,324 American men died in the Revolutionary War, approximately 6,800 from wounds suffered in battle, 8,000 from the effects of disease, the rest as prisoners of war or missing in action. Regiments of the Continental Army experienced the heaviest casualty rates, sometimes approaching 40 percent. Indeed, the casualty rate overall was higher than in any other American conflict except the Civil War. In most areas, the war claimed few civilian lives, for it was confined largely to direct engagements between armies. There were many noncombatant casualties, however, in the backcountry and the South, where Patriot and Loyalist militias waged vicious campaigns of violence.

than 25,000 were engaged at any one time. More than 100,000 served in the Continental Army, under Washington's command and the authority of the Continental Congress; the rest served in Patriot militia companies.

These militias—armed bodies of men drawn from local communities—proved important in the defense of their own areas, for they had homes as well as local reputations to protect. But the Revolutionary War was not won by citizen-soldiers who exchanged plows for guns, or backcountry riflemen who picked off British soldiers from behind trees. In the exuberant days of 1776, many Patriots did believe that militias alone could win the war against the British. As one observer noted, "the *Rage Militaire*, as the French call a passion for arms, has taken possession of the whole Continent." But because men preferred to serve with their neighbors in local companies rather than subject themselves to the discipline of the regular service, the states failed to meet their quotas for regiments in the Continental Army. Serving short terms of enlistment, often with officers of their own choosing, militiamen resisted discipline. Indeed, in the face of battle, militia companies demonstrated appalling rates of desertion.

The final victory, rather, resulted primarily from the steady struggle of the Continental Army. The American Revolution had little in common with modern national liberation movements in which armed populations engage in guerrilla warfare. Washington and his officers wanted a force that could directly engage the British, and from the beginning of the war, he argued with a skeptical Congress that victory could be won only with a full com-

Both the Continentals and the militias played important political roles as well. At a time when Americans identified most strongly with their local communities or their states, the Continental Army, through experiences like the Valley Forge winter, evolved into a powerful force for nationalist sentiment. But shortages of food and pay led to several notable army mutinies. In the most serious incident, among the Pennsylvania Line in January 1781, enlisted men killed one officer, wounded two others, and set off from their winter quarters in New Jersey for Philadelphia to ask Congress to uphold its commitments. As they marched, they were joined by British agents who encouraged them to go over to the king. Enraged at this attempt at subversion, the mutineers hanged the agents and gave up their resistance. Angry as they were at Congress, they were Americans first and hated the British. Over 100,000 men from every state served in the Continental Army, contributing mightily to the unity of purpose—the formation of a national community—that was essential to the process of nation making.

In most communities, Patriots had seized control of local government during the period of committee organizing in 1774 and 1775 (see Chapter 6), and with war imminent, they pressed the obligation to serve in a Patriot militia upon most eligible men. In Farmington, Connecticut, in 1776, eighteen men who failed to join the muster of the local militia were imprisoned "on suspicion of their being inimical to America." After individual grilling by the authorities, they petitioned for pardon. They were "penitent of their former conduct," it was reported, and understood "that there was no such thing" as remaining neutral. Probably the most important role of the Patriot militias was to force even the most apathetic of Americans to choose sides under the close scrutiny of their neighbors.

As men marched off to war, many women assumed the management of family farms and businesses. Abigail Adams, for example, ran the Adams family's farm at Quincy for years, reporting on operations in frequent letters to her husband, John, letters that included commentary on the American struggle for independence and the political structure of the new republic. Some women participated even more directly in patriotic politics. Mercy Otis Warren, sister of the Patriot James Otis Jr., turned her home into a center of Patriot political activity and published a series of satires supporting the American cause and scorning the Loyalists. Thousands of women volunteered to support the war effort by working as seamstresses, nurses, even spies.

It was common for women to travel with the armies of both sides. Some "camp followers," as they were called, were prostitutes, but most were wives, cooks, launderers, and nurses. An observer of the British army after one terrible battle noted the presence of "great numbers of women, who seemed to be the beasts of burthen, having a bushel basket on their backs, by which they were bent double. The contents seemed to be pots and kettles, various sorts of furniture, children peeping thro' gridirons and other utensils, some very young infants who were born on the road, the women [with] bare feet, cloath'd in dirty raggs. . . ." Women not only shared the hardships with the soldiers, they were present on the

battlefields carrying water, food, and supplies to the soldiers in the front lines, under cannon and musket fire. (See Out of Many Voices: A Camp Woman's Recollection of Yorktown.) Tales were later told of one "Molly Pitcher," a wife who took her husband's place at the cannon when he was killed by shrapnel. The Continental Congress later awarded a pension to Margaret Corbin, who was wounded while filling in for her mortally wounded husband. In fact, many such women won pensions for wounds suffered in battle: Mary Hays McCauley, known to the soldiers as "Sgt. McCauley," and Anna Maria Lane, wife of a Connecticut enlisted man, who "in the garb and with the courage of a soldier performed extraordinary military services and received a severe wound at the Battle of Germantown." One historian estimates that several hundred women disguised themselves as men and enlisted; one of them, Deborah Sampson of Massachusetts, was the subject of a sensational biography after the war and became the first American woman to embark on a lecture tour.

John Singleton Copley's portrait of Mercy Otis Warren captured her at the age of thirty-six, in 1765. During the Revolution, her home in Boston was a center of patriotic political activity.

SOURCE: John Singleton Copley, U.S., 1738–1815. *Mrs. James Warren (Mercy Otis)*, ca. 1763. Oil on canvas. 51¼ × 41 in. (130.1 × 104.1 cm). Bequest of Winslow Warren. Courtesy of Museum of Fine Art, Boston.

The Loyalists

Not all Americans were Patriots. Many sat on the fence, confused by the conflict, and waiting for a clear turn in the tide of the struggle before declaring their allegiance. Between a fifth and a third of the population, somewhere between half a million and a million people, remained loyal to the British crown. They called themselves Loyalists, but to Patriots were known as the Tories, the popular name for the conservative party in England, which traditionally supported the authority of the king over Parliament.

A large proportion of the Loyalists—some two-thirds of those who later filed for compensation from the British government—were relatively recent migrants to the colonies, born in England, Scotland,

OUT OF MANY VOICES

A CAMP WOMAN'S RECOLLECTION OF YORKTOWN

Young Sarah Osborn Benjamin accompanied her husband, a commissary sergeant with the Third New York Regiment, through numerous campaigns. In 1837, more than a half century later, then a woman in her eighties, she applied for (and was granted) a widow's pension from the federal government. In the deposition supporting her application, she told of participating in the Battle of Yorktown.

THEY ... MARCHED ... FOR A PLACE CALLED Williamsburg, as she thinks, deponent alternately on horseback and on foot. There arrived, they remained two days till the army all came in by land and then marched for Yorktown, or Little York as it was then called. ... Deponent was on foot and the other females above named and her said husband still on the commissary's guard. Deponent's attention was arrested by the appearance of a large plain between them and Yorktown and an entrenchment thrown up. She also saw a number of dead Negroes lying round their encampment, whom she understood the British had driven out of the town and left to starve, or were first starved and then thrown out. Deponent took her stand just back of the American tents, say about a mile from the town, and busied herself washing, mending, and cooking for the soldiers, in which she was assisted by the other females; some men washed their own clothing. She heard the roar of the artillery for a number of days, and the last night the Americans threw up entrenchments, it was a misty, foggy night, rather wet but not rainy. Every soldier threw up for himself, as she understood, and she afterwards saw and went into the entrenchments. Deponent's said husband was there throwing up entrenchments, and deponent cooked and carried in beef, and bread, and coffee (in a gallon pot) to the soldiers in the entrenchment.

On one occasion when deponent was thus employed carrying in provisions, she met General Washington, who asked her if she "was not afraid of the cannonballs?" She replied, "No, the bullets would not cheat the gallows," that "It would not do for the men to fight and starve too."

They dug entrenchments nearer and nearer to Yorktown every night or two till the last. While digging that, the enemy fired very heavy till about nine o'clock next morning, then stopped, and the drums from the enemy beat excessively....The drums continued beating, and all at once the officers hurrahed and swung their hats, and deponent asked them, "What is the matter now?" One of them replied, "Are not you soldier enough to know what it means?" Deponent replied, "No." They then replied, "The British have surrendered."

... Deponent stood on one side of the road and the American officers upon the other side when the British officers came out of the town and rode up to the American officers and delivered up [their swords, which the deponent] thinks were returned again, and the British officers rode right on before the army, who marched out beating and playing a melancholy tune, their drums covered with black handkerchiefs and their fifes with black ribbands tied around them, into an old field and there grounded their arms and then returned into town again to await their destiny. Deponent recollects seeing a great many American officers, some on horseback and some on foot, but cannot call them all by name. Washington, Lafayette, and Clinton were among the number. The British general at the head of the army was a large, portly man, full face, and the tears rolled down his cheeks as he passed along. She does not recollect his name, but it was not Cornwallis. She saw the latter afterwards and noticed his being a man of diminutive appearance and having cross eyes. ■

SOURCE: John C. Dann, ed., *The Revolution Remembered: Eyewitness Accounts of the War for Independence* (Chicago: University of Chicago Press, 1980), pp. 244–46.

or Ireland. Others, such as royal office-holders or Anglican clergymen, were dependent on the British government for their salaries. Many Loyalists were men of conservative temperament, fearful of political or social upheaval. The Loyalists included members of ethnic minorities who had been persecuted by the dominant majority, such as the Highland Scots of the Carolinas and western New York, and southern tenant farmers who had Patriot landlords. As this suggests, Loyalists were particularly strong in some colonies. They were nearly a majority in New York, and were so numerous in Pennsylvania that an officer of the Continental Army described that colony as "the enemy's country." In Georgia, Loyalists made up such a large majority that the colony would probably have abandoned the revolutionary movement had the British not surrendered at Yorktown in 1781.

Patriots passed state treason acts that prohibited speaking or writing against the Revolution. They also punished Loyalists by issuing bills of attainder, a legal process (later made illegal by the United States Constitution) by which those who refused to swear allegiance to the Patriot cause lost their civil rights as well as their property. In some areas, Loyalists faced mob violence. One favorite punishment was the "grand Tory ride," in which a crowd hauled the victim through the streets astride a sharp fence rail. Another was tarring and feathering, in which men were stripped to "buff and breeches" and their naked flesh coated liberally with heated tar and chicken feathers. One broadside recommended that Patriots "then hold a lighted Candle to the feathers, and try to set it all on fire." The torment rarely went that far, but it was brutally painful nonetheless.

The most infamous American supporter of the British cause was Benedict Arnold, whose name has become synonymous, in the United States, with treason. Arnold was a hero of the early battles of the Revolution on the American side. But in 1779, angry and resentful about what he perceived to be assignments and rank below his station, he became a paid informer of General Henry Clinton, head of the British army in New York City. In 1780, Patriots uncovered Arnold's plot to betray the strategic post at West Point on the Hudson River, which he commanded. After fleeing to the British, who paid him a handsome stipend and pension, he became a brigadier general in the British army. Benedict Arnold became the most hated man in America. In his hometown of Norwich, Connecticut, a crowd destroyed the gravestones of his family, and in cities and towns throughout America, thousands burned his effigy. During the last two years of the war, he led British raids against his home state as well as against Virginia, and after the Revolution he lived in England until his death in 1801.

The British strategy for suppressing the Revolution depended on mobilizing the Loyalists, but in most areas this proved impossible, since they were not a monolithic group, but were divided in their opinions. As many as 50,000 Loyalists, however, fought for the king during the Revolution. Many joined Loyalist militias or engaged in irregular warfare, especially in the Lower South. In 1780, when Washington's Continentals numbered about 9,000, there were 8,000 American Loyalists serving in the British army in America.

As many as 80,000 Loyalists fled the country during and after the Revolution. Many went to England or the British West Indies, but the largest number

The TORY'S Day of JUDGMENT.

A Patriot mob torments Loyalists in this print published during the Revolution. One favorite punishment was the "grand Tory ride," in which a crowd hauled the victim through the streets astride a fence rail. In another, men were stripped to "buff and breeches" and their naked flesh coated liberally with heated tar and feathers.

SOURCE: The Granger Collection.

settled in Canada; the Canadian provinces of Ontario, Nova Scotia, and New Brunswick honor Loyalist refugees as founders. Loyalist property was confiscated by the states and sold at public auction. Although the British government compensated many for their losses, most Loyalists were unhappy exiles. "I earnestly wish to spend the remainder of my days in America," wrote William Pepperell, formerly of Maine, from London in 1778. "I love the country, I love the people." Former governor Thomas Hutchinson of Massachusetts wrote that he "had rather die in a little country farm-house in New England than in the best nobleman's seat in old England." Despite their disagreement with the Patriots on essential political questions, they remained Americans, and they mourned the loss of their country.

The Campaign for New York and New Jersey

During the winter of 1775–76 the British developed a strategic plan for the war. From his base at Halifax, Nova Scotia, Sir William Howe was to take his army to New York City, which the British navy would make impregnable. From there Howe was to drive north along the Hudson, while another British army marched south from Canada to Albany. There the two armies would converge, cutting New England off from the rest of the colonies, then turn eastward to reduce the rebellious Yankees into submission. Washington, who had arrived at Boston to take command of the militia forces there in the summer of 1775, anticipated this strategy, and in the spring of 1776, he shifted his forces southward toward New York.

In early July, as Congress was taking its final vote on the Declaration of Independence, the British began their operation at New York City, landing 32,000 men, a third of them Hessian mercenaries (from the German state of Hesse), on Staten Island. The Americans, meanwhile, set up fortified positions across the harbor in Brooklyn. Attacking in late August, the British inflicted heavy casualties on the Americans, and the militia forces under Washington's command proved unreliable under fire. The Battle of Long Island ended in disaster for the Patriots, and they were forced to withdraw across the East River to Manhattan.

The British offered Congress an opportunity to negotiate, and on September 6, Benjamin Franklin, John Adams, and Edward Rutledge sat down on Staten Island with General Howe and his brother, Admiral Richard Howe. But the meeting broke up when the Howe brothers demanded repeal of the Declaration of Independence. This set the stage for another round of fighting. Six days later, the British invaded Manhattan, and only an American stand at Harlem Heights

MAP 7.1 Campaign for New York and New Jersey, 1775–77

prevented the destruction of a large portion of the Patriot army. Enjoying naval control of the harbor, the British quickly outflanked the American positions. In a series of battles over the next few months, they forced Washington back at White Plains and overran the American posts of Fort Washington and Fort Lee, on either side of the Hudson River. By November, the Americans were fleeing south across New Jersey in a frantic attempt to avoid the British under General Charles Cornwallis (see Map 7.1).

With morale desperately low, whole militia companies deserted; others, announcing the end of their terms of enlistment, left for home. American resistance seemed to be collapsing all around Washington. "Our troops will not do their duty," he wrote painfully to Congress as he crossed the Delaware River into Pennsylvania. Upon receiving his message, the delegates in Philadelphia fled to Baltimore. "I think the game is pretty near up," Washington admitted to his brother. But rather than fall back, which would surely have meant the dissolution of his entire force, he decided to risk a counterattack. On Christmas night 1776, he led 2,400 troops back across the Delaware, and the next morning defeated the Hessian forces in a surprise attack on their headquarters at Trenton, New Jersey. The Americans inflicted further heavy losses on the British at Princeton, then drove them all the way back to the environs of New York City.

Although these small victories had little strategic importance, they salvaged American morale. As Washington settled into winter headquarters at Morristown, he realized he had to pursue a defensive strategy, avoiding direct confrontations with the British while checking their advances and hurting them wherever possible. "We cannot conquer the British force at once," wrote Major General Nathaniel Greene, "but they cannot conquer us at all." This last sentiment was more a hope than a conviction, but it defined the essentially defensive American strategy of the Revolution. Most important to that strategy was the survival of the Continental Army.

The Northern Campaigns of 1777

The fighting with the American forces had prevented Howe from moving north up the Hudson River, and the British advance southward from Canada had been stalled by American resistance at Lake Champlain. In 1777, however, the British decided to replay their strategy. From Canada they dispatched General John Burgoyne with nearly 8,000 British and German troops. Howe was to move his force from New York, first taking the city of Philadelphia, the seat of the Continental Congress, and then moving north to meet Burgoyne (see Map 7.2).

Fort Ticonderoga fell to Burgoyne on July 6, but by August, the general found himself bogged down and harassed by Patriot militias in the rough country south of Lake George. After several defeats in September at the hands of an American army commanded by General Horatio Gates, Burgoyne retreated to Saratoga. There his army was surrounded by a considerably larger force of Americans, and on October 19, lacking alternatives, he surrendered his nearly 6,000 men. It would be the biggest British defeat until Yorktown, decisive because it forced the nations of Europe to recognize that the Americans had a fighting chance to win their Revolution.

The Americans were less successful against Howe. A force of 15,000 British troops left New York in July, landing a month later at the northern end of Chesapeake Bay. On September 11, the British outflanked the American defensive position at Brandywine Creek, thirty-five miles southwest of Philadelphia, inflicting heavy casualties and forcing Washington to fall back. Ten days later, the British surprised the American encampment at Paoli, only twenty-five miles from the city, leaving many Patriots dead on the field of battle. This cleared the way for the British occupation of Philadelphia, which occurred on September 26. The Continental Congress fled to the country town of York. Washington attempted a valiant counterattack at Germantown north of the city on October 4, but initial success was followed by tactical miscoordination that doomed the operation.

After this campaign, the Continentals headed into winter quarters at Valley Forge, the bitterness of their defeats muted somewhat by news of Burgoyne's surrender at Saratoga. The British had possession of Philadelphia, the most important city in North America, but it would prove of little strategic value. The Continental Congress continued to operate at York, so the unified effort suffered little disruption. At the end of two years of fighting, despite numerous military victories, the British strategy for suppressing the revolution had to be judged a failure.

The French Alliance and the Spanish Borderlands

During these two years of fighting, the Americans were sustained by loans from France and Spain, traditional allies against Great Britain. Both saw an opportunity to win back North American territories lost as a result of the Seven Years' War. The Continental Congress sent a diplomatic delegation to Paris headed by Benjamin Franklin. The urbane and cosmopolitan Franklin, who captured French hearts by dressing in homespun and wearing a "frontiersman" fur cap, established excellent relations with Comte de Vergennes, the French foreign minister. Franklin negotiated for recognition of American independence and a Franco-American alliance against the British, in addition to loans from the French to finance the Revolution. Vergennes longed to weaken the British empire any way he could, and was inclined to support the Americans. But reluctant to encourage a republican revolution against monarchy and colonialism, he hesitated.

In England, meanwhile, the Whig opposition argued strongly against the war. "The measures toward America are erroneous," declared their leader Lord Rockingham, "adherence to them is destruction." William Pitt, in the last year of his life, warned his countrymen to "beware the gathering storm" if and when France decided to support the Americans actively. When, in December 1777, news of Burgoyne's surrender reached London, British Prime Minister Frederick Lord North urgently dispatched agents to open peace discussions with Franklin in Paris. But it was too late. The victory at Saratoga, as well as fears of British conciliation with the revolutionaries, had persuaded French Foreign Minister Vergennes to tie France to the United States. In mid-December he informed Franklin that the king's council had decided to recognize American independence.

The Treaty of Alliance between France and "the United States of North America" was to take effect "should war break out" between France and Great Britain. The French pledged to "maintain effectually the liberty, sovereignty, and independence" of its ally. "Neither of the two parties," the treaty read, "shall conclude either truce or peace with Great Britain, without the formal consent of the other." France agreed to guarantee to the United States all the "northern parts of America" as well as other "conquests"

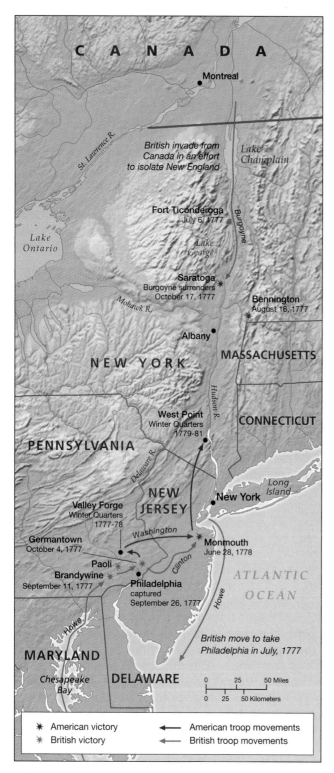

MAP 7.2 Northern Campaigns, 1777–78

Map labels:

CANADA

Montreal

St. Lawrence R.

British invade from Canada in an effort to isolate New England

Lake Champlain

Fort Ticonderoga
July 6, 1777

Lake Ontario

Lake George

Burgoyne

Saratoga
Burgoyne surrenders
October 17, 1777

Mohawk R.

Bennington
August 16, 1777

Albany

NEW YORK

MASSACHUSETTS

Hudson R.

West Point
Winter Quarters
1779-81

CONNECTICUT

PENNSYLVANIA

Delaware R.

NEW JERSEY

New York

Long Island

Valley Forge
Winter Quarters
1777-78

Washington

Clinton

Germantown
October 4, 1777

Monmouth
June 28, 1778

Paoli

Howe

ATLANTIC OCEAN

Brandywine
September 11, 1777

Philadelphia
captured
September 26, 1777

Howe

MARYLAND

British move to take
Philadelphia in July, 1777

Chesapeake Bay

DELAWARE

0   25   50 Miles
0   25   50 Kilometers

✳ American victory   ← American troop movements
✳ British victory   ← British troop movements

---

don officially informed the British government of the treaty. Fighting between the two countries broke out in June.

A year later, Spain also entered the war. Spanish officials in New Orleans were already providing substantial ammunition and provisions for American forts in the West, including supplies of beef from herds of cattle driven to New Orleans by *vaqueros* (cowboys) from Texas. In New Spain, the viceroy levied a special tax to pay for these supplies, and borderland colonists in Sonora, Texas, New Mexico, and California contributed their share. Father Junípero Serra, president of the California missions, prescribed a weekly prayer for American victory. But American attempts to establish a formal Spanish alliance met with failure. The Spanish saw the Revolution as an opportunity to regain Florida from the British and extend their control of the Mississippi Valley, but they feared the threat the Americans would pose to New Spain. "Its people are active, industrious, and aggressive," one official in Mexico wrote of the new nation, and "it would be culpable negligence on our part not to thwart their schemes for conquest."

Thus the Spanish pursued an independent strategy against the British, seizing the weakly defended Mississippi River towns of Natchez and Baton Rouge in 1779, and winning the important Gulf ports of Mobile in 1780 and Pensacola in 1781. The victory at Pensacola was achieved with the help of several companies of Florida exiles, many of them African Americans. Alarmed by the quick spread of American settlements west of the Appalachians, the Spanish attempted to establish a claim of their own to the British territory north of the Ohio; they sent an expedition into the Northwest that in 1781, succeeded in taking the minor British post of St. Joseph, in present-day Michigan.

The first French ambassador to the United States arrived with instructions to do everything he could to prevent the Americans from enlarging their territory at the expense of the Spanish borderland colonies. Like the Spanish, the French also feared the potential power of an independent American nation. Several years before, Vergennes had warned the British that if the Americans gained their independence, they "would immediately set about forming a great marine [naval armed force]," and use it in the Caribbean to "conquer both your islands and ours." Eventually they would sweep south and "not leave a foot of that hemisphere in the possession of any European power." Many American leaders did indeed have expansionist aspirations, and understood that the wartime alliance with France and tacit support of Spain were mere expedients.

Worried over the consequences of French involvement, in the spring of 1778, Lord North sent a peace

made in the war, while the United States promised to recognize French acquisitions of British islands in the West Indies. In March, the French ambassador in Lon-

commission to America with promises to repeal the parliamentary legislation that had provoked the crisis in the first place, and pledging never again to impose revenue taxes on the colonies. Three years earlier, such a pledge would surely have forestalled the movement toward independence. But the Continental Congress now declared that any person coming to terms with the British peace commission would be considered a traitor; the only possible topics of discussion were the withdrawal of British forces and the recognition of American independence.

With France in the war, the British rethought their military strategy. Considering their West Indies sugar colonies at risk, they shipped 5,000 troops from New York to the Caribbean, and succeeded in beating back a French attack. Fearing the arrival of the French fleet along the North American coast, the new British commander in America, General Henry Clinton, evacuated Philadelphia in June 1778. Washington's Continentals, fresh out of Valley Forge, went in hot pursuit. In the Battle of Monmouth, fought in stifling New Jersey heat on June 28, the British blunted the American drive and succeeded in beating an orderly retreat to New York City. The Americans, headquartered at West Point, took up defensive positions surrounding the lower Hudson River. Confidence in an impending victory now spread through the Patriot army. But after a failed American-French joint campaign against the British at Newport, Rhode Island, General Washington decided on a defensive strategy. Although the Americans enjoyed several small successes in the Northeast over the next two years, the war there went into a stall.

Indian Peoples and the Revolution in the West

At the beginning of the conflict, both sides solicited Indian support. A committee of the Continental Congress reported that "securing and preserving the friendship of Indian nations appears to be a subject of the utmost moment to these colonies." Most important was the stance of the Iroquois Confederacy—long one of the most potent political forces in colonial North America. A delegation from Congress told the Iroquois that the conflict was a "family quarrel" and urged them to keep out of it. British agents, on the other hand, pressed the Iroquois to unite against the Americans. Many Indian leaders were reluctant to get involved: "We are unwilling to join on either side of such a contest," declared an Oneida chief. "Let us Indians be all of one mind, and live with one another, and you white people settle your own disputes between yourselves."

Ultimately, however, the British proved more persuasive with their argument that a Patriot victory would mean the extension of American settlements into native homelands. Indian peoples fought in the Revolution for some of the same reasons Patriots did—political independence, cultural integrity, and the protection of their land and property—but Indian fears of American expansion led them to oppose the Patriot rhetoric of natural rights and the equality of all men. Almost all the tribes that engaged in the fighting did so on the side of the British.

British officials marshaled the support of Cherokees, Creeks, Choctaws, and Chickasaws in the South, supplying them with arms from the British arsenal at Pensacola until it was taken by the Spanish in 1781. The result was a ferocious fighting in the southern backcountry. In the summer of 1776, a large number of Cherokees, led by the warrior chief Dragging Canoe (*Tsiyu-Gunsini*), attacked dozens of American settlements. It took hard fighting before Patriot militia companies managed to drive the Cherokees into the mountains, destroying many of their towns. Although the Cherokees eventually made an official peace,

Joseph Brant, the brilliant chief of the Mohawks who sided with Great Britain during the Revolution, in a 1786 painting by the American artist Gilbert Stuart. After the Treaty of Paris, Brant led a large faction of Iroquois people north into British Canada, where they established a separate Iroquois Confederacy.

SOURCE: Gilbert Stuart. *The Mohawk Chief Joseph Brant*, 1786. Oil on canvas, 30 × 25 in. Fenimore Art Museum, Cooperstown, New York.

sporadic violence between Patriots and Indians continued along the southern frontier.

Among the Iroquois of New York, the Mohawk leader Joseph Brant (*Thayendanegea*) succeeded in bringing most Iroquois warriors into the British camp, although he was opposed by chiefs of the Oneidas and Tuscaroras, who supported the Patriots. In 1777 and 1778, Iroquois and Loyalist forces raided the northern frontiers of New York and Pennsylvania. In retaliation, an American army invaded the Iroquois homelands in 1779. Supported by Oneida and Tuscarora warriors, the Americans destroyed dozens of western villages and thousands of acres of crops. For the first time since the birth of their confederacy in the fifteenth century, the Iroquois were fighting each other (see Map 7.3).

Across the mountains, the Ohio Indians formed an effective alliance under the British at Detroit, and in 1777 and 1778, they sent warriors south against pioneer communities in western Virginia and Kentucky that had been founded in defiance of the Proclamation of 1763. Boonesborough, Kentucky, was nearly destroyed by repeated attacks, and the Americans barely held out. Virginian George Rogers Clark countered by organizing an expedition of Kentucky militia against the old French settlements in the Illinois country, which were controlled by the British. They succeeded in taking the British post at Kaskaskia in the summer of 1778, and in early 1779, in a daring winter raid on Vincennes, they captured Colonel Henry Hamilton, British commander in the West, infamously known as "the Scalp Buyer" because of the bounty he had placed on Patriots' lives.

But Clark lacked the strength to attack the strategic British garrison at Detroit. Coordinating his Iroquois forces with those in Ohio, Brant mounted a new set of offensives that cast a shadow over Clark's successes. Raids back and forth across the Ohio River by Indians and Americans claimed hundreds of lives over the next three years. The war in the West would not end with the conclusion of hostilities in the East. With barely a pause, the fighting in the trans-Appalachian West between Americans and Indians would continue for another two decades.

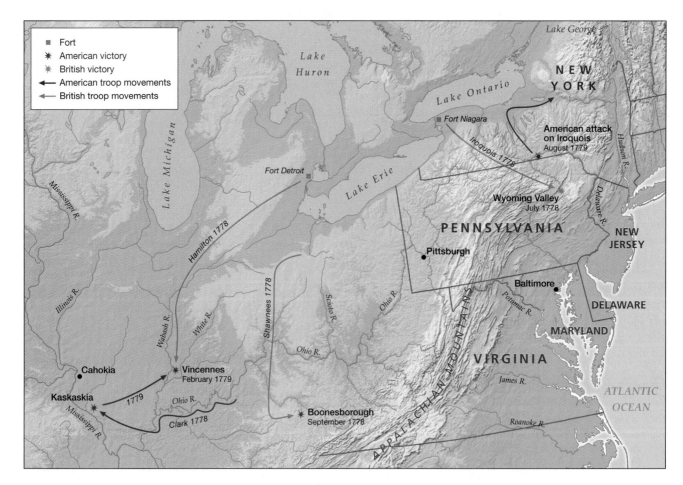

MAP 7.3 Fighting in the West, 1778–79

This American cartoon, published during the Revolution, depicts "the Scalp Buyer," Colonel Henry Hamilton, paying bounties to Indians. In fact, Indian warriors were not simply pawns of the British but fought for the same reasons the Patriots did—for political independence, cultural integrity, and protection of land and property.

SOURCE: Courtesy of the Bostonian Society/Old State House.

The War in the South

The most important fighting of the Revolution took place in the South (see Map 7.4). There the war had begun with a slave uprising. In late 1775, Lord Dunmore, the last royal governor of Virginia, issued a proclamation declaring the emancipation of all slaves and indentured servants who would desert their masters and take up arms for the British. More than 800 slaves responded to Dunmore's call. They were given uniforms emblazoned with the motto "Liberty to Slaves" and organized into an "Etheopean Corps" that fought alongside Loyalists and British troops, plundering coastal plantations and liberating more slaves. Patriots rallied, and finally routed Dunmore's army, killing many armed slaves. Many others succumbed to a virulent epidemic of smallpox. But at least 300 sailed away with Dunmore when he evacuated Virginia in July 1776.

General Clinton regained the initiative for Britain in December 1778 by sending a force from New York against Georgia, the weakest of the colonies. The British crushed the Patriot militia at Savannah and began organizing Loyalists into a fighting force in an effort to reclaim the colony. Several American counterattacks failed, including one in which they were supported by the French fleet, which bombarded Savannah. Encouraged by their success in Georgia, the British decided to apply the lessons learned there throughout the South. This involved a fundamental change from a strategy of military conquest to one of pacification. Territory would be retaken step by step, then handed over to Loyalists who would reassert colonial authority loyal to the crown. In October 1779, Clinton evacuated Rhode Island, the last British stronghold in New England, and sailed for the South with 8,000 troops. Landing at Savannah, the British force marched overland to Charleston, where they overwhelmed the American defenders and forced the surrender of more than 5,000 troops in May 1780. It was the most significant American defeat of the war. Horatio Gates, the hero of Saratoga, led a detachment of Continentals southward, but in August they were defeated by General Cornwallis at Camden, South Carolina. Patriot resistance collapsed in the Lower South, and American fortunes were suddenly at their lowest ebb since the beginning of the war.

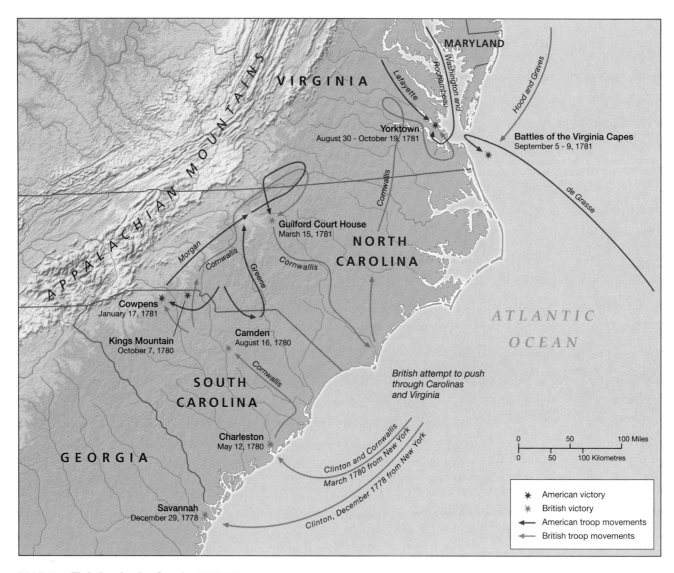

MAP 7.4 Fighting in the South, 1778–81

During the British campaign through the South, thousands of slaves responded to a British promise of liberty to those who would fight. In response, Maryland, Virginia, and North Carolina grudgingly attempted to recruit free persons of color and even slaves into their armed forces. Northern states, led by New England, had already solicited African American recruits, and Rhode Island had placed an African American regiment in the field. Some of these men served in the infantry, many more were commissary workers or teamsters. By war's end, at least 5,000 African Americans had served in Patriot militias or the Continental Army, and in the Upper South some slaves won their freedom through military service. In the Lower South, however, where the numerical superiority of slaves bred fears of rebellion among white people, there was no similar movement.

The southern campaign was marked by vicious violence between partisan militias of Patriots and Loyalists.

"The Whigs and Tories persecute each other with little less than savage fury," wrote General Greene, appointed to succeed Gates after the disaster at Camden. "There is nothing but murders and devastations in every quarter." The violence peaked in September 1780 with Cornwallis's invasion of North Carolina, where the Patriots were stronger and better organized. There the British found their southern strategy untenable: plundering towns and farms in order to feed the army in the interior had the effect of producing angry support for the Patriots. In October at King's Mountain, in the backcountry near the boundary between the Carolinas, Patriot sharpshooters outflanked and destroyed a Loyalist force, and in January 1781, Loyalists were again defeated at the Battle of the Cowpens, not far from King's Mountain.

Into 1781, the Continentals and Patriot militias waged what General Greene called a fugitive war of hit and run against the British. "I am quite tired of marching about the country in quest of adventures," Cornwallis wrote; he declared himself "totally in the dark" about what to do next. He won a victory over the Patriots at Guilford Court House in March, but, finally deciding he would not be able to hold the Carolinas as long as Virginia remained a base of support and supply for the Americans, he led his army north in the summer of 1781, establishing a base of operations at Yorktown, on Chesapeake Bay. His withdrawal from North Carolina allowed Greene to reestablish Patriot control of the Lower South.

Yorktown

While the British raged through the South, the stalemate continued in the Northeast. In the summer of 1780, taking advantage of the British evacuation of Rhode Island, the French landed 5,000 troops at Newport under the command of General Jean Baptiste Donatien de Vimeur, comte de Rochambeau. But it was not until the spring of 1781 that the general risked joining his force to Washington's Continentals north of New York City. They planned a campaign against the British in Manhattan, but in August, Washington learned that the French Caribbean fleet was headed for the Chesapeake. If he and Rochambeau could move their troops south, they might lock Cornwallis into his camp at Yorktown. Leaving a small force behind as a decoy, the two generals marched their 16,000 men overland to the Virginia shore in little more than a month.

The maneuver was a complete success. The French and Americans surrounded the British encampment and began a siege. "If you cannot relieve me very soon," Cornwallis wrote Clinton in New York, "you must expect to hear the worst." French and American heavy artillery hammered the British unmercifully until the middle of October. After the failure of a planned retreat across the York River, Cornwallis opened negotiations for the surrender of his army. Two days later, on October 19, 1781,

In 1845 Artist William Ranney depicted a famous moment during the Battle of Cowpens that took place in January 1781. Lieutenant Colonel William Washington, leader of the Patriot calvary and a relative of George Washington, was attacked by a squadron of British dragons. As Washington was about to be cut down, he was saved by his servant William Ball, who fired a pistol that wounded the attacker. Nothing more is known about Ball, but he was one of a number of African Americans who fought on the Patriot side in the battle.

SOURCE: William Ranney, *The Battle of Cowpens*. Oil on canvas. Photo by Sam Holland. Courtesy South Carolina State House.

John Trumbull's *Yorktown Surrender,* 1797. Trumbull, who prided himself on the accuracy of his work, included Cornwallis in the center of this painting. Later, when he learned that Cornwallis had not been present, he attempted to correct the error by changing the color of the uniform to blue, thereby making "Cornwallis" into an American general.

SOURCE: The Granger Collection, New York.

between lines of victorious American and French soldiers, the British troops came out from their trenches to surrender, marching to the melancholy tune of "The World Turned Upside Down":

> *If buttercups buzzed after the bee,*
> *If boats were on land, churches on sea,*
> *If summer were spring and t'other way round,*
> *Then all the world would be upside down.*

It must have seemed that way to Cornwallis. Pleading illness, he sent his second-in-command, General Charles O'Hara, to surrender. O'Hara first approached General Rochambeau, but the Frenchman waved him toward Washington. To the British, it was inconceivable that they would be required to surrender to former subordinates. Everyone knew this was an event of incalculable importance, but few guessed it was the end of the war, for the British still controlled New York.

In London, at the end of November, Lord North received the news "as he would have taken a ball in the breast," reported the colonial secretary. "Oh God!" he moaned, "it is all over!" British fortunes were at low

ebb in India, the West Indies, Florida, and the Mediterranean, the cost of the war was enormous, and there was little support among the public and members of Parliament for it. King George III wished to press on, but North submitted his resignation, and in March 1782, the king agreed to a new government headed by the Whig leader Charles Watson-Wentworth, Marquess of Rockingham, who favored granting Americans their independence.

THE UNITED STATES IN CONGRESS ASSEMBLED

The motion for independence, offered to the Continental Congress by Richard Henry Lee on June 7, 1776, called for a confederation of the states. The Articles of Confederation, the first written constitution of the United States, created a national government of sharply limited powers. This arrangement reflected the concerns of people fighting to free themselves from a coercive central government. But the weak

Confederation government had a difficult time forging the unity and assembling the resources necessary to fight the war and win the peace.

The Articles of Confederation

The debate over confederation that took place in the Continental Congress during 1776 made it clear that the delegates favoring a loose union of autonomous states outnumbered those who wanted a strong central government. A consensus finally emerged in 1777, and in November, the "Articles of Confederation" were formally adopted by the Continental Congress and sent to the states for ratification. The Articles created a national assembly, called the Congress, in which each state had a single vote. Delegates, selected annually in a manner determined by the individual state legislatures, could serve no more than three years out of six. A presiding president, elected annually by Congress, was eligible to hold office no more than one year out of three. Votes would be decided by a simple majority of the states, except for major questions, which would require the agreement of nine states.

Congress was granted national authority in the conduct of foreign affairs, matters of war and peace, and maintenance of the armed forces. It could raise loans, issue bills of credit, establish a coinage, and regulate trade with Indian nations, and it was to be the final authority in jurisdictional disputes between states. It was charged with establishing a national postal system as well as a common standard of weights and measures. Lacking the power to tax citizens directly, however, the national government was to apportion its financial burdens among the states according to the extent of their surveyed land. The Articles explicitly guaranteed the sovereignty of the individual states, reserving to them all powers not expressly delegated to Congress. Ratification or amendment required the agreement of all thirteen states. This constitution thus created a national government of specific, yet sharply circumscribed, powers.

The legislatures of twelve states soon voted in favor of the Articles, but final ratification was held up for more than three years by the government of Maryland. Claiming to represent the interests of those states without claims to lands west of the Appalachians, Maryland demanded that the eight states with western claims cede them to the Congress "for the good of the whole" (see Map 7.5). Those states were reluctant to give them up, however, creating a stalemate. Meanwhile, Congress remained an extralegal body, but it agreed to conduct business under the terms of the unratified document. It was 1781 before Virginia, the state with the most extensive western claims, broke the log-jam by promising to cede its lands. Maryland then agreed to ratification, and in March, the Articles of Confederation took effect.

The Continental Congress printed currency to finance the Revolution. Because of widespread counterfeiting, engravers attempted to incorporate complex designs, like the unique vein structure in the leaf on this eighteen-pence note. In case that wasn't enough, the engraver of this note also included the warning: "To counterfeit is Death."

SOURCE: Library of Congress.

Financing the War

Congress financed the Revolution through grants and loans from friendly foreign powers and by issuing paper currency. The total foreign subsidy by the end of the war approached $9 million, but this was insufficient to back the circulating Continental currency that Congress had authorized, the face value of which had risen to $200 million. Congress called on the states to raise taxes, payable in

MAP 7.5 State Claims to Western Lands The ratification of the Articles of Confederation in 1781 awaited settlement of the western claims of eight states. Vermont, claimed by New Hampshire and New York, was not made a state until 1791, after disputes were settled the previous year. The territory north of the Ohio River was claimed in whole or in part by Virginia, New York, Connecticut, and Massachusetts. All of them had ceded their claims by 1786, except for Connecticut, which had claimed an area just south of Lake Erie, known as the Western Reserve; Connecticut ceded this land in 1800. The territory south of the Ohio was claimed by Virginia, North Carolina, South Carolina, and Georgia; in 1802, the latter became the last state to cede its claims.

States. Into its vaults he deposited large quantities of gold and silver coin and bills of exchange obtained through loans from Holland and France. He then issued new paper currency backed by this treasure. Once confidence in the bank was established, Morris was able to supply the Continental Army through private contracts. He also began making interest payments on the debt, which in 1783 was estimated to be about $30 million.

Negotiating Independence

Peace talks between the United States and Great Britain opened in July 1782, when Benjamin Franklin sat down with the British emissary in Paris. Congress had issued its first set of war aims in 1779. The fundamental demands were recognition of American independence and withdrawal of British forces from United States territory. The American negotiators were to press for the largest territorial limits possible, including Canada, as well as guarantees of American rights to fish North Atlantic waters. As for its French ally, Congress instructed the commissioners to be guided by friendly advice, but also by "knowledge of our interests, and by your own discretion, in which we repose the fullest confidence." The French were not happy with

Continental dollars, so this currency could be retired. But most of the states were unwilling to do this. In fact, most of the states resorted to printing currency of their own, which was estimated to total another $200 million by war's end. The result of this expansion of the money supply was the rapid depreciation of Continental currency and runaway inflation. People who received fixed incomes for services—Continental soldiers, for example, as well as merchants, landlords, and other creditors—were devastated. When Robert Morris, one of the wealthiest merchants in the country, became secretary of finance in May 1781, Continental currency had ceased to circulate. Things of no value were declared "not worth a Continental."

Morris was able to turn things around. He persuaded Congress to charter a "Bank of North America" in Philadelphia, the first private commercial bank in the United

this, and in June 1781, partly as a result of French pressure, Congress issued a new set of instructions: the commissioners were to settle merely for a grant of independence and withdrawal of troops, and to be subject to the guidance and control of the French in the negotiations.

Franklin, John Jay, and John Adams, the peace commissioners in Paris, were aware of French attempts to manipulate the outcome of negotiations and place limits on American power. In direct violation of Congressional instructions and treaty obligations to France, they signed a preliminary treaty with Britain in November 1782 without consulting the French. In the treaty, Britain acknowledged the United States as "free, sovereign & independent" and agreed to withdraw its troops from all forts within American territory "with all convenient speed." They guaranteed Americans "the right to take fish" in northern waters. The American commissioners pressed the British for Canada, but settled for western territorial boundaries extending to the Mississippi River (see Map 7.6). Britain received American promises to erect "no lawful impediments" to the recovery of debts, to cease confiscating Loyalist property, and to try to persuade the states to fairly compensate Loyalist exiles. Finally, the two nations agreed to unencumbered navigation of the

Mississippi. It was an astounding coup for the Americans. The peace terms, the commissioners wrote to Congress, "appear to leave us little to complain of and not much to desire."

France was thus confronted with an accomplished fact. When French officials criticized the commissioners, the Americans responded by hinting that resistance to the treaty provisions could result in a British–American alliance. France thereupon quickly made an agreement of its own with the British.

MAP EXPLORATION

To explore an interactive version of this map, go to **www.prenhall.com/faragher5/map7.6**

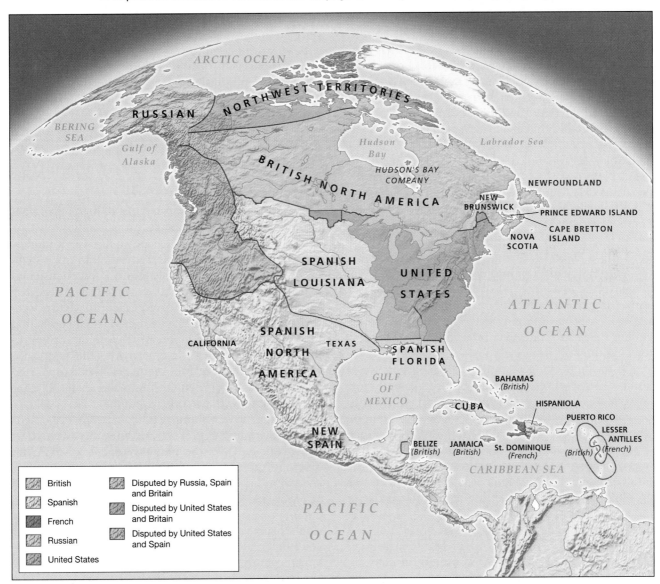

MAP 7.6 North America After the Treaty of Paris, 1783 The map of European and American claims to North America was radically altered by the results of the American Revolution.

Spain did not participate in the negotiations with the Americans. But having waged a successful campaign against the British on the Mississippi River and the Gulf Coast, its government issued a claim of sovereignty over much of the trans-Appalachian territory granted to the United States. Spain arranged a separate peace with Great Britain, in which it won the return of Florida. The final Treaty of Paris—actually a series of separate agreements among the United States, Great Britain, France, and Spain—was signed at Versailles on September 3, 1783.

The Crisis of Demobilization

During the two years between the surrender at Yorktown and the signing of the Treaty of Paris, the British continued to occupy New York City, Charleston, and a series of western posts. The Continental Army remained on wartime alert, with some 10,000 men and an estimated 1,000 women encamped at Newburgh, New York, north of West Point. The soldiers had long been awaiting their pay and were very concerned about the postwar bounties and land warrants promised them. The most serious problem, however, lay not among the enlisted men but the officer corps.

Continental officers had extracted from Congress a promise of life pensions at half pay in exchange for enlistment for the duration of the war. By 1783, however, Congress had still not made any specific provisions for officers' pensions. With peace at hand, the officers began to fear that the army would be disbanded before the problem was resolved, and they would lose whatever power they had to pressure Congress. In January 1783, a group of prominent senior officers petitioned Congress, demanding that pensions be converted to a bonus equal to five years of full pay. "Any further experiments on their patience," they warned, "may have fatal effects." Despite this barely veiled threat of military intervention, Congress rejected their petition.

With the backing of congressional nationalists, a group of army officers associated with General Horatio Gates called an extraordinary meeting of the officer corps at Newburgh. But General Washington, on whom the officers counted for support, condemned the meeting as "disorderly" and called an official meeting of his own. There was enormous tension as the officers assembled on March 15, 1783; at stake was nothing less than the possibility of a military coup at the very moment of American victory. The American Revolution was the first of many successful colonial revolutions, and in hindsight it is clear that post-independence military rule was a common outcome in many of them. Washington strode into the room and mounted the platform. Turning his back in disdain on Gates, he told the assembly that he wished to read a

statement, and then pulled a pair of glasses from his pocket. None of his officers had seen their leader wearing glasses before. "Gentlemen, you must pardon me," said Washington, noting their surprise. "I have grown gray in your service and now find myself growing blind." He then went on to denounce any resort to force. But it was his offhand remark about growing gray that had the greatest impact. Who had sacrificed more than their commander in chief? After he left, the officers adopted resolutions rejecting intervention, and a week later, on Washington's urging, Congress decided to convert the pensions to bonuses after all.

Washington's role in this crisis was one of his greatest contributions to the nation. In December 1783, he resigned his commission as general of the army despite calls for him to remain. There is little doubt that he could have assumed the role of an American dictator. Instead, by his actions and example, the principle of military subordination to civil authority was firmly established.

As for the common soldiers, they wanted simply to be discharged. In May 1783, Congress voted the soldiers three months' pay as a bonus and instructed Washington to begin dismissing them. Some troops remained at Newburgh until the British had evacuated New York in November, but by the beginning of 1784, the Continental Army had shrunk to no more than a few hundred men.

The Problem of the West

After Yorktown, the British abandoned their Indian allies in the West. When the Indians learned of the armistice, according to one British officer, they were "thunderstruck." Neither the Iroquois nor the Ohio tribes, who had fought with the British, considered themselves defeated, but the United States claimed that its victory over Great Britain should be considered a victory over the Indians as well. A heavily armed American nation now pressed for large grants of territory according to the right of conquest. Even Patriot allies were not exempt. The Oneidas, for example, who had supported the Americans, were required to make territorial concessions along with the other Iroquois.

Even as the Revolution was being fought, thousands of Americans migrated west, and after the war, settlers virtually poured over the mountains and down the Ohio River. The population of Kentucky (still part of Virginia until admitted as a state in 1792) was more than 30,000 in 1785. Five years later, at the first census of 1790, its population had grown to 74,000, while the area that would become the state of Tennessee counted another 36,000. Thousands of Americans pressed against the Indian country north of the Ohio River, and destructive violence continued along the frontier. British troops continued to occupy posts in the Northwest and encouraged Indian attacks on vulnerable settlements. Spain refused to accept the territorial settlement of the Treaty of Paris, and closed the port of New Orleans to Americans, effectively blockading the Mississippi River. Westerners, who saw that route as their primary access to markets, were outraged.

John Jay, appointed secretary for foreign affairs by the Confederation Congress in 1784, attempted to negotiate with the British for their withdrawal from the Northwest, but was told that was not possible until all outstanding debts from before the war were settled. Jay also negotiated with the Spanish for guarantees of territorial sovereignty and commercial relations, but they insisted that the Americans relinquish free navigation of the Mississippi. Congress would approve no treaty under those conditions, and some frustrated Westerners considered leaving the Confederation. A number of prominent Kentuckians advocated rejoining the British, while others, including George Rogers Clark and General James Wilkinson, secretly worked for the Spanish as informants and spies. The people of the West "stand as it were upon a pivot," Washington declared in 1784 after a trip down the Ohio. "The touch of a feather would turn them any way." In the West, local community interest continued to override the fragile development of national community sentiment.

In 1784, Congress took up the problem of extending national authority over the West. Legislation was drafted, principally by Thomas Jefferson, providing for "Government for the Western Territory." All territory outside the original thirteen states could presumably have been treated as a colonial domain, but impressed with the necessity of including Westerners in the national community, the legislation instead proposed a remarkably republican colonial policy. The western public domain would eventually be divided into states, fully the equal of the original thirteen, with guarantees of self-government and republican institutions. Once the population of a territory numbered 20,000, the residents could call a convention and establish a constitution and government of their own choosing. And once the population grew to equal that of the smallest of the original thirteen states, the territory could petition for statehood, provided it agreed to remain forever a member of the Confederation. Congress accepted these proposals, but rejected by a vote of seven to six Jefferson's clause prohibiting slavery in the West.

Passed the following year, the Land Ordinance of 1785 provided for the survey and sale of western lands. To avoid the chaos of overlapping surveys and land claims that had characterized Kentucky, the authors of the ordinance created an ordered system of survey, dividing the land into townships composed of thirty-six sections of one square mile (640 acres) each. This measure would have an enormous impact on the North American landscape, as can be seen by anyone who

has flown over the United States and looked down at the patchwork pattern. Jefferson argued that land ought to be given away to actual settlers. But, eager to establish a revenue base for the government, Congress provided for the auction of public lands for not less than one dollar per acre. In the treaties of Fort Stanwix in 1784 and Fort McIntosh in 1785, congressional commissioners forced the Iroquois and some of the Ohio Indians to cede a portion of their territory in what is now eastern Ohio, and surveyors were immediately sent there to divide up the land. These treaties were not the result of negotiation; the commissioners dictated the terms by seizing hostages and forcing compliance. The first surveyed lands were not available for sale until the fall of 1788. In the meantime, Congress, desperate for revenue, sold a tract of more than 1.5 million acres to a new land company, the Ohio Company, for a million dollars.

Thousands of Westerners chose not to wait for the official opening of the public land north of the Ohio River but settled illegally. In 1785, Congress raised troops and evicted many of them, but once the troops left, the squatters returned. The persistence of this problem convinced many congressmen to revise Jefferson's democratic territorial plan.

In the Northwest Ordinance of 1787, Congress established a system of government for the territory north of the Ohio (see Map 7.7). Three to five states were to be carved out of the giant Northwest Territory and admitted "on an equal footing with the original states in all respects whatsoever." Slavery was prohibited. But the initial guarantee of self-government in Jefferson's plan was replaced by the rule of a congressionally appointed court of judges and governor. Once the free white male population of the territory had grown to 5,000, these citizens would be permitted to choose an assembly, but the governor was given the power of absolute veto on all territorial legislation. National interest would be imposed on the localistic western communities. The Northwest Territory was a huge region that included the future states of Ohio, Indiana, Illinois, Michigan, and Wisconsin. In an early instance of government in the hands of developers, Congress chose Arthur St. Clair, president of the Ohio Company, as the first governor of the Northwest Territory.

The creation of the land system of the United States was the major achievement of the Confederation government. But there were other important accomplishments. Under the Articles of Confederation, Congress led the country through the Revolution, and its commissioners negotiated the terms of a comprehensive peace treaty. In organizing the departments of war, foreign affairs, the post office, and finance, the Confederation government created the beginnings of a national bureaucracy.

MAP EXPLORATION

To explore an interactive version of this map, go to **www.prenhall.com/faragher5/map7.7**

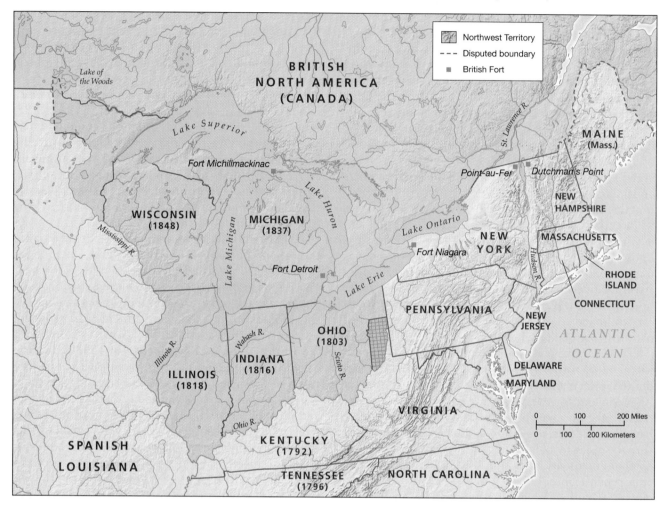

MAP 7.7 The Northwest Territory and the Land Survey System of the United States The Land Ordinance of 1785 created an ordered system of survey (revised by the Northwest Ordinance of 1787), dividing the land into townships and sections.

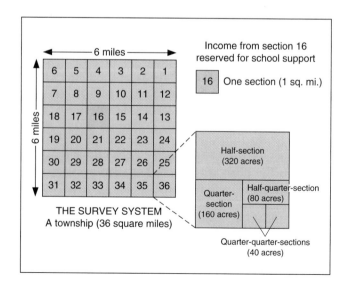

THE SURVEY SYSTEM
A township (36 square miles)

Income from section 16 reserved for school support

16   One section (1 sq. mi.)

Half-section (320 acres)

Quarter-section (160 acres)

Half-quarter-section (80 acres)

Quarter-quarter-sections (40 acres)

REVOLUTIONARY POLITICS IN THE STATES

Despite these accomplishments, most Americans focused not on the Confederation government in Philadelphia but on the governments of their own states. During the revolutionary era, most Americans identified politically and socially with their local communities rather than with the American nation. People spoke of "these United States," emphasizing the plural. The single national community feeling of the Revolution was overwhelmed by persistent localism.

The states were the setting for the most important political struggles of the Confederation period and for long afterwards.

The Broadened Base of Politics

The political mobilization that took place in 1774 and 1775 greatly broadened political participation. Mass meetings in which ordinary people expressed their opinions, voted, and gained political experience were common, not only in the cities but in small towns and rural communities as well. During these years, a greater proportion of the population began to participate in elections. Compared with the colonial assemblies, the new state legislatures included more men from rural and western districts—farmers and artisans as well as lawyers, merchants, and large landowners. Many delegates to the Massachusetts provincial congress of 1774, for example, were men from small farming communities who lacked formal education and owned little property.

This transformation was accompanied by a dramatic shift in the political debate. During the colonial period, when only the upper crust of society had been truly engaged in the political process, the principal argument followed the lines of the traditional Tory and Whig divide in British politics. The Tory position, argued by royal officials, was that colonial governments were simply convenient instruments of the king's prerogative, serving at his pleasure. The Whig position, adopted by colonial elites who sought to preserve and increase their own power, emphasized the need for a government balancing the power of a governor, an upper house, and an assembly. As a result of the Revolution, the Tory position lost all legitimacy and the Whig position was challenged by farmers, artisans, and ordinary people armed with a new and radical democratic ideology.

One of the first post-Revolution debates focused on the appropriate governmental structure for the new states. The thinking of democrats was indicated by the title of an anonymously authored New England pamphlet of 1776: *The People the Best Governors*. Power, the pamphlet argued, should be vested in a single, popularly elected assembly. There should be no property qualifications for either voting or holding office. The governor should simply execute the wishes of the people as voiced by their representatives in the assembly. Judges, too, should be popularly elected, and their decisions reviewed by the assembly. The people, in the words of this pamphlet, "best know their wants and necessities, and therefore are best able to govern themselves." The ideal form of government, according to democrats, was the community or town meeting, in which the people set their own tax rates, mustered the local militia, operated their own schools and churches, and regulated the local economy. State government was necessary only for coordination among communities.

Conservative Americans took up the Whig argument on the need for a balanced government. The "unthinking many," wrote a conservative pamphleteer, should be checked by a strong executive and an upper house. Both of these would be insulated from popular control by property qualifications and long terms in office, the latter designed to draw forth the wisdom and talent of the country's wealthiest and most accomplished men. The greatest danger, according to conservatives, was the possibility of majority tyranny, which might lead to the violation of property rights and to dictatorship. "We must take mankind as they are," one conservative wrote, "and not as we could wish them to be."

The First State Constitutions

Fourteen states—the original thirteen plus Vermont—adopted constitutions between 1776 and 1780. Each of these documents was shaped by the debate between radicals and conservatives, democrats and Whigs, and reflected a new political alignment. The constitutions of Pennsylvania, Maryland, and New York typified the political range of the times. Pennsylvania instituted a radical democracy, Maryland created a conservative set of institutions designed to keep citizens and rulers as far apart as possible, and New York adopted a system somewhere in the middle.

In Pennsylvania, a majority of the political conservatives had been Loyalists, allowing the democrats to seize power in 1776. The election of delegates to the constitutional convention was open to every man in the militia, an arrangement that further strengthened the hand of the democrats. The document this convention adopted clearly reflected a democratic agenda. It created a unicameral assembly, elected annually by all free male taxpayers. So that delegates would be responsive to their constituents, sessions of the assembly were open to the public and included roll-call votes, which had been rare in colonial assemblies. There was no governor, but rather an elected executive committee. Judges served at the pleasure of the assembly.

By contrast, the Maryland constitution, adopted the same year, was written by conservative planters who had been Patriots during the Revolution. It created property requirements for office holding that left only about 10 percent of Maryland men eligible to serve in the assembly, 7 percent in the senate. A powerful governor, elected by large property owners, controlled a highly centralized government. Judges and other high executive officers served for life. These two states, Maryland and Pennsylvania, represented the political extremes. Georgia, Vermont, and North

Carolina followed Pennsylvania's example; South Carolina's constitution was much like Maryland's.

In New York, the constitutional convention of 1777 included a large democratic faction. But conservatives such as John Jay, Gouverneur Morris, and Robert R. Livingston, managing the convention with great skill, helped produce a document that reflected Whig principles while still appealing to the people. There would be a bicameral legislature, each house having equal powers. The lower house, or assembly, was democratically elected, but there were stiff property qualifications for election to the upper house, or senate, and senators represented districts apportioned by wealth, not population. The governor, also elected by property owners, had the power of veto, which could be overridden only by a two-thirds vote of both houses. Ultraconservatives wanted a constitution more like Maryland's, but Jay argued that "another turn of the winch would have cracked the cord"; conservatives, in other words, had gotten about as much as they could without alienating the mass of voters. Other states whose constitutions blended democratic and conservative elements were New Hampshire, New Jersey, and Massachusetts.

Declarations of Rights

One of the most important innovations of the state constitutions was a guarantee of rights patterned on the Virginia Declaration of Rights of June 1776. Written by George Mason—wealthy planter, democrat, and brilliant political philosopher—the Virginia declaration set a distinct tone in its very first article: "That all men are by nature equally free and independent, and have certain inherent rights, . . . namely, the enjoyment of life and liberty, with the means of acquiring and possessing property and pursuing and obtaining happiness and safety." The fifteen articles declared, among other things, that sovereignty resided in the people, that government was the servant of the people, and that the people had the "right to reform, alter, or abolish" that government. There were guarantees of due process and trial by jury in criminal prosecutions, and prohibitions of excessive bail and "cruel and unusual punishments." Freedom of the press was guaranteed as "one of the great bulwarks of liberty," and the people were assured of "the free exercise of religion, according to the dictates of conscience."

Eight state constitutions included a general declaration of rights similar to the first article of the Virginia declaration; others incorporated specific guarantees. A number of states proclaimed the right of the people to engage in free speech and free assembly, to instruct their representatives, and to petition for the redress of grievances—rights either inadvertently or deliberately omitted from Virginia's declaration. These declarations were important precedents for the Bill of Rights, the first ten amendments to the federal Constitution. Indeed, George Mason of Virginia was a leader of the democrats who insisted that the Constitution stipulate such rights.

A Spirit of Reform

The political upheaval of the Revolution raised the possibility of other reforms in American society. The 1776 Constitution of New Jersey, by granting the vote to "all free inhabitants" who met the property requirements, enfranchised women as well as men. The number of women voters eventually led to male protests and a new state law explicitly limiting the right to vote to "free white male citizens."

By giving the vote to "all free inhabitants," the 1776 constitution of New Jersey enfranchised women as well as men who met the property requirements. The number of women voters eventually led to male protests. Wrote one: "What tho' we read, in days of yore, / The woman's occupation / Was to direct the wheel and loom, / Not to direct the nation." In 1807, a new state law explicitly limited the right of franchise to "free white male citizens."

SOURCE: Corbis/Bettmann.

The New Jersey controversy may have been an anomaly, but women's participation in the Revolution wrought subtle but important changes. In 1776, Abigail Adams wrote to her husband John Adams, away at the Continental Congress, "In the new code of laws which I suppose it will be necessary for you to make I desire you would remember the ladies, and be more generous and favourable to them than your ancestors." In the aftermath of the Revolution, there was evidence of increasing sympathy in the courts for women's property rights and fairer treatment of women's petitions for divorce. And the postwar years witnessed an increase in opportunities for women seeking an education. From a strictly legal and political point of view, the Revolution may have done little to change women's role in society, but it did seem to help change expectations. Abigail Adams's request to her husband was directed less toward the shape of the new republic than toward the structure of family life. "Do not put such unlimited powers into the hands of husbands," she wrote, "for all men would be tyrants if they could." She had in mind a new, companionate ideal of marriage that contrasted with older notions of patriarchy. Men and women ought to be more like partners, less like master and servant. This new ideal took root in America during the era of the Revolution.

The most steadfast reformer of the day was Thomas Jefferson, who after completing work on the Declaration of Independence returned to Virginia to take a seat in its House of Delegates. In 1776, he introduced a bill abolishing the law of entails, which confined inheritance to particular heirs in order that landed property remain undivided.

This portrait of the African American poet Phillis Wheatley was included in the collection of her work published in London in 1773, when she was only twenty. Kidnapped in Africa when a girl, then purchased off the Boston docks, she was more like a daughter than a slave to the Wheatley family. She later married and lived as a free woman of color before her untimely death in 1784.

SOURCE: © Bettman/CORBIS.

The majority of the land in Virginia was entailed by the mid-eighteenth century, and Jefferson believed that "entail" and "primogeniture" (inheritance of all the family property by the firstborn son)—legal customs long in effect in aristocratic England—had no place in a republican society. Jefferson's reform of inheritance law passed and had a dramatic effect. "The old families of Virginia will form connections with low people and sink into the mass," wealthy planter John Randolph complained. That was the "inevitable conclusion to which Mr. Jefferson and his leveling system has brought us." By 1798, every state had followed Virginia's lead.

Jefferson's other notable success was his Bill for Establishing Religious Freedom. Indeed, he considered this document one of his greatest accomplishments. At the beginning of the Revolution, there were established churches—denominations officially supported and funded by the government—in nine of the thirteen colonies: Congregationalists in Massachusetts, New Hampshire, and Connecticut, Anglicans in New York and the South. (See Chapter 5 for a discussion of colonial religion.) Established religion was increasingly opposed in the eighteenth century, in part because of Enlightenment criticism of the power it had over free and open inquiry, but, more important, because of the growing sectarian diversity produced by the religious revival of the Great Awakening. Many Anglican clergymen harbored Loyalist sympathies, and as part of an anti-Loyalist backlash, New York, Maryland, the Carolinas, and Georgia had little difficulty passing acts that disestablished the Anglican Church. In Virginia, however, many planters viewed Anglicanism as a bulwark against Baptist and Methodist democratic thinkers, resulting in bitter and protracted opposition to Jefferson's bill, and it did not pass until 1786.

New England Congregationalists proved even more resistant to change. Although Massachusetts, New Hampshire, and Connecticut allowed dissenting churches to receive tax support, they maintained the official relationship between church and state well into the nineteenth century. Other states, despite disestablishment, retained certain religious tests in their legal codes. Georgia, the Carolinas, and New Jersey limited office holding to Protestants; New York required legislators to renounce allegiance to the pope; and even Pennsylvania, where religious toleration had a long history, required officials to swear to a belief in the divine inspiration of the Old and New Testaments.

Jefferson proposed several more reforms of Virginia law, all of which failed to pass. He would have created a system of public education, revised the penal code to restrict capital punishment to the crimes of murder and treason, and established the gradual emancipation of slaves by law. On the whole, Jefferson and the Revolutionary generation were more successful at raising questions than at accomplishing reforms. The problems of penal reform, public education, and slavery remained for later generations of Americans to resolve.

African Americans and the Revolution

For most African Americans there was little to celebrate in the American victory, for it perpetuated the institution of slavery. Few people were surprised when thousands of black fighters and their families departed with the Loyalists and the British at the end of the war, settling in the West Indies, Canada, and Africa. Most of these refugees were fugitive slaves rather than committed Loyalists. In Virginia alone, some 30,000 slaves fled during the Revolution, including seventeen from George Washington's Mount Vernon plantation; several were recaptured, but most left the country with the British.

To many observers, there was an obvious contradiction in waging a war for liberty while continuing to support the institution of slavery. "How is it," English critic and essayist Samuel Johnson asked pointedly in 1775, "that we hear the loudest yelps for liberty among the drivers of Negroes?" The contradiction was not lost on Washington, who during the Revolution began worrying over the morality of slavery. He was not alone. Revolutionary idealism, in combination with a shift away from tobacco farming, weakened the commitment of many planters to the slave system. After the Revolution, a sizable number of Virginians granted freedom to their slaves, and there was a small but important movement to encourage gradual emancipation by convincing masters to free their slaves in their wills. George Washington was one of them, not only freeing several hundred slaves upon his death, but developing an elaborate plan for apprenticeship and tenancy for the able-bodied, and lodging and pensions for the aged. Planters in the Lower South, however, heavily dependent as they were on slave labor, resisted the growing calls for an

end to slavery. Between 1776 and 1786, all the states but South Carolina and Georgia prohibited or heavily taxed the international slave trade, and this issue became an important point of conflict at the Constitutional Convention in 1787 (see Chapter 8).

Perhaps the most important result of this development was the growth of the free African American population. From a few thousand in 1750, their number grew to more than 200,000 by the end of the century. The increase was most notable in the Upper South. The free black population of Virginia, for example, grew from fewer than 2,000 in 1780 to more than 20,000 in 1800. Largely excluded from the institutions of white Americans, the African American community now had enough strength to establish schools, churches, and other institutions of its own. At first, this development was opposed. In Williamsburg, Virginia, for instance, the leader of a black congregation was seized and whipped when he attempted to gain recognition from the Baptist Association. But by the 1790s, the Williamsburg African Church had grown to over 500 members, and the Baptist Association reluctantly recognized it. In Philadelphia, Reverend Absalom Jones established St. Thomas's African Episcopal Church. The incorporation of the word "African" in the names of churches, schools, and mutual benefit societies reflected the pride African Americans took in their heritage.

In the North, slavery was first abolished in the state constitution of Vermont in 1777, in Massachusetts in 1780, and New Hampshire in 1784. Pennsylvania, Connecticut, and Rhode Island adopted systems of gradual emancipation during these years, freeing the children of slaves at birth. (See Out of Many Voices: A Former Slave Appeals to Remain Free.) By 1804, every northern state had provided for abolition or gradual emancipation, although as late as 1810, 30,000 African Americans remained enslaved in the North.

During the era of the Revolution, a small group of African American writers rose to prominence. Benjamin Banneker, born free in Maryland, where he received an education, became one of the most accomplished mathematicians and astronomers of late eighteenth-century America. In the 1790s, he published a popular almanac that both white and black Americans consulted. Jupiter Hammon, a New York slave, took up contemporary issues in his poems and essays, one of the most important of which was his "Address to the Negroes of the State of New York," published in 1787. But the most famous African American writer was Phyllis Wheatley, who came to public attention when her *Poems on Various Subjects, Religious and Moral* appeared in London in 1773, while she was still a domestic slave in Boston. Kidnapped in Africa

OUT OF MANY VOICES

A FORMER SLAVE APPEALS TO REMAIN FREE

In 1780, the Pennsylvania legislature enacted a gradual emancipation law. By its terms any slave not registered by the deadline of November 1, 1780 would be immediately emancipated, and by the neglect of some slaveholders, a number of slaves were freed. One such person was "Cato," whose entire family was freed because their owner failed to comply with the law. In 1781, however, slaveholders pressed the legislature to extend the registration period. In response, Cato wrote the following letter, which was published in the Freedman's Journal, *September 21, 1781.*

MR. PRINTER: I AM A POOR NEGRO, WHO WITH myself and children have had the good fortune to get my freedom, by means of an act of assembly passed on the first of March, 1780, and should now with my family be as happy a set of people as any on the face of the earth, but I am told the assembly are going to pass a law to send us all back to our masters. Why dear Mr. Printer, this would be the cruelest act that ever a set of worthy good gentlemen, could be guilty of. To make a law to hang us all, would be "merciful," when compared with this law; for many of our masters would treat us with unheard barbarity, for daring to take advantage (as we have done) of the law made in our favor. Our lot in "slavery" were hard enough to bear; but having tasted the sweets of "freedom," we should now be miserable indeed. Surely no Christian gentleman can be so cruel! I cannot believe they will pass such a law. I have read the act which made me free, and I always read it with joy—and I always dwell with particular pleasure on the following words, spoken by the assembly on the top of the said law. "We esteem it a particular blessing granted to us, that we are enabled this day to add one more step to universal civilization by removing as much as possible the sorrows of those who have lived in "undeserved" bondage, and from which by the assumed authority of the kings of Great Britain, no effectual legal relief could be obtained." See it was the king of Great Britain that kept us in slavery before. Now surely, after saying so, it cannot be possible for them to make slaves of us again—nobody, but the king of England can do it—and I sincerely pray, that he may never have it in his power. It cannot be, that the assembly will take from us the liberty they have given, because a little further they go on and say, "we conceive ourselves, at this particular period, extra-ordinarily called upon, by the blessings which 'we' have received, to make manifest the sincerity of our professions, and to give a substantial proof of our gratitude." If after all this, 'we,' who by virtue of this very law (which has those very words in it which I have copied,) are now enjoying the sweets of that "substantial proof of gratitude," I say if we should be plunged back into slavery what must we think of the meaning of all those words in the beginning of said law, which seem to be a kind of creed respecting slavery, but what is more serious than all, what will our great Father think of such doings. But I pray that he may be pleased to turn the hearts of the honorable assembly from this cruel law; and that he will be pleased to make us poor blacks deserving of his mercies. CATO. ∎

SOURCE: Philip S. Foner, "A Plea Against Reenslavement," *Pennsylvania History* 39 (1972), pp. 239–241.

as a young girl and converted to Christianity during the Great Awakening, Wheatley wrote poems combining her piety and a concern for African Americans. Writing to the Mohegan Indian minister Samuel Occom in 1774, Wheatly penned a line that not only applied to her own people but to all Americans struggling to be free. "In every human breast God has implanted a principle, which we call love of freedom; it is impatient of oppression, and pants for deliverance. The same principle lives in us."

CONCLUSION

The Revolution was a tumultuous era, marked by violent conflict between Patriots and Loyalists, masters and slaves, settlers and Indian peoples. The advocates of independence emerged successful, largely because of their ability to pull together and to begin to define their national community. But fearful of the power of central authority, Americans created a relatively weak national government. People identified strongly with

CHRONOLOGY

1775	Lord Dunmore, royal governor of Virginia, appeals to slaves to support Britain
1776	July: Declaration of Independence
	August: Battle of Long Island initiates retreat of Continental Army
	September: British land on Manhattan Island
	December: George Washington counterattacks at Trenton
1777	Slavery abolished in Vermont
	September: British General William Howe captures Philadelphia
	October: British General John Burgoyne surrenders at Saratoga
	November: Continentals settle into winter quarters at Valley Forge
	December: France recognizes American independence
1778	June: France enters the war
	June: Battle of Monmouth hastens British retreat to New York
	July: George Rogers Clark captures Kaskaskia
	December: British capture Savannah

1779	Spain enters the war
1780	February: British land at Charleston
	July: French land at Newport
	September: British General Charles Cornwallis invades North Carolina
1781	February: Robert Morris appointed superintendent of finance
	March: Articles of Confederation ratified
	October: Cornwallis surrenders at Yorktown
1782	Peace talks begin
1783	March: Washington mediates issue of officer pensions
	September: Treaty of Paris signed
	November: British evacuate New York
1784	Treaty of Fort Stanwix
	Postwar depression begins
1785	Land Ordinance of 1785
	Treaty of Fort McIntosh
1786	Jefferson's Bill for Establishing Religious Freedom
	Rhode Island currency law

their local and state communities, and these governments became the site for most of the struggles over political direction that characterized the Revolution and its immediate aftermath. But not all problems, it turned out, could be solved locally. Within a very few years, the nation would sink into a serious economic depression that sorely tested the resources of local communities. By the mid-1780s, many American nationalists were paraphrasing Washington's question of 1777: "What then is to become of this nation?"

REVIEW QUESTIONS

1. Assess the relative strengths of the Patriots and the Loyalists in the American Revolution.
2. What roles did Indian peoples and African Americans play in the Revolution?
3. Describe the structure of the Articles of Confederation. What were its strengths and weaknesses?
4. How did the Revolution affect politics within the states?
5. What was the effect of the Revolution on African Americans?

RECOMMENDED READING

Wayne Bodle, *Valley Forge Winter: Civilians and Soldiers in War* (2002). The authoritative history, written by a historian who spent years on the staff at Valley Forge National Historical Park.

Thomas Fleming, *Liberty! The American Revolution* (1997). This well-written account, derived from a public television series, includes wonderful contemporary images.

Merrill Jensen, *The New Nation: A History of the United States during the Confederation, 1781–1789* (1950). Still the standard work on the 1780s.

Max M. Mintz, *Seeds of Empire: The American Revolutionary Conquest of the Iroquois* (1999). The Revolution as a war for the control of Iroquois lands in upstate New York.

Charles Patrick Neimeyer, *America Goes to War: A Social History of the Continental Army* (1996). A detailed look at the men who fought and won the Revolution.

Mary Beth Norton, *Liberty's Daughters: The Revolutionary Experience of American Women, 1750–1800* (1980). A provocative and comprehensive history of women in the Revolutionary era. Treats not only legal and institutional change but also the more subtle changes in habits and expectations.

John W. Pulis, *Moving On: Black Loyalists in the Afro-Atlantic World* (1999). Essays on their military role, but especially on their communities in Canada, Great Britain, and Africa. In each place, they remained second-class citizens.

Ray Raphael, *A People's History of the American Revolution: How Common People Shaped the Fight for Independence* (2001). Demonstrates that the Revolution was much more fractious when viewed at the level of those who did the fighting and dying.

Charles Royster, *A Revolutionary People at War* (1979). A pathbreaking study of the Continental Army and popular attitudes toward it. Emphasizes the important role played by the officer corps and the enlisted men in the formation of the first nationalist constituency.

Henry Wiencek, *Imperfect God: George Washington, His Slaves, and the Creation of America* (2003). An award-winning study of Washington's changing attitude toward slavery.

Alfred F. Young, *Masquerade: The Life and Times of Deborah Sampson, Continental Soldier* (2004). A meticulously researched account of the woman who passed for a man and served in the Continental Army. Both a biographical narrative and a discourse on the problems of writing the history of common people.

 For additional study resources for this chapter, go to the *Companion Website,* **http://www.prenhall.com/faragher**.

The New Nation

1786–1800

CHAPTER OUTLINE

A Rural Massachusetts Community Rises in Defense

Several hundred farmers from the town of Pelham and scores of other rural communities in western Massachusetts converged on the court house in Northampton, the county seat, before sunrise on Tuesday, August 29, 1786. They arrived in military formation, fifes playing and drums beating, armed with muskets, broadswords, and cudgels, the men's tricornered hats festooned with sprigs of evergreen, symbols of freedom frequently worn by Yankee soldiers during the late war for independence, which had ended only four years before. At least a third of the men and virtually all their officers were veterans. They were mustering once again in defense of their liberties.

In 1787, the country was in the midst of an economic depression that had hit farm communities particularly hard. The prices for agricultural commodities were at historic lows, yet country merchants and shopkeepers refused to advance credit, insisting that purchases and debt repayment be made in hard currency. Two-thirds of the men who marched on Northampton had been sued for debt, and many had spent time in debtor's prison. Dozens of rural towns petitioned the state government for relief, but not only did the merchant-dominated legislature reject their pleas, it raised the property tax in order to pay off the enormous debt the state had accumulated during the Revolution. The new tax was considerably more oppressive than any levied by the British before the Revolution,

and was even more odious since the revenue would go to a small group of wealthy eastern men, to whom the debt was owed.

Massachusetts farmers decided to take matters into their own hands. When outsiders threatened a man's property, they argued, the community had the right, indeed the duty, to rise up in defense. During the Revolution, armed men had marched on the courts, shutting down the operation of government, and now they were doing it again. The Northampton judges had no choice but to close the court, and that success led to similar actions in many other Massachusetts counties. "We have lately emerged from a bloody war in which liberty was the glorious prize," one man declared, "and in this glorious cause I am determined to stand with firmness and resolution."

This uprising quickly became known as Shays' Rebellion, after Daniel Shays, a decorated revolutionary officer and one of the leaders from the town of Pelham. Although rebellion was most widespread in the state of Massachusetts, similar disorders occurred in New Hampshire, Vermont, Pennsylvania, Maryland, and Virginia. Conservatives around the country were thrown into panic. The rebels, Secretary of War Henry Knox wrote to George Washington, planned to seize the property of the wealthy and redistribute it to the poor. In the opinion of Washington's former aide Colonel David Humphreys of Connecticut, the rebels were "levelers" determined to "annihilate all debts public and private." Washington agreed, and worried that rebellion threatened to break out everywhere. "There are combustibles in every State which a spark might set fire to."

Washington and other conservative leaders saw Shays' Rebellion as a class conflict that pitted poor against rich, debtor against creditor. Yet the residents of Pelham and other rural towns acted in common, without regard to rank or property. Big farmers and small farmers alike marched on the county court. They came from tight-knit

Pelham

communities, bound together by family and kinship. Among the group of one hundred Pelham residents who marched on Northampton, for example, there were twelve men from the Grey family, eight Johnsons, six McMillans. More than two-thirds of the men were accompanied by kinsmen. Whether well-to-do or poor, they considered themselves "husbandmen," and they directed their protest against "outsiders," the urban residents of Boston and other coastal towns. "I am a man that gets his living by hard labor," one rebel announced, "and I think that husbandry is as honest a calling as any in the world." The country would be a lot better off, he concluded, "if there were less white shirts and more black frocks."

The crisis ended in Massachusetts when a militia force raised by "white shirts" in the eastern part of the state, and financed by the great merchants, marched west and crushed the Shaysites in January 1787. Daniel Shays fled the state and never returned. Fifteen of the leaders were tried and sentenced to death; two were hanged before the remainder were pardoned, and some four thousand other farmers temporarily lost their right to vote, to sit on juries, or to hold office. Yet many of them considered their rebellion a success. The next year, Massachusetts voters threw out the old governor and elected a new legislature, which passed a moratorium on debts and cut taxes to only ten percent of what they had been.

The most important consequence of Shays' Rebellion, however, would be its effect on conservative nationalists unhappy with the distribution of power between the states and national government under the Articles of Confederation. "Without some alteration in our political creed," Washington wrote to James Madison, "the superstructure we have been seven years in raising, at the expence of so much blood and treasure, must fall. We are fast verging to anarchy and confusion!" The uprising "wrought prodigious changes in the minds of men respecting the powers of government," Henry Knox noted. "Everybody says they must be strengthened and that unless this shall be effected, there is no security for liberty and property." The time had come, he declared, "to clip the wings of a mad democracy."

KEY TOPICS

- The tensions and conflicts between local and national authorities in the decades after the American Revolution
- The struggle to draft the Constitution and to achieve its ratification
- Establishment of the first national government under the Constitution
- The beginning of American political parties
- The first stirrings of an authentic American national culture

---

THE CRISIS OF THE 1780s

The depression of the mid-1780s and the political protests it generated were instrumental in the development of strong nationalist sentiment among the elite circles of American life. In the aftermath of Shays' Rebellion, these sentiments coalesced into a powerful political movement dedicated to strengthening the national government.

Economic Crisis

The economic crisis had its origins in the Revolution. The shortage of goods resulting from the British blockade, the demand for supplies by the army and the militias, and the flood of paper currency issued by the Confederation Congress and the states combined to create the worst inflation in American history. United States dollars traded against Spanish dollars at the rate of 3 to

A mocking pamphlet of 1787 pictured Daniel Shays and Job Shattuck, two leaders of Shays' Rebellion. The artist gives them uniforms, a flag, and artillery, but the rebels were actually an unorganized group of farmers armed only with clubs and simple muskets. When the rebellion was crushed, Shattuck was wounded and jailed, and Shays, along with many others, left Massachusetts. He fled to a remote region of Vermont and then settled in New York.

SOURCE: National Portrait Gallery, Smithsonian Institution/Art Resource, NY.

1 in 1777, 40 to 1 in 1779, and 146 to 1 in 1781, by which time Congress had issued more than $190 million in currency (see Figure 8.1). Most of this paper money ended up in the hands of merchants who had paid only a fraction of its face value.

After the war ended, inflation gave way to depression. Political revolution could not alter economic realities: the independent United States continued to be a supplier of raw materials and an importer of manufactured products, and Great Britain remained the country's most important trading partner. In 1784, British merchants began dumping goods in the American market, offering easy terms of credit. But the production of exportable goods had been drastically reduced by the fighting, and thus the trade deficit with Britain for the period 1784–86 rose to approximately £5 million (see Figure 8.2). The deficit acted like a magnet, drawing hard currency from American accounts, leaving the country with little silver coin in circulation. Commercial banks insisted on the repayment of old loans and refused to issue new ones. By the end of 1784, the country had fallen into the grip of economic depression, and within two years, prices had fallen by 25 percent.

The depression struck while the nation was attempting to dig out from the huge mountain of debt incurred during the Revolution. Creditors were owed more than $50 million by national and state governments. Not allowed to raise taxes on its own, the Confederation Congress requisitioned the states for the funds necessary for debt repayment. The states in turn taxed their residents. At a time when there was almost no money in circulation, ordinary Americans feared being crushed by the burden of private debt and public taxes. Thus did the economic problem become a political problem.

State Remedies

In the states, radicals called for regulation of the economy. The most controversial remedies were those designed to relieve the burden on debtors and ordinary taxpayers. Farmers and debtors pressed their state governments for legal tender laws, which required creditors to accept a state's paper currency at face value (rather than market value) for all debts public and private. Despite the understandable opposition of creditors, seven states enacted such laws. For the most part, these were modest programs that worked rather well, caused little depreciation, and did not result in the problems feared by creditors.

It was the plan of the state of Rhode Island, however, that received most of the attention. A rural political party campaigning under the slogan "To Relieve the

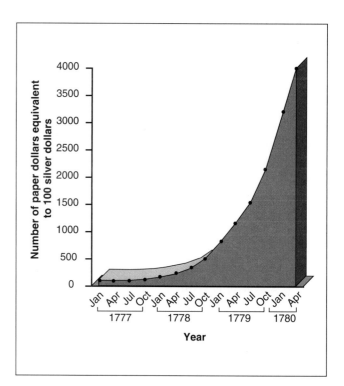

FIGURE 8.1   Postwar Inflation, 1777–80: The Depreciation of Continental Currency The flood of Continental currency issued by Congress, and the shortage of goods resulting from the British blockade, combined to create the worst inflation Americans have ever experienced. Things of no value were said to be "not worth a Continental."

SOURCE: John McCusker, "How Much Is That in Real Money?" *Proceedings of the American Antiquarian Society*, N.S. 102 (1992): 297–359.

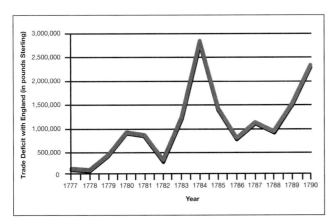

FIGURE 8.2   The Trade Deficit with Great Britain
The American trade deficit with Great Britain rose dramatically with the conclusion of the Revolution.

SOURCE: *Historical Statistics of the United States* (Washington, DC: Government Printing Office, 1976), 1176.

Distressed" captured the legislature in 1786 and enacted a radical currency law. The supply of paper money issued in relation to the population was much greater under this program than in any other state. The law declared the currency legal tender for all debts. If creditors refused to accept it, debtors were allowed to satisfy their obligations by depositing the currency with a county judge, who would then advertise the debt as paid. "In the state of *Rogue Island*," one shocked merchant wrote, "fraud and injustice" had been permitted "by solemn law." Conservatives pointed to Rhode Island as an example of the evils that accompanied unchecked democracy.

Some states erected high tariff barriers to curb imports and protect domestic industries. But foreign shippers found it easy to avoid these duties simply by unloading their cargo in states without tariffs and distributing the goods by overland transport. To be effective, commercial regulations had to be national. Local sentiment had to give way to the unity of a national community. The "means of preserving ourselves," wrote John Adams, will "never be secured entirely, until Congress shall be made supreme in foreign commerce, and shall have digested a plan for all the states."

Movement Toward a New National Government

Early in 1786, the legislature of Virginia invited all the states to appoint delegates to a convention, that they might consider political remedies for the economic crisis. The meeting was sparsely attended (only twelve delegates from five states), but the men shared their alarm over the rebellion in Massachusetts and the possibility of others like it. "What stronger evidence can be given of the want of energy in our governments than these

disorders?" Washington wrote fellow Virginian James Madison, one of the delegates. "If there exists not a power to check them, what security has a man for life, liberty, or property?" Convinced of the absolute necessity of strengthening the national government, the Annapolis convention passed a resolution requesting that the Confederation Congress call on all the states to send delegates to a national convention that they might "render the constitution of the federal government adequate to the exigencies of the union." A few weeks later, with some reluctance, the Congress voted to endorse the Philadelphia convention, to be held in May 1787, "for the sole and express purpose of revising the Articles of Confederation."

The conservatives, however, had in mind more than simply a revision of the Articles; they looked forward to a considerably strengthened national government. Louis Otto, French Charge d'Affaires in the United States, believed they were acting in the interests of their class. "Although there are no nobles in America," he informed his superiors at Versailles, "there is a class of men denominated 'gentlemen,' who by reason of their wealth, their talents, their education, their families, or the offices they hold, aspire to a preeminence which the people refuse to grant them." Believing that the consolidation of power in a strong central government would better serve their interests as merchants, bankers, and planters, the conservatives hid their motives behind the call for revision of the Articles. "The people," Otto wrote, "generally discontented with the obstacles in the way of commerce, and scarcely suspecting the secret motives of their opponents, ardently embraced this measure."

THE NEW CONSTITUTION

In late May 1787, fifty-five men from twelve states (the radical government of Rhode Island refused to send a delegation) assembled at the Pennsylvania State House in Philadelphia. A number of prominent men were missing. Thomas Jefferson and John Adams were serving as ambassadors in Europe. Patrick Henry of Virginia declared that he "smelt a rat" and stayed home. But most of America's best-known political leaders were present: George Washington, Benjamin Franklin, Alexander Hamilton, James Madison, George Mason, Robert Morris. Twenty-nine were college educated, thirty-four were lawyers, twenty-four had served in Congress, and twenty-one were veteran officers of the Revolution. At least nineteen owned slaves. Others were land speculators and merchants. But there were no ordinary farmers or artisans present, and of course, no women, African Americans, or Indians. The Constitution was framed by white men who represented America's social and economic elite.

These men were patriots, and most were republicans, committed to the idea that government must rest on the consent of the governed. But they were not democrats. They believed that the country already suffered from too much democracy. They feared that ordinary people, if given ready access to power, would enact policies against the interests of the privileged classes, and thus the nation as a whole. The specter of Shays' Rebellion hung over the proceedings.

The Constitutional Convention

On their first day of work, the delegates agreed to vote by states, as was the custom of Congress. They chose Washington to chair the meeting, and to ensure candid debate they decided to keep their sessions secret, although James Madison, a young Virginian with a profound knowledge of history and political philosophy, took voluminous notes that serve as our record of what transpired. Madison was instrumental in working with his fellow Virginians to draft what became known as the Virginia Plan. It was presented to the convention shortly after it convened, and it set the agenda.

The Virginia Plan proposed scrapping the Articles of Confederation altogether in favor of a "consolidated government" with the power to tax and to enforce its

George Washington presides over a session of the Constitutional Convention meeting in Philadelphia's State House (now known as Independence Hall) in an engraving of 1799.

SOURCE: Print and Picture Collection, The Free Library of Philadelphia.

laws directly, rather than by acting through the states. "A spirit of locality," Madison declared, was in the process of destroying "the aggregate interests of the community," by which he meant the great community of the nation. The Virginia Plan would have reduced the states to little more than administrative institutions, something like counties. According to its terms, representation in the bicameral national legislature would be based on population districts. The members of the House of Representatives would be elected by popular vote, but senators chosen indirectly by state legislators so they might be insulated from democratic pressure. The Senate would lead, controlling foreign affairs and the appointment of officials. An appointed chief executive and a national judiciary would together form a Council of Revision having the power to veto both national and state legislation.

The main opposition to the Virginia Plan came from the delegates of the small states who feared being swallowed up by the large ones. After two weeks of debate, William Paterson of New Jersey introduced an alternative, a set of "purely federal" principles that became known as the New Jersey Plan. This plan also proposed increasing the powers of the central government, but retained a single-house Congress in which the states were equally represented. After much debate and a series of votes that split the convention down the middle, the delegates finally agreed to what has been termed the Great Compromise: representation proportional to population in the House and equal representation by states in the Senate. The compromise allowed the creation of a strong national government while still providing an important role for the states.

Part of this agreement was a second, fundamental compromise that brought together the delegates from North and South. As James Madison wrote, "The real difference of interests lay, not between the large and small but between the Nothern and Southern states. The institution of slavery and its consequences formed the line of discrimination." Southern delegates wanted slavery protected by the central government, the Northern delegates wanted a central government with the power to regulate commerce, and this formed the basis of the compromise. To boost their power, Southerners wanted slaves included in the population census for the purpose of determining proportional representation, but wanted them excluded when it came to apportioning taxes. In exchange for Southern support for the "commerce clause" Northerners agreed to count five slaves as the equivalent of three freemen—the "three-fifths rule." Furthermore, the representatives of South Carolina and Georgia demanded protection for the slave trade, and after bitter debate, the delegates included a provision preventing any federal restriction on the importation of slaves for twenty years. Another article legitimized the return of fugitive slaves from free states. The word "slave" was nowhere used in the text of the Constitution (the writers employed phrases such as "persons held to labor"), but these provisions amounted to national guarantees for the preservation of Southern slavery. Although a minority of delegates were opposed to slavery, and regretted having to give in on this issue, they agreed with Madison, who wrote that "great as the evil is, a dismemberment of the union would be worse."

There was still much to decide regarding the other branches of government. Madison's Council of Revision was scratched in favor of a strong federal judiciary with the implicit power to declare unconstitutional acts of Congress. There were demands for a powerful chief executive, and Alexander Hamilton went on record that the executive should be appointed for life, raising fears that the office might prove to be, in the words of Edmund Randolph of Virginia, "the fetus of monarchy." But there was considerable support for a president with veto power to check the legislature. To keep the president independent of Congress, the delegates decided he should be elected: but fearing that ordinary voters could never "be sufficiently informed" to select wisely, they insulated the process from popular choice by creating the Electoral College. Voters in the states would not actually vote for president. Rather, each state would select a slate of "electors" equal in number to the state's total representation in the House and Senate. Following the general election, the electors in each state would meet to cast their ballots and elect the president.

In early September, the delegates turned their rough draft of the Constitution over to a Committee of Style, which shaped it into an elegant and concise document providing the general principles and basic framework of government. But Madison, known to later generations as "the Father of the Constitution," was gloomy, believing that the revisions of his original plan doomed the Union to the kind of inaction that had characterized government under the Articles of Confederation. It was left for Franklin to make the final speech to the convention. "Can a perfect production be expected?" he asked. "I consent, Sir, to this Constitution, because I expect no better, and because I am not sure that it is not the best." The delegates voted their approval on September 17, 1787, and transmitted the document to Congress, agreeing that it would become operative after ratification by nine states. Despite some congressmen who were outraged that the convention had exceeded its charge of simply modifying the Articles of Confederation, Congress called for a special ratifying convention in each of the states.

Ratifying the New Constitution

The supporters of the new Constitution immediately adopted the name Federalists to describe themselves. Their outraged opponents objected that the existing Confederation already provided for a "federal" government of balanced power between the states and the Union, and that the Constitution would replace it with a "national" government. But

in this, as in much of the subsequent process of ratification, the Federalists (or nationalists) grabbed the initiative, and their opponents had to content themselves with the label Anti-Federalists (see Map 8.1). Mercy Otis Warren, a leading critic of the new Constitution, commented on the dilemma in which the Anti-Federalists found themselves. "On the one hand," she wrote, "we stand in need of a strong federal government, founded on principles that will support the prosperity and union of the colonies. On the other, we have struggled for liberty and made costly sacrifices at her shrine and there are still many among us who revere her name too much to relinquish, beyond a certain medium, the rights of man for the dignity of government."

MAP EXPLORATION

To explore an interactive version of this map,
go to **www.prenhall.com/faragher5/map8.1**

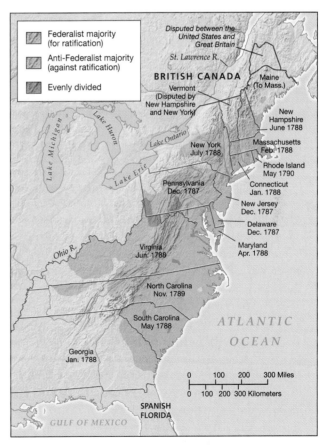

MAP 8.1 The Ratification of the Constitution, 1787–90
The distribution of the vote for the ratification of the Constitution demonstrated its wide support in sections of the country linked to the commercial economy, and its disapproval in more remote and backcountry sections. (Note that Maine remained a part of Massachusetts until admitted as a separate state in 1820.)

The critics of the Constitution were by no means a unified group. Because most of them were localists, they represented a variety of social and regional interests. Rufus King, who had been a delegate to the convention from Massachusetts wrote James Madison that the opposition in his state arose from the opinion "that the System is the production of the Rich and ambitious, . . . and that the consequence will be the establishment of two Orders in Society, one comprehending the Opulent and Great, the other the poor and illiterate." (See Out of Many Voices: Western Massachusetts Farmers Oppose Ratification.) Most Anti-Federalists believed that the Constitution granted far too much power to the central government, weakening the autonomy of communities and states. As

OUT OF MANY VOICES

WESTERN MASSACHUSETTS FARMERS OPPOSE RATIFICATION

There was much opposition to the ratification of the Constitution in Massachusetts, where in 1786–87 farmers in the western part of the state had participated in Shays' Rebellion. The western farmers who signed this letter, published in January 1788, announced their skepticism of what they called the new "aristocratick" government of the Constitution.

WHEN WE SEE THE ADHERENTS TO THIS constitution chiefly made up of civil and ecclesiastical gown men, and their dependents, the expedient they have hit upon is not likely to have the intended effect. There are many men destitute of eloquence, yet they can see and hear—They can think and judge, and are therefore not likely to be wheedled out of their senses by the sophistical reasonings of all the advocates for this new constitution in the country combined. . . . [They] tell us, that the constitution must be good, from the characters which composed the Convention that framed it. It is graced with the names of a Washington and a Franklin. Illustrious names, we allow—worthy characters in civil society. Yet we cannot suppose them, to be infallible guides, neither yet that a man must necessarily incur guilt to himself merely by dissenting from them in opinion.

We cannot think the noble general [Washington] has the same ideas with ourselves, with regard to the rules of right and wrong. We cannot think, he acts a very consistent part, or did through the whole of the contest with Great Britain: who, notwithstanding he wielded the sword in defence of American liberty, yet at the same time was, and is to this day, living upon the labours of several hundreds of miserable Africans, as free born as himself; and some of them very likely descended from parents who, in point of property and dignity in their own country, might cope with any man in America. We do not conceive we are to be overborne by the weight of any names, however revered. "ALL MEN ARE BORN FREE AND EQUAL;" if so, every man hath a natural and unalienable right to his own opinion, and, for asserting this right, ought not to be stigmatized with the epithets of tenacious and dogmatical. . . .

We do not wish to tire the publick, but would hint to those gentlemen, who would would rob the people of their liberties, that their sophistry is not like to produce the effect. We are willing to have a federal constitution. We are willing another trial should be made; this may be done without derogating from the gentlemen, who composed the late convention. In framing a constitution for this commonwealth, two trials were made before one would stick. We are willing to relinquish so much, as to have a firm, energetick government, and this we are sensible may be done, without becoming slaves, to the capricious fancies of any sett of men whatever. It is argued, that there is no danger that the proposed rulers will be disposed to exercise any powers that this constitution puts into their hands, which may enable them to deprive the people of their liberties. But in case, say they, they should make such attempts, the people may, and will rise to arms and prevent it; in answer to which, we have only to say, we have had enough of fighting in the late war, and think it more eligible, to keep our liberties in our own hands, whilst it is in our power thus to do, than to place them in the hands of fallible men, like ourselves, who may if they please, entirely deprive us of them, and so we be at last reduced to the sad alternative of losing them forever, or recovering them back by the point of the sword. The aristocratick party are sensible, that these are the sentiments of the majority of the community, and their conduct plainly evinces the truth of a well known ancient adage— "Nothing cuts like the truth." ■

SOURCE: *The Massachusetts Gazette* January 25, 1788.

local governments "will always possess a better representation of the feelings and interests of the people at large," one critic wrote, "it is obvious that these powers can be deposited with much greater safety with the state than the general government."

All the great political thinkers of the eighteenth century had argued that a republican form of government could work only for small countries. As French philosopher Montesquieu had observed, "In an extensive republic, the public good is sacrificed to a thousand private views." But in *The Federalist,* a brilliant series of essays in defense of the new Constitution written in 1787 and 1788 by James Madison, Alexander Hamilton, and John Jay, Madison stood Montesquieu's assumption on its head. Rhode Island, he argued, had demonstrated that the rights of property might not be protected in even the smallest of states. Asserting that "the most common and durable source of factions has been the various and unequal distribution of property," Madison concluded that the best way to control such factions was to "extend the sphere" of government. That way, he continued, "you take in a greater variety of parties and interests; you make it less probable that a majority of the whole will have a common motive to invade the rights of other citizens; or, if such a common motive exists, it will be more difficult for all who feel it to discover their own strength and to act in unison with each other." Rather than a disability, Madison argued, great size would be an advantage: interests would be so diverse that no single faction would be able to gain control of the state, threatening the freedoms of others.

It is doubtful whether Madison's sophisticated argument, or the arguments of the Anti-Federalists for that matter, made much of a difference in the popular voting in the states to select delegates for the state ratification conventions. The alignment of forces generally followed the lines laid down during the fights over economic issues in the years since the Revolution. Consider Pennsylvania, the first state to convene a ratification convention, in November 1787. Forty-eight percent of the Anti-Federalist delegates to the convention were farmers. By contrast, 54 percent of the Federalists were merchants, manufacturers, large landowners, or professionals. What tipped the Pennsylvania convention in favor of the Constitution was the wide support the document

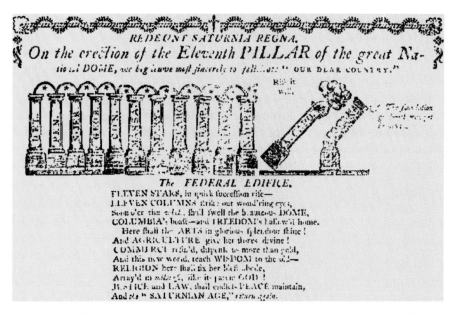

A cartoon published in July 1788, when New York became the eleventh state to ratify the Constitution. After initially voting to reject, North Carolina soon reconsidered, but radical and still reluctant Rhode Island did not join the Union until 1790.

SOURCE: The Federal Edifice "On the Erection of the Eleventh Pillar," caricature from the "Massachusetts Centinal", August 2, 1788. Neg. #33959. Collection of The New York Historical Society.

enjoyed among artisans and commercial farmers, who saw their interests tied to the growth of a commercial society. As one observer pointed out, "The counties nearest [navigable waters] were in favor of it generally, those more remote, in opposition."

Similar agrarian-localist and commercial-cosmopolitan alignments characterized most of the states. The most critical convention took place in Massachusetts in early 1788. Five states—Delaware, Pennsylvania, New Jersey, Georgia, and Connecticut—had already voted to ratify, but the states with the strongest Anti-Federalist movements had yet to convene. If the Constitution lost in Massachusetts, its fate would be in great danger. At the convention, Massachusetts opponents of ratification—which included the supporters of Shays' Rebellion—enjoyed a small majority. But several important Anti-Federalist leaders, including Governor John Hancock and Revolutionary leader Samuel Adams, were swayed by the enthusiastic support for the Constitution among Boston's townspeople. On February 16, the convention voted narrowly in favor of ratification. To no one's surprise, Rhode Island rejected the Constitution in March, but Maryland and South Carolina approved it in April and May. On June 21, New Hampshire became the ninth state to ratify.

New York, Virginia, and North Carolina were left with the decision of whether to join the new Union. Anti-Federalist support was strong in each of these states. North Carolina voted to reject. (It did not join the Union until the next year, followed by a still reluctant Rhode

Island in 1790.) In New York, the delegates were moved to vote their support by a threat from New York City to secede from the state and join the Union separately if the state convention failed to ratify. The Virginia convention was almost evenly divided, but promises to amend the Constitution to protect the people from the potential abuses of the federal government persuaded enough delegates to produce a victory for the Constitution. The promise of a Bill of Rights was important in the ratification vote of five of the states.

The Bill of Rights

The Constitutional Convention had considered a bill of rights patterned on the declarations of rights in the state constitutions (see Chapter 7), but then rejected it as superfluous. But Anti-Federalist delegates in numerous state ratification conventions had proposed a grab bag of over 200 potential amendments protecting the rights of the people against the power of the central government. In June 1789, James Madison, elected to the first Congress as a representative from Virginia, set about transforming them into a coherent series of proposals. Congress passed twelve and sent them to the states, and ten survived the ratification process to become the Bill of Rights in 1791.

The First Amendment prohibited Congress from establishing an official religion and provided for the freedom of assembly. It also ensured freedom of speech, a free press, and the right of petition. The other amendments guaranteed the right to bear arms, limit the government's power to quarter troops in private homes, and restrain the government from unreasonable searches or seizures; they assured the people their legal rights under the common law, including the prohibition of double jeopardy, the right not to be compelled to testify against oneself, and due process of law before life, liberty, or property can be taken away. Finally, the unenumerated rights of the people were protected, and the powers not delegated to the federal government were reserved to the states.

The first ten amendments to the Constitution have been a restraining influence on the growth of government power over American citizens. Their provisions have become an admired aspect of the American political tradition throughout the world. The Bill of Rights is the most important constitutional legacy of the Anti-Federalists.

THE FIRST ADMINISTRATION

Ratification of the Constitution was followed by the first federal elections—for the Congress and the presidency— and in the spring of 1789, the new federal government assumed power in the temporary capital of New York City. The inauguration of George Washington as the first president of the United States took place on April 30, 1789, on the balcony of Federal Hall, at the corner of Wall and Broad Streets. Reelected without opposition in 1792, Washington served until 1797. The first years under the new federal Constitution were especially important because they shaped the structure of the American nation-state in ways that would be enormously significant for later generations.

The Washington Presidency

Although he dressed in plain American broadcloth at his inauguration and claimed to be content with a plain republican title, Washington was counted among the nationalists. He was anything but a man of the people. By nature reserved and solemn, he chose to ride about town in a grand carriage drawn by six horses and escorted by uniformed liverymen. In the tradition of British royalty, he delivered his addresses personally to Congress and received from both houses an official reply. These customs were continued by John Adams, Washington's successor, but ended by Thomas Jefferson, who denounced them as "rags of royalty." On the other hand, Washington worked hard to adhere to the letter of the Constitution, refusing, for example, to use the veto power except where he thought the Congress had acted unconstitutionally, and personally seeking the "advice and consent" of the Senate.

Congress quickly moved to establish departments to run the executive affairs of state, and Washington soon appointed Thomas Jefferson his secretary of state, Alexander Hamilton to run the Treasury, Henry Knox the War Department, and Edmund Randolph the Justice Department, as attorney general. The president consulted each of these men regularly, and during his first term met with them as a group to discuss matters of policy. By the end of Washington's presidency, the secretaries had coalesced in what came to be known as the cabinet, an institution that has survived to the present despite the absence of constitutional authority or enabling legislation. Washington was a powerful and commanding personality, but he understood the importance of national unity, and in his style of leadership, his consultations, and his appointments, he sought to achieve a balance of conflicting political perspectives and sectional interests. These intentions would be sorely tested during the eight years of his administration.

An Active Federal Judiciary

The most important piece of legislation to emerge from the first session of Congress was the Judiciary Act of 1789; it implemented the judicial clause of the Constitution, which empowered Congress to determine the number of justices on the Supreme Court and create a system of

Two coins from the first decade of the federal republic illustrate political controversies of the period. The Washington cent was proposed by Treasury Secretary Alexander Hamilton in 1792, in the hope of enhancing popular respect for the new government by having the president's bust impressed on coins in the manner of European kings. But after long debate, Congress defeated the plan, the opponents claiming it smacked of monarchy. The Liberty coin, issued by the Mint of the United States in 1795, when under the authority of Secretary of State Thomas Jefferson, features Liberty wearing a liberty cap and bearing a marked resemblance to the French Revolutionary icon Marianne.

SOURCE: Smithsonian Institution, NNC, Douglas Mudd.

federal courts. Congress established a high court of six justices (in 1869, this was increased to nine) and established three circuit and thirteen district courts. Strong nationalists argued for a powerful federal legal system that would provide a uniform code of civil and criminal justice throughout the country. But the localists in Congress fought successfully to retain the various bodies of law that had developed in the states. They wanted to preserve local community autonomy. The act gave federal courts limited original jurisdiction, restricting them mostly to appeals from state courts. But it thereby established the principle of federal judicial review of state legislation, despite the silence of the Constitution on this point.

Under the leadership of Chief Justice John Jay, the Supreme Court heard relatively few cases during its first decade. Still, it managed to raise considerable political controversy. In *Chisholm* v. *Georgia* (1793) it ruled in favor of two South Carolina residents who had sued the state of Georgia for the recovery of confiscated property. Thus did the Court overthrow the common law principle that a sovereignty could not be sued without its consent, and it supported the Constitution's grant of federal jurisdiction over disputes "between a state and citizens of another state." Many localists feared that this nationalist ruling threatened the integrity of the states. In response, they proposed the Eleventh Amendment to the Constitution, ratified in 1798, which declared that no state could be sued by citizens from another state. The Supreme Court never-

theless established itself as the final authority on questions of law when it invalidated a Virginia statute in *Ware* v. *Hylton* (1796) and upheld the constitutionality of an act of Congress in *Hylton* v. *United States* (1796).

Hamilton's Controversial Fiscal Program

Fiscal and economic affairs pressed upon the new government. Lacking revenues, and faced with the massive national debt contracted during the Revolution, the government took power in a condition of virtual bankruptcy. Congress passed the Tariff of 1789, a compromise between advocates of protective tariffs (with duties so high that they made foreign products prohibitively expensive, thus "protecting" American products) and those who wanted moderate tariffs that produced income for the federal government. Duties on imported goods, rather than direct taxes on property or incomes, would constitute the bulk of federal revenues until the twentieth century.

In 1790, Treasury Secretary Hamilton submitted a "Report on the Public Credit," recommending that the federal government assume the obligations accumulated by the states during the previous fifteen years and redeem the national debt—owed to both domestic and foreign lenders—by agreeing to a new issue of interest-bearing bonds. By this means, Hamilton sought to inspire the confidence of domestic and foreign investors in the public credit of the new nation. Congress endorsed his plan to pay off the $11 million owed to foreign creditors, but balked at funding the domestic debt of $27 million and assuming the state debts of $25 million. Necessity had forced many individuals to sell off at deep discounts the notes, warrants, and securities the government had issued them during the Revolution. Yet Hamilton now advocated paying these obligations at face value, providing any speculator who held them with windfall profits. An even greater debate took place over the assumption of the state debts, for some states, mostly those in the South, had already arranged to liquidate them, whereas others had left theirs unpaid. Congress remained deadlocked on these issues for six months, until congressmen from Pennsylvania and Virginia arranged a compromise.

Final agreement, however, was stalled by a sectional dispute over the location of the new national capital.

Southerners supported Washington's desire to plant it on the Potomac River, but Northerners argued for Philadelphia. In return for Madison's pledge to obtain enough Southern votes to pass Hamilton's debt assumption plan—which Madison had earlier opposed as a "radically immoral" windfall for speculators—Northern congressmen agreed to a location for the new federal district on the boundary of Virginia and Maryland. In July 1790, Congress passed legislation moving the temporary capital from New York to Philadelphia until the expected completion of the federal city in the District of Columbia in 1800. Two weeks later, it adopted Hamilton's credit program. This was the first of many sectional compromises.

Hamilton now proposed the second component of his fiscal program, the establishment of a Bank of the United States. The bank, a public corporation funded by private capital, would serve as the depository of government funds and the fiscal agent of the Treasury. Congress narrowly approved it, but Madison's opposition raised doubts in the president's mind about the constitutionality of the measure, and Washington solicited the opinion of his cabinet. Here for the first time were articulated the classic interpretations of constitutional authority. Jefferson took a "strict constructionist" position, arguing that the powers of the federal government must be limited to those specifically enumerated in the Constitution. This position came closest to the basic agreement of the men who had drafted the document. Hamilton, on the other hand, reasoned that the Constitution "implied" the power to use whatever means were "necessary and proper" to carry out its enumerated powers—a loose constructionist position. Persuaded by Hamilton's opinion, Washington signed the bill, and the bank went into operation in 1791.

The final component of Hamilton's fiscal program, outlined in his famous "Report on Manufactures," was an ambitious plan, involving the use of government securities as investment capital for "infant industries," and high protective tariffs to encourage the development of an industrial economy. Many of Hamilton's specific proposals for increased tariff protection became part of a revision of duties that took place in 1792. Moreover, his fiscal program as a whole dramatically restored the financial health of the United States. Foreign investment in government securities increased and, along with domestic capital, provided the Bank of the United States with enormous reserves. Its bank notes became the most important circulating medium of the North American commercial economy, and their wide acceptance greatly stimulated business enterprise. "Our public credit," Washington declared toward the end of his

Alexander Hamilton (ca. 1804) by John Trumbull. Although Hamilton's fiscal program was controversial, it restored the financial health of the United States.

SOURCE: Art Resource, N.Y.

first term, "stands on that ground which three years ago it would have been considered as a species of madness to have foretold."

The Beginnings of Foreign Policy

The Federalist political coalition, forged during the ratification of the Constitution, was sorely strained by these debates over fiscal policy. By the middle of 1792, Jefferson, representing the Southern agrarians, and Hamilton, speaking for Northern capitalists, were locked in a full-scale feud within the Washington administration. Hamilton conducted himself more like a prime minister than a cabinet secretary, greatly offending Jefferson, who considered himself the president's heir apparent. But the dispute went deeper than a mere conflict of personalities. Hamilton stated the difference clearly when he wrote that "one side appears to believe that there is a serious plot to overturn the State governments, and substitute a monarchy to the present republican system," while "the other side firmly believes that there is a serious plot to overturn the general government and elevate the separate powers of the States upon its ruins." The conflict between Hamilton and Jefferson was to grow even more bitter over the issue of American foreign policy.

The commanding event of the Atlantic world during the 1790s was the French Revolution, which had begun in 1789. Most Americans enthusiastically welcomed the fall of the French monarchy. After the people of Paris stormed the Bastille, Lafayette sent Washington the key to its doors as a symbol of the relationship between the two revolutions. But with the beginning of the Reign of Terror in 1793, which claimed upon the guillotine the lives of hundreds of aristocrats, American conservatives began to voice their opposition. The execution of King Louis XVI, and especially the onset of war between revolutionary France and monarchical Great Britain in 1793, firmly divided American opinion.

Most at issue was whether the Franco-American alliance of 1778 required the United States to support France in its war with Britain. All of Washington's cabinet agreed on the importance of American neutrality. With France and Britain prowling for each other's vessels on the high seas, the vast colonial trade of Europe was delivered up to neutral powers, the United States prominent among them. In other words, neutrality meant windfall profits. Jefferson believed it highly unlikely that the French would call upon the Americans to honor the 1778 treaty; the administration should simply wait and see. But Hamilton argued that so great was the danger of American involvement in the war that Washington should immediately declare the treaty "temporarily and provisionally suspended."

These disagreements revealed two contrasting perspectives on the course the United States should chart in international waters. Hamilton and the nationalists believed in the necessity of an accommodation with Great Britain, the most important trading partner of the United States and the world's greatest naval power. Jefferson, Madison, and the democrats, on the other hand, looked for more international independence, less connection with the British, and thus closer relations with Britain's traditional rival, France. They pinned their hopes on the future of American western expansion.

The debate in the United States grew hotter with the arrival in early 1793 of French ambassador Edmond Genêt. Large crowds of supporters greeted him throughout the nation, and among them he solicited contributions and distributed commissions authorizing American privateering raids against the British. Understandably, a majority of Americans still nursed a hatred of imperial Britain, and these people expressed a great deal of sympathy for republican France. Conservatives such as Hamilton, however, favored a continuation of traditional commercial relations with Britain and feared the antiaristocratic violence of the French. Washing-

ton sympathized with Hamilton's position, but most of all, he wished to preserve American independence and neutrality. Knowing he must act before "Citizen" Genêt (as the ambassador was popularly known) compromised American sovereignty and involved the United States in a war with Britain, the president issued a proclamation of neutrality on April 22, 1793. In it he assured the world that the United States intended to pursue "a conduct friendly and impartial towards the belligerent powers," while continuing to do business with all sides.

Hamilton's supporters applauded the president, but Jefferson's friends were outraged. Throughout the country, those sympathetic to France organized Democratic Societies, political clubs modeled after the Sons of Liberty. Society members corresponded with each other, campaigned on behalf of candidates, and lobbied with congressmen. In a speech to Congress, President Washington denounced what he called these "self-created societies," declaring them "the most diabolical attempt to destroy the best fabric of human government and happiness."

Citizen Genêt miscalculated, however, alienating even his supporters, when he demanded that Washington call Congress into special session to debate neutrality. Jefferson, previously a confidant of the ambassador, now denounced Genêt as "hot-headed" and "indecent towards the President." But these words came too late to save his reputation in the eyes of Washington, and at the end of 1793, Jefferson left the administration. The continuing upheaval in France soon swept Genêt's party from power and he was recalled, but fearing the guillotine, he claimed sanctuary and remained in the United States. During his time in the limelight, however, he furthered the division of the Federalist coalition into a faction identifying with Washington, Hamilton, and conservative principles and a faction supporting Jefferson, Madison, democracy, and the French Revolution.

The United States and the Indian Peoples

Among the many problems of the Washington presidency, one of the most pressing concerned the West. The American attempt to treat the western tribes as conquered peoples after the Revolution had resulted only in further violence and warfare. In the Northwest Ordinance of 1787 (see Chapter 7), the Confederation Congress abandoned that premise for a new approach. "The utmost good faith shall always be observed towards the Indians," the Ordinance read. "Their lands and property shall never be taken from them without their consent." Yet the Ordinance was premised on the opening of Indian land north of the Ohio River to American settlement, its survey and sale, and the creation of new

Little Turtle, a war chief of the Miami tribe of the Ohio valley, led a large pan-Indian army to victory over the Americans in 1790 and 1791. After his forces were defeated at the Battle of Fallen Timbers in 1794, he became a friend of the United States. This lithograph is a copy of an oil portrait, which no longer survives, by the artist Gilbert Stuart.

SOURCE: Little Turtle, or Mich-i-kin-i-qua, Miami War Chief, Conqueror of Harmar and St. Clair. Lithograph made from a portrait painted in 1797 by Gilbert Stuart. Indiana Historical Society Library (negative no. C2584).

state governments. The Ordinance pointed in wildly contradictory directions.

The Constitution was silent regarding Indian policy, but the new federal government continued to pursue this inconsistent policy. In 1790, Congress passed the Intercourse Act, the basic law by which the United States would "regulate trade and intercourse with the Indian tribes." To eliminate the abuses of unscrupulous traders, the act created a federal licensing system; subsequent legislation authorized the creation of subsidized trading houses, or "factories," where Indians could obtain goods at reasonable prices. Trade abuses continued unabated for lack of adequate policing power, but these provisions indicated the best intentions of the Washington administration.

To clarify the question of Indian sovereignty, the act declared public treaties between the United States and the Indian nations to be the only legal means of obtaining Indian land. Treaty became the procedure for establishing and maintaining relations. In the twentieth century, a number of Indian tribes have successfully appealed for the return of lands obtained by states or individuals in violation of this provision of the Intercourse Act.

On the other hand, one of the federal government's highest priorities was the acquisition of western Indian land to supply a growing population of farmers (see Map 8.2). The federal government, in fact, was unable to control the flood of settlers coming down the Ohio River. An American expeditionary force was sent to evict the settlers, but inevitably they ended up fighting the Indians. In defense of their homelands, villages of Shawnees, Delawares, and other Indian peoples confederated with the Miamis under their war chief Little Turtle. In the fall of 1790, Little Turtle lured federal forces led by General Josiah Harmar into the confederacy's stronghold in Ohio and badly mauled them. In November 1791, the confederation inflicted an even more disastrous defeat on a large American force under General Arthur St. Clair, governor of the Northwest Territory. More than 900 Americans were killed or wounded, making this the worst defeat of an army by Indians in North American history.

In the aftermath of this defeat, the House of Representatives launched the first formal investigation of the executive branch undertaken by the Congress. They found St. Clair's leadership "incompetent," and he soon resigned. Yet few Americans were willing to admit to the contradiction at the heart of American policy. "We acknowledge the Indians as brothers," yet we "seize their lands," Senator Benjamin Hawkins of North Carolina wrote to President Washington. "This doctrine it might be expected would be disliked by the independent Tribes. . . . It is the source of their hostility."

Spanish Florida and British Canada

The position of the United States in the West was made even more precarious by the hostility of Spain and Great Britain, who controlled the adjoining territories. Under the dynamic leadership of King Carlos III and his able ministers, Spain introduced liberal reforms to revitalize the rule-bound economy of its American empire; as a result, the economy of New Spain grew rapidly in the 1780s. Moreover, Spain had reasserted itself in North America, acquiring the French claims to Louisiana before the end of the Seven Years' War, expanding into California, seizing the Gulf Coast during the American Revolution, and regaining Florida from Britain in the Treaty of Paris in 1783. The Spanish were deeply suspicious of the Americans. The settlers, the Spanish governor of Florida declared, "were nomadic like Arabs, . . .

MAP EXPLORATION

To explore an interactive version of this map,
go to **www.prenhall.com/faragher/map8.2**

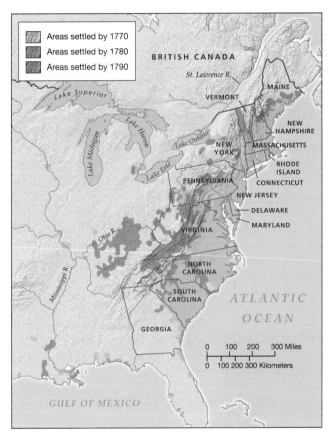

MAP 8.2 Spread of Settlement: The Backcountry Expands 1770–90 From 1770 to 1790, American settlement moved across the Appalachians for the first time. The Ohio Valley became the focus of bitter warfare between Indians and settlers.

American settlement by promoting immigration to Louisiana and Florida. They succeeded in attracting several thousand of the Acadians whom the British had deported during the Seven Years' War. Reassembling their distinctive communities in the bayou country of Louisiana, these tough emigrants became known as the Cajuns. But otherwise, the Spanish had little success with immigration and relied mostly on creating a barrier of pro-Spanish Indian nations in the lower Mississippi Valley. In the early 1790s, the Spanish constructed two new Mississippi River forts at sites that would later become the cities of Vicksburg and Memphis.

North of the Ohio River, the situation was much the same. Thousands of Loyalists had fled the United States in the aftermath of the Revolution and settled in the country north of lakes Ontario and Erie. They were understandably hostile to the new republic. In 1791, the British Parliament passed the Canada Act, creating the province of Upper Canada (later renamed Ontario) and granting the Loyalists limited self-government. To protect this province, British troops remained at a number of posts within American territory at places such as Detroit, where they supplied the Indian nations with arms and ammunition, hoping to create a buffer to

distinguished from savages only in their color, language, and the superiority of their depraved cunning and untrustworthiness." Spain claimed for itself much of the territory that today makes up the states of Tennessee, Alabama, and Mississippi, and pursued a policy designed to block the expansion of the new republic (see Map. 8.3).

Spain's anti-American policy in the West had several facets. Controlling both sides of the lower Mississippi, they closed the river to American shipping, making it impossible for western American farmers to market their crops through the port of New Orleans. They also sought to create a barrier to

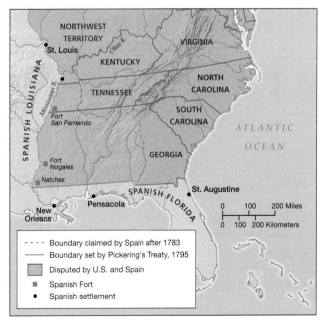

MAP 8.3 Spanish Claims to American Territory, 1783–95 Before 1795, the Spanish claimed the American territory of the Old Southwest and barred Americans from access to the port of New Orleans, effectively closing the Mississippi River. This dispute was settled by Pinckney's Treaty in 1795.

American expansion. British soldiers began constructing Fort Miami in the Maumee Valley, west of Lake Erie, well within American territory.

Domestic and International Crises

Washington faced the gravest crisis of his presidency in 1794. In the West, the inability of the federal government to subdue the Indians, eliminate the British from the northern fur trade, or arrange with the Spanish for unencumbered use of the Mississippi River stirred frontiersmen to loud protests. In the Old Northwest and Old Southwest, English and Spanish secret agents gave liberal bribes to entice American settlers to quit the Union and join themselves to Canada or Florida. In the Atlantic, Great Britain declared a blockade of France and seized vessels trading with the French West Indies. From 1793 to the beginning of 1794, the British confiscated the cargoes of more than 250 American ships, threatening hundreds of merchants with ruin. The United States was being "kicked, cuffed, and plundered all over the ocean," declared Madison, and in Congress, he introduced legislation imposing retaliatory duties on British ships and merchandise.

To make matters worse, in the summer of 1794, a rebellion broke out among farmers in western Pennsylvania. Congress had placed an excise tax on the distillation of whiskey, which many farm families produced from their surpluses of corn. Throughout rural America, farmers protested that the excise ran counter to the principles of the Revolution. "Internal taxes upon consumption," declared the citizens of Mingo Creek, in western Pennsylvania, are "most dangerous to the civil rights of freemen, and must in the end destroy the liberties of every country in which they are introduced." Hugh Henry Brackenridge, editor of the *Pittsburgh Gazette*, argued for a tax on the "unsettled lands which all around us have been purchased by speculating men, who keep them up in large bodies and obstruct the population of the country." In other words, Congress should tax land speculators, like President Washington, instead of backcountry squatters. Protest turned to riot when the Mingo Creek militia attempted to seize the tax collector, and several of their number were killed in the confrontation.

The "Whiskey Rebellion" came at a time when President Washington considered the nation to be under siege. The combination of Indian attack, international intrigue, and domestic insurrection, he believed, created the greatest threat to the nation since the Revolution. Declaring that the western disorders were "the first ripe fruit" of the democratic sentiment sweeping the country, Washington organized a federal army of 13,000 men, approximately the same size as the one he had commanded during the Revolution, and ordered the occupation of western Pennsylvania. Federal soldiers dragged half-naked men from their beds and forced them into open pens, where they remained for days in the freezing rain. Authorities arrested twenty people, and a judge convicted two of treason. The protest gradually died down. Washington pardoned the felons, sparing their lives. The president overreacted, for although there was riot and

In this 1794 painting, President George Washington reviews some 13,000 troops at Fort Cumberland on the Potomac before dispatching them to suppress the Whiskey Rebellion. Washington's mobilization of federal military power dramatically demonstrated the federal commitment to the preservation of the Union and the protection of the western boundary.

SOURCE: Francis Kemmelmeyer, *General George Washington Reviewing the Western Army at Fort Cumberland the 18th of October 1794*, after 1794. Oil on paper backed with linen. Dimensions: $18^{1}/_{8} \times 23^{1}/_{8}$. Courtesy of Winterthur Museum.

violence in western Pennsylvania, there was no organized insurrection. Nevertheless, his mobilization of federal military power dramatically demonstrated the federal commitment to the preservation of the Union, the protection of the western boundary, and the supremacy of the national over the local community.

Washington's action was reinforced by an impressive American victory against the Indian confederacy. Following the disastrous defeat of St. Clair by Little Turtle, Washington appointed General Anthony Wayne to lead a greatly strengthened American force to subdue the Indian confederacy and secure the Old Northwest. At the battle of Fallen Timbers, fought in the Maumee country of northern Ohio on August 20, 1794, Wayne crushed the Indians. Retreating, the warriors found the gates of Fort Miami closed and barred, the British inside unprepared to engage the powerful American force. The victory set the stage for the Treaty of Greenville in 1795, in which the representatives of twelve Indian nations ceded a huge territory encompassing most of present-day Ohio, much of Indiana, and other enclaves in the Northwest, including the town of Detroit and the tiny village of Chicago.

Jay's and Pinckney's Treaties

The strengthened American position in the West encouraged the British to settle their dispute with the United States so that they might concentrate on defeating republican France. In April 1794, Washington had dispatched Chief Justice John Jay to London to arrange a settlement with the British. In November, Jay and his British counterpart signed an agreement providing for British withdrawal from American soil by 1796, limited American trade with the British East and West Indies, and "most-favored-nation" status for both countries (meaning that each nation would enjoy trade benefits equal to those the other accorded any other nation-state). The treaty represented a solid gain for the young republic. With only a small army and no navy to speak of, the United States was in no position to wage war.

Details of Jay's Treaty leaked out in a piecemeal fashion that inflamed public debate. The treaty represented a victory for Hamilton's conception of American neutrality. The Jeffersonians, on the other hand, were enraged over this accommodation with Great Britain at France's expense. The absence in the treaty of any mention of compensation for the slaves who had fled to the British side during the Revolution alienated Southerners. Throughout the country Democratic Societies and Jeffersonian partisans organized protests and demonstrations. Upon his return to the United States, Jay joked, he could find his way across the country by the light of his burning effigies. Despite

these protests, the Senate, dominated by supporters of Hamilton, ratified the agreement in June 1795. In the House, a coalition of Southerners, Westerners, and friends of France attempted to stall the treaty by threatening to withhold the appropriations necessary for its implementation. They demanded that they be allowed to examine the diplomatic correspondence regarding the whole affair, but the president refused, establishing the precedent of "executive privilege" in matters of state.

The deadlock continued until late in the year, when word arrived in Philadelphia that the Spanish had abandoned their claims to the territory south of the Ohio River. Having declared war on revolutionary France, Spain had suffered a humiliating defeat. Fearing the loss of its American empire, the Spanish had suddenly found it expedient to mollify the quarrelsome Americans. In 1795, American envoy Thomas Pinckney negotiated a treaty in which Spain agreed to a boundary with the United States at the 31st parallel and to opening the Mississippi to American shipping the following year. This treaty fit the Jeffersonian conception of empire, and congressmen from the West and South were delighted with its terms. But administration supporters demanded their acquiescence in Jay's Treaty before the approval of Pinckney's Treaty.

These two important treaties finally established American sovereignty over the land west of the Appalachians and opened to American commerce a vast market extending from Atlantic ports to the Mississippi Valley. From a political standpoint, however, the events of 1794 and 1795 brought Washington down from his pedestal. Vilified by the opposition press, sick of politics, and longing to return to private life, Washington rejected the offer of a third term.

Washington's Farewell Address

During the last months of his term, Washington published his Farewell Address to the nation. "Our detached and distant situation," Washington explained, invited the nation to "defy material injury from external annoyance." He argued not for American isolation, but rather for American disinterest in the affairs of Europe. "The great rule of conduct for us in regard to foreign nations is, in extending our commercial relations to have with them as little political connection as possible." Why, he asked "entangle our peace and prosperity in the toils of European ambition, rivalship, interest, humor, or caprice?" Thomas Jefferson, in his Inaugural Address of 1801, paraphrased this first principle of American foreign policy as "peace, commerce, and honest friendship with all nations, entangling alliances with none."

FEDERALISTS AND JEFFERSONIAN REPUBLICANS

The framers of the Constitution envisioned a one-party state in which partisan distinctions would be muted by patriotism and public virtue. "Among the numerous advantages promised by a well constructed Union," Madison had written in *The Federalist*, is "its tendency to break and control the violence of faction." Not only did he fail to anticipate the rise of political parties or factions, but he saw them as potentially harmful to the new nation. Yet it was Madison who took the first steps toward organizing the opposition to the policies of the Washington administration, and it was Hamilton, who coauthored *The Federalist*, who organized administration supporters into a disciplined political faction. Despite the intentions of the framers, by the election of 1800, political factions or parties had become a fundamental part of the American system of government.

The Rise of Political Parties

The political debates of the first Washington administration pitted commercial against agrarian interests, representatives from the Atlantic seaboard against those from the frontier, Anglophiles against Francophiles. These shifting coalitions first began to polarize into political factions during the debate over Jay's Treaty in 1795, when agrarians, Westerners, Southerners, and supporters of France joined in opposition to the treaty. By the elections of 1796, people had begun to name the two factions. The supporters of Hamilton claimed the mantle of Federalism. "I am what the phraseology of politicians has denominated a FEDERALIST," declared one North Carolina candidate for office, "the friend of order, of government, and of the present administration." The opposition became known as the Republicans, a name suggesting that the Federalists were really monarchists at heart. "There are two parties at present in the United States," wrote a New York editor sympathetic to Jefferson, "aristocrats, endeavoring to lay the foundations of monarchical government, and Republicans, the real supports of independence, friends to equal rights, and warm advocates of free elective government." Historians call this opposition the Jeffersonian Republicans.

The two political factions played a fitful role in the presidential election of 1796, which pitted John Adams, Washington's vice president, against Thomas Jefferson. Partisan organization was strongest in the Middle States, where there was a real contest of political forces, weakest in New England and the South, where sectional loyalty prevailed and organized opposition was weaker. The absence of party discipline was demonstrated when the ballots of the presidential electors, cast in their respective state capitals, were counted in the Senate. Adams was victorious, but the electors chose Jefferson rather than a Federalist for vice president. The new administration was born divided.

The Adams Presidency

Adams was put in the difficult situation of facing a political opposition led by his own vice president. He nevertheless attempted to conduct his presidency along the lines laid down by Washington, and retained most of the former president's appointees. This arrangement presented Adams with another problem. Although Hamilton had

OVERVIEW

THE FIRST AMERICAN PARTY SYSTEM

Federalist Party	Organized by figures in the Washington administration who were in favor of a strong federal government, friendship with the British, and opposition to the French Revolution; its power base was among merchants, property owners, and urban workers tied to the commercial economy. A minority party after 1800, it was regionally strong only in New England.
Democratic Republican Party	Arose as the opposition to the Federalists; its adherents were in favor of limiting federal power; they were sympathetic to the French Revolution, and hostile to Great Britain; the party drew strength from Southern planters and Northern farmers. The majority party after 1800.

retired the year before, the cabinet remained committed to his advice, actively seeking his opinion and following it. As a result, Adams's authority was further undercut.

On the other hand, Adams benefited from the rising tensions between the United States and France. Angered by Jay's Treaty, the French suspended diplomatic relations at the end of 1796 and inaugurated a tough new policy toward American shipping. During the next two years, they seized more than 300 American vessels and confiscated cargoes valued at an estimated $20 million. Hoping to resolve the crisis, Adams sent an American delegation to France. But in dispatches sent back to the United States, the American envoys reported that agents of the French foreign ministry had demanded a bribe before any negotiations could be undertaken. Pressed for copies of these dispatches by suspicious Jeffersonian Republicans in Congress, in 1798, Adams released them after substituting the letters X, Y, and Z for the names of the French agents. The documents proved a major liability for the Jeffersonian Republicans, sparking powerful anti-French sentiment throughout the country. To the demand for a bribe, the American delegates had actually answered "Not a sixpence," but in the inflated rhetoric of the day, the response became the infinitely more memorable: "Millions for defense, but not one cent for tribute!" The XYZ Affair, as it became known, sent Adams's popularity soaring.

Adams and the Federalists prepared the country for war during the spring of 1798. Congress authorized tripling the size of the army, and Washington came out of retirement to command the force. Fears of a French invasion declined after word arrived of the British naval victory over the French in August 1798 at Aboukir Bay in Egypt, but the "Quasi-War" between France and the United States continued.

The Alien and Sedition Acts

In the summer of 1798, the Federalist majority in Congress, with the acquiescence of President Adams, passed four acts severely limiting both freedom of speech and the freedom of the press and threatening the liberty of foreigners in the United States. Embodying the fear that immigrants, in the words of one Massachusetts Federalist, "contaminate the purity and simplicity of the American character"

by introducing dangerous democratic and republican ideas, the Naturalization Act extended the period of residence required for citizenship from five to fourteen years. The Alien Act and the Alien Enemies Act authorized the president to order the imprisonment or deportation of suspected aliens during wartime. Finally, the Sedition Act provided heavy fines and imprisonment for anyone convicted of writing, publishing, or speaking anything of "a false, scandalous and malicious" nature against the government or any of its officers.

The Federalists intended these repressive laws as weapons to defeat the Jeffersonian Republicans. Led by Albert Gallatin, a Swiss immigrant and congressman from Pennsylvania (replacing Madison, who had retired from politics to devote his time to his plantation), the Jeffersonian Republicans contested all the Federalist war measures and acted as a genuine opposition party, complete with caucuses, floor leaders, and partisan discipline. For the first time, the two parties contested the election of Speaker of the House of Representatives, which became a partisan office. The more effective the Jeffersonian Republicans became, the more treasonous they appeared in the eyes of the Federalists. With the Revolution still fresh in memory, Americans had only a weak understanding of the concept of a loyal opposition. Disagreement

In this contemporary cartoon, *Congressional Pugilists, Congress Hall in Philadelphia, February 15, 1798,* Roger Griswold, a Connecticut Federalist, uses his cane to attack Matthew Lyon, a Vermont Democratic Republican, who retaliates with fire tongs. During the first years of the American republic, there was little understanding of the concept of a "loyal opposition," and disagreement with the policy of the Federalist administration was misconstrued as disloyalty.

SOURCE: Collection of The New York Historical Society, Neg. #33995.

with the administration was misconstrued by the Federalists as opposition to the state itself.

The Federalists thus pursued the prosecution of dissent, indicting leading Jeffersonian Republican newspaper editors and writers, fining and imprisoning at least twenty-five of them. The Sedition Act, Madison wrote, "ought to produce universal alarm, because it is levelled against the right of freely examining public characters and measures, and of free communication among the people thereon, which has ever been deemed the only effectual guardian of every other right." He and Jefferson anonymously authored resolutions, passed by the Virginia and Kentucky legislatures, declaring the Constitution nothing more than a compact among the sovereign states, and advocating the power of the states to "nullify" unconstitutional laws. When threatened with overbearing central authority, the Jeffersonian Republicans argued, the states had the right to go their own way. The Virginia and Kentucky Resolves, as they were known, had grave implications for the future of the Union, for they stamped the notion of secession with the approval of two of the founding fathers. The resolutions would later be used to justify the secession of the Southern states at the beginning of the Civil War.

The Revolution of 1800

The Alien and Sedition Acts were overthrown by the Jeffersonian Republican victory in the national elections of 1800 (see Map 8.4). As the term of President Adams drew to a close, Federalists found themselves seriously divided. In 1799, by releasing seized American ships and requesting negotiations, the French convinced Adams that they were ready to settle their dispute with the United States. The president also sensed the public mood running toward peace. But the Hamiltonian wing of the party, always scornful of public sentiment, continued to beat the drums of war. When Federalists in Congress tried to block the president's attempt to negotiate, Adams threatened to resign and turn the government over to Vice President Jefferson. "The end of war is peace," Adams declared, "and peace was offered me." Adams considered the settlement of this conflict with France to be one of the greatest accomplishments of his career, but it earned him the scorn of conservative Federalists, including Hamilton.

The Federalists divided at precisely the time when unity was necessary, allowing the Jeffersonian Republicans to capture the state governments of Pennsylvania and New York in 1799, the first important inroads of the party in the North. The presidential campaign of 1800 was the first in which Jeffersonian Republicans and Federalists operated as two national political parties. Caucuses of congressmen nominated respective slates: Adams and Charles Cotesworth Pinckney of South Carolina for the Federalists, Jefferson and Aaron Burr of New York for the Jeffersonian Republicans. Both tickets thus represented attempts at sectional balance. The Jeffersonian Republicans presented themselves as the party of traditional agrarian purity, of liberty and states' rights, of "government rigorously frugal and simple," in the words of Jefferson. They were optimistic, convinced that they were riding the wave of the future. Divided and embittered, the Federalists waged a defensive struggle for strong central government and public order, and often resorted to negative campaigning. They denounced Jefferson as an atheist, a Jacobin, and the father of mulatto children (a charge which was apparently true, according to the results of recent DNA tests, as noted in Chapter 4). One campaign placard put the issue succinctly: "GOD—AND A RELIGIOUS PRESIDENT" or "JEFFERSON—AND NO GOD!"

The balloting for presidential electors took place between October and December 1800. Adams took all the New England states while Jefferson captured the South and West. Jefferson called it "the Revolution of 1800." Party discipline was so effective that one of the provisions of the Constitution was shown to be badly outmoded. By this clause, the candidate receiving a majority of electoral votes became president and the

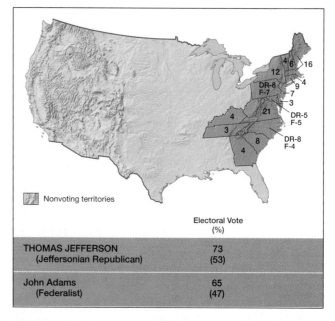

	Electoral Vote (%)
THOMAS JEFFERSON (Jeffersonian Republican)	73 (53)
John Adams (Federalist)	65 (47)

MAP 8.4 The Election of 1800 In the presidential election of 1800, Democratic Republican victories in New York and the divided vote in Pennsylvania threw the election to Jefferson. The combination of the South and these crucial Middle States would keep the Democratic Republicans in control of the federal government for the next generation.

runner-up became vice president. But by casting all their ballots for Jefferson and Burr, Jeffersonian Republican electors unintentionally created a tie and forced the election into the House of Representatives. Because the new Jeffersonian Republican–controlled Congress would not convene until March 1801, the Federalist majority was given a last chance to decide the election. They attempted to make a deal with Burr, who refused, but who also would not withdraw his name from consideration. Finally, on the thirty-fifth ballot, the Federalists gave up and arranged with their opponents to elect Jefferson without any of them having to cast a single vote in his favor. Congressman Matthew Lyon cast the symbolic final vote in a gesture of sweet revenge. The Twelfth Amendment, creating separate ballots for president and vice president, was ratified in time for the next presidential election.

The presidential election of 1800 was the first to feature campaign advertising. "T. Jefferson, President of the United States of America; John Adams—no more," reads the streamer on this election banner, illustrated with an American eagle and a portrait of Jefferson. This was mild rhetoric in a campaign characterized by wild charges. The Republicans labeled Adams a warmonger and a monarchist, while the Federalists denounced Jefferson as an atheist, Jacobin, and sexual libertine.

SOURCE: The Granger Collection.

Democratic Political Culture

Accompanying the rise of partisan politics was a transformation in popular political participation. Consider the custom of celebrating Independence Day. At the beginning of the 1790s, in many communities, the day featured demonstrations of military prowess by veteran officers, followed by banquets for leaders. Relatively few Americans played a direct role. But during the political controversies of the decade, a tradition of popular celebration developed. People took to the streets, set off fireworks, erected liberty poles, and listened to readings of the preamble of the Declaration of Independence, which more than any other document encapsulated and symbolized republican ideology. These celebrations took place first in Philadelphia, then in other large cities, and eventually spread throughout the country. By 1800, the Fourth of July had become the nation's most important holiday.

There was a corresponding increase in suffrage. In 1789, state regulations limited the franchise to a small percentage of the adult population. Women, African Americans, and Indians could not vote, but neither could a third to a half of all free adult males, who were excluded by tax-paying or property-owning requirements. Moreover, even among the eligible, the turnout was generally low. The traditional manner of voting was *viva voce*, by voice. At the polling place in each community individuals announced their selections aloud to the clerk of elections, who wrote them down. Not surprisingly, this system allowed wealthy men, landlords, and employers of the community to pressure poorer voters.

These practices changed with the increasing competition between Jeffersonian Republicans and Federalists. Popular pressure resulted in the introduction of universal white manhood suffrage in four states by 1800 and the reduction of property requirements in others. Thus was inaugurated a movement that would sweep the nation over the next quarter century. As a consequence, voter turnout increased in all the states. The growth of popular interest in politics was a transformation as important as the peaceful transition from Federalists to Jeffersonian Republicans in national government.

"THE RISING GLORY OF AMERICA"

In 1771, Philip Freneau and Hugh Henry Brackenridge addressed their graduating class at Princeton on "The Rising Glory of America." Thus far, American contributions to learning and the arts had been slim, they admitted. But they were boundlessly optimistic about the potential of their country. Indeed, judged against the literary and artistic work of individuals in the colonial period, artists and others of the Revolutionary generation accomplished a great deal in their effort to build a national culture.

American Artists

The first American to achieve prominence in the artistic world of Europe was Benjamin West, who painted portraits in his native Pennsylvania before leaving for the Continent and England, where he became popular as a painter of historical scenes. His *Death of General Wolfe* (1770) was one of the more acclaimed paintings of its day and the first to elevate an American scene to the high status of monumental historical painting. In

In this self-portrait, American artist Charles Willson Peale dramatically lifts the curtain on his Philadelphia Museum. Peale's three sons—whom he named after the artists Raphael, Rembrandt, and Titian—and two of his nieces—Anna and Sarah— also became noted painters, constituting something of a first family of American art in the early years of the new republic.

SOURCE: Charles Willson Peale, (1741-1827), *The Artist in His Museum*, 1822. Oil on canvas, 103 ¾" × 79⅞". Courtesy of the Pennsylvania Academy of the Fine Arts, Philadelphia. Gift of Mrs. Sarah Harrison. (The Joseph Harrison Jr. Collection.) ACC. no.:1878.1.2

1774, West was joined in London by John Singleton Copley, a Boston portraitist who left America because of his Loyalist sentiments. Copley's work is renowned for the truth and straightforwardness of his depictions, as in his famous portrait of Samuel Adams (1772). Both West and Copley remained in England after the Revolution. Their most promising student was Gilbert Stuart, whose work in the fashionable style of the day included a portrait of Mohawk leader Joseph Brant. Stuart returned to the United States in 1792 to paint what became the most famous portrait of President Washington.

The preeminent painter of the Revolution was Charles Willson Peale, who studied for a time with Benjamin West in London. He returned to America, however, and during the Revolution turned his talents to producing wartime propaganda. Although the almond eyes and bloated torsos of his figures suggest his technical limitations, Peale's work has a naive charm. His paintings of Washington, for example, seem more revealing of character than Stuart's placid portrait. Inspired by nationalist zeal, Peale planned a public gallery of heroes in Philadelphia that eventually grew into a famous museum of curios, reflecting his interest in natural history, archaeology, and exotic cultures. Federalists joked that its chaotic arrangement of exhibits mirrored Peale's Jeffersonian politics. Part science, part circus, the collection was purchased after Peale's death by the pioneer American entertainer P. T. Barnum.

John Trumbull of Connecticut, who had predicted America's rise to his Yale classmates, served as a soldier during the Revolution, then went to London to study with West. There he painted *The Battle of Bunker's Hill* (1785), (see Chapter 6) the first of a series of Revolutionary scenes, four of which he repainted in the Capitol rotunda in the early nineteenth century. Influenced by the grand style of eighteenth-century historical painting, Trumbull was concerned above all else with documentary detail in his scenes of the birth of America.

The Liberty of the Press

At the beginning of the Revolution in 1775, there were thirty-seven weekly or semiweekly newspapers in the thirteen colonies, only seven of which were Loyalist in sentiment. By 1789, the number of papers in the United States had grown to ninety-two, including eight dailies; three papers were being published west of the Appalachians. Relative to population, there were more newspapers in the United States than in any other country in the world—a reflection of the remarkably high literacy rate of the American people (see Chapter 5). In New England, almost 90 percent of the population could read, and even on the frontier, about two-thirds of the males were literate. During the political controversy of the 1790s, the press became the principal medium of Federalist and Jeffersonian Republican opinion, and papers came to be identified by their politics. In 1789, John Fenno, aided by Alexander Hamilton, began publication of the Federalist *Gazette of the United States*, and in 1791, Jefferson encouraged Philip Freneau to establish the competing *National Gazette*. The columns of these papers broadcast the feud between the two cabinet secretaries.

The prosecutions under the Sedition Act, however, threatened to curb the further development of the media, and in their opposition to these measures, Jeffersonian Republicans played an important role in establishing the principle of a free press. In *An Essay on Liberty of the Press* (1799), the Virginia lawyer George Hay, later appointed to the federal bench by President Jefferson, wrote that "a man may say everything which his passions suggest." Were this not true, he argued, the First Amendment would have been "the grossest absurdity that was ever conceived by the human mind." In his first Inaugural Address, Jefferson echoed this early champion of the freedom of expression. "Error of opinion may be tolerated," he declared, "where reason is left free to combat it."

The Birth of American Literature

The literature of the Revolution understandably reflected the dominating political concerns of the times. The majority of "best-sellers" during the Revolutionary era were political. The most important were Thomas Paine's *Common Sense* (1776) and his series of stirring pamphlets, published under the running title *The American Crisis* (1776–83), the first of which began with the memorable phrase "These are the times that try men's souls."

During the post-Revolutionary years there was an enormous outpouring of American publications. In the cities, the number of bookstores grew in response to the demand for reading matter. Perhaps even more significant was the appearance in the countryside of numerous book peddlers who supplied farm households with Bibles, gazettes, almanacs, sermons, and political pamphlets. Some of the most interesting American books of the postwar years examined the developing American character and proposed that the American, a product of many cultures, was a "new man" with ideas new to the world. John Filson, the author of the *Discovery, Settlement, and Present State of Kentucke* (1784), presented the narrative of one such new man, the Kentucky pioneer Daniel Boone. In doing so, he took an important step toward the creation of that most American of literary genres, the western.

But for Americans, the most important "new man" was George Washington. In 1800, an itinerant bookseller, Mason Locke Weems, published a short biography of the first president that became the new nation's first bestseller. Weem's *Life of Washington* introduced a series of popular and completely fabricated anecdotes, including the story of young Washington and the cherry tree. The book was a pioneering effort in mass culture, and Weems, as one historian puts it, was "the father of the Father of his Country." The biography was beloved by ordinary Americans of all

In this 1792 cartoon from the *Lady's Magazine*, the allegorical figure of "Columbia" receives a petition for the "Rights of Woman." In the aftermath of the Revolution, Americans debated the issue of an expanded role for women in the new republic. Many Federalists condemned "women of masculine minds," but there was general agreement among both conservatives and Democrats that the time had come for better education for American women.

SOURCE: The Library Company of Philadelphia.

political persuasions. Decades later, Abraham Lincoln recalled that he had read Weems "away back in my childhood, the earliest days of my being able to read," and had been profoundly impressed by "the struggles for the liberties of the country." Although Washington had in fact become a partisan leader of the Federalists during his second term, Weems presented him as a unifying figure for the political culture of the new nation, and that was the way he would be remembered.

Women on the Intellectual Scene

One of the most interesting literary trends of the 1790s was the growing demand for books that appealed to women readers. Susanna Haswell Rowson's *Charlotte Temple* (1791), a tale of seduction and abandonment, ran up tremendous sales and remained in print for more than a century. Other romantic works of fiction included *The Coquette* (1797) by Hannah Webster Foster. The young republic thus marked the first dramatic appearance of women writers and women readers. Although women's literacy rates continued to be lower than men's, they rose steadily as girls joined boys in common schools. This increase was one of the most important social legacies of the democratic struggles of the Revolutionary era.

Some writers argued that the new republican order ought to provide new roles for women as well as for men. The first avowed feminist in American history was Judith Sargent Murray, who publicly stated her belief that women "should be taught to depend on their own efforts, for the procurement of an establishment in life." She was greatly influenced by the English feminist Mary Wollstonecraft, but developed her line of thinking independently. Her essay "On the Equality of the Sexes," written in 1779 and published in 1790 threw down a bold challenge:

> Yes, ye lordly, ye haughty sex, our souls are by nature equal to yours: the same breath of God animates, enlivens, and invigorates us: and that we are not fallen lower than yourselves, let those witness who have greatly towered above the various discouragements by which they have been so heavily oppressed: and through I am unacquainted with the list of celebrated characters on either side, yet from the observations I have made in the contracted circle in which I have moved, I dare confidently believe, that from the commencement of time to the present day, there hath been as many females, as males, who, by the mere force of natural powers, have merited the crown of applause: who thus unassisted, have seized the wreath of fame.

"I expect to see our young women forming a new era in female history," Murray predicted. Federalists listened to such opinions with horror. "Women of masculine minds," one Boston minister sneered, "have generally masculine manners."

Judith Sargent Murray, a portrait by John Singleton Copley, completed in 1771. Born into an elite merchant family in Gloucester, Massachusetts, she became a wife and mother but also a poet, essayist, playwright, novelist, and historian. In 1779 she published an essay on the equality of the sexes that distinguished her as the first avowed feminist in American history.

SOURCE: John Singleton Copley (1738-1815), *Portrait of Mrs. John Stevens* (Judith Sargent, later Mrs. John Murray), 1770-72. Commissioned on the occasion of her first marriage, at age eighteen. Oil on canvas, 50 × 40 in. Daniel J. Terra Art Acquisition Endowment Fund, 2000.6. © Terra Foundation for American Art, Chicago / Art Resource, New York.

There seemed to be general agreement among all parties, however, that the time had come for better-educated and better-informed women. Republican institutions of self-government were widely thought to depend on the wisdom and self-discipline of the American people. Civic virtue, so indispensable for the republic, must be taught at home. By placing her learning at the service of her family, the "republican mother" was spared the criticism leveled at independent-minded women such as Murray. "A woman will have more commendation in being the mother of heroes," said a Federalist, "than in setting up, Amazon-like, for a heroine herself." Thus were women provided the opportunity to be not simply "helpmates," but people "learned and wise." But they were also expected to be content with a narrow role, not to wish for fuller participation in American democracy. (See Out of Many Voices: A Young Woman Ponders Her Choices.)

OUT OF MANY VOICES

A YOUNG WOMAN PONDERS HER CHOICES

Eliza Southgate was the nineteen-year-old daughter of a wealthy doctor, living in Portland, Maine, when she wrote this letter to her cousin, Moses Porter, on May 23, 1802. Well-educated and articulate, she satirically described the realities of career choice for women at the beginning of the nineteenth century.

I HAVE OFTEN THOUGHT WHAT PROFESSION I should choose were I a man. I might then think very differently from what I do now, yet I have always thought if I felt conscious of possessing brilliant talents, the law would be my choice. Then I might hope to arrive at an eminence which would be gratifying to my feelings. I should then hope to be a public character, respected and admired,—but unless I was convinced I possessed the talents which would distinguish me as a speaker I would be anything rather than a lawyer;—from the dry sameness of such employments as the business of an office all my feelings would revolt, but to be an eloquent speaker would be the delight of my heart. I thank Heaven I was born a woman. I have now only patiently to wait till some clever fellow shall take a fancy to me and place me in a situation, I am determined to make the best of it, let it be what it will. We ladies, you know, possess that "sweet pliability of temper" that disposes us to enjoy any situation, and we must have no choice in these things till we find what is to be our destiny, then we must consider it the best in the world. But remember, I desire to be thankful I am not a man. I should not be content with moderate abilities—nay, I should not be content with mediocrity in anything, but as a woman I am equal to the generality of my sex, and I do not feel that great desire of fame I think I should if I was a man.

I hardly know what to say to you, Cousin. I can hardly believe you serious when you say that "the enlargement of the mind will inevitably produce superciliousness and a desire of ascendancy." I should much sooner expect it from an ignorant, uncultivated mind. We cannot enlarge and improve our minds without perceiving our weakness, and wisdom is always modest and unassuming. On the contrary, a mind that has never been exerted knows not its deficiencies and presumes much more on its powers than it otherwise would. You beg me to say no more about enlarging the mind, as it is disagreeable, and you are too much prejudiced ever to listen with composure to me when I write on the subject. On what subjects shall I write you? I shall either fatigue and disgust you with feminine trifles, or shock you by stepping beyond the limits you have prescribed. ■

SOURCE: Eliza Southgate Browne, *A Girl's Life Eighty Years Ago* (New York: Scribner's Sons, 1887), p. 102.

CONCLUSION

In 1800, the population of Canada numbered about 500,000. Those of European background in New Mexico and the other Spanish North American colonies numbered approximately 25,000. And the Indian people of the continent numbered anywhere from 500,000 to a million. Overwhelming all these groups was the population of the United States, which stood at 5.3 million and was growing at the astounding annual rate of 3 percent.

During the last years of the eighteenth century, the United States had adopted a new constitution and established a new national government. It had largely repaid the debt run up during the Revolution and made peace with adversaries abroad and Indian peoples at home. Americans had begun to learn how to channel their disagreements into political struggle. The nation had withstood a first decade of stress, but tensions continued to divide the people. At the beginning of the new century, it remained uncertain whether the new nation would find a way to control and channel the energies of an expanding people.

CHRONOLOGY

1786	Annapolis Convention
1787	Constitutional Convention
1787–88	*The Federalist* published
1788	Constitution ratified
	First federal elections
1789	President George Washington inaugurated in New York City
	Judiciary Act
	French Revolution begins
1790	Agreement on site on the Potomac River for the nation's capital
	Indian Intercourse Act
	Judith Sargent Murray publishes "On the Equality of the Sexes"
1791	Bill of Rights ratified
	Bank of the United States chartered
	Alexander Hamilton's "Report on Manufactures"
	Ohio Indians defeat General Arthur St. Clair's army
1793	England and France at war; America reaps trade windfall
	Citizen Genêt affair

	President Washington proclaims American neutrality in Europe
	British confiscate American vessels
	Supreme Court asserts itself as final authority in *Chisholm* v. *Georgia*
1794	Whiskey Rebellion
	Battle of Fallen Timbers
	Jay's Treaty with the British concluded
1795	Pinckney's Treaty negotiated with the Spanish
	Treaty of Greenville
	Thomas Paine publishes *The Age of Reason*
1796	President Washington's Farewell Address
	John Adams elected president
1797–98	French seize American ships
1798	XYZ Affair
	"Quasi-war" with France
	Alien and Sedition Acts
	Kentucky and Virginia Resolves
1800	Convention of 1800
	Thomas Jefferson elected president
	Mason Locke Weems publishes *Life of Washington*

REVIEW QUESTIONS

1. Discuss the conflicting ideals of local and national authority in the debate over the Constitution.
2. What were the major crises faced by the Washington and Adams administrations?
3. Describe the roles of Madison and Hamilton in the formation of the first American political parties.
4. What did Jefferson mean when he talked of "the Revolution of 1800"?
5. Discuss the contributions of the Revolutionary generation to the construction of a national culture.

RECOMMENDED READING

Akhil Reed Amar, *The Bill of Rights: Creation and Reconstruction* (1998). A legal analysis arguing that the first ten Amendments were meant to protect the majority from the potential tyranny of the federal government.

William N. Chambers, *Political Parties in a New Nation: The American Experience, 1776–1809* (1963). An introduction to the formation of the American party system. Though several decades old, it remains essential.

Robert A. Dahl, *How Democratic is the American Constitution?* (2003). An eminent political scientist examines the anti-democratic character of the nation's defining political document.

Stanley Elkins and Eric McKitrick, *The Age of Federalism* (1993). A massive and informative account of the politics of the 1790s, from the ratification of the Constitution to the election of Jefferson.

Paul Finkelman, *Slavery and the Founders: Race and Liberty in the Age of Jefferson* (2001). A persuasive historical argument that the constitution legitimated a "slave-holders' republic."

Joanne B. Freeman, *Affairs of Honor: National Politics in the New Republic* (2001). A major reassessment of political culture in the new republic, stressing the importance of the culture of honor.

Reginald Horsman, *The Frontier in the Formative Years, 1783–1815* (1970). A sensitive survey of developments in the West, emphasizing that the "western question" was one of the most important facing the young republic.

Jackson Turner Main, *The Antifederalists: Critics of the Constitution, 1781–1788* (1961). A detailed examination of the localist tradition in early American politics. Includes a discussion of the ratification of the Constitution from the point of view of its opponents.

Simon P. Newman, *Parades and the Politics of the Street: Festive Culture in the Early American Republic* (1997). The participation of ordinary Americans in the political culture of the new republic.

Leonard L. Richards, *Shays' Rebellion: The American Revolution's Final Battle* (2002). A new interpretation that significantly broadens the meaning of the uprising of farmers in western Massachusetts.

James M. Smith, *Freedom's Fetters: The Alien and Sedition Laws and American Civil Liberties* (1966). Remains the best overview of the Federalist threat to liberty, as well as the Jeffersonian Republican counterattack.

Bernard A. Weisberger, *America Afire: Jefferson, Adams, and the Revolutionary Election of 1800* (2000). Shows that the election and the transfer of power were victories for popular self-government and that they set a major precedent for all other elections.

Gordon Wood, *The Creation of the American Republic, 1776–1787* (1969). This general survey provides the best overview of the Constitutional Convention.

 For additional study resources for this chapter, go to the *Companion Website,* http://www.prenhall.com/faragher.

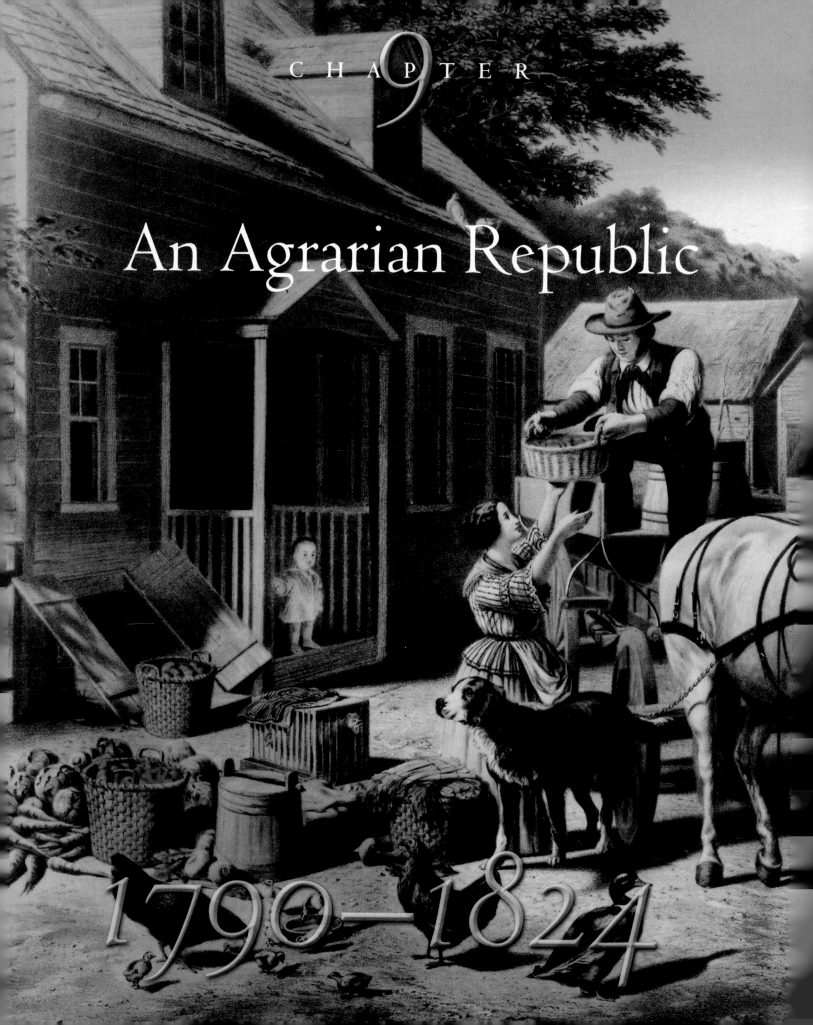

CHAPTER 9

An Agrarian Republic

1790–1824

CHAPTER OUTLINE

Expansion Touches Mandan Villages on the Upper Missouri

In mid-October 1804, news arrived at the Mandan villages, prominently situated on bluffs overlooking the upper Missouri River, that an American military party led by Meriwether Lewis and William Clark was coming up the river. The principal chiefs, hoping for expanded trade and support against their enemies the Sioux, welcomed these first American visitors. As the expedition's three boats and forty-three men approached the village, Clark wrote, "great numbers on both sides flocked down to the bank to view us." That evening, the Mandans welcomed the Americans with an enthusiastic dance and gifts of food.

Since the fourteenth century, when they had migrated from the East, the Mandans had lived along the Missouri, on the edge of the Great Plains in what is now North Dakota. They believed their homeland was "the very center of the world," and indeed it is in the heart of the North American continent. Mandan men hunted buffalo and Mandan women kept storage pits full with abundant crops of corn, beans, squash, sunflowers, and tobacco grown on the fertile soil of the river bottomlands. The Mandan villages were also the central marketplace of the northern Plains; at trading time in late summer they filled with Crows, Assiniboins, Cheyennes, Kiowas, and Arapahoes. Well before any of these people, or those of other tribes, had met a European, they were trading in kettles, knives, and guns acquired from the French and English to the east and leatherwork, glassware, and horses acquired from the Spanish in the Southwest.

Mandan
Villages

The eighteenth century had been a golden age for the Mandan, who with their closely related Hidatsa neighbors numbered about 3,000 in 1804. In each of their five villages, earth lodges surrounded a central plaza. One large ceremonial lodge was used for community gatherings, and each of the other earth lodges was home to a senior woman, her husband, her sisters (perhaps married to the same man as she, for the Mandans practiced polygamy), their daughters and their unmarried sons, along with numerous grandchildren. Matrilineal clans, the principal institution of the community, distributed food to the sick, adopted orphans, cared for the dependent elderly, and punished wrongdoers. A village council of male clan leaders selected chiefs who led by consensus and lost power when people no longer accepted their opinions.

Lewis and Clark had been sent by President Thomas Jefferson to survey the Louisiana Purchase and to find an overland route to the Pacific Ocean. They were also instructed to inform the Indians that they now owed loyalty—and trade—to the American government, thereby challenging British economic control over the lucrative North American fur trade. Meeting with the village chiefs, the Americans offered the Mandans a military and economic alliance. His people would like nothing better, responded Chief Black Cat, for the Mandans had fallen on hard times over the past decade. [Some twenty years earlier], "the smallpox destroyed the greater part of the nation," the chief said. "All the nations before this malady [were] afraid of them, [but] after they were reduced, the Sioux and other Indians waged war, and killed a great many." Black Cat was skeptical that the Americans would deter the Sioux, but Clark reassured him. "We were ready to protect them," Clark reported in his journal, "and kill those who would not listen to our good talk."

The Americans spent the winter with the Mandans, joining in their communal life and establishing firm and friendly relations with them. There were dances and joint hunting parties, frequent visits to the earth lodges, long talks around the fire, and, for many of the men, pleasant nights in the company of Mandan women. Lewis and Clark spent many hours acquiring important geographic information from the Mandans, who drew charts and maps showing the course of the Missouri, the ranges of the Rocky Mountains, and places where one could cross the Continental Divide. The information provided by the Mandans and other Indian peoples to the west was vital to the success of the expedition. Lewis and Clark's "voyage of discovery" depended largely on the willingness of Indian peoples to share their knowledge of the land with the Americans.

In need of interpreters who could help them communicate with other Indian communities on their way, the Americans hired several multilingual Frenchmen who lived with the Mandans. They also acquired the services of Sacajawea, the fifteen-year-old Lemhi wife of one of the Frenchmen, who became the only woman to join the westward journey. The presence of Sacajawea and her baby son was a signal, as Clark noted, to "all the Indians as to our friendly intentions"; everyone knew that women and children did not go on war parties.

When the party left the Mandan villages in March, Clark wrote, his men were "generally healthy, except venereal complaints which is very common amongst the natives and the men catch it from them." After an arduous journey across the Rockies, the party reached the Pacific Ocean at the mouth of the Columbia River, where they spent the winter. Overdue and feared lost, they returned in triumph to St. Louis in September 1806. Before long the Americans had established Fort Clark at the Mandan villages, giving American traders a base for challenging British dominance of the western fur trade. The permanent American presence brought increased contact, and with it much more disease. In 1837, a terrible smallpox epidemic carried away the vast majority of the Mandans, reducing the population to fewer than 150. Four Bears, a Mandan chief who had been a child at the time of the Lewis and Clark visit, spoke these last words to the remnants of his people:

"I have loved the whites," he declared. "I have lived with them ever since I was a boy." But in return for the kindness of the Mandans, the Americans had brought this plague. "I do not fear death, my friends," he said, "but to die with my face rotten, that even the wolves will shrink with horror at seeing me, and say to themselves, that is Four Bears, the friend of the whites." "They have deceived me," he pronounced with his last breath. "Those that I always considered as brothers turned out to be my worst enemies."

In sending Lewis and Clark on their "voyage of discovery" to claim the land and the loyalty of the Mandans and other western Indian communities, President Jefferson was motivated by his vision of an expanding American republic of self-sufficient farmers. During his and succeeding presidencies, expansion became a key element of national policy and pride. Yet, as the experience of the Mandans showed, what Jefferson viewed as enlargement of "the empire for liberty" had a dark side—the destruction, from disease and coerced displacement, of the communities created by America's first peoples. The effects—economic, political, and social—of continental expansion dominate the history of the United States in the first half of the nineteenth century.

KEY TOPICS

- The development of America's economy in a world of warring great powers
- The role of Jefferson's presidency and his agrarian republicanism in forging a national identity
- The ending of colonial dependency by the divisive War of 1812
- The nationalizing force of westward expansion

NORTH AMERICAN COMMUNITIES FROM COAST TO COAST

In spite of the political turmoil of the 1790s, the young United States entered the new century full of national pride and energy. But the larger issue, America's place in the world, was still uncertain, beginning with its situation on the North American continent (see Map 9.1).

The Former American Colonies

At first glance, the United States of America in 1800 was little different from the scattered colonies of the pre-Revolution era. Two-thirds of the young nation's people still lived in a long thin line of settlement within fifty miles of the Atlantic coast. From New Hampshire to Georgia, most people lived on farms or in small towns. Because they rarely traveled far from home, peoples' horizons were limited and local. Nevertheless, the new nation was already transforming itself: between 1790 and 1800, according to the

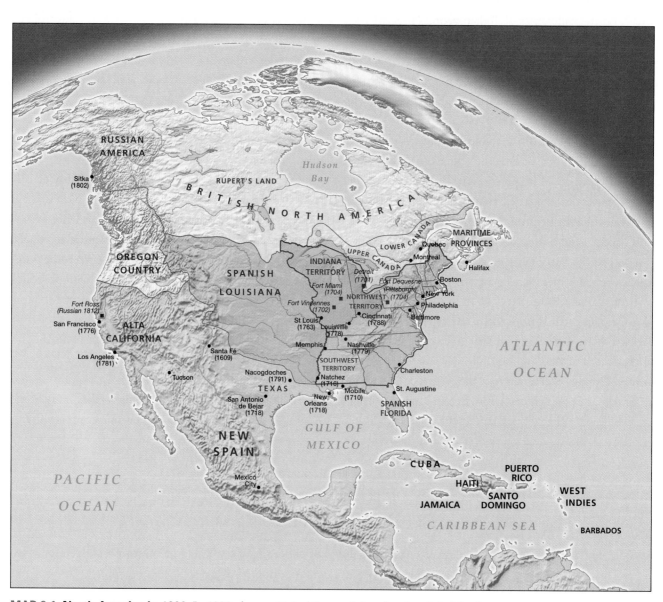

MAP 9.1 North America in 1800 In 1800, the new United States of America shared the North American continent with territories held by the European powers: British Canada, French Louisiana (secretly ceded that year to France by Spain), Spanish Florida, Spanish Mexico, and Russian Alaska, expanding southward along the Pacific coast. Few people could have imagined that by 1850, the United States would span the continent. But the American settlers who had crossed the Appalachians to the Ohio River Valley were already convinced that opportunity lay in the West.

first and second federal censuses, the American population grew from 3.9 million to 5.3 million. Growth by migration was greatest in the trans-Appalachian West, a region that was already home to approximately 100,000 Indians. From 1800 to 1850, in an extraordinary burst of territorial expansion, Americans surged westward all the way to the Pacific. In 1800, few people would have predicted that within fifty years the nation would encompass the entire continent. Then, the United States of America was a new and weak nation sharing a continent with the colonies of many of the world's great powers.

Spanish Colonies

On paper, Spain possessed most of North America, but its control crumbled rapidly in the 1790s, affecting New Spain, the richest colony in Spanish America. Mexico City, with a population of 200,000, was by far the largest and most elegant city on the continent. But there were smoldering problems. Tensions mounted between the Spanish-born *peninsulares*, high officials and bureaucrats, and the native-born *criollos* of Spanish descent, who chafed at their subordination, especially after the success of the American Revolution. In the 1790s, there were two abortive criollo conspiracies on behalf of independence in Mexico City alone. Furthermore, none of New Spain's northern provinces, created to protect the approaches to Mexico's fabulously wealthy silver mines, thrived. In all of the older settlements—San Antonio, Santa Fé, and Tucson— only a handful of persons of Spanish descent lived among a preponderantly native population. This was true even in the most recently founded northern province, Alta (Upper) California.

In 1769, in their last effort to protect their rich colony of Mexico, the Spanish established a chain of twenty-one missions in Alta California that stretched north from San Diego (1769) to Sonoma (1823). The largest of these missions was Los Angeles, which in 1800 had a largely mestizo population of 300. The town, which was the social center for the vast countryside surrounding it, functioned chiefly as a center of governmental authority (see Chapter 5). Despite Spain's desire to seal its territory from commerce with other nations, a brisk but illegal trade in otter skins, hides, and tallow developed between the United States and California after the first American ship, the *Lelia Bird*, arrived in 1803.

American traders were making inroads on Spanish-held territory along the Mississippi River as well. New Orleans, acquired by Spain from France at the end of the Seven Years' War in 1763, was becoming a thriving international port. In 1801, it shipped more than $3 million worth of tobacco, sugar, rice, cotton, fruits, and vegetables to Europe. Every year, a greater proportion of products for the New Orleans trade was supplied by Americans living some distance up the Mississippi River.

Pinckney's 1795 treaty with Spain guaranteed Americans free navigation of the Mississippi River and the right to deposit goods at the port of New Orleans. Nevertheless, Americans were uncomfortably aware that the city's crucial location at the mouth of the Mississippi meant that whatever foreign nation possessed New Orleans had the power to choke off the flourishing trade in the vast Mississippi Valley river system.

More than 600 miles north was the small trading town of St. Louis, founded by the New Orleans trader Pierre Laclède in 1763. By 1800, the town had fewer than a thousand residents, three-quarters of whom were involved in the Indian trade of the Missouri River. Spanish officials tried to supervise that trade from their offices in the town, but real control rested in the hands of the Laclèdes and other French traders. Americans visiting this shabby little place laughed at Pierre Laclède's prediction that St. Louis would become "one of the finest cities in America," but he was right.

Haiti and the Caribbean

The Caribbean posed other challenges. The rich sugar-producing islands, variously colonies of Spain (Cuba, Puerto Rico, and Santo Domingo), France (Martinique, Guadaloupe, and Saint-Domingue), and Britain (Barbados, Jamaica, and a number of smaller islands), provided 80 to 90 percent of the European supply of sugar. All the sugar plantations used enslaved Africans as the labor force. Thus, they shared with the slaveholding American South a distinctive Afro–North American society that cut across national boundaries. This world was jolted in 1791 by the revolt of black slaves in Saint-Domingue, France's richest colony. Under the leadership of Toussaint L'Ouverture, the former colony, renamed Haiti, became North America's first independent black nation. Its existence struck fear into the hearts of white slaveowners at the same time that it served as a beacon of hope to the enslaved.

British North America

British North America had been wrested from the French in the Seven Years' War (see Chapter 6). In 1800, its heart remained the former French colony of Quebec (at that time called the province of Lower Canada), with a predominantly French population of about 160,000. Most of the rest of the settlers elsewhere were American, either Loyalists driven out at the time of the Revolution or simply farmers in search of better land. British authorities, fearing civil disturbances, discouraged American immigrants from settling among the French, directing them instead either to the Maritime Provinces, dominated by Nova Scotia's great port, Halifax, or to Upper Canada, the first inland colony north of the Great Lakes, established in 1791. Farther west (and closed to settlement) lay Rupert's Land, the great stretch of the Canadian north and west that was administered by the Hudson's Bay Company. To allay popular demands stimulated by the American Revolution, Britain established legislative assemblies in Upper and Lower Canada and in the Maritimes in 1791, but, learning from their American fiasco, Britain kept the legislatures under strong executive control. British North America dominated the continental fur trade and the great succession of waterways—the St. Lawrence River, the Great Lakes, and the rivers beyond—that made it possible. Britain was on friendly terms with many of the native peoples who were part of the trade. This economic grip was a challenge and frustration to many westward-moving Americans. At the same time, the dispersed nature of the Canadian colonies made them, at least in the eyes of some Americans, ripe for conquest.

Russian America

Finally, Russian occupation of what is now Alaska posed another, rather remoter threat to the United States. Russian settlement of Alaska was an extension of its conquest of Siberia, which was driven by the fur trade. In 1741, commissioned by Tsar Peter the Great, the Danish-born naval officer Vitus Bering sailed east from Kamchatka across the sea that now bears his name, explored the Aleutian Islands, and made landfall on the southern coast of Alaska. In the aftermath of his voyages, Russian and

Siberian fur trappers, known as *promyshleniki*, became regular visitors to the Aleutian Islands and the Alaskan coast. By the late 1750s, they were shipping a steady supply of furs from Russian America.

The Russians sometimes took furs by force, holding whole villages hostage and brutalizing the native Inuit and Aleut peoples. After the Aleut Revolt of 1766, the Russian authorities promised to end the abuse, but by 1800, the precontact population of 25,000 Aleuts had been greatly reduced. At the same time, sexual relations and intermarriage between fur trappers and Aleut women created a large group of Russian creoles who assumed an increasingly prominent position in the Alaskan fur trade as navigators, explorers, clerks, and traders as the fur trade became permanent.

The Russian-American Company, chartered by the Tsar in 1799, first set up American headquarters at Kodiak. When overhunting caused a scarcity of furs, the Russians moved their headquarters south to Sitka, in what is now the southeastern panhandle of Alaska. This was the homeland of the Tlingits, a warrior society, who destroyed the Russians' first fortress in the Tlingit Revolt of 1802. The Russians reestablished Sitka by force in 1804, and over the next generation, established Russian settlements along the Pacific Coast as far south as Fort Ross, which was just north of San Francisco Bay and well within Spanish territory. The Russian presence in North America was rapidly expanding even as Spain's faltered. In 1800, however, this imperial duel was far from the consciousness of most Americans, who were more concerned about the continuing presence of the British to the north in Canada and the nearby racial powder keg in the Caribbean.

Trans-Appalachia: Cincinnati

Within the United States itself, the region of greatest growth was territory west of the Appalachian Mountains, and it was this area that was most affected by fears of continuing British influence on regional Indian peoples. By 1800, about 500,000 people (the vast majority from Virginia and North Carolina) had found rich and fertile land along the Ohio River system. Soon there was enough population for statehood. Kentucky (1792) and Tennessee (1796) were the first trans-Appalachian states admitted to the Union.

This view shows Sitka, the center of Russian activities in Alaska, in 1827. Russian architectural styles and building techniques are apparent in the Church of St. Michael the Archangel in the right background, contrasting with the Asian and Indian origins of most of Sitka's inhabitants.

SOURCE: Freidrich H. von Kittlitz, *A View of the Russian Capital*, 1827. Elmer E. Rosmusen Library Rare Books, University of Alaska, Fairbanks, from F.P. Litke, Coozy. The Charles Bunnell Collection, Acc. 12-345-678, Archives and Manuscripts, Alaska and Polar Regions Department.

Migration was a principal feature of American life. Probably 5 to 10 percent of all American households moved each year. In the rural areas of the Atlantic seaboard, a third of the households counted in the 1790 census had moved by 1800; in cities, the proportion was closer to half. Migration to the West was generally a family affair, with groups of kin moving together to a new area. One observer wrote of a caravan moving across the mountains: "They had prepared baskets made of fine hickory withe or splints, and fastening two of them together with ropes they put a child in each basket and put it across a pack saddle." Once pioneers had managed to struggle by road over the Appalachians, they gladly took to the rivers, especially the Ohio, to move farther west.

Cincinnati, strategically situated 450 miles downstream from Pittsburgh, was a particularly dramatic example of the rapid community growth and development that characterized the trans-Appalachian region. Founded in 1788, Cincinnati began life as a military fort, defending settlers in the fertile Miami River Valley of Ohio from resistance by Shawnee and Miami Indians. Conflict between these Indian peoples and the new settlers was so fierce that the district was grimly referred to as "the slaughter-house." After the battle of Fallen Timbers broke Indian resistance in 1794, Cincinnati became the point of departure for immigrants arriving by the Ohio River on their way to settle the interior of the Old Northwest: Ohio, Indiana, and Illinois. In 1800, Cincinnati had a population of about 750 people. By 1810, it had tripled in size, confirming its boast to be "the Queen City of the West."

Cincinnati merchants were soon shipping farm goods from the fertile Miami Valley down the Ohio–Mississippi River system to New Orleans, 1,500 miles away. River hazards like snags and sandbars made the downriver trip by barge or keelboat hazardous, and the return trip upriver was slow, more than three months from New Orleans to Cincinnati. Frequently, rivermen simply abandoned their flatboats in New Orleans and traveled home overland, on foot or horseback, by the long and dangerous Natchez Trace, an old Indian trail that linked Natchez on the Mississippi with Nashville, Tennessee. Nevertheless, river traffic increased yearly, and the control of New Orleans became a key concern of western farmers and merchants. If New Orleans refused to accept American goods, Cincinnati merchants and many thousands of trans-Appalachian farmers would be ruined.

Atlantic Ports: From Charleston to Boston

Although only 3 percent of the nation's population lived in cities, the Atlantic ports continued, as in the colonial era, to dominate the nation economically and politically. Seaports benefited from the advantage of relatively quick waterborne trade and communication over much slower land travel. Merchants in the seaboard cities found it easier to cross the Atlantic than to venture into their own backcountry in search of trade. In 1800, the nation's most important urban centers were all Atlantic seaports: Charleston (which had a population of 20,000), Baltimore (26,000), Philadelphia (70,000), New York (60,000), and Boston (25,000). Each had a distinctive regional identity.

Charleston, South Carolina, was the South's premier port. In colonial days, Charleston had grown rich on its links with the British West Indies and on trade with England in rice, long-staple cotton, and indigo. The social center for the great low-country plantation owners, Charleston was

When John Caspar Wild painted this view of Cincinnati in 1835, its location on the Ohio River had already established it as center for the trade in agricultural goods shipped down the river to New Orleans, first by flatboat and later by steamboat. (John Caspar Wild, *View of Cincinnati*, 1835, Museum of Fine Arts, Boston.)

SOURCE: John Caspar Wild (American, about 1804-1846), *Cincinnati, Ohio*, about 1835. Watercolor and gouache with highlights in white on paper, Image: 48.4 × 68.4 cm (19 1/16 × 26 15/16 in.), Sheet: 50.8 × 70.2 cm (20 × 27 5/8 in.) Courtesy, Museum of Fine Arts, Boston. The M. and M. Karolik Collection of American Watercolors, Drawings, and Prints, 1800-1875. Reproduced with permission. Photograph © 2006 Museum of Fine Arts, Boston. All Rights Reserved.

a multiracial city of whites, African Americans (2,000 of them free), Indian peoples, and the mixed-race offspring of these three groups. One was as likely to hear French, Spanish, or Gullah and Geeche (African-based dialects of low-country slaves) as English. This graceful, elegant city was a center for the slave trade until 1808.

Baltimore was the major port for the tobacco of the Chesapeake Bay region and thus was connected with the slave-owning aristocracy of the Upper South. But proximity to the wheat-growing regions of the Pennsylvania backcountry increasingly inclined the city's merchants to look westward and to consider ways to tap the trade of the burgeoning Ohio country.

Philadelphia, William Penn's "City of Brotherly Love," was distinguished by the commercial and banking skills of Quaker merchants. These merchants had built international trade networks for shipping the farm produce of Pennsylvania's German farmers. Philadelphia served as the nation's capital in the 1790s, and was acknowledged as its cultural and intellectual leader as well.

New York, still faintly Dutch in architecture and social customs, was soon to outgrow all the other cities. New York merchants were exceptionally aggressive in their pursuit of trade. Unlike their counterparts in Philadelphia and Boston, New Yorkers accepted the British auction system, which cut out the middleman and offered goods in large lots at wholesale prices at open auctions. Increasingly, British imports entered America through the port of New York. New York's shipping, banking, insurance, and supporting industries boomed, and as early as 1800, a quarter of all American shipping was owned by New York merchants.

Boston, the cockpit of the American Revolution, was also the capital of Massachusetts. The handsome State House, built on Beacon Hill, reflected the origins of Boston's merchant wealth: a carved wooden codfish occupied a place of honor in the new building. By the late eighteenth century, however, Boston's commercial wealth had diversified into shipbuilding, shipping, banking, and insurance.

Though small in population, these Atlantic cities led the nation socially, politically, and above all economically. In 1800, the merchants in these seaports still primarily looked across the Atlantic to Europe. In the coming half-century, however, it was the cities that developed the strongest ties with the trans-Appalachian West that were to thrive.

A NATIONAL ECONOMY

In 1800, the United States was a producer of raw materials. The new nation faced the same challenge that developing nations confront today. At the mercy of fluctuating world commodity prices they cannot control, such countries have great difficulty protecting themselves from economic dominance by stronger, more established nations.

Cotton and the Economy of the Young Republic

In 1800, the United States was predominantly rural and agricultural. According to the census, 94 of 100 Americans lived in communities of fewer than 2,500 people, and four of five families farmed the land. Farming families followed centuries-old traditions of working with hand tools and draft animals, producing most of their own food and fiber. Crops were grown for subsistence (home use) rather than for sale. Commodities such as whiskey and hogs (both easy to transport) provided small and irregular cash incomes or items for barter. As late as 1820, only 20 percent of the produce of American farms was consumed outside the local community.

In contrast, in the South, plantation agriculture based on enslaved workers was wholly commercial and international. The demand for cotton was growing rapidly in response to the boom in the industrial production of textiles in England and Europe, but extracting the seeds from the fibers of the variety of cotton that grew best in the southern interior required an enormous investment of labor. The cotton gin, which mechanized this process, was invented in 1793; soon cotton, and the slave labor system that produced it, assumed a commanding place in Southern life and in the foreign trade of the United States.

In 1790, however, increasing foreign demand for American goods and services hardly seemed likely. Trade with Britain, still the biggest customer for American raw materials, was considerably less than it had been before the Revolution. Britain and France both excluded Americans from their lucrative West Indian trade and taxed American ships with discriminatory duties. It was difficult to be independent in a world dominated by great powers.

Shipping and the Economic Boom

Despite these restrictions on American commerce, the strong shipping trade begun during the colonial era and centered in the Atlantic ports became a major asset in the 1790s, when events in Europe provided America with extraordinary opportunities. The French Revolution, which began in 1789, soon initiated nearly twenty-five years of warfare between Britain and France. All along the Atlantic seaboard, urban centers thrived as American ships carried European goods that could no longer be transported on British ships without danger of French attack (and vice versa). Because America was neutral, its merchants had the legal right to import European goods and promptly reexport them to other European countries.

Built for speed, the narrow beamed, many-sailed American clipper ships were the technological marvel of their age. In 1854, the most famous clipper ship, *Flying Cloud*, shown here, made the voyage from New York to San Francisco in 89 days.

SOURCE: ©Museum of the City of New York/CORBIS.

In spite of British and French efforts to prevent the practice (see Chapter 8), reexports amounted to half of the profits in the booming shipping trade (see Figure 9.1).

The vigorous international shipping trade had dramatic effects within the United States. The coastal cities all grew substantially from 1790 to 1820. This rapid urbanization was a sign of real economic growth (rather than a sign that poverty was pushing rural workers off the farms, as occurs in some developing countries today), for it reflected expanding opportunities in the cities. In fact, the rapid growth of cities stimulated farmers to produce the food to feed the new urban dwellers.

The long series of European wars also allowed enterprising Americans to seize such lucrative international opportunities as the China trade. In 1784, the *Empress of China* set sail from New York for Canton with forty tons of ginseng. When it returned in 1785 with a cargo of teas, silks, and chinaware, the sponsors of the voyage made a 30 percent profit. Other merchants were quick to follow. In 1787, Robert Gray left Boston in the *Columbia*, sailing south around Cape Horn, then north to the Pacific Northwest, where he bought sea otter skins cheaply from the coastal Indians. Then Gray sailed west across the Pacific to China, where he sold the furs at fabulous profits before rounding the Cape of Good Hope and returning to Boston laden with tea. In his second voyage in 1792, Gray discovered the mouth of a major Northwest river, which he named for his ship. (When

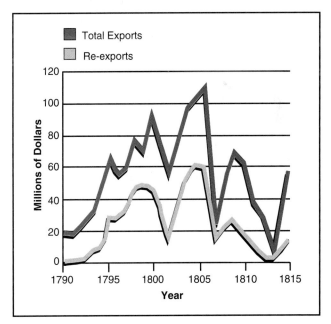

FIGURE 9.1   American Export Trade, 1790–1815 This graph shows how completely the American shipping boom was tied to European events. Exports, half of which were reexports, surged when Britain and France were at war and America could take advantage of its status as neutral. Exports slumped in the brief period of European peace in 1803–1805 and plunged following the Embargo Act of 1807 and the outbreak of the War of 1812.

SOURCE: Douglass C. North, *The Economic Growth of the United States, 1790–1860* (New York: Norton, 1966), p. 26.

Lewis and Clark ventured west in 1804, part of their task was to chart the exact path of Gray's "Columbia's River.") Soon New England so dominated the seaborne trade in furs to China that the Pacific Northwest Indians called all Americans "Bostons."

The active American participation in international trade fostered a strong and diversified shipbuilding industry. All the major Atlantic ports boasted expanding shipbuilding enterprises. Demands for speed increased as well, resulting in what many people have regarded as the flower of American shipbuilding, the clipper ship. The narrow-hulled, many-sailed clipper ships of the 1840s and 1850s set records for ships of their size. In 1854, *Flying Cloud*, built in the Boston shipyards of Donald McKay, sailed from New York to San Francisco—a 16,000-mile trip that usually took 150 to 200 days—in a mere 89 days.

THE JEFFERSON PRESIDENCY

At noon on March 4, 1801, Thomas Jefferson walked from his modest boardinghouse through the swampy streets of the new federal city of Washington to the unfinished Capitol. George Washington and John Adams had ridden in elaborate carriages to their inaugurals. Jefferson, although accepting a military honor guard, demonstrated by his actions that he rejected the elaborate, quasi-monarchical style of the two Federalist presidents and their (to his mind) autocratic style of government as well.

For all its lack of pretension, Jefferson's inauguration as the third president of the United States was a momentous occasion in American history, for it marked the peaceful transition from one political party, the Federalists, to their hated rivals, the Jeffersonian Republicans. (See Out of Many Voices: Margaret Bayard Smith Views Jefferson's Inauguration.) Beginning in an atmosphere of exceptional political bitterness, Jefferson's presidency was to demonstrate that a strongly led party system could shape national policy without leading either to dictatorship or to revolt. Jefferson's own moderation may have been the crucial factor: Setting a tone of conciliation in his inaugural address, he announced "We are all republicans; we are all federalists" and during his eight years in office he paid close attention to ways to attract moderate Federalists to the Jeffersonian Republican party.

Republican Agrarianism

Jefferson brought to the presidency a clearly defined political philosophy. Behind all the events of his administration (1801–09) and those of his successors, in what became known as the Virginia Dynasty (James Madison, 1809–17; James Monroe, 1817–25), was a clear set of beliefs that embodied Jefferson's interpretation of the meaning of republicanism for Americans.

Tall, ungainly, and diffident in manner, Thomas Jefferson was nonetheless a man of genius, an architect, naturalist, political philosopher, and politician.

SOURCE: Courtesy of the Library of Congress.

Jefferson's years as ambassador to France in the 1780s were particularly important in shaping his political thinking. Recoiling from the extremes of wealth and poverty he saw there, he came to believe that it was impossible for Europe to achieve a just society that could guarantee to most of its members the "life, liberty and . . . pursuit of happiness" of which he had written in the Declaration of Independence. Only America, he believed, provided fertile earth for the true citizenship necessary to a republican form of government. What America had, and Europe lacked, was room to grow.

Jefferson's thinking about growth was directly influenced by Englishman Thomas Malthus's deeply pessimistic and widely influential *Essay on the Principle of Population*, published in 1798. Warning of an impending population explosion, Malthus predicted that unless population growth was checked, misery and poverty would soon be widespread throughout Europe and even, Malthus warned, in America. Malthus's prediction alarmed many Americans, who had taken pride in having one of the fastest rates of population growth in the world, close to 40 percent per decade. Thomas Jefferson was not worried. He used Malthus to underline the opportunity created by America's vast land resources. The Malthusian

OUT OF MANY VOICES

Margaret Bayard Smith Views Jefferson's Inauguration

argaret Bayard Smith was the wife of the editor of the Jeffersonian National Intelligencer *newspaper. Because Washington was a very small and new town where social life and politics mixed, her own political observation and influence was considerable. In this letter to her sister-in-law, she describes how her husband's newspaper and her own network of political contacts profited from Jefferson's well-known aversion to public speaking.*

TO MISS SUSAN B. SMITH
March 4, 1801.

I have this morning witnessed one of the most interesting scenes, a free people can ever witness. The changes of administration, which in every government and in every age have most generally been epochs of confusion, villainy and bloodshed, in this our happy country take place without any species of distraction, or disorder. This day, has one of the most amiable and worthy men taken that seat to which he was called by the voice of his country. I cannot describe the agitation I felt, while I looked around on the various multitude and while I listened to an address, containing principles the most correct, sentiments the most liberal, and wishes the most benevolent, conveyed in the most appropriate and elegant language and in a manner mild as it was firm. If doubts of the integrity and talents of Mr. Jefferson ever existed in the minds of any one, methinks this address must forever eradicate them. The Senate chamber was so crowded that I believe not another creature could enter. On one side of the house the Senate sat, the other was resigned by the representatives to the ladies. The roof is arched, the room half circle, every inch of ground was occupied. It has been conjectured by several gentlemen whom I've asked, that there were near a thousand persons within the walls. The speech was delivered in so low a tone that few heard it. Mr. Jefferson had given your Brother a copy early in the morning, so that on coming out of the house, the paper was distributed immediately. Since then there has been a constant succession of persons coming for the papers. I have been interrupted several times in this letter by the gentlemen of Congress, ...; since three o'clock there has been a constant succession. ■

SOURCE: Margaret Bayard Smith, *The First Forty Years of Washington Society in the Family Letters of Margaret Bayard Smith*, ed. Gaillard Hunt (New York: Charles Scribner's Sons, 1906).

prediction need not trouble the United States, Jefferson said, as long as the country kept expanding.

Jefferson envisaged a nation of small family farms clustered together in rural communities—an agrarian republic. He believed that only a nation of roughly equal yeoman farmers, each secure in his own possessions and not dependent on someone else for his livelihood, would exhibit the concern for the community good that was essential in a republic. Indeed, Jefferson said that "those who labor in the earth are the chosen people of God," and so he viewed himself, though his "farm" was the large slave-owning plantation of Monticello.

Jefferson's vision of an expanding agrarian republic remains to this day one of our most compelling ideas about America's uniqueness and special destiny. But expansionism contained some negative aspects. The lure of the western lands fostered constant mobility and dissatisfaction rather than the stable, settled communities of yeoman farmers that Jefferson envisaged. Expansionism caused environmental damage, in particular soil exhaustion—a consequence of abandoning old lands, rather than conserving them, and moving on to new ones. Jefferson's expansionism encouraged the spread of plantations based on slave labor in the South (see Chapter 10). Finally, it bred a ruthlessness toward Indian peoples, who were pushed out of the way for white settlement or who, like the Mandans, were devastated by the diseases that accompanied European trade and contact. Jefferson's agrarianism thus bred some of the best and some of the worst traits of the developing nation.

Jefferson's Government

Thomas Jefferson came to office determined to reverse the Federalist policies of the 1790s and to ensure an agrarian "republic of virtue." Accordingly, he proposed a program of "simplicity and frugality," promising to cut all internal taxes, to reduce the size of the army (from 4,000 to 2,500 men), the navy (from twenty-five ships to seven), and the government staff, and to eliminate the entire national debt inherited from the Federalists. He kept all of these promises, even the last, although the Louisiana Purchase of 1803 cost the Treasury $15 million. This diminishment of government was a key matter of republican principle to Jefferson. If his ideal yeoman farmer was to be a truly self-governing citizen, the federal government must not, Jefferson believed, be either large or powerful. His cost-cutting measures simply carried out the pledge he had made in his inaugural address for "a wise and frugal government, which shall restrain men from injuring one another, [and] shall leave them otherwise free to regulate their own pursuits."

Perhaps one reason for Jefferson's success was that the federal government he headed was small and unimportant by today's standards. For instance, Jefferson found only 130 federal officials in Washington (a grand total of nine in the State Department, including the secretary of state). The national government's main service to ordinary people was mail delivery, and already in 1800 there were persistent complaints about slowness, unreliability, and expense in the Postal Service! Everything else—law and order, education, welfare, road maintenance, economic control—rested with state or local governments. Power and political loyalty were still local, not national.

This small national government also explains why for years, the nation's capital was so unimpressive. The French designer Pierre L'Enfant had laid out a magnificent plan of broad streets and sweeping vistas reminiscent of Paris. Congress had planned to pay for the grand buildings with money from land sales in the new city, but few people besides politicians and boardinghouse keepers (a largely female occupation) chose to live in Washington. Construction lagged: the President's House lacked a staircase to the second floor until 1808, and although the House and Senate chambers were soon completed, the central portion of the Capitol was missing. Instead of the imposing dome we know so well today, the early Capitol consisted of two white marble boxes connected by a boardwalk. It is a telling indicator of the true location of national power that a people who had no trouble building new local communities across the continent should have had such difficulty establishing their federal city.

An Independent Judiciary

Although determined to reverse Federalist fiscal policies, Jefferson was much more moderate concerning Federalist officeholders. He resisted demands by other Jeffersonian Republicans that "the board should be swept" and all Federalist officeholders replaced with party loyalists. During his term of office, Jefferson allowed 132 Federalists to remain at their posts, while placing Jeffersonian Republicans in 158 other posts. Jefferson's restraint, however, did not extend to the most notorious Federalist appointees, the so-called midnight judges.

In the last days of the Adams administration, the Federalist-dominated Congress passed several acts that created new judgeships and other positions within the federal judiciary. Jeffersonian Republicans feared that the losing Federalist Party was trying to politicize the judiciary by appointing Federalists who would use their positions to strengthen the powers of the federal government, a policy the Jeffersonians opposed. In one of his last acts in office, President Adams appointed Federalists—quickly dubbed the "midnight judges"—to these new positions. William Marbury, whom President Adams had appointed Justice of the Peace for Washington, DC, and three other appointees sued James Madison, Jefferson's secretary of state, to receive their commissions for their offices. Before the case came to trial, however, Congress, controlled by Jeffersonian Republicans, repealed the acts. This case, *Marbury v. Madison*, provoked a landmark decision from the U.S. Supreme Court.

At issue was a fundamental constitutional point: Was the judiciary independent of politics? In his celebrated 1803 decision in *Marbury v. Madison*, Chief Justice John Marshall, himself a strong Federalist and an Adams appointee, managed to find

Thomas Jefferson designed and supervised every aspect of the building and furnishing of Monticello, his classical home atop a hill near Charlottesville, Virginia. The process took almost forty years (from 1770 to 1809), for Jefferson constantly changed and refined his design, subjecting both himself and his family to years of uncomfortable living in the partially completed structure. The result, however, was one of the most civilized— and most autobiographical—houses ever built.

SOURCE: Courtesy of the Library of Congress

This symbol of the Philadelphia Society for Promoting Agriculture illustrates the principles of republican agrarianism. The yeoman farmer is ploughing his field under the approving gaze of the female figure of Columbia. His activity expresses the values of the American republic that she represents and in which Thomas Jefferson so strongly believed. As he said, "those who labor in the earth are the chosen people of God."

SOURCE: Library of Congress.

might, which was puny compared to that of the great powers, but by the distance from the fighting provided by the Atlantic Ocean. If England and France fought in North America, as they had in the Seven Years' War (see Chapter 6), America's national security would be directly threatened. Jefferson, who had once ardently supported the goals of the French Revolution, viewed Napoleon's ambitions with increasing apprehension. He feared a resumption of the political animosity of the 1790s, when Federalists and Jeffersonian Republicans had so bitterly disagreed on policy toward France (see Chapter 8).

As had his predecessors, Napoleon considered North America a potential battleground on which to fight the British. He looked first at the Caribbean where he planned to reconquer Haiti, the world's first independent black nation, reenslave its people, and use the rich profits from sugar to finance his European wars. As a first step, in 1800, France secretly reacquired the Louisiana Territory, the vast western drainage of the Mississippi and Missouri Rivers, from Spain, which had held the region since 1763. Napoleon planned to use Louisiana to grow food for sugar-producing Haiti (once it was reconquered), to act as a counterpoise to the British in Canada, and to check any American expansion that might threaten Spain's North American colonies. In 1802, he launched the plan by sending an army of 30,000 to reconquer Haiti.

In 1801, when President Jefferson first learned of the French–Spanish secret agreement about Louisiana, he was alarmed. He did not oppose the attack on the liberty of independent black Haiti, but he was concerned about the threat to American commerce on the Mississippi River. In fact, in 1802, the Spanish commander at New Orleans (the French had not yet taken formal control) closed the port to American shippers, thus disrupting commerce as far away as Cincinnati. As Jefferson feared, Federalists in Congress clamored for military action to reopen the port.

In the summer of 1802, Jefferson instructed Robert Livingston, the American ambassador to France, to negotiate to buy New Orleans and the surrounding area for $2 million (or up to $10 million, if necessary). The initial bargaining was not promising, but suddenly, in early 1803, Napoleon was ready to sell. His army of 30,000 men had

a way to please both parties. On the one hand, Marshall proclaimed that the courts had a duty "to say what the law is," thus unequivocally defending the independence of the judiciary and the principle of judicial review. On the other hand, Marshall conceded that the Supreme Court was not empowered by the Constitution to force the executive branch to give Marbury his commission. At first glance, Jefferson's government appeared to have won the battle over Adams's last-minute appointees. But in the long run, Marshall established the principle that only the federal judiciary could decide what was constitutional. This was a vital step in realizing the three-way balance of power among the branches of the federal government—executive (president), legislative (Congress), and judiciary (courts)—envisaged in the Constitution. Equally important, during his long tenure in office (1801–35), Chief Justice Marshall consistently led the Supreme Court in a series of decisions that favored the federal government over state governments. Under Marshall's direction, the Supreme Court became a powerful nationalizing force, often to the dismay of defenders of states' rights, Jefferson's Republicans among them.

Opportunity: The Louisiana Purchase

In 1800, the United States was a new and fragile democracy in a world dominated by two contending great powers: Britain and France. In 1799, the young general Napoleon Bonaparte seized control of France and began a career of military conquests. Great Britain promptly went to war against him. Following one year of peace, Britain and France were again at war in 1803, beginning a twelve-year duel that ended only with Napoleon's defeat at the battle of Waterloo in 1815. Once again, Europe was a battleground. America was protected, not by its own military

been forced to withdraw from Haiti, defeated by yellow fever and by an army of former slaves led by Toussaint L'Ouverture. Expecting the British to declare war against him again, and in need of money for European military campaigns, Napoleon suddenly offered the entire Louisiana Territory, including the crucial port of New Orleans, to the Americans for $15 million. In an age when it took at least two months for messages to cross the Atlantic, special American envoy James Monroe and Ambassador Livingston could not wait to consult Jefferson. They seized the opportunity: they bought the entire Louisiana Territory from Napoleon in Paris in April 1803. President Jefferson first learned the news two months later, on July 3rd, the eve of Independence Day. Overnight, the size of the United States more than doubled. It was the largest peaceful acquisition of territory in United States history.

At home, Jefferson suffered brief qualms. The Constitution did not authorize the president to purchase territory, and Jefferson had always rigidly insisted on a limited interpretation of executive rights. But he had also long held a sense of destiny about the West and had planned the Lewis and Clark expedition before the Louisiana Purchase was a reality. In any case, the prize was too rich to pass up. Jefferson now argued that Louisiana was vital to the nation's republican future. "By enlarging the empire of liberty," Jefferson wrote, "we . . . provide new sources of renovation, should its principles, at any time, degenerate, in those portions of our country which gave them birth." In other words, expansion was essential to liberty. But for African American slaves and Native Americans, the Louisiana Purchase simply increased the scope of their enslavement and destruction. By 1850, four of the six states in the Louisiana Purchase had entered the Union as slave states (see Chapter 10), and Indian Territory, envisaged by Jefferson as a distant refuge for beleaguered eastern Indian peoples, was surrounded by new settlements (see Chapter 15). No matter how noble Jefferson's rhetoric, neither African Americans nor American Indians shared in his "empire of liberty" (see Map. 9.2).

Incorporating Louisiana

The immediate issue following the Louisiana Purchase was how to treat the French and Spanish inhabitants of the Louisiana Territory. In 1803, when the region that is now the state of Louisiana became American property, it had a racially and ethnically diverse population of 43,000 people, of whom only 6,000 were American. French and French-speaking people were numerically and culturally dominant, especially in the city of New Orleans. New Orleans itself had a population of about 8,000, half white and half black. Two-thirds of the black population were slaves; the remainder were "free persons of color," who under French law enjoyed legal rights equal to those of

white people. The white population was a mixture of French people of European and West Indian origin. Among them were French-speaking exiles from Acadia, who became known in New Orleans as Cajuns (see Chapters 6 and 8). But there were also Spanish, Germans, English, Irish, Americans, and native-born creoles (persons of French descent), causing one observer to call the community "a veritable tower of Babel."

Many people thought that the only way to deal with a population so "foreign" was to wipe out its customs and laws and to impose American ones as quickly as possible. But the French forestalled this outcome by insisting, in the final treaty, that the inhabitants of Louisiana not only should be given the "rights, advantages and immunities of [American] citizens" as soon as possible, but that "in the mean time they shall be maintained and protected in the free enjoyment of their liberty, property and the Religion which they profess." Consequently, the incorporation of Louisiana into the American federal system became a remarkable story of adaptation between two different communities—American and French.

The effort of mutual adaptation was difficult for both sides. At a public ball held in New Orleans in January 1804, for example, American and French military officers almost came to blows over whether an English country dance or a French waltz would be played first. Officials in Washington dismissed the reported conflict as a mere frivolity, but the U.S. representative in New Orleans and governor of Lower Louisiana Territory, William Claiborne, did not. Over the next four years, Claiborne came to accept the value of French institutions to the region. As a result, with Claiborne's full support, Louisiana adopted a legal code in 1808 that was based on French civil law rather than English common law. This was not a small concession. French law differed from English law in many fundamental respects, such as in family property (communal versus male ownership), in inheritance (forced heirship versus free disposal), and even in contracts, which were much more strictly regulated in the French system. Remnants of the French legal system remain part of Louisiana state law to this day. In 1812, with the required 60,000 free inhabitants, Louisiana was admitted to the Union, becoming the first slave state in the territory of the Louisiana Purchase. New Orleans remained for years a distinctively French city, illustrating the flexibility possible under a federal system.

Texas and the Struggle for Mexican Independence

Spain objected, in vain, to Napoleon's 1803 sale of Louisiana to America. For years, Spain had attempted to seal off its rich colony of Mexico from commerce with other nations. Now, American Louisiana shared a vague and disputed

MAP EXPLORATION

To explore an interactive version of this map, go to **www.prenhall.com/faragher5/map9.2**

MAP 9.2 Louisiana Purchase The Louisiana Purchase of 1803, the largest peaceful acquisition of territory in United States history, more than doubled the size of the nation. The Lewis and Clark expedition (1804–06) was the first to survey and document the natural and human richness of the area. The American sense of expansiveness and continental destiny owes more to the extraordinary opportunity provided by the Louisiana Purchase than to other factors.

boundary with Mexico's northern province of Texas (a parcel of land already coveted by some Americans).

Soon Napoleon brought turmoil to all of Mexico. In 1808, having invaded Spain, he installed his brother Joseph Bonaparte as king, forcing Spain's king, Charles IV, to renounce his throne. For the next six years, as warfare convulsed Spain, the country's long-prized New World empire slipped away. Mexico, divided between royalists loyal to Spain and populists seeking social and economic justice for mestizos and Indians, edged bloodily toward independence. Two populist revolts—one in 1810 led by Father Miguel Hidalgo and the other in 1813 led by Father José María Morelos—were suppressed by the royalists, who executed both revolutionary leaders. In 1812, a small force, led by Mexican republican Bernardo Gutiérrez but composed mostly of American adventurers, invaded Texas, captured San Antonio, assassinated the provincial governor Manuel Salcedo, and declared Texas independent. A year later, however, the Mexican republicans were defeated by a royalist army, which then killed suspected collaborators and pillaged the province so thoroughly that the local economy was devastated. The Mexican population declined to fewer than 2,000. Under these circumstances, Mexico's difficult path toward independence seemed, at least to some Americans, to offer yet another opportunity for expansion.

RENEWED IMPERIAL RIVALRY IN NORTH AMERICA

Fresh from the triumph of the Louisiana Purchase, Jefferson scored a major victory over the Federalist Charles Cotesworth Pinckney in the presidential election of 1804, garnering 162 electoral votes to Pinckney's 14. Jefferson's shrewd wooing of moderate Federalists had been so successful that the remaining Federalists dwindled to a highly principled but sectional group, unable to attract voters outside of its home base in New England. Jefferson's Louisiana success was not repeated, however, and few other consequences of the ongoing struggle between Britain and France were so easy to solve.

Problems with Neutral Rights

In his first inaugural address in 1801, Jefferson had announced a foreign policy of "peace, commerce, and honest friendship with all nations, entangling alliances with none." This was a difficult policy to pursue after 1803, when the Napoleonic Wars resumed. By 1805, Napoleon had conquered most of Europe, but Britain, the victor at the great naval battle of Trafalgar, controlled the seas. The United States, trying to profit from trade with both countries, was caught in the middle. The British did not look kindly as their former colonists tried to evade their blockade of the French by claiming neutrality. Beginning in 1805, the British targeted the American reexport trade between the French West Indies and France by seizing American ships that were bringing French West Indian goods to Europe. Angry Americans viewed these seizures as violations of their rights as shippers of a neutral nation.

An even more contentious issue arose from the substantial desertion rate of British sailors. Many deserters promptly signed up on American ships, where they drew better pay and sometimes obtained false naturalization papers as well. The numbers involved were large: as many as a quarter of the 100,000 seamen on American ships were British. Soon the British were stopping American merchant vessels and removing any man they believed to be British, regardless of his papers. The British refusal to recognize genuine naturalization papers (on the principle "once a British subject, always a British subject") was particularly insulting to the new American sense of nationhood.

At least 6,000 innocent American citizens suffered forced impressment into the British navy from 1803 to 1812. In 1807, impressment turned bloody when the British ship *Leopard* stopped the American ship *Chesapeake* in American territorial waters and demanded to search for deserters. When the American captain refused, the *Leopard* opened fire, killing three men, wounding eighteen, and removing four deserters (three with American naturalization papers) from the damaged ship. An indignant public protested British interference and the death of innocent sailors.

The Embargo Act

Fully aware that commerce was essential to the new nation, Jefferson was determined to insist on America's right as a neutral nation to ship goods to Europe. He first tried diplomatic protests, then negotiations, and finally threats, all to no avail. In 1806, Congress passed the Non-Importation Act, hoping that a boycott of British goods, which had worked so well during the Revolutionary War, would be effective once again. It was not. Finally, in desperation, Jefferson imposed the Embargo Act in December 1807. This act forbade American ships from sailing to any foreign port, thereby cutting off all exports as well as imports. The intent of the act was to force both Britain and France to recognize neutral rights by depriving them of American-shipped raw materials.

But the results were a disaster for American trade. The commerce of the new nation, which Jefferson himself had done so much to promote, came to a standstill. Exports fell from $108 million in 1807 to $22 million in 1808, and the nation was driven into a deep depression. There was widespread evasion of the embargo. A remarkable number of ships in the coastal trade found themselves "blown off course" to the West Indies or Canada. Other ships simply left port illegally. Smuggling flourished. Pointing out that the American navy's weakness was due largely to the deep cuts Jefferson had inflicted on it, the Federalists sprang to life with a campaign of outspoken opposition to Jefferson's policy, and they found a ready audience in New England, the area hardest hit by the embargo.

Madison and the Failure of "Peaceable Coercion"

In this troubled atmosphere, Thomas Jefferson despondently ended his second term, acknowledging the failure of what he called "peaceable coercion." He was followed in office by his friend and colleague James Madison of Virginia. Although Madison defeated the Federalist candidate—again Charles Cotesworth Pinkney—by 122 electoral votes to 47, Pinckney's share of the votes was three times what it had been in 1804.

Ironically, the Embargo Act had almost no effect on its intended victims. The French used the embargo as a pretext for seizing American ships, claiming they must be British ships in disguise. The British, in the absence of American competition, developed new markets for their goods in South America. And at home, as John Randolph sarcastically remarked, the embargo was attempting "to cure corns by cutting off the toes." In March 1809, Congress admitted failure, and the Embargo Act was repealed.

But the struggle to remain neutral in the confrontation between the European giants continued. The next two years saw passage of several acts—among them the Non-Intercourse Act of 1809 and Macon's Bill Number 2 in 1810—that unsuccessfully attempted to prohibit trade with Britain and France unless they ceased their hostile treatment of U.S. shipping. Frustration with the ineffectiveness of government policy mounted.

A Contradictory Indian Policy

The United States faced other conflicts besides those with Britain and France over neutral shipping rights. In the West, the powerful Indian nations of the Ohio Valley were determined to resist the wave of expansion that had carried thousands of white settlers onto their lands. North of the Ohio River lived the Northwest Confederation of the Shawnees, Delawares, Miamis, Potawatomis, and several smaller tribes. To the south of the Ohio were the so-called "Five Civilized Tribes," the Cherokees, Chickasaws, Choctaws, Creeks, and (in Florida) the Seminoles.

According to the Indian Intercourse Act of 1790, the United States could not simply seize Indian land; it could only acquire it when the Indians ceded it by treaty. But this policy conflicted with the harsh reality of westward expansion. Commonly, settlers pushed ahead of treaty boundaries. When Indian peoples resisted the invasion of their lands, the pioneers fought back and called for military protection. Defeat of an Indian people led to further land cessions. The result for the Indians was a relentless cycle of invasion, resistance, and defeat.

Thomas Jefferson was deeply concerned with the fate of the western Indian peoples. Convinced that Indians had to give up hunting in favor of the yeoman-farmer lifestyle he so favored for all Americans, Jefferson directed the governors of the Northwest Territories to "promote energetically" his vision for civilizing the Indians, which included Christianizing them and teaching them to read. Many Indian peoples actively resisted these efforts at conversion. In addition, Jefferson's Indian civilization plan was never fully supported by territorial governors and settlers.

After the Louisiana Purchase, Jefferson offered traditionalist Indian groups new lands west of the Mississippi River, where they could live undisturbed by white settlers. But he failed to consider the pace of westward expansion. Less than twenty years later, Missouri, the first trans-Mississippi state, was admitted to the Union. Western Indians like the Mandans, who had seemed so remote, were now threatened by further westward expansion.

In fact, Jefferson's Indian policy, because it did nothing to slow down the ever-accelerating westward expansion, offered little hope to Indian peoples. The alternatives they faced were stark: acculturation, removal, or extinction. Deprived of hunting lands, decimated by disease, increasingly dependent on the white economy for trade goods and annuity payments in exchange for land cessions, many Indian peoples despaired. Like the Mandans after Lewis and Clark's visit, they came to dread the effects of white contact. Nearly every tribe found itself bitterly split between accommodationists and traditionalists. Some, like groups of Cherokees and associated tribes in the South, advocated adapting their traditional agricultural lifestyles and pursuing a pattern of peaceful accommodation. In the Northwest Territory, however, many Indians chose the path of armed resistance. (See Out of Many Voices: Red Jacket Defends Native Religion.)

Indian Resistance

The Shawnees, a seminomadic hunting and farming tribe (the men hunted, the women farmed) of the Ohio Valley, had resisted white settlement in Kentucky and Ohio since the 1750s. Anthony Wayne's decisive defeat of the

This double portrait of two Sauks Indians by John Wesley Jarvis, painted in 1833, shows the growing resistance to official American Indian policy. The father, Black Hawk, wears European dress and appears to have adapted to white ways, while the son, Whirling Thunder, stubbornly wears traditional garb.

SOURCE: John Wesley Jarvis, *Black Hawk and His Son, Whirling Thunder,* 1833. Oil on canvas. 23 1/2 × 30 in. (60.3 × 76 cm.) Gilcrease Museum, Tulsa, Oklahoma. 0126.1007.

OUT OF MANY VOICES

RED JACKET DEFENDS NATIVE RELIGION

Thomas Jefferson encouraged efforts by Protestant missionary groups to convert American Indians, but many native people resisted. Sagoyewatha, or Red Jacket, was an important leader and orator of the Seneca people of northern New York State who defended native religion against the 1805 request of a Boston missionary society to proselytize among his people. Here are some of Red Jacket's arguments:

BROTHER, OUR SEATS WERE ONCE LARGE, AND yours were very small; you have now become a great people, and we have scarcely a place left to spread our blankets; you have got our country, but are not satisfied; you want to force your religion upon us.

Brother, continue to listen. You say you are sent to instruct us how to worship the Great Spirit agreeably to his mind, and if we do not take hold of the religion which you white people teach, we shall be unhappy hereafter. You say that you are right, and we are lost; how do we know this to be true? We understand that your religion is written in a book; if it was intended for us as well as you, why has not the Great Spirit given it to us, and not only to us, but why did he not give to our forefathers the knowledge of that book, with the means of understanding it rightly? We only know what you tell us about it. How shall we know when to believe, being so often deceived by the white people?

Brother, you say there is but one way to worship and serve the Great Spirit; if there is but one religion, why do you white people differ so much about it? Why not all agree, as you can all read the book?

Brother, the Great Spirit has made us all; but he has made a great difference between his white and red children; he has given us a different complexion, and different customs; to you he has given the arts; to these he has not opened our eyes; we know these things to be true. Since he has made so great a difference between us in other things, why may we not conclude that he has given us a different religion according to our understanding. The Great Spirit does right; he knows what is best for his children; we are satisfied.

Brother, we do not wish to destroy your religion, or take it from you; we only want to enjoy our own. ■

SOURCE: Daniel Drake, *Lives of Celebrated American Indians* (Boston: Bradbury, Soden & Co., 1843), 283–87.

Indian Confederacy led by Little Turtle at Fallen Timbers (1794) and the continuing pressure of American settlement, however, had left the Shawnees divided. One group, led by Black Hoof, accepted acculturation. The rest of the tribe tried to maintain traditional ways. Most broke into small bands and tried to eke out a living by hunting, but their numbers were reduced by disease and the survivors were further demoralized by the alcohol offered them illegally by private traders. One group of traditional Shawnees, however, led by the warrior Tecumseh, sought refuge farther west.

But there was no escape from white encroachment. Between 1801 and 1809, William Henry Harrison, governor of Indiana Territory, concluded fifteen treaties with the Delawares, Potawatomis, Miamis, and other tribes. These treaties opened eastern Michigan, southern Indiana, and most of Illinois to white settlement and forced the Indians onto ever-smaller reservations. Many of these treaties were obtained by coercion, bribery, and outright trickery, and most Indians did not accept them.

In 1805, Tecumseh's brother, Tenskwatawa, known as The Prophet, began preaching a message of Indian revitalization: a rejection of all contact with the Americans, including the use of American alcohol, clothing, and trade goods, and a return to traditional practices of hunting and farming. He preached an end to quarreling, violence, and sexual promiscuity and to the accumulation of private property. Wealth was valuable only if it was given away, he said. If the Northwest Indians returned to traditional ways, Tenskwatawa promised, "the land will be overturned so that all the white people will be covered and you alone shall inhabit the land."

This was a powerful message, but it was not new. Just six years earlier, Handsome Lake had led the Seneca people of upstate New York in a similar revitalization movement. Tecumseh, however, succeeded in molding his brother's religious following into a powerful pan-Indian military resistance movement. With each new treaty that Harrison concluded, Tecumseh gained new followers among the Northwest Confederation tribes. Significantly, he also had the support of the British, who, after 1807, began sending food and guns to him from Canada.

The pan-Indian strategy was at first primarily defensive, aimed at preventing further westward expansion. But the Treaty of Fort Wayne in 1809, in which the United States gained 3 million acres of Delaware and Potawatomi land in Indiana, led to active resistance. Confronting Harrison directly, Tecumseh argued that the land belonged to the larger community of all the Indian peoples; no one tribe could give away the common property of all. He then warned that any surveyors or settlers who ventured into the 3 million acres would risk their lives.

Tecumseh took his message of common land ownership and military resistance to all the Indian peoples of the Northwest Confederacy. He was not uniformly successful, even among the Shawnees. Black Hoof, for example, refused to join. Tecumseh also recruited, with mixed success, among the tribes south of the Ohio River. In councils with Choctaws, Chickasaws, Creeks, and Cherokees, he promoted active resistance (see Map 9.3).

In November 1811, while Tecumseh was still recruiting among the southern tribes, Harrison marched to the pan-Indian village of Tippecanoe with 1,000 soldiers. The 600 to 700 Indian warriors at the town, urged on by Tenskwatawa, attacked Harrison's forces before dawn on November 7, hoping to surprise them. The attack failed, and in the battle that followed, the Americans inflicted about 150 Indian casualties, while sustaining about as many themselves. Although Harrison claimed victory, the truth was far different. Dispersed from Tippecanoe, Tecumseh's angry followers fell on American settlements in Indiana and southern Michigan, killing many pioneers and forcing the rest to flee to fortified towns. Tecumseh himself entered into a formal alliance with the British. For western settlers, the Indian threat was greater than ever.

Tecumseh, a Shawnee military leader, and his brother Tenskwatawa, a religious leader called The Prophet, led a pan-Indian revitalization and resistance movement that posed a serious threat to American westward expansion. Tecumseh traveled widely, attempting to build a military alliance on his brother's spiritual message. He achieved considerable success in the Old Northwest, but less in the Old Southwest, where many Indian peoples put their faith in accommodation. Tecumseh's death at the Battle of the Thames (1813) and British abandonment of their Shawnee allies at the end of the War of 1812 brought an end to organized Indian resistance in the Old Northwest.

SOURCE: (a) The Granger Collection, New York #A93851c. (b) Courtesy of the Library of Congress.

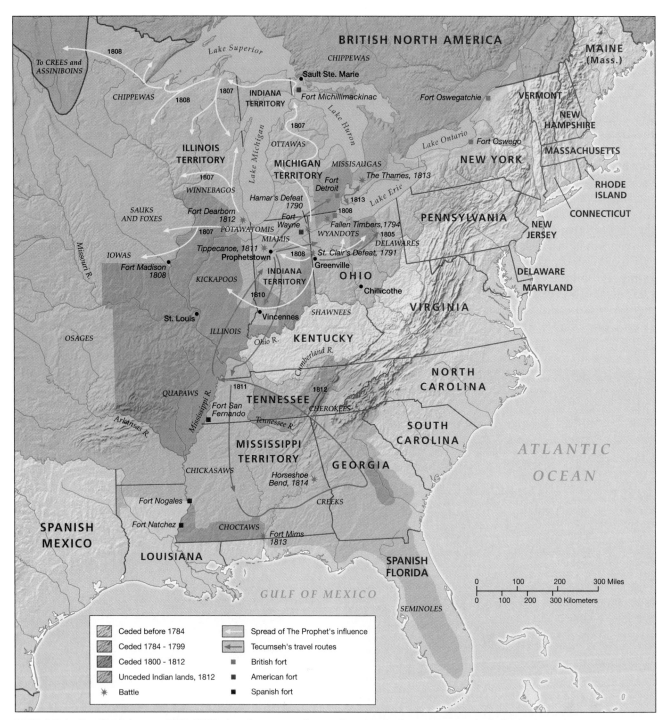

MAP 9.3 Indian Resistance, 1790–1816 American westward expansion put relentless pressure on the Indian nations in the Trans-Appalachian South and West. The Trans-Appalachian region was marked by constant warfare from the time of the earliest settlements in Kentucky in the 1780s to the War of 1812. Tecumseh's Alliance in the Old Northwest (1809–11) and the Creek Rebellion in the Old Southwest (1813–14) were the culminating struggles in Indian resistance to the American invasion of the Trans-Appalachian region. Indian resistance was a major reason for the War of 1812.

THE WAR OF 1812

Many Westerners blamed the British for Tecumseh's attacks on pioneer settlements in the Northwest. British support of western Indians and the long-standing diffi-culties over neutral shipping rights were the two griev-ances cited by President Madison when he asked Con-gress for a declaration of war against Britain on June 1, 1812. Congress obliged him on June 18. But the war had other, more general causes as well.

The War Hawks

A rising young generation of political leaders, first elected to Congress in 1810, strongly resented the continuing influence of Britain, the former mother country, on American affairs. These War Hawks, who included such future leaders as Henry Clay of Kentucky and John C. Calhoun of South Carolina, were young Jeffersonian Republicans from the West and South. They found all aspects of British interference, such as impressment of sailors and support for western Indians, intolerable. Eager to assert independence from England once and for all, these young men saw themselves finishing the job begun by the aging revolutionary generation. They also wanted to occupy Florida to prevent runaway slaves from seeking refuge with the Seminole Indians. Westerners wanted to invade Canada, hoping thereby to end threats from British-backed Indians in the Northwest, such as Tecumseh and his followers. As resentments against England and frustrations over border issues merged, the pressure for war—always a strong force for national unity—mounted.

Unaware that the British, seriously hurt by the American trade embargo, were about to adopt a more conciliatory policy, President James Madison yielded to the War Hawks' clamor for action in June 1812, and his declaration of war passed the U.S. Senate by the close vote of 19 to 13, the House by 79 to 49. All the Federalists voted against the war. (The division along party lines continued in the 1812 presidential election, in which Madison garnered 128 electoral votes to 89 for his Federalist opponent, DeWitt Clinton.) The vote was sectional, with New England and the Middle States in opposition and the West and South strongly prowar. Thus, the United States entered the War of 1812 more deeply divided along sectional lines than during any other foreign war in American history.

As a result of Jefferson's economizing, the American army and navy were small and weak. In contrast, the British, fresh from almost ten years of Napoleonic Wars, were in fighting trim. At sea, the British navy quickly established a strong blockade, harassing coastal shipping along the Atlantic seaboard and attacking coastal settlements at will. In the most humiliating attack, the British burned Washington in the summer of 1814, forcing the president and Congress to flee. Dolley Madison, the president's wife, achieved a permanent footnote in history by saving a portrait of George Washington from the White House as she fled. The indignity of the burning of Washington was somewhat assuaged in September, when Americans beat back a British attack on Baltimore and Fort McHenry. Watching the "rockets' red glare" in the battle, onlooker Francis Scott Key was moved to write the words to the "Star-Spangled Banner." There were a few American naval successes. The American frigate *Constitution*, known as "Old Ironsides," destroyed two British men-of-war, the *Guerrière* and the *Java*, in classic naval battles, but these failed to lift the British blockade (see Map 9.4).

MAP 9.4 The War of 1812 On land, the War of 1812 was fought to define the nation's boundaries. In the North, American armies attacked British forts in the Great Lakes region with little success, and the invasion of Canada was a failure. In the South, the Battle of New Orleans made a national hero of Andrew Jackson, but it occurred after the peace treaty had been signed. On the sea, with the exception of Oliver Perry's victory in the Great Lakes, Britain's dominance was so complete and its blockade so effective that British troops were able to invade the Chesapeake and burn the capital of the United States.

The Campaigns Against Northern and Southern Indians

The American goal of expansion fared badly as well. Americans envisaged a quick victory over sparsely populated British Canada that would destroy British support for Tecumseh and his Northwest Indian allies, but instead the British–Indian alliance defeated them. In July 1812, an American foray into western Canada was repulsed. A joint British and Indian force went on, in August, to capture Detroit and Fort Dearborn (site of Chicago). In September 1813, at the battle of Put-in-Bay, Captain Oliver H. Perry established American control over Lake Erie, leading to the recapture of Detroit by William Henry Harrison. Assisted by naval forces commanded by Perry, Harrison defeated British and Indian defenders in the battle of the Thames in October 1813. Among those slain in the battle was Tecumseh, fighting on the British side. Later attempts by the United States to invade Canada in the Niagara area failed, but so too did British attempts to invade the United States in the same area.

One reason for the abortive Canadian invasion, aside from failure to appreciate the strength of the British–Indian forces, was that the New England states actively opposed the war. Massachusetts, Rhode Island, and Connecticut refused to provide militia or supplies, and other New Eng-

land governors turned a blind eye to the flourishing illegal trade across the U.S.–Canadian border. Another reason was the reaction of Canadians themselves, the majority of whom were former Americans. Ironically, the most decisive effect of the American attacks was the formation of a Canadian sense of national identity and a determination never to be invaded or absorbed by the United States.

In the South, warfare similar to that waged against Tecumseh's pan-Indian resistance movement in the Northwest dramatically affected the southern Indian peoples. The first of the southern Indian peoples to battle the Americans were the Creeks, a trading nation with a long history of contacts with the Spanish and French. When white settlers began to occupy Indian lands in northwestern Georgia and central Alabama early in the nineteenth century, the Creeks, like the Shawnees in the Northwest, were divided in their response. Although many Creek bands argued for accommodation, a group known as the Red Sticks were determined to fight. During the War of 1812, the Red Sticks, allied with the British and Spanish, fought not only the Americans but other Indian groups.

In August 1813, the Red Sticks attacked Fort Mims on the Alabama River, killing more than 500 Americans and mixed-race Creeks who had gathered there for safety. Led by Andrew Jackson, troops from the Tennessee and Kentucky militias combined with the Creeks' traditional foes—the Cherokees, Choctaws, and Chickasaws— to exact revenge. Jackson's troops matched the Creeks in ferocity, shooting the Red Sticks "like dogs," one soldier reported. At the battle of Horseshoe Bend in March 1814, the Creeks were trapped between American cannon fire and their Indian enemies: more than 800 were killed, more than in any other battle in the history of Indian–white warfare.

At the end of the Creek War in 1814, Jackson demanded huge land concessions from the Creeks (including from some Creek bands that had fought on his side): 23 million acres, or more than half the Creek domain. The Treaty of Fort Jackson (1814) confirming these land concessions earned Jackson his Indian name, Sharp Knife. In early 1815 (after the peace treaty had been signed but before news of it arrived in America), Andrew Jackson achieved his best-known victory, an improbable win over veteran British troops in the battle of New Orleans.

Most of the important battles of the War of 1812 were fought on the Canadian border, on water as well as on land. This picture celebrates a rare American naval triumph in the war, the victory of Captain Oliver T. Perry over a British naval squadron on Lake Erie in September 1813.

SOURCE: © Bettman/CORBIS.

The Hartford Convention

America's occasional successes failed to diminish the angry opposition of New England Federalists to the War of 1812. Opposition to the war culminated in the Hartford Convention of 1814, where Federalist representatives from the five New England states met to discuss their grievances. At first the air was full of talk of secession from the Union, but soon cooler heads prevailed. The convention did insist, however, that a state had the right "to interpose its authority" to protect its citizens against unconstitutional federal laws. This nullification doctrine was not new; Madison and Jefferson had proposed it in the Virginia and Kentucky Resolves opposing the Alien and Sedition Acts in 1798 (see Chapter 8). In any event, the nullification threat from Hartford was ignored, for peace with Britain was announced as delegates from the convention made their way to Washington to deliver their message to Congress. There, the convention's grievances were treated not as serious business but as an anticlimactic joke.

The Treaty of Ghent

By 1814, the long Napoleonic Wars in Europe were slowly drawing to a close, and the British decided to end their war with the Americans. The peace treaty, after months of hard negotiation, was signed at Ghent, Belgium, on Christmas Eve in 1814. Like the war itself, the treaty was inconclusive. The major issues of impressment and neutral rights were not mentioned, but the British did agree to evacuate their western posts, and late in the negotiations they abandoned their insistence on a buffer state for neutral Indian peoples in the Northwest.

For all its international inconsequence, the war did have an important effect on national morale. Andrew Jackson's victory at New Orleans allowed Americans to believe that they had defeated the British. It would be more accurate to say that by not losing the war the Americans had ended their own feelings of colonial dependency. Equally important, they convinced the British government to stop thinking of America as its colony.

The War of 1812 was one of America's most divisive wars, arousing more intense opposition than any other American conflict, including Vietnam. Today, most historians regard the war as both unnecessary and a dangerous risk to new and fragile ideas of national unity. Fortunately for its future, the United States as a whole came out unscathed, and the Battle of New Orleans had provided last-minute balm for its hurt pride.

The only clear losers of the war were the Northwestern Indian nations and their Southern allies. With the death of Tecumseh at the Battle of the Thames in 1813 and the defeat of the Southern Creeks in 1814, the last hope of a united Indian resistance to white expansion perished forever. Britain's abandonment of its Indian allies in the Treaty of Ghent sealed their fate. By 1815, American settlers were on their way west again.

DEFINING THE BOUNDARIES

With the War of 1812 behind them, Americans turned, more seriously than ever before, to the tasks of expansion and national development. The so-called Era of Good Feelings (1817–23) found politicians largely in agreement on a national agenda, and a string of diplomatic achievements forged by John Quincy Adams gave the nation sharper definition. But the limits to expansion also became clear: the Panic of 1819 showed the dangers in economic growth, and the Missouri Crisis laid bare the sectional split that attended westward expansion.

Another Westward Surge

The end of the War of 1812 was followed by a westward surge to the Mississippi River that populated the Old Northwest (Ohio, Indiana, Illinois, Michigan, and Wisconsin) and the Old Southwest (western Georgia, Alabama,

Settlement of the heavily forested Old Northwest and Old Southwest required much heavy labor to clear the land. One common labor-saving method settlers learned from Indians was to "girdle" the trees (cutting the bark all around), thereby killing them. Dead trees could be more easily chopped and burned.

SOURCE: Library of Congress.

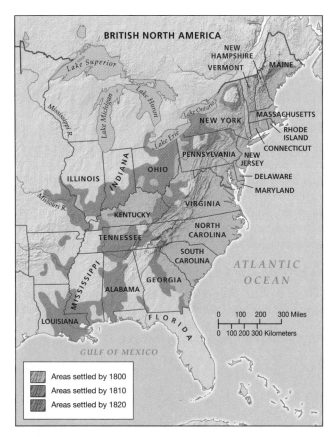

MAP 9.5 Spread of Settlement: Westward Surge, 1800–1820 Within a period of twenty years, a quarter of the nation's population had moved west of the Appalachian Mountains. The westward surge was a dynamic source of American optimism.

Mississippi, and Louisiana). The extent of the population redistribution was dramatic: in 1790, about 95 percent of the nation's population had lived in states bordering the Atlantic Ocean; by 1820 fully 25 percent of the population lived west of the Appalachians (see Map 9.5).

What accounted for this extraordinary westward surge? There were both push and pull factors. Between 1800 and 1820, the nation's population almost doubled, increasing from 5.3 million to 9.6 million. Overpopulated farmland in all of the seaboard states pushed farmers off the land, while new land pulled them westward. The defeat and removal of Indians in the War of 1812 was another important pull factor.

The most important pull factor, however, was the attractive price of western land. The Land Ordinance of 1785 priced western lands too high for all but speculators and the wealthy (see Chapter 7), but subsequent realities had slowly forced Congress to enact land laws more favorable to the small farmer. The most sustained challenge came from "squatters," who repeatedly took up land before it was officially open for sale and then claimed a "preemption" right of purchase at a lower price

that reflected the value of improvements they had made to the land. Congress sought to suppress this illegal settlement and ordered the expulsion of squatters on several occasions, but to no avail. When federal lands were officially opened for sale in Illinois in 1814, for example, there were already 13,000 settlers, forcing Congress to reverse itself and grant them all preemption rights.

Finally, in the Land Act of 1820, Congress set the price of land at $1.25 an acre, the minimum purchase at eighty acres (in contrast to the 640-acre minimum in 1785), and a down payment of $100 in cash. This was the most liberal land law yet passed in American history, but the cash requirement still favored speculators, who had more cash than most small farmers (see Figure 9.2).

There were four major migration routes. In upstate New York, the Mohawk and Genesee Turnpike led New England migrants to Lake Erie, where they traveled by boat to northern Ohio. In the Middle States region, the turnpike from Philadelphia to Pittsburgh led to the Ohio River, as did the National Road that began in Baltimore and led to Wheeling. In the South, the Wilderness Road through the Cumberland Gap led to Kentucky, and passes in the mountains of North and South Carolina led to Tennessee. The Federal Road skirted the southern edge of the Appalachians and allowed farmers from South Carolina and eastern Georgia to move directly into Alabama and Mississippi. In this way, geography facilitated lateral westward movement (Northerners tended to migrate to the Old Northwest, Southerners to the Old Southwest). Except in southern Ohio and parts

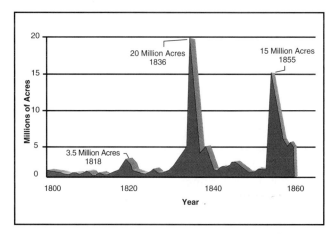

FIGURE 9.2 Western Land Sales Surges in western land sales reflect surges in westward expansion. Western land sales following the War of 1812 reached an unprecedented 3.5 million acres, but that was small in comparison with what was to come in the 1830s and 1850s. Not all land sales reflected actual settlement, however, and speculation in western lands was rampant. Collapse of the postwar speculative boom contributed to the Panic of 1819, and the abrupt end to the boom of the 1830s led to the Panic of 1837.

SOURCE: Robert Riegel and Robert Athearn, *America Moves West* (New York: Holt Rinehart 1964).

This 1816 painting by Thomas Birch shows two improvements that aided westward expansion: the lightweight but sturdy Conestoga wagon that made it possible to carry heavy loads for long distances, and the improved road—the Pennsylvania Turnpike—built by a private company that charged tolls to cover its cost.

SOURCE: Thomas Birch, (1779-1851), *Conestoga Wagon on the Pennsylvania Turnpike*, 1816. Oil on canvas, H: 21 1/4 in. × W: 28 1/2 in. © Shelburne Musueum, Shelburne, VT).

of Kentucky and Tennessee, there was very little contact among regional cultures. New Englanders carried their values and lifestyles directly west and settled largely with their own communities; Southerners did the same.

One section of northern Ohio along Lake Erie, for example, had been Connecticut's western land claim since the days of its colonial charter. Rather than give up the land when the Northwest Territory was established in 1787, Connecticut held onto the Western Reserve (as it was known) and encouraged its citizens to move there. Group settlement was common. General Moses Cleaveland of the Revolutionary War led one of the first groups of Yankees, fifty-two in all. In 1795, they settled the community that bears his name (though not his spelling of it). Many other groups followed, naming towns such as Norwalk after those they had left in Con-

necticut. These New Englanders brought to the Western Reserve their religion (Congregational), their love of learning (tiny Norwalk soon boasted a three-story academy), and their adamant opposition to slavery.

Western migration in the South was very different. On this frontier, the people clearing the land were not doing it for themselves but to create plantations for slave owners. Even before the war, plantation owners in the Natchez district of Mississippi had made fortunes growing cotton, which they shipped to Britain from New Orleans. After the war, as cotton growing expanded, hopeful slave owners from older parts of the South (Virginia, North and South Carolina, Georgia) flooded into the region, bringing their slaves with them or, increasingly, purchasing new ones supplied by the internal slave trade. The migration was like a gold rush, characterized by high hopes, land speculation, and riches—for a few. Most of the white settlers in the Old Southwest were small farm families who did not own slaves, but they hoped to, for ownership of slaves was the means to wealth. More than half of the migrants to the Old Southwest after 1812 were involuntary—enslaved African Americans. This involuntary migration of slaves tore African American families apart at the same time that white families viewed migration as a chance to replicate the lifestyle and values of older Southern states on this new frontier (see Chapter 10).

The western transplantation of distinctive regional cultures explains why, although by 1820 western states accounted for more than a third of all states (eight out of twenty-three), the West did not form a third, unified political region. Although there were common western issues—in particular, the demand for better roads and other transportation routes—communities in the Old Northwest, in general, shared New England political attitudes, whereas those in the Old Southwest shared Southern attitudes.

The Election of 1816 and the Era of Good Feelings

In 1816, James Monroe, the last of the Virginia Dynasty, was easily elected president over his Federalist opponent Rufus King (183 to 34 electoral votes). This was the last election in which Federalists ran a candidate. Monroe had no opponent in 1820 and was reelected nearly unanimously (231 to 1). The triumph of the Jeffersonian Republicans over the Federalists seemed complete.

Tall, dignified, dressed in the old-fashioned style of knee breeches and white-topped boots that Washington had worn, Monroe looked like a traditional figure. But his politics reflected changing times. When he visited Boston, as recently as 1815 the heart of a secession-minded Federalist region, he received an enthusiastic welcome, prompting the Federalist *Columbian Centinel* to proclaim an "Era of Good Feelings." The phrase has been applied to Monroe's presidency (1817–25) ever since.

The American System

Monroe sought a government of national unity, and he chose men from North and South, Jeffersonian Republicans and Federalists, for his cabinet. He selected John Quincy Adams, a former Federalist, as his secretary of state, virtually assuring that Adams, like his father, would become president. To balance Adams, Monroe picked John C. Calhoun of South Carolina, a prominent War Hawk, as secretary of war. And Monroe supported the American System, a program of national economic development that became identified with westerner Henry Clay, Speaker of the House of Representatives.

In supporting the American System, Monroe was following President Madison, who had proposed the program in his message to Congress in December 1815. Madison and Monroe broke with Jefferson's agrarianism to embrace much of the Federalist program for economic development, including the chartering of a national bank, a tax on imported goods to protect American manufacturers, and a national system of roads and canals. All three of these had first been proposed by Alexander Hamilton in the 1790s (see Chapter 8). At the time, these proposals had met with bitter Jeffersonian Republican opposition. The support that Madison and Monroe gave to Hamilton's ideas following the War of 1812 was a crucial sign of the dynamism of the American commercial economy. Many Republicans now acknowledged that the federal government had a role to play in fostering the economic and commercial conditions in which both yeoman farmer and merchant could succeed.

In 1816, Congress chartered the Second Bank of the United States for twenty years. Located in Philadelphia, the bank had a capital of $35 million, of which the government contributed $7 million. The bank was to provide the large-scale financing that the smaller state banks could not handle, and to create a strong national currency. Because they feared concentrated economic power, Jeffersonian Republicans had allowed the charter of the original Bank of the United States, founded in 1791, to expire in 1811. The Republican about-face in 1816 was a sign that the strength of commercial interests had grown to rival that of farmers, whose distrust for central banks persisted.

The Tariff of 1816 was the first substantial protective tariff in American history. In 1815, British manufacturers, who had been excluded for eight years (from the Embargo Act of 1807 to the end of the War of 1812), flooded the United States market with their products. American manufacturers complained that the British were dumping goods below cost in order to prevent the growth of American industries. Congress responded with a tariff on imported woolens and cottons, on iron, leather, hats, paper, and sugar. The measure had southern as well as northern support, although in later years, differences over the passage of higher tariffs would become one of the most persistent sources of sectional conflict.

The third item in the American System, funding for roads and canals—internal improvements, as they came to be known—was more controversial. Monroe and Madison both supported genuinely national (that is, interstate) projects such as the National Road from Cumberland, Maryland, to Vandalia, Illinois. Congressmen, however, aware of the urgent need to improve transportation in general, and sensing the political advantages that could accrue to them from directing funds to their districts, proposed spending federal money on local projects. Both Madison and Monroe vetoed such local proposals, believing them to be unconstitutional. Thus it happened that some of the most famous projects of the day, such as the Erie Canal, which lay wholly within New York State, and the early railroads, were financed by state or private money (see Chapter 12).

The support of Madison and Monroe for measures initially identified with their political opposition was an indicator of their realism. The three aspects of the American System—bank, tariff, roads—were all parts of the basic infrastructure that the American economy needed in order to develop. Briefly, during the Era of Good Feelings, politicians agreed about the need for all three. Later, each would be a source of heated partisan argument.

The Diplomacy of John Quincy Adams

The diplomatic achievements of the Era of Good Feelings were due almost entirely to the efforts of one man, John Quincy Adams, Monroe's secretary of state. Adams set himself the task of tidying up the borders of the United States. Two accords with Britain—the Rush-Bagot Treaty of 1817 and the Convention of 1818—fixed the border between the United States and Canada at the 49th parallel and resolved conflicting U.S. and British claims to Oregon with an agreement to occupy it jointly for ten (eventually twenty) years. The American claim to Oregon (present-day British Columbia, Washington, Oregon, northern Idaho, and parts of Montana) was based on China trader Robert Gray's discovery of the Columbia River in 1792 and on the Lewis and Clark expedition of 1804–06.

Adams's major diplomatic accomplishment was the Adams-Onís or Transcontinental Treaty of 1819, in which he skillfully wrested concessions from the faltering Spanish empire. Adams convinced Spain not only to cede Florida but also to drop all previous claims it had to the Louisiana Territory and Oregon. In return, the United States relinquished claims on Texas and assumed responsibility for the $5 million in claims that U.S. citizens had against Spain.

Finally, Adams picked his way through the remarkable changes occurring in Latin America, developing the policy that bears his president's name, the Monroe Doctrine. The United States was the first country outside Latin America to recognize the independence of Spain's former colonies. When the European powers (France, Austria, Russia, and Prussia) began talk of a plan to help Spain recover the lost colonies, what was the United States to do? The British, suspicious of the European powers, proposed a British–American declaration against European intervention in the hemisphere. Others might have been flattered by an approach from the British empire, but Adams would have none of it. Showing the national pride that was so characteristic of the era, Adams insisted on an independent American policy. He therefore drafted for the president the hemispheric policy that the United States has followed ever since.

On December 2, 1823, the president presented the Monroe Doctrine to Congress and the world. He called for the end of colonization of the Western Hemisphere by European nations (this was aimed as much at Russia and its Pacific coast settlements as at other European powers). Intervention by European powers in the affairs of the independent New World nations would be considered by the United States a danger to its own peace and safety. Finally, Monroe pledged that the United States would not interfere in the affairs of European countries or in the affairs of their remaining New World colonies.

All of this was a very loud bark from a very small dog. In 1823, the United States lacked the military and economic force to back up its grand statement. In fact, what kept the European powers out of Latin America was British opposition to European intervention, enforced by the Royal Navy. The Monroe Doctrine was however useful in Adams's last diplomatic achievement, the Convention of 1824, in which Russia gave up its claim to the Oregon Territory and accepted 54° 40′ north latitude as the southern border of Russian America. Thus Adams had contained another possible threat to American continental expansion (see Map 9.6).

In the short space of twenty years, the position of the United States on the North American continent had been transformed. Not only was America a much larger nation, but the Spanish presence was much diminished, Russian expansion on the West Coast contained, and peace prevailed with Britain. This string of diplomatic achievements—the treaties with Russia, Britain, and Spain and the Monroe Doctrine—represented a great personal triumph for the stubborn, principled John Quincy Adams. A committed nationalist and expansionist, he showed that reason and diplomacy were in some circumstances more effective than force. Adams's diplomatic achievements were a fitting end to the period dominated by the Virginia Dynasty, the trio of enlightened revolutionaries who did so much to shape the new nation.

The Panic of 1819

Across this impressive record of political and economic nation building fell the shadow of the Panic of 1819. A delayed reaction to the end of the War of 1812 and the Napoleonic Wars, the panic forced Americans to come to terms with their economic place in a peaceful world. As British merchant ships resumed trade on routes they had abandoned during the wars, the American shipping boom ended. And as European farm production recovered from the wars, the international demand for American foodstuffs declined and American farmers and shippers suffered.

Domestic economic conditions made matters worse. The western land boom that began in 1815 turned into a speculative frenzy. Land sales, which had totaled 1 million acres in 1815, mushroomed to 3.5 million in 1818. Some lands in Mississippi and Alabama, made valuable by the international demand for cotton, were selling for $100 an acre. Many settlers bought on credit, aided by loans from small and irresponsible "wildcat" state banks. This was not the first—or the last—speculative boom in western lands. But it ended like all the rest—with a sharp contraction of credit, begun on this occasion by the Second Bank of the United States, which in 1819 forced state banks to foreclose on many bad loans. Many small farmers were ruined, and

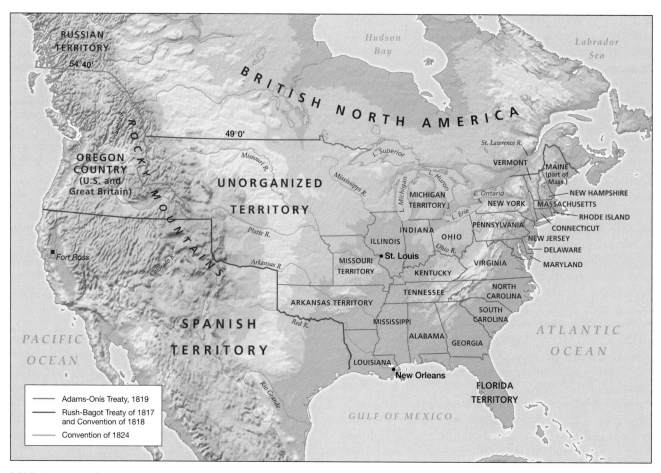

MAP 9.6 John Quincy Adams's Border Treaties John Quincy Adams, secretary of state in the Monroe administration (1817–25), solidified the nation's boundaries in several treaties with Britain and Spain. The Rush-Bagot Treaty of 1817 and the Conventions of 1818 and 1824 settled the northern boundary with Canada and the terms of a joint occupancy of Oregon. The Adams-Onís Treaty of 1819 added Florida to the United States and settled the disputed border between the American Louisiana Territory and Spanish possessions in the West.

they blamed the faraway Bank of the United States for their troubles. In the 1830s, Andrew Jackson would build a political movement on their resentment.

Urban workers suffered both from the decline in international trade and from manufacturing failures caused by competition from British imports. As they lobbied for local relief, they found themselves deeply involved in urban politics, where they could express their resentment against the merchants and owners who had laid them off. Thus developed another component of Andrew Jackson's new political coalition.

Another confrontation arose over the tariff. Southern planters, hurt by a decline in the price of cotton, began to actively protest the protective tariff, which kept the price of imported goods high even when cotton prices were low. Manufacturers, hurt by British competition, lobbied for even higher rates, which they achieved in 1824 over Southern protests. Southerners

then began to express doubts about the fairness of a political system in which they were always outvoted.

The Panic of 1819 was a symbol of this transitional time. It showed how far the country had moved since 1800, from Jefferson's republic of yeoman farmers toward a nation dominated by commerce. And the anger and resentment expressed by the groups harmed by the depression— farmers, urban workers, and Southern planters—were portents of the politics of the upcoming Jackson era.

The Missouri Compromise

In the Missouri Crisis of 1819–21, the nation confronted the momentous issue that had been buried in the general enthusiasm for expansion: as America moved west, would the largely southern system of slavery expand as well? Until 1819, this question was decided regionally. The Northwest Ordinance of 1787 explicitly banned slavery in the northern section of trans-Appalachia but made no mention of it elsewhere. Because so much of the expansion into the Old Northwest and Southwest was lateral (Northerners stayed in the north, Southerners in the south), there was little conflict over sectional differences. In 1819, however, the sections collided in Missouri, which applied for admission to the Union as a slave state (see Map 9.7).

The northern states, all of which had abolished slavery by 1819, looked askance at the extension of slavery. In addition to the moral issue of slavery, the Missouri question raised the political issue of sectional balance. Northern politicians did not want to admit another slave state. To do so would tip the balance of power in the Senate, where the 1819 count of slave and free states was eleven apiece. For their part, Southerners believed they needed an advantage in the Senate; because of faster population growth in the North, they were already outnumbered (105 to 81) in the House of Representatives. But above all, Southerners did not believe Congress had

the power to limit the expansion of slavery. They were alarmed that Northerners were considering national legislation on the matter. Slavery, in southern eyes, was a question of property, and therefore a matter for state rather than federal legislation. Thus, from the very beginning, the expansion of slavery raised constitutional issues. Indeed, the aging politician of Monticello, Thomas Jefferson, immediately grasped the seriousness of the question of the expansion of slavery. As he prophetically wrote to a friend, "This momentous question like a fire bell in the night, awakened and filled me with terror. I considered it at once the [death] knell of the Union."

In 1819, Representative James Tallmadge Jr. of New York began more than a year of congressional controversy when he demanded that Missouri agree to the gradual end of slavery as the price of entering the Union. At first, the general public paid little attention, but religious reformers (Quakers prominent among them) organized a number of

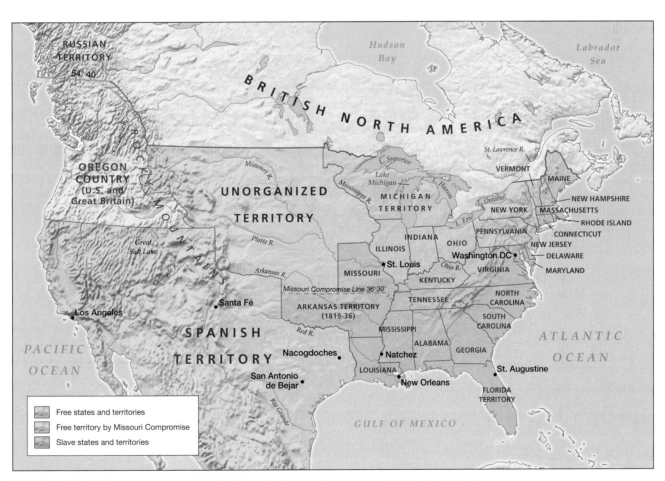

MAP 9.7 The Missouri Compromise Before the Missouri Compromise of 1820, the Ohio River was the dividing line between the free states of the Old Northwest and the slaveholding states of the Old Southwest. The compromise stipulated that Missouri would enter the Union as a slave state (balanced by Maine, a free state), but slavery would be prohibited in the Louisiana Territory north of 36° 30′ (Missouri's southern boundary). This awkward compromise lasted until 1846, when the Mexican-American War reopened the issue of the expansion of slavery.

antislavery rallies in northern cities that made politicians take notice. Former Federalists in the North who had seen their party destroyed by the achievements of Jefferson and his successors in the Virginia Dynasty eagerly seized on the Missouri issue. This was the first time that the growing northern reform impulse had intersected with sectional politics. It was also the first time that southern threats of secession were made openly in Congress.

The Senate debate over the admission of Missouri, held in the early months of 1820, was the nation's first extended debate over slavery. Observers noted the high proportion of free African Americans among the listeners in the Senate gallery. But the full realization that the future of slavery was central to the future of the nation would not become apparent to the general public until the 1850s.

In 1820, Congress achieved compromise over the sectional differences. Henry Clay forged the first of the many agreements that were to earn him the title of "the Great Pacificator" (peacemaker). The Missouri Compromise maintained the balance between free and slave states: Maine (which had been part of Massachusetts) was admitted as a free state in 1820 and Missouri as a slave state in the following year. A policy was also enacted with respect to slavery in the rest of the Louisiana Purchase: slavery was prohibited north of 36° 30′ north latitude—the southern boundary of Missouri—and permitted south of that line. This meant that the vast majority of the Louisiana Territory would be free. In reality, then, the Missouri Compromise could be only a temporary solution, because it left open the question of how the balance between slave and free states would be maintained.

CONCLUSION

In complex ways a developing economy, geographical expansion, and even a minor war helped shape American unity. Local, small, settled, face-to-face communities in both the North and the South began to send their more mobile, expectant members to new occupations in urban centers or west to form new settlements, displacing Indian communities in the process.

The westward movement was the novel element in the American national drama. Europeans believed that

CHRONOLOGY

1800	Thomas Jefferson elected president		*1814*	Treaty of Ghent
1802	Russian–American Company headquarters established at Sitka, Alaska		*1815*	Battle of New Orleans
1803	Louisiana Purchase		*1816*	James Monroe elected president
	Marbury v. *Madison*			Congress charters Second Bank of the United States
	Ohio admitted to the Union			Indiana admitted to the Union
1804	Lewis and Clark expedition leaves St. Louis		*1817*	Mississippi admitted to the Union
	Thomas Jefferson reelected president		*1818*	Illinois admitted to the Union
1807	*Chesapeake–Leopard* incident		*1819*	Panic of 1819
	Embargo Act			Adams–Onís Treaty
1808	James Madison elected president			Alabama admitted to the Union
1809	Tecumseh forms military alliance among Northwest Confederacy peoples		*1819–20*	Missouri Crisis and Compromise
1811	Battle of Tippecanoe		*1820*	James Monroe reelected president
1812	War of 1812 begins			Maine admitted to the Union
	James Madison reelected president		*1821*	Missouri admitted to the Union as a slave state
	Louisiana admitted to the Union		*1823*	Monroe Doctrine

large size and a population in motion bred instability and political disintegration. Thomas Jefferson thought otherwise, and the Louisiana Purchase was the gamble that confirmed his guess. The westward population movement dramatically changed the political landscape and Americans' view of themselves.

Expansion would not create the settled communities of yeoman farmers Jefferson had hoped for. Rather, it would breed a nation of restless and acquisitive people and, in the South, as we shall see in the next chapter, a greatly expanded community tied to cotton and to the slave labor that produced it.

REVIEW QUESTIONS

1. What economic and political problems did the United States face as a new nation in a world dominated by war between Britain and France? How successful were the efforts by the Jefferson, Madison, and Monroe administrations to solve these problems?

2. The anti-European cast of Jefferson's republican agrarianism made it appealing to many Americans who wished to believe in their nation's uniqueness, but how realistic was it?

3. Some Federalists opposed the Louisiana Purchase, warning of the dangers of westward expansion. What are arguments for and against expansion?

4. What contradictions in American Indian policy did the confrontations between Tecumseh's alliance and soldiers and settlers in the Old Northwest reveal? Can you suggest solutions to them?

5. What did the War of 1812 accomplish?

6. What were the issues that made it impossible for the Era of Good Feelings to last?

RECOMMENDED READING

Catharine Allgor, *Parlor Politics: In Which the Ladies of Washington Help Build a City and a Government* (2000). Describes the vital role that women played in the politics of the new capital city.

Stephen E. Ambrose, *Undaunted Courage: Meriwether Lewis, Thomas Jefferson, and the Opening of the American West* (1996). This heroic version of the expedition is told by a master storyteller. It ought, however, to be supplemented by the Ronda version cited below that pays attention to the Indian side of the story.

Frank Bergon, ed., *The Journals of Lewis and Clark* (1989). A handy abridgment of the fascinating history of the expedition. (For more intensive study, Gary Moulton's six-volume unabridged edition of the expedition journals is unsurpassed.)

R. David Edmunds, *Tecumseh and the Quest for Indian Leadership* (1984). A sympathetic portrait.

Joseph J. Ellis, *American Sphinx: The Character of Thomas Jefferson* (1998). An engaging exploration of Jefferson's many contradictions.

John Mack Faragher, *Sugar Creek* (1987). The fullest examination of the lives of pioneers in the Old Northwest.

Donald Hickey, *The War of 1812: A Forgotten Conflict* (1989). Takes a fresh look at the events and historiography of the war.

James Horn, Jan Ellen Lewis, and Peter S. Onuf, eds., *The Revolution of 1800: Democracy, Race and the New Republic* (2002). A collection examining Jefferson's election and presidency in the context of geopolitical and racial developments in the Atlantic world.

Jon Kukla, *A Wilderness So Immense: The Louisiana Purchase and the Destiny of America* (2003) A personality-filled account of the negotiations, and of various hopes and plans for Louisiana.

Glover Moore, *The Missouri Controversy, 1819–1821* (1953). The standard account.

Peter S. Onuf, *Jefferson's Empire* (2000). A thoughtful study of Jefferson's ideas about republicanism, empire, and nationalism.

James Ronda, *Lewis and Clark among the Indians* (1984). An innovative look at the famous explorers through the eyes of the Indian peoples they encountered.

 For additional study resources for this chapter, go to the *Companion Website,* **http://www.prenhall.com/faragher.**

WHOSE HISTORY IS IT?
IN THE FOOTSTEPS OF LEWIS AND CLARK

In March of 1805, members of the Lewis and Clark expedition left the Mandan village where they had spent the winter, and headed west, eager to face the unknown challenges that lay between them and the Pacific Ocean. Six months later, exhausted and starving, the party struggled to find their way through the mountain snow of present-day Montana and Idaho. In Idaho, a small band of Nez Perce Indians rescued the expedition, fed and housed them, helped build canoes, and served as guides for the final stage of their journey down the Columbia River to the Pacific.

Thousands of tourists have observed the bicentennial of the Lewis and Clark expedition (2003-2006) by visiting sites along the route from St. Louis to the Pacific Ocean. Many have relived the exploration by literally following in the footsteps of Lewis and Clark. Some of them have found themselves, as the explorers did 200 years ago, in Indian country. While most public attention is still focused on the heroism, accomplishment, and "undaunted courage" of Lewis and Clark, some western Indian tribes see the bicentennial as a strategic opportunity to tell the Indian side of the expedition's history.

"This time, it's about the tribes," said Gerald Baker of the National Park Service. Baker, a Hidatsa Indian, spearheaded the NPS exhibit *Corps of Discovery II* that traveled to significant sites along the explorers route on the same day, 200 years later, as the original expedition. Offering a "tent of many voices," the purpose of *Corps II* was to offer descendents of the Indian groups who first met Lewis and Clark a chance to speak of the encounter from the tribal perspective. Two hundred years ago, Lewis and Clark presented every tribe along the route with Jefferson medals inscribed with the message "Peace and Friendship." Today, tribal stories offer a grimmer viewpoint.

The determination of American Indians to have their importance to the expedition recognized was evident at the first meetings of the National Council for the Bicentennial in the early 1990s, when two council members, Allen Pinkham of the Nez Perce tribe and Jeanne Eder, Dakota Sioux, insisted on the use of the word "commemoration," rather than "celebration," to acknowledge the high price that all Indians paid for discovery, in disease, death, and cultural disruption. Since then, western tribes have chosen different ways to participate in the bicentennial commemoration. "We are the story" said Roberta Conner of the Umatilla Tribe, "but we're not just trying to say one thing. We're trying to say there are many nations, many voices, many messages."

Rather than recrimination, Pinkham sees the bicentennial as a unique opportunity to tell the remarkable story of Indian survival and adaptation. After all, says Pinkham, "After 200 years we're still here. We weren't killed off by disease and warfare." The bicentennial can serve to inform the public about modern Indian life and accomplishments. As the Nez Perce and other western Indians seize the occasion of the bicentennial to tell their own story, they hope to give a new and modern meaning to the two hands clasped together on the Jefferson medal.

This shows the medal Lewis and Clark presented to the Nez Perce Indians in 1805. One side shows a profile of Thomas Jefferson, with the description, "Th. Jefferson, President of the U.S. A.D. 1802," while the clasped hands on the other side promise Peace and Friendship.

National Park
Service Photo.

During this reenactment of the meeting of Lewis and Clark and the Nez Perce in present-day northern Idaho, tourists reach out and touch imagined history as Craig Rockwell (as Capt. William Clark) shows the group a camas plant. In reality, until the Nez Perce took them in and fed them, expedition members were too exhausted and starving to reach out to anyone. ▶

Lewiston Morning Tribune.

◀ In this horse parade, contemporary Nez Perce Indians recapture the pageantry and pride that the tribe's possession of large herds of Appaloosa horses and their renowned horsemanship brought them before white settlement.

Diana L. Jones, USDA Forest Service.

Patrick Gass, one of the soldiers on the expedition, published the first popular account, *A Journal of the Voyages and Travels of the Corps of Discovery*, in 1810. This illustration "Captains Lewis and Clark holding a Council with the Indians," depicts a frequent event, for Lewis and Clark learned the route west by consulting with local Indians. ▶

Patrick Cass, Courtesy of the Library of Congress.

1790s–1850s

Natchez-Under-the-Hill

The wharfmaster had just opened the public auction of confiscated cargoes in the center of Natchez when a great cry was heard. An angry crowd of flatboatmen, Bowie knives in hand, was storming up the bluffs from the Mississippi shouting, as the local newspaper reported, "threats of violence and death upon all who attempted to sell and buy their property." It was November 1837, and the town council had just enacted a restrictive tax of $10 per flatboat, a measure designed to rid the wharf district known as Natchez-Under-the-Hill of the most impoverished and disreputable of the flatboatmen. As the boatmen approached, merchants and onlookers shrank back in fear. But the local authorities had called out the militia, who now came marching into the square with their rifles primed and lowered. "The cold and sullen bayonets of the Guards were too hard meat for the Arkansas toothpicks," reported the local press, and "there was no fight." The boatmen sullenly turned and went back down the bluffs. It was the first confrontation in the "Flatboat Wars" that erupted as Mississippi ports tried to bring their troublesome riverfronts under regulation.

In the sixteenth century, a member of Hernando de Soto's expedition was the first European to take notice of this "land abundant in subsistence" that was "thickly peopled" by the Natchez Indians. Europeans did not settle in the area, however, until the French established the port of Fort Rosalie in the 1720s. The French destroyed the highly organized society of the Natchez Indians and the port became a major Mississippi River frontier trading center that brought peoples of different races together, leading to intermarriage and the growth of a mixed-race population.

When the Spanish took control of the territory in 1763, they laid out the new town of Natchez high on the bluffs, safe from Mississippi flooding. Fort Rosalie, rechristened Natchez-Under-the-Hill, continued to flourish as the produce grown by American farmers in Kentucky and Tennessee moved downriver on flatboats. When Americans took possession of Mississippi in 1798, the district surrounding the port became the most important center of settlement in the Old Southwest. Once again, this abundant land of rich, black soil became thickly peopled, but this time with cotton planters and their African American slaves.

Under-the-Hill gained renown as the last stop for boatmen before New Orleans. Minstrel performers sang of their exploits:

> *Den dance de boatmen dance,*
> *O dance de boatmen dance,*
> *O dance all night till broad daylight,*
> *An go home wid de gals in de morning.*

According to one traveler, "They feel the same inclination to dissipation as sailors who have long been out of port." There were often as many as 150 boats drawn up at the wharves. The crowds along the riverfront, noted John James Audubon, who visited in the 1820s, "formed a medley which it is beyond my power to describe." Mingling among American rivermen of all descriptions were trappers and hunters in fur caps, Spanish shopkeepers in bright smocks, French gentlemen from New Orleans in velvet coats, Indians wrapped in their trade blankets, African Americans both free and slave—a pageant of nations and races. Clapboard shacks and flatboats dragged on shore and converted into storefronts served as grog shops, card rooms, dance halls, and hotels. Whorehouses with women of every age and color abounded.

Natchez

On the bluffs, meanwhile, the town of Natchez had become the winter home to the southwestern planter elite. They built their mansions with commanding views of the river. A visitor attending a ball at one of these homes was dazzled by the display: "Myriads of wax candles burning in wall sconces, sparkling chandeliers, entrancing music, the scent of jasmine, rose and sweet olive, the sparkle of wine mellowed by age, the flow of wit and brilliant repartee, all were there." Sustaining this American aristocracy was the labor of thousands of enslaved men and women, who lived in the squalid quarters behind the great house and worked the endless fields of cotton.

The Natchez planters, their wealth and confidence growing with cotton's growing dominance of the local economy, found Under-the-Hill an increasing irritant. "A gentleman may game with a gambler by the hour," one resident remembered, "and yet despise him and refuse to recognize him afterward." The Under-the-Hill elite, however—gamblers, saloon keepers, and pimps—disturbed this social boundary when they began staying at hotels and even building town houses in Natchez town. And in the wake of the slave revolt led by Nat Turner in Virginia in 1831, in which fifty-five white people were killed, the planters began to feel increasingly threatened by the racial mingling of the riverfront.

In the late 1830s, rumors that their slaves were conspiring to murder them during Fourth of July celebrations while Under-the-Hill desperadoes looted their mansions reinforced the Natchez elite's growing conviction that they could no longer tolerate the polyglot community of the riverfront. The measures that ultimately provoked the flatboatmen's threats in November 1837 soon followed.

In response, the planters issued an extralegal order giving all the gamblers, pimps, and whores of Under-the-Hill twenty-four hours to evacuate the district. As the Mississippi militia sharpened their bayonets, panic swept the wharves, and that night dozens of flatboats loaded with a motley human cargo headed for the more tolerant community of New Orleans. Other river ports issued similar orders. "The towns on the river," one resident remembered, "became purified from a moral pestilence which the law could not cure." Three years later, a great tornado hit Under-the-Hill, leveling the shacks that had served so long as a rendezvous for the rivermen, and gradually the Mississippi reclaimed the old river bottom.

These two communities—Natchez, home to the rich slave-owning elite, and Natchez-Under-the-Hill, the bustling polyglot trading community—epitomize the paradox of the American South in the early nineteenth century. Enslaved African Americans laboring in the cotton fields made possible the greatest accumulations of wealth in early nineteenth-century America and the sumptuous and distinctive lifestyle of aristocratic Southern planters.

The boatmen and traders of Natchez-Under-the-Hill were vital to the planters' prosperity, but their polyglot racial and social mixing threatened the system of control, built on a rigid distinction between free white people and enslaved black people, by which the planters maintained slavery. Because the slave owners could not control the boatmen, they expelled them. This defensive reaction—to seal off the world of slavery from the wider commercial world—exposed the vulnerability of the slave system at the very moment of its greatest commercial success.

KEY TOPICS

- The domination of southern life by the slave system
- The economic implications of "King Cotton"
- The creation of African American communities under slavery
- The social structure of the white South and its increasing defensiveness

KING COTTON AND SOUTHERN EXPANSION

Slavery had long dominated southern life. African American slaves grew the great export crops of the colonial period—tobacco, rice, and indigo—on which slave owners' fortunes were made, and their presence shaped southern society and culture (see Chapter 4). Briefly, in the early days of American independence, the slave system waned, only to be revived by the immense profitability of cotton in a newly industrializing world. Cotton became the dominant crop in a rapidly expanding South that included not only the original states of Maryland, Delaware, Virginia, North and South Carolina, and Georgia, but also Kentucky, Tennessee, Missouri, Alabama, Mississippi, Louisiana, Arkansas, Florida, and Texas. The overwhelming economic success of cotton and of the slave system on which it depended created a distinctive regional culture quite different from that developing in the North.

Cotton and Expansion into the Old Southwest

Short-staple cotton had long been recognized as a crop ideally suited to southern soils and growing conditions. But it had one major drawback: the seeds were so difficult to remove from the lint that it took an entire day to hand-clean a single pound of cotton. The invention in 1793 that made cotton growing profitable was the result of collaboration between a young Northerner named Eli Whitney, recently graduated from Yale College, and Catherine Greene, a South Carolina plantation owner and widow of Revolutionary War General Nathanael Greene, who had hired Whitney to tutor her children. Whitney built a prototype cotton engine, dubbed "gin" for short, a simple device consisting of a hand-cranked cylinder with teeth that tore the lint away from the seeds. At Greene's suggestion, the teeth were made of wire. With the cotton gin, it was possible to clean more than fifty pounds of cotton a day. Soon large and small planters in the inland regions of Georgia and South Carolina had begun to grow cotton. By 1811, this area was producing 60 million pounds of cotton a year, and exporting most of it to England.

Other areas of the South quickly followed South Carolina and Georgia into cotton production. New land was wanted because cotton growing rapidly depleted the soil. The profits to be made from cotton growing drew a rush of southern farmers into the so-called black belt—an area stretching through western Georgia, Alabama, and Mississippi that was blessed with exceptionally fertile soil. Following the War of 1812, Southerners were seized by "Alabama Fever." In one of the swiftest migrations in American history, white Southerners and their slaves flooded into western Georgia and the areas that would become Alabama and Mississippi (the Old Southwest). On this frontier, African American pioneers (albeit involuntary ones) cleared the forests, drained the swamps, broke the ground, built houses and barns, and planted the first crops (see Map 10.1).

This migration caused the population of Mississippi to double (from 31,306 to 74,448) and that of Alabama to grow sixteenfold (from 9,046 to 144,317) between 1810 and 1820. This and subsequent western land booms dramatically changed the population of the original southern states as well. Nearly half of all white South Carolinians born after 1800 eventually left the state, usually to move west. By 1850, there were more than 50,000 South Carolina natives living in Georgia, almost as many in Alabama, and 26,000 in Mississippi.

Like the simultaneous expansion into the Old Northwest, settlement of the Old Southwest took place at the expense of the region's Indian population (see Chapter 9). Beginning with the defeat of the Creeks at Horseshoe Bend in 1814 and ending with the Cherokee forced migration along the "Trail of Tears" in 1838, the Five Civilized Tribes—the Cherokees, Chickasaws, Choctaws, Creeks, and Seminoles—were

SCENE ON THE LEVEE, AT NEW ORLEANS.

This 1855 illustration of black stevedores loading heavy bales of cotton onto waiting steam boats in New Orleans is an example of the South's dependence on cotton and the slave labor that produced it.

SOURCE: Copyright © The Granger Collection, New York / The Granger Collection

forced to give up their lands and move to Indian Territory (see Chapter 11).

Following the "Alabama Fever" of 1816–20, several later surges of southern expansion (1832–38, and again in the mid-1850s) carried cotton planting over the Mississippi River into Louisiana and deep into Texas. Each surge ignited feverish speculative frenzies, remembered in terms like the "Flush Times" for the heated rush of the 1830s. In the minds of the mobile, enterprising Southerners who sought their fortunes in the West, cotton profits and expansion went hand in hand. But the expansion of cotton meant the expansion of slavery.

Slavery the Mainspring— Again

The export of cotton from the South was the dynamic force in the developing American economy in the period 1790–1840. Just as the international slave trade had been the dynamic force in the Atlantic economy of the eighteenth century (see Chapter 4), southern slavery financed northern industrial development in the nineteenth century (see Figure 10.1).

MAP EXPLORATION

To explore an interactive version of this map, go to **www.prenhall.com/faragher5/map10.1**

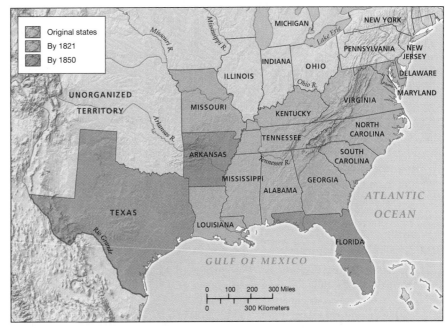

MAP 10.1 The South Expands, 1790–1850 This map shows the dramatic effect cotton production had on southern expansion. From the original six states of 1790, westward expansion, fueled by the search for new cotton lands, added another six states by 1821, and three more by 1850.

The rapid growth of cotton production was an international phenomenon, prompted by events occurring far from the American South. The insatiable demand for cotton was a result of the technological and social changes that we know today as the Industrial Revolution. Beginning early in the eighteenth century, a series of inventions resulted in the mechanized spinning and weaving of cloth in the world's first factories in the north of England. The ability of these factories to produce unprecedented amounts of cotton cloth revolutionized the world economy. The invention of the cotton gin came at just the right time. British textile manufacturers were eager to buy all the cotton that the South could produce. The figures for cotton production soared: from 720,000 bales in 1830, to 2.85 million bales in 1850, to nearly 5 million in 1860. By the time of the Civil War, cotton accounted for almost 60 percent of American exports, representing a total value of nearly $200 million a year. Cotton's central place in the national economy and its international importance led Senator James Henry Hammond of South Carolina to make a famous boast in 1858:

Without firing a gun, without drawing a sword, should they make war on us, we could bring the whole world to our feet. . . . What would happen if no cotton was furnished for three years? . . . England would topple headlong and carry the whole civilized world with her save the South. No, you dare not to make war on cotton. No power on the earth dares to make war upon it. Cotton is King.

The connection between southern slavery and northern industry was very direct. Most mercantile services associated with the cotton trade (insurance, for example) were in northern hands and, significantly, so was shipping. This economic structure was not new. In colonial times, New England ships dominated the African slave trade. Some New England families—like the Browns of Providence who made fortunes in the slave trade—invested some of their profits in the new technology of textile manufacturing in the 1790s. Other merchants—such as the Boston Associates who financed the cotton textile mills at Lowell—made their money from cotton shipping and brokerage. Thus, as cotton boomed, it provided capital for the new factories of the North.

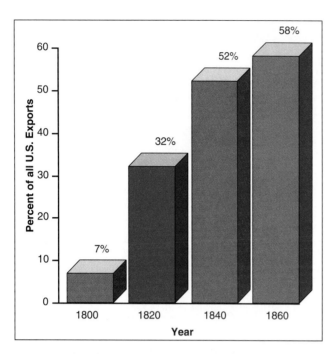

FIGURE 10.1   Cotton Exports as a Percentage of All U.S. Exports, 1800–1860 One consequence of the growth of cotton production was its importance in international trade. The growing share of the export market, and the great value (nearly $200 million in 1860) led southern slave owners to believe that "Cotton Is King." The importance of cotton to the national economy entitled the South to a commanding voice in national policy, many Southerners believed.

SOURCE: Sam Bowers Hilliard, *Atlas of Antebellum Southern Agriculture* (Baton Rouge: Louisiana State University Press, 1984), pp. 67–71.

A Slave Society in a Changing World

In the flush of freedom following the American Revolution, all the northern states abolished slavery or passed laws for gradual emancipation, and a number of slave owners in the Upper South freed their slaves (see Chapter 7). Thomas Jefferson, ever the optimist, claimed that "a total emancipation with the consent of the masters" could not be too far in the future. It was clear that national opinion found the international slave trade abhorrent. On January 1, 1808, the earliest date permitted by the Constitution, a bill to abolish the importation of slaves became law. Nevertheless, southern legislatures were unwilling to write steps toward emancipation into law, preferring to depend on the charity of individual slave owners.

But attitudes toward slavery rapidly changed in the South following the invention of the cotton gin in 1793 and the realization of the riches to be made from cotton. White Southerners believed that only African slaves could be forced to work day after day, year after year, at the rapid and brutal pace required in the cotton fields of large plantations in the steamy southern summer. As the pro-

duction of cotton climbed higher every year in response to a seemingly inexhaustible international demand, so too did the demand for slaves and the conviction of Southerners that slavery was an economic necessity.

Although cotton was far from being the only crop (the South actually devoted more acreage to corn than to cotton in 1860), its vast profitability affected all aspects of society. In the first half of the nineteenth century, King Cotton reigned supreme over an expanding domain as Southerners increasingly tied their fortunes to the slave system of cotton production. As a British tourist to Mobile wryly noted in the 1850s, the South was a place where "people live in cotton houses and ride in cotton carriages. They buy cotton, sell cotton, think cotton, eat cotton, drink cotton, and dream cotton. They marry cotton wives, and unto them are born cotton children." The South was truly in thrall to King Cotton.

As had been true since colonial times, the centrality of slavery to the economy and the need to keep slaves under firm control required the South to become a slave society, rather than merely a society with slaves, as was the case in the North. What this meant was that one particular form of social relationship, that of master and slave, (one dominant, the other subordinate) became the model for all relationships, including personal interactions between husband and wife as well as interactions in politics and at work. The profitability of cotton reconfirmed this model and extended it far beyond its original boundaries, thus creating a different kind of society in the South than the one emerging in the North.

At a time when the North was experiencing the greatest spurt of urban growth in the nation's history (see Chapter 13), most of the South remained rural: less than 3 percent of Mississippi's population lived in cities of more than 2,500 residents, and only 10 percent of Virginia's did. There was no question that concentration on plantation agriculture diverted energy and resources from the South's cities. The agrarian ideal, bolstered by the cotton boom, encouraged the antiurban and anticommercial sentiments of many white Southerners.

The South also lagged behind the North in industrialization and in canals and railroads (see Chapter 12.) In 1860, only 15 percent of the nation's factories were located in the South. Similarly, the South was also initially left behind by the transportation revolution. In 1850, only 26 percent of the nation's railroads were in the South, increasing to still only 35 percent by 1860.

The failure of the South to industrialize at the northern rate was not a matter of ignorance but of choice. Southern capital was tied up in land and slaves, and Southerners, buoyed by the world's insatiable demand for cotton, saw no reason to invest in economically risky railroads, canals, and factories. Nor were they eager to introduce the disruptive factor of free wage labor into the tightly controlled slave system. Cotton was safer. Cotton was King.

Other changes, however, could not be so easily ignored. Nationwide, the slave states were losing their political dominance because their population was not keeping pace with that of the North and the Northwest. The fear of becoming a permanent, outvoted minority was a major cause of the Nullification Crisis provoked by South Carolina in 1830 (see Chapter 11). Equally alarming, outside the South, antislavery sentiment was growing rapidly. Southerners felt directly threatened by growing abolitionist sentiment in the North, and by the 1834 action of the British Government eliminating slavery on the sugar plantations of the West Indies. The South felt increasingly hemmed in by Northern opposition to the expansion of slavery, which was evident first in the Missouri Compromise of 1820 (see Chapter 9), and later in the Congressional refusal to annex Texas in 1836, and in the battles over expansion that began with the outbreak of the Mexican American War in 1845 and continued until the Civil War in 1861 (see Chapters 14 and 15). Finally, slavery itself was not static. The changes in the system, largely caused by cotton, changed the lives of both white and black Southerners.

TO BE A SLAVE

Slavery had become distinctively southern: by 1820, as a result of laws passed after the Revolution, all of the northern states had abolished slaveholding. On January 1, 1808, the United States ended its participation in the international slave trade. Although a small number of slaves continued to be smuggled in from Africa, the growth of the slave labor force depended primarily on natural increase—that is, through births within the slave population. The slave population, estimated at 700,000 in 1790, grew to more than 4 million in 1860. A distinctive African American slave community, which had first emerged in the eighteenth century (see Chapter 4), expanded dramatically in the early years of the nineteenth century. This community was as much shaped by King Cotton as was the white South.

Cotton and the American Slave System

The explosive growth of cotton plantations changed the nature of southern slave labor. In 1850, 55 percent of all slaves were engaged in cotton growing. Another 20 percent labored to produce other crops: tobacco (10 percent), rice, sugar, and hemp. About 15 percent of all slaves were domestic servants, and the remaining 10 percent worked in mining, lumbering, industry, and construction (see Figure 10.2).

Cotton growing concentrated slaves on plantations, in contrast to the more dispersed distribution on smaller farms in earlier generations. Although more than half of all slave owners owned five slaves or fewer, 75 percent of all slaves now lived in groups of ten or more. This disproportionate distribution could have a

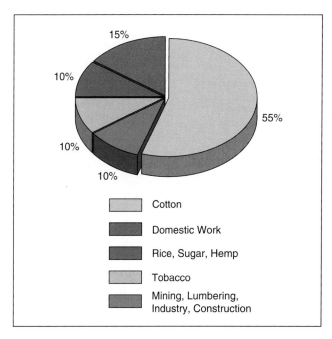

FIGURE 10.2   Distribution of Slave Labor, 1850 In 1850, 55 percent of all slaves worked in cotton, 10 percent in tobacco, and another 10 percent in rice, sugar, and hemp. Ten percent worked in mining, lumbering, industry, and construction, and 15 percent worked as domestic servants. Slaves were not generally used to grow corn, the staple crop of the yeoman farmer.

major impact on a slave's life, for it was a very different matter to be the single slave of a small farmer than to be a member of a 100-person black community on a large plantation. The size of cotton plantations fostered the growth of African American slave communities. On the other hand, the westward expansion of cotton undermined the stability of those communities. As expansion to the Southwest accelerated, so did the demand for slaves in the newly settled regions, thus fueling the internal slave trade. Slaves were increasingly clustered in the Lower South, as Upper South slave owners sold slaves "down the river" or migrated westward with their entire households. An estimated 1 million slaves migrated involuntarily to the Lower South between 1820 and 1860 (see Map 10.2).

The Internal Slave Trade

The cotton boom caused a huge increase in the domestic slave trade. Plantation owners in the Upper South (Delaware, Kentucky, Maryland, Virginia, and Tennessee) sold their slaves to meet the demand for labor in the new and expanding cotton-growing regions of the Old Southwest. In every decade after 1820, at least 150,000 slaves were uprooted either by slave trading or planter migration to the new areas, and in the expansions of the 1830s and the 1850s,

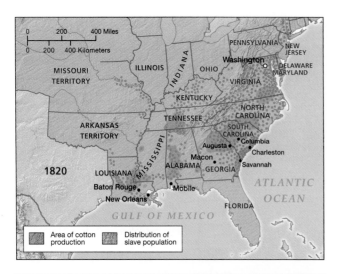

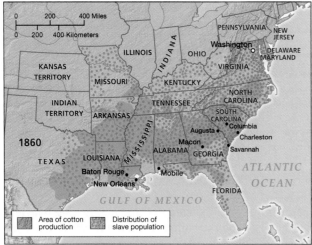

MAP 10.2 Cotton Production and the Slave Population, 1820–60 In the forty-year period from 1820 to 1860, cotton production grew dramatically in both quantity and extent. Rapid westward expansion meant that by 1860 cotton production was concentrated in the black belt (so called for its rich soils) in the Lower South. As cotton production moved west and south, so did the enslaved African American population that produced it, causing a dramatic rise in the internal slave trade.

SOURCE: Sam Bowers Hilliard, *Atlas of Antebellum Southern Agriculture* (Baton Rouge: Lousiana State University Press, 1984).

the number reached a quarter of a million. Cumulatively, between 1820 and 1860, nearly 50 percent of the slave population of the Upper South took part against their will in southern expansion. More slaves—an estimated 1 million—were uprooted by this internal slave trade and enforced migration in the early nineteenth century than were brought to North America during the entire time the international slave trade was legal (see Chapter 4).

Purchased by slave traders from owners in the Upper South, slaves were gathered together in notorious "slave pens" in places like Richmond and Charleston and then moved south by train or boat. In the interior, they were carried as cargo on steamboats on the Mississippi River, hence the dreaded phrase "sold down the river." Often slaves moved on foot, chained together in groups of fifty or more known as "coffles." Chained slaves in coffles were a common sight on southern roads, and one difficult to reconcile with the notion of slavery as a benevolent institution. Arriving at a central market in the Lower South like Natchez, New Orleans, or Mobile, the slaves, after being carefully inspected by potential buyers, were sold at auction to the highest bidder (see Map 10.3).

Although popular stereotype portrayed slave traders as unscrupulous outsiders who persuaded kind and reluctant masters to sell their slaves, the historical truth is much harsher. Traders, far from being shunned by slave-owning society, were often respected community members. One Charleston trader, Alexander McDonald, served as both an alderman and a bank president and was described as "a man of large means and responsible for all his engagements" who had "the confidence of the public." Similarly, the sheer scale of the slave trade makes it impossible to believe that slave owners only reluctantly parted with their slaves at times of economic distress. Instead, it is clear that many owners sold slaves and separated slave families not out of necessity but to increase their profits. The sheer size and profitability of the internal slave trade made a mockery of Southern claims for the benevolence of the slave system.

Sold "Down the River"

The experience of slaves who were sold or forced by their owners to migrate to the newly opened cotton lands of the Southwest (western Georgia, Alabama, Mississippi, Arkansas, and Texas) sheds light on the dynamics and tensions underlying the South's cotton-induced prosperity. Although some owners brought existing slave communities with them, the most common experience was that of individual slaves, usually still in their teens or even younger, forcibly separated from family and kin and sent alone with other strangers to a new life far away. Owners had good reason to fear the resentment of slaves who were forced into these new circumstances. For the individual slave, migration to the Southwest was a long ordeal—a Second Middle Passage.

Upper South slaveowners sold slaves to large trading firms, who collected them during the summer in slave pens in Baltimore, Richmond, Nashville, and other Northern cities. When the weather cooled,

The immense size of the internal slave trade made sights like this commonplace on southern roads. Groups of slaves, chained together in gangs called coffles, were marched from their homes in the Upper South to cities in the Lower South, where they were auctioned to new owners.

SOURCE: Library of Congress.

slaves were sent south in chains on foot in coffles, by sailing ship, or by steamboat on the Mississippi to be sold in New Orleans. There, in the streets outside of large slave pens near the French Quarter, thousands of slaves were displayed and sold each year. Dressed in new clothes provided by the traders and exhorted by the traders to walk, run, and otherwise show their stamina, slaves were presented to buyers. For their part, suspicious buyers, unsure that traders and slaves themselves were truthful, poked, prodded, and frequently stripped male and female slaves to be sure they were as healthy as the traders claimed. Aside from obvious signs of illness, buyers often looked for scars on a slave's back: too many scars were a sign of the frequent whippings that a rebellious or "uppity" slave had provoked. Most slaves were sold as individuals: with their own needs in mind, buyers rarely responded to pleas to buy an "extra" slave to keep a family together. (See Out of Many Voices: Solomon Northup Describes a New Orleans Slave Pen.)

Once sold, slaves could face a variety of conditions. A number, especially in the early years of settlement in the Old Southwest, found themselves in frontier circumstances. Young male slaves were chosen for the backbreaking work

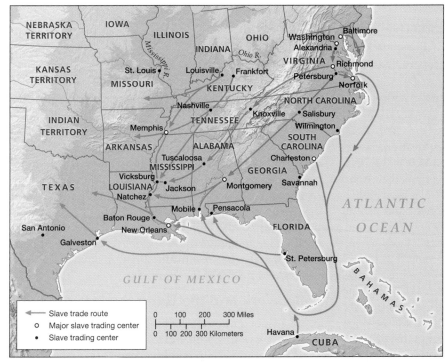

MAP 10.3 Internal Slave Trade Between 1820 and 1860, nearly 50 percent of the slave population of the Upper South was sold south to labor on the cotton plantations of the Lower South. This map shows the various routes by which they were "sold down the river," shipped by boat or marched south.

SOURCE: *Historical Atlas of the United States* (Washington: National Geographic Society, 1988).

OUT OF MANY VOICES

SOLOMON NORTHUP DESCRIBES A NEW ORLEANS SLAVE PEN

Solomon Northup, a free African American, was captured by slave traders in 1841 and shipped south to New Orleans for sale. In this passage from his autobiography, he describes his experience in a New Orleans slave pen before being sold. Northup spent twelve years as a slave before he was able to get word to northern friends, who freed him.

THE VERY AMIABLE, PIOUS-HEARTED MR. THEOPHILUS Freeman keeper of the slave pen in New-Orleans, was out among his animals early in the morning. With an occasional kick of the older men and women, and many a sharp crack of the whip about the ears of the younger slaves, it was not long before they were all astir, and wide awake. Mr. Theophilus Freeman bustled about in a very industrious manner, getting his property ready for the sales-room. . . .

In the first place we were required to wash thoroughly, and those with beards, to shave. We were then furnished with a new suit each, cheap, but clean. The men had hat, coat, shirt, pants and shoes; the women frocks of calico, and handkerchiefs to bind about their heads. We were now conducted into a large room in the front part of the building to which the yard was attached, in order to be properly trained, before the admission of customers.

The men were arranged on one side of the room, the women on the other. The tallest was placed at the head of the row, then the next tallest, and so on in the order of their respective heights. Freeman charged us to remember our places; exhorted us to appear smart and lively, —sometimes threatening, and again, holding out various inducements. During the day he exercised us in the art of "looking smart," and of moving to our places with exact precision.

Next day many customers called to examine Freeman's "new lot." The latter gentleman was very loquacious, dwelling at much length upon our several good points and qualities. He would make us hold up our heads, walk briskly back and forth, while customers would feel of our hands and arms and bodies, turn us about, ask us what we could do, make us open our mouths and show our teeth, precisely as a jockey examines a horse which he is about to barter for or purchase. Sometimes a man or woman was taken back to the small house in the yard, stripped, and inspected more minutely. Scars upon a slave's back were considered evidence of a rebellious or unruly spirit, and hurt his sale. ■

SOURCE: Solomon Northup, *Twelve Years a Slave: Narrative of Solomon Northup, a Citizen of New York, Kidnapped in Washington City in 1841, and Rescued in 1853* (Auburn NY: Derby and Miller, 1853).

---

of cutting trees and clearing land for cultivation. Some worked side by side with their owners to clear the land for small farms devoted to raising food for immediate consumption. In these circumstances, slaves were often highly self-reliant and expected by owners to hunt and fish to supplement the basic diet. This relatively cooperative and permissive attitude was also evident on larger farms where slaves engaged in the variety of tasks required in mixed farming. But uniformity and strict discipline were the rule on cotton plantations. Owners eager to clear land rapidly so as to make quick profits often drove the clearing crews at an unmerciful pace. And they attempted to impose strict discipline and a rapid pace on the work gangs that planted, hoed, and harvested cotton. Slaves from other parts of the South, used to more individual and less intense work, hated the cotton regime and most of all hated the overseers who enforced it. They also fought to retain their rights to supplement the owner-supplied diet with their own garden produce and by hunting.

Thus, the new land in the Old Southwest that appeared to offer so much opportunity for owners, bred tensions caused by forcible sale and migration, by the organization and pace of cotton cultivation, and by the owners' efforts to abrogate what slaves saw as traditional rights. Behind the owners' interest in "scientific management" of cotton must have lurked constant fear of what resentful gangs of slaves might do if freed from watchful supervision.

Field Work and the Gang System of Labor

A full 75 percent of all slaves were field workers, and it was these workers who were most directly affected by the gang labor system employed on cotton plantations (as well as in tobacco and sugar). Cotton was a crop that demanded nearly year-round labor: from planting in April, to constant hoeing and cultivation through June, to a picking season that began in August and lasted until December. The work was less skilled than on tobacco or

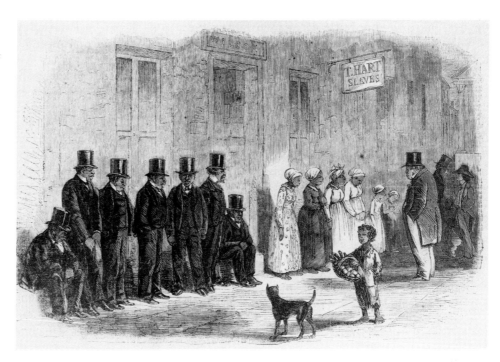

This engraving from *Harpers Weekly* shows slaves, dressed in new clothing, lined up outside a New Orleans slave pen for inspection by potential buyers before the actual auction began. They were often threatened with punishment if they did not present a good appearance and manner that would fetch a high price.

SOURCE: Courtesy of Culver Pictures, Inc.

sugar plantations, but more constant. Owners divided their slaves into gangs of twenty to twenty-five, a communal labor pattern reminiscent of parts of Africa, but with a crucial difference—these workers were supervised by overseers with whips. Field hands, both men and women, worked from "can see to can't see" (sunup to sundown) summer and winter, and frequently longer at harvest, when eighteen-hour days were common. On most plantations, the bell sounded an hour before sunup, and slaves were expected to be on their way to the fields as soon as it was light. Work continued till noon, and after an hour or so for lunch and rest, the slaves worked until nearly dark. In the evening, the women prepared dinner at the cabins and everyone snatched a few hours of unsupervised socializing before bedtime. Work days were shorter in the winter, perhaps only ten hours.

Work was tedious in the hot and humid southern fields, and the overseer's whip was never far away. Cotton growing was hard work: plowing and planting, chopping weeds with a heavy hoe, and picking the ripe cotton from the stiff and scratchy bolls, at the rate of 150 pounds a day. A strong, hardworking slave—a "prime field hand"—was valuable property, worth at least $1,000 to the master. Slaves justifiably took pride in their strength, as observed by a white Northerner traveling in Mississippi in 1854, who came across a work gang happy to be going home early because of rain:

> First came, led by an old driver carrying a whip, forty of the largest and strongest women I ever saw together . . . they carried themselves loftily, each having a hoe over the shoulder, and walking with a free, powerful stride. Behind them came the . . . [plowhands and their mules], thirty strong, mostly men, but a few of them women. . . . A lean and vigilant white overseer, on a brisk pony, brought up the rear.

That, of course, is only one side of the story. Compare former slave Solomon Northup's memory of cotton picking:

> It was rarely that a day passed by without one or more whippings. The delinquent [who had not picked enough cotton] was taken out, stripped, made to lie upon the ground, face downwards, when he received a punishment proportioned to his offence. It is the literal, unvarnished truth, that the crack of the lash, and the shrieking of the slaves, can be heard from dark till bed time, on [this] plantation, any day almost during the entire period of the cotton-picking season.

Slaves aged fast in this regime. Poor diet and heavy labor undermined health. When they were too old to work, they took on other tasks within the black community, such as caring for young children. Honored by the slave community, the elderly were tolerated by white owners, who continued to feed and clothe them until their deaths. Few actions show the hypocrisy of southern paternalism more clearly than the speed with which white owners evicted their elderly slaves in the 1860s when the end of the slave system was in sight.

House Servants

In the eighteenth century, almost all African slaves worked as field hands, but as profits from slavery grew, slaveowners diverted an increasing proportion of slave labor from the fields to the house service necessary to sustain their rich lifestyles. By one calculation, fully one-third of the female slaves in Virginia worked as house servants by 1800.

At first glance, working in the big house might seem to have been preferable to working in the fields. Physically, it was much less demanding, and house slaves were often better fed and clothed. They also had much more access to information, for white people, accustomed to servants and generally confident of their loyalty, often forgot their presence and spoke among themselves about matters of interest to the slaves: local gossip, changes in laws or attitudes, policies toward disobedient or rebellious slaves. As Benjamin Russel, a former slave in South Carolina, recalled:

> How did we get the news? Many plantations were strict about this, but the greater the precaution, the alerter became the slave, the wider they opened their ears and the more eager they became for outside information. The sources were: girls that waited on the tables, the ladies' maids and the drivers; they would pick up everything they heard and pass it on to the other slaves.

For many white people, one of the worst surprises of the Civil War was the eagerness of their house slaves to flee. Considered by their masters the best treated and the most loyal, these slaves were commonly the first to leave or to organize mass desertions. Even the Confederacy's first family, President Jefferson Davis and his wife Varina, were chagrined by the desertion of their house servants in 1864.

From the point of view of the slave, the most unpleasant thing about being a house servant (or the single slave of a small owner) was the constant presence of white people. There was no escape from white supervision. Many slaves who were personal maids and children's nurses were required to live in the big house and rarely saw their own families. Cooks and other house servants were exposed to the tempers and whims of all members of the white family, including the children, who prepared themselves for lives of mastery by practicing giving orders to slaves many times their own age. And house servants, more than any others, were forced to act grateful and ingratiating. The demeaning images of Uncle Tom and the ever-smiling mammy derive from the roles slaves learned as the price of survival. At the same time, genuine intimacy was possible, especially between black nurses and white children. But these were bonds that the white children were ultimately forced to reject as the price of joining the master class.

Artisans and Skilled Workers

A small number of slaves were skilled workers: weavers, seamstresses, carpenters, blacksmiths, mechanics. More slave men than women achieved skilled status (partly because many jobs considered appropriate for women, like cooking, were not thought of as skilled). Solomon Northup, the northern free African American kidnapped into slavery, had three owners and was hired out repeatedly as a carpenter and as a driver of other slaves in a sugar mill; he had also been hired out to clear land for a new Louisiana plantation and to cut sugar cane. Black people worked as lumberjacks (of the 16,000 lumber workers in the South, almost all were slaves), as miners, as deckhands and stokers on Mississippi riverboats, as stevedores loading cotton on the docks of Charleston, Savannah, and New Orleans, and sometimes as workers in the handful of southern factories. Because slaves were their masters' property, the wages of the slave belonged to the owner, not the slave.

The extent to which slaves made up the laboring class was most apparent in cities. A British visitor to Natchez in 1835 noted slave "mechanics, draymen, hostelers,

Thomas Jefferson used this revolving bookstand with five adjustable bookrests at Monticello. It was built of walnut in 1810 by slaves from the plantation whom Jefferson had directed to be trained as skilled carpenters.

SOURCE: Monticello/Thomas Jefferson Foundations, Inc.

labourers, hucksters and washwomen and the heterogeneous multitude of every other occupation." In the North, all these jobs were performed by white workers. In part, because the South failed to attract as much immigrant labor as the North, southern cities offered both enslaved and free black people opportunities in skilled occupations such as blacksmithing and carpentering that free African Americans in the North were denied.

THE AFRICAN AMERICAN COMMUNITY

Surely no group in American history has faced a harder job of community building than the black people of the antebellum South. Living in intimate, daily contact with their oppressors, African Americans nevertheless created an enduring culture of their own, a culture that had far-reaching and lasting influence on all of southern life and American society as a whole (see Chapter 4). Within their own communities, African American values and attitudes, and especially their own forms of Christianity, played a vital part in shaping a culture of endurance and resistance.

Few African Americans were unfortunate enough to live their lives alone among white people. Over half of all slaves lived on plantations with twenty or more other slaves, and others, on smaller farms, had links with slaves on nearby properties. Urban slaves were able to make and sustain so many secret contacts with other African Americans in cities or towns that slave owners wondered whether slave discipline could be maintained in urban settings. There can be no question that the bonds among African Americans were what sustained them during the years of slavery.

In law, slaves were property, to be bought, sold, rented, worked, and otherwise used (but not abused or killed) as the owner saw fit. But slaves were also human beings, with feelings, needs, and hopes. Even though most white Southerners believed black people to be members of an inferior, childish race, all but the most brutal masters acknowledged the humanity of their slaves. White masters learned to live with the two key institutions of African American community life: the family and the African American church, and in their turn slaves learned, however painfully, to survive slavery.

The Price of Survival

Of all the New World slave societies, the one that existed in the American South was the only one that grew by natural increase rather than through the constant importation of captured Africans. This fact alone made the African American community of the South different from the slave societies of Cuba, the Caribbean islands, and Brazil. In order to understand, we must examine the circumstances of survival and growth.

The growth of the African American slave population was not due to better treatment than in other New World slave societies, but to the higher fertility of African American women, who in 1808 (the year the international slave trade ended) had a crude birth rate of 35–40, causing a 2.2% yearly population growth. This was still below the fertility rate of white women, who had a crude birth rate of 55 and a 2.9% annual population growth. But by midcentury, the white rate had dropped to 1.99%, while the black rate remained high. The ending of African importations may have affected black population growth, for while African women usually breastfed for two years, a form of natural birth control that produced fewer births per mother, African American slave women adopted the white practice of only breastfeeding for one year, and on average gave birth to six or eight children at year-and-a-half intervals. But they also suffered from the contradictory demands of slave owners, who wanted them to work hard while still having children, for every slave baby increased the wealth of the owners.

As a result, because pregnant black women were inadequately nourished, worked too hard, or were too frequently pregnant, mortality rates for slave children under five were twice those for their white counterparts. At the time, owners often accused slave women of smothering their infants by rolling over them when asleep. When the British actress Fanny Kemble came to live on her husband's Georgia plantation in 1837, what shocked her more deeply than any other aspect of the slave system was the treatment of pregnant black women. Sensing her sympathy, pregnant slave women came to Kemble to plead for relief from field work, only to be brusquely ordered back to the fields by the overseer and Kemble's husband.

Health remained a lifelong issue for slaves. Malaria and infectious diseases such as yellow fever and cholera were endemic in the South. White people as well as black died, as the life expectancy figures for 1850 show: 40–43 years for white people and 30–33 years for African Americans. Slaves were more at risk because of the circumstances of slave life: poor housing, poor diet, and constant, usually heavy work. Sickness was chronic: 20 percent or more of the slave labor force on most plantations were sick at any one time. Many owners believed sick slaves were only "malingering." Because of the poor medical knowledge of the time, they failed to realize that adequate diet, warm housing, and basic sanitation might have prevented the pneumonia and dysentery that killed or weakened many slaves, and that exacted an especially high toll on very young children.

From Cradle to Grave

Slavery was a lifelong labor system, and the constant and inescapable issue between master and slave was how much work the slave would—or could be forced—to do. Southern white slave owners claimed that by housing, feeding, and clothing their slaves from infancy to death they were acting more humanely than northern industrialists who employed people only during their working years. But in spite of occasional instances of manumission—the freeing of a slave—the child born of a slave was destined to remain a slave.

Children lived with their parents (or with their mother if the father was a slave on another farm or plantation) in housing provided by the owner. Husband and wife cooperated in loving and sheltering their children and teaching them survival skills. From birth to about age seven, slave children played with one another and with white children, observing and learning how to survive. They saw the penalties: black adults, perhaps their own parents, whipped for disobedience; black women, perhaps their own sisters, violated by white men. And they might see one or both parents sold away as punishment or for financial gain. They would also see signs of white benevolence: special treats for children at holidays, appeals to loyalty from the master or mistress, perhaps friendship with a white child. One former slave recalled:

> Yessum, when they used to have company in the big house, Miss Ross would bring them to the door to show them us children. And, my blessed, the yard would be black with us children, all string up there next the doorstep looking up in they eyes. Old Missus would say, "Ain't I got a pretty crop of little niggers coming on?"

The children would learn slave ways of getting along: apparent acquiescence in white demands; pilfering; malingering, sabotage, and other methods of slowing the relentless work pace. Fanny Kemble, an accomplished actress, was quick to note the pretense in the "outrageous flattery" she received from her husband's slaves. But many white Southerners genuinely believed that their slaves were both less intelligent and more loyal than they really were. An escaped slave, Jermain Loguen, recalled with some distaste the charade of "servile bows and counterfeit smiles . . . and other false expressions of gladness" with which he placated his master and mistress. Frederick Douglass, whose fearless leadership of the abolitionist movement made him the most famous African American of his time, wryly noted, "As the master studies to keep the slave ignorant, the slave is cunning enough to make the master think he succeeds."

Most slaves spent their lives as field hands, working in gangs with other slaves under a white overseer, who was usually quick to use his whip to keep up the work pace. But there were other occupations. In the "big house" there were jobs for women as cooks, maids, seamstresses, laundresses, weavers, and nurses. Black men became coachmen, valets, and gardeners, or skilled craftsmen—carpenters, mechanics, and blacksmiths. Some children began learning these occupations at

Slave quarters built by slave owners, like these pictured on a Florida plantation, provided more than the basic shelter (a place to sleep and eat) that the owners intended. Slave quarters were the center of the African American community life that developed during slavery.

SOURCE: *Remains of Slave Quarters, Fort George Island, Florida,* ca. 1865. Stereograph. © Collection of The New York Historical Society. Negative no. 48163.

age seven or eight, often in an informal apprentice system. Other children, both boys and girls, were expected to take full care of younger children while the parents were working. Of course, black children had no schooling of any kind: in most of the southern states, it was against the law to teach a slave to read, although indulgent owners often rewarded their "pet" slaves by teaching them in spite of the law. At age twelve, slaves were considered full grown and put to work in the fields or in their designated occupation.

Slave Families

As had been true in the eighteenth century, families remained essential to African American culture (see Chapter 4). No southern state recognized slave marriages in law. Most owners, though, not only recognized but encouraged them, sometimes even performing a kind of wedding ceremony for the couple. Masters encouraged marriage among their slaves, believing it made the men less rebellious, and for economic reasons they were eager for the slave women to have children. Whatever marriages meant to the masters, to slaves they were a haven of love and intimacy in a cruel world, and the basis of the African American community. Husbands and wives had a chance, in their own cabins, to live their own lives among loved ones. The relationship between slave husband and wife was different from that of the white husband and wife. The master-slave system dictated that the white marriage be unequal, for the man had to be dominant and the woman dependent and submissive. Slave marriages were more equal, for husband and wife were both powerless within the slave system. Both knew that neither could protect the other from abuse at the hands of white people.

Family meant continuity. Parents made great efforts to teach their children the family history and to surround them with a supportive and protective kinship network. The strength of these ties is shown by the many husbands, wives, children, and parents who searched for each other after the Civil War when slavery came to an end. Observing African Americans' postwar migrations, a Freedmen's Bureau agent commented that "every mother's son among them seemed to be in search of his mother; every mother in search of her children." As the ads in black newspapers indicate, some family searches went on into the 1870s and 1880s, and many ended in failure.

Given the vast size of the internal slave trade, fear of separation was constant—and real. Far from being rare events prompted only by financial necessity, separations of slave families were common. One in every five slave marriages was broken, and one in every three children sold away from their families. These figures clearly show that slave owners' support for slave marriages was secondary to their desire for profits. The scale of the trade was a strong indication of the economic reality that underlay their protestations of paternalism.

In the face of constant separation, slave communities attempted to act like larger families. Following practices developed early in slavery, children were taught to respect and learn from all the elders, to call all adults of a certain age "aunt" or "uncle," and to call children of their own age "brother" or "sister" (see Chapter 4). Thus, in the absence of their own family, separated children could quickly find a place and a source of comfort in the slave community to which they had been sold.

This emphasis on family and on kinship networks had an even more fundamental purpose. The kinship of the entire community, where old people were respected and young ones cared for, represented a conscious rejection of white paternalism. The slaves' ability, in the most difficult of situations, to structure a community that expressed their values, not those of their masters, was extraordinary. Equally remarkable was the way in which African Americans reshaped Christianity to serve their needs.

African American Religion

African religions managed to survive from the earliest days of slavery in forms that white people considered as "superstition" or "folk belief," such as the medicinal use of roots by conjurers. Religious ceremonies survived, too, in late-night gatherings deep in the woods where the sound of drumming, singing, and dancing could not reach white ears (see Chapter 4). In the nineteenth century, these African traditions allowed African Americans to reshape white Christianity into their own distinctive faith that expressed their deep resistance to slavery.

The Great Awakening, which swept the South after the 1760s, introduced many slaves to Christianity, often in mixed congregations with white people (see Chapter 5). The transformation was completed by the Second Great Awakening, which took root among black and white Southerners in the 1790s. The number of African American converts, preachers, and lay teachers grew rapidly, and a distinctive form of Christianity took shape. Free African Americans founded their own independent churches and denominations. The first African American Baptist and Methodist churches were founded in Philadelphia in 1794 by the Reverend Absalom Jones and the Reverend Richard Allen. In 1816, the Reverend Allen joined with African American ministers from other cities to form the African Methodist Episcopal (AME) denomination. By the 1830s, free African American ministers like Andrew Marshall of Savannah and many more enslaved black preachers and lay ministers preached, sometimes secretly, to slaves. Their message was one of faith and love, of deliverance, of the coming of the promised land.

African Americans found in Christianity a powerful vehicle to express their longings for freedom and justice. But why did their white masters allow it? Some white people, themselves converted by the revivals, doubtless believed that they should not deny their slaves the same religious experience. But many southern slave owners expected Christianity to make their slaves obedient and peaceful. Forbidding their slaves to hold their own religious gatherings, owners insisted that their slaves attend white church services. Slaves were quick to realize the owners' purpose. As a former Texas slave recalled: "We went to church on the place and you ought to heard that preachin'. Obey your massa and missy, don't steal chickens and eggs and meat, but nary a word 'bout havin' a soul to save." On many plantations, slaves attended religious services with their masters every Sunday, sitting quietly in the back of the church or in the balcony, as the minister preached messages justifying slavery and urging obedience. But at night, away from white eyes, they held their own prayer meetings.

In churches and in spontaneous religious expressions, the black community made Christianity its own. Fusing Christian texts with African elements of group activity, such as the circle dance, the call-and-response pattern, and, above all, group singing, black people created a unique community religion full of emotion, enthusiasm, and protest. Nowhere is this spirit more compelling than in the famous spirituals: "Go Down Moses," with its mournful refrain "Let my people go"; the rousing "Didn't My Lord Deliver Daniel . . . and why not every man"; the haunting "Steal Away." Some of these spirituals became as well known to white people as to black people, but only African Americans seem to have appreciated the full meaning of their subversive messages.

Nevertheless, this was not a religion of rebellion, for that was unrealistic for most slaves. Black Christianity was an enabling religion: it helped slaves to survive, not as passive victims of white tyranny but as active opponents of an oppressive system that they daily protested in small but meaningful ways. In their faith, African Americans expressed a spiritual freedom that white people could not destroy.

Freedom and Resistance

The rapid geographical spread of cotton itself introduced a new source of tension and resistance into the slave-master relationship. Whatever their dreams, most slaves knew they would never escape. Freedom was too far away.

African cultural patterns persisted in the preference for night funerals and for solemn pageantry and song, as depicted in British artist John Antrobus's *Plantation Burial*, ca. 1860. Like other African American customs, the community care of the dead contained an implied rebuke to the masters' care of the living slaves.

SOURCE: John Antrobus, *Negro Burial*. Oil painting. The Historic New Orleans Collection #1960.46.

Almost all successful escapes in the nineteenth century (approximately 1,000 a year) were from the Upper South (Delaware, Maryland, Virginia, Kentucky, and Missouri). A slave in the Lower South or the Southwest simply had too far to go to reach freedom. In addition, white Southerners were determined to prevent escapes. Slave patrols were a common sight on southern roads. Any black person without a pass from his or her master was captured (usually roughly) and returned home to certain punishment. But despite almost certain recapture, slaves continued to flee and to help others do so. Escaped slave Harriet Tubman of Maryland, who made twelve rescue missions freeing 60–70 slaves in all (later inflated to 300 as Tubman's rescues became legendary), had extraordinary determination and skill. As a female runaway, she was unusual, too: most escapees were young men, for women often had small children they were unable to take and unwilling to leave behind.

Much more common was the practice of "running away nearby." Slaves who knew they could not reach freedom still frequently demonstrated their desire for liberty or their discontent over mistreatment by taking unauthorized leave from their plantation. Hidden in nearby forests or swamps, provided with food smuggled by other slaves from the plantation, the runaway might return home after a week or so, often to rather mild punishment. Although in reality, most slaves could have little hope of gaining freedom, even failed attempts at rebellion shook the foundations of the slave system, and thus temporary flight by any slave was a warning sign of discontent that a wise master did not ignore.

Slave Revolts

The ultimate resistance, however, was the slave revolt. Southern history was dotted with stories of former slave conspiracies and rumors of current plots (see Chapter 4). Every white Southerner knew about the last-minute failure of Gabriel Prosser's insurrection in Richmond in 1800 and the chance discovery of Denmark Vesey's plot in Charleston in 1822. But when in 1831, Nat Turner actually started a rebellion in which a number of white people were killed, southern fears were greatly magnified.

A literate man, Nat Turner was a lay preacher, but he was also a slave. It was Turner's intelligence and strong religious commitment that made him a leader in the slave community and, interestingly, these very same qualities led his master, Joseph Travis, to treat him with kindness, even though Turner had once run away for a month after being mistreated by an overseer. Turner began plotting his revolt after a religious vision in which he saw "white spirits and black spirits engaged in battle"; "the sun was darkened—the thunder rolled in the Heavens, and blood flowed in streams." Turner and five other slaves struck on the night of August 20, 1831, first killing Travis, who, Turner said, "was to me a kind master, and placed the greatest confidence in me; in fact, I had no cause to complain of his treatment of me."

Harriet Tubman was 40 years old when this photograph (later hand-tinted) was taken. Already famous for her daring rescues, she gained further fame by serving as a scout, spy and nurse during the Civil War.

SOURCE: The Granger Collection.

Moving from plantation to plantation and killing a total of fifty-five white people, the rebels numbered sixty by the next morning, when they fled from a group of armed white men. More than forty blacks were executed after the revolt, including Turner, who was captured accidentally after he had hidden for two months in the woods. Thomas R. Gray, a white lawyer to whom Turner dictated a lengthy confession before his death, was impressed by Turner's composure. "I looked on him," Gray said, "and my blood curdled in my veins." If intelligent, well-treated slaves such as Turner could plot revolts, how could white Southerners ever feel safe?

Gabriel's Rebellion, the Denmark Vesey plot, and Nat Turner's Revolt were the most prominent examples of organized slave resistance, but they were far from the only ones. Conspiracies and actual or rumored slave resistance began in colonial times (see Chapter 4) and never ceased. These

This drawing shows the moment, almost two months after the failure of his famous and bloody slave revolt, when Nat Turner was accidentally discovered in the woods near his home plantation. Turner's cool murder of his owner and methodical organization of his revolt deeply frightened many white Southerners.

SOURCE: Courtesy of the Library of Congress.

plots exposed the truth white Southerners preferred to ignore: Only force kept Africans and African Americans enslaved, and because no system of control could ever be total, white Southerners could never be completely safe from the possibility of revolt. Nat Turner brought white Southerners' fears to the surface. After 1831, the possibility of slave insurrection was never far from their minds.

Free African Americans

Another source of white disquiet was the growing number of free African Americans. By 1860, nearly 250,000 free black people lived in the South. For most, freedom dated from before 1800, when antislavery feeling among slave owners in the Upper South was widespread and cotton cultivation had yet to boom. In Virginia, for example, the number of manumitted (freed) slaves jumped tenfold in twenty years (see Chapter 7). But a new mood became apparent in 1806, when Virginia tightened its lenient manumission law: now the freed person was required to leave the state within a year or be sold back into slavery. After 1830, manumission was virtually impossible throughout the South.

Most free black people lived in the countryside of the Upper South, where they worked as tenant farmers or farm laborers. Urban African Americans were much more visible. Life was especially difficult for female-headed families, because only the most menial work—

street peddling and laundry work, for example—was available to free black women. The situation for African American males was somewhat better. Although they were discriminated against in employment and in social life, there were opportunities for skilled black craftsmen in trades such as blacksmithing and carpentry. Cities such as Charleston, Savannah, and Natchez were home to flourishing free African American communities that formed their own churches and fraternal orders.

Throughout the South in the 1830s, state legislatures tightened black codes—laws concerning free black people. Free African Americans could not carry firearms, could not purchase slaves (unless they were members of their own family), and were liable to the criminal penalties meted out to slaves (that is, whippings and summary judgments without a jury trial). They could not testify against whites, hold office, vote, or serve in the militia. In other words, except for the right to own property, free blacks had no civil rights. White people increasingly feared the influence free black people might have on slaves, for free African Americans were a living challenge to the slave system. Their very existence disproved the basic southern equations of white equals free, and black equals slave. No one believed more fervently in those equations than the South's largest population group, white people who did not own slaves.

THE WHITE MAJORITY

The pervasive influence of the slave system in the South is reflected in the startling contrast of two facts: two-thirds of all Southerners did not own slaves, yet slave owners dominated the social and political life of the region. Who were the two-thirds of white Southerners who did not

One of the ways Charleston attempted to control its African American population was to require all slaves to wear badges showing their occupation. After 1848, free black people also had to wear badges, which were decorated, ironically, with a liberty cap.

SOURCE: Courtesy of the American Numismatic Society of New York.

own slaves, and how did they live? Throughout the South, slave owners occupied the most productive land: tobacco-producing areas in Virginia and Tennessee, coastal areas of South Carolina and Georgia where rice and cotton grew, sugar lands in Louisiana, and large sections of the cotton-producing black belt, which stretched westward from South Carolina to Texas. Small farmers, usually without slaves, occupied the rest of the rural land, and a small middle class lived in the cities of the South.

The Middle Class

In the predominantly rural South, cities provided a home for a commercial middle class of merchants, bankers, factors (agents), and lawyers on whom the agricultural economy depended to sell its produce to a world market. Urban growth lagged far behind the North. The cities that grew were major shipping centers for agricultural goods: the river cities of Louisville, St. Louis, Memphis, and New Orleans, and the cotton ports of Mobile and Savannah. Formal educational institutions, libraries, and cultural activities were located in cities, and so were the beginnings of the same kind of entreprenurial and commercial spirit so evident in the North. As in the North, small industrial cities often including textile mills and heavier industry clustered along the fall line, where the rivers dropped down from the highlands to the coastal plains. Columbus, Georgia, located at the falls of the Chattahoochee River, was an example of such a small city.

The effort of William Gregg of South Carolina to establish the cotton textile industry illustrates some of the problems facing southern entrepreneurs. Gregg, a successful jeweler from Columbia, South Carolina, became convinced that textile factories were a good way to diversify the southern economy and to provide a living for poor whites who could not find work in the slave-dominated employment system. He enthusiastically publicized the findings of his tour of northern textile mills, but found a cool reception. His request to the planter-dominated South Carolina legislature for a charter of incorporation for a textile mill passed by only one vote. In 1846, he built a model mill and a company town in Graniteville, South Carolina, that attracted poor white families as employees. Gregg adapted southern paternalism to industry, providing a school and churches and prohibiting alcohol and dancing, yet paying his workers twenty percent less than northern wages. His experience in the competitive textile industry led him to favor the protective tariff, thus putting him at odds with the general attitude in South Carolina that had solidified at the time of the Nullification Crisis (see Chapter 11).

Another noteworthy exception was the Tredegar Iron Works, near Richmond, which by 1837 was the third largest foundry in the nation. Joseph Anderson, who became its manager (and later owner) in 1841 broke southern precedent by using slave labor in the mills, thus proving that enslaved workers were capable of factory work (a fact that many Southerners disputed).

Many southern planters scorned members of the commercial middle class like Joseph Anderson because they had to please their suppliers and customers, and thus lacked, in planter's eyes, true independence. This was an attitude strikingly different from that in the North, where the commercial acumen of the middle class was increasingly valued (see Chapter 12).

Poor White People

From 30 to 50 percent of all southern white people were landless, a proportion similar to that in the North. But the existence of slavery limited the opportunities for southern poor white people. Slaves made up the permanent, stable workforce in agriculture and in many skilled trades. Many poor white people led highly transient lives in search of work, such as farm labor at harvest time, which was only temporary. Others were tenant farmers working under share-tenancy arrangements that kept them in debt to the landowner. Although they farmed poorer land with less equipment than landowning farmers, most tenant farmers grew enough food to sustain their families. Like their landowning neighbors, tenant farmers aspired to independence.

Relationships between poor whites and black slaves were complex. White men and women often worked side by side with black slaves in the fields and were socially and sexually intimate with enslaved and free African Americans. White people engaged in clandestine trade to supply slaves with items like liquor that slave owners prohibited, helped slaves to escape, and even (in an 1835 Mississippi case) were executed for their participation in planning a slave revolt. At the same time, the majority of poor white people insisted, sometimes violently, on their racial superiority over blacks. For their part, many African American slaves, better dressed, better nourished, and healthier, dismissed them as "poor white trash." But the fact was that the difficult lives of poor whites, whom one contemporary described as "a third class of white people," served to blur the crucial racial distinction between independent whites and supposedly inferior, dependent black people on which the system of slavery rested. Like the boatmen whom the Natchez slave owners viewed with such alarm, poor white people posed a potential threat to the slave system.

Yeoman Values

The word "yeoman," originally a British term for a farmer who works his own land, is often applied to independent farmers of the South, most of whom lived on family-sized farms. Although yeoman farmers sometimes owned a few slaves, in general they and their families worked their land by themselves. This land ranged from adequate to poor, from depleted, once-rich regions in Virginia to the Carolina

The goal of yeoman farm families was economic independence. Their mixed farming and grazing enterprises, supported by kinship and community ties, afforded them a self-sufficiency epitomized by Carl G. von Iwonski's painting of this rough but comfortable log cabin in New Braunfels, Texas.

SOURCE: Daughters of the Republic of Texas Library. Yanaguana Society Collection.

and middle class. Large plantation owners often bought food for their slaves from small local farmers, ground the latter's corn in the plantation mill, ginned their cotton, and transported and marketed it as well. But although planters and much smaller yeomen were part of a larger community network, in the black belt the large slave owners were clearly dominant. Only in their own up-country communities did yeomen feel truly independent.

In 1828 and 1832, southern yeomen and poor white men voted overwhelmingly for Andrew Jackson. They were drawn variously to his outspoken policy of ruthless expansionism, his appeals to the common man, and his rags-to-riches ascent from poor boy to rich slave owner. It was a career many hoped to emulate. The dominance of the large planters was due at least in part to the ambition of many yeomen, especially those with two or three slaves, to expand their holdings and become rich. These farmers, enthusiastic members of the lively democratic politics of the South, supported the leaders they hoped to join.

hill country and the pine barrens of Mississippi. Typical of the yeoman-farmer community was northwestern Georgia, once home to the Creeks and Cherokees, but now populated by communities of small farmers who grew enough vegetables to feed their families, including corn, which they either ate themselves or fed to hogs. In addition, these farmers raised enough cotton every year (usually no more than one or two bales) to bring in a little cash. At least 60 percent owned their own farms.

For these yeomen, the local community was paramount. Farm men and women depended on their relatives and neighbors for assistance in large farm tasks such as planting, harvesting, and construction. Projects requiring lots of hands, like logrollings, corn shuckings, and quilting bees were community events. Farmers repaid this help, and obtained needed goods, through complex systems of barter with other members of the community. In their organization, southern farm communities were no different from northern ones, with one major exception—slavery. In the South, one of the key items in the community barter system was the labor of slaves, who were frequently loaned out to neighbors by small slave owners to fulfill an obligation to another farmer.

Where yeomen and large slave owners lived side by side, as in the Georgia black belt where cotton was the major crop, slavery again provided a link between the rich

But for a larger group of yeomen, independence and not wealth was most important. Many southern yeomen lived apart from large slaveholders, in the up-country regions where plantation agriculture was unsuitable. The very high value southern yeomen placed on freedom grew directly from their own experience as self-sufficient property-owning farmers in small, family-based communities, and from the absolute, patriarchal control they exercised over their own wives and children. This was a way of life that southern "plain folk" were determined to preserve. It made them resistant to the economic opportunities and challenges that capitalism and industrialization posed for northern farmers, which southern yeomen perceived as encroachments on their freedom.

The irony was that the freedom yeomen so prized rested on slavery. White people could count on slaves to perform the hardest and worst labor, and the degradation of slave life was a daily reminder of the freedom they enjoyed in comparison. Slavery meant that all white people, rich and poor, were equal in the sense that they were all free. This belief in white skin privilege had begun in the eighteenth century as slavery became the answer to the South's labor problem (see Chapter 4). The democratization of politics in the early nineteenth century and the enactment of nearly universal white manhood suffrage perpetuated the belief in white skin privilege, even though the gap between rich and poor white people was widening.

PLANTERS

Remarkably few slave owners fit the popular stereotype of the rich and leisured plantation owner with hundreds of acres of land and hundreds of slaves. Only 36 percent of southern white people owned slaves in 1830, and only 2.5 percent owned fifty slaves or more. Just as yeomen and poor whites were diverse, so, too, were southern slave owners (See Figure 10.3).

Small Slave Owners

The largest group of slave owners were small yeomen taking the step from subsistence agriculture to commercial production. To do this in the South's agricultural economy, they had to own slaves. But upward mobility was difficult. Owning one or two slaves increased farm production only slightly, and it was hard to accumulate the capital to buy more. One common pattern was for a slave owner to leave one or two slaves to farm while he worked another job (this arrangement usually meant that his wife had assumed responsibility for their supervision). In other cases, small farmers worked side by side with their slaves in the fields. In still other cases, owners hired out their slaves to larger slave owners.

In every case, the owner was economically vulnerable: a poor crop or a downturn in cotton prices could wipe out his gains and force him to sell his slaves. When times improved, he might buy a new slave or two and try again, but getting a secure footing on the bottom rung of the slave-owner ladder was very difficult. The rollercoaster economy of the early nineteenth century did not help matters, and the Panic of 1837 was a serious setback to many small farmers.

For a smaller group of slave owners, the economic struggle was not so hard. Middle-class professional men—lawyers, doctors, and merchants—frequently managed to become large slave owners because they already had capital (the pay from their professions) to invest in land and slaves. Sometimes they received payment for their services, not in money, but in slaves. These owners were the most likely to own skilled slaves—carpenters, blacksmiths, and other artisans—and to rent them out for profit. By steady accumulation, the most successful members of this middle class were able to buy their way into the slave-owning elite and to confirm that position by marrying their sons or daughters into the aristocracy.

The Planter Elite

The slave-owning elite, those 2.5 percent who owned fifty slaves or more, enjoyed the prestige, the political leadership, and the lifestyle to which many white Southerners aspired.

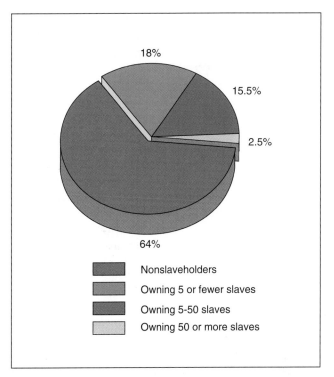

Nonslaveholders

Owning 5 or fewer slaves

Owning 5-50 slaves

Owning 50 or more slaves

FIGURE 10.3 Slaveholding and Class Structure in the South, 1830 The great mass of the southern white population were yeoman farmers. In 1830, slave owners made up only 36 percent of the southern white population; owners of more than fifty slaves constituted a tiny 2.5 percent. Yet they and the others who were middling planters dominated politics, retaining the support of yeomen who prized their freedom as white men above class-based politics.

SOURCE: U.S. Bureau of the Census.

Almost all great slave owners inherited their wealth. They were rarely self-made men, although most tried to add to the land and slaves they had inherited. Men of wealth and property had led southern politics since colonial times. Increasingly after 1820, as universal manhood suffrage spread, planters had to learn how to appeal to the popular vote, but most never acquired "the common touch." The smaller slave owners, not the great planters, formed a clear majority in every southern state legislature.

The eastern seaboard had first given rise to a class of rich planters in the colonial period, as attested by the plantations of William Byrd and Robert "King" Carter of Virginia and the cultured life of the planter elite, centered in Charleston, that had established itself in the South Carolina low country and Sea Islands. In the nineteenth century, these planters ranged from land rich but labor poor Thomas Chaplin of Tombee Plantation who grew sea-island cotton, to rice planter Nathaniel Heyward, who through wealthy marriages and land purchases amassed 45,000 acres of land and over 2,000 slaves.

As Southerners and slave owning spread westward, membership in the elite broadened to include the new wealth of Alabama, Mississippi, Louisiana, and Texas. The rich planters of the Natchez community were popularly called "nabobs" (from a Hindi word for Europeans who had amassed fabulous wealth in India). One great Natchez family, the Surgets, of French origin, traced their wealth farther back, to a Spanish land grant of 2,500 acres to Pierre Surget. In the 1850s, his grandsons Frank and James Surget controlled some 93,000 acres in Mississippi, Arkansas, and Louisiana (half of it plantation land and half bought on speculation, for resale). Each brother sold 4,000 bales of cotton a year, and between them they owned upwards of 1,000 slaves. Each also owned palatial mansions in Natchez—Cherry Hill and Clifton.

The extraordinary concentration of wealth in Natchez—in 1850, it was the richest county in the nation—fostered a self-consciously elite lifestyle that derived not from long tradition but from suddenly acquired riches. Fastidious Northerners such as Thomas Taylor, a Pennsylvania Quaker who visited Natchez in 1847, noted: "Many of the chivalric gentry whom I have been permitted to see dashing about here on highbred horses, seem to find their greatest enjoyment in recounting their bear hunts, 'great fights,' and occasional exploits with revolvers and Bowie knives—swearing 'terribly' and sucking mint juleps & cherry cobblers with straws."

Plantation Life

The urban life of the Natchez planters was unusual. Many wealthy planters, especially those on new lands in the Old Southwest, lived in isolation on their plantations with their families and slaves. Through family networks, common boarding school experience, political activity, and frequent visiting, the small new planter elite consciously worked to create and maintain a distinctive lifestyle that was modeled on that of the English aristocracy, as Southerners understood it. This entailed a large estate, a spacious, elegant mansion, and lavish hospitality. For men, the gentlemanly lifestyle meant immersion in masculine activities such as hunting, soldiering, or politics, and a touchy concern with "honor" that could lead to duels and other acts of bravado. Women of the slave-owning elite, in contrast, were expected to be gentle, charming, and always welcoming of relatives, friends, and other guests.

But this gracious image was at odds with the economic reality. Large numbers of black slaves had to be forced to work to produce the wealth that supported the planters' gracious lifestyle. Each plantation, like the yeoman farm but on a larger scale, aimed to be self-sufficient, producing not only the cash crop but most of the food and clothing for both slaves and family. There were stables full of horses for plowing, transportation, and show. There were livestock and vegetable gardens to be tended, and carpentry, blacksmithing, weaving, and sewing to be done. A large plantation was an enterprise that required many hands, many skills, and a lot of management. Large plantation

This scene is part of a larger mural, created by artist William Henry Brown in 1842, which depicts everyday life at Nitta Yuma, a Mississippi cotton plantation. The elegant white woman, here seen elaborately dressed to go riding, depended for her leisure status on the work of African American slaves, such as this one feeding her horse.

SOURCE: William Henry Brown, "*Sara Vick on Horseback*," from *Hauling the Whole Week's Picking* (detail), 1842. Watercolor and paper mounted on board. 1975.93.5. The Historic New Orleans Collection.

owners might have overseers or black drivers to supervise field work, but frequently they themselves had direct financial control of daily operations. Even if they were absentee landlords (like, for example, Thomas Chaplin in South Carolina, and the richest of the Natchez elite), planters usually required careful accounts from their overseers and often exercised the right to overrule their decisions.

The planter elite developed a paternalistic ideology to justify their rigorous insistence on the master-slave relationship. According to this ideology, each plantation was a family composed of both black and white. The master, as head of the plantation, was head of the family, and the mistress was his "helpmate." The master was obligated to provide for all of his family, both black and white, and to treat them with humanity. In return, slaves were to work properly and do as they were told, as children would. Most elite slave owners spoke of their position of privilege as a duty and a burden. (Their wives were even more outspoken about the burdensome aspects of supervising slave labor, which they bore more directly than their husbands.) John C. Calhoun spoke for many slave owners when he described the plantation as "a little community" in which the master directed all operations so that the abilities and needs of every member, black and white, were "perfectly harmonized." Convinced of their own benevolence, slave owners expected not only obedience, but gratitude from all members of their great "families."

The Plantation Mistress

The paternalistic model locked plantation mistresses into positions that bore heavy responsibility but carried no real authority. The difficulties experienced by these in some ways quite privileged women illustrate the way the master-slave relationship of a slave society affected every aspect of the personal life of slave owners.

Plantation mistresses spent most of their lives tending "family" members—including slaves—in illness and in childbirth, and supervising their slaves' performance of such daily tasks as cooking, housecleaning, weaving, and sewing. In addition, the plantation mistress often had to spend hours, even days, of behind-the-scenes preparation for the crowds of guests she was expected to welcome in her role as elegant and gracious hostess.

Despite the reality of the plantation mistress's daily supervision of an often extensive household, she did not rule it: her husband did. The plantation master was the source of authority to whom wife, children, and slaves were expected to look for both rewards and punishments. A wife who challenged her husband or sought more independence from him threatened the entire paternalistic system of control. After all, if she were not dependent and obedient, why should slaves be?

In addition to their strictly defined family roles, many southern women also suffered deeply from their isolation from friends and kin. Sometimes the isolation of life on rural plantations could be overcome by long visits, but women with many small children and extensive responsibilities found it difficult to leave. Plantation masters, on the other hand, often traveled widely for political and business reasons. John C. Calhoun, for example, who spoke so earnestly about the plantation community, spent much less time than his wife on the family plantation, Fort Hill. He spent years in Washington as a politician, while Floride Calhoun, who had accompanied him in his early career, remained at Fort Hill after the first five of their ten children were born.

Although on every plantation, black women served as nursemaids to young white children and as lifelong maids to white women, usually accompanying them when they moved as brides into their own homes, there are few historical examples of genuine sympathy and understanding of black women by white women of the slave-owning class. Few of the latter seemed to understand the sadness, frustration, and despair often experienced by their lifelong maids, who were forced to leave their own husbands and children to serve in their mistresses' new homes. A number of southern women did rail against "the curse of slavery," but few meant the inhumanity of the system; most were actually complaining about the extra work entailed by housekeeping with slaves. As one plantation mistress explained, "Slaves are a continual source of more trouble to housekeepers than all other things, vexing them, and causing much sin. We

are compelled to keep them in ignorance and much responsibility rests on us." Years later, many former slaves remembered their mistresses as being kinder than their masters, but fully a third of such accounts mention cruel whippings and other punishments by white women.

Coercion and Violence

There were generous and benevolent masters, but most large slave owners believed that constant discipline and coercion were necessary to make slaves work hard. Some slave owners used their slaves with great brutality. Owners who killed slaves were occasionally brought to trial (and usually acquitted), but no legal action was taken in the much more frequent cases of excessive punishment, general abuse, and rape. All southern slave owners, not just those who experienced the special tensions of new and isolated plantations in the Old Southwest, were engaged in a constant battle of wills with their slaves that owners frequently resolved by violence.

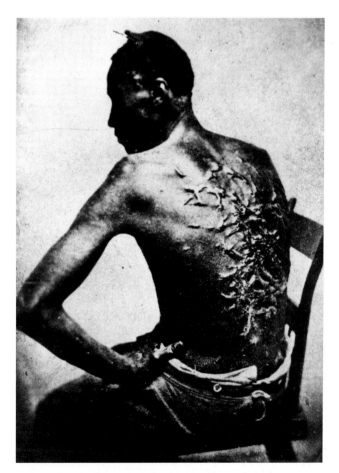

This Louisiana slave named Gordon was photographed in 1863 after he had escaped to Union lines during the Civil War. He bears the permanent scars of the violence that lay at the heart of the slave system. Few slaves were so brutally marked, but all lived with the threat of beatings if they failed to obey.

SOURCE: National Archives and Records Administration.

One of the most common violations of the paternalistic code of behavior (and of southern law) was the sexual abuse of female slaves by their masters. Usually, masters forcibly raped their women slaves at will, and slave women had little hope of defending themselves from these attacks. Sometimes, however, long-term intimate relationships between masters and slaves developed, such as the one that apparently existed between Thomas Jefferson and Sally Hemings.

It was rare for slave owners to publicly acknowledge fathering slave children or to free these children, and black women and their families were helpless to protest their treatment. Equally silenced was the master's wife, who for reasons of modesty as well as her subordinate position was not supposed to notice either her husband's infidelity or his flagrant crossing of the color lines. As Mary Boykin Chestnut, wife of a South Carolina slave owner, vehemently confided to her diary: "God forgive us, but ours is a monstrous system. . . . Like the patriarchs of old, our men live all in one house with their wives and their concubines, and the mulattoes one sees in every family partly resemble the white children. Any lady is ready to tell you who is the father of all the mulatto children in everybody's household but her own. Those, she seems to think, drop from the clouds."

An owner could do what he chose on his plantation, and his sons grew up expecting to do likewise. Unchecked power is always dangerous, and it is not surprising that it was sometimes misused. Perhaps the most surprising thing about the southern slave system is how much humanity survived despite the intolerable conditions. For that, most of the credit goes not to white paternalism, but to African Americans and the communities they created under slavery.

THE DEFENSE OF SLAVERY

"Slavery informs all our modes of life, all our habits of thought, lies at the basis of our social existence, and of our political faith," announced South Carolina planter William Henry Trescot in 1850, explaining why the South would secede from the Union before giving up slavery. Slavery bound white and black Southerners together in tortuous ways that eventually led, as Trescot had warned, to the Civil War. Population figures tell much of the story of the complex relationship between whites and blacks: of the 12 million people who lived in the South in 1860, 4 million were slaves. Indeed, in the richest agricultural regions, such as the Sea Islands of South Carolina and Georgia and parts of the black belt, black people outnumbered whites. These sheer numbers of African Americans reinforced white people's perpetual fears of black retaliation for the violence exercised by the slave master. Every rumor of slave revolts, real or imagined, kept those fears alive. The basic question was this: What might slaves do if they were not controlled? Thomas Jefferson summed up this dilemma: "We have the wolf by the ears; and we can neither hold him nor safely let him go. Justice is in one scale, and self-preservation in the other."

Developing Proslavery Arguments

Once the cotton boom began in the 1790s, Southerners increasingly sought to justify slavery. They found justifications for slavery in the Bible and in the histories of Greece and Rome, both slave-owning societies. The strongest defense was a legal one: the Constitution allowed slavery. Though never specifically mentioned in the final document, slavery had been a major issue between North and South at the Constitutional Convention in 1787. In the end, the delegates agreed that seats in the House of Representatives would be apportioned by counting all of the white population and three-fifths of the black people (Article I, Section 2, Paragraph 3); they included a clause requiring the return of runaway slaves who had crossed state lines (Article IV, Section 2, Paragraph 3); and they agreed that Congress could not abolish the international slave trade for twenty years (Article I, Section 9, Paragraph 1). There was absolutely no question: the Constitution did recognize slavery.

The Missouri Crisis of 1819–20 alarmed most Southerners, who were shocked by the evidence of widespread antislavery feeling in the North. South Carolinians viewed Denmark Vesey's conspiracy, occurring only two years after the Missouri debate, as an example of the harm that irresponsible northern antislavery talk could cause. In the wake of the Vesey conspiracy, Charlestonians turned their fear and anger outward by attempting to seal off the city from dangerous outside influences. In December 1822, the South Carolina legislature passed a bill requiring that all black seamen be seized and jailed while their ships were in Charleston harbor. Initially most alarmed about free black people from Haiti, Charlestonians soon came to believe that northern free black seamen were spreading antislavery ideas among their slaves.

After Nat Turner's revolt in 1831, Governor John Floyd of Virginia blamed the uprising on "Yankee peddlers and traders" who supposedly told slaves that "all men were born free and equal." Thus northern antislavery opinion and the fear of slave uprisings were firmly linked in southern minds. This extreme reaction, which Northerners viewed as paranoid, stemmed from the basic nature of a slave society: *anything* that challenged the master-slave relationship was viewed as a basic threat to the entire system.

After Nat Turner

In 1831, the South began to close ranks in defense of slavery. Several factors contributed to this regional solidarity. Nat Turner's revolt was important, linked as it was in the minds of many Southerners with antislavery agitation from the

North. Militant abolitionist William Lloyd Garrison began publishing the *Liberator*, the newspaper that was to become the leading antislavery organ, in 1831. The British gave notice that they would soon abolish slavery on the sugar plantations of the West Indies, an action that seemed to many Southerners much too close to home. Emancipation for West Indian slaves came in 1834. Finally, 1831 was the year before the Nullification Crisis (see Chapter 11) was resolved. Although the other southern states did not support the hotheaded South Carolinians who called for secession, they did sympathize with the argument that the federal government had no right to interfere with a state's special interest (namely, slavery). Following the crisis, other southern states joined with South Carolina in the belief that the only effective way to prevent other federal encroachment was through the militant and vehement defense of slavery.

In the 1830s, southern states began to barricade themselves against "outside" antislavery propaganda. In 1835, a crowd broke into a Charleston post office, made off with bundles of antislavery literature, and set an enormous bonfire, to fervent state and regional acclaim. By 1835, every southern legislature had tightened its laws concerning control of slaves. For example, they tried to blunt the effect of abolitionist literature by passing laws forbidding slaves to learn how to read. In only three border states—Kentucky, Tennessee, and Maryland—did slave literacy remain legal. By 1860, it is estimated, only 5 percent of all slaves could read. Slaves were forbidden to gather for dances, religious services, or any kind of organized social activity without a white person present. They were forbidden to have whiskey because it might encourage them toward revolt. The penalty for plotting insurrection was death. Other laws made manumission illegal and placed even more restrictions on the lives of free black people. In many areas, slave patrols were augmented and became more vigilant in restricting African American movement and communication between plantations.

In 1836, Southerners introduced a "gag rule" in Washington to prevent congressional consideration of abolitionist petitions. Attempts were made to stifle all open debate about slavery within the South; dissenters were pressured to remain silent or to leave. A few, such as James G. Birney and Sarah and Angelina Grimké of South Carolina, left for the North to act on their antislavery convictions, but most chose silence. Among those under the greatest pressure to

conform were Christian ministers, many of whom professed to believe that preaching obedience to slaves was a vital part of making slavery a humane system.

In addition to fueling fears of slave rebellions, the growing abolitionist sentiment of the 1830s raised the worry that southern opportunities for expansion would be cut off. Southern politicians painted melodramatic pictures of a beleaguered white South hemmed in on all sides by "fanatic" antislavery states, while at home, Southerners were forced to contemplate what might happen when they had "to let loose among them, freed from the wholesome restraints of patriarchal authority . . . an idle, worthless, profligate set of free negroes" whom they feared would "prowl the . . . streets at night and [haunt] the woods during the day armed with whatever weapons they could lay their hands on."

Finally, southern apologists moved beyond defensiveness to develop proslavery arguments. One of the first to do this was James Henry Hammond, elected a South Carolina congressman in 1834. In 1836, Hammond delivered a major address to Congress in which he denied that slavery was evil. Rather, he claimed, it had produced "the highest toned, the purest, best organization of society that has ever existed on the face of the earth." Later, in his most famous speech, Hammond claimed that a slave class—a "mudsill," he called it—was a social necessity. (See Out of Many Voices: Senator James Henry Hammond Defends Slavery.)

In 1854, another southern spokesman, George Fitzhugh, asserted that "the negro slaves of the South are

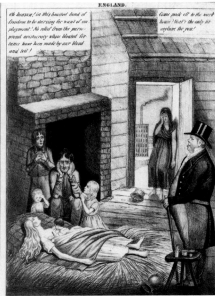

This 1841 proslavery cartoon contrasts healthy, well-cared-for African American slaves with unemployed British factory workers living in desperate poverty. The comparison between contented southern slaves and miserable northern "wage slaves" was frequently made by proslavery advocates.

SOURCE: Courtesy of Library of Congress.

OUT OF MANY VOICES

SENATOR JAMES HENRY HAMMOND DEFENDS SLAVERY

Among the many southerners who spoke and wrote in defense of slavery, few were as blunt as Senator James Henry Hammond of South Carolina, who offered this justification in a speech to the U.S. Senate, March 4, 1858.

IN ALL SOCIAL SYSTEMS THERE MUST BE A CLASS to do the menial duties, to perform the drudgery of life. That is, a class requiring but a low order of intellect and but little skill. Its requisites are vigor, docility, fidelity. Such a class you must have, or you would not have that other class which leads progress, civilization, and refinement. It constitutes the very mud-sill of society and of political government; and you might as well attempt to build a house in the air, as to build either the one or the other, except on this mud-sill. Fortunately for the South, she found a race adapted to that purpose to her hand. A race inferior to her own, but eminently qualified in temper, in vigor, in docility, in capacity to stand the climate, to answer all her purposes. We use them for our purpose, and call them slaves. . . .

The Senator from New York said yesterday that the whole world had abolished slavery. Aye, the name, but not the thing; all the powers of the earth cannot abolish that. God only can do it when he repeals the fiat, "the poor ye always have with you;" for the man who lives by daily labor, and scarcely lives at that, and who has to put out his labor in the market, and take the best he can get for it; in short, your whole hireling class of manual laborers and "operatives," as you call them, are essentially slaves. The difference between us is, that our slaves are hired for life and well compensated; there is no starvation, no begging, no want of employment among our people, and not too much employment either. Yours are hired by the day, not cared for, and scantily compensated, which may be proved in the most painful manner, at any hour in any street in any of your large towns. Why, you meet more beggars in one day, in any single street of the city of New York, than you would meet in a lifetime in the whole South. ■

SOURCE: Selection from the *Letters and Speeches of the Hon. James H. Hammond of South Carolina* (New York: John F. Trow and Co., 1866).

the happiest, and, in some sense, the freest people in the world" because all the responsibility for their care was borne by concerned white masters. Fitzhugh contrasted southern paternalism with the heartless individualism that ruled the lives of northern "wage slaves." Northern employers did not take care of their workers, Fitzhugh claimed, because "selfishness is almost the only motive of human conduct in free society, where every man is taught that it is his first duty to change and better his pecuniary situation." In contrast, Fitzhugh argued, southern masters and their slaves were bound together by a "community of interests."

Changes in the South

In spite of these defensive and repressive proslavery measures, which made the South seem monolithic in northern eyes, there were some surprising indicators of dissent. One protest occurred in the Virginia state legislature in 1832, when nonslave-holding delegates, alarmed by the Nat Turner rebellion, forced a two-week debate on the merits of gradual abolition. In the final vote, abolition was defeated 73 to 58. Although the subject was never raised again, this debate was a startling indicator of frequently unvoiced doubts about slavery that existed in the South.

But slavery was not a static system. From the 1830s on, financial changes increasingly underlined class differences among southern whites. It was much harder to become a slaveholder: from 1830 to 1860, slave owners declined from 36 to 25 percent of the population. In 1860, the average slaveholder was ten times as wealthy as the average nonslaveholder. A major reason for the shrinking number of slave owners and their increased wealth was the rapidly increasing price of slaves: a "prime field hand" was worth more than $1,500 in 1855. Such prices caused the internal slave trade to flourish: during the 1850s, slave owners from the Upper South sold some 250,000 slaves to the Lower South for handsome profits. By 1850, in the Chesapeake (Virginia, Maryland and Delaware), where American slavery had its origin, the percentage of slave owners had fallen to 28 percent, while the comparable figures for Louisiana and Mississippi were 45 percent. Agriculture was diversifying in the Upper South, while the plantation system flourished in the Lower South, as the fact that 85 percent of the great planters with more than 100 slaves lived there indicated.

Such differences in the extent of slaveholding between Upper and Lower South threatened regional political unity (see Map 10.4).

Another alarming trend was the disintegration of the slave system in southern cities. The number of urban slaves was greatly decreased because plantation owners deeply distrusted the effect of cities on the institution of slavery. Urban slaves led much more informed lives than rural ones and were often in daily contact with free blacks and urban poor whites. Many slaves were hired out and a number even hired out their own time, making them nearly indistinguishable from northern "free labor." Other urban slaves worked in commercial and industrial enterprises in jobs that were nearly indistinguishable from those of whites. Planters viewed all of these changes with suspicion, yet they also had to acknowledge that southern cities were successful and bustling centers of commerce.

Economic changes adversely affected poor whites and yeomen as well. Increased commercialization of agriculture (other than cotton) led to higher land prices that made it harder for poor whites to buy or rent land. Extensive railroad building in up-country regions during the boom of the 1850s ended the isolation of many yeomen, exposing them for the first time to the temptations and dangers of the market economy. While slave owners grew increasingly worried about threats from the abolitionist and capitalist North, yeomen worried about local threats to their independence from banks, railroads, and activist state governments. In North Carolina, disputes between slave owners and nonslaveholders erupted in print in 1857, when Hinton Helper published an attack on slavery in a book titled *The Impending Crisis*. His protest was an indicator of the growing tensions between the haves and the have-nots in the South. Equally significant, though, Helper's book was published in New York, where he was forced to move once his views became known.

In spite of these signs of tension and dissent, the main lines of the southern argument were drawn in the 1830s and remained fixed thereafter. The defense of slavery stifled debate within the South, prevented a search for alternative labor systems, and narrowed the possibility of cooperation in national politics. In time, it made compromise impossible.

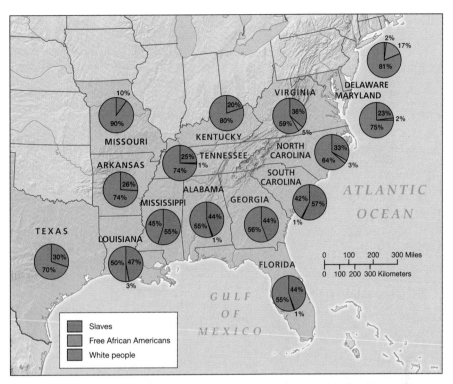

MAP 10.4 Population Patterns in the South, 1850 In South Carolina and Mississippi, the enslaved African American population outnumbered the white population; in four other Lower South states, the percentage was above 40 percent. These ratios frightened many white Southerners. White people also feared the free black population, though only three states in the Upper South and Louisiana had free black populations of over 3 percent. Six states had free black populations that were so small (less than 1 percent) as to be statistically insignificant.

CONCLUSION

The amazing growth of cotton production after 1793 transformed the South and the nation. Physically, the South expanded explosively westward: in all, seven southern states were admitted to the Union between 1800 and 1845. Cotton production fastened the slave system of labor upon the region. Although the international slave trade was abolished in 1808, the internal slave trade flourished, with devastating effects on African American families. Nationally, the profitable cotton trade fueled economic development and provided much of the original capital for the infant factory system of the North. Cotton production was based on the labor of African American slaves, who built strong communities under extremely difficult circumstances. The cohesion of African American families and the powerful faith of African American Christianity were the key community elements that bred a spirit of endurance and resistance. White Southerners, two-thirds of whom did not own slaves, denied their real dependence on slave labor by claiming equality in white skin privilege, while slave

CHRONOLOGY

1790s	Second Great Awakening		*1832*	Virginia legislature debates and defeats a measure for gradual emancipation
	Black Baptist and African Methodist Episcopal churches founded		*1834*	Britain frees slaves throughout the empire, including in its Caribbean colonies
1793	Cotton gin invented		*1835*	Charleston crowd burns abolitionist literature
1800	Gabriel Prosser's revolt discovered in Virginia			Tightening of black codes completed by southern legislatures
1806	Virginia tightens law on manumission of slaves		*1836*	Congress passes "gag rule" to prevent discussion of antislavery petitions
1808	Congress prohibits U.S. participation in the international slave trade			James Henry Hammond announces to Congress that slavery is not evil
1816–20	"Alabama Fever": migration to the Old Southwest		*1846*	William Gregg opens model textile mill at Graniteville, South Carolina
1819–20	Missouri Crisis		*1854*	George Fitzhugh publishes *Sociology for the South*, a defense of slavery
1822	Denmark Vesey's conspiracy in Charleston		*1857*	Hinton Helper publishes *The Impending Crisis*, an attack on slavery
1831	Nat Turner's revolt in Virginia			
	William Lloyd Garrison begins publishing antislavery newspaper, the *Liberator*			
1832	Nullification Crisis			
1832–38	"Flush Times": second wave of westward expansion		*1858*	James Henry Hammond's "King Cotton" speech

owners boasted of their own paternalism. But the extreme fear generated by a handful of slave revolts, the exaggerated reaction to the race mixing of Natchez-Under-the-Hill, and the growing number of free African Americans in many areas gave the lie to white claims of benevolence. In the 1830s, the South defensively closed ranks against real and perceived threats to the slave system. In this sense, the white South was nearly as trapped as the African American slaves they claimed to control. And in its growing concern for the defense of the slave system, the South's role in national politics began to change, as we shall see in the next chapter.

REVIEW QUESTIONS

1. How did cotton production after 1793 transform the social and political history of the South? How did the rest of the nation benefit? In what way was it an "international phenomenon"?

2. What were the two key institutions of the African American slave community? How did they function, and what beliefs did they express?

3. The circumstances of three very different groups—poor whites, educated and property-owning American Indians, and free African Americans—put them outside the dominant southern equations of white equals free and black equals slave. Analyze the difficulty each group encountered in the slave-owning South.

4. Who were the yeoman farmers? What was their interest in slavery?

5. Southern slaveholders claimed that their paternalism justified their ownership of slaves, but paternalism implied obligations as well as privileges. How well do you think slaveholders lived up to their paternalistic obligations?

6. How did slaveowners justify slavery? How did their defense change over time?

RECOMMENDED READING

Ira Berlin, *Generations of Captivity* (2003). A compelling survey of the changing nature of American slavery.

Charles C. Bolton, *Poor Whites of the Antebellum South: Tenants and Laborers in Central North and Northeast Mississippi* (1994). A careful consideration of a hitherto "invisible" population.

Thomas C. Buchanan, *Black Life on the Mississippi: Slaves, Free Blacks, and the Western Steamboat World* (2004). The interracial world of work on the great river.

Stephanie Camp, *Closer to Freedom: Enslaved Women and Everyday Resistance in the Plantation South* (2004). A close look at small and unspoken acts of resistance.

Steven Doyle, *Carry Me Back: The Domestic Slave Trade in American Life* (2005). An outstanding survey of the internal slave trade.

Drew Gilpin Faust, *James Henry Hammond and the Old South* (1982). This outstanding biography uses the complex and interesting story of one man's life and ambitions to tell a larger story about southern attitudes and politics.

Lacy K. Ford Jr., *Origins of Southern Radicalism: The South Carolina Upcountry, 1800–1860* (1988). One of a number of studies of up-country nonslaveholders.

Eugene Genovese, *Roll, Jordan, Roll: The World the Slaves Made* (1974). The landmark book that redirected the attention of historians from slaves as victims to the slave community as an active participant in paternalism.

Robert H. Gudmestad, *A Troublesome Commerce: The Transformation of the Interstate Slave Trade* (2003). Examines changes in the trade and the ways in which Southerners rationalized it.

Jean M. Humez, *Harriet Tubman: The Life and Life Stories* (2003). A biography that also looks at the legend.

Walter Johnson, *Soul by Soul: Life Inside the Antebellum Slave Market* (1999). A fascinating study of the workings and meanings of the New Orleans slave markets.

Peter Kolchin, *American Slavery 1619–1877* (1993). A well-written, comprehensive survey.

Stephanie McCurry, *Masters of Small Worlds: Yeoman Households, Gender Relations, and the Political Culture of the Antebellum South Carolina Low Country* (1995). A study of yeomen that links their prized political and economic independence with their strong patriarchal control over their own families.

Donald P. McNeilly, *The Old South Frontier: Cotton Plantations and the Formation of Arkansas Society, 1819–1861* (2000). Traces slavery and society in Arkansas from frontier to cotton plantations.

Michael O'Brien, *Conjectures of Order: Intellectual Life and the American South* (2004) An important two volume study of southern thought 1800–1865.

Dylan Penningroth, *The Claims of Kinfolk: African American Property and Comunity in the Nineteenth Century South* (2003). The existence, operation, and meaning of an informal system of property ownership among slaves.

Adam Rothman, *Slave Country: American Expansion and the Origins of the Deep South* (2005). Expansion into the Lower South created the most dynamic, and the most violent, slave system in the Atlantic World.

Joshua Rothman, *Notorious in the Neighborhood: Sex and Families Across the Color Line in Virginia, 1787–1861* (2003). While the law upheld white male supremacy, cross race relationships were common.

Marie Jenkins Schwartz, *Born in Bondage: Growing Up Enslaved in the Antebellum South* (2001). How slave communities sought to protect their children.

Brenda Stevenson, *Life in Black and White: Family and Community in the Slave South* (1996). A careful study of families, black and white, in Louden County, Virginia, that illustrates the difficulties both free and enslaved African American families faced.

Michael Tadman, *Speculators and Slaves: Masters, Traders, and Slaves in the Old South* (1989). Examines the extent, organization, and values of the internal slave trade.

Jeffrey Robert Young, *Domesticating Slavery: The Master Class in Georgia and South Carolina, 1670-1837* (1999). A study of changing slaveholder ideology.

Jonathhan Daniel Wells, *The Origins of the Southern Middle Class, 1800–1861* (2004). Shows how the new southern white middle class—merchants, doctors, teachers—tried to emulate that of the North while remaining committed to the slave system.

For additional study resources for this chapter, go to the *Companion Website,* http://www.prenhall.com/faragher.

The Growth of Democracy

1824–1840

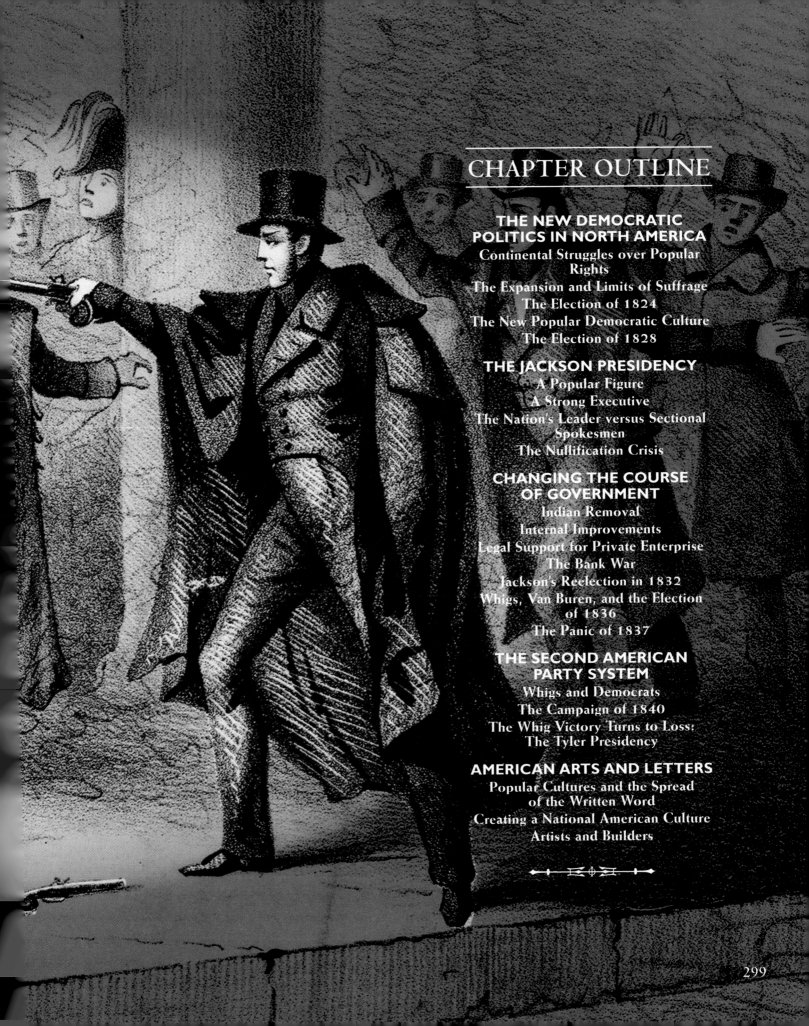

Martin Van Buren Forges
a New Kind of Political Community

When Martin Van Buren left Albany for Washington in the fall of 1821 to take up his new position as junior senator from New York, he wrote complacently: "I left the service of the state [of New York] for that of the federal government with my friends in full and almost unquestioned possession of the state government in all its branches, at peace with each other and overflowing with kindly feelings towards myself." Thus did Van Buren sum up more than ten years of intense activity in New York State politics in which he and his allies, nicknamed the Bucktails (for the Indian-inspired insignia, the tail of a buck, that members wore on their hats), created one of the first modern democratic political parties. How could it be, Washington politicians asked, that this short, invariably pleasant but rather nondescript man had triumphed over the renowned DeWitt Clinton?

Tall, handsome, arrogant DeWitt Clinton, governor of New York from 1817 to 1823 (and again from 1825 until his death in 1828), had been swept into office on a tide of enthusiasm for his plan to build a canal the length of the state. Clinton soon gained legislative approval for the project—the Erie Canal—the most ambitious and most successful canal project in an era of canal building. An aristocrat in wealth, connections, and attitude, Clinton represented old-style politics. During his first terms as governor, he ran the New York Jeffersonian Republican Party as though it were his personal property, dispensing patronage to relatives and

friends (many of whom were Federalists) on the basis of their loyalty to him, rather than their political principles.

Martin Van Buren was a new kind of politician. Born in the small, Dutch-dominated town of Kinderhook, New York, Van Buren was the son of a tavern keeper, not a member of the wealthy elite. He grew up with an enduring resentment of the aristocratic landowning families, such as the Van Schaacks and the Van Rensselaers (and, by extension, the Clintons), who disdained him when he was young. Masking his anger with charming manners, Van Buren took advantage of the growing strength of the Jeffersonian Republican Party in New York State to wrest control of the party from Clinton and forge it into a new kind of political organization. Clinton's use of patronage to reward friends at the expense of young party loyalists infuriated Van Buren and other rising politicians.

By 1819, Van Buren had gathered together enough other disgruntled Jeffersonian Republicans to form the Bucktail faction and openly challenge Clinton. Two years later, at the state constitutional convention of 1821 (where they made up three-fourths of the delegates), the Bucktails sealed their victory. Meeting in Albany to revise the out-of-date constitution of 1777, the convention voted to streamline the organization of state government and sharply curtail the patronage powers of the governor. To cement these changes, delegates enacted nearly total manhood suffrage: all adult male citizens who paid state or local taxes, served in the militia, or worked on state roads—more than four-fifths of the adult male population—were now eligible to vote directly for state legislators, governor, and members of Congress.

This dramatic democratization of politics reflected the state's changing population and new economic realities. Already, the bustling port of New York was the nation's largest city, and the state's commercial opportunities were attracting shrewd Yankee traders from New England, "whose laws, customs and usages," conservative senator Rufus King

Albany

complained, "differ from those of New York." Rising politicians like Van Buren and other Bucktails found opportunity in these changing conditions, and the old ruling families, who failed to recognize the new commercial and social values of the Yankees, gradually lost their grip on politics.

Attuned to popular feeling, the Bucktails responded to the state's growing and increasingly diverse population by creating a new kind of political community. A political party, they maintained, should be a democratic organization expressing the will of all its members, not an organization dominated by an elite group bound together by family ties and political favors. All party members, including leaders, would have to abide by majority rule, and party loyalty, rather than personal opinion or friendship, would be the bond that kept the party together. "The first man we see step to the rear," wrote Bucktail Silas Wright Jr., still smarting from the factionalism and favoritism of the Clinton years, "we cut down." In the new party system, there would be no tolerance for politicians who followed their own self-interest rather than the larger good of the party.

By the time he departed for Washington in the fall of 1821, Van Buren had established in Albany a closely knit group of friends and allies who practiced these new political principles. Party decisions, reached by discussion in legislative caucus and publicized by the party newspaper, the *Albany Argus*, were binding on all members and enforced by patronage decisions. The group, dubbed the "Albany Regency," ran New York State politics for twenty years.

In Washington, Martin Van Buren became a major architect of the new democratic politics of mass participation that has been called the Second American Party System. This movement created national political parties for the first time in American history. Van Buren believed that organization and discipline were essential, not for their own sake, but because they allowed democracy to flourish. He claimed that what made him different from DeWitt Clinton and earlier politicians was his "faith in the capacity of the masses of the people of our Country to govern themselves, and in their general integrity in the exercise of that function." This unprecedented confidence in popular opinion made American politics and politicians unique in the changing world of the early nineteenth century.

KEY TOPICS

- The role of Andrew Jackson's presidency in affirming and solidifying the new democratic politics
- The death of the American System
- Establishment of the basic two-party pattern of American political democracy
- The creation of a distinctive American cultural identity by writers, artists, and their audiences

THE NEW DEMOCRATIC POLITICS IN NORTH AMERICA

The early years of the nineteenth century were a time of extraordinary growth and change, not only for the United States, but for all the countries of North America. Seen in continental perspective, the American embrace of popular democracy was unusual. Elsewhere, crises over popular rights dominated.

Continental Struggles over Popular Rights

In 1821, after eleven years of revolts (see Chapter 9), Mexico achieved its independence from Spain.

Briefly united under the leadership of Colonel Agustin de Iturbide, Mexico declared itself a constitutional monarchy that promised equality for everyone—peninsulares, criollos, mestizos, and Indians alike. But because Spanish colonial rule had left a legacy of deep social divisions, the initial unity was short-lived.

Iturbide reigned as Emperor of Mexico for little more than a year before he was overthrown by a military junta and later executed as a traitor. The Constitution of 1824, closely modeled on the U.S. Constitution, created a federal republic, but continued a powerful political role for the Catholic Church and granted the president extraordinary powers in times of emergency. A series of weak presidents repeatedly invoked emergency powers and relied on the army, as they attempted to revive a faltering economy and reconcile the differences between the centralists—the vested interests of clergy, large landowners, and the military—and the federalists, largely criollos and mestizos, who hoped to create a liberal republic modeled on the American one. The strongest of the early presidents was General Antonio Lopez de Santa Anna, who became a national hero by saving Mexico from a Spanish invasion in 1829 and overthrowing an unpopular dictatorship in 1832. Elected to the presidency for the first time in 1833, he dominated Mexican politics for the next twenty years, during which he assumed dictatorial, centralized power, surviving the loss of Texas in 1836 and the other northern provinces in 1848 to the United States (see Chapter 15). The unresolved issue of elite versus popular rule continued to undermine the hope for unity, popular rights, and stable government in an independent Mexico.

The independence of Haiti in 1804 (see Chapter 9) set the pattern for events in many other Caribbean islands in subsequent years. Independence destroyed the sugar industry, for freed slaves asserted their popular rights by refusing to perform the killing labor demanded of them on sugar plantations. The British Caribbean islands were racked with revolts, the largest occurring on Barbados in 1816 and on Jamaica in 1831. In response, and following years of humanitarian protests at home, the British Parliament abolished slavery in all British colonies in 1834. As in Haiti, sugar production then plunged. The only island where sugar production increased was Spanish Cuba, where slavery remained legal until 1880. Elsewhere, most of the 750,000 former British slaves became poor peasants struggling to stay out of debt. The economic collapse following emancipation also destroyed the political authority of local white elites, forcing the British government to impose direct rule. Most of the British possessions in the Caribbean remained Crown Colonies until the 1920s. This sequence of events—revolt, emancipation, economic collapse, loss of local political autonomy—was closely observed by slaveowners in the American South and made them fear for their own futures.

Still a third crisis of popular rights occurred in British North America. In 1837, both Upper and Lower Canada rebelled against the limited representative government that the British government had imposed in the Constitutional Act of 1791. By far the most serious revolt was in predominantly French Lower Canada, where armed uprisings were brutally suppressed by British troops. Fearing that the true aim of the rebels was independence or, worse, becoming a part of the United States, the British government refused to recognize the French Canadian demand for their own political voice. In 1840, Britain abolished the local government of Lower Canada and joined it to Upper Canada in a union that most French Canadians opposed and in which they were a minority. In his report to the British government, Lord Durham announced that the purpose of union was to end the ethnic enmity between British and French by forcing the latter to assimilate and "abandon their vain hopes of nationality." Lord Durham suggested increased colonial self-government, but the British government, fearing further trouble, refused to grant it.

In comparison to these experiences, the rapid spread of suffrage in the United States and the growth of a vibrant but stable democratic political culture seemed all the more extraordinary. But after a brilliant start, in the 1850s the United States like its neighbors, foundered on its most basic sectional difference—slavery—that not even political democracy could reconcile (see Chapter 15).

The Expansion and Limits of Suffrage

Before 1800, most of the original thirteen states had limited the vote to property owners or taxpayers, amounting to less than half the white male population. Both locally and nationally, political control remained in the hands of the traditional elite. But westward expansion was changing the nature of American politics, first by undermining the traditional authority structures in the older states. "Old America seems to be breaking up and moving westward," an observer commented in 1817. Rapid westward expansion bolstered national pride and fostered a spirit of self-reliance. As Andrew Jackson, recruiting troops for the War of 1812, boasted, "We are the free born sons of America; the citizens of the only republic now existing in the world; and the only people on earth who possess rights, liberties, and property which they dare call their own" (see Map 11.1).

Nine new states west of the Appalachians entered the Union between 1800 and 1840. Most of the new western states extended the right to vote to all white males over the age of twenty-one. Kentucky entered the Union with universal manhood suffrage in 1792, and Tennessee (1796) and Ohio (1803) entered with low taxpayer qualifications that approached universal suffrage. By 1820, most of the older states had followed suit. In most states, the driving force behind reform was not idealistic, but very practical: competition for votes between parties or factions of parties (such as the Bucktails and the Clintonians in New York). The War of 1812 was also an important impetus to change in many states, for the propertyless men called up for militia service in that war questioned why they were eligible to fight but not to vote. There were laggards—Rhode Island, Virginia, and Louisiana did not liberalize their voting qualifications until later—but by 1840, more than 90 percent of adult white males in the nation could vote. And they could vote for more officials: governors and (most important) presidential electors were now elected by direct vote, rather than chosen by small groups of state legislators (see Map 11.2).

Universal white manhood suffrage, of course, was far from true universal suffrage: the right to vote remained barred to most of the nation's free African American males and to women of any race. Only in five New England states (Maine, New Hampshire, Vermont, Massachusetts, and Rhode Island) could free African American men vote before 1865. In the rest of the northern states, the right of free African American men to vote was restricted to only the most affluent property owners. Free African American men were denied the vote in the new western states as well. The Ohio constitution of 1802 denied them the right to vote, to hold public office, and to testify against white men in court cases. The constitutions of other western states—Illinois, Indiana, Michigan, Iowa, Wisconsin, and (later) Oregon—attempted to solve the "problem" of free African Americans by simply denying them entry into the state at all. Of course, all free black men were prohibited from voting in the slave states of the South (see Figure 11.1).

What accounted for this nearly universal denial of voting rights to free black men? Racism—the assumption that African Americans were a different and less capable people—accounted for much of it, an attitude that was strengthened by the backlash against the extremely controversial abolitionist movement of the 1830s and 1840s (see Chapter 13). Opponents also argued that enfranchisement of African American men would be a spur to free blacks to migrate out of the South, thus adding to what the North and West already regarded as an undesirable population. Finally, as party lines hardened, the Democrats, the party most closely aligned with the slave

MAP 11.1 **Population Trends: Westward Expansion, 1830** Westward population movement, a trickle in 1800, had become a flood by 1830. Between 1800 and 1830, the U.S. white and African American population more than doubled (from 5.3 million to 12.9 million), but the trans-Appalachian population grew tenfold (from 370,000 to 3.7 million). By 1830, more than a third of the nation's inhabitants lived west of the original thirteen states.

South, opposed enfranchising African American men who were almost certain to vote for their opponents.

In contrast, the reason for the denial of suffrage to white women was boringly traditional, stemming from the patriarchal belief that men headed households and represented the interests of all household members. Even wealthy single women who lived alone were considered subordinate to male relatives and denied the right to vote. (New Jersey had been an exception to this rule until it amended its constitution in 1807 to withdraw the franchise from propertied women.) Although unable to vote, women of the upper classes had long played important informal roles in national politics, and nowhere was that more true than in Washington, DC. Presidents' wives like Abigail Adams and Dolley Madison were famous for

MAP EXPLORATION

To explore an interactive version of this map, go to **www.prenhall.com/faragher5/map11.2**

MAP 11.2 The Growth of Universal White Male Suffrage Kentucky was the first western state to enact white male suffrage without tax or property qualifications. Other western states followed, and by 1820, most of the older states had dropped their suffrage restrictions as well. By 1840, more than 90 percent of the nation's white males could vote. But although voting was democratized for white men, restrictions on free African American male voters grew tighter, and women were excluded completely.

their ability to provide the social settings in which their husbands could quietly conduct political business. Another unrecognized group of skilled politicians were the women who ran the Washington boardinghouses where most congressmen lived during the legislative term. These women, longtime Washington residents, often

served as valuable sources of information and official contacts for their boarders. At the local level as well, women—often the wives of leading citizens—were accustomed to engaging informally in politics through their benevolent groups. These groups, often church-related, had since colonial times not only provided charity to the

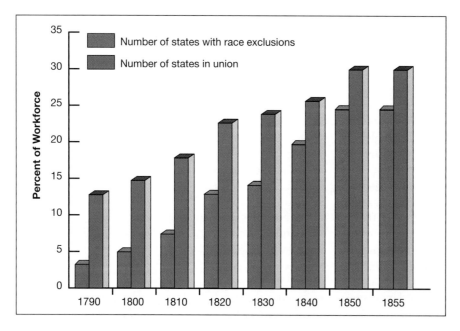

FIGURE 11.1 Race Exclusions for Suffrage: 1790–1855 This graph shows clearly that as more states entered the Union, laws excluding African American men from voting increased.

SOURCE: Alexander Keysiar, *The Right to Vote* (New York: Basic Books, 2000) p. 45.

poor but raised money to support basic community institutions such as schools, churches and libraries, in effect setting community priorities in the process.

Although the extension of suffrage to all classes of white men seemed to indicate that women had no role in public affairs, in fact women's informal involvement in politics grew along with the increasing pace of political activity. At the same time, however, as "manhood" rather than property became the qualification for voting, men began to ignore women's customary political activity and to regard their participation as inappropriate, an attitude that politically active women increasingly resented.

Thus, in a period famous for democratization and "the rise of the common man," the exclusion of important groups—African American men, and women of all races—marked the limits of liberalization. It is also true that nowhere else in the world was the right to vote as widespread as it was in the United States. The extension of suffrage to the common man marked a major step beyond the republicanism advocated by the Revolutionary generation. Thomas Jefferson had envisaged a republic of property-owning yeoman farmers. Now, however, propertyless farm workers and members of the laboring poor in the nation's cities could vote as well. European observers were curious about the democratization of voting: Could "mob rule" possibly succeed? And how would it affect traditional politics? The election of 1824 provided the first outline of the answer.

The Election of 1824

The 1824 election marked a dramatic end to the political truce that James Monroe had established in 1817. In that Era of Good Feelings, one big political party, the expanded Jeffersonian Republicans, had absorbed the remaining Federalists. This brief moment of unanimity did not survive the Panic of 1819 and the Missouri Crisis (see Chapter 9). Thus, five candidates, all of them members of the Republican Party, ran for president in the elections of 1824. The candidate chosen by the usual method of congressional caucus was William H. Crawford of Georgia. The traditional stepping stone to the presidency, however, had been the office of secretary of state, giving a strong claim to John Quincy Adams of Massachusetts, who held that position in President Monroe's administration. Adams was nominated by his state legislature, as were two other candidates, Henry Clay of Kentucky and Andrew Jackson of Tennessee. The fifth candidate, John C. Calhoun of South Carolina, Monroe's secretary of war, withdrew before the election, to run for vice president. Each candidate was clearly identified with a region: Adams with New England, Crawford and Calhoun with the South, Clay and Jackson with the West. Jackson, a latecomer to the race, was at first not taken seriously, because his record as a leg-

islator was lackluster and his political views unknown. His reputation as a military hero, however, enabled him to run as a national candidate despite his regional identification. He won 43 percent of the popular vote and 99 electoral votes—more than any other candidate. The runner-up, John Quincy Adams, won 31 percent of the popular vote and 84 electoral votes. But neither had an electoral majority, leaving it up to the House of Representatives, as in the election of 1800, to pick the winner. After some political dealing, Henry Clay threw his support to Adams, and the House elected Adams president. This was customary and proper: the Constitution gave the House the power to decide, and Clay had every right to advise his followers how to vote. But when Adams named Clay his secretary of state, the traditional stepping-stone to the highest office, Jackson's supporters promptly accused them of a "corrupt bargain." Popular opinion, the new element in politics, supported Jackson. John Quincy Adams served four miserable years as president, knowing that Jackson would challenge him, and win, in 1828 (see Map 11.3).

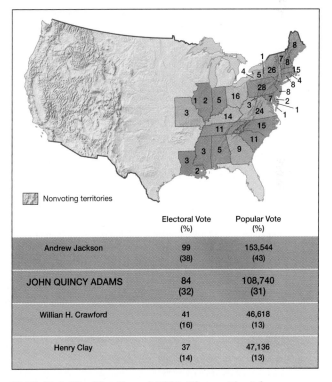

	Electoral Vote (%)	Popular Vote (%)
Andrew Jackson	99 (38)	153,544 (43)
JOHN QUINCY ADAMS	84 (32)	108,740 (31)
William H. Crawford	41 (16)	46,618 (13)
Henry Clay	37 (14)	47,136 (13)

MAP 11.3 The Election of 1824 The presidential vote of 1824 was clearly sectional. John Quincy Adams carried his native New England and little else, Henry Clay carried only his own state of Kentucky and two adjoining states, and Crawford's appeal was limited to Virginia and Georgia. Only Andrew Jackson moved beyond the regional support of the Old Southwest to wider appeal and the greatest number of electoral votes. Because no candidate had a majority, however, the election was thrown into the House of Representatives, which chose Adams.

The legislative accomplishments of Adams's presidency were scanty. Adams tried to enact the coordinated plan for economic development embodied in Henry Clay's American System (see Chapter 9) but was rebuffed by a hostile Congress, although he did succeed in obtaining funding for an extension of the National Road west from Wheeling—an issue on which he could count on western votes. Southerners blocked Adams's desire to play an important role in hemispheric affairs by refusing his request to send American delegates to a conference in Panama called by the Latin American liberator Simón Bolívar, in part because they feared it might lead to recognition of the revolutionary black republic of Haiti. Thus Adams's desire to lead the nation from a position above politics was frustrated by a political opposition that he thought illegitimate, but that was in reality an early sign of the emerging two-party system.

The New Popular Democratic Culture

In 1834, the French visitor Michel Chevalier witnessed a mile-long nighttime parade in support of Andrew Jackson. Stunned by the orderly stream of banners lit by torchlight, the portraits of George Washington, Thomas Jefferson, and Jackson, and the enthusiastic cheering of the crowd, Chevalier wrote, "These scenes belong to history. They are the episodes of a wondrous epic which will bequeath a lasting memory to posterity, that of the coming of democracy." Mass campaigns—huge political rallies, parades, and candidates with wide "name recognition," such as military heroes—were the hallmarks of the new popular democratic culture. So were less savory customs, such as the distribution of lavish food and (especially) drink at polling places, which frequently turned elections into rowdy, brawling occasions.

This well-known painting by George Caleb Bingham, *Stump Speaking*, shows a group of men (and boys, and dogs) of all social classes brought together by their common interest in politics.

SOURCE: George Caleb Bingham (American 1811–79), *Stump Speaking*, 1853–54 Oil on canvas, 42 $^1/_2$ × 58 in. The Saint Louis Art Museum, Gift of Bank of America. Photo © The Saint Louis Art Museum.

Politics, abetted by the publication of inexpensive party newspapers, was a great topic of conversation among men in early nineteenth-century America, as Richard Caton Woodville's 1845 painting *Politics in an Oyster House* suggests.

SOURCE: Richard Caton Woodville, *Politics in an Oyster House*, 1848. Oil on canvas. The Walters Art Museum.

As Chevalier noted, the spirit that motivated the new mass politics was democratic pride in participation. And as the election of 1824 showed, along with the spread of universal male suffrage went a change in popular attitudes that spelled the end of the dominance of small political elites.

Besides wider suffrage, there were other causes for the exuberance of popular democratic culture. In the nation's cities, workers had always participated in the parades and celebrations that were a part of urban life. Marching with the symbols of their trades, artisans had not only demonstrated pride in their craft, but had asserted their importance in an earlier political world ruled by elites (see Chapter 13). A print revolution had helped to democratize politics by spreading word far beyond the nation's cities about the parades, protests, and celebrations that became a basic part of popular democracy.

The print revolution had begun in 1826, when a reform organization, the American Tract Society, installed the country's first steam-powered press. Three years later, the new presses had turned out 300,000 Bibles and 6 million religious tracts, or pamphlets. The greatest growth,

however, was in newspapers that reached a mass audience. The number of newspapers soared from 376 newspapers in 1810 to 1,200 in 1835. This rise paralleled the growth of interest in politics, for most newspapers were published by political parties and were openly partisan. Packed with articles that today would be considered libelous and scandalous, newspapers were entertaining and popular reading, and they rapidly became a key part of democratic popular culture (see Figure 11.2).

Martin Van Buren was one of the first to realize the full potential of popular feeling, but politicians in other states shared Van Buren's vision of tightly organized, broad-based political groups. John C. Calhoun of South Carolina, a Virginia group known as the Richmond Junto, the Nashville Junto in Tennessee, and New Hampshire's Concord Regency all aspired to the same discipline and control as demonstrated by the Albany Regency, and each had national aspirations. The Nashville Junto led the way by nominating Andrew Jackson for president in 1824.

The new politics placed great emphasis on participation and party loyalty. Just as professional politicians such as Van Buren were expected to be loyal, so the average voter was encouraged to make a permanent commitment to a political party. One way to show that loyalty was to turn out for parades. Political processions were huge affairs, marked by the often spontaneous participation of men carrying badges and party regalia, banners and placards, and portraits of the candidates,

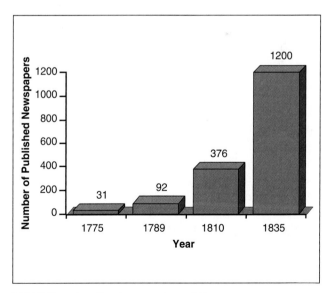

FIGURE 11.2   The Burgeoning of Newspapers
Newspapers have a long history in the United States. Even before the American Revolution, the colonies boasted 37 newspapers (see Chapter 6), and within little more than a decade, that number had nearly tripled. Toward the end of the century, however, the number of newspapers expanded rapidly, by 1835 numbering more than 30 times that of 1775.

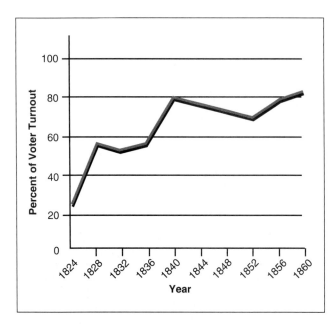

FIGURE 11.3 Pre–Civil War Voter Turnout The turnout of voters in presidential elections more than doubled from 1824 to 1828, the year Andrew Jackson was first elected. Turnout surged to 80 percent in 1840, the year the Whigs triumphed. The extension of suffrage to all white men, and heated competition between two political parties with nationwide membership, turned presidential election campaigns into events with great popular appeal.

accompanied by bands, fireworks, and the shouting and singing of party slogans and songs. The political party provided some of the same satisfactions that popular sports offer today: excitement, entertainment, and a sense of belonging. In effect, political parties functioned as giant national men's clubs. They made politics an immediate and engrossing topic of conversation and argument for men of all walks of life. In this sense, the political party was the political manifestation of a wider social impulse toward community (see Figure 11.3).

The Election of 1828

The election of 1828 was the first to demonstrate the power and effectiveness of the new popular democratic culture and party system. With the help of Martin Van Buren, his campaign manager, Andrew Jackson rode the wave of the new democratic politics to the presidency. Voter turnout in 1828 was more than twice that of 1824. Jackson's party, the Democratic Republicans (they soon dropped "Republicans" and became simply the Democrats), spoke the language of democracy, and they opposed the special privilege personified for them by President John Quincy Adams and his National Republican (as distinguished from the earlier Jeffersonian Republican) Party. Neither Jackson nor Adams campaigned on his own—that was considered undignified. But the supporters of both candidates campaigned vigorously, freely, and negatively. Jackson's supporters portrayed the campaign as a contest between "the democracy of the

country, on the one hand, and a lordly purse-proud aristocracy on the other." In their turn, Adams's supporters depicted Jackson as an illiterate backwoodsman, a murderer (he had killed several men in duels), and an adulterer (apparently unwittingly, he had married Rachel Robards before her divorce was final). Jackson's running mate for vice president was John C. Calhoun of South Carolina. Although this choice assured Jackson of valuable Southern support, it also illustrated the transitional nature of politics, for Calhoun was at the time of the election serving as vice president to John Quincy Adams, Jackson's opponent. That Calhoun was easily able to lend his support to a rival faction was a holdover from the old elite and personal politics that would soon be impossible in the new democratic political system.

Jackson won 56 percent of the popular vote (well over 80 percent in much of the South and West) and a decisive electoral majority of 178 votes to Adams's 83. The vote was interpreted as a victory for the common man. But the most important thing about Jackson's victory was the coalition that achieved it. The new democratically based political organizations—the Richmond and Nashville juntos, the Albany and Concord regencies, with help from Calhoun's organization in South Carolina—worked together to elect him. Popular appeal, which Jackson the military hero certainly possessed, was not enough to ensure victory. To be truly national, a party had to create and maintain a coalition of North, South, and West. The Democrats were the first to do this (see Map 11.4).

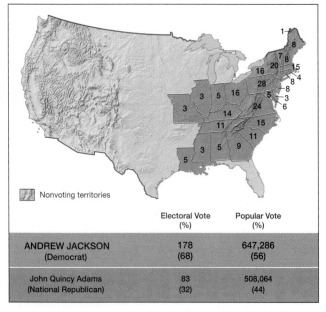

	Electoral Vote (%)	Popular Vote (%)
ANDREW JACKSON (Democrat)	178 (68)	647,286 (56)
John Quincy Adams (National Republican)	83 (32)	508,064 (44)

MAP 11.4 The Election of 1828 Andrew Jackson's victory in 1828 was the first success of the new national party system. The coalition of state parties that elected him was national, not regional. Although his support was strongest in the South and West, his ability to carry Pennsylvania and parts of New York demonstrated his national appeal.

THE JACKSON PRESIDENCY

Andrew Jackson's election ushered in a new era in American politics, an era that historians have called the "Age of the Common Man." Jackson himself, however, was no common man: he was a military hero, a rich slave owner, and an imperious and decidedly undemocratic personality. "Old Hickory," as Jackson was affectionately called, was tough and unbending, just like hickory itself, one of the hardest of woods. Yet he had a mass appeal to ordinary people, unmatched—and indeed unsought—by earlier presidents. The secret to Jackson's extraordinary appeal lies in the changing nature of American society. Jackson was the first to respond to the ways in which westward expansion and the extension of the suffrage were changing politics at the national as well as the local and state levels.

A Popular Figure

Jackson was born in 1767 and raised in North Carolina. During the American Revolution, he was captured and beaten by the British, an insult he never forgot. As a young man without wealth or family support, he moved west to the frontier station (fort) at Nashville, Tennessee, in 1788. There he made his career as a lawyer and his considerable wealth as a slave-owning planter. He had a touchy sense of pride and honor that led him into many duels. As he showed in his campaigns against the Five Civilized Tribes in the Old Southwest during the War of 1812, he was ruthless toward Indians. He first became a national hero with his underdog win against the British in the battle of New Orleans in 1815. In the popular mind, his fierce belligerence came to symbolize pioneer independence. The fact that he had little political experience, which would have made his nomination impossible under the traditional system of politics, was not a hindrance in the new age of popular politics.

On March 4, 1829, Andrew Jackson was inaugurated as president of the United States. Jackson himself was still in mourning for his beloved wife Rachel, whose recent death he attributed to the slanders of the campaign. But everyone else was celebrating. The small community of Washington was crowded with strangers, many of them Westerners and common people who had come especially for Jackson's inauguration. Jackson's brief inaugural address was almost drowned out by the cheering of the crowd, and after the ceremony the new president was mobbed by well-wishers. The same unrestrained enthusiasm was evident at a White House reception, where the crowd was large and disorderly. People stood on chairs and sofas to catch glimpses of Jackson, and shoved and pushed to reach the food and drink, which was finally carried out to the lawn. In the rush to follow, some people exited through windows rather than the doors. This was the exuberance of

Andrew Jackson was only sixty-one when he was elected president in 1828, but his lined face and white hair, captured in this early daguerreotype by Matthew Brady, perhaps explain why Margaret Bayard and others referred to him as "the old man."

SOURCE: Matthew Brady. CORBIS/Bettman.

democracy in action. It marked something new in American politics. Indeed, Jackson's administration was different from all those before it. (See Out of Many Voices: Margaret Bayard Smith Views Another Inauguration)

A Strong Executive

The mob scene that accompanied Jackson's inauguration was more than a reflection of the popular enthusiasm for Old Hickory. It also signaled a higher level of controversy in national politics. Jackson's personal style quickly stripped national politics of the polite and gentlemanly aura of cooperation it had acquired during the Era of Good Feelings and that Adams had vainly tried to maintain. Jackson had played rough all his life, and he relished controversy. His administration (1829–37) had plenty of it. Andrew Jackson dominated his administration. Except for Martin Van Buren, whom he appointed secretary of state, he mostly ignored the heads of government departments who made up his official cabinet. Instead he consulted with an informal group, dubbed the "Kitchen Cabinet," made up of Van Buren and old western friends. The Kitchen Cabinet did not include John C. Calhoun, the vice president, or either of the other two great sectional representatives,

OUT OF MANY VOICES

MARGARET BAYARD SMITH VIEWS ANOTHER INAUGURATION

Margaret Bayard Smith, who witnessed Thomas Jefferson's inauguration in 1800, was on hand to witness Andrew Jackson's inauguration 29 years account. Her account documents the changes that political democracy brought to American politics.

THOUSANDS AND THOUSANDS OF PEOPLE, without distinction of rank, collected in an immense mass round the Capitol, silent, orderly and tranquil, with their eyes fixed on the front of that edifice, waiting the appearance of the President in the portico. The door from the Rotunda opens, preceded by the marshals, surrounded by the Judges of the Supreme Court, the old man with his grey locks, that crown of glory, advances, bows to the people, who greet him with a shout that rends the air, the Cannons, from the heights around, from Alexandria and Fort Warburton proclaim the oath he has taken and all the hills reverberate the sound. . . . It was grand,—it was sublime! And had the spectacle closed here, even Europeans must have acknowledged that a free people, collected in their might, silent and tranquil, restrained solely by a moral power, without a shadow around of

military force, was majesty, rising to sublimity, and far surpassing the majesty of Kings and Princes, surrounded with armies and glittering in gold.

[After the ceremony] we set off to the President's House, but what a scene did we witness! The *Majesty of the People* had disappeared, and a rabble, a mob, of boys, negros, women, children, scrambling fighting, romping. What a pity what a pity! No arrangements had been made no police officers placed on duty and the whole house had been inundated by the rabble mob. The President, after having been *literally* nearly pressed to death and almost suffocated and torn to pieces by the people in their eagerness to shake hands with Old Hickory, had retreated through the back way. . . . This concourse had not been anticipated and therefore not provided against. Ladies and gentlemen only had been expected at this Levee, not the people en masse. But it was the People's day, and the People's President and the People would rule. God grant that one day or other, the People, do not put down all rule and rulers. ■

SOURCE: Margaret Bayard Smith. *The First Forty Years of Washington Society.* (New York: Charles Scribner's Sons, 1906).

Henry Clay and Daniel Webster. Jackson never forgave Clay for his role in the "corrupt bargain" of 1825, and he saw Daniel Webster as a representative of his favorite political target, the privileged elite.

Jackson used social distance to separate himself from other politicians. When Jackson's secretary of war, John Henry Eaton, married a beautiful woman of flamboyant reputation, he transgressed the social code of the time. It was rumored that Peggy Eaton had been Eaton's mistress, and that there were other men in her past. She was, in nineteenth-century thinking, a fallen woman and unfit for polite society. The respectable ladies of Washington shunned her. But Jackson, aroused by memories of the slanders against his own wife, defended Peggy Eaton and urged his cabinet members to force their wives to call on her. When, to a woman, they refused, Jackson called the husbands henpecked. This episode chilled the social life of cabinet members and their families and drove a wedge between Jackson and Calhoun, whose wife was a leader in the anti-Eaton group. Although

Jackson claimed to be motivated only by chivalry, he wanted to change Washington politics, and this episode helped him do it. The important although quiet role that women had played since 1800 in Washington politics came to an abrupt end. Ironically, the Eaton episode might never have occurred had Jackson not been a widower. His wife Rachel would surely have sided with Mrs. Calhoun in upholding the moral code of the time.

Jackson freely used the tools of his office to strengthen the executive branch of government at the expense of the legislature and judiciary. By using the veto more frequently than all previous presidents combined (twelve vetoes compared with nine by the first six presidents), Jackson forced Congress to constantly consider his opinions. Even more important, Jackson's "negative activism" restricted federal activity, in sharp contrast to the nationalizing tendencies of previous governments (see Chapter 9). Only Jackson's vehement and popular leadership made this sharp change of direction possible.

The Nation's Leader versus Sectional Spokesmen

Despite his western origins, Jackson was a genuinely national figure. He was more interested in asserting strong national leadership than in promoting sectional compromise. He believed that the president, who symbolized the popular will of the people, ought to dominate the government. As he put it in his first annual message, "the first principle of our system [is that] the majority is to govern." This was new. Voters were much more accustomed to thinking of politics in sectional terms. Jackson faced a Congress full of strong and immensely popular sectional figures. Three stood out: Southerner John C. Calhoun, Northerner Daniel Webster, and Westerner Henry Clay.

Intense, dogmatic, and uncompromising, John C. Calhoun of South Carolina had begun his political career as an ardent nationalist and expansionist in his early days as a War Hawk before the War of 1812. Since the debate over the Missouri Compromise in 1820, however, Calhoun had wholeheartedly identified with southern inter-ests, first and foremost among which was the expansion and preservation of slavery. As the South's minority position in Congress became clear over the years, Calhoun's defense of southern economic interests and slavery became more and more rigid. Not for nothing did he earn his nickname the "Cast-Iron Man."

Senator Daniel Webster of Massachusetts was the outstanding orator of the age. Large, dark, and stern, Webster delivered his speeches in a deep, booming voice that, listeners said, "shook the world." He was capable of pathos as well, bringing tears to the eyes of those who heard him say, while defending Dartmouth College before the Supreme Court (in the case of the same name), "It is, Sir, a small college, and yet there are those who love it." Webster, a lawyer for business interests, became the main spokesman for the new northern commercial interests, supporting a high protective tariff, a national bank, and a strong federal government. Webster's fondness for comfortable living, and especially brandy, made him less effective as he grew older, but then, as a contemporary of his remarked, "No man could be as great as Daniel Webster looked."

Two Great Sectional Leaders. The years of Jackson's presidency were also notable for the prominence of regional spokesmen, among them John C. Calhoun, who spoke for the South and slavery, and Henry Clay who spoke for the West but whose national ambitions were thwarted by Jackson's greater appeal. Clay's great personal charm is captured in this 1824 portrait (right), contrasting with Calhoun's dour expression in the later picture (left).

SOURCE: a) The Granger Collection, New York. b) Matthew H. Joulett (1788-1827), "Henry Clay," c. 1824. Oil on panel. (attr. to Joulett) © Chicago Historical Society, Chicago, USA.

In contrast with the other two, Henry Clay of Kentucky, spokesman of the West, was charming, witty, and always eager to forge political compromises. Clay held the powerful position of Speaker of the House of Representatives from 1811 to 1825 and later served several terms in the Senate. A spellbinding storyteller and well known for his ability to make a deal, Clay worked to incorporate western desires for cheap and good transportation into national politics. It was he who promoted the national plan for economic development known as the American System: a national bank, a protective tariff, and the use of substantial federal funds for internal improvements such as roads, canals, and railroads (see Chapter 9). Clay might well have forged a political alliance between the North and the West if not for the policies of President Jackson, his fellow Westerner and greatest rival. Jackson's preeminence thwarted Clay's own ambition to be president.

The prominence and popularity of these three politicians show that sectional interests remained strong even under a president as determined as Jackson to override them and disrupt "politics as usual" by imposing his own personal style. Nothing showed the power of sectional interests more clearly than the unprecedented confrontation provoked by South Carolina in Jackson's first term, the Nullification Crisis.

The Nullification Crisis

The crisis raised the fundamental question concerning national unity in a federal system: What was the correct balance between local interests—the rights of the states—and the powers of the central government? The men who wrote the federal Constitution in Philadelphia in 1787 had not been able to reach agreement on this question. Because the Constitution deliberately left the federal structure ambiguous, all sectional disagreements automatically became constitutional issues that carried a threat to national unity.

The political issue that came to symbolize the divergent sectional interests of North and South, pitting the rights of individual states against the claims of a federal majority, was the protective tariff that placed a duty (or surcharge) on imported goods. The tariff, along with internal improvements and a national bank, was a key element of Henry Clay's national economic plan that was known as The American System.

The first substantial tariff was enacted in 1816 after northern manufacturing interests clamored for protection from the ruthless British competition that followed the War of 1812 (see Chapter 9). As a group, wealthy southern planters were opposed to tariffs, both because duties raised the cost of the luxury goods they imported from Europe, and because they believed in the principle of free trade, fearing that American tariffs would cause other countries to retaliate with tariffs against southern cotton. Most southern congressmen, assured that the 1816 tariff was a temporary postwar recovery measure, voted for it. But it was not temporary.

As the North industrialized and new industries demanded protection, tariff bills in 1824 and 1828 raised rates still higher and protected more items. Southerners protested, but they were outvoted in Congress by northern and western representatives, who agreed both on the need to protect industry and on the tariff as a way to raise federal revenue. The 1828 tariff, nicknamed the "Tariff of Abominations," was a special target of southern anger, because Jackson's supporters in Congress had passed it, over Southern objections, in order to increase northern support for him in the presidential campaign of that year. It imposed especially high tariffs on imported textiles and iron; the tariffs ranged from a third to a half of the total value of those products. Southern opponents of the tariff insisted that it was not a truly national measure but a sectional one that helped only some groups while harming others. Thus, they claimed, it was unconstitutional because it violated the rights of some of the states.

South Carolina, Calhoun's home state, reacted the most forcefully to the Tariff of 1828. Of the older southern states, South Carolina had been the hardest hit by the opening of the new cotton lands in the Old Southwest, which had drained both population and commerce from the state. One index of South Carolina's changed status was the declining position of Charleston. In 1800, it was still as important a seaport as New York and Boston, but by the 1820s, it had been eclipsed by all the major northern ports as well as by Mobile and New Orleans, then the major ports for exporting cotton. To these economic woes were added the first real fears about national attitudes toward slavery. South Carolinians, who had always had close personal ties with slave owners in the Caribbean islands, were shaken by the news that the British Parliament, bowing to popular pressure at home, was planning to emancipate all the slaves in the British West Indies. If Congress had the power to impose tariffs that were harmful to some states, South Carolinians asked, what would prevent it from enacting legislation like Britain's, depriving Southerners of their slaves and, thus, of their livelihood? In this sense, although the Nullification Crisis was about the tariff, it was also about the greatest of all sectional issues, slavery.

The result of these fears was a renewed interest in the doctrine of nullification, a topic that became the subject of widespread discussion in South Carolina. The doctrine upheld the right of a state to declare a federal law null and void and to refuse to enforce it within the state. South Carolinian John C. Calhoun wrote a widely circulated defense of the doctrine, the *Exposition and Protest*, in 1828. Because Calhoun was soon to serve as

Andrew Jackson's vice president, he wrote the *Exposition* anonymously. He hoped to use his influence with Jackson, a fellow slaveowner, to gain support for nullification, but he was disappointed.

Where Calhoun saw nullification as a safeguard of the rights of the minority, Jackson saw it as a threat to national unity. As the president said at a famous exchange of toasts at the annual Jefferson Day dinner in 1830, "Our Federal Union, it must be preserved." In response to Jackson, Calhoun offered his own toast: "The Union—next to our liberty most dear. May we always remember that it can only be preserved by distributing equally the benefits and burdens of the Union." The president and the vice president were thus in open disagreement on a matter of crucial national importance. The outcome was inevitable: Calhoun lost all influence with Jackson, and two years later, he took the unusual step of resigning the vice presidency. Martin Van Buren was elected to the office for Jackson's second term. Calhoun, his presidential aspirations in ruins, became a senator from South Carolina, and in that capacity, participated in the last act of the nullification drama.

In 1832, the nullification controversy became a full-blown crisis. In passing the Tariff of 1832, Congress (in spite of Jackson's disapproval) retained high taxes on woolens, iron, and hemp, although it reduced duties on other items. South Carolina responded with a special convention and an Ordinance of Nullification, in which it rejected the tariff and refused to collect the taxes it required. The state further issued a call for a volunteer militia and threatened to secede from the Union if Jackson used force against it. Jackson responded vehemently, denouncing the nullifiers—"Disunion by armed force is treason"—and obtaining from Congress a Force Bill authorizing the federal government to collect the tariff in South Carolina at gunpoint if necessary. Intimidated, the other southern states refused to follow South Carolina's lead. More quietly, Jackson also asked Congress to revise the tariff. Henry Clay, the Great Pacificator, swung into action and soon, with Calhoun's support, had crafted the Tariff Act of 1833. The South Carolina legislature, unwilling to act without the support of other southern states, quickly accepted this face-saving compromise and repealed its nullification of the tariff of 1832. In a final burst of bravado, the legislature nullified the Force Bill, but Jackson defused the crisis by ignoring its action.

The nullification crisis was the most serious threat to national unity that the United States had ever experienced. South Carolinians, by threatening to secede, had forced concessions on a matter they believed of vital economic importance. They—and a number of other Southerners—believed that the resolution of the crisis illustrated the success of their uncompromising tactics. Most of the rest of the nation simply breathed a sigh of relief, echoing Daniel Webster's sentiment, spoken in the heat of the debate over nullification, "Liberty and Union, now and forever, one and inseparable!"

CHANGING THE COURSE OF GOVERNMENT

As Martin Van Buren later recalled, Jackson came to the presidency with a clear agenda: "First, the removal of the Indians from the vicinity of the white population and their settlement byond the Mississippi. Second, to put a stop to the abuses of the Federal government in regard to internal improvements [and] Third, to oppose as well the existing re-incorporation of the existing National Bank." As Jackson enacted his agenda, which he believed expressed the popular will, he changed the course of the federal government as decisively as Jefferson had during his presidency (see Chapter 9). But the opposition that Jackson evoked also revealed the limits of presidential authority in an age of democratic politics.

Indian Removal

The official policy of the United States government from the time of Jefferson's administration was to promote the assimilation of Indian peoples by encouraging them to adopt white ways. To Indian groups who resisted "civilization" or who needed more time to adapt, Jefferson offered the alternative of removal from settled areas in the East to the new Indian Territory west of the Mississippi River. Following this logic, at the end of the War of 1812, the federal government signed removal treaties with a number of Indian nations of the Old Northwest, thereby opening up large tracts of land for white settlement (see Chapter 9). In the Southwest, however, the Five Civilized Tribes—the Cherokees, Chickasaws, Choctaws, Creeks, and Seminoles—remained.

By the 1830s, under constant pressure from settlers, each of the five southern tribes had ceded most of its lands, but sizable self-governing groups lived in Georgia, Alabama, Mississippi, and Florida. All of these (except the Seminoles) had moved far in the direction of coexistence with whites, and they resisted suggestions that they should voluntarily remove themselves.

The Cherokees took the most extensive steps to adopt white ways. Their tribal lands in northwestern Georgia boasted prosperous farms, businesses, grain and lumber mills, and even plantations with black slaves. Intermarriage with whites and African Americans had produced an influential group of mixed-bloods within the Cherokee nation, some of whom were eager to accept white ways. Schooled by Congregationalist, Presbyterian, and Moravian missionaries, the Cherokees were almost totally literate in English.

Despite the evidence of the Cherokees' successful adaptation to the dominant white culture, in the 1820s, the legislatures of Georgia, Alabama, and Mississippi, responding to pressures from land-hungry whites, voted to invalidate federal treaties granting special self-governing status to Indian lands. Because the federal government, not the states, bore responsibility for Indian policy, these state actions constituted a sectional challenge to federal authority. In this instance, however, unlike the Nullification Crisis, the resisting states had presidential support. Living up to his reputation as a ruthless Indian fighter, Jackson determined on a federal policy of wholesale removal of the southern Indian tribes.

In 1830, at President Jackson's urging, the U.S. Congress passed the hotly debated Indian Removal Act, which appropriated funds for relocation, by force if necessary. When Jackson increased the pressure by sending federal officials to negotiate removal treaties with the southern tribes, most reluctantly signed and prepared to move. The Cherokees, however, fought their removal by using the white man's weapon—the law. At first they seemed to have won: in *Cherokee Nation* v. *Georgia* (1831) and *Worcester* v. *Georgia* (1832), Chief Justice John Marshall ruled that the Cherokees, though not a state or a foreign nation, were a "domestic dependent nation" that could not be forced by the state of Georgia to give up its land against its will. Ignoring the decision, Jackson continued his support for removal. (See Out Many Voices: "Our Hearts Are Sickened": Letter from Cherokee Chief John Ross, 1836.)

Although some Seminole bands mounted a successful resistance war in the Florida Everglades, the majority of Seminoles and members of other tribes were much less fortunate: most of the Choctaws moved west in 1830; the last of the Creeks were forcibly moved by the military in 1836, and the Chickasaws a year later. And in 1838, in the last and most infamous removal, resisting Cherokees were driven west to Oklahoma along what came to be known as the "Trail of Tears." A 7,000-man army escorting them watched thousands (perhaps a quarter of the 16,000 Cherokees) die along the way (see Map 11.5).

OUT OF MANY VOICES

"OUR HEARTS ARE SICKENED": LETTER FROM CHEROKEE CHIEF JOHN ROSS TO THE SENATE AND HOUSE OF REPRESENTATIVES, SEPTEMBER 28, 1836

In this letter John Ross, principal chief of the Cherokee, documents one stage in the Cherokee's battle to resist removal. As had Tecumseh before him (see Chapter 9), Ross protests the government tactic of reaching agreement with a few members of the tribe and then claiming that they represented the entire Cherokee nation.

[N]OW IT IS PRESENTED TO US AS A TREATY, ratified by the Senate, and approved by the President [Andrew Jackson], and our acquiescence in its requirements demanded, under the sanction of the displeasure of the United States, and the threat of summary compulsion, in case of refusal. It comes to us, not through our legitimate authorities, the known and usual medium of communication between the Government of the United States and our nation, but through the agency of a complication of powers, civil and military.

By the stipulations of this instrument, we are despoiled of our private possessions, the indefeasible property of individuals. We are stripped of every attribute of freedom and eligibility for legal self-defence. Our property may be plundered before our eyes; violence may be committed on our persons; even our lives may be taken away, and there is none to regard our complaints. We are denationalized; we are disfranchised. We are deprived of membership in the human family! We have neither land nor home, nor resting place that can be called our own. And this is effected by the provisions of a compact which assumes the venerated, the sacred appellation of treaty.

We are overwhelmed! Our hearts are sickened, our utterance is paralized, when we reflect on the condition in which we are placed, by the audacious practices of unprincipled men, who have managed their stratagems with so much dexterity as to impose on the Government of the United States, in the face of our earnest, solemn, and reiterated protestations. ∎

SOURCE: *Papers of Chief John Ross, Vol I, 1807–1839*, ed. Gary Moulton (Norman, OK: University of Oklahoma Press, 1985).

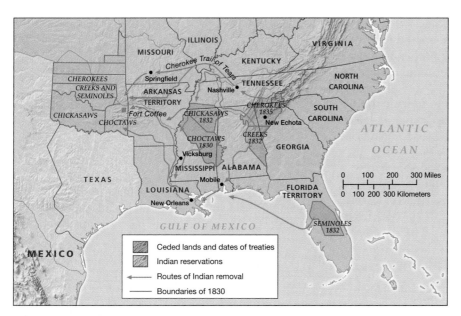

MAP 11.5 Southern Indian Cessions and Removals, 1830s Pressure on the five major southern Indian peoples—the Cherokees, Chickasaws, Choctaws, Creeks, and Seminoles—that began during the War of 1812, culminated with their removal in the 1830s. Some groups from every tribe ceded their southern homelands peacefully and moved to the newly established Indian Territory west of Arkansas and Missouri. Some, like the Seminoles, resisted by force. Others, like the Cherokees, resisted in the courts, but finally lost when President Andrew Jackson refused to enforce a Supreme Court decision in their favor. The Cherokees, the last to move, were forcibly removed by the U.S. Army along the "Trail of Tears" in 1838.

In contrast to the lesson of the Nullification Crisis, Jackson's policy on Indian removal showed how unfair majority rule could be when the minority was not strong enough to force a compromise. But just as South Carolinians were emboldened by the success of their resistance, benevolent women were encouraged by their intervention in national politics, and soon focused their petitioning skills on another cause, abolition (see Chapter 13).

Internal Improvements

Because Jackson was a Westerner, his supporters expected him to recognize the nation's urgent need for better transportation and to provide federal funding for internal improvements, especially in the West. Jackson's veto of the Maysville Road Bill of 1830 was therefore one of his most unexpected actions. Jackson refused to allow federal funding of a southern spur of the National Road in Kentucky, claiming it should be paid for by the state. Like Presidents James Madison and James Monroe before him, Jackson argued that federal funding for extensive and expensive transportation measures was unconstitutional, because it infringed on the "reserved powers" the Constitution left to the states. He also had the satisfaction of defeating a measure central to the American System proposed by his western rival, Henry Clay.

Another futile effort to resist removal, the Black Hawk "war," occurred in the Old Northwest. In 1832, Sawk and Fox Indians, led by Black Hawk, attempted to move back to their old tribal grounds in Illinois following removal, but settlers saw the move as an invasion and demanded military protection. Federal troops chased the Black Hawk band to Wisconsin, where more than 300 Indians died in a final battle, and Black Hawk himself was taken prisoner. As in the South, the last of the remaining Indians east of the Mississippi were removed by the end of the 1830s.

Indian removal was a deeply divisive national issue. President Jackson's sweeping policy undoubtedly expressed the opinion of most Southerners and Westerners. But northern opinion, led by Protestant missionaries and reform groups, was strongly opposed. Among the groups mobilized in protest were members of female benevolent societies who had a direct interest in the issue, for they had long raised money to support missionary activities aimed at assimilating, not removing, American Indians. Now, they joined together to organize the first national female petition drive. A surprised Congress was deluged by women's petitions against removal, many with hundreds of signatures (670 from Pittsburgh alone). In the end, the protest failed, but by the barest of margins: the Indian Removal Act passed the House of Representatives by only 3 votes (out of 200).

Clay's American System (which had been supported by the Monroe and Adams administrations) envisaged the role of the national government as planner and administrator of a coordinated policy involving the tariff, internal improvements and a national bank to encourage economic growth and foster the development of a national market. But since 1816, it had proved impossible to propose a nationally funded transportation plan that satisfied everyone. Repeatedly, disappointed claimants for federal funds accused each administration of favoritism and corruption. Jackson simply ended the debate over internal improvements by refusing federal funds for any of them.

But the country still needed a basic infrastructure of roads, canals, and railroads to tie the national economy together (see Chapter 12). Without federal funding and planning, the initiative passed to private developers, who turned to individual states. The states actually spent more than the federal government on internal improvements: in the 1820s, state spending for internal improvements totaled $26 million, while in the next decade, state spending for canals, railroads, and turnpikes soared to $108 million. States and towns, especially in newly populated areas of the West, competed against one another in giving land, subsidies, and other forms of encouragement to road, canal, and railroad companies to provide transportation to their particular localities. Some of these commitments were overly generous and led to financial difficulty: by 1842, nine states (Arkansas, Florida, Illinois, Indiana, Louisiana, Maryland, Michigan, Mississippi, and Pennsylvania) had defaulted on some of their transportation loans, and Ohio and New York were forced to suspend dividends to investors. This was a financially chaotic and expensive situation.

Legal Support for Private Enterprise

At the same time that funding for internal improvements passed to the states, a series of decisions by federal courts asserted broad federal powers over interstate commerce. The effect of these decisions was to vastly encourage commercial enterprise by limiting the regulatory power of the states. By preventing states from interfering with interstate commerce, the government assured entrepreneurs the freedom and security to operate in the risky new national market. Two key decisions were handed down by Chief Justice John Marshall (who had been on the bench since 1801). In *Dartmouth College* v. *Woodward* (1819), the Supreme Court prevented states from interfering in contracts, and in *Gibbons* v. *Ogden* (1824), it enjoined the state of New York from giving a monopoly over a steamboat line to Robert Fulton, inventor of the vessel. Although Fulton's invention was protected by a federal patent, its commercial application was not. Patenting thus encouraged technology, but not at the expense of competition. A decision handed down by Marshall's successor, Roger Taney, *Charles River Bridge* v. *Warren Bridge* (1837), again supported economic opportunity by denying a monopoly. All three cases involved federal reversal of decisions made at the state level, illustrating how the Supreme Court, under Marshall's leadership, weakened the powers of state governments in ways that aided the growth of private enterprise.

At the state level, another crucial commercial protection was the passage of laws concerning incorporation of businesses that had grown too large for individual proprietorship, family ownership, or limited partnership. Businesses that needed to raise large amounts of capital by attracting many investors found the contractual protections provided by incorporation to be essential. The protection investors wanted most was limited liability—the assurance that they would lose no more than what they had invested in a corporation if it were sued or went bankrupt. The net effect of state incorporation laws was to encourage large-scale economic activity and to hasten the commercialization of rural areas.

The Bank War

In the case of internal improvements, Jackson rejected, on behalf of popular democracy, the notion of coordinated economic planning by the government. His rejection set up the conditions for a speculative frenzy. Precisely the same thing resulted from his epic battle with the Second Bank of the United States.

In 1816, Congress had granted a twenty-year charter to the Second Bank of the United States. The Bank, which with thirty branches was the nation's largest, performed a variety of functions: it held the government's money (about $10 million), sold government bonds, and made commercial loans. But its most important function was the control it exercised over state banks. Because state banks tended to issue more paper money than they could back with hard currency, the Bank always demanded repayment of its loans to them in hard currency. This policy forced state banks to maintain adequate reserves and restricted speculative activities. In times of recession, the bank eased the pressure on state banks, demanding only partial payment in coin. Thus the Bank acted as a currency stabilizer by helping to control the money supply. It brought a semblance of order to what we today would consider a chaotic money system—coins of various weights and a multitude of state banknotes, many of which were discounted (not accepted at full face value) in other states.

The concept of a strong national bank was supported by the majority of the nation's merchants and businessmen and was a key element in Henry Clay's American System. Nevertheless, the Bank had many opponents. Both western farmers and urban workers had bitter memories of the Panic of 1819, which the Bank had caused (at least in part) by sharply cutting back on available credit. Many ordinary people believed that a system based on paper currency would be manipulated by bankers in unpredictable and dangerous ways. Among those who held that opinion was Andrew Jackson, who had hated and feared banks ever since the 1790s, when he had lost a great deal of money in a speculative venture.

Early in his administration, Jackson hastened to tell Nicholas Biddle, the director of the Bank: "I do not dislike your Bank any more than all banks." By 1832, Jackson's opinion had changed, and he and Biddle were locked in a personal conflict that harmed not only the national economy but the reputations of both men. Biddle, urged on by Henry Clay and Daniel Webster, precipitated the conflict by making early application for rechartering the Bank. Congress approved the application in July 1832. Jackson immediately decided on a stinging veto, announcing to Van Buren, "The bank . . . is trying to kill me, but I will kill it!"

And kill it he did that same July, with one of the strongest veto messages in American history. Denouncing the Bank as unconstitutional, harmful to states' rights, and "dangerous to the liberties of the people," Jackson presented

In this political cartoon, Jackson destroys the Second Bank of the United States by withdrawing government deposits. As the Bank crashes, it crushes the director Nicholas Biddle (depicted as the Devil), wealthy investors (with moneybags) and the newspaper editors (surrounded by paper) who opposed Jackson on this issue.

SOURCE: Courtesy of the Library of Congress.

himself as the spokesman for the majority of ordinary people and the enemy of special privilege. Nor did Jackson's veto message speak only of the sharp division between social classes. It also aroused sectional and national feelings by its allusions to the many British and eastern bank stockholders who were profiting from the debts of poor Southerners and Westerners. Jackson's message was a campaign document, written to appeal to voters. Most of the financial community was appalled, believing both the veto and the accompanying message to be reckless demagoguery.

Jackson's Reelection in 1832

Nevertheless, Jackson's veto message was a great popular success, and it set the terms for the presidential election of 1832. Henry Clay, the nominee of the anti-Jackson forces, lost the battle for popular opinion. Democrats successfully painted Clay as the defender of the Bank and of privilege. His defeat was decisive: he drew only 49 electoral votes, to Jackson's 219. A handful of votes went to the first third party in American history, the short-lived Anti-Masonic Party. This party

expressed the resentments that some new voters felt against the traditional political elite by targeting the secrecy of one fraternal group, the Masonic Order, to which many politicians (including both Jackson and Clay) belonged. The Anti-Masonic Party did make one lasting contribution to the political process. It was the first to hold a national nominating convention, an innovation quickly adopted by the other political parties.

Although the election was a triumph for Jackson, the Bank War continued, because Jackson decided to kill the Bank by transferring its $10 million in government deposits to favored state banks ("pet banks," critics called them). Cabinet members objected, as did the Senate, but Jackson responded that the election had given him a popular mandate to act against the Bank. Short of impeachment, there was nothing Congress could do to prevent Jackson from acting on his expansive—and novel—interpretation of presidential powers.

Jackson's refusal to renew the charter of the Second Bank of the United States had lasting economic and political consequences. Economically, it marked the end of Clay's

This figurehead of Andrew Jackson, carved in 1834 for the navy frigate *Constitution,* captures the unmovable resolve that made Jackson so popular early in his presidency and so reviled during the Bank War.

SOURCE: Museum of the City of New York (M52.11).

American System and inaugurated the economic policy known as *laissez faire,* where decision-making power rests with commercial interests, not with government. Politically, it so infuriated Jackson's opponents that they formed a permanent opposition party. It was from the heat of the Bank War that the now characteristic American two-party system emerged.

Whigs, Van Buren, and the Election of 1836

In 1833, as the government withdrew its deposits, Nicholas Biddle, the Bank's director, counterattacked by calling in the Bank's commercial loans, thereby causing a sharp panic and recession in the winter of 1833–34. Merchants, businessmen, and southern planters were all furious—at Jackson. His opponents, only a loose coalition up to this time, coalesced into a formal opposition party that called itself the Whigs. Evoking the memory of the Patriots who had resisted King George III in the American Revolution, the new party called on everyone to resist tyrannical "King Andrew." Just as Jackson's own calls for popular democracy had appealed to voters in all regions, so his opponents overcame their sectional differences to unite in opposition to his economic policies and arbitrary methods.

Vice President Martin Van Buren, Jackson's designated successor, won the presidential election of 1836 because the Whigs ran four sectional candidates, hoping their combined votes would deny Van Buren a majority and force the election into the House of Representatives. The strategy failed, but not by much: a shift of only 2,000 votes in Pennsylvania would have thrown the election into the House of Representatives, vindicating the Whig strategy. Their near success showed them that the basis for a united national opposition did exist. In 1840, the Whigs would prove that they had learned this lesson.

The Panic of 1837

Meanwhile, the consequences of the Bank War continued. The recession of 1833–34 was followed by a wild speculative boom, caused as much by foreign investors as by the expiration of the Bank. Many new state banks were chartered that were eager to give loans, the price of cotton rose rapidly, and speculation in western lands was feverish (in Alabama and Mississippi, the mid-1830s were known as the "Flush Times"). A government surplus of $37 million

distributed to the states in 1836 made the inflationary pressures worse. Jackson became alarmed at the widespread use of paper money (which he blamed for the inflation), and in July 1836, he issued the Specie Circular, announcing that the government would accept payment for public lands only in hard currency. At the same time, foreign investors, especially British banks, affected by a world recession, called in their American loans. The sharp contraction of credit led to the Panic of 1837 and a six-year recession, the worst the American economy had yet known.

In 1837, some 800 banks suspended business, refusing to pay out any of their $150 million in deposits. The collapse of the banking system led to business closures and outright failures. Nationwide, the unemployment rate reached more than 10 percent. In the winter of 1837–38 in New York City alone, one-third of all manual laborers were unemployed and an estimated 10,000 were living in abject poverty.

New York laborers took to the streets. Four or five thousand protesters carrying signs reading "Bread, Meat, Rent, Fuel!" gathered at City Hall on February 10, 1838, then marched to the warehouse of a leading merchant, Eli Hart. Breaking down the door, they took possession of the thousands of barrels of flour Hart had stored there rather than sell at what the mob considered a fair price. Policemen and state militia who tried to prevent the break-in were beaten by the angry mob. The Panic of 1837 lasted six long years, causing widespread misery. Not until 1843 did the economy show signs of recovery.

In neither 1837 nor 1819, did the federal government take any action to aid victims of economic recession. No banks were bailed out, no bank depositors were saved by federal insurance, no laid-off workers got unemployment payments. Nor did the government undertake any public works projects or pump money into the economy. All of these steps, today seen as essential to prevent economic collapse and to alleviate human suffering, were unheard of in 1819 and 1837. Soup kitchens and charities were mobilized in major cities, but only by private, volunteer groups, not by local or state governments. Panics and depressions were believed to be natural stages in the business cycle, and government intervention was considered unwarranted—although it was perfectly acceptable for government to intervene to promote growth. As a result, workers, farmers, and members of the new business middle class suddenly realized that participation in America's booming economy was very dangerous. The rewards could be great, but so could the penalties.

Martin Van Buren (quickly nicknamed "Van Ruin") spent a dismal four years in the White House presiding over bank failures, bankruptcies, and massive unemployment. Van Buren, who lacked Jackson's compelling

This contemporary cartoon bitterly depicts the terrible effects of the Panic of 1837 on ordinary people—bank failures, unemployment, drunkenness, and destitution—which the artist links to the insistence of the rich on payment in specie (as Jackson had required in the Species Circular of 1836). Over the scene waves the American flag, accompanied by the ironic message, "61st Anniversary of Our Independence."

SOURCE: Courtesy of the Library of Congress.

personality, could find no remedies to the depression. His misfortune gave the opposition party, the newly formed Whigs, their opportunity.

THE SECOND AMERICAN PARTY SYSTEM

The First American Party System, the confrontation between the Federalists and the Jeffersonian Republicans that began in the 1790s, had been widely viewed at the time as an unfortunate factional squabble that threatened the common good of the republic (see Chapter 8). By the 1830s, with the expansion of suffrage, attitudes had changed. The political struggles of the Jackson era, coupled with the dramatic social changes caused by expansion and economic growth, created the basic pattern of American politics: two major parties, each with at least some appeal among voters of all social

classes and in all sections of the country. That pattern, which we call the "Second American Party System," remains to this day.

Whigs and Democrats

There were genuine differences between the Whigs and the Democrats, but they were not sectional differences. Instead, the two parties reflected just-emerging class and cultural differences. The Democrats, as they themselves were quick to point out, had inherited Thomas Jefferson's belief in the democratic rights of the small, independent yeoman farmer. They had nationwide appeal, especially in the South and West, the most rural regions. As a result of Jackson's presidency, Democrats came to be identified with independence and a distaste for interference, whether from the government or from economic monopolies such as the Bank of the United States. They favored expansion, Indian removal, and the freedom to do as they chose on the frontier. Most Democratic voters

OVERVIEW

THE SECOND AMERICAN PARTY SYSTEM

Democrats	First organized to elect Andrew Jackson to the presidency in 1828. The Democratic Party spoke for Jeffersonian democracy, expansion, and the freedom of the "common man" from interference from government or from financial monopolies like the Bank of the United States. It found its power base in the rural South and West and among some northern urban workers. The Democratic Party was the majority party from 1828 to 1860.
Whigs	Organized in opposition to Andrew Jackson in the early 1830s. Heir to Federalism, the Whig Party favored a strong role for the national government in the economy (for example, it promoted Henry Clay's American System) and supported active social reform. Its power base lay in the North and Old Northwest among voters who benefited from increased commercialization and among some southern planters and urban merchants. The Whigs won the elections of 1840 and 1848.

were opposed to the rapid social and economic changes of the 1830s and 1840s.

The Whigs were themselves often the initiators and beneficiaries of economic change and were more receptive to it. Heirs of the Federalist belief in the importance of a strong federal role in the national economy (see Chapter 8), they supported Henry Clay's American System: a strong central government, the Bank of the United States, a protective tariff, and internal improvements. In fact, when it came to improvements, the Whigs wanted to improve people as well as roads. Religion was an important element in political affiliation, and many Whigs were members of evangelical reforming denominations. Reformers believed that everyone, rich and poor, was capable of the self-discipline that would lead to a good life. Thus, Whigs favored government intervention in both economic and social affairs, calling for education and social reforms, such as temperance, that aimed to improve the ordinary citizen. Many rich men were Whigs, but so were many poorer men who had a democratic faith in the perfectibility of all Americans. The Whigs' greatest strength was in New England and the northern part of the West (the Old Northwest), the areas most affected by commercial agriculture and factory work (see Chapter 13).

Yet neither party was monolithic. As has continued to be true of American political parties, both the Democrats and the Whigs were a coalition of interests affected by local and regional factors. The job of the party leader, as the Democrats' Martin Van Buren had been among the first to realize, was to forge the divergent local party interests into a winning national majority. Although Jackson's appeal was strongest in the rural South and West, the Democrats also appealed to some workers in northern cities. Urban workers cared little about rural issues, and they were less committed to the slave system than many Southerners, but they shared with Democrats from other regions a dislike of big business. On the other hand, a number of southern planters with close ties to merchant and banking interests were attracted to the Whig policy of a strong federal role in economic development, though they were less active than many northern Whigs in advocating sweeping social reform.

The Campaign of 1840

In 1840, the Whigs set out to beat the Democrats at their own game. Passing over the ever-hopeful Henry Clay, the Whigs nominated a man as much like Andrew Jackson as possible, the aging Indian fighter William Henry Harrison, former governor of the Indiana Territory from 1801 to 1812. In an effort to duplicate Jackson's winning appeal to the South as well as the West, the Whigs balanced the ticket by nominating a Southerner, John Tyler, for vice president. The campaign slogan was "Tippecanoe and Tyler too" (Tippecanoe was the site of Harrison's famous victory over Tecumseh's Indian confederation in 1811). The Whigs reached out to ordinary people with torchlight parades, barbecues, songs, coonskin caps, bottomless jugs of hard cider, and claims that Martin Van Buren, Harrison's hapless opponent, was a man of privilege and aristocratic tastes. Nothing could be farther from the truth: Van Buren was the son of a tavern keeper. But Van Buren, a short man who lacked a commanding presence, had always dressed meticulously, and now even his taste in coats and ties was used against him.

The Whig campaign tactics, added to the popular anger at Van Buren because of the continuing depression, gave Harrison a sweeping electoral victory, 234 votes to 60. Even more remarkable, the campaign achieved the greatest voter turnout up to that time (and rarely equaled since), 80 percent (see Map 11.6).

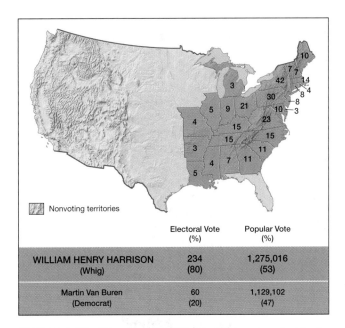

	Electoral Vote (%)	Popular Vote (%)
WILLIAM HENRY HARRISON (Whig)	234 (80)	1,275,016 (53)
Martin Van Buren (Democrat)	60 (20)	1,129,102 (47)

Nonvoting territories

MAP 11.6 The Election of 1840 The Whigs triumphed in the election of 1840 by beating the Democrats at their own game. Whigs could expect to do well in the commercializing areas of New England and the Old Northwest, but their adopted strategy of popular campaigning worked well in the largely rural South and West as well, contributing to Harrison's victory. The Whigs' choice of John Tyler as vice presidential candidate, another strategy designed to appeal to southern voters, backfired when Harrison died and Tyler, who did not share Whig principles, became America's first vice president to succeed to the presidency.

The Whig Victory Turns to Loss: The Tyler Presidency

Although the Whig victory of 1840 was a milestone in American politics, the triumph of Whig principles was short-lived. William Henry Harrison, who was sixty-eight, died of pneumonia a month after his inaugura-tion. For the first time in American history, the vice president stepped up to the presidency. Not for the last time, important differences between the dead president and his successor reshaped the direction of American politics. John Tyler of Virginia, quickly nicknamed "His Accidency," was a former Democrat who had left the party because he disagreed with Jackson's autocratic style. The Whigs had sought him primarily for his sectional appeal and had not inquired too closely into his political opinions, which turned out to be anti-Whig as well as anti-Jackson. President Tyler vetoed a series of bills embodying all the elements of Henry Clay's American System: tariffs, internal improvements, a new Bank of the United States. In exasperation, congressional Whigs forced Tyler out of the party, and his entire cabinet of Whigs resigned. To replace them, Tyler appointed former Democrats like himself. Thus, the Whig triumph of 1840, one of the clearest victories in American electoral politics, was negated by the stalemate between Tyler and the Whig majority in Congress. The Whigs were to win only one more election, that of 1848.

AMERICAN ARTS AND LETTERS

Jackson's presidency was a defining moment in the development of an American identity. His combination of western belligerency and combative individualism was the strongest statement of American distinctiveness since Thomas Jefferson's agrarianism. Did Jackson speak for all of America? The Whigs did not think so. And the definitions of American identity that were beginning to emerge in popular culture and in intellectual circles were more complex than the message coming from the White House. Throughout the nation, however, there was a widespread interest in information and literature of all kinds. The Age of the Common Man would prove to

A Regular Row in the Backwoods. The 1841 issue of the *Crockett Almanac,* named after the Tennessee backwoodsman made famous by his self-serving tall tales, portrayed a rough rural "sport." Inexpensive comic almanacs combined illustrated jokes on topical subjects with astrological and weather predictions.

SOURCE: American Antiquarian Society.

be the period when American writers and painters found the national themes that allowed them to produce the first distinctively American literature and art.

Popular Cultures and the Spread of the Written Word

The print revolution, described earlier in connection with political parties, had effects far beyond politics. Newspapers and pamphlets fostered a variety of popular cultures. For western readers, the Crockett almanacs offered a mix of humorous stories and tall tales attributed to Davy Crockett (the boisterous Tennessee "roarer" who died defending the Alamo in 1836). In New York City, the immensely popular "penny papers" (so called from their price) that began appearing in 1833 fostered a distinctive urban culture. These papers, with lurid headlines such as "Double Suicide," and "Secret Tryst," fed the same popular appetite for scandal as did other popular publications. The *Police Gazette* magazine; pamphlets about murder trials, swindlers, and pirates; and temperance dime novels such as *The Inebriate*, written in 1842 by a struggling young newspaperman named Walter (later Walt) Whitman, were read by many. Throughout the country, religious literature was still most widely read, but a small middle-class audience existed for literary magazines and, among women especially, for sentimental magazines and novels.

Accompanying all these changes in print communication was an invention that outsped them all: the telegraph, so innovative that its inventor spent years fruitlessly seeking private funds to back its application. Finally, with financing from the federal government, Samuel F. B. Morse sent his first message from Washington to Baltimore in 1844. Soon messages in Morse code would be transmitted instantaneously across the continent. The impact of this revolutionary invention, the first to separate the message from the speed at which a human messenger could travel, was immediate. The timeliness of information available to the individual, from important national news to the next train's arrival time, vastly increased. Distant events gained new and exciting immediacy. Everyone's horizon and sense of community was widened.

Creating a National American Culture

For all the improvements in communication, the United States was a provincial culture, still looking to Britain for values, standards, and lit-

erary offerings, and still mocked by the British. In a famous essay in the *Edinburgh Review* in 1820, Sidney Smith bitingly inquired, "In the four quarters of the globe, who reads an American book? or goes to an American play? or looks at an American picture or statue? What does the world yet owe to American physicians or surgeons? What new substances have their chemists discovered?" The answer was nothing—yet.

In the early years of the nineteenth century, eastern seaboard cities actively built the cultural foundation that would nurture American art and literature. Philadelphia's American Philosophical Society, founded by Benjamin Franklin in 1743, boasted a distinguished roster of scientists, including Thomas Jefferson—concurrently its president and president of the United States—and Nicholas Biddle, Jackson's opponent in the Bank War. Culturally, Boston ran a close second to Philadelphia, founding the Massachusetts General Hospital (1811) and the Boston Athenaeum (1807), a gentlemen's library and reading room. Southern cities were much less successful in supporting culture. Charleston had a Literary and Philosophical Society (founded in 1814), but the widely dispersed residences of the southern elite made urban cultural institutions difficult to sustain. Thus, unwittingly, the South ceded cultural leadership to the North.

The cultural picture was much spottier in the West. A few cities, such as Lexington, Kentucky, and Cincinnati, Ohio, had civic cultural institutions, and some transplanted New Englanders maintained connections with New England culture. A group of pioneers in Ames, Ohio, for exam-

LIBRARY OF THE ATHENÆUM.

The Boston Athenaeum was one of Boston's leading cultural institutions. The library, shown in this engraving, was probably the finest in the country in the early nineteenth century.

SOURCE: Library of the Athenaeum. Wood engraving, 1855. Collection of the Boston Athenaeum.

ple, founded a "coonskin library" composed of books purchased from Boston and paid for in coonskins. But most pioneers were at best uninterested and at worst actively hostile to traditional literary culture. This was neither from lack of literacy nor from a failure to read. Newspaper and religious journals both had large readerships in the West: the *Methodist Christian Advocate,* for example, reached 25,000 people yearly (compared with the *North American Review*'s 3,000). The frontier emphasis on the practical was hard to distinguish from anti-intellectualism.

Thus, in the early part of the nineteenth century, the gap between the intellectual and cultural horizons of a wealthy Bostonian and a frontier farmer in Michigan widened. Part of the unfinished task of building a national society was the creation of a national culture that could fill this gap. For writers and artists, the challenge was to find distinctively American themes.

Of the eastern cities, New York produced the first widely recognized American writers. In 1819, Washington Irving published *The Sketch Book,* thus immortalizing Rip Van Winkle and the Headless Horseman. Within a few years, James Fenimore Cooper's Leatherstocking novels (of which *The Last of the Mohicans,* published in 1826, is the best known) achieved wide success in both America and Europe. Cooper's novels established the experience of westward expansion, of which the conquest of the Indians was a vital part, as a serious and distinctive American literary theme. It was New England, however, that claimed to be the forge of American cultural independence from Europe. As Ralph Waldo Emerson proclaimed in "The American Scholar," a lecture he delivered in 1837 to the Harvard faculty, "Our day of dependence, our long apprenticeship to the learning of other lands, draws to a close." He went on to encourage American writers to find inspiration in the ordinary details of daily life. The stuff of literature, he declared, was to be found in "the familiar, the low . . . the milk in the pan; the ballad in the street; the news of the boat." Immensely popular, Emerson gave more than 1,500 lectures in twenty states between 1833 and 1860. "The American Scholar," his most famous lecture, carried a message of cultural self-sufficiency that Americans were eager to hear.

Asher Durand, a member of the Hudson River School of landscape painting, produced this work, *Kindred Spirits,* in 1849, as a tribute to Thomas Cole, the school's leader. Cole is one of the figures depicted standing in a romantic wilderness.

SOURCE: Asher B. Durand, "*Kindred Spirits,*" 1849. Oil on canvas. Courtesy of The New York Public Library, New York.

Artists and Builders

Artists were as successful as novelists in finding American themes. Thomas Cole, who came to America from England in 1818, painted American scenes in the style of the British romantic school of landscape painting. Cole founded the Hudson River school of American painting, a style and subject matter frankly nationalistic in tone.

The western painters—realists such as Karl Bodmer and George Catlin as well as the romantics who followed them, like Albert Bierstadt and Thomas Moran—drew on the dramatic western landscape and its peoples. Their art was an important contribution to the American sense of the land and to the nation's identity. Catlin, driven by a need to document Indian life before it disappeared, spent eight years among the tribes of the upper Missouri River. Then he assembled his collection—more than 500 paintings in all—and toured the country from 1837 to 1851 in an unsuccessful attempt to arouse public indignation about the plight of the Indian nations. George Caleb Bingham, an accomplished genre painter, produced somewhat tidied-up scenes of real-life American workers, such as flatboatmen on the Missouri River. All these painters found much to record and to celebrate in American life.

The haste and transiency of American life are nowhere as obvious as in the architectural record of this era, which is sparse. The monumental neoclassical style (complete with columns) that Jefferson had recommended for official buildings in Washington continued to be favored for public buildings elsewhere and by private concerns trying to project an imposing image, such as banks. But in general, Americans were in too much of a hurry to build for the future, and in balloon-frame construction, they found the perfect technique for the present. Balloon-frame structures—which consist of a basic frame of wooden studs fastened with crosspieces top and bottom—could be put up quickly, cheaply, and without the help of a skilled carpenter. Covering the frame with wooden siding was equally simple, and the resultant dwelling was as strong, although not as well insulated, as a house of solid timber or logs. Balloon-frame construction was first used in Chicago in the 1830s, where it created the city almost instantly. The four-room balloon-frame house, affordable to many who could not have paid for a traditionally built dwelling, became standard in that decade. This was indeed housing for the common man and his family.

CONCLUSION

Andrew Jackson's presidency witnessed the building of a strong national party system based on nearly universal white manhood suffrage. Sectionalism and localism seemed to have been replaced by a more national consciousness that was clearly expressed in the two national political parties, the Whigs and the Democrats. The Second American Party System created new democratic political communities united by common political opinions.

Culturally, American writers and artists began to establish a distinctive American identity in the arts. But as the key battles of the Jackson presidency—the Nullification Crisis, Indian removal, the Bank War—showed, the forces of sectionalism resisted the strong nationalizing tendencies of the era. As the next chapter will show, economic developments in the North were beginning to create a very different society from that of the slave South or the rural West.

CHRONOLOGY

1819	*Dartmouth College* v. *Woodward*
1821	Martin Van Buren's Bucktails defeat DeWitt Clinton in New York
	Mexican independence from Spain
1824	*Gibbons* v. *Ogden*
	John Quincy Adams elected president by the House of Representatives
1826	First American use of the steam-powered printing press
1828	Congress passes "Tariff of Abominations"
	Andrew Jackson elected president
	John C. Calhoun publishes *Exposition and Protest* anonymously
1830	Jackson vetoes Maysville Road Bill
	Congress passes Indian Removal Act
1832	Nullification Crisis begins
	Jackson vetoes renewal of Bank of the United States charter
	Jackson reelected president
1833	General Antonio Lopez de Santa Anna elected president of Mexico
1834	Whig party organized
	British abolish slavery in their Caribbean colonies
1836	Jackson issues Specie Circular
	Martin Van Buren elected president
1837	*Charles River Bridge* v. *Warren Bridge*
	Revolts against Britain in Upper and Lower Canada
	Ralph Waldo Emerson first presents "The American Scholar"
	Panic of 1837
1838	Cherokee removal along the "Trail of Tears"
1840	Whig William Henry Harrison elected president
	Act of Union merges Upper and Lower Canada
1841	John Tyler assumes presidency at the death of President Harrison
1844	Samuel F. B. Morse operates first telegraph

REVIEW QUESTIONS

1. What reasons might a person of the 1820s and 1830s give for opposing universal white manhood suffrage? Suffrage for free African American men? For women of all races?

2. Opponents believed that Andrew Jackson was unsuited in both political experience and temperament to be president of the United States, yet his presidency is considered one of the most influential in American history. Explain the changes in political organization and attitude that made his election possible.

3. Both the Nullification Crisis and Indian removal raised the constitutional issue of the rights of a minority in a nation governed by majority rule. What rights, in your opinion, does a minority have, and what kinds of laws are necessary to defend those rights?

4. Why was the issue of government support for internal improvements so controversial? What *is* the appropriate role for government in economic development?

5. What were the key differences between Whigs and Democrats? What did each party stand for? Who were their supporters? What were the links between each party's programs and party supporters?

6. What distinctive American themes did the writers, artists, and builders of the 1820s and 1830s express in their works? Are they still considered American themes today?

RECOMMENDED READING

Anne M. Boylan, The *Origins of Women's Activism: New York and Boston 1797–1840* (2002). How and why the first women's volunteer associations were formed and their political influence.

Donald B. Cole, *The Presidency of Andrew Jackson* (1993). Jackson is seen as just as influential, but less commanding and more ambiguous in his political attitudes than in earlier studies.

Ronald P. Formisano, *The Transformation of Political Culture: Massachusetts Parties, 1790s–1840s* (1983). One of many detailed studies that have contributed to our understanding of the development of the second party system.

William W. Freehling, *Prelude to Civil War* (1966). An examination of the Nullification Crisis that stresses the centrality of slavery to the dispute.

Bray Hammond, *Banks and Politics in America* (1957). The classic study of the Bank War and its consequences.

Mary Hershberger, "Mobilizing Women, Anticipating Abolition: The Struggle Against Indian Removal in the 1830s" *Journal of American History* 86:1 (June 1999).

Michael Holt, *The Rise and Fall of the American Whig Party* (1999). A massive study that covers its subject in detail.

Alexander Keyssar, *The Right to Vote: The Contested History of Democracy in the United States* (2000). A survey that examines the reasons for continual limits on the franchise.

John Lauritz Larson, *Internal Improvement: National Public Works and the Promise of Popular Government in the Early United States* (2001). Links internal improvements with political attitudes toward government, and explains how they changed.

Jean V. Matthews, *Toward a New Society: American Thought and Culture, 1800–1830* (1991). A valuable survey of American attitudes toward religion, politics, science, nature, and culture in the early nineteenth century.

Simon Newman, *Parades and the Politics of the Street* (1997). Examines how festive culture became an expression of popular political culture.

Robert Remini, *Andrew Jackson and the Source of American Freedom* (1981). An account of Jackson's White House years by his major biographer.

Kenneth Silverman, *Lightening Man: the Accursed Life of Samuel F. B. Mouse* (2003). The life of the inventor and political crank.

Alan Taylor, *William Cooper's Town: Power and Persuasion on the Frontier of the Early American Republic* (1995). An engrossing study of the effects of the democratization of politics.

Harry L. Watson, *Liberty and Power: The Politics of Jacksonian America* (1990). An excellent overview of Jacksonian politics.

 For additional study resources for this chapter, go to the *Companion Website,* **http://www.prenhall.com/faragher.**

Industry and the North

1790s–1840s

Women Factory Workers Form a Community in Lowell, Massachusetts

In the 1820s and 1830s, young farm women from all over new England flocked to Lowell to work a twelve-hour day in one of the first cotton textile factories in America. Living six to eight to a room in nearby boardinghouses, the women of Lowell earned an average of $3 a week. Some also attended inexpensive nighttime lectures or classes. Lowell, considered a model factory town, drew worldwide attention. As one admirer of its educated workers said, Lowell was less a factory than a "philanthropic manufacturing college."

The Boston investors who financed Lowell were businessmen, not philanthropists, but they wanted to keep Lowell free of the dirt, poverty, and social disorder that made English factory towns notorious. Built in 1823, Lowell boasted six neat factory buildings grouped around a central clock tower, the area pleasantly landscaped with flowers, shrubs, and trees. Housing was similarly well ordered: a Georgian mansion for the company agent; trim houses for the overseers; row houses for the mechanics and their families; and boardinghouses, each supervised by a responsible matron, for the workforce that made Lowell famous—young New England farm women.

The choice of young women as factory workers seemed shockingly unconventional. In the 1820s and 1830s, young unmarried women simply did not live alone; they lived and worked with their parents until they married. In these years of growth and westward expansion, however, America was chronically short of labor, and the Lowell manufacturers were shrewd enough to realize that young farm women were an untapped labor force. For farmers' sons, the lure of acquiring their own farms in the West was much stronger than factory wages, but for their sisters, escaping from rural isolation and earning a little money was an appealing way to spend a few years before marriage. To attract respectable young women, Lowell offered supervision both on the job and at home, with strict rules of conduct, compulsory religious services, cultural opportunities such as concerts and lectures, and cash wages.

When they first arrived in Lowell, the young women were often bewildered by the large numbers of townspeople and embarrassed by their own rural clothing and country ways. The air of the mill was hot, humid, and full of cotton lint, and the noise of the machinery—"The buzzing and hissing and whizzing of pulleys and rollers and spindles and flyers"—was constant. It was company policy for senior women to train the newcomers, and often sisters or neighbors who had preceded them to the mill helped them adjust to their new surroundings.

The work itself was simple, consisting largely of knotting broken threads on spinning machines and power looms. Most women, accustomed to the long days of farm work, enjoyed their jobs. One woman wrote home: "The work is not disagreeable. It tried my patience sadly at first, but in general I like it very much. It is easy to do, and does not require very violent exertion, as much of our farm work does."

Textile mills ran on a rigid work schedule with fines or penalties imposed on latecomers and slackers. Power-driven machinery operated at a sustained, uniform pace throughout every mill; human workers had to learn to do the same This precise work schedule represented the single largest change from preindustrial work habits, and

Lowell

it was the hardest adjustment for the workers. Moreover, each mill positioned one or two male overseers on every floor to make sure the pace was maintained. They earned more than the women who made up most of the workforce but this arrangement was unquestioned.

Why did young farm women come to Lowell? Some worked out of need, but most regarded Lowell as an opportunity: an escape from rural isolation and from parental supervision, a chance to buy the latest fashions and learn "city ways," to attend lectures and concerts, to save for a dowry or to pay for an education. As writer Lucy Larcom, one of the most famous workers, said, the women who came to Lowell sought "an opening into freer life." Working side by side and living with six to twelve other women, some of whom might be relatives or friends from home, the Lowell women built a close, supportive community for themselves.

The owners of Lowell made large profits and also drew praise for their carefully managed community, with its intelligent and independent workforce. But their success was short-lived. In the 1830s, facing competition and poor economic conditions, the owners imposed wage cuts and work speedups that their model workforce did not take lightly. Despite the system of paternalistic control

at the mills, the close bonds the women forged gave them the courage and solidarity to "turn out" in spontaneous protests, which were, however, unsuccessful in reversing the wage cuts. By 1850, the "philanthropic manufacturing college" was no more. The original Lowell workforce of New England farm girls had been replaced by poor Irish immigrants of both sexes, who earned much less than their predecessors. Now Lowell was simply another mill town.

The history of Lowell epitomizes the process by which the North (New England and the Middle Atlantic states) industrialized. A society composed largely of self-sufficient farm families (Jefferson's "yeoman farmers") changed to one of urban wage earners. Industrialization did not occur overnight. Large factories were not common until the 1880s, but long before that decade, most workers had already experienced a fundamental change in their working patterns. Once under way, the market revolution changed how people worked, how they thought, how they lived: the very basis of community. In the early years of the nineteenth century, northern communities led this transformation, fostering attitudes far different from those prevalent in the agrarian South.

KEY TOPICS

- Preindustrial ways of working and living
- The nature of the market revolution
- The effects of industrialization on workers in early factories
- Ways the market revolution changed the lives of ordinary people
- The emergence of the middle class

PREINDUSTRIAL WAYS OF WORKING

The Lowell mill was a dramatic example of the ways factories changed traditional patterns of working and living. When Lowell began operation, 97 percent of all Americans still lived on farms, and most work was done in or near the home. As had been true in colonial times,

the lives of most people were family and community based and depended on local networks of mutual obligation (see Chapter 5).

Rural and Urban Home Production

Farm families worked together to produce food and other goods for their use and for their community network. In these community exchanges, barter was customary.

Money rarely changed hands. People usually paid for a home-crafted item or a neighbor's help with a particular task, in foodstuffs or a piece of clothing or by helping the neighbor with a job he needed to have done. Thus goods and services originating in the home were part of the complicated reciprocal arrangements among community residents who knew each other well. The "just price" for an item was set by agreement among neighbors, not by some impersonal market. Another characteristic of traditional rural work was its relatively slow, unscheduled, task-oriented pace. There was no fixed production schedule or specified period of time for task completion. People did their jobs as they needed to be done, along with the daily household routine. "Home" and "work" were not separate locations or activities, but intermixed.

Likewise, in urban areas, skilled craftsmen controlled preindustrial production through the formal system of apprenticeship. Usually, the apprentice lived with the master craftsman and was treated more like a member of the family than an employee. Thus, the family-learning model used on farms was formalized in the urban apprenticeship system. At the end of the contract period, the apprentice became a journeyman craftsman. Journeymen worked for wages in the shops of master craftsmen until they had enough capital to set up shop for themselves.

Although women as well as men did task-oriented skilled work, the formal apprenticeship system was exclusively for men. Because it was assumed that women would marry, most people thought that girls only needed to learn domestic skills. Women who needed or wanted work, however, found a small niche of respectable occupations as domestic servants, laundresses, or seamstresses, often in the homes of the wealthy, or as cooks in small restaurants, or as food vendors on the street. Some owned and managed boardinghouses. Prostitution, another common female occupation (especially in seaport cities), was not respectable.

Patriarchy in Family, Work, and Society

In both rural and urban settings, working families were organized along strictly patriarchal lines. The man had unquestioned authority to direct the lives and work of family members and apprentices and to decide on occupations for his sons and marriages for his daughters. His wife had many crucial responsibilities—feeding, clothing, child rearing, taking care of apprentices, and all the other domestic affairs of the household—but in all these duties she was subject to the direction of her husband. Men were heads of families and bosses of artisanal shops; although entire families were engaged in the enterprise, the husband and father was the trained craftsman, and assistance by the family was informal and generally unrecognized.

The patriarchal organization of the family was reflected in society as a whole. Legally, men had all the power: neither women nor children had property or legal rights. For example, a married woman's property belonged to her husband, a woman could not testify on her own behalf in court, and in the rare cases of divorce, the husband kept the children, for they were considered his property. When a man died, his son or sons inherited his property. The basic principle was that the man, as head of the household, represented the common interests of everyone for

In the 1840s, Edward Hicks painted his childhood home, rendering an idealized image of rural harmony that owes more to faith in republican agrarianism than to the artist's accurate memory. The prosperous preindustrial farm had a mixed yield—sheep, cattle, dairy products, and field crops—and had an African American farm worker, (perhaps a slave) shown plowing.

SOURCE: *Residence of David Twining,* 1787. Oil on canvas. Abby Aldrich Rockefeller Folk Art Museum, Colonial Williamsburg Foundation, Williamsburg, VA.

Every small community had artisans such as blacksmiths and wheelwrights, who did such essential work as shoeing horses and mending wagons for local farmers. Artist John Neagle's heroic image of the blacksmith Pat Lyon, presents him as the very model of honest industry.

SOURCE: John Neagle (American, 1796-1865), *Pat Lyon at the Forge,* 1826-27. Oil on canvas, 93 3/4 x 68 in. (238.12 x 172.72 cm). Museum of Fine Arts Boston, Henry H. and Zoe Oliver Sherman Fund, 1975.806 Photograph © 2006 Museum of Fine Arts, Boston.

whom he was responsible—women, children, servants, apprentices. He thus controlled everything of value, and he alone could vote for political office.

The Social Order

In this preindustrial society, everyone, from the smallest yeoman farmer to the largest urban merchant, had a fixed place in the social order. The social status of artisans was below that of wealthy merchants but decidedly above that of common laborers. Yeoman farmers, less grand than large landowners, ranked above tenant farmers and farm laborers. Although men of all social ranks mingled in their daily work, they did not mingle as equals, for great importance was placed on rank and status, which were distinguished by dress and manner. Although by the 1790s many artisans who owned property were voters and vocal participants in urban politics, few directly

challenged the traditional authority of the rich and powerful to run civic affairs. The rapid spread of universal white manhood suffrage after 1800 democratized politics (see Chapter 11). At the same time, economic changes undermined the preindustrial social order. New York cabinetmaker Duncan Phyfe and sailmaker Stephen Allen amassed fortunes from their operations. Allen when he retired, was elected mayor of New York, customarily a position reserved for gentlemen. These artisans owed much of their success to the economic changes fostered by the Transportation Revolution.

THE TRANSPORTATION REVOLUTION

Between 1800 and 1840, the United States experienced truly revolutionary improvements in transportation. More than any other development, these improvements encouraged Americans to look beyond their local communities to broader ones and to foster the enterprising commercial spirit for which they became so widely known.

Improved transportation had dramatic effects, both on individual mobility and on the economy. By 1840, it was easier for people to move from one locale to another, but, even more remarkably, people now had easy access in their own cities and towns to commercial goods made in distant centers. Thus even for people who remained in one place, horizons were much broader in 1840 than they had been forty years before. The difference lay in better roads, in improvements in water transport, and in the invention and speedy development of railroads (see Map 12.1).

Roads

In 1800, travel by road was difficult for much of the year. Mud in the spring, dust in the summer, and snow in the winter all made travel by horseback or carriage uncomfortable, slow, and sometimes dangerous. Over the years, localities and states tried to improve local roads or contracted with private turnpike companies to build, maintain, and collect tolls on important stretches of road. In general, however, local roads remained poor. The federal government demonstrated its commitment to the improvement of interregional transportation by funding the National Road in 1808, at the time the greatest single federal transportation expense (its eventual cost was $7 million). Built of gravel on a stone foundation, it crossed the Appalachian Mountains at Cumberland, Maryland, thereby opening up the West. Built in stages—to Wheeling, Virginia (now West Virginia), by 1818, to Columbus, Ohio, by 1833, to Vandalia, Illinois, almost at the Mississippi River, by 1850—the National Road tied the East and the West together, strong evidence of

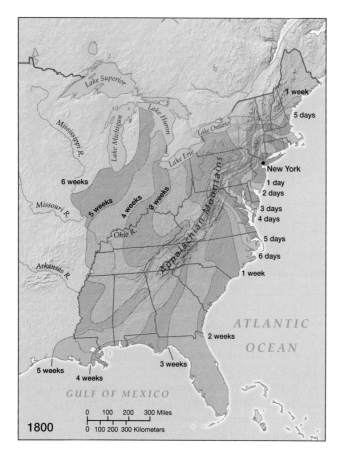

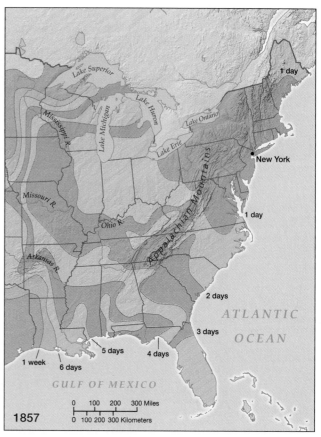

MAP 12.1 **Travel Times, 1800 and 1857** The transportation revolution dramatically reduced travel times, and vastly expanded everyone's horizons. Improved roads, canals, and the introduction of steamboats and railroads made it easier for Americans to move, and made even those who did not move less isolated. Better transportation linked the developing West to the eastern seaboard and fostered a sense of national identity and pride.

the nation's commitment to both expansion and cohesion, and helping to foster a national community.

Canals and Steamboats

However much they helped the movement of people, the National Road and other roads were unsatisfactory in a commercial sense. Shipments of bulky goods like grain were too slow and expensive by road. Waterborne transportation was much cheaper and still the major commercial link among the Atlantic seaboard states and in the Mississippi-Ohio River system. But before the 1820s, most water routes were north-south or coastal (Boston to Charleston, for example); east-west links were urgently needed. Canals turned out to be the answer.

The Erie Canal—the most famous canal of the era—was the brainchild of New York governor DeWitt Clinton, who envisioned a link between New York City and the Great Lakes through the Hudson River, and a 364-mile-long canal stretching from Albany to Buffalo.

When Clinton proposed the canal in 1817, it was derisively called "Clinton's Ditch"; the longest American canal, then in existence was only 27 miles long and had taken nine years to build. Nevertheless, Clinton convinced the New York legislature to approve a bond issue for the canal, and investors (New York and British merchants) subscribed to the tune of $7 million, an immense sum for the day.

Building the canal—40 feet wide, 4 feet deep, 364 miles long, with 83 locks and more than 300 bridges along the way—was a vast engineering and construction challenge. In the early stages, nearby farmers worked for $8 a month, but when malaria hit the workforce in the summer of 1819, many went home. They were replaced by 3,000 Irish contract laborers, who were much more expensive—50 cents a day plus room and board—but more reliable (if they survived). Local people regarded the Irish workers as different and frightening, but the importation of foreign contract labor for this job was a portent of the future. Much of the heavy

One of the Erie Canal's greatest engineering feats occured at Lockport, where the famous "combined" locks—two sets of five locks—rose side by side for 60 feet. One observer boasted, "Here the great Erie Canal has defied nature."

SOURCE: The Granger Collection, New York.

construction work on later canals and railroads was performed by immigrant labor.

DeWitt Clinton had promised, to general disbelief, that the Erie Canal would be completed in less than ten years, and he made good on his promise. The canal was the wonder of the age. On October 26, 1825, Clinton declared it open in Buffalo and sent the first boat, the *Seneca Chief*, on its way to New York at the incredible speed of four miles an hour. (Ironically, the Seneca Indians, for whom the boat was named, had been removed from the path of the canal and confined to a small reservation.) The Erie Canal provided easy passage to and from the interior, both for people and for goods. It drew settlers like a magnet, from the East and, increasingly, from overseas: by 1830, some 50,000 people a year were moving west on the canal to the rich farmland of Indiana, Illinois, and territory farther west. Earlier settlers now had a national, indeed an international, market for their produce. Moreover, farm families along the canal began purchasing household goods and cloth, formerly made at home. Indeed, one of the most dramatic illustrations of the canal's impact was a rapid decline in the production of homespun cloth in the towns and counties along its route. In 1825, the year the Erie Canal opened, New York homesteads produced 16.5 million yards of textiles. By 1835, this figure had shrunk by almost half—8.8 million yards— and by 1855, it had dropped to less than 1 million.

Towns along the canal—Utica, Rochester, Buffalo— became instant cities, each an important commercial

center in its own right. Perhaps the greatest beneficiary was New York City, which quickly established a commercial and financial supremacy no other American city could match. The Erie Canal decisively turned New York's merchants away from Europe and toward America's own heartland, building both interstate commerce and a feeling of community. As the famous song put it,

You'll always know your neighbor,
You'll always know your pal,
If you've ever navigated
On the Erie Canal.

The phenomenal success of the Erie Canal prompted other states to construct similar waterways to tap the rich interior market. Between 1820 and 1840, $200 million was invested in canal building. No other waterway achieved the success of the Erie, which collected $8.5 million in tolls in its first nine years. Nevertheless, the spurt of canal building ended the geographical isolation of much of the country.

An even more important improvement in water transportation, especially in the American interior, was the steamboat. Robert Fulton first demonstrated the commercial feasibility of steamboats in 1807, and they were soon operating in the East. Redesigned with more efficient engines and shallower, broader hulls, steamboats transformed commerce on the country's great inland river system: the Ohio, the Mississippi, the Missouri, and their tributaries. Steamboats were extremely dangerous, however; boiler explosions, fires, and sinkings were common, leading to one of the first public demands for regulation of private enterprise in 1838.

Dangerous as they were, steamboats greatly stimulated trade in the nation's interior. There had long been downstream trade on flatboats along the Mississippi River system, but it was limited by the return trip overland on the arduous and dangerous Natchez Trace. For a time, steamboats actually increased the downriver flatboat trade, because boatmen could now make more round trips in the same amount of time, traveling home by steamboat in speed and comfort. The increased river- and canal-borne trade, like the New England shipping boom of a generation earlier, stimulated urban growth and all kinds of commerce. Cities such as Cincinnati, already notable for its rapid growth, experienced a new economic surge. A frontier outpost in 1790, Cincinnati was by the 1830s a center of steamboat manufacture and machine tool production as well as a central shipping point for food for the southern market.

Railroads

Remarkable as all these transportation changes were, the most remarkable was still to come. Railroads, new in 1830 (when the Baltimore and Ohio Railroad opened with 13 miles of track), grew to an astounding 31,000 miles by 1860. By that date, New England and the Old Northwest had laid a dense network of rails, and several lines had reached west beyond the Mississippi. The South, the least industrialized section of the nation, had fewer railroads. "Railroad mania" surpassed even canal mania, as investors—as many as one-quarter of them British—rushed to profit from the new invention.

Early railroads, like the steamboat, had to overcome many technological and supply problems. For example, locomotives, to generate adequate power, had to be heavy. Heavy locomotives, in turn, required iron rather than wooden rails. The resulting demand forced America's iron industry to modernize (at first, railroad iron was imported from England). Heavy engines also required a solid gravel roadbed and strong wooden ties. Arranging steady supplies of both and the labor to lay them was a construction challenge on a new scale. Finally, there were problems of standardization: because so many early railroads were short and local, builders used any gauge (track width) that served their purposes. Thus gauges varied from place to place, forcing long-haul passengers and freight to change trains frequently. At one time, the trip from Philadelphia to Charleston involved eight gauge changes.

For some years after the introduction of the railroad, canal boats and coastal steamers carried more freight and at lower cost. It was not until the 1850s that consolidation of local railroads into larger systems began in earnest. But already it was clear that this youngest transportation innovation would have far-reaching social consequences.

The Effects of the Transportation Revolution

The new ease of transportation fueled economic growth by making distant markets accessible. The startling successes of innovations such as canals and railroads attracted large capital investments, including significant amounts from foreign investors ($500 million between 1790 and 1861), which fueled further growth. In turn, the transportation revolution fostered an optimistic, risk-taking mentality in the United States that stimulated invention and innovation. More than anything, the transportation revolution allowed people to move with unaccustomed ease. Already a restless people compared with Europeans, Americans took advantage of new transportation to move even more often—and farther away—than they had before. Disease moved with them. Epidemics that once were localized in the nation's seaports spread as travel expanded. In 1832 and 1849, cholera epidemics devastated New York City (see Chapter 13). Because of the Erie Canal and other westward travel routes, the effect of cholera was equally devastating in growing inland cities, among them St. Louis and Cincinnati, each of which lost 10 percent of their population. Cholera even stalked the Overland Trails, striking down eager goldseekers long before they reached California (see Chapter 14).

Every east-west road, canal, and railroad helped to reorient Americans away from the Atlantic and toward the heartland. This new focus was decisive in the creation of national pride and identity. Transportation improvements such as the Erie Canal and the National Road linked Americans in larger communities of interest, beyond the local communities in which they lived. And improved transportation made possible the larger market upon which commercialization and industrialization depended (see Map 12.2).

This Currier and Ives print of 1849, *The Express Train*, captures the popular awe at the speed and wonder of the new technology. This "express" probably traveled no more than 30 miles per hour.

SOURCE: The Granger Collection.

MAP EXPLORATION

To explore an interactive version of this map, go to
www.prenhall.com/faragher/map12.2

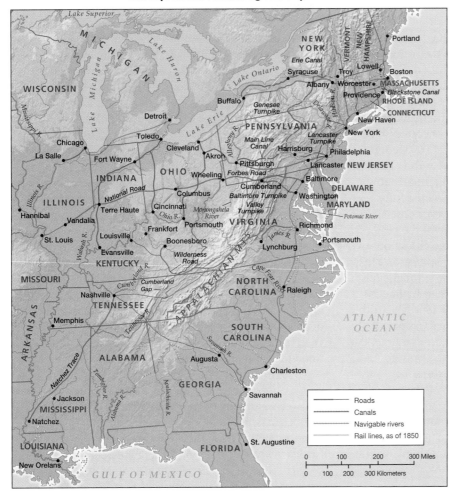

MAP 12.2 Commercial Links: Rivers, Canals, Roads, 1830 and Rail Lines, 1850
By 1830, the United States was tied together by a network of roads, canals and rivers.
This "transportation revolution" fostered a great burst of commercial activity and economic
growth. Transportation improvements accelerated the commercialization of agriculture
by getting farmers' products to wider, nonlocal markets. Access to wider markets likewise
encouraged new textile and other manufacturers to increase their scale of production.
By 1850, another revolutionary mode of transportation, the railroad, had emerged as a vital
link to the transportation infrastructure.

THE MARKET REVOLUTION

The market revolution, the most fundamental change American communities ever experienced, was the outcome of three interrelated developments: the rapid improvements in transportation just described, commercialization, and industrialization. Commercialization involved the replacement of household self-sufficiency and barter with the production of goods for a cash market. And industrialization involved the use of power-driven machinery to produce goods once made by hand.

The Accumulation of Capital

In the northern states, the business community was composed largely of merchants in the seaboard cities: Boston, Providence, New York, Philadelphia, and Baltimore. Many had made substantial profits in the international shipping boom of the period 1790–1807 (as discussed in Chapter 9). Such extraordinary opportunities attracted enterprising people. John Jacob Astor, who had arrived penniless from Germany in 1784, made his first fortune in the Pacific Northwest fur trade with China and eventually dominated the fur trade in the United States through his American Fur Company. Astor made a second fortune in New York real estate, and when he retired in 1834 with $25 million, he was reputed to be the wealthiest man in America. Many similar stories of success, though not as fabulous as Astor's, demonstrated that risk-takers might reap rich rewards in international trade.

When the early years of the nineteenth century posed difficulties for international trade, some of the nation's wealthiest men turned to local investments. In Providence, Rhode Island, Moses Brown and his son-in-law William Almy began to invest some of the profits the Brown family had reaped from a worldwide trade in iron, candles, rum, and African slaves in the new manufacture of cotton textiles. Cincinnati merchants banded together to finance the building of the first steamboats to operate on the Ohio River.

Much of the capital for the new investments came from banks, both those in seaport cities that had been established for the international trade and those, like the Lynn, Massachusetts, Mechanics Bank, founded in 1814 by a group of Lynn's Quaker merchants, that served local clients. An astonishing amount of capital, however, was raised through family connections. In the late eighteenth century, members of the business communities in the seaboard cities had begun to consolidate their position and property by intermarriage. In Boston, such a strong community developed that when Francis Cabot Lowell needed $300,000 in 1813 to build the world's first automated cotton mill in Waltham, Massachusetts (the prototype of the Lowell mills), he had only to turn to his family network (see Table 12.1).

Southern cotton provided the capital for continuing development. Because Northerners built the nation's ships, controlled the shipping trade, and provided the nation's banking, insurance, and financial services, the astounding growth in southern cotton exports enriched northern merchants almost as much as southern planters. In 1825, for example, of the 204,000 bales of cotton shipped from New Orleans, about one-third (69,000) were transshipped through the northern ports of New York, Philadelphia, and Boston. Southerners complained that their combined financial and shipping costs diverted forty cents of every dollar paid for their cotton to Northerners. Profits from cotton shipping provided some of the funds the Boston Associates made available to Francis Cabot Lowell. In another example, New York merchant Anson Phelps invested the profits he made from cotton shipping in iron mines in Pennsylvania and metalworks in Connecticut. Although imperfectly understood at the time, the truth is that the development of northern industry was paid for by southern cotton produced by enslaved African American labor. The surprising wealth that cotton brought to southern planters fostered the market revolution.

Finally, the willingness of American merchants to "think big" and risk their money in the development of a large domestic market was caused in part by American nationalism. This confidence in a future that did not yet exist was not simply a sober economic calculation but an assertion of pride in the potential of this new and expanding nation.

The Putting-Out System

Initially, the American business community invested not in machinery and factories, but in the "putting-out system" of home manufacture, thereby expanding and transforming it. In this significant departure from preindustrial work, people still produced goods at home, but under the direction of a merchant, who "put out" the raw materials to them, paid them a certain sum per finished piece, and sold the completed item to a distant market. A crucial aspect of the new putting-out system was the division of labor. In the preindustrial system, an individual worker or his household made an entire item—a shoe, for example. Now an unskilled worker often made only a part of the finished product in large quantities for low per-piece wages.

A look at the shoe industry in Lynn, Massachusetts, shows how the putting-out system transformed American manufacturing. Long a major center of the shoe industry, Lynn, in 1800, produced 400,000 pairs of shoes—enough for every fifth person in the country. The town's 200 master artisans and their families, including journeymen and apprentices, worked together in hundreds of small home workshops called "ten-footers" (from their size, about ten feet square). The artisans and journeymen cut the leather, the artisans' wives and daughters did the binding of the upper parts of the shoe, the men stitched the shoe together, and children and apprentices helped where needed. In the early days, the artisan commonly bartered his shoes for needed products. Sometimes an artisan sold his shoes to a larger retailer in Boston or Salem. Although production of shoes in Lynn increased yearly from 1780 to 1810 as markets widened, shoes continued to be manufactured in traditional artisanal ways.

The investment of merchant capital in the shoe business changed everything. In Lynn, a small group of Quaker shopkeepers and merchants, connected by family, religious, and business ties, took the lead in reorganizing the trade. Financed by the bank they founded in 1814, Lynn capitalists like Micajah Pratt built large, two-story central workshops to replace the scattered ten-footers. Pratt employed a few skilled craftsmen to cut leather for shoes, but he put out the rest of the shoemaking to less-skilled workers who were no longer connected by family ties. Individual farm women and children sewed the uppers, which, when completed, were soled by farm men and boys. Putting-out workers were paid on a piecework basis; the men and boys earned more than the women and children but much less than a master craftsman or a journeyman. This arrangement allowed the capitalist to employ much more labor for the same investment than the traditional artisan workshop. Shoe production increased enormously: the largest central shop in 1832 turned out ten times more shoes than the largest shopkeeper had sold in 1789. Gradually the putting-out system and central workshops replaced artisans' shops. Some artisans became wealthy owners of workshops, but most

TABLE 12.1	WEALTH IN BOSTON, 1687–1848			
Percent of the Population	Percent of Wealth Held			
	1687	1771	1833	1848
Top 1 percent	10%	16%	33%	37%
Top 10 percent	42	65	75	82
Lowest 80 percent	39	29	14	4

This table tracing the distribution of wealth in Boston reflects the gains made by merchants during the international shipping boom of 1790–1807 and the way in which intermarriage between wealthy families consolidated these gains.

became wage earners, and the apprenticeship system eventually disappeared.

The putting-out system moved the control of production from the individual artisan households to the merchant capitalists, who could now control labor costs, production goals, and shoe styles to fit certain markets. For example, the Lynn trade quickly monopolized the market for cheap boots for southern slaves and western farmers, leaving workshops in other cities to produce shoes for wealthier customers. This specialization of the national market—indeed, even thinking in terms of a national market—was new. Additionally, and most important from the capitalist's point of view, the owner of the business controlled the workers and could cut back or expand the labor force as economic and marketplace conditions warranted. The unaccustomed severity of economic slumps like the Panics of 1819 and 1837 made this flexibility especially desirable.

While the central workshop system prevailed in Lynn and in urban centers like New York City, the putting-out system also fostered a more dispersed form of home production. By 1810, there were an estimated 2,500 so-called outwork weavers in New England, operating handlooms in their own homes. Other crafts that rapidly became organized according to the putting-out system were flax and wool spinning, straw braiding, glove making, and the knitting of stockings. For example, the palm-leaf hat industry that supplied farm laborers and slaves in the South and West relied completely on women and children, who braided the straw for the hats at home part-time. Absorbed into families' overall domestic routines, the outwork activity seemed small, but the size of the industry itself was surprising: in 1837, 33,000 Massachusetts women braided palm-leaf hats, whereas only 20,000 worked in the state's cotton textile mills. They were producing for a large national market, made possible by the dramatic improvements in transportation that occurred between 1820 and 1840.

The Spread of Commercial Markets

Although the putting-out system meant a loss of independence for artisans such as those in Lynn, Massachusetts, New England farm families liked it. From their point of view, the work could easily be combined with domestic

Cyrus McCormick is shown demonstrating his reaper to skeptical farmers. When they saw that the machine cut four times as much wheat a day as a hand-held scythe, farmers flocked to buy McCormick's invention. Agricultural practices, little changed for centuries, were revolutionized by machines such as this.

SOURCE: *The Testing of the First Reaping Machine,* lithograph, 1831. Courtesy of the Chicago Historical Society.

work, and the pay was a new source of income that they could use to purchase mass-produced goods rather than spend the time required to make those things themselves. It was in this way that farm families moved away from the local barter system and into a larger market economy.

Commercialization, or the replacement of barter by a cash economy, did not happen immediately or uniformly throughout the nation. Fixed prices for goods produced by the new principles of specialization and division of labor appeared first along established trade routes. Rural areas in established sections of the country that were remote from trade routes continued in the old ways. Strikingly, however, western farming frontiers were commercial from the very start. The existence of a cash market was an important spur to westward expansion.

Commercial Agriculture in the Old Northwest

Every advance in transportation—better roads, canals, steamboats, railroads—made it easier for farmers to get their produce to market. Improvements in agricultural machinery increased the amount of acreage a farmer could cultivate. These two developments, added to the availability of rich, inexpensive land in the heartland, moved American farmers permanently away from subsistence agriculture and into production for sale.

The impact of the transportation revolution on the Old Northwest was particularly marked. Settlement of the region, ongoing since the 1790s, accelerated. In the 1830s, after the opening of the Erie Canal, migrants from New England streamed into northern Ohio, Illinois, Indiana, southern Wisconsin, and Michigan and began to reach into Iowa.

Government policy strongly encouraged western settlement. The easy terms of federal land sales were an important inducement: terms eased from an initial rate of $2.00 per acre for a minimum of 320 acres in 1800, to $1.25 an acre for 80 acres in 1820. Still, this was too much for most settlers to pay all at once. Some people simply squatted, taking their chances that they could make enough money to buy the land before someone else bought it. Less daring settlers relied on credit, which was extended by banks, storekeepers, speculators, promoters, and, somewhat later, railroads, which received large grants of federal lands.

The very need for cash to purchase land involved western settlers in commercial agriculture from the beginning. Farmers, and the towns and cities that grew up to supply them, needed access to markets for their crops. Canals, steamboats, and railroads ensured that access, immediately tying the individual farm into national and international commercial networks. The long period of subsistence farming that had characterized colonial New England and the early Ohio Valley frontier was superseded by commercial agriculture stimulated by the transportation revolution.

Commercial agriculture in turn encouraged regional specialization. Ohioans shipped corn and hogs first by flatboat and later by steamboat to New Orleans. Cincinnati, the center of the Ohio trade, earned the nickname "Porkopolis" because of the importance of its slaughterhouses. By 1840, the national center of wheat production had moved west of the Appalachians to Ohio. Wheat flowed from the upper Midwest along the Erie Canal to eastern cities and increasingly to Europe. Because in each new western area wheat yields were higher than in earlier ones, farmers in older regions were forced to shift away from wheat to other crops. The constant opening of new farmland encouraged mobility and wasteful soil practices. Many farmers did not wish to make a permanent commitment to their land, but rather counted on rising land prices and short-term crop profits to improve their financial situation. Prepared to move on when the price was right, they regarded their farmland not as a permanent investment but as a speculation.

At the same time, farmers who grew wheat or any other cash crop found themselves at the mercy of far-off markets, which established crop prices; distant canal or railroad companies, which set transportation rates; and the state of the national economy, which determined the availability of local credit. This direct dependence on economic forces outside the control of the local community was something new. So, too, was the dependence on technology, embodied in expensive new machines that farmers often bought on credit.

New tools made Western farmers unusually productive. John Deere's steel plow (invented in 1837) cut plowing time in half, making cultivation of larger acreages possible. Seed drills were another important advance. But the most remarkable innovation was Cyrus McCormick's reaper, patented in 1834. Earlier, harvesting had depended on manpower alone. A man could cut two or three acres of wheat a day with a cradle scythe, but with the horse-drawn reaper, he could cut twelve acres. Impressed by these figures, western farmers rushed to buy the new machines, confident that increased production would rapidly pay for them. In most years, their confidence was justified. But in bad years, farmers found that their new levels of debt could mean failure and foreclosure. They were richer, but more economically vulnerable than they had been before.

British Technology and American Industrialization

Important as were the transportation revolution and the commercialization made possible by the putting-out system, the third component of the market revolution, industrialization, brought the greatest changes to personal lives. Begun in Britain in the eighteenth century, industrialization was the result of a series of technological changes in the textile trade. In marked contrast to the putting-out system, in which capitalists had dis-

This carved and painted figure, designed as a whirligig and trade sign, shows a woman at a spinning wheel. Until cotton textile mills industrialized this work, spinning was one of the most time-consuming tasks that women and young girls did at home.

SOURCE: Library of Congress.

Island, he met Moses Brown and William Almy, who had been trying without success to duplicate British industrial technology. Having carefully committed the designs to memory before leaving England, Slater promptly built copies of the latest British machinery for Brown and Almy. Slater's mill, as it became known, began operation in 1790. It was the most advanced cotton mill in America.

Following British practice, Slater drew his workforce primarily from among young children (ages seven to twelve) and women, whom he paid much less than the handful of skilled male workers he hired to keep the machines working. The yarn spun at Slater's mill was then put out to local home weavers, who turned it into cloth on handlooms. As a result, home weaving flourished in areas near the mill, giving families a new opportunity to make money at a task with which they were already familiar.

Many other merchants and mechanics followed Slater's lead, and the rivers of New England were soon dotted with mills wherever waterpower could be tapped. Embargo and war sheltered American factories from British competition from 1807 to 1815, but when the War of 1812 ended, the British cut prices ruthlessly in an effort to drive the newcomers out of business. In 1816 Congress passed the first tariff, aimed largely against British cotton textiles, in response to the clamor by New England manufacturers for protection for their young industry.

The Lowell Mills

Another way to deal with British competition was to beat the British at their own game. With the intention of designing better machinery, a young Bostonian,

persed work into many individual households, industrialization required workers to concentrate in factories and pace themselves to the rhythms of power-driven machinery.

The simplest and quickest way for America to industrialize was to copy the British, but the British, well aware of the value of their machinery, enacted laws forbidding its export and even the emigration of skilled workers. Over the years, however, Americans managed to lure a number of British artisans to the United States.

In 1789, Samuel Slater, who had just finished an apprenticeship in the most up-to-date cotton spinning factory in England, disguised himself as a farm laborer and slipped out of England without even telling his mother good-bye. In Providence, Rhode

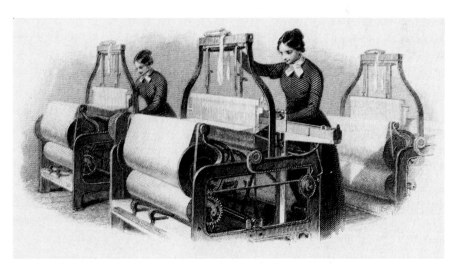

This 1850 engraving by the American Banknote company shows women tending looms at Lowell. The contrast between this industrial activity and the figure of a woman spinning at home illustrates one of the most important effects of industrialization: Now machines, not individuals, determined the pace of production.

SOURCE: Print Collection, Miriam and Ira D. Wallach Division of Art, Prints and Photographs, The New York Public Library, Astor, Lenox and Tilden Foundations.

Francis Cabot Lowell, made an apparently casual tour of British textile mills in 1810. Lowell, the founder of the Lowell mills described in the opening of this chapter, made a good impression on his English hosts, who were pleased by his interest and his intelligent questions. They did not know that each night, in his hotel room, Lowell made sketches from memory of the machines he had inspected during the day.

Lowell was more than an industrial spy, however. When he returned to the United States, he went to work with a Boston mechanic, Paul Moody, to improve on the British models. Lowell and Moody not only made the machinery for spinning cotton more efficient, but they also invented a power loom. This was a great advance, for now all aspects of textile manufacture, from the initial cleaning and carding (combing) to the production of finished lengths of cloth, could be gathered together in the same factory. Such a mill required a much larger capital investment than a small spinning mill such as Slater's, but Lowell's family network gave him access to the needed funds. In 1814, he opened the world's first integrated cotton mill in Waltham, near Boston. It was a great success: in 1815, the Boston Associates (Lowell's partners) made profits of 25 percent, and their efficiency allowed them to survive the intense British competition following the War of 1812 (see Chapter 9). Many smaller New England mills did not survive. The lesson was clear: size mattered.

The Boston Associates took the lesson to heart, and when they moved their enterprise to a new location in 1823, they thought big. They built an entire town at the junction of the Concord and Merrimack Rivers where the village of East Chelmsford stood, renaming it Lowell in memory of Francis, who had died, still a young man, in 1817. As the opening of this chapter describes, the new industrial community boasted six mills and company housing for all the workers. In 1826, the town had 2,500 inhabitants; ten years later the population was 17,000 (see Map 12.3).

Family Mills

Lowell was unique. No other textile mill was ever such a showplace. None was as large, integrated so many tasks, or relied on such a homogeneous workforce. Its location in a new town was also unusual. Much more common in the early days of industrialization were small rural spinning mills, on the model of Slater's first mill, built on swiftly running streams near existing farm communities. Because the owners of smaller mills often hired entire families, their operations came to be called family mills. The employment pattern at these mills followed that established by Slater at his first mill in 1790. Children aged eight to twelve, whose customary job was "doffing" (changing) bobbins on the spinning machines, made up 50 percent of the workforce. Women and men each made up about 25 percent of the workforce, but men had the most skilled and best-paid jobs.

Relations between these small rural mill communities and the surrounding farming communities were often difficult, as the history of the towns of Dudley and Oxford, Massachusetts, shows. Samuel Slater, now a millionaire, built three small mill communities near these towns in the early years of the nineteenth century. Each consisted of a small factory, a store, and cottages and a boardinghouse for workers. Most of Slater's workers came from outside the Dudley-Oxford area. They were a mixed group—single young farm women of the kind Lowell attracted, the poor and destitute, and workers from other factories looking for better conditions. They rarely stayed long: almost 50 percent of the workforce left every year.

Slater's mills provided a substantial amount of work for local

This early nineteenth-century watercolor shows Slater's mill, the first cotton textile mill in the United States, which depended on the waterpower of Pawtucket Falls for its energy. New England was rich in swiftly flowing streams that could provide power to spinning machines and power looms.

SOURCE: Courtesy of the Rhode Island Historical Society.

MAP EXPLORATION

To explore an interactive version of this map, go to **www.prenhall.com/faragher/map12.3**

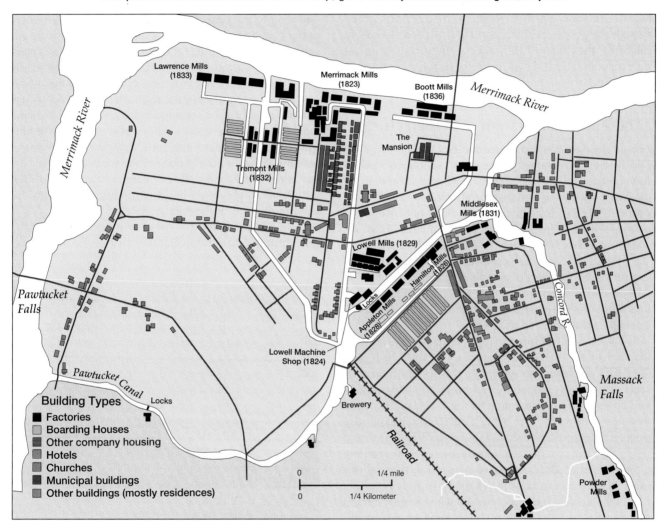

Building Types
- ■ Factories
- ▪ Boarding Houses
- ▪ Other company housing
- ▪ Hotels
- ▪ Churches
- ■ Municipal buildings
- ▪ Other buildings (mostly residences)

MAP 12.3 Lowell, Massachusetts, 1832 This town plan of Lowell, Massachusetts in 1832, illustrates the comprehensive relationship the owners envisaged between the factories and the workforce. The mills are located on the Merrimack River, while nearby are the boardinghouses for the single young female workers, row houses for the male mechanics and their families, and houses for the overseers. Somewhat farther away is the mansion of the company agent.

people, putting out to them both the initial cleaning of the raw cotton and the much more lucrative weaving of the spun yarn. But in spite of this economic link, relations between Slater and his workers on one side and the farmers and shopkeepers of the Dudley and Oxford communities on the other were stormy. They disagreed over the building of mill dams (essential for the mill power supply, these dams sometimes flooded local fields), over

taxes, over the upkeep of local roads, and over schools. The debates were so constant, and so heated, that in 1831, Slater petitioned the Massachusetts General Court to create a separate town, Webster, that would encompass his three mill communities. For their part, the residents of Dudley and Oxford became increasingly hostile to Slater's authoritarian control, which they regarded as undemocratic. Their dislike carried over to the workers as well. Disdaining the mill workers for their poverty and transiency, people in the rural communities began referring to them as "operatives," making them somehow different in their work roles from themselves. Industrial work thus led to new social distinctions. Even though the people of Dudley and Oxford benefited from the mills, they did not fully accept the social organization on which their new prosperity rested, nor did they feel a sense of community with those who did the work that led to their increased well-being.

"The American System of Manufactures"

Not all American industrial technology was copied from British inventions, for there were many home-grown inventors. Indeed, calling Americans "mechanic[s] by nature," one Frenchman observed that "in Massachusetts and Connecticut there is not a labourer who had not invented a machine or tool." By the 1840s, to take but one example, small towns like St. Johnsbury, Vermont, boasted many small industries based on local inventions, such as those by Erastus Fairbanks in scales and plows, Lemuel Hubbard in pumps, and Nicanor Kendall in guns. But perhaps most important was the pioneering American role in the development of standardized parts.

The concept of interchangeable parts, realized first in gun manufacturing, was so unusual that the British soon dubbed it the American system. In this system, a product such as a gun was broken down into its component parts and an exact mold was made for each. All pieces made from the same mold (after being hand filed by inexpensive unskilled laborers) matched a uniform standard. As a result, repairing a gun that malfunctioned required only installing a replacement for the defective part rather than laboriously making a new part or perhaps an entirely new gun.

In 1798, Eli Whitney contracted with the government to make 10,000 rifles in twenty-eight months, an incredibly short period had he been planning to produce each rifle by hand in the traditional way. Whitney's ideas far outran his performance. It took him ten years to fulfill his contract, and even then he had not managed to perfect the production of all the rifle parts. Two other New Englanders, Simeon North and John Hall, created milling machines that could grind parts to the required specifications and brought the concept to fruition, North in 1816 and Hall in 1824. When the system of interchangeable machine-made parts was adopted by the national armory at Springfield, Massachusetts, the Springfield rifle got its name.

America's early lead in interchangeable parts was a substantial source of national pride. As American gunmaker Samuel Colt boasted, "There is nothing that cannot be made by machine." Standardized production quickly revolutionized the manufacture of items as simple as nails and as complicated as clocks. By 1810, a machine had been developed that could produce 100 nails a minute, cutting the cost of nail making by two-

thirds. Finely made wooden and brass clocks, previously made (expensively) by hand, were replaced by mass-produced versions turned out in the Connecticut factories of Eli Terry, Seth Thomas, and Chauncey Jerome and sold nationwide by Yankee peddlers. Now ordinary people could keep precise time rather than estimate time by the sun, and factories could require workers to come to work on time. The need of railroads for precise timekeeping gave further support to the new system of manufacture.

Like the factory system itself, the American system spread slowly. For example, Isaac Singer's sewing machine, first patented in 1851, was not made with fully interchangeable parts until 1873, when the company was already selling 230,000 machines a year. The sewing machine revolutionized the manufacture of clothing, which up to this time had been made by women for their families at home and by hand.

American businesses mass-produced high-quality goods for ordinary people earlier than manufacturers in

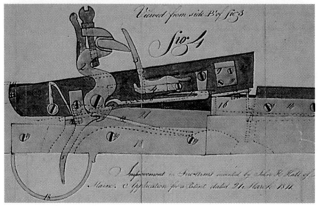

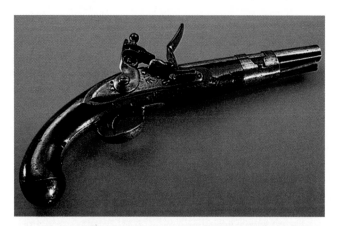

In 1816, Connecticut gunsmith Simeon North did what Eli Whitney had only hoped to do. North produced the first gun with interchangeable parts. North's invention, taken up and improved by the national armories at Springfield and Harpers Ferry, formed the basis of the American system of manufactures.

SOURCE: (top) Photograph by James L. Amos; (bottom) John H. Hall's patent for a breech-loading rifle, 1811. Both, National Geographic Image Society.

Britain or any other European country were able to do. The availability of these goods was a practical demonstration of American beliefs in democracy and equality. As historian David Potter has perceptively remarked: "European radical thought is prone to demand that the man of property be stripped of his carriage and his fine clothes. But American radical thought is likely to insist, instead, that the ordinary man is entitled to mass-produced copies, indistinguishable from the originals."

FROM ARTISAN TO WORKER

The changes wrought by the market revolution had major and lasting effects on ordinary Americans. The proportion of wage laborers in the nation's labor force rose from 12 percent in 1800 to 40 percent by 1860. Most of these workers were employed in the North, and almost half were women, performing outwork in their homes. The young farm woman who worked at Lowell for a year or two, then returned home; the master craftsman in Lynn who expanded his shop with the aid of merchant capital; the home weaver who prospered on outwork from Slater's mill—all were participating, often unknowingly, in fundamental personal and social changes.

Personal Relationships

The immense increase in productivity made possible by the principles of division of labor and specialization effectively destroyed artisan production and the apprenticeship system. For example, in New York by the mid-1820s, tailors and shoemakers were teaching apprentices only a few simple operations, in effect using them as helpers. Printers undercut the system by hiring partly trained apprentices as journeymen. In almost every trade, apprentices no longer lived with the master's family, and their parents received cash payment for the child's work. Thus, in effect, the apprenticeship system was replaced by child labor.

Although the breakdown of the family work system undoubtedly harmed independent urban artisans, it may have had a liberating effect on the women and children of farm families. About a third of the Lowell women workers did not return to their farm homes, instead remaining in town and marrying urban men or continuing to work. And of the women who did return home, fewer than half married farmers. There is no doubt that working at Lowell provided these women with new options. Women and children who earned wages by doing outwork at home may have found their voices strengthened by this evidence of their power and worth. Patriarchal control over family members was no longer absolute (see Figure 12.1).

The breakdown of the patriarchal relationship between the master craftsman and his workers became an issue in the growing political battle between the North and the South over slavery. Southern defenders of slavery compared their cradle-to-grave responsibility to their slaves with northern employers' "heartless" treatment of their "wage slaves." Certainly the new northern employer assumed less responsibility for individual workers than had the traditional artisan. Although the earliest textile manufacturers, like those at Lowell, provided housing for their workers, workers soon became responsible for their own food and housing. Moreover, northern employers felt no obligation to help or care for old or disabled workers. Southerners were right: this was a heartless system. But Northerners were also right: industrialization was certainly freer than the slave system, freer even than the hierarchical craft system, although it sometimes offered only the freedom to starve.

Mechanization and Women's Work

Industrialization posed a major threat to the status and independence of skilled male workers. In trade after trade, mechanization meant that most tasks could be performed by unskilled labor. For example, the textile mills at Lowell and elsewhere hired a mere handful of

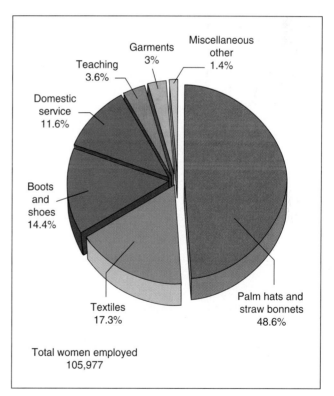

FIGURE 12.1 Occupations of Women Wage Earners in Massachusetts, 1837 This chart shows how important outwork was for women workers. Textile work in factories occupied less than 20 percent of women, while outwork in palm-leaf hats, straw bonnets, and boots and shoes accounted for over half of the total workforce. Teaching was a new occupation for women in 1837. The small percentage of 3.6 would grow in the future.

SOURCE: Based on Thomas Dublin, *Transforming Women's Work* (Ithaca, NY: Cornell University Press, 1991), Table 1.1, p. 20.

skilled mechanics; most of the rest of the workers were unskilled and lower paid. In fact, the work in the textile mills was so simple that children came to form a large part of the workforce. By 1850, in New York City, many formerly skilled trades, including shoemaking, weaving, silversmithing, pottery making, and cabinetmaking, were filled with unskilled, low-paid workers who did one specialized operation or tended machinery. Many former artisans were reduced to performing wage labor for others. Because women were so frequently hired in the putting-out system, male workers began to oppose female participation in the workforce, fearing that it would lower their own wages.

Mechanization changed the nature of women's work as well. The industrialization of textiles—first in spinning, then in weaving—relieved women of a time-consuming home occupation. To supplement family income, women now had the choice of following textile work into the factory or finding other kinds of home work. At first, these were attractive options, but negative aspects soon developed, especially in the nation's cities.

The 1820s saw the birth of the garment industry. In New York City, employers began hiring women to sew ready-made clothing, at first rough, unfitted clothing for sailors and southern slaves, but later overalls and shirts for Westerners, and finer items, such as men's shirts. Most women performed this work at low piecework rates in their homes. Although by 1860, Brooks Brothers, the famous men's clothing firm, had 70 "inside" workers in a model central workshop, the firm relied primarily on putting out sewing to 3,000 women who worked at home.

Soon the low pay and seasonal nature of the industry became notorious. Overcrowding of the market—all women could sew—led to low wages. Women were pushed into the garment trade because they were barred from many occupations considered inappropriate for them, and the oversupply of workers led to wage cutting. To make matters worse, most people believed that "respectable" women did not do factory work (Lowell in its "model" years was the exception that proved the rule), and this disparagement fostered low pay and poor working conditions.

Manufacturers in the garment trade made their profits not from efficient production but by obtaining intensive labor for very low wages. The lower the piece rate, the more each woman, sewing at home, had to produce to earn enough to live. The invention of the sewing machine only made matters worse. Manufacturers dropped their piecework rates still lower, and some women found themselves working fifteen to eighteen hours a day, producing more than they ever had but earning the same pay.

Time, Work, and Leisure

Preindustrial work had a flexibility that factory work did not, and it took factory workers a while to get accustomed to the constant pace of work. Long hours did not bother them, for they were accustomed to twelve-hour workdays and six-day weeks on the farm and in the shop. But in the early days of Slater's mill in Rhode Island, workers sometimes took a few hours off to go

This illustration of seamstresses at work, from *Sartain's Union Magazine*, January 1851, shows an early abuse created by the market revolution. Women workers were crowded into just a few occupations, thereby allowing owners to offer very low wages for very long hours of work. The women in this illustration appear to be gathered together in a central workshop, where they had each other for company. Many other women sewed alone at home, often for even lower wages.

SOURCE: Courtesy American Antiquarian Society.

berry picking or to attend to other business. And when Slater insisted on a twelve-hour day that required candles for night work, one upset father demanded that his children be sent home at sunset, the traditional end of the workday.

Factory workers gradually adjusted to having their lives regulated by the sound of the factory bell, but they did not necessarily become the docile "hands" the owners wanted. Absenteeism was common, accounting for about 15 percent of working hours, and there was much pilfering. Workers were beginning to think of themselves as a separate community whose interests differed from those of owners, and the tyranny of time over their work was certainly one reason for this.

Another adjustment required by the constant pace was that time now had to be divided into two separate activities—work and leisure. In preindustrial times, work and leisure were blended for farmers and artisans. The place of work—often the home—and the pace made it possible to stop and have a chat or a friendly drink with

a visitor. Now, however, the separation of home and workplace and the pace of production not only squeezed the fun out of the long workday but left a smaller proportion of time for leisure activities.

For many workingmen, the favored spot for after-hours and Sunday leisure became the local tavern. Community-wide celebrations and casual sociability, still common in rural areas, began to be replaced in cities by spectator sports—horse racing, boxing, and (beginning in the 1850s) baseball—and by popular entertainments, such as plays, operas, minstrel shows, concerts, and circuses. Some of these diversions, such as plays and horse racing, appealed to all social classes, but others, like parades, rowdy dance halls, and tavern games like quoits and ninepins were favored working-class amusements. The effect of these changes was to make working-class amusements more distinct, and visible, than they had been before.

The Cash Economy

Another effect of the market revolution was the transformation of a largely barter system into a cash economy. For example, a farm woman might pay in butter and eggs for a pair of shoes handmade for her by the local shoemaker. A few years later that same woman, now part of the vast New England outwork industry, might buy ready-made footwear with the cash she had earned from braiding straw for hats. Community economic ties were replaced by distant, sometimes national ones.

The pay envelope became the only direct contact between factory worker and (often absentee) owner. For workers, this change was both unsettling and liberating. On the minus side, workers were no longer part of a settled, orderly, and familiar community. On the plus side, they were now free to labor wherever they could, at whatever wages their skills or their bargaining power could command. That workers took their freedom seriously is evidenced by the very high rate of turnover—50 percent a year—in the New England textile mills.

But if moving on was a sign of increased freedom of opportunity for some workers, for others it was an unwanted consequence of the market revolution. In New England, for example, many quite prosperous artisans and farmers faced disruptive competition from factory goods and western commercial agriculture. They could remain where they were only if they were willing to become factory workers or commercial farmers. Often the more conservative choice was to move west and try to reestablish one's traditional lifestyle on the frontier.

Free Labor

At the heart of the industrializing economy was the notion of free labor. Originally, "free" referred to individual economic choice—that is, to the right of workers to move to another job rather than be held to a

TIME TABLE OF THE LOWELL MILLS,

To take effect on and after Oct. 21st, 1851.

The Standard time being that of the meridian of Lowell, as shown by the regulator clock of JOSEPH RAYNES, 43 Central Street.

	From 1st to 10th inclusive.				From 11th to 20th inclusive.				From 21st to last day of month.			
	1st Bell	2d Bell	3d Bell	Eve.Bell	1st Bell	2d Bell	3d Bell	Eve.Bell	1st Bell	2d Bell	3d Bell	Eve.Bell
January,	5.00	6.00	6.50	*7.30	5.00	6.00	6.50	*7.30	5.00	6.00	6.50	*7.30
February,	4.30	5.30	6.40	*7.30	4.30	5.30	6.25	*7.30	4.30	5.30	6.15	*7.30
March,	5.40	6.00		*7.30	5.20	5.40		*7.30	5.05	5.25		6.35
April,	4.45	5.05		6.45	4.30	4.50		6.55	4.30	4.50		7.00
May,	4.30	4.50		7.00	4.30	4.50		7.00	4.30	4.50		7.00
June,	"	"		"	"	"		"	"	"		"
July,	"	"		"	"	"		"	"	"		"
August,	"	"		"	"	"		"	"	"		"
September,	4.40	5.00		6.45	4.50	5.10		6.30	5.00	5.20		*7.30
October,	5.10	5.30		*7.30	5.20	5.40		*7.30	5.35	5.55		*7.30
November,	4.30	5.30	6.10	*7.30	4.30	5.30	6.20	*7.30	5.00	6.00	6.35	*7.30
December,	5.00	6.00	6.45	*7.30	5.00	6.00	6.50	*7.30	5.00	6.00	6.50	*7.30

* Excepting on Saturdays from Sept. 21st to March 20th inclusive, when it is rung at 20 minutes after sunset.

YARD GATES,

Will be opened at ringing of last morning bell, of meal bells, and of evening bells; and kept open Ten minutes.

MILL GATES.

Commence hoisting Mill Gates, Two minutes before commencing work.

WORK COMMENCES,

At Ten minutes after last morning bell, and at Ten minutes after bell which "rings in" from Meals.

BREAKFAST BELLS.

During March "Ring out".........at.....7.30 a. m........."Ring in" at 8:05 a. m.
April 1st to Sept. 20th inclusive.....at.....7.00 " " " .... " " at 7.35 " "
Sept. 21st to Oct. 31st inclusive.....at.....7.30 " " " .... " " at 8.05 " "
Remainder of year work commences after Breakfast.

DINNER BELLS.

" Ring out"...... ....12.30 p. m........."Ring in".... 1.05 p. m.

In all cases, the *first* stroke of the bell is considered as marking the time.

This timetable from the Lowell Mills illustrates the elaborate time schedules that the cotton textile mills expected their employees to meet. For workers, it was difficult to adjust to the regimentation imposed by clock time, in contrast to the approximate times common to preindustrial work.

SOURCE: Baker Library, Graduate School of Business Administration, Harvard University.

position by customary obligation or the formal contract of apprenticeship or journeyman labor. But "free labor" soon came to encompass as well the range of attitudes—hard work, self-discipline, and a striving for economic independence—that were necessary for success in a competitive, industrializing economy. These were profoundly individualistic attitudes, and owners cited them in opposing labor unions and the use of strikes to achieve wage goals (see Chapter 13).

For their part, many workers were inclined to define freedom more collectively, arguing that their just grievances as free American citizens were not being heard. As a group of New Hampshire female workers rhetorically asked, "Why [is] there . . . so much want, dependence and misery among us, if forsooth, we are freemen and freewomen?" Or, as the Lowell strikers of 1836 sang as they paraded through the streets:

> Oh! Isn't it a pity, such a pretty girl as I,
> Should be sent to the factory to pine away and die?
> Oh! I cannot be a slave,
> I will not be a slave,
> For I'm so fond of liberty
> That I cannot be a slave.

Early Strikes

Rural women workers led some of the first strikes in American labor history. In 1824, in one of the first of these actions, women workers at a Pawtucket, Rhode Island, textile mill led their coworkers, female and male, out on strike to protest wage cuts and longer hours.

More famous were the strikes led by the women at the model mill at Lowell. The first serious trouble came in 1834, when 800 women participated in a spontaneous turnout to protest a wage cut of 25 percent. The owners were shocked and outraged by the strike, considering it both unfeminine and ungrateful. The workers, however, were bound together by a sense of sisterhood and were protesting not just the attack on their economic independence, but the blow to their position as "daughters of freemen still." Nevertheless, the wage cuts were enforced, as were more cuts in 1836, again in the face of a turnout. Many women simply packed their clothes in disgust and returned home to the family farm.

Like these strikes, most turnouts by factory workers in the 1830s—male or female—were unsuccessful. Owners, claiming that increasing competition made wage cuts inevitable, were always able to find new workers—Irish immigrants or, after the failed 1837 revolt, French-Canadians for example—who would work at lower wages. The preindustrial notion of a community of interest between owner and workers had broken down and workers, both female and male, began to band together to act on their own behalf. (See Out of Many Voices: A "Mill Girl" Protests.)

A NEW SOCIAL ORDER

The market revolution reached into every aspect of life, down to the most personal family decisions. It also fundamentally changed the social order, creating a new middle class with distinctive habits and beliefs.

Wealth and Class

There had always been social classes in America. Since the early colonial period, planters in the South and merchants in the North had comprised a wealthy elite. Somewhere below the elite but above the mass of people were the "middling sort": a small professional group that included lawyers, ministers, schoolteachers, doctors, public officials, some prosperous farmers, prosperous urban shopkeepers and innkeepers, and a few wealthy artisans such as Boston silversmith Paul Revere. "Mechanics and farmers"—artisans and yeoman farmers—made up another large group, and the laboring poor, consisting of ordinary laborers, servants, and marginal farmers were below them. At the very bottom were the paupers—those dependent on public charity—and the enslaved. This was the "natural" social order that fixed most people in the social rank to which they were born. Although many a male servant in early America aspired to become a small farmer or artisan, he did not usually aspire to become a member of the wealthy elite, nor did serving maids often marry rich men.

The market revolution ended this stable and hierarchical social order, creating the dynamic and unstable one we recognize today: upper, middle, and working classes, whose members all share the hope of climbing as far up the social ladder as they can. This social mobility was new. In the early nineteenth century, the upper class remained about the same in size and composition. In the seacoast cities, as the example of Francis Cabot Lowell showed, the elite was a small, intermarried group, so distinctive in its superior cultural style that in Boston its members were nicknamed "Brahmins" (after the highest caste in India). The expanding opportunities of the market revolution enriched this already rich class: by the 1840s, the top 1 percent of the population owned about 40 percent of the nation's wealth. At the other extreme, fully one-third of the population possessed little more than the clothes they wore and some loose change (see Table 12.2).

The major transformation came in the lives of the "middling sort." The market revolution downgraded many independent artisans but elevated others, like Duncan Phyfe and Stephen Allen of New York. Other formerly independent artisans or farmers (or more frequently, their children) joined the rapidly growing ranks of managers and white-collar workers such as accountants, bank tellers, clerks, bookkeepers, and insurance agents. Occupational opportunities shifted dramatically in just one generation. In Utica, New York, for example, 16 percent of the city's young men held white-collar jobs in 1855, compared with only 6 per-

OUT OF MANY VOICES

A "MILL GIRL" PROTESTS

Sarah Bagley, a Lowell "mill girl" since 1836, came to prominence in 1844 when she founded and led the Lowell Female Reform Association, one of the first women's labor unions in American history. In her efforts on behalf of the ten hour day Bagley wrote for a labor newspaper, organized women's unions in at least five other New England textile mills, and testified before the Massachusetts State legislature. Although today her testimony sounds sedate, Bagley was both militant and daring for her time-in 1845, few women had ever spoken at public meetings.

THE SPECIAL COMMITTEE [OF THE MASSACHUSETTS legislature] to which was referred sundry petitions relating to the hours of labor, have considered the same and submit the following Report:

. . . On the 13th of February, the Committee held a session to hear the petitioners from the city of Lowell. Six of the female and three of the male petitioners were present, and gave in their testimony.

. . . Miss Sarah G. Bagely said she had worked in the Lowell Mills eight years and a half, six years and a half on the Hamilton Corporation, and two years on the Middlesex. She is a weaver, and works by the piece.

She worked in the mills three years before her health began to fail. She is a native of New Hampshire, and went home six weeks during the summer. Last year she was out of the mill a third of the time. She thinks the health of the operatives is not so good as the health of females who do house-work or millinery business. The chief evil, so far as health is concerned, is the shortness of time allowed for meals. The next evil is the length of time employed — not giving them time to cultivate their minds. She spoke of the high moral and intellectual character of the girls. That many were engaged as teachers in the Sunday schools. That many attended the lectures of the Lowell Institute; and she thought, if more time was allowed, that more lectures would be given and more girls attend. She thought that the girls generally were favorable to the ten hour system. She had presented a petition, same as the one before the Committee, to 132 girls, most of whom said that they would prefer to work but ten hours. In a pecuniary point of view, it would be better, as their health would be improved. They would have more time for sewing. Their intellectual, moral and religious habits would also be benefited by the change. Miss Bagely said, in addition to her labor in the mills, she had kept evening school during the winter months, for four years, and thought that this extra labor must have injured her health. ■

SOURCE: Excerpted from *Massachusetts House Document, no. 50, March of 1845.*

---

cent of their fathers. At the same time, 15 percent fewer younger men filled artisanal occupations than older men.

These new white-collar workers owed not only their jobs but their lifestyles to the new structure and organization of industry. The new economic order demanded certain habits and attitudes of workers: sobriety, responsibility, steadiness, and hard work. Inevitably, employers found themselves not only enforcing these new standards but adopting them themselves.

Religion and Personal Life

Religion, which had undergone dramatic changes since the 1790s, played a key role in the emergence of the new attitudes. The Second Great Awakening had supplanted the orderly and intellectual Puritan religion of early New England. The new evangelistic religious spirit, which stressed the achievement of salvation through personal faith, was more democratic and more enthusiastic than the earlier faith. The concept of original sin, the cornerstone of Puritan belief, was replaced by the optimistic belief that a willingness to be saved was enough to ensure salvation. Conversion and repentance were now community experiences, often taking place in huge revival meetings in which an entire congregation focused on the sinners about to be saved. The converted

TABLE 12.2	WEALTH IN NEW YORK CITY, 1828–1845	
Percent of the Population	**Percent of Wealth Held**	
	1828	**1845**
Top 1 percent	40%	50%
Top 4 percent	63	80

The impact of the market revolution on the New York City, the nation's largest seaport, is shown by the dramatic increase in wealth of the already wealthy elite in a period of less than 20 years.

bore a heavy personal responsibility to demonstrate their faith in their own daily lives through morally respectable behavior. In this way, the new religious feeling fostered individualism and self-discipline.

The Second Great Awakening had its greatest initial success on the western frontier in the 1790s, but by the 1820s, evangelical religion was reaching a new audience: the people whose lives were being changed by the market revolution and who needed help in adjusting to the demands made by the new economic conditions. In 1825, in Utica, New York, and other towns along the recently opened Erie Canal, evangelist Charles G. Finney began a series of dramatic revival meetings. His spellbinding message reached both rich and poor, converting members of all classes to the new evangelistic religion. In 1830, made famous by these gatherings, Finney was invited by businessmen to preach in Rochester. Finney preached every day for six months—three times on Sundays—and his wife, Lydia, made home visits to the unconverted and mobilized the women of Rochester for the cause. Under the Finneys' guidance and example, prayer meetings were held in schools and businesses, and impromptu religious services were held in people's homes. (See Out of Many Voices: Charles G. Finney Revives Rochester.)

Middle-class women in particular carried Finney's message by prayer and pleading to the men of their families, who found that evangelism's stress on self-discipline and individual achievement helped them adjust to new business conditions. The enthusiasm and optimism of evangelism aided what was often a profound personal transformation in the face of the market's stringent new demands. Moreover, it gave businessmen a basis for demanding the same behavior from their workers. Businessmen now argued that traditional paternalism had no role in the new business world. Because achievement depended on individual character, each worker was responsible for making his own way.

The New Middle-Class Family

The economic changes of the market revolution reshaped family roles, first in the middle class and eventually throughout the entire society. As men

OUT OF MANY VOICES

CHARLES G. FINNEY REVIVES ROCHESTER

The revival that Charles G. Finney conducted in Rochester in 1830 was so successful that it became the standard to which all subsequent revivals were compared. In his autobiography, written later, Finney describes why he designed the "anxious seat" for the middle class members of his audience.

I HAD NEVER UNTIL I WENT TO ROCHESTER, USED as a means of promoting revivals, what has since been called the anxious seat . . . From my own experience and observation I had found, that with the higher classes especially, the greatest obstacle to be overcome was their fear of being known as anxious inquirers. They were too proud to take any position that would reveal them to others as anxious for their souls.

I had found also that something was needed, to make the impression on them that they were expected at once to give up their hearts; something that would call them to act, and act as publicly before the world, as they had in their sins; something that would commit them publicly to the service of Christ. When I had called them simply to stand up in the public congregations I found that this had a very good effect; . . . [b]ut after all, I had felt for some time, that something more was necessary to bring them out from among the mass of the ungodly, to a public renunciation of their sinful ways, and a public committal of themselves to God.

At Rochester I made a call, I think for the first time, upon all that class of persons whose convictions were so ripe that they were willing to renounce their sins and give themselves to God, to come forward to certain seats which I requested to be vacated, and offer themselves up to God, while we made them subjects of prayer. A much larger number came forward than I expected, and among them was a prominent lady; and several others of her acquaintance, and belonging to the same circle of society, came forward. This increased the interest among that class of people; and it was soon seen that the Lord was aiming at the conversion of the highest classes of society. My meetings soon became thronged with that class. The lawyers, physicians, merchants, and indeed all the most intelligent people, became more and more interested, and more and more easily influenced. ■

SOURCE: Charles G. Finney, *Autobiography* (London: Hodder and Staughton, 1892).

increasingly concentrated their energies on their careers and occupations, women assumed major new responsibilities for rearing the children and inculcating in them the new attitudes necessary for success in the business world. The division of labor that occurred in industry was reflected in the middle-class home: father the breadwinner, mother the nurturer, working together in partnership to raise successful middle-class children.

When the master craftsman became a small manufacturer, or the small subsistence farmer began to manage a large-scale commercial operation, production moved away from both the family home and its members. Husbands and fathers became managers of paid workers—or workers themselves—and although they were still considered the heads of their households, they spent most of the day away from their homes and families. The husband was no longer the undisputed head of a family unit that combined work and personal life. Their wives, on the other hand, remained at home, where they were still responsible for cooking, cleaning, and other domestic tasks but no longer contributed directly to what had previously been the family enterprise. Instead, women took on a new responsibility, that of providing a quiet, well-ordered, and relaxing refuge from the pressures of the industrial world.

Catharine Beecher's *Treatise on Domestic Economy*, first published in 1841, became the standard housekeeping guide for a generation of middle-class American women. In it, Beecher combined innovative ideas for household design (especially in the kitchen, where she introduced principles of organization) with medical information, child-rearing advice, recipes, and numerous discussions of the mother's moral role in the family. The book clearly filled a need: for many pioneer women, it was the only book besides the Bible that they carried west with them.

As the work roles of middle-class men and women diverged, so did social attitudes about appropriate male and female characteristics and behavior. Men were expected to be steady, industrious, responsible, and painstakingly attentive to their business. They had little choice: in the competitive, uncertain, and rapidly changing business conditions of the early nineteenth century, these qualities were essential for men who hoped to hold their existing positions or to get ahead. In contrast, women were expected to be nurturing, gentle, kind, moral, and selflessly devoted to their families. They were expected to operate within the "woman's sphere"—the home.

The maintenance or achievement of a middle-class lifestyle required the joint efforts of husband and wife. More cooperation between them was called for than in the preindustrial, patriarchal family. The nature of the new, companionate marriage that evolved in response to the market revolution was reflected most clearly in decisions concerning children.

Family Limitation

Middle-class couples chose to have fewer children than their predecessors. Children who were being raised to succeed in the middle class placed considerable demands on family resources: They required more care, training, and education than children who could be put to work at traditional tasks at an early age. The dramatic fall in the birthrate during the nineteenth century (from an average of seven children per woman in 1800 to five in 1860) is evidence of conscious decisions about family limitation, first by members of the new middle class and later by working-class families. Few couples used mechanical methods of contraception such as the condom, partly because these were difficult to obtain and partly because most people associated their use with prostitution and the prevention of venereal disease rather than with family planning. Instead, people used birth control methods that relied on mutual consent: coitus interruptus (withdrawal before climax), the rhythm method (intercourse only during the woman's infertile period), and, most often, abstinence or infrequent intercourse.

When mutual efforts at birth control failed, married women often sought a surgical abortion, a new technique that was much more reliable than the folk remedies women had always shared among themselves. Surgical abortions were widely advertised after 1830, and widely used, especially by middle-class married women seeking to limit family size. Some historians estimate that one out of every four pregnancies was aborted in the years 1840–60 (compared to one in six in 2000). The rising rate of abortion by married women (in other words, its use as birth control) prompted the first legal bans; by 1860, twenty states had outlawed the practice.

Accompanying the interest in family limitation was a redefinition of sexuality. Doctors generally recommended that sexual urges be controlled, but they believed that men would have much more difficulty exercising such control than women, partly because they also believed, that women were uninterested in sex. (Women who were visibly interested ran the risk of being considered immoral or "fallen," and thereupon shunned by the middle class.) Medical manuals of the period suggested that it was the task of middle-class women to help their husbands and sons restrain their sexuality by appealing to their higher, moral natures. Although it is always difficult to measure the extent to which the suggestions in advice books were applied in actual practice, it seems that many middle-class women

This middle class family group, painted in 1840, illustrates the new importance of children, and of the mother-child bond.

SOURCE: Frederick Spencer, *Family Group*, 1840. © Francis G. Mayer/CORBIS.

accepted this new and limited definition of their sexuality because of their desire to limit the number of their pregnancies.

Many women of the late eighteenth century wanted to be free of the medical risks and physical debility that too-frequent childbearing brought, but they had little chance of achieving that goal until men became equally interested in family limitation. The rapid change in attitudes toward family size that occurred in the early nineteenth century has been repeated around the world as other societies undergo the dramatic experience of industrialization. It is a striking example of the ways economic changes affect our most private and personal decisions.

Middle-Class Children

Child rearing had been shared in the preindustrial household, boys learning farming or craft skills from their fathers while girls learned domestic skills from their mothers. The children of the new middle class, however, needed a new kind of upbringing, one that involved a long period of nurturing in the beliefs and personal habits necessary for success. Mothers assumed primary responsibility for this training, in part because fathers were too busy but also because people believed that women's superior qualities of gentleness, morality, and loving watchfulness were essential to the task.

Fathers retained a strong role in major decisions concerning children, but mothers commonly turned to other women for advice on daily matters. Through their churches, women formed maternal associations for help in raising their children to be religious and responsible. In Utica, New York, for example, these extremely popular organizations enabled women to form strong networks sustained by mutual advice and by publications such as *Mother's Magazine*, issued by the Presbyterian Church, and *Mother's Monthly Journal*, put out by the Baptists.

Middle-class status required another sharp break with tradition. As late as 1855, artisanal families expected all children over fifteen to work. Middle-class families, in contrast, sacrificed to keep their sons in school or in training for their chosen professions, and they often housed and fed their sons until the young men had "established" themselves financially and could marry. Mothers took the lead in an important informal activity: making sure their children had friends and contacts that would be useful when they were old enough to consider careers and marriage. Matters such as these, rarely considered by earlier generations living in small communities, now became important in the new middle-class communities of America's towns and cities.

Contrary to the growing myth of the self-made man, middle-class success was not a matter of individual achievement. Instead it was usually based on a family strategy in which fathers provided the money and mothers the nurturance. The reorganization of the family described in this section was successful: from its shelter and support emerged generations of ambitious, responsible, and individualistic middle-class men. But although boys were trained for success, this was not an acceptable goal for their sisters. Women were trained to be the nurturing, silent "support system" that undergirded male success. And women were also expected to ease the tensions of the transition to new middle-class behavior by acting as models and monitors of traditional values.

Sentimentalism

The individualistic competitiveness engendered by the market revolution caused members of the new middle class to place extraordinary emphasis on sincerity and feeling. So-called sentimentalism sprang from nostalgia for the imagined trust and security of the familiar, face-to-face life of the preindustrial village. Sermons, advice manuals, and articles now thundered warnings to young men of the dangers and deceits of urban life, and especially of fraudulent "confidence men and painted ladies" who were not what they seemed. Middle-class women were expected to counteract the impersonality and hypocrisy of the business world by the example of their own morality and sincere feeling.

For guidance in this new role, women turned to a new literary form, the sentimental novel. In contrast to older forms like sermons and learned essays, the novel was popular, accessible, and emotionally engrossing. Although denounced by ministers and scholars as frivolous, immoral, and subversive of authority, the novel found a ready audience among American women. Publishers of novels found a lucrative market, one that increased from $2.5 million in 1820 to $12.5 million in 1850. By 1850, *Harper's Magazine* estimated, four-fifths of the reading public were women, and they were reading novels written by women.

To be a "lady novelist" was a new and rather uncomfortably public occupation for women. Several authors, such as Susan Warner, were driven to

In a time before ready-made clothing was available, middle class women used *Godey's Ladies Book* as a pattern book, taking elaborate fashion illustrations such as this one from 1856 to local seamstresses, or remaking older dresses to fit the current trends.
SOURCE: © Bettmann/CORBIS

novel writing when their fathers lost their fortunes in the Panic of 1837. Novel writing could be very profitable: Warner's 1850 novel *The Wide Wide World* went through fourteen editions in two years, and works by other authors such as Lydia Maria Child, Catherine Sedgwick, and E. D. E. N. Southworth sold in the thousands of copies. Sentimental novels concentrated on private life. Religious feeling, antipathy toward the dog-eat-dog world of the commercial economy, and the need to be prepared for unforeseen troubles were common themes. Although the heroines usually married happily at the end of the story, few novels concentrated on romantic love. Most of these domestic novels, as they were known, presented readers with a vision of responsibility and community based on moral and caring family life.

Although sentimentalism originally sprang from genuine fear of the dangers individualism posed to community trust, it rapidly hardened into a rigid code of etiquette for all occasions. Moments of genuine and deep feeling, such as death, were smothered in elaborate rules concerning condolences, expressions of grief, and appropriate clothing. A widow, for example, was expected to wear "deep mourning" for a year—dresses of dull black fabrics and black bonnets covered with long, thick black veils—and in the following year "half mourning"—shiny black silk dresses, perhaps with trim of gray, violet, or white, and hats without veils. Thus sentimentalism rapidly became concerned not with feelings but social codes. Transformed into a set of rules about genteel manners to cover all occasions, sentimentalism itself became a mark of middle-class status. And it became one of the tasks of the middle-class woman to make sure her family conformed to the social code and associated only with other respectable families. In this way, women forged and enforced the distinctive social behavior of the new middle class.

Transcendentalism and Self-Reliance

As the new middle class conformed to the rules of sentimental behavior, it also sought a more general intellectual reassurance. Middle-class men, in particular, needed to feel comfortable about their public assertions of individualism and self-interest. One source of reassurance was the philosophy of transcendentalism and its well-known spokesman, Ralph Waldo Emerson. Originally a Unitarian minister, Emerson quit the pulpit in 1832 and became what one might call a secular minister. Famous as a writer and lecturer, he popularized transcendentalism, a romantic philosophical theory claiming that there was an ideal, intuitive reality transcending ordinary life. The best place to achieve that individual intuition of the Universal Being,

Emerson suggested, was not in church or in society but alone in the natural world. As he wrote in "Nature" (1836), "Standing on the bare ground—my head bathed by the blithe air, and uplifted into infinite space—all mean egotism vanishes. I become a transparent Eyeball; I am nothing; I see all; the currents of the Universal Being circulate through me; I am part and parcel of God." The same assertion of individualism rang through Emerson's stirring polemic "Self-Reliance" (1841). Announcing "Whoso would be a man, must be a nonconformist," Emerson urged that "Nothing is at last sacred but the integrity of your own mind." Inspirational but down-to-earth, Emerson was just the philosopher to inspire young businessmen of the 1830s and 1840s to achieve success in a responsible manner.

Emerson's younger friend, Henry David Thoreau, pushed the implications of individualism farther than the more conventional Emerson. Determined to live the transcendental ideal of association with nature, Thoreau lived in solitude in a primitive cabin for two years at Walden Pond, near Concord, Massachusetts,

Emerson's romantic glorification of nature included the notion of himself as a "transparent eyeball," as he wrote in "Nature" in 1836. This caricature of Emerson is from "Illustrations of the New Philosophy" by Christopher Pearce Cranch.

SOURCE: Library of Congress.

CHRONOLOGY

1790	Samuel Slater's first mill opens in Rhode Island
1793	Cotton gin invented
1798	Eli Whitney contracts with the federal government for 10,000 rifles, which he undertakes to produce with interchangeable parts
1807	Embargo Act excludes British manufactures
1810	Francis Cabot Lowell tours British textile factories
	First steamboat on the Ohio River
1812	Micajah Pratt begins his own shoe business in Lynn, Massachusetts
1813	Francis Cabot Lowell raises $300,000 to build his first cotton textile factory at Waltham, Massachusetts
1815	War of 1812 ends; British competition in manufactures resumes
1816	First protective tariff
1817	Erie Canal Construction begins
1818	National Road completed to Wheeling, Virginia (now West Virginia)
1820s	Large-scale outwork networks develop in New England
1823	Lowell mills open
1824	John Hall successfully achieves interchangeable parts at Harpers Ferry armory
	Women lead strike at Pawtucket textile mill
1825	Erie Canal opens
1830	Baltimore and Ohio Railroad opens
	Charles G. Finney's Rochester revivals
1833	National Road completed to Columbus, Ohio
1834	First strike at Lowell mills
	Cyrus McCormick patents the McCormick reaper
1837	John Deere invents steel plow
1841	Catharine Beecher's *Treatise on Domestic Economy* published
1845	New England Female Labor Reform Association formed

confronting "the essential facts of life." His experience was the basis for *Walden* (1854), a penetrating criticism of the spiritual cost of the market revolution. Denouncing the materialism that led "the mass of men [to] lead lives of quiet desperation," Thoreau recommended a simple life of subsistence living that left time for spiritual thought. Margaret Fuller, perhaps the most intellectually gifted of the transcendental circle, was patronized by Emerson because she was a woman. She expressed her sense of women's wasted potential in her pathbreaking work *Woman in the Nineteenth Century* (1845). Intellectually and emotionally, however, Fuller achieved liberation only when she moved to Europe and participated in the liberal Italian revolution of 1848. The romantic destiny she sought was tragically fulfilled when she, her Italian husband, and their child died in a shipwreck off the New York coast as they returned to America in 1850.

Although Thoreau and Fuller were too radical for many readers, Emerson's version of the romantic philosophy of transcendentalism, seemingly so at odds with the competitive and impersonal spirit of the market revolution, was in fact an essential component of it. Individualism, or, as Emerson called it, self-reliance, was at the heart of the personal transformation required by the market revolution. Sentimentalism, transcendentalism, and evangelical religion all helped the new middle class to forge values and beliefs that were appropriate to their social roles.

CONCLUSION

The three transformations of the Market Revolution: improvements in transportation, commercialization, and industrialization changed the ways people worked, and in time, changed how they thought.

For most people, the changes were gradual. Until midcentury, the lives of rural people were still determined largely by community events, although the spread of democratic politics and the availability of newspapers and other printed material increased their connection to a larger world. Wage earners made up only 40 percent of the working population in 1860, and factory workers made up an even smaller percentage.

The new middle class was most dramatically affected by the market revolution. All aspects of life, including intimate matters of family organization, gender roles, and the number and raising of children, changed. New values—evangelical religion, sentimentalism, and transcendentalism—helped the members of the new middle class in their adjustment. As the next chapter describes, the nation's cities were the first arena where old and new values collided.

REVIEW QUESTIONS

1. What changes in preindustrial life and work were caused by the market revolution?
2. This chapter argues that when people begin doing new kinds of work, their beliefs and attitudes change. Give three examples of such changes described in the chapter. Can you think of other examples?
3. Discuss the opinion offered by historian David Potter that mass production has been an important democratizing force in American politics. Do you agree? Why or why not?
4. Consider the portrait of the nineteenth-century middle-class family offered in this chapter and imagine yourself as a member of such a family. What new aspects of family relations would you welcome? Which would be difficult? Why?

RECOMMENDED READING

Christopher Clark, *The Roots of Rural Capitalism: Western Massachusetts, 1780–1860* (1990). The most thorough examination to date of how the commercial spirit changed rural life.

Ian R. Bartky, *Selling the True Time: Nineteenth-Century Timekeeping in America* (2000). How a national system of uniform time came about.

Peter L. Bernstein, *Wedding of the Waters: The Erie Canal and the Making of a Great Nation* (2005). The economic consequences of one of the first public works projects.

Martin Bruegel, *Farm, Shop, Landing: The Rise of a Market Society in the Hudson Valley, 1780–1860* (2002). Shows how one rural region made the transition to capitalism.

Alan Dawley, *Class and Community: The Industrial Revolution in Lynn* (1976). A pathbreaking study of the shift from artisanal to wage labor.

Thomas Dublin, *Transforming Women's Work: New England Lives in the Industrial Revolution* (1994). A thoughtful study of the effects of women's outwork.

Paul W. Gates, *The Farmer's Age: Agriculture, 1815–1860* (1966). The standard source on the growth of commercial agriculture.

Karen Halttunen, *Confidence Men and Painted Women: A Study of Middle-Class Culture in America* (1982). Shows the importance of sentimentalism to the new middle class.

David Houndshell, *From the American System to Mass Production, 1800–1932* (1984). How an entire network of New England "mechanics" contributed to the invention of interchangeable parts.

Paul Johnson, *Sam Patch, the Famous Jumper* (2003) Johnson uses the story of Patch, famous for plunging over Niagara Falls, to explore the bumpy transition from independent artisan to wage worker.

Jonathan Prude, *The Coming of Industrial Order: Town and Factory Life in Rural Massachusetts, 1810–1860* (1983). A major source of information on family mills.

Mary Ryan, *The Making of the Middle Class* (1981). A study of Utica, New York, demonstrating the role of women in the family strategies of the new middle class.

Charles Sellers, *The Market Revolution: Jacksonian America, 1815–1846* (1991). A synthesis of the political, religious, and economic change of the period.

Carol Sheriff, *The Artificial River: The Erie Canal and the Paradox of Progress, 1817–1862* (1996). Shows how the building of the canal changed personal lives and fostered religious beliefs in human perfectability.

Janet Siskind, *Rum and Axes: The Rise of a Connecticut Merchant Family, 1795–1850* (2002). How one merchant family became industrialists.

George Rogers Taylor, *The Transportation Revolution, 1815–1860* (1951). The indispensable book on all aspects of the American economy during this period.

 For additional study resources for this chapter, go to the *Companion Website,* http://www.prenhall.com/faragher.

Coming to Terms with the New Age

1820s–1850s

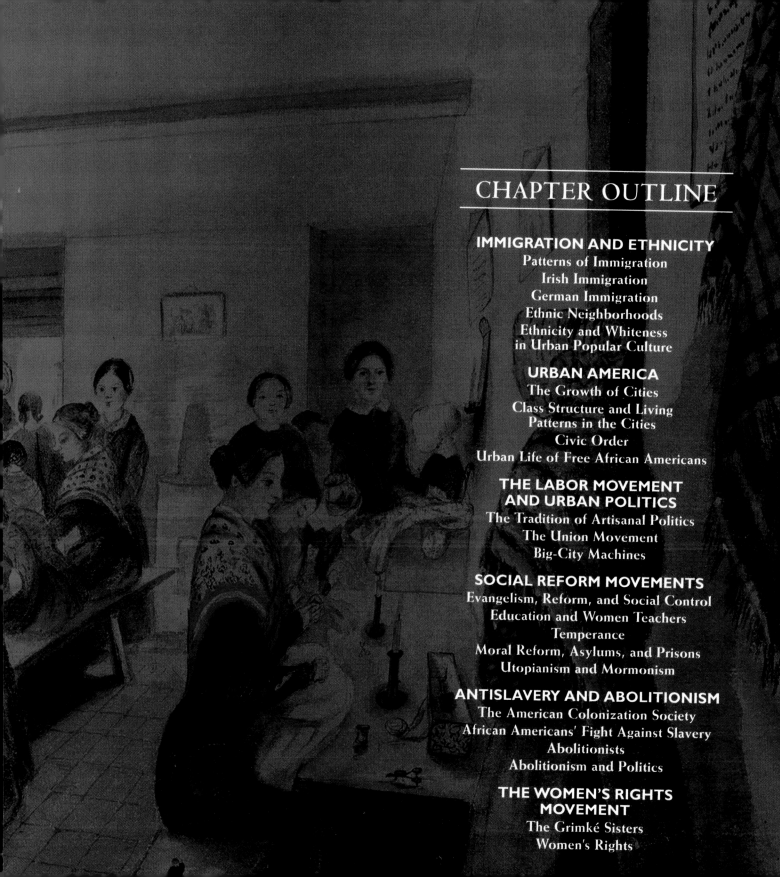

Women Reformers of Seneca Falls
Respond to the Market Revolution

In the summer of 1848, Charlotte Woodward, a nineteen-year-old glove maker who did outwork in her rural home, saw a small advertisement in an upstate New York newspaper announcing a "convention to discuss the social, civil, and religious condition and rights of woman," to be held at Seneca Falls on July 19 and 20. Woodward persuaded six friends to join her in the forty-mile journey to the convention. "At first we travelled quite alone," she recalled. "But before we had gone many miles we came on other wagon-loads of women, bound in the same direction. As we reached different crossroads we saw wagons coming from every part of the country, and long before we reached Seneca Falls we were a procession."

To the surprise of the convention organizers, almost 300 people—men as well as women—attended the two-day meeting, which focused on the Declaration of Sentiments, a petition for women's rights modeled on the Declaration of Independence. "We hold these truths to be self-evident," it announced: "That all men and women are created equal." As the Declaration of Independence detailed the oppressions King George III had imposed on the colonists, the Declaration of Sentiments detailed, in a series of resolutions, the oppressions men had imposed on women. Men had deprived women of legal rights, of the right to own their own property, of custody of their children in cases of divorce, of the right to higher education (at that time only Oberlin College and Mount Holyoke Female Seminary admitted women), of full participation in religious worship and activity, and of the right to vote.

The attendees approved all the resolutions unanimously all but the last of them, which a minority found too radical. "Why Lizzie, thee will make us ridiculous!" Quaker Lucretia Mott had exclaimed when Elizabeth Cady Stanton proposed the voting rights measure. Indeed the newspapers reporting on the convention thought the demand for the vote was ridiculously unfeminine. Undeterred, and buoyed by the success of this first women's rights convention, the group promptly planned another convention to reach new supporters and develop strategies to implement their resolutions.

The struggle for women's rights was only one of many reform movements that emerged in the United States in the wake of the economic and social disruptions of the market revolution that deeply affected regions like Seneca Falls. A farming frontier in 1800, it had been drawn into national commerce in 1828, when it was reached by an offshoot of the Erie Canal. It was drawn even further into the modern age when the railroad arrived in 1841. A village of 200 in 1824, Seneca Falls had grown to a town of over 4,000 by 1842. It was now a center for flour milling and manufacturing, and a hub of the outwork network of which Charlotte Woodward was a part. Swamped by newcomers (among them a growing number of poor Irish Catholics), the inhabitants of

Seneca Falls

to counteract the effects of industrialization, rapid growth, and the influx of newcomers.

Many reformers belonged to liberal religious groups with wide social perspectives. Perhaps a third of those attending the women's rights convention, for example, were members of the Wesleyan Methodist Society of Seneca Falls, which had broken with the national Methodist organization because it would not take a strong stand against slavery. Another quarter were Progressive Quakers of the nearby town of Waterloo, who had broken with their national organization for the same reason. Both groups were outspoken in their belief in the moral equality of all humankind and in their commitment to social activism. The Wesleyans, for example, resolved in 1847 that "we cannot identify our Christian and moral character with societies where women and colored persons are excluded." Seneca Falls had been the site of a "Temperance Reformation" in the early 1840s, and many attendees at the Women's Rights convention were also active in the temperance movement, a more limited but extremely popular reform cause dedicated to promoting abstinence from alcohol.

The idea for the Women's Rights convention emerged during a meeting in early July 1848, between Lucretia Mott—a Philadelphia Quaker and the nation's best-known woman reformer—and Elizabeth Cady Stanton of Seneca Falls, wife of a well-known antislavery orator. Reflecting her many concerns, Mott had just finished a tour of the new penitentiary at Auburn and a nearby Indian reservation, and was visiting her sister in Waterloo. Stanton renewed her acquaintance with Mott, and, in this context of friendship and shared concern for reform, the two began planning the convention.

Stanton and her family had moved from Boston, where, she remembered, they had "near neighbors, a new home with all the modern conveniences, and well-trained servants." Living in a house on the outskirts of Seneca Falls, her three children suffering from malaria, she had none of those things. "I now fully understood," she mused,

> the practical difficulties most women had to contend with. . . . The general discontent I felt with woman's portion as wife, mother, housekeeper, physician and spiritual guide, the chaotic condi-

tions into which everything fell without her constant supervision, and the wearied anxious look of the majority of women impressed me with a strong feeling that some active measures should be taken to remedy the wrongs of society in general, and of women in particular.

As she and Mott spoke of the changes that would be necessary to allow women to care for their families but have energy left over to reform "the wrongs of society," the idea of a women's rights convention was born. The women's rights movement that took shape from this convention proved exceptionally long-lasting. Stanton, soon to form a working partnership with former temperance worker Susan B. Anthony, devoted the rest of her life to women's rights.

But what of Charlotte Woodward, a local farm girl, unaware of the national reform community? Why was she there? In this age of hopefulness and change, she wanted a better life for herself. She was motivated, she said, by "all the hours that I sat and sewed gloves for a miserable pittance, which, after it was earned, could never be mine." By law and custom, her father, as head of the household, was entitled to her wages. "I wanted to work," she explained, "but I wanted to choose my task and I wanted to collect my wages." The reforming women of Seneca Falls, grouped together on behalf of social improvement, had found in the first women's rights convention a way to speak for the needs of working women such as Charlotte Woodward.

All over the North, in communities like Seneca Falls as well as in cities like New York, Americans gathered together in reform organizations to try to solve the problems that the market revolution posed for work, family life, personal and social values, and urban growth. Through these organizations, local women and men became participants in wider communities of social concern, but in spite of their best efforts, they were rarely able to settle the issues that had brought them together. The aspirations of some, among them women, free blacks, and immigrants, clashed with the social control agendas of other groups. In this fervent atmosphere of reform, many problems were raised but few were resolved.

KEY TOPICS

- The new social problems that accompanied urbanization and immigration
- The responses of reformers
- The origins and political effects of the abolitionist movement
- The involvement of women in reform efforts

IMMIGRATION AND ETHNICITY

Although the market revolution affected all aspects of American life, nowhere was its impact so noticeable as in the cities. It was primarily in cities that the startlingly large number of new immigrants clustered.

Patterns of Immigration

One of the key aspects of urban growth was a surge in immigration to the United States that began in the 1820s and accelerated dramatically after 1830. From an annual figure of about 20,000 in 1831, immigration ballooned to a record 430,000 in 1854 before declining in the years prior to the Civil War. The proportion of immigrants in the population jumped from 1.6 percent in the 1820s to 11.2 percent in 1860. In the nation's cities, the proportion was vastly larger: by 1860, nearly half of New York's population (48 percent) was foreign-born (see Map 13.1).

Most of the immigrants to the United States during this period came from Ireland and Germany. Political unrest and poor economic conditions in Germany, and the catastrophic Potato Famine of 1845–1849 in Ireland were responsible for an enormous surge in immigration from those countries between 1845 and 1854. The starving, desperate "Famine Irish" who crowded into eastern seaports were America's first large refugee group. Between them, the Germans and the Irish represented the largest influx of non-English immigrants the country had known (many Americans found the Irish dialect as strange as a foreign language). They were also the poorest: most of the Irish arrived destitute. In addition, most of the Irish and half of the Germans were Catholics, an unwelcome novelty that provoked a nativist backlash among some Protestant Americans (see Chapter 15).

It would be a mistake, however, to think that immigration was unwelcome to everyone. Industries needed willing workers, and western states, among them Wisconsin, Iowa and Minnesota, actively advertised in Europe for settlers. Many of the changes in industry and transportation that accompanied the market revolution would have been impossible without immigrants. Irish contract workers, for example, were essential to the completion of the Erie Canal in 1825. And Irish women and men kept the mills at Lowell operating when the mill operators, facing increasing competition, sought cheaper labor to replace their original labor force of farm women.

Few immigrants found life in the United States pleasant or easy. In addition to the psychological difficulties of leaving a home and familiar ways behind, most immigrants endured harsh living and working conditions. America's cities were unprepared for the social problems posed by large numbers of immigrants. Until the 1880s, the task of receiving immigrants fell completely on cities and states, not the federal government. New York City, by far the largest port of entry, did not even establish an official reception center until 1855, when Castle Garden, at the bottom of Manhattan Island (near present-day Battery Park), was so designated.

Irish Immigration

The first major immigrant wave to test American cities was caused by the catastrophic Irish Potato Famine of 1845–49. The Irish, held in unwilling colonial status by the British, subsisted poorly on small plots of farmland on which they grew grain for British landlords and potatoes for their own food. Irish emigration to the United States dated from colonial times; young people who knew they could not hope to own land in Ireland had long looked to America for better opportunities. Indeed, from 1818 to 1845, at least 10,000 Irish emigrated yearly. But in the latter year, Ireland's green fields of potato plants turned black with blight. The British government could not cope with the scale of the disaster. The Irish had two choices: starve or leave. One million people died, and another 1.5 million emigrated, the majority to the United States. Starving, diseased (thousands died of typhus during the voyage), and destitute, hundreds of thousands (250,000 in 1851 alone) disembarked in the east coast ports of New York, Philadelphia, Boston, and Baltimore. Lacking the money to go inland and begin farming, they remained in the cities. Crowded together

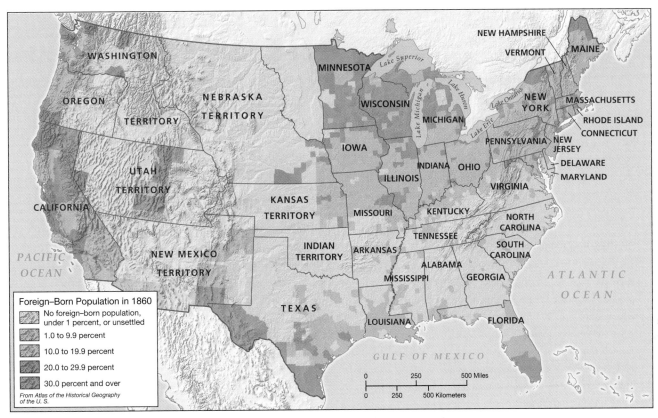

MAP 13.1 Distribution of Foreign-Born Residents of United States in 1860 The ethnic composition of the American population was increased by Irish and German immigration in the 1840s and 1850s, Chinese attraction to the California gold rush, Mormon recruitment of Scottish and English followers to Utah, and the reclassification of Mexicans after the Mexican-American War as foreigners in what had been their own lands.

in miserable housing, desperate for work at any wages, foreign in their religion and pastimes (drinking and fighting, their critics said), tenaciously nationalistic and bitterly anti-British, they created ethnic enclaves of a kind new to American cities. (See Out of Many Voices: Anna Gavin: An Irishwoman's Memories.)

The largest numbers of Irish came to New York, which managed to absorb them. But Boston, a much smaller and more homogeneous city, was overwhelmed by the Irish influx. By 1850, a quarter of Boston's population was Irish, most of them recent immigrants. Boston, the home of Puritanism and the center of American intellectualism, did not welcome illiterate Irish Catholic peasants. All over the city, in places of business and in homes normally eager for domestic servants, the signs went up: "No Irish Need Apply."

German Immigration

Germans, like the Irish, had a long history of emigration to America. William Penn, impressed by the industriousness of Germans, had taken pains to invite them to immigrate to the colony he founded, and by 1790, they

made up one-third of Pennsylvania's population. The nineteenth-century immigration of Germans began somewhat later and more slowly than that of the Irish, but by 1854, it had surpassed the Irish influx. Some German peasants, like the Irish, were driven from their homeland by potato blight in the mid-1840s. But the typical German immigrant was a small farmer or artisan dislodged by the same market forces at work in America: the industrialization of production and consolidation, and the commercialization of farming. There was also a small group of middle-class liberal intellectuals who left the German states (Germany was not yet a unified nation) after 1848 when attempts at revolution had failed. Among these individuals was Carl Schurz, who rose to become a general in the Union Army, a senator from Missouri, and secretary of the interior in the administration of Rutherford B. Hayes. On the whole, German migrants were not as poor as the Irish, and they could afford to move out of the east coast seaports to other locations. Nevertheless, like the Irish, they formed their own communities and initially encountered American hostility for their "foreign" ways.

OUT OF MANY VOICES

ANNA GAVIN: AN IRISHWOMAN'S MEMORIES

Few personal memoirs from Irish immigrants of this period survive, but the combined effects of the Famine Exodus and the hostile American reception were felt in later generations, as William Alfred's memoir of his great-grandmother Anna Maria Gavin, attests.

OF IRELAND SHE RARELY SPOKE, SAVE TO RECALL that she was often hungry there and that for her main meal she often ate cress out of the brooks on oaten bread with a bit of lard. Although she always used to say she had no desire to return to Ireland to live, she lived out of a trunk to her dying day, and taught her children to do the same. I myself, till well on in my twenties, felt that Ireland, which I had never seen, was my true country. When, over eighty, she died, it did not seem strange six months afterward to receive a slipping from an Irish newspaper, which read: "Died in Exile: Anna Maria Gavin Egan."

Of her first years here, she never tired of speaking. She and her mother landed at Castle Garden and walked up Broadway to City Hall, with bundles of clothes and pots and featherbeds in their arms. The singing of the then exposed telegraph wires frightened them, as did the bustle of the people in the streets. They lost their fear when they met an Irish policeman who directed them to a rooming house on Baxter Street.

Her training as a "manty-maker" (mantua-maker, in other words, dressmaker) gave her an advantage over other girls of her age. She got a job fast. On her way from work the first year, she nightly passed a house in whose tall, lit first-floor windows sat the most beautiful women she had ever seen, dressed to the nines, their hair as trimly curled, their faces painted fresh as new French china dolls. After weeks of gawking, she built up the courage to hazard a smile. "Come up here, you blonde bitch," one of the women called to her, "and we'll wipe that smile off your face." (It was a brothel). ■

SOURCE: William Alfred, "An Irish Integrity," in Thomas C. Wheeler, ed., *The Immigrant Experience: The Anguish of Becoming American* (New York: Viking Press, 1972).

The first two major ports of embarkation for the Germans were Bremen (in northern Germany) and Le Havre (in northern France), which were also the main ports for the importation of American tobacco and cotton. The tobacco boats bore the Bremen passengers to Baltimore, and the cotton ships took them to New Orleans, a major entry point for European immigrants until the Civil War. From these ports, many Germans made their way up the Mississippi and Ohio valleys, where they settled in Pittsburgh, Cincinnati, and St. Louis and on farms in Ohio, Indiana, Missouri, and Texas. In Texas, the nucleus of a German community began with a Mexican land grant in the 1830s. Few Germans settled either in northeastern cities or in the South.

German agricultural communities took a distinctive form that fostered cultural continuity. Immigrants formed predominantly German towns by clustering, or taking up adjoining land. A small cluster could support German churches, German-language schools, and German customs and thereby attract other Germans, some directly from Europe and some from other parts of the United States. Such communities reinforced the traditional values of German farmers, such as persistence, hard work,

and thrift. Non-German neighbors often sold out and moved on, but the Germans stayed and improved the land so they could pass it on to the next generation. They used soil conservation practices that were unusual for the time. Persistence paid: German cluster communities exist to this day in Texas, the Midwest, and the Pacific Northwest, and families of German origin are still the single largest ethnic group in agriculture.

Another area attracting immigrants in the early nineteenth century was Gold Rush California, which drew, among others, numbers of Chinese (see Chapter 14). The Chinese who came to California worked in the mines, most as independent prospectors. Other miners disliked their industriousness and their clannishness. One reporter noted groups of twenty or thirty "Chinamen, stools, tables, cooking utensils, bunks, etc., all huddled up together in indiscriminate confusion, and enwreathed with dense smoke, inhabiting close cabins, so small that one would not be of sufficient size to allow a couple of Americans to breathe in it." By the mid-1860s, Chinese workers made up 90 percent of the laborers building the Central Pacific Railroad, replacing more expensive white laborers and sowing the seeds of the long-lasting hostility of American workers toward Chinese. In the meantime, however, San Francisco's Chinatown, the oldest Chinese ethnic enclave in America, became a well-established, thriving community and a refuge in times of anti-Chinese violence.

Ethnic Neighborhoods

Ethnic neighborhoods were not limited to the Chinese. Almost all new immigrants preferred to live in neighborhoods where they could find not only family ties and familiar ways, but community support as they learned how to survive in new surroundings. Isolated partly by their own beliefs (for Catholics fully reciprocated the hatred and fear that Protestants had showed them), Irish immigrants created their own communities in Boston and New York, their major destinations. They raised the money to erect Catholic churches with Irish priests. They established parochial schools with Irish nuns as teachers and sent their children to them in preference to the openly anti-Catholic public schools. They formed mutual aid societies based on kinship or town of origin in Ireland. Men and women formed religious and social clubs, lodges, and brotherhoods and their female auxiliaries. Irishmen manned fire and militia companies as well. This dense network of associations served the same purpose that social welfare organizations do today: providing help in time of need and offering companionship in a hostile environment.

Germans who settled in urban areas also built their own ethnic enclaves—"Little Germanies"—in which they sought to duplicate the rich cultural life of German cities. In general, German immigrants were skilled workers and not as poor as the Irish. Like the Irish,

From a print loaned by the Chicago Abendpost

Wright's Grove, shown here in an 1868 illustration, was the popular picnic grounds and beer garden for the large German community on Chicago's North Side. Establishments such as this horrified American temperance advocates, who warned about the dangerous foreign notion of mixing alcohol with family fun.

SOURCE: Chicago Historical Society.

however, the Germans formed church societies, mutual benefit societies, and fire and militia companies to provide mutual support. Partly because their communities were more prosperous than those of the Irish, the Germans also formed a network of leisure organizations: singing societies, debating and political clubs, concert halls like New York's Beethoven Hall, theaters, turnvereins (gymnastics associations), and beer gardens. They published German-language newspapers as well.

Ethnic clustering, then, allowed new immigrants to hold onto aspects of their culture that they valued and to transplant them to American soil. Many native-born Americans, however, viewed ethnic neighborhoods with deep suspicion. The *Boston American* expressed the sentiments of many in 1837 when it remarked:

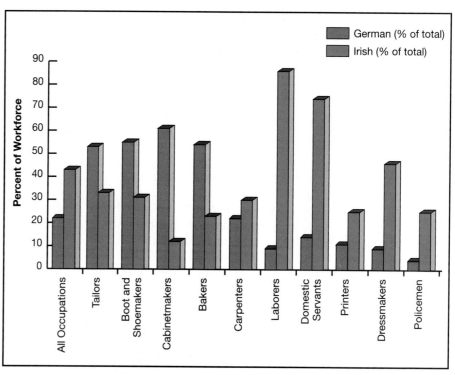

FIGURE 13.1 **Participation of Irish and German Immigrants in the New York City Workforce for Selected Occupations, 1855**

SOURCE: Robert Ernst, *Immigrant Life in New York City 1825–1863* (Syracuse: Syracuse University Press, 1994).

our foreign population are too much in the habit of retaining their own national usages, of associating too exclusively with each other, and living in groups together. It would be the part of wisdom, to ABANDON AT ONCE ALL USAGES AND ASSOCIATIONS WHICH MARK THEM AS FOREIGNERS, and to become in feeling and custom, as well as in privileges and rights, citizens of the United States.

Ethnicity and Whiteness in Urban Popular Culture

Immigrants to American cities contributed to a new urban popular culture, with New York, the largest city, leading the way. In the period 1820–60, New York experienced the replacement of artisanal labor by wagework, two serious depressions (1837–43 and 1857), and a vast influx of immigrant labor (see Figure 13.1). In response to these pressures, working-class amusements became rougher and rowdier. Taverns that served as neighborhood centers of drink and sociability were also frequent centers of brawls and riots. Community groups such as fire engine companies that had once included men of all social classes now attracted rough young laborers who formed their own youth gangs and defended "their" turf against other gangs. Some trades, such as that of

butcher, became notorious for starting fights in taverns and grog shops.

Irish immigrants, in particular, faced not only employment discrimination but persistent cultural denigration. It was common for newspapers of the time to caricature the Irish as monkeys, similar to the way cartoonists portrayed African Americans. The Irish response, which was to insist on their "whiteness," played itself out in urban popular culture in violence and mockery.

Theaters, which had been frequented by men of all social classes, provided another setting for violence. Few women, except for the prostitutes who met their customers in the third tier of the balcony, attended. In the 1820s, a long-standing tradition of small-scale rioting by poorer patrons against unpopular actors began to change into more serious violence. The Astor Place Riot of 1849 began as a theater riot by Irish immigrants and others against a British actor, but escalated into a pitched battle between the mob and the militia that left twenty-two dead.

By the 1830s, middle-class and upper-class men withdrew to more respectable theaters to which they could bring their wives and daughters, and workers found new amusements in theaters such as the Lafayette Circus, which featured dancing girls and horseback riders as well as theatrical acts. Another popular urban working-class amusement was the blackface minstrel show. White actors (often

Irish) blacked their faces and entertained audiences with songs (including the famous "Dixie," written by an Irishman as a blackface song), dances, theatrical skits, and antiblack political jokes. Cruel stereotypes such as Zip Coon, an irresponsible free black man, and Jim Crow, a slow-witted slave, entertained white audiences. Historians have speculated that the popularity of blackface expressed not only white racism but also nostalgia for the freer behavior of preindustrial life that was now impossible for white workers but that they imagined African American slaves continued to enjoy in carefree dependency.

The new working-class culture flourished especially on the Bowery, a New York City street filled with workshops, small factories, shops with cheap goods, dance halls, theaters, ice cream parlors, and oyster bars. Here working-class youth, the "Bowery b'hoys" (slang pronunciation of "boys") and "gals," found Saturday night amusements and provided it for themselves with outrageous clothing and behavior. The deliberately provocative way they dressed was, in effect, a way of thumbing their noses at the more respectable classes. The costumes worn by the characters in one long-running series of melodramas staged by the Bowery Theater imitated this style. Mose, the hero of the series, dressed more like a pirate captain than a worker, and his gal Lise wore a bright-colored, body-hugging dress that challenged the discreet, sober fashions worn by middle-class women.

URBAN AMERICA

It was within the new urban environment, with its stimulating and frightening confusion of rapid growth, occupational and ethnic change, and economic competition that new American political and social forms began to emerge.

The Growth of Cities

The market revolution dramatically increased the size of America's cities, with the great seaports leading the way. The proportion of America's population living in cities increased from only 7 percent in 1820 to almost 20 percent in 1860, a rate of growth greater than at any other time in the country's history.

The nation's five largest cities in 1850 were the same as in 1800, with one exception. New York, Philadelphia, Baltimore, and Boston still topped the list, but New Orleans had edged out Charleston (see Chapters 9 and 11). The rate of urban growth was extraordinary. All four Atlantic seaports grew at least 25 percent each decade between 1800 and

IRISH EMIGRANT.

Patrick, (just landing.) "BY MY SOWL, YOU'RE BLACK, OLD FELLOW! HOW LONG HAVE YE BIN HERE?"
Nigger, (imitatng the brogue.) "JIST THREE MONTHS, MY HONEY!"
Pat. "BY THE POWERS, I'LL GO BACK TO TIPPERARY IN A JIFFY! I'D NOT BE SO BLACK AS THAT FUR ALL THE WHISKEY IN ROSCREA!"

This cartoon encounter between a newly arrived Irishman and an African American expresses the fear of many immigrants that they would be treated like blacks and denied the privileges of whiteness.

SOURCE: *Irish Emigrant* in *Diogenes, Hys Lantern*, August 23, 1852, p. 158. From *How the Irish Became White* by Noel Ignatiev, p. 33, Routledge, ©1995.

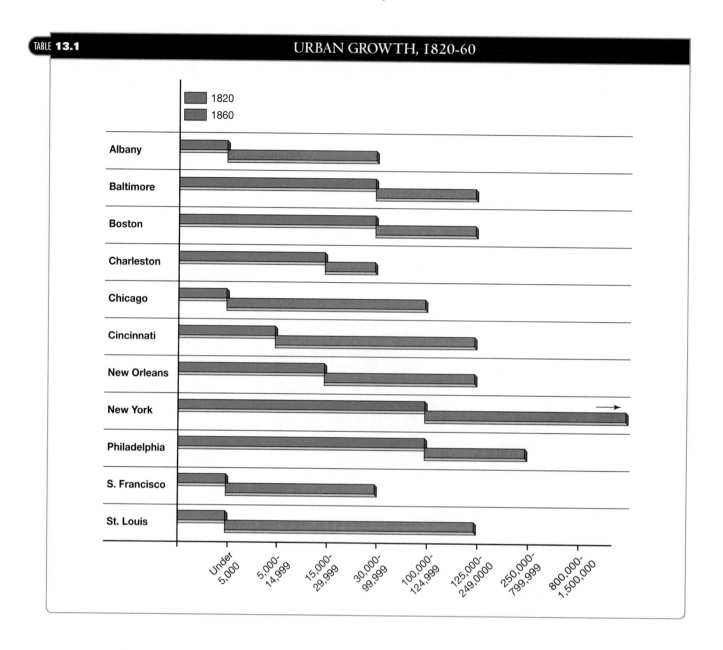

TABLE 13.1   URBAN GROWTH, 1820-60

1860, and often much more. New York, which grew from 60,000 in 1800 to 202,600 in 1830 and to more than 1 million in 1860, emerged as the nation's most populous city, its largest port, and its financial center. Between 1820 and 1830, the decade in which the Erie Canal added commerce with the American interior to the city's long-standing international trade, New York's population grew 64 percent.

Another result of the market revolution was the appearance of "instant" cities at critical points on the new transportation network. Utica, New York, once a frontier trading post, was transformed by the opening of the Erie Canal into a commercial and manufacturing center. By 1850, the city's population had reached 22,000. Chicago, on the shores of Lake Michigan, was transformed by the coming of the railroad into a major junction for water

and rail transport. By 1860, Chicago had a population of 100,000, making it the nation's eighth largest city after Cincinnati and St. Louis (see Table 13.1).

Class Structure and Living Patterns in the Cities

The preindustrial cities of eighteenth-century America had been small and compact "walking cities," in which people, rich and poor, lived near their work in a dense, small-scale housing pattern that fostered neighborliness and the mingling of social classes. The growth caused by immigration changed the character of urban life by sharpening class differences.

Although per capita income in America is estimated to have doubled between 1800 and 1850, the gap between rich and poor increased and became glaringly apparent in the nation's cities. The benefits of the market revolution were unequally distributed: by the 1840s, the top 1 percent of the population owned about 40 percent of the nation's wealth, while, at the other extreme, one-third of the population owned virtually nothing. In the cities, then, there was a very small group of wealthy people with a net worth of more than $5,000 (about 3 percent of the population), a very large group of poor people with a net worth of $100 or less (nearly 70 percent), and a middle class with incomes in between (25–30 percent).

Differences in income affected every aspect of urban life. Very poor families, including almost all new immigrants, performed unskilled labor in jobs where the future was uncertain at best, lived in cheap rented housing, moved frequently, and depended on more than one income to survive. Artisans and skilled workers with incomes of $500 or more could live adequately, though often in cramped quarters that also served as their shops.

A middle-class family with an income of more than $1,000 a year could live comfortably in a house of four to six rooms complete with carpeting, wallpaper, and good furniture. The very rich built mansions and large town houses and staffed them with many servants. In the summer, they left the cities for country estates or homes at seaside resorts such as Newport, Rhode Island, which attracted wealthy families from all over the country.

Early nineteenth-century cities lacked municipal water supplies, sewers, and garbage collection. People drank water from wells, used outdoor privies that often contaminated the water supply, and threw garbage and slop out the door to be foraged by roaming herds of pigs. Clearly, this was a recipe for disease, and every American city suffered epidemics of sanitation-related diseases such as yellow fever, cholera, and typhus. Philadelphia's yellow fever epidemic of 1793 caused 4,000 deaths and stopped all business with the outside world for more than a month. Major cholera epidemics

The Five Points neighborhood in lower Manhattan illustrates the segregated housing patterns that emerged as New York City experienced rapid growth. Immigrants, free African Americans, the poor, and criminals were crowded together in New York's most notorious slum, while wealthier people moved to more prosperous neighborhoods.

SOURCE: 1859 lithograph; The Granger Collection.

GREAT RIOT AT THE ASTOR PLACE OPERA HOUSE, NEW YORK.

ON THURSDAY EVENING MAY 10TH 1849

In 1849 a rather commonplace riot broke out at the Astor Place Theater when Irish members of the audience objected to a British actor. This riot, however, spiraled into 36 hours of violence and 22 fatalities, quelled only when city officials, for the first time, called in the Army to control it.

SOURCE: *Great Riot at the Astor Place Opera House, New York, Thursday Evening, May 10, 1849.* Publisher: N. Currier, 1849. Museum of the City of New York. The Harry T. Peters Collection. 56.300.377.

ravaged New York in 1832 and 1849, and New Orleans suffered repeated attacks of cholera and yellow fever.

Yet the cities were slow to take action. In part, this was due to poor medical understanding of disease but at least equally to expense. In response to the yellow fever epidemic, Philadelphia completed a city water system in 1801, but users had to pay a fee, and only the richest subscribed in the early days. Neither New York nor Boston had a public water system until the 1840s. Garbage collection remained a private service, and cities charged property owners for the costs of sewers, water mains, and street paving. Poorer areas of the cities could not afford the costs. When disease struck, wealthier people simply left the cities, leaving the poor to suffer the brunt of disease.

Provision of municipal services forced residential segregation. Richer people clustered in neighborhoods that had the new amenities. One of New York's first wealthy areas, Gramercy Park, was developed in 1831 by a speculator who transformed what had been Gramercy

Farm into "an ornamental private square or park, with carriageways and footwalks." Only purchasers of the surrounding lots had keys to the park; everyone else was excluded. By the 1850s, the middle class began to escape cities completely by moving to the new "streetcar suburbs," named for the new mode of urban transportation that connected these nearby areas to the city itself.

As the middle class left the city, the poor clustered in bad neighborhoods that became known as slums. The worst New York slum in the nineteenth century was Five Points, a stone's throw from City Hall. There, immigrants, free black people, and criminals were crammed into rundown buildings known in the slang of the time as "rookeries." Notorious gangs of thieves and pickpockets with names such as the Plug Uglies and the Shirt Tails dominated the district. Starvation and murder were commonplace.

With the influx of European immigrants after 1830, middle-class Americans increasingly saw slums as the home of strange and foreign people, who deserved less than American-born citizens. In this way, residential patterns came to embody larger issues of class and citizenship. Even disease itself was blamed on immigrants. When cholera epidemics, for example, disproportionately struck slum dwellers, well-to-do New Yorkers assumed that it must be the fault of the people in the slums. As banker John Pintard reasoned in 1832, the cholera epidemic must be God's judgment on "the lower classes of intemperate dissolute and filthy people huddled together like swine in their polluted habitations."

Civic Order

The challenges to middle-class respectability posed by new immigrants and unruly workers were fostered and publicized by the immensely popular "penny papers," which began publication in 1833, and by the rapidly growing number of political papers (see Chapter 11). This exuberant urban popular culture was unquestionably a part of the same new democratic political spirit that led to the great upsurge in political participation discussed in Chapter 10. And it was the inspiration for some of America's most innovative writers, foremost among them urban journalist, Democratic Party activist, and poet Walt Whitman, who distilled his passionate love for the variety and commonness of the American people in *Leaves of Grass*, a book of free-verse poems published in 1855. Regarded at the time as scandalous because of its frank language, Whitman's poetry nevertheless captured the driving energy and democratic spirit of the new urban popular culture. In a rather more sinister way, so did the writings of Edgar Allan Poe, who found the inspiration for his gothic horror stories such as "The Murders in the Rue Morgue" (1841) and "The Mystery of Marie Roget" (1842) not in Europe (as his titles might suggest), but in contemporary American crimes. Judging from its literature, Americans were apparently fascinated by their own urban violence.

Working class use of the streets for parades, celebrations, and marches was an established aspect of urban life, and perhaps nowhere so much a part of the city as in New Orleans. There, African American bands played in funeral processions, and dances drawing hundreds of slaves were regularly held in Congo Square, while elsewhere Choctaw Indians drummed and respectable middle-class men rang cowbells as they took part in rowdy street serenades in response to unpopular events.

In New York, the prosperous classes were increasingly frightened by the urban poor and by working-class rowdyism. New York City's tradition of New Year's Eve "frolics," in which laborers, apprentices, and other members of the lower classes paraded through the streets playing drums, trumpets, whistles, and other noisemakers, was an example. By 1828, the revelry had been taken over by gangs of young workers from the lower classes, 4,000 strong, who marched through the city, overturning carts, breaking windows, obstructing traffic, and harassing middle-class citizens. In the following year, the city government banned the traditional New Year's Eve parade.

In colonial days, civic disturbances had been handled informally: members of the city watch asked onlookers for such assistance as was necessary to keep the peace. New York City's first response in the 1820s and 1830s to increasing civic disorder was to hire more city watchmen and to augment them with constables and marshals. When riots occurred, the militia were called, and deaths were increasingly common as they forcibly restrained mobs. Finally, in 1845, the city created a permanent police force with a mandate to keep the poor in order. Southern cities, because of fear of slave disorder, had police forces much earlier: by the 1820s, New Orleans, Charleston, and Savannah had armed and uniformed city guards who patrolled in military fashion.

But even with police forces in place, the pressures of rapid urbanization, immigration, and the market revolution proved to be more than America's cities could contain. Beginning in the 1830s, a series of urban riots broke out against the two poorest urban groups: Catholics and free black people. As if their miserable living conditions were not enough, Irish immigrants were met with virulent anti-Catholicism. In 1834, rioters burned an Ursuline convent in Charlestown, Massachusetts; in 1844, a Philadelphia mob attacked priests and nuns and vandalized Catholic churches; in 1854, a mob destroyed an Irish neighborhood in Lawrence, Massachusetts. Often, the Irish replied in kind—for example, in an 1806 riot in New York, when they counterattacked a mob that disrupted their Christmas Eve mass in a Catholic church on Augustus Street. But the most common targets of urban violence were free African Americans.

Urban Life of Free African Americans

By 1860, there were nearly half a million free African Americans in the United States, constituting about 11 percent of the country's total black population. More than half of all free African Americans lived in the North, mostly in cities, where they competed with immigrants and native-born poor white people for jobs as day laborers and domestic servants. Their relative social position is reflected in statistics on per capita annual income in Boston in the 1850s: $91 for black people and $131 for Irish immigrants compared to $872 for the population at large. Philadelphia and New York had the largest black communities: 22,000 African Americans in Philadelphia and 12,500 in New York (another 4,313 lived just across the East River in Brooklyn). There were much smaller but still significant black communities in the New England cities of Boston, Providence, and New Haven and in Ohio cities like Cincinnati.

Free African Americans in northern cities faced residential segregation (except for the domestic servants who lived in with white families), pervasive job discrimination,

This appealing portrait of a musician, *The Bone Player*, evokes the prevalent stereotype of African Americans as innately musical, but it also clearly portrays a man who is proud of his talent.

SOURCE: William Sidney Morris (American, 1807-1868), *The Bone Player*, 1856. Oil on canvas, 91.76 x 73.98 cm (36 1/8 × 29 1.8 in.) Museum of Fine Arts, Boston Bequest of Martha C. Karolik for the M. and M. Karolik Collection of American Paintings.

segregated public schools, and severe limitations on their civil rights. In addition to these legal restrictions, there were matters of custom: African Americans of all economic classes endured daily affronts, such as exclusion from public concerts, lectures, and libraries, and segregation or exclusion from public transportation. For example, in Massachusetts—which had the reputation of being more hospitable to black people than any other northern state—the famed African American abolitionist Frederick Douglass was denied admission to a zoo on Boston Common, a public lecture and revival meeting, a restaurant, and a public omnibus, all within the space of a few days.

In common with Irish and German immigrants, African Americans created defenses against the larger hostile society by building their own community structures. They formed associations for aiding the poorest members of the community, for self-improvement, and for socializing. Tired of being insulted by the white press, African American communities supported their own newspapers. The major community organization was the black Baptist or African Methodist Episcopal (AME) church, which served, as one historian put it, as "a place of worship, a social and cultural center, a political meet-

ing place, a hiding place for fugitives, a training ground for potential community leaders, and one of the few places where blacks could express their true feelings."

Employment prospects for black men deteriorated from 1820 to 1850. Those who had held jobs as skilled artisans were forced from their positions, and their sons denied apprenticeships, by white mechanics and craftsmen who were themselves suffering from the effects of the market revolution. Limited to day labor, African Americans found themselves in direct competition with the new immigrants, especially the Irish, for jobs. On the waterfront, black men lost their jobs as carters and longshoremen to the Irish. One of the few occupations to remain open to them was that of seaman. More than 20 percent of all American sailors in 1850 were black, and over the years, their ranks included an increasing number of runaway slaves. The pay was poor and the conditions miserable, but many black men found more equality aboard ship than they did ashore. Mothers, wives, and daughters worked as domestic servants (in competition with Irishwomen), washerwomen, and seamstresses.

Free African Americans remained committed to their enslaved brethren in the South. In New York, for example, black communities rioted four times—in 1801, 1819, 1826, and 1832—against slave catchers taking escaped slaves back to slavery. But even more frequently, free African Americans were themselves targets of urban violence. An 1829 riot in Cincinnati sent a thousand black people fleeing to Canada in fear for their lives; a three-day riot in Providence in 1831 destroyed an African American district; and 1834 New York riot destroyed a black church, a school, and a dozen homes. Philadelphia, "the City of Brotherly Love," had the worst record. Home to the largest free African American community in the North, Philadelphia was repeatedly rocked by antiblack riots in the period between 1820 and 1859. Urban riots of all kinds had cost 125 lives by 1840, and more than 1,000 by 1860.

THE LABOR MOVEMENT AND URBAN POLITICS

Universal white manhood suffrage and the development of mass politics (see Chapter 11), coupled with the rapid growth of cities, changed urban politics. The traditional leadership role of the wealthy elite waned. In their place were professional politicians whose job it was to make party politics work. In New York and in other large cities, this change in politics was spurred by working-class activism.

The Tradition of Artisanal Politics

The nation's urban centers had long been strongholds of craft associations for artisans and skilled workers. These organizations, and their parades and celebrations, were recognized parts of the urban community. Groups of master craftsmen marching in community parades with

This seal of the General Society of Mechanics and Tradesmen illustrates in its motto—"By Hammer and Hand All Arts Do Stand"—the personal and community pride artisans took in their work.

SOURCE: *Seabury Champlin's June 3, 1791 Certificate of Membership in NY Mechanic Society*, Abraham Godwin, print. Courtesy, Winterthur Museum.

signs such as "By Hammer and Hand All Arts Do Stand" were visible symbols of the strength and solidarity of workers' organizations.

Also traditional were riots and demonstrations by workers (usually journeymen or apprentices, not the master artisans themselves) over matters as political and far-reaching as the American Revolution or as practical and immediate as the price of bread. In fact, protests by urban workers had been an integral part of the older social order controlled by the wealthy elite. In the eighteenth century, when only men of property could vote, such demonstrations usually indicated widespread discontent or economic difficulty among workers. They served as a warning signal that the political elite rarely ignored.

By the 1830s, the status of artisans and independent craftsmen in the nation's cities had changed (see Chapter 12). There was no safety net for workers who lost their jobs—no unemployment insurance or welfare—and no public regulation of wages and conditions of work. The members of urban workers' associations, increasingly angry over their declining status in the economic and social order, also became—tentatively at first, but then with growing conviction—active defenders of working-class interests.

What was new was the open antagonism between workers and employers. The community of interest between masters and workers in preindustrial times broke down. Workers realized they had to depend on other workers, not employers, for support. In turn, employers and members of the middle class began to take urban disorders much more seriously than their grandfathers might have done.

The Union Movement

Urban worker protest against changing conditions first took the form of party politics. The Workingmen's Party was founded in Philadelphia in 1827, and chapters quickly formed in New York and Boston as well. Using the language of class warfare—"two distinct classes . . . those that live by their own labor and they that live upon the labor of others"—the "Workies" campaigned for the ten-hour day and the preservation of the small artisanal shop. Jacksonian Democrats were quick to pick up on some of their themes, attracting many Workingmen's votes in 1832, the year Andrew Jackson campaigned against the "monster" Bank of the United States.

For their part, the Whigs wooed workers by assuring them that Henry Clay's American System, and tariff protection in particular, would be good for the economy and for workers' jobs. Nevertheless, neither major political party really spoke to the primary need of workers—for well-paid, stable jobs that assured them independence and respect. Unsatisfied with the response of political parties, workers turned to labor organization to achieve their goals.

Between 1833 and 1837, a wave of strikes in New York City cut the remaining ties between master craftsmen and the journeymen who worked for them. In 1833, journeymen carpenters struck for higher wages. Workers in fifteen other trades came to their support, and within a month the strike was won. The lesson was obvious: if skilled workers banded together across craft lines, they could improve their conditions. The same year, representatives from nine different craft groups formed the General Trades Union (GTU) of New York. By 1834, similar groups had sprung up in over a dozen cities—Boston, Louisville, and Cincinnati among them. In New York alone, the GTU helped organize almost forty strikes between 1833 and 1837, and it encouraged the formation of more than fifty unions. In 1834 also, representatives of several local GTUs met in Baltimore and organized the National Trades Union (NTU). In its founding statement the NTU criticized the "unjustifiable distribution of the wealth of society in the hands of a few individuals," which had created for working people "a humiliating, servile dependency, incompatible with . . . natural equality."

Naturally, employers disagreed with the NTU's criticism of the economic system. In Cincinnati and elsewhere, employers prevailed upon police to arrest strikers even when no violence had occurred. In another case, New York employers took striking journeymen tailors to court in 1836. Judge Ogden Edwards pronounced the strikers guilty of conspiracy and declared unions un-American. He assured the strikers that "the road of advancement is open to all" and that they would do better to strive to be masters themselves rather than "conspire" with their fellow workers. The GTU responded with a mass rally at which Judge Edwards was burned in effigy. A year later, stunned by the effects of the Panic of 1837, the GTU collapsed. The founding of these general unions, a visible sign of a class-based community of interest among workers, is generally considered to mark the beginning of the American labor movement. However, these early unions included only white men in skilled trades, who made up only a small percentage of all workers. The majority of workers—men in unskilled occupations, all free African Americans, and all women—were excluded.

Big-City Machines

Although workers were unable to create strong unions or stable political parties that spoke for their economic interests, they were able to shape urban politics. As America's cities experienced unprecedented growth, the electorate mushroomed. In New York, for example, the number of voters grew from 20,000 in 1825 to 88,900 in 1855. Furthermore, by 1855 half of the voters were foreign-born. The ease with which new immigrants gained the vote stood in marked contrast to the continuing restrictions on the voting rights of free African American men. At the time, America was the only country in the world where propertyless white men had the vote. The job of serving this white working-class electorate and

By 1855, half the voters in New York City were foreign-born. This 1858 engraving of an Irish bar in the Five Points area appeared in the influential *Harper's Weekly*. It expressed the dislike of temperance reformers for immigrants and their drinking habits, and the dismay of political reformers that immigrant saloons and taverns were such effective organizing centers for urban political machines.

SOURCE: Frank and Marie-Therese Wood Print Collections, The Picture Bank.

making the new mass political party work at the urban level fell to a new kind of career politician—the boss—and a new kind of political organization—the machine.

Just as the old system of elite leadership had mirrored the social unity of eighteenth-century cities, so the new system of machine politics reflected the class structure of the rapidly growing nineteenth-century cities. Feelings of community, which had arisen naturally out of the personal contact that characterized neighborhoods in earlier, smaller cities, now were cultivated politically. Because immigrants clustered in neighborhoods, their impact on politics could be concentrated and manipulated. Legally, three years' residence in the United States was required before one could apply for citizenship, but there was clear evidence of swifter naturalization in large cities with effective political organizations. In New York, for example, the Irish-dominated districts quickly became Democratic Party strongholds. Germans, who were less active politically than the Irish, nevertheless voted heavily for the new Republican Party in the 1850s. Between them, these two new blocs of immigrant voters destroyed the Whig Party that had controlled New York politics before the immigrants arrived.

In New York City, the Tammany Society, begun in the 1780s as a fraternal organization of artisans, slowly evolved into the key organization of the new mass politics. (Named after the Delaware chief mentioned in Chapter 3, the society met in a hall called the Wigwam and elected "sachems" as their officers.) Tammany, which was affiliated with the national Democratic Party, reached voters by using many of the techniques of mass appeal made popular earlier by craft organizations—parades, rallies, current songs, and party newspapers.

Along with these new techniques of mass appeal went new methods of organization: a tight system of political control beginning at the neighborhood level with ward committees and topped by a chairman of a citywide general committee. At the citywide level, ward leaders—bosses—bartered the loyalty and votes of their followers for positions on the city payroll for party members and community services for their neighborhood. This was machine politics. Through it, workers, although they lacked the political or organizational strength to challenge the harmful effects of the market revolution, could use their numbers to ameliorate some of its effects at the local level. Or, to be accurate, the numbers could be used by machine politicians, leading inevitably to cronyism and corruption. Nevertheless, machine politics served to mediate increasing class divisions and ethnic diversity. The machines themselves offered personal ties and loyalties—community feeling—to recent arrivals in the big cities (increasingly, immigrants from Europe) and help in hard times to workers who cast their votes correctly.

In America's big cities, the result was apparent by mid-century: the political "machine" controlled by the "boss"—the politician who represented the interests of his group and delivered their votes in exchange for patronage and favors. Critics said that big-city machines were corrupt, and indeed they often were. Antagonism between reformers, who were usually members of the upper and middle classes, and machine politicians, who spoke for the working class, was evident by the 1850s. This antagonism was to become chronic in American urban politics.

SOCIAL REFORM MOVEMENTS

The passion for reform that had become such an important part of the new middle-class thinking was focused on the problems of the nation's cities. As the opening of this chapter describes, the earliest response to the dislocations caused by the market revolution was community-based and voluntary. Middle-class people tried to deal with social changes in their communities by joining organizations devoted to reforms. The temperance movement and reforms involving education, prisons and asylums, women's rights, abolitionism, and, above all, the spread of evangelical religion were all concerns of the middle class. The reform message was vastly amplified by inventions such as the steam printing press, which made it possible to publish reform literature in great volume. Soon there were national networks of reform groups.

Evangelism, Reform, and Social Control

Evangelical religion was fundamental to social reform. Men and women who had been converted to the enthusiastic new faith assumed personal responsibility for making changes in their own lives. Personal reform quickly led to social reform. Religious converts were encouraged in their social activism by such leading revivalists as Charles G. Finney, who preached a doctrine of "perfectionism," claiming it was possible for all Christians to personally understand and live by God's will and thereby become "as perfect as God." Furthermore, Finney predicted, "the complete reformation of the whole world" could be achieved if only enough converts put their efforts into moral reform. This new religious feeling was intensely hopeful: members of evangelistic religions really did expect to convert the world and create the perfect moral and religious community on earth.

Much of America was swept by the fervor of moralistic reform, and it was the new middle class that set the agenda for reform. Reform efforts arose from the recognition that the traditional methods of small-scale local relief were no longer adequate. In colonial times, families (sometimes at the request of local government) had housed and cared for the ill or incapacitated. Small local almshouses and prisons had housed the poor and the criminal. Reformers now realized that large cities had to make large-scale provisions for social misfits and that institutional rather than private efforts were needed. This thinking was especially true of the institutional reform movements that began in the 1830s, such as the push for insane asylums. At this time, of course, the federal government provided no such relief.

A second characteristic of the reform movements was a belief in the basic goodness of human nature. All reformers believed that the condition of the unfortunate—the poor, the insane, the criminal—would improve in a wholesome environment. Thus insane asylums were built in rural areas, away from the noise and stress of the cities, and orphanages had strict rules that were meant to encourage discipline and self-reliance. Prison reform carried this sentiment to the extreme. On the theory that bad social influences were largely responsible for crime, some "model" prisons completely isolated prisoners from one another, making them eat, sleep, work, and do required Bible reading in their own cells. The failure of these prisons to achieve dramatic changes for the better in their inmates (a number of isolated prisoners went mad, and some committed suicide) or to reduce crime was one of the first indications that reform was not a simple task.

A third characteristic of the reform movements was their moralistic dogmatism. Reformers were certain they knew what was right and were determined to see their improvements enacted. It was a short step from developing individual self-discipline to imposing discipline on others. The reforms that were proposed thus took the form

of social controls. Lazy, sinful, intemperate, or unfit members of society were to be reformed for their own good, whether they wanted to be or not. This attitude was bound to cause controversy; by no means did all Americans share the reformers' beliefs, nor did those for whom it was intended always take kindly to being the targets of the reformers' concern.

Indeed, some aspects of the social reform movements were harmful. The evangelical Protestantism of the reformers promoted a dangerous hostility to Catholic immigrants from Ireland and Germany that, as noted earlier, repeatedly led to urban riots. The temperance movement, in particular, targeted immigrants for their free drinking habits. Seeking uniformity of behavior rather than tolerance, the reformers thus helped to promote the virulent nativism that infected American politics between 1840 and 1860 (see Chapter 15).

Regional and national reform organizations quickly grew from local projects to deal with social problems such as drinking, prostitution, mental illness, and crime. In 1828, for example, Congregationalist minister Lyman Beecher joined other ministers in forming a General Union for Promoting the Observance of the Christian Sabbath; the aim was to prevent business on Sundays. To achieve its goals, the General Union adopted the same methods used by political parties: lobbying, petition drives, fundraising, and special publications. These and other efforts, Beecher said,

Winslow Homer's famous painting, *The Country School*, is both affectionate and realistic, showing both the idealism of the young female teacher and the barefoot condition of many of her pupils.

SOURCE: SuperStock, Inc.

were all for the purpose of establishing "the moral government of God." Beecher was also a leader of the anti-Catholic and anti-immigrant movement, warning in 1835 of a "terrific inundation" of Catholics in the West (he meant the Ohio Valley) that threatened American democracy. His vehement sermons warning of the danger contributed to the popular anger that led to the burning of the Charlestown convent in 1834.

In effect, Beecher and similar reformers engaged in political action, but remained aloof from direct electoral politics, stressing their religious mission. In any case, sabbatarianism was controversial. Workingmen (who usually worked six days a week) were angered when the General Union forced the Sunday closure of their favorite taverns, and were quick to vote against the Whigs, the party perceived to be most sympathetic to reform thinking. But in many new western cities, sabbatarianism divided the business class itself. In Rochester, a city created by the Erie Canal, businessmen who wished to observe Sunday only in religious ways were completely unable to stop the traffic of passenger and freight boats owned by other businessmen. Other reforms likewise muddied the distinction between political and social activity. It is not surprising that women, who were barred from electoral politics but not from moral and social activism, were major supporters of reform.

Education and Women Teachers

Women became deeply involved in reform movements through their churches. It was they who did most of the fundraising for the home missionary societies that were beginning to send the evangelical message worldwide—at first by ministers alone, later by married couples. Nearly every church had a maternal association, where mothers gathered to discuss ways to raise their children as true Christians. These associations reflected a new and more positive definition of childhood. The Puritans had believed that children were born sinful and that their wills had to be broken before they could become godly. Early schools reflected these beliefs: teaching was by rote, and punishment was harsh and physical. Educational reformers, however, tended to believe that children were born innocent and needed gentle nurturing and encouragement if they were to flourish. At home, mothers began to play the central role in child rearing. Outside the home, women helped spread the new public education pioneered by Horace Mann, secretary of the Massachusetts State Board of Education.

Although literacy had long been valued, especially in New England, schooling since colonial times had been a private enterprise and a personal expense. Town grammar schools, required in Massachusetts since 1647, had been supported primarily by parents' payments, with some help from local property taxes. In 1827, Massachusetts pioneered compulsory education by legislating that public schools be supported by public taxes. Soon schooling

for white children between the ages of five and nineteen was common, although, especially in rural schools, the term might be only a month or so long. Uniformity in curriculum and teacher training, and the grading of classes by ability—measures pioneered by Horace Mann in the 1830s—quickly caught on in other states. In the North and West (the South lagged far behind), more and more children went to school, and more and more teachers, usually young single women, were hired to teach them.

The spread of public education created the first real career opportunity for women. Horace Mann insisted that to learn well, children needed schools with a pleasant and friendly atmosphere. One important way to achieve that atmosphere, Mann recommended, was to group children by ages rather than combining everyone in the traditional ungraded classroom, and to pay special attention to the needs of the youngest pupils. Who could better create the friendly atmosphere of the new classroom than women? The great champion of teacher training for women was Catharine Beecher, daughter of Lyman, who clearly saw her efforts as part of the larger work of establishing "the moral government of God." Arguing that women's moral and nurturing nature ideally suited them to be teachers, Beecher campaigned tirelessly on their behalf. Since "the mind is to be guided chiefly by means of the affections," she argued, "is not woman best fitted to accomplish these important objects?"

By 1850, women were dominant in primary school teaching, which had come to be regarded as an acceptable occupation for educated young women during the few years between their own schooling and marriage. For some women, teaching was a great adventure; they enthusiastically volunteered to be "schoolmarms" on the distant western frontiers of Wisconsin and Iowa. Still others thought globally. The young women who attended Mary Lyon's Mount Holyoke Female Seminary in Massachusetts, founded in 1837, hoped to be missionary teachers in distant lands. For others, a few years of teaching was quite enough. Low pay (half of what male schoolteachers earned) and strict community supervision (women teachers had to board with families in the community) were probably sufficient to make almost any marriage proposal look appealing.

Temperance

Reformers believed not only that children could be molded, but also that adults could change. The largest reform organization of the period, the American Society for the Promotion of Temperance, founded in 1826, boasted more than 200,000 members by the mid-1830s. Dominated by evangelicals, local chapters used revival methods—lurid temperance tracts detailing the evils of alcohol, large prayer and song meetings, and heavy group pressure—to encourage young men to stand up, confess their bad habits, and "take the pledge" not to

STEP 1. A glass with a Friend.

STEP 2. A glass to keep the cold out.

STEP 3. A glass too much.

STEP 4. Drunk and riotous.

STEP 5. The summit attained Jolly companions A confirmed drunkard.

STEP 6. Poverty and Disease.

STEP 7. Forsaken by Friends.

STEP 8. Desperation and crime.

STEP 9. Death by suicide.

LITH. & PUB. BY N. CURRIER,

33 SPRUCE ST. N.Y.

THE DRUNKARDS PROGRESS.
FROM THE FIRST GLASS TO THE GRAVE.

This Currier and Ives lithograph, *The Drunkard's Progress*, dramatically conveys the message that the first glass leads the drinker inevitably to alcoholism and finally to the grave, while his wife and child (shown under the arch) suffer.

SOURCE: Library of Congress.

drink. Here again, women played an important role (see Figure 13.2).

Excessive drinking was a national problem, and it appears to have been mostly a masculine one, for respectable women did not drink in public. (Many did, however, drink alcohol-based patent medicines. Lydia Pinkham's Vegetable Compound, marketed for "female complaints," was 19 percent alcohol.) Men drank hard cider and liquor—whiskey, rum—in abundance. Traditionally, drinking had been a basic part of men's working lives. It concluded occasions as formal as the signing of a contract and accompanied such informal activities as card games. Drink was a staple offering at political speeches, rallies, and elections. In the old artisanal workshops, drinking had been a customary pastime. Much of the drinking was well within the bounds of sociability, but the widespread use (more than seven gallons of pure alcohol, or fourteen gallons of 100-proof whiskey per capita in 1830—four times as much as today's rate) must have encouraged drunkenness.

There were many reasons to support temperance. Heavy-drinking men hurt their families economically by spending their wages on drink. Women had no recourse: the laws of the time gave men complete financial control of the household, and divorce was difficult as well as socially unacceptable. Excessive drinking also led to violence and crime, both within the family and in the larger society.

But there were other reasons as well. The new middle class, preoccupied with respectability, morality, and efficiency, found the old easygoing drinking ways unacceptable. Much of the new industrial machinery was dangerous and workers needed sobriety to be safe. As work patterns changed, employers banned alcohol at work and increasingly considered drinking men not only unreliable but also immoral. Temperance became a social and political issue. Whigs, who embraced the new morality, favored it; Democrats, who in northern cities consisted increasingly of immigrant workers, were opposed. Both German and Irish immigrants valued the social

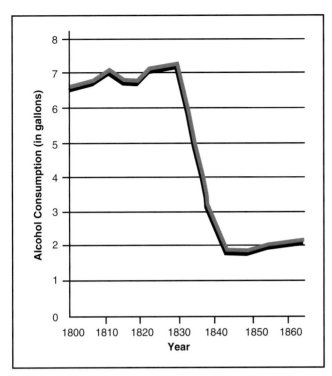

FIGURE 13.2 Per Capita Consumption of Alcohol 1800–60 The underlying cause of the dramatic fall in alcohol consumption during the 1830s was the changing nature of work brought about by the market revolution. Contributing factors were the shock of the Panic of 1837 and the untiring efforts of temperance reformers.

SOURCE: W. J. Rorabaugh, *The Alcoholic Republic: An American Tradition* (New York: Oxford University Press, 1979).

drinking that occurred in beer gardens and saloons and were hostile to temperance reform.

The Panic of 1837 affected the temperance movement. Whereas most temperance crusaders in the 1820s had been members of the middle class, the long depression of 1837–43 prompted artisans and skilled workers to give up or at least cut down substantially on drinking. Forming associations known as Washington Temperance Societies, these workers spread the word that temperance was the workingman's best chance to survive economically and to maintain his independence. Their wives, gathered together in Martha Washington Societies, were frequently even more committed to temperance than their husbands. While the men's temperance groups were often deeply involved in working-class politics, the women's groups stressed the harm that alcoholism could do to homes and families and provided financial help to distressed women and children.

Campaigns against alcohol were frequent and successful. By the mid-1840s, alcohol consumption had been more than halved, to less than two gallons per capita, about the level of today. Concern over drinking would remain constant throughout the nineteenth century and into the twentieth.

Moral Reform, Asylums, and Prisons

Alcohol was not the only "social evil" that reform groups attacked. Another was prostitution, which was common in the nation's port cities. The customary approach of evangelical reformers was to "rescue" prostitutes, offering them the salvation of religion, prayer, and temporary shelter. The success rate was not very high. As an alternative to prostitution, reformers usually offered domestic work, a low-paying and restrictive occupation that many women scorned. Nevertheless, campaigns against prostitution, generally organized by women, continued throughout the nineteenth century.

One of the earliest and most effective antiprostitution groups was the Female Moral Reform Society. Founded by evangelical women in New York in 1834 (the first president was Lydia Finney), it boasted 555 affiliates throughout the country by 1840. It was surprising that so many respectable women were willing to acknowledge the existence of something as disreputable as prostitution. Even more surprising was the speed with which the societies realized that prostitution was not as much a moral as an economic issue. The societies rapidly moved to organize charity and work for poor women and orphans. They also took direct action against the patrons of prostitutes by printing their names in local papers, and they successfully lobbied the New York state legislature for criminal penalties against the male clients as well as the women themselves.

Another dramatic example of reform was the asylum movement, spearheaded by the woman evangelist Dorothea Dix. In 1843, Dix horrified the Massachusetts state legislature with the results of her several years of study of the conditions to which insane women were subjected. She described in lurid detail how the women were incarcerated with ordinary criminals, locked up in "cages, closets, stalls, pens! Chained, naked, beaten with rods, and lashed into obedience!" Dix's efforts led to the establishment of a state asylum for the insane in Massachusetts and to similar institutions in other states. Between 1843 and 1854, Dix traveled more than 30,000 miles to publicize the movement for humane treatment of the insane. By 1860, twenty-eight states had public institutions for the insane.

Other reformers were active in related causes, such as prison reform and the establishment of orphanages, homes of refuge, and hospitals. Model penitentiaries were built in Auburn and Ossining (known as "Sing Sing"), New York, and in Philadelphia and Pittsburgh. Characterized by strict order and

Shaker Hannah Cohoon's 1845 painting of the *Tree of Life*—her effort to reproduce a vision she had seen while in a religious trance—communicates the intense spirituality of Shaker life.

SOURCE: Hannah Harrison Cohoon, *Tree of Life*, 1845. Tempera on paper. From the collection of Hancock Shaker Village, Pittsfield, Massachusetts.

discipline, these prisons were supposed to reform rather than simply incarcerate their inmates, but their regimes of silence and isolation caused despair more often than rehabilitation.

Utopianism and Mormonism

Amid all the political activism and reform fervor of the 1830s, a few people chose escape into utopian communities and new religions. The upstate New York area along the Erie Canal was the seedbed for this movement, just as it was for evangelical revivals and reform movements like the Seneca Falls convention. The area was so notable for its reform enthusiasms that it has been termed "the Burned-Over District," a reference to the waves of reform that swept through like forest fires (see Map 13.2).

Apocalyptic religions tend to spring up in places experiencing rapid social change. The Erie Canal region, which experienced the full impact of the market revolution in the early nineteenth century, was such a place. A second catalyst is hard times, and the prolonged depression that began with the Panic of 1837 led some people to embrace a belief in imminent catastrophe. The Millerites (named for their founder, William Miller) believed that the Second Coming of Christ would occur on October 22, 1843. In anticipation, members of the church sold their belongings and bought white robes for their ascension to heaven. When the Day of Judgment did not take

place as expected, most of Miller's followers drifted away. But a small group persisted. Revising their expectations, they formed the core of the Seventh-Day Adventist faith, which is still active today.

The Shakers, founded by "Mother" Ann Lee in 1774, were the oldest utopian group. An offshoot of the Quakers, the Shakers espoused a radical social philosophy that called for the abolition of the traditional family in favor of a family of brothers and sisters joined in equal fellowship. Despite its insistence on celibacy, the Shaker movement grew between 1820 and 1830, eventually reaching twenty settlements in eight states with a total membership of 6,000. The Shakers' simple and highly structured lifestyle, their isolation from the changing world, and their belief in equality drew new followers, especially among women. In contrast, another utopian community, the Oneida Community, became notorious for its sexual freedom. Founded by John Humphrey Noyes in 1848, the Oneida community, like the Shaker community, viewed itself as one family. But rather than

MAP EXPLORATION

To explore an interactive version of this map, go to **www.prenhall.com/faragher5/map13.2**

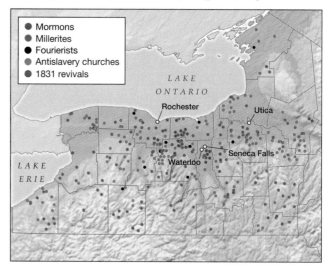

MAP 13.2 Reform Movements in the Burned-Over District The so-called Burned-Over District, the region of New York State most changed by the opening of the Erie Canal, was a seedbed of religious and reform movements. The Mormon Church originated there and Utopian groups and sects like the Millerites and the Fourierists thrived. Charles G. Finney held some of his most successful evangelical revivals in the district. Antislavery feeling was common in the region, and the women's rights movement began at Seneca Falls.

SOURCE: Whitney Cross, *The Burned-Over District* (1950; reprint, New York: Hippocrene Books, 1981).

celibacy, members practiced "complex marriage," a system of highly regulated group sexual activity. Only "spiritually advanced" males (Noyes himself and a few others) could father children, who were raised communally. These practices gave the sect a notorious reputation as a den of "free love" and "socialism," preventing Noyes from increasing its membership beyond 200.

Still other forthrightly socialist communities flourished briefly. New Harmony, Indiana, founded by the famous Scottish industrialist Robert Owen in 1825, was to be a manufacturing community without poverty and unemployment. The community survived only three years. Faring little better were the "phalanxes," huge communal buildings structured on the socialist theories of the French thinker Charles Fourier. Based on his belief that there was a rational way to divide work, Fourier suggested, for example, that children would make the best garbage collectors because they didn't mind dirt! And Louisa May Alcott (who later wrote *Little Women* and many other novels and stories) lived with her family at Fruitlands in Massachusetts, which had begun as a rural community of transcendentalists. The rapid failure of these socialist communities was due largely to inadequate planning and organization. Another reason may have been, as Alcott suggested in her satirical reminiscence, *Transcendental Wild Oats* that the women were left to do all the work while the men philosophized. Nevertheless, it is striking that at a time when so many voluntary associations successfully organized the activities of their members, so few cooperative communities succeeded.

The most successful of the nineteenth-century communitarian movements was also a product of the Burned-Over District. In 1830, a young man named Joseph Smith founded the Church of Jesus Christ of Latter-Day Saints, based on the teachings of the Book of Mormon, which he claimed to have received from an angel in a vision.

Initially, Mormonism, as the new religion became known, seemed little different from the many other new religious groups and utopian communities of the time. But under the benevolent but absolute authority of its patriarch, Joseph Smith, it rapidly gained distinction for its extraordinary unity. Close cooperation and hard work made the Mormon community successful, attracting both new followers and the animosity of neighbors, who resented Mormon exclusiveness and economic success. The Mormons were harassed in New York and driven west to Ohio and then Missouri. Finally they seemed to find an ideal home in Nauvoo, Illinois, where in 1839 they built a model community, achieving almost complete self-government and isolation from non-Mormon neighbors. But in 1844, dissension within the community over Joseph Smith's new doctrine of polygamy (marriage between one man and more than one woman,

simultaneously) gave outsiders a chance to intervene. Smith and his brother were arrested peacefully, but were killed by a mob from which their jailers failed to protect them.

The beleaguered Mormon community decided to move beyond reach of harm. Led by Brigham Young, the Mormons migrated in 1846 to the Great Salt Lake in present-day Utah. After several lean years (once, a grasshopper plague was stopped by the providential arrival of sea gulls, who ate the insects), the Mormon method of communal settlement proved successful. Their hopes of isolation were dashed, however, by the California Gold Rush of 1849.

ANTISLAVERY AND ABOLITIONISM

The antislavery feeling that was to play such an important role in the politics of the 1840s and 1850s also had its roots in the religious reform movements that began in the 1820s and 1830s. Three groups—free African Americans, Quakers, and militant white reformers—worked to bring an end to slavery, but each in different ways. Their efforts eventually turned a minor reform movement into the dominant political issue of the day.

Antislavery activity was not new. For free African Americans, the freedom of other black people had always been a major goal, but in order to achieve legal change, they needed white allies. In 1787, antislavery advocates had secured in the Constitution a clause specifying a date after which American participation in the international slave trade could be made illegal, and Congress outlawed it in 1808. By 1800, slavery had been abolished or gradual emancipation enacted in most northern states. In 1820, the Missouri Compromise prohibited slavery in most of the Louisiana Purchase lands. None of these measures, however, addressed the continuing reality of slavery in the South.

The American Colonization Society

The first attempt to "solve" the problem of slavery was a plan for gradual emancipation of slaves (with compensation to their owners) and their resettlement in Africa. This plan was the work of the American Colonization Society, formed in 1817 by northern religious reformers (Quakers prominent among them) and a number of southern slave owners, most from the Upper South and the border states (Kentuckian Henry Clay was a supporter). Northerners were especially eager to send the North's 250,000 free black people back to Africa, describing them, in the words of the society's 1829 report, as "notoriously ignorant,

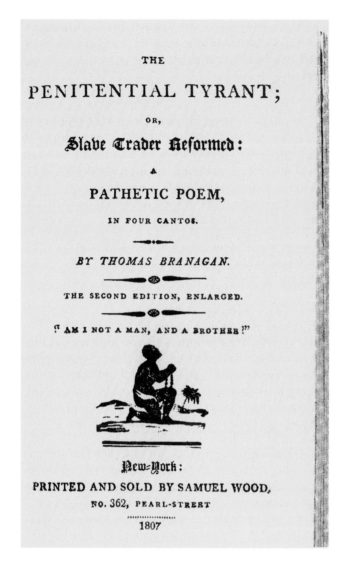

The different dates on these two widely used antislavery images are important. The title page of Thomas Branagan's 1807 book includes a then already commonly used image of a male slave. The engraving of a chained female slave was made by Patrick Reason, a black artist, in 1835. The accompanying message, "Am I Not a Woman and a Sister?" spoke particularly to white female abolitionists in the North, who were just becoming active in antislavery movements in the 1830s.

SOURCE: Courtesy of the Library of Congress.

degraded and miserable, mentally diseased, [and] broken-spirited," a characterization that completely ignored the legal and social discrimination they faced. The American Colonization Society was remarkably ineffective; by 1830, it had managed to send only 1,400 black people to a colony in Liberia, West Africa. Critics pointed out that more slaves were born in a week than the society sent back to Africa in a year.

African Americans' Fight Against Slavery

Most free African Americans rejected colonization, insisting instead on a commitment to the immediate end of slavery and the equal treatment of black people in America. "We are natives of this country," an African American minister in New York pointed out. Then he added bitterly, "We only ask that we be treated as well as foreigners." By 1830, there were at least fifty black abolitionist societies in the North. These organizations held yearly national conventions, where famous African American abolitionists like Frederick Douglass, Harriet Tubman, and Sojourner Truth spoke. The first African American newspaper, founded in 1827 by John Russwurm and Samuel Cornish, announced its antislavery position in its title, *Freedom's Journal.*

In 1829, David Walker, a free African American in Boston, wrote a widely distributed pamphlet, *Appeal to the Colored Citizens of the World,* that encouraged slave rebellion. "We must and shall be free . . . in spite of you," Walker warned whites. "And woe, woe will be it to you if we have to obtain our freedom by fighting." White Southerners blamed pamphlets such as these and the militant articles of African American journalists for stirring up trouble among southern slaves, and in particular for Nat Turner's revolt in 1831. The vehemence of white southern reaction testifies to the courage of that handful of determined free African Americans who persisted in speaking for their enslaved brothers and sisters long before most white Northerners even noticed.

Abolitionists

The third and best-known group of antislavery reformers was headed by William Lloyd Garrison. In 1831, Garrison broke with the gradualist persuaders of the American Colonization Society and began publishing his own paper, the *Liberator*. In the first issue Garrison declared, "I am in earnest—I will not equivocate—I will not excuse—I will not retreat a single inch—AND I WILL BE HEARD." Garrison, the embodiment of moral indignation, was totally incapable of compromise. His approach was to mount a sweeping crusade condemning slavery as sinful, and demanding its immediate abolishment. Garrison's crusade, like evangelical religion, was personal and moral. In reality, Garrison did not expect that all slaves would be freed immediately, but he did want and expect everyone to acknowledge the immorality of slavery. On the other hand, Garrison took the truly radical step of demanding full social equality for African Americans, referring to them individually as "a man and a brother" and "a woman and a sister." Garrison's determination electrified the antislavery movement, but his inability to compromise limited his effectiveness as a leader.

Garrison's moral vehemence radicalized northern antislavery religious groups. Theodore Weld, an evangelical minister, joined Garrison in 1833 in forming the American Anti-Slavery Society. The following year, Weld encouraged a group of students at Lane Theological Seminary in Cincinnati to form an antislavery society. When the seminary's president, Lyman Beecher, sought to suppress it, the students moved en masse to Oberlin College in northern Ohio, where they were joined by revivalist Charles Finney, who became president of the college. Oberlin soon became known as the most liberal college in the country, not only for its antislavery stance but for its acceptance of African American students and of women students as well.

Moral horror over slavery engaged many Northerners deeply in the abolitionist movement. They flocked to hear firsthand accounts of slavery by Frederick Douglass and Sojourner Truth, and by the white sisters from South Carolina, Angelina and Sarah Grimké. Northerners eagerly read slave narratives and books such as Theodore Weld's 1839 treatise *American Slavery As It Is* (based in part on the recollections of Angelina Grimké, whom Weld had married), that provided graphic details of abuse under slavery.

The style of abolitionist writings and speeches was similar to the oratorical style of the religious revivalists. Northern abolitionists believed that a full description of the evils of slavery would force southern slave owners to confront their wrongdoing and lead to a true act of repentance—freeing their slaves.

They were confrontational, denunciatory, and personal in their message, much like the evangelical preachers. Southerners, however, regarded abolitionist attacks as libelous and abusive.

Abolitionists adopted another tactic of revivalists and temperance workers when, to enhance their powers of persuasion, they began to publish great numbers of antislavery tracts. In 1835 alone, they mailed more than a million pieces of antislavery literature to southern states. This tactic also drew a backlash: southern legislatures banned abolitionist literature, encouraged the harassment and abuse of anyone distributing it, and looked the other way when (as in South Carolina) proslavery mobs seized and burned it. The Georgia legislature even offered a $5,000 reward to anyone who would kidnap William Lloyd Garrison and bring him to the South to stand trial for inciting rebellion. Most serious, the majority of southern states reacted by toughening laws concerning emancipation, freedom of movement, and all aspects of slave behavior. Hoping to prevent the spread of the abolitionist message, most southern states reinforced laws making it a crime to teach a slave how to read. Ironically, then, the immediate impact of abolitionism in the South was to stifle dissent and make the lives of slaves harder (see Chapter 10).

Even in the North, controversy over abolitionism was common. Some places were prone to antiabolitionist violence. The Ohio Valley, settled largely by Southerners, was one such place, as were northern cities experiencing the strains of rapid growth, such as Philadelphia. Immigrant Irish, who found themselves pitted against free black people for jobs, were often violently antiabolitionist. A tactic that abolitionists borrowed from revivalists—holding large and emotional meetings—opened the door to mob action. Crowds of people often disrupted such meetings, especially those addressed by Theodore Weld, whose oratorical style earned him the title of "the Most Mobbed Man in the United States." William Lloyd Garrison was stoned, dragged through the streets, and on one occasion almost hanged by a Boston mob. In a three-day New York riot of 1834, abolitionist Arthur Tappan's home and store were sacked at the same time that black churches and homes were damaged and free blacks attacked. In 1837, antislavery editor Elijah P. Lovejoy of Alton, Illinois, was killed and his press destroyed. In 1838, a mob threatened a meeting of the Philadelphia Female Anti-Slavery Society one night and, the next night, burned down the hall in which they had met.

Abolitionism and Politics

Abolitionism began as a social movement, but soon intersected with sectional interests and became a national political issue. In the 1830s, massive abolitionist petition drives gathered a total of nearly

In 1837, white abolitionist Elijah P. Lovejoy had placed the press he used to print his antislavery newspaper in an Alton, Illinois warehouse in order to protect the press against a mob. This contemporary woodcut depicts the mob's attack on the warehouse. Lovejoy died defending it.

SOURCE: The Granger Collection.

700,000 petitions requesting the abolition of slavery and the slave trade in the District of Columbia, but were rebuffed by Congress. At southern insistence and with President Andrew Jackson's approval, Congress passed a "gag rule" in 1836 that prohibited discussion of antislavery petitions.

Many Northerners viewed the gag rule and censorship of the mails, which Southerners saw as necessary defenses against abolitionist frenzy, as alarming threats to free speech. First among them was Massachusetts representative John Quincy Adams, the only former president ever to serve in Congress after leaving the executive branch. Adams so publicly and persistently denounced the gag rule as a violation of the constitutional right to petition, that it was repealed in 1844. Less well-known Northerners, like the thousands of women who canvassed their neighborhoods with petitions, made personal commitments to abolitionism that they did not intend to abandon.

John Quincy Adams was also a key figure in the abolitionists' one undoubted victory, the fight to free the fifty-three slaves on the Spanish ship *Amistad* and return them to Africa. Although the Africans successfully mutinied against the *Amistad's* crew in 1839, when the ship was found in American waters, a legal battle over their "ownership" ensued, during which the Africans themselves were held in jail. Prominent abolitionists, most notably Lewis Tappan, financed the legal fight, which went all the way to the Supreme Court, where Adams won the case for the *Amistad* defendants against the American government, which supported the Spanish claim.

Although abolitionist groups raised the nation's emotional temperature, they failed to achieve the moral unity they had hoped for, and they began to splinter.

One perhaps inevitable but nonetheless distressing split was between white and black abolitionists. Frederick Douglass and William Lloyd Garrison parted ways when Douglass, refusing to be limited to a simple recital of his life as a slave, began to make specific suggestions for improvements in the lives of free African Americans. When Douglass chose the path of political action, Garrison denounced him as "ungrateful." Douglass and other free African Americans worked under persistent discrimination, even from antislavery whites; some of the latter refused to hire black people or to meet with them as equals. For example, some Philadelphia Quaker meetings, though devoted to the antislavery cause, maintained segregated seating for black people in their churches. While many white reformers eagerly pressed for civil equality for African Americans, they did not accept the idea of social equality. On the other hand, black and white "stations" worked closely in the risky enterprise of passing fugitive slaves north over the famous Underground Railroad, as the various routes by which slaves made their way to freedom were called. Contrary to abolitionist legend, however, it was free African Americans, rather than white people, who played the major part in helping the fugitives. (See Out of Many Voices: John P. Parker, Conductor on the Underground Railroad.)

Among white abolitionists, William Lloyd Garrison remained controversial, especially after 1837, when he espoused a radical program that included women's rights, pacifism, and the abolition of the prisons and asylums that other reformers were working to establish. In 1840, the abolitionist movement formally split. The majority moved toward party politics (which Garrison abhorred), founding the Liberty Party and choosing James G. Birney (whom Theodore Weld had

OUT OF MANY VOICES

JOHN P. PARKER, CONDUCTOR ON THE UNDERGROUND RAILROAD

John P. Parker, a free African American, lived in Rowley, Ohio, and helped hundreds of slaves who escaped across the Ohio River from Kentucky. In this excerpt, he describes his rescue of a party of ten slaves stranded in Kentucky. Although he brought them safely through the woods to the Ohio River, there was still danger.

WE MADE THE RIVER ALL RIGHT, BUT THERE WAS no boat awaiting our arrival. I had no other alternative than to push straight down the bank and take my chances. My chances proved very poor, because I ran into a patrol. Seeing the size of our party he turned and ran away. I knew that the whole countryside would soon be buzzing like a hornet's nest.

Making my people throw away their bundles, I started along the bank as fast as I could go, with the fugitives following. I knew there were always boats about the ferry landing. My one hope was to beat my pursuers to them. Sure enough, at the ferry I found one lone boat. I piled the crowd into the boat, only to find it so small it would not carry all of us. Two men were left on the bank.

As I started to push off, leaving the poor fellows on the bank to their cruel fate, one of the women set up a cry that one of the men on the bank was her husband. Then I witnessed an example of heroism and self-sacrifice that made me proud of my race. For one of the single men safely in the boat, hearing the cry of the woman for her husband, arose without a word [and] walked quietly to the bank. The husband sprang into the boat as I pushed off.

As I rowed away to safety I saw dimly the silent but helpless martyr. We were still far from the Ohio shore when I saw lights around the spot where we had left the man, followed by shouts, [by] which I knew the poor fellow had been captured in sight of the promised land. ■

SOURCE: *John P. Parker, His Promised Land: The Autobiography of John P. Parker, Former Slave and Conductor on the Underground Railroad* ed. Stuart Seely Sprague (New York: W.W. Norton, 1996), 97–104.

---

converted to abolitionism) as their presidential candidate. Thus the abolitionist movement, which began as an effort at moral reform, took its first major step into politics, and this step in turn led to the formation of the Republican Party in the 1850s and to the Civil War.

For one particular group of antislavery reformers, the abolitionist movement opened up new possibilities for action. Through their participation in antislavery activity, some women came to a vivid realization of the social constraints on their activism.

THE WOMEN'S RIGHTS MOVEMENT

American women, without the vote or a role in party politics, found a field of activity in social reform movements. There was scarcely a reform movement in which women were not actively involved. Often men were the official leaders of such movements, and some women—especially those in the temperance, moral reform, and abolitionist movements—formed all-female chapters to define and implement their own policies and programs.

The majority of women did not participate in these activities, for they were fully occupied with housekeeping and child rearing (families with five children were the average). A few women—mostly members of the new middle class, who could afford servants—had the time and energy to look beyond their immediate tasks. Touched by the religious revival, these women enthusiastically joined reform movements. Led thereby to challenge social restrictions, some, like the Grimké sisters, found that their commitment carried them beyond the limits of what was considered acceptable activity for women.

The Grimké Sisters

Sarah and Angelina Grimké, members of a prominent South Carolina slaveholding family, rejected slavery out of religious conviction and moved north to join a Quaker community near Philadelphia. In the 1830s, these two sisters found themselves drawn into the growing antislavery agitation in the North. Because they knew about slavery firsthand, they were in great demand as speakers. At first they spoke to "parlor meetings" of women only, as was considered proper. But interested men kept sneaking into the talks, and soon the sisters found themselves speaking to mixed gatherings. The meetings got larger and larger, and soon the sisters realized that they had become the first female public speakers in America. In 1837 Angelina Grimké became the first woman to address a meeting of the Massachusetts state legislature (Sarah Bagley, the Lowell worker, was the second).

The sisters challenged social norms on two grounds. There was widespread disapproval of the antislavery movement, and many famous male orators were criticized by the press and mobbed at meetings. The Grimké sisters were criticized for speaking because they were women. A letter from a group of ministers cited the Bible in reprimanding the sisters for stepping out of "woman's proper sphere" of silence and subordination. Sarah Grimké answered the ministers in her 1838 *Letters on the Equality of the Sexes and the Condition of Women*, claiming that "men and women were CREATED EQUAL. . . . Whatever is right for a man to do, is right for woman." She followed with this ringing assertion: "I seek no favors for my sex. I surrender not our claim to equality. All I ask of our brethren is, that they will take their feet from off our necks and permit us to stand upright on that ground which God designed us to occupy."

Not all female assertiveness was as dramatic as Sarah Grimké's, but women in the antislavery movement found it a constant struggle to be heard. Some solved the problem of male dominance by forming their own groups, like the Philadelphia Female Anti-Slavery Society. In the antislavery movement and other reform groups as well, men accorded women a secondary role, even when—as was frequently the case—women constituted a majority of the members.

Women's Rights

The Seneca Falls Convention of 1848, the first women's rights convention in American history, was an outgrowth of almost twenty years of female activity in social reform. Every year after 1848, women gathered to hold women's rights conventions and to work for political, legal, and social equality. Over the years, in response to persistent lobbying, states passed property laws more favorable to women, and altered divorce laws to allow women to retain custody of children. Teaching positions in higher education opened up to women, as did jobs in some other occupations, and women gained the vote in some states, beginning with Wyoming Territory in 1869. In 1920, seventy-two years after universal woman suffrage was first proposed at Seneca Falls, a woman's right to vote was at

Women's gatherings, like the first women's rights convention in Seneca Falls in 1848, and this meeting of strikers in Lynn in 1860, were indicators of widespread female activism.

SOURCE: Lynn Museum.

CHRONOLOGY

1817	American Colonization Society founded
1820s	Shaker colonies grow
1825	New Harmony founded, fails three years later
1826	American Society for the Promotion of Temperance founded
1827	Workingmen's Party founded in Philadelphia
	Freedom's Journal begins publication
	Public school movement begins in Massachusetts
1829	David Walker's Appeal to the Colored Citizens of the World is published
1830	Joseph Smith founds Church of Jesus Christ of Latter-Day Saints (Mormon Church)
	Charles G. Finney's revivals in Rochester
1831	William Lloyd Garrison begins publishing antislavery newspaper, the *Liberator*
1832	Immigration begins to increase
1833	American Anti-Slavery Society founded by William Lloyd Garrison and Theodore Weld
1834	First Female Moral Reform Society founded in New York
	National Trades Union formed
1836	Congress passes "gag rule" to prevent discussion of antislavery petitions
1837	Antislavery editor Elijah P. Lovejoy killed
	Angelina Grimké addresses Massachusetts legislature
	Sarah Grimké, *Letters on the Equality of the Sexes and the Condition of Women*
	Panic begins seven-year depression
1839	Theodore Weld publishes *American Slavery As It Is*
1840s	New York and Boston complete public water systems
1840	Liberty Party founded
1843	Millerites await the end of the world
	Dorothea Dix spearheads asylum reform movement
1844	Mormon leader Joseph Smith killed by mob
1845	New York creates city police force
	Beginning of Irish Potato Famine and mass Irish immigration into the United States
1846	Mormons begin migration to the Great Salt Lake
1848	Women's Rights Convention at Seneca Falls
	John Noyes founds Oneida Community

last guaranteed in the Nineteenth Amendment to the Constitution.

Historians have only recently realized how much the reform movements of this "Age of the Common Man" were due to the efforts of the "common woman." Women played a vital role in all the social movements of the day. In doing so, they implicitly challenged the popular notion of separate spheres for men and women—the public world for him, home and family for her. The separate spheres argument, although it heaped praise on women for their allegedly superior moral qualities, was meant to exclude them from political life. The reforms discussed in this chapter show clearly that women reformers believed they had a right and a duty to propose solutions for the moral and social problems of the day. Empowered by their own religious beliefs and activism, the Seneca Falls reformers spoke for all American women when they demanded an end to the unfair restrictions they suffered as women.

CONCLUSION

Beginning in the 1820s, the market revolution changed the size and social order of America's preindustrial cities and towns. Immigration, dramatically rapid population growth, and changes in working life and class structure created a host of new urban problems ranging from sanitation to civic order. These changes occurred so rapidly that they seemed overwhelming. Older, face-to-face methods of social control no longer worked. To fill the gap, new kinds of associations—the political party, the religious crusade, the reform cause, the union movement—sprang up. These associations were new manifestations of the deep human desire for social connection, for continuity, and—especially in the growing cities—for social order. A striking aspect of these associations was the uncompromising nature of the attitudes and beliefs on which they were based. Most groups were formed of like-minded people who wanted to impose their will on others. Such intolerance boded ill for the future. If political parties, religious bodies, and reform groups were to splinter along sectional lines (as happened in the 1850s), political compromise would be very difficult. In the meantime, however, Americans came to terms with the market revolution by engaging in a passion for improvement. As a perceptive foreign observer, Francis Grund, noted, "Americans love their country not as it is but as it will be."

REVIEW QUESTIONS

1. What impact did the new immigration of the 1840s and 1850s have on American cities?
2. Why did urbanization produce so many problems?
3. What motivated the social reformers of the period? Were they benevolent helpers or dictatorial social controllers? Study several reform causes and discuss similarities and differences among them.
4. Abolitionism differed little from other reforms in its tactics, but the effects of antislavery activism were politically explosive. Why was this so?

RECOMMENDED READING

Tyler Anbinder, *Five Points* (2001). A social history of New York's most notorious slum.

Arthur Bestor, *Backwoods Utopias* (1950). The standard work on utopian communities.

W. Jeffrey Bolster, *Black Jacks: African American Seamen in the Age of Sail* (1997). Describes a major occupation for African American men.

Paul Boyer, *Urban Masses and Moral Order in America, 1820–1920* (1978). Interprets reform as an effort to reestablish the moral order of the preindustrial community.

Amy Bridges, *A City in the Republic: Antebellum New York and the Origins of Machine Politics* (1984). Describes the transition from elite political control to machine politics.

David Grimsted, *American Mobbing, 1828–1865: Toward Civil War* (1998). A national perspective on mob violence, North and South, including political violence.

James Oliver Horton and Lois E. Horton, *In Hope of Liberty: Culture, Community and Protest Among Northern Free Blacks, 1700–1860* (1997). A fine portrait that adds the perspective of change over time to earlier studies.

Gerard T. Koeppel, *Water for Gotham* (2000). How New York's municipal water system was built in spite of incompetence, corruption, and disease.

W.T. Lhaman Jr., *Jump Jim Crow* (2003). Reconstructs the impact of plays performed by the white actor Thomas D. Rice who created the blackface character, Jim Crow.

Steven Mintz, *Moralists and Modernizers: America's Pre–Civil War Reformers* (1995). A brief but inclusive study of reforms and reformers.

Benjamin Reiss, *The Showman and the Slave: Race, Death and Memory in Barnum's America* (2001). How the celebrated showman exploited a slave woman who (he claimed) had been George Washington's nurse and lived to the ripe old age of 161 to tell about it.

David Roediger, *The Wages of Whiteness* (1991). Explores the links between artisanal republicanism, labor organization, and white racism.

David Rothman, *The Discovery of the Asylum: Social Order and Disorder in the New Republic* (1971). Explores institutional reforms.

Mary Ryan, *Civic Wars: Democracy and Public Life in the American City During the Nineteenth Century* (1997). A study of New York, New Orleans, and San Francisco that argues that urban popular culture was "meeting-place democracy" in action.

Nancy Lusignan Schultz, *Fire and Roses* (2000). Uses the burning of an Ursuline convent in 1834 as an insight into women's culture in Boston.

Kathryn Sklar, *Catharine Beecher: A Study in American Domesticity* (1973). An absorbing "life and times" that explores the possibilities and limits of women's roles in the early nineteenth century.

Deborah Van Broekhoven, *The Devotion of These Women: Rhode Island in the AntiSlavery Network* (2002). Shows how informal women's activities sustained antislavery protest at the local level.

Sean Wilentz, *Chants Democratic: New York City and the Rise of the American Working Class, 1788–1850* (1983). An important book, rooted in social history, that reveals how workers acted upon their understanding of republicanism in confronting the changes wrought by the market revolution.

 For additional study resources for this chapter, go to the *Companion Website*, **http://www.prenhall.com/faragher**.

The Territorial Expansion
of the United States

1830s–1850s

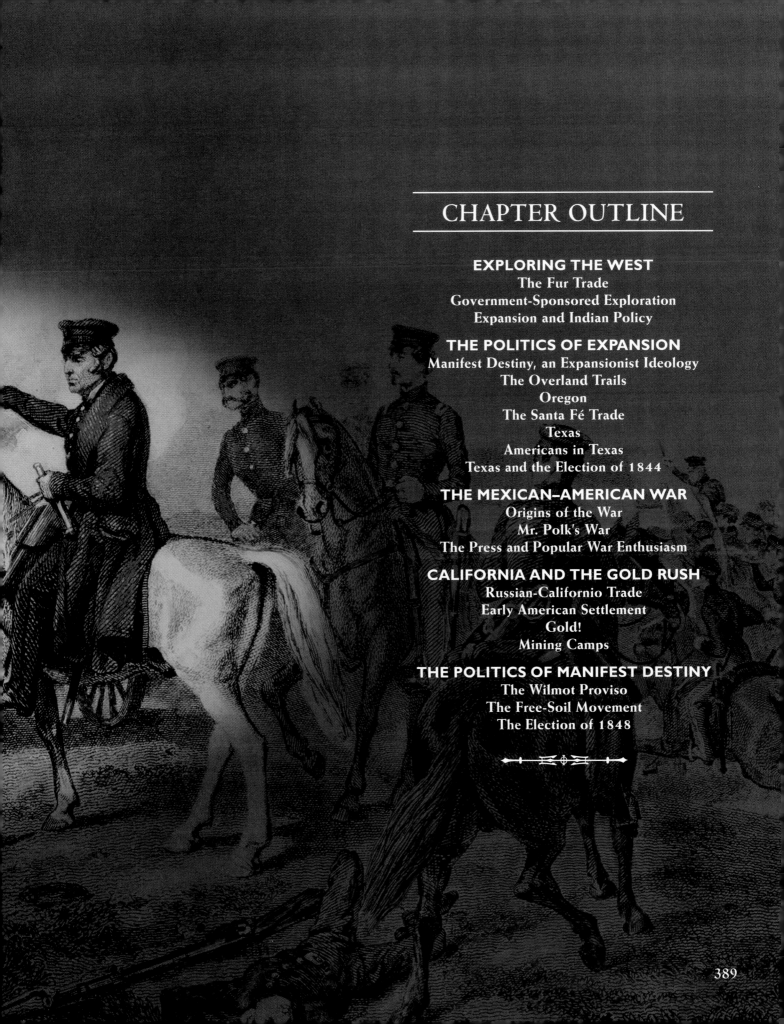

Texans and Tejanos "Remember the Alamo!"

For thirteen days in February and March 1836, a force of 187 Texans held the mission fortress known as the Alamo against a siege by 5,000 Mexican troops under General Antonio López de Santa Anna, president of Mexico. Santa Anna had come north to subdue rebellious Texas, the northernmost part of the Mexican province of Coahuila y Tejas, and to place it under central authority. On March 6 he ordered a final assault, and in brutal fighting that claimed over 1,500 Mexican lives, his army took the mission. All the defenders were killed, including Commander William Travis and the well-known frontiersmen Jim Bowie and Davy Crockett, a crushing defeat for the Texans. But the cry "Remember the Alamo!" rallied their remaining forces, which, less than two months later, routed the Mexican army and forced Santa Anna to grant Texas independence from Mexico. Today, the Alamo, in San Antonio, is one of the most cherished historic shrines in the United States.

But memory is selective: within a generation of the uprising, few remembered that many Tejanos, Spanish-speaking people born in Texas, had joined with American settlers fighting for Texas independence. During the 1820s, the Mexican government had authorized several American colonies, concentrated in the central and eastern portions of the huge Texas territory and

San Antonio

managed by *empresarios* (land agents) like Stephen F. Austin. These settler communities consisted mostly of farmers from the Mississippi Valley, who introduced slavery and cotton growing to the rich lands of coastal and upland Texas.

The Tejano community, descended from eighteenth-century Spanish and Mexican settlers, included wealthy rancheros who raised cattle on the shortgrass prairies of south Texas, as well as the cowboys known as *vaqueros* and the *peónes*, or poor tenant farmers. Although there was relatively little contact between the Americans and Tejanos, their leaders interacted in San Antonio, the center of regional government. The Tejano elite, enthusiastic about American plans for the economic development of Texas, welcomed the American immigrants. Many Americans married into elite Tejano families, who hoped that by thus assimilating and sharing power with the Americans, they could not only maintain but strengthen their community.

The Mexican state, however, was politically and socially unstable during these first years after its successful revolt against Spain in 1821. Liberals favored a loose federal union, conservatives a strong central state. As a northern frontier province, Texas did not have the benefits of statehood; as a result most Tejanos found themselves taking the liberal side in the struggle, opting for more local control over government activities. When, in 1828, the conservative centralists came to power in Mexico City and decided the Americans had too much influence in Texas, many Tejanos rose up with the Americans in opposition. In 1832, the Tejano elite of San Antonio and many prominent rancheros favored provincial autonomy and a strong role for the Americans.

As Santa Anna's army approached from the south, the wealthy ranchero Juan Nepomuceno Seguín, one of the leaders of the San Antonio community, recruited a company of Tejano volunteers and joined the American force inside the walls of the Alamo. During the siege, Commander Travis sent Seguín and some of his men for reinforcements. Stopped by Mexican troops on his way across the lines, Seguín called out, *"¡Somos paisanos!"* (We are countrymen!), confusing the guards just long enough for Seguín and his men to make their escape despite the hail of gunfire that quickly ensued. Seguín returned from his unsuccessful mission to find the burned bodies of the Alamo defenders, including seven San Antonio Tejanos. *"Texas será libre!"* (Texas shall be free!) Seguín called out as he directed the burial of the Alamo defenders. In April, Seguín led a regiment of Tejanos in the decisive battle of San Jacinto that won independence for Texas.

Pleased with independence, Tejanos played an important political role in the new Republic of Texas at first. The liberal Lorenzo de Zavala was chosen vice president, and Seguín became the mayor of San Antonio. But soon things began to change, illustrating a recurring pattern in the American occupation of new lands—a striking shift in the relations between different cultures in frontier areas. Most commonly, in the initial stage newcomers blended with native peoples, creating a "frontier of inclusion." The first hunters, trappers, and traders on every American frontier—west of the Appalachians, in the Southwest, and in the Far West—married into the local community and tried to learn native ways. Outnumbered Americans adapted to local societies as a matter of simple survival.

A second, unstable, stage occurred when the number of Americans increased and they began occupying more and more land or, as in California, "rushing" in great numbers to mine gold, overrunning native communities. This usually resulted in warfare and the rapid growth of hostility and racial prejudice—all of which was largely absent in earlier days.

A third stage—that of stable settlement—occurred when the native community had been completely "removed" or isolated. In this "frontier of exclusion," racial mixing was rare. In Texas, American settlers—initially invited in by Mexicans and Tejanos—developed an anti-Mexican passion, regarding all Spanish-speakers as their Mexican enemies rather than their Tejano allies. Tejanos were attacked and forced from their homes; some of their villages were burned to the ground. "On the pretext that they were Mexicans," Seguín wrote, Americans treated Tejanos "worse than brutes. . . . My countrymen ran to me for protection against the assaults or exactions of these adventurers." But even in his capacity as mayor, Seguín could do little, and in 1842, he and his family, like hundreds of other Tejano families, fled south to Mexico in fear for their lives.

Spanish-speaking communities in Texas, and later in New Mexico and California, like the communities of Indians throughout the West, became conquered peoples. "White folks and Mexicans were never made to live together," a Texas woman told a traveler a few years after the revolution. "The Mexicans had no business here," she said, and the Americans might "just have to get together and drive them all out of the country." The descendants of the first European settlers of the American Southwest had become foreigners in the land their people had lived in for two centuries.

KEY TOPICS

- Continental expansion and the concept of Manifest Destiny
- The contrasting examples of frontier development in Oregon, Texas, and California
- How the political effects of expansion heightened sectional tensions

EXPLORING THE WEST

There seemed to be no stopping the expansion of the American people. By 1840, they had occupied all of the land east of the Mississippi River and had organized all of it (except for Florida and Wisconsin) into states. Of the ten states admitted to the Union between 1800 and 1840, all but one were west of the Appalachian Mountains. Less than sixty years after the United States gained its independence, the majority of its population lived west of the original thirteen states. This rapid expansion was caused by the market revolution, and especially the extraordinary expansion of transportation and commerce (see Chapter 12).

The speed and success of this expansion were a source of deep national pride that whetted appetites for further expansion. Many Americans looked eagerly westward to the vast unsettled reaches of the Louisiana Purchase: to Texas, Santa Fé, to trade with Mexico, and even to the Far West, where New England sea captains had been trading for furs since the 1780s. By 1848, the United States had gained all of these coveted western lands. This chapter examines the way the United States became a continental nation, forming many frontier communities in the process. Exploring the vast continent of North America and gaining an understanding of its geography took several centuries and the efforts of many people.

The Fur Trade

The fur trade, which flourished from the 1670s to the 1840s, was an important spur to exploration on the North American continent. In the 1670s, the British Hudson's Bay Company and its French Canadian rival, Montreal's North West Company, began exploring beyond the Great Lakes in the Canadian West in search of beaver pelts. Traders and trappers for both companies depended on the goodwill and cooperation of the native peoples of the region, in particular the Assiniboins, Crees, Gros Ventres, and Blackfeet, all of whom moved freely across what later became the U.S.–Canadian border. From the marriages of European men with native women arose a distinctive mixed-race group, the "métis" (see Chapter 5). The British-dominated fur trade was an important aspect of international commerce. Americans had long coveted a part of it. Indeed, Thomas Jefferson had sent Lewis and Clark west in 1803 in part to challenge British dominance of the fur trade with western Indian peoples (see Chapter 9).

Not until the 1820s were American companies able to challenge British dominance of the trans-Mississippi fur trade. In 1824, William Henry Ashley of the Rocky Mountain Fur Company instituted the "rendezvous" system. This was a yearly trade fair, held deep in the Rocky Mountains (Green River and Jackson Hole were favored locations), to which trappers brought their catch of furs. These yearly fur rendezvous were modeled on traditional Indian trade gatherings, such as the one at the Mandan villages on the upper Missouri River and the huge gathering that took place every year at Celilo Falls on the Columbia River during the annual salmon run. Like its Indian model, the fur rendezvous was a boisterous, polyglot, many-day affair at which trappers of many nationalities—Americans and Indian peoples, French Canadians, and métis, as well as Mexicans from Santa Fé and Taos—gathered to trade, drink, and gamble.

For the "mountain men" employed by the American fur companies, the rendezvous was their only contact with American

The artist Alfred Jacob Miller, a careful observer of the western fur trade, shows a mountain man and his Indian wife in his 1837 *Bourgeois Walker & His Wife.* Walker and his wife worked together to trap and prepare beaver pelts for market, as did other European men and their Indian wives.

SOURCE: Alfred Jacob Miller, "*Bourgeois Walker and His Wife*," 1837. Watercolor. The Walters Art Museum, Baltimore (37.1940.78).

society. But most trappers, like the British and French before them, sought accommodation and friendship with Indian peoples: nearly half of them contracted long-lasting marriages with Indian women, who not only helped in the trapping and curing of furs but also acted as vital diplomatic links between the white and Indian worlds. One legendary trapper adapted so well that he became a Crow chief: the African American Jim Beckwourth, who married a Crow woman and was accepted into her tribe.

For all its adventure, the American fur trade was short-lived. By the 1840s, the population of beaver in western streams was virtually destroyed, and the day of the mountain man was over. But with daring journeys like that of Jedediah Smith, the first American to enter California over the Sierra Nevada mountains, the mountain men had helped forge a clear picture of western geography. Soon, permanent settlers would follow the trails they had blazed.

Government-Sponsored Exploration

The federal government played a major role in the exploration and development of the West. The exploratory and scientific aspects of the Lewis and Clark expedition in 1804–06 set a precedent for many government-financed quasi-military expeditions. In 1806 and 1807, Lieutenant Zebulon Pike led an expedition to the Rocky Mountains in Colorado. Major Stephen Long's exploration and mapping of the Great Plains in the years 1819–20 was part of a show of force meant to frighten British fur trappers out of the West. Then, in 1843 and 1844, another military explorer, John C. Frémont, mapped the overland trails to Oregon and California. In the 1850s, the Pacific Railroad surveys explored possible transcontinental railroad routes. The tradition of government-sponsored western exploration continued after the Civil War in the famous geological surveys, the best known of which is the 1869 Grand Canyon exploration by Major John Wesley Powell (see Map 14.1).

Beginning with Long's expedition, the results of these surveys were published by the government, complete with maps, illustrations, and, after the Civil War, photographs. These publications fed a strong popular appetite for pictures of the breathtaking scenery of the Far West and information about its inhabitants. Artists like Karl Bodmer, who accompanied a private expedition by the scientifically inclined German prince Maximilian in the years 1833–34, produced stunning portraits of American Indians. Over the next three decades, Thomas Moran, Albert Bierstadt, and other landscape artists traveled west with government expeditions and came home to paint grand (and sometimes fanciful) pictures of Yosemite Valley and the Yellowstone River region (later designated among the first national parks). All these images of the American West made a power-

ful contribution to the emerging American self-image. American pride in the land—the biggest of this, the longest of that, the most spectacular of something else—was founded on the images brought home by government surveyors and explorers.

In the wake of the pathfinders came hundreds of government geologists and botanists as well as the surveyors who mapped and plotted the West for settlement according to the Land Ordinance of 1785. The basic pattern of land survey and sale established by these measures (see Chapter 7) was followed all the way to the Pacific Ocean. The federal government sold the western public lands at low prices and, to veterans of the War of 1812, gave away land in the Old Northwest. And following policies established in the Old Northwest (see Chapter 9), the federal government also shouldered the expense of Indian removal, paying the soldiers or the officials who fought or talked Indian peoples into giving up their lands. In addition, the federal government made long-term commitments to compensate the Indian people themselves, and supported the forts and soldiers whose task was to maintain peace between settlers and Indian peoples in newly opened areas.

Expansion and Indian Policy

While American artists were painting the way of life of western Indian peoples, eastern Indian tribes were being removed from their homelands to Indian Territory (present-day Oklahoma, Kansas, and Nebraska), a region west of Arkansas, Missouri, and Iowa on the eastern edge of the Great Plains, widely regarded as unfarmable and popularly known as the Great American Desert. The justification for this western removal, as Thomas Jefferson had explained early in the century, was the creation of a space where Indian people could live undisturbed by white people while they slowly adjusted to "civilized" ways. But the government officials who negotiated the removals failed to predict the tremendous speed at which white people would settle the West (see Map 14.2).

As a result, encroachment on Indian Territory was not long in coming. The territory was crossed by the Santa Fé Trail, established in 1821; in the 1840s, the northern part was crossed by the heavily traveled Overland Trails to California, Oregon, and the Mormon community in Utah. In 1854, the government abolished the northern half of Indian Territory, establishing the Kansas and Nebraska Territories in its place and opening them to immediate white settlement. The tribes of the area—the Potawatomis, Wyandots, Kickapoos, Sauks, Foxes, Delawares, Shawnees, Kaskaskias, Peorias, Piankashaws, Weas, Miamis, Omahas, Otos, and Missouris—signed treaties accepting either vastly reduced reservations or allotments. Those who accepted allotments—sections of private land—often sold them,

MAP EXPLORATION

To explore an interactive version of this map, go to **www.prenhall.com/faragher5/map14.1**

Exploration routes:
— Lewis and Clark, 1804-06
— Zebulon Pike, 1806-07
— Thompson, 1810-11
— Stephen Long, 1819-20
— Jedediah Smith, 1822-30

MAP 14.1 Exploration of the Continent, 1804–30 Lewis and Clark's "voyage of discovery" of 1804–06 was the first of many government-sponsored western military expeditions. Crossing the Great Plains in 1806, Lieutenant Zebulon Pike was captured by the Spanish in their territory and taken to Mexico, but returned in 1807 via Texas. Major Stephen Long, who crossed the Plains in 1819–20, found them "arid and forbidding." Meanwhile, fur trappers, among them the much-traveled Jedediah Smith, became well acquainted with the West as they hunted beaver for their pelts.

under pressure, to white people. Thus, many of the Indian people who had hoped for independence and escape from white pressures in Indian Territory lost both their autonomy and their tribal identity.

The people in the southern part of Indian Territory, in what is now Oklahoma, fared somewhat better. Those members of the southern tribes—the Cherokees, Chickasaws, Choctaws, Creeks, and Seminoles—who had survived the trauma of forcible removal from the Southeast in the 1830s, quickly created impressive new communities. The five tribes divided up the territory and established self-governing nations with their own schools and churches. The societies they created were not so different from the American societies from which they had been expelled. The five tribes even carried slavery west with them: an elite economic group established plantations and shipped their cotton to New Orleans like other Southerners. Until after the Civil War, these southern tribes were able to withstand outside pressures and remain the self-governing communities that treaties had assured them they would be.

The removal of the eastern tribes did not solve "the Indian Problem," the term many Americans used to describe their relationship with the first occupants of the land. West of Indian Territory were the nomadic and warlike Indians of the Great Plains: the Sioux, Cheyennes, Arapahoes, Comanches, and Kiowas. Beyond them were the seminomadic tribes of the Rocky Mountains—the Blackfeet, Crows, Utes, Shoshonis, Nez Percé, and Salish peoples—and, in the Southwest, the farming cultures of the Pueblos, Hopis, Acomas, Zunis, Pimas, and Papagos and the migratory Apaches and Navajos. Even farther west were hundreds of

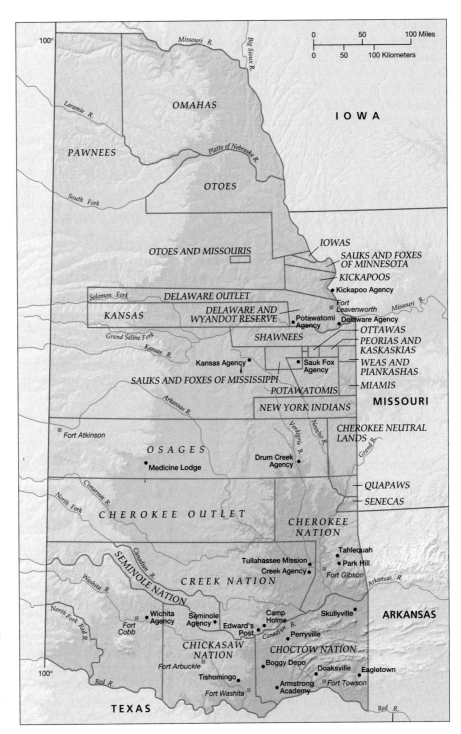

MAP 14.2 Indian Territory Before the Kansas-Nebraska Act of 1854 Indian Territory lay west of Arkansas, Missouri, and Iowa and east of Mexican Territory. Most of the Indian peoples who lived there in the 1830s and the 1840s had been "removed" from east of the Mississipi River. The southern part (now Oklahoma) was inhabited by peoples from the Old Southwest: the Cherokees, Chickasaws, Choctaws, Creeks, and Seminoles. North of that (in what is now Kansas and Nebraska) lived peoples who had been removed from the Old Northwest. All these Indian peoples had trouble adjusting not only to a new climate and a new way of life, but to the close proximity of some Indian tribes who were their traditional enemies.

small tribes in California and the Pacific Northwest. Clearly, all of these people could not be "removed," for where could they go? The first western pioneers ignored the issue. Beginning in the 1840s, they simply passed through the far western tribal lands on their way to establish new frontiers of settlement in California and Oregon. Later, after the Civil War, the government would undertake a series of Indian wars that ultimately left the remaining Indian peoples penned up on small reservations.

THE POLITICS OF EXPANSION

America's rapid expansion had many consequences, but perhaps the most significant was that it reinforced Americans' sense of themselves as pioneering people. In the 1890s, Frederick Jackson Turner, America's most famous historian, observed that the repeated experience of settling new frontiers across the continent had shaped Americans into a uniquely adventurous, optimistic, and democratic people. Other historians have disagreed with Turner, but there is no question that his view of the frontier long ago won the battle for popular opinion. Ever since the time of Daniel Boone, venturing into the wilderness has held a special place in the American imagination, seen almost as an American right.

Manifest Destiny, an Expansionist Ideology

How did Americans justify their restless expansionism? After all, the United States was already a very large country with much undeveloped land. To push beyond existing boundaries was to risk war with Great Britain, which claimed the Pacific Northwest, and with Mexico, which held what is now Texas, New Mexico, Arizona, Utah, Nevada, California, and part of Colorado. If the United States prevailed, it would be reducing 75,000 Spanish-speaking people and 150,000 Indian people to subject status. Undertaking such a conquest required a rationale.

In 1845, newspaperman John O'Sullivan provided it. It was, he wrote, "our manifest destiny to overspread the continent allotted by Providence for the free development of our yearly multiplying millions." Sullivan argued that Americans had a God-given right to bring the benefits of American democracy to other, more backward peoples—meaning Mexicans and Indians—by force, if necessary. The notion of manifest destiny summed up the powerful combination of pride in what America had achieved and missionary zeal and racist attitudes toward other peoples that lay behind the thinking of many expansionists. Americans were proud of their rapid development: the surge in population, the remarkable canals and railroads, the grand scale of the American enterprise.

Why shouldn't it be even bigger? Almost swaggering, Americans dared other countries—Great Britain in particular—to stop them.

Behind the bravado was some new international thinking about the economic future of the United States. After the devastating Panic of 1837 (see Chapter 11), many politicians became convinced that the nation's prosperity depended on vastly expanded trade with Asia. The China trade had accustomed many New Englanders to trade across the Pacific, and greater markets beckoned (see Chapter 9). Senator Thomas Hart Benton of Missouri had been advocating trade with India by way of the Missouri and Columbia Rivers since the 1820s (not the easiest of routes, as Lewis and Clark had shown). Soon Benton and others were pointing out how much Pacific trade would increase if the United States held the magnificent harbors of the west coast, among them Puget Sound in the Oregon Country, held jointly with Britain, and the bays of San Francisco and San Diego, both in Mexican-held California.

Expansionism was deeply tied to national politics. O'Sullivan, whose "manifest destiny" became the expansionist watchword, was not a neutral observer: he was the editor of the *Democratic Review*, a party newspaper. Most Democrats were wholehearted supporters of expansion, whereas many Whigs (especially in the North) opposed it. Whigs welcomed most of the changes wrought by industrialization, but advocated strong government policies that would guide growth and development within the country's existing boundaries; they feared (correctly) that expansion would raise the contentious issue of the extension of slavery to new territories.

On the other hand, many Democrats feared the industrialization that the Whigs welcomed. Where the Whigs saw economic progress, Democrats saw economic depression (the Panic of 1837 was the worst the nation had experienced), uncontrolled urban growth, and growing social unrest. For many Democrats, the answer to the nation's social ills was to continue to follow Thomas Jefferson's vision of establishing agriculture in the new territories in order to counterbalance industrialization (see Chapter 9). Another factor in the political struggle over expansion in the 1840s was that many Democrats were Southerners, for whom the continual expansion of cotton-growing lands was a matter of social faith as well as economic necessity.

These were politicians' reasons. The average farmer moved west for many other reasons: land hunger, national pride, plain and simple curiosity, and a sense of adventure.

The Overland Trails

The 2,000-mile trip on the Overland Trails from the banks of the Missouri River to Oregon and California usually took seven months, sometimes more. Travel was slow, dangerous, tedious, and exhausting. Forced to lighten their loads as animals died and winter weather threatened, pioneers often arrived at their destinations with little food and few belongings. Uprooted from family and familiar surroundings, pioneers faced the prospect of being, in the poignant and much-used biblical phrase, "strangers in a strange land." Yet despite the risks, settlers streamed west: 5,000 to Oregon by 1845 and about 3,000 to California by 1848 (before the discovery of gold) (see Map 14.3).

Pioneers had many motives for making the trip. Glowing reports from Oregon's Willamette Valley, for example, seemed to promise economic opportunity and healthy surroundings, an alluring combination to farmers in the malaria-prone Midwest who had been hard hit by the Panic of 1837. But rational motives do not tell the whole story. Many men were motivated by a sense of adventure, by a desire to experience the unknown, or, as they put it, to "see the elephant." Women were more likely to think of the trip as *A Pioneer's Search for an Ideal Home*, the title that Phoebe Judson chose for her account of her family's 1852 trip to Oregon.

Few pioneers traveled alone, partly because they feared Indian attack (which was rare), but largely because they needed help fording rivers or crossing mountains with heavy wagons. Most Oregon pioneers traveled with their families but usually also joined a larger group, forming a "train." In the earliest years, when the route was still uncertain, trains hired "pilots," generally former fur trappers. Often the men of the wagon train drew up semimilitary constitutions, electing a leader. Democratic as this process appeared, not everyone was willing to obey the leader, and many trains experienced dissension and breakups along the trail. But in essence, all pioneers—men, women, and children—were part of a new, westward-moving community in which they had to accept both the advantages and disadvantages of community membership.

Wagon trains started westward as soon as the prairies were green (thus ensuring feed for the livestock). The daily routine was soon established. Men took care of the moving equipment and the animals, while the women cooked and kept track of the children. Slowly, at a rate of about fifteen miles a day, the wagon trains moved west along the Platte River, crossing the Continental Divide at South Pass in present-day Wyoming. West of the Rockies the climate was much drier. The

long, dusty stretch along the Snake River in present-day southern Idaho finally gave way to Oregon's steep and difficult Blue Mountains and to the dangerous rafting down the Columbia River, in which many drowned and all were drenched by the cold winter rains of the Pacific Northwest. California-bound migrants faced even worse hazards: the complete lack of water in the Humbolt Sink region of northern Nevada and the looming Sierra Nevadas, which had to be crossed before the winter snows came. (Some members of the ill-fated Donner party, snowbound on the Nevada side of that range in 1846–47, resorted to cannibalism before they were rescued.)

In addition to the ever-present tedium and exhaustion, wagon trains were beset by such trail hazards as illness and accident. Danger from Indian attack, which all pioneers feared, was actually very small. It appears that unprovoked white attacks on Indians were more common than the reverse.

In contrast, cholera killed at least a thousand people a year in 1849, and in the early 1850s, when it was common

MAP 14.3 The Overland Trails, 1840 All the great trails west started at the Missouri River. The Oregon, California, and Mormon Trails followed the Platte River into Wyoming, crossed South Pass, and divided in western Wyoming. The much harsher Santa Fé Trail stretched 900 miles southwest across the Great Plains. All of the trails crossed Indian Territory and, to greater or lesser extent, Mexican possessions as well.

J. Goldsborough Bruff, one of thousands who rushed to California for gold in 1849, sketched many events in his Overland Trail journey. Here he depicts several wagons being ferried over the Platte River. The need for individuals to cooperate is obvious. Less obvious in this sketch is the danger: most river crossing points lacked ferries, and both people and livestock often drowned trying to ford them.

SOURCE: Joseph Goldsborough Bruff, *Ferriage of the Platte above the Mouth of Deer Creek, July 20, 1849.* This item is reproduced by permission of The Henry E. Huntington Library and Art Gallery, San Marino, CA (HM 8044, #50).

Both Great Britain and the United States claimed the Oregon Country by right of discovery, but in the Convention of 1818, the two nations agreed to occupy it jointly, postponing a final decision on its disposition. In reality, the British clearly dominated the region. In 1824, the Hudson's Bay Company consolidated Britain's position by establishing a major fur trading post at Fort Vancouver, on the banks of the Columbia River. Like all fur-trading ventures, the post exemplified the racial mixing of a "frontier of inclusion." Fort Vancouver housed a polyglot population of eastern Indians (Delawares and Iroquois), local Chinook Indians, French and métis from Canada, British traders, and Hawaiians. But the effect of the fur trade on native tribes in Oregon was catastrophic; suffering the fate of all Indian peoples after their initial contact with Europeans, they were decimated by European diseases.

The first permanent European settlers in Oregon were retired fur trappers and their Indian wives and families. They favored a spot in the lush and temperate

along sections of the trail along the Platte River. Spread by contaminated water, cholera caused vomiting and diarrhea, which in turn led to extreme dehydration and death, often in one night. In the afflicted regions, trailside graves were a frequent and grim sight. Drownings were not uncommon, nor were accidental ax wounds or shootings, and children sometimes fell out of wagons and were run over. The members of the wagon train community did what they could to arrange decent burials, and they provided support for survivors: men helped widows drive their wagons onward, women nursed and tended babies whose mothers were dead, and at least one parentless family, the seven Sager children, were brought to Oregon in safety.

By 1860, almost 300,000 people had traveled the Overland Trails to Oregon or California. Ruts from the wagon wheels can be seen in a number of places along the route even today. In 1869, the completion of the transcontinental railroad marked the end of the wagon train era (see Figure 14.1).

Oregon

The American settlement of Oregon provides a capsule example of the stages of frontier development. The first contacts between the region's Indian peoples and Europeans were commercial. Spanish, British, Russian, and American ships traded for sea otter skins from the 1780s to about 1810. Subsequently, land-based groups scoured the region for beaver skins as well. In this first "frontier of inclusion" there were frequent, often sexual contacts between Indians and Europeans.

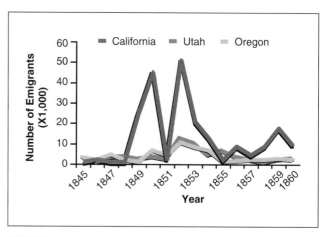

FIGURE 14.1   Overland Emigration to Oregon, California, and Utah, 1840–60 Before 1849, the westward migration consisted primarily of family groups going to Oregon or Utah. The discovery of gold in California dramatically changed the migration: through 1854, most migrants were single men "rushing" to California, which remained the favored destination up until 1860. Over the twenty-year period from 1840 to 1860, the Overland Trails were transformed from difficult and dangerous routes to well-marked and well-served thoroughfares.

SOURCE: John Unruh Jr., *The Plains Across* (Champaign-Urbana: University of Illinois Press, 1979), pp. 119–20.

Willamette Valley that became known as French Prairie, although the inhabitants were a mixed group of Americans, British, French Canadians, Indian peoples, and métis. The next to arrive were Protestant and Catholic missionaries, among them Methodist Jason Lee in 1834, Congregationalists Marcus and Narcissa Whitman in 1836, Franciscan priests Frances Blanchet and Modeste Demers in 1838, and Jesuit Pierre-Jean De Smet in 1840. None of these missionaries was very successful. Epidemics had taken the lives of many of the region's peoples, and those who were left were disinclined to give up their nomadic life and settle down as the missionaries wanted them to do. (See Out of Many Voices: Narcissa Whitman Has An Unexpected Encounter With Civilization.)

Finally, in the 1840s, came the Midwest farmers who would make up the majority of Oregon's permanent settlers, carried on the wave of enthusiasm known as "Oregon fever" and lured by free land and patriotism. By 1845, Oregon boasted 5,000 American settlers, most of them living in the Willamette Valley and laying claim to lands to which they had as yet no legal right, because neither Britain nor the United States had concluded land treaties with Oregon's Indian peoples. Their arrival signaled Oregon's shift from a "frontier of inclusion" to a "frontier of exclusion."

For these early settlers, life was at first very difficult. Most arrived in late autumn, exhausted from the strenuous overland journey. They could not begin to farm until the spring, and so they depended on the earlier settlers for their survival over the winter. In the earliest years, American settlers got vital help from the Hudson's Bay Company, even though its director, Dr. John McLoughlin, had been ordered by the British government not to encourage American settlement. McLoughlin disregarded his orders, motivated both by sympathy for the plight of the newcomers and by a keen sense of the dangers his enterprise would face if he were outnumbered by angry Americans.

The handful of American settlers in Oregon found themselves in possession of a remote frontier. One of the

OUT OF MANY VOICES

NARCISSA WHITMAN HAS AN UNEXPECTED ENCOUNTER WITH CIVILIZATION

In 1836, Narcissa Whitman, with her husband and another missionary couple, made a grueling cross-country trip to Oregon. As Whitman wrote to her mother on September 12, 1836, there was a surprise at journey's end.

WE ARE NOW IN VANCOUVER, THE NEW YORK OF the Pacific Ocean. Our first sight, as we approached the fort, was two ships lying in the harbor, one of which, the Neriade, Captain Royal, had just arrived from London. The Columbia, Captain Dandy, came last May, and has since been to the Sandwich Islands, and returned. On landing we first met Mr. Townsend, whom we saw at Walla Walla. He is from Philadelphia, and has been in the mountains two years. He is sent here by a society to collect the different species of bipeds, and quadrupeds, peculiar to this country. We brought a parcel of letters to him, the first he had received since he had left home. Mr. Townsend led us into the fort. But before we reached the home of the chief Factor, Dr. McLoughlin, we were met by several gentlemen, who came to give us a welcome, Mr. Douglas, Mr. Tolmie and Dr. McLoughlin, of the Hudson's Bay Company, who invited us in and seated us on the sofa. Soon we were introduced to Mrs. McLoughlin and Mrs. Douglas, both natives of the country—half breeds. After chatting a little we were invited to walk in the garden.

What a delightful place this is; what a contrast to the rough, barren sand plains, through which we had so recently passed. Here we find fruit of every description, apples, peaches, grapes, pears, plums, and fig trees in abundance; also cucumbers, melons, beans, peas, beets, cabbage, tomatoes and every kind of vegetable too numerous to be mentioned. Every part is very neat and tastefully arranged, with fine walks, lined on each side with strawberry vines. At the opposite end of the garden is a good summer house covered with grape vines. Here I must mention the origin of these grapes and apples. A gentlemen, twelve years ago while at a party in London, put the seeds of the grapes and apples which he ate into his vest pocket. Soon afterwards he took a voyage to this country and left them here, and now they are greatly multiplied. ∎

SOURCE: Clifford Drury, *First White Woman Over the Rockies* vol.1 (Glendale, CA: Arthur H. Clark Co., 1963): p.101.

This view of Fort Vancouver on the Columbia River shows established agriculture and thriving commerce, indicated by the large sailing ship on the river, which is probably the Hudson's Bay Company yearly supply ship from England. It was a scene like this that led Narcissa Whitman to call Fort Vancouver "the New York of the Pacific".

SOURCE: Fort Vancouver, Oregon, by unknown artist (probably John Mix Stanley), ca. 1845–48. Paul Kane Collection. WA MSS 278. Yale Collection of Western Americana, Beinecke Rare Book and Manuscript Library, Yale University.

first things they did was to draw up their own constitution, modeled on that of the State of Iowa, which one settler had brought with him. The influx of American settlers, and their efforts to establish their own government, created strains between the United States and Britain. In 1845, President James K. Polk, who was deeply anti-British, coined the belligerent slogan "Fifty-four Forty or Fight," suggesting that the United States would go to war if it didn't get control of all the territory south of 54°40′ north latitude, the border between Russian Alaska and British Canada. In office, however, Polk was willing to compromise. In June 1846, Britain and the United States concluded a treaty establishing the 49th parallel as the U.S.–Canada border, but leaving the island of Vancouver in British hands. The British then quietly wound up their declining fur trade in the region. In 1849, the Hudson's Bay Company closed

Fort Vancouver and moved its operations to Victoria, thus ending the Pacific Northwest's largely successful experience with joint occupancy. Oregon's Donation Land Claim Act of 1850 codified the practice of giving 320 acres to each white male age eighteen or over and 640 acres to each married couple to settle in the territory (African Americans, Hawaiians, and American Indians were excluded).

The white settlers realized that they had to forge strong community bonds if they hoped to survive on their distant frontier. Cooperation and mutual aid were the rule. Until well into the 1850s, residents organized yearly parties that traveled back along the last stretches of the Oregon Trail to help straggling parties making their way to the territory. Kinship networks were strong and vital: many pioneers came to join family who had migrated before them. Food sharing and mutual labor were essen-

Alfred Jabob Miller painted the busy life of Fort Laramie, a multiracial trading fort, in 1837. Bent's Fort, another multiracial trading center, would have looked much like this.

SOURCE: Alfred Jacob Miller, *The Interior of Fort Laramie,* 1858–60. The Walters Art Museum, Baltimore.

tial in the early years, when crop and livestock loss to weather or natural predators was common. Help, even to total strangers, was customary in times of illness or death.

Although this community feeling did not extend to Indian groups as a whole, relations with the small and unthreatening disease-thinned local Indian tribes were generally peaceful until 1847, when Cayuse Indians killed the missionaries Marcus and Narcissa Whitman. Their deaths triggered a series of "wars" against the remaining native people. A "frontier of exclusion" had been achieved. Nonetheless, the process by which Oregon became part of the United States (it was admitted as a state in 1859) was relatively peaceful, especially when compared with American expansion into the Spanish provinces of New Mexico and Texas.

The Santa Fé Trade

Commerce with Santa Fé, first settled by colonists from Mexico in 1609, and the center of the Spanish frontier province of New Mexico, had long been desired by American traders. But Spain had forcefully resisted American penetration. For example, Lieutenant Zebulon Pike's Great Plains and Rocky Mountain exploration of 1806–07 ended ignominiously with his capture by Spanish soldiers.

When Mexico gained its independence from Spain in 1821, this exclusionary policy changed. American traders

were now welcome in Santa Fé, but the trip over the legendary Santa Fé Trail from Independence, Missouri, was a forbidding 900 miles of arid plains, deserts, and mountains. On the Santa Fé trail, unlike the Oregon Trail, there was serious danger of Indian attack, for neither the Comanches nor the Apaches of the southern high plains tolerated trespassers. In 1825, at the urging of Senator Benton and others, Congress voted federal protection for the Santa Fé Trail, even though much of it lay in Mexican territory. The number of people venturing west in the trading caravans increased yearly because the profits were so great (the first American trader to reach Santa Fé, William Becknell, realized a thousand percent profit). By the 1840s, a few hundred American trappers and traders (called *extranjeros,* or "foreigners") lived permanently in New Mexico. In Santa Fé, some American merchants married daughters of important local families, suggesting the start of the inclusive stage of frontier contact.

Settlements and trading posts soon grew up along the long Santa Fé Trail. One of the most famous was Bent's Fort, on the Arkansas River in what is now eastern Colorado, which did a brisk trade in beaver skins and buffalo robes. Like most trading posts, it had a multiethnic population. In the 1840s, the occupants included housekeeper Josefa Tafoya of Taos, whose husband was a carpenter from Pennsylvania; an African American cook; a French tailor from New Orleans; Mexican muleteers; and a number of Indian women, including the two Cheyenne women who were the (successive) wives of William Bent, cofounder of the fort. The three small communities of Pueblo, Hardscrabble, and Greenhorn, spinoffs of Bent's Fort, were populated by men of all nationalities and their Mexican and Indian wives. All three communities lived by trapping, hunting, and a little farming. This racially and economically mixed existence was characteristic of all early trading frontiers, but another western frontier, the American agricultural settlement in Texas, was different from the start.

Texas

In 1821, when Mexico gained its independence from Spain, there were 2,240 Tejano (Spanish-speaking) residents of Texas. Established in 1716 as a buffer against possible French attack on New Spain, the main Texas

Painted by George Catlin about 1834, this scene, *Commanche Village Life*, shows how the everday life of the Comanches was tied to buffalo. The women in the foreground are scraping buffalo hide, and buffalo meat can be seen drying on racks. The men and boys may be planning their next buffalo hunt.

SOURCE: Smithsonian American Art Museum, Washington, D.C. / Art Resource, N.Y.

depended for food and clothing. Their relentless raids on the Texas settlements rose from a determination to hold onto this rich buffalo territory, for the buffalo provided all that they wanted. They had no interest in being converted by mission priests or incorporated into mixed-race trading communities.

Americans in Texas

In 1821, seeking to increase the strength of its buffer zone between the heart of Mexico and the marauding Comanches, the Mexican government granted Moses Austin of Missouri an area of 18,000 square miles within the territory of Texas. Moses died shortly thereafter, and the grant was taken up by his son Stephen F. Austin, who became the first American *empresario* (land agent). From the beginning, the American settlement of Texas differed markedly from that of other frontiers. Elsewhere, Americans frequently settled on land to which Indian peoples still held title, or, as in the case of Oregon, they occupied lands to which other countries also made claim. In contrast, the Texas settlement was fully legal: Austin and other empresarios owned their lands as a result of formal contracts with the Mexican government. In exchange, Austin agreed that he and his colonists would become Mexican citizens and would adopt the Catholic religion. It is difficult to say which of these two provisions was the more remarkable, for most nineteenth-century Americans defined their Americanness in terms of citizenship and the Protestant religion.

Additionally, in startling contrast with the usual frontier free-for-all, Austin's community was populated with hand-picked settlers, Austin insisting that "no frontiersman who has no other occupation than that of hunter will be received—no drunkard, no gambler, no profane swearer, no idler." Austin chose instead prosperous southern slaveowners eager to expand the lands devoted to cotton. Soon, Americans (including African American slaves, to whose presence the Mexican government turned a blind eye) outnumbered Tejanos by nearly two to one: in 1830, there were an estimated 7,000 Americans and 4,000 Tejanos living in Texas.

The Austin settlement of 1821 was followed by others, twenty-six in all, concentrating in the fertile river bottoms of east Texas (along the Sabine River) and south central Texas (the Brazos and the Colorado Rivers). These large settlements were highly organized farming enterprises whose principal crop was cotton, grown by African

settlements of Nacogdoches, Goliad, and San Antonio remained small, far-flung frontier outposts (see Chapter 5). As was customary throughout New Spain, communities were organized around three centers: missions and *presidios* (forts), which formed the nuclei of towns, and the large cattle-raising ranchos on which rural living depended. As elsewhere in New Spain, society was divided into two classes: the *ricos* (rich), who claimed Spanish descent, and the mixed-blood *pobres* (poor). The most colorful figures were *mestizo* (mixed-blood) *vaqueros*, renowned for their horsemanship; Americanization of their name made "buckaroos" of the American cowboys to whom they later taught their skills. Most Tejanos were neither ricos nor vaqueros but small farmers or common laborers who led hardscrabble frontier lives. But all Tejanos, rich and poor, faced the constant threat of raids by Comanche Indians.

The Comanches exemplified the revolutionary changes brought about in the lives of Plains Indians by the reintroduction of horses into the American continent (see Chapter 5). "A Comanche on his feet is out of his element . . . but the moment he lays his hands upon his horse," said artist George Catlin, "I doubt very much whether any people in the world can surpass [him]." Legendary warriors, the Comanches raided the small Texas settlements at will and even struck deep into Mexico itself. Once they raided so far south that they saw brightly plumed birds (parrots) and "tiny men with tails" (monkeys); apparently they had reached the tropical Yucatán. The nomadic Comanches followed the immense buffalo herds on which they

American slave labor and sold in the international market. By the early 1830s, Americans in Texas, ignoring the border between Mexican Texas and the United States, were sending an estimated $500,000 worth of goods (mostly cotton) yearly to New Orleans for export.

Austin's colonists and those who settled later were predominantly Southerners who viewed Texas as a natural extension of the cotton frontier in Mississippi and Louisiana (see Chapter 11). These settlers created "enclaves" (self-contained communities) that had little contact with Tejanos or Indian peoples. In fact, although they lived in Mexican territory, most Americans never bothered to learn Spanish. Nor, in spite of Austin's promises, did they become Mexican citizens or adopt the Catholic religion. Yet, because of the nature of agreements made by the empresarios, the Americans could not set up local American-style governments like the one created by settlers in Oregon. Like the immigrants who flooded into east coast cities (see Chapter 13), the Americans in Texas were immigrants to another country—but one they did not intend to adapt to.

The one exception to American exclusiveness occurred in San Antonio, the provincial government center. There, just as in Santa Fé, a handful of wealthy Americans married into the Tejano elite with ease. One such marriage in San Antonio linked wealthy Louisianan James Bowie, the legendary fighter for whom the Bowie knife is named, and Ursula Veramendi, daughter of the vice governor of Texas. With the marriage, Bowie became an honored and well-connected Mexican merchant. Only after the death of his wife and children in a cholera epidemic in 1833, did Bowie support the cause of Anglo-Texan independence, going on to fight—and die—at the Alamo.

For a brief period, Texas was big enough to hold three communities: Comanche, Tejano, and American. The nomadic Comanches rode the high plains of northern and western Texas, raiding settlements primarily for horses. The Tejanos maintained their ranchos and missions mostly in the South, while American farmers occupied the eastern and south central sections. Each group would fight to hold its land: the Comanches, their rich hunting grounds; the Mexicans, their towns and ranchos; and the newcomers, the Americans, their rich land grants.

The balance among the three communities in Texas was broken in 1828, when centrists gained control of the government in Mexico City and, in a dramatic shift of policy, decided to exercise firm control over the northern province. As the Mexican government restricted American immigration, outlawed slavery, levied customs duties and taxes, and planned other measures, Americans seethed and talked of rebellion. Bolstering their cause were as many as 20,000 additional Americans, many of them openly expansionist, who flooded into Texas after 1830. These most recent settlers did not intend to become Mexican citizens. Instead, they planned to take over Texas.

Many of the post–1830 immigrants were vehemently anti-Mexican. Statements of racial superiority were commonplace, and even Stephen Austin wrote in 1836 that he saw the Texas conflict as one of barbarism on the part of "a mongrel Spanish-Indian and negro race, against civilization and the Anglo-American race." Most recent American migrants to Texas had come from the South, and racist statements of this sort made political compromise with the Mexican government, a step favored by many of the older American settlers, impossible.

Between 1830 and 1836, in spite of the mediation efforts of Austin (who was imprisoned for eighteen months by the Mexican government for his pains), the mood on both the Mexican and the American–Texan sides became more belligerent. In the fall of 1835, war finally broke out, and a volunteer American and Tejano army assembled. After the disastrous defeat at the Alamo desbcribed in the chapter opener, Mexican general and president Antonio López de Santa Anna led his army in pursuit of the remaining army of American and Tejano volunteers commanded by General Sam Houston. On April 21, 1836, at the San Jacinto River in eastern Texas, Santa Anna thought he had Houston trapped at last. Confident of victory against the exhausted Texans, Santa Anna's army rested in the afternoon, failing even to post sentries. Although Houston advised against it, Houston's men voted to attack immediately rather than wait till the next morning. Shouting "Remember the Alamo!" for the first time, the Texans completely surprised their opponents and won an overwhelming victory. On May 14, 1836, Santa Anna signed a treaty fixing the southern boundary of the newly independent Republic of Texas at the Rio Grande. The Mexican Congress, however, repudiated the treaty and refused to recognize Texan independence. It also rejected the offer by President Andrew Jackson to solve the matter through purchase. In the eyes of the Mexicans, the American insistence on the Rio Grande boundary was little more than a blatant effort to stake a claim to New Mexico, an older and completely separate Spanish settlement. An effort by the Republic of Texas in 1841 to capture Santa Fé was easily repulsed (see Map 14.4).

Texas and the Election of 1844

The Republic of Texas was unexpectedly rebuffed in another quarter as well. The U.S. Congress refused to grant it statehood when, in 1837, Texas applied for admission to the Union. Petitions opposing the admission of a fourteenth slave state (there were then thirteen free states) poured into Congress. Congressman (and former president) John Quincy Adams of Massachusetts led the opposition to the admission of Texas. Congress debated and ultimately dropped the Texas application. President Jackson did manage to extend diplomatic recognition to

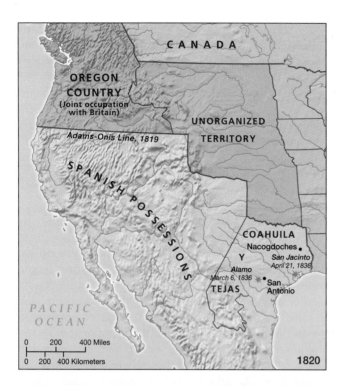

MAP 14.4 Texas: From Mexican Province to U.S. State
In the space of twenty years, Texas changed shape three times. Initially part of the Mexican province of Coahuila y Tejas, it became the Republic of Texas in 1836, following the Texas Revolt, and was annexed to the United States in that form in 1845. Finally, in the Compromise of 1850 following the Mexican-American War, it took its present shape.

the Republic of Texas, on March 3, 1837, less than twenty-four hours before he left office.

The unresolved conflict with Mexico put heavy stress on American-Tejano relations. Immediately after the revolt, San Antonio, the most important city of Mexican Texas, saw an accommodation between the old elite and the new American authorities. Although they slowly lost political power, members of the Tejano elite were not immediately dispossessed of their property. As before, ambitious Anglos married into the Tejano elite. The intermarriages made it easier for the Tejano elite to adjust to the changes in law and commerce that the Americans quickly enacted. But following a temporary recapture of San Antonio by Mexican forces in 1842, positions hardened. Many more of the Tejano elite fled to Mexico, and Americans discussed banishing or imprisoning all Tejanos until the border issue was settled. This was, of course, impossible. Culturally, San Antonio remained a Mexican city long after the Americans had declared independence. The Americans in the Republic of Texas were struggling to reconcile American ideals of democracy with the reality of subordinating those with a prior claim, the Tejanos, to the status of a conquered people.

Ethnocentric attitudes quickly triumphed. Tejanos and other Mexicans were soon being blamed by Americans for their own subordination. Senator Edward Hannegan of Indiana was one of the most outspoken: "Mexico and the United States are peopled by two distinct and utterly unhomogeneous races," he announced in 1847. "In no reasonable period could we amalgamate."

American control over the other Texas residents, the Indians, was also slow in coming. Although the coastal Indian peoples were soon killed or removed, the Comanches still rode the high plains of northern and western Texas. West of the Rio Grande, equally fierce Apache bands were in control. Both groups soon learned to distrust American promises to stay out of their territory, and they did not hesitate to raid settlements and to kill trespassers. Not until after the Civil War and major campaigns by the U.S. Army were these fierce Indian tribes conquered.

Martin Van Buren, who succeeded Andrew Jackson as president in 1837, was too cautious to raise the Texas issue during his term of office. But Texans themselves continued to press for annexation to the United States, while at the same time seeking recognition and support from Great Britain. The idea of an independent and expansionist republic on its southern border that might gain the support of America's traditional enemy alarmed many Americans. Annexation thus became an urgent matter of national politics. This issue also added to the troubles of a governing Whig Party that was already deeply divided by the policies of John Tyler, who had become president by default when William Harrison died in office (see Chapter 11). Tyler raised the issue of annexation in 1844, hoping thereby to ensure his reelection, but the strategy backfired. Presenting the annexation treaty to Congress, Secretary of State John Calhoun awakened sectional fears by connecting Texas with the urgent need of southern slave owners to extend slavery.

In a storm of antislavery protest, Whigs rejected the treaty proposed by their own president and ejected Tyler himself from the party. In his place, they chose Henry Clay, the party's longtime standard-bearer, as their presidential candidate. Clay took a noncommittal stance on Texas, favoring annexation, but only if Mexico approved. Since Mexico's emphatic disapproval was well known, Clay's position was widely interpreted as a politician's effort not to alienate voters on either side of the fence.

In contrast, in the Democratic Party, wholehearted and outspoken expansionists seized control. Sweeping aside their own senior politician, Van Buren, who like Clay tried to remain uncommitted, the Democrats nominated their first "dark horse" candidate, James K. Polk of Tennessee. Democrats enthusiastically endorsed Polk's platform, which called for "the re-occupation of Oregon and the re-annexation of Texas at the earliest practicable period." Polk won the 1844 election by the narrow margin of 40,000 popular votes (although he gained 170 electoral votes to Clay's 105). An ominous portent for the Whigs was the showing of James G. Birney of the Liberty Party, who polled 62,000 votes, largely from northern antislavery Whigs. Birney's third-party campaign was the first political sign of the growing strength of antislavery opinion. Nevertheless, the 1844

election was widely interpreted as a mandate for expansion. Thereupon, John Tyler, in one of his last actions as president, pushed through Congress a joint resolution (which did not require the two-thirds approval by the Senate necessary for treaties) for the annexation of Texas. When Texas entered the Union in December 1845, it was the twenty-eighth state and the fifteenth slave state.

THE MEXICAN–AMERICAN WAR

James K. Polk lived up to his campaign promises. In 1846, he peacefully added Oregon south of the 49th parallel to the United States; in 1848, following the Mexican-American War, he acquired Mexico's northern provinces of California and New Mexico as well. Thus, with the annexation of Texas, the United States, in the short space of three years, had added 1.5 million square miles of territory, an increase of nearly 70 percent. Polk was indeed the "manifest destiny" president.

Origins of the War

In the spring of 1846, just as the controversy over Oregon was drawing to a peaceful conclusion, tensions with Mexico grew more serious. As soon as Texas was granted statehood in 1845, the Mexican government broke diplomatic relations with the United States. In addition, because the United States supported the Texas claim of all land north of the Rio Grande, it provoked a border dispute with Mexico. In June 1845, Polk sent General Zachary Taylor to Texas, and by October, a force of 3,500 Americans were on the Nueces River with orders to defend Texas in the event of a Mexican invasion.

Polk had something bigger than border protection in mind. He coveted the continent clear to the Pacific Ocean. At the same time that he sent Taylor to Texas, Polk secretly instructed the Pacific naval squadron to seize the California ports if Mexico declared war. He also wrote the American consul in Monterey, Thomas Larkin, that a peaceful takeover of California by its residents—Spanish Mexicans and Americans alike—would not be unwelcome. When, in addition, the federally commissioned explorer John C. Frémont and a band of armed men appeared in California in the winter of 1845–46, Mexican authorities became alarmed, and ordered him to leave. After withdrawing briefly to Oregon, Frémont returned to California and was on hand in Sonoma in June to assist in the Bear Flag Revolt, in which a handful of American settlers, declaring that they were playing "the Texas game," announced California's independence from Mexico.

Meanwhile, in November 1845, Polk sent a secret envoy, John Slidell, to Mexico with an offer of $30

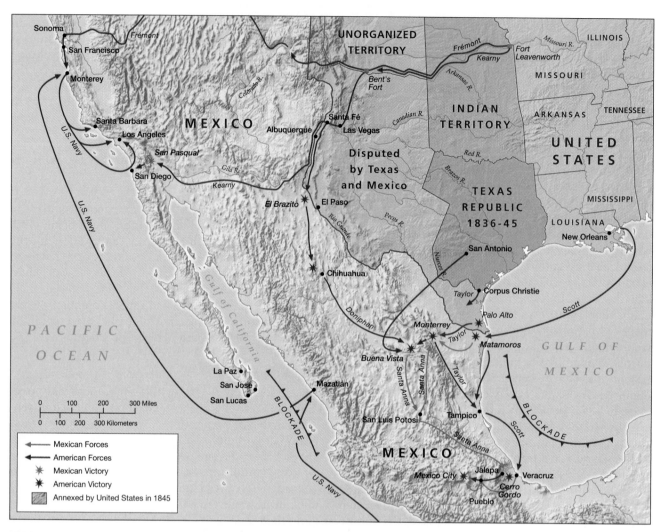

MAP 14.5 The Mexican-American War 1846–48 The Mexican-American War began with an advance by U.S. forces into the disputed area between the Nueces River and the Rio Grande in Texas. The war's major battles were fought by General Zachary Taylor in northern Mexico and General Winfield Scott in Vera Cruz and Mexico City. Meanwhile Colonel Stephen Kearny secured New Mexico and, with the help of the U.S. Navy and John C. Frémont's troops, California.

million or more for the Rio Grande border in Texas and Mexico's provinces of New Mexico and California. When the Mexican government refused even to receive Slidell, an angry Polk ordered General Taylor and his forces south to the Rio Grande, into the territory that Mexicans claimed as their soil. In April 1846, a brief skirmish between American and Mexican soldiers broke out in the disputed zone. Polk seized on the event, sending a war message to Congress: "Mexico has passed the boundary of the United States, has invaded our territory and shed American blood upon American soil. . . . War exists, and, notwithstanding all our efforts to avoid it, exists by the act of Mexico herself." This claim of President Polk's was, of course, con-

trary to fact. On May 13, 1846, Congress declared war on Mexico (see Map 14.5).

Mr. Polk's War

From the beginning, the Mexican-American War was politically divisive. Whig critics in Congress, among them a gawky young congressman from Illinois named Abraham Lincoln, questioned Polk's account of the border incident. They accused the president of misleading Congress and of maneuvering the country into an unnecessary war. The history of congressional concern over the way presidents have exercised their war powers begins here. The issue would again be prominent, for example, during the Vietnam War, in the Reagan years, and in the questions about

General Winfield Scott is shown at moment of victory, riding into Mexico City's central square in 1847
to accept the Mexican surrender. Triumphant lithographs like this were very popular with the American public,
who knew very little about the hardship and brutality of the six-month long campaign that preceded it.
SOURCE: Getty Images Inc. Hulton Archive Photos.

the reasons for war with Iraq in 2003. As the Mexican-American War dragged on and casualties and costs mounted—13,000 Americans and 50,000 Mexicans died and the United States spent $97 million—opposition increased, especially among northern antislavery Whigs. More and more people came to the opinion that the war was nothing more than a plot by Southerners to expand slavery. Many Northerners asked why Polk had been willing to settle for only a part of Oregon, but was so eager to pursue a war for slave territory. Thus expansionist dreams served to fuel sectional antagonisms.

The northern states witnessed both mass and individual protests against the war. In Massachusetts, the legislature passed a resolution condemning Polk's declaration of war as unconstitutional, and philosopher-writer Henry David Thoreau went to jail rather than pay the taxes he believed would support the war effort. Thoreau's dramatic gesture was undercut by his aunt, who paid his fine after he had spent only one night in jail. Thoreau then returned to his cabin on Walden Pond, where he wrote his classic essay "Civil Disobedience," justifying the individual's moral duty to oppose an immoral government. In the early twentieth century, the

Indian nationalist Mohandas Gandhi used Thoreau's essay to justify his campaign of "passive resistance" against British imperial rule in India. In turn, Martin Luther King and others used Gandhi's model of civil disobedience as a basis for their activities in the American civil rights movement of the 1950s and 1960s.

Whigs termed the war with Mexico "Mr. Polk's War," but the charge was not just a Whig jibe. Although he lacked a military background, Polk assumed the overall planning of the war's strategy (a practice that the critical Mr. Lincoln was to follow in the Civil War). By his personal attention to the coordination of civilian political goals and military requirements, Polk gave a new and expanded definition to the role of the president as commander-in-chief during wartime. In 1846, Polk sent General Taylor south into northeastern Mexico and Colonel Stephen Kearny to New Mexico and California. Taylor captured the northern Mexico cities of Palo Alto in May and Monterey in September 1846. Meanwhile, Kearny marched his men 900 miles to Santa Fé, which surrendered peacefully. Another march of roughly the same distance brought him by fall to southern California, which he took with the help of naval forces and Frémont's irregular troops.

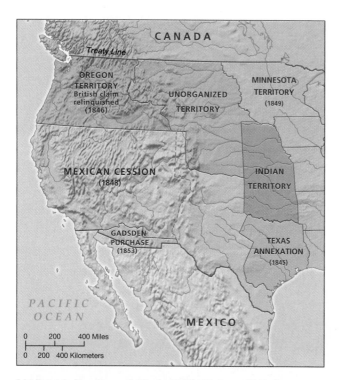

MAP 14.6 Territory Added, 1845–53 James K. Polk was elected president in 1844 on an expansionist platform. He lived up to most of his campaign rhetoric by gaining the Oregon Country (to the forty-ninth parallel) peacefully from the British, Texas by the presidential action of his predecessor John Tyler, and present-day California, Arizona, Nevada, Utah, New Mexico, and part of Colorado by war with Mexico. In the short space of three years, the size of the United States grew by 70 percent. In 1853, the Gadsden Purchase added another 30,000 square miles.

By the end of 1846, the northern provinces that Polk had coveted were now secured, but contrary to his expectations, Mexico refused to negotiate. In February 1847, General Santa Anna of Alamo fame attacked the American troops led by General Taylor at Buena Vista, but was repulsed by Taylor's small force. A month later, in March 1847, General Winfield Scott launched an amphibious attack on the coastal city of Veracruz and rapidly captured it. Americans celebrated these twin victories joyously, but they were to be the last easy victories of the war. It took Scott six months of brutal fighting against stubborn Mexican resistance on the battlefield and harassing guerrilla raids to force his way to Mexico City. American troops reacted bitterly to their high casualty rates, retaliating against Mexican citizens with acts of murder, robbery, and rape. Even General Scott himself admitted that his troops had "committed atrocities to make Heaven weep and every American of Christian morals blush for his country." In September, Scott took Mexico City, and Mexican resistance came to an end.

With the American army went a special envoy, Nicholas Trist, who delivered Polk's terms for peace. In the Treaty of Guadalupe Hidalgo, signed February 2, 1848, Mexico ceded its northern provinces of California and New Mexico (which included present-day Arizona, Utah, Nevada, and part of Colorado) and accepted the Rio Grande as the boundary of Texas. The United States agreed to pay Mexico $15 million and assume about $2 million in individual claims against that nation.

When Trist returned to Washington with the treaty, however, Polk was furious. He had actually recalled Trist after Scott's sweeping victory, intending to send a new envoy with greater demands, but Trist had ignored the recall order. "All Mexico!" had become the phrase widely used by those in favor of further expansion, Polk among them. But two very different groups opposed further expansion. The first group, composed of northern Whigs, included such notables as Ralph Waldo Emerson, who grimly warned, "The United States will conquer Mexico, but it will be as the man swallows arsenic, which brings him down in turn. Mexico will poison us." The second group was composed of Southerners who realized that Mexicans could not be kept as conquered people, but would have to be offered territorial government as

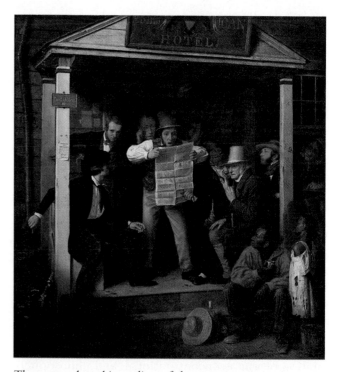

The unprecedented immediacy of the news reporting of the Mexican-American War, transmitted for the first time by telegraph, is captured here by Richard Caton Woodville in *War News from Mexico* (1848). By including an African American man and child, the artist is also voicing a political concern about the effect of the war on slavery.

SOURCE: Richard Caton Woodville, *War News from Mexico*, oil on canvas. Manovgian Foundation, on loan to the National Gallery of Art, Washington, DC.

Louisiana had been offered in 1804. Senator John C. Calhoun of South Carolina, leading the opposition, warned against admitting "colored and mixed-breed" Mexicans "on an equality with people of the United States." "We make a great mistake, sir," he argued on the floor of the Senate, "when we suppose that all people are capable of self-government." Bowing to these political protests, Polk reluctantly accepted the treaty. A later addition, the $10 million Gadsden Purchase of parts of present-day New Mexico and Arizona, added another 30,000 square miles to the United States in 1853. This purchase, made to facilitate a southern transcontinental railroad route through arid borderland, was a far cry from the rich heartland of Mexico that Polk had hoped to annex (see Map 14.6).

The Press and Popular War Enthusiasm

The Mexican-American War was the first war in which regular, on-the-scene reporting by representatives of the press caught the mass of ordinary citizens up in the war's daily events. Thanks to the recently invented telegraph, newspapers could get the latest news from their reporters, who were among the world's first war correspondents. The "penny press," with more than a decade's experience of reporting urban crime and scandals, was quick to realize that the public's appetite for sensational war news was apparently insatiable. For the first time in American history, accounts by journalists, and not the opinions of politicians, became the major shapers of popular attitudes toward a war. From beginning to end, news of the war stirred unprecedented popular excitement.

The reports from the battlefield united Americans in a new way: they became part of a temporary but highly emotional community linked by newsprint and buttressed by public gatherings. In the spring of 1846, news of Zachary Taylor's victory at Palo Alto prompted the largest meeting ever held in the cotton textile town of Lowell, Massachusetts. In May 1847, New York City celebrated the twin victories at Veracruz and Buena Vista with fireworks, illuminations, and a "grand procession" estimated at 400,000 people. Generals Taylor and Scott became overnight heroes, and in time, both became presidential candidates. Exciting, sobering, and terrible, war news had a deep hold on the popular imagination. It was a lesson newspaper publishers never forgot.

CALIFORNIA AND THE GOLD RUSH

In the early 1840s, California was inhabited by many seminomadic Indian tribes whose people numbered approximately 50,000. There were also some 7,000 *Californios*, descendants of the Spanish Mexican pioneers who had begun to settle in 1769. The American presence in California at first consisted of a few traders and settlers who often intermarried with Californios. Even American annexation at the end of the Mexican-American War changed little for the handful of Americans on this remote frontier. But then came the Gold Rush of 1849, which changed California permanently.

Russian-Californio Trade

The first outsiders to penetrate the isolation of Spanish California were not Americans, but Russians. Because the distance between California and Mexico City was so great, the Spanish had found it difficult to maintain the elaborate system of twenty-one missions first established in the eighteenth century (see Chapter 5). Nevertheless, Spanish officials in Mexico insisted on isolation, forbidding the colonists to trade with other nations. Evading Spanish regulations, Californios conducted a small illegal trade in cattle hides with American merchant ships (for the shoes made in the workshops of Massachusetts),

This drawing of the bar of a gambling saloon in San Francisco in 1855 shows the effects of the Gold Rush on California. Men from all parts of the world are gathered at this elegant bar in the large cosmopolitan city of San Francisco, which had been only a small trading post before gold was discovered in 1849.

SOURCE: Frank Marryat, *The Bar of a Gambling Saloon*, published 1855. Lithograph. Collection of the New York Historical Society, New York City (48381).

and a much larger trade with the Russian American Fur Company in Sitka, Alaska. A mutually beneficial barter of California food for iron tools and woven cloth from Russia was established in 1806. This arrangement became even brisker after the Russians settled Fort Ross (near present-day Mendocino) in 1812, and led in time to regular trade with Mission San Rafael and Mission Sonoma. That the Russians in Alaska, so far from their own capital, were better supplied with manufactured goods than the Californios is an index of the latter's isolation.

When Mexico became independent in 1821, the California trade was thrown open to ships of all nations. Nevertheless, Californios continued their special relationship with the Russians, exempting them from the taxes and inspections that they required of Americans. However, agricultural productivity declined after 1832, when the Mexican government ordered the secularization of the California missions, and the Russians regretfully turned to the rich farms of the Hudson's Bay Company in the Pacific Northwest for their food supply. In 1841, they sold Fort Ross, and the Russian-Californio connection came to an end.

Early American Settlement

It was Johann Augustus Sutter, a Swiss who had settled in California in 1839, becoming a Mexican citizen, who served as a focal point for American settlement in the 1840s. Sutter held a magnificent land grant in the Sacramento Valley. At the center of his holdings was Sutter's Fort, a walled compound that was part living quarters and part supply shop for his vast cattle ranch, which was run largely on forced Indian labor. In the 1840s, Sutter offered valuable support to the handful of American overlanders who chose California over Oregon, the destination preferred by most pioneers. Most of these Americans, keenly aware that they were interlopers in Mexican territory, settled near Sutter in California's Central Valley, away from the Californios clustered along the coast.

The 1840s immigrants made no effort to intermarry with the Californios or to conform to Spanish ways. They were bent on taking over the territory. In June 1846, these Americans banded together at Sonoma in the Bear Flag Revolt (so called because their flag bore a bear emblem), declaring independence from Mexico. The American takeover of California was not confirmed until the Treaty of Guadalupe Hidalgo in 1848. In the meantime, California was regarded by most Americans merely as a remote, sparsely populated frontier, albeit one with splendid potential. Polk and other expansionists coveted the magnificent harbors in San Diego and San Francisco as the basis for Pacific trade with Asia, but in 1848 this prospect was still only a dream.

Gold!

In January 1848, carpenter James Marshall noticed small flakes of gold in the millrace at Sutter's Mill (present-day Coloma). Soon he and all the rest of John Sutter's employees were panning for gold in California's streams. But not until the autumn of 1848 did the east coast hear the first rumors about the discovery of gold in California. The reports were confirmed in mid-November when an army courier arrived in Washington carrying a tea caddy full of gold dust and nuggets. The spirit of excitement and adventure so recently aroused by the Mexican-American War was now directed toward California, the new El Dorado. Thousands left farms and jobs and headed west, by land and by sea, to make their fortune. Later known as "forty-niners" for the year the gold rush began in earnest, these people came from all parts of the United States—and indeed, from all over the world. They trans-

Chinese first came to California in 1849 attracted by the Gold Rush. Frequently, however, they were forced off their claims by intolerant whites. Rather than enjoy an equal chance in the gold fields, they were often forced to work as servants or in other menial occupations.

SOURCE: Courtesy of the California History Room, California State Library, Sacramento, California.

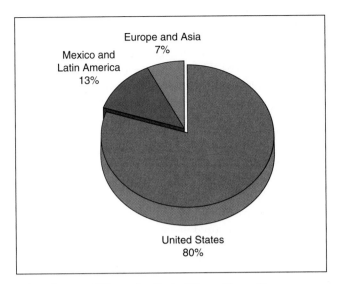

FIGURE 14.2 Where the Forty-Niners Came From
Americans drawn to the California Gold Rush of 1849 encountered a more diverse population than most had previously known. Nearly as novel to them as the 20 percent from foreign countries, was the regional variety from within the United States itself.

formed what had been a quiet ranching paradise into a teeming and tumultuous community in search of wealth in California's rivers and streams.

Eighty percent of the forty-niners were Americans. They came from every state. The Gold Rush was an eye-opening expansion of their horizons for the many who had known only their hometown folks before. The second largest group of migrants were from nearby Mexico and the west coast of Latin America (13 percent). The remainder came from Europe and Asia (see Figure 14.2).

The presence of Chinese miners surprised many Americans. Several hundred Chinese arrived in California in 1849 and 1850, and in 1852 more than 20,000 landed in San Francisco hoping to share in the wealth of "Gum Sam" (Golden Mountain). Most came, like the Americans, as temporary sojourners, intending to return home as soon as they made some money. Again, like most of the American miners, the majority of Chinese were men who left their wives at home. Dressed in their distinctive blue cotton shirts, baggy pants, and broad-brimmed hats, and with long queues hanging down their backs, hardworking Chinese miners soon became a familiar sight in the gold fields, as did the presence of "Chinatowns." The distinctive appearance of the Chinese, added to the threat of economic competition that they posed, quickly aroused American hostility. A special tax was imposed on foreign miners in 1852, and in the 1870s, Chinese immigration was sharply curtailed.

In 1849, as the gold rush began in earnest, San Francisco, the major entry port and supply point, sprang to life. From a settlement of 1,000 in 1848, it grew to a city

of 35,000 in 1850. This surge suggested that the real money to be made in California was not in panning for gold, but in feeding, clothing, housing, provisioning, and entertaining the miners. Among the first to learn that lesson was the German Jewish immigrant Levi Strauss, who sold so many tough work pants to miners that his name became synonymous with his product. And Jerusha Marshall, who opened a twenty-room boardinghouse in the city, candidly wrote to her eastern relatives: "Never was there a better field for making money than now presents itself in this place. . . . We are satisfied to dig our gold in San Francisco." From these "instant" beginnings, San Francisco stabilized to become a major American city. Meanwhile, the white population of California had jumped from an estimated pre–Gold Rush figure of 11,000 to more than 100,000 by 1852. California was admitted into the Union as a state in 1850.

Mining Camps

As had occured in San Francisco, most mining camps boomed almost instantly to life, but unlike San Francisco, they were empty again within a few years. In spite of the aura of glamour that surrounds the names of the famous camps—Poker Flat, Angels Camp, Whiskey Bar, Placerville, Mariposa—they were generally dirty and dreary places. Most miners lived in tents or hovels, unwilling to take time from mining to build themselves decent quarters. They cooked monotonous meals of beans, bread, and bacon, or, if they had money, bought meals at expensive restaurants and boardinghouses (where the table might be no more than a plank over two flour barrels). They led a cheerless, uncomfortable, and unhealthy existence, especially during the long, rainy winter months, with few distractions apart from the saloon, the gambling hall, and the prostitute's crib (see Map 14.7).

Most miners were young, unmarried, and unsuccessful. Only a small percentage ever struck it rich in California. Gold deposits that were accessible with pick and shovel were soon exhausted, and the deeper deposits required capital and machinery. Some of the workings at the Comstock Lode in Virginia City, Nevada, a later mining center, were half a mile deep. Increasingly, those who they stayed on in California had to give up the status of independent miners and become wage earners for large mining concerns.

As in San Francisco, a more reliable way to earn money in the camps was to supply the miners. Every mining community had its saloonkeepers, gamblers, prostitutes, merchants, and restauranteurs. Like the miners themselves, these people were transients, always ready to pick up and move at the word of a new gold strike. The majority of women in the early mining camps were prostitutes. Some grew rich or married respectably, but most died young of drugs, venereal disease, or violence. Most of the other women were hardworking wives of miners, and in this predominantly male society, they

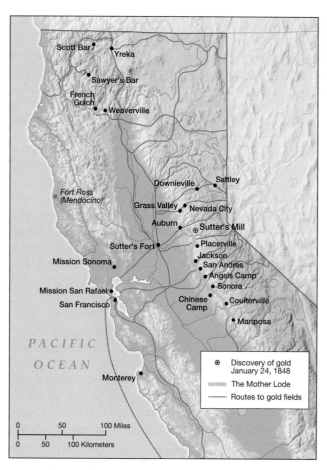

MAP 14.7 California in the Gold Rush This map shows the major gold camps along the Mother Lode in the western foothills of the Sierra Nevada mountains. Gold seekers reached the camps by crossing the Sierra Nevadas near Placerville on the Overland Trail or by sea via San Francisco. The main area of Spanish-Mexican settlement, the coastal region between Monterey and Los Angeles, was remote from the gold fields.

SOURCE: Warren A. Beck and Ynez D. Haase, *Historical Atlas of California* (Norman: University of Oklahoma Press, 1974), map 50.

for example by taking advantage of the prohibitively high mining tax on foreigners.

In the end, most mining camps were at best temporary communities. The gold "played out" and people moved on, leaving ghost towns behind. By the mid-1850s, the immediate effects of the Gold Rush had passed. California had a booming population, a thriving agriculture, and a corporate mining industry. The Gold Rush also left California with a population that was larger, more affluent, and (in urban San Francisco) more culturally sophisticated than that in other newly settled territories. And it was significantly more multicultural than the rest of the nation, for many of the Chinese and Mexicans, as well as immigrants from many European countries, remained in California after the Gold Rush subsided. But the rough equality of the early days was gone, and peoples of what were considered "lesser races" were kept in subordination.

The Gold Rush left some permanent scars, and not just on the foothills landscape: the virtual extermination of the California Indian peoples, the dispossession of many Californios who were legally deprived of their land grants, and the growth of racial animosity toward the Chinese in particular. The major characteristics of the mining frontier, evident first in the California Gold Rush and repeated many times thereafter in similar "rushes" in Colorado, Montana, Idaho, South Dakota, Arizona, and Alaska were a lack of stable communities and a worsening of racial tensions.

THE POLITICS OF MANIFEST DESTINY

In three short years, from 1845 to 1848, the territory of the United States grew an incredible 70 percent, and a continental nation took shape. This expansion, pushed by economic desires and feelings of American cultural superiority, led directly to the emergence of the divisive issue of slavery as the dominant issue in national politics.

The Wilmot Proviso

In 1846, almost all the northern members of the Whig Party opposed Democratic president James Polk's belligerent expansionism on antislavery grounds. Northern Whigs correctly feared that expansion would reopen the issue of slavery in the territories. "We appear . . . to be rushing upon perils headlong, and with our eyes all open," Daniel Webster warned in 1847. His remedy? "We want no extension of territory; we want no accession of new states. The country is already large enough." But the outpouring of popular enthusiasm for the Mexican-American War drowned Webster's words and convinced most Whig congressmen that they needed to vote military appropriations for the war in spite of their misgivings.

Ironically, it was not the Whigs, but a freshman Democratic congressman from Pennsylvania, David

made good money doing domestic work: keeping boardinghouses, cooking, doing laundry. Even the wives of professional men who in the East might have been restrained by propriety succumbed to the monetary opportunities and kept boardinghouses.

Partly because few people put any effort into building communities—they were too busy seeking gold—violence was endemic in mining areas, and much of it was racial. Discrimination, especially against Chinese, Mexicans, and African Americans, was common. Frequently miners' claims were "jumped": thieves would rob them of the gold they had accumulated, kill them, or chase them away, and then file their own claim for the victims' strike. Or unscrupulous miners might use the law to their advantage to secure the claims of others without violence—

OVERVIEW

EXPANSION CAUSES THE FIRST SPLITS IN THE SECOND AMERICAN PARTY SYSTEM

1844	Whigs reject President John Tyler's move to annex Texas, and expel him from the Whig Party.
	Southern Democrats choose expansionist James K. Polk as their presidential candidate, passing over Martin Van Buren, who is against expansion.
	Liberty Party runs abolitionist James Birney for president, attracting northern antislavery Whigs.
1846	The Wilmot Proviso, proposing to ban slavery in the territories that might be gained in the Mexican-American War, splits both parties: southern Whigs and Democrats oppose the measure; northern Whigs and Democrats support it.
1848	The new Free-Soil Party runs northern Democrat Martin Van Buren for president, gaining 10 percent of the vote from abolitionists, antislavery Whigs, and some northern Democrats. This strong showing by a third party causes Democrat Lewis Cass to lose the electoral votes of New York and Pennsylvania, allowing the Whig Zachary Taylor to win.

Wilmot, who opened the door to sectional controversy over expansion. In August 1846, only a few short months after the beginning of the Mexican-American War, Wilmot proposed, in an amendment to a military appropriations bill, that slavery be banned in all the territories acquired from Mexico. He was ready, Wilmot said, to "sustain the institutions of the South as they exist. But sir, the issue now presented is not whether slavery shall exist unmolested where it is now, but whether it shall be carried to new and distant regions, now free, where the footprint of a slave cannot be found." In the debate and voting that followed, something new and ominous occurred: southern Whigs joined southern Democrats to vote against the measure, while Northerners of both parties supported it. Sectional interest had triumphed over party loyalty. Wilmot's Proviso triggered the first breakdown of the national party system and reopened the debate about the place of slavery in the future of the nation.

The Wilmot Proviso was so controversial that it was deleted from the necessary military appropriations bills during the Mexican-American War. But in 1848, following the Treaty of Guadalupe Hidalgo, the question of the expansion of slavery could no longer be avoided or postponed. Antislavery advocates from the North argued with proslavery Southerners in a debate that was much more prolonged and bitter than in the Missouri Crisis debate of 1819. Civility quickly wore thin: threats were uttered and fistfights broke out on the floor of the House of Representatives. The Wilmot Proviso posed a fundamental challenge to both parties. Neither the Democrats nor the Whigs could take a strong stand on the amendment, because neither party could get its northern and southern wings to agree.

Decisive action, for or against, was a serious threat to party unity. Webster's fear that expansion would lead to sectional conflict had become a reality.

The Free-Soil Movement

Why did David Wilmot propose this controversial measure? Wilmot, a northern Democrat, was propelled not by ideology but by the pressure of practical politics. The dramatic rise of the Liberty Party, founded in 1840 by abolitionists, threatened to take votes away from both the Whig and the Democratic parties. The Liberty Party won 62,000 votes in the 1844 presidential election, all in the North. This was more than enough to deny victory to the Whig candidate, Henry Clay. Neither party could afford to ignore the strength of this third party.

The Liberty Party took an uncompromising stance against slavery. As articulated by Ohio's Salmon P. Chase, the party platform called for the "divorce of the federal government from slavery." The party proposed to prohibit the admission of slave states to the Union, end slavery in the District of Columbia, and abolish the interstate slave trade that was vital to the expansion of cotton growing into the Old Southwest (see Chapter 10). Liberty Party members also favored denying office to all slaveholders (a proposal that would have robbed all the southern states of their senators) and forbidding the use of slave labor on federal construction projects. In short, the party proposed to quickly strangle slavery. The popularity of this radical program among northern voters in 1844 was an indication of the moral fervor of abolitionism (see Chapter 13).

But Liberty Party doctrine was too uncompromising for the mass of northern voters, who immediately realized that the southern states would leave the Union before accepting it. Still, as the 1844 vote indicated, many Northerners opposed slavery. From this sentiment, the Free-Soil Party was born. The free-soil argument was a calculated adjustment of abolitionist principles to practical politics. It shifted the focus from the question of the morality of slavery, to the ways in which slavery posed a threat to northern expansion. The free-soil doctrine thus established a direct link between expansion, which most Americans supported, and sectional politics.

Free-soilers were willing to allow slavery to continue in the existing slave states because they supported the Union, not because they approved of slavery. They were unwilling, however, to allow the extension of slavery to new and unorganized territory. If the South were successful in extending slavery, they argued, northern farmers who moved west would find themselves competing at an economic disadvantage with large planters using slave labor. Free-soilers also insisted that the northern values of freedom and individualism would be destroyed if the slave-based southern labor system were allowed to spread.

Many free-soilers really meant "antiblack" when they said "antislavery." They proposed to ban all African American people from the new territories (a step that four states—Indiana, Illinois, Iowa, and Oregon—took, but did not always enforce). William Lloyd Garrison promptly denounced the free-soil doctrine as "white-manism," a racist effort to make the territories white. There was much truth to his charge, but there was no denying that the free-soil doctrine was popular. Although abolitionists were making headway in their claim for moral equality regardless of skin color, most Northerners were unwilling to consider social equality for African Americans, free or slave. Banning all black people from the western territories seemed a simple solution.

The Election of 1848

A swirl of emotions—pride, expansionism, sectionalism, abolitionism, free-soil sentiment—surrounded the election of 1848. The Treaty of Guadalupe Hidalgo had been signed earlier in the year, and the vast northern Mexican provinces of New Mexico and California and the former Republic of Texas had been incorporated into the United States. But the issues raised by the Wilmot Proviso remained to be resolved, and every candidate had to have an answer to the question of whether slavery should be admitted in the new territories.

Lewis Cass of Michigan, the Democratic nominee for president (Polk, in poor health, declined to run for a second term), proposed to apply the doctrine of popular sovereignty to the crucial slave–free issue. This democratic-sounding notion of leaving the decision to the citizens of each territory was based on the Jeffersonian faith in the common man's ability to vote both his own self-interest and the common good. Popular sovereignty was based on the accepted constitutional principle that decisions about slavery (like, for example, rules about suffrage) should be made at the state rather than the national level. In reality, popular sovereignty was an admission of the nation's failure to resolve sectional differences. It simply shifted decision making on the crucial issue of the expansion of slavery from national politicians to the members of territorial and state legislatures, who, belonging to different parties, were in as much disagreement as members of Congress and just as unable to resolve it.

As Cass stated it, the doctrine of popular sovereignty was deliberately vague about when a territory would choose its status. Would it do so during the territorial stage? at the point of applying for statehood? Clearly, this question was crucial, for no slave owner would invest in new land if the territory could later be declared free, and no

In 1848, the Whigs nominated a hero of the Mexican-American War, General Zachary Taylor, who ran on his military exploits. In this campaign poster, every letter of Taylor's name is decorated with scenes from the recent war, which had seized the popular imagination in a way no previous conflict had done.

SOURCE: The Granger Collection, New York.

OUT OF MANY VOICES

AN ABOLITIONIST EXPRESSES HIS DISLIKE OF POLITICS

Gerrit Smith, an ardent and wealthy New York abolitionist, explains in a letter to a friend why he supported Martin Van Buren's nomination as the Free-Soil candidate for president in 1848, but why he won't vote for him.

I HARDLY NEED SAY, THAT I AM DEEPLY INTERESTED in the present movement against the extension of slavery; and that I infinitely prefer the election of the candidates, who are identified with it, to the election of the Whig and Democratic candidates. Gen. [Zachary] Taylor and Gen. [Lewis] Cass are proslavery candidates. Mr. Van Buren and Mr. Adams are antislavery candidates. The former are the shameless tools of the slave-power. The latter bravely resist it.

It is true, that, among all the persons, whom there was the least reason to believe the Buffalo Convention [of the Free-Soil Party] would nominate for President, Mr. Van Buren was my preference. He was my preference, because I believed he would obtain a much larger vote than any of the others; and, that his nomination would go much farther than that of any of the others toward breaking up the great political parties, which, along with the ecclesiastical parties, are the chief shelters and props of slavery.

But it is not true that I shall vote for Mr. Van Buren. I can vote for no man for President of the United States, who is not an abolitionist; for no man, who votes for slaveholders, or for those, who do; for no man, whose understanding and heart would not prompt him to use the office, to the utmost, for the abolition of slavery. . . . The . . . higher ground do I take, that no man is fit for President of the United States, who does not scout the idea of the possibility of property in man, and who does not insist, that slavery is as utterly incapable of legalization, as is murder itself. Why is it not? Is it not as bad as murder? Is not, indeed, murder itself one of the elements in that matchless compound of enormous crimes? . . . There should be no surprise, that, from the day this Nation came into being until the present day, no white man has, in any one of the Southern States, been put to death, under the laws, for the murder of a slave. . . . ■

SOURCE: Sidney Mintz, (2003). The Free-Soil Party. *Digital History.* http://www.digitalhistory.uh.edu

---

abolitionist would move to a territory that was destined to become a slave state. Cass hoped his ambiguity on this point would win him votes in both North and South.

For their part, the Whigs passed over perennial candidate Henry Clay and turned to a war hero, General Zachary Taylor. Taylor, a Louisiana slaveholder, refused to take a position on the Wilmot Proviso, allowing both northern and southern voters to hope that he agreed with them. Privately, Taylor opposed the expansion of slavery. In public, he evaded the issue by running as a war hero and a national leader who was above sectional politics.

The deliberate vagueness of the two major candidates displeased many northern voters. An uneasy mixture of disaffected Democrats (among them David Wilmot) and Whigs joined former Liberty Party voters to support the candidate of the Free-Soil Party, former president Martin Van Buren. (See Out of Many Voices: An Abolitionist Expresses His Dislike of Politics.) Van Buren, angry at the Democratic Party for passing him over in 1844 and displeased with the growing southern dominance of the Demo-

cratic Party, ran as a spoiler. He knew he could not win the election, but he could divide the Democrats. In the end, Van Buren garnered 10 percent of the vote (all in the North). The vote for the Free-Soil Party cost Cass the electoral votes of New York and Pennsylvania, and General Zachary Taylor won the election with only 47 percent of the popular vote. This was the second election after 1840 that the Whigs had won by running a war hero who could duck hard questions by claiming to be above politics. Uncannily, history was to repeat itself: Taylor, like William Henry Harrison, died before his term was completed, and the chance he offered to maintain national unity—if ever it existed—was lost.

CONCLUSION

In the decade of the 1840s, westward expansion took many forms, from relatively peaceful settlement in Oregon, to war with Mexico over Texas, to the overwhelming numbers of gold rushers who changed California forever. Most of these frontiers—in Oregon,

CHRONOLOGY

1609	First Spanish settlement in New Mexico
1670s	British and French Canadians begin fur trade in western Canada
1716	First Spanish settlements in Texas
1769	First Spanish settlement in California
1780s	New England ships begin sea otter trade in Pacific Northwest
1790	First American ship visits Hawaii
1803	Louisiana Purchase
1804–06	Lewis and Clark expedition
1806	Russian-Californio trade begins
1806–07	Zebulon Pike's expedition across the Great Plains to the Rocky Mountains
1819–20	Stephen Long's expedition across the Great Plains
1821	Hudson's Bay Company gains dominance of western fur trade
	Mexico seizes independence from Spain
	Santa Fé Trail opens, soon protected by U.S. military
	Stephen F. Austin becomes first American empresario in Texas
1824	First fur rendezvous sponsored by Rocky Mountain Fur Company
	Hudson's Bay Company establishes Fort Vancouver in Oregon Country
1830	Indian Removal Act moves eastern Indians to Indian Territory

1833–34	Prince Maximilian and Karl Bodmer visit Plains Indians
1834	Jason Lee establishes first mission in Oregon Country
1835	Texas revolts against Mexico
1836	Battles of the Alamo and San Jacinto
	Republic of Texas formed
1843–44	John C. Frémont maps trails to Oregon and California
1844	Democrat James K. Polk elected president on an expansionist platform
1845	Texas annexed to the United States as a slave state
	John O'Sullivan coins the phrase "manifest destiny"
1846	Oregon question settled peacefully with Britain
	Mexican-American War begins
	Bear Flag Revolt in California
	Wilmot Proviso
1847	Cayuse War begins in Oregon
	Americans win battles of Buena Vista, Veracruz, and Mexico City
1848	Treaty of Guadalupe Hidalgo
	Free-Soil Party captures 10 percent of the popular vote in the North
	General Zachary Taylor, a Whig, elected president
1849	California Gold Rush

New Mexico, and California—began as frontiers of inclusion, in which a small number of Americans were eager for trade, accommodation, and intermarriage with the original inhabitants. Texas, with its agricultural enclaves, was the exception to this pattern. Yet on every frontier, as the number of American settlers increased, so did the sentiment for exclusion, so that by 1850, whatever their origins, the far-flung American continental settlements were more similar than different, and the success of manifest destiny seemed overwhelming.

The election of 1848, virtually a referendum on manifest destiny, yielded ironic results. James K. Polk, who presided over the unprecedented expansion, did not run for a second term, and thus the Democratic Party gained no electoral victory to match the military one. The electorate that had been so thrilled by the war news voted for a war hero—who led the antiexpansionist Whig Party. The election was decided by Martin Van Buren, the Free-Soil candidate who voiced the sentiments of the abolitionists, a reform group that had been insignificant just a few years before. The amazing expansion achieved by the Mexican-American War—America's manifest destiny—made the United States a continental nation, but stirred up the issue that was to tear it apart. Sectional rivalries and fears now dominated every aspect of politics. Expansion, once a force for unity, now divided the nation into Northerners and Southerners, who could not agree on the community they shared—the federal Union.

REVIEW QUESTIONS

1. Define and discuss the concept of manifest destiny.
2. Trace the different ways in which the frontiers in Oregon, Texas, and California moved from frontiers of inclusion to frontiers of exclusion.
3. Take different sides (Whig and Democrat) and debate the issues raised by the Mexican-American War.

4. Referring back to Chapter 13, compare the positions of the Liberty Party and the Free-Soil Party. Examine the factors that made the free-soil doctrine politically acceptable to many, and abolitionism so controversial.

RECOMMENDED READING

Sucheng Chan, *This Bittersweet Soil: The Chinese in California Agriculture 1860–1910* (1987). The Chinese in California after the Gold Rush.

Arnoldo De Leon, *The Tejano Community, 1836–1900* (1982). Traces the changing status of Tejanos after Texas came under the control of American Texans.

John Mack Faragher, *Women and Men on the Overland Trail* (1979). One of the first books to consider the experience of women on the journey west.

Paul Foos, *A Short, Offhand, Killing Affair: Soldiers and Social Conflict During the Mexican-American War* (2002). The lives and attitudes of ordinary American soldiers.

Robert V. Hine and John Mack Faragher, *The American West: A New Interpretive History* (2000). Well written, informative and beautifully illustrated.

Julie Roy Jeffrey, *Converting the West: A Biography of Narcissa Whitman* (1991). Makes a clear connection between the missionary Whitman's evangelical upbringing and her failure to understand the culture of Oregon's Cayuse Indians.

Robert W. Johannsen, *To the Halls of the Montezumas: The Mexican War in the American Imagination* (1985). A lively book that explores the impact of the Mexican-American War on public opinion.

Susan Johnson, *Roaring Camp: The Social World of the California Gold Rush* (2000). A beautifully written study of the varieties of mining camp experience.

Paul D. Lack, *The Texas Revolutionary Experience: A Political and Social History, 1835–1836* (1992). A political and social history that stresses the chaotic and discordant nature of the Texas Revolt.

Andrés Reséndez, *Changing National Identities at the Frontier: Texas and New Mexico, 1800–1850* (2004). The choices faced by Latinos, American Indians and Anglos.

Brian Roberts, *American Alchemy: The California Gold Rush and Middle-Class Culture* (2000). Its effect on middle-class men and their wives who stayed behind.

Randy Roberts and James S. Olson, *A Line in the Sand: The Alamo in Blood and Memory* (2001). How the battle became a symbol.

Malcolm Rohrbough, *Days of Gold: The California Gold Rush and the American Nation* (1997). A lively history that emphasizes the effects of this "great American epic" on the national self-image.

Kevin Starr and Richard J. Orsei, eds., *Rooted in Barbarous Soil: People, Culture and Community in Gold Rush California* (2000). Twelve historians contribute their insights.

David J. Weber, *The Mexican Frontier, 1821–1846: The American Southwest under Mexico* (1982). A fine study of the history of the Southwest before American conquest by a leading borderlands historian.

For additional study resources for this chapter, go to the *Companion Website*, http://www.prenhall.com/faragher.

WHOSE HISTORY IS IT?

REMEMBERING THE ALAMO

The Alamo, often called "The Cradle of Texas Liberty," is the number one tourist attraction in the state of Texas. Located in a small but tranquil park, remote from the noise and traffic of surrounding downtown San Antonio, the site evokes feelings of reverence and respect for the famous Anglo American heroes—William Barret Travis, Jim Bowie, and Davy Crockett—of the gallant but futile 1836 defense of the fort.

Today, the history commemorated at the Alamo remains as controversial as it was 100 years ago, when the San Antonio Chapter of the Daughters of the Texas Republic was first entrusted with its preservation. Then, the custodianship of historic sites by exclusive women's groups such as the Daughters of the American Revolution and the Mount Vernon Ladies Association was common. This meant that wealthy Anglo women controlled historic sites. But membership in the Daughters of the Republic of Texas was open to all women who could trace their ancestry to persons who settled in Texas before 1846. In the 1890s the president of the San Antonio chapter of the DRT was Adina De Zavala, granddaughter of the Tejano patriot who became the first vice-president of Texas. Adina De Zavala, with the help of another DRT member, the wealthy Clara Driscoll, led the effort to raise money to preserve the Alamo site.

This modern photograph of the Alamo chapel by the well-known landscape photographer David Muench conveys the pristine and rather nostalgic atmosphere of the site that describes itself as "the Cradle of Texas liberty."
SOURCE: © David Muench/CORBIS.

No sooner had the DRT obtained control of the Alamo than disagreement arose. In a bitter controversy sometimes called the "Second Battle of the Alamo." De Zavala wanted to retain the full history of the site as a Spanish and Mexican mission and fort, while Driscoll preferred to emphasize only the chapel as a shrine to the well-known Anglo heroes of the 1836 battle. Driscoll won: De Zavala and her supporters were legally barred from custodianship, and the Alamo chapel, surrounded by a memorial park and wall, assumed its present-day form.

Today, a century after its preservation as a historic site, the Battle of the Alamo has flared anew. The Daughters of the Republic of Texas are under attack. The most sustained protest has come from the Texans of Mexican heritage who feel that the Tejano role in defense of the Alamo has not received enough attention. In part, these protests reflect the growing political power of Mexican Americans in Texas, where in San Antonio more than sixty percent of the residents are Mexican American. This ongoing struggle reflects deeper social changes: Mexican-Americans see changes in the Alamo as a matter of equity and historical accuracy, while many Anglo-Texans oppose change in the name of tradition. This unresolved controversy reminds us that there is more than one version of the past, thus making the question of who interprets history much more than an academic matter.

Commissioned by a Dallas businessman in 1903, this famous painting hangs in the Texas governor's mansion in Austin. In this imaginary rendition of the battle, the omission of Tejano defenders from the scene allowed the artist to use light and dark to sharpen the contrast between the good Anglos and the bad Mexicans.

Robert Jenkins Onderdonk, *The Fall of the Alamo*. Friends of the Governor's Mansion, Austin.

This sculpture is part of the Alamo Cenotaph, a memorial to the slain defenders of the Alamo that was erected in Alamo Plaza in 1940. The two prominent figures are the famous defenders William B. Travis (in uniform) and Davy Crockett.

©Lee Snider/Corbis.

The so-called "Second Battle of the Alamo" occurred when these two genteel antagonists, Adina De Zavala, on the left, and Clara Driscoll on the right, disagreed over whether to include the site's Spanish and Mexican history (De Zavala) or whether, as Driscoll wished, to focus only on the Anglo heroes of the 1836 defeat. Driscoll won.

Clara Driscoll. Gift of Mrs. L. T. Barrow, 1978. Daughters of the Republic of Texas Library, CN96.2.

Because Tejano leader Juan Seguin escaped from the Alamo to rally reinforcements, he survived the battle, only to live to see the heroism of Anglo leaders commemorated in memorials like the Cenotaph, but not the Tejanos who died with them.

Texas State Preservation Board.

The Coming Crisis

the 1850s

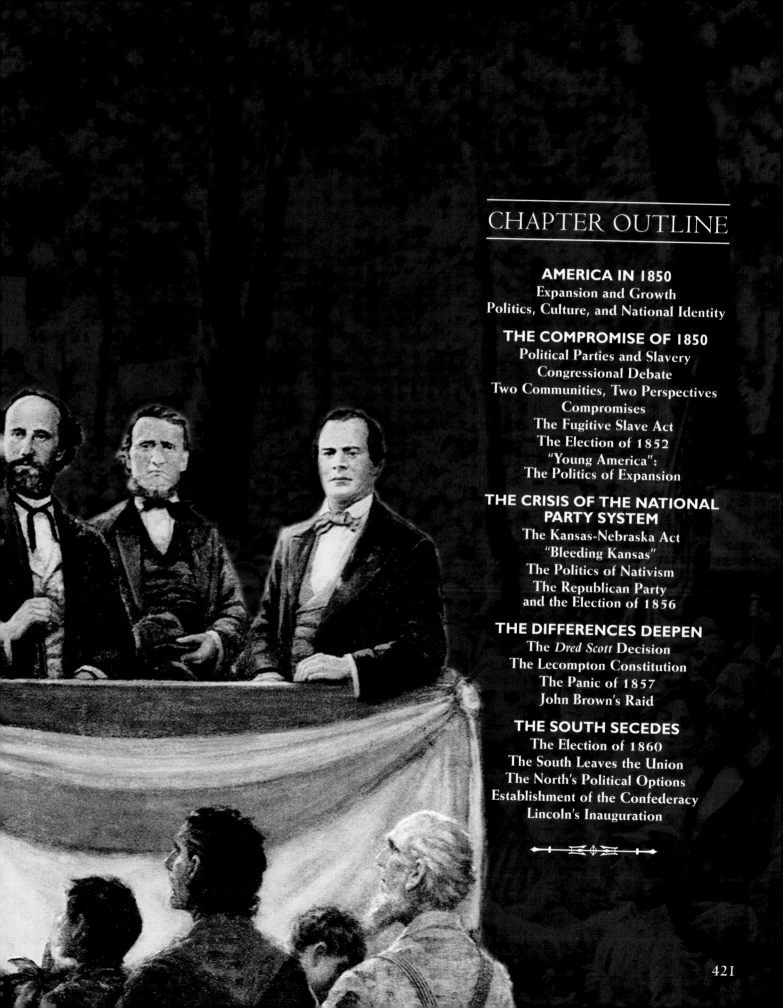

Illinois Communities Debate Slavery

On seven occasions through the late summer and autumn of 1858, in seven small Illinois towns, thousands of Illinois farmers and townspeople put aside their daily routines, climbed into carriages, farm wagons, and carts, and converged on their local town green. Entertained by brass bands, pageantry, and vast quantities of food and local gossip, they waited impatiently for the main event, the chance to take part in the Lincoln Douglas debate on the most urgent question of the day—slavery.

"The prairies are on fire," announced the *New York Evening Post* correspondent who covered the debates. "It is astonishing how deep an interest in politics these people take." The reason was clear: by 1858, the American nation was in deep political crisis. The decade-long effort to solve the problem of the future of slavery had failed. For most of this time, Washington politicians trying to build broad national parties with policies acceptable to voters in both the North and the South had done their best not to talk about slavery. That the Lincoln–Douglas debates were devoted to one issue alone—slavery and the future of the Union—showed how serious matters had become.

Democratic Senator Stephen A. Douglas of Illinois and his Republican challenger, Springfield lawyer Abraham Lincoln, presented their views in three hours of closely reasoned argument. But they did not speak alone. Cheers, boos,

groans, and shouted questions from active, engaged listeners punctuated all seven of the now famous confrontations between the two men. Thus the Lincoln–Douglas debates were community events in which Illinois citizens—who, as did Americans everywhere, held varying political beliefs—took part. Some individuals were proslavery, some antislavery, and many were undecided, but all were agreed that democratic politics gave them the means to air their opinions, to resolve their differences, and to assess the candidates who were running for a Senate seat from Illinois.

Stephen Douglas was the leading Democratic contender for the 1860 presidential nomination, but before he could mount a campaign for national office, he had first to win reelection to the Illinois seat he had held in the U.S. Senate for twelve years. His vote against allowing slavery in Kansas had alienated him from the strong Southern wing of his own party and had put him in direct conflict with its top leader, President James Buchanan. Because the crisis of the Union was so severe and Douglas's role so pivotal, his reelection campaign clearly previewed the 1860 presidential election. For the sake of its future, the Republican Party had to field a strong opponent: it found its candidate in Abraham Lincoln.

Lincoln had represented Illinois in the House of Representatives in the 1840s, but had lost political support in 1848 because he had opposed the Mexican-American War. Developing a prosperous Springfield law practice, he had been an influential member of the Illinois Republican Party since its founding in 1856. Although he had entered political life as a Whig, Lincoln was radicalized by the issue of the extension of slavery. Even though his wife's family were Kentucky slave owners, Lincoln's commitment to freedom and his resistance to the spread of slavery had now become absolute: for him, freedom and Union were inseparable.

Much less known than Douglas, Lincoln was the underdog in the 1858 Senate race. As they squared off in each

Illinois

of the seven Illinois towns, Douglas and Lincoln were an amusing sight. Douglas was short and his build was very square; his nickname was the "Little Giant." Lincoln, on the other hand, was very tall and very thin. Both were eloquent and powerful speakers. In every town, audiences of 10,000 to 15,000 listened attentively and responded vocally to each speaker's long and thought-packed arguments.

Douglas had many strengths going into the debates. He spoke for the Union, he claimed, pointing out that the Democratic Party was a national party whereas the Republican Party was only sectional. He repeatedly appealed to the racism of much of his audience with declarations such as, "I would not blot out the great inalienable rights of the white men for all the negroes that ever existed!" Calling his opponent a "Black Republican," he implied that Lincoln and his party favored the social equality of whites and blacks, even race mixing.

Lincoln did not believe in the social equality of the races, but he did believe wholeheartedly that slavery was a moral wrong. Pledging the Republican Party to the "ultimate extinction" of slavery, Lincoln continually warned that Douglas's position would lead to the opposite result: the spread of slavery everywhere. Although in this argument Lincoln was addressing the Northern fear of an expansionist "slave power," he strove at the same time to present himself as a moderate. He did not favor the breakup of the Union, but he never wavered from his antislavery stance.

The first of the seven debates, held in Ottawa on Saturday, August 21, 1858, showed not only the seriousness, but the exuberance of the democratic politics of the time. By early morning, the town was jammed with people. The clouds of dust raised by carriages driving to Ottawa, one observer complained, turned the town into "a vast smoke house." By one o'clock, the town square was filled to overflowing, and the debate enthralled an estimated 12,000 people. Ottawa, in northern Illinois, was pro-Republican, and the audience heckled Douglas unmercifully. At the second debate, a week later in Freeport, Douglas's use of the phrase "Black Republicans" drew angry shouts of "White, white" from the crowd. But as the debates moved south in the state, where Democrats predominated, the tables were turned, and Lincoln sometimes had to plead for a chance to be heard.

Although Douglas won the 1858 senatorial election in Illinois, the acclaim that Lincoln gained in the famous debates helped establish the Republicans' claim to be the only party capable of stopping the spread of slavery, and made Lincoln himself a strong contender for the Republican presidential nomination in 1860. But the true winners of the Lincoln–Douglas debates were the people of Illinois who gathered peacefully to discuss the most serious issue of their time. The young German immigrant Carl Schurz, who attended the Quincy debate, was deeply impressed by its democratic character. He noted, "There was no end of cheering and shouting and jostling on the streets of Quincy that day. But in spite of the excitement created by the political contest, the crowds remained very good-natured, and the occasional jibes flung from one side to the other were uniformly received with a laugh." The Illinois people who participated in these debates showed the strong faith Americans held in their democratic institutions and the hope—finally shattered in the election of 1860—that a lasting political solution to the problem of slavery could be found.

KEY TOPICS

- The failure of efforts by the Whigs and the Democrats to find a lasting political compromise on the issue of slavery
- The end of the Second American Party System and the rise of the Republican Party
- The secession of the Southern states following the Republican Party victory in the election of 1860

AMERICA IN 1850

The swift victory in the Mexican-American War, topped by the "prize" of California gold discussed in Chapter 14 bolstered American national pride and self-confidence. Certainly, the America of 1850 was a very different nation from the republic of 1800. Geographic expansion, population increase, economic development, and the changes wrought by the market revolution had transformed the struggling new nation. Economically, culturally, and politically Americans had forged a strong sense of national identity.

Expansion and Growth

America was now a much larger nation than it had been in 1800. Through war and diplomacy, the country had grown to continental dimensions, more than tripling in size from 890,000 to 3 million square miles. Its population had increased enormously: from 5.3 million in 1800 to more than 23 million, 4 million of whom were African American slaves and 2 million new immigrants, largely from Germany and Ireland. Comprising just sixteen states in 1800, America in 1850 had thirty-one, and more than half of the population lived west of the Appalachians. America's cities had undergone the most rapid half-century of growth they were ever to experience (see Map 15.1).

America was also much richer: it is estimated that real per capita income doubled between 1800 and 1850, moving the nation decisively out of the "developing" category. Southern cotton, which had contributed so much to American economic growth, continued to be the nation's principal export, but it was no longer the major influence on the domestic economy. The growth of manufacturing in the Northeast and the rapid opening up of rich farmlands in the Midwest assured the future of the United States as a manufacturing nation, second only to Britain, and as a major exporter of agricultural products. At home, however, the diminishing economic importance of the South's major export, cotton, diminished its political importance—at least in the eyes of many Northerners. Thus, the very success of the United States both in geographic expansion and in economic development served to question the role of the slave South in the nation's future.

Politics, Culture, and National Identity

The notion of "manifest destiny" first expressed in the expansionist fervor of the 1840s (see chapter 14), was based on a widespread belief among Americans of the superiority of their democracy. European events in 1848 also served to foster American pride. In that year, a series of democratic revolutions—in Italy, France, Germany, Hungary, and parts of the Austrian Empire—swept the Continent. Many Americans assumed that American democracy and manifest destiny were the models for these liberal revolutions. When Lajos Kossuth, the famed Hungarian revolutionary, visited the United States in 1851, he was given a hero's welcome, and Daniel Webster complacently assured him that "we shall rejoice to see our American model upon the lower Danube."

Pride in democracy was one unifying theme in a growing sense of national identity and the new middle-class values, institutions, and culture that supported it. Since the turn of the century, American writers had struggled to find distinctive American themes, and these efforts bore fruit in the 1850s in the burst of creative activity termed the "American Renaissance." Newspapers, magazines, and communication improvements of all kinds created a national audience for the American scholars and writers who emerged during this decade, among them Henry Thoreau, Nathaniel Hawthorne, Walt Whitman, Herman Melville, Emily Dickinson, and Frederick Douglass.

During the American Renaissance, American writers pioneered new literary forms. Nathaniel Hawthorne, in works like "Young Goodman Brown" (1835), raised the short story to a distinctive American literary form. Poets like Walt Whitman and Emily Dickinson experimented with unrhymed and "off-rhyme" verse. Henry David Thoreau published *Walden* in 1854. A pastoral celebration of his life at Walden Pond, in Concord, Massachusetts, the essay was also a searching meditation on the cost to the individual of the loss of contact with nature that was a consequence of the market revolution.

Indeed, although the mid-century popular mood was one of self-congratulation, most of the writers of the American Renaissance were social critics. In *The Scarlet Letter* (1850) and *The House of the Seven Gables* (1851), Nathaniel Hawthorne brilliantly exposed the repressive and hypocritical aspects of Puritan New England in the colonial period and the often impossible moral choices faced by individuals. Hawthorne's friend Herman Melville, in his great work *Moby Dick* (1851), used the story of Captain Ahab's obsessive search for the white whale to write a profound study of the nature of good and evil and a critique of American society in the 1850s. The strongest social critique, however, was Frederick Douglass's starkly simple autobiography, *Narrative of the Life of Frederick Douglass* (1845), which told of his brutal life as a slave.

The most successful American novel of the mid-nineteenth century was also about the great issue of the day, slavery. In writing *Uncle Tom's Cabin*, Harriet Beecher Stowe combined the literary style of the then-popular women's domestic novels (discussed in Chapter 12) with vivid details of slavery culled from firsthand accounts by northern abolitionists and escaped slaves. Stowe, the daughter of the reforming clergyman Lyman Beecher, had married a Congregational minister and had herself long been active in antislavery work. Stowe's famous novel told a poignant story of the Christ-like slave Uncle Tom, who patiently endured the cruel treatment of an evil white overseer,

MAP EXPLORATION

To explore an interactive version of this map, go to **www.prenhall.com/faragher5/map15.1**

MAP 15.1 U.S. Population and Settlement, 1850 By 1850, the United States was a continental nation. Its people, whom Thomas Jefferson had once thought would not reach the Mississippi River for forty generations, had not only passed the river, but leapfrogged to the west coast. In comparison to the America of 1800 (see Map 9.1 on p. 238), the growth was astounding.

Simon Legree. Published in 1851, it was a runaway best seller. More than 300,000 copies were sold in the first year, and within ten years, the book had sold more than 2 million copies, becoming the all-time American bestseller in proportion to population. Turned into a play that remained popular throughout the nineteenth century, *Uncle Tom's Cabin* reached an even wider audience. Scenes from the novel such as that of Eliza carrying her son across the ice-choked Ohio River to freedom, Tom weeping for his children as he was sold south, and the death of little Eva are among the best-known passages in all of American literature. *Uncle Tom's Cabin* was more than a heart-tugging story: it was a call to action. In 1863, when Harriet Beecher Stowe was introduced to Abraham Lincoln, the president is said to have remarked, "So you're the little woman who wrote the book that made this great war!"

THE COMPROMISE OF 1850

Stowe's novel clearly spoke to the growing concern of the American people. The year 1850 opened to the most serious political crisis the United States had ever known. The issue raised by the 1846 Wilmot Proviso—whether slavery should be extended to the new territories—could no longer be ignored (see Chapter 14).

Political Parties and Slavery

The struggle over the issue of slavery in the territories had begun in 1846 with the Wilmot Proviso, and the nation's two great political parties, the Whigs and the Democrats, had been unable to resolve it.

The Second American Party System, forged in the great controversies of Andrew Jackson's presidency

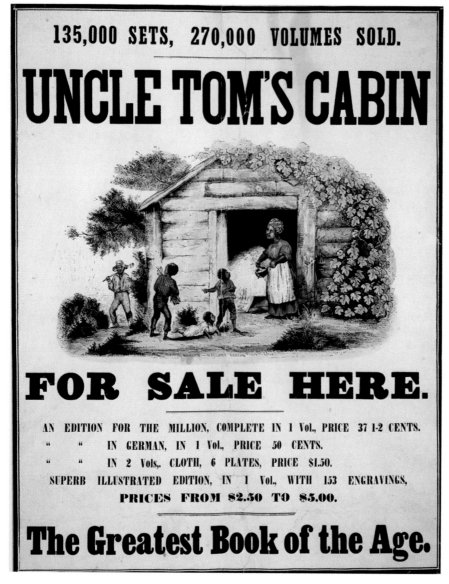

135,000 SETS, 270,000 VOLUMES SOLD.

UNCLE TOM'S CABIN

FOR SALE HERE.

AN EDITION FOR THE MILLION, COMPLETE IN 1 Vol., PRICE 37 1-2 CENTS.
"   "   IN GERMAN, IN 1 Vol., PRICE 50 CENTS.
"   "   IN 2 Vols,. CLOTH, 6 PLATES, PRICE $1.50.
SUPERB ILLUSTRATED EDITION, IN 1 Vol., WITH 153 ENGRAVINGS,
PRICES FROM $2.50 TO $5.00.

The Greatest Book of the Age.

This poster advertises *Uncle Tom's Cabin,* the bestselling novel by Harriet Beecher Stowe. This poignant story of long-suffering African American slaves had an immense impact on Northern popular opinion, swaying it decisively against slavery. In that respect, the poster's boast, "the greatest book of the age" was correct.

SOURCE: ©Bettmann/CORBIS.

by the election of 1848, sectional interests were eroding the political "glue" in both parties. Although each party still appeared united, sectional fissures already ran deep.

Political splits were preceded by divisions in other social institutions. Disagreements about slavery had already split the country's great religious organizations into northern and southern groups: the Presbyterians in 1837, the Methodists in 1844, and the Baptists in 1845. (Some of these splits turned out to be permanent. The Southern Baptist Convention, for example, is still a separate body.) Theodore Weld, the abolitionist leader, saw these splits as inevitable: "Events . . . have for years been silently but without a moment's pause, settling the basis of two great parties, the nucleus of one slavery, of the other, freedom." Indeed, the abolitionists had been posing this simple yet uncompromising choice between slavery or freedom since the 1830s. Moreover, they had been insisting on a compelling distinction: as Liberty Party spokesman Salmon P. Chase said, "Freedom is national; slavery only is local and sectional."

Congressional Debate

The debate that preceded the Compromise of 1850 was the final act in the political careers of the three aging men who in the public mind best represented America's sections: westerner Henry Clay; southerner John C. Calhoun; and Daniel Webster, spokesman for the North. It was sadly appropriate to the bitter sectional argument of 1850 that the three men contributed great words to the debate, but that the compromise itself was enacted by younger men.

In an additional irony, on July 9, 1850, in the midst of the debate, President Zachary Taylor died of acute gastroenteritis, caused by a hasty snack of fruit and cold milk at a Fourth of July celebration. A bluff military man, Taylor had been prepared to follow Andrew Jackson's precedent during the Nullification Crisis of 1832 and

(see Chapter 11), was a national party system. In their need to mobilize great masses of recently enfranchised voters to elect a president every four years, politicians created organized party structures that overrode deeply rooted sectional differences. Politicians from all sections of the country cooperated, because they knew their party could not succeed without national appeal. At a time when the ordinary person still had very strong sectional loyalties, the mass political party created a national community of like-minded voters. Yet,

simply demand that southern dissidents compromise. Vice President Millard Fillmore, who assumed the presidency, was a much weaker man, who did not seize the opportunity for presidential action.

Calhoun brought an aura of death with him to the Senate as he sat on the Senate floor for the last time, listening to the speech that he was too ill to read for himself. He died less than a month later, still insisting on the right of the South to secede if necessary, to preserve its way of life.

Calhoun argued, as he had since the Nullification Crisis (See Chapter 11) that the states rights' doctrine protected the legitimate rights of a minority in a democratic system governed by majority rule. Responding to the Wilmot Proviso, Calhoun broadened his argument to insist that Congress did not have a constitutional right to prohibit slavery in the territories. The territories, he said, were the common property of all the states, North and South, and slave owners had a constitutional right to the protection of their property wherever they moved. Of course, Calhoun's legally correct description of African American slaves as property enraged abolitionists. But on behalf of the South, Calhoun was expressing the belief—and the fear—that his interpretation of the Constitution was the only protection for slave owners, whose right to own slaves (a

fundamental right in Southern eyes) was being attacked. Calhoun's position on the territories quickly became Southern dogma: anything less than full access to the territories was unconstitutional. As Congressman Robert Toombs of Georgia put the case in 1850, the choice was stark: "Give us our just rights and we are ready to stand by the Union. Refuse [them] and for one, I will strike for independence."

Daniel Webster claimed to speak "not as a Massachusetts man, nor as a Northern man, but as an American. . . . I speak today for the preservation of the Union." He rejected Southern claims that peaceable secession was possible or desirable, and pleaded with abolitionists to compromise enough to keep the South in the Union. But he was speaking to Northerners who increasingly questioned why they should compromise when Southerners were not.

The Southern threat to secede confirmed for many Northerners the warnings of antislavery leaders that they were endangered by a menacing "slave power." Liberty Party leader James Birney, in a speech in 1844, was the first to add this phrase to the nation's political vocabulary. "The slave power," Birney explained, was a group of aristocratic slave owners who not only dominated the political and social life of the South, but conspired to control the federal government as well, posing a danger to free speech and free institutions throughout the nation.

Birney's "slave power" shone a spotlight on the increasingly defensive and monolithic response of southern representatives in national politics after 1830 (see Chapter 10). The proslavery strategy of maintaining supremacy in the Senate by having at least as many slave as free states admitted to the Union (a plan that required slavery expansion) and of maintaining control, or at least veto power, over presidential nominees seemed, in southern eyes, to be nothing less than ordinary self-defense. But to antislavery advocates, these actions looked like a conspiracy by sectional interests to control national politics. Birney's warnings about "the slave power" seemed in 1844 merely the overheated rhetoric of an extremist group of abolitionists. But the defensive Southern political strategies of the 1850s convinced an increasing number of Northern voters that "the slave power" did in fact exist. Thus in Northern eyes,

In 1850, the three men who had long represented America's three major regions attempted to resolve the political crisis brought on by the applications of California and Utah for statehood. Henry Clay is speaking; John C. Calhoun stands second from right; and Daniel Webster is seated at the left, with his head in his hand. Both Clay and Webster were ill, and Calhoun died before the Compromise of 1850 was arranged by a younger group of politicians led by Stephen A. Douglas.

SOURCE: Getty Images Inc. Hulton Archive Photos.

the South became a demonic monolith that threatened the national government.

The third of the old sectional spokesmen, Henry Clay, claiming he had "never before risen to address any assemblage so oppressed, so appalled, and so anxious," argued eloquently for compromise, but left the Senate in ill health before his plea was answered. Although Clay had assembled all the necessary parts of the bargain, it was not he, but members of a younger political generation, and in particular, the rising young Democrat from Illinois, Stephen Douglas, who drove the Compromise of 1850 through Congress.

Two Communities, Two Perspectives

Ironically, it was their common belief in expansion that made the arguments between Northerners and Southerners so irreconcilable. Southerners had been the strongest supporters of the Mexican-American War, and they still hoped to expand into Cuba, believing that the slave system must grow or wither. On the other hand, although many northern Whigs had opposed the Mexican-American War, most did so for antislavery reasons, not because they opposed expansion. The strong showing of the Free-Soil Party (which evolved out of the Liberty Party) in the election of 1848 (getting 10 percent of the popular vote) was proof of that. Basically, both North and South believed in manifest destiny, but each on its own terms.

Similarly, both North and South used the language of basic rights and liberties in the debate over expansion. But free-soilers were speaking of personal liberty, whereas Southerners meant their right to own a particular kind of property (slaves) and to maintain a way of life based on the possession of that property. In defending its own rights, each side had taken measures that infringed on the rights of the other. Southerners pointed out that abolitionists had libeled slave owners as a class and that they had bombarded the South with unwanted literature, abused the right of petition to Congress, incited slaves to rebellion, and actively helped slaves to escape. For their part, Northerners accused slave owners of censorship of the mails; imposition of the "gag rule" (repealed in 1844), which prohibited any petition against slavery from being read to or discussed by Congress; suppression of free speech in the South; and, of course, commission of the moral wrong of enslaving others in the first place.

By 1850, North and South had created fixed stereotypes of the other. To antislavery Northerners, the South was an economic backwater dominated by a small slave-owning aristocracy that lived off the profits of forced labor and deprived poor whites of their democratic rights and the fruits of honest work. The slave system was not only immoral, but a drag on the entire nation, for, in the words of Senator William Seward of New York, it subverted the "intelligence, vigor and energy" that were essen-

tial for national growth. In contrast, the dynamic and enterprising commercial North boasted a free labor ideology that offered economic opportunity to the common man and ensured his democratic rights (see Chapter 12).

Things looked very different through southern eyes. Far from being economically backward, the South, through its export of cotton, was, according to Southerners, the great engine of national economic growth from which the North benefited. Slavery was not only a blessing to an inferior race, but the cornerstone of democracy, for it ensured the freedom and independence of all white men without entailing the bitter class divisions that marked the North. Slave owners accused northern manufacturers of hypocrisy for practicing "wage slavery" without the paternal benevolence they claimed to bestow on their slaves. The North, James Henry Hammond of South Carolina charged, had eliminated the "name [of slavery], but not the thing," for "your whole hireling class of manual laborers and 'operatives' . . . are essentially slaves."

By the early 1850s, these vastly different visions of the North and the South—the result of many years of political controversy—had become fixed, and the chances of national reconciliation increasingly slim. Over the course of the decade, many Americans came to believe that the place of slavery in the nation's life had to be permanently settled. And they increasingly wondered whether their two sectional communities—one slave, one free—could continue to be part of a unitary national one.

Compromises

The Compromise of 1850 was actually five separate bills (lacking a majority for a comprehensive measure), embodying three separate compromises.

First, California was admitted as a free state, but the status of the remaining former Mexican possessions was left to be decided by popular sovereignty (a vote of the territory's inhabitants) when they applied for statehood. Utah's application for statehood was not accepted until 1896 because of controversy over the Mormon practice of polygamy. The result was, for the time being, fifteen slave states and sixteen free states. Second, Texas (a slave state) was required to cede land to New Mexico Territory (free or slave status undecided). In return, the federal government assumed $10 million of debts Texas had incurred before it became a state. Finally, the slave trade, but not slavery itself, was ended in the District of Columbia, but a stronger fugitive slave law, to be enforced in all states, was enacted (see Map 15.2).

Jubilation and relief greeted the news that compromise had been achieved. In Washington, where the anxiety and concern had been greatest, drunken crowds serenaded Congress, shouting, "The Union is saved!" That was certainly true for the moment, but analysis of the votes on the five bills that made up the compromise revealed no consistent majority. The sectional splits

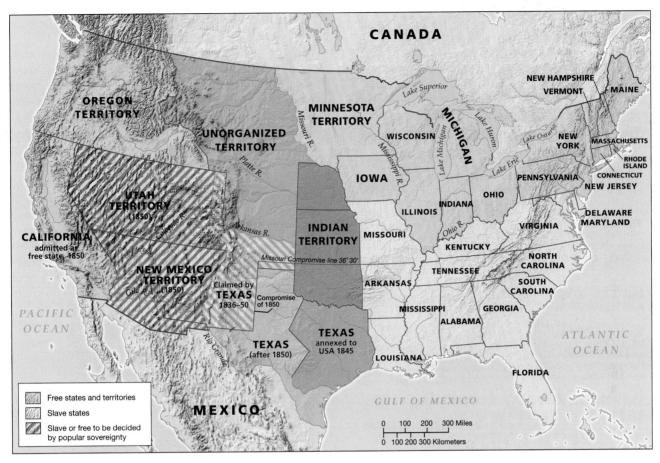

MAP 15.2 The Compromise of 1850 The Compromise of 1850, messier and more awkward than the Missouri Compromise of 1820, reflected heightened sectional tensions. California was admitted as a free state, the borders of Texas were settled, and the status of the rest of the former Mexican territory was left to be decided later by popular sovereignty. No consistent majority voted for the five separate bills that made up the compromise.

OVERVIEW

THE GREAT SECTIONAL COMPROMISES

Missouri Compromise	1820	Admits Missouri to the Union as a slave state and Maine as a free state; prohibits slavery in the rest of the Louisiana Purchase Territory north of 36°30′. Territory Covered: The entire territory of the Louisiana Purchase, exclusive of the state of Louisiana, which had been admitted to the Union in 1812.
Compromise of 1850	1850	Admits California to the Union as a free state, settles the borders of Texas (a slave state); sets no conditions concerning slavery for the rest of the territory acquired from Mexico. Enacts a national Fugitive Slave law. Territory Covered: The territory that had been part of Mexico before the end of the Mexican-American War and the Treaty of Guadalupe Hidalgo (1848): part of Texas, California, Utah Territory (now Utah, Nevada, and part of Colorado), and New Mexico Territory (now New Mexico and Arizona).

CAUTION!!
COLORED PEOPLE
OF BOSTON, ONE & ALL,

You are hereby respectfully CAUTIONED and advised, to avoid conversing with the
Watchmen and Police Officers of Boston,

For since the recent ORDER OF THE MAYOR & ALDERMEN, they are empowered to act as
KIDNAPPERS
AND
Slave Catchers,

And they have already been actually employed in KIDNAPPING, CATCHING, AND KEEPING SLAVES. Therefore, if you value your LIBERTY, and the *Welfare of the Fugitives* among you, *Shun* them in every possible manner, as so many *HOUNDS* on the track of the most unfortunate of your race.

Keep a Sharp Look Out for KIDNAPPERS, and have TOP EYE open.
APRIL 24, 1851.

This handbill warning free African Americans of danger circulated in Boston following the first of the infamous recaptures under the Fugitive Slave Law, that of Thomas Sims in 1851.

SOURCE: Library of Congress.

within each party that had existed before the compromise remained. Antislavery northern Whigs and proslavery Southern Democrats, each the larger wing of their party, were the least willing to compromise. Southern Whigs and northern Democrats were the forces for moderation, but each group was dwindling in popular appeal as sectional animosities grew.

In the country as a whole, the feeling was that the problem of slavery in the territories had been solved. The *Philadelphia Pennsylvanian* was confident that "peace and tranquillity" had been ensured, and the *Louisville Journal* said that a weight seemed to have been lifted from the heart of America. But as former Liberty Party spokesman Salmon P. Chase, now a senator from Ohio, soberly noted, "The question of slavery in the territories has been avoided. It has not been settled." And many Southerners felt that their only real gain in the contested compromise was the Fugitive Slave Law, which quickly turned out to be an inflammatory measure.

The Fugitive Slave Act

From the early days of their movement, Northern abolitionists had urged slaves to escape, promising assistance and support when they reached the North. Some free African Americans had given far more than verbal support. At great risk to themselves, they consistently offered refuge and assistance to escaped slaves. In spite of the renown of the organized network of whites and blacks known as the Underground Railroad, it rescued only a few slaves. Most escaped slaves found their most reliable help within Northern free black communities. Northerners had long been appalled by professional slave catchers, who zealously seized African Americans in the North and took them south into slavery again. Most abhorrent in northern eyes was that cap-

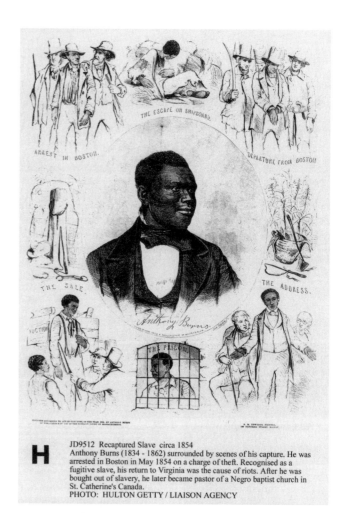

H　JD9512　Recaptured Slave circa 1854
Anthony Burns (1834 - 1862) surrounded by scenes of his capture. He was arrested in Boston in May 1854 on a charge of theft. Recognised as a fugitive slave, his return to Virginia was the cause of riots. After he was bought out of slavery, he later became pastor of a Negro baptist church in St. Catherine's Canada.
PHOTO: HULTON GETTY / LIAISON AGENCY

Escaped slave Anthony Burns, shown here surrounded by scenes of his capture in 1854, was the cause of Boston's greatest protest against the Fugitive Slave Law. The injustice of his trial and shipment back to the South converted many Bostonians to the antislavery cause.

SOURCE: Getty Images, Inc. Liaison.

tured black people were at the mercy of slave catchers because they had no legal right to defend themselves. In more than one case, a northern free African American was captured in his own community and helplessly shipped into slavery.

Solomon Northup was one such person. In his widely sold account *Twelve Years a Slave*, published in 1853, he told a harrowing tale of being kidnapped in Washington, the nation's capital, and shipped south. Northup spent twelve years as a slave before he was able to send a message to northern friends to bring the legal proof to free him. As a result of stories like Northup's, nine northern states passed personal liberty laws between 1842 and 1850, serving notice that they would not cooperate with federal recapture efforts. These northern laws enraged Southerners, who had long been convinced that all Northerners, not just abolitionists, were actively hindering efforts to reclaim their escaped slaves. At issue were two distinct definitions of "rights": Northerners were upset at the denial of legal and personal rights to escaped slaves; Southerners saw illegal infringement of their property rights. Southerners insisted that a strong federal law be part of the Compromise of 1850.

The Fugitive Slave Law, enacted in 1850, dramatically increased the power of slave owners to capture escaped slaves. The full authority of the federal government now supported slave owners, and although fugitives were guaranteed a hearing before a federal commissioner, they were not allowed to testify on their own behalf. Furthermore, the new law imposed federal penalties on citizens who protected or assisted fugitives, or who did not cooperate in their return. A number of free northern blacks, afraid that they might share Solomon Northup's fate, emigrated to Canada. Soon 30,000 to 40,000 African Americans, some formerly slave, some free, lived in Upper Canada, with the reluctant acquiescence of local authorities. Like many Americans, most Canadians were unwilling to accept black people as social equals, but they also were unwilling to force African Americans to risk recapture and return to slavery.

In Boston, the center of the American abolitionist movement, reaction to the Fugitive Slave Law was fierce. When an escaped slave named Shadrach Minkins was seized in February 1851, a group of African American men broke into the courtroom, overwhelmed the federal marshals, seized Minkins, and sent him safely to Canada. Although the action had community support—a Massachusetts jury defiantly refused to convict the perpetrators—many people, including Daniel Webster and President Fillmore, condemned it as "mob rule."

In the most famous Boston case, a biracial group of armed abolitionists led by Unitarian clergyman Thomas Wentworth Higginson stormed the federal courthouse in 1854 in an attempt to save escaped slave Anthony Burns.

The rescue effort failed, and a federal deputy marshal was killed. President Pierce sent marines, cavalry, and artillery to Boston to reinforce the guard over Burns and ordered a federal ship to be ready to deliver the fugitive back into slavery. When the effort by defense lawyers to argue for Burns's freedom failed, Bostonians raised money to buy his freedom. But the U.S. attorney, ordered by the president to enforce the Fugitive Slave Law in all circumstances, blocked the purchase. The case was lost, and Burns was marched to the docks through streets lined with sorrowing abolitionists. Buildings were shrouded in black and draped with American flags hanging upside down, while bells tolled as if for a funeral.

The Burns case radicalized many Northerners. Conservative Whig George Hilliard wrote to a friend, "When it was all over, and I was left alone in my office, I put my face in my hands and wept. I could do nothing less." During the 1850s, 322 black fugitives were sent back into slavery; only 11 were declared free. Northern popular sentiment and the Fugitive Slave Law, rigorously enforced by the federal government, were increasingly at odds.

In this volatile atmosphere, escaped African Americans wrote and lectured bravely on behalf of freedom. Frederick Douglass, the most famous and eloquent of the fugitive slaves, spoke out fearlessly in support of armed resistance. "The only way to make the Fugitive Slave Law a dead letter," he said in 1853, "is to make a half dozen or more dead kidnappers." Openly active in the underground network that helped slaves reach safety in Canada, Douglass himself had been constantly in danger of capture until his friends bought his freedom in 1847. (For another experience, see Out of Many Voices: An Escaped Slave Questions Her Freedom in the North.)

The Fugitive Slave Law brought home the reality of slavery to residents of the free states. In effect, this law forced northern communities to confront the full meaning of slavery. Although most people were still unwilling to grant social equality to the free African Americans who lived in the northern states, more and more had come to believe that the institution of slavery was wrong. The strong northern reaction against the Fugitive Slave Law also had consequences in the South. Northern protests against the Fugitive Slave Law bred suspicion in the South and encouraged secessionist thinking. These new currents of public opinion were reflected in the election of 1852.

The Election of 1852

The first sign of the weakening of the national party system in 1852 was the difficulty both parties experienced at their nominating conventions. With long-time Whig party leader Henry Clay now dead, William Seward of New York became the unofficial party head. He preferred General Winfield Scott (a military hero

OUT OF MANY VOICES

AN ESCAPED SLAVE QUESTIONS HER FREEDOM IN THE NORTH

Harriet Jacobs, who escaped to the North after seven years in hiding in the South, wrote bitterly in her Incidents in the Life of a Slave Girl *(1861) about the Fugitive Slave Law.*

"I WAS, IN FACT, A SLAVE IN NEW YORK, AS SUBJECT to slave laws as I had been in a slave state. . . . I had been chased during half my life, and it seemed as if the chase was never to end." Threatened by owners who came north for her, Jacobs was forced into hiding while northern white friends spoke to her southern owners. Informed that they were arranging her purchase, Jacobs protested: "I felt grateful for the kindness that prompted this offer, but the idea was not so pleasant to me as might have been expected. The more my mind had become enlightened, the more difficult it was for me to consider myself an article of property; and to pay money to those who had so grievously oppressed me seemed like taking from my sufferings the glory of triumph." Nevertheless, the sale went ahead. "A gentleman near me said, 'It's true; I have seen the bill of sale.' 'The bill of sale!' Those words struck me like a blow. So I was sold at last! A human being sold in the free city of New York!" ■

SOURCE: Harriet Jacobs, *Incidents in the Life of a Slave Girl*, Jean Fagan Yellin ed., (Cambridge, MA: Harvard University Press, 1987).

---

like the party's previous two candidates) to the prosouthern Fillmore, and after fifty-two ballots, managed to get him nominated. Many southern Whigs were permanently alienated by the choice; although Whigs were still elected to Congress from the South, their loyalty to the national party was strained to the breaking point. The Whigs never again fielded a presidential candidate.

The Democrats had a wider variety of candidates: Lewis Cass of popular sovereignty fame; Stephen Douglas, architect of the Compromise of 1850; and James Buchanan, described as a "Northern man with Southern principles." Cass, Douglas, and Buchanan competed for forty-nine ballots, each strong enough to block the others but not strong enough to win. Finally, the party turned to a handsome, affable nonentity, Franklin Pierce of New Hampshire, who was thought to have southern sympathies. Uniting on a platform pledging "faithful execution" of all parts of the Compromise of 1850, including the Fugitive Slave Law, Democrats polled well in the South and in the North. Most Democrats who had voted for the Free-Soil Party in 1848 voted for Pierce. So, in record numbers, did immigrant Irish and German voters, who were eligible for citizenship after three years' residence. The strong immigrant vote for Pierce was a sign of the strength of the Democratic machines in northern cities (see Chapter 13), and reformers complained, not for the last time, about widespread corruption and "vote buying" by urban bosses. Overall, however, "Genl. Apathy is the strongest candidate out here," as one Ohioan reported. Pierce easily won the 1852 election, 254 electoral votes to 42. Voter turnout was below 70 percent, lower than it had been since 1836.

"Young America": The Politics of Expansion

Pierce entered the White House in 1853 on a wave of good feeling. Massachusetts Whig Amos Lawrence reported, "Never since Washington has an administration commenced with the hearty [good] will of so large a portion of the country." This goodwill was soon strained by Pierce's support for the expansionist adventures of the "Young America" movement.

The "Young America" movement began as a group of writers and politicians in the New York Democratic Party who believed in the democratic and nationalistic promise of "manifest destiny" (a term coined by one of their members, John Sullivan). By the 1850s, however, their lofty goals had shrunk to a desire to conquer Central America and Cuba. Young America expansionists had glanced covetously southward since the end of the Mexican-American War. During the Pierce administration, several private "filibusters" (from the Spanish *filibustero*, meaning an "adventurer" or "pirate") invaded Caribbean and Central American countries, usually with the declared intention of extending slave territory. The best-known of the filibusters, William Walker, was also the most improbable. Short, slight, and soft-spoken, Walker led not one, but three invasions of Nicaragua. After the first invasion

The Japanese painting shows Commodore Matthew Perry landing in Japan in 1853. The commercial treaty Perry signed with the Japanese government, which opened a formerly closed country to American trade, was viewed in the United States as another fruit of manifest destiny.

SOURCE: *The Landing of Commodore Perry in Japan in 1853.* (Detail) Japanese, Perry's ship and procession (Ukiyo-e School) Edo period, 19th century. Handscroll; ink and color on paper, 10 $^7/_8$ × 211 $^1/_8$ in. (27.6 × 536.3 cm). Museum of Fine Arts, Boston. William Sturgis Bigelow Collection, RES.11.6054. Pho.

in 1855, Walker became ruler of the country and encouraged settlement by southern slave owners, but he was unseated by a regional revolt in 1857. His subsequent efforts to regain control of the country failed, and in his last attempt, he was captured and executed by firing squad in Honduras.

The Pierce administration, not directly involved in the filibustering, was deeply involved in an effort to obtain Cuba. In part, the effort was prompted by abortive slave revolts in Cuba in 1843–44, which led some Cuban slave owners to seek annexation to the United States so that slavery could continue. In 1854, Pierce authorized his minister to Spain, Pierre Soulé, to try to force the unwilling Spanish to sell Cuba for $130 million. Soulé met in Ostend, Belgium, with the American ministers to France and England, John Mason and James Buchanan, to compose the offer, which was a mixture of cajolements and threats. At first appealing to Spain to recognize the deep affinities between the Cubans and American southerners that made them "one people with one destiny," the document went on to threaten to "wrest" Cuba from Spain if necessary. This amazing document, which became known as the Ostend Manifesto, was supposed to be secret, but was soon leaked to the press. Deeply embarrassed, the Pierce administration was forced to repudiate it.

In another expansionist gesture in another direction, President Franklin Pierce dispatched Commodore

Matthew Perry across the Pacific to Japan, a nation famous for its insularity and hostility to outsiders. The mission resulted in 1854 in a commercial treaty that opened Japan to American trade. Perry's feat caused a newspaper in tiny Olympia, Washington, to boast, "We shall have the boundless Pacific for a market in manifest destiny. We were born to command it."

Overall, however, the complicity between the Pierce administration and proslavery expansionists was foolhardy and lost it the northern goodwill with which it had begun. The sectional crisis that preceded the Compromise of 1850 had made obvious the danger of reopening the territorial issue. Ironically, it was not the Young America expansionists, but the prime mover of the Compromise of 1850, Stephen A. Douglas, who reignited the sectional struggle over slavery expansion.

THE CRISIS OF THE NATIONAL PARTY SYSTEM

In 1854, Douglas introduced the Kansas-Nebraska Act, proposing to open those lands that had been the northern part of Indian Territory to American settlers under the principle of popular sovereignty. He thereby reopened the question of slavery in the territories. Douglas knew he was taking a political risk, but he believed he could satisfy both his expansionist aims and his presidential ambitions. He was wrong. Instead, he pushed the national party system into crisis, first killing the Whigs and then destroying the Democrats.

The Kansas-Nebraska Act

In a stunning example of the expansionist pressures generated by the market revolution, Stephen Douglas introduced the Kansas-Nebraska Act to further the construction of a transcontinental railroad across what was still considered the "Great American Desert" to California. Douglas wanted the rail line to terminate in Chicago, in his own state of Illinois, rather than in the rival St. Louis, but for that to happen, the land west of Iowa and Missouri had to be organized into territories (the first step toward statehood). To get Congress to agree to the organization of the territories, however, Douglas needed the votes of southern Democrats, who were unwilling to support him unless the territories were open to slavery.

Douglas thought he was solving his problem by proposing that the status of slavery in the new territories be governed by the principle of popular sovereignty. Democratic politicians had favored this democratic-sounding slogan, vague enough to appeal to both proslavery and antislavery voters, ever since 1848. Douglas thought Southerners would support his bill because of its popular sovereignty provision, and Northerners because it favored a northern route for the transcontinental railroad. Douglas chose also to downplay the price he had to pay for southern support—by allowing the possibility of slavery in the new territories, his bill in effect repealed the Missouri Compromise of 1820, which barred slavery north of latitude 36°30′ (see Map 15.3).

The Kansas-Nebraska bill passed, but it badly strained the major political parties. Southern Whigs voted with southern Democrats in favor of the measure, northern Whigs rejected it absolutely, creating an irreconcilable split that left Whigs unable to field a presidential candidate in 1856. The damage to the Democratic Party was almost as great. In the congressional elections of 1854, northern Democrats lost two-thirds of their seats (a drop from ninety-one to twenty-five), giving the southern Democrats (who were solidly in favor of slavery extension) the dominant voice both in Congress and within the party.

Douglas had committed one of the greatest miscalculations in American political history. A storm of protest arose throughout the North. More than 300 large anti-Nebraska rallies occurred during congressional consideration of the bill, and the anger did not subside. Douglas, who confidently believed that "the people of the North will sustain the measure when they come to understand it," found himself shouted down more than once at public rallies when he tried to explain the bill.

The Kansas-Nebraska bill shifted a crucial sector of northern opinion: the wealthy merchants, bankers, and manufacturers, called the "Cotton Whigs," who had economic ties with southern slave owners and had always disapproved of abolitionist activity. Convinced that the bill would encourage antislavery feeling in the North, Cotton Whigs urged southern politicians to vote against it, only to be ignored. Passage of the Kansas-Nebraska Act convinced many northern Whigs that compromise with the South was impossible. Even as sober a newspaper as the *New York Times* regarded the act as "part of this great scheme for extending and perpetuating the supremacy of the Slave Power." In Kansas in 1854, hasty treaties were concluded with the Indian tribes who owned the land. Some, such as the Kickapoos, Shawnees, Sauks, and Foxes, agreed to relocate to small reservations. Others, like the Delawares, Weas, and Iowas, agreed to sell their lands to whites. Still others, such as the Cheyennes and Sioux, kept the western part of Kansas Territory (now Colorado)—until gold was discovered there in 1859. Once the treaties were signed, both proslavery and antislavery white settlers began to pour in, and the battle was on.

"Bleeding Kansas"

The first to claim land in Kansas were residents of nearby Missouri, itself a slave state. Missourians took up land claims, established proslavery strongholds such as the towns of Leavenworth, Kickapoo, and Atchison, and repeatedly and blatantly swamped Kansas elections with Missouri votes. In 1855, in the second of several notoriously fraudulent elections, 6,307 ballots were cast in a territory that had fewer than 3,000 eligible voters. Most of the proslavery votes were cast by "border ruffians," as they proudly called themselves, from Missouri. These were frontiersmen, fond of boasting that they could "scream louder, jump higher, shoot closer, get drunker at night and wake up soberer in the morning than any man this side of the Rocky Mountains."

Northerners quickly responded. The first party of New Englanders arrived in the summer of 1854 and established the free-soil town of Lawrence, named for former "Cotton Whig" Amos Lawrence, who financed them. More than a thousand others had joined them by the following summer. Among those who responded were Rev. Samuel Adair and his wife Florella. Florella Brown and Samuel Adair had met and married in the early 1840s when they were students at Oberlin College, a stronghold of abolitionist sentiment. In 1854, Rev. Adair wrote to the American Missionary Association asking to be sent to Kansas: "[F]or many years my heart has rather been with the West; but my wife has been rather disinclined to go to the new settlements. But since the 'Nebraska Iniquity' has been perpetuated she has entirely changed her mind & thinks now is the time to strike." They settled in Osawatomie, a Kansas free-soil stronghold, in March of 1855. Like the Adairs, the other migrants were free-soilers, and many were religious reformers as well. The contrast of values between them

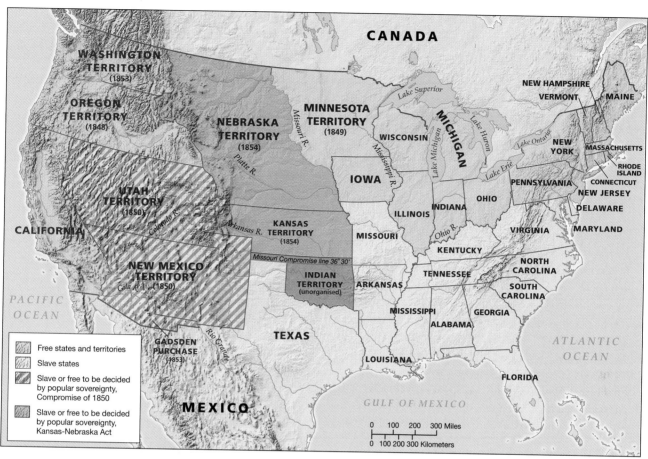

MAP 15.3 The Kansas-Nebraska Act, 1854 The Kansas-Nebraska Act, proposed by Steven A. Douglas in 1854, opened the central and northern Great Plains to settlement. The act had two major faults: it robbed Indian peoples of half the territory guaranteed to them by treaty, and, because it repealed the Missouri Compromise line, it opened up the lands to warring proslavery and antislavery factions.

and the border ruffians was almost total. When non-drinking William Phillips stiffly refused a friendly offer of a drink from a Missourian, the border ruffian burst out, "That's just it! This thing of temperance and abolitionism and the Emigrant Aid Society are all the same kind of thing."

Kansas soon became a bloody battleground as the two factions struggled to secure the mandate of "popular sovereignty." Free-Soilers in Lawrence received shipments of heavy crates, innocuously marked "BOOKS" but actually containing Sharps repeating rifles, sent by eastern supporters. For their part, the border ruffians—already heavily armed, with Bowie knives in their boots, revolvers at their waists, rifles slung from their shoulders, and swords at their sides—called for reinforcements. Senator David Atchison of Missouri exhorted Alabamans: "Let your young men come forth to Missouri and Kansas! Let them come well armed!"

In the summer of 1856, these lethal preparations exploded into open warfare. First, proslavery forces burned and looted the town of Lawrence. In retaliation, a grim old man named John Brown led his sons in a raid on the proslavery settlers of Pottawatomie Creek, killing five unarmed people. A wave of violence ensued. Armed bands roamed the countryside, and burnings and killings became commonplace. John Brown and his followers were just one of many bands of marauding murderers who were never arrested, never brought to trial, and never stopped from committing further violence. Peaceful residents of large sections of rural Kansas were repeatedly forced to flee to the safety of military forts when rumors of one or another armed band reached them. (See Out of Many Voices: An Abolitionist Couple Attempts to Live Their Principles in Bleeding Kansas.)

The rest of the nation watched in horror as the residents of Kansas slaughtered each other in the pursuit of sectional goals. Americans' pride in their nation's great achievements was threatened by the endless violence in one small part—but a part that increasingly seemed to represent the divisions of the whole.

OUT OF MANY VOICES

AN ABOLITIONIST COUPLE ATTEMPTS TO LIVE THEIR PRINCIPLES IN BLEEDING KANSAS

ev. Samuel Adair and his wife Florella Brown Adair set-tled in Osawatomie in March of 1855 and were soon joined by other family members. Florella's brother John and a number of his sons settled nearby, but their violent antislav-ery views contributed to the Kansas turmoil. As Florella wrote to her sister early in 1856, "you ask in one of your letters if we have any fear of our lives. I think now we are constantly exposed and we have almost no protection." In September, John Brown perpe-trated the Potowatomie massacre. Florella described the retaliation in a letter to her sister.

FIFTEEN OR TWENTY CAME DASHING DOWN TO our house and up to the door yelling out who lives here, and where is the man. A sick woman and three little children having fled to us for protection commenced screaming and crying don't kill us, don't burn the house down over us while I stood in the door and begged they would spare our lives and they might have all they could find in the house or on the place. Seeing us frightened almost to death, the Captain said hold on boys there is nobody here but women and children and we are Gentlemen, we never abuse women and children, don't be frightened Ladies we won't hurt you, "but if we get the men we will put the rope over their heads mighty quick." ■

SOURCE: Adair letters quoted in Gerald W. McFarland, *A Scattered People* (New York: Random House, 1985) pp 140–149.

The Politics of Nativism

The violence in Kansas was echoed by increasing vio-lence in the nation's cities. Serious violence marred the elections of 1854 and 1856 in New York. In New Orleans, anger over corrupt elections caused a self-appointed vig-ilance committee to attempt a takeover of the city gov-ernment. The vigilantes recruited several hundred men to erect barricades in Jackson Square in the heart of the city, where they skirmished for five days with an oppos-ing force composed largely of Catholics and immigrants. In Chicago, riots started in 1855, when the mayor attempted to close the saloons on Sunday. German work-ingmen joined by Irishmen and Swedes paraded in protest and were met by 200 men of the National Guard, militia, and special police. The ensuing "Lager Beer Riots" ended with the imposition of martial law on the entire city.

This urban violence, like that in Kansas, was caused by the breakdown of the two-party system. The breakup of the Whig Party left a political vacuum that was filled by one of the strongest bursts of nativism, or antiimmi-grant feeling, in American history, and by the rapid growth of the new American Party, which formed in 1850 to give political expression to nativism. The new

This night-time meeting of supporters of the Know-Nothing Party in New York City was dramatically spotlighted by a new device borrowed from the theater, an incandescent calcium light, popularly called a limelight.

SOURCE: Getty Images Inc. Hulton Archive Photos.

BATTLE OF HICKORY POINT, 25 MILES NORTH OF LAWRENCE.

This lithograph shows the Battle of Hickory Point, 1856, one of the many battles between proslavery fighters and free-soilers that gave the territory its dreadful nickname, Bleeding Kansas.

SOURCE: W. Breyman, *Battle of Hickory Point*, Courtesy of Anne S. K. Brown Military Collection, John Hay Library, Brown University.

party was in part a reaction to the Democratic Party's success in capturing the support of the rapidly growing population of mostly Catholic foreign-born voters. Irish immigrants in particular voted Democratic, both in reaction to Whig hostility (as in Boston) and because of their own antiblack prejudices. Frequently in competition with free African Americans for low-paying jobs, Irish immigrants were more likely to share the attitudes of Southerners than those of abolitionists.

The reformist and individualistic attitudes of many Whigs inclined them toward nativism. Many Whigs disapproved of the new immigrants because they were poor, Catholic, and often disdainful of the temperance movement. The Catholic Church's opposition to the liberal European revolutions of 1848 also fueled anti-Catholic fears. If America's new Catholic immigrants opposed the revolutions in which other Americans took such pride (believing them to be modeled on the American example), how could the future of America's own democracy be ensured? Finally, nativist Whigs held immigration to be solely responsible for the increases in crime and the rising cost of relief for the

poor that accompanied the astoundingly rapid urban growth of the 1830s and 1840s (see Chapter 13).

Nativism drew former Whigs, especially young men in white-collar and skilled blue-collar occupations, to the new American Party. At the core of the party were several secret fraternal societies open only to native-born Protestants who pledged never to vote for a Catholic, on the grounds that all Catholics took their orders straight from the pope in Rome. When questioned about their beliefs, party members maintained secrecy by answering, "I know nothing"—hence the popular name for American Party members, the Know-Nothings.

Know-Nothings scored startling victories in northern state elections in 1854, winning control of the legislature in Massachusetts and polling 40 percent of the vote in Pennsylvania. No wonder one Pennsylvania Democrat reported, "Nearly everybody seems to have gone altogether deranged on Nativism." The American Party initially polled well in the South, attracting the votes of many former southern Whigs. But in the 1850s, no party could ignore slavery, and in 1855, the American Party split into northern (antislavery) and southern (proslavery) wings. Soon after this split, many people who had voted for the Know-Nothings shifted their support to another new party, one that combined many characteristics of the Whigs with a westward-looking, expansionist, free-soil policy. This was the Republican Party, founded in 1854.

The Republican Party and the Election of 1856

Many constituencies found room in the new Republican Party. Its supporters included many former northern Whigs who opposed slavery absolutely, many Free-Soil Party supporters who opposed the expansion of slavery, but were willing to tolerate it in the South, and many northern reformers concerned about temperance and Catholicism. The Republicans also attracted the economic core of the old Whig Party—the merchants and industrialists who wanted a strong national government to promote economic growth by supporting a protective tariff, transportation improvements, and cheap land for western farmers. In quieter times, it would have taken this party a while to sort out all its differences and become a true political community. But because of the sectional crisis, the fledgling party nearly won its very first presidential election.

The immediate question facing the nation in 1856 was which new party, the Know-Nothings or the Republicans, would emerge the stronger. But the more important question was whether the Democratic Party could hold together. The two strongest contenders for the Democratic nomination were President Pierce and Stephen A. Douglas. Douglas had proposed the Kansas-Nebraska Act and Pierce had actively supported it. Both men therefore had the support of the southern wing of the party. But it was precisely

their support of this act that made Northerners oppose both of them. The Kansas-Nebraska Act's divisive effect on the Democratic Party now became clear: no one who had voted on the bill, either for or against, could satisfy both wings of the party. A compromise candidate was found in James Buchanan of Pennsylvania, the "Northern man with Southern principles." Luckily for him, he had been ambassador to Great Britain at the time of the Kansas-Nebraska Act and thus had not had to commit himself.

The election of 1856 appeared to be a three-way contest that pitted Buchanan against explorer John C. Frémont of the Republican Party and the American (Know-Nothing) Party's candidate, former president Millard Fillmore. In fact, the election was two separate contests, one in the North and one in the South. The northern race was between Buchanan and Fremont, the southern one between Buchanan and Fillmore. Frémont's name appeared on the ballot in only four southern states, all in the Upper South, and even there he polled almost no votes. Although he carried only the state of Maryland, Fillmore attracted more than 40 percent of the vote in ten other slave states. Frémont decisively defeated Buchanan in the North, winning eleven of sixteen free states. Buchanan, however, won the election with only 45 percent of the popular vote, because he was the only national candidate. But the Republicans, after studying the election returns, claimed "victorious defeat," for they realized that in 1860, the addition of just two more northern states to their total would mean victory. Furthermore, the Republican Party had clearly defeated the American Party in the battle to win designation as a major party. These were grounds for great optimism—and for great concern, for the Republican Party was a sectional, rather

SOUTHERN CHIVALRY — ARGUMENT versus CLUB'S.

The beating of Senator Charles Sumner by Congressman Preston Brooks on the floor of the U.S. Senate attracted the horrified attention of northerners but won the approval of southerners.

SOURCE: The Granger Collection.

OVERVIEW

POLITICAL PARTIES SPLIT AND REALIGN

Whig Party	Ran its last presidential candidate in 1852. The candidate, General Winfield Scott, alienated many southern Whigs, and the party was so split it could not field a candidate in 1856.
Democratic Party	Remained a national party through 1856, but Buchanan's actions as president made southern domination of the party so clear that many northern Democrats were alienated. Stephen Douglas, running as a northern Democrat in 1860, won 29 percent of the popular vote; John Breckinridge, running as a Southern Democrat, won 18 percent.
Liberty Party	Antislavery party; ran James G. Birney for president in 1844. He won 62,000 votes, largely from northern antislavery Whigs.
Free-Soil Party	Ran Martin Van Buren, former Democratic president, in 1848. Gained 10 percent of the popular vote, largely from Whigs but also from some northern Democrats.
American (Know-Nothing) Party	Nativist party made striking gains in 1854 congressional elections, attracting both northern and southern Whigs. In 1856, its presidential candidate, Millard Fillmore, won 21 percent of the popular vote.
Republican Party	Founded in 1854. Attracted many northern Whigs and northern Democrats. Presidential candidate John C. Frémont won 33 percent of the popular vote in 1856; in 1860, Abraham Lincoln won 40 percent and was elected in a four-way race.

than a national, party; it drew almost all its support from the North. Southerners viewed its very existence as an attack on their vital interests. Thus the rapid rise of the Republicans posed a growing threat to national unity.

The election of 1856 attracted one of the highest voter turnouts in American history—79 percent. Ordinary people had come to share the politicians' concern about the growing sectional rift. The combined popular vote for Buchanan and Fillmore (67 percent) showed that most voters, north and south, favored politicians who at least claimed to speak for national rather than sectional interests. The northern returns also showed something else. Northerners had decided that the threat posed by the expansion of slavery was greater than that posed by the new immigrants; although it never disappeared, nativism subsided (see Map 15.4).

THE DIFFERENCES DEEPEN

In one dreadful week in 1856, the people of the United States heard, in quick succession, about the looting and burning of Lawrence, Kansas, about John Brown's retaliatory massacre at Pottawatomie, and about unprecedented violence on the Senate floor. In the last of these incidents, Senator Charles Sumner of Massachusetts suffered permanent injury in a vicious attack by Congressman Preston Brooks of South Carolina. Trapped at his desk, Sumner was helpless as Brooks beat him so

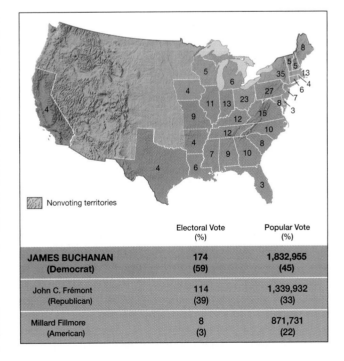

Nonvoting territories

	Electoral Vote (%)	Popular Vote (%)
JAMES BUCHANAN (Democrat)	**174** **(59)**	**1,832,955** **(45)**
John C. Frémont (Republican)	114 (39)	1,339,932 (33)
Millard Fillmore (American)	8 (3)	871,731 (22)

MAP 15.4 The Election of 1856 Because three parties contested the 1856 election, Democrat James Buchanan was a minority president. Although Buchanan alone had national support, Republican John Frémont won most of the free states, and Millard Fillmore of the American Party gained 40 percent of the vote in most of the slave states.

hard with his cane that it broke. A few days earlier, Sumner had given an insulting antislavery speech. Using the abusive, accusatory style favored by abolitionists, he had singled out for ridicule Senator Andrew Butler of South Carolina, charging him with choosing "the harlot, slavery" as his mistress. Senator Butler was Preston Brooks's uncle; in Brooks's mind, he was simply avenging an intolerable affront to his uncle's honor. So far had the behavioral codes of North and South diverged, that each man found his own action perfectly justifiable and the action of the other outrageous. Their attitudes were mirrored in their respective sections.

The *Dred Scott* Decision

Although James Buchanan firmly believed that he alone could hold together the nation so riven by hatred and violence, his self-confidence outran his abilities. He was so deeply indebted to the strong southern wing of the Democratic Party, that he could not take the impartial actions necessary to heal "Bleeding Kansas." And his support for a momentous pro-southern decision by the Supreme Court further aggravated sectional differences.

In *Dred Scott* v. *Sandford*, decided on March 6, 1857, two days after James Buchanan was sworn in, a southern-dominated Supreme Court attempted—and failed—to solve the political controversy over slavery. Dred Scott had been a slave all his life. His owner, army surgeon John Emerson, had taken Scott on his military assignments during the 1830s to Illinois (a free state) and Wisconsin Territory (a free territory, north of the Missouri Compromise line). During that time, Scott married another slave, Harriet, and their daughter Eliza was born in free territory. Emerson and the Scotts then returned to Missouri (a slave state) and there, in 1846, Dred Scott sued for his freedom and that of his wife and his daughter born in Wisconsin Territory (who as women had no legal standing of their own) on the grounds that residence in free lands had made them free. It took eleven years for the case to reach the Supreme Court, and by then its importance was obvious to everyone.

Chief Justice Roger B. Taney, of Maryland, seventy-nine years old, hard of hearing and failing of sight, insisted on reading his majority opinion in its entirety, a process that took four excruciating hours. Declaring the Missouri Compromise unconstitutional, Taney asserted that the federal government had no right to interfere with the free movement of property throughout the territories. Taney was in effect making John C. Calhoun's states' rights position, always considered an extremist southern position, the law of the land. He then dismissed the *Dred Scott* case on the grounds that only citizens could bring suits before federal courts and that black people—slave or free—were not citizens. With this bold judicial intervention into the most heated issue of the day, Taney intended to settle the controversy over the expansion of slavery once and for all. Instead, he inflamed the conflict.

The five southern members of the Supreme Court concurred in Taney's decision, as did one Northerner, Robert C. Grier. Historians have found that President-elect Buchanan had pressured Grier, a fellow Pennsylvanian, to support the majority. Two of the three other Northerners vigorously dissented, and the last voiced other objections. This was clearly a sectional decision, and the response to it was sectional. Southerners expressed great satisfaction and strong support for the Court. The *Georgia Constitutionalist* announced, "Southern opinion upon the subject of southern slavery . . . is now the supreme law of the land . . . and opposition to southern opinion upon this subject is now opposition to the Constitution, and morally treason against the Government."

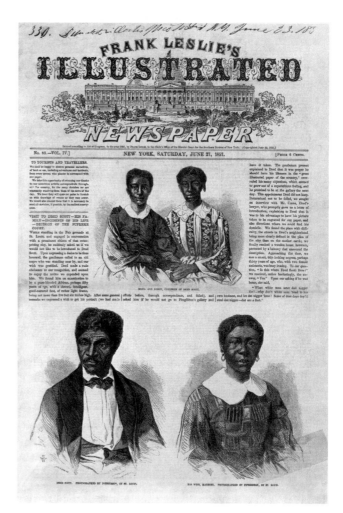

These sympathetic portraits of Harriet and Dred Scott and their daughters in 1857 helped to shape the northern reaction to the Supreme Court's decision that denied the Scotts' claim to freedom. The infamous *Dred Scott* decision was intended to resolve the issue of slavery expansion, but instead heightened angry feelings in both North and South.

SOURCE: *Frank Leslie's Illustrated Newspaper*, June 27, 1857. Library of Congress. © CORBIS

Northerners disagreed. Many were so troubled by the *Dred Scott* decision that for the first time, they found themselves seriously questioning the power of the Supreme Court to establish the "law of the land." The New York legislature passed a resolution declaring that the Supreme Court had lost the confidence and respect of the people of that state, and another resolution refusing to allow slavery within its borders "in any form or under any pretense, or for any time, however short." New York Republicans also proposed an equal suffrage amendment for free African Americans, who were largely disenfranchised by a stringent property qualification for voting. But this was too liberal for the state's voters, who defeated it. This racist attitude was a bitter blow to free African Americans in the North. Frederick Douglass was so disheartened that he seriously considered emigrating to Haiti.

For the Republican Party, the *Dred Scott* decision represented a formidable challenge. By invalidating the Missouri Compromise, the decision swept away the free-soil foundation of the party. But to directly challenge a Supreme Court decision was a weighty matter. The most sensational Republican counterattack—made by both Abraham Lincoln and William Seward—was the accusation that President Buchanan had conspired with the southern Supreme Court justices to subvert the American political system by withholding the decision until after the presidential election. Lincoln also raised the frightening possibility that "the next *Dred Scott* decision" would legalize slavery even in free states that abhorred it. President Buchanan's response to events in Kansas, including the drafting of a proslavery constitution, also stoked sectional antagonisms.

The Lecompton Constitution

In Kansas, the doctrine of popular sovereignty led to continuing civil strife and the political travesty of two territorial governments. The first election of officers to a territorial government in 1855 produced a lopsided proslavery outcome that was clearly the result of illegal voting by Missouri border ruffians. Free-Soilers protested by forming their own government, giving Kansas both a proslavery territorial legislature in Lecompton and a Free-Soil government in Topeka. Free-Soil voters boycotted a June 1857 election of representatives to a convention called to write a constitution for the territory once it reached statehood. As a result, the convention had a proslavery majority that wrote the proslavery Lecompton constitution and then applied to Congress for admission to the Union under its terms. In the meantime, in October, Free-Soil voters had participated in relatively honest elections for the territorial legislature, elections that returned a clear Free-Soil majority. Nevertheless, Buchanan, in the single most disastrous mistake of his administration, endorsed the proslavery constitution, because he feared the loss of the support of southern Democrats. It seemed that Kansas would

enter the Union as a sixteenth slave state, making the number of slave and free states equal.

Unexpected congressional opposition came from none other than Stephen Douglas, author of the legislation that had begun the Kansas troubles in 1854. Now, in 1857, in what was surely the bravest step of his political career, Douglas opposed the Lecompton constitution on the grounds that it violated the principle of popular sovereignty. He insisted that the Lecompton constitution must be voted on by Kansas voters in honest elections. Defying James Buchanan, the president of his own party, Douglas voted with the majority in Congress in April 1858 to refuse admission to Kansas under the Lecompton constitution. In a new referendum, the people of Kansas also rejected the Lecompton constitution, 11,300 to 1,788. Kansas was finally admitted as a free state in January 1861.

The defeat of the Lecompton constitution did not come easily. There was more bloodshed in Kansas: sporadic ambushes and killings, including a mass shooting of nine free-soilers. And there was more violence in Congress: a free-for-all involving almost thirty congressmen broke out in the House late one night after an exchange of insults between Republicans and southern Democrats. And the Democratic Party was breaking apart. Douglas had intended to preserve the Democrats as a national party, but instead, he lost the support of the southern wing. Summing up these events, Congressman Alexander Stephens of Georgia wrote glumly to his brother: "All things here are tending my mind to the conclusion that the Union cannot and will not last long."

The Panic of 1857

Adding to the growing political tensions was the short, but sharp, depression of 1857 and 1858. Technology played a part. In August 1857, the failure of an Ohio investment house—the kind of event that had formerly taken weeks to be widely known—was the subject of a news story flashed immediately over telegraph wires to Wall Street and other financial markets. A wave of panic selling ensued, leading to business failures and slowdowns that threw thousands out of work. The major cause of the panic was a sharp, but temporary, downturn in agricultural exports to Britain, and recovery was well under way by early 1859.

Because it affected cotton exports less than northern exports, the Panic of 1857 was less harmful to the South than to the North. Southerners took this as proof of the superiority of their economic system to the free-labor system of the North, and some could not resist the chance to gloat. Senator James Henry Hammond of South Carolina drove home the point in his celebrated "King Cotton" speech of March 1858:

> When the abuse of credit had destroyed credit and annihilated confidence; when thousands of the strongest commercial houses in the world were coming down . . . when you came to a deadlock, and revolutions were threatened, what brought you up? . . .

This painting by Charles G. Rosenberg and James H. Cafferty shows a worried crowd exchanging the latest news on Wall Street during the Panic of 1857. This was the first economic depression in which the telegraph played a part by carrying bad financial news in the West to New York much more rapidly than in the past.

SOURCE: Painting by J. Cafferty & C. Rosenberg. Courtesy of the Museum of the City of New York.

> We have poured in upon you one million six hundred thousand bales of cotton just at the moment to save you from destruction. . . . We have sold it for $65,000,000, and saved you.

It seemed that all matters of political discussion were being drawn into the sectional dispute. The next step toward disunion was an act of violence perpetrated by the grim abolitionist from Kansas, John Brown.

John Brown's Raid

In the heated political mood of the late 1850s, some improbable people became heroes. None was more improbable than John Brown, the self-appointed avenger who had slaughtered unarmed proslavery men in Kansas in 1856. In 1859, Brown proposed a wild scheme to raid the South and start a general slave uprising. He believed, as did most northern abolitionists, that discontent among Southern slaves was so great that such an uprising needed only a spark to get going. Significantly, free African Americans—among them Frederick Douglass—did not

support Brown, thinking his plan to raid the federal arsenal at Harpers Ferry, Virginia, was doomed to failure. They were right. On October 16, 1859, Brown led a group of twenty-two white and African American men against the arsenal. However, he had made no provision for escape. Even more incredible, he had not notified the Virginia slaves whose uprising it was supposed to initiate. In less than a day, the raid was over. Eight of Brown's men (including two of his sons) were dead, no slaves had joined the fight, and Brown himself was captured. Moving quickly to prevent a lynching by local mobs, the state of Virginia tried and convicted Brown (while he was still weak from the wounds of battle) of treason, murder, and fomenting insurrection.

Ludicrous in life, possibly insane, Brown was nevertheless a noble martyr. In his closing speech prior to sentencing, Brown was magnificently eloquent: "Now, if it is deemed necessary that I should forfeit my life for the furtherance of the end of justice, and mingle my blood further with the blood of my children and with the blood of millions in this slave country whose rights are disregarded by wicked, cruel, and unjust enactments, I say, let it be done."

Brown's death by hanging on December 2, 1859, was marked throughout northern communities with public rites of mourning not seen since the death of George Washington. Church bells tolled, buildings were draped in black, ministers preached sermons, prayer meetings were held, abolitionists issued eulogies. Ralph Waldo Emerson said that Brown would "make the gallows as glorious as the cross," and Henry David Thoreau called him "an angel of light." Naturally, not all Northerners supported Brown's action. Northern Democrats and conservative opinion generally repudiated him. But many people, while rejecting Brown's raid, did support the antislavery cause that he represented.

Brown's raid shocked the South because it aroused the greatest fear, that of slave rebellion. Southerners believed that northern abolitionists were provoking slave revolts, a suspicion apparently confirmed when documents captured at Harpers Ferry revealed that Brown had the financial support of half a dozen members of the northern elite. These "Secret Six"—Gerrit Smith, George Stearns, Franklin Sanborn, Thomas Wentworth Higginson, Theodore Parker, and Samuel Gridley Howe—had been willing to finance armed attacks on the slave system.

Even more shocking to Southerners than the raid itself, was the extent of northern mourning for Brown's death. Although the Republican Party disavowed Brown's actions, Southerners simply did not believe the party's statements. Southerners wondered how they could stay in the Union in the face of "Northern insolence." The *Richmond Enquirer* reported, "The Harpers Ferry invasion has advanced the cause of disunion more than any other event that has happened since the formation of [the] government." Looking to the presidential race, Senator Robert Toombs of Georgia warned that the South would "never permit this Fed-

The execution by hanging of John Brown, December 2, 1859 is depicted in this popular image in a northern newspaper as a solemn military occasion. Southerners were angered and alarmed by popular northern opinion that regarded Brown as a martyr rather than as a terrorist.

SOURCE: *Frank Leslie's Illustrated Newspaper*, December 10, 1859. Library of Congress.

eral government to pass into the traitorous hands of the Black Republican party." Talk of secession as the only possible response became common throughout the South.

THE SOUTH SECEDES

By 1860, sectional differences had caused one national party, the Whigs, to collapse. The second national party, the Democrats, stood on the brink of dissolution. Not only the politicians, but ordinary people in both the North and the South were coming to believe there was no way to avoid what in 1858 William Seward (once a Whig, now a Republican) had called an "irrepressible conflict."

The Election of 1860

The split of the Democratic Party into northern and southern wings that had occurred during President Buchanan's tenure became official at the Democratic nominating conventions in 1860. The party convened first in Charleston, South Carolina, the center of secessionist agitation. It was the worst possible location in which to attempt to reach unity. Although Stephen Douglas had the support of the plurality of delegates, he did not have the two-thirds majority necessary for nomination. As the price of their support, Southerners insisted that Douglas support a federal slave code—a guarantee that slavery would be protected in the territories. Douglas could not agree without violating his own belief in popular sovereignty and losing his northern support. After

ten days, fifty-nine ballots, and two southern walkouts, the convention ended where it had begun: deadlocked. Northern supporters of Douglas were angry and bitter: "I never heard Abolitionists talk more uncharitably and rancorously of the people of the South than the Douglas men," one reporter wrote. "They say they do not care a damn where the South goes."

In June, the Democrats met again in Baltimore. The Douglasites, recognizing the need for a united party, were eager to compromise wherever they could, but most southern Democrats were not. More than a third of the delegates bolted. Later, holding a convention of their own, they nominated Buchanan's vice president, John C. Breckinridge of Kentucky. The remaining two-thirds of the Democrats nominated Douglas, but everyone knew that a Republican victory was inevitable. To make matters worse, some southern Whigs joined with some border-state nativists to form the Constitutional Union Party, which nominated John Bell of Tennessee.

Republican strategy was built on the lessons of the 1856 "victorious defeat." The Republicans planned to carry all the states Frémont had won, plus Pennsylvania, Illinois, and Indiana. The two leading Republican contenders were Senator William H. Seward of New York and Abraham Lincoln of Illinois. Seward, the party's best-known figure, had enemies among party moderates, who thought he was too radical, and among nativists with whom he had clashed in the New York Whig Party. Lincoln, on the other hand, appeared new, impressive, more moderate than Seward, and certain to carry Illinois. Lincoln won the nomination on the third ballot.

The election of 1860 presented voters with one of the clearest choices in American history. On the key issue of slavery, Breckinridge supported its extension to the territories; Lincoln stood firmly for its exclusion. Douglas attempted to hold the middle ground with his principle of popular sovereignty; Bell vaguely favored compromise as well. The Republicans offered other platform planks designed to appeal to northern voters: support for a homestead act (free western lands), for a transcontinental railroad, for other internal improvements, and for a higher tariff. Although they spoke clearly against the extension of slavery, Republicans sought to dispel their radical abolitionist image. The Republican platform condemned John Brown's raid as "the gravest of crimes," repeatedly denied that Republicans favored the social equality of black people, and strenuously affirmed that they sought to preserve the Union. In reality, Republicans simply did not believe the South would secede if Lincoln won. In this, the Republicans were not alone; few Northerners believed southern threats—Southerners had threatened too many times before.

Breckinridge insisted that he and his supporters were loyal to the Union—as long as their needs concerning slavery were met. The only candidate who spoke urgently and openly about the impending threat of secession was Douglas. Breaking with convention, Douglas campaigned personally, in both the North and, bravely, in the hostile South, warning of the danger of dissolution and presenting himself as the only truly national candidate. Realizing his own chances for election were slight, he told his private secretary, "Mr. Lincoln is the next President. We must try to save the Union. I will go South."

In accordance with tradition, Lincoln did not campaign for himself, but many other Republicans spoke for him. The Republicans did not campaign in the South; Breckinridge did not campaign in the North. Each side was therefore free to believe the worst about the other. All parties, North and South, campaigned with oratory, parades and rallies, free food and drink. Even in the face of looming crisis, this presidential campaign was the best entertainment of the day.

The mood in the Deep South was close to mass hysteria. Rumors of slave revolts—in Texas, Alabama, and South Carolina—swept the region, and vigilance committees sprang up to counter the supposed threat. In the South Carolina upcountry, the question of secession dominated races for the state legislature. Candidates such as A. S. Wallace of York, who advocated "patriotic forbearance" if Lincoln won, were soundly defeated. The very passion and excitement of the election campaign moved Southerners toward extremism. Even the weather—the worst drought and heat wave the South had known for years—contributed to the tension.

The election of 1860 produced the second highest voter turnout in U.S. history (81.2 percent, topped only by 81.8 percent in 1876). The election turned out to be two regional contests: Breckinridge versus Bell in the South, Lincoln versus Douglas in the North. Breckinridge carried eleven slave states with 18 percent of the popular vote; Bell carried Virginia, Tennessee, and Kentucky with 13 percent of the popular vote. Lincoln won all eighteen of the free states (he split New Jersey with Douglas) and almost 40 percent of the popular vote. Douglas carried only Missouri, but gained nearly 30 percent of the popular vote. Lincoln's electoral vote total was overwhelming: 180 to a combined 123 for the other three candidates. But although Lincoln had won 54 percent of the vote in the northern states, his name had not even appeared on the ballot in ten southern states. The true winner of the 1860 election was sectionalism (see Map 15.5).

The South Leaves the Union

Charles Francis Adams, son and grandson of presidents, wrote in his diary on the day Lincoln was elected, "The

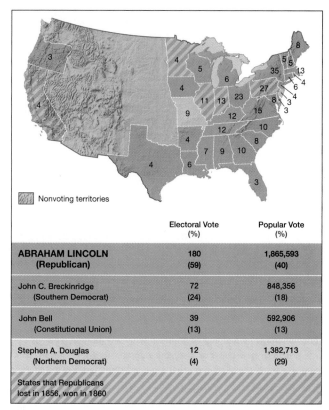

	Electoral Vote (%)	Popular Vote (%)
ABRAHAM LINCOLN (Republican)	180 (59)	1,865,593 (40)
John C. Breckinridge (Southern Democrat)	72 (24)	848,356 (18)
John Bell (Constitutional Union)	39 (13)	592,906 (13)
Stephen A. Douglas (Northern Democrat)	12 (4)	1,382,713 (29)

States that Republicans lost in 1856, won in 1860

MAP 15.5 The Election of 1860 The election of 1860 was a sectional election. Lincoln won no votes in the South, Breckinridge none in the North. The contest in the North was between Lincoln and Douglas, and although Lincoln swept the electoral vote, Douglas's popular vote was uncomfortably close. The large number of northern Democratic voters opposed to Lincoln was a source of political trouble for him during the Civil War.

great revolution has actually taken place. . . . The country has once and for all thrown off the domination of the Slaveholders." That was precisely what the South feared.

The results of the election shocked Southerners. They were humiliated and frightened by the prospect of becoming a permanent minority in a political system dominated by a party pledged to the elimination of slavery. In southern eyes, the Republican triumph meant they would become unequal partners in the federal enterprise, their way of life (the slave system) existing on borrowed time. As a Georgia newspaper said ten days after Lincoln's election, "African slavery, though panoplied by the Federal Constitution, is doomed to a war of extermination. All the powers of a Government which has so long sheltered it will be turned to its destruction. The only hope for its preservation, therefore, is out of the Union." And Mary Boykin Chesnut, member of a well-connected South Carolina family, confided to her diary, "The die is cast—no more vain regrets—sad forebodings are useless. The stake is life or death."

The governors of South Carolina, Alabama, and Mississippi, each of whom had committed his state to secession

OVERVIEW

THE IRREPRESSIBLE CONFLICT

Declaration of Independence	*1776*	Thomas Jefferson's denunciation of slavery deleted from the final version.
Northwest Ordinance	*1787*	Slavery prohibited in the Northwest Territory (north of the Ohio River).
Constitution	*1787*	Slavery unmentioned but acknowledged in Article I, Section 2, counting three-fifths of all African Americans, slave and free, in a state's population; and in Article I, Section 9, which barred Congress from prohibiting the international slave trade for twenty years.
Louisiana Purchase	*1803*	Louisiana admitted as a slave state in 1812; no decision about the rest of Louisiana Purchase.
Missouri Compromise	*1820*	Missouri admitted as a slave state, but slavery prohibited in Louisiana Purchase north of 36°30′.
Wilmot Proviso	*1846*	Proposal to prohibit slavery in territory that might be gained in Mexican-American War causes splits in national parties.
Compromise of 1850	*1850*	California admitted as free state; Texas (already admitted in 1845) is a slave state; the rest of Mexican Cession to be decided by popular sovereignty. Ends the slave trade in the District of Columbia, but a stronger Fugitive Slave Law, leading to a number of violent recaptures, arouses northern antislavery opinion.
Kansas-Nebraska Act	*1854*	At the urging of Stephen A. Douglas, Congress opens Kansas and Nebraska Territories for settlement under popular sovereignty. Open warfare between proslavery and antislavery factions breaks out in Kansas.
Lecompton Constitution	*1857*	President James Buchanan's decision to admit Kansas to the Union with a proslavery constitution is defeated in Congress.
***Dred Scott* Decision**	*1857*	The Supreme Court's denial of Dred Scott's case for freedom is welcomed in the South, condemned in the North.
John Brown's Raid and Execution	*1859*	Northern support for John Brown shocks the South.
Democratic Party Nominating Conventions	*1860*	The Democrats are unable to agree on a candidate; two candidates, one northern (Stephen A. Douglas) and one southern (John C. Breckinridge) split the party and the vote, thus allowing Republican Abraham Lincoln to win.

if Lincoln were elected, immediately issued calls for special state conventions. At the same time, calls went out to southern communities to form vigilance committees and volunteer militia companies. A visiting Northerner, Sereno Watson, wrote to his brother in amazement: "This people is apparently gone crazy. I do not know how to account for it & have no idea what might be the end of it. Union men, Douglas men, Breckinridge men are alike in their loud denunciation of submission to Lincoln's administration. There are of course those who think differently but they scarcely dare or are suffered to open their mouths." In the face of this frenzy, cooperationists (the term used for those opposed to immediate secession) were either intimidated into silence or simply left behind by the speed of events.

On December 20, 1860, a state convention in South Carolina, accompanied by all the hoopla and excitement of bands, fireworks displays, and huge rallies, voted unanimously to secede from the Union. In the weeks that followed, conventions in six other Southern states (Mississippi, Florida, Alabama, Georgia, Louisiana, and Texas) followed suit, with the support, on average, of 80 percent of their delegates.

The succession of rapid, state by state conventions was a deliberate strategy developed by secessionists, who feared that a single convention of all the southern states would move too slowly, allowing cooperationists time to organize. There was genuine division of opinion in the Deep South, especially in Georgia and Alabama, along customary up-country–low-country lines. Yeoman farmers who did not own slaves and workers in the cities of the South were most likely to favor compromise with the North. But secessionists constantly reminded both groups that the Republican victory would lead to the emancipation of the slaves and the end of white privilege (see

Chapter 10). And all Southerners, most of whom were deeply loyal to their state and region, believed that Northerners threatened their way of life. In reality, although class divisions among them were very real, none of the Deep South states held anywhere near the number of Unionists that Republicans had hoped. Throughout the South, secession occurred because Southerners no longer believed they had a choice. "Secession is a desperate remedy," acknowledged South Carolina's David Harris, "but of the two evils I do think it is the lesser" (see Map 15.6).

In every state that seceded, the joyous scenes of South Carolina were repeated as the decisiveness of action replaced the long years of anxiety and tension. People danced in the streets, most believing the North had no choice but to accept secession peacefully. They ignored the fact that eight other slave states—Delaware, Maryland, Kentucky, Missouri, Virginia, North Carolina, Tennessee, and Arkansas—had not acted—though the latter four states would secede after war broke out. Just as Republicans had miscalculated in thinking southern threats a mere bluff, so secessionists now miscalculated in believing they would be able to leave the Union in peace.

The North's Political Options

What should the North do? Buchanan, indecisive as always, did nothing. The decision thus rested with Abraham Lincoln, even before he officially became president. One possibility was compromise, and many proposals were suggested, ranging from full adoption of the Breckinridge campaign platform to reinstatement of

MAP EXPLORATION

To explore an interactive version of this map, go to **www.prenhall.com/faragher5/map15.6**

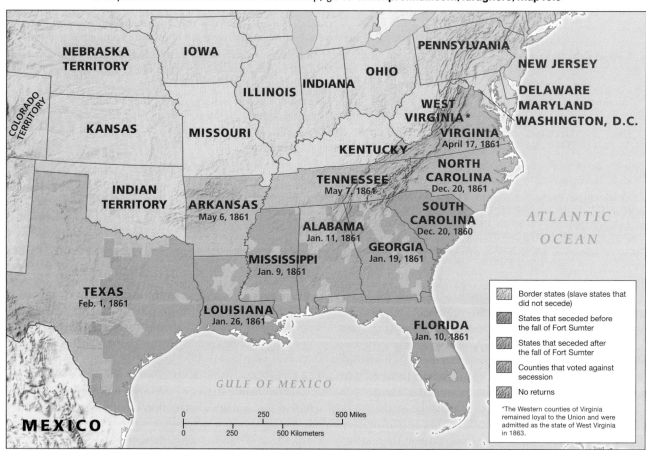

MAP 15.6 The South Secedes The southern states that would constitute the Confederacy seceded in two stages. The states of the Lower South seceded before Lincoln took office. Arkansas and three states of the Upper South—Virginia, North Carolina, and Tennessee—waited until after the South fired on Fort Sumter. And four border slave states—Delaware, Maryland, Kentucky and Missouri—chose not to secede. Every Southern state (except South Carolina) was divided on the issue of secession, generally along up-country–low-country lines. In Virginia, this division was so extreme, that West Virginia split off to become a separate nonslave state and was admitted to the Union in 1863.

the Missouri Compromise line. Lincoln cautiously refused them all, making it clear that he would not compromise on the extension of slavery, which was the South's key demand. He hoped, by appearing firm but moderate, to discourage additional southern states from seceding, while giving pro-Union Southerners time to organize. He succeeded in his first aim, but not in the second. Lincoln and most of the Republican Party had seriously overestimated the strength of pro-Union sentiment in the South.

A second possibility, suggested by Horace Greeley of the *New York Tribune*, was to let the seven seceding states "go in peace." This is what many secessionists expected, but too many Northerners—including Lincoln himself—believed in the Union for this to happen. As Lincoln said, what was at stake was "the necessity of proving that popular government is not an absurdity. We must settle this question now, whether in a free government the minority have the right to break up the government whenever they choose." At stake was all the accumulated American pride in the federal government as a model for democracies the world over.

The third possibility was force, and this was the crux of the dilemma. Although he believed their action was wrong, Lincoln was loath to go to war to force the seceding states back into the Union. On the other hand, he refused to give up federal powers over military forts and customs posts in the South. These were precisely the powers the seceding states had to command if they were to function as an independent nation. A confrontation was bound to come. Abraham Lincoln, not for the last time, was prepared to wait for the other side to strike the first blow.

Establishment of the Confederacy

In February, delegates from the seven seceding states met in Montgomery, Alabama, and created the Confederate States of America. They wrote a constitution that was identical to the Constitution of the United States, with a few crucial exceptions: it strongly supported states' rights and made the abolition of slavery practically impossible. These two clauses did much to define the Confederate enterprise. It was difficult to avoid the conclusion that the structure of the new Confederacy had been decided by the southern dependence on slave labor. L. W. Spratt of South Carolina confessed as much in 1859: "We stand committed to the South, but we stand more vitally committed to the cause of slavery. It is, indeed, to be doubted whether the South [has] any cause apart from the institution which affects her." The South's entire defense of slavery was built on a commitment to individualism and decentralization: the rights of the slave owner over his slaves; the right of freedom claimed by all white men; and the rights of individual states versus the federal government. The military defense of the South, however, would require a strong central government. This was to be the South's basic dilemma throughout the Civil War.

The Montgomery convention passed over the fire-eaters—the men who had been the first to urge secession—

and chose Jefferson Davis of Mississippi as president and Alexander Stephens of Georgia as vice president of the new nation. Both men were known as moderates. Davis, a slave owner who had been a general in the Mexican-American War and secretary of war in the Pierce administration, and who was currently a senator from Mississippi, had expressed his own uncertainties by retaining his Senate seat for two weeks after Mississippi seceded. Stephens, a former leader in the Whig Party, had been a cooperationist delegate to Georgia's convention, where he urged that secession not be undertaken hastily.

The choice of moderates was deliberate, for the strategy of the new Confederate state was to argue that secession was a normal, responsible, and expectable course of action, and nothing for the North to get upset about. This was the theme that President Jefferson Davis of the Confederate States of America struck in his Inaugural Address, delivered to a crowd of 10,000 from the steps of the State Capitol at Montgomery, Alabama, on February 18, 1861. "We have changed the constituent parts," Davis said, "but not the system of our Government." Secession was a legal and peaceful step that, Davis said, quoting from the Declaration of Independence, "illustrates the American idea that governments rest on the consent of the governed . . . and that it is the right of the people to alter or abolish them at will whenever they become destructive of the ends for which they were established." After insisting that "a just perception of mutual interest [should] permit us peaceably to pursue our separate political [course]," Davis concluded, "Obstacles may retard, but they cannot long prevent, the progress of a movement sanctified by its justice and sustained by a virtuous people." This impressive inaugural prompted a deeply moved correspondent for the *New York Herald* to report, "God does not permit evil to be done with such earnest solemnity, such all-pervading trust in His Providence, as was exhibited by the whole people on that day."

Lincoln's Inauguration

The country as a whole waited to see what Abraham Lincoln would do, which at first appeared to be very little. In Springfield, Lincoln refused to issue public statements before his inaugural (although he sent many private messages to Congress and to key military officers), for fear of making a delicate situation worse. Similarly, during a twelve-day whistle-stopping railroad trip east from Springfield, he was careful to say nothing controversial. Eastern intellectuals, already suspicious of a mere "prairie lawyer," were not impressed. Finally, hard evidence of an assassination plot forced Lincoln to abandon his whistle-stops at Harrisburg and, protected by Pinkerton detectives, he traveled incognito into Washington, "like a thief in the night," as he complained. These signs of moderation and caution did not appeal to an American public with a penchant for electing military heroes. Americans wanted leadership and action.

Lincoln continued, however, to offer nonbelligerent firmness and moderation. And at the end of his Inaugural Address on March 4, 1861, as he stood ringed by federal troops called out in case of a Confederate attack, the new president offered unexpected eloquence:

> I am loath to close. We are not enemies, but friends. We must not be enemies. Though passion may have strained, it must not break our bonds of affection. The mystic chords of memory, stretching from every battlefield, and patriot grave, to every living heart and hearthstone, all over this broad land, will yet swell the chorus of the Union, when again touched, as surely they will be, by the better angels of our nature.

CONCLUSION

Americans had much to boast about in 1850. Their nation was vastly larger, richer, and more powerful than it had been in 1800. But the issue of slavery was slowly dividing the North and the South, two communities with similar origins and many common bonds. The following decade was marked by frantic efforts at political compromise, beginning with the Compromise of 1850, continuing with the Kansas-Nebraska Act of 1854, and culminating in the Supreme Court's 1859 decision in the *Dred Scott* case. Increasingly, the ordinary people of the two regions demanded resolution of the crisis. The two great parties of the Second American Party System, the Democrats and the Whigs, unable to find a solution, were destroyed. Two new sectional parties—the Republican Party and a southern party devoted to the defense of slavery—fought the 1860 election, but Southerners refused to accept the national verdict. Politics had failed: the issue of slavery was irreconcilable. The only remaining recourse was war. But although Americans were divided, they were still one people. That made the war, when it came, all the more terrible.

CHRONOLOGY

1820	Missouri Compromise		Republican Party formed as Whig Party dissolves
1828–32	Nullification Crisis	*1855*	William Walker leads his first filibustering expedition to Nicaragua
1846	Wilmot Proviso	*1856*	Burning and looting of Lawrence, Kansas
1848	Treaty of Guadalupe Hidalgo ends Mexican-American War		John Brown leads Pottawatomie massacre
	Zachary Taylor elected president		Attack on Senator Charles Sumner
	Free-Soil Party formed		James Buchanan elected president
1849	California and Utah seek admission to the Union as free states	*1857*	*Dred Scott* decision
			President Buchanan accepts proslavery Lecompton constitution in Kansas
1850	Compromise of 1850		Panic of 1857
	California admitted as a free state	*1858*	Congress rejects Lecompton constitution
	American (Know-Nothing) Party formed		Lincoln-Douglas debates
	Zachary Taylor dies, Millard Fillmore becomes president	*1859*	John Brown's raid on Harpers Ferry
1851	North reacts to Fugitive Slave Law	*1860*	Four parties run presidential candidates
	Harriet Beecher Stowe's *Uncle Tom's Cabin* published		Abraham Lincoln elected president
1852	Franklin Pierce elected president		South Carolina secedes from Union
1854	Ostend Manifesto	*1861*	Six other Deep South states secede
	Kansas-Nebraska Act		Confederate States of America formed
	Treaties with Indians in northern part of Indian Territory renegotiated		Lincoln takes office

REVIEW QUESTIONS

1. What aspects of the remarkable economic development of the United States in the first half of the nineteenth century contributed to the sectional crisis of the 1850s?

2. How might the violent efforts by abolitionists to free escaped slaves who had been recaptured, and the federal armed enforcement of the Fugitive Slave Act have been viewed differently by Northern merchants (the so-called Cotton Whigs), Irish immigrants, and abolitionists?

3. Consider the course of events in "Bloody Kansas" from Douglas's Kansas-Nebraska Act to the congressional rejection of the Lecompton constitution. Were these events the inevitable result of the political impasse in Washington, or could

other decisions have been made that would have changed the outcome?

4. The nativism of the 1850s that surfaced so strongly in the Know-Nothing Party was eclipsed by the crisis over slavery. But nativist sentiment has been a recurring theme in American politics. Discuss why it was strong in the 1850s and why it has emerged periodically since then.

5. Evaluate the character and actions of John Brown. Was he the hero proclaimed by northern supporters or the terrorist condemned by the South?

6. Imagine that you lived in Illinois, home state to both Douglas and Lincoln, in 1860. How would you have voted in the presidential election, and why?

RECOMMENDED READING

William L. Barney, *The Secessionist Impulse: Alabama and Mississippi in 1860* (1974). Covers the election of 1860 and the subsequent conventions that led to secession.

Robert F. Engs and Randall M. Miller, eds., *The Birth of the Grand Old Party: The Republicans' First Generation*, (2002). Six major historians consider the party's beginnings.

Nicole Etcheson, *Bleeding Kansas: Contested Liberty in the Civil War Era* (2004). A look at the Kansas issue from the perspective of white settlers.

Don E. Fehrenbacher, *The Dred Scott Case: Its Significance in American Law and Politics* (1978). A major study by the leading historian on this controversial decision.

Don E. Fehrenbacher and Ward M. McAfee, *The Slave-owning Republic* (2002). This revisionist book suggests that the authors of the Constitution believed slavery should be regulated by the states, but that over time Northerners allowed the more national Southern argument to prevail.

Eric Foner, *Free Soil, Free Labor, Free Men: The Ideology of the Republican Party before the Civil War* (1970). One of the first studies to focus on the free labor ideology of the North and its importance in the political disputes of the 1850s.

Lacey K. Ford Jr., *Origins of Southern Radicalism: The South Carolina Upcountry, 1800–1860* (1988). One of a number of studies of the attitudes of up-country farmers in South Carolina who supported secession wholeheartedly.

William A. Link, *Roots of Secession: Slavery and Politics in Antebellum Virginia* (2003). Draws connections between the changing circumstances of slavery and politics in the 1850s.

Robert E. May, *Manifest Destiny's Underworld: Filibustering in Antebellum America* (2002). A study of the activities and attitudes toward the adventurers.

David S. Reynolds, *John Brown, Abolitionist* (2005). Argues that Brown's extremism became the Civil War norm.

Leonard L. Richards, *The Slave Power: The Free North and Southern Domination 1780–1860* (2000). A study of the reaction to the political role of the slave South in national politics.

Anne C. Rose, *Voices of the Marketplace: American Thought and Culture, 1830–1860* (1995). A study that considers the effects of the concepts of Christianity, democracy, and capitalism on American cultural life.

Kenneth M. Stampp, *America in 1857: A Nation on the Brink* (1990). A study of the "crucial" year by a leading southern historian.

John Stauffer, *The Black Hearts of Men: Radical Abolitionists and the Transformation of Race* (2001). Argues that radical abolitionists rejected the gender and racial conventions of their day.

Albert J. Von Frank, *The Trials of Anthony Burns: Freedom and Slavery in Emerson's Boston* (1998). An eloquent study of the trial and the links between transcendentalist and abolitionist opinion.

Edward L. Widmer, *Young America: The Flowering of Democracy in New York City* (1999). Recovers the idealism of the early years of this literary/political movement and traces its decline.

 For additional study resources for this chapter, go to the *Companion Website*, **http://www.prenhall.com/faragher**.

The Civil War

1861–1865

CHAPTER OUTLINE

Mother Bickerdyke Connects Northern Communities to Their Boys at War

In May 1861, the Reverend Edward Beecher interrupted his customary Sunday service at Brick Congregational Church in Galesburg, Illinois, to read a disturbing letter to the congregation. Two months earlier, Galesburg had proudly sent 500 of its young men off to join the Union army. They had not yet been in battle. Yet, the letter reported, an alarming number were dying of diseases caused by inadequate food, medical care, and sanitation at the crowded military camp in Cairo, Illinois. Most army doctors were surgeons trained to operate and amputate on the battlefield. They were not prepared to treat soldiers sick with dysentery, pneumonia, typhoid, measles—all serious, frequently fatal diseases that could often be cured with careful nursing. The letter writer, appalled by the squalor and misery he saw around him, complained of abuses by the army. The Union army, however, was overwhelmed with the task of readying recruits for battle, and had made few provisions for their health when they were not in combat.

The shocked and grieving members of Beecher's congregation quickly decided to send not only supplies, but one of their number to inspect the conditions at the Cairo camp and to take action. In spite of warnings that army regulations excluded women from encampments, the congregation voted to send their most qualified member, Mary Ann Bickerdyke, a middle-aged widow who made her

Illinois

living as a "botanic physician." This simple gesture of community concern launched the remarkable Civil War career of "the Cyclone in Calico," who defied medical officers and generals alike in her unceasing efforts on behalf of ill, wounded, and convalescent Union soldiers.

"Mother" Bickerdyke, as she was called, let nothing stand in the way of helping her "boys." When she arrived in Cairo, she immediately set to work cleaning the hospital tents and the soldiers themselves, and finding and cooking nourishing food for them. The hospital director, who resented her interference, ordered her to leave, but she blandly continued her work. When he reported her to the commanding officer, General Benjamin Prentiss, she quickly convinced the general to let her stay. "I talked sense to him," she later said.

From a peacetime point of view, what Mother Bickerdyke was doing was not unusual. Every civilian hospital had a matron, who made sure patients were supplied with clean bed linen and bandages and were fed the proper convalescent diet. But in the context of the war—the sheer number of soldiers, the constant need to set up new field hospitals and commandeer scarce food for an army on the move—it was unusual indeed and required an unusual person. A plain-spoken, hardworking woman, totally unfazed by rank or tender masculine egos, Mother Bickerdyke single-mindedly devoted herself to what she called "the Lord's work." The ordinary soldiers loved her; wise generals supported her. Once, when an indignant officer's wife complained about Bickerdyke's rudeness, General William Tecumseh Sherman joked, "You've picked the one person around here who outranks me. If you want to lodge a complaint against her, you'll have to take it to President Lincoln."

Other communities all over the North rallied to make up for the Army's shortcomings with supplies and assistance. By their actions, Mother Bickerdyke and others like her exposed the War Department's inability to meet the needs of the nation's first mass army. The efforts of women on the local level—for example, to make clothing for men from their communities who had gone off to the war—quickly took on national dimensions. The Women's Central Association of Relief (WCAR), whose organizers were mostly reformers in the abolitionist, temperance, and education movements, eventually had 7,000 chapters throughout the North. Its volunteers raised funds, made and collected food, clothes, medicine, bandages, and more than 250,000 quilts and comforters, and sent them to army camps and hospitals. All told, association chapters supplied an estimated $15 million worth of goods to the Union troops.

In June 1861, responding to requests by officials of the WCAR for formal recognition of the organization, President Abraham Lincoln created the United States Sanitary Commission and gave it the power to investigate and advise the Medical Bureau. The commission's more than 500 "sanitary inspectors" (usually men) instructed soldiers in such matters as water supply, placement of latrines, and safe cooking.

Although at first she worked independently and remained suspicious of all organizations (and even of many other relief workers), in 1862, Mother Bickerdyke was persuaded to become an official agent of "the Sanitary," as it was known. The advantage to her was access to the commission's warehouses and the ability to order from them precisely what she needed. The advantage to the Sanitary was that Mother Bickerdyke was an unequaled fundraiser. In speaking tours throughout Illinois, she touched her female listeners with moving stories of wounded boys whom she had cared for as if they were her own sons. Her words to men were more forceful. It was a man's business to fight, she said. If he was too old or ill to fight with a gun, he should fight with his dollars. With the help of Bickerdyke's blunt appeals, the Sanitary raised $50 million for the Union war effort.

As the Civil War continued, Mother Bickerdyke became a key figure in the medical support for General Ulysses S. Grant's campaigns along the Mississippi River. She was with the army at Shiloh, and as Grant slowly fought his way to Vicksburg, she set up convalescent hospitals in Memphis. Grant authorized her to commandeer any army wagons she needed to transport supplies. Between fifty and seventy "contrabands" (escaped former slaves) worked on her laundry crew. On the civilian side, the Sanitary Commission authorized her to draw on its supply depots in Memphis, Cairo, Chicago, and elsewhere. In a practical sense a vital "middlewoman" between the home front and the battlefield, she was also, in a symbolic and emotional sense, a stand-in for all mothers who had sent their sons to war.

The Civil War was a national tragedy, ripping apart the political fabric of the country, and causing more casualties than any other war in the nation's history. The death toll of approximately 620,000 exceeded the number of dead in all the other wars from the Revolution through the Vietnam War. Yet in another sense, it was a community triumph. Local communities directly supported and sustained their soldiers on a massive scale in unprecedented ways. As national unity failed, the strength of local communities, symbolized by Mother Bickerdyke, endured.

KEY TOPICS

- The social and political changes created by the unprecedented nature and scale of the Civil War
- The major military campaigns of the war
- The central importance of the end of slavery to the war efforts of North and South

COMMUNITIES MOBILIZE FOR WAR

A neutral observer in March 1861 might have seen ominous similarities. Two nations—the United States of America (shorn of seven states in the Deep South) and the Confederate States of America—each blamed the other for the breakup of the Union. Two new presidents—Abraham Lincoln and Jefferson Davis—each faced the challenging task of building and maintaining national unity. Two regions—North and South—scorned each other and boasted of their own superiority. But the most basic similarity was not yet apparent: both sides were unprepared for the ordeal that lay ahead.

Fort Sumter: The War Begins

In their Inaugural Addresses, both Abraham Lincoln and Jefferson Davis prayed for peace, but positioned themselves for war. Careful listeners to both addresses realized that the two men were on a collision course. Jefferson Davis claimed that the Confederacy would be forced to "appeal to arms . . . if . . . the integrity of our territory and jurisdiction [is] assailed." Lincoln said, "The power confided to me will be used to hold, occupy, and possess the property and places belonging to the government." One of those places, Fort Sumter, in South Carolina, was claimed by both sides.

Fort Sumter, a major federal military installation, sat on a granite island at the entrance to Charleston harbor. So long as it remained in Union hands, Charleston,

the center of secessionist sentiment, would be immobilized. Thus it was hardly surprising that Fort Sumter would provide President Lincoln with his first crisis.

With the fort dangerously low on supplies, Lincoln had to decide whether to abandon it or risk the fight that might ensue if he ordered it resupplied. On April 6, Lincoln took cautious and careful action, notifying the governor of South Carolina that he was sending a relief force to the fort carrying only food and no military supplies. Now the decision rested with Jefferson Davis, who opted for decisive action. On April 10, he ordered General P. G. T. Beauregard to demand the surrender of Fort Sumter and to attack it if the garrison did not comply. On April 12, as Lincoln's relief force neared Charleston harbor, Beauregard opened fire. Two days later, the defenders surrendered and the Confederate Stars and Bars rose over Fort Sumter. The people of Charleston celebrated wildly. "I did not know," wrote Mary Boykin Chesnut in her diary, "that one could live such days of excitement."

The Call to Arms

Even before the attack on Fort Sumter, the Confederate Congress had authorized a volunteer army of 100,000 men to serve for twelve months. There was no difficulty finding volunteers. Men flocked to enlist, and their communities sent them off in ceremonies featuring bands, bonfires, and belligerent oratory. Most of that oratory, like Jefferson Davis's Inaugural Address (see Chapter 15), evoked the Revolutionary War and the right of free people to resist tyranny. Exhilarated by their own rapid mobilization, most Southerners believed that Unionists were cowards who would not be able to face up to southern bravery. "Just throw three or four shells among those blue-bellied Yankees," one North Carolinian boasted, "and they'll scatter like sheep." The cry of "On to Washington!" was raised throughout the South, and orators confidently predicted that the city would be captured and the war concluded within sixty days. For these early recruits, war was a patriotic adventure.

The "thunderclap of Sumter" startled the North into an angry response. The apathy and uncertainty that had prevailed since Lincoln's election disappeared, to be replaced by strong feelings of patriotism. On April 15, Lincoln issued a proclamation calling for 75,000 state militiamen to serve in the federal army for ninety days. Enlistment offices were swamped with so many enthusiastic

This Currier and Ives lithograph shows the opening moment of the Civil War. On April 12, 1861, Confederate General P.G.T. Beauregard ordered the shelling of Fort Sumter in Charleston harbor. Two days later, Union Major Robert Anderson surrendered, and mobilization began for what turned out to be the most devastating war in American history.

SOURCE: The Granger Collection, New York.

volunteers that many men were sent home. Free African Americans, among the most eager to serve, were turned away: this was not yet a war for or by black people.

Public outpourings of patriotism were common. New Yorker George Templeton Strong recorded one example on April 18: "Went to the [City] Hall. The [Sixth] Massachusetts Regiment, which arrived here last night, was marching down on its way to Washington. Immense crowd; immense cheering. My eyes filled with tears, and I was half choked in sympathy with the contagious excitement. God be praised for the unity of feeling here! It is beyond, very far beyond, anything I hoped for."

The mobilization in Chester, Pennsylvania, was typical of the northern response to the outbreak of war. A patriotic rally was held at which a company of volunteers (the first of many from the region) calling themselves the "Union Blues" were mustered into the Ninth Regiment of Pennsylvania Volunteers amid cheers and band music. As they marched off to Washington (the gathering place for the Union army), companies of home guards were organized by the men who remained behind. Within a month, the women of Chester had organized a countywide system of war relief that sent a stream of clothing, blankets, bandages, and other supplies to the local troops and provided assistance to their families at home. Such relief organizations, some formally organized, some informal, emerged in every community, North and South, that sent soldiers off to the Civil War. These

organizations not only played a vital role in supplying the troops, but maintained the human, local link on which so many soldiers depended. In this sense, every American community accompanied its young men to war.

The Border States

The first secession, between December 20, 1860, and February 1, 1861, had taken seven Deep South states out of the Union. Now, in April, the firing on Fort Sumter and Lincoln's call for state militias forced the other southern states to take sides. Courted—and pressured—by both North and South, four states of the Upper South (Virginia, Arkansas, Tennessee, and North Carolina) joined the original seven in April and May 1861. Virginia's secession tipped the other three toward the Confederacy. The capital of the Confederacy was now moved to Richmond. This meant that the two capitals—Richmond and Washington—were less than 100 miles apart.

Still undecided was the loyalty of the northernmost tier of slave-owning states: Missouri, Kentucky, Maryland, and Delaware. Each controlled vital strategic assets. Missouri not only bordered the Mississippi River, but controlled the routes to the west. Kentucky controlled the Ohio River. The main railroad link with the West ran through Maryland and the hill region of western Virginia (which split from Virginia to become the free state of West Virginia in 1863). Delaware controlled access to Philadelphia. Finally, were Maryland to secede, the nation's capital would be completely surrounded by Confederate territory.

Delaware was loyal to the Union (less than 2 percent of its population were slaves), but Maryland's loyalty was divided, as an ugly incident on April 19 showed. When the Sixth Massachusetts Regiment (the one George Templeton Strong had cheered in New York) marched through Baltimore, a hostile crowd of 10,000 southern sympathizers, carrying Confederate flags, pelted the troops with bricks, paving stones, and bullets. Finally, in desperation, the troops fired on the crowd, killing twelve people and wounding others. In retaliation, southern sympathizers burned the railroad bridges to the North and destroyed the telegraph line to Washington, cutting off communication between the capital and the rest of the Union for six days.

Lincoln's response was swift and stern. He stationed Union troops along Maryland's crucial railroads, declared martial law in Baltimore, and arrested the suspected

This patriotic painting shows the departure of New York's Seventh Regiment for Washington in mid-April of 1861. Stirring scenes like this occured across the nation following "the thunderclap of Sumter" as communities mobilized for war.

SOURCE: *Departure of the 7th Regiment, N.Y.S.M., April 19, 1861*, George Hayward. (American, born England, 1800-72?), Graphite pencil, transparent and opaque watercolor on paper, Sheet: 36.7 × 51.3 cm (14 7/16 × 20 3/16 in.). Museum of Fine Arts, Boston.

ringleaders of the pro-Confederate mob and held them without trial. In July, he ordered the detention of thirty-two secessionist legislators and many sympathizers. Thus was Maryland's loyalty to the Union ensured. The arrests in Maryland were the first of a number of violations of basic civil rights during the war, all of which the president justified on the basis of national security.

As in Maryland, the loyalties of the other border states were also divided. Missouri was plagued by guerrilla battles (reminiscent of the prewar "Bleeding Kansas") throughout the war. In Kentucky, division took the form of a huge illegal trade with the Confederacy through neighboring Tennessee, to which Lincoln, determined to keep Kentucky in the Union, turned a blind eye. The conflicting loyalties of the border states were often mirrored within families. Kentucky Senator John J. Crittenden had two sons who were major generals, one in the Union army and the other in the Confederate army.

That Delaware, Maryland, Missouri, and Kentucky chose to stay in the Union was a severe blow to the Confederacy. Among them, the four states could have added 45 percent to the white population and military manpower of the Confederacy and 80 percent to its manufacturing capacity. Almost as damaging, the decision of four slave states to stay in the Union punched a huge hole in the Confederate argument that the southern states were forced to secede to protect their right to own slaves.

The Battle of Bull Run

Once sides had been chosen and the initial flush of enthusiasm had passed, the nature of the war, and the mistaken notions about it, soon became clear. The event that shattered the illusions was the First Battle of Bull Run, at Manassas Creek in Virginia in July 1861. Confident of a quick victory, a Union army of 35,000 men marched south, crying "On to Richmond!" So lighthearted and unprepared was the Washington community, that the troops were accompanied not only by journalists, but by a crowd of politicians and sightseers. At first the Union troops held their ground against the 25,000 Confederate troops commanded by General P. G. T. Beauregard (of Fort Sumter fame). But when 2,300 fresh Confederate troops arrived as reinforcements, the untrained northern troops broke ranks in an uncontrolled retreat that swept up the frightened sightseers as well. Soldiers and civilians alike retreated in disarray to Washington. Confederate Mary Boykin Chesnut recorded in her diary, "We might have walked into Washington any day for a week after Manassas, such was the consternation and confusion there."

Bull Run was sobering—and prophetic. The Civil War was the most lethal military conflict in American history, leaving a legacy of devastation on the battlefield and desolation at home. It claimed the lives of nearly 620,000 soldiers, more than the the First and Second World Wars combined. One out of every four soldiers who fought in the war never returned home.

The Relative Strengths of North and South

Overall, in terms of both population and productive capacity, the Union seemed to have a commanding edge over the Confederacy. The North had two and a half times the South's population (22 million to 9 million, of whom 3.5 million were slaves) and enjoyed an even greater advantage in industrial capacity (nine times that of the South). The North produced almost all of the nation's firearms (97 percent), had 71 percent of its railroad mileage, and produced 94 percent of its cloth and 90 percent of its footwear. The North seemed able to feed, clothe, arm, and transport all the soldiers it chose. The North's wholehearted commitment to the market revolution, shown in particular in its superior ability to organize its economic advantage, was ultimately to prove decisive: by the end of the war, the Union had managed to field and equip more than 2 million soldiers as compared to the Confederacy's 800,000. But in the short term, the South had important assets to counter the advantage of the North.

The first was the nature of the struggle. For the South, this was a defensive war, in which the most basic principle of the defense of home and community united almost all white citizens, regardless of their views about slavery. The North would have to invade the South and then control it against guerrilla opposition in order to win. The parallels with the Revolutionary War were unmistakable. Most white Southerners were confident that the North, like Great Britain in its attempt to subdue the rebellious colonies, would turn out to be a lumbering giant against whom they could secure their independence.

Second, the military disparity was less extreme than it appeared. Although the North had manpower, its troops were mostly untrained. The professional federal army numbered only 16,000, and most of its experience had been gained in small Indian wars. Moreover, the South, because of its tradition of honor and belligerence (see Chapter 10), appeared to have an advantage in military leadership. More than a quarter of all the regular army officers chose to side with the South. The most notable was Robert E. Lee. Offered command of the Union army by President Lincoln, Lee hesitated, but finally decided to follow his native state, Virginia, into the Confederacy, saying, "I have been unable to make up my mind to raise my hand against my native state, my relatives, my children, and my home."

Finally, it was widely believed that slavery would work to the South's advantage, for slaves could continue to do the vital plantation work while their masters went off to war. But above all, the South had the weapon of cotton. "Cotton is King," James Henry Hammond had announced in 1858, at the height of the cotton boom that made the 1850s the most profitable decade in southern history.

Because of the crucial role of cotton in industrialization, Southerners were confident that the British and French need for southern cotton would soon bring those countries to recognize the Confederacy as a separate nation.

GOVERNMENTS ORGANIZE FOR WAR

The Civil War forced the federal government to assume powers unimaginable just a few years before. Abraham Lincoln took as his primary task leading and unifying the nation in his role as commander-in-chief. He found the challenge almost insurmountable. Jefferson Davis's challenge was even greater. He had to create a Confederate nation out of a loose grouping of eleven states, each believing strongly in states' rights. Yet in the Confederacy, as in the Union, the conduct of the war required central direction.

Lincoln Takes Charge

Lincoln's first task as president was to assert control over his own cabinet. Because he had few national contacts outside the Republican Party, Lincoln chose to staff his cabinet with other Republicans, including, most unusually, several who had been his rivals for the presidential nomination. Secretary of State William Seward, widely regarded as the leader of the Republican Party, at first expected to "manage" Lincoln as he had Zachary Taylor in 1848, but he soon became the president's willing partner. On the other hand, Treasury Secretary Salmon P. Chase, a staunch abolitionist, adamantly opposed concessions to the South and considered Lincoln too conciliatory; he remained a vocal and dangerous critic. That the Republican Party was a not-quite-jelled mix of former Whigs, abolitionists, moderate Free-Soilers, and even some prowar Democrats, made Lincoln's task as party leader much more difficult than it might otherwise have been.

After the fall of Fort Sumter, military necessity prompted Lincoln to call up the state militias, order a naval blockade of the South, and vastly expand the military budget. Breaking with precedent, he took these actions without congressional sanction because Congress was not in session. Military necessity—the need to hold the border states—likewise prompted other early actions, such as the suspension of habeas corpus and the acceptance of Kentucky's ambiguous neutrality. Over howls of protest from abolitionists, the president also repudiated an unauthorized declaration issued by General John C. Frémont, military commander in Missouri, in August 1861 that would have freed Missouri's slaves. Lincoln feared that such an action would lead to the secession of Kentucky and Maryland.

Although James K. Polk had assumed responsibility for overall American military strategy during the Mexican-

This photograph, taken a month before his inauguration, shows Lincoln looking presidential. It was clearly intended to reassure a public still doubtful about his abilities.

SOURCE: Corbis/Bettmann.

American War (see Chapter 14), Lincoln was the first president to act as commander-in-chief in both a practical and a symbolic way. He actively directed military policy, because he realized that a civil war presented problems different from those of a foreign war of conquest. Lincoln wanted above all to persuade the South to rejoin the Union, and his every military order was dictated by the hope of eventual reconciliation—hence his cautiousness, and his acute sense of the role of public opinion. Today, we recognize Lincoln's exceptional abilities and eloquent language, but in his own time, some of his most moving statements fell on deaf ears. His first priority had to be to keep the Union unified. He always had to step carefully as he tried to find common ground across a wide spectrum of opinions from militant abolitionist to southern sympathizer. At the same time, he presided over a vast expansion of the powers of the federal government.

Expanding the Power of the Federal Government

The greatest expansion in government power during the war was in the War Department, which by early 1862 was faced with the unprecedented challenge of feeding, clothing, and arming 700,000 Union soldiers. Initially, the government relied on the individual states to equip and supply their vastly expanded militias. States often contracted directly with textile mills and shoe factories to clothe their troops. In many northern cities, volunteer groups sprang up to recruit regiments, buy them weapons, and send them to Washington. Other such community groups, like the one in Chester, Pennsylvania, focused on clothing and providing medical care to soldiers. By January 1862, the War Department, under the able direction of Edwin M. Stanton, a former Democrat from Ohio, was able to perform many basic functions of procurement and supply without too much delay or corruption. But the size of the Union army and the complexity of fully supplying it demanded constant efforts at all levels—government, state, and community—throughout the war. Thus, in the matter of procurement and supply, as in mobilization, the battlefront was related to the home front on a scale that Americans had not previously experienced.

The need for money for the vast war effort was pressing. Treasury Secretary Chase worked closely with Congress to develop ways to finance the war. They naturally turned to the nation's economic experts—private bankers, merchants, and managers of large businesses. With the help of Philadelphia financier Jay Cooke, the Treasury used patriotic appeals to sell war bonds to ordinary people in amounts as small as $50. Cooke sold $400 million in bonds, taking for himself what he considered a "fair commission." By the war's end, the United States had borrowed $2.6 billion for the war effort, the first example in American history of the mass financing of war. Additional sources of revenue were sales taxes and the first federal income tax (of 3 percent). Imposed in August 1861, the income tax affected only the affluent: anyone with an annual income under $800 was exempt.

Most radical of all was Chase's decision—which was authorized only after a bitter congressional fight—to print and distribute Treasury notes (paper money). Until then, the money in circulation had been a mixture of coins and state bank notes issued by 1,500 different state banks. The Legal Tender Act of February 1862 created a national currency. Because of its color, the paper bank notes were popularly known as "greenbacks." In 1863, Congress passed the National Bank Act, which prohibited state banks from issuing their own notes and forced them to apply for federal charters. Thus was the first uniform national currency created, at the expense of the independence that many state banks had prized. "These are extraordinary times, and extraordinary measures must be resorted to in order to save our Government and preserve our nationality," pleaded Congressman Elbridge G. Spaulding, sponsor of the legislation. Only through this appeal to wartime necessity were Spaulding and his allies able to overcome the opposition, for the switch to a national currency was widely recognized as a major step toward centralization of economic power in the hands of the federal government. Such a measure would have been unthinkable if southern Democrats had still been part of the national government.

The absence of southern Democrats also made possible passage of a number of Republican economic measures not directly related to the war.

Although the outbreak of war overshadowed everything else, the Republican Party in Congress was determined to fulfill its campaign pledge of a comprehensive program of economic development. Republicans quickly passed the Morrill Tariff Act (1861); by 1864, this and subsequent measures had raised tariffs to more than double their prewar rate. In 1862 and 1864, Congress created two federally chartered corporations to build a transcontinental railroad—the Union Pacific Railroad Company, to lay track westward from Omaha, and the Central Pacific, to lay track eastward from California—thus fulfilling the dreams of the many expansionists who believed America's economic future lay in trade with Asia across the Pacific Ocean. Two other measures, both passed in 1862, had long been sought by Westerners. The Homestead Act gave 160 acres of public land to any citizen who agreed to live on the land for five years, improve it by building a house and cultivating some of the land, and pay a small fee. The Morrill Land Grant Act gave states public land that would allow them to finance land-grant colleges offering education to ordinary citizens in practical skills such as agriculture, engineering, and military science. Coupled with this act, the establishment of a federal Department of Agriculture in 1862 gave American farmers a big push toward modern commercial agriculture.

This package revealed the Whig origins of many Republicans, for in essence, the measures amounted to an updated version of Henry Clay's American System of national economic development, illustrating yet again the unstoppable nature of the market revolution. They were to have a powerful nationalizing effect, connecting ordinary people to the federal government in new ways. As much as the extraordinary war measures, the enactment of the Republican program increased the role of the federal government in national life. Although many of the executive war powers lapsed when the battles ended, the accumulation of strength by the federal government, which southern Democrats would have opposed had they been in Congress, was never reversed.

Diplomatic Objectives

To Secretary of State William Seward fell the job of making sure that Britain and France did not extend diplomatic recognition to the Confederacy. Although Southerners had been certain that King Cotton would gain them European support, they were wrong. British public opinion, which had strongly supported the abolition of slavery within the British Empire in the 1830s, would not now countenance the recognition of a new nation based on slavery. British cotton manufacturers found economic alternatives, first using up their backlog of southern cotton and then turning to Egypt and India for new supplies. In spite of Union protests, however, both Britain and France did allow Confederate vessels to use their ports, and British shipyards sold six ships to the Confederacy. But in 1863, when the Confederacy commissioned Britain's Laird shipyard to build two iron-clad ships with pointed prows for ramming Union ships, the Union threatened war, and the British government made sure that the Laird ironclads were never delivered. Seward had wanted to threaten Britain with war earlier, in 1861, when the prospect of diplomatic recognition for the Confederacy seemed most likely, but Lincoln had overruled him, cautioning, "One war at a time."

Nonbelligerence was also the Union response in 1861, when a bankrupt Mexico suffered the ignominy of a joint invasion by British, Spanish, and French troops determined to collect the substantial debts owed by Mexico to their nations. This was a serious violation of Mexican independence, just the kind of European intervention that the Monroe Doctrine had been formulated to prevent (see Chapter 9). When it became clear that France was bent on conquest, Britian and Spain withdrew, and Mexican forces repelled the French troops on May 5, 1862. Ever since, Mexico has celebrated *El Cinco de Mayo*. France eventually prevailed, and installed the Austrian archduke Maximilian as emperor. In normal times, the French conquest could have led to war, but fearing that France might recognize the Confederacy or invade Texas, Seward had to content himself with refusing to recognize the new Mexican government. In the meantime, he directed Union troops to gain a stronghold in Texas as soon as possible. In November, five months after the French marched into Mexico City, Union troops seized Brownsville, a town on the Texas-Mexico border, sending a clear signal to the French to go no farther. In 1866, after the Civil War, strong diplomatic pressure from Seward convinced the French to withdraw from Mexico. The following year, the hapless Maximilian was captured and shot during a revolt led by a future Mexican president, Benito Juárez. To him fell the task of reviving Mexico after a disastrous decade that included civil war (see Chapter 14), and economic collapse, as well as foreign invasion.

Although the goal of Seward's diplomacy— preventing recognition of the Confederacy by the European powers—was always clear, its achievement was uncertain for more than two years. Northern fears and southern hopes seesawed with the fortunes of battle. Not until the victories at Vicksburg and Gettysburg in July 1863, could Seward be reasonably confident of success.

Jefferson Davis Tries to Unify the Confederacy

Although Jefferson Davis had held national cabinet rank (as secretary of war under President Franklin Pierce), had experience as an administrator, and was a former military man (none of which was true of Abraham Lincoln), he was unable to hold the Confederacy together. Perhaps no one could have.

Davis's first cabinet of six men, appointed in February 1861, included a representative from each of the states of the first secession except Mississippi, which was represented by Davis himself. This careful attention to the equality of the states pointed to the fundamental problem that Davis was unable to overcome. For all of its drama, secession was a conservative strategy for preserving the slavery-based social and political structure that existed in every southern state. A shared belief in states' rights—that is, in their own autonomy—was a poor basis on which to build a unified nation. Davis, who would have preferred to be a

This painting by William C. Washington, *Jackson Entering the City of Winchester,* shows the dashing Confederate General "Stonewall" Jackson saving the Virginia town from Union capture in 1862. Jackson and other Confederate generals evoked fierce loyalty to the Confederacy. Unfortunately, by the time this victory was commemorated, Jackson himself was dead, killed by friendly fire at the Battle of Chancellorsville in May of 1863.

SOURCE: William Washington, *Stonewall Jackson Entering the City of Winchester, Virginia.* Oil painting. Valentine Museum Library, Richmond, Virginia.

The contrast between the hope and valor of these young southern volunteer soldiers, photographed shortly before the first battle of Bull Run, and the later advertisements for substitutes (at right), is marked. Southern exemptions for slave owners and lavish payment for substitutes increasingly bred resentment among the ordinary people of the South.

SOURCE: Cook Collection. Valentine Museum Library/Richmond History Center.

SUBSTITUTE NOTICES.

WANTED—A SUBSTITUTE for a conscript, to serve during the war. Any good man over the age of 35 years, not a resident of Virginia, or a foreigner, may hear of a good situation by calling at Mr. GEORGE BAGBY'S office, Shockoe Slip, to-day, between the hours of 9 and 11 A. M. [jy 9—1t*] A COUNTRYMAN.

WANTED—Two SUBSTITUTES—one for artillery, the other for infantry or cavalry service. Also, to sell, a trained, thoroughbred cavalry HORSE. Apply to DR. BROOCKS, Corner Main and 12th streets, or to T. T. BROOCKS,
jy 9—3t* Petersburg, Va.

WANTED—Immediately, a SUBSTITUTE. A man over 35 years old, or under 18, can get a good price by making immediate application to Room No. 50, Monument Hotel, or by addressing "J. W.," through Richmond P. O. jy 9—1t*

WANTED—A SUBSTITUTE, to go into the 24th North Carolina State troops, for which a liberal price will be paid. Apply to me at Dispatch office this evening at 4 o'clock P. M.
jy 9—1t* R. R. MOORE.

WANTED—A SUBSTITUTE, to go in a first-rate Georgia company of infantry, under the heroic Jackson. A gentleman whose health is impaired, will give a fair price for a substitute. Apply immediately at ROOM, No. 13, Post-Office Department, third story, between the hours of 10 and 3 o'clock. jy 9—6t*

WANTED—Two SUBSTITUTES for the war. A good bonus will be given. None need apply except those exempt from Conscript. Apply to-day at GEORGE I. HERRING'S,
jy 9—1t* Grocery store, No. 56 Main st.

general rather than a president, lacked Lincoln's persuasive skills and political astuteness. Although he saw the need for unity, he was unable to impose it. Soon his autonomous style of leadership—he wanted to decide every detail himself—angered his generals, alienated cabinet members, and gave southern governors reason to resist his orders. By the second year of the war, when rich slave owners were refusing to give up their privileges for the war effort, Davis no longer had the public confidence and support he needed to coerce them. After the first flush of patriotism had passed, the Confederacy never lived up to its hope of becoming a unified nation.

Confederate Disappointments

The failure of "cotton diplomacy" was a crushing blow. White Southerners were stunned that Britain and France would not recognize their claim to independence. Well into 1863, the South hoped that a decisive battlefield victory would change the minds of cautious Europeans. In the meantime, plantations continued to grow cotton, but were directed to withhold it from market, in the hope that lack of raw material for their textile mills would lead the British

and French to recognize the Confederacy. The British reacted indignantly, claiming that the withholding of cotton was economic blackmail and that to yield "would be ignominious beyond measure," as Lord Russell put it. Because British textile manufacturers had found new sources of cotton, when the Confederacy ended the embargo in 1862 and began to ship its great surplus, the world price of cotton plunged. Then too, the Union naval blockade, weak at first, began to take effect. Cotton turned out to be not so powerful a diplomatic weapon after all.

Perhaps the greatest southern failure was in the area of finances. At first, the Confederate government tried to raise money from the states, but governors refused to impose new taxes. By the time uniform taxes were levied in 1863, it was too late. Heavy borrowing and the printing of great sums of paper money produced runaway inflation (a ruinous rate of 9,000 percent by 1865, compared with 80 percent in the North). Inflation, in turn, caused incalculable damage to morale and prospects for unity.

After the initial surge of volunteers, enlistment in the military fell off, as it did in the North also. In April 1862, the Confederate Congress passed the first draft law in

American history, and the Union Congress followed suit in March 1863. The southern law declared that all able-bodied men between eighteen and thirty-five were eligible for three years of military service. Purchase of substitutes was allowed, as in the North, but in the South the price was uncontrolled, rising eventually to $10,000 in Confederate money. The most disliked part of the draft law was a provision exempting one white man on each plantation with twenty or more slaves. This provision not only seemed to disprove the earlier claim that slavery freed white men to fight, but it aroused class resentments. A bitter phrase of the time complained, "It's a rich man's war but a poor man's fight."

Contradictions of Southern Nationalism

In the early days of the war, Jefferson Davis successfully mobilized feelings of regional identity and patriotism. Many Southerners felt part of a beleaguered region that had been forced to resist northern tyranny. But most Southerners felt loyalty to their own state and local communities, not to a Confederate nation. The strong belief in states' rights and aristocratic privilege undermined the Confederate cause. Some Southern governors resisted potentially unifying actions such as moving militias outside their home states. Broader measures, such as general taxation, were widely evaded by rich and poor alike. The inequitable draft was only one of many things that convinced the ordinary people of the South that this was a war for privileged slave owners, not for them. With its leaders and citizens fearing (perhaps correctly) that centralization would destroy what was distinctively southern, the Confederacy was unable to mobilize the resources—financial, human, and otherwise—that might have prevented its destruction by northern armies.

THE FIGHTING THROUGH 1862

Just as political decisions were often driven by military necessity, the basic northern and southern military strategies were affected by political considerations as much as by military ones. The initial policy of limited war, thought to be the best route to ultimate reconciliation, ran into difficulties because of the public's impatience for victories. But victories, as the mounting slaughter made clear, were not easy to achieve.

The War in Northern Virginia

The initial Northern strategy, dubbed by critics the Anaconda Plan (after the constrictor snake), envisaged slowly squeezing the South with a blockade at sea and on the Mississippi River. Proposed by the general-in-chief, Winfield Scott, a native of Virginia, it avoided invasion and conquest in the hope that a strained South would recognize the inevitability of defeat and thus surrender. Lincoln accepted

the basics of the plan, but public clamor for a fight pushed him to agree to the disastrous Battle of Bull Run and then to a major buildup of Union troops in northern Virginia under General George B. McClellan (see Map 16.1).

Dashing in appearance, McClellan was extremely cautious in battle. In March 1862, after almost a year spent drilling the raw Union recruits and after repeated exhortations by an impatient Lincoln, McClellan committed 120,000 troops to what became known as the Peninsular campaign. The objective was to capture Richmond, the Confederate capital. McClellan had his troops and their supplies ferried in 400 ships from Washington to Fortress Monroe, near the mouth of the James River, an effort that took three weeks. Inching up the James Peninsula toward Richmond, he tried to avoid battle, hoping his overwhelming numbers would convince the South to surrender. By June, McClellan's troops were close enough to Richmond to hear the church bells ringing—but not close enough for victory. In a series of battles known as the Seven Days, Robert E. Lee (who had just assumed command of the Confederacy's Army of Northern Virginia) boldly counterattacked, repeatedly catching McClellan off guard. Taking heavy losses as well as inflicting them, Lee drove McClellan back. In August, Lee routed another Union army, commanded by General John Pope, at the Second Battle of Bull Rull (Second Manassas). Lincoln, alarmed at the threat to Washington and disappointed by McClellan's inaction, ordered him to abandon the Peninsular campaign and return to the capital.

Jefferson Davis, like Abraham Lincoln, was an active commander-in-chief. And like Lincoln, he responded to a public that clamored for more action than a strictly defensive war entailed. After the Seven Days victories, Davis supported a Confederate attack on Maryland. At the same time, he issued a proclamation urging the people of Maryland to make a separate peace. But in the brutal battle of Antietam on September 17, 1862, which claimed more than 5,000 dead and 19,000 wounded, McClellan's army checked Lee's advance. Lee retreated to Virginia, inflicting terrible losses on northern troops at Fredricksburg when they again made a thrust toward Richmond in December 1862. The war in northern Virginia was stalemated: neither side was strong enough to win, but each was too strong to be defeated (see Map 16.2).

Shiloh and the War for the Mississippi

Although most public attention was focused on the fighting in Virginia, battles in Tennessee and along the Mississippi River proved to be the key to eventual Union victory. The rising military figure in the West was Ulysses S. Grant, who had once resigned from the service because of a drinking problem. Reenlisting as a colonel after the fall of Fort Sumter, Grant was promoted to brigadier general within two months. In February 1862, Grant captured Fort Henry and Fort Donelson, on the Tennessee

MAP EXPLORATION

To explore an interactive version of this map, go to **www.prenhall.com/faragher5/map16.1**

1861–62

Area controlled by Union
Area gained by Union
Area controlled by Confederacy

← Union advance
✳ Union victory
✳ Confederate victory

1863

1864–65

MAP 16.1 Overall Strategy of the Civil War The initial Northern strategy for subduing the South, the so-called Anaconda Plan, entailed strangling it by a blockade at sea and obtaining control of the Mississippi River. But at the end of 1862, it was clear that the South's defensive strategy could only be broken by the invasion of Southern territory. In 1864, Sherman's "March to the Sea" and Grant's hammering tactics in northern Virginia brought the war home to the South. Lee's surrender to Grant at Appomattox Courthouse on April 9, 1865, ended the bloodiest war in the nation's history.

and Cumberland Rivers, establishing Union control of much of Tennessee and forcing Confederate troops to retreat into northern Mississippi.

Moving south with 28,000 men, Grant met a 40,000-man Confederate force commanded by General Albert Sidney Johnston at Shiloh Church in April 1862. Seriously outnumbered on the first day, Grant's forces were reinforced by the arrival of 35,000 troops under the command of General Don Carlos Buell. After two days of bitter and bloody fighting in the rain, the Confederates withdrew. The losses on both sides were enormous: the North lost 13,000 men, the South 11,000, including General Johnston, who bled to death. McClellan's Peninsular campaign was already under way when Grant won at Shiloh, and Jefferson Davis, concerned about the defense of Richmond, refused to reinforce the generals who were trying to stop Grant. Consequently, Union forces kept moving, capturing Memphis in June and beginning a campaign to eventually capture Vicksburg, "the Gibraltar of

the Mississippi." Grant and other Union generals faced strong Confederate resistance, and progress was slow. Earlier that year, naval forces under Admiral David Farragut had captured New Orleans and then continued up the Mississippi River. By the end of 1862, it was clearly only a matter of time before the entire river would be in Union hands. Arkansas, Louisiana, and Texas would then be cut off from the rest of the Confederacy (see Map 16.3).

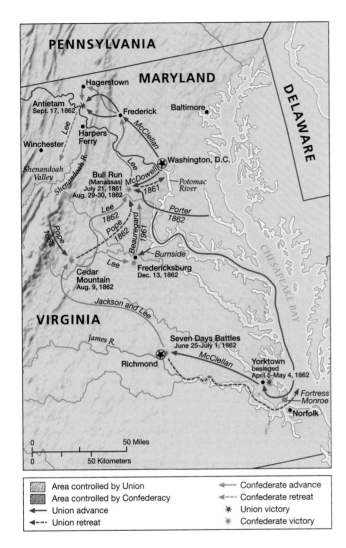

MAP 16.2 Major Battles in the East, 1861–62 Northern Virginia was the most crucial and the most constant theater of battle. The prizes were the two opposing capitals, Washington and Richmond, only 70 miles apart. By the summer of 1862, George B. McClellan, famously cautious, had achieved only stalemate in the Peninsular campaign. He did, however, turn back Robert E. Lee at Antietam in September.

The War in the Trans–Mississippi West

Although only one western state, Texas, seceded from the Union, the Civil War was fought in small ways in many parts of the West. Southern hopes for the extension of slavery into the Southwest were reignited by the war, and the just-announced discovery of gold in Colorado impelled the Confederacy to attempt to capture it. Texans mounted an attack on New Mexico, which they had long coveted, and kept their eyes on the larger prizes of Arizona and California. A Confederate force led by General Henry H. Sibley occupied Santa Fé and Albuquerque early in 1862 without resistance, thus posing a serious Confederate threat to the entire Southwest. Confederate hopes were dashed,

however, by a ragtag group of 950 miners and adventurers organized into the first Colorado Volunteer Infantry Regiment. After an epic march of 400 miles from Denver, which was completed in thirteen days despite snow and high winds, the Colorado militia stopped the unsuspecting Confederate troops in the Battle of Glorieta Pass on March 26–28, 1862. This dashing action, coupled with the efforts of California militias to safeguard Arizona and Utah from seizure by Confederate sympathizers, secured the Far West for the Union.

Other military action in the West was less decisive. The chronic fighting along the Kansas-Missouri border set a record for brutality when Confederate William Quantrill's Raiders made a predawn attack on Lawrence, Kansas, in August 1863, massacring 150 inhabitants and burning the town. Another civil war took place in Indian Territory, south of Kansas. The southern Indian tribes who had been removed there from the Old Southwest in the 1830s included many who were still bitter over the horrors of their removal by federal troops, and they sympathized with the Confederacy. John Ross, leader of the majority pro-Union Cherokee fullbloods, at first tried to assure the safety of his people by proclaiming their neutrality, but later in 1861, bordered by Confederate states and lacking support from Washington, he signed a treaty of alliance with the Confederates. The Confederacy actively sought Indian support by offering Indian people representation in the Confederate Congress. Consequently, many Indians fought for the South, among them Stand Watie, who became a Confederate military officer. Union victories at Pea Ridge (in northwestern Arkansas) in 1862 and near Fort Gibson (in Indian Territory) in 1863 secured the area for the Union, but did little to stop dissension among the Indian groups themselves. Ross, captured in 1862 and held at Fort Leavenworth in Kansas, never returned to his tribe, which factionalized badly after his departure. After the Civil War, the victorious federal government used the tribes' wartime support for the Confederacy as a justification for demanding further land cessions.

Elsewhere in the West, other groups of Indians found themselves caught up in the wider war. An uprising by the Santee Sioux in Minnesota occurred in August 1862, just as McClellan conceded defeat in the Peninsular campaign in Virginia. Alarmed whites, certain that the uprising was a Confederate plot, ignored legitimate Sioux grievances and responded in kind to Sioux ferocity. In little more than a month, 500 to 800 white settlers and an even greater number of Sioux were killed. Thirty-eight Indians were hanged in a mass execution in Mankato on December 26, 1862, and subsequently all Sioux were expelled from Minnesota. In 1863, U.S. Army Colonel Kit Carson invaded Navajo country in Arizona in retaliation for Indian raids on U.S. troops. Eight thousand Navajos were forced on the brutal "Long Walk" to Bosque Redondo on the Pecos River in New Mexico, where they were held prisoner until a treaty between the United States and the Navajos was signed in 1868.

The hostilities in the West showed that no part of the country, and none of its inhabitants, could remain untouched by the Civil War.

The Naval War

The Union's naval blockade of the South, intended to cut off commerce between the Confederacy and the rest of the world, was initially unsuccessful. The U.S. Navy had only thirty-three ships with which to blockade 189 ports along 3,500 miles of coastline. Southern blockade runners evaded Union ships with ease: only an estimated one-eighth of all Confederate shipping was stopped in 1862. Moreover, the Confederacy licensed British-made privateers to strike at northern shipping. In a two-year period, one such Confederate raider, the *Alabama*, destroyed sixty-nine Union

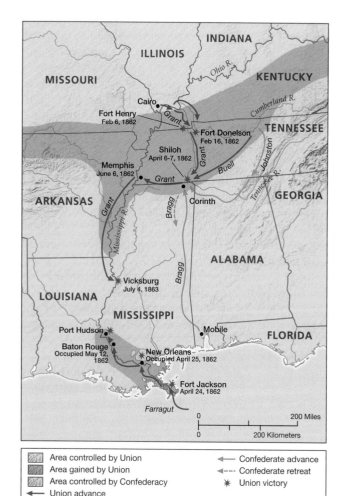

MAP 16.3 Major Battles in the Interior, 1862–63
Ulysses S. Grant waged a mobile war, winning at Fort Henry and Fort Donelson in Tennessee in February 1862, and at Shiloh in April, and capturing Memphis in June. He then laid siege to Vicksburg, as Admiral David Farragut captured New Orleans and began to advance up the Mississippi River.

ships with cargoes valued at $6 million. Beginning in 1863, however, as the Union navy became larger, the blockade began to take effect. In 1864, a third of the blockade runners were captured, and in 1865, half of them. As a result, fewer and fewer supplies reached the South.

North and South also engaged in a brief duel featuring the revolutionary new technology of ironcladding. The Confederacy refitted a scuttled Union vessel, the *Merrimac*, with iron plating and renamed it the *Virginia*. On March 8, 1862, as McClellan began his Peninsular campaign, the *Virginia* steamed out of Norfolk harbor to challenge the Union blockade. The iron plating protected the *Virginia* from the fire of the Union ships, which found themselves defenseless against its ram and its powerful guns. Two Union ships went down, and the blockade seemed about to be broken. But the North had an experimental ironclad of its own, the *Monitor*, which was waiting for the *Virginia* when it emerged from port on March 9. The *Monitor*, which looked like "an immense shingle floating on the water, with a gigantic cheese box rising from its center," was the ship of the future, for the "cheese box" was a revolving turret, a basic component of battleships to come. The historic duel between these first two ironclads was inconclusive, and primitive technology together with limited resources made them of little consequence for the rest of the war. But this brief duel prefigured the naval and land battles of the world wars of the twentieth century as much as did the massing of huge armies on the battlefield.

For the Union, the most successful naval operation in the first two years of the war was not the blockade, but the seizing of exposed coastal areas. The Sea Islands of South Carolina were taken, as were some of the North Carolina islands and Fort Pulaski, which commanded the harbor of Savannah, Georgia. Most damaging to the South, was the capture of New Orleans.

The Black Response

The capture of Port Royal in the South Carolina Sea Islands in 1861 was important for another reason. Whites fled at the Union advance, but 10,000 slaves greeted the troops with jubilation and shouts of gratitude. Union troops had unwittingly freed these slaves in advance of any official Union policy on the status of slaves in captured territory.

Early in the war, an irate Southerner who saw three of his slaves disappear behind Union lines at Fortress Monroe, Virginia, demanded the return of his property, citing the Fugitive Slave Law. The Union commander, Benjamin Butler, replied that the Fugitive Slave Law no longer applied and that the escaped slaves were "contraband of war." News of Butler's decision spread rapidly among the slaves in the region of Fortress Monroe. Two days later, eight runaway slaves appeared; the next day, fifty-nine black men and women arrived at the fort. Union commanders had found an effective way to rob the South of its basic workforce. The "contrabands," as they were known, were put to work building fortifications and doing other useful work in northern camps. Washington, DC, became a refuge for contraband blacks, who crowded into the capital to join the free black people who lived there (at 9,000 people, they were one of the largest urban black populations outside the Confederacy). Many destitute contrabands received help from the Contraband Relief Association. Modeled on the Sanitary Commission, the association was founded by former slave Elizabeth Keckley, seamstress to Mary Todd Lincoln, the president's wife.

As Union troops drove deeper into the South, the black response grew. When Union General William Tecumseh Sherman marched his army through Georgia in 1864, 18,000 slaves—entire families, people of all ages—flocked to the Union lines. By the war's end, nearly a million black people, fully a quarter of all the slaves in the South, had "voted with their feet" for the Union.

THE DEATH OF SLAVERY

The overwhelming response of black slaves to the Union advance changed the nature of the war. As increasing numbers of slaves flocked to Union lines, the conclusion that the South refused to face was unmistakable: the southern war to defend the slave system did not have the support of slaves themselves. Any northern policy that ignored the issue of slavery and the wishes of the slaves was unrealistic.

The Politics of Emancipation

In 1862, as the issue of slavery loomed ever larger, Abraham Lincoln, acutely aware of divided northern opinion, inched his way toward a declaration of emancipation. Lincoln was correct to be worried about the unity of opinion in the North. Before the war, within the Republican Party, only a small group of abolitionists had favored freeing the slaves. Most Republicans were more concerned about the expansion of slavery than they were about the lives of slaves themselves. For their part, most northern Democrats were openly antiblack. Irish workers in northern cities had rioted against free African Americans, with whom they often competed for jobs. There was also the question of what would become of slaves who were freed. Northern Democrats effectively played on racial fears in the 1862 congressional elections, warning that freed slaves would pour into northern cities and take jobs from white laborers.

Nevertheless, the necessities of war demanded that Lincoln adopt a policy to end slavery. In March 1862, he proposed that every state undertake gradual, compensated emancipation, after which former slaves would be resettled in Haiti and Panama (neither of which was under U.S. control). This unrealistic colonization scheme doomed the proposal.

Even as Radical Republicans chafed at Lincoln's slow pace, he was edging toward a new position. Following the Union victory at Antietam in September 1862, Lincoln issued a preliminary decree: unless the rebellious states returned to the Union by January 1, 1863, he would declare their slaves "forever free." The decree increased the pressure on the South by directly linking the slave system to the war effort. Thus the freedom of black people became part of the struggle. Frederick Douglass, the voice of black America, wrote, "We shout for joy that we live to record this righteous decree."

On January 1, 1863, Lincoln duly issued the final Emancipation Proclamation, which turned out to be less than sweeping. The proclamation freed the slaves in the areas of rebellion—the areas the Union did not control—but specifically exempted slaves in the border states and in former Confederate areas conquered by the Union. Lincoln's purpose was to meet the abolitionist demand for a war against slavery while not losing the support of conservatives, especially in the border states. But the proclamation was so equivocal that Lincoln's own secretary of state, William Seward, remarked sarcastically, "We show our sympathy with slavery by emancipating slaves where we cannot reach them and holding them in bondage where we can set them free."

One group greeted the Emancipation Proclamation with open celebration. On New Year's Day, hundreds of African Americans gathered outside the White House and cheered the president. They called to him, as pastor Henry M. Turner recalled, that "if he would come out of that palace, they would hug him to death." Free African Americans predicted that the news would encourage southern slaves either to flee to Union lines or refuse to work for their masters. Both of these things were already happening as African Americans seized on wartime changes to reshape white-black relations in the South. In one sense, then, the Emancipation Proclamation simply gave a name to a process already in motion.

Abolitionists set about moving Lincoln beyond his careful stance in the Emancipation Proclamation. Reformers such as Elizabeth Cady Stanton and Susan B. Anthony lobbied and petitioned for a constitutional amendment outlawing slavery. Congress, at Lincoln's urging, approved and sent to the states a statement banning slavery throughout the United States. Quickly ratified by the Union states in 1865, the statement became the Thirteenth Amendment to the Constitution. (The southern states, being in a state of rebellion, could not vote.) Lincoln's firm support for this amendment is a good indicator of his true feelings about slavery when he was freed of the kinds of military and political considerations necessarily taken into account in the Emancipation Proclamation.

Black Fighting Men

As part of the Emancipation Proclamation, Lincoln gave his support for the first time to the recruitment of black soldiers. Early in the war, eager black volunteers had been bitterly disappointed at being turned away. Many, like Robert Fitzgerald, a free African American from Pennsylvania, found other ways to serve the Union cause. Fitzgerald first drove a wagon and mule for the Quartermaster Corps, and later, in spite of persistent seasickness, he served in the Union navy. After the Emancipation Proclamation, however, Fitzgerald was able to do what he had wanted to do all along: be a soldier. He enlisted in the Fifth Massachusetts Cavalry, a regiment that, like all the units in which black soldiers served, was 100 percent African American, but commanded by white officers.

In Fitzgerald's company of eighty-three men, half came from slave states and had run away to enlist; the other half came mostly from the North but also from Canada, the West Indies, and France. Other regiments had volunteers from Africa. The proportion of volunteers from the loyal border states (where slavery was still legal) was upwards of 25 percent—a lethal blow to the slave system in those states.

After a scant two months of training, Fitzgerald's company was sent on to Washington and thence to battle in northern Virginia. Uncertain of the reception they would receive in northern cities with their history of

antiblack riots, Fitzgerald and his comrades were pleasantly surprised. "We are cheered in every town we pass through," he wrote in his diary. "I was surprised to see a great many white people weeping as the train moved South." White people had reason to cheer: black volunteers, eager and willing to fight, made up 10 percent of the Union army. Nearly 200,000 African Americans (one out of every five black males in the nation) served in the Union army or navy. A fifth of them—37,000—died defending their own freedom and the Union.

Military service was something no black man could take lightly. African American soldiers faced prejudice within the army and had to prove themselves in battle. The performance of black soldiers under fire helped to change the minds of the Union army command. "The bravery of the blacks . . . completely revolutionized the sentiment of the army with regard to the employment of negro troops," wrote Charles Dana, assistant secretary of war. "I heard prominent officers who formerly in private had sneered at the idea of negroes fighting express themselves after that as heartily in favor of it."

However, the Confederates hated and feared African American troops and threatened to treat any captured black soldier as an escaped slave subject to execution. On at least one occasion, the threats were carried out. In 1864, Confederate soldiers massacred 262 black soldiers at Fort Pillow, Tennessee, after they had surrendered. Although large-scale episodes such as this were rare (especially after President Lincoln threatened retaliation), smaller ones were not. On duty near Petersburg, Virginia, Robert Fitzgerald's company lost a picket to Confederate hatred: wounded in the leg, he was unable to escape from Confederate soldiers, who smashed his skull with their musket butts.

Another extraordinary part of the story of the African American soldiers was their reception by black people in the South, who were overjoyed at the sight of armed black men, many of them former slaves themselves, wearing the uniform of the Union army. As his regiment entered Wilmington, North Carolina, one soldier wrote, "Men and women, old and young, were running throughout the streets, shouting and praising God. We could then truly see what we have been fighting for."

COME AND JOIN US BROTHERS.
PUBLISHED BY THE SUPERVISORY COMMITTEE FOR RECRUITING COLORED REGIMENTS
1210 CHESTNUT ST. PHILADELPHIA.

This recruiting poster for African Americans in 1863 (they were barred from enlistment before then) depicts a regiment of black union soldiers adjacent to their white commander. Nearly 200,000 African American men—1 in 5—served in the Union army or navy.

SOURCE: Lithograph; ICHi-22051; *Come and join us brothers* Civil War; Philadelphia, PA; ca. 1863. Creator P. S. Duval & Son. Chicago Historical Society.

Robert Fitzgerald's own army career was brief. Just five months after he enlisted, he caught typhoid fever. Hearing of his illness, Fitzgerald's mother traveled from Pennsylvania and nursed him, probably saving his life. Eventually, 117 members of his regiment died of disease—and only 7 in battle. Eight months after he had enlisted, Fitzgerald was discharged for poor eyesight. His short military career nevertheless gave him, in the words of a granddaughter, the distinguished lawyer Pauli Murray, "a pride which would be felt throughout his family for the next century."

African American soldiers were not treated equally by the Union army. They were segregated in camp, given the worst jobs, and paid less than white soldiers ($10 a month rather than $13). Although they might not be able to do much about the other kinds of discrimination, the men of the Fifty-fourth Massachusetts found an unusual way to protest their unequal pay: they refused to accept it, preferring to serve the army for free until it decided to treat them as free men. The protest was effective; in June 1864, the War Department equal-

ized the wages of black and white soldiers. (See Out of Many Voices: Soldier James Henry Gooding Protests Unequal Pay for Black Soldiers, 1863.)

In other ways the army service of black men made a dent in northern white racism. Massachusetts, the state where abolitionist feeling was the strongest, went the farthest by enacting the first law forbidding discrimination against African Americans in public facilities. Some major cities, among them San Francisco, Cincinnati, Cleveland, and New York, desegregated their streetcars. Some states—Ohio, California, Illinois—repealed statutes that had barred black people from testifying in court or serving on juries. But above all, as Frederick Douglass acutely saw, military service permanently changed the status of African Americans. "Once let the black man get upon his person the brass letters, U.S., let him get an eagle on his button and a musket on his shoulder and bullets in his pocket," Douglass said, and "there is no power on earth that can deny that he has earned the right to citizenship."

OUT OF MANY VOICES

SOLDIER JAMES HENRY GOODING PROTESTS UNEQUAL PAY FOR BLACK SOLDIERS, 1863

After the Emancipation Proclamation, African American men were allowed to enlist in the Union army, but they did not find the equal treatment that they doubtless hoped for. In September 1863, only nine months after he was allowed to enlist, African American soldier James Henry Gooding wrote a passionate letter to President Lincoln protesting unequal treatment:

YOUR EXCELLENCY, ABRAHAM LINCOLN:

[W]hen the war trumpet sounded o'er the land, when men knew not the Friend from the Traitor, the black man laid his life at the altar of the Nation,—and he was refused. When the arms of the Union were beaten, in the first year of the war, and the Executive called for more food for its ravenous maw, again the black man begged the privilege of aiding his country in her need, to be again refused.

And now he is in the War, and how has he conducted himself? Let their dusky forms rise up, out of the mires of James Island, and give the answer. Let the rich mould around Wagner's

parapet be upturned, and there will be found an eloquent answer. Obedient and patient and solid as a wall are they. All we lack is a paler hue and a better acquaintance with the alphabet.

Now the main question is, are we Soldiers, or are we Laborers? We are fully armed, and equipped, have done all the various duties pertaining to a Soldier's life, have conducted ourselves to the complete satisfaction of General Officers, who were, if anything, prejudiced against us, but who now accord us all the encouragement and honors due us . . .

Now your Excellency, we have done a Soldier's duty. Why can't we have a Soldier's pay? You caution the Rebel chieftain, that the United States knows no distinction in her soldiers. She insists on having all her soldiers of whatever creed or color, to be treated according to the usages of War. Now if the United States exacts uniformity of treatment of her soldiers from the insurgents, would it not be well and consistent to set the example herself by paying all her soldiers alike? ■

SOURCE: Herbert Aptheker, ed., *A Documentary History of the Negro People in the United States* (New York: Citadel Press, 1951), 482–484.

THE FRONT LINES AND THE HOME FRONT

Civil War soldiers wrote millions of letters home, more proportionately than in any American war. Their letters and the ones they received in return were links between the front lines and the home front, between the soldiers and their home communities. They are a testament to the patriotism of both Union and Confederate troops, for the story they tell is frequently one of slaughter and horror.

The Toll of War

In spite of early hopes for what one might call a "brotherly" war, one that avoided excessive brutality, Civil War battles were appallingly deadly (see Figure 16.1). One reason was technology: improved weapons, particularly modern rifles, had much greater range and accuracy than the muskets they replaced. The Mexican-American War had been fought with smooth-bore muskets, which were slow to reload and accurate only at short distances. As Ulysses Grant said, "At a distance of a few hundred yards, a man could fire at you all day [with a musket] without your finding out." The new Springfield and Enfield rifles were accurate for a quarter of a mile or more.

Civil War generals, however, were slow to adjust to this new reality. Almost all Union and Confederate generals remained committed to the conventional military doctrine of massed infantry offensives—the "Jomini doctrine"—that they had learned in their military classes at West Point. Part of this strategy had been to "soften up" a defensive line with artillery before an infantry assault, but now the range of the new rifles made artillery itself vulnerable to attack. As a result, generals relied less on "softening up" than on immense numbers of infantrymen, hoping that enough of them would survive the withering rifle fire to overwhelm the enemy line. Enormous casualties were a consequence of this basic strategy.

Medical ignorance was another factor in the casualty rate. Because the use of antiseptic procedures was in its infancy, men often died because minor wounds became infected. Gangrene was a common cause of death. Disease was an even more frequent killer, taking twice as many men as were lost in battle. The overcrowded and unsanitary conditions of many camps were breeding grounds for smallpox, dysentery, typhoid, pneumonia, and, in the summer, malaria.

Both North and South were completely unprepared to handle the supply and health needs of their large armies. Twenty-four hours after the battle of Shiloh, most

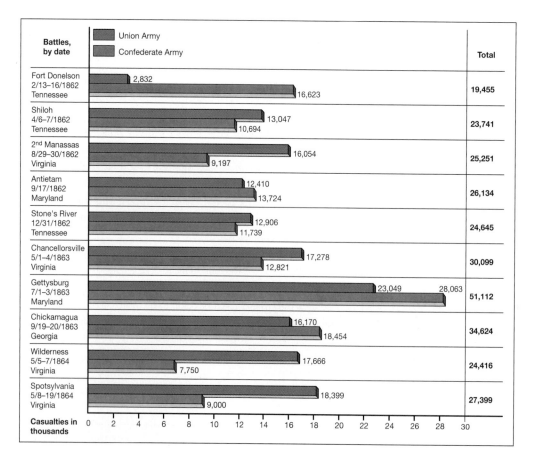

Battles, by date	Union Army — Confederate Army	Total
Fort Donelson 2/13–16/1862 Tennessee	2,832 / 16,623	**19,455**
Shiloh 4/6–7/1862 Tennessee	13,047 / 10,694	**23,741**
2nd Manassas 8/29–30/1862 Virginia	16,054 / 9,197	**25,251**
Antietam 9/17/1862 Maryland	12,410 / 13,724	**26,134**
Stone's River 12/31/1862 Tennessee	12,906 / 11,739	**24,645**
Chancellorsville 5/1–4/1863 Virginia	17,278 / 12,821	**30,099**
Gettysburg 7/1–3/1863 Maryland	23,049 / 28,063	**51,112**
Chickamagua 9/19–20/1863 Georgia	16,170 / 18,454	**34,624**
Wilderness 5/5–7/1864 Virginia	17,666 / 7,750	**24,416**
Spotsylvania 5/8–19/1864 Virginia	18,399 / 9,000	**27,399**

Casualties in thousands: 0 2 4 6 8 10 12 14 16 18 20 22 24 26 28 30

FIGURE 16.1 The Casualties Mount up
This chart of the ten costliest battles of the Civil War shows the relentless toll of casualties (killed, wounded, missing, captured) on both the Union and Confederate sides.

of the wounded still lay on the field in the rain. Many died of exposure; some, unable to help themselves, drowned. Nor were the combatants prepared to deal with masses of war prisoners, as the shocking example of the Confederate prison camp at Andersonville in northern Georgia demonstrated. Andersonville was an open stockade with no shade or shelter, erected early in 1864 to hold 10,000 northern prisoners. But by midsummer, it held 33,000. During the worst weeks of that summer, 100 prisoners died of disease, exposure, or malnutrition each day.

Army Nurses

Many medical supplies that the armies were unable to provide were donated by the United States Sanitary Commission in the North, as described in the opening of this chapter, and by women's volunteer groups in the South. But in addition to supplies, there was also an urgent need for skilled nurses to care for wounded and convalescent soldiers. Nursing within a family context was widely considered to be women's work. Caring for sick family members was a key domestic responsibility for women, and most had considerable experience with it. But taking care of strange men in hospitals was another thing. There were strong objections that such work was "unseemly" for respectable women.

Under the pressure of wartime necessity, and over the objections of most army doctors—who resented the challenge to their authority from people no different than their daughters or wives—women became army nurses. Hospital nursing, previously considered a job only disreputable women would undertake, now became a suitable vocation for middle-class women. Under the leadership of veteran reformer Dorothea Dix of the asylum movement (see Chapter 13), and in cooperation with the Sanitary Commission (and with the vocal support of Mother Bickerdyke), by the war's end more than 3,000 northern women had worked as paid army nurses and many more as volunteers. Other women organized volunteer efforts outside the Sanitary Commission umbrella. Perhaps the best known was Clara Barton, who had been a government clerk before the war and consequently knew a number of influential members of Congress. Barton organized nursing and the distribution of medical supplies; she also used her congressional contacts to force reforms in army medical practice, of which she was very critical.

Southern women were also active in nursing and otherwise aiding soldiers, though the South never boasted a single large-scale organization like the Sanitary Commission. The women of Richmond volunteered when they found the war on their doorstep in the summer of 1862. During the Seven Days Battles, thousands of wounded poured into Richmond; many died in the streets, because there was no room for them in hospitals. Richmond women first established informal "roadside hospitals" to meet the need, and their activities expanded from there. As in the North, middle-class women at first faced strong resistance from army doctors and even their own families, who believed that a field hospital was "no place for a refined lady." Kate Cumming of Mobile, who nursed in Corinth, Mississippi, after the Battle of Shiloh, faced down such reproofs, though she confided to her diary that nursing wounded men was very difficult: "Nothing that I had ever heard or read had given me the faintest idea of the horrors witnessed here." She and her companion nurses persisted and became an important part of the Confederate medical services. For southern women, who had been much less active in the public life of their communities than their northern reforming sisters, this Civil War activity marked an important break with prewar tradition.

Although women had made important advances, most army nurses and medical support staff were men. One volunteer nurse was the poet Walt Whitman, who visited wounded soldiers in the hospital in

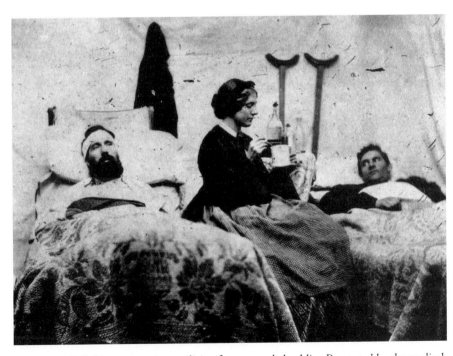

Nurse Ann Bell shown preparing medicine for a wounded soldier. Prompted by the medical crisis of the war, women such as Bell and "Mother" Bickerdyke actively participated in the war effort as nurses.

SOURCE: Center of Military History, U.S. Army.

Washington, DC. Horrified at the suffering he saw, Whitman also formed a deep admiration for the "incredible dauntlessness" of the common soldier in the face of slaughter and privation. While never denying the senselessness of the slaughter, Whitman nevertheless found hope in the determined spirit of the common man and woman.

The Life of the Common Soldier

The conditions experienced by the eager young volunteers of the Union and Confederate armies included massive, terrifying, and bloody battles, apparently unending, with no sign of victory in sight. Soldiers suffered from the uncertainty of supply, which left troops, especially in the South, without uniforms, tents, and sometimes even food. They endured long marches over muddy, rutted roads while carrying packs weighing fifty or sixty pounds. Disease was rampant in their dirty, verminous, and unsanitary camps, and hospitals were so dreadful that more men left them dead than alive. As a result, desertion was common: an estimated one of every nine Confederate soldiers and one of every seven Union soldiers deserted. Unauthorized absence was another problem. At Antietam, Robert E. Lee estimated that unauthorized absence reduced his strength by a third to a half. In October 1861, a Louisiana man wrote to his brother-in-law: "You spoke as if you had some notion of volunteering. I advise you to stay at home." Once the initial patriotic fervor had waned, attitudes such as his were increasingly common, both on the battlefield and at home.

Wartime Politics

In the earliest days of the war, Northerners had joined together in support of the war effort. Democrat Stephen A. Douglas, Lincoln's defeated rival, paid a visit to the White House to offer Lincoln his support, then traveled home to Illinois, where he addressed a huge rally of Democrats in Chicago: "There can be no neutrals in this war, only patriots—or traitors!" Within a month, Douglas was dead at age forty-eight. The Democrats had lost the leadership of a broad-minded man who might have done much on behalf of northern unity. By 1862, Democrats had split into two factions: the War Democrats and the Peace Democrats, derogatorily called "Copperheads" (from the poisonous snake).

Despite the split in the party in 1860 and the secession of the South, the Democratic Party remained a powerful force in northern politics. It had received 44 percent of the popular vote in the North in the 1860 election and its united opposition to the emancipation of slaves explains much of Lincoln's equivocal action on this issue. But the Peace Democrats went far beyond opposition to emancipation, denouncing the draft, martial law, and the high-handed actions of "King Abraham."

The leader of the Copperheads, Clement Vallandigham, a former Ohio congressman, advocated an armistice and a negotiated peace that would "look only to the welfare, peace and safety of the white race, without reference to the effect that settlement may have on the African." Western Democrats, he threatened, might form their own union with the South, excluding New England with its radical abolitionists and high-tariff industrialists. Lincoln could not afford to take Vallandigham's threats lightly. Besides, he was convinced that some Peace Democrats were members of secret societies—the Knights of the Golden Circle and the Sons of Liberty—that had been conspiring with the Confederacy. In 1862, Lincoln proclaimed that all people who discouraged enlistments in the army or otherwise engaged in disloyal practices would be subject to martial law. In all, 13,000 people were arrested and imprisoned, including Vallandigham, who was exiled to the Confederacy. Lincoln rejected all protests, claiming that his arbitrary actions were necessary for national security.

Lincoln also faced challenges from the radical faction of his own party. As the war continued, the Radicals gained strength: it was they who pushed for emancipation in the early days of the war and for harsh treatment of the defeated South after it ended. The most troublesome Radical was Salmon P. Chase, who in December 1862, caused a cabinet crisis when he encouraged Senate Republicans to complain that Secretary of State William Seward was "lukewarm" in his support for emancipation. This Radical challenge was a portent of the party's difficulties after the war, which Lincoln did not live to see—or prevent.

Economic and Social Strains on the North

Wartime needs caused a surge in northern economic growth, but the gains were unequally distributed. Early in the war, some industries suffered: textile manufacturers could not get cotton, and shoe factories that had made cheap shoes for slaves were without a market. But other industries boomed—boot making, shipbuilding, and the manufacture of woolen goods such as blankets and uniforms, to give just three examples. Coal mining expanded, as did ironmaking, especially the manufacture of iron rails for railroads. Agricultural goods were in great demand, promoting further mechanization of farming. The McCormick brothers grew rich from sales of their reapers. Once scorned as a "metal grasshopper," the ungainly-looking McCormick reaper made hand harvesting of grain a thing of the past and led to great savings in manpower. Women, left to tend the family farm while the men went to war, found that with mechanized equipment, they could manage the demanding task of harvesting.

Meeting wartime needs enriched some people honestly, but speculators and profiteers also flourished, as they have in every war. By the end of the war, government contracts had exceeded $1 billion. Not all of this business was free from corruption. New wealth was evident in every northern city. Many people were appalled

A black man is lynched during the New York City Draft Riots in July 1863. Free black people and their institutions were major victims of the worst rioting in American history until then. The riots were more than a protest against the draft; they were also an outburst of frustration over urban problems that had been festering for decades.

SOURCE: Culver Pictures, Inc.

Another major source of social tension was conscription. The Union introduced a draft in March 1863. Especially unpopular was a provision in the draft law that allowed the hiring of substitutes or the payment of a commutation fee of $300. Substitutes were mostly recent immigrants who had not yet filed for citizenship and were thus not yet eligible to be drafted. It is estimated that immigrants (some of whom were citizens) made up 20 percent of the Union army. Substitution had been accepted in all previous European and American wars. It was so common that President Lincoln, though overage, tried to set an example by paying for a substitute himself. The Democratic Party, however, made substitution an inflammatory issue. Pointing out that $300 was almost a year's wages for an unskilled laborer, they denounced the draft law (88 percent of Democratic congressmen had voted against it). They appealed to popular resentment by calling it "aristocratic legislation" and to fear, by running headlines such as "Three Hundred Dollars or Your Life."

at the spectacle of wealth in the midst of wartime suffering. Still, some of the new wealth went to good causes. Of the more than $3 million raised by the female volunteers of the United States Sanitary Commission, some came from gala Sanitary Fairs designed to attract those with money to spend.

For most people, however, the war brought the day-to-day hardship of inflation. During the four years of the war, the North suffered an inflation rate of 80 percent, or nearly 15 percent a year. This annual rate, three times what is generally considered tolerable, did much to inflame social tensions. Wages rose only half as much as prices, and workers responded by joining unions and striking. Thirteen occupational groups, among them tailors, coal miners, and railroad engineers, formed unions during the Civil War. Manufacturers, bitterly opposed to unions, freely hired strikebreakers (many of whom were African Americans, women, or immigrants) and formed organizations of their own to prevent further unionization and to blacklist union organizers. Thus both capital and labor moved far beyond the small, localized confrontations of the early industrial period. The formation of large-scale organizations, fostered by wartime demand, laid the groundwork for the national battle between workers and manufacturers that would dominate the last part of the nineteenth century.

As practiced in the local communities, conscription was indeed often marred by favoritism and prejudice. Local officials called up many more poor than rich men and selected a higher proportion of immigrants than non-immigrants. In reality, however, only 7 percent of all men called to serve actually did so. About 25 percent hired a substitute, another 45 percent were exempted for "cause" (usually health reasons), and another 20–25 percent simply failed to report to the community draft office. Nevertheless, by 1863, many northern urban workers believed that the slogan "a rich man's war but a poor man's fight," though coined in the South, applied to them as well.

The New York City Draft Riots

In the spring of 1863, there were protests against the draft throughout the North. Riots and disturbances broke out in many cities, and several federal enrollment officers were killed. The greatest trouble occurred in New York City between July 13 and July 16, 1863, where a wave of working-class looting, fighting, and lynching claimed the lives of 105 people, many of them African American. The rioting, the worst up to that time in American history, was quelled only when five units of the U.S. Army were rushed from the battlefield at Gettysburg, where they had been fighting Confederates the week before.

The riots had several causes. Anger at the draft and racial prejudice were what most contemporaries saw. From a historical perspective, however, the riots were at least as much about the urban growth and tensions described in Chapter 13. The Civil War made urban problems worse and heightened the visible contrast between the lives of the rich and those of the poor. These tensions exploded, but were not solved, during those hot days in the summer of 1863.

Ironically, African American men, a favorite target of the rioters' anger, were a major force in easing the national crisis over the draft. Though they had been barred from service until 1863, in the later stages of the war, African American volunteers filled much of the manpower gap that the controversial draft was meant to address.

The Failure of Southern Nationalism

The war brought even greater changes to the South. As in the North, war needs led to expansion and centralization of government control over the economy. In many cases, Jefferson Davis himself initiated government control (over railroads, shipping, and war production, for example), often in the face of protest or inaction by governors who favored states' rights. The expansion of government brought sudden urbanization, a new experience for the predominantly rural South. The population of Richmond, the Confederate capital, almost tripled, in large part because the Confederate bureaucracy grew to 70,000 people. Because of the need for military manpower, a good part of the Confederate bureaucracy consisted of women, who were referred to as "government girls." All of this—government control, urban growth, women in the paid workforce—was new to Southerners, and not all of it was welcomed.

Even more than in the North, the voracious need for soldiers fostered class antagonisms. When small yeoman farmers went off to war, their wives and families struggled to farm on their own, without the help of mechanization, which they could not afford, and without the help of slaves, which they had never owned. But wealthy men could be exempted from the draft if they had more than twenty slaves. Furthermore, many upper-class Southerners—at least 50,000—avoided military service by paying liberally ($5,000 and more) for substitutes. In the face of these inequities, desertions from the Confederate army soared.

Worst of all was the starvation. The North's blockade and the breakdown of the South's transportation system restricted the availability of food in the South, and these problems were vastly magnified by runaway inflation. Prices in the South rose by an unbelievable 9,000 percent from 1861 to 1865. Speculation and hoarding by the rich made matters even worse. In the spring of 1863, food riots broke out in four Georgia cities (Atlanta among

them) and in North Carolina. In Richmond, more than a thousand people, mostly women, broke into bakeries and snatched loaves of bread, crying "Bread! Bread! Our children are starving while the rich roll in wealth!" When the bread riot threatened to turn into general looting, Jefferson Davis himself appealed to the crowd to disperse—but found he had to threaten the rioters with gunfire before they would leave. A year later, Richmond stores sold eggs for $6 a dozen and butter for $25 a pound. One woman wept, "My God! How can I pay such prices? I have seven children; what shall I do?"

Increasingly, the ordinary people of the South, preoccupied with staying alive, refused to pay taxes, to provide food, or to serve in the army. Soldiers were drawn home by the desperation of their families as well as by the discouraging course of the war. By January 1865, the desertion rate had climbed to 8 percent a month.

At the same time, the life of the southern ruling class was irrevocably altered by the changing nature of slavery. By the end of the war, one-quarter of all slaves had fled to the Union lines, and those who remained often stood in a different relationship to their owners. As white masters and overseers left to join the army, white women were left behind on the plantation to cope with shortages, grow crops, and manage the labor of slaves. Lacking the patriarchal authority of their husbands, white women found that white-black relationships shifted, sometimes drastically (as when slaves fled) and sometimes more subtly. Slaves increasingly made their own decisions about when and how they would work, and they refused to accept the punishments that would have accompanied this insubordination in prewar years. One black woman, implored by her mistress not to reveal the location of a trunk of money and silver plate when the invading Yankees arrived, looked her in the eye and said, "Mistress, I can't lie over that; you bought that silver plate when you sold my three children."

Peace movements in the South were motivated by a confused mixture of realism, war weariness, and the animosity of those who supported states' rights and opposed Jefferson Davis. The anti-Davis faction was led by his own vice president, Alexander Stephens, who early in 1864, suggested a negotiated peace. Peace sentiment was especially strong in North Carolina, where more than a hundred public meetings in support of negotiations were held in the summer of 1863. Davis would have none of it, and he commanded enough votes in the Confederate Congress to enforce his will and to suggest that peace sentiment was traitorous.

THE TIDE TURNS

As Lincoln's timin of the Emancipation Proclamation showed, by 1863 the nature of the war was changing. The proclamation freeing the slaves struck directly at the southern home front and the civilian workforce.

That same year, the nature of the battlefield war changed as well. The Civil War became the first total war.

The Turning Point of 1863

In the summer of 1863, the moment finally arrived when the North could begin to hope for victory. But for the Union army, the year opened with stalemate in the East and slow and costly progress in the West. For the South, 1863 represented its highest hopes for military success and for diplomatic recognition by Britain or France.

Attempting to break the stalemate in northern Virginia, General Joseph "Fighting Joe" Hooker and a Union army of 130,000 men attacked a Confederate army half that size at Chancellorsville in May. In response, Robert E. Lee daringly divided his forces, sending General Thomas "Stonewall" Jackson and 30,000 men on a day-long flanking movement that caught the Union troops by surprise. Although Jackson was killed (shot by his own men by mistake), Chancellorsville was a great Confederate victory; there were 17,000 Union losses. However, Confederate losses were also great: 13,000 men, representing more than 20 percent of Lee's army.

Though weakened, Lee moved to the attack. In June, in his second and most dangerous single thrust into Union territory, he moved north into Maryland and Pennsylvania. His purpose was as much political as military: he hoped that a great Confederate victory would lead Britain and France to intervene in the war and demand a negotiated peace. The ensuing Battle of Gettysburg, July 1–3, 1863, was another horrible slaughter. On the last day, Lee sent 15,000 men, commanded by George Pickett, to attack the heavily defended Union center. The charge was suicidal. When the Union forces opened fire at 700 yards, one southern officer reported, "Pickett's division just seemed to melt away. . . . Nothing but stragglers came back."

Lee retreated from the field, leaving more than one-third of his army behind—28,000 men killed, wounded, or missing. Union general George Meade elected not to pursue with his battered Union army (23,000 casualties). "We had them in our grasp," Lincoln said in bitter frustration. "We had only to stretch forth our arms and they were ours. And nothing I could say or do could make the Army move." Nevertheless, Lee's great gamble had failed; he never again mounted a major offensive (see Map 16.4).

The next day, July 4, 1863, Ulysses S. Grant took Vicksburg, Mississippi, after a costly siege. The combined news of Gettysburg and Vicksburg dissuaded Britain and France from recognizing the Confederacy and checked the northern peace movement. It also tightened the North's grip on the South, for the Union now controlled the entire Mississippi River. In November, Generals Grant and Sherman broke the Confederate hold on Chattanooga, Tennessee, thereby opening the way to Atlanta.

MAP EXPLORATION

To explore an interactive version of this map, go to
www.prenhall.com/faragher5/map16.4

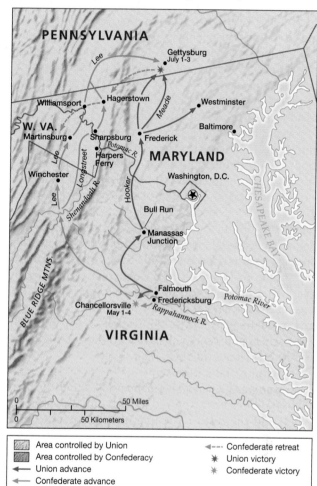

MAP 16.4 The Turning Point: 1863 In June, Lee boldly struck north into Maryland and Pennsylvania, hoping for a victory that would cause Britain and France to demand a negotiated peace on Confederate terms. Instead, he lost the hard-fought battle of Gettysburg, July 1–3. The very next day, Grant's long siege of Vicksburg succeeded. These two great Fourth of July victories turned the tide in favor of the Union. The Confederates never again mounted a major offensive. Total Union control of the Mississippi now exposed the Lower South to attack.

Grant and Sherman

In March 1864, President Lincoln called Grant east and appointed him general-in-chief of all the Union forces. Lincoln's critics were appalled. Grant was an uncouth Westerner (like the president) and (unlike the president) was rumored to have a drinking problem. Lincoln replied that if he knew the general's brand of whiskey, he would send a barrel of it to every commander in the Union army.

Grant devised a plan of strangulation and annihilation. While he took on Lee in northern Virginia, he sent General William Tecumseh Sherman to defeat Confederate general Joe Johnston's Army of Tennessee, which was defending the approach to Atlanta. Both Grant and Sherman exemplified the new kind of warfare. They aimed to inflict maximum damage on the fabric of southern life, hoping that the South would choose to surrender rather than face total destruction. This decision to broaden the war so that it directly affected civilians was new in American military history, and prefigured the total wars of the twentieth century.

In northern Virginia, Grant pursued a policy of destroying civilian supplies. He said he "regarded it as humane to both sides to protect the persons of those found at their homes, but to consume everything that could be used to support or supply armies." One of those supports was slaves. Grant welcomed fleeing slaves to Union lines and encouraged army efforts to put them to work or enlist them as soldiers. He also cooperated with the efforts of groups like the New England Freedmen's Aid Society, which sent northern volunteers (many of them women) into Union-occupied parts of the South to educate former slaves. The Freedmen's Bureau, authorized by Congress in March 1865, continued this work into Reconstruction. One of the northern teachers who went south in 1866 to work for the bureau was Robert Fitzgerald, the former soldier.

The most famous example of the new strategy of total war was General Sherman's 1864 march through Georgia. Sherman captured Atlanta on September 2, 1864, and the rest of Georgia now lay open to him. Gloom enveloped the South. "Since Atlanta I have felt as if all were dead within me, forever," Mary Boykin Chesnut wrote in her diary. "We are going to be wiped off the earth" (see Map 16.5).

In November, Sherman set out to march the 285 miles to the coastal city of Savannah, living off the land and destroying everything in his path. His military purpose was to tighten the noose around Robert E. Lee's army in northern Virginia by cutting off Mississippi, Alabama, and Georgia from the rest of the Confederacy. But his second purpose, openly stated, was to "make war so terrible" to the people of the South, to "make them so sick of war that generations would pass away before they would again appeal to it." Accordingly, he told his men to seize, burn, or destroy everything in their path (but, significantly, not to harm civilians).

It was estimated that Sherman's army did $100 million worth of damage. "They say no living thing is found in Sherman's track," Mary Boykin Chesnut wrote, "only chimneys, like telegraph poles, to carry the news of [his] attack backwards." (See Out of Many Voices: A Georgia Plantation Mistress Laments Her Losses.)

Terrifying to white southern civilians, Sherman was initially hostile to black Southerners as well. In the interests of speed and efficiency, his army turned away many of the 18,000 slaves who flocked to it in Georgia, causing a number to be recaptured and reenslaved. This callous action caused such a scandal in Washington that Secretary of War Edwin Stanton arranged a special meeting in Georgia with Sherman and twenty African American ministers who spoke for the freed slaves. This meeting in itself was extraordinary: no one had ever before asked slaves what they wanted. Equally extraordinary was Sherman's response in Special Field Order 15, issued in January 1865: he set aside more than 400,000 acres of Confederate land to be given to the freed slaves in forty-acre parcels. This was war of a kind that white Southerners had never imagined.

Far to the North, a much smaller unimaginable event occurred in October, when twenty-six Confederate sympathizers invaded St. Albans, Vermont, robbing three banks, setting fires, killing a man—and then escaping over the border into Canada. When a Montreal magistrate released the men on a technicality, American military authorities threatened retaliation if Canadian authorities ever again allowed such an event. The St. Albans inci-

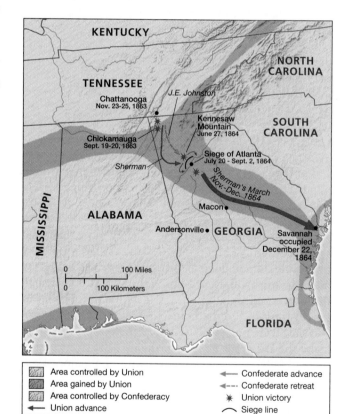

MAP 16.5 Sherman's Campaign in Georgia, 1864
Ulysses S. Grant and William Tecumseh Sherman, two like-minded generals, commanded the Union's armies in the final push to victory. While Grant hammered away at Lee in northern Virginia, Sherman captured Atlanta in September (a victory that may have been vital to Lincoln's reelection) and began his March to the Sea in November 1864.

OUT OF MANY VOICES

A GEORGIA PLANTATION MISTRESS LAMENTS HER LOSSES

Dolly Burge, a widowed Georgia slaveowner, describes what happened when Sherman's Army reached her plantation on November 19, 1864.

[L]IKE DEMONS THEY [SHERMAN'S TROOPS] RUSH in! My yards are full. To my smokehouse, my dairy, pantry, kitchen, and cellar, like famished wolves they come, breaking locks and whatever is in their way. The thousand pounds of meat in my smoke-house is gone in a twinkling, my flour, my meat, my lard, butter, eggs, pickles of various kinds—both in vinegar and brine—wine, jars, and jugs are all gone. My eighteen fat turkeys, my hens, chickens, and fowls, my young pigs, are shot down in my yard and hunted as if they were rebels themselves. Utterly powerless I ran out and appealed to the guard.

"I cannot help you, Madam; it is orders."

Alas! little did I think while trying to save my house from plunder and fire that they were forcing my boys [her young male slaves] from home at the point of the bayonet. One, Newton, jumped into bed in his cabin, and declared himself sick. Another crawled under the floor—a lame boy he was,—but they pulled him out, placed him on a horse, and drove him off . . . James Arnold, in trying to escape from a back window, was captured and marched off. Henry, too, was taken; I know not how or when, but probably when he and Bob went after the mules. I had not believed they would force from their homes the poor, doomed negroes, but such has been the fact here, cursing them and saying that "Jeff Davis wanted to put them in his army, but that they should not fight for him, but for the Union." No! Indeed no! They are not friends to the slave. We have never made the poor, cowardly negro fight, and it is strange, passing strange, that the all-powerful Yankee nation with the whole world to back them, their ports open, their armies filled with soldiers from all nations, should at last take the poor negro to help them out against this little Confederacy which was to have been brought back into the Union in sixty days' time!

My poor boys! My poor boys! What unknown trials are before you! How you have clung to your mistress and assisted her in every way you knew. ■

SOURCE: *A Woman's Wartime Journal: An Account of the Passage over Georgia's Plantation of Sherman's Army on the March to the Sea, as Recorded in the Diary of Dolly Sumner Lunt (Mrs. Thomas Burge)* (Electronic Edition, Davis Library, University of North Carolina at Chapel Hill, www.docsouth.unc.edu/burge/lunt.html).

dent, minor in itself, caused both the British government and Canadian officials to think seriously about how to defend against the possibility of future American invasions. The answer was obvious: the Canadian provinces, which by 1860 stretched from one coast to the other, would need to be united. In 1867, all of the Canadian provinces joined in confederation and henceforth were known as the Dominion of Canada. In this way, a small Confederate pinprick helped to foster the unity of America's large northern neighbor.

The 1864 Election

The war complicated the 1864 presidential election. Lincoln was renominated during a period when the war was going badly. Opposed by the Radicals, who thought he was too conciliatory toward the South, and by Republican conservatives, who disapproved of the Emancipation Proclamation, Lincoln had little support within his own party.

In contrast, the Democrats had an appealing candidate: General George McClellan, a war hero (always a favorite with American voters) who was known to be sympathetic to the South. Democrats played shamelessly on the racist fears of the urban working class, accusing Republicans of being "negro-lovers" and warning that racial mixing lay ahead.

A deeply depressed Lincoln fully expected to lose the election. "I am going to be beaten," he told an army officer in August 1864, "and unless some great change takes place badly beaten." A great change did take place: Sherman captured Atlanta on September 2. Jubilation swept the North: some cities celebrated with 100-gun salutes. Lincoln won the election with 55 percent of the popular vote. Seventy-eight percent of the soldiers voted for him rather than for their former commander. The vote probably saved the Republican Party from extinction. Ordinary people and war-weary soldiers had voted to continue a difficult and divisive conflict. The election was important evidence of northern support for Lincoln's policy of unconditional surrender for the South. There would be no negotiated peace; the war would continue.

Nearing the End

As Sherman devastated the lower South, Grant was locked in struggle with Lee in northern Virginia. Grant did not favor subtle strategies. He bluntly said, "The art of war is simple enough. Find out where your enemy is. Get at him as soon as you can. Strike at him as hard as you can, and keep moving on." Following this plan, Grant eventually hammered Lee into submission, but at enormous cost. Lee had learned the art of defensive warfare (his troops called him "the King of Spades" because he made them dig trenches so often), and he inflicted heavy losses on the Union army in a succession of bloody encounters in the spring and summer of 1864: almost 18,000 at the battle of the Wilderness, more than 8,000 at Spotsylvania, and 12,000 at Cold Harbor. At Cold Harbor, Union troops wrote their names and addresses on scraps of paper and pinned them to their backs, so certain were they of being killed or wounded in battle. Grim and terrible as Grant's strategy was, it proved effective. Rather than pulling back after his failed assaults, he kept moving South, finally settling in for a prolonged siege of Lee's forces at Petersburg. The North's great advantage in population finally began to tell. There were more Union soldiers to replace those lost in battle, but there were no more white Confederates (see Map 16.6).

In desperation, the South turned to what had hitherto been unthinkable: arming slaves to serve as soldiers in the Confederate army. As Jefferson Davis said in February 1865, "We are reduced to choosing whether the negroes shall fight for or against us." But—and this was the bitter irony—the African American soldiers and their families would have to be promised freedom or they would desert to the Union at the first chance they had. Even though Davis's proposal had the support of General Robert E. Lee, the Confederate Congress balked at first. As one member said, the idea was "revolting to Southern sentiment, Southern pride, and Southern honor." Another candidly admitted, "If slaves make good soldiers our whole theory of slavery is wrong." Finally, on March 13, the Confederate Congress authorized a draft of black soldiers—without mentioning freedom. Although two regiments of African American soldiers were immediately organized in Richmond, it was too late. The South never had to publicly acknowledge the paradox of having to offer slaves freedom so that they would fight to defend slavery.

By the spring of 1865, public support for the war simply disintegrated in the South. Starvation, inflation, dissension, and the prospect of military defeat were too much. In February, Jefferson Davis sent his vice president, Alexander Stephens, to negotiate terms at a peace conference at Hampton Roads. Lincoln would not countenance anything less than full surrender, although he did offer gradual emancipation with compensation for slave owners. Davis, however, insisted on southern independence at all costs. Consequently, the Hampton Roads conference failed and southern resistance faded away. In March 1865, Mary Boykin Chesnut recorded in her diary: "I am sure our army is silently dispersing. Men are going the wrong way all the time. They slip by now with no songs nor shouts. They have given the thing up."

Appomattox

Grant's hammering tactics worked—slowly. In the spring of 1865, Lee and his remaining troops, outnumbered two to one, still held Petersburg and Richmond. Starving, short of ammunition, and losing men in battle or to desertion every day, Lee retreated from Petersburg on April 2. The Confederate government fled Richmond, stripping

This striking photograph by Thomas C. Roche shows a dead Confederate soldier, killed at Petersburg on April 3, 1865, only six days before the surrender at Appomattox. The new medium of photography conveyed the horror of the war with a gruesome reality to the American public.
SOURCE: Courtesy of the Library of Congress.

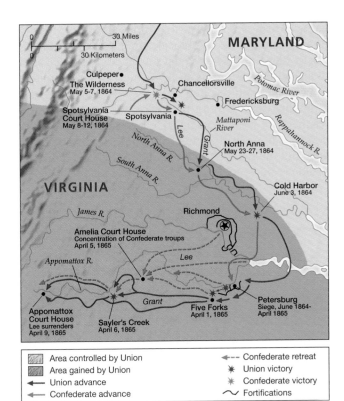

MAP 16.6 The Final Battles in Virginia 1864–65 In the war's final phase early in 1865, Sherman closed one arm of a pincers by marching north from Savannah, while Grant attacked Lee's last defensive positions in Petersburg and Richmond. Lee retreated from them on April 2 and surrendered at Appomattox Court House on April 9, 1865.

and burning the city. Seven days later, Lee and his 25,000 troops surrendered to Grant at Appomattox Court House. Grant treated Lee with great respect and set a historic precedent by giving the Confederate troops parole. This meant they could not subsequently be prosecuted for treason. Grant then sent the starving army on its way with three days' rations for every man. Jefferson Davis, who had hoped to set up a new government in Texas, was captured in Georgia on May 10. The war was finally over.

Death of a President

Sensing that the war was near its end, Abraham Lincoln visited Grant's troops when Lee withdrew from Petersburg on April 2. Thus it was that Lincoln came to visit Richmond, and to sit briefly in Jefferson Davis's presidential office, soon after Davis had left it. As Lincoln walked the streets of the burned and pillaged city, black people poured out to see him and surround him, shouting "Glory to God! Glory! Glory! Glory!" Lincoln in turn, said to Admiral David Porter:

"Thank God I have lived to see this. It seems to me that I have been dreaming a horrid dream for four years, and now the nightmare is gone." Lincoln had only the briefest time to savor the victory. On the night of April 14, President and Mrs. Lincoln went to Ford's Theater in Washington. There, Lincoln was shot at point-blank range by John Wilkes Booth, a Confederate sympathizer. He died the next day. For the people of the Union, the joy of victory was muted by mourning for their great leader. After a week of observances in Washington, Lincoln's coffin was loaded on a funeral train that slowly carried him back to Springfield. All along the railroad route, day and night, in small towns and large, people gathered to see the train pass and to pay their last respects. At that moment, the Washington community and the larger Union community were one and the same.

The nation as a whole was left with Lincoln's vision for the coming peace, expressed in the unforgettable words of his Second Inaugural Address:

> With malice toward none, with charity for all, with firmness in the right as God gives us to see the right, let us strive on to finish the work we are in, to bind up the nation's wounds, to care for him who shall have borne the battle and for his widow and his orphan, to do all which may achieve and cherish a just and lasting peace among ourselves and with all nations.

Abraham Lincoln toured Richmond, the Confederate capital, just hours after Jefferson Davis had fled. This photograph, taken April 4, 1865, shows Yankee cavalry horses in the foreground, and the smoldering city in the background. It gives a sense of the devastation suffered by the South and the immense task of rebuilding and reconciliation that Lincoln did not live to accomplish.

SOURCE: Library of Congress.

CONCLUSION

In 1865, a divided people had been forcibly reunited by battle. Their nation, the United States of America, had been permanently changed by civil war. Devastating losses among the young men of the country—the greatest such losses the nation was ever to suffer—would affect not only their families but all of postwar society. Politically, the deepest irony of the Civil War was that only by fighting it had America become completely a nation. For it was the war that broke down local isolation. Ordinary citizens in local communities, North and South, developed a national perspective as they sent their sons and brothers to be soldiers, their daughters to be nurses and teachers. Then, too, the federal government, vastly strengthened by wartime necessity, reached the lives of ordinary citizens more than ever before. The question now was whether this strengthened but divided national community, forged in battle, could create a just peace.

CHRONOLOGY

1861
March: Morrill Tariff Act

April: Fort Sumter falls; war begins

April: Mobilization begins

April–May: Virginia, Arkansas, Tennessee, and North Carolina secede

June: United States Sanitary Commission established

July: First Battle of Bull Run

December: French troops arrive in Mexico, followed by British and Spanish forces in January.

1862
February: Legal Tender Act

February: Battles of Fort Henry and Fort Donelson

March: Battle of Pea Ridge

March: Battle of the *Monitor* and the *Merrimack* (renamed the *Virginia*)

March–August: George B. McClellan's Peninsular campaign

March: Battle of Glorieta Pass

April: Battle of Shiloh

April: Confederate Conscription Act

April: David Farragut captures New Orleans

May: *Cinqo de Mayo*: Mexican troops repel Franch invaders

May: Homestead Act

June–July: Seven Days Battles

July: Pacific Railway Act

July: Morrill Land Grant Act

August: Santee Sioux Uprising, Minnesota

September: Battle of Antietam

December: Battle of Fredericksburg

1863
January: Emancipation Proclamation

February: National Bank Act

March: Draft introduced in the North

March: Colonel Kit Carson sends 8,000 Navajos on the "Long Walk" to Bosque Redondo, New Mexico Territory

April: Richmond bread riot

May: Battle of Chancellorsville

June: French occupy Mexico City

July: Battle of Gettysburg

July: Surrender of Vicksburg

July: New York City Draft Riots

November: Battle of Chattanooga

November: Union troops capture Brownsville, Texas

1864
March: Ulysses S. Grant becomes general-in-chief of Union forces

April: Fort Pillow massacre

May: Battle of the Wilderness

May: Battle of Spotsylvania

June: Battle of Cold Harbor

June: Maximilian becomes Emperor of Mexico

September: Atlanta falls

October: St. Albans incident

November: Abraham Lincoln reelected president

November–December: William Tecumseh Sherman's March to the Sea

1865
April: Richmond falls

April: Robert E. Lee surrenders at Appomattox

April: Lincoln assassinated

December: Thirteenth Amendment to the Constitution becomes law

REVIEW QUESTIONS

1. At the outset of the Civil War, what were the relative advantages of the North and the South, and how did they affect the final outcome?

2. In the absence of the southern Democrats, in the early 1860s, the new Republican Congress was able to pass a number of party measures with little opposition. What do these measures tell you about the historical roots of the Republican Party? More generally, how do you think we should view legislation passed in the absence of the customary opposition, debate, and compromise?

3. The greatest problem facing Jefferson Davis and the Confederacy was the need to develop a true feeling of nationalism. Can the failure of this effort be blamed on Davis's weakness as a leader alone, or are there other causes?

4. In what ways can it be said that the actions of African Americans, both slave and free, came to determine the course of the Civil War?

5. Wars always have unexpected consequences. List some of those consequences both for soldiers and for civilians in the North and in the South.

6. Today, Abraham Lincoln is considered one of our greatest presidents, but he did not enjoy such approval at the time. List some of the contemporary criticisms of Lincoln, and evaluate them.

RECOMMENDED READING

Edward Ayers, *In the Presence of Mine Enemies: War in the Heart of America, 1859–1863* (2003). A study of two counties, one Confederate, one Union, in the war.

Joan Cashin, ed., *The War Was You and Me: Civilians in the American Civil War* (2002). Focuses on the connections between the front line and the home front.

Paul A. Cimbala and Randall M. Miller, *Union Soldiers and the Northern Home Front: Wartime Experiences, Postwar Adjustments* (2002). The effects of the Civil War on ordinary people.

Laura F. Edwards, *Scarlett Doesn't Live Here Anymore: Southern Women in the Civil War Era* (2000). A brief but comprehensive survey.

Paul Escott, *After Secession: Jefferson Davis and the Failure of Confederate Nationalism* (1978). A thoughtful study of Davis's record as president of the Confederacy.

Drew Gilpin Faust, *Mothers of Invention: Women of the Slaveholding South in the American Civil War* (1996). A major study that considers the importance of gender at the white South's "moment of truth."

Bryan and Nelson Langford, eds., *Eye of the Storm: A Civil War Odyssey* (2000). The richly illustrated diary of a Union soldier, including his captivity at Andersonville.

James M. Mc Pherson, *Battle Cry of Freedom: The Civil War Era* (1988). An acclaimed, highly readable synthesis of much scholarship on the war.

———, *The Atlas of the Civil War* (1994). Detailed battle diagrams with clear descriptions.

Pauli Murray, *Proud Shoes: The Story of an American Family* (1956). Murray tells the proud story of her African American family and her grandfather, Robert Fitzgerald.

Phillip Shaw Paludan, *"A People's Contest": The Union at War, 1861–1865* (1988). A highly successful social history of the North during the war.

Nina Silbar, *Daughters of the Union: Northern Women Fight the Civil War* (2005). Argues that women found a new sense of self and citizenship in wartime.

John David Smith, ed. *Black Soldiers in Blue: African American Troops in the Civil War Era* (2002). Fourteen essays on many different aspects of military service.

David Williams, Teresa Crisp Williams, and David Carlson, *Plain Folk in a Rich Man's War: Class and Dissent in Confederate Georgia* (2002). Focus on class divisions during the war.

Keith P. Wilson, *Campfires of Freedom: The Camp Life of Black Soldiers During the Civil War* (2002). Camp life examined to show the soldiers' personal transition from slavery to freedom.

 For additional study resources for this chapter, go to the *Companion Website,* **http://www.prenhall.com/faragher.**

Reconstruction

1863–1877

CHAPTER OUTLINE

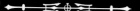

Hale County, Alabama: From Slavery to Freedom in a Black Belt Community

On a bright Saturday morning in May 1867, 4,000 former slaves eagerly streamed into the town of Greensboro, bustling seat of Hale County in west-central Alabama. They came to hear speeches from two delegates to a recent freedmen's convention in Mobile and to find out about the political status of black people under the Reconstruction Act just passed by Congress. Tensions mounted in the days following this unprecedented gathering, as military authorities began supervising voter registration for elections to the upcoming constitutional convention that would rewrite the laws of Alabama. On June 13, John Orrick, a local white, confronted Alex Webb, a politically active freedman, on the streets of Greensboro. Webb had recently been appointed a voter registrar for the district. Orrick swore he would never be registered by a black man, and shot Webb dead. Hundreds of armed and angry freedmen formed a posse to search for Orrick, but failed to find him. Galvanized by Webb's murder, 500 local freedmen formed a chapter of the Union League, the Republican Party's organizational arm in the South. The chapter functioned as both a militia company and a forum to agitate for political rights.

Violent political encounters between black people and white people were common in Southern communities in the wake of the Civil War. Communities throughout the South struggled over the meaning of freedom in ways that reflected their particular circumstances. The 4 million freed people constituted roughly one-third of the total Southern population, but the black–white ratio in individual communities varied enormously. In some places, the Union army had been a strong presence during the war, hastening the collapse of the slave system and encouraging experiments in free labor. Other areas had remained relatively untouched by the fighting. In some areas, small farms prevailed; in others, including Hale County, large plantations dominated economic and political life.

West-central Alabama had emerged as a fertile center of cotton production just two decades before the Civil War. There, African Americans, as throughout the South's black belt, constituted more than three-quarters of the population. With the arrival of federal troops in the spring of 1865, African Americans in Hale County, like their counterparts elsewhere, began to challenge the traditional organization of plantation labor.

One owner, Henry Watson, found that his entire workforce had deserted him at the end of 1865. "I am in the midst of a large and fertile cotton growing country," Watson wrote to a partner. "Many plantations are entirely without labor, many plantations have insufficient labor, and upon none are the laborers doing their former accustomed work." Black women refused to work in the fields, preferring to stay home with their children and tend garden plots. Nor would male field hands do any work, such as caring for hogs, that did not directly increase their share of the cotton crop.

Above all, freed people wanted more autonomy. Overseers and owners thus grudgingly allowed them to work the land "in families," letting them choose their own supervisors and find their own provisions. The result was a shift from the gang labor characteristic of the antebellum period,

Greensboro

in which large groups of slaves worked under the harsh and constant supervision of white overseers, to the sharecropping system, in which African American families worked small plots of land in exchange for a small share of the crop. This shift represented less of a victory for newly freed African Americans than a defeat for plantation owners, who resented even the limited economic independence it forced them to concede to their black workforce.

Only a small fraction—perhaps 15 percent—of African American families were fortunate enough to be able to buy land. The majority settled for some version of sharecropping, while others managed to rent land from owners, becoming tenant farmers. Still, planters throughout Hale County had to change the old routines of plantation labor. Local African Americans also organized politically. In 1866, Congress had passed the Civil Rights Act and sent the Fourteenth Amendment to the Constitution to the states for ratification; both promised full citizenship rights to former slaves. Hale County freedmen joined the Republican Party and local Union League chapters. They used their new political power to press for better labor contracts, demand greater autonomy for the black workforce, and agitate for the more radical goal of land confiscation and redistribution. "The colored people are very anxious to get land of their own to live upon independently; and they want money to buy stock to make crops," reported one black Union League organizer. "The only way to get these necessaries is to give our votes to the [Republican] party." Two Hale County former slaves, Brister Reese and James K. Green, won election to the Alabama state legislature in 1869.

It was not long before these economic and political gains prompted a white counterattack. In the spring of 1868, the Ku Klux Klan—a secret organization devoted to terrorizing and intimidating African Americans and their white Republican allies—came to Hale County. Disguised in white sheets, armed with guns and whips, and making nighttime raids on horseback, Klansmen flogged, beat, and murdered freed people. They intimidated voters and silenced political activists. Planters used Klan terror to dissuade former slaves from leaving plantations or organizing for higher wages.

With the passage of the Ku Klux Klan Act in 1871, the federal government cracked down on the Klan, breaking its power temporarily in parts of the former Confederacy. But no serious effort was made to stop Klan terror in the west Alabama black belt, and planters there succeeded in reestablishing much of their social and political control.

The events in Hale County illustrate the struggles that beset communities throughout the South during the Reconstruction era after the Civil War. The destruction of slavery and the Confederacy forced African Americans and white people to renegotiate their old economic and political roles. These community battles both shaped and were shaped by the victorious and newly expansive federal government in Washington. In the end, Reconstruction was only partially successful. Not until the "Second Reconstruction" of the twentieth-century civil rights movement would the descendants of Hale County's African Americans begin to enjoy the full fruits of freedom—and even then not without challenge.

KEY TOPICS

- Competing political plans for reconstructing the defeated Confederacy
- Difficult transition from slavery to freedom for African Americans
- The political and social legacy of Reconstruction in the Southern states
- Post–Civil War transformations in the economic and political life of the North

THE POLITICS OF RECONSTRUCTION

When General Robert E. Lee's men stacked their guns at Appomattox, the bloodiest war in American history ended. More than 600,000 soldiers had died during the four years of fighting, 360,000 Union and 260,000 Confederate. Another 275,000 Union and 190,000 Confederate troops had been wounded. Although President Abraham Lincoln insisted early on that the purpose of the war was to preserve the Union, by 1863, it had evolved as well into a struggle for African American liberation. Indeed, the political, economic, and moral issues posed by slavery were the root cause of the Civil War, and the war ultimately destroyed slavery, although not racism, once and for all.

The Civil War also settled the Constitutional crisis provoked by the secession of the Confederacy and its justification in appeals to states' rights. The name "United States" would from now on be understood as a singular rather than a plural noun, signaling an important change in the meaning of American nationality. The old notion of the United States as a voluntary union of sovereign states gave way to the new reality of a single nation, in which the federal government took precedence over the individual states. The key historical developments of the Reconstruction era revolved around precisely how the newly strengthened national government would define its relationship with the defeated Confederate states and the 4 million newly freed slaves.

The Defeated South

The white South paid an extremely high price for secession, war, and defeat. In addition to the battlefield casualties, the Confederate states sustained deep material and psychological wounds. Much of the best agricultural land lay waste, including the rich fields of northern Virginia, the Shenandoah Valley, and large sections of Tennessee, Mississippi, Georgia, and South Carolina. Many towns and cities—including Richmond, Atlanta, and Columbia, South Carolina—were in ruins. By 1865, the South's most precious commodities, cotton and African American slaves, no longer were measures of wealth and prestige. Retreating Confederates destroyed most of the South's cotton to prevent its capture by federal troops. What remained was confiscated by Union agents as contraband of war. The former slaves, many of whom had fled to Union lines during the latter stages of the war, were determined to chart their own course in the reconstructed South as free men and women.

It would take the South's economy a generation to overcome the severe blows dealt by the war. In 1860, the South held roughly 25 percent of the nation's wealth; a decade later it controlled only 12 percent. Many white Southerners resented their conquered status, and white notions of race, class, and "honor" died hard. A white North Carolinian, for example, who had lost almost everything dear to him in the war—his sons, home, and slaves—recalled in 1865 that in spite of all his tragedy he still retained one thing. "They've left me one inestimable privilege—to hate 'em. I git up at half-past four in the morning, and sit up till twelve at night, to hate 'em."

Emancipation proved the most bitter pill for white Southerners to swallow, especially the planter elite. Conquered and degraded, and in their view robbed of their slave property, white people responded by regarding African Americans more than ever as inferior to themselves. In the antebellum South, white skin had defined a social bond

Decorating the Graves of Rebel Soldiers, *Harper's Weekly,* August 17, 1867. After the Civil War, both Southerners and Northerners created public mourning ceremonies honoring fallen soldiers. Women led the memorial movement in the South which, by establishing cemeteries and erecting monuments, offered the first cultural expression of the Confederate tradition. This engraving depicts citizens of Richmond, Virginia, decorating thousands of Confederate graves with flowers at the Hollywood Memorial Cemetery on the James River. A local women's group raised enough funds to transfer over 16,000 Confederate dead from Northern cemeteries for reburial in Richmond.

SOURCE: The Granger Collection, New York.

that transcended economic class. It gave even the lowliest poor white a badge of superiority over even the most skilled slave or prosperous free African American. Emancipation, however, forced white people to redefine their world. The specter of political power and social equality for African Americans made racial order the consuming passion of most white Southerners during the Reconstruction years. In fact, racism can be seen as one of the major forces driving Reconstruction and, ultimately, undermining it.

Abraham Lincoln's Plan

By late 1863, Union military victories had convinced President Lincoln of the need to fashion a plan for the reconstruction of the South (see Chapter 16). Lincoln based his reconstruction program on bringing the seceded states back into the Union as quickly as possible. He was determined to respect private property (except in the case of slave property), and he opposed imposing harsh punishments for rebellion. His Proclamation of Amnesty and Reconstruction of December 1863 offered "full pardon" and the restoration of property, not including slaves, to white Southerners willing to swear an oath of allegiance to the United States and its laws, including the Emancipation Proclamation. Prominent Confederate military and civil leaders were excluded from Lincoln's offer, though he indicated that he would freely pardon them.

The president also proposed that when the number of any Confederate state's voters who took the oath of allegiance reached 10 percent of the number who had voted in the election of 1860, this group could establish a state government that Lincoln would recognize as legitimate. Fundamental to this Ten Percent Plan was acceptance by the reconstructed governments of the abolition of slavery. Lincoln's plan was designed less as a blueprint for Reconstruction than as a way to shorten the war and gain white people's support for emancipation. It angered those Republicans—known as Radical Republicans—who advocated not only equal rights for the freedmen but a tougher stance toward the white South.

In July 1864, Senator Benjamin F. Wade of Ohio and Congressman Henry W. Davis of Maryland, both Radicals, proposed a harsher alternative to the Ten Percent Plan. The Wade-Davis bill required 50 percent of a seceding state's white male citizens to take a loyalty oath before elections could be held for a convention to rewrite the state's constitution. The bill also guaranteed equality before the law (although not suffrage) for former slaves. Unlike the president, the Radical Republicans saw Reconstruction as a chance to effect a fundamental transformation of Southern society. They thus wanted to delay the process until war's end and to limit participation to a small number of Southern Unionists. Lincoln viewed Reconstruction as part of the larger effort to win the war and abolish slavery. He wanted to weaken the Confederacy by creating new state governments that could win broad support from Southern white people. The Wade-Davis bill threatened his efforts to build political consensus within the Southern states, and Lincoln therefore pocket-vetoed it, by refusing to sign it within ten days of the adjournment of Congress.

Redistribution of Southern land among former slaves posed another thorny issue for Lincoln, Congress, and federal military officers. As Union armies occupied parts of the South, commanders had improvised a variety of arrangements involving confiscated plantations and the African American labor force. For example, in 1862, General Benjamin F. Butler began a policy of transforming slaves on Louisiana sugar plantations into wage laborers under the close supervision of occupying federal troops. Butler's policy required slaves to remain on the estates of loyal planters, where they would receive wages according to a fixed schedule, as well as food and medical care for the aged and sick. Abandoned plantations would be leased to Northern investors. By 1864, some 50,000 African American laborers on nearly 1,500 Louisiana estates worked either directly for the government or for individual planters under contracts supervised by the army.

In January 1865, General William T. Sherman issued Special Field Order 15, setting aside the Sea Islands off the Georgia coast and a portion of the South Carolina low-country rice fields for the exclusive settlement of freed people. Each family would receive forty acres of land and the loan of mules from the army—the origin, perhaps, of the famous call for "forty acres and a mule" that would soon capture the imagination of African Americans throughout the South. Sherman's intent was not to revolutionize Southern society, but to relieve the demands placed on his army by the thousands of impoverished African Americans who followed his march to the sea. By the summer of 1865, some 40,000 freed people, eager to take advantage of the general's order, had been settled on 400,000 acres of "Sherman land."

Conflicts within the Republican Party prevented the development of a systematic land distribution program. Still, Lincoln and the Republican Congress supported other measures to aid the emancipated slaves. In March 1865, Congress established the Freedmen's Bureau. Along with providing food, clothing, and fuel to destitute former slaves, the bureau was charged with supervising and managing "all the abandoned lands in the South and the control of all subjects relating to refugees and freedmen." The act that established the bureau also stated that forty acres of abandoned or confiscated land could be leased to freed slaves or white Unionists, who would have an option to purchase after three years and "such title thereto as the United States can convey."

At the time of Lincoln's assassination, his Reconstruction policy remained unsettled and incomplete. In its broad outlines, the president's plans had seemed to favor a speedy restoration of the Southern states to the

Photography pioneer Timothy O'Sullivan took this portrait of a multigenerational African American family on the J.J. Smith plantation in Beaufort, South Carolina, 1862. Many white plantation owners in the area had fled, allowing slaves like these to begin an early transition to freedom before the end of the Civil War.

SOURCE: Corbis/Bettmann.

Union and a minimum of federal intervention in their affairs. But with his death, the specifics of postwar Reconstruction had to be hammered out by a new president, Andrew Johnson of Tennessee, a man whose personality, political background, and racist leanings put him at odds with the Republican-controlled Congress.

Andrew Johnson and Presidential Reconstruction

Andrew Johnson, a Democrat and former slaveholder, was a most unlikely successor to the martyred Lincoln. By trade a tailor, educated by his wife, Johnson overcame his impoverished background and served as state legislator, governor, and U.S. senator. Throughout his career, Johnson had championed yeoman farmers and viewed the South's plantation aristocrats with contempt. He was the only Southern member of the U.S. Senate to remain loyal to the Union, and he held the planter elite responsible for secession and defeat. In 1862, Lincoln appointed Johnson to the difficult post of military governor of Tennessee. There he successfully began wartime Reconstruction and cultivated Unionist support in the mountainous eastern districts of that state.

In 1864, the Republicans, in an appeal to Northern and border state "War Democrats," nominated Johnson for vice president. But despite Johnson's success in Ten-

nessee and in the 1864 campaign, many Radical Republicans distrusted him, and the hardscrabble Tennessean remained a political outsider in Republican circles. In the immediate aftermath of Lincoln's murder, however, Johnson appeared to side with those Radical Republicans who sought to treat the South as a conquered province. The new president hinted at indicting prominent Confederate officials for treason, disfranchising them, and confiscating their property. Such tough talk appealed to Radical Republicans. But support for Johnson quickly faded as the new president's policies unfolded. Johnson defined Reconstruction as the province of the executive, not the legislative branch, and he planned to restore the Union as quickly as possible. He blamed individual Southerners—the planter elite—rather than entire states for leading the South down the disastrous road to secession. In line with this philosophy, Johnson outlined mild terms for reentry to the Union.

In the spring of 1865, Johnson granted amnesty and pardon, including restoration of property rights except slaves, to all Confederates who pledged loyalty to the Union and support for emancipation. Fourteen classes of Southerners, mostly major Confederate officials and wealthy landowners, were excluded. But these men could apply individually for presidential pardons. During his tenure Johnson pardoned roughly 90 percent of those who applied. Significantly, Johnson instituted this plan while Congress was not in session.

By the fall of 1865, ten of the eleven Confederate states claimed to have met Johnson's requirements to reenter the Union. On December 6, 1865, in his first annual message to Congress, the president declared the "restoration" of the Union virtually complete. But a serious division within the federal government was taking shape, for the Congress was not about to allow the president free rein in determining the conditions of Southern readmission.

Andrew Johnson used the term "restoration" rather than "reconstruction." A lifelong Democrat with ambitions to be elected president on his own in 1868, Johnson hoped to build a new political coalition composed of Northern Democrats, conservative Republicans, and Southern Unionists. Firmly committed to white supremacy, he opposed political rights for the freedmen. Johnson's open sympathy for his fellow white Southerners, his antiblack bias, and his determination to control the course of Reconstruction placed him on a collision course with the powerful Radical wing of the Republican Party.

The Radical Republican Vision

Most Radicals were men whose careers had been shaped by the slavery controversy. At the core of their thinking lay a deep belief in equal political rights and equal economic opportunity, both guaranteed by a powerful national government. They argued that once free labor, universal education, and equal rights were implanted in the South, that region would be able to share in the North's material wealth, progress, and fluid social mobility. Representative George W. Julian of Indiana typified the Radical vision for the South. He called for elimination of the region's "large estates, widely scattered settlements, wasteful agriculture, popular ignorance, social degradation, the decline of manufactures, contempt for honest labor, and a pampered oligarchy." This process would allow Republicans to develop "small farms, thrifty tillage, free schools, social independence, flourishing manufactures and the arts, respect for honest labor, and equality of political rights."

In the Radicals' view, the power of the federal government would be central to the remaking of Southern society, especially in guaranteeing civil rights and suffrage for freedmen. In the most far-reaching proposal, Representative Thaddeus Stevens of Pennsylvania called for the confiscation of 400 million acres belonging to the wealthiest 10 percent of Southerners, to be redistributed to black and white yeomen and Northern land buyers. "The whole fabric of Southern society must be changed," Stevens told Pennsylvania Republicans in September 1865, "and never can it be done if this opportunity is lost. How can republican institutions, free schools, free churches, free social intercourse exist in a mingled community of nabobs and serfs?"

Northern Republicans were especially outraged by the stringent "black codes" passed by South Carolina, Mississippi, Louisiana, and other states. These were designed to restrict the freedom of the black labor force and keep freed people as close to slave status as possible. Laborers who left their jobs before contracts expired would forfeit wages already earned and be subject to arrest by any white citizen. Vagrancy, very broadly defined, was punishable by fines and involuntary plantation labor. Apprenticeship clauses obliged black children to work without pay for employers. Some states attempted to bar African Americans from land ownership. Other laws specifically denied African Americans equality with white people in civil rights, excluding them from juries and prohibiting interracial marriages.

The black codes underscored the unwillingness of white Southerners to accept the full meaning of freedom for African Americans. The Radicals, although not a majority of their party, were joined by moderate Republicans, as growing numbers of Northerners grew suspicious of white Southern intransigence and the denial of political rights to freedmen. When the Thirty-ninth Congress convened in December 1865, the large Republican majority prevented the seating of the white Southerners elected to Congress under President Johnson's provisional state governments. Republicans also established the Joint Committee on Reconstruction. After hearing extensive testimony from a broad range of witnesses, it concluded that not only were old Confederates back in power in the South but that black codes and racial violence required increased protection for African Americans.

As a result, in the spring of 1866, Congress passed two important bills designed to aid African Americans. The landmark Civil Rights bill, which bestowed full citizenship on African Americans, overturned the 1857 *Dred Scott* decision and the black codes. It defined all persons born in the United States (except Indian peoples) as national citizens, and it enumerated various rights, including the rights to make and enforce contracts, to sue, to give evidence, and to buy and sell property. Under this bill, African Americans acquired "full and equal benefit of all

Office of the Freedmen's Bureau, Memphis, Tennessee, *Harper's Weekly*, June 2, 1866. Established by Congress in 1865, the Freedmen's Bureau provided economic, educational, and legal assistance to former slaves in the post–Civil War years. Bureau agents were often called upon to settle disputes between black and white Southerners over wages, labor contracts, political rights, and violence. While most Southern whites only grudgingly acknowledged the Bureau's legitimacy, freed people gained important legal and psychological support through testimony at public hearings like this one.

SOURCE: Library of Congress.

laws and proceedings for the security of person and property as is enjoyed by white citizens."

Congress also voted to enlarge the scope of the Freedmen's Bureau, empowering it to build schools and pay teachers, and also to establish courts to prosecute those charged with depriving African Americans of their civil rights. The bureau achieved important, if limited, success in aiding African Americans. Bureau-run schools helped lay the foundation for Southern public education. The bureau's network of courts allowed freed people to bring suits against white people in disputes involving violence, nonpayment of wages, or unfair division of crops. The very existence of courts hearing public testimony by African Americans provided an important psychological challenge to traditional notions of white racial domination.

But an angry President Johnson vetoed both of these bills. In opposing the Civil Rights bill, Johnson denounced the assertion of national power to protect African American civil rights, claiming it was a "stride toward centralization, and the concentration of all legislative powers in the national Government." But Johnson's intemperate attacks on the Radicals—he damned them as traitors unwilling to restore the Union—united moderate and Radical Republicans and they succeeded in overriding the vetoes. Congressional Republicans, led by the Radical faction, were now unified in challenging the president's power to direct Reconstruction and in using national authority to define and protect the rights of citizens.

In June 1866, fearful that the Civil Rights Act might be declared unconstitutional, and eager to settle the basis for the seating of Southern representatives, Congress passed the Fourteenth Amendment. The amendment defined national citizenship to include former slaves ("all persons born or naturalized in the United States") and prohibited the states from violating the privileges of citizens without due process of law. It also empowered Congress to reduce the representation of any state that denied the suffrage to males over twenty-one. Republicans adopted the Fourteenth Amendment as their platform for the 1866 congressional elections and suggested that Southern states would have to ratify it as a condition of readmission. President Johnson, meanwhile, took to the stump in August to support conservative Democratic and Republican candidates. His unrestrained speeches often degenerated into harangues, alienating many voters and aiding the Republican cause.

For their part, the Republicans skillfully portrayed Johnson and Northern Democrats as disloyal and white Southerners as unregenerate. Republicans began an effective campaign tradition known as "waving the bloody shirt"—reminding Northern voters of the hundreds of thousands of Yankee soldiers left dead or maimed by the war. In the November 1866 elections, the Republicans increased their majority in both the House and the Senate and gained control of all the Northern states. The stage was now set for a battle between the president and Congress. Was it to be Johnson's "restoration" or Congressional Reconstruction?

Congressional Reconstruction and the Impeachment Crisis

United against Johnson, Radical and moderate Republicans took control of Reconstruction early in 1867. In March, Congress passed the First Reconstruction Act over Johnson's veto. This act divided the South into five military districts subject to martial law. To achieve restoration, Southern states were first required to call new constitutional conventions, elected by universal manhood suffrage. Once these states had drafted new constitutions, guaranteed African American voting rights, and ratified the Fourteenth Amendment, they were eligible for readmission to the Union. Supplementary legislation, also passed over the president's veto, invalidated the provisional governments established by Johnson, empowered the military to administer voter registration, and required an oath of loyalty to the United States (see Map 17.1).

Congress also passed several laws aimed at limiting Johnson's power. One of these, the Tenure of Office Act, stipulated that any officeholder appointed by the president with the Senate's advice and consent could not be removed until the Senate had approved a successor. In this way, congressional leaders could protect Republicans, such as Secretary of War Edwin M. Stanton, entrusted with implementing Congressional Reconstruction. In August 1867, with Congress adjourned, Johnson suspended Stanton and appointed General Ulysses S. Grant interim secretary of war. This move enabled the president to remove generals in the field that he judged to be too radical and replace them with men who were sympathetic to his own views. It also served as a challenge to the Tenure of Office Act. In January 1868, when the Senate overruled Stanton's suspension, Grant broke openly with Johnson and vacated the office. Stanton resumed his position and barricaded himself in his office when Johnson attempted to remove him once again.

Outraged by Johnson's relentless obstructionism, and seizing upon his violation of the Tenure of Office Act as a pretext, Radical and moderate Republicans in the House of Representatives again joined forces and voted to impeach the president by a vote of 126 to 47 on February 24, 1868, charging him with eleven counts of high crimes and misdemeanors. To ensure the support of moderate Republicans, the articles of impeachment focused on violations of the Tenure of Office Act. The case against Johnson would have to be made on the basis of willful violation of the law. Left unstated were the Republicans' real reasons for wanting the president removed: Johnson's political views and his opposition to the Reconstruction Acts.

MAP EXPLORATION

To explore an interactive version of this map,
go to **www.prenhall.com/faragher5/map17.1**

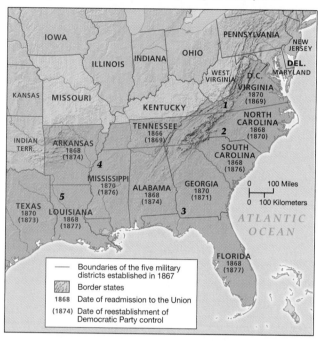

MAP 17.1 Reconstruction of the South, 1866–77 Dates
for the readmission of former Confederate states to the Union
and the return of Democrats to power varied according
to the specific political situations in those states.

An influential group of moderate Senate Republicans feared the damage a conviction might do to the constitutional separation of powers. They also worried about the political and economic policies that might be pursued by Benjamin Wade, the president pro tem of the Senate and a leader of the Radical Republicans, who, because there was no vice president, would succeed to the presidency if Johnson were removed from office. Behind the scenes during his Senate trial, Johnson agreed to abide by the Reconstruction Acts. In May, the Senate voted 35 for conviction, 19 for acquittal—one vote shy of the two-thirds necessary for removal from office. Johnson's narrow acquittal established the precedent that only criminal actions by a president—not political disagreements—warranted removal from office.

The Election of 1868

By the summer of 1868, seven former Confederate states (Alabama, Arkansas, Florida, Louisiana, North Carolina, South Carolina, and Tennessee) had ratified the revised constitutions, elected Republican governments, and ratified the Fourteenth Amendment. They had thereby earned read-

mission to the Union. Though Georgia, Mississippi, Texas, and Virginia still awaited readmission, the presidential election of 1868 offered some hope that the Civil War's legacy of sectional hate and racial tension might finally ease.

Republicans nominated Ulysses S. Grant, the North's foremost military hero. An Ohio native, Grant had graduated from West Point in 1843, served in the Mexican War, and resigned from the army in 1854. Unhappy in civilian life, Grant received a second chance during the Civil War. He rose quickly to become commander in the western theater, and he later destroyed Lee's army in Virginia. Although his armies suffered terrible losses, Grant enjoyed tremendous popularity after the war, especially when he broke with Johnson. Totally lacking in political experience, Grant admitted, after receiving the nomination, that he had been forced into it in spite of himself.

Significantly, at the very moment that the South was being forced to enfranchise former slaves as a prerequisite for readmission to the Union, the Republicans rejected a campaign plank endorsing black suffrage in the North. Their platform left "the question of suffrage in all the loyal States . . . to the people of those States." State referendums calling for black suffrage failed in eight Northern states between 1865 and 1868, succeeding only in Iowa and Minnesota. The Democrats, determined to reverse Congressional Reconstruction, nominated Horatio Seymour, former governor of New York and a long-time foe of emancipation and supporter of states' rights.

The Ku Klux Klan, founded as a Tennessee social club in 1866, emerged as a potent instrument of terror (see the opening of this chapter). In Louisiana, Arkansas, Georgia, and South Carolina the Klan threatened, whipped, and murdered black and white Republicans to prevent them from voting. This terrorism enabled the Democrats to carry Georgia and Louisiana, but it ultimately cost the Democrats votes in the North. In the final tally, Grant carried twenty-six of the thirty-four states for an electoral college victory of 214 to 80. But he received a popular majority of less than 53 percent, beating Seymour by only 306,000 votes. Significantly, more than 500,000 African American voters cast their ballots for Grant, demonstrating their overwhelming support for the Republican Party. The Republicans also retained large majorities in both houses of Congress.

In February 1869, Congress passed the Fifteenth Amendment, providing that "the right of citizens of the United States to vote shall be denied or abridged on account of race, color, or previous condition of servitude." To enhance the chances of ratification, Congress required the three remaining unreconstructed states—Mississippi, Texas, and Virginia—to ratify both the Fourteenth and Fifteenth Amendments before readmission. They did so, and rejoined the Union in early 1870. The Fifteenth Amendment was ratified in February 1870. In the

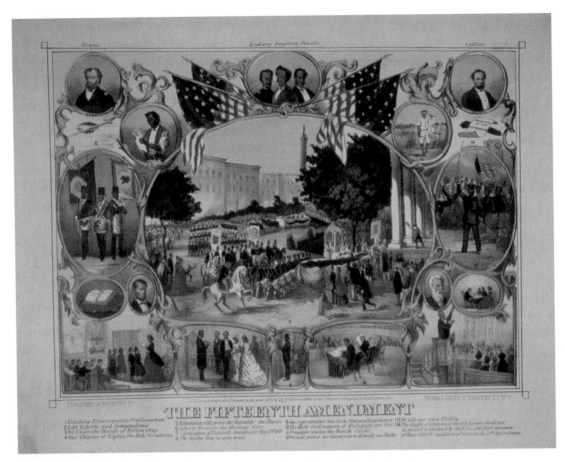

The Fifteenth Amendment, 1870. The Fifteenth Amendment, ratified in 1870, stipulated that the right to vote could not be denied "on account of race, color, or previous condition of servitude." This illustration expressed the optimism and hopes of African Americans generated by this Consitutional landmark aimed at protecting black political rights. Note the various political figures (Abraham Lincoln, John Brown, Frederick Douglass) and movements (abolitionism, black education) invoked here, providing a sense of how the amendement culminated a long historical struggle.

SOURCE: Courtesy of the Library of Congress.

narrow sense of simply readmitting the former Confederate states to the Union, Reconstruction was complete.

Woman Suffrage and Reconstruction

The battles over the political status of African Americans proved an important turning point for women as well. The Fourteenth and Fifteenth Amendments, which granted citizenship and the vote to freedmen, both inspired and frustrated women's rights activists. Many of these women had long been active in the abolitionist movement. During the war, they had actively supported the Union cause through their work in the National Woman's Loyal League and the United States Sanitary Commission. Elizabeth Cady Stanton and Susan B. Anthony, two leaders with long involvement in both the antislavery and feminist movements, objected to the inclusion of the word "male" in the Fourteenth Amendment. "If that word 'male' be inserted," Stanton predicted in 1866, "it will take us a century at least to get it out."

Insisting that the causes of the African American vote and the women's vote were linked, Stanton, Anthony, and Lucy Stone founded the American Equal Rights Association in 1866. The group launched a series of lobbying and petition campaigns to remove racial and sexual restrictions on voting from state constitutions. Throughout the nation, the old abolitionist organizations and the Republican Party emphasized passage of the Fourteenth and Fifteenth Amendments and withdrew funds and support from the cause of woman suffrage. Disagreements over these amendments divided suffragists for decades.

OVERVIEW

RECONSTRUCTION AMENDMENTS TO THE CONSTITUTION, 1865–1870

Amendment and Date Passed by Congress	Main Provisions	Ratification Process (3/4 of all states including ex- Confederate states required)
13 (January 1865)	• Prohibited slavery in the United States	December 1865 (27 states, including 8 Southern states)
14 (June 1866)	• Conferred national citizenship on all persons born or naturalized in the United States • Reduced state representation in Congress proportionally for any state disfranchising male citizens • Denied former Confederates the right to hold state or national office • Repudiated Confederate debt	July 1868 (after Congress made ratification a prerequisite for readmission of ex-Confederate states to the Union)
15 (February 1869)	• Prohibited denial of suffrage because of race, color, or previous condition of servitude	March 1870 (ratification required for readmission of Virginia, Texas, Mississippi, and Georgia)

The radical wing, led by Stanton and Anthony, opposed the Fifteenth Amendment, arguing that ratification would establish an "aristocracy of sex," enfranchising all men while leaving women without political privileges. In arguing for a Sixteenth Amendment that would secure the vote for women, they used racist and elitist appeals. They urged "American women of wealth, education, virtue, and refinement" to support the vote for women and oppose the Fifteenth Amendment "if you do not wish the lower orders of Chinese, Africans, Germans, and Irish, with their low ideas of womanhood to make laws for you and your daughters." Other women's rights activists, including Lucy Stone and Frederick Douglass, asserted that "this hour belongs to the Negro." They feared a debate over woman suffrage at the national level would jeopardize passage of the two amendments.

By 1869, woman suffragists had split into two competing organizations. The moderate American Woman Suffrage Association (AWSA), led by Lucy Stone, Julia Ward Howe, and Henry Blackwell, focused on achieving woman suffrage at the state level. It maintained close ties with the Republican Party and the old abolitionist networks, worked for the Fifteenth Amendment, and actively sought the support of men. The more radical wing founded the all-female National Woman Suffrage Association (NWSA). For the NWSA, the vote represented only one part of a broad spectrum of goals inherited from the Declaration of Sentiments manifesto

adopted at the first women's rights convention held in 1848 at Seneca Falls, New York (see Chapter 13).

Women did not win the vote in this period, but they did establish an independent suffrage movement that eventually drew millions of women into political life. The NWSA in particular demonstrated that self-government and democratic participation in the public sphere were crucial for women's emancipation. The failure of woman suffrage after the Civil War was less a result of factional fighting than of the larger defeat of Radical Reconstruction and the ideal of expanded citizenship.

THE MEANING OF FREEDOM

For 4 million slaves, freedom arrived in various ways in different parts of the South. In many areas, slavery had collapsed long before Lee's surrender at Appomattox. In regions far removed from the presence of federal troops, African Americans did not learn of slavery's end until the spring of 1865. There were thousands of sharply contrasting stories, many of which revealed the need for freed slaves to confront their owners. One Virginia slave, hired out to another family during the war, had been working in the fields when a friend told her she was now free. "Is dat so?" she exclaimed. Dropping her hoe, she ran the seven miles to her old place, confronted her former mistress, and shouted, "I'se free! Yes, I'se free! Ain't got to work fo' you no mo'." But regardless of specific regional circumstances,

Susan B. Anthony (1820–1906) and Elizabeth Cady Stanton (1815–1902), the two most influential leaders of the woman suffrage movement, ca. 1892. Anthony and Stanton broke with their longtime abolitionist allies after the Civil War, when they opposed the Fifteenth Amendment. They argued that the doctrine of universal manhood suffrage it embodied would give consitutional authority to the claim that men were the social and political superiors of women. As founders of the militant National Woman Suffrage Association, Stanton and Anthony established an independent woman suffrage movement with a broader spectrum of goals for women's rights, and drew millions of women into public life during the late nineteenth century.

SOURCE: Courtesy of the Susan B. Anthony House, Rochester, NY www.susanbanthonyhouse.org.

the meaning of "freedom" would be contested for years to come. The deep desire for independence from white control formed the underlying aspiration of newly freed slaves. For their part, most Southern white people sought to restrict the boundaries of that independence. As individuals and as members of communities transformed by emancipation, former slaves struggled to establish economic, political, and cultural autonomy. They built on the twin pillars of slave culture—the family and the church—to consolidate and expand African American institutions and thereby laid the foundation for the modern African American community.

Emancipation greatly expanded the choices available to African Americans. It helped build confidence in their ability to effect change without deferring to white people. Freedom also meant greater uncertainty and risk. But the vast majority of African Americans were more than willing to take their chances.

Moving About

The first impulse of many emancipated slaves was to test their freedom. The simplest, most obvious way to do this involved leaving home. Throughout the summer and fall of 1865, observers in the South noted enormous numbers of freed people on the move. One former slave squatting in an abandoned tent outside Selma, Alabama, explained his feeling to a Northern journalist: "I's want to be free man, cum when I please, and nobody say nuffin to me, nor order me roun'." When urged to stay on with the South Carolina family she had served for years as a cook, a slave woman replied firmly: "No, Miss, I must go. If I stay here I'll never know I am free."

Yet many who left their old neighborhoods returned soon afterward to seek work in the general vicinity, or even on the plantation they had left. Many wanted to separate themselves from former owners, but not from familial ties and friendships. Others moved away altogether, seeking jobs in nearby towns and cities. Many former slaves left predominantly white counties, where they felt more vulnerable and isolated, for new lives in the relative comfort of predominantly black communities. In most Southern states, there was a significant population shift toward black belt plantation counties and towns after the war. Many African Americans, attracted by schools, churches, and fraternal societies as well as the army, preferred the city. Between 1865 and 1870, the African American population of the South's ten largest cities doubled, while the white population increased by only 10 percent.

Disgruntled planters had difficulty accepting African American independence. During slavery, they had expected obedience, submission, and loyalty from African Americans. Now many could not understand why so many former slaves wanted to leave, despite urgent pleas to continue working at the old place. The deference and humility white people expected from African Americans could no longer be taken for granted. Indeed, many freed people went out of their way to reject the old subservience. Moving about freely was one way of doing this, as was refusing to tip one's hat to white people, ignoring former masters or mistresses in the streets, and refusing to step aside on sidewalks. When freed people staged parades, dances, and picnics to celebrate their new freedom, as they did, for example, when commemorating the Emancipation Proclamation, white people invariably condemned them angrily for "insolence," "outrageous spectacles," or "putting on airs."

The African American Family

Emancipation allowed freed people to strengthen family ties. For many former slaves, freedom meant the opportunity to reunite with long-lost family members. To track down relatives, freed people trekked to faraway places, put ads in newspapers, sought the help of Freedmen's Bureau agents, and questioned anyone who might have information about loved ones. Many thousands of family reunions, each with its own story, took place after the war. One North Carolina slave, who had seen his parents separated by sale, recalled many years later what for him had been the most significant aspect of freedom. "I has got thirteen great-gran' chilluns an' I know whar dey ever'one am. In slavery times dey'd have been on de block long time ago. "Thousands of African American couples who had lived together under slavery streamed to military and civilian authorities and demanded to be legally married. By 1870, the two-parent household was the norm for a large majority of African Americans. For many freed people, the attempt to find lost relatives dragged on for years. Searches often proved frustrating, exhausting, and ultimately disappointing. Some "reunions" ended painfully with the discovery that spouses had found new partners and started new families.

Emancipation brought changes to gender roles within the African American family as well. By serving in the Union army, African American men played a more direct role than women in the fight for freedom. In the political sphere, black men could now serve on juries, vote, and hold office; black women, like their white counterparts, could not. Freedmen's Bureau agents designated the husband as household head and established lower wage scales for women laborers. African American editors, preachers, and politicians regularly quoted the biblical injunction that wives submit to their husbands.

African American men asserted their male authority, denied under slavery, by insisting their wives work at home instead of in the fields. African American women generally wanted to devote more time than they had under slavery to caring for their children and to performing such domestic chores as cooking, sewing, gardening, and laundering. Yet African American women continued to work outside the home, engaging in seasonal field labor for wages or working a family's rented plot. Most rural black families barely eked out a living, and thus the labor of every family member was essential to survival. The key difference from slave times was that African American families themselves, not white masters and overseers, decided when and where women and children worked.

African American Churches and Schools

The creation of separate African American churches proved the most lasting and important element of the energetic institution building that went on in post-emancipation years. Before the Civil War, Southern Protestant churches had relegated slaves and free African Americans to second-class membership. Black worshipers were required to sit in the back during services, they were denied any role in church governance, and they were excluded from Sunday schools. Even in larger cities, where all-black congregations sometimes built their own churches, the law required white pastors. In rural areas, slaves preferred their own preachers to the sermons of local white ministers, who quoted Scripture to justify slavery and white supremacy. "That old white preachin' wasn't nothin'," former slave Nancy Williams recalled. "Old white preachers used to talk with their tongues without sayin' nothin', but Jesus told us slaves to talk with our hearts."

In communities around the South, African Americans now pooled their resources to buy land and build their own churches. Before these structures were completed, they might hold services in a railroad boxcar, where Atlanta's First Baptist Church began, or in an outdoor arbor, the original site of the First Baptist Church of Memphis. By late 1866, Charleston's African American community could boast of eleven churches in the city—five Methodist, two Presbyterian, two Episcopalian, one Baptist, and one Congregational. In rural areas, different denominations frequently shared the same church building. Churches became the center not only for religious life, but for many other activities that defined the African American community: schools, picnics, festivals, and political meetings.

The church became the first social institution fully controlled by African Americans. In nearly every community, ministers, respected for their speaking and organizational skills, were among the most influential leaders. By 1877, the great majority of black Southerners had withdrawn from white-dominated churches. In South Carolina, for example, only a few hundred black Methodists attended biracial churches, down from over 40,000 in 1865. Black Baptist churches, with their decentralized and democratic structure and more emotional services, attracted the greatest number of freed people. By the end of Reconstruction, the vast majority of African American Christians belonged to black Baptist or Methodist churches.

The rapid spread of schools reflected African Americans' thirst for self-improvement. Southern states had prohibited education for slaves. But many free black people managed to attend school, and a few slaves had been able to educate themselves. Still, over 90 percent of the South's adult African American population was illiterate in 1860. Access to education thus became a central part of the meaning of freedom. Freedmen's Bureau agents repeatedly expressed amazement at the number of makeshift classrooms organized by African Americans in rural areas. A bureau officer described these "wayside schools": "A negro riding on a loaded wagon, or sitting on a hack waiting for a train, or by the cabin door, is often seen, book in hand delving after the rudiments of knowledge. A group on the platform of a depot,

An overflow congregation crowds into Richmond's First African Baptist Church in 1874. Despite their poverty, freed people struggled to save, buy land, and erect new buildings as they organized hundreds of new black churches during Reconstruction. As the most important African American institution outside the family, the black church, in addition to tending to spiritual needs, played a key role in the educational and political life of the community.

SOURCE: The Granger Collection.

after carefully conning an old spelling book, resolves itself into a class."

African American communities received important educational aid from outside organizations. By 1869, the Freedmen's Bureau was supervising nearly 3,000 schools serving over 150,000 students throughout the South. Over half the roughly 3,300 teachers in these schools were African Americans, many of whom had been free before the Civil War. Other teachers included dedicated Northern white women, volunteers sponsored by the American Missionary Association (AMA). The bureau and the AMA also assisted in the founding of several black colleges, including Tougaloo, Hampton, and Fisk, designed to train black teachers. Black self-help proved crucial to the education effort. Throughout the South in 1865 and 1866, African Americans raised money to build schoolhouses, buy supplies, and pay teachers. Black artisans donated labor for construction, and black families offered room and board to teachers.

Land and Labor After Slavery

Most newly emancipated African Americans aspired to quit the plantations and to make new lives for themselves. Leaving the plantation was not as simple as walking off. Some freed people did find jobs in railroad building, mining, ranching, or construction work. Others raised subsistence crops and tended vegetable gardens as squatters. White planters, however, tried to retain African Americans as permanent agricultural laborers. Restricting the employment of former slaves was an important goal of the black codes. For example, South Carolina legislation in 1865 provided that "no person of color shall pursue or practice the art, trade, or business of an artisan, mechanic, or shopkeeper, or any other

trade employment, or business, besides that of husbandry, or that of a servant under contract for service or labor" without a special and costly permit.

The majority of African Americans hoped to become self-sufficient farmers. Many former slaves believed they were entitled to the land they had worked throughout their lives. General Oliver O. Howard, chief commissioner of the Freedmen's Bureau, observed that many "supposed that the Government [would] divide among them the lands of the conquered owners, and furnish them with all that might be necessary to begin life as an independent farmer." This perception was not merely a wishful fantasy. Frequent reference in the Congress and the press to the question of land distribution made the idea of "forty acres and a mule" not just a pipe dream but a matter of serious public debate.

Above all, African Americans sought economic autonomy, and ownership of land promised the most independence. "Give us our own land and we take care of ourselves," was how one former slave saw it. "But widout land, de ole massas can hire us or starve us, as dey please." At the Colored Convention in Montgomery, Alabama, in May 1867, delegates argued that the property now owned by planters had been "nearly all earned by the sweat of our brows, not theirs. It has been forfeited to the government by the treason of its owners, and is liable to be confiscated whenever the Republican Party demands it." But by 1866, the federal government had already pulled back from the various wartime experiments involving the breaking up of large plantations and the leasing of small plots to individual families. President Johnson directed General Howard of the Freedmen's Bureau to evict tens of thousands of freed people settled on confiscated and abandoned land in southeastern Virginia, southern Louisiana, and the Georgia and South Carolina low country. These evictions created a deep sense of betrayal among African Americans. A former Mississippi slave, Merrimon Howard, bitterly noted that African Americans had been left with "no land, no house, not so much as a place to lay our head. . . . We were friends on the march, brothers on the battlefield, but in the peaceful pursuits of life it seems that we are strangers." (See Map 17.2.)

By the late 1860s, sharecropping had emerged as the dominant form of working the land. Sharecropping represented a compromise between planters and former slaves. Under sharecropping arrangements that were usually very detailed, individual families contracted with landowners to be responsible for a specific plot. Large plantations were thus broken into family-sized farms. Gen-

erally, sharecropper families received one-third of the year's crop if the owner furnished implements, seed, and draft animals, or one-half if they provided their own supplies. African Americans preferred sharecropping to gang labor, as it allowed families to set their own hours and tasks and offered freedom from white supervision and control. For planters, the system stabilized the workforce by requiring sharecroppers to remain until the harvest and to employ all family members. It also offered a way around the chronic shortage of cash and credit that plagued the postwar South. (See Out of Many Voices: "Sharecropping Contract.")

Freed people did not aspire to sharecropping. Owning land outright or tenant farming (renting land) were both more desirable. But though black sharecroppers clearly enjoyed more autonomy than in the past, the vast

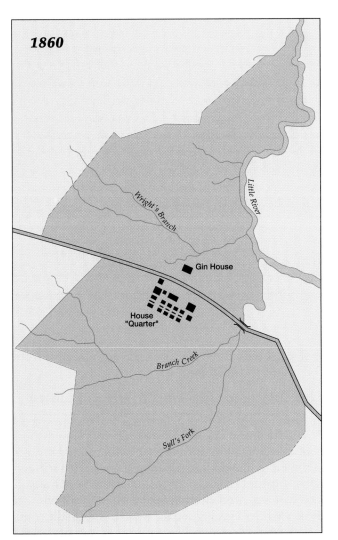

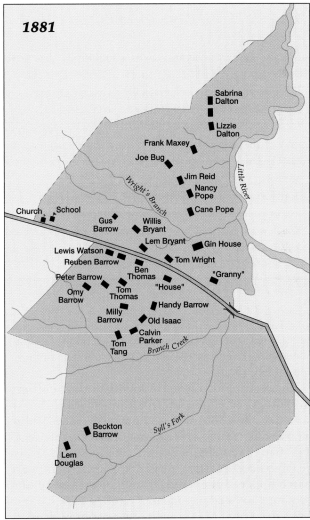

MAP 17.2 The Barrow Plantation, Oglethorpe County, Georgia, 1860 and 1881 (approx. 2,000 acres) These two maps, based on drawings from *Scribner's Monthly,* April 1881, show some of the changes brought by emancipation. In 1860, the plantation's entire black population lived in the communal slave quarters, right next to the white master's house. In 1881, black sharecropper and tenant families lived on individual plots, spread out across the land. The former slaves had also built their own school and church.

OUT OF MANY VOICES

SHARECROPPING CONTRACT BETWEEN REUBEN GOULDIN AND D. KUNKLE, AUGUSTA COUNTY VIRGINIA, JANUARY 1, 1867

*A*mong the most important and controversial activities of the Freedmen's Bureau was the effort to regulate labor relations in the post-Emancipation South. Planters and former slaves improvised a variety of sharecropping arrangements, and work contracts were often overseen by local Freedmen's Bureau agents. The following agreement was placed on file at the Freedmen's Bureau in Augusta County, Virginia, in early 1867. Note the highly detailed account of mutual obligations established for both the sharecropper and the land owner.

MEMO OF CONTRACT FOR CROPPING ON THE shares this year entered into this 1st day of January 1867 between D. Kunkle and Reuben Gouldin as follows. Gouldin is to work himself and furnish the necessary labour to put in at least say twenty-five acres each corn, wheat and oats, and cultivate the same in such fields on the place upon which he resides as Kunkle may designate and Gouldin is to take good care of and feed all the stock on the premises, to haul and chop ready for use the firewood for Kunkle, work his garden and one additional acre, in cane and potatoes or a part of each and to mend up and renew the fences in such way as Kunkle may direct, so as to secure the crops, and is to use energy and industry in carrying on the business—and Gouldin is to have one

eighth (1/8) of all the field crops raised—namely of the corn, wheat and oats, to have his house rent, garden and firewood free of charge and after the 1st of April the use of one milk cow and for any other work pertaining to the crop, done by Gouldin or his family for Kunkle or his family—Gouldin is to have a fair remuneration—to be settled up at least once each month, and it is understood they are to do all such work when called upon—Gouldin is to have one eighth of the wheat crop now in the ground and is to sow [and put in] as much and leave it should he remain but one year and he is to prepare all the crops raised for mill or market. It is further understood that should Kunkle become dissatisfied with Gouldin's way of doing business, he may at any time cancel this contract by giving Gouldin thirty days notice and paying him at the rate of twelve dollars per month for his services—in lieu of any part of the crop, provided however that should Kunkle not give such notice before the 1st day of August Gouldin shall remain the year out and receive a part of the crop as herein before provided, Kunkle to furnish the horse, seed, and all the tools necessary for carrying on the business. ■

SOURCE: Edward L. Ayers, comp., *The Valley of the Shadow: Two Communities in the American Civil War*, http://valley.vcdh.virginia.edu/, © 1993–2004.

---

majority never achieved economic independence or land ownership. They remained a largely subordinate agricultural labor force.

Sharecropping came to dominate the Southern agricultural economy and African American life in particular. By 1880, about 80 percent of the land in the black belt states—Mississippi, Alabama, and Georgia—had been divided into family-sized farms. Nearly three-quarters of black Southerners were sharecroppers. Often several families worked adjoining parcels of land in common, pooling their labor in order to get by. Men usually oversaw crop production. Women went to the fields seasonally during planting or harvesting, but they mainly tended to household chores and child care. In addition, women frequently held jobs that might bring in cash, such as raising chickens or taking in laundry. The cotton har-

vest engaged all members of the community, from the oldest to the youngest.

The Origins of African American Politics

Inclusion, rather than separation, was the objective of early African American political activity. The greatest political activity by African Americans occurred in areas occupied by Union forces during the war. In 1865 and 1866, African Americans throughout the South organized scores of mass meetings, parades, and petitions that demanded civil equality and the right to vote. In the cities, the growing web of churches and fraternal societies helped bolster early efforts at political organization. (See Out Many Voices: "An Address to the Loyal Citizens and Congress of the United States")

Hundreds of African American delegates, selected by local meetings or churches, attended statewide political conventions held throughout the South in 1865 and 1866. Previously free African Americans, as well as black ministers, artisans, and veterans of the Union army, tended to dominate these proceedings, setting a pattern that would hold throughout Reconstruction. Convention debates sometimes reflected the tensions within African American communities, such as friction between poorer former slaves and better-off free black people, or between lighter- and darker-skinned African Americans. But most of these state gatherings concentrated on passing resolutions on issues that united all African Americans. The central concerns were suffrage and equality before the law. As the delegates to an Alabama convention asserted in 1867: "We claim exactly the same rights, privileges and immunities as are enjoyed by white men—we ask nothing more and will be content with nothing less. . . . The law no longer knows white nor black, but simply men, and consequently we are entitled to ride in public conveyances, hold office, sit on juries and do everything else which we have in the past been prevented from doing solely on the ground of color."

The passage of the First Reconstruction Act in 1867 encouraged even more political activity among African Americans. The military started registering the South's electorate, ultimately enrolling approximately 735,000 black and 635,000 white voters in the ten unreconstructed states. Five states—Alabama, Florida, Louisiana, Mississippi, and South Carolina—had black electoral majorities. Fewer than half the registered white voters

OUT OF MANY VOICES

AN ADDRESS TO THE LOYAL CITIZENS AND CONGRESS OF THE UNITED STATES, CONVENTION OF COLORED CITIZENS, ALEXANDRIA, VIRGINIA, AUGUST 2–5, 1865

After the Civil War, thousands of recently freed slaves and free blacks took part in grassroots political meetings all over the South. The resolution excerpted below illustrates the deep concerns expressed by delegates over the lenient Reconstruction policies pursued by President Johnson. In particular, they feared the quick return to power of defeated Confederate forces, and worried that African American political rights would be quickly crushed without a Federal military presence.

WE, THE UNDERSIGNED MEMBERS OF A CONVENTION of colored citizens of the State of Virginia, would respectfully represent that, although we have been held as slaves, and denied all recognition as a constituent of your nationality for almost the entire period of the duration of your Government, and that by your permission we have been denied either home or country, and deprived of the dearest rights of human nature: yet when you and our immediate oppressors met in deadly conflict upon the field of battle—the one to destroy and the other to save your Government and nationality, we, with scarce an exception, in our inmost souls espoused your cause, and watched, and prayed, and waited, and labored for your success.

Well, the war is over, the rebellion is "put down," and we are declared free! Four fifths of our enemies are paroled or amnestied, and the other fifth are being pardoned, and the President has, in his efforts at the reconstruction of the civil government of the States, late in rebellion, left us entirely at the mercy of these subjugated but unconverted rebels, in everything save the privilege of bringing us, our wives and little ones, to the auction block.

We warn you in time that our only safety is in keeping them under Governors of the military persuasion until you have so amended the Federal Constitution that it will prohibit the States from making any distinction between citizens on account of race or color. In one word, the only salvation for us besides the power of the Government, is in the possession of the ballot. Give us this, and we will protect ourselves. We are "sheep in the midst of wolves," and nothing but the military arm of the Government prevents us and all the truly loyal white men from being driven from the land of our birth. Do not then, we beseech you, give to one of these "wayward sisters" the rights they abandoned and forfeited when they rebelled until you have secured our rights by the aforementioned amendment to the Constitution. ■

SOURCE: Paul Halsall, comp., *Internet Modern History Sourcebook*, http://www.fordham.edu/halsall/mod/modsbook27.html (halsall@fordham.edu, 1997, rev. 2001).

W. L. Sheppard, "Electioneering at the South," *Harper's Weekly*, July 25, 1868. Throughout the Reconstruction-era South, newly freed slaves took a keen interest in both local and national political affairs. The presence of women and children at these campaign gatherings illustrates the importance of contemporary political issues to the entire African American community.

SOURCE: Library of Congress.

participated in the elections for state constitutional conventions in 1867 and 1868. In contrast, four-fifths of the registered black voters cast ballots in these elections. Much of this new African American political activism was channeled through local Union League chapters throughout the South. However, as the fate of Alex Webb in Hale County, Alabama, again makes clear, few whites welcomed this activism.

Begun during the war as a Northern, largely white middle-class patriotic club, the Union League now became the political voice of the former slaves. Union League chapters brought together local African Americans, soldiers, and Freedmen's Bureau agents to demand the vote and an end to legal discrimination against African Americans. It brought out African American voters, instructed freedmen in the rights and duties of citizenship, and promoted Republican candidates. Not surprisingly, newly enfranchised freedmen voted Republican and formed the core of the Republican Party in the South. For most ordinary African Americans, politics was inseparable from economic issues, especially the land question. Grass-roots political organizations frequently intervened in local disputes with planters over the terms of labor contracts. African American political groups closely followed the congressional debates over Reconstruction policy and agitated for land confiscation and distribution. Perhaps most important, politics was the only arena where black and white Southerners might engage each other on an equal basis.

SOUTHERN POLITICS AND SOCIETY

By the summer of 1868, when the South had returned to the Union, the majority of Republicans believed the task of Reconstruction to be finished. Ultimately, they put their faith in a political solution to the problems facing the vanquished South. That meant nurturing a viable two-party system in the Southern states, where no Republican Party had ever existed. If that could be accomplished, Republicans and Democrats would compete for votes, offices, and influence, just as they did in Northern states. Most Republican congressmen were moderates, conceiving Reconstruction in limited terms. They rejected radical calls for confiscation and redistribution of land, as well as permanent military rule of the South. The Reconstruction Acts of 1867 and 1868 laid out the requirements for the readmission of Southern states, along with the procedures for forming and electing new governments.

Yet over the next decade, the political structure created in the Southern states proved too restricted and fragile to sustain itself. To most Southern whites, the active participation of African Americans in politics seemed extremely dangerous. Federal troops were needed to protect Republican governments and their supporters from violent opposition. Congressional action to monitor Southern elections and protect black voting rights became routine. Despite initial successes, Southern Republicanism proved an unstable coalition of often conflicting elements, unable to sustain effective power for very long. By 1877, Democrats had regained political control of all the former Confederate states.

Southern Republicans

Three major groups composed the fledgling Republican coalition in the postwar South. African American voters made up a large majority of Southern Republicans throughout the Reconstruction era. Yet African Americans outnumbered whites in only three Southern states; thus, Republicans would have to attract white support to win elections and sustain power.

A second group consisted of white Northerners, derisively called "carpetbaggers" by native white Southerners. Most carpetbaggers combined a desire for personal gain with a commitment to reform the "unprogressive" South by developing its material resources and introducing Yankee institutions, such as free labor and free public schools. Most were veterans of the Union army who stayed in the South after the war. Others included Freedmen's Bureau agents and businessmen who had invested capital in cotton plantations and other enterprises.

Carpetbaggers tended to be well educated and from the middle class. Albert Morgan, for example, was an army veteran from Ohio who settled in Mississippi after the war.

When he and his brother failed at running a cotton plantation and sawmill, Morgan became active in Republican politics as a way to earn a living. He won election to the state constitutional convention, became a power in the state legislature, and risked his life to keep the Republican organization alive in the Mississippi Delta region. Although they made up a tiny percentage of the population, carpetbaggers played a disproportionately large role in Southern politics. They won a large share of Reconstruction offices, particularly in Florida, South Carolina, and Louisiana and in areas with large African American constituencies.

The third major group of Southern Republicans were the native whites pejoratively termed "scalawags." They had even more diverse backgrounds and motives than the Northern-born Republicans. Some were prominent prewar Whigs who saw the Republican Party as their best chance to regain political influence. Others viewed the party as an agent of modernization and economic expansion. "Yankees and Yankee notions are just what we want in this country," argued Thomas Settle of North Carolina. "We want their capital to build factories and workshops. We want their intelligence, their energy and enterprise." Loyalists during the war and traditional enemies of the planter elite (most were small farmers), these white Southerners looked to the Republican Party for help in settling old scores and relief from debt and wartime devastation.

Yet few white Southerners identified with the political and economic aspirations of African Americans. Moderate elements more concerned with maintaining white control of the party, and encouraging economic investment in the region, outnumbered and defeated "confiscation radicals" who focused on obtaining land for African Americans.

Reconstructing the States: A Mixed Record

With the old Confederate leaders barred from political participation, and with carpetbaggers and newly enfranchised African Americans representing many of the plantation districts, Republicans managed to dominate the ten Southern constitutional conventions of 1867–69.

Most of the conventions produced constitutions that expanded democracy and the public role of the state. The new documents guaranteed the political and civil rights of African Americans, and they abolished property qualifications for officeholding and jury service, as well as imprisonment for debt. They created the first state-funded systems of education in the South, to be administered by state commissioners. The new constitutions also mandated establishment of orphanages, penitentiaries, and homes for the insane. The changes wrought in the South's political landscape seemed quite radical to many. In 1868, only three years after the end of the war, Republicans came to power in most of the Southern states. By 1869, new constitutions had been ratified in all the old Confederate states. "These constitutions and governments," one South Carolina

Democratic newspaper vowed bitterly, "will last just as long as the bayonets which ushered them into being, shall keep them in existence, and not one day longer."

Republican governments in the South faced a continual crisis of legitimacy that limited their ability to legislate change. They had to balance reform against the need to gain acceptance, especially by white Southerners. Their achievements were thus mixed. In the realm of race relations there was a clear thrust toward equal rights and against discrimination. Republican legislatures followed up the federal Civil Rights Act of 1866 with various antidiscrimination clauses in new constitutions and laws prescribing harsh penalties for civil rights violations. While most African Americans supported autonomous African American churches, fraternal societies, and schools, they insisted that the state be "color-blind." African Americans could now be employed in police forces and fire departments, serve on juries, school boards, and city councils, and they could hold public office at all levels of government.

Segregation, though, became the norm in public school systems. African American leaders often accepted segregation because they feared that insistence on integrated education would jeopardize funding for the new school systems. They generally agreed with Frederick Douglass that separate schools were "infinitely superior" to no schools at all. So while they opposed constitutional language requiring racial segregation in schools, most African Americans were less interested in the abstract ideal of integrated education than in ensuring educational opportunities for their children and employment for African American teachers.

Demands by African Americans to prohibit segregation in railroad cars, steamboats, theaters, and other public spaces revealed and heightened the divisions within the Republican Party. Moderate white Republicans feared such laws would only further alienate potential white supporters. But by the early 1870s, as black influence and assertiveness grew, laws guaranteeing equal access to transportation and public accommodation were passed in many states. By and large, though, such civil rights laws were difficult to enforce in local communities.

In economic matters, Republican governments failed to fulfill African Americans' hopes of obtaining land. Few former slaves possessed the cash to buy land in the open market, and they looked to the state for help. Republicans tried to weaken the plantation system and promote black ownership by raising taxes on land. Yet, even when state governments seized land for nonpayment of taxes, the property was never used to help create black homesteads. In Mississippi, for example, 6 million acres, or about 20 percent of the land, had been forfeited by 1875. Yet virtually all of it found its way back to the original owners after they paid minimal penalties.

Republican leaders envisioned promoting Northern-style capitalist development—factories, large towns, and diversified agriculture—through state aid. Much Republican state lawmaking was devoted to encouraging railroad construction. This government backing gave railroad companies credibility and helped them raise capital. In exchange, states received liens on railroads as security against defaults on payments to bondholders.

Between 1868 and 1872, the Southern railroad system was rebuilt and over 3,000 new miles of track added, an increase of almost 40 percent. But in spite of all the new laws, it proved impossible to attract significant amounts of Northern and European investment capital. The obsession with railroads withdrew resources from education and other programs. As in the North, it also opened the doors to widespread corruption and bribery of public officials. Railroad failures eroded public confidence in the Republicans' ability to govern. The "gospel of prosperity" ultimately failed to modernize the economy or solidify the Republican Party in the South.

White Resistance and "Redemption"

The emergence of a Republican Party in the reconstructed South brought two parties, but not a two-party system, to the region. The opponents of Reconstruction, the Democrats, refused to acknowledge Republicans' right to participate in Southern political life. In their view, the Republican Party, supported primarily by the votes of former slaves, was the partisan instrument of the Northern Congress. Since Republicans controlled state governments, this denial of legitimacy meant, in effect, a rejection of state authority itself. In each state, Republicans were split between those who urged conciliation in an effort to gain white acceptance and those who emphasized consolidating the party under the protection of the military.

From 1870 to 1872, the Ku Klux Klan fought an ongoing terrorist campaign against Reconstruction governments and local leaders. Although not centrally organized, the Klan was a powerful presence in nearly every Southern state. It acted as a kind of guerrilla military force in the service of the Democratic Party, the planter class, and all those who sought the restoration of white supremacy. Planters sometimes employed Klansmen to enforce labor discipline by driving African Americans off plantations to deprive them of their harvest share.

In October 1870, after Republicans carried Laurens County in South Carolina, bands of white people drove 150 African Americans from their homes and murdered 13 black and white Republican activists. In March 1871, three African Americans were arrested in Meridian, Mississippi, for giving "incendiary" speeches. At their court hearing, Klansmen killed two of the defendants and the Republican judge, and thirty more African Americans were murdered in a day of rioting. The single bloodiest episode of Reconstruction era violence took place in Colfax, Louisiana, on Easter Sunday 1873. Nearly 100 African Americans were murdered after they failed to hold a besieged courthouse during a contested election.

Southern Republicans looked to Washington for help. In 1870 and 1871, Congress passed three Enforcement Acts designed to counter racial terrorism. These declared that interference with voting was a federal offense. The acts provided for federal supervision of voting, and authorized the president to send the army and to suspend the writ of habeas corpus in districts declared to be in a state of insurrection. The most sweeping measure was the Ku Klux Klan Act of April 1871, which made the violent infringement of civil and political rights a federal crime punishable by the national government. Attorney General Amos T. Akerman prosecuted hundreds of Klansmen in North Carolina and Mississippi. In October 1871, President Grant sent federal troops to occupy nine South Carolina counties; they rounded up thousands of Klan members. By the election of 1872, the federal government's intervention had helped break the Klan and restore a semblance of law and order.

The Civil Rights Act of 1875 outlawed racial discrimination in theaters, hotels, railroads, and other public places. But the law proved more an assertion of principle than a direct federal intervention in Southern affairs. Enforcement required African Americans to take their cases to the federal courts, a costly and time-consuming procedure.

As wartime idealism faded, Northern Republicans became less inclined toward direct intervention in Southern affairs. They had enough trouble retaining political control in the North. In 1874, the Democrats gained a majority in the House of Representatives for the first time since 1856. Key Northern states also began to fall to the Democrats. Northern Republicans slowly abandoned the freedmen and their white allies in the South. Southern Democrats were also able to exploit a deepening fiscal crisis by blaming Republicans for excessive extension of public credit and the sharp increase in tax rates. Republican governments had indeed spent public money for new state school systems, orphanages, roads, and other internal improvements.

Gradually, conservative Democrats "redeemed" one state after another. Virginia and Tennessee led the way in 1869, North Carolina in 1870, Georgia in 1871, Texas in 1873, and Alabama and Arkansas in 1874. In Mississippi, white conservatives employed violence and intimidation to wrest control in 1875 and "redeemed" the state the following year. Republican infighting in Louisiana in 1873 and 1874 led to a series of contested election results, including bloody clashes between black militia and armed whites, and finally to "redemption" by the Democrats in 1877. Once these states returned to Democratic rule, African Americans faced obstacles to voting, more stringent controls on plantation labor, and deep cuts in social services.

Several Supreme Court rulings involving the Fourteenth and Fifteenth Amendments effectively constrained federal protection of African American civil rights. In the

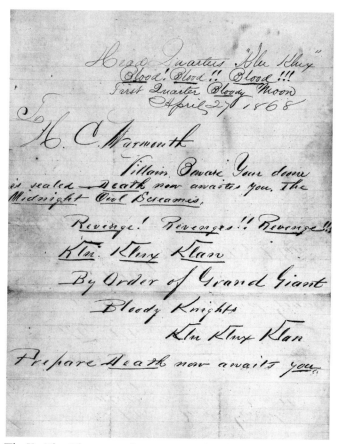

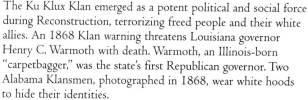

The Ku Klux Klan emerged as a potent political and social force during Reconstruction, terrorizing freed people and their white allies. An 1868 Klan warning threatens Louisiana governor Henry C. Warmoth with death. Warmoth, an Illinois-born "carpetbagger," was the state's first Republican governor. Two Alabama Klansmen, photographed in 1868, wear white hoods to hide their identities.

SOURCE: (a) From The Henry Clay Warmoth Papers # 752, Southern Historical Collection, Wilson Library, University of North Carolina at Chapel Hill; (b) Rutherford B. Hayes Presidential Center.

so-called Slaughterhouse cases of 1873, the Court issued its first ruling on the Fourteenth Amendment. The cases involved a Louisiana charter that gave a New Orleans meat-packing company a monopoly over the city's butchering business on the grounds of protecting public health. A rival group of butchers had sued, claiming the law violated the Fourteenth Amendment, which prohibited states from depriving any person of life, liberty, or property without due process of law. The Court held that the Fourteenth Amendment protected only the former slaves, not butchers, and that it protected only national citizenship rights, not the regulatory powers of states. The ruling in effect denied the original intent of the Fourteenth Amendment— to protect against state infringement of national citizenship rights as spelled out in the Bill of Rights.

Three other decisions curtailed federal protection of black civil rights. In *United States* v. *Reese* (1876) and *United*

States v. *Cruikshank* (1876), the Court restricted congressional power to enforce the Ku Klux Klan Act. Future prosecution would depend on the states, rather than on federal authorities. In these rulings, the Court held that the Fourteenth Amendment extended the federal power to protect civil rights only in cases involving discrimination by states; discrimination by individuals or groups was not covered. The Court also ruled that the Fifteenth Amendment did not guarantee a citizen's right to vote; it only barred certain specific grounds for denying suffrage— "race, color, or previous condition of servitude." This interpretation opened the door for Southern states to disfranchise African Americans for allegedly nonracial reasons. States back under Democratic control began to limit African American voting by passing laws restricting voter eligibility through poll taxes and property requirements.

Finally, in the 1883 Civil Rights Cases decision, the Court declared the Civil Rights Act of 1875 unconstitutional, holding that the Fourteenth Amendment gave Congress the power to outlaw discrimination by states, but not by private individuals. The majority opinion held that black people must no longer "be the special favorite of the laws." Together, these Supreme Court decisions marked the end of federal attempts to protect African American rights until well into the next century.

White Yeomen, White Merchants, and "King Cotton"

The Republicans' vision of a "New South" remade along the lines of the Northern economy failed to materialize. Instead, the South declined into the country's poorest agricultural region. Unlike Midwestern and Western farm towns burgeoning from trade in wheat, corn, and livestock, Southern communities found themselves almost entirely dependent on the price of one commodity. In the post–Civil War years, "King Cotton" expanded its realm, as greater numbers of small white farmers found

themselves forced to switch from subsistence crops to growing cotton for the market (see Map 17.3).

A chronic shortage of capital and banking institutions made local merchants and planters the sole source of credit. They advanced loans and supplies to small owners, tenant farmers, and sharecroppers in exchange for a lien, or claim, on the year's cotton crop. They often charged usurious interest rates on advances, while marking up the prices of the goods sold in their stores. Taking advantage of the high illiteracy rates among poor Southerners, landlords and merchants easily altered their books to inflate the figures. At the end of the year, sharecroppers and tenants found themselves deep in debt to stores for seed, supplies, and clothing. Despite hard work and even bountiful harvests, few small farmers could escape from heavy debt.

MAP EXPLORATION

To explore an interactive version of this map, go to **www.prenhall.com/faragher/map17.3**

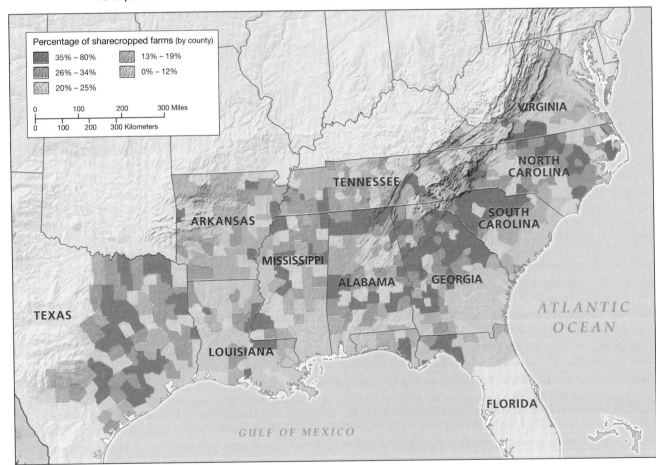

MAP 17.3 Southern Sharecropping and the Cotton Belt, 1880 The economic depression of the 1870s forced increasing numbers of Southern farmers, both white and black, into sharecropping arrangements. Sharecropping was most pervasive in the cotton belt regions of South Carolina, Georgia, Alabama, Mississippi, and east Texas.

The spread of the "crop lien" system as the South's main form of agricultural credit forced more and more farmers into cotton growing. The transition to cotton dependency developed unevenly, at different speeds in different parts of the South. Penetration by railroads, the availability of commercial fertilizers, and the opening up of new lands to cultivation were key factors in transforming communities from diversified, locally oriented farming to the market-oriented production of cotton.

The pent-up demand for cotton following the war brought high prices (as much as 43 cents per pound) through the late 1860s. But as the "crop lien" system spread, and as more and more farmers turned to cotton growing as the only way to obtain credit, expanding production depressed prices. Competition from new cotton centers in the world market, such as Egypt and India, accelerated the downward spiral. As cotton prices declined alarmingly, to roughly 11 cents per pound in 1875 to 5 cents by the early 1890s, per capita wealth in the South fell steadily, equaling only one-third that of the East, Midwest, or West by the 1890s. Small farmers caught up in a vicious cycle of low cotton prices, debt, and dwindling food crops found their old ideal of independence sacrificed to the cruel logic of the cotton market.

By 1880, nearly 40 percent of all Southern farms were operated by tenants and sharecroppers. About one-third of the white farmers and nearly three-quarters of the African American farmers in the cotton states were sharecroppers or tenants. To obtain precious credit, most found themselves forced to produce cotton for market, and thus became enmeshed in the debt-ridden crop lien system. In traditional cotton producing areas, especially the black belt, landless farmers growing cotton had replaced slaves growing cotton. In the upcountry and newer areas of cultivation, cotton-dominated commercial agriculture, with landless tenants and sharecroppers as the main workforce, had replaced the more diversified subsistence economy of the antebellum era.

One class of white Southerners benefiting from these arrangements were local merchants. As hundreds of new villages (communities of less than 2,500 people) sprang up in every corner of the South, especially in the new upcountry and Piedmont settlements, local merchants provided both goods and credit for local farmers. With their power based on control of credit and marketing, merchants emerged as a new economic elite unconnected to the antebellum planters whose power had rested on the ownership of land and slaves. But within both the new towns and the old planter elite, white families increasingly defined their social position by celebrating a certain type of ideal household. Women found meaning in their role as upholders of domestic virtue by creating a comfortable home environment and tending to the needs of children and husbands. Men were to be of strong moral fiber and to provide material support for the family. These elite ideals, articulated in magazines, schools, sermons, and other public discourse, rested on a belief that one's ability to reach the standards of womanhood and manhood rested solely upon moral character and individual choice.

RECONSTRUCTING THE NORTH

Abraham Lincoln liked to cite his own rise as proof of the superiority of the Northern system of "free labor" over slavery. "There is no permanent class of hired laborers amongst us," Lincoln asserted. "Twenty-five years ago, I was a hired laborer. The hired laborer of yesterday, labors on his own account today; and will hire others to labor for him tomorrow. Advancement—improvement in condition—is the order of things in a society of equals." But the triumph of the North brought with it fundamental changes in the economy, labor relations, and politics that brought Lincoln's ideal vision into question. The spread of the factory system, the growth of large and powerful corporations, and the rapid expansion of capitalist enterprise all hastened the development of a large unskilled and routinized workforce. Rather than becoming independent producers, more and more workers found themselves consigned permanently to wage labor.

The old Republican ideal of a society bound by a harmony of interests had become overshadowed by a grimmer reality of class conflict. A violent national railroad strike in 1877 was broken only with the direct intervention of federal troops. That conflict struck many Americans as a turning point. Northern society, like the society of the South, appeared more hierarchical than equal. That same year, the last federal troops withdrew from their Southern posts, marking the end of the Reconstruction Era. By then, the North had undergone its own "reconstruction" as well.

The Age of Capital

In the decade following Appomattox, the North's economy continued the industrial boom begun during the Civil War. By 1873, America's industrial production had grown 75 percent over the 1865 level. By that time, too, the number of nonagricultural workers in the North had surpassed the number of farmers. Between 1860 and 1880, the number of wage earners in manufacturing and construction more than doubled, from 2 million to over 4 million. Only Great Britain boasted a larger manufacturing economy than the United States. During the same period, nearly 3 million immigrants arrived in America, almost all of whom settled in the North and West.

The railroad business both symbolized and advanced the new industrial order. Shortly before the Civil War, enthusiasm mounted for a transcontinental line. Private companies took on the huge and expensive job of construction, but the federal government funded the project, providing the largest subsidy in American history. The Pacific Railway Act of 1862 granted the Union Pacific and the Central Pacific rights to a broad swath of land extending from Omaha, Nebraska, to Sacramento, California. An 1864 act bestowed a subsidy of $15,000 per mile of track laid over smooth plains country and varying larger amounts up to $48,000 per mile in the foothills and mountains of the Far West. The Union Pacific employed gangs of Irish American and African American workers to lay track heading west from Omaha.

Meanwhile the Central Pacific, pushing east from California, had a tougher time finding workers, and began recruiting thousands of men from China. In 1868, the Senate ratified the Burlingame Treaty, giving Chinese the right to emigrate to the U.S., while specifiying that "nothing contained herein shall be held to confer naturalization." The right to work in America, in other words, did not bestow any right to citizenship. Some 12,000 Chinese laborers (about 90 percent of the workforce) bore the brunt of the difficult conditions in the Sierra Nevada mountains, where blizzards, landslides, and steep rock faces took an awful toll. Chinese workers earned a reputation for toughness and efficiency. "If we found we were in a hurry for a job of work," wrote one of the Central Pacific's superintendents, "it was better to put on Chinese at once". Working in baskets suspended by ropes, Chinese laborers chipped away at solid granite walls and became expert in the use of nitroglycerin for blasting through the mountains. But after completion of the transcontinental line threw thousands of Chinese railroad workers onto the California labor market, the open door immigration pledge in the Burlingame Treaty would soon be eclipsed by a virulent tide of anti-Chinese agitation among Western politicians and labor unions. In 1882, Congress passed the Chinese Exclusion Act, suspending any further Chinese immigration for ten years.

On May 10, 1869, Leland Stanford, the former governor of California and president of the Central Pacific Railroad, traveled to Promontory Point in Utah Territory to hammer a ceremonial golden spike, marking the finish of the first transcontinental line. Other railroads went up with less fanfare. The Southern Pacific, chartered by the state of California, stretched from San Francisco to Los Angeles, and on through Arizona and New Mexico to connections with New Orleans. The Atchison, Topeka, and Santa Fe reached the Pacific in 1887 by way of a southerly route across the Rocky Mountains. The Great Northern, one of the few lines financed by private capital, extended west from St. Paul, Minnesota, to Washington's Puget Sound.

Railroad corporations became America's first big businesses. Railroads required huge outlays of investment capital, and their growth increased the economic power of banks and investment houses centered in Wall Street. Bankers often gained seats on the boards of directors of these railroad companies, and their access to capital sometimes gave them the real control of railways. By the early 1870s the Pennsylvania Railroad stood as the nation's largest single company, with more than 20,000 employees. A new breed of aggressive entrepreneur sought to ease cutthroat competition by absorbing smaller companies and forming "pools" that set rates and divided the market. A small group of railroad executives, including Cornelius Vanderbilt, Jay Gould, Collis P. Huntington, and James J. Hill, amassed unheard-of fortunes. When he died in 1877, Vanderbilt

Chinese immigrants, like these section gang workers, provided labor and skills critical to the successful completion of the first transcontinental railroad. This photo was taken in Promontory, Utah Territory, in 1869.

SOURCE: The Denver Public Library, Western History Collection.

left his son $100 million. By comparison, a decent annual wage for working a six-day week was around $350.

Railroad promoters, lawyers, and lobbyists became ubiquitous figures in Washington and state capitals, wielding enormous influence among lawmakers. "The galleries and lobbies of every legislature," one Republican leader noted, "are thronged with men seeking . . . an advantage." Railroads benefited enormously from government subsidies. Between 1862 and 1872, Congress alone awarded more than 100 million acres of public lands to railroad companies and provided them over $64 million in loans and tax incentives.

Some of the nation's most prominent politicians routinely accepted railroad largesse. Republican senator William M. Stewart of Nevada, a member of the Committee on Pacific Railroads, received a gift of 50,000 acres of land from the Central Pacific for his services. The worst scandal of the Grant administration grew out of corruption involving railroad promotion. As a way of diverting funds for the building of the Union Pacific Railroad, an inner circle of Union Pacific stockholders created the dummy Crédit Mobilier construction company. In return for political favors, a group of prominent Republicans received stock in the company. When the scandal broke in 1872, it politically ruined Vice President Schuyler Colfax and led to the censure of two congressmen.

Other industries also boomed in this period, especially those engaged in extracting minerals and processing natural resources. Railroad growth stimulated expansion in the production of coal, iron, stone, and lumber, and these also received significant government aid. For example, under the National Mineral Act of 1866, mining companies received millions of acres of free public land. Oil refining enjoyed a huge expansion in the 1860s and 1870s. As with railroads, an early period of fierce competition soon gave way to concentration. By the late 1870s, John D. Rockefeller's Standard Oil Company controlled almost 90 percent of the nation's oil-refining capacity.

Liberal Republicans and the Election of 1872

With the rapid growth of large-scale, capital-intensive enterprises, Republicans increasingly identified with the interests of business rather than the rights of freedmen or the antebellum ideology of "free labor." The old Civil War–era Radical Republicans had declined in influence. State Republican parties now organized themselves around the spoils of federal patronage rather than grand causes such as preserving the Union or ending slavery. Despite the Crédit Mobilier affair, Republicans had no monopoly on political scandal. In 1871, New York City newspapers reported the shocking story of how Democratic Party boss William M. Tweed and his friends had systematically stolen tens of millions from the city treasury. The "Tweed Ring" had received enormous bribes and kickbacks from city contractors and businessmen. Grotesquely caricatured by Thomas Nast's cartoons in *Harper's Weekly*, Tweed emerged as the preeminent national symbol of increasingly degraded and dishonest urban politics. But to many, the scandal represented only the most extreme case of the routine corruption that now plagued American political life.

By the end of President Grant's first term, a large number of disaffected Republicans sought an alternative. The Liberal Republicans, as they called themselves, shared several core values. First, they emphasized the doctrines of classical economics, stressing the law of supply and demand, free trade, defense of property rights, and individualism. They called for a return to limited government, arguing that bribery, scandal, and high taxes all flowed from excessive state interference in the economy.

Liberal Republicans were also suspicious of expanding democracy. "Universal suffrage," Charles Francis Adams Jr. wrote in 1869, "can only mean in plain English the government of ignorance and vice—it means a European, and especially Celtic, proletariat on the Atlantic coast, an African proletariat on the shores of the Gulf, and a Chinese proletariat on the Pacific." Liberal Republicans believed that politics ought to be the province of "the best men"—educated and well-to-do men like themselves, devoted to the "science of government." They proposed civil service reform as the best way to break the hold of party machines on patronage.

Although most Liberal Republicans had enthusiastically supported abolition, the Union cause, and equal rights for freedmen, they now opposed continued federal intervention in the South. The national government had done all it could for the former slaves; they must now take care of themselves. "Root, Hog, or Die" was the harsh advice offered by Horace Greeley, editor of the *New York Tribune*. In the spring of 1872, a diverse collection of Liberal Republicans nominated Greeley to run for president. A longtime foe of the Democratic Party, Greeley nonetheless won that party's presidential nomination as well. He made a new policy for the South the center of his campaign against Grant. The "best men" of both sections, he argued, should support a more generous Reconstruction policy based on "universal amnesty and impartial suffrage." All Americans, Greeley urged, must put the Civil War behind them and "clasp hands across the bloody chasm."

Grant easily defeated Greeley, carrying every state in the North and winning 56 percent of the popular vote. Most Republicans were not willing to abandon the regular party organization, and "waving the bloody shirt" was still a potent vote-getter. But the 1872 election accelerated the trend toward federal abandonment of African American citizenship rights. The Liberal Republicans quickly faded as an organized political force. But their ideas helped define a growing conservative consciousness among the Northern public. For the rest of the century, their political and economic views attracted a growing number of middle-class professionals and businessmen. This agenda included retreat from the ideal of racial justice, hostility toward trade unions, suspicion of working-class and immigrant political power, celebration of competitive individualism, and opposition to government intervention in economic affairs.

The Depression of 1873

In the fall of 1873, the postwar boom came to an abrupt halt as a severe financial panic triggered a deep economic depression. The collapse resulted from commercial overexpansion, especially, speculative investing in the nation's railroad system. The investment banking house of Jay Cooke and Company failed in September 1873, when it found itself unable to market millions of dollars in Northern Pacific Railroad bonds. Soon, other banks and brokerage houses, especially those dealing in railroad securities, caved in as well, and the New York Stock Exchange suspended operations. By 1876, half the nation's railroads had defaulted on their bonds. Over the next two years, more than 100 banks folded and 18,000 businesses shut their doors. The depression that began in 1873 lasted sixty-five months—the longest economic contraction in the nation's history until then.

The human toll of the depression was enormous. As factories began to close across the nation, the unemployment rate soared to about 15 percent. In many cities, the jobless rate was much higher; roughly one-quarter of New York City workers were unemployed in 1874. Many thousands of men took to the road in search of work, and the "tramp" emerged as a new and menacing figure on the social landscape. The Pennsylvania Bureau of Labor Statistics noted that never before had "so many of the working classes, skilled and unskilled . . . been moving from place to place seeking employment that was not to be had." Farmers were also hard hit by the depression. Agricultural output continued to grow, but prices and land values fell sharply.

Mass meetings of workers in New York and other cities issued calls to government officials to create jobs through public works. But these appeals were rejected. Indeed, many business leaders and political figures denounced even meager efforts at charity. E. L. Godkin wrote in the Christmas 1875 issue of *The Nation* that "free soup must be prohibited, and all classes must learn that soup of any kind, beef or turtle, can be had only by being paid for." Men such as Godkin saw the depression as a natural, if painful, part of the business cycle, one that would allow only the strongest enterprises (and workers) to survive. They dismissed any attempts at government interference, in the form of either job creation or relief for the poor.

The depression of the 1870s prompted many workers and farmers to question the old free-labor ideology that celebrated a harmony of interests in Northern society. More people voiced anger at and distrust of large corporations that exercised great economic power from outside their communities. Businessmen and merchants, meanwhile, especially in large cities, became more conscious of their own class interests. New political organizations, such as Chicago's Citizens' Association, united businessmen in campaigns for fiscal conservatism and defense of property rights. In national politics, the persistent depression made the Republican Party, North and South, more vulnerable than ever.

"The Tramp," *Harper's Weekly*, September 2, 1876. The depression that began in 1873 forced many thousands of unemployed workers to go "on the tramp" in search of jobs. Men wandered from town to town, walking or riding railroad cars, desperate for a chance to work for wages or simply for room and board. The "tramp" became a powerful symbol of the misery caused by industrial depression and, as in this drawing, an image that evoked fear and nervousness among the nation's middle class.

SOURCE: The Picture Bank, Frank & Marie-Therese Wood Print Collection.

The Electoral Crisis of 1876

With the economy mired in depression, Democrats looked forward to capturing the White House in 1876.

New scandals plaguing the Grant administration also weakened the Republican Party. In 1875, a conspiracy surfaced between distillers and U.S. revenue agents to cheat the government out of millions in tax revenues. The government secured indictments against more than 200 members of this "Whiskey Ring," including Orville E. Babcock, Grant's private secretary. Though acquitted, thanks to Grant's intervention, Babcock resigned in disgrace. In 1876, Secretary of War William W. Belknap was impeached for receiving bribes for the sale of trading posts in Indian Territory, and he resigned to avoid conviction (see Map 17.4).

Democrats hammered away at the Grant administration's low standard of honesty in government, and for president, they nominated Governor Samuel J. Tilden of New York, who brought impeccable reform credentials to his candidacy. In 1871, he had helped expose and prosecute the "Tweed Ring" in New York City. As governor, he had toppled the "Canal Ring," a graft-ridden scheme involving inflated contracts for repairs on the Erie Canal. In their platform, the Democrats linked the issue of corruption to an attack on Reconstruction policies. They blamed the Republicans for instituting "a corrupt centralism" that subjected Southern states to "the rapacity of carpetbag tyrannies," riddled the national government "with incapacity, waste, and fraud," and "locked fast the prosperity of an industrious people in the paralysis of hard times."

Republican nominee Rutherford B. Hayes, governor of Ohio, also sought the high ground. As a lawyer in Cincinnati, he had defended runaway slaves. Later, he had distinguished himself as a general in the Union army. Republicans charged Tilden with disloyalty during the war, income tax evasion, and close relations with powerful railroad interests. Hayes promised, if elected, to support an efficient civil service system, to vigorously prosecute officials who betrayed the public trust, and to introduce a system of free universal education.

On an election day marred by widespread vote fraud and violent intimidation, Tilden received 250,000 more popular votes than Hayes. But Republicans refused to concede victory, challenging the vote totals in the electoral college. Tilden garnered 184 uncontested electoral votes, one shy of the majority required to win, while Hayes received 165. The problem centered in 20 disputed votes from Florida, Louisiana, South Carolina, and Oregon. In each of the three Southern states two sets of electoral votes were returned. In Oregon, which Hayes had unquestionably carried, the Democratic governor nevertheless replaced a disputed Republican elector with a Democrat.

The crisis was unprecedented. In January 1877, Congress moved to settle the deadlock, establishing an Electoral Commission composed of five senators, five representatives, and five Supreme Court justices; eight were Republicans and seven were Democrats. The commission voted along strict partisan lines to award all the contested electoral votes to Hayes. Outraged by this

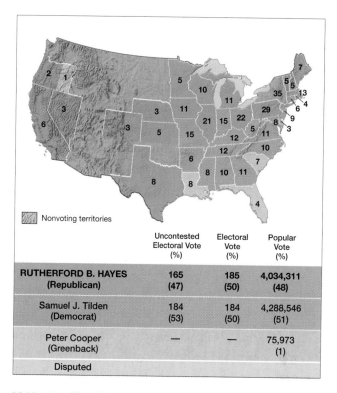

	Uncontested Electoral Vote (%)	Electoral Vote (%)	Popular Vote (%)
RUTHERFORD B. HAYES (Republican)	165 (47)	185 (50)	4,034,311 (48)
Samuel J. Tilden (Democrat)	184 (53)	184 (50)	4,288,546 (51)
Peter Cooper (Greenback)	—	—	75,973 (1)
Disputed			

Nonvoting territories

MAP 17.4 The Election of 1876 The presidential election of 1876 left the nation without a clear-cut winner.

decision, Democratic congressmen threatened a filibuster to block Hayes's inauguration. Violence and stalemate were avoided when Democrats and Republicans struck a compromise in February. In return for Hayes's ascendance to the presidency, the Republicans promised to appropriate more money for Southern internal improvements, to appoint a Southerner to Hayes's cabinet, and to pursue a policy of noninterference ("home rule") in Southern affairs.

Shortly after assuming office, Hayes ordered removal of the remaining federal troops in Louisiana and South Carolina. Without this military presence to sustain them, the Republican governors of those two states quickly lost power to Democrats. "Home rule" meant Republican abandonment of freed people, Radicals, carpetbaggers, and scalawags. It also effectively nullified the Fourteenth and Fifteenth Amendments and the Civil Rights Act of 1866. The "Compromise of 1877" completed repudiation of the idea, born during the Civil War and pursued during Congressional Reconstruction, of a powerful federal government protecting the rights of all American citizens. As one black Louisianan lamented, "The whole South—every state in the South—had got into the hands of the very men that held us slaves." Other voices hailed this turning point in policy. "The negro," declared *The Nation*, "will disappear from the field of national politics. Henceforth, the nation, as a nation, will have nothing more to do with him."

CONCLUSION

Reconstruction succeeded in the limited political sense of reuniting a nation torn apart by the Civil War. The Radical Republican vision, emphasizing racial justice, equal civil and political rights guaranteed by the Fourteenth and Fifteenth Amendments, and a new Southern economy organized around independent small farmers, never enjoyed the support of the majority of its party or the Northern public. By 1877, the political force of these ideals was spent, and the national retreat from them nearly complete.

The end of Reconstruction left the way open for the return of white domination in the South. The freed people's political and civil equality proved only temporary. It would take a "Second Reconstruction," the civil rights movement of the next century, to establish full black citizenship rights once and for all.

The federal government's failure to pursue land reform left former slaves without the economic independence needed for full emancipation. Yet the newly autonomous black family, along with black-controlled churches, schools, and other social institutions, provided the foundations for the modern African American community. If the federal government was not yet fully committed to protecting equal rights in local communities, the Reconstruction Era at least pointed to how that goal might be achieved. Even as the federal government retreated from the defense of equal rights for black people, it took a more aggressive stance as the protector of business interests. The Hayes administration responded decisively to one of the worst outbreaks of class violence in American history by dispatching federal troops to several Northern cities to break the Great Railroad Strike of 1877. In the aftermath of Reconstruction, the struggle

CHRONOLOGY

1865	Freedmen's Bureau established
	Abraham Lincoln assassinated
	Andrew Johnson begins Presidential Reconstruction
	Black codes begin to be enacted in Southern states
	Thirteenth Amendment ratified
1866	Civil Rights Act passed
	Congress approves Fourteenth Amendment
	Ku Klux Klan founded
1867	Reconstruction Acts, passed over President Johnson's veto, begin Congressional Reconstruction
	Tenure of Office Act
	Southern states call constitutional conventions
1868	President Johnson impeached by the House, but acquitted in Senate trial
	Fourteenth Amendment ratified
	Most Southern states readmitted to the Union
	Ulysses S. Grant elected president
1869	Congress approves Fifteenth Amendment
	Union Pacific and Central Pacific tracks meet at Promontory Point in Utah Territory
	Suffragists split into National Woman Suffrage Association and American Woman Suffrage Association
1870	Fifteenth Amendment ratified
1871	Ku Klux Klan Act passed
	"Tweed Ring" in New York City exposed
1872	Liberal Republicans break with Grant and Radicals, nominate Horace Greeley for president
	Crédit Mobilier scandal
	Grant reelected president
1873	Financial panic and beginning of economic depression
	Slaughterhouse cases
1874	Democrats gain control of House for first time since 1856
1875	Civil Rights Act
1876	Disputed election between Samuel Tilden and Rutherford B. Hayes
1877	Electoral Commission elects Hayes president
	President Hayes dispatches federal troops to break Great Railroad Strike and withdraws last remaining federal troops from the South

between capital and labor had clearly replaced "the Southern question" as the number one political issue of the day. "The overwhelming labor question has dwarfed all other questions into nothing," wrote an Ohio Republican. "We have home questions enough to occupy attention now."

REVIEW QUESTIONS

1. How did various visions of a "reconstructed" South differ? How did these visions reflect the old political and social divisions that had led to the Civil War?
2. What key changes did emancipation make in the political and economic status of African Americans? Discuss the expansion of citizenship rights in the post–Civil War years. To what extent did women share in the gains made by African Americans?
3. What role did such institutions as the family, the church, the schools, and the political parties play in the African American transition to freedom?
4. How did white Southerners attempt to limit the freedom of former slaves? How did these efforts succeed, and how did they fail?
5. Evaluate the achievements and failures of Reconstruction governments in the Southern states.
6. What were the crucial economic changes occurring in the North and South during the Reconstruction era?

RECOMMENDED READING

David W. Blight, *Race and Reunion: The Civil War in American Memory* (2001). An elegantly written and deeply researched inquiry into how Americans "remembered" the Civil War in the half century after Appomattox, arguing that sectional reconciliation came at the cost of racial division.

Paul A. Cimbala and Randall M. Miller, eds., *The Freedmen's Bureau and Reconstruction* (1999). A wide ranging collection of the latest scholarship, with special attention to recapturing the historical voices of freed people.

Jane Dailey, *Before Jim Crow: The Politics of Race in Postemancipation Virginia* (2000). A fine study that focuses on the tension between the drive to establish white supremacy and the struggle for biracial coalitions in post–Civil War Virginia politics.

Laura F. Edwards, *Gendered Strife & Confusion: The Political Culture of Reconstruction* (1997). An ambitious analysis of how gender ideologies played a key role in shaping the party politics and social relations of the Reconstruction-Era South.

Michael W. Fitzgerald, *The Union League Movement in the Deep South* (1989). Uses the Union League as a lens through which to examine race relations and the close connections between politics and economic change in the post–Civil War South.

Eric Foner, *Reconstruction: America's Unfinished Revolution, 1863–1877* (1988). The most comprehensive and thoroughly researched overview of the Reconstruction Era.

Jacqueline Jones, *Labor of Love, Labor of Sorrow* (1985). Includes excellent material on the work and family lives of African American women in slavery and freedom.

Leon Litwack, *Been in the Storm So Long: The Aftermath of Slavery* (1979). A richly detailed analysis of the transition from slavery to freedom; excellent use of African American sources.

Elizabeth Regosin, *Freedom's Promise: Ex-Slave Families and Citizenship in the Age of Emancipation* (2002). A thoughtful analysis of how freedmen and freedwomen asserted familial relationships as a means to claiming citizenship rights after emancipation, based on research into federal pension applications made by dependent survivors of Civil War soldiers.

Scott Reynolds Nelson, *Iron Confederacies: Southern Railways, Klan Violence, and Reconstruction* (1999). Pathbreaking analysis of how conservative Southern and Northern business interests rebuilt the South's railroad system and also achieved enormous political power within individual states.

 For additional study resources for this chapter, go to the *Companion Website*, http://www.prenhall.com/faragher.

WHOSE HISTORY IS IT?

FLYING THE STARS AND BARS:
THE CONTESTED MEANING OF THE CONFEDERATE FLAG

In March 2000, thousands of demonstrators rallied outside the Capitol in Montgomery, Alabama, calling on state officials to once again fly the Confederate flag over the building. This rally was organized by the League of the South, a group dedicated to celebrating white Southern history and culture. But are displays of the Confederate flag reflections of the fierce pride many white Southerners have for the "Lost Cause" or a reaction to the progress African-Americans have made since the Civil Rights movement of the 1950s and 1960s? The flag is the same design as the battle flag carried in the field by Confederate troops during the Civil War. Throughout the South, the revived use of the Confederate flag began as part of the white backlash against the campaign to end legal segregation. In 1963 Alabama Gov. George C. Wallace ordered the Confederate battle flag to fly on top of the Montgomery state capitol to protest a visit by Attorney General Robert F. Kennedy, who had come to town to discuss desegregation of the state's schools.

Since that time, many Americans around the country have adopted it as an all-purpose symbol of rebellion and resistance to authority, displayed on posters, clothing, bumper stickers, and featured in music videos. But for most African-Americans the Confederate flag meant something quite different. In the summer of 1988 fourteen black Alabama state legislators were arrested for trespassing on state property when they attempted to scale a chain-link fence and remove the flag. Rep. Alvin Holmes, one of those arrested, said, "When I walk up the Capitol steps, instead of seeing the American flag, the flag that

This 1871 painting by Richard Norris Brooke depicts Confederate soldiers at the end of the Civil War, furling the rebel battle flag for the last time. In the postwar Reconstruction years, the Ku Klux Klan adapted it as a symbol of white supremacy and resistance to Federal authority.

AP Wide World Photos.

I served under when I was in the United States Army, I see a flag that represents treason, sedition, slavery, and oppression toward my people."

Many whites insisted the old flag was about regional identity and pride, not race, a "symbol of heritage" somehow divorced from the historical brutality of slavery. John Napier, a retired Air Force colonel and leader of the Sons of Confederate veterans argued, "We celebrate our civil rights history. There are those of us who feel the earlier struggle should be commemorated historically, too. While we're running around naming streets for Rosa Parks, which I have no problem with, you're getting into removing all the symbols of the Confederacy." African-Americans, for whom the flag symbolized slavery, racism, segregation, and violence, tried to distinguish between private and public displays. "I see nothing wrong with someone flying the Confederate flag even on their front lawn or putting it on their bumper stickers," said Earl Shinhoster, an official of the NAACP. "I do, however, see something wrong when the state promotes something that many people find offensive." In a 2001 referendum, Mississippi, voters overwhelmingly approved retaining the Confederate symbol as part of the state flag. In South Carolina, the NAACP led an effective economic boycott against the state to protest continued flying of the Stars and Bars over the capitol. A compromise solution removed the flag from the capitol, but kept it flying nearby. As long as private and public displays of the Confederate flag persist, so will the highly charged debates over the historical meanings it embodies.

Although the University of Mississippi officially disassociated itself from the Confederate flag in 1981, it continued to fly among fans at this 1995 Ole Miss football game in Oxford. ▶

AP Wide World Photos.

💧 Demonstrators from the Harriet Tubman Freedom House burn the Confederate flag in this 2000 protest against the Stars and Bars flying over the state capitol in Columbia, South Carolina.

AP Wide World Photos.

Two years after Mississippi voters decided to keep the Confederate battle emblem as part of the state flag, the issue remained politically charged. This yard sign from the 2003 governor's race expresses support for Republican candidate Haley Barbour, who attacked Democratic Governor Ronnie Musgrove for insisting on giving voters a chance to decide the state flag's design. 💧

AP Wide World Photos.

Confederate flags are frequently used as all purpose symbols of cultural rebellion. This one appears on a stock car at the North Florida Speedway in Wewahitchka, 2002. ▶

Richard Bickel, CORBIS-NY.

💧 NAACP march near Ft. Mill, South Carolina in April 2002, supporting an economic boycott of South Carolina over the continued presence of the Confederate flag at the state house in Columbia.

AP Wide World Photos.

APPENDIX

THE DECLARATION OF INDEPENDENCE

When in the course of human events it becomes necessary for one people to dissolve the political bands which have connected them with another and to assume, among the powers of the earth, the separate and equal station to which the laws of nature and of nature's God entitle them, a decent respect to the opinions of mankind requires that they should declare the causes which impel them to the separation.

We hold these truths to be self-evident, that all men are created equal; that they are endowed by their Creator with certain unalienable rights; that among these are life, liberty, and the pursuit of happiness. That, to secure these rights, governments are instituted among men, deriving their just powers from the consent of the governed; that, whenever any form of government becomes destructive of these ends, it is the right of the people to alter or to abolish it, and to institute a new government, laying its foundation on such principles, and organizing its powers in such form, as to them shall seem most likely to effect their safety and happiness. Prudence, indeed, will dictate that governments long established should not be changed for light and transient causes; and, accordingly, all experience hath shown that mankind are more disposed to suffer, while evils are sufferable, than to right themselves by abolishing the forms to which they are accustomed. But when a long train of abuses and usurpations, pursuing invariably the same object, evinces a design to reduce them under absolute despotism, it is their right, it is their duty, to throw off such government and to provide new guards for their future security. Such has been the patient sufferance of these colonies, and such is now the necessity which constrains them to alter their former systems of government. The history of the present King of Great Britain is a history of repeated injuries and usurpations, all having, in direct object, the establishment of an absolute tyranny over these States. To prove this, let facts be submitted to a candid world:

He has refused his assent to laws the most wholesome and necessary for the public good.

He has forbidden his governors to pass laws of immediate and pressing importance, unless suspended in their operation till his assent should be obtained; and, when so suspended, he has utterly neglected to attend to them.

He has refused to pass other laws for the accommodation of large districts of people, unless those people would relinquish the right of representation in the legislature, a right inestimable to them and formidable to tyrants only.

He has called together legislative bodies at places unusual, uncomfortable, and distant from the depository of their public records, for the sole purpose of fatiguing them into compliance with his measures.

He has dissolved representative houses, repeatedly for opposing, with manly firmness, his invasions on the rights of the people.

He has refused, for a long time after such dissolutions, to cause others to be elected; whereby the legislative powers, incapable of annihilation, have returned to the people at large for their exercise; the state remaining, in the meantime, exposed to all the danger of invasion from without and convulsions within.

He has endeavored to prevent the population of these States; for that purpose, obstructing the laws for naturalization of foreigners, refusing to pass others to encourage their migration hither, and raising the conditions of new appropriations of lands.

He has obstructed the administration of justice by refusing his assent to laws for establishing judiciary powers.

He has made judges dependent on his will alone for the tenure of their offices and the amount and payment of their salaries.

He has erected a multitude of new offices and sent hither swarms of officers to harass our people and eat out their substance.

He has kept among us, in time of peace, standing armies, without the consent of our legislatures.

He has affected to render the military independent of, and superior to, the civil power.

He has combined with others to subject us to a jurisdiction foreign to our Constitution and unacknowledged by our laws, giving his assent to their acts of pretended legislation—

For quartering large bodies of armed troops among us;

For protecting them by mock trial, from punishment for any murders which they should commit on the inhabitants of these States;

For cutting off our trade with all parts of the world;

For imposing taxes on us without our consent;

For depriving us, in many cases, of the benefit of trial by jury;

For transporting us beyond seas to be tried for pretended offences;

For abolishing the free system of English laws in a neighboring province, establishing therein an arbitrary government, and enlarging its boundaries, so as to render it at once an example and fit instrument for introducing the same absolute rule into these colonies;

For taking away our charters, abolishing our most valuable laws, and altering, fundamentally, the powers of our governments.

For suspending our own legislatures and declaring themselves invested with power to legislate for us in all cases whatsoever.

He has abdicated government here by declaring us out of his protection and waging war against us.

He has plundered our seas, ravaged our coasts, burnt our towns, and destroyed the lives of our people.

He is, at this time, transporting large armies of foreign mercenaries to complete the works of death, desolation, and tyranny already begun with circumstances of cruelty and perfidy scarcely paralleled in the most barbarous ages, and totally unworthy the head of a civilized nation.

He has constrained our fellow citizens, taken captive on the high seas, to bear arms against their country, to become the executioners of their friends and brethren, or to fall themselves by their hands.

He has excited domestic insurrections amongst us and has endeavored to bring on the inhabitants of our frontiers, the merciless Indian savages, whose known rule of warfare is an undistinguished destruction of all ages, sexes, and conditions.

In every stage of these oppressions, we have petitioned for redress in the most humble terms; our repeated petitions have been answered only by repeated injury. A prince whose character is thus marked by every act which may define a tyrant is unfit to be the ruler of a free people.

Nor have we been wanting in attention to our British brethren. We have warned them, from time to time, of attempts made by their legislature to extend an unwarrantable jurisdiction over us. We have reminded them of the circumstances of our emigration and settlement here. We have appealed to their native justice and magnanimity, and we have conjured them, by the ties of our common kindred, to disavow these usurpations, which would inevitably interrupt our connections and correspondence. They, too, have been deaf to the voice of justice and consanguinity. We must, therefore, acquiesce in the necessity which denounces our separation, and hold them, as we hold the rest of mankind, enemies in war, in peace, friends.

We, therefore, the representatives of the United States of America, in general Congress assembled, appealing to the Supreme Judge of the world for the rectitude of our intentions, do, in the name and by the authority of the good people of these colonies, solemnly publish and declare, that these united colonies are, and of right ought to be, free and independent states: that they are absolved from all allegiance to the British Crown, and that all political connection between them and the state of Great Britain is, and ought to be, totally dissolved; and that, as free and independent states, they have full power to levy war, conclude peace, contract alliances, establish commerce, and to do all other acts and things which independent states may of right do. And, for the support of this declaration, with a firm reliance on the protection of Divine Providence, we mutually pledge to each other our lives, our fortunes, and our sacred honor.

THE CONSTITUTION OF THE UNITED STATES OF AMERICA

We the people of the United States, in order to form a more perfect union, establish justice, insure domestic tranquillity, provide for the common defense, promote the general welfare, and secure the blessings of liberty to ourselves and our posterity, do ordain and establish this Constitution for the United States of America.

Article I

Section 1. All legislative powers herein granted shall be vested in a Congress of the United States, which shall consist of a Senate and House of Representatives.

Section 2. 1. The House of Representatives shall be composed of members chosen every second year by the people of the several States, and the electors in each State shall have the qualifications requisite for electors of the most numerous branch of the State legislature.

2. No person shall be a representative who shall not have attained to the age of twenty-five years, and been seven years a citizen of the United States, and who shall not, when elected, be an inhabitant of that State in which he shall be chosen.

3. Representatives and direct taxes[1] shall be apportioned among the several States which may be included within this Union, according to their respective numbers, which shall be determined by adding to the whole number of free persons, including those bound to service for a term of years, and excluding Indians not taxed, three fifths of all other persons.[2] The actual enumeration shall be made within three years after the first meeting of the Congress of the United States, and within every subsequent term of ten years, in such manner as they shall by law direct. The number of representatives shall not exceed one for every thirty thousand, but each State shall have at least one representative; and until such enumeration shall be made, the State of New Hampshire shall be entitled to choose three, Massachusetts eight, Rhode Island and Providence Plantations one, Connecticut five, New York six, New Jersey four, Pennsylvania eight, Delaware one, Maryland six, Virginia ten, North Carolina five, South Carolina five, and Georgia three.

4. When vacancies happen in the representation from any State, the executive authority thereof shall issue writs of election to fill such vacancies.

5. The House of Representatives shall choose their speaker and other officers; and shall have the sole power of impeachment.

Section 3. 1. The Senate of the United States shall be composed of two senators from each State, chosen by the legislature thereof,[3] for six years; and each senator shall have one vote.

2. Immediately after they shall be assembled in consequence of the first election, they shall be divided as equally as may be into three classes. The seats of the senators of the first class shall be vacated at the expiration of the second year, of the second class at the expiration of the fourth year, and of the third class at the expiration of the sixth year, so that one third may be chosen every second year; and if vacancies happen by resignation, or otherwise, during the recess of the legislature of any State, the executive thereof may make temporary appointments until the next meeting of the legislature, which shall then fill such vacancies.[4]

3. No person shall be a senator who shall not have attained to the age of thirty years, and been nine years a citizen of the United States, and who shall not, when elected, be an inhabitant of that State for which he shall be chosen.

4. The Vice President of the United States shall be President of the Senate, but shall have no vote, unless they be equally divided.

5. The Senate shall choose their other officers, and also a president pro tempore, in the absence of the Vice President, or when he shall exercise the office of the President of the United States.

6. The Senate shall have the sole power to try all impeachments. When sitting for that purpose, they shall be on oath or affirmation. When the President of the United States is tried, the chief justice shall preside: and no person shall be convicted without the concurrence of two thirds of the members present.

7. Judgment in cases of impeachment shall not extend further than to removal from office, and disqualification to hold and enjoy any office of honor, trust or profit under the United States: but the party convicted shall nevertheless be liable and subject to indictment, trial, judgment and punishment, according to law.

Section 4. 1. The times, places, and manner of holding elections for senators and representatives, shall be prescribed in each State by the legislature thereof; but the Congress may at any time by law make or alter such regulations, except as to the places of choosing senators.

2. The Congress shall assemble at least once in every year, and such meeting shall be on the first Monday in December, unless they shall by law appoint a different day.

Section 5. 1. Each House shall be the judge of the elections, returns and qualifications of its own members, and a majority of each shall constitute a quorum to do business; but a smaller number may adjourn from day to day, and may be authorized to compel the attendance of absent members, in such manner, and under such penalties as each House may provide.

2. Each House may determine the rules of its proceedings, punish its members for disorderly behavior, and, with the concurrence of two thirds, expel a member.

3. Each House shall keep a journal of its proceedings, and from time to time publish the same, excepting such parts as may in their judgment require secrecy; and the yeas and nays of the members of either House on any question

---

[1] See the Sixteenth Amendment.
[2] See the Fourteenth Amendment.
[3] See the Seventeenth Amendment.

[4] See the Seventeenth Amendment.

shall, at the desire of one fifth of those present, be entered on the journal.

4. Neither House, during the session of Congress, shall, without the consent of the other, adjourn for more than three days, nor to any other place than that in which the two Houses shall be sitting.

Section 6. 1. The senators and representatives shall receive a compensation for their services, to be ascertained by law, and paid out of the Treasury of the United States. They shall in all cases, except treason, felony, and breach of the peace, be privileged from arrest during their attendance at the session of their respective Houses, and in going to and returning from the same; and for any speech or debate in either House, they shall not be questioned in any other place.

2. No senator or representative shall, during the time for which he was elected, be appointed to any civil office under the authority of the United States, which shall have been created, or the emoluments whereof shall have been increased, during such time; and no person holding any office under the United States shall be a member of either House during his continuance in office.

Section 7. 1. All bills for raising revenue shall originate in the House of Representatives; but the Senate may propose or concur with amendments as on other bills.

2. Every bill which shall have passed the House of Representatives and the Senate, shall, before it become a law, be presented to the President of the United States; If he approves he shall sign it, but if not he shall return it, with his objections, to that House in which it shall have originated, who shall enter the objections at large on their journal, and proceed to reconsider it. If after such reconsideration two thirds of that House shall agree to pass the bill, it shall be sent, together with the objections, to the other House, by which it shall likewise be reconsidered, and if approved by two thirds of that House, it shall become a law. But in all such cases the votes of both Houses shall be determined by yeas and nays, and the names of the persons voting for and against the bill shall be entered on the journal of each House respectively. If any bill shall not be returned by the President within ten days (Sundays excepted) after it shall have been presented to him, the same shall be a law, in like manner as if he had signed it, unless the Congress by their adjournment prevent its return, in which case it shall not be a law.

3. Every order, resolution, or vote to which the concurrence of the Senate and the House of Representatives may be necessary (except on a question of adjournment) shall be presented to the President of the United States; and before the same shall take effect, shall be approved by him, or being disapproved by him, shall be repassed by two thirds of the Senate and House of Representatives, according to the rules and limitations prescribed in the case of a bill.

Section 8. 1. The Congress shall have the power

1. To lay and collect taxes, duties, imposts, and excises, to pay the debts and provide for the common defense and general welfare of the United States; but all duties, imposts, and excises shall be uniform throughout the United States.

2. To borrow money on the credit of the United States;

3. To regulate commerce with foreign nations, and among the several States, and with the Indian tribes;

4. To establish a uniform rule of naturalization, and uniform laws on the subject of bankruptcies throughout the United States;

5. To coin money, regulate the value thereof, and of foreign coin, and fix the standard of weights and measures;

6. To provide for the punishment of counterfeiting the securities and current coin of the United States;

7. To establish post offices and post roads;

8. To promote the progress of science and useful arts, by securing for limited times to authors and inventors the exclusive right to their respective writings and discoveries;

9. To constitute tribunals inferior to the Supreme Court;

10. To define and punish piracies and felonies committed on the high seas, and offenses against the law of nations;

11. To declare war, grant letters of marque and reprisal, and make rules concerning captures on land and water;

12. To raise and support armies, but no appropriation of money to that use shall be for a longer term than two years;

13. To provide and maintain a navy;

14. To make rules for the government and regulation of the land and naval forces;

15. To provide for calling forth the militia to execute the laws of the Union, suppress insurrections and repel invasions;

16. To provide for organizing, arming, and disciplining the militia, and for governing such part of them as may be employed in the service of the United States, reserving to the States respectively, the appointment of the officers, and the authority of training the militia according to the discipline prescribed by Congress;

17. To exercise exclusive legislation in all cases whatsoever, over such district (not exceeding ten miles square) as may, by cession of particular States, and the acceptance of Congress, become the seat of the government of the United States, and to exercise like authority over all places purchased by the consent of the legislature of the State in which the same shall be, for the erection of forts, magazines, arsenals, dockyards, and other needful buildings; and

18. To make all laws which shall be necessary and proper for carrying into execution the foregoing powers, and all other powers vested by this Constitution in the government of the United States, or any department or officer thereof.

Section 9. 1. The migration or importation of such persons as any of the States now existing shall think proper to admit, shall not be prohibited by the Congress prior to the year one thousand eight hundred and eight, but a tax or duty may be imposed on such importation, not exceeding ten dollars for each person.

2. The privilege of the writ of habeas corpus shall not be suspended, unless when in cases of rebellion or invasion the public safety may require it.

3. No bill of attainder or ex post facto law shall be passed.

4. No capitation, or other direct, tax shall be laid, unless in proportion to the census or enumeration hereinbefore directed to be taken.[5]

5. No tax or duty shall be laid on articles exported from any State.

6. No preference shall be given by any regulation of commerce or revenue to the ports of one State over those of another: nor shall vessels bound to, or from, one State be obliged to enter, clear, or pay duties in another.

7. No money shall be drawn from the treasury, but in consequence of appropriations made by law; and a regular statement and account of the receipts and expenditures of all public money shall be published from time to time.

8. No title of nobility shall be granted by the United States: and no person holding any office of profit or trust under them, shall, without the consent of the Congress, accept of any present, emolument, office, or title, of any kind whatever, from any king, prince, or foreign State.

Section 10. 1. No State shall enter into any treaty, alliance, or confederation; grant letters of marque and reprisal; coin money; emit bills of credit; make any thing but gold and silver coin a tender in payment of debts; pass any bill of attainder, ex post facto law, or law impairing the obligation of contracts, or grant, any title of nobility.

2. No State shall, without the consent of the Congress, lay any imposts or duties on imports or exports, except what may be absolutely necessary for executing its inspection laws: and the net produce of all duties and imposts laid by any State on imports or exports, shall be for the use of the treasury of the United States; and all such laws shall be subject to the revision and control of the Congress.

3. No State shall, without the consent of the Congress, lay any duty of tonnage, keep troops, or ships of war in time of peace, enter into any agreement or compact with another State, or with a foreign power, or engage in war, unless actually invaded, or in such imminent danger as will not admit of delay.

Article II

Section 1. 1. The executive power shall be vested in a President of the United States of America. He shall hold his office during the term of four years, and, together with the Vice President, chosen for the same term, be elected, as follows:

2. Each State shall appoint, in such manner as the legislature thereof may direct, a number of electors, equal to the whole number of senators and representatives to which the State may be entitled in the Congress: but no senator or representative, or person holding any office of trust or profit under the United States, shall be appointed an elector.

The electors shall meet in their respective States, and vote by ballot for two persons, of whom one at least shall not be an inhabitant of the same State with themselves. And they shall make a list of all the persons voted for, and of the number of votes for each; which list they shall sign and certify, and transmit sealed to the seat of the government of the United States, directed to the president of the Senate. The president of the Senate shall, in the presence of the Senate and House of Representatives, open all the certificates, and the votes shall then be counted. The person having the greatest number of votes shall be the President, if such number be a majority of the whole number of electors appointed; and if there be more than one who have such majority, and have an equal number of votes, then the House of Representatives shall immediately choose by ballot one of them for President; and if no person have a majority, then from the five highest on the list the said House shall in like manner choose the President. But in choosing the President, the votes shall be taken by States, the representation from each State having one vote; a quorum for this purpose shall consist of a member or members from two thirds of the States, and a majority of all the States shall be necessary to a choice. In every case after the choice of the President, the person having the greatest number of votes of the electors shall be the Vice President. But if there should remain two or more who have equal votes, the Senate shall choose from them by ballot the Vice President.[6]

3. The Congress may determine the time of choosing the electors, and the day on which they shall give their votes; which day shall be the same throughout the United States.

4. No person except a natural born citizen, or a citizen of the United States, at the time of the adoption of this Constitution, shall be eligible to the office of President; neither shall any person be eligible to the office who shall not have attained to the age of thirty-five years, and been fourteen years a resident within the United States.

5. In case of the removal of the President from office, or of his death, resignation, or inability to discharge the powers and duties of the said office, the same shall devolve on the Vice President, and the congress may by law provide for the case of removal, death, resignation or inability, both of the President and Vice President, declaring what officer shall then act as President, and such officer shall act accordingly until the disability be removed, or a President shall be elected.

6. The President shall, at stated times, receive for his services a compensation which shall neither be increased nor diminished during the period for which he shall have been elected, and he shall not receive within that period any other emolument from the United States, or any of them.

7. Before he enter on the execution of his office, he shall take the following oath or affirmation:—"I do solemnly swear (or affirm) that I will faithfully execute the

---

[5]See the Sixteenth Amendment.

[6]Superseded by the Twelfth Amendment.

office of President of the United States, and will to the best of my ability, preserve, protect and defend the Constitution of the United States."

Section 2.   1. The President shall be commander in chief of the army and navy of the United States, and of the militia of the several States, when called into the actual service of the United States; he may require the opinion in writing, of the principal officer in each of the executive departments, upon any subject relating to the duties of their respective offices, and he shall have power to grant reprieves and pardons for offenses against the United States, except in cases of impeachment.

2. He shall have power, by and with the advice and consent of the Senate, to make treaties, provided two thirds of the senators present concur; and he shall nominate, and by and with the advice and consent of the Senate, shall appoint ambassadors, other public ministers and consuls, judges of the Supreme Court, and all other officers of the United States, whose appointments are not herein otherwise provided for, and which shall be established by law; but the Congress may by law vest the appointment of such inferior officers, as they think proper, in the President alone, in the courts of laws, or in the heads of departments.

3. The President shall have power to fill up all vacancies that may happen during the recess of the Senate, by granting commissions which shall expire at the end of their next session.

Section 3.   He shall from time to time give to the Congress information of the state of the Union, and recommend to their consideration such measures as he shall judge necessary and expedient; he may, on extraordinary occasions, convene both Houses, or either of them, and in case of disagreement between them with respect to the time of adjournment, he may adjourn them to such time as he shall think proper; he shall receive ambassadors and other public ministers; he shall take care that the laws be faithfully executed, and shall commission all the officers of the United States.

Section 4.   The President, Vice President, and all civil officers of the United States, shall be removed from office on impeachment for, and conviction of, treason, bribery, or other high crimes and misdemeanors.

Article III

Section 1.   The judicial power of the United States shall be vested in one Supreme Court, and in such inferior courts as the Congress may from time to time ordain and establish. The judges, both of the Supreme and inferior courts, shall hold their offices during good behavior, and shall, at stated times, receive for their services, a compensation, which shall not be diminished during their continuance in office.

Section 2.   1. The judicial power shall extend to all cases, in law and equity, arising under this Constitution, the laws of the United States, and treaties made, or which shall be made, under their authority;—to all cases of admiralty and maritime jurisdiction;—to controversies to which the United States shall be a party;[7]—

to controversies between two or more States;—between a State and citizens of another State;—between citizens of different States;—between citizens of the same State claiming lands under grants of different States, and between a State, or the citizens thereof, and foreign States, citizens or subjects.

2. In all cases affecting ambassadors, other public ministers and consuls, and those in which a State shall be party, the Supreme Court shall have original jurisdiction. In all the other cases before mentioned, the Supreme Court shall have appellate jurisdiction, both as to law and fact, with such exceptions, and under such regulations as the Congress shall make.

3. The trial of all crimes, except in cases of impeachment, shall be by jury; and such trial shall be held in the State where the said crimes shall have been committed; but when not committed within any State, the trial shall be such place or places as the congress may by law have directed.

Section 3.   1. Treason against the United States shall consist only in levying war against them, or in adhering to their enemies, giving them aid and comfort. No person shall be convicted of treason unless on the testimony of two witnesses to the same overt act, or on confession in open court.

2. The Congress shall have power to declare the punishment of treason, but no attainder of treason shall work corruption of blood, or forfeiture except during the life of the person attained.

Article IV

Section 1.   Full faith and credit shall be given in each State to the public acts, records, and judicial proceedings of every other State. And the Congress may by general laws prescribe the manner in which such acts, records and proceedings shall be proved, and the effect thereof.

Section 2.   1. The citizens of each State shall be entitled to all privileges and immunities of citizens in the several States.[8]

2. A person charged in any State with treason, felony, or other crime, who shall flee from justice, and be found in another State, shall on demand of the executive authority of the State from which he fled, be delivered up to be removed to the State having jurisdiction of the crime.

3. No person held to service or labor in one State under the laws thereof, escaping into another, shall, in consequence of any law or regulation therein, be discharged from such service or labor, but shall be delivered up on claim of the party to whom such service or labor may be due.[9]

Section 3.   1. New States may be admitted by the Congress into this Union; but no new State shall be formed or erected within the jurisdiction of any other State, nor any State be formed by the junction of two or more States, or parts of States, without the consent of the legislatures of the States concerned as well as of the Congress.

---

[7]See the Eleventh Amendment.

[8]See the Fourteenth Amendment, Sec. 1.
[9]See the Thirteenth Amendment.

2. The Congress shall have power to dispose of and make all needful rules and regulations respecting the territory or other property belonging to the United States; and nothing in this Constitution shall be so construed as to prejudice any claims of the United States, or of any particular State.

Section 4.   The United States shall guarantee to every State in this Union a republican form of government, and shall protect each of them against invasion; and on application of the legislature, or of the executive (when the legislature cannot be convened) against domestic violence.

Article V

The Congress, whenever two thirds of both Houses shall deem it necessary, shall propose amendments to this Constitution, or, on the application of the legislatures of two thirds of the several States, shall call a convention for proposing amendments, which in either case shall be valid to all intents and purposes, as part of this Constitution, when ratified by the legislatures of three fourths of the several States, or by conventions in three fourths thereof, as the one or the other mode of ratification may be proposed by the Congress; Provided that no amendment which may be made prior to the year one thousand eight hundred and eight shall in any manner affect the first and fourth clauses in the ninth section of the first article; and that no State, without its consent, shall be deprived of its equal suffrage in the Senate.

Article VI

1. All debts contracted and engagements entered into, before the adoption of this Constitution, shall be as valid against the United States under this Constitution, as under the Confederation.[10]

2. This Constitution, and the laws of the United States which shall be made in pursuance thereof; and all treaties made, or which shall be made, under the authority of the United States, shall be the supreme law of the land; and the judges in every State shall be bound thereby, any thing in the Constitution or laws of any State to the contrary notwithstanding.

3. The senators and representatives before mentioned, and the members of the several State legislatures, and all executive and judicial officers, both of the United States and of the several States, shall be bound by oath or affirmation to support this Constitution; but no religious test shall ever be required as a qualification to any office or public trust under the United States.

Article VII

The ratification of the conventions of nine States shall be sufficient for the establishment of this Constitution between the States so ratifying the same.

Done in Convention by the unanimous consent of the States present the seventeenth day of September in the year of our Lord one thousand seven hundred and eighty-seven, and of the independence of the United States of

---

[10]See the Fourteenth Amendment, Sec. 4.

America the twelfth. In witness whereof we have hereunto subscribed our names.

[Signatories' names omitted]

* * *

Articles in addition to, and amendment of, the Constitution of the United States of America, proposed by Congress, and ratified by the legislatures of the several States, pursuant to the fifth article of the original Constitution.

Amendment I
[First ten amendments ratified December 15, 1791]

Congress shall make no law respecting an establishment of religion, or prohibiting the free exercise thereof; or abridging the freedom of speech, or of the press; or the right of the people peaceably to assemble, and to petition the government for a redress of grievances.

Amendment II

A well regulated militia, being necessary to the security of a free State, the right of the people to keep and bear arms, shall not be infringed.

Amendment III

No soldier shall, in time of peace be quartered in any house, without the consent of the owner, nor in time of war, but in a manner to be prescribed by law.

Amendment IV

The right of the people to be secure in their persons, houses, papers, and effects, against unreasonable searches and seizures, shall not be violated, and no warrants shall issue, but upon probable cause, supported by oath or affirmation, and particularly describing the place to be searched, and the persons or things to be seized.

Amendment V

No person shall be held to answer for a capital or otherwise infamous crime, unless on a presentment or indictment of a grand jury, except in cases arising in the land or naval forces, or in the militia, when in actual service in time of war or public danger; nor shall any person be subject for the same offense to be twice put in jeopardy of life or limb; nor shall be compelled in any criminal case to be a witness against himself, nor be deprived of life, liberty, or property, without due process of law; nor shall private property be taken for public use, without just compensation.

Amendment VI

In all criminal prosecutions, the accused shall enjoy the right to a speedy and public trial, by an impartial jury of the State and district wherein the crime shall have been committed, which district shall have been previously ascertained by law, and to be informed of the nature and cause of the accusation; to be confronted with the witnesses against him; to have compulsory process for obtaining witnesses in his favor, and to have the assistance of counsel for his defense.

Amendment VII

In suits at common law, where the value in controversy shall exceed twenty dollars, the right of trial by jury shall be preserved, and no fact tried by a jury shall be otherwise reexamined in any court of the United States, than according to the rules of the common law.

Amendment VIII

Excessive bail shall not be required, nor excessive fines imposed, nor cruel and unusual punishments inflicted.

Amendment IX

The enumeration in the Constitution of certain rights shall not be construed to deny or disparage others retained by the people.

Amendment X

The powers not delegated to the United States by the Constitution, nor prohibited by it to the States, are reserved to the States respectively, or to the people.

Amendment XI [January 8, 1798]

The judicial power of the United States shall not be construed to extend to any suit in law or equity, commended or prosecuted against one of the United States by citizens of another State, or by citizens or subjects of any foreign State.

Amendment XII [September 25, 1804]

The electors shall meet in their respective States, and vote by ballot for President and Vice President, one of whom, at least, shall not be an inhabitant of the same State with themselves; they shall name in their ballots the person voted for as President, and in distinct ballots, the person voted for as Vice President, and they shall make distinct lists of all persons voted for as President and of all persons voted for as Vice President, and of the number of votes for each, which lists they shall sign and certify, and transmit sealed to the seat of the government of the United States, directed to the President of the Senate;—The President of the Senate shall, in the presence of the Senate and House of Representatives, open all the certificates and the votes shall then be counted;—The person having the greatest number of votes for President, shall be the President, if such number be a majority of the whole number of electors appointed; and if no person have such majority, then from the persons having the highest numbers not exceeding three on the list of those voted for as President, the House of Representatives shall choose immediately, by ballot, the President. But in choosing the President, the votes shall be taken by States, the representation from each State having one vote; a quorum for this purpose shall consist of a member or members from two thirds of the States, and a majority of all the States shall be necessary to a choice. And if the House of Representatives shall not choose a President whenever the right of choice shall devolve upon them, before the fourth day of March next following, then the Vice President shall act as President,

as in the case of the death or other constitutional disability of the President. The person having the greatest number of votes as Vice President shall be the Vice President, if such number be a majority of the whole number of electors appointed, and if no person have a majority, then from the two highest numbers on the list, the Senate shall choose the Vice President; a quorum for the purpose shall consist of two thirds of the whole number of Senators, and a majority of the whole number shall be necessary to a choice. But no person constitutionally ineligible to the office of President shall be eligible to that of Vice President of the United States.

Amendment XIII [December 18, 1865]

Section 1. Neither slavery nor involuntary servitude, except as a punishment for crime whereof the party shall have been duly convicted, shall exist within the United States, or any place subject to their jurisdiction.

Section 2. Congress shall have power to enforce this article by appropriate legislation.

Amendment XIV [July 28, 1868]

Section 1. All persons born or naturalized in the United States, and subject to the jurisdiction thereof, are citizens of the United States and of the State wherein they reside. No State shall make or enforce any law which shall abridge the privileges or immunities of citizens of the United States; nor shall any State deprive any person of life, liberty, or property, without due process of law; nor deny to any person within its jurisdiction the equal protection of the laws.

Section 2. Representatives shall be apportioned among the several States according to their respective numbers, counting the whole number of persons in each State, excluding Indians not taxed. But when the right to vote at any election for the choice of electors for President and Vice President of the United States, representatives in Congress, the executive and judicial officers of a State, or the members of the legislature thereof, is denied to any of the male inhabitants of such State, being twenty-one years of age, and citizens of the United States, or in any way abridged, except for participating in rebellion, or other crime, the basis of representation there shall be reduced in the proportion which the number of such male citizens shall bear to the whole number of male citizens twenty-one years of age in such State.

Section 3. No person shall be a senator or representative in Congress, or elector of President and Vice President, or hold any office, civil or military, under the United States, or under any State, who having previously taken an oath, as a member of Congress, or as an officer of the United States, or as a member of any State legislature, or as an executive or judicial officer of any State, to support the Constitution of the United States, shall have engaged in insurrection or rebellion against the same, or given aid or comfort to the enemies thereof. But Congress may by a vote of two thirds of each House, remove such disability.

Section 4. The validity of the public debt of the United States, authorized by law, including debts incurred for payment of pensions and bounties for services in suppressing insurrection or rebellion, shall not be questioned. But neither the United States nor any State shall assume or pay any debt or obligation incurred in aid of insurrection or rebellion against the United States, or any claim for the loss or emancipation of any slave; but all such debts, obligations, and claims shall be held illegal and void.

Section 5. The Congress shall have the power to enforce, by appropriate legislation, the provisions of this article.

Amendment XV [March 30, 1870]

Section 1. The right of citizens of the United States to vote shall not be denied or abridged by the United States or by any State on account of race, color, or previous condition of servitude.

Section 2. The Congress shall have power to enforce this article by appropriate legislation.

Amendment XVI [February 25, 1913]

The Congress shall have power to lay and collect taxes on incomes, from whatever source derived, without apportionment among the several States, and without regard to any census or enumeration.

Amendment XVII [May 31, 1913]

The Senate of the United States shall be composed of two senators from each State, elected by the people thereof, for six years; and each senator shall have one vote. The electors in each State shall have the qualifications requisite for electors of the most numerous branch of the State legislature.

When vacancies happen in the representation of any State in the Senate, the executive authority of such State shall issue writs of election to fill such vacancies: Provided, That the legislature of any State may empower the executive thereof to make temporary appointments until the people fill the vacancies by election as the legislature may direct.

This amendment shall not be so construed as to affect the election or term of any senator chosen before it becomes valid as part of the Constitution.

Amendment XVIII [11] [January 29, 1919]

After one year from the ratification of this article, the manufacture, sale, or transportation of intoxicating liquors within, the importation thereof into, or the exportation thereof from the United States and all territory subject to the jurisdiction thereof for beverage purposes is thereby prohibited.

The Congress and the several States shall have concurrent power to enforce this article by appropriate legislation.

This article shall be inoperative unless it shall have been ratified as an amendment to the Constitution by the legislatures of the several States, as provided in the constitution, within seven years from the date of the submission hereof to the States by Congress.

---

[11] Repealed by the Twenty-first Amendment.

Amendment XIX [August 26, 1920]

The right of citizens of the United States to vote shall not be denied or abridged by the United States or by any State on account of sex.

Congress shall have the power to enforce this article by appropriate legislation.

Amendment XX [January 23, 1933]

Section 1. The terms of the President and Vice President shall end at noon on the 20th day of January and the terms of Senators and Representatives at noon on the 3d day of January, of the years in which such terms would have ended if this article had not been ratified; and the terms of their successors shall then begin.

Section 2. The Congress shall assemble at least once in every year, and such meeting shall begin at noon on the 3d day of January, unless they shall by law appoint a different day.

Section 3. If, at the time fixed for the beginning of the term of President, the President-elect shall have died, the Vice President-elect shall become President. If a President shall not have been chosen before the time fixed for the beginning of his term, or if the President-elect shall have failed to qualify, then the Vice President-elect shall act as President until a President shall have qualified; and the Congress may by law provide for the case wherein neither a President-elect nor a Vice President-elect shall have qualified, declaring who shall then act as President, or the manner in which one who is to act shall be selected, and such person shall act accordingly until a President or Vice President shall have qualified.

Section 4. The Congress may by law provide for the case of the death of any of the persons from whom, the House of Representatives may choose a President whenever the right of choice shall have devolved upon them, and for the case of the death of any of the persons from whom the Senate may choose a Vice President whenever the right of choice shall have devolved upon them.

Section 5. Sections 1 and 2 shall take effect on the 15th day of October following the ratification of this article.

Section 6. This article shall be inoperative unless it shall have been ratified as an amendment to the Constitution by the legislatures of three-fourths of the several States within seven years from the date of its submission.

Amendment XXI [December 5, 1933]

Section 1. The Eighteenth Article of amendment to the Constitution of the United States is hereby repealed.

Section 2. The transportation or importation into any State, Territory, or possession of the United States for delivery or use therein of intoxicating liquors in violation of the laws thereof, is hereby prohibited.

Section 3. This article shall be inoperative unless it shall have been ratified as an amendment to the Constitution by conventions in the several States, as provided in the Constitution, within seven years from the date of the submission thereof to the States by the Congress.

Amendment XXII [March 1, 1951]

No person shall be elected to the office of the President more than twice, and no person who has held the office of President, or acted as President, for more than two years of a term to which some other person was elected President shall be elected to the office of the President more than once.

But this article shall not apply to any person holding the office of President when this article was proposed by the Congress, and shall not prevent any person who may be holding the office of President, or acting as President, during the term within which this article becomes operative from holding the office of President or acting as President during the remainder of such term.

This article shall be inoperative unless it shall have been ratified as an amendment to the Constitution by the legislatures of three-fourths of the several States within seven years from the date of its submission to the States by the Congress.

Amendment XXIII [March 29, 1961]

Section 1.   The District constituting the seat of Government of the United States shall appoint in such manner as the Congress may direct.

A number of electors of President and Vice President equal to the whole number of Senators and Representatives in Congress to which the District would be entitled if it were a State, but in no event more than the least populous State; they shall be in addition to those appointed by the States, but they shall be considered, for the purposes of the election of President and Vice President, to be electors appointed by a State; and they shall meet in the District and perform such duties as provided by the twelfth article of amendment.

Section 2.   The Congress shall have power to enforce this article by appropriate legislation.

Amendment XXIV [January 23, 1964]

Section 1.   The right of citizens of the United States to vote in any primary or other election for President or Vice President, for electors for President or Vice President, or for Senator or Representative in Congress, shall not be denied or abridged by the United States or any State by reason of failure to pay any poll tax or other tax.

Section 2.   The Congress shall have power to enforce this article by appropriate legislation.

Amendment XXV [February 10, 1967]

Section 1.   In case of the removal of the President from office or of his death or resignation, the Vice President shall become President.

Section 2.   Whenever there is a vacancy in the office of the Vice President, the President shall nominate a Vice President who shall take office upon confirmation by a majority of both Houses of Congress.

Section 3.   Whenever the President transmits to the President pro tempore of the Senate and the Speaker of the House of Representatives his written declaration that he is unable to discharge the powers and duties of his office, and until he transmits to them a written declaration to the contrary, such powers and duties shall be discharged by the Vice President as Acting President.

Section 4.   Whenever the Vice President and a majority of either the principal officers of the executive departments or of such other body as Congress may by law provide, transmit to the President pro tempore of the Senate and the Speaker of the House of Representatives their written declaration that the President is unable to discharge the powers and duties of his office, the Vice President shall immediately assume the powers and duties of the office as Acting President.

Thereafter, when the President transmits to the President pro tempore of the Senate and the Speaker of the House of Representatives his written declaration that no inability exists, he shall resume the powers and duties of his office unless the Vice President and a majority of either the principal officers of the executive departments or of such other body as Congress may by law provide, transmit within four days to the President pro tempore of the Senate and the Speaker of the House of Representatives their written declaration that the President is unable to discharge the powers and duties of his office. Thereupon Congress shall decide the issue, assembling within forty-eight hours for that purpose if not in session. If the Congress, within twenty-one days after receipt of the latter written declaration, or, if Congress is not in session, within twenty-one days after Congress is required to assemble, determines by two-thirds vote of both Houses that the President is unable to discharge the powers and duties of his office, the Vice President shall continue to discharge the same as Acting President; otherwise, the President shall resume the powers and duties of his office.

Amendment XXVI [June 30, 1971]

Section 1.   The right of citizens of the United States who are eighteen years of age or older to vote shall not be denied or abridged by the United States or by any State on account of age.

Section 2.   The Congress shall have power to enforce this article by appropriate legislation.

Amendment XXVII[12] [May 7, 1992]

No law, varying the compensation for services of the Senators and Representatives, shall take effect until an election of Representatives shall have intervened.

---

[12]James Madison proposed this amendment in 1789 together with the ten amendments that were adopted as the Bill of Rights, but it failed to win ratification at the time. Congress, however, had set no deadline for its ratification, and over the years—particularly in the 1980s and 1990s—many states voted to add it to the Constitution. With the ratification of Michigan in 1992 it passed the threshold of 3/4ths of the states required for adoption, but because the process took more than 200 years, its validity remains in doubt.

PRESIDENTS AND VICE PRESIDENTS

1. George Washington (1789)
   John Adams (1789)

2. John Adams (1797)
   Thomas Jefferson (1797)

3. Thomas Jefferson (1801)
   Aaron Burr (1801)
   George Clinton (1805)

4. James Madison (1809)
   George Clinton (1809)
   Elbridge Gerry (1813)

5. James Monroe (1817)
   Daniel D. Thompkins (1817)

6. John Quincy Adams (1825)
   John C. Calhoun (1825)

7. Andrew Jackson (1829)
   John C. Calhoun (1829)
   Martin Van Buren (1833)

8. Martin Van Buren (1837)
   Richard M. Johnson (1837)

9. William H. Harrison (1841)
   John Tyler (1841)

10. John Tyler (1841)

11. James K. Polk (1845)
    George M. Dallas (1845)

12. Zachary Taylor (1849)
    Millard Fillmore (1849)

13. Millard Fillmore (1850)

14. Franklin Pierce (1853)
    William R. King (1853)

15. James Buchanan (1857)
    John C. Breckinridge (1857)

16. Abraham Lincoln (1861)
    Hannibal Hamlin (1861)
    Andrew Johnson (1865)

17. Andrew Johnson (1865)

18. Ulysses S. Grant (1869)
    Schuyler Colfax (1869)
    Henry Wilson (1873)

19. Rutherford B. Hayes (1877)
    William A. Wheeler (1877)

20. James A. Garfield (1881)
    Chester A. Arthur (1881)

21. Chester A. Arthur (1881)

22. Grover Cleveland (1885)
    T. A. Hendricks (1885)

23. Benjamin Harrison (1889)
    Levi P. Morgan (1889)

24. Grover Cleveland (1893)
    Adlai E. Stevenson (1893)

25. William McKinley (1897)
    Garret A. Hobart (1897)
    Theodore Roosevelt (1901)

26. Theodore Roosevelt (1901)
    Charles Fairbanks (1905)

27. William H. Taft (1909)
    James S. Sherman (1909)

28. Woodrow Wilson (1913)
    Thomas R. Marshall (1913)

29. Warren G. Harding (1921)
    Calvin Coolidge (1921)

30. Calvin Coolidge (1923)
    Charles G. Dawes (1925)

31. Herbert C. Hoover (1929)
    Charles Curtis (1929)

32. Franklin D. Roosevelt (1933)
    John Nance Garner (1933)
    Henry A. Wallace (1941)
    Harry S Truman (1945)

33. Harry S Truman (1945)
    Alben W. Barkley (1949)

34. Dwight D. Eisenhower (1953)
    Richard M. Nixon (1953)

35. John F. Kennedy (1961)
    Lyndon B. Johnson (1961)

36. Lyndon B. Johnson (1963)
    Hubert H. Humphrey (1965)

37. Richard M. Nixon (1969)
    Spiro T. Agnew (1969)
    Gerald R. Ford (1973)

38. Gerald R. Ford (1974)
    Nelson A. Rockefeller (1974)

39. James E. Carter Jr. (1977)
    Walter F. Mondale (1977)

40. Ronald W. Reagan (1981)
    George H. W. Bush (1981)

41. George H. W. Bush (1989)
    James D. Quayle III (1989)

42. William J. Clinton (1993)
    Albert Gore (1993)

43. George W. Bush (2001)
    Richard Cheney (2001)

PRESIDENTIAL ELECTIONS

Year	Number of States	Candidates	Party	Popular Vote	Electoral Vote[†]	Percentage of Popular Vote*
1789	11	GEORGE WASHINGTON	No party designations		69	
		John Adams			34	
		Other Candidates			35	
1792	15	GEORGE WASHINGTON	No party designations		132	
		John Adams			77	
		George Clinton			50	
		Other Candidates			5	
1796	16	JOHN ADAMS	Federalist		71	
		Thomas Jefferson	Democratic-Republican		68	
		Thomas Pinckney	Federalist		59	
		Aaron Burr	Democratic-Republican		30	
		Other Candidates			48	
1800	16	THOMAS JEFFERSON	Democratic-Republican		73	
		Aaron Burr	Democratic-Republican		73	
		John Adams	Federalist		65	
		Charles C. Pinckney	Federalist		64	
		John Jay	Federalist		1	
1804	17	THOMAS JEFFERSON	Democratic-Republican		162	
		Charles C. Pinckney	Federalist		14	
1808	17	JAMES MADISON	Democratic-Republican		122	
		Charles C. Pinckney	Federalist		47	
		George Clinton	Democratic-Republican		6	
1812	18	JAMES MADISON	Democratic-Republican		128	
		DeWitt Clinton	Federalist		89	
1816	19	JAMES MONROE	Democratic-Republican		183	
		Rufus King	Federalist		34	
1820	24	JAMES MONROE	Democratic-Republican		231	
		John Quincy Adams	Independent-Republican		1	
1824	24	JOHN QUINCY ADAMS	Democratic-Republican	108,740	84	30.5
		Andrew Jackson	Democratic-Republican	153,544	99	43.1
		William H. Crawford	Democratic-Republican	46,618	41	13.1
		Henry Clay	Democratic-Republican	47,136	37	13.2
1828	24	ANDREW JACKSON	Democrat	647,286	178	56.0
		John Quincy Adams	National-Republican	508,064	83	44.0
1832	24	ANDREW JACKSON	Democrat	687,502	219	55.0
		Henry Clay	National-Republican	530,189	49	42.4
		William Wirt	Anti-Masonic	} 33,108	7	
		John Floyd	National-Republican		11	2.6

*Percentage of popular vote given for any election year may not total 100 percent because candidates receiving less than 1 percent of the popular vote have been omitted.

[†]Prior to the passage of the Twelfth Amendment in 1904, the electoral college voted for two presidential candidates; the runner-up became Vice-President. Data from *Historical Statistics of the United States, Colonial Times to 1957* (1961), pp. 682–683, and *The World Almanac.*

PRESIDENTIAL ELECTIONS (continued)

Year	Number of States	Candidates	Party	Popular Vote	Electoral Vote	Percentage of Popular Vote
1836	26	MARTIN VAN BUREN	Democrat	765,483	170	50.9
		William H. Harrison	Whig		73	
		Hugh L. White	Whig		26	
		Daniel Webster	Whig	739,795	14	49.1
		W. P. Mangum	Whig		11	
1840	26	WILLIAM H. HARRISON	Whig	1,274,624	234	53.1
		Martin Van Buren	Democrat	1,127,781	60	46.9
1844	26	JAMES K. POLK	Democrat	1,338,464	170	49.6
		Henry Clay	Whig	1,300,097	105	48.1
		James G. Birney	Liberty	62,300		2.3
1848	30	ZACHARY TAYLOR	Whig	1,360,967	163	47.4
		Lewis Cass	Democrat	1,222,342	127	42.5
		Martin Van Buren	Free-Soil	291,263		10.1
1852	31	FRANKLIN PIERCE	Democrat	1,601,117	254	50.9
		Winfield Scott	Whig	1,385,453	42	44.1
		John P. Hale	Free-Soil	155,825		5.0
1856	31	JAMES BUCHANAN	Democrat	1,832,955	174	45.3
		John C. Frémont	Republican	1,339,932	114	33.1
		Millard Fillmore	American ("Know Nothing")	871,731	8	21.6
1860	33	ABRAHAM LINCOLN	Republican	1,865,593	180	39.8
		Stephen A. Douglas	Democrat	1,382,713	12	29.5
		John C. Breckinridge	Democrat	848,356	72	18.1
		John Bell	Constitutional Union	592,906	39	12.6
1864	36	ABRAHAM LINCOLN	Republican	2,206,938	212	55.0
		George B. McClellan	Democrat	1,803,787	21	45.0
1868	37	ULYSSES S. GRANT	Republican	3,013,421	214	52.7
		Horatio Seymour	Democrat	2,706,829	80	47.3
1872	37	ULYSSES S. GRANT	Republican	3,596,745	286	55.6
		Horace Greeley	Democrat	2,843,446	*	43.9
1876	38	RUTHERFORD B. HAYES	Republican	4,036,572	185	48.0
		Samuel J. Tilden	Democrat	4,284,020	184	51.0
1880	38	JAMES A. GARFIELD	Republican	4,453,295	214	48.5
		Winfield S. Hancock	Democrat	4,414,082	155	48.1
		James B. Weaver	Greenback-Labor	308,578		3.4
1884	38	GROVER CLEVELAND	Democrat	4,879,507	219	48.5
		James G. Blaine	Republican	4,850,293	182	48.2
		Benjamin F. Butler	Greenback-Labor	175,370		1.8
		John P. St. John	Prohibition	150,369		1.5
1888	38	BENJAMIN HARRISON	Republican	5,447,129	233	47.9
		Grover Cleveland	Democrat	5,537,857	168	48.6
		Clinton B. Fisk	Prohibition	249,506		2.2
		Anson J. Streeter	Union Labor	146,935		1.3

*Because of the death of Greeley, Democratic electors scattered their votes.

PRESIDENTIAL ELECTIONS (continued)

Year	Number of States	Candidates	Party	Popular Vote	Electoral Vote	Percentage of Popular Vote
1892	44	GROVER CLEVELAND	Democrat	5,555,426	277	46.1
		Benjamin Harrison	Republican	5,182,690	145	43.0
		James B. Weaver	People's	1,029,846	22	8.5
		John Bidwell	Prohibition	264,133		2.2
1896	45	WILLIAM MCKINLEY	Republican	7,102,246	271	51.1
		William J. Bryan	Democrat	6,492,559	176	47.7
1900	45	WILLIAM MCKINLEY	Republican	7,218,491	292	51.7
		William J. Bryan	Democrat; Populist	6,356,734	155	45.5
		John C. Woolley	Prohibition	208,914		1.5
1904	45	THEODORE ROOSEVELT	Republican	7,628,461	336	57.4
		Alton B. Parker	Democrat	5,084,223	140	37.6
		Eugene V. Debs	Socialist	402,283		3.0
		Silas C. Swallow	Prohibition	258,536		1.9
1908	46	WILLIAM H. TAFT	Republican	7,675,320	321	51.6
		William J. Bryan	Democrat	6,412,294	162	43.1
		Eugene V. Debs	Socialist	420,793		2.8
		Eugene W. Chafin	Prohibition	253,840		1.7
1912	48	WOODROW WILSON	Democrat	6,296,547	435	41.9
		Theodore Roosevelt	Progressive	4,118,571	88	27.4
		William H. Taft	Republican	3,486,720	8	23.2
		Eugene V. Debs	Socialist	900,672		6.0
		Eugene W. Chafin	Prohibition	206,275		1.4
1916	48	WOODROW WILSON	Democrat	9,127,695	277	49.4
		Charles E. Hughes	Republican	8,533,507	254	46.2
		A. L. Benson	Socialist	585,113		3.2
		J. Frank Hanly	Prohibition	220,506		1.2
1920	48	WARREN G. HARDING	Republican	16,143,407	404	60.4
		James M. Cox	Democrat	9,130,328	127	34.2
		Eugene V. Debs	Socialist	919,799		3.4
		P. P. Christensen	Farmer-Labor	265,411		1.0
1924	48	CALVIN COOLIDGE	Republican	15,718,211	382	54.0
		John W. Davis	Democrat	8,385,283	136	28.8
		Robert M. La Follette	Progressive	4,831,289	13	16.6
1928	48	HERBERT C. HOOVER	Republican	21,391,993	444	58.2
		Alfred E. Smith	Democrat	15,016,169	87	40.9
1932	48	FRANKLIN D. ROOSEVELT	Democrat	22,809,638	472	57.4
		Herbert C. Hoover	Republican	15,758,901	59	39.7
		Norman Thomas	Socialist	881,951		2.2
1936	48	FRANKLIN D. ROOSEVELT	Democrat	27,752,869	523	60.8
		Alfred M. Landon	Republican	16,674,665	8	36.5
		William Lemke	Union	882,479		1.9
1940	48	FRANKLIN D. ROOSEVELT	Democrat	27,307,819	449	54.8
		Wendell L. Willkie	Republican	22,321,018	82	44.8
1944	48	FRANKLIN D. ROOSEVELT	Democrat	25,606,585	432	53.5
		Thomas E. Dewey	Republican	22,014,745	99	46.0

PRESIDENTIAL ELECTIONS (continued)

Year	Number of States	Candidates	Party	Popular Vote	Electoral Vote	Percentage of Popular Vote
1948	48	HARRY S TRUMAN	Democrat	24,105,812	303	49.5
		Thomas E. Dewey	Republican	21,970,065	189	45.1
		J. Strom Thurmond	States' Rights	1,169,063	39	2.4
		Henry A. Wallace	Progressive	1,157,172		2.4
1952	48	DWIGHT D. EISENHOWER	Republican	33,936,234	442	55.1
		Adlai E. Stevenson	Democrat	27,314,992	89	44.4
1956	48	DWIGHT D. EISENHOWER	Republican	35,590,472	457[*]	57.6
		Adlai E. Stevenson	Democrat	26,022,752	73	42.1
1960	50	JOHN F. KENNEDY	Democrat	34,227,096	303[†]	49.9
		Richard M. Nixon	Republican	34,108,546	219	49.6
1964	50	LYNDON B. JOHNSON	Democrat	42,676,220	486	61.3
		Barry M. Goldwater	Republican	26,860,314	52	38.5
1968	50	RICHARD M. NIXON	Republican	31,785,480	301	43.4
		Hubert H. Humphrey	Democrat	31,275,165	191	42.7
		George C. Wallace	American Independent	9,906,473	46	13.5
1972	50	RICHARD M. NIXON[‡]	Republican	47,165,234	520	60.6
		George S. McGovern	Democrat	29,168,110	17	37.5
1976	50	JAMES E. CARTER JR.	Democrat	40,828,929	297	50.1
		Gerald R. Ford	Republican	39,148,940	240	47.9
		Eugene McCarthy	Independent	739,256		
1980	50	RONALD W. REAGAN	Republican	43,201,220	489	50.9
		James E. Carter Jr.	Democrat	34,913,332	49	41.2
		John B. Anderson	Independent	5,581,379		
1984	50	RONALD W. REAGAN	Republican	53,428,357	525	59.0
		Walter F. Mondale	Democrat	36,930,923	13	41.0
1988	50	GEORGE H. W. BUSH	Republican	48,901,046	426	53.4
		Michael Dukakis	Democrat	41,809,030	111	45.6
1992	50	WILLIAM J. CLINTON	Democrat	43,728,275	370	43.2
		George H. W. Bush	Republican	38,167,416	168	37.7
		H. Ross Perot	United We Stand, America	19,237,247		19.0
1996	50	WILLIAM J. CLINTON	Democrat	45,590,703	379	49.0
		Robert Dole	Republican	37,816,307	159	41.0
		H. Ross Perot	Reform	7,874,283		8.0
2000	50	GEORGE W. BUSH	Republican	50,459,624	271	47.9
		Albert Gore	Democrat	51,003,328	266	49.4
		Ralph Nader	Green	2,882,985	0	2.7
2004	50	GEORGE W. BUSH	Republican	59,117,523	286	51.1
		John Kerry	Democrat	55,557,584	252	48.0
		Ralph Nader	Green	405,623	0	0.3

[*]Walter B. Jones received 1 electoral vote.

[†]Harry F. Byrd received 15 electoral votes.

[‡]Resigned August 9, 1974: Vice President Gerald R. Ford became President.

ADMISSION OF STATES INTO THE UNION

	State	Date of Admission		State	Date of Admission
1.	Delaware	December 7, 1787	26.	Michigan	January 26, 1837
2.	Pennsylvania	December 12, 1787	27.	Florida	March 3, 1845
3.	New Jersey	December 18, 1787	28.	Texas	December 29, 1845
4.	Georgia	January 2, 1788	29.	Iowa	December 28, 1846
5.	Connecticut	January 9, 1788	30.	Wisconsin	May 29, 1848
6.	Massachusetts	February 6, 1788	31.	California	September 9, 1850
7.	Maryland	April 28, 1788	32.	Minnesota	May 11, 1858
8.	South Carolina	May 23, 1788	33.	Oregon	February 14, 1859
9.	New Hampshire	June 21, 1788	34.	Kansas	January 29, 1861
10.	Virginia	June 25, 1788	35.	West Virginia	June 20, 1863
11.	New York	July 26, 1788	36.	Nevada	October 31, 1864
12.	North Carolina	November 21, 1789	37.	Nebraska	March 1, 1867
13	Rhode Island	May 29, 1790	38.	Colorado	August 1, 1876
14.	Vermont	March 4, 1791	39.	North Dakota	November 2, 1889
15.	Kentucky	June 1, 1792	40.	South Dakota	November 2, 1889
16.	Tennessee	June 1, 1796	41.	Montana	November 8, 1889
17.	Ohio	March 1, 1803	42.	Washington	November 11, 1889
18.	Louisiana	April 30, 1812	43.	Idaho	July 3, 1890
19.	Indiana	December 11, 1816	44.	Wyoming	July 10, 1890
20.	Mississippi	December 10, 1817	45.	Utah	January 4, 1896
21.	Illinois	December 3, 1818	46.	Oklahoma	November 16, 1907
22.	Alabama	December 14, 1819	47.	New Mexico	January 6, 1912
23.	Maine	March 15, 1820	48.	Arizona	February 14, 1912
24.	Missouri	August 10, 1821	49.	Alaska	January 3, 1959
25.	Arkansas	June 15, 1836	50.	Hawaii	August 21, 1959

DEMOGRAPHICS OF THE UNITED STATES

POPULATION GROWTH

Year	Population	Percent Increase
1630	4,600	
1640	26,600	478.3
1650	50,400	90.8
1660	75,100	49.0
1670	111,900	49.0
1680	151,500	35.4
1690	210,400	38.9
1700	250,900	19.2
1710	331,700	32.2
1720	466,200	40.5
1730	629,400	35.0
1740	905,600	43.9
1750	1,170,800	29.3
1760	1,593,600	36.1
1770	2,148,100	34.8
1780	2,780,400	29.4
1790	3,929,214	41.3
1800	5,308,483	35.1
1810	7,239,881	36.4
1820	9,638,453	33.1
1830	12,866,020	33.5
1840	17,069,453	32.7
1850	23,191,876	35.9
1860	31,443,321	35.6
1870	39,818,449	26.6
1880	50,155,783	26.0
1890	62,947,714	25.5
1900	75,994,575	20.7
1910	91,972,266	21.0
1920	105,710,620	14.9
1930	122,775,046	16.1
1940	131,669,275	7.2
1950	150,697,361	14.5
1960	179,323,175	18.5
1970	203,302,031	13.4
1980	226,542,199	11.4
1990	248,718,301	9.8
2000	281,421,906	13.1

Source: Historical Statistics of the United States (1975); Statistical Abstract of the United States (2001).

Note: Figures for 1630–1780 include British colonies within limits of present United States only; Native American population included only in 1930 and thereafter.

WORKFORCE

Year	Total Number Workers (1000s)	Farmers as % of Total	Women as % of Total	% Workers in Unions
1810	2,330	84	(NA)	(NA)
1840	5,660	75	(NA)	(NA)
1860	11,110	53	(NA)	(NA)
1870	12,506	53	15	(NA)
1880	17,392	52	15	(NA)
1890	23,318	43	17	(NA)
1900	29,073	40	18	3
1910	38,167	31	21	6
1920	41,614	26	21	12
1930	48,830	22	22	7
1940	53,011	17	24	27
1950	59,643	12	28	25
1960	69,877	8	32	26
1970	82,049	4	37	25
1980	106,940	3	43	23
1990	125,840	3	45	16
2000	140,863	2	47	12

Source: Historical Statistics of the United States (1975); Statistical Abstract of the United States (2001).

VITAL STATISTICS
(in thousands)

Year	Births	Deaths	Marriages	Divorces
1800	55	(NA)	(NA)	(NA)
1810	54.3	(NA)	(NA)	(NA)
1820	55.2	(NA)	(NA)	(NA)
1830	51.4	(NA)	(NA)	(NA)
1840	51.8	(NA)	(NA)	(NA)
1850	43.3	(NA)	(NA)	(NA)
1860	44.3	(NA)	(NA)	(NA)
1870	38.3	(NA)	9.6 (1867)	0.3 (1867)
1880	39.8	(NA)	9.1 (1875)	0.3 (1875)
1890	31.5	(NA)	9.0	0.5
1900	32.3	17.2	9.3	0.7
1910	30.1	14.7	10.3	0.9
1920	27.7	13.0	12.0	1.6
1930	21.3	11.3	9.2	1.6
1940	19.4	10.8	12.1	2.0
1950	24.1	9.6	11.1	2.6
1960	23.7	9.5	8.5	2.2
1970	18.4	9.5	10.6	3.5
1980	15.9	8.8	10.6	5.2
1990	16.7	8.6	9.8	4.7
1997	14.6	8.6	8.9	4.3

Source: *Historical Statistics of the United States* (1975); *Statistical Abstract of the United States* (1999). Population Estimates Program, Population Division, U.S. Census Bureau, January 2001.

RACIAL COMPOSITION OF THE POPULATION
(in thousands)

Year	White	Black	Indian	Hispanic	Asian
1790	3,172	757	(NA)	(NA)	(NA)
1800	4,306	1,002	(NA)	(NA)	(NA)
1820	7,867	1,772	(NA)	(NA)	(NA)
1840	14,196	2,874	(NA)	(NA)	(NA)
1860	26,923	4,442	(NA)	(NA)	(NA)
1880	43,403	6,581	(NA)	(NA)	(NA)
1900	66,809	8,834	(NA)	(NA)	(NA)
1910	81,732	9,828	(NA)	(NA)	(NA)
1920	94,821	10,463	(NA)	(NA)	(NA)
1930	110,287	11,891	(NA)	(NA)	(NA)
1940	118,215	12,866	(NA)	(NA)	(NA)
1950	134,942	15,042	(NA)	(NA)	(NA)
1960	158,832	18,872	(NA)	(NA)	(NA)
1970	178,098	22,581	(NA)	(NA)	(NA)
1980	194,713	26,683	1,420	14,609	3,729
1990	208,727	30,511	2,065	22,372	2,462
2000	211,461	34,658	2,476	35,306	10,642

Source: U.S. Bureau of the Census, *U.S. Census of Population: 1940,* vol. II, part 1, and vol. IV, part 1; *1950,* vol. II, part 1; *1960,* vol. I, part 1; *1970,* vol. I, part B; and *Current Population Reports,* P25-1095 and P25-1104; *Statistical Abstract of the United States* (2001).

IMMIGRATION, BY ORIGIN
(in thousands)

Period	Europe	Americas	Asia
1820–30	106	12	—
1831–40	496	33	—
1841–50	1,597	62	—
1851–60	2,453	75	42
1861–70	2,065	167	65
1871–80	2,272	404	70
1881–90	4,735	427	70
1891–1900	3,555	39	75
1901–10	8,065	362	324
1911–20	4,322	1,144	247
1921–30	2,463	1,517	112
1931–40	348	160	16
1941–50	621	355	32
1951–60	1,326	997	150
1961–70	1,123	1,716	590
1971–80	800	1,983	1,588
1981–90	762	3,616	2,738
1991–2000	1,100	3,800	2,200

Source: *Historical Statistics of the United States* (1975); *Statistical Abstract of the United States* (1991); Population Estimates Program, Population Division, U.S. Census Bureau, April 2001.

BIBLIOGRAPHY

CHAPTER 1

Settling the Continent

Larry D. Agenbroad, et al., eds., *Megafauna and Man* (1990)

John Bierhorst, ed., *The Red Swan: Myths and Tales of the American Indians* (1976)

Robson Bonnichsen and Karen L. Turnmire, *Ice Age People of North America: Environments, Origins, and Adaptations* (1999)

Michael H. Crawford, *The Origins of Native Americans: Evidence from Anthropological Genetics* (1998)

Tom D. Dillehay, *The Settling of the Americas: A New Prehistory* (2000)

E. James Dixon, *Bones, Boats, and Bison: Archaeology and the First Colonization of Western North America* (2000)

Richard Erdoes and Alfonso Ortiz, eds., *American Indian Myths and Legends* (1984)

Guy Gibbon, *Archaeology of Prehistoric Native America: An Encyclopedia* (1998)

Lee Eldridge Huddleston, *Origins of the American Indians: European Concepts, 1492–1729* (1967)

George Kubler, *Esthetic Recognition of Ancient Amerindian Art* (1991)

Hanns J. Prem, *The Ancient Americas: A Brief History and Guide to Research* (1997)

Heather Anne Pringle, *In Search of Ancient North America: An Archaeological Journey to Forgotten Cultures* (1996)

Richard F. Townsend, ed., *The Ancient Americas: Art from Sacred Landscapes* (1992)

Frederick Hadleigh West, ed., *American Beginnings: The Prehistory and Palaeoecology of Beringia* (1996)

New Ways of Living on the Land

Kenneth M. Ames and Herbert D. G. Mascher, *Peoples of the Northwest Coast: Their Archaeology and Prehistory* (2000)

Leonard W. Blake and Hugh C. Cutler, *Plants from the Past* (2001)

David S. Brose, et al., *Ancient Art of the American Woodland Indians* (1985)

Thomas E. Emerson, et al., eds. *Late Woodland Societies: Tradition and Transformation Across the Midcontinent* (2000)

Richard I. Ford, ed., *Prehistoric Food Production in North America* (1985)

Sarah W. Neusius, *Foraging, Collecting, and Harvesting: Archaic Period Subsistence and Settlement in the Eastern Woodlands* (1986)

James L. Phillips and James A. Brown, eds., *Archaic Hunters and Gatherers in the American Midwest* (1983)

Richard H. Steckel and Jerome C. Rose, *The Backbone of History: Health and Nutrition in the Western Hemisphere* (2002)

The Development of Farming

Frances R. Berdan, *The Aztecs of Central Mexico* (1982)

David S. Brose and N'omi Greber, eds., *Hopewell Archaeology* (1979)

David Carrasco, et al., eds., *Mesoamerica's Classic Heritage: From Teotihuacan to the Aztecs* (2000)

William S. Dancey and Paul J Pacheco, eds., *Ohio Hopewell Community Organization* (1997)

Emil W. Haury, *The Hohokam* (1976)

Ted Hirschfield, *Middle Mississippians: Encounters with the Prehistoric Amerindians* (1996)

Rosemary Joyce, *Gender and Power in Prehispanic Mesoamerica* (2000)

William F. Keegan, ed., *Emergent Horticultural Economies of the Eastern Woodlands* (1987)

R. Barry Lewis and Charles Stout, eds., *Mississippian Towns and Sacred Spaces* (1998)

George R. Milner, *The Cahokia Chiefdom: The Archaeology of a Mississippian Society* (1998)

Warren King Moorehead, *The Cahokia Mounds* (2000)

Barker H. Morrow and V. B. Price, eds., *Anasazi Architecture and American Design* (1997)

Timothy R. Pauketat and Thomas E. Emerson, eds., *Cahokia: Domination and Ideology in the Mississippian World* (1997)

Stephen Plog, *Ancient Peoples of the American Southwest* (1998)

Paul F. Reed, ed., *Foundations of Anasazi Culture: The Basketmaker-Pueblo Transition* (2000)

Bruce D. Smith, *The Mississippian Emergence* (1990)

David E. Stuart, *Anasazi America: Seventeen Centuries on the Road from Center Place* (2000)

Christy G. Turner, *Man Corn: Cannibalism and Violence in the Prehistoric American Southwest* (2000)

W. H. Wills, *Early Prehistoric Agriculture* (1988)

Biloine W. Young and Melvin L. Fowler, *Cahokia, The Great Native American Metropolis* (2000)

Cultural Regions of North America on the Eve of Colonization

Michael A. Adler, ed., *The Prehistoric Pueblo World*, A.D. 1150–1350 (1996)

Kenneth M. Ames and Herbert D. G. Mascher, *Peoples of the Northwest Coast: Their Archaeology and Prehistory* (2000)

Elizabeth M. Brunfiel and John W. Fox, *Factional Competition and Political Development in the New World* (1993)

Catherine M. Cameron, *Hopi Dwellings: Architecture at Oryi* (1999)

Lyle Campbell and Marianne Mithun, eds., *The Languages of Native America* (1979)

Paul H. Carlson, *The Plains Indians* (1999)

James Taylor Carson, *Searching for the Bright Path: The Mississippi Choctaws from Prehistory to Removal* (1999)

May Castleberry, *The New World's Old World: Photographic Views of Ancient America* (2003)

Cheryl Claassen and Rosemary A. Joyce, eds., *Women in Prehistory: North America and Mesoamerica* (1997)

Olive P. Dickason, *Canada's First Nations: A History of Founding Peoples* (1992)

Michelle Hegmon, ed., *The Archaeology of Regional Interaction: Religion, Warfare, and Exchange Across the American Southwest* (1999)

June Helm, *The People of Denendah: Ethnohistory of the Indians of Canada's Northwest Territories* (2000)

David LaVere, *The Caddo Chiefdoms: Caddo Economics and Politics, 700–1835* (1998)

Steven A. LeBlanc, *Prehistoric Warfare in the American Southwest* (1999)

Stephen H. Lekson, *The Chaco Meridian: Centers of Political Power in the Ancient Southwest* (1999)

Jill E. Neitzel, ed., *Great Towns and Regional Politics: In the Prehistoric American Southwest and Southeast* (1999)

Mallory McCane O'Connor, *Lost Cities of the Ancient Southeast* (1995)

Alfonso Ortiz, ed., *New Perspectives on the Pueblos* (1972)

Howard S. Russell, *Indian New England Before the* Mayflower (1980)

Frank G. Speck, *Penobscot Man* (1940)

Bruce Trigger, *The Children of Aataentsic: A History of the Huron People to 1660* (1976)

CHAPTER 2

The Expansion of Europe

James M. Blaut, *1492: The Debate on Colonialism, Eurocentrism, and History* (1992)

Fernand Braudel, *The Mediterranean and the Mediterranean World in the Age of Philip II* (1972)

Carol Cipolla, *Before the Industrial Revolution: European Society and Economy, 1100–1700* (1976)

Patrick Collinson, *The Religion of Protestants: The Church in English Society, 1559–1625* (1982)

Andre Gunder Frank, *World Accumulation, 1492–1789* (1978)

Giancarlo Masini and Iacopo Gari, *How Florence Invented America: Vespucci, Verranzano, and Mazzei and Their Contribution to the Conception of the New World* (1998)

Douglass North, *The Rise of the Western World: A New Economic History* (1973)

José Casas Pardo, ed., *Economic Effects of the European Expansion, 1492–1824* (1992)

J. H. Parry, *The Age of Reconnaissance* (1963)

———, *Europe and a Wider World: The Establishment of the European Hegemony: Trade and Expansion in the Age of the Renaissance* (1966)

Geoffrey Vaughn Scannell, *The First Imperial Age: European Overseas Expansion c. 1400–1715* (1989)

The Spanish in the Americas

Fredi Chiapelli, ed., *First Images of America: The Impact of the New World on the Old* (1976)

Kathleen Deagan and José María Cruxent, *Columbus's Outpost among the Taínos: Spain and America at La Isabela, 1493–1498* (2002)

Henry F. Dobyns, *Their Number Become Thinned: Native American Population Dynamics in Eastern North America* (1983)

J. H. Elliott, *The Old World and the New, 1492–1650* (1970)

Anthony Grafton, *New Worlds, Ancient Texts: The Power of Tradition and the Shock of Discovery* (1992)

John H. Hann, *A History of the Timucua Indians and Missions* (1996)

Hugh Honour, *New Golden Land: European Images of America from the Discoveries to the Present Time* (1975)

Charles Hudson and Carmen Chaves Tesser, eds., *The Forgotten Centuries: Indians and Europeans in the American South, 1521–1704* (1994)

René Jara and Nicholas Spadaccini, eds., *Amerindian Images and the Legacy of Columbus* (1992)

Elizabeth A. H. John, *Storms Brewed in Other Men's Worlds: The Confrontation of Indians, Spanish, and French in the Southwest, 1540–1795* (1975)

James Lang, *Conquest and Commerce: Spain and England in the Americas* (1975)

James Lockhart and Stuart B. Schwartz, *Early Latin America: A History of Colonial Spanish America and Brazil* (1983)

Albert Mauncy, *Sixteenth-Century St. Augustine: The People and Their Homes* (1997)

Jerald T. Milanich, *Laboring in the Fields of the Lord: Spanish Missions and Southeastern Indians* (1999)

Jerald T. Milanich and Charles Hudson, *Hernando de Soto and the Indians of Florida* (1993)

James Howlett O'Donnell III, *Southeastern Frontiers: Europeans, Africans, and American Indians, 1513–1840: A Critical Bibliography* (1982)

Edmundo O'Gorman, *The Invention of America: An Inquiry into the Historical Nature of the New World and the Meaning of its History* (1961)

Stuart B. Schwartz, *Victors and Vanquished: Spanish and Nahua Views of the Conquest of Mexico* (2000)

David M. Traboulay, *Columbus and Las Casas: The Conquest and Christianization of America, 1492–1566* (1994)

Northern Explorations and Encounters

Alfred Goldsworthy Bailey, *The Conflict of European and Eastern Algonkian Cultures, 1504–1700* (1969)

Peter T. Bradley, *British Maritime Enterprise in the New World: From the Late Fifteenth to the Mid-Eighteenth Century* (1999)

Carl Bridenbaugh, *Vexed and Troubled Englishmen, 1590–1642* (1968)

Susan Danforth, *Encountering the New World, 1493–1800* (1991)

Philip J. Deloria and Neal Salisbury, eds., *A Companion to American Indian History* (2002)

G. R. Elton, *England under the Tudors* (1974)

C. H. George and Katherine George, *The Protestant Mind of the English Reformation* (1961)

John Guy, *Tudor England* (1988)

R. J. Knecht, *The French Civil Wars, 1562–1598* (2000)

Karen Ordahl Kupperman, *Indians and English: Facing Off in Early America* (2000)

Peter Laslett, *The World We Have Lost* (1965)

Anthony McFarlane, *The British in the Americas, 1480–1815* (1994)

Lee Miller, *Roanoke: Solving the Mystery of England's Lost Colony* (2000)

James S. Pritchard, *In Search of Empire: The French in the Americas, 1670–1730* (2004)

David B. Quinn, *North America from Earliest Discovery to First Settlements* (1977)

————, *The Roanoke Voyages, 1584–1590*, 2 vols. (1955)

Bernard W. Sheehan, *Savagism and Civility: Indians and Englishmen in Colonial Virginia* (1980)

Russell Thornton, *American Indian Holocaust and Survival* (1987)

Margo Todd, ed., *Reformation to Revolution: Politics and Religion in Early Modern England* (1995)

Marcel Trudel, *The Beginnings of New France, 1524–1663* (1973)

Keith Wrightson, *English Society, 1580–1680* (1982)

Biography

Miles H. Davidson, *Columbus Then and Now: A Life Reexamined* (1997)

David A. Howard, *Conquistador in Chains: Cabeza de Vaca and the Indians of the Americas* (1997)

Harry Kelsey, *Sir Francis Drake: The Queen's Pirate* (1998)

Carole Levin, *The Heart and Stomach of a King: Elizabeth I and the Politics of Sex and Power* (1994)

Richard Lee Marks, *Cortés: The Great Adventurer and the Fate of Aztec Mexico* (1993)

James McDermott, *Martin Frobisher: Elizabethan Privateer* (2001)

P. E. Russell, *Prince Henry the Navigator: A Life* (2000)

David Starkey, *Elizabeth: The Struggle for the Throne* (2000)

Henry Raup Wagner, *The Life and Writings of Bartolomé de las Casas* (1967)

CHAPTER 3

Spain and Its Competitors in North America

Gary Clayton Anderson, *The Indian Southwest, 1580–1830: Ethnogenesis and Reinvention* (1999)

James Axtell, *The Invasion Within: The Contest of Culture in Colonial North America* (1985)

Denys Delâge, *Bitter Feast: Amerindians and Europeans in Northeastern North America, 1600–64* (1993)

W. J. Eccles, *The Canadian Frontier, 1534–1760* (1983)

Carl J. Ekberg, *French Roots in the Illinois Country: The Mississippi Frontier in Colonial Times* (1998)

Eric Hinderaker and Peter C. Mancall, *At the Edge of Empire: The Backcountry in British North America* (2003)

J. R. Jones, *The Anglo–-Dutch Wars of the Seventeenth Century* (1996)

Cathy D. Matson, *Merchants and Empire: Trading in Colonial New York* (1998)

Peter Moogk, *La Nouvelle France: The Making of French Canada, a Cultural History* (2000)

Daniel Paul, *We Were Not the Savages: A Mi'kmaq Perspective on the Collision Between European and Native American Civilizations* (2000)

Oliver Rink, *Holland on the Hudson: An Economic and Social History of Dutch New York* (1986)

Sylvia Van Kirk, *Many Tender Ties: Women in Fur-Trade Society in Western Canada, 1670–1870* (1999)

England in the Chesapeake

Edward L. Bond, *Damned Souls in a Tobacco Colony: Religion in Seventeenth-Century Virginia* (2000)

Kathleen M. Brown, *Good Wives, Nasty Wenches, and Anxious Patriarchs: Gender, Race, and Power in Colonial Virginia* (1996)

Wesley F. Craven, *White, Red, and Black: The Seventeenth Century Virginian* (1971)

April Lee Hatfield, *Atlantic Virginia: Intercolonial Relations in the Seventeenth Century* (2004)

Ronald Hoffman, *Princes of Ireland, Planters of Maryland: A Carroll Saga, 1500–1782* (2000)

Karen Ordahl Kupperman, *Settling with the Indians: The Meeting of English and Indian Cultures in America, 1580–1640* (1980)

Gloria L. Main, *Tobacco Colony: Life in Early Maryland, 1650–1720* (1982)

Michael Leroy Oberg, *Dominion and Civility: English Imperialism and Native America, 1585–1685* (1999)

The New England Colonies

David Grayson Allen, *In English Ways: The Movement of Societies and the Transferal of English Local Law and Custom* (1981)

Bernard Bailyn, *The New England Merchants in the Seventeenth Century* (1955)

Carl Bridenbaugh, *Fat Mutton and Liberty of Conscience: Society in Rhode Island, 1636–1690* (1974)

Joyce E. Chaplin, *Subject Matter: Technology, the Body, and Science on the Anglo–American Frontier, 1500–1676* (2001)

David Cressy, *Coming Over: Migration and Communication between England and New England in the Seventeenth Century* (1987)

William Cronon, *Changes in the Land: Indians, Colonists, and the Ecology of New England* (1983)

John Demos, *A Little Commonwealth: Family Life in Plymouth Colony* (1970)

David D. Hall, ed., *Puritans in the New World: A Critical Anthology* (2004)

Timothy Hall, *Separating Church and State: Roger Williams and Religious Liberty* (1998)

Francis Jennings, *The Invasion of America: Indians, Colonialism, and the Cant of Conquest* (1975)

Benjamin W. Labaree, *America and the Sea: A Maritime History* (1998)

Amy Scrager Lang, *Prophetic Women: Anne Hutchinson and the Problem of Dissent in the Literature of New England* (1987)

Elizabeth Reis, *Damned Women: Sinners and Witches in Puritan New England* (1997)

The Restoration Colonies

Wesley F. Craven, *The Southern Colonies in the Seventeenth Century, 1607–1689* (1949)

Michael Kammen, *Colonial New York: A History* (1975)

Sung Bok Kim, *Landlord and Tenant in Colonial New York: Manorial Society, 1664–1775* (1978)

H. T. Merrens, *Colonial North Carolina* (1964)

Donna Merwick, *Death of a Notary: Conquest and Change in Colonial New York* (1999)

Gary B. Nash, *Quakers and Politics: Pennsylvania, 1681–1726* (1968)

M. Eugene Sirmans, *Colonial South Carolina: A Political History, 1663–1763* (1966)

Jack M. Sosin, *English America and the Restoration Monarchy of Charles II: Transatlantic Politics, Commerce, and Kinship* (1980)

Conflict and War

Thomas J. Archdeacon, *New York City, 1664–1710* (1976)

Paul Boyer and Stephen Nissenbaum, *Salem Possessed* (1974)

Colin G. Calloway, ed., *After King Philip's War: Presence and Persistence in Indian New England* (1997)

Guy Chet, *Conquering the American Wilderness: The Triumph of European Warfare in the Colonial Northeast* (2003)

Eveline Cruickshanks, *The Glorious Revolution* (2000)

James D. Drake, *King Philip's War: Civil War in New England, 1675–1676* (1999)

Ramón A. Gutiérrez, *When Jesus Came, the Corn Mothers Went Away: Marriage, Sexuality, and Power in New Mexico, 1500–1846* (1991)

Richard R. Johnson, *Adjustment to Empire: The New England Colonies, 1675–1715* (1981)

D. W. Jordan, *Maryland's Revolution of Government, 1689–1692* (1974)

Carol F. Karlsen, *The Devil in the Shape of a Woman: Witchcraft in Colonial New England* (1987)

Karen Ordahl Kupperman, *Indians and English: Facing Off in Early America* (2000)

Almon Wheeler Lauber, *Indian Slavery in Colonial Times within the Present Limits of the United States* (1913)

Jill Lepore, *The Name of War: King Philip's War and the Origins of American Identity* (1998)

David S. Lovejoy, *The Glorious Revolution in America* (1972)

Nancy Shoemaker, *A Strange Likeness: Becoming Red and White in Eighteenth-Century North America* (2004)

Wilcomb E. Washburn, *The Governor and the Rebel: A History of Bacon's Rebellion in Virginia* (1957)

Stephen S. Webb, *1676: The End of American Independence* (1980)

Biography

Mary K. Geiter, *Willlam Penn* (2000)

J. A. Leo Lemay, *The American Dream of Captain John Smith* (1991)

Edmund S. Morgan, *Puritan Dilemma: The Story of John Winthrop* (1958)

Ann Sanford, *Anne Bradstreet, the Worldly Puritan* (1974)

Marc Simmons, *The Last Conquistador: Juan de Oñate and the Settling of the Far Southwest* (1991)

Robert S. Tilton, *Pocahontas: The Evolution of an American Narrative* (1994)

Alvin Gardner Weeks, *Massasoit of the Pokanokets* (1919)

Selma R. Williams, *Divine Rebel: The Life of Anne Marbury Hutchinson* (1981)

CHAPTER 4

The African Slave Trade

Jay Coughtry, *The Notorious Triangle: Rhode Island and the African Slave Trade, 1799–1807* (1981)

Philip D. Curtin, *Economic Change in Precolonial Africa: Senegambia in the Era of the Slave Trade* (1975)

Basil Davidson, *The African Slave Trade* (1980)

Benedict G. Der, *The Slave Trade in Northern Ghana* (1998)

Elizabeth Donnan, ed., *Documents Illustrative of the History of the Slave Trade to America*, 4 vols. (1930–35)

David Eltis, et al., eds., *Slavery in the Development of the Americas* (2004)

Eli Faber, *Jews, Slaves, and the Slave Trade: Setting the Record Straight* (1998)

Philip Gould, *Barbaric Traffic: Commerce and Antislavery in the Eighteenth-Century Atlantic World* (2003)

Robert W. Harms, *The Diligent: A Voyage through the Worlds of the Slave Trade* (2001)

J. E. Inikori, *Forced Migration: The Impact of the Export Slave Trade on African Societies* (1982)

Robert W. July, *A History of the African People* (1992)

Herbert S. Klein, *The Middle Passage: Comparative Studies in the Atlantic Slave Trade* (1978)

Robin Law, *The Slave Coast of West Africa, 1550–1750: The Impact of the Atlantic Slave Trade on an African Society* (1991)

Paul E. Lovejoy, ed., *Africans in Bondage: Studies in Slavery and the Slave Trade* (1986)

Daniel P. Mannix and Malcolm Crowley, *Black Cargoes: A History of the Atlantic Slave Trade* (1962)

David Northrup, ed., *The Atlantic Slave Trade* (1994)

J. A. Rawley, *The Transatlantic Slave Trade* (1981)

Edward Reynolds, *Stand the Storm: A History of the Atlantic Slave Trade* (1985)

A. C. de C. M. Saunders, *A Social History of Black Slaves and Freemen in Portugal, 1441–1555* (1982)

Randy J. Sparks, *Two Princes of Calabar: An Eighteenth-Century Atlantic Odyssey* (2004)

Jon Vogt, *Portuguese Rule on the Gold Coast, 1469–1682* (1979)

James Walvin, *Making the Black Atlantic: Britain and the African Diaspora* (2000)

The Development of North American Slave Societies

L. R. Bailey, *Indian Slave Trade in the Southwest: A Study of Slave-Taking and the Traffic in Indian Captives* (1966)

Ira Berlin, *Generations of Captivity: A History of African-American Slaves* (2003)

T. H. Breen and Stephen Innes, *"Myne Owne Ground": Race and Freedom on Virginia's Eastern Shore* (1980)

Verner W. Crane, *The Southern Frontier, 1670–1732* (1929)

Richard S. Dunn, *Sugar and Slaves: The Rise of the Planter Class in the English West Indies, 1624–1713* (1972)

David Eltis, *The Rise of African Slavery in the Americas* (2000)

Sharla M. Fett, *Working Cures: Healing, Health, and Power on Southern Slave Plantations* (2002)

Laura Foner and Eugene D. Genovese, eds., *Slavery in the New World: A Reader in Comparative History* (1969)

Allan Gallay, *The Indian Slave Trade: The Rise of the English Empire in the American South, 1670–1717* (2002)

Graham Russell Hodges, *Root and Branch: African Americans in New York and East Jersey, 1613–1863* (1999)

Thomas N. Ingersoll, *Mammon and Manon in Early New Orleans: The First Slave Society in the Deep South, 1718–1819* (1999)

Charles Joyner, *Down by the Riverside: A South Carolina Slave Community* (1984)

Alan Kulikoff, *Tobacco and Slaves: The Development of Southern Cultures in the Chesapeake, 1680–1800* (1986)

Jane Landers, *Black Society in Spanish Florida* (1999)

Daniel Littlefield, *Rice and Slaves: Ethnicity and the Slave Trade in Colonial South Carolina* (1981)

Paul E. Lovejoy, *Transformations in Slavery: A History of Slavery in Africa* (1983)

Edgar J. McManus, *Black Bondage in the North* (1973)

Gary B. Nash, *Red, White, and Black: The Peoples of Early North America* (1992)

Julia Floyd Smith, *Slavery and Rice Culture in Low Country Georgia, 1750–1860* (1985)

Peter H. Wood, *Black Majority: Negroes in Colonial South Carolina from 1670 through the Stono Rebellion* (1974)

African to African American

John B. Boles, *Black Southerners, 1619–1869* (1984)

Alex Bontemps, *The Punished Self: Surviving Slavery in the Colonial South* (2001)

Sylviane A. Diouf, *Servants of Allah: African Muslims Enslaved in the Americas* (1998)

John Hope Franklin and Loren Schweniger, *Runaway Slaves: Rebels in the Plantation* (1999)

Michael Gomez, *Exchanging Our Country Marks: The Transformation of African Identities in the Colonial and Antebellum South* (1998)

Annette Gordon-Reed, *Thomas Jefferson and Sally Hemings: An American Controversy* (1997)

Herbert G. Gutman, *The Black Family in Slavery and Freedom, 1750–1925* (1976).

Joseph E. Harris, ed., *Global Dimensions of the African Diaspora* (1982)

Gerald W. Mullin, *Flight and Rebellion: Slave Resistance in Eighteenth-Century Virginia* (1972)

Orlando Patterson, *Slavery and Social Death: A Comparative Study* (1982)

Mark M. Smith, *Mastered by the Clock: Time, Slavery, and Freedom in the American South* (1997)

Sterling Stuckey, *Slave Culture: Nationalist Theory and the Foundations of Black America* (1987).

V. B. Thompson, *The Making of the African Diaspora in the Americas, 1441–1900* (1984)

Slavery and Empire

Joyce O. Appleby, *Economic Thought and Ideology in Seventeenth-Century England* (1978)

Heather Cateau and S. H. H. Carrington, eds., *Capitalism and Slavery Fifty Years Later: Eric Eustace Williams—A Reassessment of the Man and His Work* (2000)

Eugene Genovese and Elizabeth Fox-Genovese, *Fruits of Merchant Capital: Slavery and Bourgeois Property in the Rise and Expansion of Capitalism* (1983)

E. J. Hobsbawn, *Industry and Empire: The Making of Modern English Society, 1750 to the Present Day* (1968)

Michael Kammen, *Empire and Interest: The American Colonies and the Politics of Mercantilism* (1970)

John J. McCusker and Russell R. Menard, *The Economy of British America, 1607–1787* (1985)

Barbara L. Solow, ed., *Slavery and the Rise of the Atlantic System* (1991)

Eric Williams, *Capitalism and Slavery* (1944)

Slavery and Freedom

David Brion Davis, *The Problem of Slavery in Western Culture* (1966)

Carl N. Degler, *Neither Black nor White: Slavery and Race Relations in Brazil and the United States* (1971)

Edmund S. Morgan, *American Slavery, American Freedom: The Ordeal of Colonial Virginia* (1975)

Joel Williamson, *New People: Miscegenation and Mulattoes in the United States* (1980)

Biography

Philip D. Curtin, ed., *Africa Remembered: Narratives of West Africans from the Era of the Slave Trade* (1967)

Paul Edwards, ed., *The Interesting Narrative of the Life of Olaudah Equiano, or Gustavus Vassa, the African, written by himself* (1987)

James B. Hedges, *The Browns of Providence Plantation* (1952)

Kenneth A. Lockridge, *The Diary and Life of William Byrd II of Virginia, 1674–1744* (1987)

Phinizy Spalding, *Oglethorpe in America* (1977)

CHAPTER 5

North American Regions

Patricia Albers and Beatrice Medicine, eds., *The Hidden Half: Studies of Plains Indian Women* (1983)

Carole Blackburn, *Harvest of Souls: The Jesuit Missions and Colonialism in North America, 1632–1650* (2000)

Richard L. Bushman, *From Puritan to Yankee: Character and the Social Order in Connecticut, 1690–1765* (1967)

David Bussiert and Steven G. Reinhardt, eds., *Creolization in the Americas* (2000)

Edward D. Castillo, ed., *Native American Perspectives on the Hispanic Colonization of Alta California* (1992)

Andrew R. L. Cayton and Frederika J. Teute, eds., *Contact Points: American Frontiers from the Mohawk Valley to the Mississippi, 1750–1830* (1998)

Cornelia Hughes Dayton, *Women before the Bar: Gender, Law, and Society in Connecticut, 1639–1789* (1995)

Brian Leigh Dunnigan, *Frontier Metropolis: Picturing Early Detroit, 1701–1838* (2001)

John C. Ewers, *The Horse in Blackfoot Indian Culture* (1955)

David Hackett Fischer and James C. Kelly, *Bound Away: Virginia and the Westward Movement* (2000)

Joseph W. Glass, *The Pennsylvania Culture Region: A View from the Barn* (1986)

Robert F. Heizer, *The Destruction of California Indians* (1974)

Donald A. Hutslar, *The Architecture of Migration: Log Construction in the Ohio Country, 1750–1850* (1986)

Christine Leigh Hyrman, *Commerce and Culture: The Maritime Communities of Colonial Massachusetts* (1984)

Rhys Isaac, *Worlds of Experience: Communities in Colonial Virginia* (1987)

Robert H. Jackson, *Indian Population Decline: The Missions of Northwestern New Spain, 1687–1840* (1994)

———, *From Savages to Subjects: Missions in the History of the American Southwest* (2000)

Francis Jennings, *The Ambiguous Iroquois Empire* (1984)

Terry G. Jordan and Matti Kaups, *The American Backwoods Frontier: An Ethnic and Ecological Interpretation* (1988)

Lyle Kohler, *A Search for Power: "The Weaker Sex" in Seventeenth-Century New England, 1650–1750* (1982)

James T. Lemon, *The Best Poor Man's Country: A Geographical Study of Early Southeastern Pennsylvania* (1972)

Kenneth Lockridge, *Literacy in Colonial New England* (1974)

James H. Merrell, *The Indians' New World: Catawbas and Their Neighbors from European Contact through the Era of Removal* (1989)

———, *Into the American Woods: Negotiators on the Pennsylvania Frontier* (1999)

Jane T. Merritt, *At the Crossroads: Indians and Empires on a Mid-Atlantic Frontier, 1700–1763* (2003)

Gary B. Nash, *The Urban Crucible* (1979)

Jacqueline Peterson and Jennifer S. H. Brown, eds., *The New Peoples: Being and Becoming Métis in North America* (1985)

Daniel K. Richter, *The Ordeal of the Longhouse: The Peoples of the Iroquois League in the Era of European Colonization* (1992)

Darrett B. Rutman and Anita H. Rutman, *A Place in Time: Middlesex County, Virginia, 1650–1750* (1984)

Marylynn Salmon, *Women and the Law of Property in Early America* (1986)

Sally Schwartz, *A Mixed Multitude: The Struggle for Toleration in Colonial Pennsylvania* (1987)

William S. Simmons, *Spirit of the New England Tribes: Indian History and Folklore, 1620–1984* (1986)

Daniel Blake Smith, *Inside the Great House: Planter Family Life in Eighteenth-Century Chesapeake Society* (1980)

Laurel T. Ulrich, *Good Wives: Image and Reality in the Lives of Women in Northern New England, 1650–1750* (1982)

Daniel H. Usner Jr., *Indians, Settlers, and Slaves in a Frontier Exchange Economy: The Lower Mississippi Valley before 1783* (1992)

Diverging Social and Political Patterns

James E. Block, *Nation of Agents: The American Path to a Modern Self and Society* (2002)

Bernard Bailyn, *The Peopling of British North America: An Introduction* (1986)

Bruce C. Daniels, ed., *Power and Status: Essays on Officeholding in Colonial America* (1986)

Robert J. Dinkin, *Voting in Provincial America: A Study of Elections in the Thirteen Colonies, 1680–1776* (1977)

A. Roger Ekirch, *Bound for America: The Transportation of British Convicts to the Colonies, 1718–1775* (1987)

Carla Gardina Pestana and Sharon V. Salinger, eds., *Inequality in Early America* (1999)

Thomas L. Purvis, *Proprietors, Patronage, and Paper Money: Legislative Politics in New Jersey, 1703–1776* (1986)

Sharon V. Salinger, *"To Serve Well and Faithfully": Labor and Indentured Servants in Pennsylvania, 1682–1800* (1987)

The Cultural Transformation of British North America

Linda Baumgarten, *What Clothes Reveal: The Language of Clothing in Colonial and Federal America: The Colonial Williamsburg Collection* (2002)

Patricia U. Bonomi, *Under the Cope of Heaven: Religion, Society, and Politics in Colonial America* (1986)

Henry Steele Commager, *The Empire of Reason: How Europe Imagined and America Realized the Enlightenment* (1977)

Patricia Crain, *The Story of A: The Alphabetization of America from "The New England Primer" to "The Scarlet Letter"* (2000)

John Demos, *Circles and Lines: The Shape of Life in Early America* (2004)

Nancy Isenberg and Andrew Burstein, eds., *Mortal Remains: Death in Early America* (2003)

Ned C. Landsman, *From Colonials to Provincials: American Thought and Culture, 1680–1760* (1997)

Jackson Turner Main, *The Social Structure of Revolutionary America* (1965)

Barbara B. Oberg and Harry S. Stout, eds., *Benjamin Franklin, Jonathan Edwards, and the Representation of American Culture* (1993)

Mark A. Peterson, *The Price of Redemption: The Spiritual Economy of Puritan New England* (1997)

Nina Reid-Mahoney, *Philadelphia's Enlightenment, 1740–1800: Kingdom of Christ, Empire of Reason* (2001)

Frank Shuffelton, ed., *The American Enlightenment* (1993)

Biography

Verner W. Crane, *Benjamin Franklin and a Rising People* (1952)

Harry Kelsey, *Juan Rodriguez Cabrillo* (1986)

Gerald R. McDermott, *Jonathan Edwards Confronts the Gods* (2000)

Robert Middlekauff, *The Mathers: Three Generations of Puritan Intellectuals, 1596–1728* (1999)

Martin J. Morgado, *Junípero Serra's Legacy* (1987)

Harry S. Stout, *The Divine Dramatist: George Whitefield and the Rise of Modern Evangelicalism* (1991)

Laurel Ulrich, *A Midwife's Tale: The Life of Martha Ballard, Based on Her Diary, 1785–1812* (1990)

CHAPTER 6

The Seven Years' War in America

Fred Anderson, *A People's Army: Massachusetts Soldiers and Society in the Seven Years' War* (1984)

Frank W. Brecher, *Losing a Continent: France's North American Policy, 1753–1763* (1998)

Gregory Evans Dowd, *War Under Heaven: Pontiac, the Indian Nations, and the British Empire* (2002)

Sylvia R. Frey, *The British Soldier in America: A Social History of Military Life in the Colonial Period* (1981)

Dougles E. Leach, *Roots of Conflict: British Armed Forces and Colonial Americans, 1677–1763* (1986)

Richard Middleton, *The Bells of Victory: The Pitt–Newcastle Ministry and the Conduct of the Seven Years' War, 1757–1762* (1985)

Robert C. Newbold, *The Albany Congress and Plan of Union of 1754* (1955)

William Pencak, *War, Politics, and Revolution in Provincial Massachusetts* (1981)

Tom Pocock, *Battle for Empire: The Very First World War, 1756–63* (1998)

Alan Rogers, *Empire and Liberty* (1974)

David Curtis Skaggs and Larry L. Nelson, eds., *The Sixty Years' War for the Great Lakes, 1754–1814* (2001)

Noel T. St. John Williams, *Redcoats along the Hudson* (1997)

Richard White, *The Middle Ground: Indians, Empires, and Republics in the Great Lakes Region, 1650–1815* (1991)

Imperial Crisis in British North America

Stuart Andrews, *The Rediscovery of America: Transatlantic Crosscurrents in an Age of Revolution* (1998)

Thomas C. Barrow, *Trade and Empire: The British Customs Service in Colonial America* (1967)

Don Cook, *The Long Fuse: How England Lost the American Colonies, 1760–1785* (1995)

Theodore Draper, *A Struggle for Power: The American Revolution* (1996)

Marc Egnal, *A Mighty Empire: The Origins of the American Revolution* (1988)

Eliga H. Gould, *The Persistence of Empire: British Political Culture in the Age of the American Revolution* (2000)

Woody Holton, *Forced Founders: Indians, Debtors, Slaves, and the Making of the American Revolution in Virginia* (1999)

Alice Hanson Jones, *The Wealth of a Nation to Be* (1980)

John J. McCusker, *Rum and the American Revolution* (1989)

Philip James McFarland, *The Brave Bostonians: Hutchinson, Quincy, Franklin, and the Coming of the American Revolution* (1998)

J. G. A. Pocock, *The Machiavellian Moment: Florentine Political Thought and the Atlantic Republican Tradition* (1975)

William Lowell Putnam, *John Peter Zenger and the Fundamental Freedom* (1997)

Caroline Robbins, *The Eighteenth-Century Commonwealthman* (1959)

Arthur M. Schlesinger, *The Colonial Merchants and the American Revolution* (1917)

John W. Tyler, *Smugglers and Patriots: Boston Merchants and the Advent of the American Revolution* (1986)

Carl Ubbelohde, *The Vice-Admiralty Courts and the American Revolution* (1960)

Kathleen Wilson, *Island Race: Englishness, Empire, and Gender in the Eighteenth Century* (2003)

From Resistance to Rebellion

David Ammerman, *In the Common Cause: American Response to the Coercive Acts of 1774* (1974)

T. H. Breen, *Tobacco Culture: The Mentality of the Great Tidewater Planters on the Eve of Revolution* (1985)

Richard D. Brown, *Revolutionary Politics in Massachusetts: The Boston Committee of Correspondence and the Towns, 1772–1774* (1970)

Richard L. Bushman, *King and People in Provincial Massachusetts* (1985)

H. Trevor Colbourn, *The Lamp of Experience: Whig History and the Intellectual Origins of the American Revolution* (1965)

Light Townsend Cummins, *Spanish Observers and the American Revolution, 1775–1783* (1991)

Derek Davis, *Religion and the Continental Congress, 1774–1789: Contributions to Original Intent* (2000)

Bernard Donoughue, *British Politics and the American Revolution: The Path to War, 1773–1775* (1964)

Gregory T. Edgar, *Reluctant Break with Britain: From Stamp Act to Bunker Hill* (1997)

Jack P. Greene, *Understanding the American Revolution: Issues and Actors* (1995)

Benjamin W. Labaree, *The Boston Tea Party* (1974)

Pauline Maier, *From Resistance to Rebellion* (1972)

Edmund S. Morgan, *The Birth of the Republic, 1763–1789* (1956)

Ray Raphael, *First American Revolution: Before Lexington and Concord* (2002)

Jackson O'Shaughnessy, *An Empire Divided: The American Revolution and the British Caribbean* (2000)

John Shy, *Toward Lexington: The Role of the British Army in the Coming of the American Revolution* (1965)

Peter David Garner Thomas, *Tea Party to Independence: The Third Phase of the American Revolution, 1773–1776* (1991)

Morton White, *The Philosophy of the American Revolution* (1978)

Gary Wills, *Inventing America* (1978)

Biography

Bernard Bailyn, *The Ordeal of Thomas Hutchinson* (1974)

Della Gray Barthelmas, *The Signers of the Declaration of Independence* (1997)

Richard R. Beeman, *Patrick Henry: A Biography* (1974)

Jeremy Black, *Pitt the Elder* (1992)

John Brooke, *King George III* (1974)

John E. Ferling, *The Loyalist Mind: Joseph Galloway and the American Revolution* (1977)

———, *Setting the World Ablaze: Washington, Adams, and Jefferson and the American Revolution* (2000)

William M. Fowler, Jr., *The Baron of Beacon Hill: A Biography of John Hancock* (1979)

———, *Samuel Adams: Radical Puritan* (1997)

Rhys Isaac, *Landon Carter's Uneasy Kingdom: Revolution and Rebellion on a Virginia Plantation* (2004)

David A. McCants, *Patrick Henry, the Orator* (1990)

Colin Nicolson, "Infamas Govener" Francis Bernard and the Origins of the American Revolution (2001)

Peter Shaw, The Character of John Adams (1976)

Peter D. G. Thomas, Lord North (1974)

Andrew S. Walmsley, Thomas Hutchinson and the Origins of the American Revolution (1999)

Gordon S. Wood, Americanization of Benjamin Franklin (2004)

CHAPTER 7

The War for Independence

Ian Barnes, The Historical Atlas of the American Revolution (2000)

Ira Berlin and Ronald Hoffman, eds., Slavery and Freedom in the Age of the American Revolution (1983)

Wayne Bodle, Valley Forge Winter: Civilians and Soldiers in War (2002)

T.H. Breen, Marketplace of Revolution: How Consumer Politics Shaped American Independence (2004)

Charles E. Claghorn, Women Patriots of the American Revolution (1991)

Stephen Conway, British Isles and the War of American Independence (2000)

Lawrence D. Cress, Citizens in Arms: The Army and the Militia in American Society to the War of 1812 (1982)

Paul Finkleman, ed., Slavery, Revolutionary America, and the New Nation (1989)

William M. Fowler Jr., Rebels Under Sail: The American Navy During the Revolution (1976)

Francis Fox, Sweet Land of Liberty: The Ordeal of the American Revolution in Northampton County, Pennsylvania (2000)

Barbara Graymont, The Iroquois in the American Revolution (1972)

Leslie Hall, Land and Allegiance in Revolutionary Georgia (2001)

David C. Hendrickson, Peace Pact: The Lost World of the American Founding (2003)

Ronald Hoffman and Peter J. Albert, eds., Arms and Independence: The Military Character of the American Revolution (1984)

———— eds., Women in the Age of the American Revolution (1989)

Ronald Hoffman and Thad W. Tate, eds., An Uncivil War: The Southern Backcountry during the American Revolution (1985)

Francis Jennings, The Creation of America: Through Revolution to Empire (2000)

Mark E. Kann, A Republic of Men: The American Founders, Gendered Language, and Patriarchial Politics (1998)

Cynthia A. Kierner, Southern Women in Revolution, 1776–1800 (1998)

Arthur S. Lefkowitz, The Long Retreat: The Calamitous American Defense of New Jersey, 1776 (1999)

Paul C. Nagel, The Adams Women: Abigail and Louise Adams, Their Sisters and Daughters (1987)

Gary B. Nash, Race and Revolution (1990)

Mary Beth Norton, The British Americans: The Loyalist Exiles in England, 1774–1789 (1972)

James O'Donnell, Southern Indians in the American Revolution (1973)

Andrew Jackson O'Shaughnessy, An Empire Divided: The American Revolution and the British Caribbean (2000)

Howard W. Peckham, The Toll of Independence: Engagements and Battle Casualties of the American Revolution (1974)

Elizabeth Perkins, Border Life: Experience and Memory in the Revolutionary Ohio Valley (1998)

Benjamin Quarles, The Negro in the American Revolution, rev. ed. (1996)

David Lee Russell, The American Revolution in the Southern Colonies (2000)

James W. St. G. Walker, The Black Loyalists (1976)

Anthony F. C. Wallace, The Death and Rebirth of the Seneca (1970)

Alfred F. Young, ed., The American Revolution: Explorations in American Radicalism (1976).

The United States in Congress Assembled

Joyce Appleby, Inheriting the Revolution: The First Generation of Americans (2000)

Richard Beeman, et al., eds., Beyond Confederation: Origins of the Constitution and American National Identity (1987)

E. Wayne Carp, To Starve the Army at Pleasure: Continental Army Administration and American Political Culture, 1774–1783 (1984)

E. J. Ferguson, The Power of the Purse: A History of American Public Finance, 1776–1790 (1960)

Calvin C. Jillson, Congressional Dynamics: Structure, Coordination, and Choice in the First American Congress, 1774–1789 (1994)

Jackson Turner Main, Political Parties before the Constitution (1973)

Jack N. Rakove, The Beginnings of National Politics: An Interpretive History of the Continental Congress (1979)

Gerald Sourzh, Benjamin Franklin and American Foreign Policy (1969)

Gordon S. Wood, The Creation of the American Republic, 1776–1787 (1969)

Revolutionary Politics in the States

Willi Paul Adams, The First American Constitutions: Republican Ideology and the Making of the State Constitutions (1980)

Roger H. Brown, Redeeming the Republic: Federalists, Taxation, and the Origins of the Constitution (1993)

Donald S. Lutz, Popular Consent and Popular Control: Whig Political Theory in the Early State Constitutions (1980)

Jackson Turner Main, The Sovereign States, 1775–1789 (1973)

Biography

William Howard Adams, Gouverneur Morris: An Independent Life (2003)

Silvio A. Bedini, The Life of Benjamin Banneker (1972)

Patricia Cleary, Elizabeth Murray: A Woman's Pursuit of Independence in Eighteenth-Century America (2000)

John Mack Faragher, Daniel Boone: The Life and Legend of an American Pioneer (1992)

Douglas Southall Freeman, George Washington, 7 vols. (1948–57)

Lowell Hayes Harrison, George Rogers Clark and the War in the West (1976)

John W. Hartmann, The American Partisan: Henry Lee and the Struggle for Independence, 1776–1780 (2000)

Isabel Thompson Kelsay, *Joseph Brant, 1743–1807: Man of Two Worlds* (1984)

James Kirby Martin, *Benedict Arnold, Revolutionary Hero* (1997)

Gregory D. Massey, *John Laurens and the American Revolution* (2000)

William Henry Robinson, *Phillis Wheatley and Her Writings* (1984)

Susan Burgess Shenstone, *So Obstinately Loyal: James Moody, 1744–1809* (2000)

Henry Wiencek, *Imperfect God: George Washington, His Slaves, and the Creation of America* (2003)

Alfred F. Young, *Masquerade: The Life and Times of Deborah Sampson, Continental Soldier* (2004)

Rosemarie Zagarri, *A Woman's Dilemma: Mercy Otis Warren and the American Revolution* (1995)

CHAPTER 8

The Crisis of the 1780s

Roger H. Brown, *Redeeming the Republic: Federalists, Taxation, and the Origin of the Constitution* (1993)

Keith L. Dougherty, *Collective Action Under the Articles of Confederation* (2001)

Ronald Hoffman and Peter J. Albert, eds., *Soverign States in an Age of Uncertainty* (1982)

Robert A. Gross, eds., *In Debt to Shays: The Bicentennial of an Agrarian Rebellion* (1993)

Merrill Jensen, *The New Nation: A History of the United States during the Confederation, 1781–1789* (1950)

Leonard L. Richards, *Shay's Rebellion: The American Revolution's Final Battle* (2002)

David Szatmary, *Shay's Rebellion: The Making of an Agrarian Insurrection* (1980)

The New Constitution

Douglass Adair, *Fame and the Founding Fathers*, ed. Trevor Colbourn (1974)

Bernard Bailyn, *To Begin the World Anew: The Genius and Ambiguities of the American Founders* (2003)

Charles A. Beard, *An Economic Interpretation of the Constitution of the United States* (1913)

Saul Cornell, *The Other Founders: Anti-Federalism and the Dissenting Tradition in America, 1788–1828* (1999)

Robert A. Dahl, *How Democratic Is the American Constitution?* (2003)

Max Farrand, ed., *Records of the Federal Convention of 1787*, 4 vols. (1911–37)

Paul Finkelman, *Slavery and the Founders: Race and Liberty in the Age of Jefferson* (2001)

John P. Kaminski and Gaspare J. Saladino, eds., *The Documentary History of the Ratification of the Constitution* (1982)

Mark E. Kann, *A Republic of Men: The American Founders, Gendered Language, and Patriarchal Politics* (1998)

Leonard W. Levy, *Origins of the Bill of Rights* (1999)

James H. Read, *Power Versus Liberty: Madison, Hamilton, Wilson, and Jefferson* (2000)

Gary Rosen, *American Compact: James Madison and the Problem of Founding* (1999)

Herbert J. Storing, ed., *The Complete Anti-Federalist*, 7 vols. (1981)

The New Nation

Kenneth R. Bowling and Donald R. Kennon, eds., *Neither Separate Nor Equal: Congress in the 1790s* (2000)

Collin G. Calloway, *Crown and Calumet: British-Indian Relations, 1783–1815* (1987)

Noble E. Cunningham, *Jefferson vs. Hamilton: Confrontations That Shaped a Nation* (2000)

Wilbur Edel, *Kekionga! The Worst Defeat in the History of the U.S. Army* (1997)

James Horn et al., eds., *Revolution of 1800: Democracy, Race, and the New Republic* (2002)

Edward S. Kaplan, *The Bank of the United States and the American Economy* (1999)

Peter McNamara, *Political Economy and Statesmanship: Smith, Hamilton, and the Foundation of the Commercial Republic* (1998)

Mark J. Rozell, et al., eds., *George Washington and the Origins of the American Presidency* (2000)

Garrett Ward Sheldon, *The Political Philosophy of James Madison* (2001)

Wiley Sword, *President Washington's Indian War: The Struggle for the Old Northwest, 1790–1795* (1985)

Garry Wills, *Negro President: Jefferson and the Slave Power* (2003)

Federalists and Jeffersonian Republicans

Doron Ben-Atar and Barbara B. Oberg, eds., *Federalists Reconsidered* (1998)

Alexander De Conde, *The Quasi-War: Politics and Diplomacy of the Undeclared War with France, 1797–1801* (1966)

Andrew Lenner, *The Federal Principle in American Politics, 1790–1833* (2001)

Forrest McDonald, *States' Rights and the Union: Imperium in Imperio, 1776–1876* (2000)

Michael A. Palmer, *Stoddert's War: Naval Operations During the Quasi-War with France, 1798–1801* (2000)

Andrew W. Robertson, *The Language of Democracy: Political Rhetoric in the United States and Britain, 1790–1900* (1995)

James Roger Sharp, *American Politics in the Early Republic: The New Nation in Crisis* (1993)

David Waldsteicher, *In the Midst of Perpetual Fetes: The Making of American Nationalism, 1776–1820* (1997)

"The Rising Glory of America"

R. A. Burchell, ed., *The End of Anglo–America: Historical Essays in the Study of Cultural Divergence* (1991)

Andrew Burstein, *Sentimental Democracy: The Evolution of America's Romantic Self-Image* (1999)

Ellen Fernandez-Sacco, *Spectacular Masculinities: The Museums of Peale, Baker, and Bowen in the Early Republic* (1998)

Linda Kerber, *Women of the Republic: Intellect and Ideology in Revolutionary America* (1980)

Biography

Gay Wilson Allen, *St. John de Crèvecoeur: The Life of an American Farmer* (1987)

Aleine Austin, *Matthew Lyon, "New Man" of the Democratic Revolution, 1749–1822* (1981)

Lance Banning, *The Sacred Fire of Liberty: James Madison and the Founding of the Federal Republic* (1995)

R. B. Bernstein, *Thomas Jefferson* (2003)

Richard Brookhiser, *Alexander Hamilton, American* (1999)

Harvey Lewis Carter, *The Life and Times of Little Turtle: First Sagamore of the Wabash* (1987)

Helen A. Cooper, *John Trumbull: The Hand and Spirit of a Painter* (1982)

John Patrick Diggins, *John Adams* (2003)

Dorinda Evans, *The Genius of Gilbert Stuart* (1999)

Roger G. Kennedy, *Burr, Hamilton, and Jefferson: A Study in Character* (2000)

David McCullough, *John Adams* (2001)

David Micklethwait, *Noah Webster and the American Dictionary* (2000)

Jules David Prown, *John Singleton Copley* (1966)

William M. S. Rasmussen and Robert S. Tilton, *George Washington: The Man Behind the Myths* (1999)

Sheila L. Skemp, *Judith Sargent Murray: A Brief Biography with Documents* (1998)

K. Alan Synder, *Defining Noah Webster: Mind and Morals in the Early Republic* (1990)

Harlow G. Unger, *Noah Webster: The Life and Times of an American Patriot* (1998)

Mason Locke Weems, *The Life of Washington*, ed. Marcus Cunliffe (1962)

CHAPTER 9

North American Communities from Coast to Coast

James Gibson, *Imperial Russia in Frontier America* (1976)

Marcel Giraud, *A History of French Louisiana, 1698–1715* (1974)

Barbara Sweetland Smith and Redmond Barnett, eds., *Russian America* (1990)

David Weber, *The Spanish Frontier in North America* (1993)

The National Economy

W. Eliot Brownlee, *Dynamics of Ascent: A History of the American Economy* (1979)

Stuart Bruchey, *The Roots of American Economic Growth, 1607–1861* (1965)

Curtis P. Nettels, *The Emergence of a National Economy, 1775–1815* (1962)

Douglass C. North, *The Economic Growth of the United States, 1790–1860* (1966)

The Jefferson Presidency

Henry Adams, *The United States in 1800* (1955)

Robert Lowry Clinton, *Marbury v. Madison and Judicial Review* (1989)

Noble E. Cunningham, *The Jeffersonian Republicans and Power: Party Operations, 1801–1809* (1963)

George Drago, *Jefferson's Louisiana: Politics and the Clash of Legal Traditions* (1975)

Burton Spivak, *Jefferson's English Crisis: Commerce, Embargo, and the Republican Revolution* (1979)

Robert W. Tucker and David Hendrickson, *Empire of Liberty: The Statecraft of Thomas Jefferson* (1990)

G. Edward White, *The Marshall Court and Cultural Change, 1815–1835*, abridged ed. (1991)

James S. Young, *The Washington Community, 1800–1828* (1966)

Renewed Imperial Rivalry in North America

Henry Warner Bowden, *American Indians and Christian Missions: Studies in Cultural Conflict* (1981)

Gregory Evans Dowd, *A Spirited Resistance: The North American Indian Struggle for Unity, 1745–1815*

Reginald Horsman, *Expansion and American Indian Policy, 1783–1812* (1967)

Drew R. McCoy, *The Last of the Fathers: James Madison and the Republican Legacy* (1989)

Francis Paul Prucha, *The Great Father: The United States Government and the American Indians*, 2 vols. (1984)

Defining the Boundaries

John Boles, *Religion in Antebellum Kentucky* (1976)

Andrew Cayton, *The Frontier Republic: Ideology and Politics in the Ohio Country, 1789–1812* (1986)

———, *Frontier Indiana* (1996)

George Dangerfield, *The Era of Good Feelings* (1952)

Anita Shafer Goodstein, *Nashville, 1780–1860: From Frontier to City* (1989)

Christine Leigh Heyrman, *Southern Cross: The Beginnings of the Bible Belt* (1997)

Walter LaFeber, ed., *John Quincy Adams and the American Continental Empire* (1965)

Malcolm J. Rohrbough, *The Land Office Business* (1968)

———, *The Trans-Appalachian Frontier: Peoples, Societies, and Institutions, 1775–1850* (1978)

Richard Slotkin, *Regeneration through Violence: The Mythology of the American Frontier* (1973)

Richard C. Wade, *The Urban Frontier: The Rise of Western Cities, 1790–1850* (1973)

CHAPTER 10

King Cotton and Southern Expansion

Bruce Levine, *Half Slave and Half Free: The Roots of Civil War* (1992).

Daniel S. Dupre, *Transforming the Cotton Frontier, Madison County, Alabama, 1800–1840* (1997)

Robert W. Fogel and Stanley Engerman, *Time on the Cross: The Economics of American Negro Slavery* (1974)

Joseph P. Reidy, *From Slavery to Agrarian Capitalism in the Cotton Plantation South: Central Georgia, 1800–1880* (1992)

Gavin Wright, *The Political Economy of the Cotton South: Households, Markets, and Wealth in the Nineteenth Century* (1978)

Slavery and African American Communities

Ira Berlin and Philip D. Morgan, eds., *Cultivation and Culture: Labor and the Shaping of Slave Life in the Americas* (1993)

John Blassingame, *The Slave Community*, rev. ed. (1979)

Randolph B. Campbell, *An Empire for Slavery: The Peculiar Institution in Texas, 1821–1865* (1989)

Charles B. Dew, *Bond of Iron: Master and Slave at Buffalo Forge* (1994)

Douglas Egerton, *Gabriel's Rebellion: The Virginia Slave Conspiracies of 1800 and 1802* (1993)

Barbara Field, *Slavery on the Middle Ground: Maryland during the Nineteenth Century* (1985)

Eugene D. Genovese, *From Rebellion to Revolution: Afro-American Slave Revolts in the Making of the Modern World* (1979)

Charles Joyner, *Down by the Riverside: A South Carolina Slave Community* (1984)

Lawrence W. Levine, *Black Culture and Black Consciousness: Afro-American Folk Thought from Slavery to Freedom* (1977)

Ann Patton Malone, *Sweet Chariot: Slave Family and Household Structure in Nineteenth-Century Louisiana* (1992)

Albert Raboteau, *Slave Religion: The "Invisible Institution" in the Antebellum South* (1978)

Kenneth Stampp, *The Peculiar Institution* (1956)

Sterling Stuckey, *Slave Culture: Nationalist Theory and the Foundation of Black America* (1987)

Richard C. Wade, *Slavery in the Cities: The South 1820–1860* (1964)

Deborah Gray White, *Arn't I a Woman?* (1985)

Yeomen, Planters, and the Defense of Slavery

David T. Bailey, *Shadow on the Church: Southwestern Evangelical Religion and the Issue of Slavery, 1783–1860* (1985)

F. N. Boney, *Southerners All* (1990)

Joan Cashin, *A Family Venture: Men and Women on the Southern Frontier* (1991)

Bill Cecil-Fronsman, *Common White: Class and Culture in Antebellum North Carolina* (1992)

William J. Cooper, *The South and the Politics of Slavery, 1829–1856* (1978)

Clement Eaton, *The Freedom of Thought Struggle in the Old South* (1964)

Drew Gilpin Faust, ed., *The Ideology of Slavery: Proslavery Thought in the Antebellum South, 1830–1860* (1981)

Elizabeth Fox-Genovese, *Within the Plantation Household* (1988)

Jean Friedman, *The Enclosed Garden: Women and Community in the Evangelical South, 1830–1900* (1985)

J. William Harris, *Plain Folk and Gentry in a Slave Society: White Liberty and Black Slavery in Augusta's Hinterlands* (1985)

Christopher Morris, *Becoming Southern: The Evolution of a Way of Life, Warren County and Vicksburg, Mississippi, 1770–1860* (1995)

Michael Wayne, *Death of an Overseer* (2001)

Bertram Wyatt-Brown, *Southern Honor: Ethics and Behavior in the Old South* (1982)

CHAPTER 11

The New Democratic Politics and Jackson Presidency

Glenn C. Altschuler and Stuart M. Blumin, *Rude Republic: Americans and Their Politics in the Nineteenth Century* (2000)

William L. Anderson, *Cherokee Removal: Before and After* (1991)

Steven C. Bullock, *Revolutionary Brotherhood: Freemasonry and the Transformation of the American Social Order, 1730–1840* (1996)

John Ehle, *Trail of Tears* (1988)

Lucy Maddox, *Removals: Nineteenth-Century American Literature and the Politics of Indian Affairs* (1991)

Reeve Huston, *Land and Freedom: Rural Society, Popular Protest, and Party Politics in Antebellum New York* (2000).

Arthur M. Schlesinger Jr., *The Age of Jackson* (1945)

John Ward, *Andrew Jackson: Symbol for an Age* (1955)

Chilton Williamson, *American Suffrage: From Property to Democracy, 1760–1860* (1960)

The Rise of the Whigs and the Second American Party System

Daniel W. Howe, *The Political Culture of the American Whigs* (1980)

Lawrence F. Kohl, *The Politics of Individualism: Parties and the American Character in the Jacksonian Era* (1989)

Richard P. McCormick, *The Second American Party System: Party Formation in the Jacksonian Era* (1966)

Joel H. Sibley, *The Partisan Imperative: The Dynamics of American Politics before the Civil War* (1985)

American Arts and Letters

Richard D. Brown, *Knowledge Is Power: The Diffusion of Information in Early America, 1700–1865* (1989)

Cathy N. Davidson, *Revolution and the Word: The Rise of the Novel in America* (1986)

Nathan O. Hatch, *The Democratization of American Christianity* (1989)

Barbara Novak, *Nature and Culture: American Landscape Painting 1825–1875* (1982)

Gwendolyn Wright, *Building the Dream: A Social History of Housing in America* (1981)

CHAPTER 12

The Transportation Revolution

Clarence Danhof, *Changes in Agriculture: The Northern United States, 1820–1870* (1969)

E. M. Dodd, *American Business Corporations until 1860* (1954)

Albert Fishlow, *American Railroads and the Transformation of the Ante-Bellum Economy* (1965)

John Denis Haeger, *The Investment Frontier: New York Businessmen and the Economic Development of the Old Northwest* (1981)

Thomas Dublin, *Women at Work: The Transformation of Work and Community in Lowell, Massachusetts, 1826–1860* (1979).

Oscar Handlin and Mary Handlin, *Commonwealth: A Study of the Role of Government in the American Economy: Massachusetts, 1774–1861* (1947)

Morton J. Horwitz, *The Transformation of American Law, 1780–1860* (1977)

Karl Raitz, ed., *The National Road* (1995)

Ronald E. Shaw, *Canals for a Nation: The Canal Era in the United States, 1790–1860* (1990)

Peter Way, *Common Labour: Workers and the Digging of North American Canals, 1780–1860* (1993)

The Market Revolution

Thomas C. Cochran, *Frontiers of Change: Early Industrialism in America* (1981)

Robert F. Dalzell Jr., *Enterprising Elite: The Boston Associates and the World They Made* (1987)

David J. Jeremy, *Transatlantic Industrial Revolution: The Diffusion of Textile Technology between Britain and America* (1981)

Paul Johnson, *A Shopkeeper's Millennium: Society and Revivals in Rochester, New York, 1815–1837* (1978)

Bruce Laurie, *Artisans into Workers: Labor in Nineteenth-Century America* (1989)

Walter Licht, *Industrializing America: The Nineteenth Century* (1995)

Merritt R. Smith, *Harpers Ferry Armory and the New Technology* (1977)

Melvyn Stokes and Stephen Conway, eds., *The Market Revolution in America: Social, Political and Religious Expressions 1800–1880* (1996)

Barbara Tucker, *Samuel Slater and the Origins of the American Textile Industry, 1790–1860* (1984)

From Artisan to Worker

Mary H. Blewett, *Men, Women, and Work: Class, Gender, and Protest in the New England Shoe Industry, 1780–1910* (1988)

Paul G. Faler, *Mechanics and Manufacturers in the Early Industrial Revolution: Lynn, Massachusetts* (1981)

Michael H. Glickstein, *Concepts of Free Labor in Antebellum America* (1991)

Joan M. Jensen, *Loosening the Bonds: Mid-Atlantic Farm Women, 1750–1850* (1986)

Bruce Laurie, *Working People of Philadelphia, 1800–1850* (1980)

W. J. Rorabaugh, *The Craft Apprentice: From Franklin to the Machine Age in America* (1986)

A New Social Order

Stuart M. Blumin, *The Emergence of the Middle Class: Social Experience in the American City* (1989)

Jeanne Boydston, *Home and Work* (1990)

Janet Farrell Brodie, *Contraception and Abortion in Nineteenth-Century America* (1994)

Nancy E. Cott, *The Bonds of Womanhood: "Woman's Sphere" in New England, 1780–1835* (1977)

Anthony F. C. Wallace, *Rockdale: The Growth of an American Village in the Early Industrial Revolution* (1977)

Middle-Class Culture

Barbara A. Bardes and Suzanne Gossett, *Declarations of Independence: Women and Political Power in Nineteenth-Century American Fiction* (1990)

John F. Kasson, *Rudeness and Civility: Manners in Nineteenth-Century America* (1990)

Walter Benn Michaels and Donald E. Pease, eds., *The American Renaissance Reconsidered* (1985)

Lewis Perry, *Intellectual Life in America* (1984)

Ann Rose, *Transcendentalism as a Social Movement* (1981)

Richard Teichgraeber III, *Sublime Thoughts/Penny Wisdom: Situating Emerson and Thoreau in the American Market* (1995)

Jane Tompkins, *Sensational Designs: The Cultural World of American Fiction, 1790–1860* (1986)

Steven J. Ross, *Workers on the Edge: Work, Leisure and Politics in Industrializing Cincinnati, 1788–1890* (1985). Studies the growth of wage labor in a major western city.

CHAPTER 13

Immigration and Ethnicity

Oscar Handlin, *The Uprooted* (1951; 2nd ed. 1973)

Noel Ignatiev, *How the Irish Became White* (1995)

Kerby A. Miller, *Emigrants and Exiles: Ireland and the Irish Exodus to North America* (1985)

Stanley Nadel, *Little Germany: Ethnicity, Religion, and Class in New York City, 1845–1880* (1990)

Dennis P. Ryan, *Beyond the Ballot Box: A Social History of the Boston Irish, 1845–1917* (1989)

Urban America

Oliver E. Allen, *The Tiger: The Rise and Fall of Tammany Hall* (1995)

John Duffy, *The Sanitarians* (1990)

Paul A. Gilje, *The Road to Mobocracy: Popular Disorder in New York City, 1763–1834* (1987)

Herbert G. Gutman, *Work, Culture, and Society in Industrializing America: Essays in American Working-Class History* (1976)

James Oliver Horton, *Free People of Color: Inside the African American Community* (1993)

Gary B. Nash, *Forging Freedom: Philadelphia's Black Community, 1720–1840* (1988)

Charles E. Rosenberg, *The Cholera Years* (1962)

Dennis C. Rousey, *Policing the Southern City, New Orleans 1805–1889* (1997)

Sam Bass Warner, *The Private City: Philadelphia in Three Periods of Its Growth* (1968)

Religion, Reform, and Utopianism

Lawrence Cremin, *American Education: The National Experience, 1783–1861* (1981)

Whitney R. Cross, *The Burned-Over District: The Social and Intellectual History of Enthusiastic Religion in Western New York, 1800–1850* (1950)

Barbara Epstein, *The Politics of Domesticity: Women, Evangelism, and Temperance in Nineteenth Century America* (1981)

Lori D. Ginzberg, *Women and the Work of Benevolence: Morality, Politics, and Class in the Nineteenth-Century United States* (1990)

Carl F. Kaestle, *Pillars of the Republic: Common Schools and American Society, 1780–1860* (1983)

W. J. Rorabaugh, *The Alcoholic Republic: An American Tradition* (1979)

Abolitionism

David Brion Davis, *The Problem of Slavery in the Age of Revolution, 1770–1823* (1975)

Frederick Douglass, *The Narrative of the Life of Frederick Douglass, An American Slave* (1845)

Peter P. Hinks, *To Awaken My Afflicted Brethren: David Walker and the Problem of Antebellum Slave Resistance* (1997)

Howard Jones, *Mutiny on the* Amistad (1987)

Jean Fagan Yellin, *Women and Sisters: The Antislavery Feminists in American Culture* (1989)

Women's Rights

Ellen C. DuBois, *Feminism and Suffrage: The Emergence of an Independent Women's Movement in America, 1848–1869* (1978)

Gerda Lerner, *The Grimké Sisters from South Carolina: Pioneers for Women's Rights and Abolition* (1967)

Sandra S. Weber, *Special History Study, Women's Rights National Historical Park, Seneca Falls, New York* (1985)

CHAPTER 14

Exploration and Expansion

Jennifer S. H. Brown, *Strangers in Blood: Fur Trade Company Families in Indian Country* (1980)

William H. Goetzmann, *Army Exploration in the American West, 1803–1863* (1959)

William H. Goetzmann and William N. Goetzmann, *The West of the Imagination* (1986)

Norman A. Graebner, *Empire on the Pacific: A Study in American Continental Expansion* (1955)

LeRoy R. Hafen, ed., *The Mountain Men and the Fur Trade of the Far West*, 10 vols. (1968–72)

Sam W. Haynes, *James Polk and the Expansionist Impulse*, (1997)

Thomas R. Hietala, *Manifest Design: Anxious Aggrandizement in Late Jacksonian America* (1985)

Reginald Horsman, *Race and Manifest Destiny* (1981)

Theodore J. Karaminski, *Fur Trade and Exploration: Opening of the Far Northwest, 1821–1852* (1983)

Patricia Nelson Limerick, *The Legacy of Conquest: The Unbroken Past of the Unbroken West* (1987)

Frederick Merk, *Manifest Destiny and Mission in American History: A Reinterpretation* (1963)

———, *History of the Westward Movement* (1978)

Dale Morgan, *Jedediah Smith and the Opening of the West* (1982)

Peter Nabakov, ed., *Native American Testimony: An Anthology of Indian and White Relations* (1978)

James P. Ronda, *Astoria and Empire* (1990)

Charles G. Sellers, *James K. Polk: Jacksonian, 1795–1843* (1957)

———, *James K. Polk: Continentalist, 1843–1846* (1966)

Henry Nash Smith, *Virgin Land: The American West as Symbol and Myth* (1950)

Edward H. Spicer, *Cycles of Conquest: The Impact of Spain, Mexico, and the United States on the Indians of the Southwest, 1533–1960* (1981)

Robert A. Trennert, *Alternative to Extinction: Federal Indian Policy and the Beginnings of the Reservation System, 1846–1851* (1975)

Sylvia Van Kirk, *"Many Tender Ties": Women in Fur Trade Society in Western Canada, 1670–1870* (1980)

Albert K. Weinberg, *Manifest Destiny: A Study of Nationalist Expansionism in American History* (1957)

Peter Booth Wiley with Korogi Ichiro, *Yankees in the Land of the Gods: Commodore Perry and the Opening of Japan* (1990)

David J. Wishart, *The Fur Trade of the American West, 1807–1840: A Geographic Synthesis* (1979)

California and Oregon

John W. Caughey, *The California Gold Rush* (1975)

Malcolm Clark Jr., *Eden Seekers: The Settlement of Oregon, 1818–1862* (1981)

Douglas H. Daniels, *Pioneer Urbanites: A Social and Cultural History of Black San Francisco* (1980)

James R. Gibson, *Farming the Frontier: The Agricultural Opening of Oregon Country, 1786–1846* (1985)

Ramon Gutierrez and Richard J. Orsi, *Contested Eden: California Before the Gold Rush* (1998)

Albert L. Hurtado, *Indian Survival on the California Frontier* (1988)

Julie Roy Jeffrey, *Frontier Women: Civilizing The West? 1840–1860* (1998)

Marquis James, *The Raven: The Story of Sam Houston* (1929)

David Johnson, *Founding the Far West: California, Oregon, and Nevada, 1840–1890* (1992)

Alvin Josephy, *The Nez Percé and the Opening of the Northwest* (1965)

Rodman W. Paul, *California Gold: The Beginning of Mining in the Far West* (1974)

Leonard Pitt, *The Decline of the Californios: A Social History of the Spanish-Speaking Californians, 1846–1890* (1966)

James J. Rawls, *Indians of California: The Changing Image* (1984)

Brian Roberts, *American Alchemy: The California Gold Rush and Middle-Class Culture* (2000)

Kevin Starr, *Americans and the California Dream, 1850–1915* (1973)

John I. Unruh Jr., *The Plains Across: Overland Emigrants and the Trans–Mississippi West, 1840–1860* (1979)

Texas and the Mexican–American War

K. Jack Bauer, *The Mexican War, 1846–1848* (1974)

William C. Binkley, *The Texas Revolution* (1952)

Gene M. Brack, *Mexico Views Manifest Destiny* (1976)

Holly Beachley Brear, *Inherit the Alamo: Myth and Ritual at an American Shrine* (1995)

Donald E. Chipman, *Spanish Texas, 1519–1821* (1992)

Seymour Conner and Odie Faulk, *North America Divided: The Mexican War, 1846–1848* (1971)

Arnoldo De León, *They Called Them Greasers: Anglo Attitudes toward Mexicans in Texas, 1821–1900* (1983)

John S. D. Eisenhower, *So Far from God: The U.S. War with Mexico 1846–1848* (1989)

Neil Harlow, *California Conquered: War and Peace on the Pacific, 1846–1850* (1982)

Ernest McPherson Lander Jr., *Reluctant Imperialist: Calhoun, South Carolina, and the Mexican War* (1980)

Timothy Matovina, *Tejano Religion and Ethnicity: San Antonio, 1921–1860* (1995)

Frederick Merk, *Slavery and the Annexation of Texas* (1972)

David Montejano, *Anglos and Mexicans in the Making of Texas, 1836–1986* (1987)

Stanley Noyes, *Los Comanches: The Horse People, 1751–1845* (1994)

David Pletcher, *The Diplomacy of Annexation: Texas, Oregon, and the Mexican War* (1973)

Andreas V. Reichstein, *Rise of the Lone Star: The Making of Texas* (1989)

Susan Scholwer, *Alamo Images: Changing Perceptions of a Texas Experience* (1985)

John H. Schroeder, *Mr. Polk's War: American Opposition and Dissent, 1846–1848* (1971)

Otis A. Singletary, *The Mexican War* (1960)

Jésus F. de la Teja, *San Antonio de Béxar: A Community on New Spain's Northern Frontier* (1995)

The Politics of Manifest Destiny

Chaplain W. Morrison, *Democratic Politics and Sectionalism: The Wilmot Proviso Controversy* (1967)

Michael Morrison, *Slavery and the American West: The Eclipse of Manifest Destiny and the Coming of the Civil War* (1997).

Joseph G. Raybeck, *Free Soil: The Election of 1848* (1970)

Joel H. Sibley, *The Shrine of Party: Congressional Voting Behavior, 1841–1852* (1967)

CHAPTER 15

The Crisis over Slavery

Richard H. Abbott, *Cotton and Capital: Boston Businessmen and Antislavery Reform, 1854–1868* (1991)

Gary Collison, *Shadrach Minkins: From Fugitive Slave to Citizen* (1997)

W. Ehrlich, *They Have No Rights: Dred Scott's Struggle for Freedom* (1979)

C. C. Goen, *Broken Churches, Broken Nation* (1985)

Thomas F. Grossett, *Uncle Tom's Cabin and American Culture* (1985)

William Lee Miller, *Arguing About Slavery: The Great Battle in the United States Congress* (1996)

H. Craig Miner and William E. Unrau, *The End of Indian Kansas* (1978)

Stephen Oates, *To Purge This Land with Blood: A Biography of John Brown* (1970)

J. Rossbach, *Ambivalent Conspirators: John Brown, the Secret Six and a Theory of Black Political Violence* (1982)

Thomas P. Slaughter, *Bloody Dawn: The Christiana Riots and Racial Violence in the Antebellum North* (1991)

Gerald W. Wolff, *The Kansas-Nebraska Bill: Party, Section, and the Coming of the Civil War* (1977)

Bertram Wyatt-Brown, *Yankee Saints and Southern Sinners* (1985)

The Crisis of the National Party System

Tyler Anbinder, *Nativism and Slavery: The Northern Know-Nothings and the Politics of the 1850s* (1992)

J. H. Baker, *Affairs of Party: The Political Culture of Northern Democrats in the Mid-Nineteenth Century* (1983)

Ronald Formisano, *The Birth of Mass Political Parties: Michigan, 1827–1861* (1971)

William E. Gienapp, *The Origins of the Republican Party, 1852–1856* (1987)

Michael Holt, *The Political Crisis of the 1850s* (1978)

Robert W. Johannsen, *The Lincoln-Douglas Debates* (1965)

John Mayfield, *Rehearsal for Republicanism: Free Soil and the Politics of Antislavery* (1980)

The South Secedes

William. L. Barney, *The Road to Secession* (1972)

Charles H. Brown, *Agents of Manifest Destiny: The Lives and Times of the Filibusters* (1980)

Steven A. Channing, *Crisis of Fear: Secession in South Carolina* (1970)

William J. Cooper, *The South and the Politics of Slavery* (1978)

Avery O. Craven, *The Growth of Southern Nationalism 1848–1861* (1953)

William W. Freehling, *The Road to Disunion*, Vol. I: *Secessionists at Bay, 1776–1854* (1991)

Michael P. Johnson, *Secession and Conservatism in the Lower South: The Social and Ideological Bases of Secession in Georgia, 1860–1861* (1983)

Robert E. May, *The Southern Dream of a Caribbean Empire, 1854–1861* (1973)

John McCardell, *The Idea of a Southern Nation: Southern Nationalists and Southern Nationalism, 1830–1861* (1979)

K. M. Stampp, *And the War Came: The North and the Secession Crisis 1860–1861* (1950)

Joe A. Stout, *The Liberators: Filibustering Expeditions into Mexico, 1848–1862, and the Last Thrust of Manifest Destiny* (1973)

Ronald L. Takaki, *A Proslavery Crusade: The Agitation to Reopen the African Slave Trade* (1971)

J. Mills Thornton, *Politics and Power in a Slavery Society* (1978)

Eric H. Walter, *The Fire-Eaters* (1992)

CHAPTER 16

The Lincoln Presidency and the Northern Home Front

Jeanie Attie, *Patriotic Toil: Northern Women and the American Civil War* (1998)

Richard Franklin Bensel, *Yankee Leviathan: The Origins of Central State Authority in America, 1859–1877* (1991)

George M. Frederickson, *The Inner Civil War: Northern Intellectuals and the Crisis of the Union* (1965)

J. Matthew Gallman, *The North Fights the Civil War: The Home Front* (1994)

Ernest A. McKay, *The Civil War and New York City* (1990)

James M. McPherson, *Abraham Lincoln and the Second American Revolution* (1990)

Mark E. Neely, *The Fate of Liberty: Abraham Lincoln and Civil Liberties* (1991)

Thomas H. O'Connor, *Civil War Boston: Homefront and Battlefield* (1997)

Phillip Shaw Paludan, *The Presidency of Abraham Lincoln* (1994)

Heather Cox Richardson, *The Greatest Nation of the Earth: Republican Economic Policies during the Civil War* (1997)

Anne C. Rose, *Victorian America and the Civil War* (1992)

Joel Sibley, *A Respectable Minority: The Democratic Party in the Civil War Era, 1860–1868* (1977)

Lyde Cullen Sizer, *The Political Work of Northern Women Writers and the Civil War* (2000)

Bell I. Wiley, *The Life of Johnny Reb* (1943)

———, *The Life of Billy Yank* (1952)

The Death of Slavery

Ira Berlin et al. eds., *Freedom, A Documentary History of Emancipation, 1861–1867*, Series 1, Volume I: *The Destruction of Slavery* (1985)

———, eds., *Freedom, A Documentary History of Emancipation, 1861–1867*, Series 1, Volume II: *The Wartime Genesis of Free Labor: The Upper South* (1993)

———, eds. *Freedom, A Documentary History of Emancipation, 1861–1867*, Series 1, Volume III: *The Wartime Genesis of Free Labor: The Lower South* (1990)

———, eds. *Freedom, A Documentary History of Emancipation, 1861–1867*, Series 2: *The Black Military Experience* (1988)

John Hope Franklin, *The Emancipation Proclamation* (1963)

Willie Lee Rose, *Rehearsal for Reconstruction: The Port Royal Experiment* (1964)

The Confederacy and the Southern Home Front

Steven V. Ash, *When the Yankees Came: Conflict and Chaos in the Occupied South 1861–1865* (1995)

William Blair, *Virginia's Private War: Feeding Body and Soul in the Confederacy, 1861–1865* (1998)

Daniel W. Crofts, *Reluctant Confederates: Upper South Unionists in the Secession Crisis* (1989)

William C. Davis, *"A Government of Our Own": The Making of the Confederacy* (1994)

Wayne K. Durrill, *War of Another Kind: A Southern Community in the Great Rebellion* (1990)

Drew Gilpin Faust, *The Creation of Confederate Nationalism* (1988)

———, *The Confederate Republic: A Revolution against Politics* (1994)

William W. Freehling, *The South vs. The South: How Anti-Confederate Southerners Shaped the Course of the Civil War.*

James L. Roark, *Masters without Slaves: Southern Planters in the Civil War and Reconstruction* (1978)

William Rogers, *Confederate Home Front: Montgomery During the Civil War* (1999)

Daniel E. Sutherland, *Seasons of War: The Ordeal of a Confederate Community 1861–1865* (1995)

LeeAnn Whites, *The Civil War as a Crisis in Gender: Augusta, Georgia, 1860–1890* (1995)

The Fighting

Michael Barton, *Good Men: The Character of Civil War Soldiers* (1981)

Ken Burns, *The Civil War* (1990)

Bruce Catton, *A Stillness at Appomattox* (1953)

David Eocher, *The Longest Night* (2001)

Shelby Foote, *The Civil War: A Narrative*, 3 vols. (1958–1974)

Joseph T. Glatthaar, *Forged in Battle: The Civil War Alliance of Black Soldiers and White Officers* (1990)

———, *The March to the Sea and Beyond: Sherman's Troops in the Savannah and Carolinas Campaign* (1985)

Mark Grimsley, *The Hard Hand of War: Union Policy toward Southern Civilians, 1861–1865* (1995)

Edward Hagerman, *The American Civil War and the Origins of Modern Warfare* (1988)

Alvin Josephy, *The Civil War in the West* (1992)

Gerald F. Linderman, *Embattled Courage: The Experience of Combat in the American Civil War* (1987)

Edwin S. Redkey, ed., *A Grand Army of Black Men: Letters from African-American Soldiers in the Union Army, 1861–1865* (1992)

Charles Royster, *The Destructive War: William Tecumseh Sherman, Stonewall Jackson, and the Americans* (1991)

CHAPTER 17

The Politics of Reconstruction

Richard H. Abbott, *The Republican Party and the South, 1855–1877* (1986)

Herman Belz, *Emancipation and Equal Rights* (1978)

Michael Les Benedict, *A Compromise of Principle: Congressional Republicans and Reconstruction* (1974)

———, *The Impeachment and Trial of Andrew Johnson* (1973)

Michael Kent Curtis, *No State Shall Abridge: The Fourteenth Amendment and the Bill of Rights* (1990)

Ellen Carol DuBois, *Feminism and Suffrage* (1978)

Eric Foner, *Politics and Ideology in the Age of the Civil War* (1980)

William C. Harris, *With Charity for All: Lincoln and the Restoration of the Union* (1997)

Robert Kaczorowski, *The Politics of Judicial Interpretation: The Federal Courts, Department of Justice, and Civil Rights, 1866–1876* (1985)

James McPherson, *Ordeal by Fire: The Civil War and Reconstruction* (1982)

Michael Perman, *Emancipation and Reconstruction, 1862–1879* (1987)

Brooks D. Simpson, *The Reconstruction Presidents* (1998)

Kenneth M. Stampp, *The Era of Reconstruction, 1865–1877* (1965)

The Meaning of Freedom

Ira Berlin et al., eds., *Freedom: A Documentary History*, 3 vols. (1985–91)

W. E. B. DuBois, *Black Reconstruction* (1935)

Barbara J. Fields, *Slavery and Freedom on the Middle Ground* (1985)

Eric Foner, *Freedom's Lawmakers: A Directory of Black Officeholders during Reconstruction* (1996)

Noralee Frankel, *Freedom's Women: Black Women and Families in Civil War Era Mississippi* (1999)

Herbert G. Gutman, *The Black Family in Slavery and Freedom* (1976)

Sharon Ann Holt, *Making Freedom Pay: North Carolina Freedpeople Working For Themselves, 1865–1900* (2000)

Thomas Holt, *Black over White: Negro Political Leadership in South Carolina during Reconstruction* (1977)

Lynda J. Morgan, *Emancipation in Virginia's Tobacco Belt* (1992)

Nell Irvin Painter, *Exodusters* (1977)

Howard N. Rabinowitz, *Race Relations in the Urban South, 1865–1890* (1978)

Roger L. Ransom and Richard Sutch, *One Kind of Freedom: The Economic Consequences of Emancipation* (1977)

Edward Royce, *The Origins of Southern Sharecropping* (1993).

Leslie A. Schwalm, *A Hard Fight for We: Women's Transition from Slavery to Freedom in South Carolina* (1997)

Southern Politics and Society

James A. Baggett, *The Scalawags: Southern Dissenters in the Civil War and Reconstruction* (2003)

Pamela Brandwein, *Reconstructing Reconstruction: The Supreme Court and the Production of Historical Truth* (1999)

Dan T. Carter, *When the War Was Over: The Failure of Self Reconstruction in the South, 1865–1877* (1985)

Richard N. Current, *Those Terrible Carpetbaggers* (1988)

Stephen Hahn, *The Roots of Southern Populism* (1983)

Sally McMillen, *To Raise Up the South: Sunday Schools in Black and White Churches, 1865–1915* (2001)

Scott Reynolds Nelson, *Iron Confederacies: Southern Railroads, Klan Violence, and Reconstruction* (1999)

Michael S. Perman, *The Road to Redemption: Southern Politics, 1868–1979* (1984)

Daniel W. Stowell, *Rebuilding Zion: The Religious Reconstruction of the South, 1863–1877* (1998)

Allen W. Trelease, *White Terror: The Ku Klux Klan Conspiracy and Southern Reconstruction* (1971)

Jonathan M. Wiener, *Social Origins of the New South* (1978)

Reconstructing the North

Stephen Buechler, *The Transformation of the Woman Suffrage Movement* (1986)

Morton Keller, *Affairs of State* (1977)

David Montgomery, *Beyond Equality: Labor and the Radical Republicans, 1862–1872* (1967)

Keith I. Polakoff, *The Politics of Inertia: The Election of 1876 and the End of Reconstruction* (1973)

Heather Cox Richardson, *The Death of Reconstruction: Race, Labor, and Politics in the Post Civil War North, 1865–1901* (2001)

Amy Dru Stanley, *From Bondage to Contract: Wage Labor, Marriage, and the Market in the Age of Slave Emancipation* (1998)

Mark W. Summers, *Railroads, Reconstruction, and the Gospel of Prosperity* (1984)

———, *The Era of Good Stealings* (1993)

Xi Wang, *The Trial of Democracy: Black Suffrage and Northern Republicans, 1860–1910* (1997)

C. Vann Woodward, *Reunion and Reaction: The Compromise of 1877 and the End of Reconstruction* (1956)

Biography

David Donald, *Charles Sumner and the Rights of Man* (1970)

Russell Duncan, *Freedom's Shore: Tunis Campbell and the Georgia Freedmen* (1986)

William S. McFeely, *Frederick Douglass* (1989)

———, *Grant: A Biography* (1981)

———, *Yankee Stepfather: General O. O. Howard and the Freedmen* (1968)

Hans L. Trefousse, *Andrew Johnson* (1989)

———, *Thaddeus Stevens: Nineteenth Century Egalitarian* (1997)

CHAPTER 18

Indian Peoples and Indian–White Relations

David Wallace Adams, *Education for Extinction: American Indians and the Boarding School Experience, 1875–1928* (1995)

Morris W. Foster, *Being Comanche: A Social History of an American Indian Community* (1991)

Lisbeth Haas, *Conquests and Historical Identities in California, 1769–1936* (1995)

Shelley Bowen Hatfield, *Chasing Shadows: Indians Along the United States–Mexico Border, 1876–1911* (1998)

Frederick E. Hoxie, *A Final Promise: The Campaign to Assimilate the Indians, 1880–1920* (1984, 2001)

Albert L. Hurtado, *Indian Survival on the California Frontier* (1988)

Patricia Nelson Limerick, *The Legacy of Conquest: The Unbroken Past of the American West* (1987)

John D. McDermott, *A Guide to the Indian Wars of the West* (1998)

Devon Abbott Mihesuah, *Cultivating the Rosebuds: The Education of Women at the Cherokee Female Seminary, 1851–1909* (1993)

Theda Perdue, ed., *Sifters: Native American Women's Lives* (2001)

Catherine Price, *The Oglala People, 1841–1879* (1996)

Glenda Riley, *Women and Indians on the Frontier, 1825–1915* (1984)

Elliott West, *The Way to the West: Essays on the Central Plains* (1995)

Richard White, *The Roots of Dependency: Subsistence, Environment, and Social Change among the Choctaws, Pawnees, and Navajos* (1983)

Murray R. Wickett, *Contested Territory: Whites, Native Americans, and African Americans in Oklahoma, 1865–1907* (2000)

Internal Empire

Armando C. Alonzo, *Tejano Legacy: Rancheros and Settlers in South Texas, 1734–1900* (1998)

Susan Armitage and Elizabeth Jameson, eds., *The Women's West* (1987)

Susan Armitage, Ruth B. Moynihan, and Christiane Fischer Dichamp, eds., *So Much to Be Done: Women Settlers on the Mining and Ranching Frontier* (1990)

Arnoldo De Leon, *Racial Frontiers: Africans, Chinese, and Mexicans in Western America, 1848–1890* (2002)

Sarah Deutsch, *No Separate Refuge: Culture, Class and Gender on an Anglo-Hispanic Frontier in the American Southwest, 1880–1940* (1987)

David M. Emmons, *The Butte Irish: Class and Ethnicity in an American Mining Town, 1875–1925* (1989)

Sarah Barringer Gordon, *The Mormon Question: Polygamy and Constitutional Conflict in Nineteenth-Century America* (2002)

Douglas Monroy, *Thrown among Strangers: The Making of Mexican Culture in Frontier California* (1990)

Katherine G. Morrissey, *Mental Territories: Mapping the Inland Empire* (1997)

Gunter Peck, *Reinventing Free Labor: Padrones and Immigrant Workers in the North American West, 1880–1930* (2000)

William G. Robbins, *Colony and Empire: The Capitalist Transformation of the American West* (1994)

Quintard Taylor, *In Search of the Racial Frontier: African Americans in the American West, 1528–1990* (1998)

Sally Zanjani, *A Mine of Her Own: Women Prospectors in the American West, 1850–1950* (1997)

Ranching and Farming

Allan G. Bogue, *From Prairie to Corn Belt: Farming on the Illinois and Iowa Prairies in the Nineteenth Century* (1963)

Sucheng Chan, *This Bitter-Sweet Soil: The Chinese in California Agriculture, 1860–1910* (1986)

Philip Durham and Everett L. Jones, *The Negro Cowboys* (1965)

Mark Fiege, *Irrigated Eden: the Making of an Agricultural Landscape in the American West* (1999)

Dee Garceau, *The Important Things of Life: Women, Work, and Family in Sweetwater County, Wyoming, 1880–1929* (1997)

C. Robert Haywood, *Victorian West: Class and Culture in Kansas Cattle Towns* (1991)

Stan Hoig, *The Oklahoma Land Rush of 1889* (1984)

Lawrence Jelinek, *Harvest Empire: A History of California Agriculture*, 2d ed. (1982)

Frederick C. Luebke, ed., *European Immigrants in the American West: Community Histories* (1998)

David Vaught, *Cultivating California: Growers, Specialty Crops, and Labor, 1875–1920* (1999)

Paul I. Wellman, *The Trampling Herd: The Story of the Cattle Range in America* (1988)

The Western Landscape

Alfred L. Bush and Lee Clark Mitchell, *The Photograph and the American Indian* (1994)

William Cronon, George Miles, and Jay Gitlin, eds., *Under an Open Sky: Rethinking America's Western Past* (1992).

Mick Gidley, *Edward S. Curtis and the North American Indian, Incorporated* (1998)

William H. Goetzmann and William N. Goetzmann, *The West of the Imagination* (1986)

Joy S. Kasson, *Buffalo Bill's Wild West: Celebrity, Memory, and Popular History* (2000)

Chris J. Magoc, *Yellowstone: The Creation and Selling of an American Landscape, 1870–1903* (1999)

Walter Nugent and Martin Ridge, eds., *The American West: The Reader* (1999)

Paul Reddin, *Wild West Shows* (1999)

Richard Slotkin, *Gunfighter Nation: The Myth of the Frontier in 20th-Century America* (1992)

Mark David Spence, *Dispossessing the Wilderness: Indian Removal and the Making of the National Parks* (1999)

Richard White, *"It's Your Misfortune and None of My Own": A History of the American West* (1991)

Richard White and Patricia Nelson Limerick, *The Frontier in American Culture* (1994)

Donald Worster, *An Unsettled Country: Changing Landscapes of the American West* (1994)

David M. Wrobel, *Promised Lands: Promotion, Memory, and the Creation of the American West* (2002)

Biography

Matthew Baigell, *Albert Bierstadt* (1981)

Louise Barnett, *Touched by Fire: The Life, Death, and Mythic Afterlife of George Armstrong Custer* (1996)

Robert W. Larson, *Red Cloud: Warrior-Statesman of the Lakota Sioux* (1997)

Joan T. Mark, *A Stranger in Her Native Land: Alice Fletcher and the American Indians* (1988)

Sara R. Massey, ed., *Black Cowboys of Texas* (2000)

Valerie Mathes, *Helen Hunt Jackson and Her Indian Reform Legacy* (1990)

Elinore Pruitt Stewart, *Letters of a Woman Homesteader* (1914, 1989)

Edwin R. Sweeney, *Cochise, Chiricahua Apache Chief* (1991)

Jerry D. Thompson, ed., *Juan Cortina and the Texas-Mexico Frontier, 1859–1877* (1994)

Benson Tong, *Susan La Flesche Picotte, M.D.: Omaha Indian Leader and Reformer* (1999)

Robert M. Utley, *The Lance and the Shield: The Life and Times of Sitting Bull* (1993)

Donald Worster, *A River Running West: The Life of John Wesley Powell* (2001)

Sally Zanjani, *Sarah Winnemucca* (2001)

CHAPTER 19

Science, Technology, and Industry

Alfred D. Chandler Jr., *The Visible Hand: The Managerial Revolution in American Business* (1977)

David A. Hounshell, *From the American System to Mass Production, 1800–1932* (1984)

Walter Licht, *Industrializing America: The Nineteenth Century* (1995)

A. J. Millard, *Edison and the Business of Innovation* (1990)

William S. Pretzer, ed., *Working at Inventing: Thomas A. Edison and the Menlo Park Experience* (2001)

Leonard S. Reich, *The Making of American Industrial Research: Science and Business at G. E. and Bell, 1876–1926* (1985)

Business and the Economy

Wendy Gamber, *The Female Economy: The Millinery and Dressmaking Trades, 1860–1930* (1997)

Pamela Walker Laird, *Advertising Progress: American Business and the Rise of Consumer Marketing* (1998)

Naomi R. Lamoreaux, *The Great Merger Movement in American Business, 1895–1904* (1985)

Daniel Nelson, *Managers and Workers: Origins of the Factory System in the United States, 1880–1920* (1975)

Sarah Lyons Watts, *Order against Chaos: Business Culture and Labor Ideology in America, 1800–1915* (1991)

Olivier Zunz, *Making America Corporate, 1870–1920* (1990)

Working Class and Labor

Eric Arnesen, *Waterfront Workers of New Orleans: Race, Class, and Politics, 1863–1923* (1991)

John Bodnar, *Immigration and Industrialization: Ethnicity in an American Mill Town* (1977)

Lisa M. Fine, *The Souls of the Skyscraper: Female Clerical Workers in Chicago, 1870–1930* (1990)

Herbert G. Gutman, *Work, Culture and Society in Industrializing America: Essays in American Working-Class and Social History* (1977)

David M. Katzman, *Seven Days a Week: Women and Domestic Service in Industrializing America* (1978)

Joanne Meyerowitz, *Women Adrift: Industrial Wage Earners in Chicago, 1880–1930* (1988)

David Montgomery, *The Fall of the House of Labor: The Workplace, the State, and American Labor Activism, 1865–1925* (1987)

Daniel T. Rodgers, *The Work Ethic in Industrial America, 1850–1920* (1978)

Roy Rosenzweig, *Eight Hours for What We Will: Workers and Leisure in an Industrial City, 1870–1920* (1983)

Robert E. Weir, *Beyond Labor's Veil: The Culture of the Knights of Labor* (1996)

The Industrial City

John S. Garner, ed., *The Midwest in American Architecture* (1991)

Dolores Hayden, *The Grand Domestic Revolution: A History of Feminist Designs for American Homes, Neighborhoods, and Cities* (1981)

Scott Molloy, *Trolley Wars: Streetcar Workers on the Line* (1996)

Mark H. Rose, *Cities of Light and Heat: Domesticating Gas and Electricity in Urban America* (1995)

Carl Smith, *Urban Disorder and the Shape of Belief: The Great Chicago Fire, the Haymarket Bomb, and the Model Town of Pullman* (1995)

John R. Stilgoe, *Borderland: Origins of the American Suburb, 1820–1939* (1988)

The New South

Edward L. Ayers, *The Promise of the New South* (1992)

Don Doyle, *New Men, New Cities, New South* (1990)

Jacquelyn Dowd Hall, et al., *Like a Family: The Making of a Southern Cotton Mill World* (1987, 2000)

Gerald D. Jaynes, *Branches without Roots: Genesis of the Black Working Class in the American South, 1862–1882* (1986)

Lawrence H. Larsen, *The Rise of the Urban South* (1985)

Cathy McHugh, *Mill Family: The Labor System in the Southern Textile Industry, 1880–1915* (1988)

Karin A. Shapiro, *A New South Rebellion: The Battle Against Convict Labor in the Tennessee Coalfields, 1871–1896* (1998)

Rise of Consumer Society

Elaine S. Abelson, *When Ladies Go A-Thieving* (1989)

Stuart Blumin, *The Emergence of the Middle Class* (1989)

Sarah Burns, *Inventing the Modern Artist: Art and Culture in Gilded Age America* (1996)

Yong Chen, *Chinese San Francisco, 1850–1943* (2000)

Priscilla Ferguson Clement, *Growing Pains: Children in the Industrial Age, 1850–1890* (1997)

Steven Conn, *Museums and American Intellectual Life, 1876–1926* (1998)

Perry Duis, *Challenging Chicago: Coping with Everyday Life, 1837–1920* (1998)

Warren Goldstein, *Playing for Keeps: A History of Early Baseball* (1989)

Katherine C. Grier, *Culture and Comfort: Parlor Making and Middle-Class Identity, 1850–1930* (1988, 1997)

Judy Hilkey, *Character Is Capital: Success Manuals and Manhood in Gilded Age America* (1997)

John F. Kasson, *Amusing the Millions: Coney Island at the Turn of the Century* (1978)

Lawrence W. Levine, *Highbrow/Lowbrow: The Emergence of Cultural Hierarchy in America* (1988)

Patricia Marks, *Bicycles, Bangs, and Bloomers: The New Woman in the Popular Press* (1990)

Madelon Powers, *Faces along the Bar: Lore and Order in the Working-Man's Saloon, 1870–1920* (1998)

Steven A. Riess, *City Games: The Evolution of American Urban Society and the Rise of Sports* (1989)

Leigh Eric Schmidt, *Consumer Rites: The Buying and Selling of American Holidays* (1995)

Biography

Ron Chernow, *Titan: The Life of John D. Rockefeller, Sr.* (1998)

Helen Lefkowitz Horowitz, *The Power and Passion of M. Carey Thomas* (1994)

Paul Israel, *Edison: A Life of Invention* (1998)

Harold Livesay, *Andrew Carnegie and the Rise of Big Business*, 2d ed. (2000)

Craig Phelan, *Grand Master Workman: Terence Powderly and the Knights of Labor* (2000)

Jean Strouse, *Morgan: American Financier* (1999)

Robert C. Twombly, *Louis Sullivan* (1986)

Michael Zuckerman, *Almost Chosen People: Oblique Biographies in the American Grain* (1993)

CHAPTER 20

The Nation and Politics

Paula C. Baker, *The Moral Frameworks of Public Life: Gender, Politics and the State in Rural New York, 1870–1930* (1991)

Michael Lewis Goldberg, *An Army of Women: Gender and Politics in Gilded Age Kansas* (1997)

J. William Harris, *Deep Souths: Delta, Piedmont, and Sea Island Society in the Age of Segregation* (2001)

Erika Lee, *At America's Gates: Chinese Immigration during the Exclusion Era, 1882–1943* (2003)

Gwendolyn Mink, *Old Labor and New Immigrants in American Political Development* (1986)

Nell Irvin Painter, *Standing at Armageddon: The United States, 1877–1919* (1987)

Douglas Steeples and David O. Whitten, *Democracy in Desperation: The Depression of 1893* (1998)

Brook Thomas, Plessy v. Ferguson: A Brief History with Documents (1997)

David Traxel, 1898: The Birth of the American Century (1998)

C. Vann Woodward, The Strange Career of Jim Crow, 3rd rev. ed. (1974)

Populism

Peter Argersinger, The Limits of Agrarian Radicalism: Western Populism and American Politics (1995)

Lawrence Goodwyn, Democratic Promise: The Populist Moment in America (1976)

Steven Hahn, The Roots of Southern Populism (1983)

Robert C. McMath, American Populism: A Social History (1993)

Scott G. McNall, The Road to Rebellion: Class Formation and Kansas Populism 1865–1900 (1988)

Norman Pollack, The Humane Economy: Populism, Capitalism and Democracy (1990)

Protest and Reform Movements

Ruth Bordin, Woman and Temperance: The Quest for Power and Liberty, 1873–1900 (1981)

Susan Curtis, A Consuming Faith: The Social Gospel and Modern American Culture (1991)

Barbara Leslie Epstein, The Politics of Domesticity: Women, Evangelism, and Temperance in Nineteenth-Century America (1981)

Paul Krause, The Battle for Homestead, 1880–1892 (1992)

Ralph E. Luker, The Social Gospel in Black and White (1991)

Alison M. Parker, Purifying America: Women, Cultural Reform, and Pro-Censorship Activism, 1873–1933 (1997)

Gretchen Ritter, Goldbugs and Greenbacks: The Antimonopoly Tradition and the Politics of Finance in America, 1865–1896 (1997)

Richard Schneirov, Shelton Stromquist, and Nick Salvatore, eds., The Pullman Strike and the Crisis of the 1890s: Essays on Labor and Politics (1999)

Carlos A. Schwantes, Coxey's Army (1985)

Gary Scott Smith, The Search for Social Salvation: Social Christianity and America, 1880–1925 (2000)

Imperialism and Empire

Tunde Adeleke, Unafrican Americans: Nineteenth-Century Black Nationalists and the Civilizing Mission (1998)

Nupur Chaudhuri and Margaret Strobel, eds., Western Women and Imperialism (1992)

Willard B. Gatewood, Jr., Black Americans and the White Man's Burden (1975)

Patricia Hill, The World Their Household: The American Women's Foreign Mission Movement and Cultural Transformation, 1870–1920 (1985)

Amy Kaplan and Donald E. Pease, eds., Cultures of United States Imperialism (1993)

Emily S. Rosenberg, Spreading the American Dream: American Economic and Cultural Expansion, 1890–1945 (1982)

Robert W. Rydell, All the World's a Fair: Vision of Empire at the American International Expositions, 1876–1916 (1984)

Anders Stephanson, Manifest Destiny: American Expansion and the Empire of Right (1995)

Spanish–American War and the Philippines

Virginia M. Bouvier, ed., Whose America? The War of 1898 and the Battles to Define the Nation (2001)

H. W. Brands, Bound to Empire: The United States and the Philippines (1992)

Kristin L. Hoganson, Fighting for American Manhood: How Gender Politics Provoked the Spanish–American and Philippine–American Wars (1998)

Brian McAllister Linn, The Philippine War, 1899–1902 (2000)

Stuart Creighton Miller, "Benevolent Assimilation": The American Conquest of the Philippines, 1899–1903 (1982)

Ivan Musicant, Empire By Default: The Spanish-American War and the Dawn of the American Century (1998)

Louis A. Perez, Jr., The War of 1898: The United States and Cuba in History and Historiography (1998)

Harvey Rosenfeld, Diary of a Dirty Little War: The Spanish–American War of 1898 (2000)

Angel Smith and Emma Davila-Cox, eds., The Crisis of 1898: Colonial Redistribution and Nationalist Mobilization (1999)

Biography

Ruth Bordin, Frances Willard: A Biography (1986)

Mari Jo Buhle, Paul Buhle, and Harvey J. Kaye, eds., The American Radical (1995)

Edward P. Crapol, James G. Blaine: Architect of Empire (2000)

Bruce J. Evensen, God's Man for the Gilded Age: D.L. Moody and the Rise of Modern Mass Evangelism (2003)

Jane Taylor Nelsen, A Prairie Populist: The Memoirs of Luna Kellie (1992)

Allan Peskin, Garfield: A Biography (1978)

Ben Procter, William Randolph Hearst: The Early Years, 1863–1910 (1998)

Nick Salvatore, Eugene V. Debs (1982)

Peggy Samuels and Harold Samuels, Teddy Roosevelt at San Juan: The Making of a President (1997)

Patricia A. Schechter, Ida B. Wells-Barnett and American Reform, 1880–1930 (2001)

C. Van Woodward, Tom Watson (1963)

CHAPTER 21

The Currents of Progressivism

Walter M. Brasch, Forerunners of Revolution: Muckrakers and the American Social Conscience (1990)

John D. Buenker, Urban Liberalism and Progressive Reform (1973)

Mina Carson, Settlement Folk: Social Thought and the American Settlement Movement, 1885–1930 (1990)

Nancy Cohen, Reconstruction of American Liberalism, 1865–1914 (2002)

Leon Fink, Progressive Intellectuals and the Dilemmas of Democratic Commitment (1997)

Richard Hofstadter, The Age of Reform: From Bryan to FDR (1955)

Robert D. Johnston, The Radical Middle Class: Populist Democracy and the Question of Capitalism in Progressive Era Portland, Oregon (2003)

James T. Kloppenberg, *Uncertain Victory: Social Democracy and Progressivism in European and American Thought, 1870–1920* (1986)

William A. Link, *The Paradox of Southern Progressivism, 1880–1930* (1992)

Richard McCormick, *The Party Period and Public Policy* (1986)

Robert Wiebe, *The Search for Order, 1877–1920* (1967)

Social Control and Its Limits

Paul M. Boyer, *Urban Masses and Moral Order in America, 1820–1920* (1978)

Eldon J. Eisenach, *The Lost Promise of Progressivism* (1994)

Randy D. McBee, *Dance Hall Days: Intimacy and Leisure Among Working-Class Immigrants in the United States* (2000)

Ruth Rosen, *The Lost Sisterhood: Prostitutes in America, 1900–1918* (1982)

Andrea Tone, *The Business of Benevolence: Industrial Paternalism in Progressive America* (1997)

Working-Class Communities and Protest

John Bodnar, *The Transplanted* (1985)

Susan A. Glenn, *Daughters of the Shtetl: Life and Labor in the Immigrant Generation* (1990).

James R. Green, *The World of the Worker: Labor in Twentieth-Century America* (1980)

Alice Kessler-Harris, *Out to Work: A History of Wage-Earning Women in the United States* (1982)

David Montgomery, *The Fall of the House of Labor* (1987)

Kathy Peiss, *Cheap Amusements: Working Women and Leisure in Turn-of-the-Century New York* (1986)

Roy Rosenzweig, *Eight Hours for What We Will* (1983)

Ronald Takaki, *Strangers from a Different Shore: A History of Asian Americans* (1989)

Women's Movements and Black Awakening

Paula Baker, *The Moral Frameworks of Public Life* (1991)

Mari Jo Buhle, *Women and American Socialism* (1983)

Rebecca Edwards, *Angels in the Machinery: Gender in American Party Politics from the Civil War to the Progressive Era* (1997)

Linda Gordon, *Woman's Body, Woman's Right: A Social History of Birth Control* (1976)

Molly Ladd-Taylor, *Mother Work: Women, Child Welfare, and the State, 1890–1930* (1994)

National Progressivism

Kendrick A. Clements, *The Presidency of Woodrow Wilson* (1992)

John M. Cooper Jr., *The Warrior and the Priest: Theodore Roosevelt and Woodrow Wilson* (1983)

Lewis L. Gould, *The Presidency of Theodore Roosevelt* (1991)

Biography

Ellen Chesler, *Woman of Valor: Margaret Sanger and the Birth Control Movement in America* (1992)

Louis R. Harlan, *Booker T. Washington: Wizard of Tuskegee, 1901–1915* (1983)

J. Joseph Huthmacher, *Senator Robert F. Wagner and the Rise of Urban Liberalism* (1971)

Stephen Kantrowitz, *Ben Tillman and the Reconstruction of White Supremacy* (2000)

David Levering Lewis, *W.E.B. Du Bois: Biography of a Race, 1868–1919* (1993)

Nick Salvatore, *Eugene V. Debs: Citizen and Socialist* (1982)

Patricia A. Schechter, *Ida B. Wells-Barnett and American Reform, 1880–1930* (2001)

Kathryn Kish Sklar, *Florence Kelley and the Nation's Work* (1995)

Bernard A. Weisberger, *The LaFollettes of Wisconsin* (1994)

Robert Westbrook, *John Dewey and American Democracy* (1991)

CHAPTER 22

Becoming a World Power

Richard H. Collin, *Theodore Roosevelt's Caribbean* (1990)

John M. Hart, *Empire and Revolution: The Americans in Mexico Since the Civil War* (2002).

Walter LaFeber, *The Panama Canal* (1978)

Lester E. Langley, *The Banana Wars: An Inner History of American Empire, 1900–1934* (1983)

Mary A. Renda, *Taking Haiti: Military Occupation and the Culture of U.S. Imperialism, 1915–1940* (2001)

The Great War

Lloyd E. Ambrosius, *Woodrow Wilson and the American Diplomatic Tradition* (1987)

Paul Fussell, *The Great War and Modern Memory* (1973)

Martin Gilbert, *The First World War: A Complete History* (1994)

James Joll, *The Origins of the First World War* (1984)

American Mobilization

A. E. Barbeau and Florette Henri, *The Unknown Soldiers: Black American Troops in World War I* (1974)

John W. Chambers, *To Raise an Army: The Draft in Modern America* (1987)

Nancy Gentile Ford, *Americans All! Foreign Born Soldiers in World War I* (2001).

Stephen Vaughn, *Holding Fast the Inner Lines: Democracy, Nationalism, and the Committee on Public Information* (1980)

Over Here

Allen J. Brandt, *No Magic Bullet: A Social History of Venereal Disease in the United States since 1880* (1985)

Leslie M. DeBauche, *Reel Patriotism: The Movies and World War I* (1997)

Frances R. Early, *A World Without War: How U.S. Feminists and Pacifists Resisted World War I* (1997)

Margaret Mary Finnegan, *Selling Suffrage: Consumer Culture and Votes for Women* (1999)

Maureen Greenwald, *Women, War, and Work* (1980)

Ellis W. Hawley, *The Great War and the Search for Modern Order,* 2d ed. (1992)

Jeffrey Haydu, *Making American Industries Safe for Democracy* (1997)

David M. Kennedy, *Over Here* (1980)

Barbara Steinson, *American Women's Activism in World War I* (1982)

Neil A. Wynn, *From Progressivism to Prosperity: World War I and American Society* (1986)

Repression and Reaction

James P. Grossman, *Land of Hope: Chicago, Black Southerners, and the Great Migration* (1989)

Frederick C. Luebke, *Bonds of Loyalty: German Americans and World War I* (1974)

Regin Schmidt, *Red Scare: The FBI and the Origins of Anticommunism in the United States, 1919–1943* (2000)

Mark Robert Schneider, *"We Return Fighting": The Civil Rights Movement in the Jazz Age* (2002).

An Uneasy Peace

Dana Frank, *Purchasing Power: Consumer Organizing, Gender, and the Seattle Labor Movement, 1919–1929* (1994)

Lloyd Gardner, *Safe for Democracy: The Anglo-American Response to Revolution, 1913–1923* (1984)

Robert D. Johnson, *The Peace Progressives and American Foreign Relations* (1995)

Carol Wilcox Melton, *Between War and Peace: Woodrow Wilson and the American Expeditionary Force in Siberia, 1918–1921* (2002).

Richard Polenberg, *Fighting Faiths: The Abrams Case, the Supreme Court, and Free Speech* (1987)

Daniel D. Stid, *The President As Statesman: Woodrow Wilson and the Constitution* (1998)

Biography

Kendrick Clements, *Woodrow Wilson: World Statesman* (1987)

Ellen Carol DuBois, *Harriot Stanton Blatch and the Winning of Woman Suffrage* (1997)

Frank E. Vandiver, *Black Jack: The Life and Times of John J. Pershing* (1977)

Jacqueline van Voris, *Carrie Chapman Catt* (1987)

Warren Zimmerman, *First Great Triumph: How Five Americans Made Their Country A World Power* (2002).

CHAPTER 23

Postwar Prosperity and Its Price

David Brody, *Workers in Industrial America* (1980)

Gilbert C. Fite, *Cotton Fields No More: Southern Agriculture, 1865–1980* (1984)

Ellis W. Hawley, *The Great War and the Search for Modern Order* (1979).

Kenneth T. Jackson, *Crabgrass Frontier* (1985)

William Leuchtenberg, *The Perils of Prosperity, 1914–1932* (1958)

Clay McShane, *Down the Asphalt Path* (1994)

Gwendolyn Wright, *Building the American Dream* (1981)

Gerald Zahavi, *Workers, Managers, and Welfare Capitalism* (1988)

The New Mass Culture

Beth A. Bailey, *From Front Porch to Back Seat: Courtship in Twentieth-Century America* (1988)

Douglas B. Craig, *Fireside Politics: Radio and Political Culture in the United States, 1920–1940* (2000)

Daniel J. Czitrom, *Media and the American Mind* (1982)

John D'Emilio and Estelle B. Freedman, *Intimate Matters: A History of Sexuality in America* (1988)

Susan J. Douglas, *Listening In: Radio and the American Imagination* (1999)

Pamela Walker Laird, *Advertising Progress: American Business and the Rise of Consumer Marketing* (1998)

Jackson Lears, *Fables of Abundance: A Cultural History of Advertising in America* (1994)

Roland Marchand, *Advertising the American Dream: Making Way for Modernity, 1920–1940* (1985).

Steven J. Ross, *Working Class Hollywood: Silent Film and the Shaping of Class in America* (1998)

Robert Sklar, *Movie Made America*, rev. ed. (1995)

Resistance to Modernity

Katherine M. Blee, *Women and the Klan: Racism and Gender in the 1920s* (1991)

John Higham, *Strangers in the Land: Patterns of American Nativism, 1860–1925* (1955)

Edward J. Larson, *Summer of the Gods: The Scopes Trial and America's Continuing Debate Over Science* (1997)

Mae M. Ngai, *Impossible Subjects: Illegal Aliens and the Making of Modern America* (2004)

Thomas R. Pegram, *Battling Demon Rum: The Struggle for a Dry America, 1800–1933* (1998)

Daniel J. Tichenor, *Dividing Lines: Immigration Control in America* (2002)

The State, the Economy, and Business

Kendrick A. Clements, *Hoover, Conservation, and Consumerism: Engineering the Good Life* (2000)

Warren I. Cohen, *Empire without Tears* (1987)

Louis Galambos and Joseph Pratt, *The Rise of the Corporate Commonwealth* (1988)

John Earl Haynes, ed., *Calvin Coolidge and the Coolidge Era* (1998)

Roland Marchand, *Creating the Corporate Soul: The Rise of Public Relations and Corporate Imagery in American Big Business* (1998)

Charles L. Mee, *The Ohio Gang: The World of Warren G. Harding* (1981)

Emily S. Rosenberg, *Spreading the American Dream* (1982)

Promises Postponed

Nancy F. Cott, *The Grounding of American Feminism* (1987)

Ann Douglas, *Terrible Honesty: Mongrel Manhattan in the 1920s* (1995)

Nathan I. Huggins, *Harlem Renaissance* (1971)

Cary D. Mintz, *Black Culture and the Harlem Renaissance* (1988)

Kathy H. Ogren, *The Jazz Revolution: Twenties America and the Meaning of Jazz* (1989)

George J. Sanchez, *Becoming Mexican American* (1993)

Mark Robert Schneider, *"We Return Fighting": The Civil Rights Movement in the Jazz Age* (2002)

Judith Stein, *The World of Marcus Garvey* (1985)

Biography

Edith L. Blumhofer, *Aimee Semple McPherson* (1993)

David Burner, *Herbert Hoover: The Public Life* (1979)

Robert Creamer, *Babe: The Legend Comes to Life* (1975)

Neal Gabler, *Winchell: Gossip, Power, and the Culture of Celebrity* (1994)

Fred Hobson, *Mencken: A Life* (1994)

David Levering Lewis, *W. E. B. DuBois: The Fight for Equality and the American Century, 1919–1963* (2000)

David Nasaw, *The Chief: The Life of William Randolph Hearst* (2000)

Arnold Rampersad, *The Life of Langston Hughes*, 2 vols. (1986–88)

Robert A. Slayton, *Empire Statesman: The Rise and Redemption of Al Smith* (2001)

CHAPTER 24

Hard Times

Michael A. Bernstein, *The Great Depression* (1987)

Michael D. Bordo, et al., eds., *The Defining Moment: The Great Depression and the American Economy in the Twentieth Century* (1998)

John A. Garraty, *The Great Depression* (1986)

Robert S. McElvaine, ed., *Down and Out in the Great Depression* (1983)

Janet Poppendieck, *Breadlines Knee-Deep in Wheat* (1986)

Jeff Singleton, *The American Dole: Unemployment Relief and the Welfare State in the Great Depression* (2000)

Studs Terkel, *Hard Times* (1970)

T.H. Watkins, *The Hungry Years: A Narrative History of the Great Depression in America* (1999)

Elmos Wicker, *The Banking Panics of the Great Depression* (1996)

FDR and the First New Deal

Paul K. Conkin, *The New Deal*, 2d ed. (1975)

Steve Fraser and Gary Gerstle, eds., *The Rise and Fall of the New Deal Order* (1988)

Ellis Hawley, *The New Deal and the Problem of Monopoly* (1966)

William Leuchtenberg, *The FDR Years* (1995)

George McJimsey, *The Presidency of Franklin Delano Roosevelt* (2000)

James S. Olson, *Saving Capitalism* (1988)

Albert U. Romasco, *The Politics of Recovery: Roosevelt's New Deal* (1983)

Theodore M. Saloutos, *The American Farmer and the New Deal* (1982)

Left Turn and the Second New Deal

Kristi Andersen, *The Creation of a Democratic Majority, 1928–1936* (1979)

Irving Bernstein, *The Turbulent Years: A History of the American Worker, 1933–1941* (1970)

John Braeman et al., eds., *The New Deal: The State and Local Levels* (1975).

Alan Brinkley, *Voices of Protest: Huey Long, Father Coughlin, and the New Deal* (1982)

Peter Friedlander, *The Emergence of a UAW Local* (1975)

Gary Gerstle, *Working Class Americanism* (1989)

Kenneth J. Heineman, *A Catholic New Deal: Religion and Reform in Depression Pittsburgh* (1999)

Robin D. G. Kelley, *Hammer and Hoe: Alabama Communists during the Great Depression* (1990)

Joseph P. Lash, *Dealers and Dreamers* (1988)

Roy Lubove, *The Struggle for Social Security* (1968)

Robert H. Zieger, *The CIO, 1935–1955* (1995)

The New Deal and the West

James M. Gregory, *American Exodus: The Dust Bowl Migration and Okie Culture in California* (1989)

Norris Hundley Jr., *The Great Thirst: California and Water, 1770s–1990s* (1992)

Laurence Kelly, *The Assault on Assimilation: John Collier and the Origins of Indian Policy Reform, 1920–1954* (1983)

Vicki Ruiz, *Cannery Women/Cannery Lives: Mexican Women, Unionization, and the California Food Processing Industry, 1930–1950* (1987)

Charles J. Shindo, *Dust Bowl Migrants in the American Imagination* (1997)

Kevin Starr, *Endangered Dreams: The Great Depression in California* (1996)

Graham D. Taylor, *The New Deal and American Indian Tribalism* (1980)

Donald Worster, *Dust Bowl* (1979)

Depression-Era Culture

Thomas P. Doherty, *Pre-Code Hollywood: Sex, Immorality, and Insurrection in American Cinema, 1930–1934* (1999)

Lewis A. Erenberg, *Swingin' the Dream: Big Band Jazz and the Rebirth of American Culture* (1998)

Vivian Gornick, *The Romance of American Communism* (1976)

Harvey Klehr, *The Heyday of American Communism* (1984)

Anthony W. Lee, *Painting on the Left* (1999)

J. Fred MacDonald, *Don't Touch That Dial* (1979)

Richard McKinzie, *The New Deal for Artists* (1973)

Barbara Melosh, *Engendering Culture: Manhood and Womanhood in New Deal Public Art and Theater* (1991)

David P. Peeler, *Hope among Us Yet* (1987)

Richard H. Pells, *Radical Visions and American Dreams: Culture and Social Thought in the Depression Years* (1973)

Thomas Schatz, *The Genius of the System: Hollywood Filmmaking in the Studio Era* (1988)

William Stott, *Documentary Expression and Thirties America* (1973).

The Limits of Reform

Francisco E. Balderrama, *Decade of Betrayal: Mexican Repatriation in the 1930s* (1995)

Suzanne Mettler, *Dividing Citizens: Gender and Federalism in New Deal Public Works* (1998)

Mark Naison, *Communists in Harlem during the Depression* (1983)

James T. Patterson, *Congressional Conservatism and the New Deal* (1967)

Landon R.Y. Storrs, *Civilizing Capitalism: The National Consumers' League, Women's Activism, and Labor Standards in the New Deal Era* (2000)

Patricia Sullivan, *Days of Hope: Race and Democracy in the New Deal Era* (1996)

Susan Ware, *Beyond Suffrage: Women in the New Deal* (1981)

———, *Partner and I: Molly Dewson, Feminism, and New Deal Politics* (1987)

Nancy J. Weiss, *Farewell to the Party of Lincoln: Black Politics in the Age of FDR* (1983)

G. Edward White, *The Constitution and the New Deal* (2000)

Robert L. Zangrando, *The NAACP Crusade against Lynching* (1980)

Biography

David Burner, *Herbert Hoover* (1978)

Blanche W. Cook, *Eleanor Roosevelt: A Life* (1992)

Kenneth S. Davis, *FDR*, 4 vols. (1972, 1975, 1986, 1992)

Steven Fraser, *Labor Will Rule: Sidney Hillman and the Rise of American Labor* (1991)

Dorothy Healey and Maurice Isserman, *California Red: A Life in the American Communist Party* (1990)

June Hopkins, *Harry Hopkins: Sudden Hero, Brash Reformer* (1999)

J. Joseph Huthmacher, *Robert F. Wagner and the Rise of Urban Liberalism* (1968)

Nelson Lichtenstein, *The Most Dangerous Man in Detroit: Walter Reuther and the Fate of American Labor* (1995)

Karen Becker Ohrn, *Dorothea Lange and the Documentary Tradition* (1980)

Naomi E. Pasachoff, *Frances Perkins: Champion of the New Deal* (1999)

Lois Scharf, *Eleanor Roosevelt* (1987)

Robert Zieger, *John L. Lewis* (1988)

CHAPTER 25

Coming of World War II

Justus D. Doenecke, *Storm on the Horizon: The Challenge to American Intervention, 1939–1941* (2000)

Akira Iriye, *The Origins of the Second World War in Asia and the Pacific* (1987)

Deborah Lipstadt, *Beyond Belief: The American Press and the Coming of the Holocaust, 1933–1945* (1986)

Ernest Mandel, *The Meaning of the Second World War* (1986)

Geoffrey S. Smith, *To Save a Nation* (1992)

Robert B. Stinnett, *Day of Deceit: The Truth about FDR and Pearl Harbor* (2000)

Arsenal of Democracy and the Home Front

Karen Anderson, *Wartime Women* (1981)

Amy Bentley, *Eating for Victory: Food Rationing and the Politics of Domesticity* (1998)

Alison R. Bernstein, *American Indians and World War II* (1991)

Dominic J. Capeci and Martha Wilkerson, *Layered Violence: The Detroit Rioters of 1943* (1991)

Paul D. Casdorph, *Let the Good Times Roll: Life at Home in America During World War II* (1989)

Charles D. Chamberlain, *Victory at Home: Manpower and Race in the American South during World War II* (2003)

Roger Daniels, *Concentration Camps USA: Japanese Americans and World War II* (1971)

Thomas Doherty, *Projections of War: Hollywood, American Culture and World War II* (1993)

Lewis A. Erenberg and Susan E. Hirsch, eds., *The War in American Culture: Society and Consciousness During World War II* (1996)

Sherna Berger Gluck, *Rosie the Riveter Revisited: Women, the War, and Social Change* (1987).

Rachel Waltner Goosen, *Women Against the Good War: Conscientious Objection and Gender on the American Home Front, 1941–1947* (1997)

Maureen Honey, *Bitter Fruit: African American Women in World War II* (1999)

Daniel Kryder, *Divided Arsenal: Race and the American State during World War II* (2000)

Roger W. Lotchin, *The Bad City in the Good War: San Francisco, Los Angeles, Oakland, and San Diego* (2003)

Gary Y. Okihiro, *Whispered Silences: Japanese Americans and World War II* (1996)

Greg Robinson, *By Order of the President: FDR and the Internment of Japanese Americans* (2001)

George H. Roeder, *The Censored War: American Visual Experience during World War II* (1993)

Lawrence R. Samuel, *Pledging Allegiance: American Identity and the Bond Drive of World War II* (1997)

Bartholomew H. Sparrow, *From the Outside In: World War II and the American State* (1996)

Kevin Starr, *Embattled Dreams: California in War and Peace, 1940–1950* (2002)

William M. Tuttle Jr., *"Daddy's Gone to War": The Second World War in the Lives of America's Children* (1993)

World at War

William H. Bartsch, *December 8, 1941: MacArthur's Pearl Harbor* (2003)

Alison Bernstein, *American Indians and World War II* (1991)

Conrad C. Crane, *Bombs, Cities, and Civilians* (1993)

John W. Dower, *War without Mercy* (1986)

Akira Iriye, *Power and Culture: The Japanese-American War, 1941–1945* (1981)

Lee Kennett, *G.I.: The American Soldier in World War II* (1987)

Eric Markusen and David Kopf, *The Holocaust and Strategic Bombing: Genocide and Total War in the Twentieth Century* (1995)

Peter Maslowski, *Armed with Cameras: The American Military Photographers of World War II* (1993)

Brenda L. Moore, *Serving Our Country: Japanese American Women in the Military during World War II* (2003)

Williamson Murray and Allan R. Millett, *A War to be Won: Fighting the Second World War* (2000)

Barbara Brooks Tomblin, *G.I. Nightingales: The Army Nurse Corps in World War II* (1996)

David S. Wyman, *The Abandonment of the Jews: America and the Holocaust, 1941–1945* (1984)

Last Stages of War

John D. Chappell, *Before the Bomb: How America Approached the End of the Pacific War* (1997)

David P. Colley, *Blood for Dignity: The Story of the First Integrated Combat Unit in the U.S. Army* (2003)

Paul Fussell, *The Boy's Crusade: The American Infantry in Northwestern Europe, 1944–1945* (2003)

Lloyd C. Gardner, *Spheres of Influence: The Great Powers Partition Europe, from Munich to Yalta* (1993)

Peter Schrijvers, *The Crash of Ruin: American Combat Soldiers in Europe during World War II* (1998)

Michael S. Sherry, *The Rise of American Air Power* (1987)

Atomic Bomb

Gar Alperovitz, *The Decision to Use the Atomic Bomb and the Architecture of an American Myth* (1995)

Paul Boyer, *By the Bomb's Early Light: American Thought and Culture at the Dawn of the Atomic Age* (1985)

Peter Bacon Hales, *Atomic Spaces: Living on the Manhattan Project* (1997)

Ruth H. Howes, *Their Day in the Sun: Women of the Manhattan Project* (1999)

J. Samuel Walker, *Prompt and Utter Destruction: Truman and the Use of Atomic Bombs against Japan* (1997)

Eileen Welsome, *The Plutonium Files: America's Secret Medical Experiments in the Cold War* (1999)

Biography/Memoir

Mark M. Anderson, ed., *Hitler's Exiles: Personal Stories of the Flight from Nazi Germany to America* (1998)

Jeremy Bernstein, *Oppenheimer: Portrait of an Enigma* (2004)

Carlo D'Este, *Patton: A Genius for War* (1995)

Preston John Hubbard, *Apocalypse Undone: My Survival of Japanese Imprisonment during World War II* (1990)

Paula F. Pfeffer, *A. Philip Randolph* (1990)

Robert Underhill, *FDR and Harry: Unparalleled Lives* (1996)

CHAPTER 26

Global Insecurities and the Policy of Containment

Christian G. Appy, ed., *Cold War Constructions: The Political Culture of United States Imperialism, 1945–1966* (2000)

H. W. Brands Jr., *The Devil We Knew: Americans and the Cold War* (1993)

Warren I. Cohen, *America in the Age of Soviet Power, 1945–1991* (1993)

John Gaddis, *We Now Know: Rethinking Cold War History* (1997)

Walter Hixson, *Parting the Curtain: Propaganda, Culture, and the Cold War, 1945–1961* (1997)

Townsend Hoopes and Douglas Brinkley, *FDR and the Creation of the U.N.* (1997)

Walter LaFeber, *America, Russia, and the Cold War, 1945–1992*, 7th ed. (1993)

Arnold A. Offner, *Another Such Victory: President Truman and the Cold War* (2002)

Arch Puddington, *Broadcasting Freedom: The Cold War Triumph of Radio Free Europe and Radio Liberty* (2000)

Richard Rhodes, *Dark Sun: The Making of the Hydrogen Bomb* (1995)

David F. Rudgers, *Creating the Secret State: The Origins of the Central Intelligence Angency, 1943–1947* (2000)

Michael Schaller, *American Occupation of Japan: The Origins of the Cold War in Asia* (1985)

The Truman Presidency

Gary A. Donaldson, *Truman Defeats Dewey* (1999)

Michael R. Gardner, *Harry Truman and Civil Rights* (2002)

Zachary Karabell, *The Last Campaign: How Harry Truman Won the 1948 Election* (2000)

Melvyn P. Leffler, *A Preponderance of Power: National Security, the Truman Administration, and the Cold War* (1992)

Steve Neal, ed., *HST: Memories of the Truman Years* (2003)

Sean J. Savage, *Truman and the Democratic Party* (1997)

The Cold War at Home

Larry Ceplair and Steven Englund, *The Inquisition in Hollywood: Politics in the Film Community, 1930–1960* (1980)

Noam Chomsky, ed., *The Cold War and the University: Toward an Intellectual History of the Postwar Years* (1997)

Sigmund Diamond, *Compromised Campus: The Collaboration of Universities with the Intelligence Community, 1945–1995* (1992)

Andrew D. Grossman, *Neither Dead Nor Red: Civilian Defense and American Political Development During the Early Cold War* (2001)

Michael J. Hogan, *A Cross of Iron: Harry S Truman and the Origins of the National Security State, 1945–1954* (1998)

Scott Lucas, *Freedom's War: The American Crusade Against the Soviet Union* (1999)

Patrick McGilligan and Paul Buhle, *Tender Comrades: A Backstory of the Hollywood Blacklist* (1997).

Lisle A. Rose, *The Cold War Comes to Main Street: America in 1950* (1999)

Ellen Schrecker, *Many Are the Crimes: McCarthyism in America* (1998)

Ellen W. Schrecker, *No Ivory Tower: McCarthyism and the Universities* (1986)

Cold War Culture

Michael Barson, *"Better Dead Than Red!" A Nostalgic Look at the Golden Years of Russiaphobia, Red-Baiting, and Other Commie Madness* (1992)

Paul Buhle and Dave Wagner, *Radical Hollywood* (2002)

George Lipsitz, *A Rainbow at Midnight: Labor and Culture in the 1940s* (1994).

Lary May, ed., *Recasting America: Culture and Politics in the Age of the Cold War* (1989)

Elaine McClarnand and Steve Goodson, eds., *The Impact of the Cold War on American Popular Culture* (1999)

John L. Rudolph, *Scientists in the Classroom: the Cold War Reconstruction of American Science Education* (2002)

David Seed, *American Science Fiction and the Cold War* (1999)

Joanne P. Sharp, *Condensing the Cold War: Reader's Digest and American Identity* (2000)

Jessica Wang, *American Science in an Age of Anxiety: Scientists, Anticommunism, and the Cold War* (1999)

Korean War

Bevin Alexander, *Korea: The First War We Lost*, rev. ed., 2000

William T. Bowers, William M. Hammond, George L. MacGarrigle, *Black Solider, White Army: The 24th Infantry Regiment in Korea* (1996)

Albert E. Cowdrey, *The Medics' War* (1987)

Stephen Endicott and Edward Hagerman, *The United States and Biological Warfare: Secrets from the Early Cold War and Korea* (1998)

Paul G. Pierpaoli Jr., *Truman and Korea: The Political Culture of the Early Cold War* (1999)

Ron Robin, *The Making of the Cold War Enemy* (2001)

Stanley Sandler, *The Korean War: No Victors, No Vanquished* (1999)

Biography

Allida M. Black, *Casting Her Own Shadow: Eleanor Roosevelt and the Shaping of Postwar Liberalism* (1996)

John C. Culver, *American Dreamer: The Life and Times of Henry A. Wallace* (2000)

Martin Bauml Duberman, *Paul Robeson* (1988)

Curt Gentry, *J. Edgar Hoover: The Man and the Secrets* (1991)

Alonzo L. Hamby, *Man of the People: A Life of Harry S Truman* (1995)

Arthur Herman, *Joseph McCarthy: Reexamining the Life and Legacy of America's Most Hated Senator* (1999)

Robert M. Lichtman, *Deadly Farce: Harvey Matusow and the Informer System in the McCarthy Era* (2004)

David G. McCullough, *Truman* (1992)

Wilson D. Miscamble, *George F. Kennan and the Making of American Foreign Policy, 1947–1950* (1992)

Geoffrey Perret, *Old Soldiers Never Die: The Life of Douglas MacArthur* (1996)

CHAPTER 27

American Society at Midcentury

Roslayn Fraad Baxandall and Elizabeth Ewen, *Picture Windows: How the Suburbs Happened* (2000)

Stephanie Coontz, *The Way We Never Were* (1992)

John P. Diggins, *The Proud Decades: America in War and Peace, 1941–1960* (1988)

Benita Eisler, *Private Lives: Men and Women of the Fifties* (1986)

Adam Ward Rome, *The Bulldozer in the Countryside: Suburban Sprawl and the Rise of American Environmentalism* (2001)

Jessica Weiss, *To Have and to Hold: Marriage, the Baby Boom and Social Change* (2000)

Youth Culture

Wini Breines, *Young, White, and Miserable: Growing Up Female in the Fifties* (1992)

Thomas Doherty, *Teen Pics* (1994)

Nelson George, *The Death of Rhythm and Blues* (1988)

James B. Gilbert, *A Cycle of Outrage: America's Reaction to the Juvenile Delinquent in the 1950s* (1986)

Kirse Granat May, *Golden State, Golden Youth: The California Image in Popular Culture* (2002)

Jim Miller, *Flowers in the Dustbin: The Rise of Rock and Roll, 1947–1977* (1999)

Mass Culture and Its Discontents

Erik Barnouw, *Tube of Plenty* (1982)

Nancy E. Bernhard, *U.S. Television News and Cold War Propaganda, 1947–1960* (1999)

Joel Foreman, ed., *The Other Fifties: Interrogating Midcentury American Icons* (1997)

George Lipsitz, *Time Passages* (1990).

J. Fred MacDonald, *Television and the Red Menace* (1985)

David Marc, *Demographic Vistas: Television and American Culture* (1984)

Lynn Spigel, *Make Room for TV* (1992)

Stephen J. Whitfield, *The Culture of the Cold War* (1991)

The Cold War Continued

James G. Blight and Peter Kornbluh, eds., *Politics of Illusion: The Bay of Pigs Invasion Reexamined* (1999)

Robert R. Bowie, *Waging Peace: How Eisenhower Shaped an Enduring Cold War Strategy* (1998)

Nick Cullather, *Secret History: The CIA's Classified Account of its Operations in Guatemala, 1952–1954* (1999)

Paul Dickson, *Sputnik: The Shock of the Century* (2001)

Piero Gleijeses, *Shattered Hope: The Guatemalan Revolution and the United States, 1944–1954* (1991)

Zachary Karabell, *Architects of Intervention: The United States, the Third World, and the Cold War, 1946–1962* (1999)

Richard A. Melanson and David A. Mayers, eds., *Reevaluating Eisenhower* (1986)

John F. Kennedy and the New Frontier

Trumbull Higgins, *The Perfect Failure: Kennedy, Eisenhower, and the CIA at the Bay of Pigs* (1988)

Walter LaFeber, *Inevitable Revolutions* (1983)

Thomas G. Paterson, ed., *Kennedy's Quest for Victory* (1989)

Gerald L. Posner, *Case Closed: Lee Harvey Oswald and the Assassination of JFK* (1993)

Sheldon M. Stern, *Averting 'The Final Failure': John F. Kennedy and the Secret Cuban Missile Crisis Meetings* (2003)

Richard E. Welch Jr., *Response to Revolution: The United States and Cuba, 1959–1961* (1985)

Garry Wills, *The Kennedy Imprisonment* (1983)

Biography

Chuck Berry, *Chuck Berry: The Autobiography* (1987)

Robert Dallek, *An Unfinished Life: John F. Kennedy, 1917–1963* (2003)

Carol George, *God's Salesman: Norman Vincent Peale and the Power of Positive Thinking* (1993)

Peter Guralnick, *Last Train to Memphis: The Rise of Elvis Presley* (1994)

Daniel Horowitz, *Betty Friedan and the Making of the Feminine Mystique* (1998)

Barry Miles, *Allen Ginsberg* (1989)

Gerald Nicosia, *Memory Babe: A Critical Biography of Jack Kerouac* (1983)

Geoffrey Perret, *Eisenhower* (1999)

CHAPTER 28

Origins of the Movements

Michael R. Belknap, *Federal Law and Southern Order* (1987)

Scott DeVeaux, *The Birth of BeBop* (1998)

Grace Elizabeth Hale, *Making Whiteness: The Culture of Segregation in the South, 1890–1940* (1998)

Charles P. Henry, *Ralph Bunche: Model Negro or American Other* (1999)

Grace Williams O'Brien, *The Color of the Law: Race, Violence, and Justice in the Post–World War II South* (1999)

James T. Patterson, *Brown v. Board of Education: A Civil Rights Milestone and Its Troubled Legacy* (2001)

Bernard Schwartz, *The NAACP's Legal Strategy against Segregated Education* (1987)

Mark Tushnet, *Making Civil Rights Law: Thurgood Marshall and the Supreme Court, 1936–1961* (1994)

No Easy Road to Freedom, 1957–62

Clayborne Carson, *In Struggle: SNCC and the Black Awakening of the 1960s* (1981)

William Chafe, *Civilities and Civil Rights: Greensboro, North Carolina, and the Black Struggle for Equality* (1980)

Constance Curry, et al., *Deep In Our Hearts: Nine White Women in the Freedom Movement* (2000)

John Dittmer, *Local People: The Struggle for Civil Rights in Mississippi* (1994)

James Farmer, *Lay Bare the Heart* (1985)

David J. Garrow, *The FBI and Martin Luther King, Jr.* (1983)

Cheryl L. Greenberg, ed., *A Circle of Trust: Remembering SNCC* (1998)

Charles M. Payne, *I've Got the Light of Freedom: The Organizing Tradition and the Mississippi Freedom Struggle* (1995)

Miles Wolff, *Lunch at the 5&10* (1990)

The Movement at High Tide, 1963–65

Seth Cagin and Philip Dray, *We Are Not Afraid* (1988)

Sara Evans, *Personal Politics: The Roots of Women's Liberation in the Civil Rights Movement and the New Left* (1979)

Henry Hampton and Steve Fayer, *Voices of Freedom: An Oral History of the Civil Rights Movement* (1990)

Doug McAdam, *Freedom Summer* (1988)

Diane McWhorter, *Carry Me Home: Birmingham, Alabama: The Climax of the Civil Rights Revolution* (2001)

Belinda Robnett, *How Long? How Long? African American Women in the Struggle for Civil Rights* (1997)

Clive Webb, *Fight Against Fear: Southern Jews and Black Civil Rights* (2001)

Robert Weisbrot, *Freedom Bound: A History of America's Civil Rights Movement* (1990).

Civil Rights Beyond Black and White

Thomas W. Conger, *The National Congress of American Indians* (1999)

Donald Fixico, *Termination and Relocation: Federal Indian Policy, 1945–1960* (1986)

Manuel G. Gonzalez, *Mexicanos: A History of Mexicans in the United States* (1999)

David G. Gutierrez, *Walls and Mirrors: Mexican Americans, Mexican Immigrants, and the Politics of Ethnicity* (1998)

Gabriel Haslip-Viera, et al., eds, *Boricuans in Gotham : Puerto Ricans and the Making of New York City* (2004)

Mae M. Ngai, *Impossible Subjects: Illegal Aliens and the Making of Modern America* (2004)

David Palumbo-Liu, *Asian Americans: Historical Crossings of a Racial Frontier* (1999)

Maria E. Perez y Gonzalez, *Puerto Ricans in the United States* (2000)

Kenneth R. Philip, *Termination Revisited: American Indians on the Trail to Self Determination, 1933–1953* (1999)

Carmen Theresa Whalen, *From Puerto Rico to Philadelphia: Puerto Rican Workers and Postwar Economies* (2001)

Biography

Robert Dallek, *Flawed Giant: Lyndon B. Johnson and His Times, 1961–1973* (1998)

John D'Emilio, *Lost Prophet: The Life and Times of Bayard Rustin* (2003)

Michael Eric Dyson, *I May Not Get There With You: The True Martin Luther King, Jr.* (2000)

James Forman, *The Making of Black Revolutionaries* (1985)

David J. Garrow, *Bearing the Cross: Martin Luther King, Jr., and the Southern Christian Leadership Conference* (1986)

Chana Kai Lee, *For Freedom's Sake: The Life of Fannie Lou Hamer* (1999)

John Lewis, *Walking With the Wind: A Memoir of the Movement* (1998)

Barbara Ramsey, *Ella Baker and the Black Freedom Movement* (2003)

Jo Ann Gibson Robinson, *The Montgomery Bus Boycott and the Women Who Started It* (1987)

Malcolm X, with Alex Haley, *The Autobiography of Malcolm X* (1965)

CHAPTER 29

Vietnam: America's Longest War

David L. Anderson, *The Columbia Guide to the Vietnam War* (2002)

Christian G. Appy, *Working-Class War: American Combat Soldiers in Vietnam* (1993)

Larry Berman, *No Peace, No Honor: Nixon, Kissinger, and Betrayal in Vietnam* (2001)

Robert Buzzanco, *Vietnam and the Transformation of American Life* (1999)

Kenton J. Clymer, *The Vietnam War: Its History, Literature and Music* (1998)

Gerald J. DeGroot, *A Noble Cause? America and the Vietnam War* (1999)

Michael S. Foley, *Confronting the War Machine: Draft Resistance during the Vietnam War* (2003)

Herman Graham III, *The Brothers' War: Black Power, Manhood, and the Military Experience* (2003)

William M Hammond, *Reporting Vietnam: Media and Military at War* (1998)

George C. Herring, *America's Longest War: The United States and Vietnam, 1950–1975*, 3rd ed. (1996)

————, ed., *The Pentagon Papers*, abridged ed. (1993)

Andrew E. Hunt, *The Turning: A History of Vietnam Veterans Against the War* (1999)

David Kaiser, *American Tragedy: Kennedy, Johnson, and the Origins of the Vietnam War* (2000)

Jeffrey Kimball, *Nixon's Vietnam War* (1998)

Fredrik Logevall, *Choosing War: The Lost Chance for Peace and the Escalation of War in Vietnam* (1999)

Robert Mann, *A Grand Illusion: America's Descent into Vietnam* (2001)

James S. Olson and Randy Roberts, *My Lai: A Brief History with Documents* (1998)

Randy Shilts, *Conduct Unbecoming: Lesbians and Gays in the U.S. Military, Vietnam to the Persian Gulf* (1993)

Fred Turner, *Echoes of Combat: The Vietnam War in American Memory* (1996)

James E. Westheider, *Fighting on Two Fronts: African Americans and the Vietnam War* (1997)

Marilyn B. Young, *The Vietnam Wars, 1945–1990* (1991)

A Generation in Conflict

David Allyn, *Make Love, Not War: The Sexual Revolution, Unfettered History* (2000)

Beth Bailey, *Sex in the Heartland* (1999)

Alexander Bloom and Wini Breines, eds., *Takin' It to the Streets: A Sixties Reader* (1995)

Aniko Bodroghkozy, *Groove Tube: Sixties Television and the Youth Rebellion* (2001)

Peter Braunstein and Michael William Doyle, eds., *Imagine Nation: The American Counterculture of the 1960s and '70s* (2002)

Howard Brick, *Age of Contradiction: American Thought and Culture in the 1960s* (1998)

Paul Buhle and John McMillian, eds., *The New Left Revisited* (2003)

David Farber, *The Age of Great Dreams: America in the 1960s* (1994)

James J. Farrell, *The Spirit of the Sixties: The Making of Postwar Radicalism* (1997)

Jennifer Frost, *"An Interracial Movement of the Poor": Community Organizing and the New Left in the 1960s* (2001)

Maurice Isserman and Michael Kazin, *America Divided: The Civil War of the 1960s* (2000)

Paul Lyons, *New Left, New Right, and the Legacy of the Sixties* (1996)

John C. McWilliams, *The 1960s Cultural Revolution* (2000)

Timothy Miller, *The 60s Communes: Hippies and Beyond* (1999)

Mark Oppenheimer, *Knocking on Heaven's Door: American Religion in the Age of Counterculture* (2003)

George Rising, *Clean for Gene: Eugene McCarthy's 1968 Presidential Campaign* (1997)

William L. Van Deburg, *New Day in Babylon: The Black Power Movement and American Culture, 1965–1975* (1992)

Mary Ann Wynkoop, *Dissent in the Heartland: The Sixties at Indiana University* (2002)

The Politics of Identity

Kathleen C. Berkeley, *The Women's Liberation Movement in America* (1999)

Dudley Clendinen and Adam Nagourney, *Out for Good: The Struggle to Build a Gay Rights Movement in America* (1999)

Rachel Blau De Plessis and Ann Snitow, *The Feminist Memoir Project: Voices from Women's Liberation* (1998)

Susan J. Douglas, *Where the Girls Are: Growing Up Female with the Mass Media* (1994)

Martin Duberman, *Stonewall* (1993)

Gerald Horne, *Fire This Time: The Watts Uprising and the 1960s* (1995)

Blance Linden-Ward and Carol Hurd Green, *American Women in the 1960s* (1993)

Marguerite V. Marin, *Social Protest in an Urban Barrio: A Study of the Chicano Movement, 1966–1974* (1991)

Peter Matthiessen, *In the Spirit of Crazy Horse* (1992)

Joane Nagel, *American Indian Ethnic Renewal: Red Power and the Resurgence of Identity and Culture* (1996)

Armando Navarro, *Mexican American Youth Organization: Avant-Garde of the Chicano Movement in Texas* (1995)

Joy Ann Williamson, *Black Power on Campus* (2003)

The Nixon Presidency and Watergate

Mary C. Brennan, *Turning Right in the Sixties: The Conservative Capture of the GOP* (1995)

J. Brooks Flippen, *Nixon and the Environment* (2000)

Leonard Garment, *In Search of Deep Throat: The Greatest Political Mystery of Our Time* (2000)

Lewis L. Gould, *1968: The Election That Changed America* (1993)

Dean J. Kotlowski, *Nixon's Civil Rights: Politics, Principle, and Policy* (2001)

Allen J. Matusow, *Nixon's Economy: Booms, Busts, Dollars and Votes* (1998)

Keith W. Olson, *Watergate: The Presidential Scandal that Shook America* (2003)

Richard Reeves, *President Nixon: Alone in the White House* (2001)

Biography

David L. Anderson, ed., *The Human Tradition in the Vietnam Era* (2000)

Elaine Brown, *A Taste of Power: A Black Woman's Story* (1992)

Jody Carlson, *George C. Wallace and the Politics of Powerlessness* (1981)

Robert Dallek, *Flawed Giant: Lyndon Johnson and His Times, 1961–1973* (1998)

Adam Fortunate Eagle, *Heart of the Rock: The Indian Invasion of Alcatraz* (2002)

Robert Alan Goldberg, *Barry Goldwater* (1995)

Elliot Gorn, ed., *Muhammed Ali: The People's Champ* (1996)

Joan Hoff, *Nixon Reconsidered* (1994)

Daniel Horowitz, *Betty Friedan and the Making of the Feminine Mystique: The American Left, the Cold War, and Modern Feminism* (1998)

Maurice Isserman, *The Other American: The Life of Michael Harrington* (2000)

Joseph A. Palermo, *In His Own Right: The Political Odyssey of Senator Robert F. Kennedy* (2001)

Jonah Raskin, *For the Hell of It: The Life and Times of Abbie Hoffman* (1996)

Kenneth S. Stern, *Loud Hawk: The United States versus the American Indian Movement* (1994)

Evan Thomas, *Robert Kennedy: His Life* (2000)

Jack Todd, *Desertion: In the Time of Vietnam* (2001)

Irwin Unger and Debi Unger, *LBJ: A Life* (1999)

CHAPTER 30

The Overextended Society

Michael A. Bernstein and David E. Adler, eds., *Understanding American Economic Decline* (1994)

W. Carl Biven, *Jimmy Carter's Economy: Policy in an Age of Limits* (2002)

Gordon L. Clark, *Unions and Communities Under Siege* (1989)

Claudia Goldin, *Understanding the Gender Gap: An Economic History of American Women* (1990)

Burton I. Kaufman, *The Arab Middle East and the United States: Inter-Arab Rivalry and Superpower Diplomacy* (1996)

Paul Krugman, *Peddling Prosperity: Economic Sense and Nonsense in the Age of Diminished Expectations* (1994)

Bruce J. Schulman, *From Cotton Belt to Sunbelt* (1991)

Jon Teaford, *Cities of the Heartland: The Rise and Fall of the Industrial Midwest* (1993)

Daniel Yergin, *The Prize: The Epic Quest for Oil, Money, and Power* (1990)

"Lean Year" Presidents

George C. Edwards III, *At the Margins: Presidential Leadership of Congress* (1989)

Gary M. Fink and Hugh Davis Graham, eds., *The Carter Presidency: Policy Choices in the Post–New Deal Era* (1998)

John Robert Greene, *The Presidency of Gerald R. Ford* (1995)

Gary Sick, *October Surprise: America's Hostages in Iran and the Election of Ronald Reagan* (1991)

The New Conservatism

William C. Berman, *America's Right Turn: From Nixon to Clinton* (1998)

Joel A. Carpenter, *Revive Us Again: The Reawakening of American Fundamentalism* (1997)

Dan T. Carter, *From George Wallace to Newt Gingrich: Race in the Conservative Counterrevolution, 1963–1994* (1996)

Betty A. Dobratz and Stephanie L. Shanks-Meile, *"White Power, White Pride!" The White Separatist Movement in the United States* (1997)

Susan Faludi, *Backlash: The Undeclared War Against American Women* (1991)

Angela Howard and Sasha Ranae Adams Tarrant, eds., *Reaction to the Modern Women's Movement, 1963 to the present* (1997)

William Martin, *With God on Our Side: The Rise of the Religious Right in America* (1996)

Grass-Roots Politics

Henry F. Bedford, *Seabrook Station: Citizen Politics and Nuclear Power* (1990)

Nicholas Dagen Bloom, *Suburban Alchemy: 1960s New Towns and the Transformation of the American Dream* (2001)

Craig Cox, *Storefront Revolution: Food Co-ops and the Counterculture* (1994)

David Frum, *How We Got Here: The 70s, The Decade That Brought You Modern Life (For Better or Worse)* (2000)

Lois Gibbs, *Love Canal: The Story Continues* (1998)

Gerald Markowitz and David Rosner, *Deceit and Denial: The Deadly Politics of Industrial Pollution* (2002)

Donald G. Mathews and Jane S. De Hart, *Sex, Gender, and the Politics of ERA* (1990)

Stephen Paul Miller, *The Seventies Now: Culture as Surveillance* (1999)

Gordana Rabrenovic, *Community Builders: A Tale of Neighborhood Mobilization in Two Cities* (1996)

David Brian Robertson, ed., *Loss of Confidence: Politics and Policy in the 1970s* (1998)

Suzanne Staggenborg, *The Pro-Choice Movement: Organization and Activism in the Abortion Conflict* (1991)

Foreign Policy

William J. Broad, *Teller's War: The Top-Secret Story Behind the Star Wars Deception* (1992)

Beth A. Fischer, *The Reagan Reversal: Foreign Policy and the End of the Cold War* (1997)

Mark Gasiorowski, *U.S. Foreign Policy and the Shah* (1991)

Christopher Hemmer, *Which Lessons Matter? American Foreign Policy Decision Making in the Middle East, 1979–1987* (2000)

William M. LeoGrande, *Our Own Backyard: The United States in Central America, 1977–1992* (1998)

Timothy P. Maga, *The World of Jimmy Carter: U.S. Foreign Policy, 1977–1981* (1994)

Jack F. Matlock Jr., *Reagan and Gorbachev: How the Cold War Ended* (2004)

Morris H. Morley, *Washington, Somoza, and the Sandinistas: State and Regime in U.S. Policy Toward Nicaragua, 1969–1981* (1994)

Bob Woodward, *Veil: The Secret Wars of the CIA* (1987)

The Reagan Revolution

Robert M. Collins, *More: The Politics of Economic Growth in Postwar America* (2000)

Matthew Dallek, *The Right Moment: Ronald Reagan's First Victory and the Decisive Turning Point in American Politics* (2000, 2004)

Nicholas Laham, *Ronald Reagan and the Politics of Immigration Reform* (2000)

Michael Schaller, *Reckoning with Reagan* (1992)

John W. Sloan, *The Reagan Effect: Economics and Presidential Leadership* (1999)

Best of Times, Worst of Times

James D. Cockcroft, *Outlaws in the Promised Land: Mexican Immigrant Workers and America's Future* (1986)

Barbara Ehrenreich, *Fear of Falling: The Inner Life of the Middle Class* (1989)

Elizabeth Fee and Daniel M. Fox, eds., *AIDS: The Making of a Chronic Disease* (1992)

Jacqueline Jones, *The Dispossessed: America's Underclasses from the Civil War to the Present* (1992)

Michael B. Katz, ed., *The "Underclass" Debate* (1993)

Hilda Scott, *Working Your Way to the Bottom: The Feminization of Poverty* (1985)

Randy Shilts, *And the Band Played On: Politics, People, and the AIDS Epidemic* (1987)

Ruth Sidel, *Women and Children Last: The Plight of Poor Women in Affluent America* (1986)

Lenore J. Weitzman, *The Divorce Revolution: The Unexpected Social and Economic Consequences for Women and Children in America* (1985)

Richard White, *Rude Awakenings: What the Homeless Crisis Tells Us* (1992)

Biography

Peter G. Bourne, *Jimmy Carter: A Comprehensive Biography From Plains to Postpresidency* (1997)

Jimmy Carter, *Keeping Faith: Memoirs of a President* (1982, 1995)

Rosalynn Carter, *First Lady from Plains* (1984)

Adam Clymer, *Edward M. Kennedy: A Biography* (1999)

Jim Cullen, *Born in the U.S.A.: Bruce Springsteen and the American Tradition* (1997, 2005)

Betty Ford, with Chris Chase, *Betty, A Glad Awakening* (1987)

Marshall Frady, *Jesse: The Life and Pilgrimage of Jesse Jackson* (1996)

Ernest B. Furgurson, *The Hard Right: The Rise of Jesse Helms* (1986)

Steven M. Gillon, *The Democrats' Dilemma: Walter F. Mondale and the Legacy of Liberalism* (1992)

Kitty Kelley, *Nancy Reagan* (1991)

Linda J. Lear, *Rachel Carson* (1997)

Peter Meyer, *Defiant Patriot: The Life and Exploits of Lt. Colonel Oliver L. North* (1987)

Edmund Morris, *Dutch: A Memoir of Ronald Reagan* (1999)

William E. Pemberton, *Exit with Honor: The Life and Presidency of Ronald Reagan* (1997)

Wilbur C. Rich, *Coleman Young and Detroit Politics* (1989)

CHAPTER 31

"A Kinder, Gentler Nation"

Meena Bose and Rosanna Perotti, eds., *From Cold War to New World Order: The Foreign Policy of George H.W. Bush* (2002)

Stephen F. Cohen, *Failed Crusade: America and the Tragedy of Post-Communist Russia* (2000)

John L. Gaddis, *The United States and the End of the Cold War* (1992)

David Halberstam, *War in a Time of Peace: Bush, Clinton, and the Generals* (2001)

William G. Hyland, *Clinton's World: Remaking American Foreign Policy* (1999)

Robert D. Kaplan, *The Coming Anarchy: Shattering the Dreams of the Post–Cold War* (2000)

Tomas W. Lippman, *Madeleine Albright and the New American Diplomacy* (2000)

Robert Litwak, *Rogue States and U.S. Foreign Policy: Containment After the Cold War* (2000)

David Mosler and Bob Catley, *Global America: Imposing Liberalism on a Recalcitrant World* (2000)

Micah L. Sifry and Christopher Cerf, eds., *The Gulf War Reader* (1991)

Jeff Wheelwright, *The Irritable Heart: The Medical Mystery of the Gulf War* (2001)

The Clinton Presidency

Lauren Berlant and Lisa Duggan, eds., *Our Monica, Ourselves: The Clinton Affair and the National Interest* (2001)

Sidney Blumenthal, *The Clinton Wars* (2003)

James Carville, *Stickin': The Case for Loyalty* (2000)

Joe Conason and Gene Lyons, *The Hunting of the President: The Ten-Year Campaign to Destroy Bill and Hillary Clinton* (2000)

Richard A. Posner, *An Affair of State: The Investigation, Impeachment, and Trial of President Clinton* (1999)

Alvin Z. Rubinstein, Albina Shayevich, and Boris Zlotnikov, eds., *The Clinton Foreign Policy Reader: Presidential Speeches with Commentary* (2000)

Steven E. Schier, ed., *The Postmodern Presidency: Bill Clinton's Legacy in U.S. Politics* (2000)

Susan Schmidt and Michael Weisskopf, *Truth at Any Cost: Ken Starr and the Unmaking of Bill Clinton* (2000)

Hanes Walton Jr., *Reelection: William Jefferson Clinton as a Native-Son Presidential Candidate* (2000)

Alex Waddan, *Clinton's Legacy: A New Democrat in Governance* (2001)

Changing American Communities

David Brooks, *Bobos in Paradise: The New Upper Class and How They Got There* (2000)

Sara M. Evans, *Tidal Wave: How Women Changed America at Century's End* (2003).

Helen Hayes, *U.S. Immigration and the Undocumented: Ambivalent Lives, Furtive Lives* (2001)

Denis Lynn Daly Heyck, ed., *Barrios and Borderlands: Cultures of Latinos and Latinas in the United States* (1994)

Bill Ong Hing, *Making and Remaking Asian America through Immigration Policy, 1850–1990* (1993)

Godfrey Hodgson, *More Equal Than Others: America from Nixon to the New Century* (2004).

Ted G. Lewis, *Microsoft Rising: . . . and Other Tales of Silicon Valley* (1999)

New York Times, The Downsizing of America (1996)

J. Eric Oliver, *Democracy in Suburbia* (2001)

Howard Rheingold, *The Virtual Community* (1994).

Adam Ward Rome, *The Bulldozer in the Countryside: Suburban Sprawl and the Rise of American Environmentalism* (2001)

Reed Ueda, *Postwar Immigrant America* (1994)

A New Age of Anxiety

Jewelle Taylor Gibbs, *Race and Justice: Rodney King and O. J. Simpson in a House Divided* (1996)

Mark S. Hamm, *Apocalypse in Oklahoma: Waco and Ruby Ridge Revenged* (1997)

Chester Hartman, ed., *Double Exposure: Poverty and Race in America* (1997)

Randall Kennedy, *Race, Crime, and the Law* (1997)

Lawrence Levine, *The Opening of the American Mind: Canons, Culture, and History* (1996)

Joanne Meyerowitz, ed. *History and September 11th* (2003)

Christian Parenti, *Lockdown America: Police and Prisons in the Age of Crisis* (1999)

David M. Reimers, *Unwelcome Strangers: American Identity and the Turn Against Immigration* (1998)

Roger Simon, *Divided We Stand: How Al Gore Beat George Bush and Lost the Presidency* (2001)

Robert C. Smith, *Racism in the Post–Civil Rights Era* (1995)

James D. Tabor and Eugene V. Gallagher, *Why Waco? Cults and the Battle for Religious Freedom in America* (1995)

The New Millennium

Walden Bello, *The Future in the Balance* (2001)

Jeremy Brecher, Tim Costello, and Brendan Smith, *Globalization From Below* (2000)

Alexander Cockburn, Jeffrey St. Clair, and Alan Sekula, *Five Days That Shook the World: Seattle and Beyond* (2000)

Anthony Giddens, *Runaway World* (1999)

Michael Hardt and Antonio Negri, *Empire* (2000)

David Held, ed., *A Globalizing World? Culture, Economics, Politics* (2000).

Edward S. Herman and Robert W. McChesney, *The Global Media: The New Missionaries of Corporate Capitalism* (1997)

Joshua Karliner, *The Corporate Planet: Ecology and Politics in the Age of Globalization* (1997)

Margaret Keck and Kathryn Sikkink, *Activists Beyond Borders: Advocacy Networks in International Politics* (1998)

Michael T. Klare, Blood and Oil: *The Dangers and Consequences of America's Growing Dependency* (2004)

Amory Starr, *Naming the Enemy: Anti-Corporate Movements Confront Globalization* (2000)

John D. Wirth, *Smelter Smoke in North America: The Politics of Transborder Pollution* (2000)

Biography

Barbara Bush, *Reflections: Life After the White House* (2003)

Bill Clinton, *My Life* (2004)

Karlene Faith, *Madonna, Brawdy & Soul* (1997)

John Robert Greene, *The Presidency of George Bush* (2000)

Nigel Hamilton, *Bill Clinton: An American Journey* (2003)

Molly Ivins and Lou Dubose Shrub: *The Short But Happy Political Life of George W. Bush* (2000)

Joyce Milton, *The First Partner: Hillary Rodham Clinton* (1999)

Kevin Phillips, *American Dynasty* (2004)

Gerald L. Posner, *Citizen Perot: His Life and Times* (1996)

Richard A. Serrano, *One of Ours: Timothy McVeigh and the Oklahoma City Bombing* (1998)

Mel Steely, *The Gentleman from Georgia: The Biography of Newt Gingrich* (2000)

Tom Wicker, *George Herbert Walker Bush* (2004)

Text Credits

Chapter 1: Page 9 Emergence Song, William Brandon, The Magic World: American Indian Songs and Poems, 1971. **Page 12** Winnebago Song: This Newly Created World, from the Winnebago Medicine Rite as Recoded in Raul Radin, The Road to Life and Death: A Ritual Drama of the American Indians, Princeton University Press © 1945.

Chapter 2: Figure 2.2 The African, Indian and European Population of the Americas, from Colin McEvedy and Richard Jones Atlas of World Population History, Allen Lane © 1978. Curtis Brown.

Chapter 4: Figure 4.1 Reproduced from *The American Colonies: From Settlement to Independence* Copyright © R.C. Simmons 1976 by permission of PFD (www.pfd.co.uk) on behalf of Professor Richard Simmons. **Figure 4.2** Africans as a Percentage of Total Population of the British Colonies, 1650–1977, from Robert W. Fogel and Stanley L. Engerman, *Time on the Cross: The Economics of American Negro Slavery*, 1974, p.21. **Page 90** Courtesy of The Historical Society of Pennsylvania.

Chapter 5: Figure 5.1 Sobel, Mechal. *The World They Made Together*, © 1987 Princeton University Press, 1989 paperback edition. Reprinted by permission of Princeton University Press. **Table 5.2** Main Jackson, Turner. *Social Structure of Revolutionary America* © 1965 Princeton University Press, 1993 renewed PUP. Reprinted by permission of Princeton University Press.

Chapter 7: Page 203 "A Former Slave Appeals to Remain Free Philip S. Fonre, *A Plea Against Reenslavement*, Pennsylvania History, 39 (1972), pp. 239–41".

Chapter 8: Figure 8.1 Postwar Inflation 1777–1780 The Depreciation of Continental Currency from John McCusker, *How Much is That in Real Money?*, *Proceedings of the American Antiquarian Society*, NS 102 © 1992 Courstesy, American Antiquarian Society.

Chapter 9: Figure 9.1 American Export Trade 1790–1815, Douglas C. North, The Economic Growth of the United States 1790–1860, Norton, 1966, p. 26. **Figure 9.2** Western Land Sales, Robert Riegel & Robert Athearn, American Moves West, © 1964.

Chapter 11: Figure 11.1 Race Exclusion for Suffrage, 1790–1855, Alexander Keysiar, The Right to Vote, Basic Books, 2000, p. 45 Perseus Books. **Page 314** Our Hearts are Sickened: Letter from Cherokee Chief John Ross to the Senate and House of Representatives, Sept. 28, 1836, Papers of Chief John Ross, University of Oklahoma Press, 1985.

Chapter 12: Figure 12.1 Occupation of Women Wage Earners in Massachusetts, 1837, based on Thomas Dublin, Transforming Women's Work, © 1994 T1.1, p. 20.

Chapter 13: Figure 13.1 Participation of Irish and German Immigrants in the New York City Work Force for Selected Occupations in 1855, Robert Ernst, *Immigrant Life in New York City 1825–1863* © 1994. Reprinted by permission of the estate of Robert Ernst. **Figure 13.2** From *The Alcoholic Republic: An American Tradition* by W.J. Rarabaugh, Copyright © 1979 by Oxford Univeristy Press, Inc. Used by permission of Oxford University Press, Inc. **Map 13.2** Reprinted from Whitney R. Cross, *The Burned-Over District: The Social and Intellectual History of Enthusiastic Religion in Western New*

York 1800–1850. Copyright © 1950 by Cornell University. Used with permission of the publisher, Cornell University Press.

Chapter 14: Figure 14.1 From *The Plains Across: The Overland Emigrants and the Trans-Mississippi West, 1840–60.* Copyright 1979 by the Board of Trustees of the University of Illinois. Used with permission of the University of Illinois Press. **Map 14.7** From *Historical Atlas of California*, by Warren A. Beck and Ynez D. Haase. Copyright © 1974 by The University of Oklahoma Press, Norman. Reprinted by permission of the publisher. All rights reserved.

Chapter 16: Page 475 Lunt, Dolly Summer. *A Woman's Wartime Journal: An Account of Passage over Georgia's Plantation of Sherman's Army on the March of the Sea, Documenting the American South.* University Library, The University of North Carolina at Chapel Hill, 1996 http://docsouth.unc. edu/burge/lunt.html

Chapter 17: Page 496 Freedmen's Bureau Records: Contract Between D. Kunkle and Reuben Gouldin, January 1, 1867

Chapter 18: Map 18.1 From *Historical Atlas of Oklahoma*, 3rd edition, by John W. Morris, Charles R. Goins and Edwin C. McReynolds. Copyright © 1965, 1976, 1986 by the University of Oklahoma Press, Norman. Reprinted by permission of the publisher. All rights reserved. **Map 18.4** Mormon Cultural Diffusion, ca. 1883, Donald W. Meinig, *The Geography of the American West, 1847–1964* from The Annals of the Association of American Geographers 55, no. 2, June 1965. **Page. 533** "Memories of Calvary Life Mrs. Orsemus Boyd, Calvary Life in the Tent and Field, (New York: J. Selwin Tait & Son) 1894 as reprinted in Christiane Fischer, ed. *Let Them Speak for Themselves: Women in the America West, 1849–1900*, EJP Dutton, 1978, pp. 11–12, 116."

Chapter 19: Map 19.2 Population of Foreign Birth by Region, 1880, Clifford L. Lord and Elizabeth H. Lord, ed., Lord & Lord Historical Atlas of the United States, 1953.

Chapter 20: Map 20.1 Strikes by State, 1880, Carville Earle, Geography Inquiry and American Historical Problems, Copyright © 1992 Stanford University Press.

Chapter 22: Map 22.3 Women Suffrage by State, 1869–1914, Barbara C. Shortridge, *Atlas of American Women*, Macmillan 1987. **Page 665** Letters From the Great Migration, 1917 *Journal of Negro History*, Vol. IV, 1919, pp. 317.

Chapter 23: Page 689 "To Bob or Not to Bob: Changing Fashion and The New Woman of the 1920s." Mary Garden Pictorial Review, April 1927, 8FF. Hearst.

Chapter 24: Page 723 "I Was Able to Make My Voice Really Ring Out" http:www.historicalvoices.org/flint. Oral history courtesy of Sherna Gluck, Feminist History Project.

Chapter 25: Figure 25.1 From The Gallup Poll, 1835–1971 by George Gallup, Copyright © 1972 by the American Institute of Public Opinion. Used by permission of Random House. **Page 758** From *The Collected Poems of Langston Hughes* by Langston Hughes, Copyright © 1994 by The Estate of Langston Hughes. Used by permission of Alfred A. Knopf, a division of Random House, Inc.

U.S. History Documents CD-ROM

Over 300 Primary Source Documents

INDEX

A

Abenakis Indians, 74
Abernathy, Ralph, 854
Abolitionism, 381
  abolitionists, 381
  African American support for, 379–80
  American Colonization Society, 379
  politics and, 381–83
Abominations, Tariff of, 312
Abortion, 933–34, 975
  as birth control method, 349
  embryonic stem cell research and, 977
Abraham Lincoln Brigade, 734
Abrams v. United States, 663
Abu Ghraib, 987
Acadia, 106, 123, 148
  expulsion of Acadians, 150
Accomodationist philosophy, racism and, 631
Acheson, Dean, 794
Ackerman, Nathan, 715
Acoma Indians, 21, 58, 395
Acosta, Joseph de, 7
Acosta, Oscar Zeta, 905
Act of Trade and Navigation (1651), 72
Adair, Samuel, 434
Adams, Abigail, 146–47, 181, 201, 303
Adams, Charles Francis, Jr., 444, 505, 605
Adams, John, 164
  American Revolution, 184
  Continental Congress, 172
  economy and, 211
  election of 1796, 224
  election of 1800, 226–27
  First Continental Congress, 146–47
  midnight judges, 236
  as peace commissioner, 194
  presidency, 216, 224–25
  Second Continental Congress, 167–68, 169
Adams, John Quincy, 258
  Amistad mutiny, 382
  election of 1824, 305, *305*
  gag rule, 382
  presidency, 306
  as Secretary of State, 260, 261
  Texas and, 403
Adams-Onís Treaty, 261
Adams, Samuel, 146, 156, 160, 161, 162, 164, 215
Addams, Jane, 611, 612–13, 650, 653

Adena culture, 16
Administration of Justice Act (1774), 164
Advertising industry, 554, 684–85, 825
Affirmative action programs, 945, 976–77
Affluent Society, The (Galbraith), 814
Afghanistan: Soviet invasion of, 937
  war on terrorism and, 983–84
Africa. *See also* Slave trade: Cold War in, 830
African Americans, 557. *See also* Civil rights movement
  Slavery; Slaves; abolitionism and, 379–80
  accomodationist philosophy, 631
  African heritage, 99–100
  Africanization of South, 100–1
  American Revolution, 178, 202–4
  birth patterns, colonial period, 128
  black awakening, 631–32
  Black Power movement, 900–1
  black women's activism, 631–32
  burial practices, 100
  Civil War, 455, 465–67, 471
  as communists, 734
  communities of, under slavery, 281–86
  as cowboys, 529
  culture of, understanding, 99–100
  discrimination against, 369–70
  discriminatory labor practices, 557
  disenfranchisement, in South, 616
  education, 493–94, 573
  Emancipation Proclamation, 465–66
  Great Migration, 663–65, 680
  housing discrimination, 816
  Jim Crow laws, 594
  land/labor and, 494–95
  language and, 100
  literature, 202–3
  music, 573, 822, 849–50
  New Deal, 738–39
  "New Negro," 700–2
  in New South workforce, 561–62
  in Oregon settlement, 402–3
  population growth, 202
  poverty and, 944
  racial violence/riots, 500, 595, 664–65, 757–58
  religion, 202, 283–84, 592
  representation in Congress, *595*
  social gospel movement, 592
  in sports, 573, 688
  in 19th century cities, 286, 369–70

  in Union army, 465–66
  Vietnam War and, 890
  voting/voting rights, 227, 303, 305, 595
  westward expansion and, 275
  women, in New South workforce, 561–62
  World War I, 654–55, 680
  World War II, 751, 756–57, 761
African Americans, Reconstruction era:Amendments, 488
  black codes, 487
  education, 493–94
  family life, 493
  Freedmen's Bureau, 485, 488
  freedom, 491–92
  increasing mobility, 493
  land/labor and, 482–83, 485
  politics of, 496–98
  racial violence/riots, 500, 501
  religion, 493
  sharecropping, 483, 495, 497, *502*
African Methodist Episcopal (AME) denomination, 283, 370
Age of Anxiety, 972–78
Age of the Common Man, 309
  arts and letters in, 321–24
Agnew, Spiro T., 908
Agrarianism, Republican, 244–45
Agrarian Tradition, 15–16
Agribusiness, in California, 536–37
Agricultural Adjustment Administration (AAA), 719
Agriculture. *See also* specific crops:
  agribusiness, 536–37
  colonial period, 129
  commercial, beginnings of, 338
  development of, 12–18
  Dust Bowl, 727–29
  in early Mexico, 12, 13
  in early Southwest, 14–15
  in eastern Woodlands, 16
  farmer-labor unity, 587–88
  farmers' alliances, 585–86
  Grange movement, 584–85
  Great Plains farming communities, 531–34
  Mississippian, 16–18
  new production technologies, 535
  plantation, 82, 93, 94, 127
  producing for market, 535
  revolution, 14
  in 1920s, 681–82

U